Ethical Theory and Business

Tenth Edition

For forty years, successive editions of *Ethical Theory and Business* have helped to define the field of business ethics. The tenth edition reflects the current, multidisciplinary nature of the field by explicitly embracing a variety of perspectives on business ethics, including philosophy, management, and legal studies. Chapters integrate theoretical readings, case studies, and summaries of key legal cases to guide students to a rich understanding of business ethics, corporate responsibility, and sustainability. The tenth edition has been entirely updated, ensuring that students are exposed to key ethical questions in the current business environment. New chapters cover the ethics of IT, ethical markets, and ethical management and leadership. Coverage includes climate change, sustainability, international business ethics, sexual harassment, diversity, and LGBTQ discrimination. New case studies draw students directly into recent business ethics controversies, such as sexual harassment at Fox News, consumer fraud at Wells Fargo, and business practices at Uber.

Denis G. Arnold is the Surtman Distinguished Professor of Business Ethics at the University of North Carolina, Charlotte. One of the world's leading experts in business ethics, he is a former Editor in Chief of the prestigious scholarly journal *Business Ethics Quarterly*, published by Cambridge University Press, and a past president of the Society for Business Ethics. His research includes scores of articles and chapters and several books. A distinguished teacher praised by students at the undergraduate, MBA, doctoral, and executive levels, he has provided ethics training for leaders at Fortune 500 companies, smaller enterprises, and non-profit organizations.

Tom L. Beauchamp holds graduate degrees from Yale University and Johns Hopkins University, where he received his Ph.D. in 1970. He then joined the faculty of the Philosophy Department at Georgetown University, Washington, DC and a joint appointment at the Kennedy Institute of Ethics as Senior Research Scholar. He is the author of *Case Studies in Business, Society, and Ethics* (2003) and *Philosophical Ethics* (2001). He is co-author of *The Human Use of Animals* (2008), *Principles of Biomedical Ethics* (2012), and *A History and Theory of Informed Consent* (1986). Many of his articles were republished under the title *Standing on Principles: Collected Works*.

Norman E. Bowie is the author or editor of eighteen books in business ethics, ethics, and political philosophy. His *Business Ethics: A Kantian Perspective* (Cambridge, 2017), which has been translated into Japanese and Chinese, has just appeared in a much revised and expanded second edition. Other books include *Business Ethics in the 21st Century* (2013) and *Business Ethics for Dummies* (2011). He is past president of the Society for Business Ethics and former Executive Director of the American Philosophical Association. In 2009, the Society for Business Ethics honored him with an award for scholarly achievement. The festschrift *Kantian Business Ethics* was devoted to his work.

ETHICAL THEORY AND BUSINESS

Tenth Edition

DENIS G. ARNOLD

University of North Carolina, Charlotte

TOM L. BEAUCHAMP

Georgetown University, Washington DC

NORMAN E. BOWIE

University of Minnesota

CAMBRIDGE
UNIVERSITY PRESS

CAMBRIDGE
UNIVERSITY PRESS

University Printing House, Cambridge CB2 8BS, United Kingdom

One Liberty Plaza, 20th Floor, New York, NY 10006, USA

477 Williamstown Road, Port Melbourne, VIC 3207, Australia

314–321, 3rd Floor, Plot 3, Splendor Forum, Jasola District Centre,
New Delhi – 110025, India

79 Anson Road, #06–04/06, Singapore 079906

Cambridge University Press is part of the University of Cambridge.

It furthers the University's mission by disseminating knowledge in the pursuit of
education, learning, and research at the highest international levels of excellence.

www.cambridge.org
Information on this title: www.cambridge.org/9781108422970
DOI: 10.1017/9781108386128

Ninth edition © Pearson Education Limited 2014
Tenth edition © Denis G. Arnold, Tom L. Beauchamp, and Norman E. Bowie 2020

This book was previously published by Pearson Education, Inc. 2014
Tenth edition published by Cambridge University Press 2020

A catalogue record for this publication is available from the British Library.

Library of Congress Cataloging-in-Publication Data
Names: Arnold, Denis Gordon, editor. | Beauchamp, Tom L., editor. | Bowie, Norman E., 1942– editor.
Title: Ethical theory and business / [edited by] Denis G. Arnold, Tom L. Beauchamp, Norman E. Bowie.
Description: Tenth edition. | New York : Cambridge University Press, 2019. | Revised edition of Ethical theory and business, c2013.
Identifiers: LCCN 2019005967| ISBN 9781108422970 (hardback) | ISBN 9781108435260 (paperback)
Subjects: LCSH: Business ethics – United States. | Business ethics – United States – Case studies. | Industries – Social aspects –
United States. | Industries – Social aspects – United States – Case studies. | Commercial crimes – United States – Cases. | Consumer
protection – Law and legislation – United States – Cases.
Classification: LCC HF5387 .E82 2019 | DDC 174/.4–dc23
LC record available at https://lccn.loc.gov/2019005967

ISBN 978-1-108-42297-0 Hardback
ISBN 978-1-108-43526-0 Paperback

Additional resources for this publication at www.cambridge.org/arnold10ed

Brief Contents

List of Cases   *page* xiii
Preface   xvii

1 Ethical Theory and Business Practice   1

2 The Rights and Responsibilities of Employees   42

3 Managing, Leading, and Governing   88

4 Diversity, Discrimination, and Harassment in the Workplace   159

5 Corporate Social Responsibility   204

6 Ethics and Information Technology   261

7 Marketing Ethics   295

8 Environmental Sustainability   369

9 Ethical Issues in International Business   432

10 Ethical Markets   492

11 Economic and Global Justice   542

   Index   589

Contents

List of Cases   *page* xiii
Preface   xvii

1 Ethical Theory and Business Practice   1
1.1 Introduction   1
1.2 Fundamental Concepts   1
1.3 Fundamental Problems   7
1.4 Normative Ethical Theory   15
1.5 A Multi-Step Ethical Decision Procedure   34

Cases   39
Case 1: The Training Program   39
Case 2: Should Company Policy Apply to All?   39
Case 3: Deceiving Student Loan Borrowers Drives Profits at Navient   40

2 The Rights and Responsibilities of Employees   42
2.1 Introduction   42
2.2 Ethical Consideration of Employees   45
   Treating Employees with Respect, *Norman E. Bowie*   45
   Decency Means More than "Always Low Prices": A Comparison of Costco
      to Walmart's Sam's Club, *Wayne F. Cascio*   49
2.3 The Hiring and Firing of Employees   56
   In Defense of the Contract at Will, *Richard A. Epstein*   56
   Employment at Will and Due Process, *Patricia H. Werhane and Tara J. Radin*   61
2.4 Health and Safety   68
   Occupational Health and Safety, *John R. Boatright*   68
   Safety Culture in High Risk Industries, *Mark A. Cohen, Madeline Gottlieb,*
      Joshua Linn, and Nathan Richardson   75

Legal Perspective   80
Supreme Court of the United States, *Automobile Workers v. Johnson Controls, Inc.* (1991)   80

Cases   81
Case 1: Outsourcing at Any Cost? Do Corporations Ever Have a Moral Obligation
      Not to Outsource?   81
Case 2: Sexism in the City of London   83
Case 3: Off-Duty Smoking   84
Case 4: Fired for Drinking the Wrong Brand of Beer   84
Case 5: The Other Side of Manufacturing in the United States   85
Case 6: BP's Disastrous Safety Culture   86

3 Managing, Leading, and Governing   88

3.1 Introduction   88
3.2 Ethical Culture and Leadership   92
     Ethics and Effectiveness: The Nature of Good Leadership, *Joanne B. Ciulla* 92
     Ethics as Organizational Culture, *Linda Treviño and Katherine Nelson* 95
3.3 Governance   106
     Good Directors and Bad Behavior, *Robert A. Prentice*   106
     Ethics and Executive Compensation, *Robert W. Kolb*   112
     Do CEOs Get Paid Too Much?, *Jeffrey Moriarty*   117
3.4 Whistleblowing   124
     Whistleblowing and Employee Loyalty, *Ronald Duska*   124
     Whistleblowing, Moral Integrity, and Organizational Ethics, *George G. Brenkert* 128
     After the Wrongdoing: What Managers Should Know about Whistleblowing,
          Janet P. Near and Marcia P. Miceli   138

Legal Perspectives   145
Superior Court of New Jersey, *Warthen v. Toms River Community Memorial
     Hospital* (1985)   145
Superior Court of New Jersey, *Potter v. Village Bank of New Jersey* (1988) 145

Cases   147
Case 1: Uber's Ethical Leadership Vacuum   147
Case 2: The Bachelor Party   149
Case 3: Wells Fargo's Corporate Culture   149
Case 4: Shareholder Losses and Executive Gains: Bank of America's Acquisition
     of Merrill Lynch   153
Case 5: Roger Boisjoly and the *Challenger* Disaster: Disloyal Employee or Courageous
     Whistleblower?   156
Case 6: Tainted Medicine   157

4 Diversity, Discrimination, and Harassment in the Workplace   159

4.1 Introduction   159
4.2 Diversity in the Workplace   165
     Affirmative Action and Diversity Goals in Hiring and Promotion, *Tom L. Beauchamp* 165
4.3 Sexual Harassment   170
     Sex Discrimination Claims under Title VII of the Civil Rights Act of 1964,
          Crystal Liu, Elizabeth Macgill, and Apeksha Vora   170
     Reconceptualizing Sexual Harassment, Again, *Vicki Schultz*   178
4.4 LGBT Rights at Work   186
     The Social and Economic Imperative of Lesbian, Gay, Bisexual, and Transgendered
          Supportive Organizational Policies, *Eden B. King and José M. Cortina* 186

Legal Perspectives   192
Supreme Court of the United States, *Meritor Savings Bank, FSB v. Vinson, et al.* (1986) 192
Supreme Court of the United States, *Teresa Harris, Petitioner v. Forklift Systems, Inc.* (1993) 193

Cases   194
Case 1: Hiring Discrimination at Bass Pro Shops   194
Case 2: Promotions at Uptown Bottling and Canning Company   195

Case 3: Sexism in Silicon Valley 196
Case 4: A Culture of Sexism and Harassment at Fox News 198
Case 5: Freedom of Expression at American Plastics Products 200
Case 6: Harassment at Brademore Electric 200
Case 7: Gay and Lesbian Rights at Friendly Motors 201
Case 8: A Matter of Integrity? 202

5 Corporate Social Responsibility 204
5.1 Introduction 204
5.2 Shareholder Management versus Stakeholder Management 207
The Social Responsibility of Business Is to Increase Its Profits, *Milton Friedman* 207
The Error at the Heart of Corporate Leadership, *Joseph L. Bower and Lynn S. Paine* 211
Managing for Stakeholders, *R. Edward Freeman* 220
Putting a Stake in Stakeholder Theory, *Eric W. Orts and Alan Strudler* 229
Toward a Theory of Business, *Thomas Donaldson and James P. Walsh* 235

Legal Perspectives 247
Supreme Court of New Jersey, *A. P. Smith Manufacturing Co. v. Barlow* (1953) 247
United States Supreme Court, *Citizens United v. Federal Election Commission* (2010) 247
United States Supreme Court, *Burwell v. Hobby Lobby Stores Inc., et al.* (2014) 248
Johnson & Johnson: Our Credo 249
Republic of India, The Companies Act of 2013 249

Cases 251
Case 1: The 5,000 Percent Price Hike: Turing Pharmaceuticals' Acquisition of Daraprim 251
Case 2: The NYSEG Corporate Responsibility Program 253
Case 3: H. B. Fuller in Honduras: Street Children and Substance Abuse 255
Case 4: Merck and River Blindness 256
Case 5: From Tension to Cooperative Dialogue: Holcim 258
Case 6: ITC's Vocational Training Program 259

6 Ethics and Information Technology 261
6.1 Introduction 261
6.2 Consumer Privacy 263
The Meaning and Value of Privacy, *Daniel J. Solove* 263
Information Technology, Privacy, and the Protection of Personal Data,
Jeroen van den Hoven 267
The Privacy Merchants: What Is to Be Done?, *Amitai Etzioni* 273
6.3 Complicity 279
Internet Content Providers and Complicity in Human Rights Abuse, *Jeffery D. Smith* 279

Cases 289
Case 1: Privacy at MyFriends.Com 289
Case 2: Implanting Microchips in Workers: Improving Efficiency or Invading Privacy? 290
Case 3: Social Media and the Modern Worker: The Use of Facebook as an Organizational
Monitoring and Management Tool 291
Case 4: Facebook's Emotional Contagion Study 293
Case 5: Doing Business in China 294

7 Marketing Ethics   295

7.1 Introduction   295

7.2 Autonomy and Marketing   302

Advertising and Behavior Control, *Robert L. Arrington*   302

Marketing and the Vulnerable, *George G. Brenkert*   308

7.3 Deception and Commercial Speech   315

The Perils of Ignoring History: Big Tobacco Played Dirty and Millions Died. How Similar Is Big Food?, *Kelly D. Brownell and Kenneth E. Warner*   315

Persistent Threats to Commercial Speech, *Jonathan H. Adler*   325

7.4 Pharmaceutical Marketing   330

The Drug Pushers, *Carl Elliott*   330

The Ethics of Direct to Consumer Pharmaceutical Advertising, *Denis G. Arnold*   337

Legal Perspectives   346

United States Court of Appeals for the Seventh Circuit, *B. Sanfield, Inc. v. Finlay Fine Jewelry Corp.* (1999)   346

United States Court of Appeals for the Second Circuit, *Coca-Cola Company v. Tropicana Products, Inc.* (1982)   346

Supreme Court of California, *Kasky v. Nike, Inc.* (2002)   347

United States Supreme Court, *Central Hudson Gas and Electric Corp. v. Public Service Commission* (1980)   348

Cases   349

Case 1: Advice for Sale: How Companies Pay TV Experts for On-Air Product Mentions   349

Case 2: Hucksters in the Classroom   352

Case 3: The Exposure of Children to Erectile Dysfunction Advertising   354

Case 4: Kraft Foods, Inc.: The Cost of Advertising on Children's Waistlines   355

Case 5: Let Them Drink Soda: Coca-Cola's Effort to Influence Public Health Research   359

Case 6: Merck & Company: The Vioxx Recall   361

Case 7: Pfizer: Repeat Offender   365

8 Environmental Sustainability   369

8.1 Introduction   369

8.2 Sustainability and Natural Capitalism   375

Sustainability, *Alan Holland*   375

Natural Capitalism: The Next Industrial Revolution, *Paul Hawken, Amory Lovins, and L. Hunter Lovins*   381

Is It Time to Jump Off the Sustainability Bandwagon?, *Joseph DesJardins*   390

8.3 Corporate Environmental Misconduct   398

Corporate Responsibility, Democracy, and Climate Change, *Denis G. Arnold*   398

Actions Speak Louder than Words: Greenwashing in Corporate America, *Jacob Vos*   404

Legal Perspectives   413

United States Supreme Court, *United States v. Best Foods et al.* (1998)   413

United States Supreme Court, *Whitman v. American Trucking Associations, Inc.* (2001)   413

Cases   415

Case 1: The Cruise Industry: Exotic Promises and Toxic Waters   415

Case 2: Texaco in the Ecuadorean Amazon   417

Case 3: Interface Corporation and Sustainable Business   419
Case 4: What Does It Mean to Be Truly Green? Environmental Sustainability at Frito-Lay
    North America   420
Case 5: Driving Sustainability at Tesla   427
Case 6: The Dirty Truth: Volkswagen's Diesel Deception   429

9 Ethical Issues in International Business   432
  9.1 Introduction   432
  9.2 Relativism vs. Human Rights   436
      Relativism and the Moral Obligations of Multinational Corporations,
        Norman E. Bowie   436
      Corporate Human Rights Obligations, *Denis G. Arnold*   440
  9.3 Sweatshops and Bribery   448
      Sweatshops, *Laura P. Hartman*   448
      Can Global Brands Create Just Supply Chains?, *Richard M. Locke*   453
      Corruption and the Multinational Corporation, *David Hess*   459

  Legal Perspectives   467
  Supreme Court of Texas, *Dow Chemical Company and Shell Oil Company v. Domingo
    Castro Alfaro et al.* (1990)   467
  United States Court of Appeals, Ninth Circuit, *John Doe I, et al. v. Unocal Corp., et al.*
    (2002)   468
  United States Supreme Court, *Kiobel v. Royal Dutch Petroleum Co.* (2013)   468
  The United Nations, *Global Compact*   469
  The United Nations, *Protect, Respect and Remedy Framework for Business and Human
    Rights*   470
  The United Kingdom Bribery Act (2010) and the United States Foreign Corrupt
    Practices Act (1977)   474

  Cases   475
  Case 1: Foreign Assignment   475
  Case 2: Blood, Sweat, and Tears: Child Labor in the Chocolate Supply Chain   476
  Case 3: Chrysler and Gao Feng: Corporate Responsibility for Religious and Political
    Freedom in China   477
  Case 4: Should Walmart Do More? A Case Study in Global Supply Chain Ethics   479
  Case 5: The Hidden Price of Low Cost: Subcontracting in Bangladesh's Garment Industry   481
  Case 6: FIFA's Red Card: Corruption and World Cup Soccer   487
  Case 7: Walmart de México: Millions in Bribes Fuel Growth   489

10 Ethical Markets   492
  10.1 Introduction   492
  10.2 Should Everything Be for Sale?   496
      Noxious Markets, *Deborah Satz*   496
      Markets without Limits, *Jason Brennan and Peter M. Jaworski*   502
      Markets in Utopia, *James Stacey Taylor*   507
  10.3 Price Gouging   512
      The Ethics of Price Gouging, *Matt Zwolinski*   512
      What's the Matter with Price Gouging?, *Jeremy Snyder*   516

10.4 Financial Markets   520
       Ethical Issues in Financial Services, *John R. Boatright*   520
       The Moral Problem of Insider Trading, *Alan Strudler*   527

Legal Perspective   531
United States Supreme Court, *United States, Petitioner v. James Herman O'Hagan*
       (1997)   531

Cases   532
Case 1: Should Everything Be for Sale?   532
Case 2: Like Taking Candy from a Baby? Mylan's Pricing of the EpiPen   533
Case 3: The Big Fix: How Big Banks Colluded to Rig Interest Rates   535
Case 4: Predatory Lending at Countrywide Financial   536
Case 5: Martha Stewart Living Omnimedia, Inc.: An Accusation of Insider Trading   539

11 Economic and Global Justice   542
11.1 Introduction   542
11.2 Economic Justice   549
       An Egalitarian Theory of Justice, *John Rawls*   549
       The Entitlement Theory, *Robert Nozick*   554
       Rich and Poor, *Peter Singer*   557
       Freedom and the Foundations of Justice, *Amartya Sen*   561
11.3 Global Justice   564
       Why Globalization Works, *Martin Wolf*   564
       Globalization Moralized, *Richard W. Miller*   570

Legal Perspective   580
Universal Declaration of Human Rights   580

Cases   583
Case 1: Sapora's Patriarchal Society   583
Case 2: Cocaine at the Fortune 500 Level   584
Case 3: Surviving (?) on a Minimum Wage   585
Case 4: Wages of Failure: The Ethics of Executive Compensation   586
Case 5: SC Johnson: Pyrethrum Sourcing from Kenya   587

Index   589

Cases

Chapter 1

Case 1: The Training Program   39
Case 2: Should Company Policy Apply to All?   39
Case 3: Deceiving Student Loan Borrowers Drives Profits at Navient   40

Chapter 2

Case 1: Outsourcing at Any Cost? Do Corporations Ever Have a Moral Obligation
    Not to Outsource?   81
Case 2: Sexism in the City of London   83
Case 3: Off-Duty Smoking   84
Case 4: Fired for Drinking the Wrong Brand of Beer   84
Case 5: The Other Side of Manufacturing in the United States   85
Case 6: BP's Disastrous Safety Culture   86

Chapter 3

Case 1: Uber's Ethical Leadership Vacuum   147
Case 2: The Bachelor Party   149
Case 3: Wells Fargo's Corporate Culture   149
Case 4: Shareholder Losses and Executive Gains: Bank of America's Acquisition of Merrill Lynch   153
Case 5: Roger Boisjoly and the *Challenger* Disaster: Disloyal Employee or Courageous
    Whistleblower?   156
Case 6: Tainted Medicine   157

Chapter 4

Case 1: Hiring Discrimination at Bass Pro Shops   194
Case 2: Promotions at Uptown Bottling and Canning Company   195
Case 3: Sexism in Silicon Valley   196
Case 4: A Culture of Sexism and Harassment at Fox News   198
Case 5: Freedom of Expression at American Plastics Products   200
Case 6: Harassment at Brademore Electric   200
Case 7: Gay and Lesbian Rights at Friendly Motors   201
Case 8: A Matter of Integrity?   202

Chapter 5

Case 1: The 5,000 Percent Price Hike: Turing Pharmaceuticals' Acquisition of Daraprim   251
Case 2: The NYSEG Corporate Responsibility Program   253
Case 3: H. B. Fuller in Honduras: Street Children and Substance Abuse   255
Case 4: Merck and River Blindness   256
Case 5: From Tension to Cooperative Dialogue: Holcim   258
Case: 6: ITC's Vocational Training Program   259

Chapter 6

Case 1: Privacy at MyFriends.Com 289
Case 2: Implanting Microchips in Workers: Improving Efficiency or Invading Privacy? 290
Case 3: Social Media and the Modern Worker: The Use of Facebook as an Organizational Monitoring and Management Tool 291
Case 4: Facebook's Emotional Contagion Study 293
Case 5: Doing Business in China 294

Chapter 7

Case 1: Advice for Sale: How Companies Pay TV Experts for On-Air Product Mentions 349
Case 2: Hucksters in the Classroom 352
Case 3: The Exposure of Children to Erectile Dysfunction Advertising 354
Case 4: Kraft Foods, Inc.: The Cost of Advertising on Children's Waistlines 355
Case 5: Let Them Drink Soda: Coca-Cola's Effort to Influence Public Health Research 359
Case 6: Merck & Company: The Vioxx Recall 361
Case 7: Pfizer: Repeat Offender 365

Chapter 8

Case 1: The Cruise Industry: Exotic Promises and Toxic Waters 415
Case 2: Texaco in the Ecuadorean Amazon 417
Case 3: Interface Corporation and Sustainable Business 419
Case 4: What Does It Mean to Be Truly Green? Environmental Sustainability at Frito-Lay North America 420
Case 5: Driving Sustainability at Tesla 427
Case 6: The Dirty Truth: Volkswagen's Diesel Deception 429

Chapter 9

Case 1: Foreign Assignment 475
Case 2: Blood, Sweat, and Tears: Child Labor in the Chocolate Supply Chain 476
Case 3: Chrysler and Gao Feng: Corporate Responsibility for Religious and Political Freedom in China 477
Case 4: Should Walmart Do More? A Case Study in Global Supply Chain Ethics 479
Case 5: The Hidden Price of Low Cost: Subcontracting in Bangladesh's Garment Industry 481
Case 6: FIFA's Red Card: Corruption and World Cup Soccer 487
Case 7: Walmart de México: Millions in Bribes Fuel Growth 489

Chapter 10

Case 1: Should Everything Be for Sale? 532
Case 2: Like Taking Candy from a Baby? Mylan's Pricing of the EpiPen 533
Case 3: The Big Fix: How Big Banks Colluded to Rig Interest Rates 535
Case 4: Predatory Lending at Countrywide Financial 536
Case 5: Martha Stewart Living Omnimedia, Inc.: An Accusation of Insider Trading 539

Chapter 11

Case 1: Sapora's Patriarchal Society 583
Case 2: Cocaine at the Fortune 500 Level 584
Case 3: Surviving (?) on a Minimum Wage 585
Case 4: Wages of Failure: The Ethics of Executive Compensation 586
Case 5: SC Johnson: Pyrethrum Sourcing from Kenya 587

Preface

It has been forty years since the publication of the first edition of *Ethical Theory and Business* by Norm Bowie and Tom Beauchamp. At that point in time, the book helped to originate and define the academic field of business ethics. Ethical issues have become even more complex and firm misconduct has not abated; unfortunately, this tenth edition is just as relevant now as it was forty years ago. Subjects covered in the book should be of considerable interest and assistance in addressing the many challenging ethical issues confronted by contemporary business.

In 1979 business ethics was primarily a philosophical field and philosophers were the primary teachers of business ethics courses in colleges and universities. Today, business ethics is a multidisciplinary field with scholars from the social sciences making some of the most important contributions to the field and in the classroom. Social scientists have made particularly important contributions to our understanding of the causes of firm misconduct and to understanding the features of organizational design that hinder or enhance ethical business practices. The tenth edition reflects the multidisciplinary nature of the field by including social scientific as well as philosophical perspectives. The textbook can be readily used by teachers from any field, and will provide students in all majors with cutting edge, multidisciplinary perspectives on the most important ethical issues confronting contemporary business.

With this edition, Cambridge University Press has taken over the publication of the book. As one of the world's leading academic presses, Cambridge will allow the book to remain focused on the needs of faculty and students. This edition contains over twenty new case studies on the many ethical issues in business that have made headlines since the ninth edition was published. Legal perspectives, which our former publisher had placed online and charged a fee for students to access, reappear in this edition in the physical textbook. The legal perspectives have been transformed by the editors into summaries (rather than the previous, edited excerpts from court decisions) making them even more user friendly for students. The book has been expanded to include new material, including stand-alone chapters on management, leadership, and governance, and on the ethical limits of markets. The book has more material than is likely to be used in a single course, and this feature allows faculty to tailor the course to their own needs. Most of the case studies can be used with multiple readings, and not merely with the readings in the chapters in which they appear. Faculty may wish to assign all of the opening chapter to students, or only excerpts from that chapter, something that is facilitated by major section breaks. The great variety of topics in the book is a reflection both of the complex environments in which businesses operate and the growth of the literature in the field. It is hoped that you enjoy the range and variety of subjects that are covered in the following pages.

Denis G. Arnold

1

Ethical Theory and Business Practice

1.1 INTRODUCTION

Can business organizations be just? Should the chief obligation of managers be to look out for the bottom line, or do managers also have obligations to other stakeholders such as customers and employees? Should business organizations be environmentally sustainable? Do global business organizations have obligations to protect human rights wherever they do business? How much influence can businesses legitimately exert over public policy? These are some of the many questions that permeate discussions of the role of ethics in business.

The essays and cases in this book provide an opportunity to discuss these questions by reading and reflecting on influential arguments that have been made on these subjects by leading experts. The goal of this first chapter is to provide a foundation in ethical theory sufficient for reading and critically evaluating the material in the ensuing chapters.

1.2 FUNDAMENTAL CONCEPTS

MORALITY AND ETHICAL THEORY

A distinction between morality and ethical theory is employed in several essays in this volume. *Morality* is concerned with social practices defining right and wrong. These practices – together with other kinds of customs, rules, and mores – are transmitted within cultures and institutions from generation to generation. Similar to political constitutions and natural languages, morality exists prior to the acceptance (or rejection) of its standards by particular individuals. In this respect, morality cannot be purely a personal policy or code and is certainly not confined to the rules in professional codes of conduct adopted by corporations and professional associations.

In contrast with *morality*, the terms *ethical theory* and *moral philosophy* point to reflection on the nature and justification of right actions. These words refer to attempts to introduce clarity, substance, and precision of argument into the domain of morality. Although many people go through life with an understanding of morality dictated by their culture or religion, other persons are not satisfied to merely conform to their upbringing or the doctrines that have been passed on to them. They want difficult ethical questions answered in ways that can be rationally explained and justified and can be coherently linked with other justified beliefs.

Ethical theorists seek to put moral beliefs and social practices of morality into a unified and defensible shape. Sometimes this task involves challenging conventional moral beliefs by assessing the quality of moral arguments and suggesting modifications in existing beliefs. Other times it involves the application of ethical theory to new problems such as privacy in the Internet era, climate change, or pharmaceutical marketing. Morality, we might say, consists of what persons ought to do in order to conform to society's norms of behavior, whereas ethical theory concerns the philosophical reasons for and against aspects of social morality. Usually the latter effort centers on *justification*: philosophers seek to justify a system of standards or some moral point of view on the basis of carefully analyzed and defended concepts and principles such as respect for autonomy, distributive justice, equal treatment, human rights, beneficence, and truthfulness.

Social scientists, on the other hand, are primarily concerned with understanding why individuals, groups, and organizations behave in certain ways. Why are some people more susceptible to peer pressure than others? How can leaders encourage ethical conduct on the part of followers? What do employees perceive to be a just organizational environment, and what do they perceive to be unjust? What types of organizational systems and processes support ethical conduct, and what types support misconduct? These types of questions, and the empirical studies that are designed to answer them, are at the heart of the study of behavioral business ethics. While philosophical ethics is an ancient field of study dating back to at least ancient Greek philosophers such as Socrates, Plato, and Aristotle, behavioral business ethics is a new field of applied psychology and management studies dating from the 1990s. This books includes both subjects.

Most moral principles are already embedded in public morality, but usually in a vague and underanalyzed form. Justice is a good example. Recurrent topics in the pages of the *Wall Street Journal, Fortune, Businessweek*, and other leading business outlets, often discuss the justice of the present system of corporate and individual taxation as well as the salaries and bonuses paid to executives, especially at firms that lost money for shareholders or that require taxpayer bailouts to survive, and the offshore outsourcing of jobs from one country to another. However, an extended or detailed analysis of principles of justice is virtually never provided in the media. Such matters are left at an intuitive level, where the correctness of a particular moral point of view is assumed, without argument.

Yet, the failure to provide anything more than a superficial justification, in terms of intuitive principles learned from parents or peers, leaves people unable to defend their principles when challenged or to persuade others of their position. In a society with many diverse views of morality, one can be fairly sure that one's principles will be challenged. A business person who asserts that a particular practice is morally wrong (or right) can expect to be challenged within her organization by colleagues who disagree. She will have little influence within her organization if she cannot also explain *why* she believes that action is wrong (or right). To defend her assertion she must be able to *justify* her position by providing reasoned arguments. The tools of ethics, then, can be of significant value to students of business, managers, and leaders.

MORALITY AND PRUDENCE

Most students do not encounter ethics as an academic topic of study until college or graduate school. Morality, however, is learned by virtually every young child as part of the acculturation process. The first step in this process is learning to distinguish moral rules from rules of prudence (self-interest). This task can be difficult, because the two kinds of rules are taught simultaneously, without being distinguished by the children's teachers. For example, people are constantly reminded in their early years to observe rules such as "Don't touch the hot stove," "Don't cross the street without looking both ways," "Brush your teeth after meals," and "Eat your vegetables." Most of these "oughts" and "ought nots" are instructions in self-interest – that is, rules of prudence, but moral rules are taught at the same time. Parents, teachers, and peers teach that certain things *ought not* to be done because they are "wrong" (morally) and that certain things *ought* to be done because they are "right" (morally): "Don't pull your sister's hair." "Don't take money from your mother's pocketbook." "Share your toys." "Write a thank-you note to Grandma." These moral instructions seek to control actions that affect the interests of other people. As people mature, they learn what society expects of them in terms of taking into account the interests of other people.

One common observation in business is that self-interest and good ethics generally coincide, because it is usually in one's interest to act morally. We continually hear that good ethics is good business. This fact makes evaluating another's conduct difficult and may tend to confuse moral reasoning with prudential reasoning. An example of how moral and prudential reasoning can run together is evident in the decision BB&T bank made about its home lending practices. During the subprime mortgage lending craze that led to the credit crisis and the great recession, banks and other lenders issued lucrative mortgages to borrowers who could not hope to repay the loans, often using deceptive or predatory means. In the short term, borrowers were able to own homes they could not otherwise afford, and lenders made a lot of money. But in the end many borrowers lost their homes and lenders became unprofitable, went out of business, or required the government to bail them out. North Carolina-based BB&T, with 1,800 regional banking outlets, declined to issue these bad loans and remained profitable throughout the years of the credit crisis and the great recession. In explaining their lending practices, John Allison, the retired CEO of BB&T, said, "Absolutely never do anything that is bad for your client. Maybe you'll make a profit in the short term, but it will come back to haunt you … We knew that housing prices wouldn't go up forever, and we were setting up a lot of young people to have serious economic problems."[1]

Another example of moral and prudential reasoning running together in business is found in the decision of the Marriott Corporation to make a concerted effort to hire persons who had been on welfare. These individuals had often been considered high risk as employees, but changes in the US welfare system forced many welfare recipients to seek work. Marriott was one of the few major companies to take the initiative to hire them in large numbers. Such behavior might be considered an example of moral goodwill and ethical altruism. Although corporate officials at Marriott clearly believed that their decision was ethically sound and promoted the public good, they also believed that their initiative to hire former welfare recipients was good business. J. W. Marriott, Jr., said, "We're getting good employees for the long term, but we're also helping these communities. If we don't step up in these inner cities and provide work, they'll never pull out of it. But it makes bottom line sense. If it didn't, we wouldn't do it."[2]

The mixture of moral language with the language of prudence is often harmless. Many people are more concerned about the *actions* businesses take than with their *motivations* to perform those actions. These people will be indifferent as to whether businesses use the language of prudence or the language of morality to justify what they do, as long as they do the right thing. This distinction between motives and actions is very important to philosophers, however, because a business practice that might be prudentially justified also might lack moral merit or might even be morally wrong. History has shown that some actions that were long accepted or at least condoned in the business community were eventually condemned as morally dubious. Examples include pollution of the air and water, forced labor, deceitful marketing, and large political contributions and lobbying directed at people of political influence.

Business people often reflect on the morality of their actions not because it is prudent to do so but because it is right to do so. For example, Elo TouchSystems Inc., a subsidiary of Raychem Corporation that manufactures computer and other monitors, decided to relocate the company from Oak Ridge, Tennessee, to Freemont, California. As a matter of fidelity to its 300 employees, the company attempted to find new jobs for them in the Oak Ridge area by placing advertisements, sponsoring job fairs, and the like. It also offered generous bonuses for those who would relocate to California. In light of the pool of talent known to the company to be available in California, none of this activity in Tennessee seemed in the company's prudential interest. It simply seemed the morally appropriate policy.

It is widely believed that acting morally is in the interest of business, and thus prudence seems to be one strong motive – perhaps the main motive – for acting ethically. However, throughout this text we will repeatedly see that prudence often dictates a different business decision than does morality. In other words, business people must frequently choose between doing the right thing and doing what is good for business. This conflict informs many of the readings and cases in this book.

MORALITY AND LAW

Business ethics is currently involved in an entangled, complex, and mutually stimulating relationship with the law in various countries and international agreements. Morality and law share concerns over matters of basic social importance and often have in common certain principles, obligations, and criteria of evidence. Law is the public's agency for translating morality into explicit social guidelines and practices and for stipulating punishments for offenses. Several selections in this book mention case law (judge-made laws expressed in court decisions), statutory law (federal and state statutes and their accompanying administrative regulations), and international law (treaties and agreements among nations). In these forms, law has forced vital issues before the public and is frequently the source of emerging issues in business ethics. Case law, in particular, has established influential precedents in the United States that provide material for reflection on both legal and moral questions.

Some have said that corporate concern about business ethics can be reduced or eliminated by turning problems over to the legal department. The operative idea is "Let the lawyers decide; if it's legal, it's moral." Although this tactic would simplify matters, moral evaluation needs to be distinguished from legal evaluation. Despite an intersection between morals and law, the law is not the sole repository of a society's moral standards and values, even when the law is directly concerned with moral problems. A law-abiding person is not necessarily morally sensitive or virtuous, and the fact that something is legally acceptable does not imply that it is morally acceptable. For example, forced labor and slavery have been legal in many nations and are still sanctioned in some rogue nations but are clearly unjust. In Saudi Arabia current laws systematically discriminate against women. "If you're a Saudi woman, you can't board an airplane, get a job, go to school or get married without the permission of a male 'guardian,' whether a husband, father or, if they're both out of the picture, your son."[3] Currently "at-will" employees in the United States and "casual workers" in Australia can be legally fired for morally unacceptable reasons. Many questions are raised in subsequent chapters about the morality of business actions such as plant relocation, outsourcing, and mergers that cause unemployment, even though such actions are not illegal.

Consider the following examples: It was perfectly legal when beer distributor CJW Inc. fired its employee 24-year-old Isac Aguero of Racine, Wisconsin, for drinking a Bud Light at a local bar after work. CJW is the local distributor of Miller beer, and Aguero's bosses disliked his supporting the competition. Because Aguero was an "at-will" employee, he had no legal recourse (see Chapter 2).[4] So too, it was legal when Houston financier Charles E. Hurwitz doubled the rate of tree cutting in the nation's largest privately owned virgin redwood forest. He did so to reduce the debt he incurred when his company, the Maxxam Group, borrowed money to complete a hostile takeover of Pacific Lumber Company, which owned the redwoods. Before the takeover, Pacific Lumber had followed a sustainable cutting policy but nonetheless had consistently operated at a profit. Despite the legality of the new clear-cutting policy initiated by the new owner, it has been criticized as immoral.[5] Lastly, it may have been legal for Merrill Lynch executives to pay themselves millions of dollars in bonuses after losing billions of dollars in shareholder value by making imprudent investments, but most outside observers believe this compensation was unfair (see Chapter 11).

A related problem involves the belief that a person found guilty under law is therefore morally guilty. Such judgments are not necessarily correct, as they depend on either the intention of the agents or the moral acceptability of the law on which the judgment has been reached. For example, if a chemical company is legally liable for polluting the environment, or a pharmaceutical firm is liable for a drug that has harmed certain patients, it does not follow that any form of moral wrongdoing, culpability, or guilt is associated with the activity.

Asbestos litigation is a well-known example. Because of the strength, durability, and fire resistance of asbestos, it was used in thousands of consumer, automotive, scientific, industrial, and maritime processes and products. Virtually no serious social attention was paid to asbestos in the United States until 1964, when a strong link was established between asbestos dust and disease. As many as 27 million US workers may have been exposed to this fiber, and 100 million people may have been exposed to asbestos in buildings. Manufacturers did not know about these problems of disease until around 1964; but beginning with the 1982 bankruptcy of the Johns-Manville Corporation, many corporations were successfully sued. The problem continues to escalate today, especially owing to cases brought by mesothelioma patients and by persons who worked with asbestos but actually have no asbestos-related illness. Over the years of litigation, at least 8,000 companies have been sued, 95 corporations have been bankrupted, and costs have exceeded $70 billion. Although asbestos manufacturers and their customers originally had good intentions and good products, they paid a steep price under the law.[6]

Furthermore, the courts have often been accused of causing moral inequities through court judgments rendered against corporations.[7] For example, Dow Corning was successfully sued by plaintiffs alleging that personal injuries resulted from Dow's silicone breast implants, leading the company to file bankruptcy. After an exhaustive study, the US Food and Drug Administration concluded that there is no evidence that silicone breast implants present health risks. In another case, Chevron Oil was successfully sued for mislabeling its cans of the herbicide paraquat, although the offending label conformed exactly to federal regulations, which permitted no other form of label to be used. In both cases it is easy to understand why critics have considered various regulations, legislation, and case-law decisions unjustified.

Taken together, these considerations lead to the following conclusions: If something is legal, it is not necessarily moral; if something is illegal, it is not necessarily immoral. To discharge one's legal obligations is not necessarily to discharge one's moral obligations.

THE RULE OF CONSCIENCE

The slogan "Let your conscience be your guide" has long been, for many, what morality is all about. Yet, despite their admiration for persons of conscience, ethicists have typically judged appeals to conscience alone as insufficient and untrustworthy for ethical judgment. Consciences vary radically from person to person and time to time; moreover, they are often altered by circumstance, religious belief, childhood, and training. One example is found in the action of

Stanley Kresge, the son of the founder of S. S. Kresge Company – now known as the K-Mart Corporation – who is a teetotaler for religious reasons. When the company started selling beer and wine, Kresge sold all his stock. His conscience, he said, would not let him make a profit on alcohol. The company, though, dismissed his objection as "his own business" and said that it saw nothing wrong with earning profits on alcohol.[8] A second example is that of factory farming animals in confined conditions that cause them significant pain and suffering and that require the use of antibiotics to prevent disease. Many consumers don't believe there is anything morally objectionable about these practices since it provides them with inexpensive protein, but increasing numbers of consumers believe that the pain caused to animals is unjustified and that the use of antibiotics is harmful to human health. Their consciences lead them to choose pasture farmed animal products or to adopt vegetarian diets. The consciences of some people lead them to take further action and to join activist groups and to protest factory farming. In rare cases, activists have physically destroyed factory farm facilities.

In any given classroom, the consciences of students will lead them to have different views about the moral legitimacy of using marijuana, hacking, or lying on one's résumé. The reliability of conscience, in short, is not self-certifying. Moral justification must be based on a source external to individual conscience.

APPROACHES TO THE STUDY OF ETHICS

Morality and ethical theory can be studied and developed by a variety of methods, but three general approaches have dominated the literature. Two of these approaches describe and analyze morality, presumably without taking moral positions. The other approach takes a moral position and appeals to morality or ethical theory to underwrite judgments. These three approaches are (1) descriptive, (2) conceptual, and (3) normative (prescriptive). These categories do not express rigid and always clearly distinguishable approaches. Nonetheless, when understood as broad positions, they can serve as models of inquiry and as valuable distinctions.

Social scientists often refer to the first approach as the *descriptive approach*, or the *scientific study* of ethics. Factual description and explanation of moral behavior and beliefs of employees, managers, leaders, and organizations, as performed by management and organization science scholars, are typical of this approach. The second approach involves the *conceptual study* of significant terms in ethics. Here, the meanings of terms such as *right, obligation, justice, good, virtue*, and *responsibility* are analyzed. Crucial terms in business ethics such as *liability, deception, corporate intention*, and *stakeholder* can be given this same kind of careful conceptual attention. The proper analysis of the term *morality* (as defined at the beginning of this chapter) and the distinction between the moral and the nonmoral are typical examples of these conceptual problems.

The third approach, *normative (prescriptive) ethics*, is a prescriptive study attempting to formulate and defend basic moral norms. Normative business ethics aims at determining what *ought* to be done, which needs to be distinguished from what *is*, in fact, practiced. Ideally, an ethical theory provides reasons for adopting a whole system of moral principles or virtues. *Utilitarianism* and *Kantianism* are the two most influential theories and a basic understanding of them is essential for all university students. Utilitarians argue that there is but a single fundamental principle determining right action, which can be roughly stated as follows: "An action is morally right if and only if it produces at least as great a balance of value over disvalue as any available alternative action." Kantians, by contrast, have argued for principles that specify obligations rather than a balance of value. For example, one of Kant's best-known principles of obligation is "Never treat another person merely as a means to your own goals," even if doing so creates a net balance of positive value. Both forms of these theories, together with other dimensions of ethical theory, are examined later in this chapter.

Principles of normative ethics are commonly used to treat specific moral problems such as fairness in contracts, conflicts of interest, environmental pollution, mistreatment of animals, and racial and sexual discrimination. This use of ethical theory is often referred to, somewhat misleadingly, as *applied ethics*. Philosophical treatment of business ethics involves the focused analysis of a moral problem and the use of careful reasoning that employs general ethical principles to attempt to resolve problems that commonly arise in the professions.

Substantially the same general ethical principles apply to the problems across professional fields, such as engineering and medicine, and in areas beyond professional ethics as well. One might appeal to principles of justice, for example, to illuminate and resolve issues of taxation, healthcare distribution, responsibility for environmental harm, criminal punishment, and racial discrimination. Similarly, principles of veracity (truthfulness) apply to debates about secrecy and deception in international politics, misleading advertisements in business ethics, balanced reporting in journalistic ethics, and disclosure of illness to a patient in medical ethics. Increased clarity about the general conditions under which truth must be told and when it may be withheld would presumably enhance understanding of moral requirements in each of these areas.

The exercise of sound judgment in business practice together with appeals to ethical theory are central in the essays and cases in this volume. Rarely is there a straightforward "application" of principles that mechanically resolves problems. Principles are more commonly *specified*, that is, made more concrete for the context, than applied. Much of the best work in contemporary business ethics involves arguments for how to specify principles to handle particular problems.

1.3 FUNDAMENTAL PROBLEMS

RELATIVISM AND OBJECTIVITY OF BELIEF

Some writers have contended that moral views simply express the ways in which a culture both limits and accommodates the desires of its people. In the early part of the twentieth century, defenders of relativism used the discoveries of anthropologists in the South Sea Islands, Africa, and South America as evidence of a diversity of moral practices throughout the world. Their empirical discoveries about what is the case led them to the conclusion that moral rightness is contingent on cultural beliefs and that the concepts of rightness and wrongness are meaningless apart from the specific historical and cultural contexts in which they arise. The claim is that patterns of culture can be understood only as unique wholes and that moral beliefs about moral behavior are closely connected in a culture.

Descriptive claims about what *is* the case in cultures have often been used by relativists to justify a *normative* position as to what *should* be the case or what *ought* to be believed. That is, some ethical relativists assert that whatever a culture thinks is right or wrong really is right or wrong for the members of that culture. This thesis is normative, because it makes a value judgment; it delineates *which standards or norms correctly determine right and wrong behavior*. Thus, if the Swedish tradition allows abortion, then abortion really is morally permissible in Sweden. If the Mexican tradition forbids abortion, then abortion really is wrong in Mexico.

Ethical relativism provides a theoretical basis for those who challenge what they consider to be the imposition of Western values on the rest of the world. Specifically, some spokespersons in Asia have criticized what they regard as the attempts of Westerners to impose their values (as the normatively correct values) on Asian societies. For example, it is argued that Asians give more significant value than do Westerners to the welfare of society when it is in conflict with the welfare of the individual. However, it has also been pointed out that because of the range of values embraced by and within Asian nations it is all but impossible to say that there is such an entity as "Asian values." Secular Asian societies such as India, for example, have long traditions of respect for individual rights and embrace values consonant with Western societies. Also, younger generations tend to have significantly different views about the rights of individuals from those of older generations.

Despite the influence of relativism and multiculturalism, there have been many recent attempts by government agencies, non-governmental organizations, and multinational corporations to promulgate international codes of business conduct that surmount relativism (see Chapter 9). In the era of economic globalization, these efforts are increasing rather than diminishing.

Ethical theorists have tended to reject relativism, and it is important to understand why. First, we need to ask: What does the argument from the fact of cultural diversity reveal? When early anthropologists probed beneath surface "moral" disagreements, they often discovered agreement at deeper levels on more basic values. For example, one anthropologist discovered a tribe in which parents, after raising their children and when still in a relatively healthy state, would climb a high tree. Their children would then shake the tree until the parents fell to the ground and died. This cultural practice seems vastly different from Western practices. The anthropologist discovered, however, that the tribe believed that people went into the afterlife in the same bodily state in which they left this life. Their children, who wanted them to enter the afterlife in a healthy state, were no less concerned about their parents than are children in Western cultures. Although cultural disagreement exists concerning the afterlife (a disagreement about what is or is not the case), there is no ultimate *moral* disagreement over the moral principles determining how children should treat their parents.

A contemporary business example can also help illustrate this point. Bribery is widely used by businesses to obtain contracts in Afghanistan and Russia, but is regarded as an unacceptable means to secure contracts in Canada and Australia. This might be taken to show that bribery really is morally permissible in Afghanistan and Russia and wrong in Canada and Australia. However, the fact that bribery is widely practiced in Afghanistan and Russia does not necessarily mean that it is regarded as morally acceptable behavior by most people in those nations. It is more likely the case that those who engage in bribery simply have greater power than do most people in those nations and so can engage in the behavior without repercussions.

Despite their many obvious differences of practice and belief, people often do actually agree about what may be called *ultimate moral standards*. For example, both Germany and the United States have laws to protect consumers from the adverse effects of new drugs and to bring drugs to the market as quickly as possible so that lives are saved. Yet, Germany and the United States have different standards for making the trade-off between protecting consumers from side-effects and saving lives as soon as possible. This suggests that two cultures may agree about basic principles of morality yet disagree about how to implement those principles in particular situations.

In many "moral controversies," people seem to differ only because they have different *factual* beliefs. For instance, individuals often differ over appropriate actions to protect the environment, not because they have different sets of standards about environmental ethics, but because they hold different factual views about how certain discharges of chemicals and airborne particles will or will not harm the environment. Climate change is a good example (see Chapter 8). A warming climate will cause harm to many people through, for example, droughts in some areas and rising seas in other areas. The vast majority of climate scientists, as well as scientists in related fields, believe that currently occurring climate change is caused by human greenhouse gas emissions (for example, the use of fossil fuels) and deforestation. However, many politicians claim that the science is inconclusive and that current climate change is a natural phenomenon. This difference in factual beliefs leads to differences about what public policies and business policies should be followed. Identical sets of normative standards may be invoked in their arguments about environmental protection, yet different policies and actions may be recommended.

It is therefore important to distinguish *relativism of judgments* from *relativism of standards*. Differing judgments may rely on the same general standards for their justification. Relativism of judgment is so pervasive in human social life that it would be foolish to deny it. People may differ in their judgments about whether one policy regarding keeping sensitive customer information confidential is more acceptable than another, but it does not follow that they have different moral standards regarding confidentiality. The people may hold the same moral standard(s) on protecting confidentiality but differ over how to implement the standard(s).

However, these observations do not determine whether a relativism of standards provides the most adequate account of morality. If moral conflict did turn out to be a matter of a fundamental conflict of moral *standards*, such conflict could not be removed even if there were perfect agreement about the facts, concepts, and background beliefs of a case. Suppose, then, that disagreement does in fact exist at the deepest level of moral thinking – that is, suppose that two cultures disagree on basic or fundamental norms. It does not follow even from this *relativity of standards* that there is no ultimate norm or set of norms in which everyone *ought* to believe. To see why, consider the following analogy to religious disagreement: From the fact that people have incompatible religious or atheistic beliefs, it does not follow that there is no single correct set of religious or atheistic propositions. Nothing more than skepticism seems justified by the facts about religion that are adduced by anthropology. Similarly, nothing more than such skepticism about the moral standards would be justified if fundamental conflicts of *moral standards* were discovered in ethics.

The evident inconsistency of ethical relativism with many of our most cherished moral beliefs is another reason to be doubtful of it. No general theory of ethical relativism is likely to convince us that a belief is acceptable merely because others believe in it strongly enough, although that is exactly the commitment of this theory. At least some moral views seem relatively more enlightened, no matter how great the variability of beliefs. The idea that practices such as slavery, forced labor, sexual exploitation under severe threat, employment discrimination against women, and grossly inequitable salaries cannot be evaluated across cultures by some common standard seems morally unacceptable, not morally enlightened. It is one thing to suggest that such beliefs might be *excused* (and persons found nonculpable), still another to suggest that they are *right*.

When two parties argue about some serious, divisive, and contested moral issue – for example, conflicts of interest in business – people tend to think that some fair and justified judgment may be reached. People seldom infer from the mere fact of a conflict between beliefs that there is no way to judge one view as correct or as better argued or more reasonable than the other. The more absurd the position advanced by one party, the more convinced others become that some views are mistaken, unreasonable, or require supplementation.

MORAL DISAGREEMENTS

Whether or not ethical relativism is a tenable theory, we must confront the indisputable fact of moral disagreement. In any pluralistic culture many conflicts of value exist. In this volume a number of controversies and dilemmas are examined, including trade-offs between cost-cutting and protecting workers, blowing the whistle on the unethical or illegal activities of one's company versus company loyalty, deceptive marketing versus lower profits, insider trading, exploitation of labor in sweatshops, and the like. Although disagreements run deep in these controversies, there are ways to resolve them or at least to reduce levels of conflict. Several methods have been employed in the past to deal constructively with moral disagreements, each of which deserves recognition as a method of easing disagreement and conflict.

Obtaining Objective Information. Many moral disagreements can be at least partially resolved by obtaining additional factual information on which moral controversies turn. Earlier it was shown how useful such information can be in trying to ascertain whether cultural variations in belief are fundamental. It has often been assumed that moral disputes are by definition produced solely by differences over moral principles or their application and not by a lack of scientific or factual information. This assumption is misleading inasmuch as moral disputes – that is, disputes over what morally ought or ought not to be done – often have nonmoral elements as their main ingredients. For example, debates over the allocation of tax dollars to prevent accidents or disease in the workplace often become bogged down in factual issues of whether particular measures such as the use of protective masks or lower levels of toxic chemicals actually function better to prevent death and disease.

Another example is provided by the dispute between Greenpeace and Royal Dutch Shell. After lengthy investigation, Royal Dutch Shell proposed to sink a loading and storage buoy for oil deep in the North Sea (off the coast of England). Despite evidence that such an operation posed no environmental danger, Greenpeace conducted protests and even used a group of small boats to thwart the attempt. Royal Dutch Shell yielded to its critics, and the buoy was cut up and made into a quay in Norway. Later, however, Greenpeace came to the conclusion that new facts indicated that there had never been any serious environmental danger. Furthermore, it appears that Greenpeace's recommended method of disposing of the buoy caused environmental harm that would have been avoided by sinking it, as Shell had originally planned.

Controversial issues such as the following are laced with issues of both values and facts: how satisfactorily toxic substances are monitored in the workplace; how a start-up company has "appropriated" an established company's trade secrets; what effects access to pornography through the Internet produces; whether an extension of current copyright laws would reduce sharing of copyrighted recordings on the Internet; and how vaccines for medical use should be manufactured, disseminated, and advertised. The arguments used by disagreeing parties may turn on a dispute about liberty, harm, or justice and therefore may be primarily moral; but they may also rest on factual disagreements over, for example, the effects of a product, service, or activity. Information may thus have only a limited bearing on the resolution of some controversies, yet it may have a direct and almost overpowering influence in others.

Definitional Clarity. Sometimes, controversies have been settled by reaching conceptual or definitional agreement over the language used by disputing parties. Controversies discussed in Chapter 4 about ethical issues regarding diversity and sexual harassment, for example, are often needlessly complicated because different senses of these expressions are employed, and yet disputing parties may have a great deal invested in their particular definitions. If there is no common point of contention in such cases, parties will be addressing entirely separate issues through their conceptual assumptions. Often, these parties will not have a bona fide moral disagreement but, rather, a purely conceptual one.

Although conceptual agreement provides no guarantee that a dispute will be settled, it will facilitate direct discussion of the outstanding issues. For this reason, many essays in this volume dwell at some length on problems of conceptual clarity.

Analysis of Arguments and Positions. Finally, an important method of inquiry is that of exposing the inadequacies in and unexpected consequences of arguments and positions. A moral argument that leads to conclusions that a proponent is not prepared to defend and did not previously anticipate will have to be changed, and the distance between those who disagree will perhaps be reduced by this process. Inconsistencies not only in reasoning but in organizational schemes or pronouncements can be uncovered. However, in a context of controversy, sharp attacks or critiques are unlikely to eventuate in an agreement unless a climate of reason prevails. A fundamental axiom of successful negotiation is "reason and be open to reason." The axiom holds for moral discussion as well as for any other disagreement.

No contention is made here that moral disagreements can always be resolved or that every reasonable person must accept the same method for approaching disagreement. Many moral problems may not be resolvable by any of the four methods that have been discussed. A single ethical theory or method may never be developed to resolve all disagreements adequately, and the pluralism of cultural beliefs often presents a barrier to the resolution of issues. Given the possibility of continual disagreement, the resolution of cross-cultural conflicts such as those faced by multinational corporations may prove especially elusive. However, if something is to be done about these problems, a resolution seems more likely to occur if the methods outlined in this section are used.

THE PROBLEM OF EGOISM

Attitudes in business have often been deemed fundamentally egoistic. Executives and corporations are said to act purely from prudence – that is, each business is out to promote solely its own interest in a context of competition. Some people say that the corporation has no other interest, because its goal is to be as economically successful in competition as possible.

The philosophical theory called *egoism* has familiar origins. We have all been confronted with occasions on which we must make a choice between spending money on ourselves or on some worthy charitable enterprise. When one elects to purchase new clothes for oneself rather than contribute to famine relief in Africa, one is giving priority to self-interest over the interests of others. Egoism generalizes beyond these occasions to all human choices. The egoist contends that all choices either do involve or should involve self-promotion as their sole objective. Thus, a person's or a corporation's goal and perhaps only obligation is self-promotion. No sacrifice or obligation is owed to others.

There are two main varieties of egoism: psychological egoism and ethical egoism. We will discuss each in turn.

Psychological Egoism. Psychological egoism is the view that everyone is always motivated to act in his or her perceived self-interest. This factual theory regarding human motivation offers an *explanation* of human conduct, in contrast with a *justification* of human conduct. It claims that people always do what pleases them or what is in their interest. Popular ways of expressing this viewpoint include the following: "People are at heart selfish, even if they appear to be unselfish"; "People look out for Number One first"; "In the long run, everybody does what he or she wants to do"; and "No matter what a person says, he or she acts for the sake of personal satisfaction."

If psychological egoism is true it would present a serious challenge to normative moral philosophy. If this theory is correct, there is no purely altruistic moral motivation. Yet, normative ethics appears to presuppose that people ought to behave in accordance with the demands of morality, whether or not such behavior promotes their own interests. If people *must act* in their own interest, to ask them to sacrifice for others would be absurd. Accordingly, if psychological egoism is true, the whole enterprise of normative ethics is futile. However, psychologists have shown that humans act on a variety of motives.

Those who accept psychological egoism are convinced that their theory of motivation is correct. Conversely, those who reject the theory do so not only because they see many examples of altruistic behavior in the lives of friends, colleagues, saints, heroes, and public servants, but also because contemporary anthropology, psychology, and biology offer some compelling studies of sacrificial behavior. Even if people are basically selfish, critics of egoism maintain that there are at least some compelling examples of preeminently unselfish actions such as corporations that reduce profits to provide services to communities in need (see Chapter 5) and employees who "blow the whistle" on unsafe or otherwise improper business practices even though they could lose their jobs and suffer social ostracism (see Chapter 3).

The defender of psychological egoism is not impressed by the exemplary lives of saints and heroes or by social practices of corporate sacrifice. The psychological egoist maintains that all who expend effort to help others, to promote fairness in competition, to promote the general welfare, or to risk their lives for the welfare of others are, underneath it all, acting to promote themselves. By sacrificing for their children, parents seek the satisfaction that comes from their children's development or achievements. By following society's moral and legal codes, people avoid both the police and social ostracism.

Egoists maintain that no matter how self-sacrificing one's behavior may at times seem, the desire behind the action is self-regarding. One is ultimately out for oneself, whether in the long or the short run, and whether one realizes it or not. Egoists view self-promoting actions as perfectly compatible with behavior that others categorize as altruistic. For example, many corporations have adopted "enlightened self-interest" policies through which they respond to community needs and promote worker satisfaction to promote their corporate image and ultimately their earnings. The clever person or corporation can appear to be unselfish, but the action's true character depends on the *motivation* behind the appearance. Honest corporate leaders will, in the view of the egoist, emulate General Electric chairman and CEO Jeffery Immelt, who announced GE's new "ecoimagination" environmental initiative, saying, "we can improve the environment and make money doing it. We see that green is green."[9] According to the egoist, apparently altruistic agents who are less honest than Immelt may simply believe that an unselfish appearance best promotes their long-range interests. From the egoist's point of view, the fact that some (pseudo?) sacrifices may be necessary in the short run does not count against egoism.

Consider the following example. Since the late 1980s, the pharmaceutical company Merck has spent hundreds of millions of dollars to help eradicate diseases such as river blindness (onchocerciasis) and elephantiasis (lymphatic filariasis) in the developing world (see Chapter 5). Partly as a result of these activities, Merck had enjoyed a "sterling reputation" as "the most ethical of the major drug companies."[10] However, in 2004 Merck's chairman and CEO, Raymond Gilmartin, was called before the US Senate Finance Committee to testify about his company's problematic arthritis drug Vioxx (rofecoxib) which was subsequently withdrawn from the market (see Chapter 7). Observers noted that Gilmartin was treated gently – even kindly – by the senators. They attributed the gentle treatment to Merck's past record of ethical leadership. (This treatment contrasted significantly with the harsh criticism executives at companies involved in the financial crisis of 2008 received from Congress.) From the perspective of egoists, Merck's efforts at combating diseases in the developing world should be understood entirely as self-interested activity. As evidence of this claim they point to the favorable treatment Merck received by Congress as a direct result of those and other allegedly altruistic activities.

Even if Merck's behavior is best explained as motivated by self-interest, it need not follow that all human behavior can be best explained as motivated by self-interest. The question remains: Is psychological egoism correct? At one level this question can be answered only by empirical data – by looking at the facts. Significantly, there is a large body of evidence both from observations of daily practice and from experiments in psychological laboratories that counts against the universality of egoistic motivation. The evidence from daily practice is not limited to heroic action but includes such mundane practices as voting and leaving tips in restaurants and hotels where a person does not expect to return and has nothing to gain.

It is tempting for the psychological egoist to make the theory *necessarily* true because of the difficulties in proving it to be *empirically* true. When confronted with what look like altruistic acts, egoists may appeal to unconscious motives of self-interest or claim that every act is based on some desire of the person performing the act. For example, the egoist will note that people will feel good after performing allegedly altruistic acts and then claim that it is the desire to feel good that motivated the person in the first place.

The latter explanation seems to be a conceptual or verbal trick: the egoist has changed the meaning of *self-interest*. At first, *self-interest* meant "acting exclusively on behalf of one's own self-serving interest." Now the word has been redefined to mean "acting on any interest one has." In other words, the egoist has conceptualized "interest" to always entail self-interested motivation. If psychological egoists are right, we never intend impartially to help a child, loved one, friend, or colleague but only to achieve our own satisfaction. But even if an act brings satisfaction, it does not follow that one was motivated by the goal of satisfaction or intended some form of satisfaction. Finally, notice one other feature about psychological egoism. If it is an accurate description of human nature, then humans are *incapable* of acting out of any interest but self-interest. Principled actions based on motives, such as respect for other persons, the greater good, or justice, are not, in this view, motives humans are capable of acting from.

Ethical Egoism. Ethical egoism is a theory stating that the supreme principle of conduct is to promote one's well-being above everyone else's. Whereas psychological egoism is a *descriptive*, psychological theory about human motivation, ethical egoism is a *normative* theory about what people ought to do. According to psychological egoism, people always *do* act on the basis of perceived self-interest. According to ethical egoism, people always *ought* to act on the basis of self-interest.

Ethical egoism contrasts sharply with common moral beliefs. Consider the maxim "You're a sucker if you don't put yourself first and others second." This maxim is generally thought morally unacceptable, because morality obligates people to return a lost wallet to an owner and to correct a bank loan officer's errors in their favor. Nevertheless, questions about why people should look out for the interests of others on such occasions have troubled many reflective persons. Some have concluded that acting against one's interest is contrary to reason. These thinkers, who regard conventional morality as tinged with irrational sentiment and indefensible constraints on the individual, are the supporters of ethical egoism. It is not their view that one should always ignore the interests of others but, rather, that one should take account of and act on the interests of others only if it suits one's own interests to do so.

What would society be like if ethical egoism were the conventional, prevailing theory of proper conduct? Some philosophers and political theorists have argued that anarchism and chaos would result unless preventive measures were adopted. A classic statement of this position was made by the philosopher Thomas Hobbes (1588–1679). Imagine a world with limited resources, he said, where persons are approximately equal in their ability to harm one another and where everyone acts exclusively in his or her interest. Hobbes argued that in such a world everyone would be at everyone else's throat, and society would be plagued by anxiety, violence, and constant danger. As Hobbes declared, life would be "solitary, poor, nasty, brutish, and short."[11] However, Hobbes also assumed that human beings are sufficiently rational to recognize their interests. To avoid the war of all against all, he urged his readers to form a powerful government to protect themselves.

Egoists accept Hobbes's view in the following form: Any clever person will realize that she or he has no moral obligations to others besides those obligations she or he voluntarily assumes because it is in one's own interest to agree to abide by them. Each person should accept moral rules and assume specific obligations only when doing so promotes one's self-interest. In agreeing to live under laws of the state that are binding on everyone, one should obey these laws only to protect oneself and to create a situation of communal living that is personally advantageous. One should also back out of an obligation whenever it becomes clear that it is to one's long-range disadvantage to fulfill the obligation. When confronted by a social revolution, the questionable trustworthiness of a colleague, or an incompetent administration at one's place of employment, no one is under an obligation to obey the law, fulfill contracts, or tell the truth. These obligations exist only because one assumes them, and one ought to assume them only as long as doing so promotes one's own interest.

An arrangement whereby everyone acted on more or less fixed rules such as those found in conventional moral and legal systems would produce the most desirable state of affairs for each individual from an egoistic point of view. The reason is that such rules arbitrate conflicts and make social life more agreeable. These rules would include, for example, familiar moral and legal principles of justice that are intended to make everyone's situation more secure and stable.

Only an unduly narrow conception of self-interest, the egoist might argue, leads critics to conclude that the egoist would not willingly observe conventional rules of justice. If society can be structured to resolve personal conflicts through courts and other peaceful means, egoists will view it as in their interest to accept those binding social arrangements, just as they will perceive it as prudent to treat other individuals favorably in personal contexts.

The egoist is not saying that his or her interests are served by promoting the good of others but, rather, is claiming that his or her personal interests are served by observing impartial rules that protect one's interest, irrespective of the outcome for others. Egoists do not care about the welfare of others unless it affects their welfare, and this desire for personal well-being alone motivates acceptance of the conventional rules of morality.

Egoistic Business Practices and Utilitarian Results. A different view from that of Hobbes, and one that has been influential in some parts of the business community, is found in Adam Smith's (1723–90) economic and moral writings. Smith believed that the public good – especially in the commercial world – evolves out of a suitably restrained clash of competing individual interests. As individuals pursue their self-interest, the interactive process is guided by an "invisible hand," ensuring that the public interest is achieved. Ironically, according to Smith, egoism in commercial transactions leads not to the war of all against all but, rather, to a utilitarian outcome – that is, to the largest number of benefits for the largest number of persons. The free market is, Smith thought, a better method of achieving the public good, however inadvertently, than the highly visible hand of Hobbes's all-powerful sovereign state.

Smith believed that government should be limited in order to protect individual freedom. At the same time, he recognized that concern with freedom and self-interest could get out of control. Hence, he proposed that minimal state regulatory activity is needed to provide and enforce the rules of the competitive game. Smith's picture of a restrained egoistic world has captivated many people interested in the business and economic community.[12] They, like Smith, do not picture themselves as selfish and indifferent to the interests of others, and they recognize that a certain element of cooperation is essential if their interests are to flourish. They recognize that when their interests conflict with the interests of others, they should pursue their interests within the established rules of the competitive game. (Smith was writing about small businesses and privately held companies, since the modern, publicly held corporation did not yet exist.)

Such a restrained egoism is one form of defense of a free-market economy; competition among individual firms advances the utilitarian good of society as a whole. Hence, a popular view of business ethics is captured by the phrase "Ethical egoism leads to utilitarian outcomes." As Smith said, corporations and individuals pursuing their individual interests thereby promote the public good, so long as they abide by the rules that protect the public.

Some people believe that a contemporary example is found in the way world hunger can be alleviated as a result of capitalistic behavior (see Chapter 9). They claim that capitalistic investment and productivity increase jobs, social welfare, social cooperation, wealth in society, and morally responsible behavior. The thesis is that these benefits accrue widely across the society, affecting both poor and wealthy, even if the goal of capitalists is purely their own economic gain.[13]

Critics of this argument note that although global capitalism can generate significant benefits, the ability to generate many of those benefits presumes that certain regulatory controls are in place in the nations in which business is conducted. At the very least, there must be regulation to ensure that there is a free market. Also, developing nations often lack the framework of laws, policing authorities, and judicial review presumed by Smith. In such circumstances, the unrestrained pursuit of self-interest can result in the exploitation of workers, and environmental practices that are harmful to human welfare and increase rather than decrease poverty. For example, a business may take advantage of the fact that a developing nation has no means of occupational safety enforcement and, to save money, may choose not to put in place standards for protecting workers from injury by exposure to toxic chemicals or poorly maintained machinery.

An important and neglected aspect of Smith's defense of capitalism is that it was predicated on his theory of ethics.[14] (Smith held the Chair in Moral Philosophy at the University of Glasgow for over ten years.) Egoists typically neglect important features of Smith's thinking about ethics and human behavior. Smith did argue that *prudence*, or the careful pursuit of one's self-interest, is a virtue. But he also argued that *benevolence*, or actions directed at the good of others, is an equally important virtue, one that is necessary for social welfare. And he warned against the self-interested partiality in our judgments. A minimal regulatory environment for business was possible without resulting in the anarchy predicted by Hobbes, Smith argued, because of the sympathetic nature of persons and our capacity for benevolence.

1.4 NORMATIVE ETHICAL THEORY

The central question discussed in this section is: What constitutes an acceptable ethical standard for business practice, and by what authority is the standard acceptable? One time-honored answer is that the acceptability of a moral standard is determined by prevailing practices in business or by authoritative, profession-generated documents such as codes. Many business persons find this viewpoint congenial and therefore do not see the need for revisions in practices that they find already comfortable and adequate.

Professional standards do play a role in business ethics and will be discussed in later chapters in this book. Ultimately, however, the internal morality of business does not supply a comprehensive framework for the many pressing questions of business ethics. Morality in the world of business evolves in the face of social change and critical philosophical argument; it cannot rely entirely on its own historical traditions. Its standards therefore need to be justified in terms of independent ethical standards such as those of public opinion, law, and philosophical ethics – just as the moral norms of a culture need to be justified by more than an appeal to those norms themselves. The following two parts of this section are devoted to two ethical theories that have been particularly influential in moral philosophy: utilitarianism and Kantianism. Some knowledge of these theories is indispensable for reflective study in business ethics, because a sizable part of the field's literature draws on methods and conclusions found in these theories.

UTILITARIAN THEORIES

Utilitarian theories hold that the moral worth of actions or practices is determined by their consequences. An action or practice is right if it leads to the best possible balance of good consequences over bad consequences for all the parties affected. In taking this perspective, utilitarians believe that the purpose or function of ethics is to promote human welfare by minimizing harms and maximizing benefits.

The first developed philosophical writings that made the category of "utility" central in moral philosophy were those of David Hume (1711–76), Jeremy Bentham (1748–1832), and John Stuart Mill (1806–73). Mill's *Utilitarianism* (1863) is still today considered the standard statement of this theory. Mill discusses two foundations or sources of utilitarian thinking: a *normative* foundation in the "principle of utility" and a *psychological* foundation in human nature. He proposes his principle of utility – the "greatest happiness principle" – as the foundation of normative ethical theory. *Actions are right*, Mill says, *in proportion to their tendency to promote happiness or absence of pain, and wrong insofar as they tend to produce pain or displeasure.* According to Mill, pleasure and freedom from pain are alone desirable as ends. All desirable things (which are numerous) are desirable either for the pleasure inherent in them or as means to promote pleasure and prevent pain.

Mill's second foundation derives from his belief that most persons, and perhaps all, have a basic desire for unity and harmony with their fellow human beings. Just as people feel horror at crimes, he says, they have a basic moral sensitivity to the needs of others. Mill sees the purpose of morality as tapping natural human sympathies to benefit others while controlling unsympathetic attitudes that cause harm to others. The principle of utility is conceived as the best means to these basic human goals.

Essential Features of Utilitarianism. Several essential features of utilitarianism are present in the theories of Mill and other utilitarians. First, utilitarianism is committed to the maximization of the good and the minimization of harm and evil. It asserts that society ought always to produce the greatest possible balance of positive value or the minimum balance of disvalue for all persons affected. The means to maximization is efficiency, a goal that persons in business find congenial, because it is highly prized throughout the economic sector. Efficiency is a means to higher profits and lower prices, and the struggle to be maximally profitable seeks to obtain maximum production from limited economic resources. The utilitarian commitment to the principle of optimal productivity through efficiency is, in this regard, an essential part of the traditional business conception of society and a standard part of business practice.

Many businesses, as well as government agencies, have adopted specific tools such as cost–benefit analysis, risk assessment, or management by objectives – all of which are strongly influenced by a utilitarian philosophy. Other businesses do not employ such specific tools but make utilitarian judgments about the benefits and costs of having layoffs, conducting advertising campaigns, hiring lobbyists, paying CEOs, and providing employee benefits. Though unpopular in the short term, many adjustments are often welcomed because they are directed at long-term financial improvement, favorable government regulation, and job security. In this respect, business harbors a fundamentally utilitarian conception of the goals of its enterprise. Much the same is true of the goals of public policy in many countries.

A second essential feature of the utilitarian theory is a *theory of the good*. Efficiency itself is simply an instrumental good; that is, it is valuable strictly as a means to something else. Even growth and profit maximization are only means to the end of intrinsic goods. But what is "good" according to the utilitarian? An answer to this question can be formed by considering the New York stock market. Daily results on Wall Street are not intrinsically good. They are extrinsically good as a means to other ends, such as financial security and happiness. Utilitarians believe that people ought to orient their lives and frame their goals around conditions that are good in themselves without reference to further consequences. Health, friendship, and freedom from pain are among such values.

However, utilitarians disagree concerning what constitutes the complete range of things or states that are good. Bentham and Mill are hedonists. They believe that only pleasure or happiness (synonymous for the purposes of this discussion) can be intrinsically good. Everything besides pleasure is instrumentally good to the end of pleasure. *Hedonistic* utilitarians, then, believe that any act or practice that maximizes pleasure (when compared with any alternative act or practice) is right. Later utilitarian philosophers have argued that other values besides pleasure possess intrinsic worth, for example, friendship, knowledge, courage, health, and beauty. Utilitarians who believe in multiple intrinsic values are referred to as *pluralistic* utilitarians.

In recent philosophy, economics, and psychology, neither the approach of the hedonists nor that of the pluralists has prevailed. Both approaches have seemed relatively unhelpful for purposes of objectively stating and arraying basic goods. Another and competitive theory appeals to individual preferences. From this perspective, the concept of utility is understood not in terms of states of affairs such as happiness or friendship, but in terms of the satisfaction of individual preferences, as determined by a person's behavior. In the language of business, utility is measured by a person's purchases. More generally, utility may be said to be measurable by starting with a person's actual pursuits. To maximize a person's utility is to provide that which he or she has chosen or would choose from among the available alternatives. To maximize the utility of all persons affected by an action or a policy is to maximize the utility of the aggregate group.

Although the *preference* utilitarian approach to value has been viewed by many as superior to its predecessors, it is not trouble free as an ethical theory. A major problem arises over morally unacceptable preferences. For example, an airline pilot may prefer to have a few beers before going to work, or an employment officer may prefer to discriminate against women, yet such preferences are morally intolerable. Utilitarianism based purely on subjective preferences is satisfactory, then, only if a range of acceptable preferences can be formulated. This latter task has proved difficult in theory, and it may be inconsistent with a pure preference approach. Should products such as cigarettes, fireworks, heroin, and automatic rifles be legally prohibited because they cause harm, even though many people would prefer to purchase them? How could a preference utilitarian answer this question?

One possible utilitarian response is to ask whether society is better off as a whole when these preferences are prohibited and when the choices of those desiring them are frustrated. If these products work against the larger objectives of utilitarianism (maximal public welfare) by creating unhappiness and pain, the utilitarian could argue that preferences for these products should not be counted in the calculus of preferences. Preferences that serve to frustrate the preferences of others would then be ruled out by the goal of utilitarianism. But would the resulting theory be one entirely based on preferences and only preferences?

A third essential feature of utilitarianism is its commitment to the measurement and comparison of goods. In a hedonistic theory, people must be able to measure pleasurable and painful states and be able to compare one person's pleasures with another's to decide which is greater. Bentham, for example, worked out a measurement device that he called the *hedonic calculus*. He thought he could add the quantitative units of individual pleasure, subtract the units of individual displeasure, and thereby arrive at a total measure of pleasure (or happiness). By the use of this system it is allegedly possible to determine the act or practice that will provide the greatest happiness to the greatest number of people.

When Bentham's hedonic calculus turned out to be of limited practical value, Mill shifted to a criterion that we would today call a panel of experts (persons of requisite experience). Because Mill believed that some pleasures were better or higher order than others, a device was needed to decide which pleasures were in fact better. The experts were designated to fill that role. Subsequently, this idea of Mill's also turned out to be of limited practical value, and notions like that of *consumer choice* were substituted in some utilitarian theories. Consumer behavior, in this conception, can be empirically observed as prices change in the market. If one assumes that consumers seek to rationally order and maximize their preferences, given a set of prices, an objective measurement of utility is possible.

Act and Rule Utilitarianism. Utilitarian moral philosophers are conventionally divided into two types – act utilitarians and rule utilitarians. An *act utilitarian* argues that in all situations one ought to perform that act that leads to the greatest good for the greatest number. The act utilitarian regards rules such as "You ought to tell the truth in making contracts" and "You ought not to manipulate persons through advertising" as useful guidelines but also as expendable in business and other relationships. An act utilitarian would not hesitate to break a moral rule if breaking it would lead to the greatest good for the greatest number in a particular case. *Rule utilitarians*, however, reserve a more significant place for rules, which they do not regard as expendable on grounds that utility is maximized in a particular circumstance.

There are many applications of both types of utilitarianism in business ethics.[15] Consider the following case in which US business practices and standards run up against the quite different practices of the Italian business community. The case involves the tax problems encountered by an Italian subsidiary of a major US bank. In Italy the practices of corporate taxation typically involve elaborate negotiations among hired company representatives and the Italian tax service, and the tax statement initially submitted by a corporation is regarded as a dramatically understated bid intended only as a starting point for the negotiating process. In the case in question, the US manager of the Italian banking subsidiary decided, against the advice of locally experienced lawyers and tax consultants, to ignore the native Italian practices and file a conventional US-style tax statement (that is, one in which the subsidiary's profits for the year were not dramatically understated). His reasons for this decision included his belief that the local customs violated the moral rule of truth telling.[16]

An act utilitarian might well take exception to this conclusion. Admittedly, to file an Italian-style tax statement would be to violate a moral rule of truth telling; but the act utilitarian would argue that such a rule is only a guideline and can justifiably be violated to produce the greatest good. In the present case, the greatest good would evidently be done by following the local consultants' advice to conform to Italian practices. Only by following those practices would the appropriate amount of tax be paid. This conclusion is strengthened by the ultimate outcome of the present case: The Italian authorities forced the bank to enter into the customary negotiations, a process in which the original, truthful tax statement was treated as an understated opening bid, and a dramatically excessive tax payment was consequently exacted.

In contrast with the position of act utilitarians, rule utilitarians hold that rules have a central position in morality that cannot be compromised by the demands of particular situations. Compromise threatens the general effectiveness of the rules, the observance of which maximizes social utility. For the rule utilitarian, then, actions are justified by appeal to abstract rules such as "Don't kill," "Don't bribe," and "Don't break promises." These rules, in turn, are justified by an appeal to the principle of utility. The rule utilitarian believes this position can avoid the objections of act utilitarianism, because rules are not subject to change by the demands of individual circumstances. Utilitarian rules are in theory firm and protective of all classes of individuals, just as human rights are rigidly protective of all individuals regardless of social convenience and momentary need.

Act utilitarians have a reply to these criticisms. They argue that there is a third option beyond ignoring rules and strictly obeying them, which is that the rules should be regarded as "rules of thumb" to be obeyed *only sometimes*. In cases in which adhering to the rule of thumb will result in a decline in overall welfare, the rule should be ignored.

Criticisms of Utilitarianism. A major problem for utilitarianism is whether preference units or some other utilitarian value such as happiness can be measured and compared to determine the best action among the alternatives. For example, in deciding whether to open a pristine Alaskan wildlife preserve to oil exploration and drilling, how does one compare the combined value of an increase in the oil supply, jobs, and consumer purchasing power with the value of wildlife preservation and environmental protection? How does a responsible official – at, say, the Bill and Melinda Gates Foundation – decide how to distribute limited funds allocated for charitable contributions (for example, as this foundation has decided, to international vaccination and children's health programs)? If a corporate social audit (an evaluation of the company's acts of social responsibility) were attempted, how could the auditor measure and compare a corporation's ethical assets and liabilities?

The utilitarian reply is that the alleged problem is either a pseudo-problem or a problem that affects all ethical theories. People make crude, rough-and-ready comparisons of values every day, including those of pleasures and dislikes. For example, workers decide to go as a group to a bar rather than have an office party because they think the bar function will satisfy more members of the group. Utilitarians acknowledge that accurate measurements of others' goods or preferences can seldom be provided because of limited knowledge and time. In everyday affairs such as purchasing supplies, administering business, or making legislative decisions, severely limited knowledge regarding the consequences of one's actions is often all that is available.

Utilitarianism has also been criticized on the grounds that it ignores nonutilitarian factors that are needed to make moral decisions. The most prominent omission cited is a consideration of justice: the action that produces the greatest balance of value for the greatest number of people may bring about unjustified treatment of a minority. Suppose society decides that the public interest is served by denying health insurance to those testing positive for the AIDS virus. Moreover, in the interest of efficiency, suppose insurance companies are allowed to weed out those covered because they have some characteristics that are statistically associated with an enhanced risk of injury or disease – for example, genetic disorders. Suppose such policies would, on balance, serve the public's financial interest by lowering insurance costs. Utilitarianism seems to *require* that public law and insurance companies deny coverage to persons with genetic disorders and to many others at higher risk of disease or injury. If so, would not this denial be unjust to those who are at high risk through no fault of their own?

Utilitarians insist, against such criticisms, that all entailed costs and benefits of an action or practice must be weighed, including, for example, the costs that would occur from modifying a statement of basic rights. In a decision that affects employee and consumer safety, for example, the costs often include protests from labor and consumer groups, public criticism from the press, further alienation of employees from executives, the loss of customers to competitors, and the like. Also, rule utilitarians deny that narrow cost–benefit determinations are acceptable. They argue that general rules of justice (which are themselves justified by broad considerations of utility) ought to constrain particular actions and uses of cost–benefit calculations. Rule utilitarians maintain that the criticisms of utilitarianism previously noted are shortsighted because they focus on injustices that might be caused through a superficial or short-term application of the principle of utility. In a long-range view, utilitarians argue, promoting utility does not eventuate in overall unjust outcomes.

KANTIAN ETHICS

CNN reported that online shoppers who visited the Internet auction site eBay were surprised to find a "fully functional kidney" for sale by a man giving his home as "Sunrise, Florida." He was proposing to sell one of his two kidneys. The price had been bid up to more than $5.7 million before eBay intervened and terminated the (illegal) auction.[17] Although it was never determined whether this auction was genuine, it is known that kidneys are for sale in some parts of Asia, notably India. One study showed, after locating 305 sellers, that Indians who sold their kidneys actually worsened rather than bettered their financial position as a result of the sale; the study also showed that some men forced their wives to sell a kidney and that many sellers suffered a permanent decline in health.[18] Irrespective of the consequences of a kidney sale, many people look with moral indignation on the idea of selling a kidney, whether in the United States or in India.[19] They see it as wrongful exploitation, rather than opportunity, and they don't care whether it has strong utilitarian benefits for society. What is it about selling a kidney that provokes this sense of moral unfairness, and can a moral theory capture the perceived wrongness?

Kantian Respect for Persons. Many have thought that Immanuel Kant's (1724–1804) ethical theory helps clarify the basis of such moral concern as well as what should be done about it. A follower of Kant could argue that using human organs as commodities is to treat human beings as though they were merely machines or capital, and so to deny people the respect appropriate to their dignity as rational human beings. Kant argued that persons should be treated as ends and never purely as means to the ends of others. That is, failure to respect persons is to treat another as a means in accordance with one's *own* ends, and thus as if they were not independent agents. To exhibit a lack of respect for a person is either to reject the person's considered judgments, to ignore the person's concerns and needs, or to deny the person the liberty to act on those judgments. For example, manipulative advertising that attempts to make sales by interfering with the potential buyer's reflective choice violates the principle of respect for persons. In the case of kidney sales, almost all sellers are in desperate poverty and desperate need. Potentially all organ "donations" will come from the poor while the rich avoid donating their kidneys even to their relatives. In effect, the organ is treated as a commodity and the owner of the organ as merely a means to a purchaser's ends.

In Kantian theories, respect for the human being is said to be necessary – not just as an option or at one's discretion – because human beings possess a moral dignity and therefore should not be treated as if they had merely the conditional value possessed by machinery, industrial plants, robots, and capital. This idea of "respect for persons" has sometimes been expressed in corporate contexts as "respect for the individual."

An example in business ethics is found in the practices of Southwest Airlines, which has the reputation of treating its employees and customers with unusual respect. Employees report that they feel free to express themselves as individuals and that they feel a strong loyalty to the airline.

Following the terrorist attacks of September 11, 2001, Southwest was the only airline that did not lay off employees or reduce its flight schedule. As a consequence, some employees offered to work overtime, without pay, to save the company money until people resumed flying.[20] The firm prides itself on a relationship with all stakeholders that is a relationship of persons, rather than simply a relationship of economic transactions.

Another example is found at Motorola, where respect for individual persons is one of the "key beliefs" that has served as a foundation for their Code of Conduct for decades. As understood by Motorola, "Constant respect for people means we treat everyone with dignity, as we would like to be treated ourselves. Constant respect applies to every individual we interact with around the world."[21] The Motorola Code of Conduct specifies how this principle should be applied to "Motorolans," customers, business partners, shareholders, competitors, communities, and governments. All employees at Motorola are evaluated, in part, on the extent to which they demonstrate respect for each of these stakeholders.

Some have interpreted Kant to hold categorically that people can never treat other persons as a means to their ends. This interpretation is mistaken. Kant did not categorically prohibit the use of persons as means to the ends of other people. He argued only that people must not treat another *exclusively* as a means to their ends. An example is found in circumstances in which employees are ordered to perform odious tasks. Clearly, they are being treated as a means to an employer's or a supervisor's ends, but the employees are not exclusively used for others' purposes because they are not mere servants or objects. In an economic exchange, suppose that Jones is using Smith to achieve her end, but similarly Smith is using Jones to achieve her end. So long as the exchange is freely entered into without coercion or deception by either party, neither party has used the other merely for her end. Thus even in a hierarchical organization an employer can be the boss without exploiting the employee, so long as the employee freely entered into that relationship. The key to not using others merely as a means is to respect their dignity.

This interpretation suggests that the example of the kidney sale does not necessarily show any disrespect for persons. Kant seems to require only that each individual *will the acceptance* of those principles on which he or she is acting. If a person freely accepts a certain form of action and it is not intrinsically immoral, that person is a free being and has a right to so choose. Selling a kidney might fall into this category. It is conceivable, for example, that if as a condition of the exchange, kidney sellers were guaranteed first-rate medical care for the rest of their lives to help prevent sickness and death from complications related to transplant surgery, purchasing a kidney might be regarded as permissible.[22] However, because kidney sellers are seldom provided with such care, they develop serious medical complications and their lifespan is often reduced as a result. In this way they are literally regarded as disposable. It is this judgment that informs the assessment some Kantians make today that unregulated kidney sales are immoral.

Respecting others does not merely entail a negative obligation to refrain from treating others as mere objects; it also entails positive obligations to help ensure the development of rational and moral capacities. For example, some Kantians argue today that employers of low-skill workers in the developing world have obligations to ensure that the workers enjoy sufficient free time and the wages to develop their capacities to function as moral agents. Accordingly, workers who are paid more than they would make if they were living on the street, but not enough to live decent human lives, are treated with impermissible disrespect.

Kant's theory finds *motives* for actions to be of the highest importance, in that it expects persons to make the right decisions *for the right reasons*. If persons are honest only because they believe that honesty pays, their "honesty" is cheapened. It seems like no honesty at all, only an action that appears to be honest. For example, when corporate executives announce that the reason they made the morally correct decision was because it was good for their business, this reason seems to have nothing to do with morality. According to Kantian thinking, if a corporation does the right thing only when (and for the reason that) it is profitable or when it will enjoy good publicity, its decision is prudential, not moral.

Consider the following three examples of three people making personal sacrifices to raise money to help pay for a cancer-stricken co-worker to receive an extremely expensive new drug therapy that is not covered by health insurance. Fred makes the sacrifices only because he fears the criticism that would result if he failed to do so. He hates doing it and secretly resents being involved. Sam, by contrast, derives no personal satisfaction from helping raise money. He would rather be doing other things and makes the sacrifice purely from a sense of obligation. Bill, by contrast, is a kindhearted person. He does not view his actions as a sacrifice and is motivated by the satisfaction that comes from helping others. Assume in these three cases that the consequences of all the sacrificial actions are equally good and that the co-worker receives the drug therapy, as each agent intends. The question to consider is which persons are behaving in a morally praiseworthy manner. If utilitarian theory is used, this question may be hard to answer, especially if act utilitarianism is the theory in question, because the good consequences in each case are identical. The Kantian believes, however, that motives – in particular, motives of moral obligation – count substantially in moral evaluation.

It appears that Fred's motives are not moral motives but motives of prudence that spring from fear. Although his actions have good consequences, Fred does not deserve any moral credit for his acts because they are not morally motivated. To recognize the prudential basis of an action does not detract from the goodness of any consequences it may have. Given the purpose or function of the business enterprise, a motive of self-interest may be the most appropriate motive to ensure good consequences. The point, however, is that a business executive derives no special moral credit for acting in the corporate self-interest, even if society is benefited by and satisfied with the action.

If Fred's motive is not moral, what about Bill's and Sam's? Here moral philosophers disagree. Kant maintained that moral action must be motivated by a maxim (rule) of moral obligation. From this perspective, Sam is the only individual whose actions may be appropriately described as moral. Bill deserves no more credit than Fred, because Bill is motivated by the emotions of sympathy and compassion, not by obligation. Bill is naturally kindhearted and has been well socialized by his family, but this motivation merits no moral praise from a Kantian, who believes that actions motivated by self-interest alone or compassion alone cannot be morally praiseworthy. To be deserving of moral praise, a person must act from obligation.

To elaborate this point, Kant insisted that all persons must act for the *sake of* obligation – not merely *in accordance with* obligation. That is, the person's motive for action must involve a recognition of the duty to act. Kant tried to establish the ultimate basis for the validity of rules of obligation in pure reason, not in intuition, conscience, utility, or compassion. Morality provides a rational framework of principles and rules that constrain and guide all people, independent of their personal goals and preferences. He believed that all considerations of utility and self-interest are secondary, because the moral worth of an agent's action depends exclusively on the moral acceptability of the rule according to which the person is acting.

An action has moral worth only if performed by an agent who possesses what Kant called a "good will." A person has a good will only if the motive for action is moral obligation, as determined by a universal rule of obligation. Kant developed this notion into a fundamental moral law: "I ought never to act except in such a way that I can also will that my maxim should become a universal law." Kant called this principle the *categorical imperative*. It is categorical because it admits of no exceptions and is absolutely binding. It is imperative because it gives instruction about how one must act. He gave several examples of imperative moral maxims: "Help others in distress," "Do not commit suicide," and "Work to develop your abilities."

Universalizability. Kant's strategy was to show that the acceptance of certain kinds of action is self-defeating, because *universal* participation in such behavior undermines the action. Some of the clearest cases involve persons who make a unique exception for themselves for purely selfish reasons. Suppose a person considers breaking a promise to a co-worker that would be inconvenient to keep. According to Kant, the person must first formulate her or his reason as a universal rule. The rule would say, "Everyone should break a promise whenever keeping it is inconvenient." Such a rule is contradictory, Kant held, because if it were consistently recommended that all individuals should break their promises when it was convenient for them to do so, the practice of making promises would be senseless. Given the nature of a promise, a rule allowing people to break promises when it becomes convenient makes the institution of promise-making unintelligible. A rule that allows cheating on an exam similarly negates the purpose of testing.

Kant's belief was that the conduct stipulated in these rules could not be made universal without the emergence of some form of contradiction. During the run-up to the US housing bubble, Beazer Homes USA used deceptive and illegal lending practices to sell more houses to consumers who could not afford the mortgages. Beazer eventually settled with the US Justice Department and agreed to pay $50 million in restitution and its CEO agreed to return $6.5 million in compensation and tens of thousands of shares of the company.[23] In this example, the company made an exception of itself by engaging in predatory lending, thereby cheating the system, which is established by certain lending rules that help ensure most borrowers can pay back their loans. This conduct, if carried out by other corporations, violates the rules presupposed by the system, thereby rendering the system inconsistent. Because many companies *did* engage in predatory lending practices and passed on bad loans to other investors, a housing bubble was created and eventually burst, undermining the global financial system and causing massive hardship. Kant's point was not that such practices lead to bad consequences, although they often do, but that such conduct constitutes making an unfair exception of oneself. Kant's view was that actions involving invasion of privacy, theft, line cutting, cheating, kick-backs, bribes, and the like are contradictory in that they are not consistent with the institutions or practices they presuppose.

Criticisms of Kantianism. Despite Kant's contributions to moral philosophy, his theories have been criticized as narrow and inadequate to handle various problems in the moral life. He had little to say regarding moral emotions or sentiments such as sympathy and caring. Some people also think that Kant emphasized universal obligations (obligations common to all people) at the expense of particular obligations (obligations that fall only on those in particular relationships or who occupy certain roles, such as those of a business manager). Whereas the obligation to keep a promise is a universal obligation, the obligation to grade students fairly falls only on teachers responsible for submitting grades.

Many managerial obligations result from special roles played in business. For example, business persons tend to treat customers according to the history of their relationship. If a person is a regular customer and the merchandise being sold is in short supply, the regular customer will be given preferential treatment because a relationship of commitment and trust has already been established. Japanese business practice has conventionally extended this notion to relations with suppliers and employees: after a trial period, the regular employee has a job for life at many firms. Also, the bidding system is used less frequently in Japan than in the West. Once a supplier has a history with a firm, the firm is loyal to its supplier, and each trusts the other not to exploit the relationship.

However, particular obligations and special relationships may not be inconsistent with Kantianism, because they may not violate any universal ethical norms. Although Kant wrote little about such particular duties, he would agree that a complete explanation of moral agency in terms of duty requires an account of *both* universal *and* particular duties.

A related aspect of Kant's ethical theory that has been scrutinized by philosophers is his view that moral motivation involves *impartial* principles. Impartial motivation may be distinguished from the motivation that a person might have for treating a second person in a certain way because the first person has a particular interest in the well-being of the second person (a spouse or valued customer, for example). A conventional interpretation of Kant's work suggests that if conflicts arise between one's obligation and one's other motivations – such as friendship, reciprocation, or love – the motive of obligation should always prevail. In arguing against this moral view, critics maintain that persons are entitled to show favoritism to their loved ones. This criticism suggests that Kantianism (and utilitarianism as well) has too broadly cast the requirement of impartiality and does not adequately account for those parts of the moral life involving partial, intimate, and special relationships.

Special relationships with a unique history are often recognized in business. For instance, the Unocal Corporation sharply criticized its principal bank, Security Pacific Corporation, for knowingly making loans of $185 million to a group that intended to use the money to buy shares in Unocal for a hostile takeover. Fred Hartley, chairman and president of Unocal, argued that the banks and investment bankers were "playing both sides of the game." Hartley said that Security Pacific had promised him that it would not finance such takeover attempts three months before doing so and that it had acted under conditions "in which the bank [has] continually received [for the last 40 years] confidential financial, geological, and engineering information from the company."[24] A 40-year history in which the bank stockpiled confidential information should not simply be cast aside for larger goals. Security Pacific had violated a special relationship it had with Unocal.

Nonetheless, impartiality seems at some level an irreplaceable moral concept, and ethical theory should recognize its centrality in many business relationships. The essence of rules governing banks – to the extent explicit rules exist – is that banks can lend money to insiders if and only if insiders are treated exactly as outsiders are treated. Here the rule of impartiality is an essential moral constraint. By contrast, 75 percent of America's 1,500 largest corporations made insider loans strictly on the basis of partiality; most loans were made for stock purchases. This partiality massively backfired in 2000–2003, and many companies had to "forgive" or "pardon" the loans and charge off millions of dollars. Loans at Tyco, Lucent, Mattel, Microsoft, and Webvan became famous cases.[25] For example, WorldCom loaned then-CEO Bernie Ebbers $160 million for his personal "stock purchase/retention." And Anglo Irish Bank CEO Sean Fitzpatrick resigned suddenly in 2008 after it was revealed that he authorized £150 million in loans to himself and other insiders, most of which he hid from auditors.[26] The bank was subsequently nationalized.

The need for impartiality is also important in healthcare, especially because of the efforts of the pharmaceutical and medical device industry to influence physician behavior. Medical professionals who are paid large sums by industry for consulting and other services have been criticized for failing to provide care that is in the best interest of patients because of their financial ties to drug and device companies (see Chapter 7). Recently the Cleveland Clinic, a leading medical center, began electronically publishing all of its physicians' and researchers' financial ties to industry in an effort to emphasize the importance of impartial medical advice.[27]

Corporate America continues to suffer from major business scandals, many of which end in the criminal prosecution of corporate executives and the dissolution of the company. Violations of the demand for impartiality and fair dealing are virtually always present in these scandals. Here are three examples. First, in a notorious case, the accounting firm of Arthur Andersen had such a close and partial relationship with its client Enron that it could not perform an objective audit of the firm. Enron was treated with a deference, partiality, and favoritism that contrasted sharply with the auditing of other firms, who were treated with the conventional impartiality expected of an auditing firm. Second, executives at many US companies have been discovered to be "backdating" their stock options. *Backdating* is the practice of looking back in time for the date on which one's company stock price was at its lowest and granting the purchase on that date. Typically this is done when the stock value is much higher so that the executive can immediately cash in the stock and make a substantial profit. For example, the former CEO of Take-Two Interactive Software Inc., the maker of the video game "Grand Theft Auto," pleaded guilty to granting undisclosed, backdated options to himself and others.[28] More than 80 companies have revealed that they are investigating instances of backdating as a result of prompting from regulators and internal audit committees. Third, many knowledgeable observers believe that the recent financial crisis that resulted from the collapse of the housing bubble in the United States was partly due to the cozy relationship between credit rating agencies and the investment banks whose products they were supposed to be objectively evaluating on behalf of investors. The credit rating agencies gave their highest-grade investment ratings to investment bank products that were toxic, all the while receiving fees from the banks for their services.

Unfair treatment does not only take place among executives. An assistant restaurant manager in charge of scheduling can unfairly give her friends on the staff the best shifts, rather than the most competent waiters or cooks. And a retail manager can unfairly enforce rules (for example, no personal calls while at work) by allowing favorite employees to break the rule while enforcing the rule on other employees.

CONTEMPORARY TRENDS IN ETHICAL THEORY

Thus far only utilitarian and Kantian theories have been examined. Both meld a variety of moral considerations into a surprisingly systematized framework, centered around a single major principle. Much is attractive in these theories, and they were the dominant models in ethical theory throughout much of the twentieth century. In fact they have sometimes been presented as the only types of ethical theory, as if there were no available alternatives from which to choose. However, much recent philosophical writing has focused on defects in these theories and on ways in which the two theories actually affirm a similar conception of the moral life oriented around universal principles and rules.

These critics promote alternatives to the utilitarian and Kantian models. They believe that "master principle theories" do not merit the attention they have received and the lofty position they have occupied. Three popular replacements for, or perhaps supplements to, Kantian and utilitarian theories are (1) rights theories (which are based on human rights); (2) virtue theories (which are based on character traits); and (3) common morality theories (which are generally obligation-based). These theories are the topics of the next three sections.

Each of these three types of theories has treated some problems well and has supplied insights not found in utilitarian and Kantian theories. Although it may seem as if there is an endless array of disagreements across the theories, these theories are not in all respects competitive, and in some ways they are even complementary. The reader may profitably look for convergent insights in these theories.

RIGHTS THEORIES

Terms from moral discourse such as *value, goal,* and *obligation* have thus far in this chapter dominated the discussion. *Principles* and *rules* in Kantian and utilitarian theories have been understood as statements of obligation. Yet, many assertions that will be encountered throughout this volume are claims to rights, and public policy issues often concern rights or attempts to secure rights. Many current controversies in professional ethics, business, and public policy involve the rights to property, work, privacy, a healthy environment, and the like. This section presents theories that give rights a distinctive character in ethical theory and yet allow rights to be connected to the obligations that we have previously examined.

In recent years, public discussions about moral protections for persons vulnerable to abuse, enslavement, or neglect have typically been stated in terms of rights. Many believe that these rights transcend national boundaries and particular governments. For example, we have seen several controversies over exploitative labor conditions in factories (so-called sweatshop conditions) that manufacture products for Nike, Reebok, Abercrombie and Fitch, Target, Gap, J. C. Penney, Liz Claiborne, L.L.Bean, Walmart, Apple, Microsoft, Sony, Dell, and many other companies. At stake are the human rights of millions of workers around the globe, including rights to safe working conditions, payment of all legally required wages, protections against mandated overtime work, collective bargaining agreements, codes of conduct for industries, open-factory inspections, and new monitoring systems.[29] In addition, activists have urged that American companies not do business in countries that have a record of extensive violation of human rights. China, Nigeria, and Myanmar have all come under severe criticism. (These issues, and others surrounding violations of human rights in sweatshops, are discussed in Chapter 9.)

Unlike legal rights, human rights are held independently of membership in a state or other social organization. Historically, human rights evolved from the notion of natural rights. As formulated by John Locke and others in early modern philosophy, natural rights are claims that individuals have against the state. If the state does not honor these rights, its legitimacy is in question. Natural rights were thought to consist primarily of rights to be free of interference, or liberty rights. Proclamations of rights to life, liberty, property, a speedy trial, and the pursuit of happiness subsequently formed the core of major Western political and legal documents. These rights came to be understood as powerful assertions demanding respect and status.

A number of influential philosophers have maintained that ethical theory or some part of it must be "rights-based."[30] They seek to ground ethical theory in an account of rights that is not reducible to a theory of obligations or virtues. Consider a theory to be discussed in Chapter 10 that takes liberty rights to be basic. One representative of this theory, Robert Nozick, refers to his social philosophy as an "entitlement theory." The appropriateness of that description is apparent from this provocative line with which his book begins: "Individuals have rights, and there are things no person or group may do to them (without violating their rights)." Nozick grounds this right in Kant's arguments regarding respect for persons. Starting from this assumption, Nozick builds a political theory in which government action is justified only if it protects the fundamental rights of its citizens.

This political theory is also an ethical theory. Nozick takes the following moral rule to be basic: All persons have a right to be left free to do as they choose. The moral obligation not to interfere with a person follows from this right. That the obligation *follows* from the right is a clear indication of the priority of rights over obligations; that is, in this theory the obligation is derived from the right, not the other way around.

Many rights-based theories hold that rights form the justifying basis of obligations because they best express the purpose of morality, which is the securing of liberties or other benefits for a right-holder.[31] However, few rights-based theories *deny* the importance of obligations (or duties), which they regard as central to morality. They make this point by holding that there is a correlativity between obligations and rights: "*X* has a right to do or to have *Y*" means that the moral system of rules (or the legal system, if appropriate) imposes an obligation on someone to act or to refrain from acting so that X is enabled to do or have Y.[32]

These obligations are of two types: *negative obligations* are those that require that we not interfere with the liberty of others (thus securing liberty rights); *positive obligations* require that certain people or institutions provide benefits or services (thus securing benefit rights or welfare rights).[33] Correlatively, a *negative right* is a valid claim to liberty, that is, a right not to be interfered with, and a *positive right* is a valid claim on goods or services. The rights not to be beaten, subjected to unwanted surgery, or sold into slavery are examples of negative or liberty rights. Rights to food, medical care, and insurance are examples of positive or benefit rights.

The right to liberty is here said to be "negative" because no one has to act to honor it. Presumably, all that must be done is to leave people alone. The same is not true regarding positive rights; to honor these rights, someone has to provide something. For example, if a starving person has a human right to well-being, someone has an obligation to provide that person with food. As has often been pointed out, positive rights place an obligation to provide something on others, who can respond that this requirement interferes with their property rights to use their resources for their chosen ends. The distinction between positive and negative rights has often led those who would include various rights to well-being (to food, housing, healthcare, etc.) on the list of human rights to argue that the obligation to provide for positive rights falls on the political state. This distinction has intuitive appeal to many business persons, because they wish to limit both the responsibilities of their firms and the number of rights conflicts they must address. This point has recently become more compelling in light of the rise of theories of justice that address global poverty. Assuming, as the United Nations does, that humans have a fundamental right to have access to basic goods including housing, food, and healthcare, it can be argued that ensuring these rights to basic goods requires that coercive institutions such as governments, the World Health Organization, and the World Bank be designed to guarantee these rights to everyone.

A conflict involving negative rights is illustrated by the debate surrounding attempts by employers to control the lifestyle of their employees. Some employers will not accept employees who smoke. Some will not permit employees to engage in dangerous activities such as skydiving, auto racing, or mountain climbing. By making these rules, one can argue that employers are violating the liberty rights of the employees as well as the employees' right to privacy. Conversely, the employer can argue that he or she has a right to run the business as he or she sees fit. Thus, both sides invoke negative rights to make a moral case.

Theories of moral rights have not traditionally been a major focus of business ethics, but this situation is changing at present. For example, employees traditionally could be fired for what superiors considered disloyal conduct, and employees have had no right to "blow the whistle" on corporate misconduct. When members of minority groups complain about discriminatory hiring practices that violate their human dignity and self-respect, one plausible interpretation of these complaints is that those who register them believe that their moral rights are being infringed. Current theories of employee, consumer, and stockholder rights all provide frameworks for debates about rights within business ethics.

The language of moral rights is greeted by some with skepticism because of the apparently absurd proliferation of rights and the conflict among diverse claims to rights (especially in recent political debates). For example, some parties claim that a pregnant woman has a right to have an abortion, whereas others claim that fetuses have a right to life that precludes the right to have an abortion. As we shall see throughout this volume, rights language has been extended to include such controversial rights as the right to financial privacy, rights of workers to obtain various forms of information about their employer, the right to work in a pollution-free environment, the right to hold a job, and the right to healthcare.

Many writers in ethics now agree that a person can legitimately exercise a right to something only if sufficient justification exists – that is, when a right has an overriding status. Rights such as a right to equal economic opportunity, a right to do with one's property as one wishes, and a right to be saved from starvation may have to compete with other rights. The fact that rights theorists have failed to provide a hierarchy for rights claims may indicate that rights, like obligations, are not absolute moral demands but rather ones that can be overridden in particular circumstances by more stringent competing moral claims.

The idea of grounding duties or obligations in correlative rights is attractive to managers of many large global corporations because it provides a transcultural and transnational set of ethical norms that apply in all nations and can be used as the basis for uniform global corporate policies. For example, pharmaceutical companies that conduct research with human subjects in 30 countries would like to be able to apply the same moral rules in all 30 countries. Otherwise, chaos and inconsistency constantly threaten.

Because of this interest in human rights on the part of many global managers, but also because of vocal critics of some global business activities, the United Nations Human Rights Council approved Guiding Principles on Business and Human Rights in 2011. These principles are intended to provide a global standard for identifying the human rights responsibilities of businesses (see Chapter 9).

VIRTUE ETHICS

Virtue ethics descends from the classical Hellenistic tradition represented by Plato and Aristotle, in which the cultivation of a virtuous character is viewed as morality's primary function. Aristotle held that virtue is neither a feeling nor an innate capacity but a disposition bred from an innate capacity properly trained and exercised. People acquire virtues much as they do skills such as carpentry, playing a musical instrument, or cooking. They become just by performing just actions and become temperate by performing temperate actions. Virtuous character, says Aristotle, is neither natural nor unnatural; it is cultivated and made a part of the individual, much like a language or tradition.

But an ethics of virtue is more than habitual training. This approach relies even more than does Kant's theory on the importance of having a correct *motivational structure*. A just person, for example, has not only a psychological disposition to act fairly but also a morally appropriate desire to act justly. The person characteristically has a moral concern and reservation about acting in a way that would be unfair. Having only the motive to act in accordance with a rule of obligation (Kant's only demand) is not morally sufficient for virtue. Imagine a person who always performs his or her obligation because it is an obligation but who intensely dislikes having to allow the interests of others to be taken into account. Such a person does not cherish, feel congenial toward, or think fondly of others, and this person respects others only because obligation requires it. This person can, nonetheless, on a theory of moral obligation such as Kant's or Mill's, perform a morally right action, have an ingrained disposition to perform that action, and act with obligation as the foremost motive. The virtue theorist's criticism is that if the desire is not right, a necessary condition of virtue is lacking.

Consider an encounter you might have with a tire salesperson. You tell the salesperson that safety is most important and that you want to be sure to get an all-weather tire. He listens carefully and then sells you exactly what you want, because he has been well trained by his manager to see his primary obligation as that of meeting the customer's needs. Acting in this way has been deeply ingrained in this salesperson by his manager's training. There is no more typical encounter in the world of retail sales than this one. However, suppose now that we go behind the salesperson's behavior to his underlying motives and desires. We find that this man detests his job and hates having to spend time with every customer who comes through the door. He cares not at all about being of service to people or creating a better environment in the office. All he really wants is to watch the television set in the waiting lounge and to pick up his paycheck. Although this man meets his moral obligations, something in his character is morally defective.

When people engage in business or take jobs simply for the profit or wages that will result, they may meet their obligations and yet not be engaged in their work in a morally appropriate manner. However, if persons start a business because they believe in a quality product – a new, healthier and environmentally friendly food, for example – and deeply desire to sell that product, their character is more in tune with our moral expectations. Entrepreneurs often exhibit this enthusiasm and commitment. The practice of business is morally better if it is sustained by persons whose character manifests enthusiasm, truthfulness, compassion, respectfulness, and patience. Of course, the ability of employees to exhibit these virtues depends on the ability and desire of senior managers to cultivate an appropriate organizational culture. Employees who work in "sweatshop" conditions or with unscrupulous mangers who demand sales above all other considerations are unlikely to be able to cultivate such virtues.

Interesting discussions in business ethics now center on the appropriate virtues of managers, employees, and other participants in business activity, as will be seen many times in this book. Among the many virtues that have been discussed are integrity, truthfulness, courage, and compassion. However, some alleged "virtues" of business life have been sharply contested in recent years, and various "virtues" of the business person have seemed not to be *moral* virtues at all. Competitiveness and toughness are two examples. *Fortune* has long published a list of the toughest bosses. For many years before he was fired as CEO of Sunbeam, Al Dunlap was perennially on the list. He had earned the nickname "Chainsaw Al" for his propensity to fire people and shut down plants even when they were marginally profitable. Dunlap made stock price and profitability the only worthy goals of a business enterprise. In his case business toughness was eventually judged a moral vice. This example suggests that some alleged business virtues may not turn out to be virtues at all.

There is another reason why virtue ethics may be important for business ethics. A morally good person with the right desires or motivations is more likely to understand what should be done, more likely to be motivated to perform required acts, and more likely to form and act on moral ideals than would a morally bad person. A person who is ordinarily trusted is one who has an ingrained motivation and desire to perform right actions and who characteristically cares about morally appropriate responses. A person who simply follows rules of obligation and who otherwise exhibits no special moral character may not be trustworthy. It is not the rule follower but the person disposed by character to be generous, caring, compassionate, sympathetic, and fair who should be the one recommended, admired, praised, and held up as a moral model. Many experienced business persons say that such trust is the moral cement of the business world.

Furthermore, studies indicate that for employees to take corporate ethics policies seriously, they need to perceive executives both as personally virtuous and as consistent enforcers of ethics policies throughout the organization.[34]

COMMON MORALITY THEORIES

Finally, the view that there is a common morality that all people share by virtue of communal life, and that this morality is ultimately the source of all theories of morality, is known as *common morality theory*. This view is especially influential in contemporary biomedical ethics, an area of applied ethics that shares many topics of concern with business ethics.[35] According to this approach, virtually all people in all cultures grow up with an understanding of the basic demands of morality. Its norms are familiar and unobjectionable to those deeply committed to a moral life. They know not to lie, not to steal, to keep promises, to honor the rights of others, not to kill or cause harm to innocent persons, and the like. The common morality is simply the set of norms shared by all persons who are seriously committed to the objectives of morality. This morality is not merely *a* morality that differs from *other* moralities.[36] It is applicable to all persons in all places, and all human conduct is rightly judged by its standards.

The following are examples of *standards of action* (rules of obligation) in the common morality: (1) "Don't kill," (2) "Don't cause pain or suffering to others," (3) "Prevent evil or harm from occurring," and (4) "Tell the truth." There are also many examples of *moral character traits* (virtues) recognized in the common morality, including (1) nonmalevolence, (2) honesty, (3) integrity, and (4) conscientiousness. These virtues are universally admired traits of character, and a person is regarded as deficient in moral character if he or she lacks such traits.

The thesis that there are universal moral standards is rooted in (1) a theory of the objectives of the social institution of morality and (2) a hypothesis about the sorts of norms that are required to achieve those objectives. Philosophers such as Thomas Hobbes and David Hume pointed out that centuries of experience demonstrate that the human condition tends to deteriorate into misery, confusion, violence, and distrust unless norms such as those listed earlier – the norms of the common morality – are observed. These norms prevent or minimize the threat of social deterioration.

It would be an overstatement to maintain that these norms are necessary for the *survival* of a society (as various philosophers and social scientists have maintained),[37] but it is not too much to claim that these norms are necessary to *ameliorate or counteract the tendency for the quality of people's lives to worsen or for social relationships to disintegrate*.[38] In every well-functioning society norms are in place to prohibit lying, breaking promises, causing bodily harm, stealing, committing fraud, taking of life, neglecting children, failing to keep contracts, and the like.[39] These norms are what they are, and not some other set of norms, because they have proven that they successfully achieve the objectives of morality. This success in the service of human flourishing accounts for their moral authority, and there is no more basic explanation of or justification for their moral authority. Thus, defenders of common morality maintain that there is no philosophical ethical theory that uproots or takes priority over the common morality; indeed, all *philosophical* theories start out from an understanding of the common morality and build a theory on top of this understanding.

These theories do not assume that every person accepts the norms in the common morality. It would be implausible to maintain that all persons in all societies do in fact accept moral norms. Unanimity is not the issue. Many amoral, immoral, or selectively moral persons do not care about or identify with various demands of the common morality. Some persons are morally weak; others are morally depraved. It would also be implausible to hold that a *customary* set of norms or a *consensus* set of norms in a society qualifies, as such, for inclusion in the *common* morality. The notion that moral justification is ultimately grounded in the customs and consensus agreements of particular groups is a moral travesty. Any given society's customary or consensus position may be a distorted outlook that functions to block awareness of common morality requirements. Some societies are in the influential grip of leaders who promote religious zealotries or political ideologies that depart profoundly from the common morality.

From the perspective of those who emphasize the common morality, only universally valid norms warrant our making intercultural and cross-cultural judgments about moral depravity, morally misguided beliefs, savage cruelty, and other moral failures. If we did not have recourse to universal norms, we could not make basic distinctions between moral and immoral behavior and therefore could not be positioned to criticize even outrageous human actions, some of which are themselves proclaimed in the name of morality. This takes us to the subject of how *particular* moralities are viewed in common morality theories.

Many justifiable moral norms are particular to cultures, groups, and even individuals. The common morality contains only general moral standards. Its norms are abstract, universal, and content thin. Particular moralities tend to be the reverse: concrete, nonuniversal, and content rich. These moralities may contain norms that are often comprehensive and detailed. Business ethics, and indeed all professional ethics, are examples of particular moralities. Many examples are found in codes of professional practice, institutional codes of ethics, government regulations, and the like.

Business ethics is fundamentally an attempt to make the moral life specific and practical. The reason why the norms of business ethics in particular cultures often differ from those of another culture is that the abstract starting points in the common morality can be coherently applied in a variety of ways to create norms that take the form of specific guidelines, institutional and public policies, and conflict resolutions. Universal norms are simply not appropriate instruments to determine practice or policy or to resolve conflicts unless they are made sufficiently specific to take account of financial constraints, social efficiency, cultural pluralism, political procedures, uncertainty about risk, and the like.

General moral norms must be *specified* to make them sufficiently concrete so that they can function as practical guidelines in particular contexts. Specification is not a process of producing general norms such as those in the common morality; it assumes that they are already available. Specification reduces the indeterminateness and abstractness of general norms to give them increased action-guiding capacity, without loss of the moral commitments in the original norm(s).[40] For example, the norm that we must "respect the autonomous judgment of competent persons" cannot, unless it is specified, handle complicated problems of whether workers have a right to know about potential dangers in a chemical plant. This will have to be specified in light of the dangers in the plant (or in that type of plant). The process of specification will have to become increasingly concrete as new problems emerge. That is, even already specified rules, guidelines, policies, and codes will almost always have to be specified further to handle new or unanticipated circumstances.

As defenders of the common morality theory see it, this is the way business ethics actually works, and it is through this progressive specification that we retain the common morality and make moral progress by creating new norms. The common morality can be extended as far as we need to extend it to meet practical objectives. There is, of course, always the possibility of developing more than one line of specification when confronting practical problems and moral disagreements. It is to be expected – indeed, it is unavoidable – that different persons and groups will offer conflicting specifications to resolve conflicts or vagueness. In any given problematic case, several competing specifications may be offered by reasonable and fair-minded parties, all of whom are serious about maintaining fidelity to the common morality. For example, while it may be commonly understood that people must be respected, there are likely many different but equally reasonable ways of demonstrating respect for customers or employees.

This diversity does not distress defenders of a common morality theory, because they believe that all that we can ask of moral agents is that they impartially and faithfully specify the norms of the common morality with an eye to overall moral coherence.

Another challenge to common morality theory comes from those who argue that reasonable people from disparate cultures *disagree* about what constitutes the common morality itself and that there are therefore a variety of different and inconsistent common moralities.[41] This particular criticism is not compelling, however, because it has never been shown and even seems inconceivable that some morally committed cultures do not accept rules against lying, breaking promises, stealing, and the like. This is what would have to be shown to prove that common morality theories do not hold universally.

A PROLOGUE TO THEORIES OF JUSTICE

The concluding chapter (Chapter 11) of this book focuses on justice in relation to business. Many rules and principles form the terms of cooperation in society. Society is laced with implicit and explicit arrangements and agreements under which individuals are obligated to cooperate or abstain from interfering with others. Philosophers are interested in the justice of these terms of cooperation. They pose questions such as these: What gives one person or group of people the right to expect cooperation from another person or group of people in some societal interchange (especially an economic one) if the former benefit and the latter do not? Is it just for some citizens to have more property than others? Is it fair for one person to gain an economic advantage over another, if both abide strictly by existing societal rules?

In their attempts to answer such questions, some philosophers believe that diverse human judgments and beliefs about justice can be brought into systematic unity through a general theory of justice. Justice has been analyzed differently, however, in rival and often incompatible theories. Some features of these general normative theories of justice are treated in Chapter 11. Here we need note only that a key distinction between just *procedures* and just *results* exists in the literature on justice.

Ideally, it is preferable to have both, but this is not always possible. For example, a person might achieve a just result in redistributing wealth but might use an unjust procedure to achieve that result, such as undeserved taxation of certain groups. By contrast, just procedures sometimes eventuate in unjust results, as when a fair trial finds an innocent person guilty. Some writers in business ethics are concerned with issues of procedural justice when they discuss such concerns as the use of ombudsmen, grievance procedures, peer review, and arbitration procedures.

Many problems of justice that a cooperative society must handle involve some system or set of procedures that foster, but do not ensure, just outcomes. Once there is agreement on appropriate procedures, the outcome must be accepted as just, even if it produces inequalities that seem unjust by other standards. If procedural justice is the best that can be attained – as, for example, is claimed in the criminal justice system – society should accept the results of its system with a certain amount of humility and perhaps make allowances for inevitable inequalities and even inequities and misfortunes.

In the age of globalization, questions of global justice have been given more attention by political philosophers. The facts that inspire much contemporary work on global justice are well known. Nearly 1 billion people are malnourished and without access to safe drinking water, and 50,000 humans die each day owing to poverty-related causes. Approximately 2.6 billion people live on $2 a day or less. Additionally, increases in global warming, caused primarily by a long history of disproportionate carbon emissions per capita by industrialized nations, are expected to worsen the situation of the world's poorest people this century.

Political philosophers are attempting to work out the obligations of the world's advantaged peoples to the world's poorest peoples. One common view taken by many economists is that rapid economic liberalization in the interest of job creation in the world's poorest nations is the best means of promoting a just global distribution of wealth. In reply, many theorists of global justice argue that rapid economic liberalization by itself may be insufficient or may introduce more problems than it solves. So-called Cosmopolitan theorists argue instead for adherence to careful economic development strategies that adhere to core ethical norms such as basic human rights. More recently, they have also begun to argue for an ethical obligation to reduce carbon emissions to curb climate change given its anticipated harmful impacts on human populations, especially the poor who are least able to adapt.

THE MORAL POINT OF VIEW

A student whose first introduction to ethical theory is this introductory chapter would not be unjustified in feeling a little frustrated at this point. "How," one might ask, "am I supposed to decide which of the normative theories presented thus far – utilitarianism, Kantian ethics, rights theory, virtue ethics, and common morality theory – is the most appropriate basis for making sound ethical decisions regarding business decisions?" This is a reasonable concern. Our response is threefold. First, moral philosophy is a 2,500-year-old tradition. It is not surprising that there should be a significant body of work that merits careful attention. To ignore or downplay this tradition would impoverish any discussion of the ethical practice of business. Second, not all these theories are incompatible. Although some of these views, most notably the Kantian and utilitarian traditions, seem to stand in opposition to one another, other views are more compatible. For example, Kant recognized and discussed at length the importance of the virtues in the life of moral agents, and common morality theories welcome the idea of universally important virtues. Scholars are now beginning to pay more attention to Kant's writings on virtue as well as to the compatibility of virtue theory with a number of other kinds of theory. So too, many of the most prominent rights theories can be grounded in various theories of obligation, including both Kantian ethics and rule utilitarianism. So we can see that several types of theories – or *elements* of the theories such as justice, nonmalevolence, honesty, or integrity – may be compatible. Different theorists tend to emphasize different ideas, but at least in the case of these views, we can see that a resourceful student of ethics will be able to draw some elements from each view without falling into inconsistency.

The third response is more complicated. All the theories discussed in this chapter share certain elements that could be referred to as the right attitude to take in ethics. This is often referred to as "the moral point of view." When we take the moral point of view, we seek to adjudicate disputes rationally; we take an appropriately impartial stance; we assume that other persons are neither more nor less important than ourselves (so that our own claims will be considered alongside and not above those of others). These components of the moral point of view are respectively concerned with rationality, impartiality, and universalizability.

The moral point of view is *rational* in the sense that it involves the application of reason rather than feeling or mere inclination. This is not to denigrate the great importance of the moral emotions and sentiments (for example, love, devotion, and compassion), but moral issues also frequently invoke unwarranted emotional responses in individuals. The attempt to justify a moral stance by appeal to reasons that may be publicly considered and evaluated by other persons facilitates a process whereby individuals with distinctly different emotional responses to a moral issue may seek mutual understanding and, perhaps, agreement. In business the fact that one person wields more economic power than another person cannot by itself outweigh the needs for both parties to offer a rational basis for their competing moral perspectives.

The moral point of view is *universal* in the sense that the principles or propositions reached from that perspective apply to all persons and to all relevantly similar circumstances. Thus, if a moral principle or proposition is valid, no persons are exempt from its strictures. The notion of universalizability has particular relevance in the era of economic globalization. It requires that we regard all persons as equal in dignity and as such that we respect them in our business dealings wherever they may live or work. It is not reasonable to expect highly concrete and practical standards that are universal (for example, "Don't permit the lobbying of political officials"), but it is hoped that the basic principles on which such concrete rules are erected can be shown to apply to all persons (for example, "Avoid conflicts of interest").

The moral point of view is *impartial* in the sense that a moral judgment is formed without regard to particular advantaging or disadvantaging properties of persons. Moral judgments are formed behind what John Rawls has called the "veil of ignorance": A judgment should be formed without regard to the particular fortuitous advantages or disadvantages of persons such as special talents or handicaps, because these properties are morally arbitrary. The ideal, then, is an unbiased evaluation without regard to a person's race, sex, nationality, and economic circumstances, which cannot be regarded as legitimate bases for treating persons differently from other persons. Impartiality is important in many business contexts, including human resource management, where such considerations may interfere with the fair evaluation, promotion, or dismissal of employees.

This understanding of the moral point of view does not exclude *partiality* as if it were illicit. Favoring the interests of one party over another is justified when there are overriding reasons for ranking the specific interests of one party over another. Such partiality is most likely to occur in contexts of familial, professional, or contractual responsibilities.

This point is of obvious importance to business managers who must discharge distinct moral and legal obligations to their employers. The challenge of the ethical manager is to determine when the interests of his or her employers trump those of other stakeholders, and when the interests of those stakeholders override the interests of his or her employers.

To sum up, a business person or business organization that is solely guided by economic considerations is an amoral or unethical organization. The ethical business person or organization, in contrast, is one in which managers and employees alike recognize the importance of moral considerations in their everyday business activities, as well as in their strategic planning, and act accordingly.[42]

1.5 A MULTI-STEP ETHICAL DECISION PROCEDURE

Some ethical issues at work are relatively simple to resolve, especially in an organization with clear policies and a strong ethical culture. In such organizations, it may be simply a matter of applying existing policies consistently. However, many ethical issues in business are complicated and there are not always readily apparent answers to the challenges that arise. For example, Facebook's business model is built around acquiring and selling user data; its business partners will be more profitable if Facebook users act in certain ways. Facebook users can be readily manipulated for business ends or for political ends. Facebook largely ignored the ethical dimensions of its business model, but was forced to confront them because of extensive criticism from external stakeholders. Consider three of these ethical issues: During the 2016 US election cycle, Russian agents, among others, spread misinformation on Facebook in order to manipulate users and thereby influence the outcome of the 2016 presidential election in a manner favorable to its authoritarian government. The Russians favored Donald Trump over Hillary Clinton and succeeded in sowing disinformation on the platform in support of Trump. Critics charge that Facebook failed to adequately identify and remove fake content from its feeds. Users could not differentiate false stories from stories from credible news sources. Facebook has also been criticized for misusing user information by releasing user data to third parties without appropriate permission. In addition, Facebook was criticized for manipulating the emotions of hundreds of thousands of its users (including adolescents aged 13–17) without their informed consent. The goal of the manipulation was to test the power of Facebook's influence. A *New York Times* investigative report in 2018 indicated that Facebook's leaders were focused on growth and gave these challenging ethical issues minimal attention. In characterizing Facebook's behavior, one executive for one of the world's largest advertising companies concludes that "Facebook will do whatever it takes to make money. They have absolutely no morals."[43]

It should be noted that there is nothing unique about business issues that are complex and without an easy answer. How should a board of directors respond to a takeover offer? When should a company diversify its product line or bring a new product to market? How much should a firm invest in research? Despite the complexity and lack of a clear answer, these decisions get made and they get made because there is a procedure for making them. However, what is frequently overlooked is that most business decisions contain an ethical element, and sometimes the ethical element is the single most important element. To ignore or downplay ethical issues is to invite future difficulties as Facebook discovered. Here we provide a multi-step ethical decision-making procedure that takes into account the concepts and theories discussed in these chapters and serves as a practical means for managers and leaders to resolve ethical issues in business.

1. ***Get the facts***: First, the management team must be sure it has the relevant facts. Getting the problem correctly identified is the appropriate starting point. If the problem is misidentified, or important elements of the problem are overlooked, any proposed solution is likely to fail to solve the problem. An analysis may show that there are multiple problems that require attention, or that the problem is more simple or more complex, or potentially much worse or less serious, than initially understood.

2. ***Identify stakeholders***: To take the moral point of view, a person must consider the impact of his or her actions on those affected by one's actions. In the context of business, those affected by a business decision are often called "stakeholders." Some stakeholders have special salience because the support of these stakeholders is necessary to the survival of the firm. Customers, employees, suppliers, and the local community are prominent examples. It seems as if managers and government regulatory agencies are essential stakeholders in this sense as well. Treating these stakeholders with respect and fairness is both an ethical requirement and a requirement of prudence. But management decisions almost always impact individuals whose support is not necessary to the survival of the firm. Externalities, or firm actions that impact third parties who are not a party to a contract or transaction, are a prime example. To see this, consider that the actions of firms often impact the environment in negative ways that harm individuals (e.g., via air or water pollution) with no business relationship to the firm. An ethical decision requires that the management team consider the adverse impact of its actions on all those affected by a company's decision.

3. ***Act with integrity***: "Integrity" is sometimes used as a synonym for "honesty," but its richer meaning is that one's actions are consistent with one's stated or professed values. Organizational integrity means staying true to the stated values of the organization. There is near unanimous agreement in the corporate community regarding the value of fidelity to the rule of law. There is widespread agreement regarding the importance of the values of honesty, fidelity to contracts, and fair dealing. We recognize that management sometimes does break the law or act in violation of these fundamental norms. However, such actions are widely condemned in the business community and the discussion of ethical theory in this chapter has provided reasons for firms to endorse the rule of law and these fundamental ethical norms. Normally, these values are the moral bedrock of a firm. Many firms also explicitly endorse values that emphasize a basic consideration for people, such as care and

respect. As we have seen earlier in this chapter, such consideration can be regarded as a minimum moral expectation.

Such values are not, however, exhaustive of the values that must be considered in a business decision. Most businesses explicitly endorse values that are associated with the particular industry they are in. The banking industry is committed to the value of privacy and has the confidentiality of client financial information as a priority. Safety is a fundamental value in the oil, mining, and construction industries. Patient welfare is a core value in the healthcare and pharmaceutical industries. In making decisions, the management team should be true to the values of the organization it manages and employees should be commended for taking such values into account in the actions they perform on behalf of the firm.

4. ***Consider the consequences***: Assess the consequences of potential courses of action on different stakeholders. It is easy to ignore the consequences of an action on the less powerful and those that appear to have little or no influence on firm revenues. For example, many corporations have been criticized because their management team seems to focus only on the impact of their decisions on short-term stock valuation (which is typically tied to their compensation). An overemphasis on the short-term stock price, while potentially valuable to current stock owners, is bad ethics and typically bad management, even if it results in enhanced compensation for executives. An ethical perspective requires managers and leaders to take into account the broader consequences of their decision. This does not mean that the interests of all affected parties necessarily have the same weight, but that the interests of diverse stakeholders need to be weighed.

5. ***Make a sound decision***: Firm leaders or managers must eventually decide how to proceed. Decisions that contain important ethical dimensions should be justified by reference to the preceding steps. For complex problems it is important to think creatively, and not merely as if there are only two options that one can choose from. Managers frequently operate with bounded rationality that limits their ability to think creatively outside their normal patterns or habits. For important decisions, consulting stakeholders can provide invaluable insight and new ways of thinking that can inform the ultimate decision.

The chapters that follow will delve more deeply into the practices of business, identify those affected by business activities, and emphasize important ethical principles and values that can help managers and leaders make ethically sound decisions. We will also consider what features of organizations, what types of leaders, and what industry practices can support the ethical conduct of business.

Notes

1. Christina Rexrode, "Bankers and Ethics: Is It Time to Talk?" *Charlotte Observer* (December 13, 2010).
2. Dana Milbank, "Hiring Welfare People, Hotel Chain Finds, Is Tough but Rewarding," *Wall Street Journal* (October 31, 1996), pp. A1–A2.
3. Borzou Daragahi, "Saudi Arabia: A Nightmare for Women," *Los Angeles Times* (April 22, 2008).
4. Dustin Block, "He Had a Bud Light; Now He Doesn't Have a Job," *Journal Times* (February 9, 2007).
5. Robert Lindsey, "Ancient Redwood Trees Fall to a Wall Street Takeover," *The New York Times* (March 2, 1988).
6. Insurance Information Institute, "Asbestos Liability" (New York, January 15, 2003): www.iii.org/media/hottopics/ insurance/asbestos/; and Mark D. Plevin et al., "Where Are They Now, Part 5: An Update on Developments in Asbestos-Related Bankruptcy Cases," *Mealey's Asbestos Bankruptcy Report* 8, no. 8 (March, 2009): www.crowell.com /Practices/Bankruptcy/History-of-Asbestos-Bankruptcies.
7. Taken from Peter Huber, "The Press Gets off Easy in Tort Law," *Wall Street Journal* (July 24, 1985), editorial page.
8. "Principle Sale," *Wall Street Journal* (May 22, 1985), p. 35.

9. Jeff Immelt, "Global Environmental Challenges." Lecture delivered at George Washington School of Business (Washington, DC, May 9, 2005).

10. Alex Berenson, "For Merck Chief, Credibility at the Capitol," *The New York Times* (November 19, 2004), p. C1; and John Simons and David Stipp, "Will Merck Survive Vioxx?" *Fortune* (November 1, 2004), pp. 91–104. See also Roy Vagelos and Louis Galambos, *The Moral Corporation: Merck Experiences* (Cambridge University Press, 2006).

11. Thomas Hobbes, *Leviathan*, pt. 1, chap. 13, par. 9.

12. Smith's economic work focused primarily on businesses such as sole proprietorships and small companies, and almost not at all on corporations or what he called "joint stock companies." Although a few joint stock companies existed in his time, he could hardly have imagined the economic dominance and power of modern corporations in the twenty-first century. For this reason, caution is in order when one applies Smith's views to modern economic relations. See Adam Smith, *An Inquiry into the Nature and the Causes of the Wealth of Nations* (Indianapolis, IN: Liberty Fund, 1981). See, especially, vol. 2, bk. 5, chap. 1, pt. 3.

13. This thesis is argued (without reference to philosophical theories of egoism) by Wolfgang Sauer, "Also a Concrete Self-Interest," *United Nations Chronicle* (issue on "Global Sustainable Development: The Corporate Responsibility"), online edition (2002): www.un.org/pubs/chronicle/2002/issue3.

14. Smith's classic work on the subject is *The Theory of Moral Sentiments* (Indianapolis, IN: Liberty Fund, 1982), the sixth and final edition of which appeared in 1790 shortly before his death.

15. For an act-utilitarian example in business ethics, see R. M. Hare, "Commentary on Beauchamp's Manipulative Advertising," *Business and Professional Ethics Journal* 3 (1984): 23–28; for a rule-utilitarian example, see Robert Almeder, "In Defense of Sharks: Moral Issues in Hostile Liquidating Takeovers," *Journal of Business Ethics* 10 (1991): 471–84.

16. Tom L. Beauchamp, ed., *Case Studies in Business, Society, and Ethics*, 5th ed. (Upper Saddle River, NJ: Prentice Hall, 2004), chap. 3.

17. CNN.com (September 3, 1999), "Online Shoppers Bid Millions for Human Kidney."

18. Madhav Goyal, Ravindra Mehta, Lawrence Schneiderman, and Ashwini Sehgal, "Economic and Health Consequences of Selling a Kidney in India," *Journal of the American Medical Association* 288 (October 2, 2002): 1589–93.

19. For discussion of these issues, see Mark J. Cherry, *Kidney for Sale: Human Organs, Transplantation, and the Market* (Washington, DC: Georgetown University Press, 2005).

20. Mary Schlangenstein, "Workers Chip in to Help: Southwest Employees Offer Free Labor," *Seattle Times* (September 26, 2001), p. E1.

21. Motorola, "Code of Business Conduct" (revised September 29, 2004): www.motorola.com/content.jsp?globalObjectId=75–107.

22. For a defense of a similar view, see James S. Taylor, *Stakes and Kidneys: Why Markets in Human Body Parts are Morally Imperative* (Burlington, VT: Ashgate, 2005).

23. Diana B. Henriques, "Beazer Homes Reaches Deal on Fraud Charges," *The New York Times* (July 1, 2009); and Robbie Whelan and Joann S. Lublin, "Beazer CEO Will Give Back Incentive Pay," *Wall Street Journal* (March 4, 2011).

24. See Jennifer Hull, "Unocal Sues," *Wall Street Journal* (March 13, 1985), p. 22; and Charles McCoy, "Mesa Petroleum Alleges Unocal Coerced Banks," *Wall Street Journal* (March 22, 1985), p. 6.

25. Ralph King, "Insider Loans: Everyone Was Doing It," *Business 2.0* (as posted January 15, 2003): www.business2.com/articles/mag.

26. "Anglo Irish Bank Chief Quits after Hiding £87m Loans," *Belfast Telegraph* (December 19, 2008).

27. Reed Abelson, "Cleveland Clinic Discloses Doctors' Industry Ties," *The New York Times* (December 2, 2008).

28. Reuters, "Ex-CEO Pleads Guilty in Backdating Probe," *Los Angeles Times* (February 15, 2007).

29. For a landmark agreement on the island of Saipan (a class-action settlement), see *Legal Intelligencer* 227, no. 64 (September 30, 2002), National News Section, p. 4. For discussion of contemporary labor practice problems at the largest contract manufacturer in the world, see the *Bloomberg Businessweek* cover story, "Inside Foxconn" (September 13, 2010).

30. Ronald Dworkin argues that political morality is rights-based in *Taking Rights Seriously* (London: Duckworth, 1977), p. 171. John Mackie has applied this thesis to *morality generally* in "Can There Be a Right-Based Moral Theory?" *Midwest Studies in Philosophy* 3 (1978): 350–59, esp. p. 350. Henry Shue has defended this view as it applies to foreign policy and development in *Basic Rights: Subsistence, Affluence, and U.S. Foreign Policy*, 2nd ed. (Princeton University Press, 1996). See further Judith Jarvis Thomson, *The Realm of Rights* (Cambridge, MA: Harvard University Press, 1990), pp. 122ff.

31. See further Alan Gewirth, "Why Rights Are Indispensable," *Mind* 95 (1986): 329–44, p. 333, and Gewirth's later book, *The Community of Rights* (University of Chicago Press, 1996).

32. See David Braybrooke, "The Firm but Untidy Correlativity of Rights and Obligations," *Canadian Journal of Philosophy* 1 (1972): 351–63; and Carl P. Wellman, *Real Rights* (Oxford University Press, 1995).

33. See the treatment of these distinctions in Eric Mack, ed., *Positive and Negative Duties* (New Orleans: Tulane University Press, 1985).

34. Linda Klebe Treviño and Michael E. Brown, "Managing to Be Ethical: Debunking Five Business Ethics Myths," *Academy of Management Executive* 18 (2004): 69–81.

35. See, for example, Tom L. Beauchamp and James F. Childress, *Principles of Biomedical Ethics*, 6th ed. (Oxford University Press, 2008), esp. chap. 10; and Bernard Gert, Charles M. Culver, and Danner K. Clouser, *Bioethics: A Return to Fundamentals* (Oxford University Press, 1997).

36. Although there is only a single, universal common morality, there is more than one theory of the common morality. The common morality is universally shared; it is not a theory of what is universally shared. For examples of diverse theories of the common morality, see Alan Donagan, *The Theory of Morality* (University of Chicago Press, 1977); Gert, Culver, and Clouser, *Bioethics: A Return to Fundamentals*; and W. D. Ross, *The Foundations of Ethics* (Oxford University Press, 1939).

37. See Sissela Bok, *Common Values* (Columbia: University of Missouri Press, 1995), pp. 13–23, 50–59. She cites a body of influential writers on the subject.

38. Compare the arguments in G. J. Warnock, *The Object of Morality* (London: Methuen, 1971), esp. pp. 15–26; John Mackie, *Ethics: Inventing Right and Wrong* (London: Penguin, 1977), pp. 107ff.

39. Such norms are referred to as "hypernorms" by Thomas Donaldson and Thomas Dunfee. See their *Ties That Bind: A Social Contracts Approach to Business Ethics* (Boston, MA: Harvard Business School Press, 1999). Donaldson and Dunfee's social contracts approach to business ethics is influential among social science scholars but less so among philosophers and practitioners.

40. See Henry Richardson, "Specifying Norms as a Way to Resolve Concrete Ethical Problems," *Philosophy and Public Affairs* 19 (1990): 279–310; Richardson, "Specifying, Balancing, and Interpreting Bioethical Principles," *Journal of Medicine and Philosophy* 25 (2000): 285–307.

41. See, for example, Leigh Turner, "Zones of Consensus and Zones of Conflict: Questioning the 'Common Morality' Presumption in Bioethics," *Kennedy Institute of Ethics Journal* 13, no. 3 (2003): 193–218; and Turner, "An Anthropological Exploration of Contemporary Bioethics: The Varieties of Common Sense," *Journal of Medical Ethics* 24 (1998): 127–33; David DeGrazia, "Common Morality, Coherence, and the Principles of Biomedical Ethics," *Kennedy Institute of Ethics Journal* 13 (2003): 219–30; Ronald A. Lindsay, "Slaves, Embryos, and Nonhuman Animals: Moral Status and the Limitations of Common Morality Theory," *Kennedy Institute of Ethics Journal* 15, no. 4 (December 2005): 323–46.

42. Elements of this final section are excerpted and reprinted, with the permission of the publisher, from Denis G. Arnold, "Moral Reasoning, Human Rights, and Global Labor Practices," in *Rising Above Sweatshops: Innovative Approaches to Global Labor Challenges* (Westport, CT: Praeger, 2003).

43. Sapna Maheshwari, "'No Morals': Advertisers React to Facebook Report," *The New York Times* (November 15, 2018).

CASES

Case 1: The Training Program

DENIS G. ARNOLD

Rajiv recently graduated from an American university with a major in management and a minor in computer science. His student visa will expire soon, and in order to remain in the United States he needs a job. Good jobs in his home country are scarce.

Rajiv was invited to join a free eight-week software training program. After the training program, the company has promised to place him in a company that will sponsor his work visa, which international students need in order to work in the United States. The hiring companies will provide the training program company with a fee for every hire they make. The firm offering the training program is a start-up company. Rajiv accepted the offer and has attended training along with five other trainees.

Rajiv and his fellow trainees are learning SAP software, which is a database software implemented mainly in very large multinational corporations. Usually, when large companies want to implement this software, they hire consulting firms such as Deloitte, IBM, or Accenture to undertake the projects. These consulting firms in turn hire employees from smaller companies like the one Rajiv is training with on a project-by-project basis.

The owner of the company instructed Rajiv and the other trainees to produce a résumé with three to four years of fake work experience using SAP software on projects for large companies. Their résumés will be forwarded to staffing agencies that specialize in finding people with such skill sets for big consulting firms.

After doing some research online and talking to family and friends who are familiar with the IT industry, Rajiv came to the conclusion that faking work experience on the résumé is common practice among those seeking US work visas and that it is very difficult to find an entry level position in this field without faking a previous work record.

Rajiv explained to the owner of the start-up company that he is not comfortable lying on his résumé. The owner advised him to not think too much about it and explained to him that "Everybody does it" and "There is nothing wrong with it." He said, "Just get onto a project and you will learn on the job because you will be working on large teams; people will help you out if you do not know what you are doing."

On the one hand, Rajiv does not want to lie on his résumé. On the other hand, he has no other job lined up and it is very difficult to find an employer who is willing to hire an international student and sponsor a work visa. If he does not find a job in the next three months he will be forced to go back to his home country because his student visa will expire. The other five students in the training program are also international students and they have agreed to inflate their résumés. They say that "there is no other choice" because none of them are finding employment anywhere else. Rajiv must make a decision about what to do within a few days. What should he do?

Discussion Questions

1. If you were in Rajiv's position, what would you do? Why?
2. Do you agree with Rajiv's fellow trainees that they have no choice but to lie on their résumés? Why, or why not?
3. Based on your reading thus far, what ethical concepts or theories are most relevant to analyzing this case? Why? Explain.
4. What do you think would happen if a lie on one's résumé about "three to four years of work experience" were discovered later in one's career? Explain.

Case 2: Should Company Policy Apply to All?

DENIS G. ARNOLD

Sam manages the men's department in a large department store. His star salesperson is Jessica, a recent college graduate who has been unable to find work elsewhere. Jessica has an outgoing personality, is extremely friendly and warm with customers, and dresses in fashionable, form fitting clothing. Customers tend to follow her suggestions regarding what looks good on them and often return to shop with her. Jessica is especially good at getting customers to apply for company credit cards and to purchase more expensive items than they had originally intended to buy. While working, Jessica will often talk with her friends on her personal mobile phone. Customers can overhear these personal conversations. Having personal phone conversations while working is strictly prohibited by company policy (company policy does allow employees to make such calls on breaks). However, Sam lets Jessica have these conversations while on duty because of her excellent productivity. As long as she is increasing his department's sales, he does not want to bother her about the policy violations.

Robert is another salesperson and he has been working in the men's department for several years. He lost his job in the banking industry, and took this sales job to make ends meet. He is polite to customers, but not especially chatty. He usually helps customers locate what they came to the store to purchase rather than try to sell them more expensive products that they may not be able to afford. Because of his experience in banking with customers who ran up bills on high interest credit cards that they could not afford to pay down, he does not push company credit card sales very hard. His sales are good, but not near the lofty levels attained by Jessica. Robert has never used his mobile phone while working, but his wife is pregnant with their first child,

and recently he took some nervous calls from her while he was working. On both occasions Sam happened to hear him on the phone and on both occasions Sam made him hang up and reminded him of the company policy about mobile phone use while on duty. On the second occasion, Robert confronted Sam and stated that he allowed Jessica to use her mobile phone while on duty so he should also allow him to use his phone – at least for important calls. Sam ignored this comment and told Robert to "get in line" and follow company policy or he would have to write up a policy violation letter for his personnel file.

Later that night, however, Sam wondered whether he was doing the right thing by disciplining Robert. He had to enforce the policy at least some of the time, he thought, and he couldn't afford to offend Jessica, but something still troubled him about the situation.

Discussion Questions

1. Does Robert have a legitimate complaint? Why, or why not?

2. Is Sam acting in an ethically appropriate manner? Why, or why not?

3. Based on your reading thus far, what ethical concepts or theories are most relevant to analyzing this case? How are they relevant? Explain.

4. Should managers consistently enforce company policies? Why, or why not?

Case 3: Deceiving Student Loan Borrowers Drives Profits at Navient

ROXANNE ROSS AND DENIS G. ARNOLD

About 70 percent of recent graduates leave college with student loans. The average debt per borrower is approximately $30,000. Cumulatively, US student loan debt is over $1.4 trillion, surpassing credit card and auto loan debt. Of the 44 million Americans with student loans, 8 million, or about one in six, are in default, meaning they have not made a payment in over nine months. The amount owed for those in default is $130 billion. Many others struggle to make payments.

Legislation was changed to help those struggling to manage their debt. The changes allowed borrowers to

make payment plans based on their income. Borrowers meeting certain thresholds for income and family size could pay as little as $0 per month. It also meant the federal government would pay interest charges for some. Eligible borrowers could also receive loan forgiveness after 20 years of monthly payments. These repayment options were intended to be a lifeline for floundering borrowers.

However, the Consumer Financial Protection Bureau (CFPB) found that many borrowers did not take advantage of the changes because Navient, the largest service provider of student loans, purposefully withheld information about lower cost repayment options. According to the CFPB, Navient convinced borrowers to enroll in plans that were more profitable for the firm at the borrower's expense. Navient, once part of Sallie Mae, services 12 million borrowers with over $300 billion in loans. One in four borrowers pays their loans through Navient. The company serves as a link between borrowers and banks actually holding the debt. Navient is supposed to help students manage debt. However, the CFPB maintained that Navient intentionally deceived borrowers, stating that the service provider was "systematically and illegally failing borrowers at every stage of repayment."

The CFPB sued Navient for deceiving borrowers. Specifically, the suit states Navient violated the Dodd-Frank Wall Street Reform and Consumer Protection Act, the Fair Credit Reporting Act, and the Fair Debt Collections Practices Act. Navient processed payments incorrectly, neglected to respond to borrowers' complaints, encouraged borrowers to enroll in plans that would cost them more, deceived borrowers about requirements to release cosigners, and wrongly harmed the credit of disabled borrowers, including injured veterans. Navient also financially rewarded customer service representatives for signing up borrowers for more costly repayment options.

The amount lost for individual borrowers is difficult to estimate, as it would vary from person to person. Some borrowers were not affected at all. Others face financial troubles that could have been avoided had they been properly informed about their repayment options. For instance, disabled veterans who cannot work qualify to have their loans discharged. Those veterans may have permanently damaged credit records. Such avoidable damage could hold people back from buying a house or paying off other loans. The CFPB estimates that $4 billion in additional interest was illegally charged to debtor accounts. In response to litigation filed by the CFPB, Navient stated that "There is no expectation that the servicer [Navient] will act in the interest of the consumer." Instead, Navient claims its responsibility was to the creditors whose loans it is servicing.

Discussion Questions

1. From an ethical perspective, how would you assess Navient's behavior toward student loan borrowers in this case? Explain.

2. How do you assess Navient's claim that it has no obligation to act on behalf of the student loan borrowers whose loans it services? Explain.

3. Apply the multi-step ethical decision procedure to this case. What sound decisions would be required by Navient leaders? How would Navient's behavior need to change if the decision procedure were to be applied? Explain.

This case was written for classroom discussion and is based on the following sources: "CFPB Sues Nation's Largest Student Loan Company Navient for Failing Borrowers at Every Stage of Repayment" (January 18, 2017). Retrieved August 11, 2017 from www.consumerfinance.gov/about-us/newsroom/cfpb-sues-nations-largest-student-loan-company-navient-failing-borrowers-every-stage-repayment/.

S. Cowley and J. Silver-Greenberg, "Student Loan Collector Cheated Millions, Lawsuits Say," *The New York Times* (January 18, 2017). Retrieved from www.nytimes.com/2017/01/18/business/dealbook/student-loans-navient-lawsuit.html.

Student Loan Debt Statistics 2017. Retrieved August 11, 2017 from https://studentloans.net/student-loan-debt-statistics/.

S. Nasiripour, "Student Debt Giant Navient to Borrowers: You're on Your Own," *Bloomberg.com* (April 3, 2017). Retrieved August 15, 2017 from www.bloomberg.com/news/articles/2017–04-03/student-debt-giant-navient-to-borrowers-you-re-on-your-own.

2

The Rights and Responsibilities of Employees

2.1 INTRODUCTION

Traditionally, business firms are organized hierarchically, with production line or customer service employees at the bottom and the CEO at the top. Typically, the interests of the owners or stockholders are given priority over the interests of employees. However, much recent literature presents a challenge to these arrangements, especially to underlying classic economic assumptions whereby labor is treated as analogous to land, capital, and machinery, that is, as a replaceable input and a mere means to profit. Employees want to be treated as persons who are appropriately valued in the business enterprise. They want decent salaries and a safe working environment, as well as appreciation from supervisors, a sense of accomplishment, and fair opportunities to display their talents. Many employees are also interested in participating in planning the future directions of the company, defining the public responsibilities of the corporation, evaluating the role and quality of management, and – most especially – helping to set the tasks assigned to their jobs. These new developments in labor relations are all to the good, but they must be understood in light of a very different tradition whereby an employee is clearly subordinate to the employer, is legally obligated to obey the employer's orders, and has few rights except the right to quit.

ETHICAL CONSIDERATION OF EMPLOYEES

Why should employees be treated with respect and consideration? In a tight labor market an economist might argue that doing so will attract employees, but are there reasons for respecting employees other than economic ones? In his contribution to this chapter, "Treating Employees with Respect," Norman E. Bowie argues that there are compelling ethical reasons for thinking that employees should be treated with respect, and not as mere disposable inputs in the cogs of production. Bowie emphasizes the Kantian idea of respect for person, the idea that because people are rational creatures that can pursue their own ends (as opposed to being driven merely by instinct) they have unique dignity. Because they have unique dignity, they are entitled to be treated as more than mere instruments of production and are entitled to respect. Bowie provides a powerful analysis that helps us to understand the fundamental obligations of employers to employees.

The next article in this section by Wayne F. Cascio, "Decency Means More than 'Always Low Prices': A Comparison of Costco to Walmart's Sam's Club," compares the management of Sam's Club, a warehouse retailer that is part of Walmart, and its competitor Costco. Walmart and Sam's Club are famous for low prices that make products affordable for customers who lack ample financial resources. However, Walmart has come under sustained criticism in recent years for allegedly unfair and illegal labor practices such as underpayment of earnings, sexual discrimination against women, the use of illegal alien workers, and transferring the burden of employee healthcare costs to taxpayers. Cascio points out that Costco is an aggressive and highly successful competitor to Walmart. Over a five-year period, Costco's stock rose 55 percent while Walmart's declined 10 percent. At the same time, Costco was taking extraordinarily good care of its employees and customers. Cascio argues that if Costco can be profitable while ensuring that all its employees and other stakeholders are treated well, Walmart should be able to do the same.

THE HIRING AND FIRING OF EMPLOYEES

In the traditional view, the freedom of the employee to quit, the freedom of the employer to fire, and the right of the employer to order the employee to do his or her bidding define the essence of the employment contract. In the United States the legal principle behind the traditional view is called the *employment-at-will principle*. This principle says that in the absence of a specific contract or law, an employer may hire, fire, demote, or promote an employee whenever the employer wishes. Moreover, the employer may act with justification, with inadequate justification, or with no justification at all. Scholars from the law and economics school have continued to support the traditional employment-at-will doctrine. For example, Richard A. Epstein argues in his contribution to this chapter, "In Defense of the Contract at Will," that employment-at-will is both fair and efficient. Spokespersons from the law and economics school take efficiency concerns very seriously, and Epstein spends considerable time developing some of these concerns.

Over the years this master–servant relationship, which is at the core of the employment-at-will doctrine, has been legally constrained. Once unions were given legal protection, collective bargaining produced contracts that constrained the right of employers to fire at will. Employees who were protected by union contracts usually could be fired only for just cause and then only after a lengthy grievance process. During the height of the union movement, the chief protection against an unjust firing was the union-negotiated contract. However, during the 1980s and 1990s the percentage of the US workforce belonging to unions fell into the teens, and as a result the protection offered by the union-negotiated contract covers millions fewer workers.

Some might argue that the decline in the number of US workers who belong to unions has not significantly increased the number of employees who are at risk of an unjust dismissal. These people argue that a large number of enlightened companies have adopted policies that provide the same type of protection against unjust dismissal as was previously found in union-negotiated contracts. Moreover, where such policies exist they have the force of law. For example, in 1985 the New Jersey Supreme Court held that Hoffman-LaRoche Inc. was bound by job security assurances that were implied in an employee manual. The manual seemed to pledge that employees could be fired only for just cause and then only if certain procedures were followed. Hoffman-LaRoche argued that although the company manual gave company policy, adherence to it was voluntary and not legally enforceable. The Court, however, said employers cannot have it both ways without acting unfairly and, so, illegally. Hoffman-LaRoche had to reinstate an employee who had been fired on grounds that his supervisor had lost confidence in his work.

In response to this and similar rulings, a number of corporations have taken steps to make it more difficult for employees to use company manuals and policy statements to protect their jobs. Some are simply eliminating the manuals and dismantling their grievance procedure apparatus. Sears Roebuck and other employers have their employees sign a form declaring that they can be fired "with or without just cause." Patricia H. Werhane and Tara J. Radin consider several arguments for the employment-at-will doctrine and find them wanting. In "Employment at Will and Due Process" they argue that a just workplace will include both substantive and procedural due process for employees.

Others point out that during the 1980s and early 1990s, certain grounds for firing employees were made illegal by federal or state law. Anti-discrimination statutes protect workers from being fired because of their race or sex, because they are handicapped, or because of age. Federal law also protects workers from being fired because they resist sexual advances from their bosses or refuse to date them. The protection given employees from this and other forms of sexual harassment is discussed in Chapter 4.

HEALTH AND SAFETY

Critics of business and government have long contended that uninformed workers are routinely, and often knowingly, exposed to dangerous conditions. For example, employers did not tell asbestos workers for many years of the known dangers of contracting asbestosis. Although little is currently understood about the knowledge and comprehension of workers, evidence from at least some industries indicates that ignorance is a causal factor in occupational illness or injury. The simplest solution is to ban hazardous products from use, but to do so would involve shutting down a large segment of industrial manufacturing. Hundreds of products still contain asbestos either because no functional substitute is available or replacement is not cost efficient.

The implications of worker ignorance are chillingly present in the following worker's testimony before an Occupational Safety and Health Administration (OSHA) hearing on the toxic agent DBCP (1,2-dibromo-3-chloropropane):

> We had no warning that DBCP exposure might cause sterility, testicular atrophy, and perhaps cancer. If we had known that these fumes could possibly cause the damage that we have found out it probably does cause, we would have worn equipment to protect ourselves. As it was, we didn't have enough knowledge to give us the proper respect for DBCP.[1]

The regulation of workplace risks has consistently sought to determine an objective level of acceptable risk and then to ban or limit exposure above that level. However, the goal of safety is not the primary justification for disclosures of risk. Individuals need the information upon which the objective standard is based to determine whether the risk it declares acceptable is *acceptable to them*. Here a subjective standard of acceptable risk seems more appropriate than an objective standard established by "experts." Choosing to risk testicular atrophy seems rightly a worker's personal choice, one not fully decidable by health and safety standards established for groups of workers. Even given objective standards, substantial ambiguity prevails when the experts are uncertain about the risks, and dangerous dose levels cannot be established.

Problems also surface about the strategy of information disclosure and the strategy of protective schemes – especially if one or the other is used in isolation. Often, there are no meaningful figures to define the relationship between acceptable risk and the ease with which the risk can be eliminated or controlled. There also may be no consensus about which levels of probability of serious harm, such as death, constitute risks sufficiently high to require that steps be taken to reduce or eliminate the risk or to provide information to those affected.

John R. Boatright focuses on the worker's right to receive information from employers and the effectiveness of the current system in "Occupational Health and Safety." He also looks at the worker's right to refuse to work and the government's obligation to regulate the workplace. He concentrates on particularly controversial regulatory programs and policies and how they affect the rights to know and refuse. Also included in the legal perspectives section of this chapter is the case of *Automobile Workers v. Johnson Controls, Inc.*, which determined that employers cannot legally adopt "fetal protection policies" that exclude women of childbearing age from a hazardous workplace, because such policies involve illegal sex discrimination.

Major industrial disasters, such as the *Deepwater Horizon* explosion and fire that killed 11 and injured 17 oil workers in the Gulf of Mexico, continue to be an occupational risk. Yet BP had a poor record of safety compared to other major oil firms during the same time period. As Mark A. Cohen and his co-authors point out in "Safety Culture in High Risk Industries," best practices for the management of health and safety in dangerous industries are well understood. What are required to help ensure the safety of workers are leader commitment, resources, and training. When these are in place, a safety culture that protects the lives and bodily integrity of workers can be maintained. Without these, injury and death are nearly inevitable.

Note

1. Occupational Safety and Health Administration, "Access to Employee Exposure and Medical Records – Final Rules," *Federal Register* (May 23, 1980), p. 35222.

2.2 ETHICAL CONSIDERATION OF EMPLOYEES

Treating Employees with Respect

NORMAN E. BOWIE

If the average person has a second moral principle to supplement the Golden Rule, it is probably a principle that says we should respect people. Just as the first formulation of the categorical imperative provided a more rigorous formulation of the Golden Rule, Kant's second formulation of the categorical imperative, "Always act so that you treat the humanity in a person, whether in your own person or in that of another, always as an end and never as a means only,"[1] is a more rigorous formulation of the principle that one should respect people.

Respecting people is thoroughly interwoven into the fabric of contemporary life. A "respect-for-persons" principle, like a "golden rule" principle, could claim the status of a universal moral principle. People demand respect, and when they don't feel respected, the results can be tragic, as we have seen. In the United States, there are numerous instances where people have been shot dead because they allegedly did not "respect" the shooter.

Moreover, there is no one in the business community who has challenged the respect-for-persons principle as a principle in business ethics. Yet ironically, many of the moral criticisms of business practice are directed against policies that do not respect persons – for example, that business human relations policies often invade privacy or relegate people to dead-end jobs where they cannot grow professionally. In addition, there is considerable controversy, even among ethicists, as to what a respect-for-persons principle requires.

In this chapter I shall develop Kant's respect-for-persons principle and show the implications of that principle for business practice. I believe that if Kant's respect-for-persons principle were honored, business practice would look very different. Thus, the application of Kantian ethics here calls for a fairly radical reform of business practice. Nonetheless, I shall argue that such reform may actually

Parts of this essay are excerpted from Norman E. Bowie, *Business Ethics: A Kantian Perspective* (Cambridge University Press, 2017).

enhance the bottom line, rather than hurt it as business-people often suppose.

I want to begin by describing a misunderstanding or misuse of the respect-for-persons principle. I recall from my undergraduate days in the early 1960s, when I first developed my interest in Kant, we addressed the issue of whether buying a product like vegetables in the supermarket violated the respect-for-persons requirement of the second formulation of the categorical imperative. In buying our groceries, did we use the clerk who in those days rang up our purchases on a cash register? Did we use the clerk as a means merely? First, we decided that we did not *merely* use people in business transactions because we could accomplish our goal – buying carrots or potatoes – and still show respect to those on the other end of the transactions. We could speak to them, wish them a good day, thank them for their service, and things like that. A casual observer in a supermarket can distinguish those patrons who treat the cashiers with respect from those who do not.

However, we wondered if all Kant's respect-for-persons principle required was that we be nice to people. Undergraduate economics courses provide an analysis of how a manager should treat the various factors of production. The most efficient manager is one that rearranges capital, land, machines, and workers so that their proportional marginal productivity is equal. The requirement of equal proportional marginal productivity works as follows: If the price of machines rises with respect to labor, substitute labor for machines until the marginal productivity of each is equal. If the price of labor rises with respect to machines, substitute machines for labor until the marginal productivity for both is equal. For the economists these substitutions are morally equivalent.

At first glance it looks as if a Kantian would say that the two substitutions are not morally equivalent. The first, substituting labor for machines, is morally permissible; the second, substituting machines for labor, is not morally permissible. In the latter case it looks as if the employees are used as a means merely for the enhancement of the profits of the stockholders. It is morally permissible to use machines that way, but it is not morally permissible to use people that way. Unlike the grocery store example, the managers who act on behalf of the stockholders – at least in publicly held corporations of any size – are not in a personal face-to-face relationship with the employees and thus cannot avoid the charge of merely using the employees by saying that in the transaction they treated the other party to the transaction with respect. It doesn't matter if managers were nice to the employees when they laid them off. Since some layoffs are

handled in a degrading and cruel way, there is a moral distinction among various practices for laying people off. However, being enlightened rather than degrading and cruel does not get the enlightened managers off the moral hook completely. The real issue, under the respect-for-persons principle, is whether people can be fired at all just because labor becomes more expensive relative to machines. What would a Kantian, using Kant's respect-for-persons principle, say about that? To answer that question, some explanation of Kant's respect-for-persons principle is in order.

The Respect-for-Persons Principle

Kant did not simply assert that human beings are entitled to respect; he has an elaborate argument for it. Human beings ought to be respected because human beings have dignity. For Kant, an object that has dignity is beyond price. That's what's wrong with the principle that says a manager should adjust the inputs of production to the point where the marginal productivity of each is equal. And further, the denial of dignity is what makes much downsizing unjust. In these cases, that which is without price – human beings – are treated as simply exchangeable with that which has a price. Human employees have a dignity that machines and capital do not. Thus, it looks like managers cannot manage their corporate resources in the most efficient manner without violating the respect-for-persons principle. Whether that is the correct implication remains to be seen.

But first, why do persons possess a dignity that is beyond all price? They have dignity because human beings are capable of autonomy and thus are capable of self-governance. As autonomous beings capable of self-governance, they are also responsible beings, since autonomy and self-governance are conditions for responsibility. A person who is not autonomous and who is not capable of self-governance is not responsible. That's why little children or the mentally ill are not considered responsible beings. Thus, there is a conceptual link between being a human being, being an autonomous being, being capable of self-governance, and being a responsible being.

Autonomous responsible beings are capable of making and following their own laws; they are not simply subject to the causal laws of nature. Human beings are different from billiard balls. Anyone who recognizes that she is autonomous should recognize that she is responsible for her actions and thus she should recognize that she is a moral being. From this Kant argues that the fact that one is a moral being enables us to say that such a being possesses dignity: "Morality is the condition under which alone a rational being can be an end in himself because only through it is it possible to be a lawgiving member in the realm of ends. Thus morality, and humanity, insofar as it is capable of morality, alone have dignity."[2] This emphasis on dignity and respect undercuts the notion that Kant's ethics is primarily an austere ethic of duty. As T. E. Hill puts it, "[For Kant] moral conduct is the practical exercise of the noble capacity to be rational and self-governing; a capacity which sets us apart from the lower animals and gives us dignity. Kant's ethics is as much an ethics of self-esteem as it is an ethics of duty."[3]

Now, as a point of logic, a person who recognizes that he or she is responsible and thus has dignity should ascribe dignity to other people who have the same capacity to be autonomous and responsible beings. As Kant says:

> Rational nature exists as an end in itself. Man necessarily thinks of his own existence in this way, and thus far it is a subjective principle of human actions. Also every rational being thinks of his existence on the same rational ground which holds also for myself; thus it is at the same time an objective principle from which, as a supreme practical ground, it must be possible to derive all laws of the will.[4]

This quotation provides Kant's argument for the necessity of including all other persons within the scope of the respect-for-persons principle (treating the humanity in a person as an end and never as a means only). The argument is based on consistency. What we say about ourselves we must say about similar cases, namely about other human beings. Kant's focus is on the person as moral agent. Freedom and the ability to make laws (as opposed to being simply subjected to causal laws) are necessary conditions for moral agency. Rationality is a result of our freedom and enables us to be moral beings; rationality allows us to act on laws we have made rather than being simply subjected to causal laws.

This quotation emphasizing the relationship between freedom and rationality provides the basis for an overall critique of some standard business practices. In other words, contrary to what critics of Kant's respect-for-persons principle say, the principle is not overly abstract and sentimental. It means much more than being nice to people in business transactions.

Employment at Will

The business practice of employment at will receives considerable attention in this chapter. Employment at will is prevalent in the United States and many employees actually sign a statement acknowledging that they are "at-will" employees. In signing these documents, employees acknowledge that, in the absence of a contract or specific legislative protection, they may be fired for any reason, good reason, bad reason, or even no reason at all. But firing a person for a bad reason or no reason at all is an assault on rationality itself, the very foundation of respect for persons. Bad reasons might include presenting a threat to a mediocre supervisor's job security by being extremely competent and hardworking, following company policies that a supervisor does not like, or asserting one's rights under the law. Thus, the practice of employment at will seems to violate the respect-for-persons principle in tolerating dismissals. If this is true, a common US business practice with respect to employees is morally deficient.

One might respond by noting that many employees sign "at-will" contracts and thus they are accepting that condition of employment. These employees are exercising their freedom and it would be disrespectful to deny them that right. However, many would argue that this argument is flawed. First, and especially in a tight labor market, employees need to sign that employment at-will acknowledgment if they are to be employed. They really do not have a choice and are victims of economic institutional coercion. This response is controversial and cannot be examined in detail here, but if the argument is successful, it shows that employment at will fails the respect-for-persons test. After all, coercion is an assault on freedom and rationality – which are the foundations of respect for employees. But even if the employment at-will contract is not coercive, it fails the Kantian respect-for-persons test for another reason. Persons not only have an obligation to respect the humanity of others, they have an obligation to respect humanity in themselves. Signing a contract that challenges your freedom and rationality violates the respect-for-persons principle. As an extreme example of this idea, the respect-for-persons principle obligates you not to sign a contract that allows you to be enslaved. The employment at-will practice is wrong when it violates the obligation to respect the rationality and freedom of an employee, such as when an employee is fired for a bad reason or no reason at all.

Health and Safety

The obligation of an employer to provide a safe and healthy environment is another important issue in this chapter. Kant was clear in arguing that respecting persons requires more than not coercing them. We not only must not use people, but we must treat them as ends in themselves. Sometimes we must take positive action to enable people to achieve their ends or goals. An environment that protects a person's health and safety is a necessary condition for anyone to achieve his or her ends. Denying a person a necessary condition for achieving his or her goals and purposes is to show a lack of respect for their personhood.

Fair enough. But how far does the employer's obligation extend? For a utilitarian, the answer is provided by a cost–benefit analysis. The employer's obligation extends up to the point where the cost of providing a healthy and safe environment exceeds the benefits such a healthy and safe environment provides to society. A Kantian does not look at the issue that way. For any given job situation, the Kantian would ask "Who has the responsibility in this case?" and "What does respect for persons entail?" For example, at a construction site, the construction company needs to steer pedestrians away from the site, put scaffolding over the sidewalk, and require hard hats and other appropriate safety gear for employees. But pedestrians have an obligation to follow walkway signs and instructions; workers have an obligation to wear hard hats at the job site, eye protection when needed for safety, and not smoke in areas where smoking is prohibited because of a fire hazard. A utilitarian looks at costs and benefits to society. A Kantian emphasizes responsibilities and obligations to respect personhood.

Harassment and Discrimination

The "me too" movement has sparked a renewed and intense interest in sexual harassment and members of the LGBT community complain of overt and covert discrimination in numerous business transactions from rental housing to buying a wedding cake. Sexual harassment and discrimination based on sex or sexual orientation, or other arbitrary characteristics, such as race or ethnicity, are clear violations of Kant's respect-for-persons principle. Sexism in general regards women as generally inferior to men and is often grounded in ignorance and false perceptions of reality such as the belief that women cannot reason as well as men. Sexual harassment involves treating a person as a means merely, as an object of sexual gratification. Sexual harassment often involves an abuse of power where the victim feels coerced as when sexual gratification is demanded for a job or a promotion. Similarly, a hostile work environment undermines the dignity of certain members of the business organization.

Discrimination against members of the LGBT community, as with discrimination against members of racial or ethnic minorities, is an affront to their dignity and self-respect. Economists such as Milton Friedman have hailed business transactions as an ideal of nondiscrimination. Discrimination is inefficient. Kantians point out that,

additionally, such discrimination is unfair because it takes a characteristic like sexual orientation that is irrelevant to a business transaction and makes it determinant as to whether the business transaction will take place at all. This places an unfair burden on members of the LGBT community and undermines dignity and self-respect in members of that community.

Privacy

The respect-for-persons principle has implications for business practice and conduct that go far beyond the issues considered in this chapter. Another example concerns the obligation of the business community to protect the privacy of employees and also the obligation not to impede the legitimate privacy rights of individuals. The Kantian ideals of autonomy and self-respect provide the grounding for this business obligation. Privacy is an important, and perhaps a necessary, condition for the development of a self-concept as an autonomous individual. Most importantly privacy enables us to draw distinctions in our relationships; it allows us to have acquaintances, friends, and intimate partners. Individuals do not want information that they share in confidence with a spouse or intimate friend to be shared with others. Keeping information that we have about another private is a way of maintaining their autonomy and showing respect.

It follows from this analysis that a business has an obligation to protect the privacy of employees and other stakeholders such as customers. In the digital age this obligation to protect privacy is just as stringent as the obligation to provide a healthy and safe work environment. The occurrence of security failures, leading to massive privacy breaches, in business sectors such as in the banking and credit industries, is a moral failure as well as a public relations disaster.

Kant's emphasis on the categorical obligation to respect the humanity of persons in others, and in oneself, fits well with common sense morality and provides a principle for guiding business practice and, where necessary, its reform.

Notes

1. Immanuel Kant, *Foundations of the Metaphysics of Morals (1785),* trans. L. W. Beck (New York: Macmillan, 1990), p. 46.
2. Ibid., p. 52.
3. T. E. Hill, Jr., *Dignity and Practical Reason in Kant's Moral Theory* (Ithaca, NY: Cornell University Press, 1992), pp. 36–37.
4. Kant, *Foundations of the Metaphysics of Morals,* p. 36.

Decency Means More than "Always Low Prices": A Comparison of Costco to Walmart's Sam's Club

WAYNE F. CASCIO

To be sure, Walmart wields its awesome power for just one purpose: to bring the lowest possible prices to its customers. Sam Walton, affectionately known as "Mr. Sam" by Walmart associates, embodied a number of admirable values that he instilled in the company he founded: hard work, discipline, modesty, unpretentiousness, and frugality. By all accounts he also wanted his employees to be motivated, inspired, and happy to work for Walmart. At the same time, however, he was driven, tireless, and determined to drive a hard bargain. His brilliance lay in his ability to execute a singularly powerful idea: Sell stuff that people need every day, just a little cheaper than everyone else, sell it at that low price all the time, and customers will flock to you. Walmart's mission is found as a slogan printed on every Walmart bag: "Always low prices. *Always.*" Walmart's obsessive focus on that single core value created what has become the largest and most powerful company in history.

The company espouses those same core values today, but ironically, their application is quite different from that in the 1960s, the 1970s, even the 1980s. Today, the very characteristics that allowed Walmart to prosper and grow are the source of unrelenting criticism. As Charles Fishman notes, the company's core values seem to have become inverted, for they now sometimes drive behavior that is not only exploitive but, in some cases, illegal as well.[1] Consider the pressure on store managers to control labor costs. As noted in its 2005 annual report, Walmart is a defendant in numerous class-action lawsuits involving employment-related issues as varied as failure to pay required overtime to hourly employees, challenges to exempt (from overtime) status by assistant store managers, and allegations of gender-based discrimination in pay, promotions, job transfers, training, job assignments, and healthcare coverage.

There is another aspect of the Walmart effect that is more troubling, and it concerns how Walmart gets those low prices: low wages for its employees, unrelenting pressure on suppliers, products cheap in quality as well as price, offshoring jobs.

Wal-Mart has the power to squeeze profit-killing concessions from suppliers, many of whom are willing to do almost anything to keep the retailer happy, in part because Wal-Mart now dominates consumer markets so thoroughly that they have no choice . . . Wal-Mart's price pressure can leave so little profit that there is little left for innovation . . . [As a result] decisions made in Bentonville routinely close factories as well as open them.[2]

This paper focuses on a company that is already more than "always low prices." That company is warehouse-retailer Costco – one that may provide an alternative to the Walmart model by delivering low prices to consumers, but not at the cost of employees' wages or quality of life. In the following sections we will begin by providing some background on the company, including its history, its business model, its ethical principles, core beliefs, and values. Then we will consider some typical Wall Street analysts' assessments of this approach, followed by a systematic comparison of the financial performance of Costco with that of Sam's Club, a warehouse retailer that is part of Walmart.

Costco: A Brief History

The company's co-founder and chief executive officer, Jim Sinegal, is the son of a coal miner and steelworker. In 1954, as an 18-year-old student at San Diego Community College, a friend asked him to help unload mattresses for a month-old discounter called Fed-Mart. What he thought would be a one-day job turned into a career. He rose to executive Vice-President for Merchandising, and became a protégé of Fed-Mart's chairman, Sol Price. Mr. Price is credited with inventing the idea of high-volume warehouse stores that sell a limited number of products.

Sol Price sold Fed-Mart to a German retailer in 1975, and was fired soon after. Mr. Sinegal then left and helped Mr. Price start a new warehouse company, Price Club. Its huge success led others to enter the business: Walmart started Sam's Club, Zayre's started BJ's Wholesale Club, and in 1983 a Seattle entrepreneur, Jeffrey Brotman, helped Mr. Sinegal to found Costco Wholesale Corporation. The company began with a single store in Issaquah, Washington, outside of Seattle. At the end of fiscal 2005, as the fourth

From *Academy of Management Perspectives*, August 2006. Reprinted with permission.

largest retailer in the United States and the ninth largest in the world, it had a total of 460 warehouses in 37 US states, Puerto Rico, and several additional countries: Canada, Mexico, United Kingdom, Taiwan, South Korea, and Japan. Costco and Price Club merged in 1993.

Ethical Principles, Core Beliefs, and Values

In their most recent letter to shareholders, co-founders Jeff Brotman and Jim Sinegal wrote: "We remain committed to running our company and living conscientiously by our Code of Ethics every day: to obey the law; take care of our members; take care of our employees; respect our suppliers; and reward you, our shareholders."[3] Note the modern-day heresy in Costco's numbered code of ethics: taking care of customers and employees takes precedence over rewarding shareholders. As we will see below, this has not escaped the critical appraisal of Wall Street analysts.

In contrast to Walmart, which believes, as many other companies do, that shareholders are best served if employers do all they can to hold down costs, including the costs of labor, Costco's approach is decidedly different. In terms of how it treats its workers, Mr. Sinegal says, "It absolutely makes good business sense. Most people agree that we're the lowest-cost provider. Yet we pay the highest wages. So it must mean we get better productivity. It's axiomatic in our business – you get what you pay for."[4]

Wages at Costco start at $10 an hour, rising to $18.32, excluding *twice*-a-year bonuses of between $2,000 and $3,000 for those at the top wage for more than a year. Its average hourly wage is $17 an hour. Walmart does not share its wage scale, and does not break down separately the pay of its Sam's Club workers, but the average pay of a full-time worker at Walmart is $10.11 an hour. The pay scale of unionized grocery clerks in the Puget Sound area, very good jobs as far as retail goes, provides a further comparison. Those jobs start at $7.73 an hour and top out at $18.

Labor costs at Costco are expensive, accounting for about 70 percent of the company's total cost of operations, and they are more than 40 percent higher than those at Walmart. So how can the company compete based on cost leadership and still pay such high wages? According to co-founder Sinegal: "It's just good business. I mean obviously anyone who is a business person thinks about the importance of people to their operation. You've got to want to get the very best people that you can, and you want to be able to keep them and provide some job security for them. That's not just altruism, it's good business."[5]

Turning Over Inventory Faster than People

Costco's wages help keep turnover unusually low, 17 percent overall and just 6 percent after the first year. In contrast, turnover at Walmart is 44 percent per year, close to the retail-industry average. "We're trying to turn our inventory faster than our people," says Mr. Sinegal. "Obviously it's not just wages that motivate people. How much they are respected, and whether they feel they can have a career at a company, are also important."[6]

Toward that end, Costco also has some rules about discipline and promotion. An employee with more than two years of service cannot be fired without the approval of a senior company officer. (It used to be that only one of the co-founders, Sinegal or Brotman, could issue this approval.) The company also requires itself to promote internally for 86 percent of its openings in top positions. "In truth, it turns out to be 98 percent" according to Mr. Sinegal.[7] By comparison, and this is also very high, 76 percent of all store managers at Walmart started their careers in hourly positions.

Costco's chief financial officer, Richard Galanti, speaks the same language. "One of the things Wall Street chided us on is that we're too good to our employees ... We don't think that's possible." In his office, he keeps a memo from Sol Price, dated August 8, 1967, posted on his bulletin board. It reads: "Although we are all interested in margin, it must never be done at the expense of our philosophy." To Galanti, there is an object lesson in that approach with respect to employee relations: "Costco is not going to make money at the expense of what's right."[8]

The View from Wall Street Analysts

How is Costco's treatment of employees received on Wall Street? Not everyone is happy with this business strategy. Some Wall Street analysts argue that Mr. Sinegal is overly generous, not only to Costco's customers, but to its employees as well. They worry that the company's operating expenses could get out of hand. In the opinion of Deutsche Bank Securities, Inc. analyst Bill Dreher, "At Costco, it's better to be an employee or a customer than a shareholder."[9] Sanford C. Bernstein & Co. analyst Ian Gordon argued similarly: "Whatever goes to employees comes out of the pockets of shareholders."[10]

Another Sanford C. Bernstein & Co. analyst, Emme Kozloff, faulted Mr. Sinegal for being too generous to his employees. She noted that when analysts complained that Costco's workers were paying just 4 percent toward their healthcare costs, he raised that percentage only to 8 percent, when the retail average is 25 percent. "He has been too benevolent," she said. "He's right that a happy employee is a productive, long-term employee, but he could force employees to pick up a little more of the burden."[11] She added, "Their benefits are amazing, but shareholders get frustrated from a stock perspective."[12]

Like other companies, public and private, small and large, surging healthcare costs forced Costco to move aggressively to control expenses. The increase in Costco employees' contribution to 8 percent was the company's first increase in employee health premiums in eight years. According to CEO Jim Sinegal, the company held off from boosting premiums for as long as it could, and it did not give in until it had lowered its earnings forecast twice.[13]

Analyst Bill Dreher agrees with Emme Kozloff. "From the perspective of investors, Costco's benefits are overly generous. Public companies need to care for shareholders first. Costco runs its business like it is a private company."[14] According to Mr. Dreher, Costco's unusually high wages and benefits contribute to investor concerns that profit margins at Costco aren't as high as they should be.

Analyst Ian Gordon also noted another Costco sin: It treats its customers too well. Its bargain-basement prices are legendary, and, as a result, customers flock to its stores. At about the same time that these analysts were commenting on Costco, the company was planning to add staff at checkouts in order to shorten lines. While business schools often teach that caring for customers is a cardinal rule for business success, Wall Street tended to put a different spin on the company's customer-care initiative, as analyst Gordon noted: "It was spending what could have been shareholders' profit on making a better experience for customers."[15]

What is Costco's response to this criticism? According to CEO Sinegal: "On Wall Street they're in the business of making money between now and next Thursday. I don't say that with any bitterness, but we can't take that view. We want to build a company that will still be here 50 and 60 years from now."[16]

If shareholders mind Mr. Sinegal's philosophy, it is not obvious. Consider a five-year comparison of the performance of Costco's and Walmart's common stock, as of May 1, 2006. Based on an index value of 100 on May 1, 2001, Costco's stock has risen 55 percent during that time period, while Walmart's has fallen 10 percent. According to Forbes.com, on May 20, 2006, Costco shares traded at 24.8 times expected earnings. At Walmart the multiple was 17.4.

If anything, Costco's approach shows that when it comes to wages and benefits, a cost-leadership strategy need not be a race to the bottom. In the words of CEO Sinegal, "We pay much better than Walmart. That's not altruism, that's good

business."[17] The contrast is stark and the stakes are high. Which model of competition will predominate in the United States? As we shall see below, Costco's magic lies in its ability to lift productivity, to compete on employee smarts, management savvy, and constant innovation, rather than to skimp on pay and benefits.

Costco's Merchandise and Pricing Strategy

It starts with the buyers. Companies that do business with Sam's Club and Costco, like Mag Instrument, Inc., the manufacturer of Maglite brand flashlights, notice that the warehouse clubs' buyers have far different approaches to selecting merchandise. Sam's Club buyers tend to think about value – meaning price – while Costco's buyers tend to think about value – meaning quality. John Wyatt, Vice-President of Sales at Mag Instrument says, "There's just a different mentality, a safer mentality at Sam's, less cutting-edge. Costco's buyers have full authority to do what they want. They're given freedom to make mistakes."[18]

Costco CFO Richard Galanti linked the company's employees to the company's popularity with customers. "We certainly believe that the quality of our employees is one very important reason – realizing they're ambassadors to the customer – for our success."[19] The fact that Costco rewards workers for treating customers well, through its bonus program, is something you don't see on the shelves, yet it contributes to the stores' popularity. So also does its pricing policy.

To appreciate the pricing policy, consider a single item, men's all-cotton button-down shirts that bear Costco's signature brand name, Kirkland. They sell for $12.99 each. A few years ago they sold for $17.99, a bargain even then. Costco had committed to the manufacturer that it would buy at least 100,000 a year. Two years ago, however, it was selling a million per year. So it negotiated a better price with the manufacturer. As a result, Costco dropped the price it charges customers by $5 a shirt.[20]

Acknowledging the temptation to charge a little more, CEO Sinegal asks, "Who the hell's going to notice if you charge $14.99 instead of $12? Well, we're going to know. It's an attitudinal thing – you always give the customer the best deal."[21] That is the essence of Costco's pricing strategy: Wow consumers with unbelievably low prices so they keep coming in.

In fact, Costco sets a strict cap on its profit margin per item: 14 percent for all goods except Kirkland-brand items, which have a 15 percent cap. Department stores typically mark up items by 30 percent or more. That cap on markup stays the same no matter how great the demand or how limited the supply.

Relations with Suppliers

Fishman and others have described Walmart's legendary squeeze plays on its suppliers. Costco takes a slightly different, but no less tough, approach toward its suppliers. It simply warns suppliers not to offer other retailers lower prices than Costco gets.

When a frozen-food supplier mistakenly sent Costco an invoice meant for Walmart, Mr. Sinegal discovered that Walmart was getting a better price. Costco has not brought that supplier back. Costco has to be flinty, because the competition is so fierce. Says Mr. Sinegal, "We have to be competitive against the biggest competitor in the world. We cannot afford to be timid."[22]

Nor can Costco allow personal relationships to get in the way. As an example, consider what happened when Starbucks did not pass on savings from a drop in coffee-bean prices. Although Mr. Sinegal is a friend of Starbucks Chairman Howard Schultz, Mr. Sinegal warned that he would remove Starbucks coffee from his stores unless it cut its prices. Starbucks relented. According to Tim Rose, Costco's Senior Vice-President for food merchandising, "Howard said, 'Who do you think you are, the price police?'" Mr. Sinegal replied emphatically that he was.

To sum up the previous two sections, a reasonable conclusion is that Costco offers high-quality merchandise at low prices, and it does not hesitate to lean on its suppliers – all of its suppliers – to ensure that it is getting as good a deal as any other retailer. What it sacrifices in margin it makes up in volume. Such frugality extends to the chief executive officer's pay, but when it comes to Costco employees, generous benefits and accommodation to labor unions set Costco apart from almost any other retailer.

CEO Pay and Employee Benefits at Costco

For the last three years, CEO Sinegal has received a salary of $350,000, excluding stock options. That is very low for a CEO of a $52 billion-per-year business. By comparison, the typical CEO of a large American company makes more than 430 times the pay of the average worker. In a 2005 interview with *ABC News* Mr. Sinegal said, "I figured that if I was making something like 12 times more than the typical person working on the floor, that was a fair salary." Of course, as a co-founder of the company, Sinegal owns a lot of Costco stock – more than $150 million worth. He's rich, but only on paper.[23]

In terms of employee benefits, Costco contributes generously to its workers' 401(k) plans, starting with 3 percent of salary the second year, and rising to 9 percent after 25 years. Its insurance programs absorb most dental expenses. Costco

workers pay 8 percent of their health premiums. Full-time workers are eligible for health insurance after three months, and part-timers after six months. The retail-industry average is 23 percent. Eighty-five percent of Costco employees have health-insurance coverage, compared to less than half at Walmart and Target.

Perhaps Chief Financial Officer Richard Galanti best sums up Costco's philosophy of employee relations. "From day one, we've run the company with the philosophy that if we pay better than average, provide a salary people can live on, have a positive environment and good benefits, we'll be able to hire better people, they'll stay longer, and be more efficient."[24]

In return for all of its largesse, Costco does enjoy low employee turnover, as we mentioned earlier, but it also reaps a less obvious benefit: low inventory shrinkage. Shrinkage is a combination of employee theft, shoplifting, vendor fraud, and administrative error. Of these four components, employee theft is by far the largest contributor. How much does shrinkage cost? A 2002 study by Ernst & Young of 55 of the largest and most successful American retailers operating an average of 1,076 stores with mean revenues of approximately $8.8 billion, revealed that the average loss was 1.7 percent of sales, or roughly $19 million annually. At a national level that amounts to more than $31 billion, costing the average family of four more than $440 a year in higher prices. Costco's inventory shrinkage is the lowest in the industry, well below 0.20 percent of sales for fiscal 2005. That also keeps prices low for consumers.

Relations with Unions

When 70,000 employees of the nation's three largest grocery chains, Kroger, Safeway, and Albertson's, went on strike in Southern California in 2004, Costco avoided the fray, quietly renegotiating a separate contract with its union employees there. The three-year deal, which was ratified by more than 90 percent of the workers, included higher wages and increased company contributions to employee pension plans.

In contrast, the strike at the supermarket chains lasted four months before a settlement was reached on February 29, 2004. It resulted in cuts in wages and benefits for new workers, thereby creating a two-tier system in which new workers coming in do not have the same wages and benefits as older workers.

About 13 percent of Costco's employees belong to unions (in California, Maryland, New Jersey, New York, and Virginia), and they work at warehouses that were previously Price Club locations. The relative labor peace is symbolic of the company's relations with its employees. According to Rome Aloise, an international union representative for the Teamsters, Costco is one of the better companies he deals with. "They gave us the best agreement of any retailer in the country." The contract guarantees employees at least 25 hours of work a week, and requires that at least half of a store's employees be full time.[25]

Walmart takes a different tack. Its official stance, as stated on its website, Walmartfacts.com, is as follows:

> Our Wal-Mart union stance is simple. There has never been a need for a Wal-Mart union due to the familiar, special relationship between Wal-Mart associates and their managers. Wal-Mart has encouraging and advantageous relationships with both our loyal and happy associates on the floor of each Wal-Mart facility and our wonderful manage-rial staff. There has yet to be a standard in Wal-Mart union history for a union to be needed.

According to the *Los Angeles Times*, at the first sign of union activity, Walmart managers are supposed to call a hotline, prompting a visit from a special team from Walmart headquarters. Walmart spokesperson Mona Williams told the *Times* that such teams do exist, but that their purpose is merely to help managers respond effectively and legally to union organizing activity. Judges have ruled in cases across the country that Walmart has illegally influenced employees seeking to organize.

A few Walmart employees have succeeded in organizing. A Walmart store in Jonquière, Canada, was certified as a union shop, represented by the United Food & Commercial Workers (UFCW), in August 2004. Two months later, just as the UFCW and Walmart representatives were preparing to begin mandatory contract negotiations, Walmart Canada issued an ominous press release from its headquarters near Toronto. "The Jonquière store is not meeting its business plan, and the company is concerned about the economic viability of the store." In February, 2005, before a collective-bargaining agreement was reached, Walmart closed the store.

In 2000, ten butchers at a Walmart Supercenter in Jacksonville, Texas, voted to join a union. Less than a month later, Walmart switched to pre-packaged meats, eliminating jobs for butchers from its stores nationwide.

Having examined business models, pricing strategies, and employment policies at Costco and some of its competitors, it is appropriate to look at their relative financial and operating performance in the marketplace. To do that, we will compare some relevant operating and financial-performance statistics of warehouse retailer Sam's Club, a business unit of Walmart, to those of Costco.

Costco versus Sam's Club: A Test of High- and Low-Wage Strategies

All data in this section come from the 2005 annual reports of Costco and Walmart, unless otherwise noted. In 2005 Costco employed approximately 67,600 workers at its 338 warehouses in the United States, while Sam's Club employed approximately 110,200 at its 551 US warehouses.[26] In terms of wages alone, a Costco employee earned, on average, $35,360 ($17 per hour). The average Sam's Club employee earned $21,028 ($10.11 per hour).[27] Labor rates at Costco are therefore more than 40 percent higher than those at Sam's Club. One important effect of high versus low wages is on employee turnover, and the financial effects of such turnover. These effects are quite different at Costco and Sam's Club.

The fully loaded cost of replacing a worker who leaves (separation, replacement, and training costs), depending on the level of the job, typically varies from 1.5 to 2.5 times the annual salary paid for that job, excluding lost productivity.[28] To be extremely conservative, let us assume that the fully loaded cost to replace an hourly employee at Costco or Sam's Club costs only 60 percent of his or her annual salary.

If a Costco employee quits voluntarily, the fully loaded cost to replace him or her is therefore $21,216. If a Sam's Club employee leaves, the cost is $12,617. At first glance it may look like the low-wage strategy at Sam's Club yields greater savings in turnover. But wait. Employee turnover at Costco is 17 percent per year (11,492 employees), excluding seasonal workers. At Sam's Club it is more than 2.5 times higher, 44 percent a year (48,488 employees). The total annual cost to Costco is therefore $21,216 × 11,492 = $243.81 million, while the total annual cost to Sam's Club is $12,617 × 48,488 = $611.77 million.

Of course the overall costs and numbers of employees who leave at Sam's Club is higher, because it employs more people. If Costco had an annual employee-turnover rate equivalent to that of Sam's Club (44 percent), that is, 29,744 employees who leave, its annual cost would be $631.05 million. Costco's opportunity savings (costs not incurred) therefore are $387.24 million *per year*.[29] Averaged over the total number of employees at each firm, however, the per-employee cost at Sam's Club is still higher, $5,274.41 versus $3,628.11 at Costco. High employee-turnover rates are expensive any way you look at it.

Wages are not the only distinguishing characteristic between the two retailers. At Costco, 85 percent of employees are covered by the company's healthcare insurance plan, with the company paying an average of $5,735 per worker. Sam's Club covers 47 percent of its workers, at an average annual outlay of $3,500. Fully 91 percent of Costco's employees are covered by retirement plans, with the company contributing an average of $1,330 per employee, versus 64 percent of employees at Sam's Club, with the company contributing an average of $747 per employee.

In return for all of its generosity, Costco gets one of the most loyal and productive workforces in all of retailing. While Sam's Club's 110,200 employees generated some $37.1 billion in US sales in 2005, Costco did $43.05 billion in US sales with 38 percent fewer employees. As a result, Costco generated $21,805 in US operating profit per hourly employee, compared to $11,615 at Sam's Club.[30]

Costco's productive workforce more than offsets its higher costs. Labor and overhead costs at Costco (selling, general, and administrative expenses, or SG&A) were 9.73 percent of sales in 2005. Walmart does not break out SG&A at Sam's Club, but it is likely higher than at Costco, but lower than Walmart's 17 percent of sales. By comparison, it was 24 percent at Target Stores. Costco's motivated employees also sell more: $886 of sales per square foot, versus only $525 of sales per square foot at Sam's Club, and $461 at BJ's Wholesale Club, its other primary club rival.[31]

These figures illustrate nicely the common fallacy that labor rates equal labor costs. Costco's hourly labor rates are more than 40 percent higher than those at Sam's Club ($17 versus $10.11), but when employee productivity is considered (sales per employee), Costco's labor costs are lower than those at Sam's Club (5.55 percent at Costco versus 6.25 percent at Sam's Club).[32]

Conclusions

As Holmes and Zellner noted, "Given Costco's performance, the question for Wall Street shouldn't be why Costco isn't more like Walmart. Rather, why can't Walmart deliver high shareholder returns and high living standards for its workforce?"[33] Says Costco CEO James Sinegal: "Paying your employees well is not only the right thing to do, but it makes for good business."[34]

To make its high-wage strategy pay off, however, Costco is constantly looking for ways to increase efficiency, such as by repackaging goods into bulk items to reduce labor, speeding up Costco's just-in-time inventory and distribution system, and boosting sales per square foot. Nor have rivals been able to match Costco's innovative packaging or

merchandising mix. For example, Costco was the first wholesale club to offer fresh meat, pharmacies, and photo labs.

Defenders of Walmart's low-wage strategy focus on the undeniable benefits its low prices bring to consumers, but the broader question is this: Which model of competition will predominate in the United States? While shareholders may do just as well with either strategy over the long run, it is important to note that the cheap-labor model is costly in many ways. It can lead to poverty and related social problems, and transfer costs to other companies and taxpayers, who indirectly pay the healthcare costs of all the workers not insured by their frugal employers.

Fishman described the extent to which Walmart shifts the burden of payments for healthcare to taxpayers in Georgia and Tennessee. Those are not the only states where this has occurred. According to a study by the Institute for Labor and Employment at the University of California, Berkeley, California, taxpayers subsidized $20.5 million for medical care for Walmart employees in that state alone.

At a broader level, the Democratic Staff of the Committee on Education and the Workforce estimates that one 200-person Walmart store may result in a cost to federal taxpayers of $420,750 per year– about $2,103 per employee.[35] Those additional public costs stem from items such as the following for qualifying Walmart employees and their families: free and reduced lunches, housing assistance, federal tax credits and deductions for low-income families, additional federal healthcare costs of moving into state children's health-insurance programs, and low-income energy assistance.

If a large number of employers adopted the same low-wage strategy, their policies would certainly reduce the wages of US workers, along with their purchasing power and standards of living. Such a low-wage strategy would crimp consumer spending, and constrict economic growth. In that sense, Walmart is a problem, but also an opportunity. Consumer sentiment may provide some encouragement. Thus, in a recent survey, 89 percent of consumers said they would be willing to spend "a little extra" for products that are produced by companies that pay workers good wages and have good working conditions. Only 10 percent of respondents answered "no" to that item, and 1 percent were unsure. Costco's strategy of combining high wages and benefits with innovative ideas and a productive workforce shows that consumers, workers, and shareholders all can benefit from a cost-leadership strategy.

Notes

1. Charles Fishman, *The Wal-Mart Effect* (New York: Penguin, 2006).

2. Ibid., p. 89.

3. Costco Wholesale Corp., Annual Report 2005, p. 5.

4. N. Shapiro, "Company for the People," *Seattle Weekly* (December 15, 2004). Retrieved May 1, 2006 from www.seattleweekly.com/generic/show_print.php.

5. C. Frey, "Costco's Love of Labor: Employees' Well-being Key to Its Success," *Seattle Post-Intelligencer* (March 29, 2004). Retrieved May 1, 2006 from www.seattlepi.nwsource.com.

6. Shapiro, "Company for the People."

7. Ibid.

8. Ibid.

9. S. Holmes and W. Zellner, "The Costco Way," *Businessweek* (April 12, 2004), p. 76.

10. Shapiro, "Company for the People."

11. S. Greenhouse, "How Costco Became the Anti-Wal-Mart," *The New York Times* (July 17, 2005). Retrieved May 1, 2006 from www.nytimes.com/2005/07/17/business/yourmoney/17costco.html.

12. A. Zimmerman, "Costco's Dilemma: Is Treating Employees Well Unacceptable for a Publicly-Traded Corporation?" *Wall Street Journal* (March 26, 2004). Retrieved May 1, 2006 from www.reclaimdemocracy.org/articles_2004/costco_employee_benefits_walmart.html.

13. Ibid.

14. Ibid.

15. Shapiro, "Company for the People."

16. Greenhouse, "How Costco Became the Anti-Wal-Mart."

17. M. Shields, "Treating Workers Justly Pays off," *CNN.com* (September 5, 2005). Retrieved May 1, 2006 from www.cnn.com/2005/POLITICS/09/05/treating.workers.right/.

18. L. Coleman-Lochner, "Costco Service Key to Outpacing Rival Sam's Club," *Denver Post* (March 4, 2006), p. 8C.

19. Ibid.

20. Shapiro, "Company for the People."

21. Ibid.

22. Greenhouse, "How Costco Became the Anti-Wal-Mart."

23. A. B. Goldberg and B. Ritter, "Costco CEO Finds Pro-Worker Means Profitability," *ABC News* (December 2, 2005). Retrieved April 24, 2006 from http://abcnews.go.com/2020.

24. Zimmerman, "Costco's Dilemma."

25. Greenhouse, "How Costco Became the Anti-Wal-Mart."

26. These figures were derived under the assumption that each warehouse at Sam's Club and Costco employs an average of 200 workers. In 2005 Costco had 338 warehouses in the United States. In 2005 Sam's Club had 551 US warehouses.

27. The average wage rate for Costco employees was reported in Coleman-Lochner, "Costco Service Key to Outpacing Rival Sam's Club." The average wage rate for Sam's Club employees is based on the average wage rate for Walmart's hourly workers. The company does not identify the pay rate of Sam's Club employees separately. Annual wages are computed by multiplying 2,080 (40 hours per week × 52 weeks) times the average employee's hourly wage in each company.

28. W. F. Cascio, *Costing Human Resources: The Financial Impact of Behavior in Organizations*, 4th ed. (Cincinnati, OH: South-Western University Press, 2000).

29. $631.05 million (costs that would be incurred with a 44 percent turnover rate) minus $243.81 million (costs actually incurred with a 17 percent turnover rate) = $387.24 million.

30. Walmart measures the profit of each of its segments, of which Sam's Club is one, as "segment operating income," which is defined as income from continuing operations before net income expense, income taxes, and minority interest (Wal-Mart 2005 Annual Report, p. 48). Sam's Club's operating income for 2005 was $1.28 billion. At Costco, it was $1.474 billion. When Sam's Club's operating income is divided by the number of employees (110,200) it equals $11,615.25. When Costco's operating income is divided by the number of employees (67,600) it equals $21,804.73.

31. In its 2005 Annual Report, Costco reported that each of its warehouses averaged $124 million in sales, and that each warehouse averaged 140,000 square feet. Wal-Mart's 2005 Annual Report showed Sam's Club's total square footage as 70.7 million, with $37.119 billion in sales. Information for BJ's Wholesale Club for 2005 comes from the five-year financial-information summary presented at www.bjsinvestor.com/factsheet.cfm.

32. These figures were computed as follows. Costco generates $636,849 in annual sales per employee, and it pays each employee an average of $35,360 in wages. That is 5.55 percent of the sales generated. Sam's Club generates $336,660 in annual sales per employee, and it pays each employee an average of $21,028 in wages. That is 6.25 percent of the sales generated.

33. Holmes and Zellner, "The Costco Way."

34. Costco Annual Report, 2005, p. 77.

35. Democratic Staff of the Committee on Education and the Workforce, "Everyday Low Wages: The Hidden Price We All Pay for Wal-Mart," *in Taking Sides: Clashing Views on Economic Issues*, 12th ed., ed. F. J. Bonello (Dubuque, IA: McGraw-Hill/Dushkin, 2006), pp. 162–78.

2.3 THE HIRING AND FIRING OF EMPLOYEES

In Defense of the Contract at Will

RICHARD A. EPSTEIN

The persistent tension between private ordering and government regulation exists in virtually every area known to the law, and in none has that tension been more pronounced than in the law of employer and employee relations. During the last 50 years, the balance of power has shifted heavily in favor of direct public regulation, which has been thought strictly necessary to redress the perceived imbalance between the individual and the firm. In particular the employment relationship has been the subject of at least two major statutory revolutions. The first, which culminated in the passage of the National Labor Relations Act in 1935, set the basic structure for collective bargaining that persists to the current time. The second, which is embodied in Title VII of the Civil Rights Act of 1964, offers extensive protection to all individuals against discrimination on the basis of race, sex, religion, or national origin. The effect of these two statutes is so pervasive that it is easy to forget that, even after their passage, large portions of the employment relation remain subject to the traditional common-law rules, which when all was said and done set their face in support of freedom of contract and the system of voluntary exchange. One manifestation of that position was the prominent place that the common law, especially as it developed in the nineteenth century, gave to the contract at will. The basic position was set out in an oft-quoted passage from *Payne v. Western & Atlantic Railroad*:

> [M]en must be left, without interference to buy and sell where they please, and to discharge or retain employees at will for good cause or for no cause, or even for bad cause without thereby being guilty of an unlawful act *per se*. It is a right which an employee may exercise in the same way, to the same extent, for the same cause or want of cause as the employer.[1]

In the remainder of this paper, I examine the arguments that can be made for and against the contract at will. I hope to show that it is adopted not because it allows the employer to exploit the employee, but rather because over a very broad range of circumstances it works to the mutual benefit of both parties, where the benefits are measured, as ever, at the time of the contract's formation and not at the time of dispute. To justify this result, I examine the contract in light of the three dominant standards that have emerged as the test of the soundness of any legal doctrine: intrinsic fairness, effects upon utility or wealth, and distributional consequences. I conclude that the first two tests point strongly to the maintenance of the at-will rule, while the third, if it offers any guidance at all, points in the same direction.

The Fairness of the Contract at Will

The first way to argue for the contract at will is to insist upon the importance of freedom of contract as an end in itself. Freedom of contract is an aspect of individual liberty, every bit as much as freedom of speech, or freedom in the selection of marriage partners or in the adoption of religious beliefs or affiliations. Just as it is regarded as *prima facie* unjust to abridge these liberties, so too is it presumptively unjust to abridge the economic liberties of individuals. The desire to make one's own choices about employment may be as strong as it is with respect to marriage or participation in religious activities, and it is doubtless more pervasive than the desire to participate in political activity. Indeed for most people, their own health and comfort, and that of their families, depend critically upon their ability to earn a living by entering the employment market. If government regulation is inappropriate for personal, religious, or political activities, then what makes it intrinsically desirable for employment relations?

It is one thing to set aside the occasional transaction that reflects only the momentary aberrations of particular parties who are overwhelmed by major personal and social dislocations. It is quite another to announce that a rule to which vast numbers of individuals adhere is so fundamentally corrupt that it does not deserve the minimum respect of the law. With employment contracts we are not dealing with the widow who has sold her inheritance for a song to a man with a thin mustache. Instead we are dealing with the routine stuff of ordinary life; people who are competent enough to marry, vote, and pray are not unable to protect themselves in their day-to-day business transactions.

Courts and legislatures have intervened so often in private contractual relations that it may seem almost quixotic to insist that they bear a heavy burden of justification every time they wish to substitute their own judgment for that of the immediate parties to the transactions. Yet it is hardly likely that remote public bodies have better information about individual ·preferences than the parties who hold them. This basic principle of autonomy, moreover, is not limited to some areas of individual conduct and wholly inapplicable to others. It covers all these activities as a piece and admits no ad hoc exceptions, but only principled limitations.

This general proposition applies to the particular contract term in question. Any attack on the contract at will in the name of individual freedom is fundamentally misguided. As the Tennessee Supreme Court rightly stressed in *Payne*, the contract at will is sought by both persons.[2] Any limitation upon the freedom to enter into such contracts limits the power of workers as well as employers and must therefore be justified before it can be accepted. In this context the appeal is often to an image of employer coercion. To be sure, freedom of contract is not an absolute in the employment context, any more than it is elsewhere. Thus the principle must be understood against a backdrop that prohibits the use of private contracts to trench upon third-party rights, including uses that interfere with some clear mandate of public policy, as in cases of contracts to commit murder or perjury.

In addition, the principle of freedom of contract also rules out the use of force or fraud in obtaining advantages during contractual negotiations; and it limits taking advantage of the young, the feeble-minded, and the insane. But the recent wrongful discharge cases do not purport to deal with the delicate situations where contracts have been formed by improper means or where individual defects of capacity or will are involved. Fraud is not a frequent occurrence in employment contracts, especially where workers and employers engage in repeat transactions. Nor is there any reason to believe that such contracts are marred by misapprehensions, since employers and employees know the footing on which they have contracted: the phrase "at will" is two words long and has the convenient virtue of meaning just what it says, no more and no less.

An employee who knows that he can quit at will understands what it means to be fired at will, even though he may not like it after the fact. So long as it is accepted that the employer is the full owner of his capital and the employee is the full owner of his labor, the two are free to exchange on whatever terms and conditions they see fit, within the limited constraints just noted. If the arrangement turns out to be disastrous to one side, that is his problem; and once cautioned, he probably will not make the same mistake a second time. More to the point, employers and employees are unlikely to make the same mistake once. It is hardly plausible that contracts at will could be so pervasive in all businesses and at all levels if they did not serve the interests of employees as well as employers. The argument from fairness then is very simple, but not for that reason unpersuasive.

The Utility of the Contract at Will

The strong fairness argument in favor of freedom of contract makes short work of the various for-cause and good-faith restrictions upon private contracts. Yet the argument is incomplete in several respects. In particular, it does not explain why the presumption in the case of silence should be in favor of the contract at will. Nor does it give a descriptive account of *why* the contract at will is so commonly found in all trades and professions. Nor does the argument meet on their own terms the concerns voiced most frequently by the critics of the contract at will. Thus, the commonplace belief today (at least outside the actual world of business) is that the contract at will is so unfair and one-sided that it cannot be the outcome of a rational set of bargaining processes any more than, to take the extreme case, a contract for total slavery. While we may not, the criticism continues, be able to observe them, defects in capacity at contract formation nonetheless must be present: the ban upon the contract at will is an effective way to reach abuses that are pervasive but difficult to detect, so that modest government interference only strengthens the operation of market forces.

In order to rebut this charge, it is necessary to do more than insist that individuals as a general matter know how to govern their own lives. It is also necessary to display the structural strengths of the contract at will that explain why rational people would enter into such a contract, if not all the time, then at least most of it. The implicit assumption in this argument is that contracts are typically for the mutual benefit of both parties. Yet it is hard to see what other assumption makes any sense in analyzing institutional arrangements (arguably in contradistinction to idiosyncratic, nonrepetitive transactions). To be sure, there are occasional cases of regret after the fact, especially after an infrequent, but costly, contingency comes to pass. There will be cases in which parties are naïve, befuddled, or worse. Yet in framing either a rule of policy or a rule of construction, the focus cannot be on that biased set of cases in which the contract aborts and litigation ensues. Instead, attention must be directed to standard repetitive transactions, where the centralizing tendency powerfully promotes expected mutual gain. It is simply incredible to postulate that either employers or employees, motivated as they are by self-interest, would enter routinely into a transaction that leaves them worse off than they were before, or even worse off than their next best alternative.

From this perspective, then, the task is to explain how and why the at-will contracting arrangement (in sharp contrast to slavery) typically works to the mutual advantage of the parties. Here, as is common in economic matters, it does not matter that the parties themselves often cannot articulate the reasons that render their judgment sound and breathe life into legal arrangements that are fragile in form but durable in practice. The inquiry into mutual benefit in turn requires an examination of the full range of costs and benefits that arise from collaborative ventures. It is just at this point that the nineteenth-century view is superior to the emerging modern conception. The modern view tends to lay heavy emphasis on the need to control employer abuse. Yet, as the passage from *Payne* indicates, the rights under the contract at will are fully bilateral, so that the employee can use the contract as a means to control the firm, just as the firm uses it to control the worker.

The issue for the parties, properly framed, is not how to minimize employer abuse, but rather how to maximize the gain from the relationship, which in part depends upon minimizing the sum of employer and employee abuse. Viewed in this way the private contracting problem is far more complex. How does each party create incentives for the proper behavior of the other? How does each side insure against certain risks? How do both sides minimize the administrative costs of their contracting practices? . . .

1. Monitoring Behavior. The shift in the internal structure of the firm from a partnership to an employment relation eliminates neither bilateral opportunism nor the conflicts of interest between employer and employee. Begin for the moment with the fears of the firm, for it is the firm's right to maintain at-will power that is now being called into question. In all too many cases, the firm must contend with the recurrent problem of employee theft and with the related problems of unauthorized use of firm equipment and employee kickback arrangements. . . . [The] proper concerns of the firm are not limited to obvious

forms of criminal misconduct. The employee on a fixed wage can, at the margin, capture only a portion of the gain from his labor, and therefore has a tendency to reduce output. The employee who receives a commission equal to half the firm's profit attributable to his labor may work hard, but probably not quite as hard as he would if he received the entire profit from the completed sale, an arrangement that would solve the agency-cost problem only by undoing the firm. . . .

The problem of management then is to identify the forms of social control that are best able to minimize these agency costs. . . . One obvious form of control is the force of law. The state can be brought in to punish cases of embezzlement or fraud. But this mode of control requires extensive cooperation with public officials and may well be frustrated by the need to prove the criminal offense (including *mens rea*) beyond a reasonable doubt, so that vast amounts of abuse will go unchecked. Private litigation instituted by the firm may well be used in cases of major grievances, either to recover the property that has been misappropriated or to prevent the individual employee from further diverting firm business to his own account. But private litigation, like public prosecution, is too blunt an instrument to counter employee shirking or the minor but persistent use of firm assets for private business. . . .

Internal auditors may help control some forms of abuse, and simple observation by co-workers may well monitor employee activities. (There are some very subtle trade-offs to be considered when the firm decides whether to use partitions or separate offices for its employees.) Promotions, bonuses, and wages are also critical in shaping the level of employee performance. But the carrot cannot be used to the exclusion of the stick. In order to maintain internal discipline, the firm may have to resort to sanctions against individual employees. It is far easier to use those powers that can be unilaterally exercised: to fire, to demote, to withhold wages, or to reprimand. These devices can visit very powerful losses upon individual employees without the need to resort to legal action, and they permit the firm to monitor employee performance continually in order to identify both strong and weak workers and to compensate them accordingly. The principles here are constant, whether we speak of senior officials or lowly subordinates, and it is for just this reason that the contract at will is found at all levels in private markets. . . .

In addition, within the employment context firing does not require a disruption of firm operations, much less an expensive division of its assets. It is instead a clean break with consequences that are immediately clear to both sides.

The lower cost of both firing and quitting, therefore, helps account for the very widespread popularity of employment-at-will contracts. There is no need to resort to any theory of economic domination or inequality of bargaining power to explain at-will contracting, which appears with the same tenacity in relations between economic equals and subordinates and is found in many complex commercial arrangements, including franchise agreements, except where limited by statutes.

Thus far, the analysis generally has focused on the position of the employer. Yet for the contract at will to be adopted ex ante, it must work for the benefit of workers as well. And indeed it does, for the contract at will also contains powerful limitations on employers' abuses of power. To see the importance of the contract at will to the employee, it is useful to distinguish between two cases. In the first, the employer pays a fixed sum of money to the worker and is then free to demand of the employee whatever services he wants for some fixed period of time. In the second case, there is no fixed period of employment. The employer is free to demand whatever he wants of the employee, who in turn is free to withdraw for good reason, bad reason, or no reason at all.

The first arrangement invites abuse by the employer, who can now make enormous demands upon the worker without having to take into account either the worker's disutility during the period of service or the value of the worker's labor at contract termination. A fixed-period contract that leaves the worker's obligations unspecified thereby creates a sharp tension between the parties, since the employer receives all the marginal benefits and the employee bears all the marginal costs.

Matters are very different where the employer makes increased demands under a contract at will. Now the worker can quit whenever the net value of the employment contract turns negative. As with the employer's power to fire or demote, the threat to quit (or at a lower level to come late or leave early) is one that can be exercised without resort to litigation. Furthermore, that threat turns out to be most effective when the employer's opportunistic behavior is the greatest because the situation is one in which the worker has least to lose. To be sure, the worker will not necessarily make a threat whenever the employer insists that the worker accept a less favorable set of contractual terms, for sometimes the changes may be accepted as an uneventful adjustment in the total compensation level attributable to a change in the market price of labor. This point counts, however, only as an additional strength of the contract at will, which allows for small adjustments *in both directions* in ongoing contractual arrangements with a minimum of bother and confusion. . . .

2. Reputational Losses. Another reason why employees are often willing to enter into at-will employment contracts stems from the asymmetry of reputational losses. Any party who cheats may well obtain a bad reputation that will induce others to avoid dealing with him. The size of these losses tends to differ systematically between employers and employees – to the advantage of the employee. Thus in the usual situation there are many workers and a single employer. The disparity in number is apt to be greatest in large industrial concerns, where the at-will contract is commonly, if mistakenly, thought to be most unsatisfactory because of the supposed inequality of bargaining power. The employer who decides to act for bad reason or no reason at all may not face any legal liability under the classical common-law rule. But he faces very powerful adverse economic consequences. If co-workers perceive the dismissal as arbitrary, they will take fresh stock of their own prospects, for they can no longer be certain that their faithful performance will ensure their security and advancement. The uncertain prospects created by arbitrary employer behavior is functionally indistinguishable from a reduction in wages unilaterally imposed by the employer. At the margin some workers will look elsewhere, and typically the best workers will have the greatest opportunities. By the same token the large employer has more to gain if he dismisses undesirable employees, for this ordinarily acts as an implicit increase in wages to the other employees, who are no longer burdened with uncooperative or obtuse co-workers.

The existence of both positive and negative reputational effects is thus brought back to bear on the employer. The law may tolerate arbitrary behavior, but private pressures effectively limit its scope. Inferior employers will be at a perpetual competitive disadvantage with enlightened ones and will continue to lose in market share and hence in relative social importance. The lack of legal protection to the employees is therefore in part explained by the increased informal protections that they obtain by working in large concerns.

3. Risk Diversification and Imperfect Information. The contract at will also helps workers deal with the problem of risk diversification. . . . Ordinarily, employees cannot work more than one, or perhaps two, jobs at the same time. Thereafter the level of performance falls dramatically, so that diversification brings in its wake a low return on labor. The contract at will is designed in part to offset the concentration of individual investment in a single job by allowing diversification among employers *over time*. The employee is not locked into an unfortunate contract if he finds better opportunities elsewhere or if he detects some weakness in the internal structure of the firm. A similar analysis applies on the employer's side where he is a sole proprietor, though ordinary diversification is possible when ownership of the firm is widely held in publicly traded shares.

The contract at will is also a sensible private adaptation to the problem of imperfect information over time. In sharp contrast to the purchase of standard goods, an inspection of the job before acceptance is far less likely to guarantee its quality thereafter. The future is not clearly known. More important, employees, like employers, *know what they do not know*. They are not faced with a bolt from the blue, with an "unknown unknown." Rather they face a known unknown for which they can plan. The at-will contract is an essential part of that planning because it allows both sides to take a wait-and-see attitude to their relationship so their new and more accurate choices can be made on the strength of improved information. ("You can start Tuesday and we'll see how the job works out" is a highly intelligent response to uncertainty.) To be sure, employment relationships are more personal and hence often stormier than those that exist in financial markets, but that is no warrant for replacing the contract at will with a for-cause contract provision. The proper question is: Will the shift in methods of control work a change for the benefit of both parties, or will it only make a difficult situation worse?

4. Administrative Costs. There is one last way in which the contract at will has an enormous advantage over its rivals. It is very cheap to administer. Any effort to use a for-cause rule will in principle allow all, or at least a substantial fraction of, dismissals to generate litigation. Because motive will be a critical element in these cases, the chances that either side will obtain summary judgment will be negligible. Similarly, the broad modern rules of discovery will allow exploration into every aspect of the employment relation. Indeed, a little imagination will allow the plaintiff's lawyer to delve into the general employment policies of the firm, the treatment of similar cases, and a review of the individual file. The employer for his part will be able to examine every aspect of the employee's performance and personal life in order to bolster the case for dismissal. . . .

Distributional Concerns

Enough has been said to show that there is no principled reason of fairness or utility to disturb the common law's longstanding presumption in favor of the contract at will. It remains to be asked whether there are some hitherto unmentioned distributional consequences sufficient to throw that conclusion into doubt. . . .

The proposed reforms in the at-will doctrine cannot hope to transfer wealth systematically from rich to poor on the model of comprehensive systems of taxation or welfare benefits. Indeed it is very difficult to identify in advance any deserving group of recipients that stands to gain unambiguously from the universal abrogation of the at-will contract. The proposed rules cover the whole range from senior executives to manual labor. At every wage level, there is presumably some differential in worker's output. Those who tend to slack off seem on balance to be most vulnerable to dismissal under the at-will rule; yet it is very hard to imagine why some special concession should be made in their favor at the expense of their more diligent fellow workers.

The distributional issues, moreover, become further clouded once it is recognized that any individual employee will have interests on both sides of the employment relation. Individual workers participate heavily in pension plans, where the value of the holdings depends in part upon the efficiency of the legal rules that govern the companies in which they own shares. If the regulation of the contract at will diminishes the overall level of wealth, the losses are apt to be spread far and wide, which makes it doubtful that there are any gains to the worst off in society that justify somewhat greater losses to those who are better off. The usual concern with maldistribution gives us situations in which one person has one hundred while each of one hundred has one and asks us to compare that distribution with an even distribution of, say, two per person. But the stark form of the numerical example does not explain how the skewed distribution is tied to the concrete choice between different rules governing employment relations. Set in this concrete context, the choices about the proposed new regulation of the employment contract do not set the one against the many but set the many against each other, all in the context of a shrinking overall pie. The possible gains from redistribution, even on the most favorable of assumptions about the diminishing marginal utility of money, are simply not present.

If this is the case, one puzzle still remains: Who should be in favor of the proposed legislation? One possibility is that support for the change in common-law rules rests largely on ideological and political grounds, so that the legislation has the public support of persons who may well be hurt by it in their private capacities. Another possible explanation could identify the hand of interest-group politics in some subtle form. For example, the lawyers and government officials called upon to administer the new legislation may expect to obtain increased income and power, although this explanation seems insufficient to account for the current pressure. A more uncertain line of inquiry could ask whether labor unions stand to benefit from the creation of a cause of action for wrongful discharge. Unions, after all, have some skill in working with for-cause contracts under the labor statutes that prohibit firing for union activities, and they might be able to promote their own growth by selling their services to the presently nonunionized sector. In addition, the for-cause rule might give employers one less reason to resist unionization, since they would be unable to retain the absolute power to hire and fire in any event. Yet, by the same token, it is possible that workers would be less inclined to pay the costs of union membership if they received some purported benefit by the force of law without unionization. The ultimate weight of these considerations is an empirical question to which no easy answers appear. What is clear, however, is that even if one could show that the shift in the rule either benefits or hurts unions and their members, the answer would not justify the rule, for it would not explain why the legal system should try to skew the balance one way or the other. The bottom line therefore remains unchanged. The case for a legal requirement that renders employment contracts terminable only for cause is as weak after distributional considerations are taken into account as before. . . .

Conclusion

The recent trend toward expanding the legal remedies for wrongful discharge has been greeted with wide approval in judicial, academic, and popular circles. In this paper, I have argued that the modern trend rests in large measure upon a misunderstanding of the contractual processes and the ends served by the contract at will. No system of regulation can hope to match the benefits that the contract at will affords in employment relations. The flexibility afforded by the contract at will permits the ceaseless marginal adjustments that are necessary in any ongoing productive activity conducted, as all activities are, in conditions of technological and business change. The strength of the contract at will should not be judged by the occasional cases in which it is said to produce unfortunate results, but rather by the vast run of cases where it provides a sensible private response to the many and varied problems in labor contracting. All too often the case for a wrongful discharge doctrine rests upon the identification of possible employer abuses, as if they were all that mattered. But the proper goal is to find the set of comprehensive arrangements that will minimize the frequency and severity of abuses by employers and employees alike. Any effort to drive employer abuses to zero can only increase the difficulties inherent in the employment relation. Here, a full analysis of the relevant costs and benefits shows why the constant minor imperfections of the market, far from being a reason to oust private agreements, offer the most powerful reason for respecting them. The doctrine of wrongful discharge is the problem and not the solution. This is one of the many situations in which courts and legislatures should leave well enough alone.

Notes

1. *Payne v. Western & Atlantic R.R.*, 81 Tenn. 507, 518–19 (1884), overruled on other grounds; *Hutton v. Watters*, 132 Tenn. 527, 544, 179 S.W. 134, 138 (1915).
2. Ibid.

Employment at Will and Due Process

PATRICIA H. WERHANE AND TARA J. RADIN

In 1980, Howard Smith III was hired by the American Greetings Corporation as a materials handler at the plant in Osceola, Arkansas. He was promoted to forklift driver and held that job until 1989, when he became involved in a dispute with his shift leader. According to Smith, he had a dispute with his shift leader at work. After work he tried to

© 1995 Patricia H. Werhane and Tara J. Radin: 1995a, "Employment at Will and Due Process," in Thomas Donaldson and Patricia H. Werhane (eds.), *Ethical Issues in Business, 5th edition*. (Prentice-Hall, Englewood Cliffs, NJ), pp. 364–374. Reprinted by permission of the authors.

discuss the matter, but according to Smith, the shift leader hit him. The next day Smith was fired.

Smith was an "at-will" employee. He did not belong to, nor was he protected by, any union or union agreement. He did not have any special legal protection, for there was no apparent question of age, gender, race, or handicap discrimination. And he was not alleging any type of problem with worker safety on the job. The American Greetings Employee Handbook stated that "We believe in working and thinking and planning to provide a stable and growing business, to give such service to our customers that we may provide maximum job security for our employees." It did not state that employees could not be fired without due process or reasonable cause. According to the common-law principle of employment at will (EAW), Smith's job at American Greetings could, therefore, legitimately be terminated at any time without cause, by either Smith or his employer, as long as that termination did not violate any law, agreement, or public policy.

Smith challenged his firing in the Arkansas court system as a "tort of outrage." A "tort of outrage" occurs when an employer engages in "extreme or outrageous conduct" or intentionally inflicts terrible emotional stress. If such a tort is found to have occurred, the action, in this case, the dismissal, can be overturned.

Smith's case went to the Supreme Court of Arkansas in 1991. In court the management of American Greetings argued that Smith was fired for provoking management into a fight. The court held that the firing was not in violation of law or a public policy, that the employee handbook did not specify restrictions on at-will terminations, and that the alleged altercation between Smith and his shift leader "did not come close to meeting" criteria for a tort of outrage. Howard Smith lost his case and his job.[1]

The principle of EAW is a common-law doctrine that states that in the absence of law or contract, employers have the right to hire, promote, demote, and fire whomever and whenever they please. In 1887, the principle was stated explicitly in a document by H. G. Wood entitled *Master and Servant*. According to Wood, "a general or indefinite hiring is prima facie a hiring at will."[2] Although the term *master-servant*, a medieval expression, was once used to characterize employment relationships, it has been dropped from most of the recent literature on employment.[3]

In the United States, EAW has been interpreted as the rule that when employees are not specifically covered by union agreement, legal statute, public policy, or contract, employers "may dismiss their employees at will … for good cause, for no cause, *or even for causes morally wrong*, without being thereby guilty of legal wrong."[4] At the same time, at-will employees enjoy rights parallel to employer prerogatives, because employees may quit their jobs for any reason whatsoever (or no reason) without having to give any notice to their employers. At-will employees range from part-time contract workers to CEOs, including all those workers and managers in the private sector of the economy not covered by agreements, statutes, or contracts. Today at least 60 percent of all employees in the private sector in the United States are "at-will" employees. These employees have no rights to due process or to appeal employment decisions, and the employer does not have any obligation to give reasons for demotions, transfers, or dismissals. Interestingly, while employees in the *private sector* of the economy tend to be regarded as at-will employees, *public sector* employees have guaranteed rights, including due process, and are protected from demotion, transfer, or firing without cause.

Due process is a means by which a person can appeal a decision in order to get an explanation of that action and an opportunity to argue against it. Procedural due process is the right to a hearing, trial, grievance procedure, or appeal when a decision is made concerning oneself. Due process is also substantive. It is the demand for rationality and fairness: for good reasons for decisions. EAW has been widely interpreted as allowing employees to be demoted, transferred, or dismissed without due process, that is, without having a hearing and without requirement of good reasons or "cause" for the employment decision. This is not to say that employers do not have reasons, usually good reasons, for their decisions. But there is no moral or legal obligation to state or defend them. EAW thus sidesteps the requirement of procedural and substantive due process in the workplace, but it does not preclude the institution of such procedures or the existence of good reasons for employment decisions.

EAW is still upheld in the state and federal courts of this country, as the Howard Smith case illustrates, although exceptions are made when violations of public policy and law are at issue. According to the *Wall Street Journal*, the court has decided in favor of the employees in 67 percent of the wrongful discharge suits that have taken place during the past three years. These suits were won not on the basis of a rejection of the principle of EAW but, rather, on the basis of breach of contract, lack of just cause for dismissal when a company policy was in place, or violations of public policy. The court has carved out the "public policy" exception so as not to encourage fraudulent or wrongful behavior on the part of employers, such as in cases where employees are asked to break a law or to violate state public policies, and in cases where employees are not allowed to exercise fundamental rights, such as the rights to vote, to serve on a jury, and to collect workers' compensation. For example, in one case, the court reinstated an employee who was fired for reporting theft at his plant on the grounds that criminal conduct requires such reporting.[5]

During the last ten years, a number of positive trends have become apparent in employment practices and in state and federal court adjudications of employment disputes. Shortages of skilled managers, fear of legal repercussions, and a more genuine interest in employee rights claims and reciprocal obligations have resulted in a more careful spelling out of employment contracts, the development of elaborate grievance procedures, and in general less arbitrariness in employee treatment.[6] While there has not been a universal revolution in thinking about employee rights, an increasing number of companies have qualified their EAW prerogatives with restrictions in firing without cause. Many companies have developed grievance procedures and other means for employee complaint and redress.

Interestingly, substantive due process, the notion that employers should give good reasons for their employment actions, previously dismissed as legal and philosophical nonsense, has also recently developed positive advocates. Some courts have found that it is a breach of contract to fire a long-term employee when there is not sufficient cause – under normal economic conditions even when the contract is only a verbal one. In California, for example, 50 percent of the implied contract cases (and there have been over 200) during the last five years have been decided in favor of the employee, again, without challenging EAW.[7] In light of this recognition of implicit contractual obligations between employees and employers, in some unprecedented court cases *employees* have been held liable for good faith breaches of contract, particularly in cases of quitting without notice in the middle of a project and/or taking technology or other ideas to another job.[8]

These are all positive developments. At the same time, there has been neither an across-the-board institution of due process procedures in all corporations nor any direct challenges to the *principle* (although there have been challenges to the practice) of EAW as a justifiable and legitimate approach to employment practices. Moreover, as a result of mergers, downsizing, and restructuring, hundreds of thousands of employees have been laid off summarily without being able to appeal those decisions.

At-will employees, then, have no rights to demand an appeal to such employment decisions except through the court system. In addition, no form of due process is a requirement preceding any of these actions. Moreover, unless public policy is violated, the law has traditionally protected employers from employee retaliation in such actions. It is true that the scope of what is defined as "public policy" has been enlarged so that at-will dismissals without good reason have been greatly reduced. It is also true that many companies have grievance procedures in place for at-will employees. But such procedures are voluntary, procedural due process is not *required*, and companies need not give any reasons for their employment decisions.

In what follows we shall present a series of arguments defending the claim that the right to procedural and substantive due process should be extended to all employees in the private sector of the economy. We will defend the claim partly on the basis of human rights. We shall also argue that the public/private distinction that precludes the application of constitutional guarantees in the private sector has sufficiently broken down so that the absence of a due process requirement in the workplace is an anomaly.

Employment at Will

EAW is often justified for one or more of the following reasons:

1. The proprietary rights of employers guarantee that they may employ or dismiss whomever and whenever they wish.
2. EAW defends employee and employer rights equally, in particular the right to freedom of contract, because an employee voluntarily contracts to be hired and can quit at any time.
3. In choosing to take a job, an employee voluntarily commits herself to certain responsibilities and company loyalty, including the knowledge that she is an at-will employee.
4. Extending due process rights in the workplace often interferes with the efficiency and productivity of the business organization.
5. Legislation and/or regulation of employment relationships further undermine an already overregulated economy.

Let us examine each of these arguments in more detail. The principle of EAW is sometimes maintained purely on the basis of proprietary rights of employers and corporations. In dismissing or demoting employees, the employer is not denying rights to *persons*. Rather, the employer is simply excluding that person's *labor* from the organization.

This is not a bad argument. Nevertheless, accepting it necessitates consideration of the proprietary rights of employees as well. To understand what is meant by "proprietary rights of employees" it is useful to consider first what is meant by the term *labor*. *Labor* is sometimes used collectively to refer to the workforce as a whole. It also refers to the activity of working. Other times it refers to the productivity or "fruits" of that activity. Productivity, labor in the third sense, might be thought of as a form of property or at least as something convertible into property, because the productivity of working is what is traded for remuneration in employee–employer work agreements. For example, suppose an advertising agency hires an expert known for her creativity in developing new commercials. This person trades her ideas, the product of her work (thinking), for pay. The ideas are not literally property, but they are tradable items because, when presented on paper or on television, they are sellable by their creator and generate income. But the activity of working (thinking in this case) cannot be sold or transferred.

Caution is necessary, though, in relating productivity to tangible property, because there is an obvious difference between productivity and material property. Productivity requires the past or present activity of working, and thus the presence of the person performing this activity. Person, property, labor, and productivity are all different in this important sense. A person can be distinguished from his possessions, a distinction that allows for the creation of legally fictional persons such as corporations or trusts that can "own" property. Persons cannot, however, be distinguished from their working, and this activity is necessary for creating productivity, a tradable product of one's working.

In dismissing an employee, a well-intentioned employer aims to rid the corporation of the costs of generating that employee's work products. In ordinary employment situations, however, terminating that cost entails terminating that employee. In those cases the justification for the at-will firing is presumably proprietary. But treating an employee "at will" is analogous to considering her a piece of property at the disposal of the employer or corporation. Arbitrary firings treat people as things. When I "fire" a robot, I do not have to give reasons, because a robot is not a rational being. It has no use for reasons. On the other hand, if I fire a person arbitrarily, I am making the assumption that she does not need reasons either. If I have hired people, then, in firing them, I should treat them as such, with respect, throughout the termination process. This does not preclude firing. It merely asks employers to give reasons for their actions, because

reasons are appropriate when people are dealing with other people.

This reasoning leads to a second defense and critique of EAW. It is contended that EAW defends employee and employer rights equally. An employer's right to hire and fire at will is balanced by a worker's right to accept or reject employment. The institution of any employee right that restricts at-will hiring and firing would be unfair unless this restriction was balanced by a similar restriction controlling employee job choice in the workplace. Either program would do irreparable damage by preventing both employees and employers from continuing in voluntary employment arrangements. These arrangements are guaranteed by "freedom of contract," the right of persons or organizations to enter into any voluntary agreement with which all parties of the agreement are in accord.[9] Limiting EAW practices or requiring due process would negatively affect freedom of contract. Both are thus clearly coercive, because in either case persons and organizations are forced to accept behavioral restraints that place unnecessary constraints on voluntary employment agreements.[10]

This second line of reasoning defending EAW, like the first, presents some solid arguments. A basic presupposition upon which EAW is grounded is that of protecting equal freedoms of both employees and employers. The purpose of EAW is to provide a guaranteed balance of these freedoms. But arbitrary treatment of employees extends prerogatives to managers that are not equally available to employees, and such treatment may unduly interfere with a fired employee's prospects for future employment if that employee has no avenue for defense or appeal. This is also sometimes true when an employee quits without notice or good reason. Arbitrary treatment of employees *or* employers therefore violates the spirit of EAW – that of protecting the freedoms of both the employees and employers.

The third justification of EAW defends the voluntariness of employment contracts. If these are agreements between moral agents, however, such agreements imply reciprocal obligations between the parties in question for which both are accountable. It is obvious that in an employment contract, people are rewarded for their performance. What is seldom noticed is that if part of the employment contract is an expectation of loyalty, trust, and respect on the part of an employee, the employer must, in return, treat the employee with respect as well. The obligations required by employment agreements, if these are free and noncoercive agreements, must be equally obligatory and mutually restrictive on both parties. Otherwise one party cannot expect – morally expect – loyalty, trust, or respect from the other.

EAW is most often defended on practical grounds. From a utilitarian perspective, hiring and firing at will is deemed necessary in productive organizations to ensure maximum efficiency and productivity, the goals of such organizations. In the absence of EAW, unproductive employees, workers who are no longer needed, and even troublemakers, would be able to keep their jobs. Even if a business *could* rid itself of undesirable employees, the lengthy procedure of due process required by an extension of employee rights would be costly and time-consuming, and would likely prove distracting to other employees. This would likely slow production and, more likely than not, prove harmful to the morale of other employees.

This argument is defended by Ian Maitland, who contends

> [I]f employers were generally to heed business ethicists and institute workplace due process in cases of dismissals and take the increased costs or reduced efficiency out of workers' paychecks – then they would expose themselves to the pirating of their workers by other employers who would give workers what they wanted instead of respecting their rights in the workplace. ... In short, there is good reason for concluding that the prevalence of EAW does accurately reflect workers' preferences for wages over contractually guaranteed protections against unfair dismissal.[11]

Such an argument assumes (a) that due process increases costs and reduces efficiency, a contention that is not documented by the many corporations that have grievance procedures, and (b) that workers will generally give up some basic rights for other benefits, such as money. The latter is certainly sometimes true, but not always so, particularly when there are questions of unfair dismissals or job security. Maitland also assumes that an employee is on the same level and possesses the same power as her manager, so that an employee can choose her benefit package in which grievance procedures, whistleblowing protections, or other rights are included. Maitland implies that employers might include in that package of benefits their rights to practice the policy of unfair dismissals in return for increased pay. He also at least implicitly suggests that due process precludes dismissals and layoffs. But this is not true. Procedural due process demands a means of appeal, and substantive due process demands good reasons, both of which are requirements for other managerial decisions and judgments. Neither demands benevolence or lifetime employment, or prevents dismissals. In fact, having good reasons gives an employer a justification for getting rid of poor employees.

In summary, arbitrariness, although not prohibited by EAW, violates the managerial ideal of rationality and consistency. These are independent grounds for not abusing EAW. Even if EAW itself is justifiable, the practice of EAW, when interpreted as condoning arbitrary employment decisions, is not justifiable. Both procedural and substantive due process are consistent with, and a moral requirement of, EAW. The former is part of recognizing obligations implied by freedom of contract, and the latter, substantive due process, conforms with the ideal of managerial rationality that is implied by a consistent application of this common-law principle.

Employment at Will, Due Process, and the Public/Private Distinction

The strongest reasons for allowing abuses of EAW and for not instituting a full set of employee rights in the workplace, at least in the private sector of the economy, have to do with the nature of business in a free society. Businesses are privately owned voluntary organizations of all sizes from small entrepreneurships to large corporations. As such, they are not subject to the restrictions governing public and political institutions. Political procedures such as due process, needed to safeguard the public against the arbitrary exercise of power by the state, do not apply to private organizations. Guaranteeing such rights in the workplace would require restrictive legislation and regulation. Voluntary market arrangements, so vital to free enterprise and guaranteed by freedom of contract, would be sacrificed for the alleged public interest of employee claims.

In the law, courts traditionally have recognized the right of corporations to due process, although they have not required due process for employees in the private sector of the economy. The justification put forward for this is that since corporations are public entities acting in the public interest, they, like people, should be afforded the right to due process.

Due process is also guaranteed for permanent full-time workers in the public sector of the economy, that is, for workers in local, state, and national government positions. The Fifth and Fourteenth Amendments protect liberty and property rights such that any alleged violations or deprivation of those rights may be challenged by some form of due process. According to recent Supreme Court decisions, when a state worker is a permanent employee, he has a property interest in his employment. Because a person's productivity contributes to the place of employment, a public worker is entitled to his job unless there is good reason to question it, such as poor work habits, habitual absences, and the like. Moreover, if a discharge would prevent him from obtaining other employment, which often is the case with state employees who, if fired, cannot find further government employment, that employee has a right to due process before being terminated.[12]

This justification for extending due process protections to public employees is grounded in the public employee's proprietary interest in his job. If that argument makes sense, it is curious that private employees do not have similar rights. The basis for this distinction stems from a tradition in Western thinking that distinguishes between the public and private spheres of life. The public sphere contains that part of a person's life that lies within the bounds of government regulation, whereas the private sphere contains that part of a person's life that lies outside those bounds. The argument is that the portion of a person's life that influences only that person should remain private and outside the purview of law and regulation, while the portion that influences the public welfare should be subject to the authority of the law.

Although interpersonal relationships on any level – personal, family, social, or employee–employer – are protected by statutes and common law, they are not constitutionally protected unless there is a violation of some citizen claim against the state. Because entrepreneurships and corporations are privately owned, and since employees are free to make or break employment contracts of their choice, employee–employer relationships, like family relationships, are treated as "private." In a family, even if there are no due process procedures, the state does not interfere, except when there is obvious harm or abuse. Similarly, employment relationships are considered private relationships contracted between free adults, and so long as no gross violations occur, positive constitutional guarantees such as due process are not enforceable.

The public/private distinction was originally developed to distinguish individuals from the state and to protect individuals and private property from public – i.e., governmental – intrusion. The distinction, however, has been extended to distinguish not merely between the individual or the family and the state but also between universal rights claims and national sovereignty, public and private ownership, free enterprise and public policy, publicly and privately held corporations, and even between public and private employees. Indeed, this distinction plays a role in national and international affairs. Boutros Boutros-Ghali, the head of the United Nations [1991–96], confronted a dilemma in deciding whether to go into Somalia without an invitation. His initial reaction was to stay out and to respect Somalia's right to "private" national sovereignty. It was only when he decided that Somalia had fallen apart as an independent state that he approved UN intervention. His dilemma parallels that of a state, which must decide whether to intervene in a family quarrel, the alleged abuse of a spouse or child, the inoculation of a Christian Scientist, or the blood transfusion for a Seventh-Day Adventist.

There are some questions, however, with the justification of the absence of due process with regard to the public/private distinction. Our economic system is allegedly based on private property, but it is unclear where "private" property and ownership end and "public" property and ownership begin. In the workplace, ownership and control is often divided. Corporate assets are held by an ever-changing group of individual and institutional shareholders. It is no longer true that owners exercise any real sense of control over their property and its management. Some do, but many do not. Moreover, such complex property relationships are spelled out and guaranteed by the state. This has prompted at least one thinker to argue that "private property" should be defined as "certain patterns of human interaction underwritten by public power."[13]

This fuzziness about the "privacy" of property becomes exacerbated by the way we use the term *public* in analyzing the status of businesses and in particular corporations. For example, we distinguish between privately owned business corporations and government-owned or -controlled public institutions. Among those companies that are not government owned, we distinguish between regulated "public" utilities whose stock is owned by private individuals and institutions; "publicly held" corporations whose stock is traded publicly, who are governed by special SEC regulations, and whose financial statements are public knowledge; and privately held corporations and entrepreneurships, companies, and smaller businesses that are owned by an individual or group of individuals and not available for public stock purchase.

There are similarities between government-owned public institutions and privately owned organizations. When the air controllers went on strike in the 1980s, Ronald Reagan fired them and declared that, as public employees, they could not strike because it jeopardized the public safety. Nevertheless, both private and public institutions run transportation, control banks, and own property. While the goals of private and public institutions differ in that public institutions are allegedly supposed to place the public good ahead of profitability, the simultaneous call for businesses to become socially responsible and the demand for governmental organizations to become efficient and accountable further question the dichotomy between "public" and "private."

Many business situations reinforce the view that the traditional public/private dichotomy has been eroded, if not entirely, at least in large part. For example, in 1981, General Motors (GM) wanted to expand by building a plant in what is called the "Poletown" area of Detroit. Poletown is an old Detroit Polish neighborhood. The site was favorable because it was near transportation facilities and there was a good supply of labor. To build the plant, however, GM had to displace residents in a nine-block area. The Poletown Neighborhood Council objected, but the Supreme Court of Michigan decided in favor of GM and held that the state could condemn property for private use, with proper compensation to owners, when it was in the public good. What is particularly interesting about this case is that GM is not a government-owned corporation; its primary goal is *profitability*, not the common good. The Supreme Court nevertheless decided that it was in the *public* interest for Detroit to use its authority to allow a company to take over property despite the protesting of the property owners. In this case the public/private distinction was thoroughly scrambled.

The overlap between private enterprise and public interests is such that at least one legal scholar argues that "developments in the twentieth century have significantly undermined the 'privateness' of the modern business corporations, with the result that the traditional bases for distinguishing them from public corporations have largely disappeared."[14] Nevertheless, despite the blurring of the public and private in terms of property rights and the status and functions of corporations, the subject of employee rights appears to remain immune from conflation.

The expansion of employee protections to what we would consider just claims to due process gives to the state and the courts more opportunity to interfere with the private economy and might thus further skew what is seen by some as a precarious but delicate balance between the private economic sector and public policy. We agree. But if the distinction between public and private institutions is no longer clear-cut, and the traditional separation of the public and private spheres is no longer in place, might it not then be better to recognize and extend constitutional guarantees so as to protect all citizens equally? If due process is crucial to political relationships between the individual and the state, why is it not central in relationships between employees and corporations, since at least some of the companies in question are as large and powerful as small nations? Is it not in fact inconsistent with our democratic tradition *not* to mandate such rights?

The philosopher T. M. Scanlon summarizes our intuitions about due process. Scanlon says:

> The requirement of due process is one of the conditions of the moral acceptability of those institutions that give some people power to control or intervene in the lives of others.[15]

The institution of due process in the workplace is a moral requirement consistent with rationality and the consistency expected in management decision-making. It is not precluded by EAW, and it is compatible with the overlap between the public and private sectors of the economy. Convincing business of the moral necessity of due process, however, is a task yet to be completed.

Notes

1. *Howard Smith III v. American Greetings Corporation*, 304 Ark. 596; 804 S.W. 2d 683.
2. H. G. Wood, *A Treatise on the Law of Master and Servant* (Albany, NY: John D. Parsons, Jr., 1877), p. 134.
3. Until the end of 1980 the *Index of Legal Periodicals* indexed employee–employer relationships under this rubric.
4. Lawrence E. Blades, "Employment at Will versus Individual Freedom: On Limiting the Abusive Exercise of Employer Power," *Columbia Law Review* 67 (1967): 1405, quoted from *Payne v. Western*, 81 Tenn. 507 (1884), and *Hutton v. Watters*, 132 Tenn. 527, S.W. 134 (1915).
5. *Palmateer v. International Harvester Corporation*, 85 Ill. App. 2d 124 (1981).
6. See David Ewing, *Justice on the Job: Resolving Grievances in the Nonunion Workplace* (Boston, MA: Harvard Business School Press, 1989).
7. See R. M. Bastress, "A Synthesis and a Proposal for Reform of the Employment at Will Doctrine," *West Virginia Law Review* 90 (1988): 319–51.
8. See "Employees' Good Faith Duties," *Hastings Law Journal* 39 (1988). See also *Hudson v. Moore Business Forms* 609 Supp. 467 (N.D. Cal. 1985).
9. See *Lockner v. New York*, 198 U.S. (1905) and Adina Schwartz, "Autonomy in the Workplace," in *Just Business*, ed. Tom Regan (New York: Random House, 1984), pp. 129–40.
10. Eric Mack, "Natural and Contractual Rights," *Ethics* 87 (1977): 153–59.
11. Ian Maitland, "Rights in the Workplace: A Nozickian Argument," in *Taking Sides*, ed. Lisa Newton and Maureen Ford (Guilford, CT: Dushkin Publishing Group, 1990), pp. 34–35.
12. Richard Wallace, "Union Waiver of Public Employees' Due Process Rights," *Industrial Relations Law Journal* 8 (1986): 583–87.
13. Morris Cohen, "Dialogue on Private Property," *Rutgers Law Review* 9 (1954): 357. See also Morris Cohen, *Law and the*

Social Order (New York: Harcourt Brace, 1933) and
Robert Hale, "Coercion and Distribution in a Supposedly
Non-Coercive State," *Political Science Quarterly* 38 (1923):
470; John Brest, "State Action and Liberal Theory," *University
of Pennsylvania Law Review* 130 (1982): 1296–329.

14. Gerald Frug, "The City as a Legal Concept," *Harvard Law
Review* 93 (1980): 1129.
15. T. M. Scanlon, "Due Process," in *Nomos XVIII: Due Process*,
ed. J. Roland Pennock and John W. Chapman (New York
University Press, 1977), p. 94.

2.4 HEALTH AND SAFETY

Occupational Health and Safety

JOHN R. BOATRIGHT

The Scope of the Problem

Many Americans live with the possibility of serious injury and death every working day. For some workers, the threat comes from a major industrial accident, such as the collapse of a mine or a refinery explosion, or from widespread exposure to a hazardous substance, such as asbestos, which is estimated to have caused more than 350,000 cancer deaths since 1940.[1] The greatest toll on the workforce is exacted, however, by little-publicized injuries to individual workers, some of which are gradual, such as hearing loss from constant noise or nerve damage from repetitive motions. Some of the leading causes of death, such as heart disease, cancer, and respiratory conditions, are thought to be job-related, although causal connections are often difficult to make. Even stress on the job is now being recognized as a workplace hazard that is responsible for headaches, back and chest pains, stomach ailments, and a variety of emotional disorders.

The Distinction between Safety and Health

Although the term *safety* is often used to encompass all workplace hazards, it is useful to make a distinction between *safety* and *health*. Safety hazards generally involve loss of limbs, burns, broken bones, electrical shocks, cuts, sprains, bruises, and impairment of sight or hearing. These injuries are usually the result of sudden and often violent events involving industrial equipment or the physical environment of the workplace. . . .

Health hazards are factors in the workplace that cause illnesses and other conditions that develop over a lifetime of exposure. Many diseases associated with specific occupations have long been known. In 1567, Paracelsus identified pneumoconiosis, or black lung disease, in a book entitled *Miners' Sickness and Other Miners' Diseases.* . . . Mercury poisoning, once common among felt workers, produces tremors, known as "the hatters' shakes," and delusions and hallucinations, which gave rise to the phrase "mad as a hatter."

In the modern workplace, most occupational health problems result from routine exposure to hazardous substances. Among these substances are fine particles, such as asbestos, . . . heavy metals, gases, . . . solvents, . . . and certain classes of chemicals. Pesticides pose a serious threat to agricultural workers, and radiation is an occupational hazard to X-ray technicians and workers in the nuclear industry.

Because occupationally related diseases result from long-term exposure and not from identifiable events on the job, employers have generally not been held liable for them, and they have not, until recently, been recognized in workers' compensation programs. The fact that the onset of many diseases occurs years after the initial exposure – 30 or 40 years in the case of asbestos – hides the causal connection. The links are further obscured by a multiplicity of causes. The textile industry, for example, claims that byssinosis among its workers results from their own decision to smoke and not from inhaling cotton dust on the job. Lack of knowledge, especially about cancer, adds to the difficulty of establishing causal connections.

Regulation of Occupational Health and Safety

Prior to the passage of the Occupational Safety and Health Act (OSH Act) in 1970, government regulation of

Ethics and the Conduct of Business, 5th ed., by John R. Boatright. Adapted by permission of Pearson Education Inc., Upper Saddle River, NJ.

occupational health and safety was almost entirely the province of the states. Understaffed and underfunded, the agencies charged with protecting workers in most states were not very effective. Only a small percentage of workers in many states were even under the jurisdiction of regulatory agencies; often, powerful economic interests were able to influence their activities. Because the agencies lacked the resources to set standards for exposure to hazardous substances, they relied heavily on private standard-setting organizations and the industries themselves. The emphasis in most states was on education and training, and prosecutions for violations were rare. State regulatory agencies were also concerned almost exclusively with safety rather than with health.

States still play a major role in occupational health and safety through workers' compensation systems, but in 1970, primary responsibility for the regulation of working conditions passed to the federal government. The "general duty clause" of the OSH Act requires employers "to furnish to each of his employees employment and a place of employment which are free from recognized hazards that are causing or are likely to cause death or serious injury."[2] In addition, employers have a specific duty to comply with all the occupational safety and health standards that OSHA is empowered to make. Employees also have a duty, under Section 5(b), to "comply with occupational safety and health standards and all rules, regulations, and orders issued pursuant to this Act which are applicable to his own actions and conduct." OSHA regulates occupational health and safety primarily by issuing standards, which are commonly enforced by workplace inspections. Examples of standards are permissible exposure limits (PELs) for toxic substances and specifications for equipment and facilities, such as guards on saws and the height and strength of railings.

The Right to a Safe and Healthy Workplace

At first glance, the right of employees to a safe and healthy workplace might seem to be too obvious to need any justification. This right – and the corresponding obligation of employers to provide working conditions free of recognized hazards – appears to follow from a more fundamental right – namely, the right of survival. Patricia H. Werhane writes, for example, "Dangerous working conditions threaten the very existence of employees and cannot be countenanced when they are avoidable." Without this right, she argues, all other rights lose their significance.[3] Some other writers base a right to a safe and healthy workplace on the Kantian ground that persons ought to be treated as ends rather than as means. Mark MacCarthy has described this view as follows:

People have rights that protect them from others who would enslave them or otherwise use them for their own purposes. In bringing this idea to bear on the problem of occupational safety, many people have thought that workers have an inalienable right to earn their living free from the ravages of job-caused death, disease, and injury.[4]

Congress, in passing the OSH Act granting the right to all employees of a safe and healthy workplace, was apparently relying on a cost–benefit analysis, balancing the cost to industry with the savings to the economy as a whole. Congress, in other words, appears to have been employing essentially utilitarian reasoning. Regardless of the ethical reasoning used, though, workers have an undeniable right not to be injured or killed on the job.

It is not clear, though, what specific protection workers are entitled to or what specific obligations employers have with respect to occupational health and safety. One position, recognized in common law, is that workers have a right to be protected against harm resulting directly from the actions of employers where the employer is at fault in some way. Consider the case of the owner of a drilling company in Los Angeles who had a 23-year-old worker lowered into a 33-foot-deep, 18-inch-wide hole that was being dug for an elevator shaft. No test was made of the air at the bottom of the hole, and while he was being lowered, the worker began to have difficulty breathing. Rescue workers were hampered by the lack of shoring, and the worker died before he could be pulled to the surface. The owner of the drilling company was convicted of manslaughter, sentenced to 45 days in jail, and ordered to pay $12,000 in compensation to the family of the victim. A prosecutor in the Los Angeles County district attorney's office explained the decision to bring criminal charges with the words, "Our opinion is you can't risk somebody's life to save a few bucks. That's the bottom line."

Few people would hesitate to say that the owner of the company in this case violated an employee's rights by recklessly endangering his life. In most workplace accidents, however, employers can defend themselves against the charge of violating the rights of workers with two arguments. One is that their actions were not the *direct cause* of the death or injury, and the other is that the worker *voluntarily assumed the risk*. These defenses are considered in turn.

The Concept of a Direct Cause

Two factors enable employers to deny that their actions are a direct cause of an accident in the workplace. One factor is that industrial accidents are typically caused by a combination of factors, frequently including the actions of workers themselves. When there is such a multiplicity of causes, it is difficult to assign responsibility to any one person. The legal treatment of industrial accidents in the United States incorporates this factor by recognizing two common-law defenses for employers: that a workplace accident was caused in part by (1) lack of care on the part of the employee (the doctrine of "contributory negligence") or by (2) the negligence of co-workers (the "fellow-servant rule"). As long as employers are not negligent in meeting minimal obligations, they are not generally held liable for deaths or injuries resulting from industrial accidents.

The second factor is that it is often not practical to reduce the probability of harm any further. It is reasonable to hold an employer responsible for the incidence of cancer in workers who are exposed to high levels of a known carcinogen, especially when the exposure is avoidable. But a small number of cancer deaths can be statistically predicted to result from very low exposure levels to some widely used chemicals. Is it reasonable to hold employers responsible when workers contract cancer from exposure to carcinogens at levels that are considered to pose only a slight risk? The so-called Delaney amendment, for example, forbids the use of any food additive found to cause cancer. Such an absolute prohibition is practicable for food additives, because substitutes are usually readily available. But when union and public-interest groups petitioned OSHA in 1972 to set zero tolerance levels for ten powerful carcinogens, the agency refused on the ground that workers should be protected from carcinogens "to the maximum extent practicable *consistent with continued use*."[5] The position of OSHA, apparently, was that it is unreasonable to forgo the benefit of useful chemicals when there are no ready substitutes and the probability of cancer can be kept low by strict controls. This is also the position of philosopher Alan Gewirth, who argues that the right of persons not to have cancer inflicted on them is not absolute. He concluded, "Whether the use of or exposure to some substance should be prohibited should depend on the degree to which it poses the risk of cancer. . . . If the risks are very slight . . . and if no substitutes are available, then use of it may be permitted, subject to stringent safeguards."[6] . . .

The Voluntary Assumption of Risk
A further common-law defense is that employees voluntarily assume the risk inherent in work. Some jobs, such as coal mining, construction, longshoring, and meatpacking, are well known for their high accident rates, and yet some individuals freely choose these lines of work, even when

safer employment is available. The risk itself is sometimes part of the allure, but more often the fact that hazardous jobs offer a wage premium in order to compensate for the greater risk leads workers to prefer them to less hazardous, less well-paying jobs. Like people who choose to engage in risky recreational activities, such as mountain climbing, workers in hazardous occupations, according to the argument, knowingly accept the risk in return for benefits that cannot be obtained without it. Injury and even death are part of the price they may have to pay. And except when an employer or a fellow employee is negligent in some way, workers who have chosen to work under dangerous conditions have no one to blame but themselves.

A related argument is that occupational health and safety ought not to be regulated because it interferes with the freedom of individuals to choose the kind of work that they want to perform. Workers who prefer the higher wages of hazardous work ought to be free to accept such employment, and those with a greater aversion to risk ought to be free to choose other kinds of employment or to bargain for more safety, presumably with lower pay. To deny workers this freedom of choice is to treat them as persons incapable of looking after their own welfare. . . .

The argument that employees assume the risk of work can be challenged on several grounds. First, workers need to possess a sufficient amount of information about the hazards involved. They cannot be said to assume the risk of performing dangerous work when they do not know what the risks are. Also, they cannot exercise the right to bargain for safer working conditions without access to the relevant information. Yet, employers have generally been reluctant to notify workers or their bargaining agents of dangerous conditions or to release documents in their possession. Oftentimes, hazards in the workplace are not known by the employer or the employee until after the harm has been done. In order for employers to be relieved of responsibility for injury or death in the workplace, though, it is necessary that employees have adequate information *at the time they make a choice*.

Second, the choice of employees must be truly free. When workers are forced to perform dangerous work for lack of acceptable alternatives, they cannot be said to assume the risk. For many people with few skills and limited mobility in economically depressed areas, the only work available is often in a local slaughterhouse or textile mill, where they run great risks. Whether they are coerced into accepting work of this kind is a controversial question. Individuals are free in one sense to accept or decline whatever employment is available, but the alternatives of unemployment or work at poverty-level wages may be so unacceptable that people lack freedom of choice in any significant sense.

Risk and Coercion

In order to determine whether workers assume the risk of employment by their free choice, we need some account of the concept of coercion. A paradigm example is the mugger who says with a gun in hand, "Your money or your life." The "choice" offered by the mugger contains an undesirable set of alternatives that are imposed on the victim by a threat of dire consequences. A standard analysis of coercion that is suggested by this example involves two elements: (1) getting a person to choose an alternative that he or she does not want, and (2) issuing a threat to make the person worse off if he or she does not choose that alternative.

Consider the case of an employer who offers a worker who already holds a satisfactory job higher wages in return for taking on new duties involving a greater amount of risk. The employer's offer is not coercive because there is no threat involved. The worker may welcome the offer, but declining it leaves the worker still in possession of an acceptable position. Is an employer acting like a mugger, however, when the offer of higher pay for more dangerous work is accompanied by the threat of dismissal? Is "Do this hazardous work or be fired!" like or unlike the "choice" offered by the mugger? The question is even more difficult when the only "threat" is not to hire a person. Is it coercive to say, "Accept this dangerous job or stay unemployed!" because the alternative of remaining out of work leaves the person in exactly the same position as before? Remaining unemployed, moreover, is unlike getting fired, in that it is not something that an employer inflicts on a person.

In order to answer these questions, the standard analysis of coercion needs to be supplemented by an account of what it means to issue a threat. A threat involves a stated intention of making a person worse off in some way. To fire a person from a job is usually to make that person worse off, but we would not say that an employer is coercing a worker by threatening dismissal for failure to perform the normal duties of a job. Similarly, we would not say that an employer is making a threat in not hiring a person who refuses to carry out the same normal duties. A person who turns down a job because the office is not provided with air conditioning, for example, is not being made worse off by the employer. So why would we say that a person who chooses to remain unemployed rather than work in a coal mine that lacks adequate ventilation is being coerced?

The answer of some philosophers is that providing employees with air conditioning is not morally required; however, maintaining a safe mine is. Whether a threat is coercive because it would make a person worse off can be determined only if there is some baseline that answers the question, worse off compared with what? Robert Nozick gives an example of an abusive slave owner who offers not to give a slave his daily beating if the slave will perform some disagreeable task the slave owner wants done.[7] Even though the slave might welcome the offer, it is still coercive, because the daily beating involves treating the slave in an immoral manner. For Nozick and others, what is *morally required* is the relevant baseline for determining whether a person would be made worse off by a threatened course of action.

It follows from this analysis that coercion is an inherently ethical concept that can be applied only after determining what is morally required in a given situation. As a result, the argument that the assumption of risk by employees relieves employers of responsibility involves circular reasoning. Employers are freed from responsibility for workplace injuries on the ground that workers assume the risk of employment only if they are not coerced into accepting hazardous work. But whether workers are coerced depends on the right of employees to a safe and healthy workplace – and the obligation of employers to provide it. . . .

Whirlpool Corporation

The Whirlpool Corporation operates a plant in Marion, Ohio, for the assembly of household appliances.[8] Components for the appliances are carried throughout the plant by an elaborate system of overhead conveyors. To protect workers from the objects that occasionally fall from the conveyors, a huge wire mesh screen was installed approximately 20 feet above the floor. The screen is attached to an angle-iron frame suspended from the ceiling of the building. Maintenance employees at the plant spend several hours every week retrieving fallen objects from the screen. Their job also includes replacing paper that is spread on the screen to catch dripping grease from the conveyors, and occasionally they do maintenance work on the conveyors themselves. Workers are usually able to stand on the frame to perform these tasks, but occasionally it is necessary to step on to the screen.

In 1973, several workers fell partway through the screen, and one worker fell completely through to the floor of the plant below but survived. Afterward, Whirlpool began replacing the screen with heavier wire mesh, but on June 28, 1974, a maintenance employee fell to his death through a portion of the screen that had not been replaced. The company responded by making additional repairs and forbidding employees to stand on the angle-iron frame or step on to the screen. An alternative method for retrieving objects was devised using hooks.

Two maintenance employees at the Marion plant, Virgil Deemer and Thomas Cornwell, were still not satisfied. On July 7, 1974, they met with the maintenance supervisor at the plant to express their concern about the safety of the screen. At a meeting two days later with the plant safety director, they requested the name, address, and telephone number of a representative in the local office of the Occupational Safety and Health Administration. The safety director warned the men that they "had better stop and think about what they were doing," but he gave them the requested information. Deemer called the OSHA representative later that day to discuss the problem.

When Deemer and Cornwell reported for the night shift at 10:45 p.m. the next day, July 10, they were ordered by the foreman to perform routine maintenance duties above an old section of the screen. They refused, claiming that the work was unsafe, whereupon the foreman ordered the two employees to punch out. In addition to losing wages for the six hours they did not work that night, Deemer and Cornwell received written reprimands, which were placed in their personnel files.

The Right To Know about and Refuse Hazardous Work

The *Whirlpool* case illustrates a cruel dilemma faced by many American workers. If they stay on the job and perform hazardous work, then they risk serious injury and even death. On the other hand, if they refuse to work as directed, then they risk disciplinary action, which can include loss of wages, unfavorable evaluation, demotion, and dismissal. Many people believe that it is unjust for workers to be put into the position of having to choose between safety and their job. Rather, employees ought to be able to refuse orders to perform hazardous work without fear of suffering adverse consequences. Even worse are situations in which workers face hazards of which they are unaware. Kept in the dark about dangers lurking in the workplace, employees have no reason to refuse hazardous work and are unable to take other steps to protect themselves.

Features of the Right to Know and Refuse

The right to refuse hazardous work is different from a right to a safe and healthy workplace. If it is unsafe to work above the old screen, as Deemer and Cornwell contended, then their right to a safe and healthy workplace was violated.

A right to refuse hazardous work, however, is only one of several alternatives that workers have for securing the right to a safe and healthy workplace. Victims of racial or sexual discrimination, for example, also suffer a violation of their rights, but it does not follow that they have a right to disobey orders or to walk off the job in an effort to avoid discrimination. Other means are available for ending discrimination and for receiving compensation for the harm done. The same is true for the right to a safe and healthy workplace.

The right to know is actually an aggregation of several rights. Thomas O. McGarity classifies these rights by the correlative duties that they impose on employers. These are (1) the duty to *reveal* information already possessed; (2) the duty to *communicate* information about hazards through labeling, written communications, and training programs; (3) the duty to *seek out* existing information from the scientific literature and other sources; and (4) the duty to *produce* new information (for example, through animal testing) relevant to employee health.[9] Advocates of the right of workers to know need to specify which of these particular rights are included in their claim.

Disagreement also arises over questions about what information workers have a right to know and which workers have a right to know it. In particular, does the information that employers have a duty to reveal include information about the past exposure of workers to hazardous substances? Do employers have a duty to notify past as well as present employees? The issue at stake in these questions is a part of the "right to know" controversy commonly called *worker notification*.

The main argument for denying workers a right to refuse hazardous work is that such a right conflicts with the obligation of employees to obey all reasonable directives from an employer. An order for a worker to perform some especially dangerous task may not be reasonable, however. The foreman in the *Whirlpool* case, for example, was acting contrary to a company rule forbidding workers to step on the screen. Still, a common-law principle is that employees should obey even an improper order and file a grievance afterward, if a grievance procedure is in place, or seek whatever other recourse is available. The rationale for this principle is that employees may be mistaken about whether an order is proper, and chaos would result if employees could stop work until the question is decided. It is better for workers to obey now and correct any violation of their rights later.

The fatal flaw in this argument is that later may be too late. The right to a safe and healthy workplace, unlike the right not to be discriminated against, can effectively provide protection for workers only if violations of the right are prevented in the first place. Debilitating injury and death cannot be corrected later; neither can workers and their families ever be adequately compensated for a loss of this kind. The right to refuse hazardous work, therefore, is necessary for the existence of the right to a safe and healthy workplace.

The Justification for Refusing Hazardous Work

A right to a safe and healthy workplace is empty unless workers have a right in some circumstances to refuse hazardous work, but there is a tremendous amount of controversy over what these circumstances are. In the *Whirlpool* case, the Supreme Court cited two factors as relevant for justifying a refusal to work. These are (1) that the employee reasonably believes that the working conditions pose an imminent risk of death or serious injury, and (2) that the employee has reason to believe that the risk cannot be avoided by any less disruptive course of action. Employees have a right to refuse hazardous work, in other words, only as a last resort – when it is not possible to bring unsafe working conditions to the attention of the employer or to request an OSHA inspection. Also, the hazards that employees believe to exist must involve a high degree of risk of serious harm. Refusing to work because of a slight chance of minor injury is less likely to be justified. The fact that a number of workers had already fallen through the screen at the Whirlpool plant, for example, and that one had been killed strengthens the claim that the two employees had a right to refuse their foreman's order to step on to it.

The pivotal question, of course, is the proper standard for a reasonable belief. How much evidence should employees be required to have in order to be justified in refusing to work? Or should the relevant standard be the actual existence of a workplace hazard rather than the belief of employees, no matter how reasonable? A minimal requirement, which has been insisted on by the courts, is that employees act in *good faith*. Generally, acting in good faith means that employees have an honest belief that a hazard exists and that their only intention is to protect themselves from the hazard. The "good faith" requirement serves primarily to exclude refusals based on deliberately false charges of unsafe working conditions or on sabotage by employees. Whether a refusal is in good faith does not depend on the reasonableness or correctness of the employees' beliefs about the hazards in the workplace. Thus, employees who refuse an order to fill a tank with a dangerous chemical in the mistaken but sincere belief that a valve is faulty are acting in good faith, but employees who use the same excuse to conduct a work stoppage for other reasons are not acting in good faith, even if it should turn out that the valve is faulty. . . .

The Justification of a Right to Know

Unlike the right to refuse hazardous work, the right to know about workplace hazards is not necessary for the right to a safe and healthy workplace. This latter right is fully protected as long as employers succeed in ridding the workplace of significant hazards. Some argue that the right to know is still an effective, if not an absolutely essential, means for securing the right to a safe and healthy workplace. Others maintain, however, that the right to know is not dependent for its justification on the right to a safe and healthy workplace; that is, even employees who are adequately protected by their employers against occupational injury and disease still have a right to be told what substances they are handling, what dangers they pose, what precautions to take, and so on.

The Argument from Autonomy. The most common argument for the right to know is one based on autonomy. This argument begins with the premise that autonomous individuals are those who are able to exercise free choice in matters that affect their welfare most deeply. Sometimes this premise is expressed by saying that autonomous individuals are those who are able to *participate* in decision-making about these matters. One matter that profoundly affects the welfare of workers is the amount of risk that they assume in the course of earning a living. Autonomy requires, therefore, that workers be free to avoid hazardous work, if they so choose, or have the opportunity to accept greater risks in return for higher pay, if that is their choice. In order to choose freely, however, or to participate in decision-making, it is necessary to possess relevant information. In the matter of risk assumption, the relevant information includes knowledge of the hazards present in the workplace. Workers can be autonomous, therefore, only if they have a right to know.

In response, employers maintain that they can protect workers from hazards more effectively than workers can themselves without informing workers of the nature of those hazards. Such a paternalistic concern, even when it is sincere and well founded, is incompatible, however, with a respect for the autonomy of workers. A similar argument is sometimes used to justify paternalism in the doctor–patient relation. For a doctor to conceal information from a patient even in cases where exclusive reliance on the doctor's greater training and experience would result in better medical care is now generally regarded as unjustified. If paternalism is morally unacceptable in the doctor–patient relation, where doctors have an obligation to act in the patient's interest, then it is all the more suspect in the employer–employee relation, where employers have no such obligation.[10]

Although autonomy is a value, it does not follow that employers have an obligation to further it in their dealings with employees. The autonomy of buyers in market transactions is also increased by having more information, but the sellers of a product are not generally required to provide this information except when concealment constitutes fraud. The gain of autonomy for employees must be balanced, moreover, against the not inconsiderable cost to employers of implementing a "right to know" policy in the workplace. In addition to the direct cost of assembling information, attaching warning labels, training workers, and so on, there are also indirect costs. Employees who are aware of the risk they are taking are more likely to demand higher wages or else safer working conditions. They are more likely to avail themselves of workers' compensation benefits and to sue employers over occupational injury and disease. Finally, companies are concerned about the loss of valuable trade secrets that could occur from informing workers about the hazards of certain substances.

Bargaining over Information. An alternative to a right to know policy that respects the autonomy of both parties is to allow bargaining over information. Thomas O. McGarity has described this alternative in the following way:

> Because acquiring information costs money, employees desiring information about workplace risks should be willing to pay the employer (in reduced wages) or someone else to produce or gather the relevant information. A straightforward economic analysis would suggest that employees would be willing to pay for health and safety information up to the point at which the value in wage negotiations of the last piece of information purchased equaled the cost of that additional information.[11]

Although promising in theory, this alternative is not practical. It creates a disincentive for employers, who possess most of the information, to yield any of it without some concession by employees, even when it could be provided at little or no cost. Bargaining is feasible for large unions with expertise in safety matters, but reliance on it would leave members of other unions and nonunionized workers without adequate means of protection. In the absence of a market for information, neither employers nor employees would have a basis for determining the value of information in advance of negotiations. Finally, there are costs associated with using the bargaining process to decide any matter – what economists call "transaction costs" – and these are apt to be quite high in negotiations over safety

issues. It is unlikely, therefore, that either autonomy or worker health and safety would be well served by the alternative of bargaining over matters of occupational health and safety.

Utilitarian Arguments for a Right to Know

There are two arguments for the right to know as a means to greater worker health and safety. Both are broadly utilitarian in character. One argument is based on the plausible assumption that workers who are aware of hazards in the workplace will be better equipped to protect themselves. Warning labels or rules requiring protective clothing and respirators are more likely to be effective when workers fully appreciate the nature and extent of the risks they are taking. Also, merely revealing information about hazardous substances in the workplace is not apt to be effective without extensive training in the procedures for handling them safely and responding to accidents. Finally, workers who are aware of the consequences of exposure to hazardous substances will also be more likely to spot symptoms of occupational diseases and seek early treatment.

The second utilitarian argument is offered by economists who hold that overall welfare is best achieved by allowing market forces to determine the level of acceptable risk. In a free market, wages are determined in part by the willingness of workers to accept risks in return for wages. Employers can attract a sufficient supply of workers to perform hazardous work either by spending money to make the workplace safer, thereby reducing the risks, or by increasing wages to compensate workers for the greater risks. The choice is determined by the marginal utility of each kind of investment. Thus, an employer will make the workplace safer up to the point that the last dollar spent equals the increase in wages that would otherwise be required to induce workers to accept the risks. At that point, workers indicate their preference for accepting the remaining risks rather than forgoing a loss of wages in return for a safer workplace.

Unlike the autonomy argument, in which workers bargain over risk information, this argument proposes that workers bargain over the trade-off between risks and wages. In order for a free market to determine this trade-off in a way that achieves overall welfare, it is necessary for workers to have a sufficient amount of information about the hazards in the workplace. Thomas O. McGarity has expressed this point as follows:

> A crucial component of the free market model of wage and risk determination is its assumption that workers

are fully informed about the risks that they face as they bargain over wages. To the extent that risks are unknown to employees, they will undervalue overall workplace risks in wage negotiations. The result will be lower wages and an inadequate incentive to employers to install health and safety devices. In addition, to the extent that employees can avoid risks by taking action, uninformed employees will fail to do so. Society will then under invest in wages and risk prevention, and overall societal wealth will decline. Moreover, a humane society is not likely to require diseased or injured workers to suffer without proper medical attention. In many cases, society will pick up the tab.[12] . . .

Although these two utilitarian arguments provide strong support for the right to know, they are both open to the objection that there might be more efficient means, such as more extensive OSHA regulation, for securing the goal of worker health and safety. Could the resources devoted to complying with a right-to-know law, for example, be better spent on formulating and enforcing more stringent standards on permissible exposure limits and on developing technologies to achieve these standards? Could the cost of producing, gathering, and disseminating information be better borne by a government agency than by individual employers? These are difficult empirical questions for which conclusive evidence is largely lacking.

Notes

1. The estimate is made in W. J. Nicholson, "Failure to Regulate – Asbestos: A Lethal Legacy," US Congress, Committee of Government Operations, 1980.
2. Sec. 5(a) (1).
3. Patricia H. Werhane, *Persons, Rights, and Corporations* (Upper Saddle River, NJ: Prentice Hall, 1985), p. 132.
4. Mark MacCarthy, "A Review of Some Normative and Conceptual Issues in Occupational Safety and Health," *Environmental Affairs* 9 (1981): 782–83.
5. *Federal Register* 39, no. 20 (January 29, 1974): 3758. Emphasis added.
6. Alan Gewirth, "Human Rights and the Prevention of Cancer," in *Human Rights: Essays on Justification and Applications* (University of Chicago Press, 1982), p. 189.
7. Robert Nozick, "Coercion," in *Philosophy, Science and Method*, ed. Sidney Morgenbesser, Patrick Suppes, and Morton White (New York: St. Martin's Press, 1969), pp. 440–72.
8. *Whirlpool Corporation v. Marshall*, 445 U.S. 1 (1980).
9. Thomas O. McGarity, "The New OSHA Rules and the Worker's Right to Know," *Hastings Center Report* 14 (August 1984), pp. 38–39.
10. This point is made in Ruth R. Faden and Tom L. Beauchamp, "The Right to Risk Information and the Right to Refuse Health Hazards in the Workplace," in *Ethical Theory and Business*, 4th ed., ed. Tom L. Beauchamp and Norman E. Bowie (Upper Saddle River, NJ: Prentice Hall, 1993), p. 205.
11. McGarity, "The New OSHA Rules and the Worker's Right to Know," p. 40.
12. Ibid., p. 41.

Safety Culture in High Risk Industries

MARK A. COHEN, MADELINE GOTTLIEB, JOSHUA LINN, AND NATHAN RICHARDSON

Studies of past major accidents in different industries have given rise to a substantial management literature on safety culture. Researchers have examined a range of "high reliability" industries and tried to identify the characteristics most commonly associated with firms that have strong safety cultures. One definition of safety culture in this literature is *the set of values promoted by the firm's policies that lead employees to prioritize health, safety, and the environment.*[1] Many policies, initiatives, and procedures affect a firm's safety culture and thereby affect employees' actions that could cause a spill. Examples include providing worker training and using a compensation structure that encourages individuals to make decisions that increase safety.

Safety culture can be understood within the context of *corporate culture*, defined as "the ways work and authority are organized, the ways people are rewarded and controlled, as well as organizational features such as customs, taboos, company slogans, heroes and social rituals."[2] Safety culture refers to the features of a firm's culture that specifically affect safety, both that of individual workers and that of processes that relate to the release of dangerous or environmentally

Excerpted from: Mark A. Cohen, Madeline Gottlieb, Joshua Linn, and Nathan Richardson, "Deepwater Drilling: Law, Policy, and Economics of Firm Organization and Safety," *Vanderbilt Law Review* 64 (2011): 1851.

harmful materials (sometimes called process safety).[3] After the nuclear explosion at Chernobyl in 1986, an entire body of literature developed on the importance of a strong safety culture in high-risk industries).[4] Specifically, that work focused on the underlying causes of catastrophic accidents and ways to avoid them.[5]

We present an overview of the safety culture literature and give a few examples of policies that indicate a strong safety culture in industries outside of the oil and gas context. We then outline a theoretical structure for understanding why a firm selects a particular level of safety culture, and we provide the economic justification for government policy intervention.

Organizations with a Strong Safety Culture

Organizations that operate relatively error free in high-risk industries over a long period of time are termed high-reliability organizations ("HROs").[6] Several researchers have identified characteristics of HROs through a combination of empirical studies, case studies, and application of theoretical frameworks to specific examples. Weick and Sutcliffe compiled a comprehensive list of qualities that HROs exhibit, including preoccupation with failure, reluctance to simplify interpretations, sensitivity to operations, commitment to resilience, and deference to expertise. Weick and Sutcliffe provide examples of HROs, such as aircraft carriers and nuclear power plants.

Hopkins focuses on three of the attributes listed above, citing constant worry about failure, reluctance to draw quick conclusions, and sensitivity to the experience of frontline operators as important components of safety culture.[7] Roberts and Bea expand on these elements and assert that HROs also aggressively seek out information, design their reward and incentive systems to recognize costs and benefits of failure versus reliability, and consistently foster communication among employees about the organization's mission and where the employees fit in.[8] As discussed in the following section, the importance of information flows, as well as flexible decision-making, are crucial to successful HROs.

A nuclear power plant is one example of a hazardous worksite where awareness of risk is central to avoiding catastrophes. The Diablo Canyon nuclear power plant, for example, exhibits qualities of an HRO by mandating that employees spend one week of every four in training. Frequent training prevents employees from becoming complacent and reinforces the idea that the organization strives to learn what it does not know.

Aviation is another high-risk industry in which some organizations operate with high reliability. Many airlines behave as HROs, as evidenced by the expensive precautions they take to minimize risk. It is a subject of debate whether this is because airlines internally value a strong safety culture or because they are just complying with legal requirements. Laws mandate that there be two qualified pilots in the cockpit of a large commercial aircraft, and the Federal Aviation Administration requires that air traffic controllers develop a Safety Management System. These and other legal provisions force firms to adopt some HRO-type behaviors, which they may or may not have adopted otherwise. Scarlett et al. find that the Federal Aviation Administration's "[s]ite-specific and general environmental and safety management systems aim to strengthen safety cultures and accountability within firms ... [but these systems] require periodic independent audits of their substance, implementation, and effectiveness in improving safety results."[9]

Aircraft carriers operate in extremely dangerous conditions with little margin for error. To avoid disasters, US Navy aircraft carriers build redundancy into their operations, such that there are more than twenty communications devices on board to ensure that the landing-signal officer is always connected to a commander in the control tower.[10] Organizations such as the Navy "spend money to create redundancy, there is no question in anyone's mind that the organization believes it can't know everything and must take the possibility of accidents seriously," and thus a strong safety culture emerges.[11]

Organizations with a Weak Safety Culture

Commonly agreed-upon characteristics of low-reliability organizations, or organizations prone to catastrophe, are cost-cutting, lack of training, poor communication, poor supervision, and fatigue.[12] Some studies also cite disaggregation of responsibility and inflexible decision-making as contributing factors to disasters. A strong safety culture requires a balance between centralization and decentralization of decision-making, such that a "delegated capacity for local detection must be held simultaneously with a centralized capacity that maintains the organization's larger awareness of its vulnerability and serves to coordinate responses and learning that occur at the local level."[13] Weick and Sutcliffe find that an HRO must have flexible decision-making that allows for decisions to come from the top-level managers during stable times and from further down the ladder during emergencies. Hopkins argues that complete decentralization does not allow operations managers to learn from incidents that top management might have stored away for future institutional reference.[14]

In theory, organizations could have avoided numerous disasters had they incorporated HRO tactics into their operations. For example, in 2006, an airplane crashed after taking off from the wrong runway in Lexington, Kentucky, because of confusion about taxi patterns due to construction.[15] "A small group of aircraft maintenance workers told the investigators that they had also experienced confusion when taxiing to conduct engine tests – they worried that an accident could happen, but did not know how to effectively notify people who could make a difference."[16] This example demonstrates the importance of information flows.

Another avoidable incident occurred in 1986 when the space shuttle *Challenger* fell apart within the first two minutes of its flight. Hopkins finds that "the decision to launch the *Challenger* space shuttle was made against the advice of the expert engineers."[17] Hopkins believes that had NASA employed flexible decision-making, which is crucial to HROs, the accident would have been avoided.

Weick and Sutcliffe use the example of the Union Pacific–Southern Pacific railroad merger to illustrate potential repercussions of a weak safety culture.[18] Union Pacific experienced several accidents, some fatal, directly after the merger when its safety culture was in flux.[19] At that time, errors were underreported or ignored until they were almost irreversible, top management was composed of people with homogeneous backgrounds who wanted to simplify operations, and any employee who relied on expertise to make decisions without explicit permission from supervisors was deemed insubordinate. Thus, Union Pacific failed to follow many of the essential HRO practices. ...

Marais et al. further argue that the simultaneously centralized and decentralized decision-making recommended for HROs "can lead to major accidents in complex socio-technical systems."[20] For instance, before a ferry disaster in Zeebrugge, Belgium, "those making decisions about vessel design, harbor design, cargo management, passenger management, traffic scheduling, and vessel operation were unaware of the impact of their decisions on the others and the overall impact on the process," even though they were all making their decisions properly according to HRO theory.[21] These examples suggest that becoming an HRO is more difficult than simply adopting each individual policy and procedure that the literature advocates.

Why Aren't All Firms HROs?

The preceding discussion raises the question as to why all firms are not HROs. Hopkins suggests that organizations do not always behave in their best interest because

"organizations themselves don't act – individuals within them do," an observation that makes failure to invest in safety more understandable.[22] In many cases, employees do not have the proper incentives to behave in manners consistent with an HRO. Executives may be pressured to perform quickly and cheaply and may perceive safety as less important.

Information flow between individuals, particularly up and down the hierarchy, has also prevented firms from engaging in HRO behaviors. According to Hopkins, "[r]esearch shows that, prior to every major accident, information was available somewhere in the organization pointing to the fact that trouble was brewing, but this information failed to make its way upwards to people with the capacity and inclination to take effective action."[23] Top managers need to convey to all employees the importance of reporting all information, both positive and negative. Thus, the literature suggests that some firms may not be HROs because upper management does not provide the correct incentives for employees to report all information. In order to provide correct incentives, upper management may need to make trade-offs between short-run costs and long-term safety. Roberts and Bea note that HROs

> seek to establish reward and incentive systems that balance the costs of potentially unsafe but short-run profitable strategies with the benefits of safe and long-run profitable strategies . They make it politically and economically possible for people to make decisions that are both short-run safe and long-run profitable. This is important to ensure that the focus of the organization is fixed on accident avoidance. When organizations focus on today's profits without consideration of tomorrow's problems, the likelihood of accidents increases.[24]

Hopkins asserts that employees are driven not only by financial incentives but also by praise and criticism.[25] It is widely acknowledged within the management literature that to instill a particular culture, performance evaluations and rewards must reinforce that culture. Hence, if cost-cutting is more important than safety in a manager's evaluation and reward structure, then it would not be surprising to see safety taking second place to cost-cutting.

Summary of the Safety Culture Literature

Here we list a few specific policies and procedures that researchers have suggested indicate a strong safety culture in other industries. These safety culture indicators may or may not apply to deepwater drilling, but they help ground the theoretical discussion that follows.

The literature emphasizes that safety culture must be advocated by upper management. Consider a few specific policies and procedures that are adopted at firms with strong safety cultures: (1) redundancy; (2) compensation schemes, including bonuses, that emphasize safety performance; (3) the employment of appropriately trained individuals with the provision of continual on-the-job training; and (4) regular analysis of how changes affect safety (i.e., management of change).

Redundancy should be built into emergency preparation and day-to-day operations. A firm could achieve a stronger safety culture by requiring more than one qualified person to assess operations and having a variety of people at different management levels sign off on all operational changes. This would also guarantee a smooth information flow between senior executives, managers, and frontline workers.

Compensation schemes play a central role in promoting a strong safety culture. Consider a firm whose managers' compensation depends exclusively on the operating profits of their business units. Each manager will try to reduce costs even if doing so increases the number of accidents within the unit (as long as the accidents do not result in a larger increase in costs).

Hiring well-trained workers and providing on-the-job training is also consistent with a strong safety culture. Many decisions made by employees affect safety, although the effects of these decisions are not readily apparent. Analyzing the effects of such decisions is costly to the firm, in terms of time and money. A willingness to pay the costs and undertake the analysis represents a prioritization of safety over costs and is thus indicative of an HRO.

Notes

1. Terry L. Von Thaden and Alyssa M. Gibbons, "The Safety Culture Indicator Scale Measurement System." Final Report, Office of Aviation Research and Development, Washington, DC (2008). Numerous definitions, often closely related, are available in the literature. For example, James Reason has defined safety culture as "the product of individual and group values, attitudes, competencies, and patterns of behavior that determine the commitment to, and the style and proficiency of, an organization's health and safety programmes." Karl E. Weick and Kathleen M. Sutcliffe, *Managing the Unexpected: Resilient Performance in an Age of Uncertainty* (New York: John Wiley, 2001), pp. 127–28 (citing James T. Reason, *Managing the Risks of Organizational Accidents* (Aldershot: Ashgate, 1997),

p. 194). In general, "a culture of safety" means that the culture is centered on safety as the main priority. The term "safety culture" denotes that every organization has a culture of safety that sits on a spectrum from weak to strong. Organizations with exceptionally strong safety cultures that effectively minimize accidents are often referred to as "high-reliability organizations" (HROs). For purposes of this article, we use "strong safety culture" to indicate the qualities of an HRO.

2. James A. Brickley, Clifford W. Smith, Jr., and Jerold L. Zimmerman, *Managerial Economics and Organizational Architecture*, 5th ed. (New York: McGraw-Hill, 2009), p. 291.

3. James A. Baker, III et al., "Report of the BP U.S. Refineries Independent Safety Review Panel" (2007). Retrieved from www.bp.com/liveassetslbp_internet/globalbp/globalbp_u k_english/SP/STAGING/local_assets/assets/pdfs/ Baker_panel_report.pdf.

4. See generally Weick and Sutcliffe, *Managing the Unexpected*; Kathryn Mearns, Sean M. Whitaker, and Rhona Flin, "Safety Climate, Safety Management Practice and Safety Performance in Offshore Environments," *Safety Science* 41 (2003): 641–80; Karlene H. Roberts and Robert Bea, "Must Accidents Happen? Lessons from High-Reliability Organizations," *Academy of Management Executive* 15 (2001): 70–78.

5. See generally Weick and Sutcliffe, *Managing the Unexpected*: Mearns et al., "Safety Climate, Safety Management Practice and Safety Performance in Offshore Environments"; Roberts and Bea, "Must Accidents Happen?"

6. Weick and Sutcliffe, *Managing the Unexpected*, p. 3.

7. Andrew Hopkins, *Failure to Learn: The BP Texas City Refinery Disaster* (Sydney: CCH Australia, 2008), p. 13.

8. Roberts and Bea, "Must Accidents Happen?," p. 71.

9. Lynn Scarlett, Arthur Fraas, Richard Morgenstern, and Timothy Murphy, "Managing Environmental, Health, and Safety Risks: A Comparative Assessment of the Minerals Management Service and Other Agencies" (Resources for the Future, Discussion Paper No. 10-64, 2011), p. 4. Retrieved from www.rff.org/documents/RFF-DP-10-64.pdf.

10. Roberts and Bea, "Must Accidents Happen?," p. 73.

11. Ibid., pp. 73–74.

12. See, for example, Deepwater Horizon Study Group, Center for Catastrophic Risk Management, "Progress Report 2" (2010), p. 1. Retrieved from http://ccrm.berkeley.edu/pdfs_papers/ bea_pdfs/DHSG_July_Report-Final.pdf ("[F]ailures to contain, control, mitigate, plan, and clean up ... appear to be deeply rooted in a multi-decade history of organizational malfunction and shortsightedness").

13. Weick and Sutcliffe, *Managing the Unexpected*, p. 170.

14. Hopkins, *Failure to Learn*, pp. 91–106.

15. Matthew L. Wald, "Crew Sensed Trouble Seconds Before Crash," *The New York Times* (January 17, 2007). Retrieved from www.nytimes.com/2007/01/18/us/18crash.html? adxnnl=l&adxnnlx=1315754099-UKLDQJFdJp 0H_GE02bjDgLA.

16. Nancy G. Leveson, *Engineering a Safer World: Systems Thinking Applied to Safety* (Cambridge, MA: MIT Press, 2011), p. 352.

17. Andrew Hopkins, "The Problem of Defining High Reliability Organisations" (National Research Center for Occupational Health and Safety Regulation, Australian National University Working Paper No. 51, 2007), p. 11.

18. Weick and Sutcliffe, *Managing the Unexpected*, p. 4.

19. Charles Boisseau and David Ivanovich, "Union Pacific Put under Safety Review: 33 Cars Derail in Texas Town in Latest of a String of Accidents," *Houston Chronicle* (August 27, 2007), p. A1. Retrieved from www.chron.com/CDA/archives/archive .mpl/1997_1432888/union-pacific-put-under-safety-review -33-cars-dera.html.

20. Karen Marais, Nicolas Dulac, and Nancy Leveson, "Beyond Normal Accidents and High Reliability Organizations: The Need for an Alternative Approach to Safety in Complex Systems (Massachusetts Institute of Technology, Working Paper, 2004), p. 1.

21. Ibid.

22. Hopkins, *Failure to Learn*, p. 83.

23. Ibid., p. 114.

24. Roberts and Bea, "Must Accidents Happen?," p. 74.

25. Hopkins, *Failure to Learn*, p. 84.

LEGAL PERSPECTIVE

Supreme Court of the United States, *Automobile Workers v. Johnson Controls, Inc.* (1991)

The question before the Court was whether an employer could exclude a fertile female employee from certain jobs out of concern for the health of a fetus that might be conceived. Johnson Controls, Inc. (Johnson Controls) manufactures batteries and prior to the passage of the Civil Rights Act of 1964 had never employed females in a battery manufacturing job. At that point women were hired although Johnson Controls was extremely concerned about fertile women being exposed to lead and warned women to avoid jobs that might result in lead exposure. Between 1979 and 1983 eight employees who became pregnant had blood level lead exposure of 30 micrograms per deciliter. Johnson Controls responded with a policy that included a broad exclusion of women from jobs that exposed them to lead.

In its ruling the Court pointed out that the policy excluded women but not men who wished to risk their reproductive health for a particular job. The policy explicitly discriminates against women on the basis of their sex. Earlier an Appeals Courts had supported the legality of the policy because the discrimination was benign, that is, it was designed to protect women and any fetus that might be conceived. In disagreeing with the Appeals Courts, Justice Blackman pointed out that the policy was based on gender and childbearing capacity and not on fertility alone since there was considerable evidence that exposure to lead had debilitating effects on "the male reproductive system." Blackman cited the Pregnancy Discrimination Act of 1978 that stated that "discrimination based on a woman's prepregnancy is, on its face, discrimination because of her sex." The Court then considered whether the Johnson Controls policy was protected by a BFOQ exception (BFOQ is a bona fide occupational qualification). However, the Court found no BFOQ because fertile women could perform the job as well as men and did so. Finally, the Court added, "Decisions about the welfare of future children must be left to the parents who conceive, bear, support, and raise them rather to the employers who hire those parents."

CASES

Case 1: Outsourcing at Any Cost? Do Corporations Ever Have a Moral Obligation Not to Outsource?

JULIAN FRIEDLAND

In 1997, when Galaxywire.net, a successful Internet service provider, was looking for a new central office location, it found a very receptive community in Green Fork, Illinois. With the unemployment rate hovering at 16 percent, the city was ready to offer the company a great deal in return for moving there. Galaxywire planned to hire 3,000 in its first year, primarily in customer service, software engineering, and Web design.

City development officials offered a $300,000 low-interest loan for employee training, a 50 percent tax abatement for the first ten years, and even landed a federal grant to construct a new $2.3 million secondary building for day care and executive suites. With Green Fork only about an hour's drive from Chicago, it seemed this small city of 30,000 with plenty of willing and able workers was the perfect spot for Galaxywire's home office.

The company accepted the offer and at the official announcement ceremony, CEO Dale Horner predicted a bright future. For 35 years, Green Fork's largest employer was Freedman Steel, but the company left town after a lengthy and bitter labor dispute. Since then, locals had grown distrustful of large corporations. Acknowledging this, Horner made a substantial commitment to the residents: "We plan to stay and be an integral part of the community," he promised. "Our employees are really a family. Across the board, everyone is considered as important as the highest executive. Lots of companies say that, but as I hope you'll come to see, we're rather different from most companies."

Seven years later, Galaxywire was thriving. Not only was the home office extremely productive, the company had expanded considerably, opening dozens of offices across the country. Nevertheless, top management was considering closing the Green Fork office and moving its customer service, software engineering, and Web design units to India. The company stood to save at least $10 million a year by doing so. Customer service employees earning $10–15 an hour in the United States earn only $2–4 in India. Similarly, Web designers and software engineers earning $60–70 an hour here earn only $6–8 an hour there.

Furthermore, new research by the Software Engineering Institute (SEI) at Carnegie Mellon University had shown that 85 Indian software companies had received a level 5 Compatibility Maturation Model Rating (CMM) which is the highest rating of engineering excellence. By comparison, only 42 other organizations worldwide had achieved that rating. So management realized that India offered a highly skilled, English-speaking workforce particularly competitive in information technology at a bargain-basement price. And to top it off, the company could deduct the cost of moving from its taxable income as a business expense. As a result, most of Galaxywire's competitors were already outsourcing to Southeast Asia. This trend was making it more difficult for American customer service agents and IT professionals to find work. Many were seeking new careers in non-outsourceable service sectors such as restaurants, retail sales, tourism, construction, and teaching.

Galaxywire decided to let its employees know immediately of its intention to close the home office before the media could get hold of the story, giving the workers ten months' notice – eight months more than federal law requires for mass layoffs. It also provided severance packages of a month's full pay and extended health insurance coverage for five months. However, none of the top executives based in Green Fork would be laid off. They would move to smaller offices in California and were likely to receive particularly high year-end bonuses as a result of the savings outsourcing would bring.

Upon hearing the news of the closure, the workers and the city tried to find a solution that would have allowed the company to stay and still recoup most of the money it hoped to save by moving. With the unemployment rate still at 10 percent, the town simply could not afford to lose its largest employer. Negotiators proposed a deal that would save the company $7 million in the first year, $8 million

Reprinted by permission of the author.

the second, and $9 million yearly thereafter. The city extended the tax abatement for another decade, increasing the yearly reduction to 60 percent.

The employees agreed to a 15 percent pay-cut and a considerable reduction in benefits. But still, the company would not stay. So the workers went back to the drawing board, cutting another 5 percent of their wages, slashing a third of their vacation days, and doubling their health insurance premiums. The city increased the tax reduction by another 5 percent. The resulting deal saved the company $10 million in the first year, $11 million the next, and $12 million yearly thereafter. This time, the company took several days to review the offer seriously.

The top executives met the next day to discuss this new offer. They realized that this deal did have a number of advantages:

1. Deciding not to move would increase employee loyalty and make good on the promise they initially made to stay.
2. There was already a highly skilled and dedicated workforce in Green Fork.
3. The workforce in India had not been fully tested. And several companies had already brought their customer service centers back from India, where the agents did not always master American colloquialisms, frustrating many customers, especially those hostile to outsourcing.
4. If they accepted this offer, they might be able to influence other cities where their offices were located to give them similar deals and thus avoid the risk and hassle of moving altogether.
5. If they decided not to move, they might be able to save a good deal on marketing since staying could provide a lucrative advertising angle such as: "Galaxywire.net is working to keep jobs in America."
6. They could still move their executive suites to sunny California.

But there were also some potential negatives to accepting the offer:

1. There might be growing resentment in the community about Galaxywire forcing its employees and the city to bend over backwards, creating a dangerous precedent that could further strip the community of tax support from other businesses and lower the salaries and benefits of employees elsewhere.
2. It seemed unlikely that the employees and city would be prepared to continue making such extensive sacrifices indefinitely. Eventually, the workers might unionize and make things more difficult.

These negatives made one executive suggest rejecting the offer, but make amends for breaking the promise to stay in the community by covering tuition for employee retraining. Another suggested exploring the possibility of staying in Green Fork, but in order to stem the tide of negative press and morale, to accept the original offer, which seemed to preserve most of the advantages of the second offer but without the disadvantages. The first offer would save them close to as much as the second but also allow them to retain a truly appreciative and non-resentful staff, and even provide the company with a potentially potent advertising campaign that could keep Galaxywire in a leadership position in a competitive market which had suffered negative press over outsourcing.

But by then it was time to go home and think about all the options. What should the board decide?

Discussion Questions

1. Does Galaxywire.net have a moral duty to keep its promise to stay in Green Fork so long as it can do so profitably? Why, or why not? Explain. If so, is accepting even the first offer from the city and workers too much to ask? Why, or why not? Explain.
2. Should the employees simply take this loss as a valuable opportunity to seek new careers instead of assuming they would be able to keep one career all their lives despite a rapidly changing global economy? Explain.
3. Corporate incentives, such as tax abatements and low-interest loans, are sometimes described as "corporate welfare" since they are government subsidies. Critics charge that such programs unfairly burden communities and taxpayers and constitute morally illegitimate extortion on the part of companies. Do you tend to agree or disagree with this assessment? Explain.
4. Should the community have focused its attention instead on the state and federal government, asking it to discourage outsourcing? Why, or why not? Explain.

Case 2: Sexism in the City of London

SABRINA SPEIGHTS AND DENIS G. ARNOLD

The financial services industry based in the City of London is characterized by high demands, high stakes, and high stress.[1] Demanding work schedules and extensive traveling are cited as reasons why there are so few female executives in financial service firms. Several initiatives have been designed to improve women's representation in the sector. The data show, however, that even when well-educated, ambitious women attain positions in financial services, discrimination persists. According to the UK's Equality and Human Rights Commission, the starting salaries of women in finance are 37 percent lower than their male counterparts' and the average bonus for men is five times that of women (£14,554 vs. £2,875). These statistics help make financial services the leader in gender pay gaps in the UK economy. Not only do women in the financial services sector receive lower starting salaries and smaller bonuses, according to a survey conducted by the *Financial Times*, one in five women in the global asset management industry has suffered a sexual assault at work. The *Financial Times* also found that while women make up 50 percent of overall staff they make up less than 20 percent of leadership.

With few women in senior leadership positions, hostile work environments with toxic organizational cultures continue to inhibit the advancement of women. For example, Julie Bower left her job at Schroder Securities after her boss unapologetically tried to find ways to get her to leave despite Bower meeting her sales goals while battling ovarian cancer. Svetlana Lokhova (in the London office of the Russian investment bank, Sberbank) also left her job because of harassment and bullying. Lokhova's boss, David Longmuir, would routinely send emails to her co-workers and clients referring to her as "Miss Bonkers" and "Crazy Miss Cokehead." This "macho" culture – often dismissed as joking banter – can leave women isolated, deny their earned rewards, and make them more susceptible to sexual assault. This was the case for Penny Duncombe, an equities specialist at one of London's most elite banks. Penny was considered an "ice queen" by her colleagues because drinking with them made her uncomfortable. When she decided to attend a social gathering, a colleague spiked her glass of wine and assaulted her. She passed out and woke up on the street outside her office.

What can women do when they are subjected to this treatment? Svetlana Lokhova chose to file suit; but this choice was not without consequences. Although she was paid a large settlement of £3 million, the loss of income, exorbitant legal fees, opportunity costs, and mental and emotional anguish left her feeling less than victorious. It took 18 months of court battles for Lokhova to be awarded damages about which she concluded, "people who think you come out of court as a victor – that's just not true. Everyone loses out. What a waste of three years of my life, a waste of health, a waste of money."

Note

1. The City of London is two square miles within Greater London and is home to the Bank of England and many financial services firms.

Discussion Questions

1. Is the treatment described in the case disrespectful in the Kantian sense, or merely joking banter of the sort that is to be expected in industries where there are a disproportionate number of men? Why? Explain.
2. From the perspective of a woman, how might it feel to work in an environment such as that described in the case? Explain.
3. Can the behavior be justified from an ethical perspective? Explain.
4. What might explain the persistence of such behavior in modern workplaces staffed by well-educated men? Explain.

This case was written for classroom discussion and is based on the following sources: L. Cooper, "Sexism in the City: In London, Female Bankers' Bonuses Are 80 percent Lower," *Finance AOL .com* (September 8, 2009). Retrieved from www.aol.com/2009/09/08/sexism-in-the-city-in-london-female-bankers-bonuses-are-80-pe/.

L. Eccles and R. Taylor, "Banker Dubbed 'Crazy Miss Cokehead' by Her Bosses Claims Her £3 Million Pay-Out for Sexual Harassment Was Not Worth the Stress of the Legal Battle," *Daily Mail* (April 30, 2015). Retrieved from www.dailymail.co.uk/news/article-3062954/Banker-dubbed-Crazy-Miss-Cokehead-bosses-claims-3million-pay-sexual-harassment-not-worth-stress-legal-battle.html.

"Sexism and the City," *Financial Times* (January 16, 2015). Retrieved from www.ft.com/content/7c182ab8-9c33-11e4-b9f8-00144feabdc0.

P. Markham, "Victim of Sexism in the City to Get £1 m Payout," *Daily Mail* (n.d.). Retrieved from www.dailymail.co .uk/news/article-37241/Victim-sexism-City-1 m-payout.html.

Case 3: Off-Duty Smoking

JESSICA PIERCE

Rob, the Personnel Manager at the ShopRight Super Store, interviewed two candidates for a floor manager position. The candidates had similar resumes – both had about ten years of relevant experience, and good references – and both interviewed well. When Rob interviewed Cathy, the second candidate, he noticed that she was a smoker. He could tell by the smell of her clothes and breath, and he noticed a pack of Camel Lights in her purse when she opened it to find a pen. He decided to hire Jen, the first candidate.

Since both candidates were good, Rob had to go with what he called "soft" reasons, the central one of which was that Cathy was a smoker. Rob didn't like smoking – he considered it disgusting, and a sign of weakness of character; anyone with a strong personality would have the determination to quit. In the back of his mind, Rob also felt that he was doing his employer a favor. The company had a good health plan – for the moment. But smokers and other unhealthy people were putting increasing strain on employer-sponsored health insurance plans.

According to the National Workrights Institute, 25 percent of those surveyed would be less likely to hire someone who was a smoker.[1] Although employer health expenditures for smokers are indeed higher on average than for nonsmo-

kers, other "modifiable" risk factors such as depression, stress, and obesity actually may cost employers more.[2]

Notes

1. National Workrights Institute, "Lifestyle Discrimination: Employer Control of Legal Off Duty Employee Activities" (2005). Retrieved August 30, 2005 from www.workrights.org.
2. Health Enhancement Research Organization, "Research" (2005). Retrieved September 19, 1995 from www.thehero.org /research.htm.

Discussion Questions

1. Was Rob's choice justified? Why or why not?
2. Is it fair for an employer to refuse to hire a smoker? What about an overweight person? (Are there any relevant differences between a smoker and an overweight person?) Be sure to define what you mean by "fair."
3. Does the job position being filled – floor manager – make any relevant difference in this case? If not, can you think of a position where smoking would be relevant?
4. Should employers be free not to hire employees whose personal behaviors are considered high risk?
5. Should employers be able to restrict employees' high-risk behaviors? Why or why not?

Reprinted with permission of the author.

Case 4: Fired for Drinking the Wrong Brand of Beer

DENIS G. ARNOLD

Ross Hopkins, 41, ordered a Budweiser at a Denver bar while relaxing on a Saturday night. The waitress mistakenly brought him a Coors. Not wanting to wait, he sipped the Coors. Also at the bar that night was the son-in-law of the majority shareholder of his employer, American Eagle Distribution Company. The next Monday Hopkins was fired. American Eagle is the local distributor of Budweiser,

and Hopkins's bosses did not like his supporting the competition. They stated that he failed to avoid a conflict of interest with his responsibilities at American Eagle. Isac Aguero, 24, can empathize with Hopkins, since he was fired from CJW, Inc. for the same reason. Aguero was a forklift operator at CJW, the local Miller Brewing Co. distributor in Racine, Wisconsin. Aguero was photographed during Racine's annual Mardi Crawl enjoying a Bud Light, and the photo appeared in the "On the Town" section of the local newspaper. His bosses saw the photo and fired him the following Monday. Aguero claims that he was never told not to drink Budweiser and that nothing in the employee handbook said he should avoid certain drinks. His employer would not comment on the circumstances of his dismissal.

Discussion Questions

1. Is it morally permissible for employers to fire at-will employees for legal behavior off duty? Why, or why not? Explain.

2. Were American Eagle and CJW justified in terminating Hopkins and Aguero? Why, or why not? Explain.

3. Should there be legal protection for workers to prevent them from being fired for legal, off-duty behavior? Why, or why not? Explain.

4. How might an ethical organization more fairly impose a restriction on employees utilizing competitors' products? Explain.

This case was prepared for classroom discussion and is based on the following sources: Associated Press, "Wrong Beer Costs Man His Job" (May 18, 2005) and Dustin Block, "He Had a Bud Light; Now He Doesn't Have a Job," *Journal Times* (February 11, 2005).

Case 5: The Other Side of Manufacturing in the United States

NORMAN E. BOWIE

For the past 30 years many Americans have been concerned about the decline of manufacturing jobs. The issue has drawn the concern of politicians and has been a central concern of Donald Trump. Various states have eagerly competed to attract manufacturing jobs and used a number of devices such as extensive tax breaks to do so. However, there are severe costs in employee safety that come with some of these manufacturing jobs. Few states had competed more aggressively and successfully than Alabama, having provided a quarter billion dollars in tax breaks and other benefits in order to attract Mercedes Benz, Toyota, Honda, and Hyundai. Auto parts companies followed. Employees at these plants do not enjoy the benefits and protections of unionization, as do automobile workers in Michigan.

Tax breaks turned out not to be the only costs. In Alabama and surrounding southern states, there were human costs as well. Southern states were competing against Mexico, Bangladesh, and parts of Asia. The foreign auto manufactures put unrealistic quotas on their suppliers. The suppliers responded by increasing the quotas that workers were supposed to meet, increasing the hours of employees, and short-cutting training. Documented incidents include the following:

- At the Nakanishi Manufacturing bearing plant a maintenance worker was engulfed in flames from a flash fire in a dust collection system. There had been four previous fires.
- At the HP Helzer Automotive Systems plant a woman scorched her hand inside an oven used for baking foam rubber linings for BMW hoods. She had slipped on a puddle of oil on the floor in front of the oven.

- At the WKW-Erbsloeh Automotive plant a worker was seriously scalded when he fell into a vat of sulfuric and phosphoric acid. Working above the vats, his job was to haul hoses, tools, and 50 pound bags of caustic soda. There were no gangways, cables, or handrails. The time allotted for doing his job had been cut from 24 hours to 14–16 and as few as 6 hours.
- At Matsu Alabama a worker was hired through a temporary employment agency as a janitor. One night he was forced to work on the assembly line in order to meet a production quota. He had no training. Leaning inside a machine, the die that stamps metal bolts slammed against him. He lost three fingers of his left hand; his right hand was severed at the wrist and eventually his right forearm needed to be amputated.

But the case of Regina Elsea was the most tragic of all. Elsea, age 20, had gone to work for Ajin USA, a parts supplier for Hyundai and Kia located in Cusseta Alabama for $8.75 an hour. She had a boyfriend and went to work for Ajin to save money for an apartment they could rent together. She worked 12-hour shifts seven days a week. On June 18, 2016, the assembly line stopped because a machine that mounted pillars for sideview mirrors on dashboard frames had jammed. Maintenance did not show up. Concerned about making their quota, Elsea and two co-workers took the task on themselves. Elsea grabbed a tool and tried to break the jam. She had no training for this task. The machine suddenly started again crushing Elsea against a steel dashboard frame impaling her with a pair of welding tips. The emergency shutoff was activated and maintenance finally arrived. The Korean maintenance worker could do nothing, panicked, and fled. Elsea was still alive when emergency crews arrived and had her flown to a trauma center in Birmingham. She died the next day. Ajin sent a single artificial flower to her funeral.[1]

Note

1. The facts surrounding this case are all taken from Peter Waldman, "Inside Alabama's Auto Jobs Boom: Cheap Wages, Little Training, Crushed Limbs," *Businessweek* (March 23, 2017).

Discussion Questions

1. Why do you think workplace injuries are so common in Alabama's automotive factories? Explain.
2. Should these workplace risks just be expected as an unfortunate feature of low-wage jobs? Why, or why not? Explain.
3. Do employers have an ethical obligation to improve working conditions to prevent such injuries? Why, or why not? Explain.
4. What specific ideas from Boatright's discussion of occupational safety seem most relevant to this case? Why? Explain.

Case 6: BP's Disastrous Safety Culture

DENIS G. ARNOLD

BP is one of the largest oil companies in the world. It operates the third largest oil refinery in the United States in Texas City, Texas. In 2005 the health, safety, and environment manager at the Texas City refinery warned leaders that safety incidents are a problem, "I would like for us to make these incidents our No. 1 priority . . . I truly believe that we are on the verge of something bigger happening and that we must make critical decisions tomorrow morning over getting the workforce's attention around safety." This warning came after years of cost-cutting, reduced safety training, and neglected maintenance at the facility. One month later a catastrophic explosion at the plant killed 15 workers and seriously injured over 180 more. Among those killed were workers whose temporary office trailers were placed next to dangerous plant operations where intensive chemical operations were used to refine hydrocarbons. On the morning of the explosion, a dangerous start-up operation at the plant was undertaken without three critical pieces of safety equipment in functioning order. These included the hydrocarbon level indicator, the level alarm which would be triggered in the event of unsafe conditions, and an emergency control valve which would be used to shut down the flow. In addition, the Pre-Startup Safety Review procedure which would have detected these problems and ensured that non-essential personnel were not present was not undertaken. After the disaster a panel convened by the US Chemical Safety and Hazard Investigation Board identified the following causes of the disaster at BP.

1. Ineffective leadership regarding safety processes.
2. Poor communication with workers.
3. Inadequate resources.
4. Lack of accountability on the part of senior executives.
5. Lack of a uniform safety culture.

The government made a series of recommendations to improve the safety performance at the company, including more resources for safety training and equipment maintenance and accountability for safety on the part of executives.

In 2006 an oil spill from a BP pipeline in Alaska released in the range of 213,000–267,000 gallons of crude oil into Prudhoe Bay, Alaska. The leak occurred in a decaying section of the pipeline built in the 1970s. The federal government found that BP failed to adequately maintain the pipeline as a result of cost-cutting measures. BP reached a $255 million settlement with the state of Alaska and paid a $20 million fine to the federal government. The government estimated that BP saved $9.6 million by failing to inspect and maintain the pipeline over an eight-year period. BP's net profit for 2006 was $22 billion.

In 2010 BP's Macondo 18,000 foot deep well in the Gulf of Mexico experienced a blowout leading to a massive explosion on board the *Deepwater Horizon* oil drilling rig. The disaster killed 11 workers and resulted in the largest oil spill in US history. It took 87 days to control the flow of oil and in that time it is estimated that it spilled 4 million barrels of oil into the Gulf of Mexico, seriously harming ocean life, commercial fishing, and tourism throughout the region. A joint investigation by the US Bureau of Ocean Energy Management and the Coast Guard found that "The loss of life at the Macondo site on April 20, 2010, and the subsequent pollution of the Gulf of Mexico through the summer of 2010 were the result of poor risk management, last-minute changes to plans, failure to observe and respond to critical indicators, inadequate well control response and insufficient emergency bridge response training by companies and individuals responsible for drilling at the Macondo well and for the operation of the *Deepwater Horizon*." While investigators found that BP contractors Transocean and Halliburton shared blame, they found that BP was ultimately responsible for the disaster. BP lost $3.6 billion in 2010 but returned to profitability in 2011 earning profits over $25.6 billion. Through 2018, BP has paid out more than $65 billion in penalties and claims for the disaster.

Discussion Questions

1. How would you characterize the organizational safety culture at BP? Explain.
2. Are accidents like these just the cost of doing business in the oil industry? Why, or why not? Explain.
3. How would you characterize the stance of BP toward its employees based on their safety record? Explain.

4. What recommendations would Cohen, Gottlieb, Linn, and Richardson have for improving the safety performance at BP? Explain.

This case was written for the purposes of classroom discussion and is based on the following sources: US Chemical Safety and Hazard Investigation Board, Investigation Report, Report No. 2005-04-I-TX, *Refinery Explosion and Fire*, Texas City, Texas (2007). Retrieved from www.hsdl.org/?view&did=234995.

Andrew Hopkins, "The Problem of Defining High Reliability Organisations" (National Research Center for Occupational Health and Safety Regulation, Australian National University Working Paper No. 51, 2007).

Yereth Rosen, "Alaska to Collect $255 Million for 2006 BP Pipeline Leaks," *Reuters* (November 8, 2012). Retrieved from www.reuters.com/article/us-bp-alaskaspill/alaska-to-collect-255-million-for-2006-bp-pipeline-leaks-idUSBRE8A800M20121109.

Jeanette Lee, "BP Alaska Unit Pleads Guilty in Spill," AP (November 29, 2007). Retrieved from www.washingtonpost.com/wp-dyn/content/article/2007/11/29/AR2007112901583.html.

John M. Broder, "BP Shortcuts Lead to Gulf Oil Spill, Report Says," *The New York Times* (September 14, 2011).

Ron Bousso, "BP Deepwater Horizon Costs Balloon to $65 Billion," *Reuters* (January 16, 2018).

3

Managing, Leading, and Governing

3.1 INTRODUCTION

At the organizational level, the level of the firm, we speak of some corporations as good corporations, or socially responsible corporations, and other corporations as bad corporations, or socially irresponsible corporations. What makes them so? What are the causes of bad organizational behavior? How should managers lead organizations to avoid bad behavior and irresponsible conduct ? What are the characteristics of an ethical leader? What are the responsibilities of a corporate board of directors with respect to business ethics and corporate responsibility? These are the questions upon which we will focus in this chapter.

ETHICAL CULTURE AND LEADERSHIP

A natural impulse is to look to the top, to the leaders of an organization. After all, leaders are supposed to set an example. But what makes a good leader. In her contribution "Ethics and Effectiveness: The Nature of Good Leadership," Joanne B. Ciulla defends the thesis that an unethical leader is not a real leader. Her view is informed by the commonly accepted intuition that Hitler, despite his power and influence over history, was not a leader. Applying her insight to business, Ciulla would maintain that an unethical CEO is not a leader. Ciulla recognizes that a leader must be effective – the leader must get things done. However, a real leader is not only effective, but ethical as well. In his classic treatise on political leadership, Machiavelli advises the prince on how to be effective, but often Machiavelli's advice is unethical. The ideal leader finds a way to be both ethical and effective or to make ethics effective. Indeed, society expects business leaders to be successful within the bounds of the law and while avoiding harm. Too often, leaders achieve short-term economic success through misconduct or exempt themselves from the normal ethical rules that apply to everyone.

Ciulla argues that the real leader must live up to ethical standards, but she is realistic with respect to the stringency of these standards. Set the standards too low and people will be cynical about their leaders. Simply following the law is not enough. However, if the standards are set too high, good, but imperfect people may not accept leadership positions. We need to be careful if we ask leaders to act according to a higher standard. To be a leader, perfection or saintliness is not required, but a strong moral compass is needed.

One way that business leaders can help create and maintain ethically praiseworthy business practices is by cultivating an ethical culture within their organizations. Most medium and large-sized businesses have values or mission statements that serve to clarify for employees and others the core beliefs of the organization. Most companies also have employee codes of conduct. However, the relative importance of the stated values and code of conduct of an organization differs from company to company. Some companies screen for employees compatible with their values, train employees to adhere to the company's values, and evaluate employees partly in compliance with the organization's values. Many companies also employee a Chief Ethics Officer, or Director of Ethics and Compliance, whose job it is to mentor other managers on ethics and compliance issues, train employees, establish and maintain employee hotlines for internal reporting of ethical lapses, and in general foster an ethical culture within an organization. Such companies may be said to have integrity.

On the other hand, some companies may create a values statement largely for its public relations value and altogether ignore it in the day-to-day operations and strategic planning of the organization; Enron is a famous example of such a company and Wells Fargo is a recent example. At such companies, employee code violations may be ignored in cases where employees bring in substantial revenues or otherwise gain favor with management. Simultaneously, employees who adhere to the code or act in a manner consistent with corporate values may be penalized or even fired. Such a company lacks integrity.

In their contribution included in this chapter "Ethics as Organizational Culture," Linda Treviño and Katherine Nelson explain that organizational cultures can be strong or weak, ethical or unethical, depending on a range of formal and informal organizational systems. They emphasize the importance of codes of conduct, orientation and training programs, and incentive structures and evaluation systems in cultivating a strong ethical culture within organizations. They argue that without such systems in place, employees are likely to make organizational decisions driven by their own values rather than organizational values. They show that ethical leadership on the part of executives is essential to the maintenance of a strong ethical culture, and that hypocritical leaders who fail to "walk the talk" encourage unethical employee behavior.

GOVERNANCE

Although the public focuses on the leadership qualities of executives, it is the corporate board of directors who are ultimately responsible for ensuring the moral integrity of the corporation. Robert A. Prentice believes that insights from behavioral ethics will give us insights into why business leaders do bad things. In his contribution to this chapter, "Good Directors and Bad Behavior," he argues that behavioral ethics helps explain why corporate boards of directors are not always good overseers of management. Otherwise good people, including both executives and employees, can make ethically bad decisions due to such factors as a desire to please those in authority, a desire to fit into the group, and when they fear a loss. This latter factor is called loss aversion. An example is the fact that someone is more likely to do something wrong to keep a job compared to obtaining the job in the first place.

However, CEOs and other executives face special ethical challenges including overconfidence, the tendency to interpret information in a self-serving way, a tendency to think that the good one has done balances out the bad one has done, a tendency to act impulsively and then rationalize after the fact, and finally the tendency that power seems to stimulate sexual misconduct. With this knowledge from behavioral ethics before it, one might think a corporate board of directors could be a good watchdog. However, several reasons explain why this is often not the case. First on a strictly rational basis, individual members of a board of directors are seldom sued and in any case are usually protected by board and officer insurance. Simply put, they are seldom held individually responsible for their actions. In addition, the fact that the board has hired the chief executive officer and the chief financial officer means that the board of directors is susceptible to psychology biases themselves. For example, they are more likely to think that the people they hired are good people, they will tend to overlook evidence to the contrary, they find it more difficult to detect lies, and they can be starstruck by charismatic CEOs. Ignorance of these psychological factors helps explain the poor record of some boards in dealing with misconduct. Awareness of these psychological factors should make boards of directors better watchdogs.

One of the most important decisions that a board of directors makes is setting the salary of the CEO. Many in the public believe that boards, especially in the United States, have done a terrible job in this regard by overpaying CEOs and exacerbating the increasing inequality in the United States over the past 30 or more years. Every year American business magazines, such as *Fortune* and *Businessweek*, run exposés on excessive executive compensation. The editors argue that in the worst cases – poor corporate performances together with excessive executive compensation – there is no possible justification other than greed, and that in many cases with good corporate performance, the salaries are still excessive.

Robert W. Kolb provides an overview of the debate that swirls around executive compensation in "Ethics and Executive Compensation." After providing some data that include international comparisons and explaining some of the complexities surrounding what counts as compensation, he considers the ethical arguments for and against the current system of executive compensation. Arguments in favor of the current system are based on claims that high executive compensation is deserved, that it results from the exercise of a free contract, and that the current system is efficient in providing the maximum of goods and services. Opponents of the current system of executive compensation often appeal to the injustice of the wide divergence between executive pay and ordinary worker pay and point to the stress this inequality puts on the community in general and institutions within the community. Kolb elucidates each of these positions and provides a critical response to each as well.

In his contribution to this chapter, "Do CEOs Get Paid Too Much?" Jeffrey Moriarty assesses executive compensation packages and considers various arguments that might be used to justify them. He argues that none of the three standard defenses of current executive compensation levels – a free market defense, a defense grounded in what executives deserve as a result of their labors, and a utility-based argument – justifies present compensation levels. His conclusion is that the popular view that CEOs are greatly overpaid is correct.

WHISTLEBLOWING

Some corporations have unethical corporate cultures, others have generally ethical cultures but managers or employees or groups of employees who are willing to engage in unethical or illegal behavior because it is in their interest to do so. When a good employee observes illegal or unethical behavior in a company, what should that employee do?

Early ethics scholarship on whistleblowing – the practice of informing third parties such as law enforcement or the media about wrongdoing in an organization – focused on the conditions that constitute justified whistleblowing. That focus was caused in large part by the belief that whistleblowing breached a duty of loyalty of the employee to the employer. As a result of that analysis, a fairly standard list of conditions was drawn up that needed to be met if whistleblowing was morally justifiable. Two authors in this chapter challenge the standard view in two very different ways. In "Whistleblowing and Employee Loyalty," Ronald Duska challenges the assumption that the employee has a duty of loyalty to the employer. He argues that loyalty can apply only in a relationship that transcends self-interest and must be based on a stable relationship of trust and confidence. The relationship of an employee to the corporation is not that kind of relationship, in his view, because it is a relationship of mutual self-interest. In this form of relationship, the employee does not have an obligation of loyalty to the employer.

In his article, "Whistleblowing, Moral Integrity, and Organizational Ethics," George G. Brenkert argues that the core justification of whistleblowing is that it allows employees, relative to their positions of responsibility within the organization, to act with integrity rather than being complicit in wrongdoing. When an employee knows that a company is engaged in wrongdoing and is failing to redress the situation internally, the employee is justified in reporting the wrongdoing to parties outside the organization. Ideally, self-correcting organizations would address internal problems so that they acted in a manner consistent with their stated values, the law, and ordinary moral norms, thereby obviating the need for whistleblowers.

Janet P. Near and Marcia P. Miceli help managers to understand how they can avoid the need for whistleblowing in "After the Wrongdoing: What Managers Should Know about Whistleblowing." They note that most whistleblowers are normal, good employees who observe or are asked to participate in actions that are unethical or contrary to their conscience. In addition, most whistle-blowers begin by raising their concerns internally, within the organization itself. In other words whistleblowers are not simply disgruntled employees. Of course not every employee who observes wrongdoing blows the whistle either internally or externally. Indeed it may be that few employees are would-be whistleblowers. Why is that? Near and Miceli believe the fear of retaliation is a major reason. However, the circumstances are also important. As they point out with respect to internal whistle-blowing, "the choice to blow the whistle is correlated with the seriousness of the observed wrong-doing, the strength of evidence of wrongdoing, having supportive supervisors, and working in an organization whose culture is supportive of whistleblowing." Thus a supportive management team, and a supportive organizational culture, can keep whistleblowing in-house and thus prevent external whistleblowing and the organizational harm that results. As Near and Miceli point out, retaliation against an internal whistleblower increases the likelihood that the internal whistleblower will go public.

When a whistleblower goes public, even in cases where the whistleblower is morally justified in his or her actions, the practical result is that whistleblowers typically suffer economically and often psychologically for their moral stand. Well-publicized cases of whistleblowing bring public acclaim to the whistleblower but little else. The whistleblower finds it nearly impossible to get an equivalent job in the same industry and difficult to get another job at all.

Given this reality, governmental efforts have been made to protect whistleblowers. In the United States, whistleblowers may notify the government when a contractor or supplier (for example, in the pharmaceutical or military sectors) engages in wrongful action and collects a percentage of the fine levied by the government against the company engaged in wrongdoing under the False Claims Act. In 1986 Congress strengthened the False Claims Act to pay rewards of 15 to 30 percent of recovered funds. This has resulted in an increase in occurrences of whistleblowing with some whistleblowers receiving payments in the tens of millions of dollars. In 1999 the United Kingdom adopted the Public Interest Disclosure Act that provides financial compensation for whistleblowers who act in the public interest. In 2002 *Time* named three whistleblowers as persons of the year and whistleblowers received some protection under the Sarbanes–Oxley Act passed by Congress in the summer of 2002. In 2009 and again in 2010 Congress strengthened the False Claims Act to make it easier to bring charges against companies for retaining overpayments and for providing kick-backs. In 2011, in direct response to wrongdoing on Wall Street and the resulting Dodd-Frank Act, the US Securities and Exchange Commission put in place stronger whistleblower rules that provide for larger payments to whistleblowers for a much wider range of securities violations.

In conclusion, many of the moral grounds for employee loyalty have been destroyed. Commentators refer to the collapse of the social contract between a company and its employees.

Yet there are some minimum requirements of loyalty based in law. However, whistleblowing often involves speaking out on behalf of the public good when, for example, the government is being fraudulently charged for services or products. Recent changes in whistleblowing laws have made it easier for employees to blow the whistle and at the same time made it potentially financially rewarding. Cheryl Eckard, a quality-assurance manager at GlaxoSmithKline, tried repeatedly to get the company to fix contaminated production lines and incorrect labeling of drugs at one of its plants that manufactures pharmaceuticals. After being rebuffed by the company and eventually terminated, Eckard reported the problems to the US Food and Drug Administration. GlaxoSmithKline settled for $750 million and Eckard received a $96 million payout from the settlement.

3.2 ETHICAL CULTURE AND LEADERSHIP

Ethics and Effectiveness: The Nature of Good Leadership

JOANNE B. CIULLA

The moral triumphs and failures of leaders carry a greater weight and volume than those of most other people.[1] In leadership, we see morality and immorality magnified, which is why the study of ethics is fundamental to the study of leadership. The study of ethics concentrates on the nature of right and wrong and good and evil. It examines the relationships of people with each other and with other living things. Ethics explores questions related to what we should do and what we should be like as individuals, as members of a group or society, and in the different roles that we play in life. The role of a leader entails a distinctive type of human relationship. Some hallmarks of this relationship are power and/or influence, vision, obligation, and responsibility. By understanding the ethics of this relationship, we gain a better understanding of leadership because some of the central issues in ethics are also the central issues of leadership. They include personal challenges such as self-knowledge, self-interest, and self-discipline, and moral obligations related to justice, duty, competence, and the greatest good.

The Hitler Problem

Some scholars would argue that bullies and tyrants are not leaders, which takes us to what I have called "the Hitler problem."[2] The Hitler problem is based on how you answer the question: Was Hitler a leader? According to the morally unattractive definitions, he was a leader, perhaps even a great leader, albeit an immoral one. Heifetz argued that, under the "great man" and trait theories of leadership, you can put Hitler, Lincoln, and Gandhi in the same category because the underlying idea of the theory is that leadership is influence over history.[3] However, when your concept of leadership includes ethical considerations, Hitler was not a leader at all. He was a bully or tyrant – or simply the head of Germany.

We see how ingrained ethical ideas are in the concept of a leader when scholars differentiate between leaders and "real leaders" or "true leaders." Burns and Bass suggest that many leaders – transactional ones – are competent in that they promote exchanges among subordinates in their pursuit of collective outcomes, but that only transformational leaders are leaders in a strong moral sense. Extending this distinction, Burns and Bass attempt to separate leaders who fit the description of a transformational leader but are not ethical, from ethical leaders by distinguishing between transformational and pseudotransformational leaders or authentic transformational leaders.[4] Brown, Treviño, and Harrison make this distinction between common leadership and ethical leadership explicit in their concept of ethical leadership: "the demonstration of normatively appropriate conduct through personal actions and interpersonal relations, and the promotion of such conduct to followers through two-way communication, reinforcement, and decision-making."[5] Using Bennis and Nanus's characterization of leadership – "Managers are people who do things right and leaders are people who do right things"[6] – one could argue that Hitler was neither unethical nor a leader. (Maybe he was a manager?) Bennis and Nanus are among those scholars who sometimes slip into using the term leader to mean a morally good leader. However, what appears to be behind this in Bennis and Nanus's comment is the idea that leaders are or should be a head above everyone else morally. . . .

The Relationship between Ethics and Effectiveness

History defines successful leaders largely in terms of their ability to bring about change for better or worse. As a result, great leaders in history include everyone from Gandhi to Hitler. Machiavelli was disgusted by Cesare Borgia the man, but impressed by Borgia as the resolute, ferocious, and cunning prince.[7] Whereas leaders usually bring about change or are successful at doing something, the ethical questions waiting in the wings are always these: Was the change itself good? How did the leader go about bringing change? And what were the leader's intentions? A full analysis of the ethics and effectiveness of any action requires one to ask: Was it the right thing to do? Was it done the right way? Was it done for the right reason? In my own work, I have argued that a good leader is an ethical and an effective leader.[8] Whereas, this may seem like stating the obvious, the problem we face is that we do not always find ethics and effectiveness in the same leader. Some leaders are highly ethical but not very effective. Others are very effective at serving the needs of their constituents or organizations but not very ethical. United States Senator Trent Lott, who was forced to step down from his position as Senate majority leader because of his insensitive racial comments, is a compelling example of the latter. Some of his African-American constituents said that they would vote for him again, regardless of his racist comments because Lott had used his power and influence in Washington to bring jobs and money to the state. In politics, the old saying "He may be a son-of-a-bitch, but he's *our* son-of-a-bitch," captures the trade-off between ethics and effectiveness. In other words, as long as Lott gets the job done, we do not care about his ethics.

This distinction between ethics and effectiveness is not always a crisp one. Sometimes being ethical is being effective and sometimes being effective is being ethical. In other words, ethics is effectiveness in certain instances. There are times when simply being regarded as ethical and trustworthy makes a leader effective and other times when being highly effective makes a leader ethical. Given the limited power and resources of the secretary-general of the United Nations, it would be very difficult for someone in this position to be effective in the job if he or she did not behave ethically. The same is true for organizations. In the famous Tylenol case, Johnson & Johnson actually increased sales of Tylenol by pulling Tylenol bottles off their shelves after someone poisoned some of them. The leaders at Johnson & Johnson were effective because they were ethical.

The criteria that we use to judge the effectiveness of a leader are also not morally neutral. For a while, Wall Street and the business press lionized Al Dunlap ("Chainsaw Al") as a great business leader. Their admiration was based on his ability to downsize a company and raise the price of its stock. Dunlap apparently knew little about the nuts and bolts of running a business. When he failed to deliver profits at Sunbeam, he tried to cover up his losses and was fired. In this case and in many business cases, the criteria for effectiveness are practically and morally limited. It does not take great skill to get rid of employees, and taking away a person's livelihood requires a moral and a practical argument. Also, one of the most striking aspects of professional ethics is that often what seems right in the short run is not right in the long run or what seems right for a group or organization is not right when placed in a broader context. For example, Mafia families may have very strong internal ethical systems, but they are highly unethical in any larger context of society.

There are also cases when the sheer competence of a leader has a moral impact. For instance, there were many examples of heroism in the aftermath of the September 2001 terrorist attacks on the World Trade Center. The most inspiring and frequently cited were the altruistic acts of rescue workers. Yet consider the case of Alan S. Weil, whose law firm Sidley, Austin, Brown, & Wood occupied five floors of the World Trade Center. Immediately after watching the Trade Center towers fall to the ground and checking to see if his employees got out safely, Weil got on the phone and within three hours had rented four floors of another building for his employees. By the end of the day, he had arranged for an immediate delivery of 800 desks and 300 computers. The next day, the firm was open for business with desks for almost every employee.[9] We do not know if Mr. Weil's motives were altruistic or avaricious, but his focus on doing his job allowed the firm to fulfill its obligations to all of its stakeholders, from clients to employees. . . .

Deontological and Teleological Theories

The ethics-and-effectiveness question parallels the perspectives of deontological and teleological theories in ethics. From the deontological point of view, intentions are the morally relevant aspects of an act. As long as the leader acts according to his or her duty or on moral principles, then the leader acts ethically, regardless of the consequences. From the teleological perspective, what really matters is that the leader's actions result in bringing about something morally good or "the greatest good." Deontological theories locate the ethics of an action in the moral intent of the leader and his or her moral justification for the action, whereas teleological theories locate the ethics of the action in its results. We need both deontological and teleological theories to account for the ethics of leaders. Just as a good leader has to be ethical and effective, he or she also has to act according to duty and with some notion of the greatest good in mind.

In modernity, we often separate the inner person from the outer person and a person from his or her actions. Ancient Greek theories of ethics based on virtue do not have this problem. In virtue theories, you basically are what you do. The utilitarian John Stuart Mill saw this split between the ethics of the person and the ethics of his or her actions clearly.[10] He said the intentions or reasons for an act tell us something about the morality of the person, but the ends of an act tell us about the morality of the action. This solution does not really solve the ethics-and-effectiveness problem. It simply reinforces the split between the personal morality of a leader and what he or she does as a leader.

Going back to an earlier example, Mr. Weil may have worked quickly to keep his law firm going because he was so greedy he did not want to lose a day of billings, but in doing so, he also produced the greatest good for various stakeholders. We may not like his personal reasons for acting, but in this particular case, the various stakeholders may not care because they also benefited. If the various stakeholders knew that Weil had selfish intentions, they would, as Mill said, think less of him but not less of his actions. This is often the case with business. When a business runs a campaign to raise money for the homeless, it may be doing it to sell more of its goods and improve its public image. Yet it would seem a bit harsh to say that the business should not have the charity drive and deny needed funds for the homeless. One might argue that it is sometimes very unethical to demand perfect moral intentions. Nonetheless, personally unethical leaders who do good things for their constituents are still problematic. Even though they provide for the greatest good, their people can never really trust them.

Moral Standards

People often say that leaders should be held to "a higher moral standard," but does that make sense? If true, would it then be acceptable for everyone else to live by lower moral standards? The curious thing about morality is that if you set the moral standards for leaders too high, requiring something close to moral perfection, then few people will be qualified to be leaders or will want to be leaders. For example, how many of us could live up to the standard of having never lied, said an unkind word, or reneged on a promise? Ironically, when we set moral standards for leaders too high, we become even more dissatisfied with our leaders because few are able to live up to our expectations. We set moral standards for leaders too low, however, when we reduce them to nothing more than following the law or, worse, simply not being as unethical as their predecessors. A business leader may follow all laws and yet be highly immoral in the way he or she runs a business. Laws are supposed to be either morally neutral or moral minimums about what is right. They do not and cannot capture the scope and complexity of morality. For example, an elected official may be law abiding and, unlike his or her predecessor, live by "strong family values." The official may also have little concern for the disadvantaged. Not caring about the poor and the sick is not against the law, but is such a leader ethical? So where does this leave us? On one hand, it is admirable to aspire to high moral standards, but on the other hand, if the standards are unreachable, then people give up trying to reach them.[11] If the standards are too high, we may become more disillusioned with our leaders for failing to reach them. We might also end up with a shortage of competent people who are willing to take on leadership positions because we expect too much from them ethically. Some highly qualified people stay out of politics because they do not want their private lives aired in public. If the standards are too low, we become cynical about our leaders because we have lost faith in their ability to rise above the moral minimum.

History is littered with leaders who did not think they were subject to the same moral standards of honesty, propriety, and so forth, as the rest of society. One explanation for this is so obvious that it has become a cliché – power corrupts. Winter's and McClelland's works on power motives and on socialized and personalized charisma offer psychological accounts of this kind of leader behavior.[12] Maccoby and a host of others have talked about narcissistic leaders who, on the bright side, are exceptional and, on the dark side, consider themselves exceptions to the rules.[13]

Hollander's work on social exchange demonstrates how emerging leaders who are loyal to and competent at attaining group goals gain "idiosyncrasy credits" that allow them to deviate from the groups' norms to suit common goals.[14] As Price has argued, given the fact that we often grant leaders permission to deviate or be an exception to the rules, it is not difficult to see why leaders sometimes make themselves exceptions to moral constraints.[15] This is why

I think we should not hold leaders to higher *moral* standards than ourselves. If anything, we have to make sure that we hold them to the same standards as the rest of society. What we should expect and hope is that our leaders will fail less than most people at meeting ethical standards, while pursuing and achieving the goals of their constituents. The really interesting question for leadership development, organizational, and political theory is: What can we do to keep leaders from the moral failures that stem from being in a leadership role?

Notes

1. See Joanna B. Cuilla, *The Ethics of Leadership* (Belmont, CA: Wadsworth, 2003).
2. See Joanna B. Cuilla, "Leadership Ethics: Mapping the Territory," *Business Ethics Quarterly* 5 (1995): 5–24.
3. Ronald A. Heifetz, *Leadership without Easy Answers* (Cambridge, MA: Harvard University Press, 1994).
4. James M. Burns, *Leadership* (New York: Harper & Row, 1978); Bernard M. Bass, "Does the Transactional-Transformational Leadership Paradigm Transcend Organizational and National Boundaries?," *American Psychologist* 52 (1997): 130–39; Bernard M. Bass and Paul Steidlmeier, "Ethics, Character, and Authentic Transformational Leader Behavior," *The Leadership Quarterly* 10 (1999): 181–217.
5. Michael E. Brown, Linda K. Treviño, and David A. Harrison, "Ethical Leadership: A Social Learning Perspective for Construct Development and Testing," *Organizational Behavior and Human Decision Processes* 97 (2005): 117–34 (p. 120).
6. Warren Bennis and Burt Nanus, *Leaders: Strategies for Taking Charge* (New York: HarperCollins, 1985), p. 21.
7. Giuseppe Prezzolini, *Nicolo Machiavelli, the Florentine*, trans. R. Roeder (New York: Brentano's, 1928), p. 11.
8. Cuilla, "Leadership Ethics: Mapping the Territory."
9. John Schwartz, "Up from the Ashes, One Firm Rebuilds," *The New York Times* (September 16, 2001), sec. 3, p. 1.
10. John Stuart Mill, "What Utilitarianism Is," in *Utilitarianism and Other Essays*, ed. A. Ryan (New York: Penguin Books, 1987), pp. 272–338.
11. Joanna B. Cuilla, "Casuistry and the Case for Business Ethics," in *Business as a Humanity*, ed. T. Donaldson and R. E. Freeman (Oxford University Press, 1994), pp. 167–83.
12. D. G. Winter, "The Motivational Dimensions of Leadership: Power, Achievement, Affiliation," in *Multiple Intelligences and Leadership*, ed. R. E. Riggio, S. E. Murphy, and F. J. Pirozzolo (Mahwah, NJ: Lawrence Erlbaum Associates, 2002), pp. 118–38; David C. McClelland, *Power: The Inner Experience* (New York: Halsted, 1975).
13. Michael Maccoby, "Narcissistic Leaders," *Harvard Business Review* 78 (2000): 69–75.
14. Edwin Hollander, *Leaders, Groups, and Influence* (Oxford University Press, 1964).
15. Terry Price, "Explaining Ethical Failures of Leadership," *The Leadership and Organizational Development Journal* 21 (2000): 177–84.

Ethics as Organizational Culture

LINDA TREVIÑO AND KATHERINE NELSON

What Is Culture?

Anthropologists define culture as a body of learned beliefs, traditions, and guides for behavior shared among members of a group.[1] This idea of culture has been particularly useful for understanding and differentiating among work organizations and the behavior of people in them.[2] It's a way of differentiating one organization's "personality" from another. The organizational culture expresses shared assumptions, values, and beliefs[3] and is manifested in many ways, including formal rules and policies, norms of daily behavior, physical settings, modes of dress, special language, myths, rituals, heroes, and stories.[4] To assess and understand an organization's culture requires knowledge of the organization's history and values, along with a systematic analysis of multiple formal and informal organizational systems.

Organizational cultures can vary widely, even within the same industry (consider Walmart, Target, and Costco – all big-box retailers that have very different cultures). In the computer industry, IBM was known for many years for its relative formality, exemplified by a dress code that mandated dark suits, white shirts, and polished shoes. Apple Computer, on the other hand, was known for its informality. Particularly in its early days, T-shirts, jeans, and tennis shoes were the expected Apple "costume." *Fortune* magazine described IBM as "the sensible, wingtip, Armonk, New York computer company, not part of that sneaker-wearing, tofu-eating Silicon Valley crowd."[5] Although that characterization was made a long time ago, it's still pretty applicable today.

Strong versus Weak Cultures

Organizational cultures can be strong or weak.[6] In a strong culture, standards and guidelines are widely shared within the organization, providing common direction for day-to-day behavior. This is likely because all cultural systems, formal and informal, are aligned to provide consistent direction and to point behavior in the same direction. In the 1980s, Citicorp's culture was so strong that when Katherine Nelson, a co-author of this article and former vice-president and head of human resources communications at Citicorp, traveled to the firm's offices in the Far East to deliver ethics training, she felt right at home (despite huge differences in national culture). "You could tell that you were in a Citicorp facility," she said, "whether you were in London, Tokyo, or New York." When Nelson facilitated an ethics training session for Japanese managers, she presented them with a common ethical dilemma: What do you do if you have raised an important ethical issue with your manager and nothing is done? Moreover, the manager discourages you from pursuing the issue. The potential answers included do nothing, go around the manager to the next level, raise the issue in writing to the manager, or take the issue to a staff department such as human resources.

The Japanese managers unanimously gave the "correct" answer according to Citicorp culture and policies at the time. They said they would go around their manager and take the issue to the next level. Nelson was surprised at their response, thinking that it conflicted with the wider Japanese culture's deference to authority and seniority. So she asked these managers, "Doesn't this conflict with Japanese culture?" To which they responded, "You forget – we are much more Citicorp than we are Japanese." Citicorp's culture proved to be so strong that standards and guidelines spanned continents and superseded national culture. (Citicorp merged with Travelers in 1998 to form Citigroup, and its culture has changed significantly since then.) This type of experience has since been verified by some of our international students who worked for US-based multinationals before returning to school for their MBA degree. For example, one student worked for Baxter Healthcare in a country known for corruption and bribery. Baxter's strong ethical culture didn't allow such conduct,

and employees were proud to be a part of such an organization and happy to comply (even or perhaps especially in the midst of a corrupt business culture).

In a weak organizational culture, strong subcultures exist and guide behavior that differs from one subculture to another. Many large public universities can be thought of as having weak cultures. For example, for faculty, departmental subcultures are often stronger than the overall university culture; the romance languages department differs from the accounting department. Among students at a large state university, the fraternity-sorority subculture coexists with the political activist subculture, the devout Christian subculture, the jock subculture, and many other subcultures, and behavior is quite different within each. It's important to note that weak doesn't necessarily mean bad. In some situations, weak cultures are desirable. They allow for strong subcultures featuring diversity of thought and action. However, in a weak culture, behavioral consistency across the organization is tough to achieve. Look around your own school or work organization. Would you characterize its culture as strong or weak?

How Culture Influences Behavior: Socialization and Internalization

Employees are brought into the organization's culture through a process called enculturation, or *socialization*.[7] Through socialization, employees learn "the ropes." Socialization can occur through formal training or mentoring, or through more informal transmission of norms of daily behavior by peers and superiors. New members learn from observing how others behave or through informally transmitted messages. When effectively socialized into a strong culture, employees behave in ways that are consistent with expectations of the culture (or subculture). They know how to dress, what to say, and what to do.

With socialization, people behave in ways that are consistent with the culture because they feel they are expected to do so. Their behavior may have nothing to do with their personal beliefs, but they behave as they are expected to behave in order to fit into the context and to be approved by peers and superiors.[8] As an example, the president of a huge financial firm once took a young, high-potential manager out to lunch and walked him right over to Brooks Brothers for a new suit. "You can't get where you're going in a cheap suit," the president told the young man, who continued to buy his suits at Brooks Brothers.

But individuals may behave according to the culture for another reason – because they have internalized cultural expectations. With *internalization*, individuals have adopted the external cultural standards as their own. Their behavior, though consistent with the culture, also accords with their own beliefs. They may come into the organization sharing its values and expectations, thus making for a very smooth transition. Or, they may internalize cultural expectations over time. In the above example, the young manager may have initially bought the Brooks Brothers suit because he felt compelled to; but over time, he continued to buy those suits perhaps because he had internalized the expectation and wanted to do so.

The concepts of socialization and internalization apply to understanding why employees behave ethically or unethically in an organization. Most people prefer to behave ethically. When they join an organization with a strong ethical culture, the messages about honesty and respect resonate with their personal beliefs and are easily internalized. They act ethically because it's natural for them to do so and consistent with the cultural messages they're receiving. But unfortunately, most employees can be socialized into behaving unethically, especially if they have little work experience to contrast with the messages being sent by the current unethical culture. If everyone around them is lying to customers, they're likely to do the same as long as they remain a member of the organization.

Ethical Culture: A Multisystem Framework

We said earlier that ethical culture can be conceptualized as representing a slice of the organization's broader culture. Ethical culture is created and maintained through a complex interplay of formal and informal organizational systems (Figure 3.1). Formally, executive leader communications, selection systems, orientation and training programs, rules, policies and codes, performance management systems, organizational structures, and formal decision-making processes

all contribute to creating and maintaining ethical culture. Informally, heroes and role models; norms of daily behavior; rituals, myths, and stories; and language indicate whether the formal ethics-related systems represent reality or facade. In the following we provide examples of each of these important ethical culture systems. Although we discuss these systems separately, keep in mind that they are all interconnected.

Alignment of Ethical Culture Systems

To create a consistent ethical culture message, the formal and informal systems must be *aligned* (work together) to support ethical behavior. To have a fully aligned ethical culture, the multiple formal and informal systems must all be sending employees consistent messages that point in the direction of ethical behavior. For example, imagine a company whose formal corporate values statement and ethics code tell employees that honesty is highly valued in the organization and that employees should always be truthful with customers and each other. Consistent with that values statement, the selection system does background checks on potential employees, incorporates ethics-related questions in interviews, and highlights the company's values to recruits. Once hired, new employees are further oriented into the ethical culture by learning about the values of the founder, how the history of the company supports those values, and how the current executive team is carrying on that tradition. They're also trained in the specific kinds of ethical issues they could face in their jobs and how to handle them ethically. They learn that the performance management system will assess them on values-related criteria, including honest and trustworthy interactions, and that these assessments will be important to decisions about compensation and promotion. They are also encouraged to take personal responsibility and speak up about any ethical

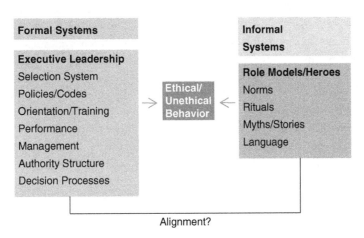

Figure 3.1 A multisystem ethical culture framework

concerns. On the informal side, they learn that high-level managers routinely tell customers the truth about the company's ability to meet their needs and that the company celebrates employees of exemplary integrity at an annual awards dinner. Employees in such an organization receive a consistent message about the organization's commitment to honesty, and their behavior is likely to be honest as well because these formal and informal systems are aligned and supporting their ethical behavior.

But opportunities for misalignment abound in these complex systems. For example, if the same organization touts its honesty in its values statement but regularly deceives customers in order to land a sale, and the organization gives a highly "successful" but highly deceptive sales representative the firm's sales award, the organization's formal and informal systems are out of alignment. The formal statements say one thing while company actions and rituals say quite another. Employees perceive that deceit is what the organization is really about, despite what the ethics code says. Cultures can range from strongly aligned ethical cultures (where all systems are aligned to support ethical behavior) to strongly aligned unethical cultures (where all systems are aligned to support unethical behavior) to those that are misaligned because employees get somewhat mixed messages due to conflicts between the formal and informal systems.

Leaders should be interested in creating a strongly aligned ethical culture because American employees strongly prefer working for such an organization. A 2006 study found that 82 percent of Americans would actually prefer to be paid less but work for an ethical company than be paid more but work for an unethical company. Importantly, more than a third of people say that they've left a job because they disagreed with the company's ethical standards. So having a strong ethical culture is an important way to retain the best employees.[9]

Another reason leaders need to create and maintain a strongly aligned ethical culture is that the US Sentencing Commission revised its guidelines for sentencing organizational defendants in 2004 (see www.ussc.gov for more information about these guidelines). When the US Sentencing Commission (www.ussc.gov) evaluated the effect of the original 1991 guidelines, it noted that many organizations seemed to be engaging in a kind of "check-off approach" to the guidelines. In responding to guideline requirements to qualify for reduced sentencing and fines, these organizations would establish formal ethics and/or legal compliance programs, including ethics offices, codes of conduct, training programs, and reporting systems. But the commission learned that many of these formal programs were perceived to be only "window dressing" by employees because they were inconsistent with the employees' day-to-day organizational experiences. The commission subsequently revised its guidelines to call for developing and maintaining a strong ethical culture. As a result, many companies are now assessing their cultures to determine how they're doing in relation to ethics so if they do get into legal trouble, they can demonstrate that they have been making sincere efforts to guide their employees toward ethical conduct.

Ethical Leadership

Executive Leaders Create Culture

Executive leaders affect culture in both formal and informal ways. Senior leaders can create, maintain, or change formal and informal cultural systems by what they say, do, or support.[10] Formally, their communications send a powerful message about what's important in the organization. They influence a number of other formal culture dimensions by creating and supporting formal policies and programs, and they influence informal culture by role modeling, the language they use, and the norms their messages and actions appear to support.

The founder of a new organization is thought to play a particularly important culture-creating role.[11] Often, the founder has a vision for what the new organization should be. He or she often personifies the culture's values, providing a role model for others to observe and follow, and guides decision-making at all organizational levels. For example, Thomas Jefferson founded the University of Virginia. Although he's long gone, it's said even today that when the governing board of the university is faced with a difficult decision, they're still guided by "what Mr. Jefferson would do." Founders of small businesses frequently play this culture-creating role.

Herb Kelleher is the legendary founder of Southwest Airlines, often cited as the best-run US airline. The no-frills airline started in 1971 and has been growing and flying pretty high ever since, despite many difficulties in its industry. Southwest Airlines has never served a meal, and its planes are in and out of the gate in 20 minutes. During Kelleher's tenure as CEO and chairman, other airlines went bankrupt, suffered strikes, or disappeared. But Southwest continued to succeed even after the terrorist attacks of September 11, 2001, that sent the entire industry reeling. The secret is thought to be the company's culture and an *esprit de corps* inspired by Kelleher – he believes in serving the needs of employees, who then take great care of customers and ultimately provide shareholder returns. . . .

Current executive leaders can also influence culture in a number of ways.[12] They can help maintain the current culture, or they can change it by articulating a new vision and values; by paying attention to, measuring, and controlling certain things; by making critical policy decisions; by recruiting and hiring personnel who fit their vision of the organization; and by holding people accountable for their actions.

Sometimes new leaders significantly change longstanding corporate culture. Jack Welch, retired CEO of General Electric Company, radically changed the formerly staid bureaucratic culture of GE into a lean and highly competitive organization during his leadership tenure. Welch began the culture change effort by clearly articulating his vision that the new GE would be number one or number two in the world in each of its businesses. Businesses that could not measure up would be sold.

Traditional GE employees had been attracted to the job security of the old GE. But Welch wanted to encourage competitiveness, risk taking, creativity, self-confidence, and dynamism. He recruited managers who were interested in doing a great job and then moving on, if GE no longer needed them. Many of the old-line GE employees found themselves unhappy, out of sync – and, frequently, out of a job.

Welch also focused on identifying and eliminating unproductive work in the organization. He told managers to eliminate reports, reviews, and forecasts; to speed decision cycles; and to move information more quickly through the organization by eliminating unnecessary bureaucratic layers. All of this contributed to the "leaner and meaner" GE culture he created.

Welch's successor, Jeff Immelt (who became CEO in 2001), has changed the GE culture yet again. He announced in 2004 that four things would be required to keep the company on top: execution, growth, great people, and virtue. The first three were consistent with the GE everyone knew.

However, most people don't expect the word *virtue* to be associated with a company that earns billions in revenue. But Immelt had learned that people perceived GE to be "a laggard" on the social responsibility front, and he vowed to change that. He has said that, in a world of business ethics scandals, people don't admire business as they used to and that the gulf between rich and poor is growing. As a result, he believes that companies are obligated to provide solutions to the world's problems – not to just make money for shareholders and obey the law. "Good leaders give back. . . . It's up to us to use our platform to be a good citizen."[13] In line with this new focus on virtue, Immelt appointed GE's first vice-president for corporate citizenship and has been publishing corporate citizenship annual reports. The company is committing itself to becoming a leader in environmental cleanup and a catalyst for change. You're probably familiar with its "Ecoimagination" initiative that focuses on green initiatives and concern about climate change. This initiative even has its own devoted website (www.ecoimagination.com), as does the GE Citizenship initiative more generally (www.ge.com /citizenship). The company also now audits suppliers in developing countries to ensure compliance with labor, environmental, and health and safety standards. And the company has increased its focus on diversity, including granting domestic partner health benefits to employees, and has entered into dialogue with socially responsible mutual funds. In response to a request from African-American employees to do more in Africa, GE is working with the public health service in Ghana, where it has provided equipment, water treatment, and leadership training. . . .

Ethical Leadership and Ethical Culture. Clearly, employees take their cues from the messages sent by those in formal leadership roles. But most employees don't know

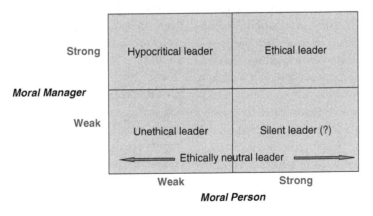

Figure 3.2 Executive ethical leadership

the senior executives of their organization personally. They only know what they can make sense of from afar. Therefore senior executives must develop a "reputation" for ethical leadership by being visible on ethics issues and communicating a strong ethics message. A recent study[14] found that such a reputation rests upon dual dimensions that work together: a moral person dimension and a moral manager dimension (see Figures 3.1 and 3.2). In this section, first we explain what each dimension represents and then we combine these dimensions into a matrix that shows how leaders can develop a reputation for ethical leadership, unethical leadership, hypocritical leadership, or ethically neutral leadership.

The moral person dimension represents the "ethical" part of the term *ethical leadership* and is vital to developing a reputation for ethical leadership among employees. As a moral person, the executive is seen first as demonstrating certain individual traits (integrity, honesty, and trustworthiness). For example, one executive described ethical leaders as "squeaky clean." But probably more important are visible behaviors.

These include doing the right thing, showing concern for people and treating them with dignity and respect, being open and listening, and living a personally moral life. To some extent, senior executives live in glass houses. They are often public figures who are active in their communities. So they need to be particularly careful about their private behavior. Rumors can begin quickly and taint an otherwise solid reputation. Finally, an important contributor to being perceived as a moral person is to make decisions in a particular way – decisions that are explicitly based on values, fairness, concern for society, and other ethical decision rules.

But being a moral person is not in itself enough to be perceived as an ethical leader. Being a moral person tells employees how the leader is likely to behave, but it doesn't tell them how the leader expects them to behave. So to complete the ethical leadership picture, executives must also act as "moral managers" – they must focus on the "leadership" part of the term *ethical leadership* by making ethics and values an important part of their leadership message and by shaping the firm's ethical culture. They do that by conveying the importance of ethical conduct in a variety of ways. Most of the messages employees receive in business are about bottom-line goals. Therefore, senior executives must make ethics a priority of their leadership if ethics is to get attention from employees. Moral managers do this by being visible role models of ethical conduct, by communicating openly and regularly with employees about ethics and values, and by using the reward system to hold everyone accountable to the standards.

When Paul O'Neill first became CEO at Alcoa, he brought with him a profound concern for worker safety. Although Alcoa already had an enviable safety record at the time based on industry standards, O'Neill created a goal of zero lost work days from accidents – a goal that flabbergasted even the safety director. When O'Neill visited plants, he told employees that the company was no longer going to budget for safety – if a hazard was fixable, they should do it and the company would pay for it, no questions asked. Then he gave the hourly workforce his telephone number at home and told them to call him directly about safety problems. He created an accident reporting system that required reporting within 24 hours of any accident, no matter how small, and he used the reports as an opportunity for learning so that future accidents could be avoided. He also got on an airplane and visited employees who had been seriously hurt, no matter where in the world they were. Safety messages were everywhere, including woven into the carpets at some Alcoa sites. And when employees in the Pittsburgh headquarters crossed the street, they were careful not to jaywalk because it was "unsafe." Years after O'Neill retired, Alcoa continued to improve until it became the safest company in the world.

In the completely different arena of diversity, O'Neill again stood out for his principled leadership. In his first week on the job, his secretary asked him to sign papers to join a country club. This had been standard procedure in the past because CEO membership was required in order for other Alcoa executives to join and use the club. Upon asking for certification that the club did not discriminate, he learned that the club did not have an open membership policy. O'Neill refused to sign the papers and developed a new policy saying that Alcoa would not reimburse any employee expenses at a place that did not allow admission to anyone who wanted it. O'Neill was encouraged not to rock the boat and to wait before making such a huge change. His response was, "What excuse am I going to use six or twelve months from now? I've just discovered my principles? They were on vacation . . . when I first came?" He explained that you have to have the courage of your convictions and insist on them all of the time, not just when it's convenient.[15]

Unethical Leadership. Unfortunately, unethical leaders can just as strongly influence the development of an unethical culture. In terms of our matrix, unethical leaders have reputations as weak moral persons and weak moral managers. In interviews, senior executives cited Al Dunlap as a senior executive with a reputation for unethical leadership. John Byrne of *BusinessWeek* wrote a book about Dunlap (*Mean Business*, 1997) and published excerpts in the magazine. According to Byrne, Dunlap became famous for turning struggling companies around. When hired at Sunbeam, he was considered such a celebrity CEO that the stock price spiked 49 percent in one day. But while at Sunbeam, he was also known for "emotional abuse" of employees – being "condescending, belligerent and disrespectful." "At his worst, he became viciously profane, even violent. Executives said he would throw papers or furniture, bang his hands on his desk, and shout so ferociously that a manager's hair would be blown back by the stream of air that rushed from Dunlap's mouth." Dunlap also demanded that employees make the numbers at all costs, and he rewarded them handsomely for doing so. As a result, they felt pressure to use questionable accounting and sales techniques. Dunlap also lied to Wall Street, assuring them that the firm was making its projections and would continue to reach even higher. After just a couple of years, Dunlap couldn't cover up the real state of affairs, and Sunbeam's board fired him in 1998. But he left the company crippled.[16] In 2002, Dunlap settled a civil suit filed by the Securities and Exchange Commission (SEC). He paid a $500,000 fine and agreed that never again would he be an officer or a director of a public company. Investigators learned that allegations of accounting fraud on Dunlap's watch go back to the 1970s and follow him through a number of companies.

Hypocritical Leadership. Perhaps nothing can make us more cynical than a leader who talks incessantly about integrity and ethical values but then engages in unethical conduct, encourages others to do so either explicitly or implicitly, rewards only bottom-line results, and fails to discipline misconduct. This leader is strong on the communication aspect of moral management but clearly isn't an ethical person – doesn't "walk the talk." It's a "do as I say, not as I do" approach. Al Dunlap made no pretense about ethics. All that mattered was the bottom line, and he didn't pretend to be a nice guy. But hypocritical leadership is all about ethical pretense. The problem is that by putting the spotlight on integrity, the leader raises expectations and awareness of ethical issues. At the same time, employees realize that they can't trust anything the leader says. That leads to cynicism, and employees are likely to disregard ethical standards themselves if they see the leader doing so.

An example of hypocritical leadership is Lord John Browne, formerly the CEO of BP. Under Browne's leadership, the company launched a $200 million "Beyond Petroleum" campaign to promote its image as a highly socially responsible company that would deliver performance without trading off worker safety or environmental concerns. But when BP's

Texas City plant exploded (killing 15 workers and injuring many more) and two big oil spills occurred in Alaska, regulators and employees cited cost-cutting on safety and negligence in pipeline corrosion prevention as causes. It seemed that the Beyond Petroleum campaign was more about words than action. Greenpeace awarded Browne the "Best Impression of an Environmentalist" award in 2005, and the CEO was finally asked to resign in 2007 after a scandal in his personal life surfaced.[17] The lesson is pretty clear. If leaders are going to talk ethics and social responsibility (as they should), they had better "walk the talk" or risk cynicism or worse.

Ethically Neutral or "Silent" Leadership. The fact is that many top managers are not strong leaders either ethically or unethically. They fall into what employees perceive to be an ethically "neutral" or ethically "silent" leadership zone. They simply don't provide explicit leadership in the crucial area of ethics. They are perceived to be silent on this issue, and employees aren't sure what the leaders think about ethics, if anything. This may be because the leader doesn't realize how important executive ethical leadership is to the organization's ethical culture, isn't comfortable with talking about ethics issues, or just doesn't care that much. On the moral person dimension, the ethically neutral leader is not clearly unethical but is perceived to be more self-centered than people-oriented. On the moral manager dimension, the ethically neutral leader is thought to focus on the bottom line without setting complementary ethical goals. Little or no ethics message is coming from the top. But it turns out that silence represents an important message. In the context of all the other bottom-line-oriented messages being sent in a highly competitive business environment, employees are likely to interpret silence to mean that the top executive really doesn't care how business goals are met (only that they are met), and they'll act on that message.[18] . . .

Research has found that executive ethical leadership is critical to employees. Unethical behavior is lower, and employees are more committed to their organization, more ethically aware, and more likely to engage in positive helping behaviors (including reporting problems to management) in firms that have an ethical culture characterized by top executives who are strong ethical leaders.[19] Research has also found evidence that executive ethical leadership flows down through the organization, affecting supervisors' ethical leadership behavior and finally employee behavior.[20] But interestingly, senior executives are often not aware of how important their ethical leadership is. Many believe that being an ethical person who makes ethical decisions is enough. But it isn't enough. Executives must lead on this issue (be moral managers) if it is to register with employees. In a highly competitive environment of intense focus on the bottom line, employees need to know that the executive leaders in their organization care about ethics at least as much as financial performance. An ethical leader makes it clear that strong bottom-line results are expected, but only if they can be delivered in a highly ethical manner. Leaders may talk in terms of reputation or use other language they find comfortable. But the message must be that the firm's long-term reputation is an asset that everyone must protect.

Other Formal Cultural Systems

Selection Systems

When considering the ethical culture, organizations can avoid ethical problems by recruiting the right people and by building a reputation that precedes the organization's representatives wherever they go. Companies can conduct background checks, check references, administer integrity tests, and survey applicants. Interviewers can also ask ethics-related questions in interviews, for example, by asking candidates about ethical issues they've confronted in the past and how they've handled them.

In an article entitled, "Can You Interview for Integrity?" William Byham[21] offered a series of questions an interviewer concerned about ethics might ask a recruit. Here are adaptations of some of them:

1. We sometimes have to choose between what we think is right and what's best for the company. Can you give an example of such a time and tell how you handled it?
2. Can you describe your current employer's ethics? Are there things you feel good about? bad about?
3. Please provide an example of an ethical decision you've made at work and tell how you handled it. What factors did you consider?
4. Can you provide an example of some past work behavior that you've regretted? How would you behave differently today?
5. Have you ever felt the need to exaggerate or bend the truth to make a sale?
6. Have you ever observed someone else stretching the rules at work? What did you do, if anything?
7. People are often tempted to make something seem better than it is. Have you ever been in such a situation?
8. Have you ever had to go against company policies in order to accomplish something?
9. Have you ever managed someone who misled a client? How did you handle it?
10. What's your philosophy of how to think about policies? Are they guidelines, to be followed to the letter?

Our students have been asked similar types of questions in interviews with the best companies. Are you prepared to answer questions like these?

Recruiters can also inform prospective employees about the importance of integrity in their organization and what happens to those who break the rules. Companies that are serious about integrity can include statements about their values and expectations in recruiting literature, in the scripts recruiters use when interviewing job candidates, in offer letters to candidates, and in new-hire orientation programs. . . .

Values and Mission Statements

Once employees are on board, many organizations aim to guide employees' behavior through formal organizational value statements, mission statements, credos, policies, and formal codes of ethical conduct. Value and mission statements and credos are general statements of guiding beliefs. Most companies have them, but it's important that the values and mission statement be closely aligned with other dimensions of the culture. According to James Collins, co-author of *Built to Last: Successful Habits of Visionary Companies*, "the words matter far less than how they are brought to life. The mistake most companies make . . . is not setting up procedures to make sure the mission is carried out." If the policies and codes are followed in daily behavior and people are held accountable to them, this is another example of a strong ethical culture in alignment. . . .

Policies and Codes

Formal ethics policies (often called codes of ethics or codes of conduct) are longer and more detailed than broad values and mission statements. They provide guidance about behavior in multiple specific areas. For example, most ethics codes address issues of respectful treatment of others, conflicts of interest, expense reporting, and the appropriateness of giving and receiving gifts. Policy manuals are even lengthier than codes and include more detailed lists of rules covering a multitude of job situations that are specific to the industry, organization, and type of job.

Most ethics codes were introduced within the past 30 years. A mid-1990s study of the *Fortune* 1000 found that 98 percent of these large firms reported addressing ethics and conduct issues in formal documents. Of those 98 percent, 78 percent had codes of ethics.[22] In a 2005 Ethics Resource Center study, 86 percent of respondents from a wide variety of employers across the United States reported that the private sector, public sector, and not-for-profit organizations they work for have formal ethics policy standards.[23]So it's fair to say that most employers are making an effort to provide formal guidance to their employees regarding ethical and legal conduct. It's also important to note that these codes are living documents that are revised regularly in response to changing conditions. For example, early ethics codes said nothing about Internet privacy or social networking guidelines, but these topics are much more common in today's codes.

Most companies with codes now distribute them quite widely. A 1995 survey of *Fortune* 1000 firms found that 75 percent of responding companies reported distributing their code or policy to at least 80 percent of their employees.[24] This finding may be a by-product of the US Sentencing Guidelines which specify communication of compliance standards to all employees as a guiding principle. Research has found that when employees are familiar with the code and refer to it for guidance, they are less likely to engage in unethical behavior, more likely to seek advice about ethical issues, and more likely to report ethical rule violations.[25] But, to have real influence on behavior, a code must be enforced.[26] Otherwise, codes of conduct are more likely to be viewed as mere "window dressing" rather than guides for actual behavior. . . .

Managers, especially middle managers, want to have a stated organizational policy or code when it comes to serious ethical matters. Remember, cognitive moral development research tells us that most people are looking outside themselves for guidance, and stated organizational policy can be an important source of that guidance. To determine where policy is needed, the organization can survey managers about areas of ethical concern and their perception of the need for policy in each area. In one study, managers made it clear that policy was needed in such areas as expense claims, gifts and bribes, and treatment of competitor information.[27]

Orientation and Training Programs

Socialization into the ethical culture is often begun through formal orientation programs for new employees and is reinforced through ongoing training. The organization's cultural values and guiding principles can be communicated in orientation programs. Employees often receive an introduction to the values and mission statements as well as the company's history and current code of conduct. But new employees are so overwhelmed with information that it's important to follow up with training programs that offer more specific guidance. An increasing number of firms have added ethics to their list of training programs. Some have done so as a result of the revision of the US Sentencing Commission Guidelines and the Sarbanes–Oxley legislation that requires public companies to conduct compliance training at all levels, including senior executives and the board of directors. Most *Fortune* 1000 firms provide some ethics training,[28] and many of them do so annually. In the 2005 Ethics Resource Center study,[29] 69 percent of people surveyed said that their employers provide ethics training and that this training is generally mandatory. Some companies use online ethics training; others use classroom face-to-face training.

It's important to note that the ethics training must be consistent with other ethical culture systems, because a training program that is out of alignment with other culture systems is thought of, at best, as a pleasant day away from the office. At its worst, the ethics training is seen as an obstacle to getting "real" work done – or even as a joke. For example, a young man who worked in mortgage lending in 2006 said that his company had provided a high-quality weeklong training program to prepare him for his job. Among other more technical aspects of his job, he was taught to advise clients to be sure that they could afford their payments and to avoid incurring additional credit card debt. He felt that this was smart and caring advice, and he felt good about his new role. But when he returned to the office, his "mentor" (who had been in the job only six months longer than he had) told him that all that mattered was closing the deal and making money for himself and the company, and that "advising" clients was a waste of time. If his "advisor" role had been reinforced by his mentor, the cultural message would have been entirely different. Perhaps the company's fate would have been different as well – it no longer exists.

Performance Management Systems

Performance management systems involve the formal process of articulating employee goals, identifying performance metrics, and then providing a compensation structure that rewards individual – and frequently team – effort in relation to those goals. Performance management systems also include formal disciplinary systems that are designed to address performance problems when they arise. An effective performance management system is a key component of the ethical culture. The system plays an essential role in alignment or misalignment of the ethical culture because people pay attention to what is measured, rewarded, and disciplined. So if employees with integrity are the ones who get ahead, and unethical behavior is disciplined, that process goes a long way toward promoting an ethical culture.

Designing a Performance Management Process That Supports Ethical Conduct. Because people "do what's measured and rewarded," the best way for an organization to design a comprehensive performance management system is to spend time identifying which factors drive the results the organization strives to achieve. This type of corporate soul-searching generally results in a list of these factors, both financial and nonfinancial. Just as *Fortune* magazine considers reputation when designing its famed "lists" of admired companies, many sophisticated companies understand that reputation, in many cases, drives long-term financial results. However, many companies continue to design performance management programs that consider only financial results. They ignore the nonfinancial drivers that can actually serve as the underpinning of the numbers. These companies focus on *what* business results are delivered, and they ignore *how* those results were achieved. That is probably the fastest way for an organization's ethical culture to get out of alignment.

Here's how performance management systems can be designed to get great results the right way. First, an organization needs to focus on the mechanics. For example, once an organization understands what is necessary to drive results, it needs to set goals to achieve those desired results and metrics to determine whether the goals are being met. Real success in this area comes when organizations effectively communicate those goals to every employee, helping employees identify how each person can create value for the organization and then rewarding employees fairly for their contribution to achieving those corporate goals. Once the mechanics are in place, the next challenge is to marry the *what* with the *how*, and that's where an organization's articulated values come in. Those values – probably concerning the importance of people, integrity, diversity, customer service, and so forth – need to be translated into behavior metrics that every employee is held accountable for. When such a process is in place, high fliers who exceed all of their numbers can be held accountable for *how* they met those numbers because this step is built right into their performance expectations and rewards process. A good example is an account executive with a leading consulting company who managed her firm's relationship with many of the largest companies in New York City. Her clients generated revenues in the millions for her firm, and that fact alone would ordinarily be enough to ensure that she was named a partner in the firm. However, the senior management team was so upset at how she trounced the firm's stated value of "treating people with respect" – she was extremely abusive to her co-workers – that they repeatedly denied her promotion. Of course, one could argue that she shouldn't have a job at all. But at least her behavior – the *how* involved in attaining her huge results – prevented her from being promoted and esteemed as a partner.

American Express has tied its performance appraisal system directly to its values and code of conduct. The values are associated with a culture that focuses on long-term results as well as the desire to be an "employer of choice." The company's ethics code states the expectation that leaders will be ethical role models who exhibit the highest standards of integrity, develop employees, communicate the company's ethical expectations and their own support for those expectations, and create an open environment so that employees feel free to express their concerns. The company's 360-degree performance management process for senior leaders then identifies a number of leadership competencies, including explicit examples of high performance such as the following:

- Treats others with respect at all times; is fair and objective.
- Actively listens and incorporates input from others.
- Acts with integrity.
- Inspires the trust of the team, is reliable and consistent.
- Talks openly and honestly – says it as it is.

Examples of poor performance are also part of the system (e.g., "breaks promises, is inconsistent, fails to show respect for others").

The ratings of these competencies are weighted substantially in promotion and compensation decisions, thus making it difficult to get promoted if one is rated poorly on these ethical leadership competencies and important to be rated highly if an employee wants to advance. Finally, the company is investing resources in providing leaders with the necessary skills so that they can effectively fulfill the company's expectations consistent with its values.[30]

Alignment of the goals and rewards with the organization's values is essential because employees will generally do what's measured and rewarded, and they'll assume that the behaviors that are rewarded represent the "real" ethical culture. So, in the American Express example, behavior consistent with the company's stated values is measured and rewarded with promotions and compensation. This is a great example of ethical culture alignment.

But misalignment of rewards with other aspects of the ethical culture is quite common. For example, imagine an organization where everyone knows that the top sales representative's sales depend on lying to customers about delivery dates despite an ethics code that talks about customer satisfaction as a key value. Not only does the unethical conduct go undisciplined, but the sales representative receives large bonuses, expensive vacations, and recognition at annual sales meetings. Members of the sales force recognize that information about what is rewarded carries the "real" cultural message, and so the code becomes meaningless – or worse yet, an example of top management's hypocrisy.

For an ethical culture to be in alignment, poor performance against stated ethical goals must also be addressed quickly and fairly. For example, dishonest or disrespectful behavior (or any behavior inconsistent with ethical values) should be disciplined using a progressive disciplinary system that employees perceive to be fair. For example, a first offense (unless it is particularly serious) is usually addressed in a constructive manner that gives the employee the opportunity to provide input and to change the behavior. Subsequent misconduct is addressed more severely, and dismissal is the ultimate outcome for repeat or serious offenses. It's also important that employees be disciplined equally across organizational and performance levels. That means the successful star executive as well as the lower-level employee must be disciplined for knowingly breaking the rules. In fact, at that higher level, the discipline should probably be quicker and harsher because the higher in the organization one goes, the more responsibility one holds, and the more one is a role model for others. As a result of recent scandals and increased scrutiny by regulators, companies are taking discipline more seriously. Even the perception of unethical behavior can lead companies to dismiss high-level executives in the current environment. . . .

The bottom line is that performance management systems are important in themselves because they provide guidance about expected behavior, but they're particularly important in the sense that people look to them to reflect the "real" message about what is valued in the organization. The essential question is whether consistency exists between what the organization says (e.g., values statements, codes) and what it actually measures, rewards, and punishes.

Notes

1. R. A. Barrett, *Culture and Conduct: An Excursion in Anthropology* (Belmont, CA: Wadsworth, 1984).
2. T. E. Deal and A. A. Kennedy, *Corporate Cultures* (Reading, MA: Addison-Wesley, 1982); M. R. Louis, "A Cultural Perspective on Organizations: The Need for and Consequences of Viewing Organizations as Culture-Bearing Milieux," *Human Systems Management* 2 (1981): 246–58; J. Martin and C. Siehl, "Organizational Culture and Counterculture: An Uneasy Symbiosis," *Organizational Dynamics* (Autumn 1983): 52–64; A. M. Pettigrew, "On Studying Organizational Cultures," *Administrative Science Quarterly* 24 (1979): 570–80; E. H. Schein, *Organizational Culture and Leadership* (San Francisco, CA: Jossey-Bass, 1985); L. Smircich, "Concepts of Culture and Organizational Analysis," *Administrative Science Quarterly* 28 (1983): 339–58.
3. Smircich, "Concepts of Culture and Organizational Analysis."
4. Deal and Kennedy, *Corporate Cultures*.
5. B. Morris, "He's Smart. He's Not Nice. He's Saving Big Blue," *Fortune* (April 14, 1997): 68–81.
6. Deal and Kennedy, *Corporate Cultures*.
7. J. Van Maanen and E. H. Schein, "Toward a Theory of Organizational Socialization," in *Research in Organizational Behavior*, vol. 1, ed. L. Cummings and B. Staw (New York: JAI Press, 1979), pp. 209–64; C. D. Fisher, "Organizational Socialization: An Integrative Review," in *Research in Personnel and Human Resources Management*, vol. 4, ed. K. Rowland and G. Ferris (Greenwich, CT: JAI Press, 1986), pp. 101–45.
8. Barrett, *Culture and Conduct*.
9. "The Business Effect of Ethics on Employee Engagement." LRN Ethics Study, 2006, www.lrn.com.
10. Schein, *Organizational Culture and Leadership*.
11. Pettigrew, "On Studying Organizational Cultures"; E. H. Schein, "How Culture Forms, Develops, and Changes," in *Gaining Control of the Corporate Culture*, ed. R. H. Kilmann, M. J. Saxtion, and R. Serpa (San Francisco, CA: Jossey-Bass, 1985), pp. 17–43; P. Selznick, *Leadership in Administration* (New York: Harper & Row, 1957).
12. Schein, "How Culture Forms, Develops, and Changes"; Selznick, *Leadership in Administration*.
13. M. Gunther, "Money and Morals at GE," *Fortune* (November 15, 2004): 177–78.
14. Ibid.
15. P. O'Neill, "O'Neill on Ethics and Leadership," speech at the Berg Center for Ethics and Leadership, Katz Graduate School of Business, University of Pittsburgh, 2002.
16. J. A. Byrne, "Chainsaw," *Businessweek* (October 18, 1999): 128–49.
17. J. Sonnenfeld, "The Real Scandal at BP," *Businessweek* (May 14, 2007): 98.
18. L. K. Treviño, G. R. Weaver, D. G. Gibson, and B. L. Toffler, "Managing Ethics and Legal Compliance: What Works and What Hurts," *California Management Review* 41, no. 2 (1999): 131–51.
19. Ibid.
20. D. Mayer, M. Kuenzi, R. Greenbaum, M. Bardes, and R. Salvador, "How Does Ethical Leadership Flow? Test of a Trickle-Down Model," *Organizational Behavior and Human Decision Processes* 108 (2008): 1–13.
21. W. C. Byham, "Can You Interview for Integrity?," *Across the Board* (March–April, 2004): 34–38.
22. G. R. Weaver, L. K. Treviño, and P. L. Cochran, "Corporate Ethics Practices in the Mid-1990s: An Empirical Study of the Fortune 1000," *Journal of Business Ethics* 18, no. 3 (1999): 283–94.

23. *2005 National Business Ethics Survey* (Washington, DC: Ethics Resource Center, 2005).

24. Weaver et al., "Corporate Ethics Practices in the Mid-1990s."

25. Treviño et al., "Managing Ethics and Legal Compliance."

26. J. Kish-Gephart, D. Harrison, and L. K. Treviño, "Bad Apples, Bad Cases, and Bad Barrels: Meta-Analytic Evidence about Sources of Unethical Decisions at Work – Understanding Calculated and Impulsive Pathways," *Journal of Applied Psychology* 95 (2010): 1–31.

27. D. Nel, L. Pitt, and R. Watson, "Business Ethics: Defining the Twilight Zone," *Journal of Business Ethics* 8 (1989): 781–91.

28. Weaver et al., "Corporate Ethics Practices in the Mid-1990s."

29. *2005 National Business Ethics Survey.*

30. G. Weaver, L. K. Treviño, and B. Agie, "Somebody I Look up to: Ethical Role Models in Organizations," *Organizational Dynamics* 34, no. 4 (2005): 313–30.

3.3 GOVERNANCE

Good Directors and Bad Behavior

ROBERT A. PRENTICE

The Gathering Ethical Storm

Having cleaned house three years ago by replacing a sleepy, unambitious management team with a dynamic new CEO (Tom Chan) and a creative new CFO (Sally Marsh), Turon Industries' board of directors was feeling pretty good about things. Tom and Sally had wowed the board during the interview process. They were experienced, articulate, likable, and seemingly quite trustworthy. But now the directors have received a communication from Turon's outside auditor that an emergency board meeting is needed and that it would be best if Tom and Sally did not attend. Over the past two years, several of the directors have heard vague scuttlebutt about aggressive accounting, but their positive impressions of Tom and Sally have allayed all fears. Surely the board has nothing serious to worry about. Or does it?

Because financial frauds are not uncommon, and CEOs and CFOs are most often directly involved in them,[1] Turon's board does indeed have grounds for concern. This is the case for three primary reasons. First, due to a variety of organizational pressures and decision-making missteps, even people who wish to be "good" – as Tom and Sally presumably do – often make serious ethical missteps. Second, top corporate officers like Tom and Sally are particularly susceptible to making several of these errors. And third, for various psychological reasons, corporate directors often will find it difficult to adequately police those officers. Among many examples would be the Enron board, and, more recently, that of the News Corporation.[2]

Why Do Good People Do Bad Things?

A persistent question among business ethicists is why good people do bad things. Although the occasional psychopath will climb into the ranks of elite corporate officers,[3] most CEOs and CFOs – like the majority of people, in general – wish to act ethically and properly. But inside a corporate organization, doing so is often difficult for a variety of reasons.

Behavioral ethics is a comparatively recent field of study concerned with why moral transgressions occur and how they can be prevented.[4] Ethical missteps can easily result in ruined careers or even prison sentences, yet they occur with unsettling frequency. The organizational and psychological causes are quite numerous.[5] While an article of this size cannot possibly catalogue them all, please consider the following examples.

Obedience to Authority

Most people derive psychological satisfaction from pleasing authority figures. Humans are hard-wired to desire to please their parents, their teachers, and – as they grow up – their bosses, even when doing so violates their conscience.[6] Indeed, individuals are often so focused on pleasing persons in a position of authority that they may follow orders without recognizing any related ethically questionable conduct.

In his famous obedience studies, Stanley Milgram found that people would administer to others what they believed were painful electric shocks, just because a stranger in a gray lab coat – who appeared to be in charge of an experiment –

From Robert A. Prentice, "Good Directors and Bad Behavior," *Business Horizons* 55, no. 6, November–December (2012) 535–41. Reproduced with permission of Elsevier via Copyright Clearance Center.

told them to do so. They were uneasy and clearly did not wish to administer the currents, yet they did when urged by a person with no real authority over them.[7] In a workplace where the person in authority is a respected friend and someone who really does have the subordinate's professional future in his or her hands, it is easy to imagine how difficult it must be to muster the courage to act ethically, when to do so contradicts the superior's directives.

Conformity Bias

Just as people generally desire to please those in authority, they also wish to fit in with their group. Individuals tend to adopt the views and to copy the conduct of their peers. It is not only high school students who would jump off a cliff if their friends did; the vast majority of people in business feel this same pressure. Indeed, organizations often exhibit moral contagion, as patterns of behavior – both ethical and unethical – can spread throughout a company as employees emulate other employees, especially their superiors.[8]

Most adults do not carry an adequate internal moral compass, and therefore look to others in their organizational environment for guidance regarding how to act ethically. It is not surprising, then, that unethical behavior by seemingly ethical people in strong ethical environments can have a profound effect upon others in an organization, leading them to often view unethical behavior as acceptable.[9] Unfortunately, negative behaviors and unethical actions are more likely to be modeled or reciprocated by others than are positive behaviors and ethical actions.[10]

Loss Aversion

People suffer from losses roughly twice as much as they enjoy gains. Therefore, they are willing to take risks to avoid losses that they would not take to achieve gains.[11] Moreover, individuals judge actions such as cutting employees' pay as fairer if it is done to avoid corporate losses rather than augment corporate profits.[12]

Importantly, people will take unethical actions to avoid losses that they would not take to garner gains. Consider Dave Bliss, former basketball coach at Baylor University. As a scandal unfolded in his basketball program, Bliss was willing to falsely label as a drug dealer one of his players who had been murdered by a teammate.[13] Bliss was trying to cover up illegal payments he had made to the player. It seems unimaginable that Bliss would have told such a cruel lie to obtain his job in the first place, but he was willing to do so to keep his job once he had it. Studies show that most earnings management is not done to achieve record profits, but instead to avoid announcing losses.[14]

Although these three phenomena – obedience to authority, conformity bias, and loss aversion – represent just a small sampling of the ways in which organizational pressures and other contextual features can adversely impact individuals' ethical decision-making, they hint at a well-established truth: "Human cognitive faculties, social pressures, institutional norms, and structural features all conspire to lead well-intentioned people to do harm. We human beings are products of forces that often elude our control – and even our notice."[15]

The Peculiar Susceptibility of Corporate Titans

People are not equally susceptible to these psychological influences. Human nature is too variable for that. However, there is evidence that the types of people who become top corporate officers and the settings in which they find themselves can combine to create unusual susceptibility to committing ethical errors.

Overconfidence

Surveys demonstrate that, in mathematically impossible percentages, most people are overconfident in their abilities. They believe they are better drivers, better teachers, better auditors, and better pretty-much-everything-else than their peers. David Brooks calls the human mind "an overconfidence machine."[16] This tendency toward overconfidence extends to the ethical realm, where 92 percent of Americans are comfortable with their character, and most believe that they are more ethical than their peers and even are more likely to go to heaven than Mother Theresa.[17]

Unfortunately, if people are too comfortable with their own character and too confident in their moral judgments, they become vulnerable to making ethical decisions without adequate reflection. Any reader of the various tell-all books written about the Enron disaster can see how the overweening confidence of these "smartest guys in the room" led them to just assume the decisions they made were wise and ethical.[18] Enron executives were not given to self-doubt.

Indeed, there is substantial evidence that the types of people who rise to the top of corporate organizations are often particularly confident in their abilities and their character.[19] They have experienced much success in their lives, or else they wouldn't be where they are. They tend to think that they are ethical, and this belief is reinforced by people around them constantly telling these leaders that they are right, and smart, and good.

Consider Enron's Kenneth (Ken) Lay. As a minister's son, a captain of industry, and a recognized philanthropist, Lay had every reason to be – and, apparently was – supremely confident in his ability to make ethical decisions. Yet his errors were large and legion, and his denial was nearly absolute. He was certain that the press was at fault for the bad financial and ethical news that finally surfaced.[20] This is a common pattern for people like Tom and Sally who have risen to the top ranks of corporate organizations like Turon Industries.

Self-Serving Bias

Evidence indicates that people have great difficulty being objective when their well-being is at stake or their deeply-held views are at issue. Their psychological need to look out for themselves and to maintain consistency in their views strongly affects how they gather information, process information, and even remember information. Conservatives will tend to watch Fox News and liberals will tend to watch MSNBC because each group, along with most everyone else, wants to hear information that confirms – rather than contradicts – its beliefs.

Shown identical information, groups holding dissimilar views will likely perceive it differently. In one study, the same document was interpreted as supporting capital punishment (by individuals who already endorsed the practice) and undermining the case for capital punishment (by those who already opposed the practice). The same facts were processed in diametrically opposite ways. Asked months later what they remembered about the document, study participants tended to recall facts that supported their particular point of view rather than details that undermined it.[21]

The self-serving bias is ubiquitous and particularly potent. It can cause people to sincerely believe that whatever course of action is best for them, personally, is ethically permissible. Leaders are particularly vulnerable to this effect. Studies even show an *instant entitlement bias*; that is, given resources to distribute among a group of strangers, most people will dole them out evenly – *unless* they are casually told that they have been appointed leader of the group, in which case they tend to give themselves a much larger share, though they've done nothing to merit the status of leader.[22] In their minds, simply being labeled as such is enough to legitimize unfair allocation behavior.

When considering Tyco CEO Dennis Kozlowski's $6,000 shower curtain, $15,000 umbrella stand, and $2 million birthday party for his wife – all paid for by Tyco shareholders – it is difficult not to detect a sense of entitlement that affected Kozlowski's sense of fairness.[23] Recent behavior of CEOs in a series of acquisitions similarly points to narcissism that adversely affects corporate behavior.[24]

Moral License

Most people think of themselves as good folks and want to be so regarded by others. To that end, individuals tend to keep a running scoreboard in their head that matches their actions to their self-perceptions. If they do something they realize was a little sketchy, they typically look for ways to "make it up" in a process known as *moral compensation*. If people are reminded of some incident where they did not live up to their own moral standards and are soon thereafter given an opportunity to donate to charity or to volunteer for a good cause, they will tend to participate in these endeavors more fully than people who have not been so reminded, and who therefore do not feel the need to compensate for their moral lapse.[25]

The flip side of moral compensation is *moral licensing*: the tendency of people who have done something good, and who have therefore added "points" to their moral scoreboard, to allow themselves a little leeway to depart from their own ethical standards. If people are reminded of times they have acted morally and then are given the opportunity to donate or volunteer, they will tend to participate less fully than individuals who have not been prompted to remember what good people they are.[26]

Numerous studies document moral compensation and moral licensing which collectively comprise *moral equilibrium*. Obviously, of the two components, moral licensing seems particularly dangerous – and it is, especially for corporate leaders. Again, consider Ken Lay, who received Philanthropist of the Year awards. It would have been easy for Lay to have given himself moral license to fail to meet his own standards. Importantly, this is a subconscious process; people usually do not realize how their earlier actions are affecting their current decisions.

For years, Johnson & Johnson was lauded as one of America's most ethical companies for its handling of the 1982 Tylenol recall.[27] Could that have caused the firm to grant itself moral license, leading to its recent highly publicized ethical troubles? British Petroleum re-branded itself as a progressive energy company and its CEO, Lord John Browne, became the world's most recognized spokesman for corporate social responsibility.[28] Could that have caused BP to grant itself moral license leading to its numerous refinery accidents and the *Deepwater Horizon* debacle? The evidence suggests that the answer could easily be yes.

Moral Rationalization

Recent research indicates that a surprising proportion of human decision-making is relatively automatic, with little cognitive input. Often times, decisions are driven by emotion. It is easy to set up hypothetical scenarios of, for example, a brother and sister deciding to have sex with one another – in a situation where pregnancy could not possibly result – that will cause most people to immediately conclude the act is immoral, but be unable to rationally explain why.[29] Frequently, when people believe that they are reasoning through to an ethical conclusion, it turns out all they are doing is rationalizing a decision their brain made nearly automatically, based primarily upon emotions such as anger and disgust.

Psychological studies show that the people who become top executives of large corporations tend to be extroverts who behave more impulsively than the average person.[30] Therefore, leaders are even more likely to decide ethically-tinged issues quickly and decisively, and then resort to post-decision rationalizing in order to justify their choices to themselves and others. Again, this is a largely subconscious process that people are unaware they are engaging in.

Bathsheba Syndrome

Corporate leaders and other successful individuals often act in a sexually forward manner (e.g., William Aramony, Mark Hurd, Tiger Woods, Bill Clinton, David Letterman, John Edwards, Herman Cain, Elliott Spitzer, Bobby Petrino), act profligately (e.g., Dennis Kozlowski, Bernie Ebbers), and are utterly tone deaf regarding ethical issues (e.g., Jeff Skilling, Chainsaw Al Dunlap, Donald Trump).

It is quite surprising how elite corporate officers (e.g., Bernie Ebbers), top government officials (e.g., Eliot Spitzer), and other successful figures (e.g., Tiger Woods) come to believe that the rules which apply to everyone else do not apply to them. Habitually, they do outrageous things, with little or no effort to hide their wrongdoings because they become convinced of their importance to the firm's mission; this, in their minds, justifies exempting themselves from legal and ethical standards that apply to others.[31]

Ludwig and Longenecker made the point almost two decades ago that much wrongdoing is perpetrated not by top officers lacking a moral code or subject to fierce competitive pressures, but instead by men and women of strong integrity and intelligence who are unable to handle success.[32] The scholars coined the term the *Bathsheba Syndrome* after concluding that like biblical King David of Israel – who, after many admirable successes, suffered a stunning moral lapse – some successful people seem to throw "it all away by engaging in an activity which is wrong, which they know is wrong, which they know [will] lead to their downfall if discovered, and which they mistakenly believe they have the power to conceal."[33] Success, they posit, often leads successful people to lose focus; gain privileged access to information, people, or objects which can be very tempting; obtain largely unconstrained control over organizational resources; and gain an almost magical belief in their own ability to manipulate outcomes and therefore to conceal their wrongdoing.

All this may be exacerbated by simple greed. A recent study indicates that people of higher social class, which would certainly include CEOs and CFOs, tend to act more unethically than people of lower social class. The key factor is their more favorable attitude toward greed, which is a strong determinant of unethical behavior.[34]

Boards: It's Hard to Be a Watchdog

If organizational pressures and psychological factors often cause "good" people to act unethically, and if captains of industry are uniquely susceptible to many of these situational factors, then corporate boards of directors should be extraordinarily attentive when monitoring the actions of company executives. Careful monitoring by boards is critical to avoiding the impact of the Bathsheba Syndrome and other problems of top corporate officers.[35] And yet, boards often fall short. Why?

There are rational economic reasons, of course, why boards of directors often fail to adequately monitor CEOs and CFOs. They are not sued particularly often, and when they are, they are usually protected by D&O insurance. Directors, especially outside directors, are also given various protections under federal securities law. Ultimately, directors virtually never pay judgments out of their own pockets.[36]

However, there are also not-so-rational psychological factors that can cause directors to fail to monitor as closely as they should. Directors must be aware of these and guard against them.

False Attribution Error

The first psychological factor is the *false attribution error*. When directors – indeed, when most humans – read in the newspaper that an individual has done a bad thing, they tend to assume the actor was a bad person; likewise, when they read that an individual has done a good thing, they assume he/she was a good person.[37] And because they will typically have selected the CEO, directors will usually believe that he or she is a good person who would not do a bad thing. As noted earlier, though, organizational pressures and psychological shortcomings can cause decent folks to exhibit less than admirable behaviors. The situational can overwhelm the dispositional.

Overconfidence and the Personal Positivity Bias

Directors who have chosen top officers will usually trust the quality of character of those officers. Part of the reason for this is natural *overconfidence* in their own ability to size up others. Furthermore, the judgments people make about individuals tend to be favorable rather than unfavorable, in part because of the *personal positivity bias*.[38] Although people think increasingly ill of politicians in general, their view toward their own representatives tends to be much more favorable.

Confirmation Bias and Cognitive Dissonance

Having selected people they believe to be honest, directors will then tend to look for evidence which supports that conclusion and ignore contradictory information. In a process known as *confirmation bias*, directors will seek out and remember evidence consistent with their assumptions ("Our CEO is a good person who would not do bad things") while glossing over inconsistencies until they become nearly overwhelming.[39] Furthermore, the concept of *cognitive dissonance* means that once directors have placed their confidence in the honesty of a CEO, they will be extremely reluctant to reach the conclusion that they made a mistake, even when contrary evidence begins to come to light.[40]

False Consensus Effect and Vulnerability to Deception

Directors will often ignore information indicating dishonesty by top officers when fed even implausible explanations by the same. The *false consensus effect*, which causes people to generally believe others see the world as they do,[41] prompts honest directors to expect that the officers they deal with will also act honestly. Individuals who are not particularly trustworthy themselves trust others less, while individuals who are trustworthy tend to trust others more, leaving the latter especially vulnerable to deception.[42]

Directors are further hindered by the fact that it is difficult for them to tell when they are being lied to. While it is common for humans to believe they are adept at detecting deception, overconfidence again rears its ugly head, as the evidence shows few people truly are good lie detectors.[43] We all bear a *vulnerability to deception*. Shell noted that "human perception overall is not a reliable defense to opportunistic behavior."[44] And Baier observed that because the feelings, beliefs, and intentions upon which we often base our trust "sometimes can be faked, [trust] is a notoriously vulnerable good."[45]

Cult of the CEO

Finally, director gullibility is exacerbated by the fact that, like everyone else, directors can be star-struck. People tend to worship celebrities, and the *cult of the CEO* heightens this phenomenon.[46] Humans are often so enamored of corporate titans that they let them get by with decisions and actions they would condemn in other people. And when leaders are continually given a pass in this way by those around them, it only reinforces any dishonest tendencies they may have. As articulated by Luban: "Our culture is more willing to tolerate stylish scoundrels who come out on top than honorable, rule-following losers."[47]

The Bottom Line

Directors owe a fiduciary duty to shareholders to adequately monitor their company's officers, especially as regards unethical and/or illegal conduct. The lessons of this brief article are that good people sometimes do bad things; that corporate officers are often examples of this; and that for a variety of reasons, many psychological in nature, directors often have a difficult time acting as effective monitors to stop officers' illegal and unethical behavior.

There is no easy answer to this challenge, but directors need to be aware of officers' psychological tendencies, as well as their own. They must recognize their unique vulnerability, given that officers typically set the agenda for board meetings and provide most of the information upon which directors rely.[48]

Directors are not auditors, who owe shareholders an obligation to be skeptical. They are, in fact, legally entitled to presume the honesty and accuracy of the information given them by officers – at least, absent some sort of red flag. Nonetheless, directors must keep their ethical antennae up and be ready to act upon reliable information that would disconfirm a previously-held opinion regarding officer integrity.

Organizational pressures and psychological vulnerabilities are explanations for why directors often fail to effectively monitor officer abuses. That said, these explanations are not excuses.

Notes

1. Deloitte Forensic Center, *Ten Things about Financial Statement Fraud*, 3rd ed. (2009). Retrieved May 9, 2012 from www.deloitte.com/assets/Dcom-UnitedStates/Local%20Assets/Documents/FAS_ForensicCenter_us_fas-us_dfc/us_dfc_ten_things_about_financial_statement_fraud_241109.pdf.
2. E. N. Veasey, "Policy and Legal Overview of Best Corporate Governance Practices," *SMU Law Review* 56, no. 4 (2003):

2135–47; D. Carr, "News Corp. Board's Cozy Compliance," *The New York Times* (May 7, 2012), p. B1.

3. P. Babiak and R. D. Hard, *Snakes in Suits: When Psychopaths Go to Work* (New York: Harper, 2006).

4. R. Cropanzano and F. O. Walumbwa, "Moral Leadership: A Short Primer on Competing Perspectives," in *Managerial Ethics*, ed. M. Schminke (New York: Routledge, 2010), pp. 21–52.

5. M. H. Bazerman and A. E. Tenbrunsel, *Blind Spots* (Princeton University Press, 2011).

6. M. Stout, *The Sociopath Next Door* (New York: Broadway Books, 2006).

7. S. Milgram, "Behavioral Study of Obedience," *Journal of Abnormal and Social Psychology* 67, no. 4 (1963): 371–78.

8. "CEOs: Back to Ethical Basics," *Christian Science Monitor* (July 2, 2002). Retrieved from www.csmonitor.com/2002/0702/p08s01-comv.html.

9. Cropanzano and Walumbwa, "Moral Leadership."

10. D. de Cremer, "On the Psychology of Preventing and Dealing with Ethical Failures: A Behavioral Ethics Approach," in *Managerial Ethics*, ed. Schminke, pp. 111–25.

11. A. Tversky and K. Kahneman, "Advances in Prospect Theory: Cumulative Representations of Uncertainty," *Journal of Risk and Uncertainty* 5, no. 4 (1992): 297–323.

12. J. Margolis and A. Molinsky, "Three Practical Challenges of Moral Leadership," in *Moral Leadership*, ed. D. Rhode (San Francisco, CA: Jossey-Bass, 2006), pp. 77–93.

13. G. Bishop, "After Rising from Lowest Depths, Baylor Crafts a Powerhouse," *International Herald Tribune* (February 28, 2012), p. 14.

14. A. S. Pinello and R. Dusenbury, "The Role of Cognition and Ethical Conviction in Earnings Management Behavior" (2006). Retrieved April 19, 2012 from http://ssrn.com/abstract=711422.

15. Margolis and Molinsky, "Three Practical Challenges of Moral Leadership," pp. 77–78.

16. D. Brooks, *The Social Animal* (New York: Random House, 2011), p. 218.

17. M. Jennings, "Ethics and Investment Management: True Reform," *Financial Analysts Journal* 61, no. 3 (2005): 45–58.

18. B. Cruver, *Anatomy of Greed* (New York: Carroll & Graf, 2002); B. McLean and P. Elkin, *The Smartest Guys in the Room* (New York: Penguin Group, 2006).

19. D. C. Langevoort, "The Behavioral Economics of Mergers and Acquisitions" (2010). Retrieved April 19, 2012 from http://ssrn.com/abstract=1692777.

20. D. Messick, "Ethical Judgment and Moral Leadership," in *Moral Leadership*, ed. Rhode, pp. 95–110.

21. C. G. Lord, L. Ross, and M. R. Lepper, "Biased Assimilation and Attitude Polarization: The Effects of Prior Theories on Subsequently Considered Evidence," *Journal of Personality and Social Psychology* 37, no. 11 (1979): 2098–109.

22. D. de Cremer, E. van Dijk, and C. P. Reinders Folmer, "Why Leaders Feel Entitled to Take More," in *Psychological Perspectives on Ethical Behavior and Decision Making*, ed. D. de Cremer (Charlotte, NC: Information Age Publishing, 2009), pp. 107–19.

23. F. Norris, "Why His Peers Say Kozlowski Got off Easy," *The New York Times* (September 23, 2005), p. C1.

24. S. M. Davidoff, "For Some CEOs, a Mirror Can Become a Dangerous Tool," *The New York Times* (March 7, 2012), p. B9.

25. U. Khan and R. Dhar, "Licensing Effect in Consumer Choice," *Journal of Marketing Research* 43, no. 2 (2006): 259–66.

26. S. Sachdeva, R. Iliev, and D. L. Medin, "Sinning Saints and Saintly Sinners: The Paradox of Moral Self-Regulation," *Psychological Science* 20, no. 4 (2009): 523–28.

27. R. Sisodia, J. Sheth, and D. B. Wolfe, *Firms of Endearment* (Upper Saddle River, NJ: Wharton School Publishing, 2007).

28. K. T. Jackson, *Building Reputational Capital* (Oxford University Press, 2004).

29. J. Haidt, *The Righteous Mind* (New York: Pantheon, 2012).

30. D. Keltner, C. A. Langner, and M. L. Allison, "Power and Moral Leadership," in *Moral Leadership*, ed. Rhode, pp. 177–94.

31. T. L. Price, *Understanding Ethical Failures in Leadership* (Cambridge University Press, 2005).

32. D. C. Ludwig and C. O. Longenecker, "The Bathsheba Syndrome: The Ethical Failure of Successful Leaders," *Journal of Business Ethics* 12, no. 4 (1993): 265–73.

33. Ibid., p. 267.

34. P. K. Piff, D. M. Stancato, S. Côté, R. Mendoza-Denton, and D. Keltner, "Higher Social Class Predicts Increased Unethical Behavior," *Proceedings of the National Academy of Sciences* 109, no. 11 (2012): 1086–91.

35. Ludwig and Longenecker, "The Bathsheba Syndrome."

36. B. Black, B. Cheffins, and M. Klausner, "Outside Director Liability," *Stanford Law Review* 58, no. 4 (2006): 1055–159.

37. N. R. Feigenson, "Merciful Damages: Some Remarks on Forgiveness, Mercy, and Tort Law," *Fordham Urban Law Journal* 27, no. 4 (2000): 1633–50.

38. S. Plous, *The Psychology of Judgment and Decision Making* (New York: McGraw-Hill, 1993).

39. J. Groopman, *How Doctors Think* (New York: Houghton Mifflin, 2007).

40. L. Festinger, *A Theory of Cognitive Dissonance* (Stanford University Press, 1957).

41. L. Ross, D. Greene, and P. House, "The 'False Consensus Effect': An Egocentric Bias in Social Perception and Attribution Processes," *Journal of Experimental Social Psychology* 13, no. 3 (1977): 279–301.

42. D. C. Langevoort, "Where Were the Lawyers? A Behavioral Inquiry into Lawyers' Responsibility for Clients' Fraud," *Vanderbilt Law Review* 46, no. 1 (1993): 75–119.

43. P. Ekman, *Telling Lies* (New York: W. W. Norton, 2001).

44. G. R. Shell, "Opportunism and Trust in the Negotiation of Commercial Contracts: Toward a New Cause of Action," *Vanderbilt Law Review* 44, no. 2 (1991): 221–82 (p. 238).

45. A. C. Baier, "Trust and Its Vulnerabilities," in *The Tanner Lectures on Human Values*, ed. G. B. Peterson (Salt Lake City, UT: University of Utah Press, 1992), p. 109.

46. G. Haigh, *Fat Cats: The Strange Cult of the CEO* (New York: Thunder's Mouth Press, 2005).

47. D. Luban, "Making Sense of Moral Meltdowns," in *Moral Leadership*, ed. Rhode, pp. 57–75 (p. 63).

48. N. F. Sharpe, "The Cosmetic Independence of Corporate Boards," *Seattle University Law Review* 34, no. 4 (2011): 1435–56.

Ethics and Executive Compensation

ROBERT W. KOLB

Executive compensation refers to the total reward provided by the firm to the top level of executives in a corporation, such as the chief executive officer (CEO), the chief operations officer (COO), the chief financial officer (CFO), and a handful of other executives who occupy the very highest level of management. At this level in the firm, total compensation generally takes many forms, including any or all of the following: salaries, bonuses, incentive payments, deferred compensation plans, stock options, and the direct provision of goods and services. Unlike direct cash payments of salaries and bonuses, the other forms of compensation can be relatively large and less visible. For example, stock options granted to executives are not generally visible to the public, yet they may be worth more than the direct cash payments the executive receives. Similarly, many executives receive quite valuable packages of perquisites ("perks"), such as apartments, personal staff, personal transportation, and the payment by the firm of many other expenses that most employees would have to bear themselves.

Social and Ethical Issues

Many observers see the size and form of executive compensation as a pressing social and ethical issue. These concerns have become particularly poignant in recent years as the public has become aware of the absolute magnitude and generosity of some pay packages. Furthermore, public attention has focused on numerous instances in which executives were rewarded very handsomely even as the firms they were leading floundered. Public indignation has arisen at the picture of very handsomely rewarded executives coupled with a firm that is experiencing financial losses, closure of facilities, and employee dislocations in the form of cuts in pay and benefits and enforced layoffs.

One of the most emotional aspects of the executive compensation issue is the absolute magnitude of executive compensations. For large firms in the United States, compensation for top executives can run into many millions of dollars per year. Some celebrated situations have arisen in which compensation for a single year can push toward $100 million, particularly if stock options are granted in that year. To some observers, the very size of this compensation seems totally inappropriate and even obscene.

Criticism of executive compensation has focused most intensely on practices in the United States, and critics of the present executive compensation practices often point to both domestic and international comparisons with the present level and structure of executive compensation that prevails in US firms. Within the United States, critics of executive compensation point to trends in executive compensation relative to the total pay packages received by rank-and-file employees in the same firm. Most studies suggest that the ratio of executive compensation to that of ordinary workers has increased dramatically in the past few decades. In other words, executive pay seems to be rising much more rapidly than worker pay, and these critics present these data as evidence of a system gone wrong.

Two types of international comparisons play a prominent role in the executive compensation debate. First, executive compensation in US firms appears to be more generous than in comparable non-US firms. Studies have examined the absolute magnitude of compensation internationally as well as the ratio of executive compensation to ordinary worker compensation across countries. In general, studies have found that top executives in US-based companies receive a higher level of absolute compensation (i.e., the actual dollar worth of the entire pay package) than similarly placed executives in non-US firms. As a second type of international comparison, researchers examine the ratio of executive compensation to the pay of ordinary workers in US firms versus the same ratio in non-US firms. Most studies find a large difference in this ratio, with the executives of US firms receiving a much higher wage relative to that of ordinary workers than is the case in comparable non-US firms. Again, critics take this disparity as evidence of a flaw in the system in the United States.

Defenders of the present arrangement of executive compensation generally acknowledge the overall accuracy of the empirical claims summarized above and grant that executive compensation in US firms is higher than it is abroad and also that executive pay in the United States has been rising faster than that of workers. These defenders of the present level and system of compensation often argue that these trends by themselves constitute no evidence that the present level is wrong or that the trend is moving in the wrong direction. To make such an argument, they assert, merely assumes that the previous levels were correct and that recent departures are in error. However, what if the previous levels of absolute or relative compensation were too low? Then, the movement toward higher executive compensation would be a movement toward a more appropriate level of pay. Similarly, international comparisons might carry little weight by themselves. If US pay levels are high compared with those that prevail in other countries, it might just mean that the other countries have it wrong.

These reflections suggest that the issue must be examined at a deeper level to make real progress in understanding the social and ethical aspects of executive compensation. In particular, a more sophisticated examination of the issue might attempt to answer questions such as the following. Do executives deserve the compensation they receive? Does the present system of executive compensation serve the interest of society as a whole? Does the present level of executive compensation lead to an unjust allocation of a society's resources? Is the present arrangement of executive compensation simply the result of individuals and firms that exercise freedoms and make decisions that rightly lie within their control? Finally, what are the effects on society as a whole of a system in which some receive relatively so much and others so little? Most of the remainder of this essay considers these issues in turn, but before turning to these matters, it is important to

be aware of the economic complexity of executive compensation arrangements.

The Complexity of Executive Compensation

One possible explanation for the perceived largesse of executive compensation turns on its inefficiency. That is, that the pay has to be large in order to encourage the executive to manage in a way that maximizes firm value. The typical executive has much of her human capital tied to the fortunes of the firm she leads. If she is risk averse, she will prefer a bureaucratic approach to managing the firm, taking no chances, and producing mediocre results. However, stock investors should hold well-diversified portfolios, thereby insulating themselves from the risk of particular firms. Consequently, shareholders would prefer that the firm take more risks in the hope of producing outsized results. This reflects a principal–agent conflict between shareholders and firm managers.

To induce executives to take risks with the firm that maximize firm value, the firm needs to structure executive compensation in a way that aligns the risk-taking behavior of managers with the desires of the firm's shareholders. As a result, the firm might wisely offer managers pay packages loaded with incentive features, such as stock options, that pay little or nothing for mediocre results, yet pay off extremely well for truly good firm performance. However, receiving incentive compensation has less value to a risk-averse manager than the actual dollar cost of the compensation expended by the firm – the risk-averse manager would prefer a dollar of cash to a dollar's worth of options. This is the inefficiency of incentive compensation. Yet, from the firm's point of view, this inefficient form of payment may be exactly the best strategy. In other words, the firm might do well to embrace a costly and inefficient form of payment to get the executive to behave as the shareholders wish. If paying an executive $10 million "extra" gets the executive to produce an additional half-percent of returns on $50 billion of assets, this creates $250 million of additional firm value, making the $10 million of "excess" compensation a very wise decision, even if it appears to unjustly reward an executive. We now turn to a direct consideration of the social and ethical dimensions of executive compensation.

Desert

Could it be that executives deserve the compensation they receive? Top executives of large corporations control the deployment of vast resources in the form of the firm's financial worth, the work of thousands of employees, and even the use of the land and natural resources to which the firm has access. These executives make decisions that have extremely important social consequences. Committing the firm to the wrong investments can waste billions of dollars of wealth, destroy the livelihood of thousands of employees, and even drive the entire firm into bankruptcy. Similarly, the value of correct decisions at this level is gigantic. For example, IBM's decision to create the IBM PC in 1981 spawned an industry that revolutionized work around the world, created any number of related industries and firms, and sowed the seeds of some of the greatest individual fortunes the world has ever seen.

A gifted executive who could make the right decisions at these levels would create value for society that would dwarf even the most lavish executive pay package. Does such an individual deserve very high compensation for exercising his or her talents in a manner that is so socially beneficial? Many think that the answer to this question is clearly affirmative, and they tend to see firms as perpetually engaged in a search for such talent. According to this analysis, it is extremely wise to pay $100 million annually to an executive who can make decisions that would create $100 billion in wealth. Surely such individuals are rare and difficult to identify, but perhaps the hunt for and competition for those with this kind of potential is justified?

Critics of this desert argument reply by pointing out that actual executives seldom display such genius, and it is in fact easy to identify very highly paid executives who seem much more adept at making wrong choices and destroying value than making brilliant decisions and creating benefits. Beyond pointing out situations in which the actual performance does not seem to deserve high compensation, critics of the desert argument often maintain that no one could merit such compensation no matter how brilliant one's decisions. They argue that it is wrong for any individual to take so much for himself or herself, no matter how much benefit that individual might create for others.

Freedom

Some view the level of executive compensation as essentially unproblematic no matter what the level, subject to the basic constraints that compensation be determined simply by economic actors exercising their freedom to arrive at a contract. Here, the argument goes as follows: An executive, like any other worker, seeks the best employment contract available. The firm seeks the best managers it can find, subject to its own ideas about its willingness to pay and the perceived qualities of the potential executive. Both sides of the bargain, firm and executive, merely exercise their basic freedoms as economic actors in a free market and reach an agreement on that basis. As a result, the process is fair and leads to employment compensation that is fair simply due to its being the result of a market process that is seen to be a fair process by its very nature.

Furthermore, those who emphasize the importance of freedom of contract point out that freedom of contract benefits society, because the capitalist economic system works by allowing firms to make their own choices and to compete. For the executive, the freedoms being exercised are even more basic than they are for the firm, because the executive sells his or her own labor, so the sphere of freedom being exercised is very basic indeed.

In rebuttal to this line of argument, critics of the present system of executive compensation assert that the model of two independent agents striking an arm's-length bargain does not describe the situation very well at all, so the emphasis on freedom is misplaced. These critics point out that executive compensation is typically determined by the compensation committee, which comprises members of the firm's board of directors. However, membership in many boards is conferred directly or indirectly by the CEO of the firm. As a result, the very people administering the compensation of a CEO may owe their directors' seats to the same CEO, whose compensation they are supposed to judge and control.

Furthermore, top executives and board members are often friends, sometimes old friends of close standing. In addition, many directors serve on the boards of several companies, and CEOs of one firm often serve on the boards of other firms. This arrangement creates a class of directors and CEOs who flourish in a club-like atmosphere. As a result, the employment contract with the firm's top executive may not be a fair bargain struck by two completely independent parties. Instead, these critics argue, it may well be an arrangement of mutual advantage reached among friends, or at least it may be a situation in which directors are naturally empathetic toward CEOs who are part of the same managerial class. The result of this intimacy is a set of employment contracts for top executives that is the result not of a pure and free market process, these critics charge, but of an impure process tainted by ties of friendship or mutual appreciation.

Utility Maximization and Social Goals

Some observers of executive compensation focus on the overall benefits, or overall utility, of the present policy of executive compensation. These thinkers believe that the best approach to such an issue turns on the question of what arrangement will create the highest total societal benefit. As such, they are less concerned with what an executive might receive or deserve and instead ask, What system of executive compensation will create the greatest overall benefit for society? For them, the best system of executive compensation is the one that achieves the goal of maximizing social utility, which we may restrict to the narrower range of social wealth for conceptual convenience.

Even though these thinkers approach the issue from within a framework that emphasizes utility, they can often differ in the solutions they favor, because they disagree on which policies will contribute to utility. One group of thinkers attempting to defend the basic structure of executive compensation arrangements approaches the issue from the point of view of designing contracts. These thinkers analyze the problem in the following terms. The top executives of a firm are agents of the shareholders, who are the principals. The executives choose how to deploy the assets of the firm. The perfect agent would allocate those funds just as the principals would desire were they themselves present and able to make decisions. However, executives are not only agents of the shareholders but also persons in their own right, and thus, in their decisions as executives, they are torn between the pursuit of their own desires and the fulfillment of their role as agents of the shareholders.

This conflicted loyalty suggests that shareholders might achieve the best result for the firm by designing contracts with the firm's executives that align the incentives of the executives with those of the firm. This is the approach of *incentive compatibility* – making the incentives that the executives are offered compatible with the goals of the firm. The well-designed employment contract allows the executive to prosper when, and only when, the firm prospers. One tool for aligning incentives is the granting of stock options to the firm's executives. The properly structured option in this case is worth very little or nothing when the firm does poorly, but it is worth a great deal when the firm performs well. For example, a stock option given to an executive might pay off handsomely if the stock price of the firm rises by 50 percent over the next three years, but it might be worth very little otherwise. Under this model, the level of executive compensation is of relatively little importance. Instead, the goal is to structure executive compensation so that the executive acts to create more wealth for the firm even when the executive acts selfishly.

Critics of this line of argument charge that these kinds of arrangements abound in *contracting defects* – the failure of the compensation scheme to align the incentives of the executive and the firm. These critics point to numerous and well-publicized cases in which executives have been rewarded very handsomely even when the firm suffered horribly. When this happens, these critics protest, the incentives have not been aligned, and the result is a failure from the point of view of maximizing utility or the interests of society. As a result, opponents of the present structure of executive compensation still believe that allowing executives to absorb so much wealth diminishes overall utility.

However, merely saying that the present structuring of executive compensation has failed, in fact, to achieve compatible incentives is only a technical argument. It does not yet attack the central idea of attempting to align incentives, and it is clear that these critics are not merely calling for a technical rearrangement of contract terms. They very much believe that the entire level and structure of compensation is deeply flawed or even evil. While these deeper disagreements over utility and contract design may not have been fully defined, the terms of debate seem to be moving toward clarification.

Distributive Justice

While utilitarian arguments about executive compensation generally concentrate on the total utility effect of compensation arrangements, other critics of executive compensation approach the problem in terms of the distribution of societal resources. For them, the issue is not merely the total amount of wealth but how that wealth is distributed across persons and groups in society. Some critics maintain that the present levels of executive compensation offend against the principles of distributive justice. They maintain that a just society is one in which the distribution of wealth, goods, privileges, and positions across society meets certain conditions. These critics maintain that concentrating so much wealth in the hands of these few executives constitutes an unjust distribution of society's wealth and that justice requires new social arrangements aimed at preventing that concentration.

There are many alternative conceptions of distributive justice, and different theorists arrive at different principles of a just distribution, with radically divergent prescriptions for the allocation of the goods in a society. Considering one sample position on the issue of distributive justice can make the charge against the present mode of executive compensation more concrete by considering *egalitarianism* – the view that a just distribution of goods in a society is one of perfect equality. Egalitarians see the vast gap in wealth between executives and others in society and conclude that such a distribution offends against justice because the distribution is not equal. The egalitarian view resembles that of many distributive justice theorists who believe that a just distribution is one that can be measured against a particular paradigm of a just distribution. Egalitarians take equality as their paradigm, but other theorists allow for much more inequality and much more flexibility. However, it is fair to say that most of those social observers who focus on issues of distributive justice would be highly critical of the present mode of executive compensation.

In contrast, some reject the very idea that justice might require some particular pattern of distribution. They often argue that any actual distribution that results from processes of exchange that are free from coercion and deception is by its very nature a just distribution. These theorists tend to emphasize freedom of individual action and economic freedom rather than being concerned about how wealth actually comes to be distributed. As such, they regard the very concept of distributive justice as bogus, at least as it is framed by those who wish to maintain that there is some standard of justice to which the distribution of goods in a just society must conform.

Communitarianism

Communitarian critics of executive compensation argue that the present system harms the community. They tend to see society as a community held together by social bonds in a way that allows citizens to form an organic whole. Extremely high levels of executive compensation place a gulf between a patrician class of executives and the citizenry of workers. As such, this gulf breaks down the bonds of community, weakens society, and works toward a fractured community that is resolved into persons as atoms, unconnected and out of touch with each other.

The remedy for this situation, as far as executive compensation goes, is a system that strengthens the community of executives and workers, a result that can only be achieved by reducing the gap in pay that alienates the two groups from each other. This criticism differs from a focus on utility or distributive justice because it tends to give greater weight to organic wholes – firms, communities, or entire societies – instead of placing so much emphasis on individual persons. In contrast, while those who emphasize utility and distributive justice may agree with the communitarians on policy prescriptions, their concern with utility and distributive justice is still highly compatible with an emphasis on the individual.

Philosophers who take freedom of the individual as a prime value are the natural opponents of communitarians. Against the communitarians, they argue that attempts to build stronger communities by interfering with free contracting of firms with executives tramples on individual rights in a way that is impermissible. Instead, they believe that the right of free action for individuals has a primacy that trumps the pursuit of any social goal, whether it be the maximization of utility, the achievement of some distribution that others might deem to be just, or the building of strong community ties.

Conclusion

Executive compensation continues to attract public attention and to generate a lively debate. The lifestyles of executives made possible by the compensation they receive cannot fail to generate interest and even envy. The admittedly large gap between executive pay and that of workers is bound to support the continuing view that something is amiss with the system and that some injustice must account for the difference. However, this entry has attempted to indicate some of the complexity of the issue. Finding a proper solution to the issue of executive compensation will involve the same concepts that arise in the criticism of almost all social arrangements: desert, freedom, utility maximization or wealth creation, the distribution of wealth in a society, and the effects of all social arrangements on the structure and health of communities.

Do CEOs Get Paid Too Much?

JEFFREY MORIARTY

America's corporate executives get paid huge sums of money. *Businessweek*[1] estimates that, in 2003, CEOs of the 365 largest US corporations were paid on average $8 million, 301 times as much as factory workers.[2] CEOs' pay packages, including salary, bonus, and restricted stock and stock option grants, increased by 340 percent from 1991 to 2001, while workers' paychecks increased by only 36 percent.[3] What, if anything, is wrong with this?

Although it has received a great deal of attention in management and economics journals and in the popular press, the topic of executive compensation has been virtually ignored by philosophers. As a result, its normative dimensions have been largely ignored. Organizational theorists and economists tend to be more interested in what the determinants of CEO pay *are* than in what they *should be*. What is needed, I suggest, is a general ethical framework for thinking about justice in pay. After elaborating this framework, I will argue that CEOs get paid too much.

Three Views of Justice in Wages

To determine whether CEOs get paid too much, we first need to consider what, in general, makes a wage just. In this section, I will sketch three views of justice in wages, each of which is based on a widely recognized moral value. I do not claim that these are the only views of justice in wages possible. But the values from which they derive are the ones most frequently appealed to in the debates about CEO pay. It is unlikely that any other view would be as attractive.

According to what I will call the "agreement view," just prices for goods are obtained through arm's-length negotiations between informed buyers and informed sellers. In our case, the good is the CEO's services, the seller is the CEO, and the buyer(s) is (are) the company's owner(s). Provided there are no imperfections (e.g., fraud, coercion) in the bargaining process, the agreement view says, the wage that comes out of it is just. Owners are free to do what they want with their money, and CEOs are free to do what they want with their services.

The "desert view" appeals to independent standards for justice in wages. It says that people deserve certain wages for performing certain jobs, whatever they might agree to accept for performing them. The wages people deserve may depend on facts about their jobs (e.g., their difficulty or degree of responsibility), people's performances in them (e.g., how much effort they expend, how much they contribute to the firm), or both. According to the desert view, the CEO should be paid $8 million per year if and only if he deserves to be paid $8 million per year.

What I will call the "utility view" conceives of wages not as rewards for past work, but as incentives for future work. The purpose of wages on this view is to maximize firm wealth by attracting, retaining, and motivating talented workers. If, in our case, the CEO's position is not compensated adequately, few talented candidates will apply or remain on the job for long, and the company as a whole will suffer. On the other hand, an expensive CEO can easily earn his keep through even small increases in the price of the company's stock. According to the utility view, then, a compensation package of $8 million per year is just if and only if it maximizes firm wealth by attracting, retaining, and optimally motivating a talented CEO.[4]

Too often in discussions of executive compensation, the separateness of these views is overlooked. But if we do not distinguish among them, we run the risk of talking past each other. P's belief that CEOs do not deserve, by any standard of deservingness, $8 million per year may lead him to the conclusion that CEOs make too much money. Q's belief that the pay negotiations between CEOs and owners are fair may lead him to the conclusion that CEOs do not make too much money. In fact, both P and Q may agree that CEOs do not deserve $8 million per year and that the pay negotiations between CEOs and owners are fair. They may simply disagree about what is morally more important: deserts or agreements. Understanding this, of course, does not solve the debate. But it does help to clarify what it might be about.

To solve the debate about CEO pay, we must determine which view of justice in wages is correct. It is unlikely (for reasons given below) that agreement theorists, desert theorists, and utility theorists will all come to the same conclusion about how much CEOs should be paid. I will not try to do this here. There is deep disagreement about the relative importance of these values. A full defense of one of them against the others is beyond the scope of this paper. Fortunately, it is not necessary to determine which view of justice in wages is correct to draw *any* conclusions about CEO pay. Below I will argue that its current level cannot be justified by the agreement view, the desert view, or the utility view. No matter which one is correct, CEOs get paid too much. It is possible, as I indicated, that new theories of justice in wages will be developed. But the theories we have sketched are based on the most common moral values, and it is not at all clear what these new theories would look like. Until it is, we have reason to believe that the current level of CEO pay cannot be justified *simpliciter*.

The Agreement View

According to this view, a just price for the CEO's services is one that results from an arm's-length negotiation between an informed CEO and informed owners. I will show that these negotiations are not, in general, conducted at arm's length. If they were, CEOs would be paid on average less than $8 million per year.[5]

The problem occurs mainly on the "buy" side of the equation, so we will focus our attention there. Traditionally, shareholders are represented in negotiations with the CEO by a subset of the members of the company's board of directors. This may seem promising to those who would appeal to the agreement view to justify the current level of CEO compensation. Since directors are elected by shareholders, they might say, it is likely that the directors who negotiate with the CEO – those who form the board's "compensation committee" – are in fact independent and informed. If shareholders did not elect independent and informed directors, they would risk paying too much to an incompetent CEO, or too little to an exceptional one.

This hope is unfounded. It is well known that shareholders do not, in fact, elect directors in any meaningful way. When a seat on the board opens up, usually there is just one person who "runs" in the "election." Once a candidate is nominated, her election is a formality. The group that controls the nomination process, then, controls the board's membership. In most cases this is not the shareholders but the board itself, whose chairman in 84 percent of American firms is the firm's CEO.[6] Although there has been a trend away from direct CEO involvement in the nominating process in recent years, most CEOs still wield considerable informal influence over it.[7]

This is worrisome. Whereas shareholders may elect, out of apathy or ignorance, directors who are unfamiliar with the industry and friendly with the CEO, CEOs can encourage the appointment of such directors. Do they? The fact that CEOs who are appointed *before* the appointment of their compensation committee chairs are paid more, on average, than CEOs who are appointed *after* suggests that they do.[8] Examining the composition of boards of directors more carefully, we see that, in general, directors may be informed, but they are not independent.

Three factors compromise directors' independence from their CEOs. The first is gratitude. The board member's job is prestigious, lucrative, and undemanding. Directors of the 200 largest American corporations receive on average $179,000 for 20 days of work per year.[9] They may also be given life and medical insurance, retirement benefits, and the use of company property such as automobiles and vacation homes. In addition, there is the considerable "social capital" directors acquire in the form of connections with influential people. Thus getting an appointment to a board is like getting a large gift. This is problematic, for it is natural for gift-recipients to feel grateful to gift-givers. The larger the gift is, the more grateful, and more inclined to "return the favor," the gift-recipient will be. Since CEOs have a great deal of influence over who gets appointed to the board, the directors will feel grateful to him. To represent properly shareholders' interests, then, they will have to fight against this feeling. There is reason to believe they have not been successful. Recent research shows a positive correlation between director and CEO pay.[10]

Self-interest is the second factor compromising the independence of directors in pay negotiations with CEOs. To determine how much to pay their CEO, the board will usually find out how much CEOs of comparable firms are being paid. The more those CEOs make, the more the board will pay their CEO.[11] The problem is that many boards have members who are CEOs of comparable firms.[12] This is good from the point of view of having knowledgeable directors. But CEO-directors have a self-interested reason to increase the pay of the CEO with whom they are negotiating. Suppose CEO A sits on CEO B's board, and A and B run comparable firms. The more pay A agrees to give to B, the more pay A himself will later receive. For, when it comes time to determine A's pay package, B's pay package will be used as one of the reference points.

The third factor is not a reason directors have to favor CEOs; it is the absence of a reason directors should have to favor shareholders. Since they are paying with their own money, shareholders have a powerful incentive not to overpay the CEO. The more they pay the CEO, the less they have for themselves. Directors, by contrast, are not paying with their own money. Although they are often given shares in the company as compensation, directors are rarely required to buy them. So their incentive not to overpay the CEO is less powerful. It might be wondered whether shareholders can make it more powerful by threatening to recall overly generous directors. They cannot. Shareholders in most firms lack this power. In fact, not only will directors have nothing to fear if they *do* overpay the CEO, they will have something to fear if they *do not*. Shareholders cannot recall generous directors, but CEOs can use their power to force them out.

Let me sum up. According to the agreement view, a wage of $8 million per year is just if and only if it results from an arm's-length negotiation between an informed CEO and an informed group of owners. We argued that these negotiations are not, in general, conducted at arm's length. It follows that $8 million per year is not a just (average) wage. Because the independence condition is violated in a way that favors the CEO, we can be confident that the just average wage on this view is less than $8 million per year. Speculation about how much less, however, would be premature. A different view of justice in wages may be correct, and it may justify the current level of CEO pay. In the next section I will examine the desert view.

The Desert View

A familiar complaint about CEO pay is that it has increased in years when firms have performed badly. This complaint is grounded in the desert view of justice in wages. It assumes that a CEO should get the wage he deserves, that the wage a CEO deserves is determined by his contribution to the firm, and that the proper measure of contribution is firm performance. If the firm performs worse in year two than in year one, the argument goes, the CEO deserves to make less, and therefore should make less, in year two than in year one. The agreement and utility views of justice in wages cannot account, except indirectly, for this intuition.[13]

Determining how much pay CEOs deserve involves us in two difficulties. The first is identifying the standard(s) for deservingness. Above I noted that economic contribution is often taken to be the basis of desert of wages. But a variety of others have been offered, including (i) the physical effort exerted by the worker, (ii) the amount of ability, skill, or training his job requires, (iii) its difficulty, stress, dangerousness, or unpleasantness, and (iv) its degree of responsibility or importance. Desert may be determined by one or several of these factors. The second problem is connected to the first. Once we identify the desert base(s) for wages, then we must find a way of matching desert levels to pay levels. Suppose contribution is the basis of desert, and suppose, as a direct result of key decisions by the CEO, the firm's profits increase 20 percent in a year. We might think that the CEO's desert level increases by 20 percent and therefore that he deserves a 20 percent raise. But what should his initial salary have been? Without a way of matching desert levels to pay levels, we cannot answer this question. However, from the point of view of desert, the absolute amount of the CEO's pay rise matters as much as its percentage increase.

For the purposes of this paper, both of these problems may be avoided. The first questions our ability to identify the base(s) of desert. In response, I will assume, as most parties to the debate about CEO pay do, that the basis for desert of pay is contribution. Indeed, of all the desert bases mentioned above, this is the one most likely to justify the current level of CEO pay. The second questions our ability to identify what it is exactly that people deserve. In response, I will not argue that CEOs deserve to make less than $8 million per year *absolutely*. Instead, I will argue that they deserve to make less than $8 million per year *given that* their employees make on average $27,000 per year. CEOs are not 301 times as deserving as their employees.

Under the assumption that contribution is the sole desert base for pay, the CEO deserves to be paid 301 times what the average worker is paid if and only if his contribution is 301 times as valuable as the worker's. For every $1 in revenue the worker generates, the CEO must generate $301. If the worker generates $100,000 in a year, the CEO must generate $30.1 million. Does this happen?

Some will deny that this question can be answered. They will say that employees are not Robinson Crusoes, each at work on their own self-contained projects. Instead, many people work together on the same complex projects. As a result, it is difficult or impossible to tell where one person's contribution ends and another's begins.

This is not, of course, an objection that will be advanced by those who appeal to the desert view to justify the current level of CEO pay. They need a way to measure contribution accurately. If the stronger form of this objection is true, however, and we cannot tell how much each employee contributes to the firm, then we cannot tell how much each deserves to be paid. So this conclusion is not unwelcome from the point of view of this paper. But it is weak. A thoroughgoing skepticism about the accuracy of contribution measurements yields the conclusion that we *cannot tell* whether CEOs deserve to make 301 times as much as their employees, not that they *do not* deserve to make this much. As far as this view is concerned, CEOs may deserve to make *more* than 301 times as much as their employees.

This kind of skepticism about the accuracy of contribution measurements is, I believe, unwarranted. Although it may be impossible to determine exactly how much each employee contributes to the firm, rough estimates are possible. The popular view, of course, is that CEOs matter enormously to their firms. The CEOs of successful corporations are glorified in news stories and biographies. Witness, for example, the flurry of books written by and about Jack Welch, the former chief executive of General Electric. If we accept this view, we will conclude that CEOs' contributions are at least 301 times as valuable as their employees'.

But we should not. To be sure, some scholars endorse the popular view, but an increasing number reject it. Summarizing the current state of the debate, Khurana says the "overall evidence" points to "at best a contingent and relatively minor cause-and-effect relationship between CEOs and firm performance."[14] He explains: "a variety of internal and external constraints inhibit CEOs' abilities to affect firm performance ... [including] internal politics, previous investments in fixed assets and particular markets, organizational norms, and external forces such as competitive pressures and barriers to exit and entry."[15] It cannot be denied that CEOs' decisions at times make a difference to firm performance. These leaders may deserve bonuses for strategic thinking. But, if Khurana is right, cases such as these are exceptions to the rule. Factors outside of the CEO's control normally "contribute" more to the firm's success than the CEO does.

Some will reject the research on which this result is founded. Others will point out that it is compatible with the claim that CEOs contribute 301 times as much to their firms as their employees. These claims are not irrational. No theorist is willing to say exactly how much, compared with the average employee, the average CEO contributes. But they are unreasonable. There is mounting evidence that CEOs are not as important as they were once thought to be, and average employees are far from useless. We have ample evidence for a negative conclusion, namely, the claim that CEOs deserve to be paid 301 times as much as their employees is *unjustified*. But I think the evidence licenses a tentative positive conclusion as well, namely, that CEOs are *less* than 301 times as deserving as their employees, and so deserve *less* than 301 times as much pay. The desert view clearly does not support, and probably condemns, the current level of CEO pay.

The Utility View

Having considered the agreement and desert views of justice in wages, let us now turn to the utility view. To recall, this view says that a just wage for a CEO is one that maximizes firm wealth by attracting, retaining, and motivating a talented leader. This is perhaps the most important of the three views of justice in wages. Boards of directors frequently appeal to utility-based arguments to defend the pay packages they give to their CEOs. I will argue that these defenses fail. I begin by discussing pay as a tool of attraction and retention. I then consider its role in motivation.

Attraction and Retention

Several of the desert bases discussed above might be cited as reasons an employer has to pay more to fill a certain job. The most important of these are effort, skill, and difficulty (including stress, dangerousness, and unpleasantness).[16] Since, other things equal, an employee will choose an easier job over a harder job, employers will have to make other things unequal, by offering higher wages for the harder job. Similarly, employers will offer higher wages for jobs that require rare and valuable skills or long periods of training, and for jobs that are comparatively difficult.[17]

The CEO's job has some of these characteristics. It does not require much physical effort, but it requires skill and training, and it is difficult and stressful. The question, of course, is not *if* the CEO's job has these characteristics, but *to what degree* it has them. Is the CEO's job *so* difficult and stressful, and does it require *so* much skill and training, that offering $8 million per year is necessary to get talented people to become CEOs? Those convinced by my argument that CEOs do not deserve to be paid 301 times what their employees are paid may think not. But notice we are now asking a different question: not what people deserve for performing the CEO's job, but what would make them willing to perform it.

The answer, however, is similar. There is no evidence that offering $8 million per year is necessary to get talented people to become CEOs. Indeed, we have reason to believe that much less will do. Consider the jobs of university presidents and US military generals. They are no less difficult, and require no less skill and training, than the jobs of CEOs. But the wages offered to presidents and generals are many times lower than the wages offered to CEOs. The median compensation of presidents of private research universities is $385,000 per year;[18] US military generals earn $143,000 per year.[19] Despite this, there is no shortage of talented university presidents and military generals. The fact that people can be attracted to difficult, specialized, and high-skill managerial jobs that pay "only" several hundred thousand dollars per year suggests that talented people will still want to become CEOs even if they are paid less than $8 million per year.

Three objections might be advanced against this conclusion. It might be admitted that the CEO's job is about as difficult, and requires about as much skill and training, as the university president's job or the military general's job. But, it might be said, the CEO's job is in one important way more unpleasant than these jobs. Military generals get, in addition to a paycheck, the satisfaction of knowing that they are protecting their country. University presidents get, in addition to a paycheck, the satisfaction of knowing that they are helping to increase human understanding. There is no comparable benefit, according to this objection, for CEOs.

I suspect that many CEOs find their jobs immensely intrinsically rewarding, and would find this suggestion mildly insulting. But let us grant, for the sake of argument, that CEOs' jobs are less intrinsically rewarding than university presidents' and military generals' jobs. Are they *that* much less rewarding – as many as 21 times so? For the objection to succeed, they would have to be. But it is implausible to suppose that they are. While the extra unpleasantness of the CEO's job may make it necessary to offer more than $385,000 per year to attract talented candidates, it is hardly plausible to suppose that it makes it necessary to offer $8 million.

The second objection grants that talented people would still be attracted to the CEO's job even if they were offered less than $8 million per year. But, it says, when this much pay is offered, truly exceptional people become interested. Analogously, the people who are now university presidents are talented, but truly exceptional people would become university presidents if they were offered, instead of several hundred thousand dollars per year, several million dollars per year.

Pay does matter to people when they are choosing a profession. So it is reasonable to assume that the people who become CEOs because corporations offer $8 million per year are, on average, more talented than the people who would become CEOs if corporations offered $1 million per year. But there are two reasons to think that they are not *that much* more talented, and so not worth the extra pay. First, the spectrum of managerial talent is only so wide. And $1 million per year is more than enough to attract a talented person to a difficult and important managerial job, as is demonstrated by the high talent level found among military generals and university presidents. Thus the $8 million-per-year CEO simply *cannot be* that much more talented than the $1 million-per-year CEO. Second, as we said in our discussion of the desert view, firms' performances do not usually depend heavily on the contributions of their CEOs. So it is unlikely that the modest difference in talent between

the $8 million-per-year CEO and the $1 million-per-year CEO will translate into a $7 million difference in firm performance. In support of this, note that while American CEOs significantly outearn Japanese and British CEOs, American firms do not generally outperform Japanese and British firms.[20]

It might be said – as a third objection – that I am missing the point. The fact is that the going rate *now* for CEOs is $8 million per year. In this market, it is necessary for any one firm to offer $8 million per year to get a talented person to become its CEO. This argument defies free-market economic sense. It says, in effect, that the market cannot correct itself. This is pessimistic.

Our discussion has focused on attraction; we have said nothing about retention. Could it be the case that while $8 million per year is not necessary to *attract* talented people to the CEO's job, it is necessary to *retain* them in the face of competing offers? The answer is no. In the first place, it is unlikely that there will be many competing offers. According to a study by Challenger, Gray, and Christmas Inc., of the 67 CEO departures in December 2003, in only one case was "position elsewhere" given as the reason for the departure. If CEOs were paid less, this number might increase. But even if it did, firms should not be alarmed. The difficulty of retention is a function of the difficulty of attraction. If it is not difficult to get a qualified person to take the CEO's job in the first place, it will not be difficult – or, more to the point, necessary – to retain him in the face of competing offers. The company can simply hire a new one.[21]

Motivation

Attraction and retention are not the only utility-based reasons for paying employees certain wages. There is also motivation. Employees who are talented *and* motivated create more wealth for their firms than employees who are only talented. There are three ways paying CEOs $8 million per year might be thought – mistakenly, I will argue – to maximize firm wealth through motivation.

First, it might motivate the CEO himself. The CEO knows that if he does not do an excellent job, he will be fired. Since he wants to keep making $8 million per year, he will work as hard as he can. If CEOs were paid less money, they would work less hard, and firms would be worse off.

In this respect also, pay matters. It motivates people to work hard. It is thus arguable that the CEO who is paid $8 million per year will work harder than the CEO who is paid $1 million per year. But this, as we know by now, is not what needs to be shown. What needs to be shown is that the extra amount of hard work put in by the $8 million-per-year

CEO is worth an extra $7 million. It is unlikely that it is. There is no guarantee that extra hard work will translate into extra revenue, and there is only so hard an executive can work. One might think that an extra $7 million per year would be worth it if one thought that CEOs would put in very little effort if they were paid only $1 million per year. But this takes a pessimistic view of CEOs' characters, as if only money – and only a lot of it – could get them to do anything. There is no empirical evidence to support this view. To the contrary, studies show that money is not the only, or even the primary, reason people work hard.[22] Instead of trying to further motivate their CEOs with more money, then, firms would do better to use the extra money to increase revenue in other ways, such as advertising more.

The second motivation-based reason for paying CEOs $8 million per year is, in effect, a slightly different version of the first. It has been said that CEOs' compensation packages should be structured so that CEOs' and owners' interests are *aligned*.[23] Owners want the stock price to go up. So CEOs should be paid in a way that makes them want the stock price to go up. This is typically achieved by paying CEOs mostly in restricted stock and stock options. Since, it is assumed, the CEO wants to make more money rather than less, this will give him an incentive to try to make the company's stock price go up. The idea is not just to make sure that CEOs do what investors want; it is to make sure that they do *only* what investors want. If the CEO is paid mostly in stock, he has little to gain from pursuing alternative courses of action.

Let us grant, for the sake of argument, that CEOs' interests should be aligned exclusively with investors' interests. Let us also grant that offering CEOs $5 million per year in restricted stock and stock options accomplishes this.[24] Does this prove that CEOs should be paid $5 million in stock? It does only if there is no cheaper way of achieving this goal. But there is: monitoring and dismissal. The interests of most employees are aligned with investors' interests this way. Employees are monitored. If they promote interests other than those (ultimately) of the investors, they are dismissed. Would anyone seriously propose, as an alternative to this practice, giving each employee several million dollars in stock options? To be sure, doing so would align their interests with investors' interests. But it is expensive and unnecessary. The same is true of paying CEOs $5 million in stock. There is no reason to give away so much of the firm's wealth when the CEO can simply be fired for poor performance. Owners could secure the same level of loyalty at a fraction of the price.

We have examined two ways that paying CEOs $8 million per year might maximize firm wealth through motivation. Both focus on the effects of high pay on the CEO. The third focuses on the effects of high pay on other employees. According to some, a firm's job hierarchy can be seen as a tournament, with the CEO's job as top prize. Many of the firm's employees, they say, want this prize and will work hard to get it. The better the prize is, the harder they will work. If the CEO is paid $8 million per year, the rest of the employees will work very hard indeed. The consequent increase in productivity will be good for the firm as a whole. Ehrenberg and Bognanno find evidence for this hypothesis in the field of professional golf.[25] They observe that golfers' scores are negatively correlated with potential earnings. The larger the tournament's purse is, and hence the more money the golfers could win, the better they play.

This is the most sophisticated of the utility-based attempts to justify the current level of CEO pay. Still, the argument in its present form has several problems. In the first place, not every employee wants to be CEO, no matter how much the job pays. So paying the CEO $8 million per year provides an incentive to work hard to only some of the firm's employees. Second, there is evidence that this practice will have unintended negative effects. Since there is only one CEO's job, employees must compete with each other to get it. The more the job pays, the more intense the competition will be. This is problematic, for competition fosters jealousy and hostility, which can hinder communication and cooperation.[26] This will not matter to golfers; they play alone. But employees often work together; a decline in communication and cooperation may lead to a decline in productivity. In support of this, Cowherd and Levine find that pay inequality between workers and managers is negatively correlated with product quality.[27] Thus, while paying CEOs $8 million per year may increase hard work, it may also increase competition. The benefit of the former may be outweighed by the cost of the latter.

Even if it is not, this does not suffice to prove that CEOs should be paid $8 million per year. My objection is familiar. That is, while paying CEOs $8 million per year might be an effective motivational tool, it is likely not a *cost*-effective one. Above we said that the $8 million-per-year CEO is likely to be only slightly more productive than the $1 million-per-year CEO. Similar reasoning suggests that $8 million-per-year CEO hopefuls are likely to be only slightly more productive than $1 million-per-year CEO hopefuls. From the point of view of utility, then, firms would do better to use the extra $7 million to increase revenue in other ways.

Conclusion

To structure the debate about executive compensation, I distinguished three views of justice in wages: the agreement view, the desert view, and the utility view. No matter which one is right, I argued, CEO pay is too high. Owners may "agree" to pay CEOs $8 million per year, but the negotiations are not conducted at arm's length. If they were, CEOs would be paid less. The evidence suggests also that CEOs do not deserve to make 301 times what workers make, and that paying CEOs $8 million per year does not maximize firm wealth. New evidence may emerge that challenges these conclusions. Alternatively, new theories of justice in wages may be developed. Until then, it is reasonable to believe that CEO pay is too high.

This result is important. It supports the popular suspicion that CEOs are overpaid. But our inquiry leaves an important question unanswered, namely, exactly how much should CEOs be paid? Answering this question will truly be an interdisciplinary effort. First, we must determine what the correct view of justice in wages is. That is, we must determine which of these values, in this context, is most important. Here the writings of moral and political philosophers will be relevant. Second, we must apply the correct theory of justice in wages to the problem of CEO pay. That is, we must identify the wage that maximizes firm wealth, gives the CEO what he deserves, or would be the result of an arm's-length negotiation between the CEO and the owners. Here the writings of economists and organizational theorists will be relevant. Each of these tasks will be difficult and will require a full discussion of its own. In the meantime, what should be done? CEO pay should be kept from increasing; ideally, it should decrease. Space considerations prevent a detailed discussion of how this can be accomplished. I conclude, however, with two preliminary suggestions.

First, CEOs should be removed from the director election process. Directors feel obligated to those who put them on the board. If this is the CEO, they will feel obligated to him, and be more inclined to overpay him. Directors should feel obligated to the people they are actually representing: the shareholders. Letting shareholders elect them will help to create this feeling. It is possible that it will also make being a director a more demanding job. It may end the era in which an individual can serve on several corporate boards and still hold a full-time job. This would be a good thing. Being a director is an important job: directors oversee entities whose actions can impact the welfare of thousands of people. It should feel like one.

Second, directors should be required to make meaningful investments in the firms that they direct. They need not all own a certain percentage of the firm's total stock. What matters is that they own an amount that is meaningful for them. This promotes the first objective: directors will feel more obligated to shareholders if they are themselves shareholders. It is useful for another reason as well. Above we said that a problem with the pay negotiations between directors and CEOs is that directors feel as if they are not paying with their own money. Making them buy stock would help to ameliorate this problem. An implication of this view is that other kinds of compensation that seem "free" to directors should be eliminated. This includes stock options insofar as they are not counted against firm earnings. If options are given as compensation, they should be expensed.[28]

Notes

1. L. Lavelle, "Executive Pay," *Businessweek* (April 19, 2004): 106–19.
2. For convenience, the figures for average CEO pay and average factory worker pay are rounded off in the text. The more precise figures – $8.1 million and $26,899, respectively – are used in the calculation of the ratio of CEO pay to worker pay.
3. J. A. Byrne, "How to Fix Corporate Governance," *Businessweek* (May 6, 2002): 68–75.
4. Some might deny that it makes sense to speak of an "agreement view" or "utility view" of *justice* in wages. We can talk about whether utility or agreements should determine the wages workers get, all things considered. But, according to this objection, justice is *defined* in terms of desert; the just wage, by definition, is the wage the worker deserves. I do not want to engage in a terminological dispute. What the objection describes as a debate about the wages workers should get, all things considered, *just is* what I describe as a debate about justice in wages.
5. More precisely, CEOs would be paid *on average* less than $8 million per year. It is possible that some CEOs are not overpaid according to any of the three views of justice in wages. But even if some – or as I suspect, most – are, it follows that average CEO pay is too high.
6. A. Shivdasani and D. Yermack, "CEO Involvement in the Selection of New Board Members: An Empirical Analysis," *Journal of Finance* 54 (1999): 1829–53.
7. B. G. Main, C. A. O'Reilly, and J. B. Wade, "The CEO, the Board of Directors and Executive Compensation: Economic and Psychological Perspectives," *Industrial and Corporate Change* 4 (1995): 292–332.
8. Ibid.
9. M. Jaffe, "Average CEO Pay at Big Firms Held Steady at $11.3 Million," *Mercury News* (December 30, 2003): www.mercurynews.com/mld/mercurynews/business/7597346.htm.

10. This contradicts the intuitively plausible view that since most directors are rich already, the money they get paid for being a director will not influence them. B. K. Boyd, "Board Control and CEO Compensation," *Strategic Management Journal* 15 (1994): 335–44.

11. M. Ezzamel and R. Watson, "Market Comparison Earnings and the Bidding-up of Executive Cash Compensation: Evidence from the United Kingdom," *Academy of Management Journal* 41 (1998): 221–31.

12. Main et al., "The CEO, the Board of Directors and Executive Compensation."

13. Most researchers believe CEO pay is not, in fact, tied closely to performance. See, for example, M. C. Jensen and K. J. Murphy, "Performance Pay and Top Management Incentives," *Journal of Political Economy* 98 (1990): 225–64.

14. R. Khurana, *Searching for a Corporate Savior: The Irrational Quest for Charismatic CEOs* (Princeton University Press), p. 23.

15. Ibid., p. 22.

16. I do not include on this list degree of responsibility. While some people may not want to hold jobs in which they could have a significant impact on people's lives, I suspect there are equally many, if not more, who do. I also do not include contribution. Instead I understand "skill" expansively to include all of the talents and traits taken by firms to be positively correlated with contribution.

17. Nichols and Subramanian suggest that high CEO pay is justified, in part, because CEOs' jobs are risky. When the company performs poorly, CEOs are more likely than average workers to be fired. But this ignores the fact that CEOs have less to fear from job loss than average workers. CEOs are wealthy, whereas most employees cannot afford to be out of work for long. D. Nichols and C. Subramanian, "Executive Compensation: Excessive or Equitable?," *Journal of Business Ethics* 29 (2001): 339–51.

18. J. Basinger, "Soaring Pay, Big Questions," *Chronicle of Higher Education* 50, no. 12 (2003): S9–S11.

19. Bureau of Labor Statistics, *Occupational Outlook Handbook, 2004–05* (Washington, DC: US Department of Labor, 2004).

20. J. M. Abowd and D. S. Kaplan, "Executive Compensation: Six Questions That Need Answering," *Journal of Economic Perspectives* 13 (1999): 145–68.

21. This is not to suggest that companies should make *no* effort to keep their CEOs. There is debate about whether CEO succession events disrupt firm performance, but most writers agree that they tend to lower the price of the firm's stock.

22. D. B. Annis and L. F. Annis, "Merit Pay, Utilitarianism, and Desert," *Journal of Applied Philosophy* 3 (1986): 33–41.

23. Jensen and Murphy, "Performance Pay and Top Management Incentives."

24. Khurana, *Searching for a Corporate Savior*.

25. R. Ehrenberg and M. L. Bognanno, "Do Tournaments Have Incentive Effects?" *Journal of Political Economy* 98 (1990): 1307–24.

26. Annis and Annis, "Merit Pay, Utilitarianism, and Desert."

27. D. M. Cowherd and D. I. Levine, "Product Quality and Pay Equity between Lower-Level Employees and Top Management: An Investigation of Distributive Justice Theory," *Administrative Science Quarterly* 37 (1992): 302–20.

28. A draft of this paper was presented at Georgetown University. I wish to thank members of that audience, and also George Brenkert, Edwin Hartman, Kelly Moriarty, Jeffrey Wilder, and two anonymous *Business Ethics Quarterly* referees for helpful comments and discussion.

3.4 WHISTLEBLOWING

Whistleblowing and Employee Loyalty

RONALD DUSKA

There are proponents on both sides of the issue – those who praise whistleblowers as civic heroes and those who condemn them as "finks." Maxwell Glen and Cody Shearer, who wrote about the whistleblowers at Three Mile Island nuclear power plant say, "Without the *courageous* breed of assorted company insiders known as whistle-blowers – workers who often risk their livelihoods to disclose information about construction and design flaws – the Nuclear Regulatory Commission itself would be nearly as idle as Three Mile Island ... That whistle-blowers deserve both gratitude and protection is beyond disagreement."[1] In 2002 *Time Magazine* named the whistle-blowers in high profile scandals as its Person of the Year. In 2017 it named the Silence Breakers, women who blew the whistle on sexual harassment, to that same honor.

Still, while some praise whistleblowers, others vociferously condemn them. For example, in a now infamous

Reprinted by permission of the author.

quote, James Roche, the former president of General Motors said:

> Some critics are now busy eroding another support of free enterprise – the loyalty of a management team, with its unifying values and cooperative work. Some of the enemies of business now encourage an employee to be *disloyal* to the enterprise. They want to create suspicion and disharmony, and pry into the proprietary interests of the business. However this is labeled – industrial espionage, whistle-blowing, or professional responsibility – it is another tactic for spreading disunity and creating conflict.[2]

From Roche's point of view, not only is whistleblowing not "courageous" and not deserving of "gratitude and protection" as Glen and Shearer would have it, it is corrosive and impermissible.

Discussions of the ethics of whistleblowing generally revolve around two topics: (1) debates about whether and when whistleblowing is permissible, and (2) debates about whether and when one has an obligation to blow the whistle. In this contribution I want to focus on the first problem, because I find it somewhat disconcerting that there is a problem at all. When I first looked into the ethics of whistleblowing it seemed to me that whistleblowing was a good thing, and yet I found in the literature claim after claim that it was in need of defense, that there was something wrong with it, namely that it was an act of disloyalty.

If whistleblowing is a disloyal act, it deserves disapproval, and ultimately any action of whistleblowing needs justification. This disturbs me. It is as if the act of a good Samaritan is being condemned as an act of interference, as if the prevention of a suicide needs to be justified.

In his classic book *Business Ethics*, Norman Bowie claims that "whistle-blowing ... violate(s) a *prima facie* duty of loyalty to one's employer." According to Bowie, there is a duty of loyalty that prohibits one from reporting one's employer or company. Bowie, of course, recognizes that this is only a *prima facie* duty, that is, one that can be overridden by a higher duty to the public good. Nevertheless, the axiom that whistleblowing is disloyal is Bowie's starting point.[3]

Bowie is not alone. Sissela Bok sees "whistleblowing" as an instance of disloyalty:

> The whistle-blower hopes to stop the game; but since he is neither referee nor coach, and since he blows the whistle on his own team, his act is seen as a *violation of loyalty*. In holding his position, he has assumed certain obligations to his colleagues and clients. He may even have subscribed to a loyalty oath or a promise of confidentiality ... Loyalty to colleagues and to clients comes to be pitted against loyalty to the public interest, to those who may be injured unless the revelation is made.[4]

Bowie and Bok end up defending whistleblowing in certain contexts, so I don't necessarily disagree with their conclusions. However, I fail to see how one has an obligation of loyalty to one's company, so I disagree with their perception of the problem and their starting point. I want to argue that one does not have an obligation of loyalty to a company, even a *prima facie* one, because companies are not the kind of things that are properly objects of loyalty. To make them objects of loyalty gives them a moral status they do not deserve and in raising their status, one lowers the status of the individuals who work for the companies. Thus, the difference in perception is important because those who think employees have an obligation of loyalty to a company fail to take into account a relevant moral difference between persons and corporations.

But why aren't companies the kind of things that can be objects of loyalty? To answer that we have to ask what are proper objects of loyalty. John Ladd states the problem this way, "Granted that loyalty is the wholehearted devotion to an object of some kind, what kind of thing is the object? Is it an abstract entity, such as an idea or a collective being? Or is it a person or group of persons?"[5] Philosophers fall into three camps on the question. On one side are the idealists who hold that loyalty is devotion to something more than persons, to some cause or abstract entity. On the other side are what Ladd calls "social atomists," and these include empiricists and utilitarians, who think that at most one can only be loyal to individuals and that loyalty can ultimately be explained away as some other obligation that holds between two people. Finally, there is a moderate position that holds that although idealists go too far in postulating some superpersonal entity as an object of loyalty, loyalty is still an important and real relation that holds between people, one that cannot be dismissed by reducing it to some other relation.

There does seem to be a view of loyalty that is not extreme. According to Ladd, "'loyalty' is taken to refer to a relationship between persons – for instance, between a lord and his vassal, between a parent and his children, or between friends. Thus the object of loyalty is ordinarily taken to be a person or a group of persons."[6]

But this raises a problem that Ladd glosses over. There is a difference between a person or a group of persons, and aside from instances of loyalty that relate two people such as lord/vassal, parent/child, or friend/friend, there are instances of loyalty relating a person to a group, such as a person to his family, a person to this team, and a person to his country. Families, countries, and teams are presumably groups of persons. They are certainly ordinarily construed as objects of loyalty.

But to what am I loyal in such a group? In being loyal to the group am I being loyal to the whole group or to its members? It is easy to see the object of loyalty in the case of an individual person. It is simply the individual. But to whom am I loyal in a group? To whom am I loyal in a family? Am I loyal to each and every individual or to something larger, and if to something larger, what is it? We are tempted to think of a group as an entity of its own, an individual in its own right, having an identity of its own.

To avoid the problem of individuals existing for the sake of the group, the atomists insist that a group is nothing more than the individuals who comprise it, nothing other than a mental fiction by which we refer to a group of individuals. It is certainly not a reality or entity over and above the sum of its parts, and consequently is not a proper object of loyalty. Under such a position, of course, no loyalty would be owed to a company because a company is a mere mental fiction, since it is a group. One would have obligations to the individual members of the company, but one could never be justified in overriding those obligations for the sake of the "group" taken collectively. A company has no moral status except in terms of the individual members who comprise it. It is not a proper object of loyalty. But the atomists go too far. Some groups, such as a family, do have a reality of their own, whereas groups of people walking down the street do not. From Ladd's point of view the social atomist is wrong because he fails to recognize the kinds of groups that are held together by "the ties that bind." The atomist tries to reduce these groups to simple sets of individuals bound together by some externally imposed criteria. This seems wrong.

There do seem to be groups in which the relationships and interactions create a new force or entity. A group takes on an identity and a reality of its own that is determined by its purpose, and this purpose defines the various relationships and roles set up within the group. There is a division of labor into roles necessary for the fulfillment of the purposes of the group. The membership, then, is not of individuals who are the same but of individuals who have specific relationships to one another determined by the aim of the group. Thus we get specific relationships like parent/child, coach/player, and so on, that don't occur in other groups. It seems then that an atomist account of loyalty that restricts loyalty merely to individuals and does not include loyalty to groups might be inadequate.

But once I have admitted that we can have loyalty to a group, do I not open myself up to criticism from the proponent of loyalty to the company? Might not the proponent of loyalty to business say: "Very well. I agree with you. The atomists are shortsighted. Groups have some sort of reality and they can be proper objects of loyalty. But companies are groups. Therefore companies are proper objects of loyalty."

The point seems well taken, except for the fact that the kinds of relationships that loyalty requires are just the kind that one does not find in business. As Ladd says, "The ties that bind the persons together provide the basis of loyalty." But all sorts of ties bind people together. I am a member of a group of fans if I go to a ball game. I am a member of a group if I merely walk down the street. What binds people together in a business is not sufficient to require loyalty.

A business or corporation does two things in the free enterprise system: It produces a good or service and it makes a profit. The making of a profit, however, is the primary function of a business as a business, for if the production of the good or service is not profitable, the business would be out of business. Thus non-profitable goods or services are a means to an end. People bound together in a business are bound together not for mutual fulfillment and support, but to divide labor or make a profit. Thus, while we can jokingly refer to a family as a place where "they have to take you in no matter what," we cannot refer to a company in that way. If a worker does not produce in a company or if cheaper laborers are available, the company – in order to fulfill its purpose – should get rid of the worker. A company feels no obligation of loyalty. The saying "You can't buy loyalty" is true. Loyalty depends on ties that demand self-sacrifice with no expectation of reward. Business functions on the basis of enlightened self-interest. I am devoted to a company not because it is like a parent to me; it is not. Attempts of some companies to create "one big happy family" ought to be looked on with suspicion. I am not devoted to it at all, nor should I be. I work for it because it pays me. I am not in a family to get paid, I am in a company to get paid.

The cold hard truth is that the goal of profit is what gives birth to a company and forms that particular group. Money is what ties the group together. But in such a commercialized venture, with such a goal, there is no loyalty, or at least none need be expected. An employer will release an employee and an employee will walk away from an employer when it is profitable for either one to do so.

Not only is loyalty to a corporation not required, it more than likely is misguided. There is nothing as pathetic as the story of the loyal employee who, having given above and beyond the call of duty, is let go in the restructuring of the company. He feels betrayed because he mistakenly viewed the company as an object of his loyalty. Getting rid of such foolish romanticism and coming to grips with this hard but accurate assessment should ultimately benefit everyone.

To think we owe a company or corporation loyalty requires us to think of that company as a person or as a group with a goal of human fulfillment. If we think of it in this way we can be loyal. But this is the wrong way to think. A company is not a person. A company is an instrument, and an instrument with a specific purpose, the making of profit. To treat an instrument as an end in itself, like a person, may not be as bad as treating an end as an instrument, but it does give the instrument a moral status it does not deserve; and by elevating the instrument we lower the end. All things, instruments and ends, become alike.

Remember that Roche refers to the "management team" and Bok sees the name "whistleblowing" coming from the instance of a referee blowing a whistle in the presence of a foul. What is perceived as bad about whistleblowing in business from this perspective is that one blows the whistle on one's own team, thereby violating team loyalty. If the company can get its employees to view it as a team they belong to, it is easier to demand loyalty. Then the rules governing teamwork and team loyalty will apply. One reason the appeal to a team and team loyalty works so well in business is that businesses are in competition with one another. Effective motivation turns business practices into a game and instills teamwork.

But businesses differ from teams in very important respects, which makes the analogy between business and a team dangerous. Loyalty to a team is loyalty within the context of sport or a competition. Teamwork and team loyalty require that in the circumscribed activity of the game I cooperate with my fellow players, so that pulling all together, we may win. The object of (most) sports is victory. But winning in sports is a social convention, divorced from the usual goings on of society. Such a winning is most times a harmless, morally neutral diversion.

But the fact that this victory in sports, within the rules enforced by a referee (whistleblower), is a socially developed convention taking place within a larger social context makes it quite different from competition in business, which, rather than being defined by a context, permeates the whole of society in its influence. Competition leads not only to victory but to losers. One can lose at sport with precious few consequences. The consequences of losing at business are much larger. Further, the losers in business can be those who are not in the game voluntarily (we are all forced to participate) but who are still affected by business decisions. People cannot choose to participate in business. It permeates everyone's lives.

The team model, then, fits very well with the model of the free market system, because there competition is said to be the name of the game. Rival companies compete and their object is to win. To call a foul on one's own teammate is to jeopardize one's chances of winning and is viewed as disloyalty.

But isn't it time to stop viewing corporate machinations as games? These games are not controlled and are not ended after a specific time. The activities of business affect the lives of everyone, not just the game players. The analogy of the corporation to a team and the consequent appeal to team loyalty, although understandable, is seriously misleading, at least in the moral sphere where competition is not the prevailing virtue.

If my analysis is correct, the issue of the permissibility of whistleblowing is not a real issue since there is no obligation of loyalty to a company. Whistleblowing is not only permissible but expected when a company is harming society. The issue is not one of disloyalty to the company, but of whether the whistleblower has an obligation to society if blowing the whistle will bring him retaliation.

Notes

1. Maxwell Glen and Cody Shearer, "Going after the Whistle-Blowers," *Philadelphia Inquirer* (August 2, 1983), Op-Ed, p. 11A.
2. James M. Roche, "The Competitive System, to Work, to Preserve, and to Protect," *Vital Speeches of the Day* (May 1971), p. 445.
3. Norman Bowie, *Business Ethics* (Englewood Cliffs, NJ: Prentice Hall, 1982), pp. 140–43.
4. Sissela Bok, "Whistleblowing and Professional Responsibilities," *New York University Education Quarterly* 2 (1980): 3.
5. John Ladd, "Loyalty," in *Encyclopedia of Philosophy* (vol. 5), ed. Paul Edwards (New York: Macmillan, 1967), p. 97.
6. Ibid.

Whistleblowing, Moral Integrity, and Organizational Ethics

GEORGE G. BRENKERT

Whistleblowing has attracted considerable interest, both popular and academic, during the past one hundred years. Although one can find examples of whistleblowing prior to the twentieth century, whistleblowing is largely a contemporary phenomenon that has increased in frequency and extent. Changes in job structures, attitudes toward authority, and the size and complexity of organizations are among the reasons cited for this increase. Many definitions of whistleblowing have been offered over the past half century. Some are relatively informal and careless in their formulation, others more meticulous. The following paragraphs offer a resolution of these differences in the pursuit of a coherent account of the concept of whistleblowing.

First, whistleblowers do not have to be current members of the organization. They can be former members, applicants, suppliers, or auditors. The Sarbanes–Oxley Act of 2002, a federal law enacted in response to corporate and accounting scandals, recognizes both present and former employees, as well as applicants, as whistleblowers. More generally, it seems that the whistleblower is a person "with privileged access to an organization's data or information"[1] that he has gained due to his official relationship with the organization. Because of one's relationship with the organization, one is assumed to have obligations of confidentiality and loyalty to the organization. Thus a potential whistleblower must be bound by norms of confidentiality, privacy, and loyalty that govern the operations of that organization.

Second, whistleblowing may occur inside or outside an organization. Some reject this view and argue that whistleblowing within an organization involves processes and procedures that are part of the organization. Thus, one who reports internally is not whistleblowing but only following standard procedures. This view is mistaken. There are many examples in which people have blown the whistle within their organizations – Cynthia Cooper blew the whistle internally on accounting practices at WorldCom. The mistake made by those who oppose the notion of internal whistleblowing is the failure to see that one can report "bad" information internally in ways that do not follow the normal chain of command and which are not, therefore, simply standard procedures. When I inform my supervisor that something wrong or harmful is going on, that is

fulfilling my role responsibility. When I have to circumvent my supervisor because he will not do something to correct a harm or wrong, but tries to block the information from getting to appropriate individuals, then a situation of internal whistleblowing arises. Accordingly, Sarbanes–Oxley speaks of whistleblowing in an internal context.

Third, whistleblowing is a deliberate act. One does not blow the whistle by accident. Instead, one must decide and initiate a course of action to release confidential information in order to correct a wrong the whistleblower believes someone in the organization is committing. If an employee accidentally left a document detailing wrongdoing within an organization on the desk of a journalist or a top executive in the organization who might redress that wrongdoing, it would not be a case of whistleblowing.

Even though whistleblowing must be a deliberate act, any particular whistleblower might not want his or her name associated with the act of whistleblowing. He or she may seek to blow the whistle anonymously. Sarbanes–Oxley explicitly mandates the possibility of anonymous whistleblowing. The implications of anonymity for the justification of any particular case of whistleblowing are strongly disputed. Particularly in Europe, anonymous whistleblowing has been viewed as unjustified. Whichever route one takes to blow the whistle may have practical consequences for the whistleblower and the charges brought against him or her, but it does not alter the fact that he or she has engaged in an act of whistleblowing.

Fourth, the wrongdoing that is the object of whistleblowing must be substantial. Very minor transgressions in a firm or organization might be the occasion for someone to report their occurrence to someone outside the chain of command or even to people outside the organization. For example, suppose someone goes to a person higher in the hierarchy or to the press with a report that someone has taken a few pencils home from work, charging that this act is theft and ought to be stopped. The person revealing this action does what a whistleblower would do, but the object of the action lacks the significance whistleblowing requires. To begin with, the wrong is a common one, and though organizations oppose employees taking company property home for their personal use, this is not the appropriate occasion for

From George G. Brenkert and Tom L. Beauchamp, eds., *The Oxford Handbook of Business Ethics* (Oxford University Press, 2009). Reprinted with permission.

complaining to higher officials or the press. It is too minor. Further, whistleblowing occurs within a context in which the act and/or information regarding the act is not public or open. Indeed it is viewed as confidential or secret to the organization. The potential whistleblower is viewed as having an obligation not to make the information known to the public. In trivial matters such confidentiality and obligations are themselves trivial or nonexistent. The situation does not rise to the level of whistleblowing. However, this does not mean that there are any sharp lines here. There are not.

Fifth, in blowing the whistle, an individual must direct his or her report at some person or organization (e.g., a newspaper) that the whistleblower believes can do something to correct the purported wrongdoing. Since what one divulges may relate to past, present, or future wrongdoings, the whistleblower's report seeks to stop, prevent, or rectify some wrongdoing. In any case, the report must be to someone the whistleblower believes can set in process changes that will accomplish these aims. Hence, whistleblowing need not be to someone in authority, though frequently it will be. It would not be whistleblowing if one simply told one's spouse or a friend.

An ironical result of this analysis is that whistleblowing, so understood, is a complex phenomenon that has evolved away from its simpler origins in sporting activities, where the referee or umpire "blows the whistle" to stop some infraction. In sports, it is the role of the officials to blow the whistle; they are (in general) respected parts of the game; they are not members of a team, but outsiders, hired by the league; what they "reveal" is not something hidden or confidential, but something that has occurred in public that they have witnessed and any careful spectator might also have seen. Though whistleblowers do still try to stop infractions, the preceding characteristics of officials in sports are not replicated in whistleblowing as we know it today. . . .

An Integrity Theory of Whistleblowing

In formulating an integrity theory, I will begin by focusing on the notion of wrongdoing and the responsibilities one has to report wrongdoing associated with the organization of which one is a member. Through one's association or membership with an organization, one takes on certain responsibilities one would not otherwise have. In considering this role or position, I concentrate on wrongdoing rather than harm that occurs through one's organization, since some harm might be justifiably imposed on others. For an example, a supervisor might desire to learn certain intimate details about an employee's private life, but though this desire is harmed when it is blocked, still it is justified to

block that desire. The supervisor has not been wronged. Such incidents are not an occasion for whistleblowing. Instead, it is unjustified harms, or wrongs that raise the issue of whistleblowing. The action or policy that is the object of whistleblowing must violate some important rule, law, or value according to which the business, or those within the business, should operate.

In such a context, I will argue that in accordance with a Principle of Positional Responsibility (PPR) a person has a responsibility to blow the whistle. The scope and stringency of this responsibility is dependent, in part, upon one's other responsibilities to the organization, the possibility of effectively reporting the wrongdoing, and the risks to oneself, one's other responsibilities and projects. However, only some whistleblowing is obligatory. Other acts of whistleblowing are supererogatory. Whether one is justified in blowing the whistle, all things considered, depends on how one's responsibility under the PPR coheres with other responsibilities and ideal forms of behavior to which the person is also committed. Which are most important? Which should take precedence? In acting in accord with the Principle of Positional Responsibility or other responsibilities and values one holds, how may one best maintain one's integrity? In each situation potentially involving whistleblowing, one must not simply consider whether there are good moral reasons to blow the whistle but also whether one should, all things considered, blow the whistle given the balance of responsibilities and ideal forms of behavior to which he or she is committed. This is a question of one's integrity. Thus, this account is a two-part, mixed account of justified whistleblowing: a Principle of Positional Responsibility and the integrity considerations of one's commitment to PPR and other normative demands and values that define one.

Duties of Employees

To develop an account of the Principle of Positional Responsibility it will be helpful to begin by considering what responsibility a person, qua employee, has to report a serious wrongdoing occurring within or through one's organization. By exploring these employee responsibilities we can seek to determine whether an employee has a responsibility not only to report serious wrongdoings to his or her superiors but also to do so under circumstances that would constitute whistleblowing.

The employer/employee relationship has both legal and moral aspects. Since both the law and applications of moral standards differ from society to society, these differences will have an impact on the justification of whistleblowing in different societies. For this chapter, I have assumed an Anglo-American setting. In this context, one crucial aspect is that people have agreed to work for the business and have (thereby) acquired various responsibilities. This is a historically developed relation that involves various norms and expectations. Among the responsibilities most relevant to the present discussion are the following: confidentiality, loyalty, obedience, and reporting to proper superiors or authorities.

Each employee has a duty of confidentiality with regard to legitimately private matters within the organization for which one works. There are certain matters that are private or confidential in any such relationship. Sometimes this is interpreted in the sense that "what happens here, stays here." However, regardless of how strongly some insist on this duty, the duty of confidentiality is *prima facie* not unconditioned or absolute. In some instances, it can and should be overridden, for example, when doing so may prevent serious wrongdoing.

As an employee, one also has duties of loyalty to the business for which one works. With regard to one's employer, the Restatement of Agency says that "one has a duty to his principal to act solely for the benefit of the principal in all matters connected with his agency."[2] Again, this is best taken as a *prima facie* duty. However, one also has duties of loyalty to one's fellow employees. One learns things about them one could not otherwise know, for example, certain vulnerabilities they have. One becomes part of a team or a group whose performance depends upon what one does. Any action that might jeopardize their jobs or the company may be viewed as disloyal and undercutting what they hold important. A person of integrity would seriously regard each of these duties.

In addition, the Third Restatement of Agency also specifies a "duty to provide information." This says that

> an agent has a duty to use reasonable effort to provide the principal with facts that the agent knows, has reason to know, or should know when (1) the agent knows or has reason to know that the principal would wish to have the facts; or, subject to any manifestation by the principal, the facts are material to the agent's duties to the principal; and (2) the facts can be provided to the principal without violating a duty owed by the agent to another person.[3]

If we assume that the principal would want to know about wrongdoing so that he or she could correct it, then an employee would be justified, on the basis of this job responsibility, to report the wrongdoing to his principal. If an employee saw someone breaking into the business, setting fire to the business's property, or taking goods out the front door, that person has a responsibility to say something to her supervisor or to someone who might correct this situation. Similarly, if an employee knows that someone from outside the business is stealing the organization's property or resources, they would have a responsibility to make this known to some appropriate person who can address this situation.

But what if the principal did not want to know certain facts? Does the agent then not have a responsibility to provide that information? What if the supervisor tells one to forget what one saw or learned and to mind one's own business? In such a case, when this duty to report is interpreted to refer to what a supervisor wants to hear, there is no responsibility to report anything other than what the principal would wish to have.

In fact, it is this situation that raises the question of whistleblowing. If one simply reports to one's supervisor some wrongdoing, one is not, as such, whistleblowing. One is doing one's job, though perhaps exceeding even that. Still, it need not be whistleblowing. Instead, whistleblowing occurs when the person one reports to has rejected one's notice regarding some wrongdoing. Perhaps the potential whistleblower is urged to be a team player; she is instructed that there "really" is not a problem; or she is told to just stick to her job. In this situation, the whistleblower potentially faces a double failure. There is the wrongdoing itself and the refusal by one's supervisor to deal with it. This means that if one were to report the wrongdoing in question to anyone else, one would be challenging the power and authority of the supervisor, if not the organization. One would be engaging in both an act of disclosure as well as one of disobedience. Such disobedience is generally taken to be a sign of disloyalty. Thus, whistleblowing only occurs when one does not follow the usual hierarchical order of reporting. If one breaks ranks, as it were, to inform someone not in one's usual line of reporting – someone in upper-level management, say – one then becomes a whistleblower. One must consider whether such further action is warranted and what that justification might be. . . .

The Integrity Theory
The Principle of Positional Responsibility

Underlying our responsibility to report wrongdoing is a Principle of Positional Responsibility. This principle morally obliges people to report wrongdoings to those who might prevent or rectify them, when the wrongdoings are of a significant nature (either individually or collectively), when one has special knowledge due to one's circumstances that others lack, when one has a privileged relationship with the organization through which the wrongdoing is occurring (or has occurred), and when others are not attempting to correct the wrongdoing.

This is not a general principle of doing good or even preventing harm. It is a limited principle of reporting wrongdoing, under specific circumstances and conditions, with the intention of preventing or stopping it. We do not have a general duty to correct the wrongs of the world. If we did, we would be constantly involved in the affairs of others in order to fulfill our moral obligations. And, since we have limited time, abilities, and means, we would also need some means to distinguish among the various wrongs that deserved our attention. However, the Principle of Positional Responsibility tells us that due to a special organizational or situational position we occupy involving knowledge of wrongdoing, as well as our ability to have an effect on correcting a wrong of some importance through making it known, a person acquires a responsibility to speak out. That is, through these special circumstances we have a specific duty or responsibility to take steps that will lead to the correction of wrongs.

This principle concerns wrongdoings that are of a serious nature. Though this notion lacks specificity and precision, so too does much of life in business. Still, we can differentiate between those wrongs that might regard small or inconsequential matters and those involving matters of great importance and/or harm to large numbers of people. The elevator inspector who shut down poorly operating elevators that were improperly licensed was addressing a serious wrongdoing. An employee who reports on improper city road contracts is also concerned about serious matters, as was the FAA flight controller who worried about colliding planes. Sometimes the wrongdoing is much more abstract as when it involves accounting procedures. For example, at WorldCom various expenditures were treated as capital expenditures rather than ordinary expenses. This different accounting approach allowed WorldCom to record significant profits when, according to ordinary accounting rules, it was losing money. Part of the reason that the wrongdoing must be serious is that if a person sought to report a trivial matter, for example, a few missing pencils, to someone in upper management or to the media, he would be viewed as an annoyance, rather than a whistleblower. If the wrongdoing were very minor, it would not rise to the level of whistleblowing, whether or not it was justified in the particular case.

The Principle of Positional Responsibility requires, it should be noted, that one is connected with the organization (or situation) through which one or more people are engaged in wrongdoing. It does not tell us, absent this connection, that one has any particular responsibilities. In short, it is this connection that gives a person the position or "standing" to reveal and attempt to correct the wrongs of others. This "standing" arises because as a member of the organization (or one who has privileged access) one supports the organization through one's actions (or even sometimes one's inactions), one is more likely to have verifiable knowledge unavailable to others through such an association, and by having access to officials in the organization there may be an initial presumption one may more easily and effectively bring about change. It is true that through the media and the Internet one might become aware of a host of wrongdoings around the world. But that knowledge is not part of the special circumstances in which one is a member of an organization through which wrongdoing is taking place.

Finally, this principle requires that we can have some effect to stop the wrongdoing or to correct it, though we need not be able to do this directly or individually. It is sufficient that the whistleblower provide the impetus or the occasion that may lead, through others, to the correction of this wrongdoing. The whistleblower need not be able to change the situation all by herself. However, by shining the light of day upon the wrongdoing, her reporting may play a crucial role in the correction process.

It is worth noting that the Principle of Positional Responsibility is compatible with widely held views regarding an individual's responsibility to report and, if possible, prevent wrongdoings associated with one's position, knowledge, and abilities. Some of this is captured in the law. For example, as earlier noted, one might be accused of a "misprision of a felony" if one fails to report felonious behavior of which one is aware.

Nonlegal, moral examples would include our responsibility to alert our neighbors and the police if we know that someone is breaking into our neighbor's house. Under these circumstances we have a responsibility to report crimes in our neighborhoods in the city. Crime Awareness campaigns and Neighborhood Crime Reports build on this notion of responsibility to report wrongs of which one becomes aware. These are responsibilities we have both as moral agents and as members of society.

In contrast to a general principle of beneficence, a Principle of Positional Responsibility would prioritize the wrongs to be addressed based upon the above contextual conditions of organizational membership, knowledge, and ability to have an effect on correcting the alleged wrongs. As a moral agent employed by a business, one occupies a special position that others do not have. Employees are subject to the Principle of Positional Responsibility and have an obligation to report wrongdoing. Recognizing this principle helps to explain the moral outrage people express when they learn that someone knew of some important wrong he might have helped stop by calling attention to it, but did nothing. It is for this reason that we are morally troubled when we learn that executives at the Johns-Manville Corporation knew about the asbestos dangers to its employees in the 1930s, 1940s, and 1950s but not only did not tell them but also hid the dangers from them. We wonder why someone did not "blow the whistle" during these years. Hence, a special responsibility falls on one due to the circumstances defined by Principle of Positional Responsibility.

Implications of the Principle of Positional Responsibility

Still, we need to ask more specifically about the responsibilities that flow from this principle with regard to the employee reporting of wrongdoings. What are its implications for the employee whose supervisor has proven to be an obstacle? Does one have a responsibility to report further up the organization outside of standard hierarchical routes? Must one exhaust all internal sources to which one might report? When should one report externally?

By itself, the Principle of Positional Responsibility does not answer such questions. Instead, we must interpret this principle within two related contexts that relate to the scope or extent of the principle, on the one hand, and its weight or stringency, on the other.

First, in order to define the *scope* or extent of this principle, we must look to other relevant principles and values. PPR is a second-order principle. Rather than telling us not to lie or not to harm other people, it tells us that we should report the wrongdoings of others under certain circumstances as part of an effort to prevent or to correct those wrongs. But how far we should take this and in what manner, it does not say. For this we require, in part, other principles and values, for example, the value of loyalty to an organization; principles of responsibility to friends and family; the public interest.

Second, PPR lays out a responsibility we have within its own narrow framework, but does not define the weight or *stringency* we should attribute to it. This framework must be further determined by one's abilities and what might reasonably be expected of a person in a whistleblowing situation. How should we weigh significant threats to potential whistleblowers that may ruin their careers, destroy their family, alienate them from their peers, conflict with other important responsibilities, and/or bankrupt them? Ethicists commonly distinguish between obligations we have and admirable actions that go beyond our duties. Ideal and even heroic acts are termed *supererogatory*. Might not some whistleblowing acts fall into this category rather than being strictly obligatory? These are issues of the stringency of the Principle of Positional Responsibility that we must also consider.

The Scope of the Principle of Positional Responsibility

Previously, I have identified an employee-based responsibility to inform or report to one's supervisor, as well as duties of loyalty, obedience, and confidentiality. How do these norms relate to the Principle of Positional Responsibility when one's supervisor has told one that one's concerns regarding some putative wrongdoing are not serious or relevant and that one should get back to work? What does this principle direct one to do? How far should one proceed in reporting? This is one way to approach questions of the scope or extent of this principle.

We may begin by assuming that some serious wrong is being done to someone or some group and that all the conditions for PPR are relevantly fulfilled. *Prima facie*, one ought to report the wrongdoing. Similarly, one's other duties of loyalty, obedience, as well as respect for those one works for are also *prima facie*. They can be overridden in serious cases. Consequently, PPR might, given appropriate circumstances, override them.

One's obligation to report should be directed internally (at least initially and subject to overriding conditions) because the source of the wrongdoing comes through the organization. One's loyalty is not simply to one's supervisor but also to the organization. The wrongdoing may also have significant implications for the organization (loss of reputation, legal fees, fines). Under these circumstances, to permit those closest to the wrongdoing (and responsible to correct it) the opportunity to do so is to respect their authority and self-determination. To report externally, as long as there were other reasonable internal venues, would be to undercut their responsibilities and not give them a chance to do what they should do. In addition, the internal route might also be the most efficient way to address the situation. The organization could then deal with the fact that a serious legal or moral wrong has been done. In the case of a serious legal wrongdoing, the corporation would have to self-report the problem to legal authorities. This inside approach would give the leadership of the organization a chance to know about the problem before the media or court system does, to announce the problem to the responsible legal officials, and to begin to address the organizational dimensions of the problem even before a full legal accounting took place. In general, this would be desirable both practically and ethically for an organization. However, should the internal route pose significant danger to the potential whistleblower or the strong likelihood of a pointless result, then one's obligation to report would be to external agents.

An employee does not have a responsibility to challenge insurmountable barriers. He or she does not have a responsibility to reform the organization so that reports of wrongdoing make it to the top levels. If each person the whistleblower goes to in the hierarchy does not act on the information but resists and punishes the whistleblower, then there is something wrong with the organization, its processes, and procedures. Though many organizations have rules and policies requiring employees to report wrongdoing, still, the de facto corporate culture may oppose such reporting as a form of snitching or betrayal. The more a business undercuts the conditions required for the fulfillment of one's responsibility to report internally, the weaker is this responsibility to the organization. It is not surprising that one of the reasons empirical accounts report why people do not blow the whistle is that they believe nothing will be done. This is a direct reflection on the failure of the organization's internal mechanisms and culture.

If under these circumstances, an employee continues to try to report up the corporate chain of command, then they go above and beyond the call of duty. Doing so may even be foolish. It may also be that one's actions are of a supererogatory nature, presenting us with an ideal, if not heroic, form of loyalty. However, morality does not require that one take such steps or that one uselessly sacrifice oneself in this manner, even if the aim is noble. Instead, one's reporting responsibility is to make genuine efforts to report the wrongdoing to responsible officials. When it becomes clear that the organizational response is not going to change, it would be unreasonable to require one to go through each level of the organization. Instead, the Principle of Positional Responsibility and loyalty require that one give the organization a fair and meaningful chance to address the charges and to correct the problem.

If internal reporting has failed or is certain to fail, when would one's responsibility to report require that one report externally? The answer is not that one needs additionally strong evidence. Even to report internally one should have reasonable evidence that wrongdoing has taken place.

Whether one reports internally or externally one should not be reporting rumors or hunches. Instead, one must consider the significance of the wrongdoing and the possibility that this wrong can be corrected. The more serious the wrongdoing and the greater the chance that reporting will correct the situation, the stronger is one's obligation to report it.

Should one also consider potential risks to the organization from reporting? For example, the revelation of the wrongs committed by some employees of Arthur Andersen and its subsequent indictment and conviction in the Enron auditing case, led to the demise of Arthur Andersen. The actions of a handful of people resulted in tens of thousands of others being thrown out of their jobs. This appears to many to be a case in which justice was done, though the heavens fell. However, for a whistleblower to make such judgments he would have to know whether the wrongdoing he knows about is a single instance, or part of a pattern. He would have to know about the future actions of the media, the courts, and top executives. This is not something any whistleblower is in a situation to know. This means that though the whistleblower must act on the basis of a known wrongdoing, he can do so with only a very limited comprehension of the full situation. It is this that, in part, makes whistleblowing a risky and dangerous undertaking for others as well as the whistleblower himself. It does not mean that he does not have a responsibility to report serious wrongdoings externally. However, it does emphasize the importance of being accurate in the charges one brings.

The Stringency of the Principle of Positional Responsibility

The question of the weight or stringency that one should attribute to the Principle of Positional Responsibility arises also with regard to risks to oneself. There are different studies on this topic, but there is certainly the possibility that one will suffer – perhaps even dramatically – if one reports wrongdoing, but particularly if one does so externally. Some businesses have responded with a viciousness that is appalling. The treatment of Dan Gellert by Eastern Airlines is a good example. As a pilot at Eastern Airlines, Gellert became aware of a defect in the autopilot control system on Lockheed 1011 aircraft. At times it would disengage in a manner that could lead to a crash. In fact, one plane did crash. Others had near crashes. For his efforts to bring this situation to the attention of management and get it corrected, he was given flight schedules that tested his physical well-being, mental exams that challenged his psychological fitness, told to appear in courtrooms in other cities in a time frame that was impossible, and so on. All this was part of an effort to discredit him. In short, what a whistleblower should know is that her life will change – and may change significantly – as a result of her report.

This risk to oneself directly affects one's moral responsibility to blow the whistle since it may negatively affect many of one's other responsibilities, important interests, and projects. One has multiple responsibilities and interests that have defined one's life prior to this unexpected event. One has built up relationships at work and outside of work that depend upon one fulfilling the responsibilities that constitute these other relationships. Will one act consistently on these principles, or will one compromise some of them? Which principles and values are most important? How courageous is one prepared to be? How courageous is one capable of being? How would other moral agents who are courageous act, and what risks would they undertake, in this situation? What about one's duty of confidentiality and obedience that are part of one's job? What about one's responsibilities to one's peers and one's family? The Principle of Positional Responsibility, by itself, cannot answer these questions.

The extent of one's responsibilities under this principle will be difficult to determine in any particular case and certainly cannot be ascertained precisely in many cases. A soldier's responsibilities may include placing himself in harm's way such that he might possibly be killed. A physician has a responsibility to his patients that may involve contracting life-threatening sicknesses. However, employees do not, ordinarily, have a responsibility – unless they so choose – to sacrifice their health, lives, or futures for a business by helping to prevent the damage that the wrongdoing of others may do to them. Rather, their whistleblowing responsibilities are tied, most closely, to those who are wronged (or may be wronged) by the employees of the business for which they work.

Assuming that some serious wrongdoing has taken (or will take) place, that the person has reasonable evidence of this wrongdoing, that the agents normally responsible are not fulfilling their duties, and that one has a reasonable prospect of effectively changing the situation, one has a responsibility to proceed with bringing the wrongdoing to the attention of others who can do something about it. And, particularly, if whistleblowing would have very minimal, short-term effects on one's life, but correct a serious wrong, then an employee has a responsibility to try to make the information public.

However, if the chance of success is limited and the implications for the whistleblower are themselves so significant that his or her life will be dramatically injured as a result, it is much less obvious that the person is responsible to blow the whistle. After all, the wrongdoing is not itself a failure of the potential whistleblower, but of others in the organization. Further, it is plausible that a person does not have an obligation to report the wrongdoings of others when doing so will destroy himself or turn him simply into a means whereby the organization's wrongs are corrected.

Accordingly, a person doing his duty by blowing the whistle may at the same time justifiably seek to avoid grave risks to himself. Some whistleblowers have anonymously blown the whistle. However, this option is not always available – in some cases if one says anything, it will be quite clear to others who spoke up. Further, it is often said that anonymous reporting is viewed as less authoritative and less persuasive than when a person places her name on the report. It is easier then to judge its authenticity and the motivations of the person doing the reporting.

How should we respond when the harsh consequences for the whistleblower cannot be avoided? In general, the greater the seriousness of the wrongdoing, the more certain the evidence of such wrongdoing, and the greater the likelihood that publicly reporting it will correct the wrongdoing, the greater will be one's responsibility to make it known. However, there will be a point, due to the negative effects on the whistleblower – and this may differ for individuals – when we may say that blowing the whistle is beyond the call of ordinary duty. It is not a moral requirement that one is obliged to fulfill. One is not blameworthy if one does not do it. In such cases, whistleblowing may be supererogatory. It constitutes an ideal or heroic action that is admirable, but beyond what is morally demanded. It makes sense to encourage such actions in a society. It is important to protect those who engage in them. We should even, on many occasions, seek to emulate such actions and encourage others to do so as well. Nevertheless, they are not morally obligatory in the sense that if a person does not do them he or she is morally blameworthy and should be condemned or morally punished. Those who do blow the whistle in such circumstances have displayed great moral courage. But in destroying their family, losing their house, incurring large debts to support their efforts, they have clearly gone beyond any call of ordinary moral duty.

In making these decisions regarding whistleblowing, one must place the Principle of Positional Responsibility within the context of other values and norms one justifiably stands for. We are concerned in whistleblowing situations with one's faithfulness or commitment not only to this principle but also to other important values, norms, and ideals that define one. Is one prepared to act and live by them even when confronted with situations that impose threats and costs – sometimes even of a considerable nature – on one? These are considerations of integrity, inasmuch as a person of integrity will defend her values and norms even when doing so is inconvenient or difficult. As Lynn Sharp Paine says, "persons of integrity have a set of anchoring beliefs or principles that define who they are and what they believe in. They stand for something and remain steadfast when confronted with adversity or temptation."[4]

Beyond this, assuming that our values, responsibilities, and ideals may conflict at times, a person of integrity will integrate these normative facets of her life into some reasonably coherent whole. Those responsibilities and values of greatest importance will receive the greatest priority. Integrity, we are told, "involves recognition that some desires are more important and more desirable than others; that some commitments make a greater claim upon us than others; that some values are deeper than others; and that some principles take priority over others."[5] Which of these principles, ideals, and values are the most important ones to support and at what cost to oneself as well as others? To which values and norms is one prepared to remain faithful? Is one prepared to sacrifice other important values (e.g., family, career) to correct the wrongdoing one has discovered?

When an instance of whistleblowing arises, the justified course of action will be filtered through these different normative dimensions of one's justified values and norms. Does this area central to who a person is shrink, at such times, to a small island focused simply on protecting oneself? Does it encompass others and the full range of one's values, norms, and ideals? The decision one makes on implementing the Principle of Positional Responsibility will be a decision regarding one's integrity as one decides what one justifiably stands for. One might say that this situation is the flip side of complicity. It is not because one is involved in wrongdoing that one must decide whether or not one will blow the whistle, but because one must choose between the different principles of obligation and duty that pertain to one, the ideals by which one lives, and the kind of person one wishes to be. Even with internal whistleblowing, one must decide to step outside the security, protections, and relative anonymity of the normal hierarchy to make a moral stand for what ought to be done. It is inherently a situation that requires courage and commitment to one's values and principles.

Consider then an employee, Debra, who knows of wrongdoing in the business for which she works; others who work there are afraid to say anything. Her supervisor and peers say that she ought to forget it about it: "That's just the way things are done around here." Debra is certain that wrongdoing is going on and has evidence to back up her view. This wrongdoing bothers her greatly; she understands the implications of PPR. Thus, Debra takes her information to top management or goes to an outside source to change things, even knowing that there are considerable risks. However, in doing so she does not blow the whistle simply because this is the implication of PPR, but because it fits with her ongoing concerns for honesty, for not wronging others, and for accountability. These values and norms have defined Debra's life and her relations with others. Not to blow the whistle would be to retreat and compromise these, as well as PPR. It is a question of integrity – of knowing what was going on, of having certain values and views, and of living them. Contrariwise, if she had these values, norms, and character traits and did not act on them, she would be a hypocrite and her integrity tarnished.

Contrast this with Jim, who comes to know of serious wrongdoing that is going on regarding accounting measures at his firm. No one is being physically harmed, but the company is misreporting its financial status and various activities. When this fraud becomes known, this will affect investors and possibly employees and suppliers. Jim reports his knowledge of the wrongdoing to his supervisor, who says that he will take care of it and that Jim should stick to his own job. There are suggestions that if he does not do this he will be in trouble. Jim is convinced that the supervisor will do nothing, and if he (Jim) does not do anything else, this wrongdoing will continue (at least for the present). Though there are other people (with authority) in the organization who know the wrongdoing is going on, there is a conspiracy of silence amongst a small group of people. Jim is aware of the implications of PPR, but Jim has other important responsibilities as well that have shaped his life. He is the sole provider for his family. He is also the chairperson of a regional group that focuses on providing disadvantaged children with educational support. His role has been critical in moving this group from one that is largely ineffective to one that makes an important impact on children in the area. Since this area is conservative, Jim believes that if he became involved in revealing the corporate wrongdoing his position in this regional organization would be jeopardized and the aid they are providing disrupted. He is also not certain that if he blew the whistle anyone would listen. He knows about the retaliation against other whistleblowers, and he has his family to think about. He decides that there are other, more important things he should be doing than correcting this particular wrong in his company by whistleblowing. He also has other, more direct responsibilities that would be crippled if he blew the whistle. Ideally, of course, he would do both. But this is not an ideal world. He can maintain his integrity by resigning, even if it means taking a lower-paying job, while fulfilling the other important responsibilities he has undertaken and which are crucial to him and those to whom he is responsible.

In each of these cases, the integrity of those involved has played a role in how the Principle of Positional Responsibility is applied. If one's responsibility to blow the whistle does not significantly disrupt one's other responsibilities and projects, one has a responsibility to blow the whistle. One would be wrong not to do so, whether internally or, if necessary, externally. However, all too frequently, in deciding to blow the whistle, one may be making a life-altering decision that will affect oneself as well as others. It is not like calling the police to report a neighborhood crime, which may take a few minutes or few hours, after which it will be over. Due to the responses of fellow workers, the recrimination to which one may render oneself vulnerable, the amount of time and money one must expend to defend one's claims, the pressures it will place on one's personal life and family relationships, whistleblowing may simply change the course of one's life. It is too easy to say, abstractly considered, one has a moral obligation to blow the whistle without placing this obligation within the broader context of the other responsibilities, values, and practical implications for the whistleblower. One cannot appropriately respond to PPR by simply considering this principle itself, separated from the rest of one's life. Instead, one's response must arise out of how this principle, in a particular set of circumstances, coheres with the rest of who we are, namely, our other values, principles, and ideals as we have integrated them into our lives. The question is not simply and abstractly, "Would it be justified for some person or other to blow the whistle in this situation?" But rather the question is, "Would it be justified for this person in this situation to blow the whistle?" Here the risks a person must take play a legitimate role in her decision as well as how this action coheres with other values and norms she supports. In answering these questions, one defines what kind of person one is and reaffirms (or undercuts) one's integrity.

Hence, the present account of justified whistleblowing is a mixed one. The Principle of Positional Responsibility and integrity play joint roles. But because PPR plays its role within the broader context of our integrity, I have called it the Integrity Theory.

Whistleblowing and the Design of Organizations

The preceding accounts of whistleblowing ask what justifies an individual engaging in whistleblowing. The Integrity Theory, I believe, is the best response to that question.

However, focusing on this question distracts us from the underlying problem of the misconduct occurring in (or through) organizations that organizations themselves fail to identify and correct. Whistleblowers have played a vital role in bringing to light many of these wrongdoings. They have provided an admirable service to the public. For this they deserve protection. However, depending on the measures adopted, this way of correcting wrongdoing may not be very successful. In any case, such an approach treats the symptoms and not the underlying problems. It is a Band-Aid approach.

Accordingly, we should also be asking about the situation that gives rise to the need for individual whistleblowing. What, in short, is the problem to which whistleblowing is the supposed answer? What is the design problem to which blowing the whistle is the answer? The unsurprising, but important, answer is that whistleblowing is necessary when there has been a failure within the organization. It is one way by which we discover and seek to correct important wrongs or abuses by organizations when some of their members do not wish to recognize or correct them. In short, the wrongdoing whistleblowers target is both an individual and an organizational failure.

There are two striking features of this answer. First, this answer tends to imperil, and sometimes destroy, the people who report the wrongdoing. There are numerous reports of the terrible retaliation whistleblowers have experienced. And though the empirical evidence does not demonstrate that all whistleblowers suffer significant retaliation, far too many do. Second, whistleblowing is, often, not terribly effective. The evidence regarding how often claims of whistleblowing successfully result in the wrongs or harms reported being corrected is extremely difficult to come by, given the nature of these actions. One measure is to consider those who have filed under the Whistleblower Protection Act. On this score, whistleblowers have had "a minuscule success rate. Only 1 percent of such cases since 2001 was referred to agency heads for investigation. Of the last 95 such cases that reached the federal circuit court of appeals, only one whistleblower won."[6] Accordingly, whistleblowing as a response to wrongdoing by organizations and the people in them has considerable weaknesses. The whistleblowing answer to our design problem is not an obviously good answer – even if an individual is justified in blowing the whistle. Those who blow the whistle are themselves often wronged or abused. And the result of their efforts is quite frequently that needed changes do not take place. Yet these changes were the point of the whistleblowing. As such, the current focus on individual whistleblowing is often the justification of sacrificial victims on behalf of ineffective efforts.

This suggests that we need more discussion of organizational conditions that would forestall the necessity of whistleblowing. If organizations were designed to obviate the necessity of whistleblowing, then the gut-wrenching stories of the fate of whistleblowers might be considerably reduced and the occasions of individual whistleblowing become much more infrequent. In short, the discussion of organizational designs that would reduce or eliminate the need for whistleblowing should be primary, and any justification of individual whistleblowing should be secondary. *The real ethical problem whistleblowing raises is how do we create self-correcting organizations that catch violations by themselves and do not rely on individuals (who experience retaliation) to identify and demand their correction?*

The relevant design question regarding organizations is not simply a matter of trying to protect whistleblowers but of creating organizations in which external whistleblowing is not necessary (or at the least minimized), and in which internal whistleblowing (should it be necessary) is received with a positive response. Such organizations must be able to detect and acknowledge mistakes or wrongful acts, receive bad news, and take steps to correct those problems. Unless organizations are serious about this, we cannot be serious about whistleblowing. If they were serious, they would be self-regulating and self-enforcing organizations. Such organizations would, thereby, be faithful to their own values, purposes, and legitimating bases. They would be organizations of integrity.

Self-Correcting Organizations

What features would characterize a self-correcting organization?

First, they would seek information regarding problems and violations from all those who are members of (or who have a privileged relation with) the organization. They cannot rely simply on monitors, auditors, or the like. If an organization's self-correcting method is dependent simply on monitors or auditors to detect its problems, then it will always be inadequate since such an approach can never have a monitor in each office and for every action.

Second, the members of organizations must also have an acknowledged responsibility to come forward when they see misconduct. Organizations can seek to capture this responsibility in codes of ethics, through ethics and compliance programs, and those in charge of overseeing ethical and legal complaints. Nevertheless, these methods will not be adequate unless this responsibility is acknowledged through a corporate culture that values, rather than denigrates, the reporting of bad news and misconduct. The most direct way for this to occur is for those involved to self-report problems, errors, wrongful acts, and so on. As in experimental sciences, these failures may be the occasion of important learning and redirection of the individuals, departments, and businesses involved.

Third, there must be means to receive the reports and to initiate examination of them and, as appropriate, institute needed changes. The point, after all, of bringing such charges forward is, when warranted, to make changes. At the same time, there are stories about employees being told they have a responsibility to report misconduct and then not being protected when they do. Both these situations suggest the importance of structural and cultural changes. These do not, however, take place spontaneously. They require the good will of management and executives, the "buy-in" of employees, but also the need of the law, social pressures, and stakeholder pressures on behalf of such behavior. The law must play an important role here, giving not only some measure of protection to whistleblowers but also incentives to organizations to be self-correcting.

Fourth, self-correcting organizations would have to institute measures to foster an attitude among employees willing to push back against directions to engage in illegal or unethical behaviors. They would have to encourage them to fulfill their responsibilities to identify substantive wrongdoings and to resist efforts to remain quiet. This would require important cultural changes for many organizations and individuals. In particular, cultural changes are necessary to address the situation that has often been reported of insiders who see wrong things being done but tend not to report them.

The other side of this equation would require that organizations be structured, and their members trained, to accept bad news, to confront wrongdoing, and seek ways to change it. To encourage these attitudes it is necessary to address negative attitudes employees and supervisors may have regarding resistance to their views and the reporting of misconduct. This involves, but is not limited to, integrating ethics into performance evaluations and feedback surveys, linking the value of loyalty to the legitimating bases of the organization, and protecting and commending those who identify problems and misconduct. This involves programs and initiatives far beyond whistleblowing situations. These initiatives speak to a general condition for how those who have power and authority over others should treat those subordinate to them when the latter inform their leaders of illegal, immoral, or illegitimate activities going on in the organization. The organizational dimension of this question is the fundamental ethical issue that whistleblowing raises.

Finally, since an organization is not a wholly self-contained system but exists only within the political, economic, social, and legal context of its time, there is a role for the broader social and political system in the preceding, for example, for the government to provide penalties for harming or harassing whistleblowers and incentives for whistleblowers to come forward with valuable information. Since we are dealing with "the crooked timber" of humanity, there must always be means, internally and externally, for people in an organization to circumvent wrongdoers when these are the people to whom one would ordinarily report the wrongdoing. More generally, however, we should work to create organizations and a social and political system that renders whistleblowing and such sacrifices unnecessary. We need to transform organizations that shape and form our lives so that the wrong, the harms, and the abuses that occur through them can be identified and corrected. We may not be able to ensure that this is always the case, but we can do a better job than we have.

This is the project on which those truly concerned about whistleblowing should be focused. It is this project of revising corporate activities that will address the real problem that lies behind whistleblowing.

Notes

1. Peter B. Jubb, "Whistleblowing: A Restrictive Definition and Interpretation," *Journal of Business Ethics* 21 (1999): 77–94 (p. 83).
2. Richard Degeorge, *Business Ethics*, 6th rev. ed. (Upper Saddle River, NJ: Pearson, 2006), p. 302.
3. Ibid.
4. Lynn Sharp Paine, "Integrity," in *The Blackwell Encyclopedic Dictionary of Business Ethics*, ed. Patricia H. Werhane and R. Edward Freeman (Malden, MA: Blackwell, 1997), p. 335.
5. Damian Cox Marguerite La Caza, and Michael P. Levine, *Integrity and the Fragile Self* (Aldershot: Ashgate, 2003), p. 8.
6. Mark Clayton, "Hard Job of Blowing the Whistle Gets Harder," *The Christian Science Monitor* (January 20, 2005).

After the Wrongdoing: What Managers Should Know about Whistleblowing

JANET P. NEAR AND MARCIA P. MICELI

Whistleblowing

Serious wrongdoing never occurs in some organizations – but this may not prevent employees from misperceiving that wrongdoing has occurred. Other firms may engage in wrongdoing unknowingly or a small rogue group of employees may commit illegal actions much to their managers' surprise. In some firms, of course, wrongdoing may be a part of business as usual. Whether perceived or real, managers often learn of wrongdoing in their organizations only when an employee blows the whistle about that wrongdoing. Clearly, managers would prefer that the whistleblowing be internal and limited to the confines of the organization rather than publicized through external channels such as the media or law enforcement agencies. Ironically, research shows that the actions managers may take in order to prevent whistleblowers from going external turn out to be precisely the actions that drive them to do so.

For example, at Peanut Corporation of America, plant manager Kenneth Kendrick reported to the CEO, Stewart Parnell, that plant conditions were unsanitary. In response, Kendrick was told by Parnell to ship peanuts despite contamination due to a leaking roof that let dirt and bird feces enter the production facility. Kendrick then emailed the Texas State Department of Health but received no response. Finally, as Kendrick learned that salmonella outbreaks were sickening many people and killing several others, he went on *Good Morning America* and explained that he felt compelled to complain to the media when his own granddaughter had become ill from eating the contaminated peanut butter.[1] As a result of these events, Peanut Corporation of America went bankrupt and executives and plant managers were indicted on 76 charges.[2] On Monday, September 21, 2015, former CEO Stewart Parnell was sentenced to 28 years in prison, the "toughest penalty ever for a corporate executive in a food poisoning outbreak."[3]

In this article we summarize what has been learned about whistleblowers from three decades of research and suggest strategies that managers can use to deal effectively with whistleblowing events. Along the way, we will provide brief

From *Business Horizons* 59 (2016).

answers to several questions based on what has been learned from the research:

- Why does whistleblowing matter?
- Where does whistleblowing happen?
- What is whistleblowing?
- Who blows the whistle and when do they do so?
- When and why do whistleblowers suffer reprisal?

The answers are often unexpected or surprising, but knowing those answers can provide the best strategies for responding effectively to internal whistleblowing – and for dealing with the aftermath of external whistleblowing if concerns are made public. Our concern is not with judging the complexity of ethical issues associated with whistleblowing, although those are certainly important; instead we focus on the pragmatic lessons that have been learned about the whistleblowing process from systematic research about whistleblowers, managers, and retaliation.

Why Does Whistleblowing Matter to Managers and Organizations?

The organization incurs many potential costs when organizational wrongdoing occurs. These might be financial when revenue or funds are lost, such as in cases of employee embezzlement. They might be reputational, as when lawsuits are filed (e.g., over product recalls, employee discrimination cases, any of a myriad of alleged illegal behaviors). There may be increased visibility as a result of media reports of perceived wrongdoing or even mere improprieties. Such unwanted attention may lead to perceptions of low corporate social responsibility among stakeholders, or perhaps to additional regulations from lawmakers or enhanced scrutiny on the part of law enforcement agents. Even when firms are not bankrupted by allegations of wrongdoing, at least some employees will almost certainly react with reduced organizational commitment, which could lead to higher turnover rates and perhaps lower productivity. If managers will follow through with careful investigation, internal whistleblowers can help organizations avoid or reduce these kinds of costs by alerting managers to allegations of wrongdoing before they are made public.[4] Doing so has two benefits: (1) It resolves the current problem, hopefully before external stakeholders learn about it, and (2) it signals to employees that managers are open to dissent and wish to learn about problems before they escalate. Employees will then be more willing to share timely information about wrongdoing with managers in the future, thus preventing the nightmare of negative publicity in the media, social or otherwise.

The stories of three well-known whistleblowers who were selected as Persons of the Year by *Time* magazine in 2002 illustrate these issues.[5] Normally *Time* features only one Person of the Year, so putting three faces on the cover was unusual in and of itself. This was also the first time that whistleblowers had been selected for the honor, which is perhaps not surprising because the term "whistleblower" had been coined only 30 years before by Ralph Nader.[6] There have been many famous whistleblowers in subsequent years, but we begin with these three cases precisely because they were so notorious and because they are quite representative of the whistleblowing process.

All three whistleblowers were women and two were in the accounting areas of their organizations: Sherron Watkins of Enron, Coleen Rowley of the FBI, and Cynthia Cooper of WorldCom. Watkins, a vice-president of accounting, warned Enron chairman Kenneth Lay about improper accounting methods being used in several areas of the firm.[7] Congress subsequently released Watkins's letter to Lay as part of its investigation of Enron and the internal whistleblower was outed. Rowley, an FBI staff attorney in Minneapolis, sent a memo to FBI Director Robert Mueller about her concerns regarding Zacarias Moussaoui, one of the September 11 co-conspirators; these warnings to the FBI were ignored. She later testified to the Senate Judiciary Committee on some of the endemic problems facing the FBI and the intelligence community that she believed interfered with "connecting the dots."[8] Cooper, a vice-president of internal audit at WorldCom, informed its board that the company had covered up $3.8 billion in losses.[9] WorldCom CEO Bernard Ebbers and other executives eventually received prison sentences. The *Time* cover story focused attention on whistleblowers, and these cases – among others – led to legal and social changes; all three whistleblowers were also affected, as they left their organizations (Rowley) or their firms went bankrupt (Watkins and Cooper). We begin with these three older cases because they typify key aspects of the whistleblowing process that we will consider as follows:

- All whistleblowing cases involve multiple parties, including one or more wrongdoers, whistleblowers, and complaint recipients (e.g., internal or external auditors) who receive the whistleblower's allegation of wrongdoing.
- The vast majority of whistleblowers start by reporting the wrongdoing internally to the organization, often to their direct manager, and use external channels only if the internal reports prove unsatisfactory.

• Many whistleblowers find their experiences difficult, although not all suffer retaliation.

Where Does Whistleblowing Happen?

The short answer to this question is: in all kinds of organizations. Wrongdoing happens everywhere and will probably come to an organization near you sometime in your managerial lifetime. Of course, rates of wrongdoing, whistleblowing, and retaliation vary over time, industry, type of job, and type of organization, as we will discuss. But the fact is that wrongdoing and therefore whistleblowing can happen in the best managed of organizations. One employee intent on personal but illegitimate gain may cause such events to unfold, as may one employee who inadvertently or unwittingly engages in behavior that offends or harms other employees. The employee who knowingly engages in cover-up (e.g., of defective parts or products) in order to protect the firm is also engaging in wrongdoing, even if that individual's motivations are altruistic. In short, the motivations that cause employees to engage in wrongdoing – whether in support of themselves, their work unit, or the entire organization – are varied and unpredictable. For example, in the case of GM's recent problems with faulty ignition switches, many employees and engineers seem to have noticed the safety issue but did not report it to anyone, for reasons that remain unclear.[10] Only when multiple deaths were reported did GM recall the faulty switches. As a result, GM CEO Mary Barra fired 15 employees for not reporting the problem.

As with wrongdoers, the motivations of whistleblowers are diverse and difficult to anticipate. All kinds of organization members engage in whistleblowing, for different reasons and under different circumstances. As we will explain, whistleblowers tend *not* to be disloyal employees out to harm the organization. Often, they are the long-term and loyal employees who care most about their organizations and are trying to protect them from continuing on a dangerous path. What we have learned from consistent research findings over many years is that whistleblowers are made, not born; they are normal employees who find themselves in the wrong place at the wrong time and therefore observe events that they believe are wrongful, and want to share that information with someone who can put a stop to the events.[11]

In almost all cases, employees first blow the whistle internally, usually to their direct supervisor or other managers.[12] Whistleblowers then move to external whistleblowing only in rare cases, usually if the internal whistleblowing was unsuccessful or produced reprisal. Again, we will present the numbers to document this statement.

In summary: Wrongdoing can happen anywhere; whistleblowing often follows; and wrongdoing is usually reported internally first, giving managers a great opportunity to respond to the allegations of wrongdoing. This response may involve proving to whistleblowers that the events they thought they observed were not actually wrongful, or it may mean dealing with actual wrongdoing in a way that resolves the current problem and prevents future actions. It is critical that managers understand their response will influence what whistleblowers do next: If whistleblowers feel their concerns have not been heard or dealt with, they are more likely to take their case to the media or to law enforcement, as illustrated by Kenneth Kendrick's actions. Retaliation against the whistleblower also increases the chance that the employee will go public with the information.[13] This may be counterintuitive to managers' expectations, but again, this effect has been well documented by research. Before discussing this, however, we spend some time defining "whistleblowing." This is a term fraught with ambiguity; only by explaining our working definition will we be able to move ahead to discuss the research results based on this definition.

What Is Whistleblowing?

Much of the social science research concerning whistleblowing has used a standard definition,[14] which we developed in the early 1980s[15] because we found that the media were using varying definitions which could lead to imprecision and confusion in usage. Whistleblowing has subsequently been conceptually defined and operationally measured fairly consistently by researchers; as a result, we can draw direct conclusions about whistleblowing and whistleblowers. Formally, we define whistleblowing as: "The disclosure by organization members (former or current) of illegal, immoral, or illegitimate practices under the control of their employers, to persons or organizations that may be able to effect action."[16]

For example, journalists often limit their use of the term "whistleblowing" to the reporting of wrongdoing through external channels (e.g., the media or law enforcement). In contrast, researchers have used a broad definition including both internal and external whistleblowers so that their actions might be compared empirically. Carefully designed field studies of actual whistleblowers have shown that most whistleblowers use internal channels first.[17] Only a small number of these individuals go on to subsequently use external channels, and this due to the response they receive from the managers to whom they report the wrongdoing. For example, the Ethics Resource Center surveyed thousands of mostly private sector employees and found that only 18 percent ever used external channels for reporting wrongdoing and 84 percent of all employees did so only after reporting internally first.[18] We will discuss the reasons for this. This information would not have been known if researchers had focused only on external whistleblowers.

This definition also limits the specification of whistleblowers to current employees such as Sherron Watkins at Enron[19] or former employees such as Sally Ride, who no longer worked for NASA at the time she reported her concerns about its problematic operations,[20] or Edward Snowden, who no longer worked for the NSA (but instead worked for an NSA contractor) when he went public with information about its surveillance programs.[21] Of course, organizational wrongdoing may be reported by outsiders rather than insiders,[22] but in actuality insiders are more likely to have clear information about wrongdoing in an age when organizational operations are more complex and often more hidden than in the past. We do not include outsiders (e.g., journalists) in our definition of whistleblowers because they cannot be subject to the same kinds of organizational response (e.g., retaliation or firing) that may confront whistleblowers who are current or former employees of an organization. Perhaps the quintessential insider was Dr. Jeff Wigand, a scientist who blew the whistle on the use of addictive additives at Brown and Williamson, a large firm in the tobacco industry.[23] The 1999 feature film *The Insider*, starring Russell Crowe, told the story of Wigand, who tried to persuade top management at Brown and Williamson to remove the chemicals Wigand believed had been added to enhance the addictive effects of nicotine – and was fired for his efforts. Subsequently, Wigand discussed his concerns on *60 Minutes* despite threats of reprisal. It is unlikely that anyone other than an employee or former employee would have been able to access the information Wigand learned about in his job; even if an outsider had gained this sort of sensitive information, he/she would not have been subject to the pressures Brown and Williamson could bring to bear on Wigand as a former employee, who still relied on health insurance benefits from the firm as part of his severance package – and was threatened with discontinuation of the benefits if he went public with his allegations. This case illustrates why it is important to distinguish insiders from outsiders when studying whistleblowers.

According to our definition, the purpose of whistleblowing is to get the wrongdoing stopped by reporting it to someone (internal or external) with the authority or power to make this happen. Thus, whistleblowing differs from what is sometimes referred to as "employee voice," which occurs when employees recommend changes in the organization with the intent to improve operations or otherwise benefit the organization. . . .

Who Blows the Whistle and When Do They Do So?

Studies indicate that while most employees do not observe wrongdoing in their organizations in a given year, some clearly do, and this may be higher in organizations where whistleblowing is not encouraged either by legal means or by the organization's culture. Moreover, most employees who observe wrongdoing do not blow the whistle. Why is this?

Firstly, fear of retaliation is part of the story. The rates of whistleblowing in US federal agencies increased when employees gained greater protection under the law from reprisal following whistleblowing. This is not to say that all whistleblowers avoided retaliation. In fact, as the rate of whistleblowing increased among US federal employees who observed wrongdoing, so did the one-year rate of retaliation among those whistleblowers who were not anonymous – from 16 percent in 1980 to 21 percent in 1983 to 33 percent in 1992.[24] The two-year rate in Australia in 2005 was 22 percent among state and federal employees.[25]

Even though employees of the US government receive some protection from firing or the most serious of reprisals, they often suffer other punishments. For example, Peter Van Buren, an employee of the Foreign Service for 23 years, reported wasteful spending in Iraq in his book *We Meant Well*, which had been cleared by the State Department for publication; subsequently, however, Van Buren lost his security clearance and was told to work from home, telecommuting on a job that had no real duties. He joined the ranks of the "hallwalkers": employees of government agencies who effectively lose the right to execute their jobs and instead lose their desks and wander the halls of their agencies or work from home.[26] Presumably, the rate of retaliation would be higher among employees of business firms or nonprofits, as this group does not enjoy the same types of legal protection from reprisal as do government employees, as we will discuss.

But this is not the whole story because employees who observe wrongdoing and choose to blow the whistle differ somewhat from employees who choose not to blow the whistle. Based on results from multiple studies, they tend to be older, with more years of education and of service to the organization; they are more likely to be supervisors and have higher pay levels; and they say that they have both knowledge of appropriate internal channels for reporting wrongdoing and a feeling of responsibility for reporting wrongdoing.[27]

Secondly, the conditions matter; in fact, they may be even more important than the characteristics of the employee in distinguishing those who choose to blow the whistle from those who do not. Specifically, the choice to blow the whistle is correlated with the seriousness of the observed wrongdoing, the strength of evidence of wrongdoing, having supportive supervisors, and working in an organization whose culture is supportive of whistleblowing.[28] Employees who observe wrongdoing under these conditions are more likely to blow the whistle than are other employees, regardless of their own personal characteristics. In short, employees tend to report wrongdoing when they think it is especially egregious and they are quite sure that what they observed was actually wrongful behavior; they tend not to blow the whistle when the wrongdoing seems minor or when their evidence is weak. Furthermore, employees report wrongdoing when they think that supervisors want to learn about the wrongdoing, presumably in order to make changes if changes are warranted. When asked why they had not reported wrongdoing they had observed, employees most frequently answered that it was because they knew their managers could not or would not make changes and the wrongdoing would continue unabated; the second most frequent response was that they feared reprisal.[29] In sum, if managers want to learn about wrongdoing from internal whistleblowers, and not in the media, there are specific steps to be taken in order to encourage employees to provide this information rather than go public with it. Those steps are clear:

- provide support for internal whistleblowers;
- investigate allegations of wrongdoing and share the results of the investigation with employees; and
- do not allow reprisal against internal whistleblowers because it sends the signal that information from employees is not valued.

When and Why Do Whistleblowers Suffer Reprisal?

As indicated previously, most whistleblowers in random samples of employees from known organizations do not suffer reprisal, contrary to the picture that may be presented in media reports of individual whistleblowers – almost all of whom seem to have been the victims of retaliation. But this is one area in which the numbers may lead to misleading conclusions, because even though the rate of retaliation may be low, the consequences appear significant.

Once again, definitions matter. Retaliation has been defined as "undesirable action taken against a whistleblower – and in direct response to the whistleblowing – who reported wrongdoing internally (i.e., within the organization) or externally (i.e., outside the organization)."[30] Retaliation may take many forms in addition to outright firing. For example, at a large military base where both civilian and military employees completed an anonymous questionnaire with a checklist of 22 types of reprisal, the most common forms of retaliation were poor performance appraisal (15 percent), tighter scrutiny of daily activities by management (14 percent), and verbal harassment or intimidation (12 percent). None of the employees reported firing, demotion, or suspension, suggesting that managers turned to more creative forms of reprisal when their options were constrained by regulation or managerial practice.[31]

Interestingly, retaliation in most studies tended to occur when the wrongdoing reported was serious – precisely when employees were most likely to blow the whistle. Retaliation also tended to be correlated with low support from managers and a culture unsupportive of whistleblowing. Finally, in several studies, retaliation was correlated with external whistleblowing.[32] It should be recalled that whistleblowers rarely turn to external channels and usually do so only after they have first used internal channels for reporting the wrongdoing. As we noted, this means that in many cases the process plays out in three steps:

1. The employee reports the wrongdoing internally.
2. The manager retaliates against the whistleblower.
3. The whistleblower then reports the wrongdoing externally, in the media, to the union, or to law enforcement.

Managers who think they can circumvent the process by retaliating against the internal whistleblower, and thereby discouraging further action, may in fact achieve just the opposite. Based on findings from past research on whistleblowers, internal whistleblowers who suffer reprisal are likely to then report the wrongdoing externally. Clearly, managers who do not want to read negative publicity about their organization in the media should prevent wrongdoing; but if or when wrongdoing occurs, they may still avoid unwanted notoriety if they take the whistleblower seriously, investigate the allegations, and prevent supervisors from engaging in reprisal against the whistleblower.

Increasingly, US employees of private firms – and not just government workers – are being offered legal protection from retaliation or even a bounty for reporting wrongdoing. For example, Cheryl Eckard warned her senior managers at GlaxoSmithKline that defective drugs were being produced at the company's plant in Puerto Rico.

Instead of resolving the problems, they fired her. Eckard filed a lawsuit. Ultimately, GlaxoSmithKline paid $750 million to the US government to settle criminal and civil complaints that the company knowingly sold contaminated drugs; of this amount, Eckard received $96 million.[33] Federal laws protect some employees of private firms from retaliation when they report some types of wrongdoing;[34] for example, employees who report safety problems to OSHA are explicitly protected from retaliation.[35] In some situations, such as Eckard's, the federal regulations also provide a bounty or reward to whistle-blowers who are successful in helping the US government recover funds lost to fraud or abuse, especially through the SEC and Sarbanes–Oxley regulations.[36] As of 2011, 49 states offered protection from retaliation against whistle-blowers under some conditions,[37] but the variation among states has historically been huge; for example, in some states whistleblowers must first report internally in order to enjoy protection from reprisal, but in others the opposite is true.[38] The laws are changing quickly and in ways that make retaliation against whistleblowers much riskier for managers.

Conclusions

We read about sensational cases of organizational wrongdoing and contentious whistleblowing cases in media outlets and often assume that this is typical of all organizations and all whistleblowers. In fact, findings from systematic social science research using random samples of employees from specified organizations, completed over the past 30 years, have been remarkably consistent and imply specific recommendations for managers. Many managers will at some point observe wrongdoing, and some will blow the whistle themselves – or they will serve as the official complaint recipient when one of their subordinates or colleagues wants to report wrongdoing in the organization. Either way, managers who know something about the typical whistleblowing process will be forewarned and forearmed.

Usually, whistleblowers are *not* malcontents seeking to spread negative rumors about the firm or organization; they are employees who think they have observed serious wrongdoing and would like to see it stopped – and in most cases they believe their bosses will thank them for bringing forward this vital piece of information. The majority of employees who observe wrongdoing will not report it, but they tend to do so if the wrongdoing is serious, the evidence is clear, and management provides a culture that is supportive of hearing and acknowledging bad news. Most whistleblowers do not suffer reprisal, but those who do often

make their allegations public; again, this is most likely when the wrongdoing observed is especially serious or if the reporting employee thinks that management is not supportive of whistleblowers (perhaps rightly so, because they were after all the victims of retaliation). To avoid external whistleblowing, which entails all sorts of costs for the organization, managers may take clear, sometimes uncomfortable actions:

- Listen to employees who allege wrongdoing and carefully investigate the allegations.
- Make the results of the investigation known to those who were aware of the alleged wrongdoing, whether this is a small group of employees or all employees.
- Correct the problem if one is found and do so transparently (e.g., a change in policy or firing the wrongdoer).
- Treat whistleblowers with respect and care, and ensure that other co-workers and managers do not punish them for their actions.

These actions can increase the chance that information about organizational wrongdoing stays inside the organization, where it may be remedied, instead of being aired in social media, legal records, or other public venues.

Notes

1. D. Harris and K. Barrett, "Former Manager Says Peanut Plant Complaints Ignored," *ABC News* (February 16, 2009). Retrieved from http://abcnews.go.com/GMA/story?id=6888169.
2. G. Goetz, "Peanut Corporation of America from Inception to Indictment: A Timeline," *Food Safety News* (February 22, 2013). Retrieved from www.foodsafetynews.com/2013/02/peanut-corporation-of-america-from-inception-to-indictment-a-timeline/#.VbknGvlVhHw.
3. M. Basu, "28 Years for Salmonella: Peanut Exec Gets Groundbreaking Sentence," *CNN.com* (September 22, 2015). Retrieved from www.cnn.com/2015/09/21/us/salmonella-peanut-exec-sentenced/index.html.
4. M. P. Miceli, J. P. Near, and T. M. Dworkin, *Whistle-Blowing in Organizations* (New York: Psychology Press, 2008).
5. R. Lacayo and A. Ripley, "Persons of the Year 2002: Cynthia Cooper, Coleen Rowley, and Sherron Watkins," *Time* 160 (December 30, 2002): 30–33.
6. R. Nader, P. J. Petkas, and K. Blackwell, *Whistle-Blowing: The Report on the Conference on Professional Responsibility* (New York: Grossman, 1972).
7. G. Beenen and J. Pinto, "Resisting Organizational-Level Corruption: An Interview with Sherron Watkins," *Academy of Management Learning and Education* 8, no. 2 (2009): 275–89.
8. Lacayo and Ripley, "Persons of the Year 2002."

9. C. Cooper, *Extraordinary Circumstances: The Journey of a Corporate Whistleblower* (Hoboken, NJ: John Wiley & Sons, 2008).

10. B. Kennedy, "CEO Mary Barra Outlines GM's 'Enormously Painful' Ignition Switch Recall Report," *Yahoo! Finance* (June 5, 2014). Retrieved from http://finance.yahoo.com/news/ceo-mary-barra-outlines-gms-184629164.html.

11. J. P. Near and M. P. Miceli, "Whistle-Blowing: Myth and Reality," *Journal of Management* 22, no. 3 (1996): 507–26.

12. Miceli et al., *Whistle-Blowing in Organizations.*

13. Ibid.

14. G. King, III, "The Effects of Interpersonal Closeness and Issue Seriousness on Blowing the Whistle," *Journal of Business Communication* 34, no. 4 (1997): 419–36.

15. M. P. Miceli and J. P. Near, "The Relationship among Beliefs, Organizational Position, and Whistle-Blowing Status: A Discriminant Analysis," *Academy of Management Journal* 27, no. 4 (1984): 687–705; J. P. Near and M. P. Miceli, "Organizational Dissidence: The Case of Whistle-Blowing," *Journal of Business Ethics* 4, no. 1 (1985): 1–16.

16. Near and Miceli, "Organizational Dissidence," p. 4.

17. A. J. Brown, *Whistleblowing in the Australian Public Sector: Enhancing the Theory and Practice of Internal Witness Management in Public Sector Organizations.* Australia and New Zealand School of Government Research Series (Canberra: ANU E-Press, 2008); Ethics Resource Center, *Inside the Mind of a Whistleblower: A Supplemental Report of the 2011 National Business Ethics Survey* (2012). Retrieved from www.corporatecomplianceinsights.com/wp-content/uploads/2012/05/inside-the-mind-of-a-whistleblower-NBES.pdf; Miceli et al., *Whistle-Blowing in Organizations.*

18. Ethics Resource Center, *Inside the Mind of a Whistleblower.*

19. Beenen and Pinto, "Resisting Organizational-Level Corruption."

20. L. Sherr, *Sally Ride: America's First Woman in Space* (New York: Simon & Schuster, 2014).

21. M. Scherer, "Edward Snowden, The Dark Prophet," *Time* (December 11, 2013). Retrieved from http://poy.time.com/2013/12/11/runner-up-edward-snowden-the-dark-prophet/.

22. M. P. Miceli, S. Dreyfus, and J. P. Near, "Outsider 'Whistle-Blowers': Conceptualising and Distinguishing Bell-Ringing Behavior," in *International Handbook on Whistle-Blowing Research*, ed. A. J. Brown, D. Lewis, R. Moberly, and W. Vandekerckhove (Cheltenham: Edward Elgar, 2014), pp. 71–84.

23. A. Armenakis, "Making a Difference by Speaking Out: Jeff Wigand Says Exactly What's on His Mind," *Journal of Management Inquiry* 13, no. 4 (2004): 355–62; A. Ripley, "Ten Questions for Jeffrey Wigand," *Time* 165, no. 7 (2005): 8.

24. J. P. Near and M. P. Miceli, "Wrongdoing, Whistle-Blowing, and Retaliation in the U.S. Government: What Have Researchers Learned from the Merit Systems Protection Board (MSPB) Survey Results?," *Review of Public Personnel Administration* 28, no. 3 (2008): 263–81.

25. Brown, *Whistleblowing in the Australian Public Sector.*

26. G. Raz, "'Hallwalkers': The Ghosts of the State Department." Radio broadcast. *All Things Considered*, 2012. Washington, DC National Public Radio.

27. Miceli et al., *Whistle-Blowing in Organizations.*

28. Ibid.

29. J. P. Near, J. R. Van Scotter, M. T. Rehg, and M. P. Miceli, "Does Type of Wrongdoing Affect the Whistle-Blowing Process?," *Business Ethics Quarterly* 14, no. 2 (2004): 219–42.

30. M. T. Rehg, M. P. Miceli, J. P. Near, and J. R. Van Scotter, "Antecedents and Outcomes of Retaliation against Whistle-Blowers: Gender Difference, and Power Relationships," *Organization Science* 19, no. 2 (2008): 221–40 (p. 222).

31. Ibid.

32. Miceli et al., *Whistle-Blowing in Organizations.*

33. D. Meinert, "Whistle-Blowers: Threat or Asset?," *HR Magazine* 56, no. 4 (2011): 27–32.

34. J. Deschenaux, "Government Focus on Whistleblowers Impacts Private Sector" (August 14, 2012). Retrieved from Society for Human Resource Management website: www.shrm.org/legalissues/federalresources/pages/whistle-blowers-private-sector.aspx.

35. United States Department of Labor, *The Whistleblower Protection Programs* (2015). Retrieved from www.whistleblowers.gov/.

36. T. M. Dworkin, "SOX and Whistleblowing," *Michigan Law Review* 105, no. 8 (2007): 1757–80; Meinert, "Whistle-Blowers: Threat or Asset?"; A. Rose, "Better Bounty Hunting: How the SEC's New Whistleblower Program Changes the Securities Fraud Class Action Debate," *Northwestern University Law Review* 108, no. 4 (2014): 1235–302.

37. Meinert, "Whistle-Blowers: Threat or Asset?"

38. Miceli et al., *Whistle-Blowing in Organizations.*

LEGAL PERSPECTIVES

Superior Court of New Jersey, *Warthen v. Toms River Community Memorial Hospital* (1985)

Corrine Warthen, a registered nurse at Toms River Community Memorial Hospital, was terminated after 11 years of service. The grounds for termination were that nurse Warthen refused to dialyze a patient who was a double amputee and suffered from a number of ailments. Warthen based her refusal to dialyze on the following: On two previous occasions, she had to cease treatment because the patient suffered cardiac arrest and severe internal hemorrhaging during the dialysis procedure and the patient was terminally ill and the procedure was causing additional health complications. Warthen had asked to be, and had been, reassigned to avoid doing a procedure in a situation she considered morally, medically, and philosophically objectionable. Despite the initial reassignment, Warthen was again asked to dialyze the patient. In speaking with the treating physician she was told that the family wished him kept alive through dialysis and that he would not survive without it. The head nurse told Warthen she must do the procedure or be terminated. Warthen did refuse and was terminated as a result.

Warthen filed suit. Tom River Community Memorial Hospital then filed a motion for summary judgment, or dismissal, which was granted on the grounds that, while a nurse is permitted to have a personal moral judgment, "it does not rise to a public policy in the face of the general public policies that patients must be cared for in hospitals and patients must be treated basically by doctors and doctors' orders must be carried out." Warthen appealed, disputing the trial court's interpretation of the public policy issues.

Warthen argued that she was justified as a matter of law in bringing suit because the question of whether adherence to the Code for Nurses, a code of ethics of the American Nurses Association, constituted a public policy defense was a question of fact that should be decided by a jury. The Superior Court rejected this argument on the following grounds: (1) the issue of whether the Code for Nurses represented a clear expression of public policy did not present a genuine issue of material fact precluding summary judgment; (2) that the provision in the Code upon which Warthen relied – a provision that nurses provide services that respect human dignity – "should not be at the expense of the patient's life or contrary to the family's wishes; (3) the State Supreme Court has confirmed the State's basic interest in the preservation of life. This public policy mandate overrides any policy favoring the right of a nurse to refuse to participate in treatments she believes threatens human dignity; (4) the public cannot wonder whether a person will or will not receive treatment based on a nurse's personal ethical belief; and (5) that Warthen had justified her decision not to treat on moral, medical, and philosophical grounds rather than on the Code for Nurses. Thus the original judgment *against* Warthen was affirmed.

Superior Court of New Jersey, *Potter v. Village Bank of New Jersey* (1988)

Dale J. Potter became president and chairman of the board of Village Bank of New Jersey in 1982. During the course of his work, he noted that many cash deposits between $8,000 and $9,000 were made into the accounts of several officers, including the president of Em Kay Equities. Em Kay Holding Corporation (Em Kay) owned 93 percent of the stock of Village Bank. Em Kay itself was owned by the Em Kay group, Mory Kraselnick and Moises Kroitoro, headquartered in Panama City, Panama. On March 24, Potter learned that his job was being advertised in the *Wall Street Journal*. Potter confronted Kraselnick, only to be told that "he was not as outspoken and enthusiastic as I want you to be when you meet me." Seven days later on March 31, 1983 seven deposits of $9,000 each were made into accounts, including Kraselnick's, of Em Kay related companies. Potter suspected the laundering of money and called the New Jersey Commissioner of Banking to report the transactions. Before meeting with the Commissioner, another $50,000 in cash deposits were made. When Potter inquired, he was told they were lease payments. After meeting with the Commissioner, Potter was told to remain anonymous and that a bank examination would be undertaken. Bank audits began around the end of April or the beginning of May, 1983. In July Potter informed the board of Village Bank of the audits but did not inform them of his meetings with the Commissioner.

Sometime between July and December 1983 Potter informed the secretary to the board of directors of his meeting with the Commissioner. When confronted by an angry Kraselnick as to why Potter went to the Commissioner, Potter said, "I thought that it was drug money," and Kraselnick replied, "you're probably right." From that point on Potter felt that he was being isolated and not being allowed to efficiently run the bank. Potter was told that he was about to be fired and on May 22, 1984, Potter wrote a letter to Kraselnick indicating that he believed himself to be "de facto" fired and at this point to be "essentially terminated." Potter rejected a proposed settlement letter of

June 1, 1984 and when he and his attorney tried to attend the June 11 board meeting they were turned away.

A lawsuit ensued where it was determined that Potter had been wrongfully discharged and was awarded $50,000 in compensatory damages and $100,000 in punitive damages. The verdict was appealed to the New Jersey Supreme Court. In ruling to uphold the appeal on the grounds of a public policy protection for at-will employees, the Court said, "Potter's termination relates to the public policy designed to encourage citizens to report suspected criminal violations to the proper authorities in order to ensure proper enforcement of both state and federal penal laws . . . Nowhere in our society is the need for protection greater than in protecting well motivated citizens who blow the whistle on suspected white-collar and street-level criminal activities." Blowing the whistle on one or more bank directors suspected of laundering money from illegal activities protects employees, including bank presidents, from retaliatory discharge and permits them to recover economic and noneconomic losses.

CASES

Case 1: Uber's Ethical Leadership Vacuum

ROXANNE ROSS AND DENIS G. ARNOLD

Uber has grown into a $72 billion company just ten years after its inception. The company holds market dominance in ride sharing services and is one of the most valuable privately owned tech start-ups in the world. Uber serves as a virtual marketplace that matches its hundreds of thousands of drivers with millions of passengers using a sophisticated pricing algorithm that adjusts prices according to demand. Although Uber earns several billion dollars each year, the company is not yet profitable. In 2017 Uber's gross revenue was $37 billion while its net losses were $4.5 billion. Despite the losses, Uber's gross bookings multiplied twenty-fold in just three years and its valuation is based on the expectation that Uber will achieve profitability in the near future.

While Uber is known for its rapid expansion, the start-up is also known for a business model that has caused problems with key stakeholders. Major problems have arisen regarding driver welfare, passenger safety, poor customer service, poor driver support, and the sexual harassment of employees at Uber's corporate offices. Because of concerns about driver welfare, passenger safety, and regulatory compliance, Uber's services have been banned in some form (i.e., temporary, partial, or full suspension of operations) in many jurisdictions throughout the world.

Uber's problems are frequently attributed to the leadership of CEO Travis Kalanick. He is known to be personally combative and disdainful of others, to brag about sexual exploits, and to flout the law. Employees who have had experience with him generally have a negative view. In trying to persuade Kalanick to change his ways, Uber President Jeff Jones argued that the data showed that "Uber's riders and drivers viewed the company as made up of a bunch of greedy, self-centered jerks." For example, Kalanick was recorded in the back seat of an UberBlack during Superbowl weekend berating the driver for complaining about fares. Kalanick can be heard yelling at the driver, "Some people don't like to take responsibility for their own shit! They blame everything in their life on somebody else!"

The video was posted on the Internet and widely covered in the media.

Uber has a long history of lawsuits with its drivers regarding their treatment. Most of the tension is derived from Uber's classification of its drivers as independent contractors which greatly reduces labor costs for the company. Uber uses the contractor classification to recruit new members to their fleet with the slogan, "Be Your Own Boss." However, only half of the drivers surveyed by National Public Radio (n = 927) said they actually felt this statement rang true. One survey response stated that the only aspect of their job that drivers control is when they sign on and off. Former Department of Labor division head David Weil commented on Uber's driver classification as follows, "You know, I can't just declare a pigeon a duck because I think it should be a duck." He went on to say that the driver–company relationship looks like a traditional employee–employer relationship. Unlike other contract workers in the gig economy, Uber drivers do not decide the prices they charge or the services they offer. Because they are independent contractors, Uber drivers do not receive benefits that typical employees receive such as health insurance, disability insurance, and overtime pay. Unlike employees, they pay their own payroll taxes, insurance, and costs to operate a vehicle. Additionally, Uber bears significantly less risk when issues arise with drivers because of the contractor classification. Some estimates suggest that it would cost Uber an additional $4.1 billion annually (or $13 k per driver) to change the status of drivers to that of employees. The additional costs would be for insurance, workers' compensation, vacation time, social security, mileage reimbursement, and unemployment benefits.

Many lawsuits have also been filed against Uber by their passengers, mainly due to rider safety issues. Several passengers report being raped and assaulted by drivers. A woman in New Delhi was assaulted and raped by her driver, who had a history of sex crimes. Critics charge that Uber should have conducted a thorough background check that would have discovered his past. After the case was made public, an Uber executive illegally obtained the victim's medical records and shared them with Kalanick because of suspicions about her motives (the driver was later convicted and sentenced to life in prison). In West Hollywood, a woman was drugged by the free water provided in the vehicle and woke up naked in her apartment. Yet another account involved a woman in Boston being locked inside the driver's car and then asked for sex. Uber responded by giving her a $30 credit.

Uber drivers have fewer hurdles to clear than their taxi driver counterparts when it comes to background checks. The company's resistance to more stringent checks on drivers is thought to be due to concerns about slowing the driver onboarding process which facilitates rapid expansion. For several of the court proceedings regarding rider endangerment, Uber rejected responsibility for the drivers' acts, citing their contractor status to support their claim for attenuated liability. Some reports suggest there are thousands of customer complaints involving the words "rape" or "sexual assault." Uber conducted its own investigation and found 170 instances of some form of sexual misconduct between its drivers and passengers.

The list of constituents who reported problems with Uber grew when a former employee at Uber, software engineer Susan Fowler, wrote a blog post detailing widespread sexual harassment at Uber's corporate offices. Among other examples, Fowler explained that her manager requested to have sex with her on her first day under his supervision. Fowler brought the issue to Uber's Human Resource department, yet her complaints were dismissed because the manager was a "high performer." Uber hired a prominent law firm to investigate approximately 200 complaints regarding sexism and sexual harassment and confirmed the accounts of Fowler and other employees.

This turmoil led to Kalanick taking a leave of absence which evolved into the founder stepping down as CEO. Major Uber investors eventually decided the mistakes were intolerable and asked Kalanick to resign. At the time of Kalanick's departure, his net worth was valued at $6.7 billion.

Discussion Questions

1. Is Kalanick an ethical leader (effective + ethical) as defined by Ciulla? Why, or why not? Explain.

2. Is Kalanick an ethical leader (moral manager + moral person) as defined by Treviño and Nelson? Why, or why not? Explain.

3. Do you believe that the board provided appropriate oversight for Uber's CEO and the company itself? Why, or why not? If not, why might this have been the case? Explain.

4. Consider the situation at Uber under Kalanick. Would those firm behaviors cause you to not use Uber transportation? Why, or why not? Explain. Would you want to work for Uber? Why, or why not? Explain.

This case was written for classroom discussion and is based on the following sources: S. Gandel, "The Cost of Turning Uber Drivers into Employees: $4.1 Billion," *Fortune* (September 17, 2015). Retrieved June 22, 2017 from http://fortune.com/2015/09/17/ubernomics/.

H. Kelly, "Uber and its Never-Ending Stream of Lawsuits," *CNN* (August 11, 2016). Retrieved June 19, 2017 from https://money.cnn.com/2016/08/11/technology/uber-lawsuits/.

E. Grant Simran Khosla, "Here's Everywhere Uber Is Banned around the World" (April 8, 2015). Retrieved June 24, 2017 from www.businessinsider.com/heres-everywhere-uber-is-banned-around-the-world-2015–4.

A. Lashinsky, "How Having Female Editors Shaped My Book on Uber," *Fortune* (May 23, 2017). Retrieved June 22, 2017 from https://fortune.com/2017/05/23/uber-book-sexual-harassment/.

M. Isaac and S. Chira, "David Bonderman Resigns from Uber Board after Sexist Remark," *The New York Times* (June 13, 2017). Retrieved from www.nytimes.com/2017/06/13/technology/uber-sexual-harassment-huffington-bonderman.html.

E. Newcomer, "Uber CEO Travis Kalanick Has Resigned," *Bloomberg.com* (June 21, 2017). Retrieved from www.bloomberg.com/news/articles/2017-06-21/uber-chief-executive-travis-kalanick-resigns-ny-times-reports.

E. Newcomer, "Uber, Lifting Financial Veil, Says Sales Growth Outpaces Losses," *Bloomberg.com* (April 14, 2017). Retrieved from www.bloomberg.com/news/articles/2017–04-14/embattled-uber-reports-strong-sales-growth-as-losses-continue.

A. Shahani, "The Faceless Boss: A Look into the Uber Driver Workplace," *National Public Radio* (June 9, 2017). Retrieved June 19, 2017 from www.npr.org/sections/alltechconsidered/2017/06/09/531642304/the-faceless-boss-a-look-into-the-uber-driver-workplace; www.bloomberg.com/opinion/articles/2017-03-16/uber-needs-to-get-real-about-that-69-billion-price-tag.

Eric Newcomer and Brad Stone, "The Fall of Travis Kalanick Was a Lot Weirder and Darker than You Thought," *Businessweek* (January 18, 2018).

Case 2: **The Bachelor Party**

DENIS G. ARNOLD

Sam recently graduated and was thrilled to accept a job on the team of a charismatic mutual fund manager at a large investment firm that manages billions of dollars in mutual funds and other investments for individuals, companies, universities, and public pension funds. Gordon, the charismatic manager, is one of the most successful fund managers at the firm. A few months after Sam started working at the company, Gordon invited him and other male co-workers in his group to his bachelor party. Their female co-workers were not invited. Sam agreed to go. On Friday, Sam, Gordon, and a group of their male colleagues took a flight to Miami on a private jet where they were picked up in a limo by several Wall Street traders with whom their company does business. The traders execute buy and sell orders for the mutual funds under Gordon's management. Sam knows that the traders are not the most competitive from the standpoint of prompt execution of trades or cost, but they are friendly and have a reputation as great hosts. Sam also knows that mutual fund companies are barred by SEC regulations from accepting gifts from traders, since the choice of traders is supposed to be governed by the best interests of investors. There is also a self-imposed, $100 limit at the company on the value of gifts to employees. But Gordon and other co-workers have gone on other junkets paid for by traders in the past, so he assumes it's okay. Besides, he's already in Miami.

The Wall Street traders let everyone know how pleased they are that their company is hosting the party. Everyone ends up at a private harbor where they board a yacht. On board the yacht are several young women who are pretty clearly paid "escorts" or prostitutes. The yacht is stocked with fine food, alcohol, and the drug ecstasy. After a few hours, the yacht leaves the dock and cruises about a half-mile offshore. A good time is had by all and some business deals are done with the paperwork to be done later.

When Sam gets back to town and is in the comfort of his own apartment, he begins to reflect on the past weekend. It was a great time, but he wonders what will happen if people outside Gordon's group find out. On Tuesday he has lunch with his college friend, Laura, who works for a traditional, "straitlaced," and "by-the-book" fund manager at the same firm. He tells her about the party, and asks what she thinks. Laura points out that it is clearly stated in the company code of conduct that legal compliance is expected, that taking gifts from traders is prohibited, and that violations should be reported to supervisors. She also reports that nothing like this takes place in her group at the firm. Sam points out that Gordon is his supervisor. He also points out that the same traders he partied with told him that they gave a senior executive at the firm hard-to-get tickets to sporting events like the US Open and the Ryder Cup on several occasions.

Discussion Questions

1. What, if anything, is ethically or legally objectionable about Sam's actions in relation to his work at the mutual fund company? Explain.
2. Should Sam report the party to someone at the company? To the SEC? Why, or why not? Explain.
3. Should Laura report what she has heard about the party to her boss? To someone else? Why, or why not? Explain.
4. Using resources from Treviño and Nelson, how would you characterize the ethical culture and ethics programs at this company? Explain.

Case 3: **Wells Fargo's Corporate Culture**

ROXANNE ROSS AND DENIS G. ARNOLD

Wells Fargo is a Fortune 100 company and one of the world's largest banks, with $2 trillion in assets and over 250,000 employees. Its 2017 revenue was $88.4 billion (non-interest income of $38.8 billion) with net income of $22.2 billion. The US Consumer Financial Protection Bureau (CFPB) has found that the bank's employees opened millions of unauthorized accounts on behalf of unsuspecting customers. Evidence suggests that senior executives at Wells

Fargo were aware of the issue of the fake accounts long before the CFPB investigation. Employees opened more than 3.5 million sham bank and credit card accounts under customers' names without their knowledge. Forensic accounting investigations by independent auditors remain underway, and the number of fake accounts may prove much larger. Employees were creating the fraudulent accounts in order to meet unrealistic sales goals imposed on them by senior leadership in the Community Bank division. The employees were typically required to sell eight new banking products a day. For their January sales push, they were required to sell 20 new products daily. Wells Fargo customers had, on average, 6.7 different banking products – double the industry standard. As a result of the unauthorized accounts, customers were charged fees and had their credit scores impacted without their knowledge or consent. The scandal has resulted in significant damage to the bank's reputation and has cost millions of dollars in lost business, legal fees, and refunds. Over 5,300 employees have been fired, at least some for blowing the whistle on illegal activity.

Much of the blame for the scandal has been placed on John Stumpf, former Chairman and CEO of Wells Fargo, and Carrie Tolstedt, former head of the Community Banking division. Tolstedt was identified as the primary driver of the aggressive sales practices. Her inability, or unwillingness, to recognize the inherent flaws in her sales model was described in an internal report as contributing to the widespread use of deceptive and fraudulent practices by employees. As information regarding the scandal unfolded, Tolstedt is said to have hidden the number of employees who had been fired for creating fake accounts. Stumpf was criticized for his slow reactions to the cutthroat sales tactics, his lackadaisical approach to investigating claims of wrongdoing, and his failure to implement strong ethics and compliance programs at the bank. Both Stumpf and Tolstedt have denied wrongdoing.

During the time period that these activities occurred, the company's stock rose 67 percent. By the time the public became aware of the scandal, Tolstedt was on the verge of retiring with over $124 million in stock options and was estimated to have made over $200 million. Before the scandal came to light, Stumpf was paid an annual salary of $19.3 million, but the bulk of his compensation came in the form of stock options. As the investigation into the fraudulent accounts proceeded, and before the CFPB concluded its initial investigation, Stumpf exercised Wells Fargo stock options worth $65.4 million. He retains 2.5 million shares estimated to be valued at $137 million as well as millions of dollars in additional retirement benefits.

In a report commissioned by the board, and based on interviews with 100 current and former employees and the review of millions of internal documents, a prominent law firm found that decentralized management that gave Tolstedt near complete authority over the Community Bank was a major reason why the problem went unaddressed. According to the report, "She resisted and rejected the near unanimous view of senior regional bank leaders that the sales goals were unreasonable and led to negative outcomes and improper behavior." Stumpf himself was warned by employees and customers for years about the sales practices but took no action. In response to their part in the misconduct, the bank's board of directors used "claw back" provisions in their contracts to require that Stumpf surrender $69 million in compensation and that Tolstedt surrender $67 million in compensation.

The culture of the consumer banking division at Wells Fargo during Tolstedt's leadership has been described as toxic by investigators and employees alike. Reports have surfaced of tearful employees, who did not want to engage in fraud, cracking under the pressure of formal warnings and closed door meetings with managers. One employee describes being physically ill from stress while at work. Some of the employees who created fake accounts would target immigrants who struggled with the English language or elderly adults with memory problems. Other employees moved money in and out of fake accounts to avoid suspicion. For their sales push in January, legitimate customer requests for new accounts that should have been opened in December were sometimes stockpiled for weeks to help employees meet their goal of 20 new products a day. Employees describe the constant threat of being fired for failing to meet the required daily goals and being told to meet those goals by any means necessary.

The Federal Sentencing Guidelines for Organizations require all organizations to have ethics and compliance programs proportional to their size and resources. Many employees who reported consumer fraud internally claim that they were fired as a result. The Occupational Safety and Health Administration (OSHA) has stated that there is evidence that Wells Fargo broke federal law for firing whistleblowers. Human resources personnel at the bank verified that the bank purposefully retaliated against whistleblowers who tried to alert company leaders about fraudulent practices. According to a former employee, whistleblowers were closely monitored after calling the internal ethics hotline so that they could be fired later for other reasons, such as arriving a few minutes late to work. One employee described reporting the fake accounts to the internal ethics hotline after a lack of response from reporting through other internal channels. Shortly after calling the ethics hotline, the employee was terminated for inappropriate workplace behavior. OSHA's investigators report that there is no compelling evidence that this was the actual reason for the firing. One whistleblower reported both to the internal ethics hotline and human resources that he had been instructed by his manager to open unwarranted debit cards and secretly enroll customers in online banking. Eight days later, the whistleblower was fired for being late. Other employees have come forward to report that they were similarly retaliated against for whistleblowing.

The circumstances surrounding whistleblower retaliation are further complicated by required U5 reports (Uniform Termination Notice for Securities Industry Registration) that must be filed when certain bank employees leave their position. These reports serve as an inter-organization employee database used to relay information about employees between banks. Negative comments regarding the reasons an employee left or was fired are visible to other banks and essentially serve to blacklist employees from banking jobs. Wells Fargo employees stated that these forms were used as a technique to discourage whistleblowers from coming forward. These claims coincide with suspect information on the forms regarding the reasons whistleblowers had been fired. The fake account issue appears to have been downplayed on the forms, indicating intentional concealment by the bank's management. An internal report dated over a decade earlier foreshadowed the problem of the fraudulent accounts. The report stated that there was evidence of employees tampering with customers' accounts to meet sales goals. Despite knowledge of the creation of such fake accounts, no systematic changes occurred between the earlier report and when the scandal first came to light in 2016 aside from the firing of low-level employees.

Subsequent investigations revealed that Wells Fargo permitted many other forms of extracting fees from customers via illegitimate means. These included:

1. Charging between 570,000 and 800,000 automobile loan borrowers for auto insurance they did not need (because borrowers already had insurance of their own). The insurance charges contributed to approximately 20,000–25,000 wrongful vehicle repossessions, including many active duty military personnel.
2. Charging 110,000 mortgage customers approximately $98 million in illegitimate fees to extend guaranteed interest rates until the sale of a home was finalized. In these cases, the delay in closing the home sale was primarily caused by Well Fargo itself. The deceptive practice only came to light after four former Wells Fargo employees notified Congress in a letter.
3. Selling tens of millions of dollars of add-on services to consumers utilizing deceptive techniques. Federal investigators maintain that consumers did not fully understand or know how to use the products and that the billing was opaque or hidden. These products included pet insurance, legal services, home warranties, and debt-protection.[1]
4. Selling investment products that wealth advisors did not understand and that were almost guaranteed to result in losses for clients. Representatives from Wells Fargo Advisors, the bank's brokerage and wealth management unit, recommended "volatility-linked" products that regulators say the advisors did not understand. The products were sold to clients as a hedge against a downturn in markets, when in fact they were never intended for this purpose or even for retail sale. One of the most popular options lost 99.7 percent of its value since it was introduced in 2009. "It is absolutely evil. Obviously, Wells Fargo had no idea what they were selling," said Joe Saluzzi, co-head of trading at Themis Trading. Regulators ordered the bank to repay $3.4 million to investors.

Patricia McCoy, former official at the CFPB, summarized the views of many critics when she said, "Wells Fargo had a business model, until all of this came to light, that emphasized generating fees charged to consumers under duplicitous circumstances simply for the sake of padding revenue."

In the second quarter of 2018 Wells Fargo took a $619 million charge against earnings to refund customers it overcharged. The bank faces multiple lawsuits filed on behalf of consumers, employees, and shareholders. Thus far it has settled class-action lawsuits with customers for $142 million and with shareholders for $480 million. Among those being sued are the board of directors. The board has taken the highly unusual step of hiring lobbyists to represent the board in Washington in the face of Congressional investigations. It has spent $600,000 of corporate funds to represent itself before Congress. Lawyers representing current and former executives argue that they should not be held personally liable for the fraudulent and illegal practices. In denying their claim, US District Judge John Tigar wrote that it was reasonable to believe that "senior executives knew about, or at least recklessly turned a blind eye to, the stream of red flags" and has permitted the lawsuits to go forward.

The CFPB initially fined Wells Fargo $185 million for the fake accounts. Later, the CFPB and the Office of the

Comptroller of the Currency reached a $1 billion settlement with the bank for its failure to implement adequate ethics and compliance programs (often referred to as "risk management" programs in the financial services industry). Subsequently, the Department of Justice reached a $2.09 billion settlement with the bank for selling mortgage-backed securities that misstated the income of borrowers and mispresented the quality of the products. These practices were widespread in the years preceding the financial crisis of 2008–2009 and other banks have paid similar penalties. In addition, as a direct result of the activities described above, the Federal Reserve Board of Governors' Division of Banking Supervision and Regulation stated that in the wake of "ineffective oversight" it was replacing four of the 16 directors from the board (eight current board members were holdovers from when the scandal came to public light). It also announced that it was freezing the amount of assets the bank could have on its books at the current level of approximately $2 trillion, until the bank could demonstrate that it has in place an effective ethics and compliance program consistent with its size and scope. The restrictions prevent the bank from growing and keeping pace with its peers. As a direct result of reputational harm and financial costs of misconduct, analysts believe that share values of Wells Fargo are performing well below the share value of peer banks. Numerous federal and state investigations into the bank's past practices are continuing.

Note

1. The *Wall Street Journal* reports that Bank of America and Citigroup paid more than $700 million each to settle similar claims with regulators in 2014 and 2015.

Discussion Questions

1. How would you describe the corporate culture at Well Fargo? Explain.
2. Why do you believe the fake accounts scam persisted so long at Wells Fargo? Explain.
3. What roles did leaders play in misconduct at Wells Fargo? Explain.
4. If you were to help select new executive leadership for Wells Fargo, what traits or qualities would you look for in candidates (aside from business acumen)?
5. If you were asked to implement new management systems at Wells Fargo, what might you want to change? Explain.

This case was written by Roxanne Ross and Denis G. Arnold for the purposes of classroom discussion. It is based on the following sources: C. Arnold, "Former Wells Fargo Employees Describe Toxic Sales Culture, Even at HQ," *National Public Radio* (October 4, 2016). Retrieved May 23, 2017 from www.npr.org/ 2016/10/04/496508361/former-wells-fargo-employees-describe-toxic-sales-culture-even-at-hq.

B. Chappell, "Wells Fargo Claws Back $75 Million More from 2 Executives over Fake Accounts," *National Public Radio* (April 10, 2017). Retrieved May 23, 2017 from www.npr.org/sections/thetwo-way/2017/04/10/523254069/wells-fargo-claws-back-75-million-more-from-2-executives-over-fake-accounts.

J. A. Kingson and S. Cowley (April 10, 2017). "Wells Fargo to Claw Back $75 Million from 2 Former Executives Accounts," *The New York Times* (April 10, 2017). Retrieved May 23, 2017 from www.nytimes.com/2017/04/10/business/wells-fargo-pay-executives-accounts-scandal.html.

S. Cowley, "Wells Fargo Faces Scrutiny for Black Marks on Ex-Employee Files," *The New York Times* (November 3, 2016). Retrieved May 23, 2017 from www.nytimes.com/2016/11/04/business/dealbook/wells-fargo-faces-scrutiny-for-black-marks-on-ex-employee-files.html.

M. Egan, "Wells Fargo Workers: I Called the Ethics Line and Was Fired," *CNN Money* (September 21, 2016). Retrieved May 24, 2017 from https://money.cnn.com/2016/09/21/investing/wells-fargo-fired-workers-retaliation-fake-accounts/index.html.

M. Egan, "Wells Fargo's Whistleblower Problem Worsens," *CNN Money* (April 6, 2017). Retrieved May 23, 2017 from https://money.cnn.com/2017/04/06/investing/wells-fargo-whistleblower-retaliation-osha/index.html.

D. Ivory, "Wells Fargo's Regulator Admits It Missed Red Flags," *The New York Times* (April 19, 2017). Retrieved from www.nytimes.com/2017/04/19/business/dealbook/wells-fargo-fraud-office-of-comptroller-currency.html.

J. A. Kingson and S. Cowley, "At Wells Fargo, Crushing Pressure and Lax Oversight Produced a Scandal," *The New York Times* (April 10, 2017). Retrieved from www.nytimes.com/2017/04/10/business/dealbook/11wells-fargo-account-scandal.html.

S. Cowley, "Wells Fargo Review Finds 1.4 Million More Suspect Accounts," *The New York Times* (August 31, 2017). Retrieved from www.nytimes.com/2017/08/31/business/dealbook/wells-fargo-accounts.html.

G. Morgenson, "Wells Fargo Forced Unwanted Auto Insurance on Borrowers," *The New York Times* (July 27, 2017). Retrieved August 1, 2017 from www.nytimes.com/2017/07/27/business/wells-fargo-unwanted-auto-insurance.html.

M. Eagan, "Wells Fargo Wrongly Hit Homebuyers with Fees to Lock in Mortgage Rates," *CNN Money* (October 4, 2017).

E. Glazer, "Wells Fargo's Latest Challenge: Refunds for Pet Insurance, Legal Services," *Wall Street Journal* (July 19, 2018).

M. Egan, "Wells Fargo Sold Dangerous Investments It Didn't Understand, Regulators Say," *CNN Money* (October 16, 2017).

M. Egan, "The Two-Year Wells Fargo Horror Story Just Won't End," *CNN Money* (September 7, 2018). Retrieved September 10, 2018 from https://money.cnn.com/2018/09/07/news/companies/wells-fargo-scandal-two-years/index.html.

Case 4: Shareholder Losses and Executive Gains: Bank of America's Acquisition of Merrill Lynch

REBECCA WATERS AND DENIS G. ARNOLD

Founded in 1914, Merrill Lynch had long been regarded as a leader and mainstay in the financial markets. In the 1990s and 2000s, Merrill Lynch developed two separate but successful businesses under the same roof: fixed income trading and wealth management. The bond trading operations focused on subprime mortgages: high risk and return vehicles. In 2007 and 2008, the subprime mortgage market, which had increasingly moved toward the heart of Merrill Lynch's and other Wall Street banks' balance sheets, fell as housing prices dropped and subprime securities lost value.[1] In October of 2007, Merrill Lynch posted losses of $8.4 billion because of subprime mortgages. In July of 2008, in the midst of a financial crisis that was quickly spreading from the United States to markets across the globe, Merrill Lynch sold $31 billion worth of subprime securities for "pennies on the dollar" in hopes of freeing the company's balance sheet from the toxic assets. Two other Wall Street investment banking staples, Bear Stearns and Lehman Brothers, went bankrupt. In order to avoid a similar fate, Merrill Lynch entered into merger talks with Bank of America in early September. On September 12, 2009, John Thain and Kenneth Lewis, the Chief Executive Officers of Merrill Lynch and Bank of America respectively, announced Bank of America's offer to buy Merrill Lynch for $29 a share or $50.3 billion in stock.

On December 5, 2008, Bank of America shareholders affirmatively voted to merge with Merrill Lynch.[2] At the time, Bank of America was viewed by the public as a "white knight" for not allowing Merrill Lynch to fail as Lehman Brothers and Bear Stearns had done just months before.[3] However, during December 2008, Merrill Lynch's losses increased exponentially, and at the end of the year, billions of dollars in bonuses were paid out to Merrill Lynch executives. In January of 2009, the Securities and Exchange Commission filed a lawsuit against Bank of America for withholding information from shareholders.[4] Subsequently, by March of 2009, Bank of America's stock had dropped from $33 a share to $3.14 a share on March 6 following its purchase of Merrill Lynch.[5] In April of 2009, Bank of America shareholders voted to restrict the authority of the bank's Chief Executive Officer, Kenneth Lewis, by separating the roles of CEO and Chairman of the Board. The splitting of these roles

was a highly unusual reprimand.[6] It was at this time that Lewis announced his resignation, effective at the end of the year.[7] How did Bank of America and Lewis fall from their position of "white knight" to being sued by the federal government for misleading shareholders?

Merrill Lynch's Executive Bonuses

In late December of 2008, Merrill Lynch executives and employees received bonuses totaling $3.5 billion.[8] Just after Bank of America shareholders agreed to purchase Merrill Lynch, 149 Merrill Lynch employees received end-of-the-year bonuses of $3 million or more, and 11 executives received bonuses of $10 million in stock and cash.[9] While these bonuses are enormous by most standards, many Wall Street firms claim they must pay at least this much to maintain their top talent. Why did Merrill Lynch executives get paid such high bonuses for bankrupting the company? Merrill Lynch executives claim that their bonuses were not about "performance," but rather represented "fees" for successfully completing the merger.[10] However, according to documents held by the Committee on Oversight and Government Reform, the Merrill Lynch executive bonuses were performance bonuses, not fees, and thus not locked in by pre-existing contracts.[11] Investigations by the government revealed that $3.62 billion in bonuses were paid to executives at Merrill Lynch less than a month before Bank of America received $25 billion in federal aid to help with the merger. The bonus funds allocated to executives at Merrill Lynch included more than a third of the Toxic Asset Relief Program (TARP) monies that Merrill Lynch received, and thus, Merrill Lynch executives' bonuses were paid with government money. The bonuses provided to Merrill Lynch executives were quite high: 22 times greater than those awarded to AIG executives ($3,620 million versus $165 million) for the year 2009.

Before the Bank of America and Merrill Lynch merger was finalized, John Thain and both companies' lawyers agreed upon the size of Merrill Lynch's employees' bonuses.[12] Originally, Bank of America consented to Merrill Lynch's request for up to $5.8 billion in bonuses with $40 million going to Thain; all with 60 percent in cash and 40 percent in

Written by Rebecca Waters under the supervision of Denis Arnold. Revised by Denis Arnold. © 2018 Denis G. Arnold.

stock. However, after Merrill Lynch's increased fourth quarter losses, top Bank of America officials requested that Thain decrease Merrill's bonus pool to $3.5 billion. By the end of December, Merrill Lynch's losses had become fully public. At this point, Thain downsized his request for a $40 million bonus to a $5 or $10 million bonus. It was only after shareholders and the general public vehemently rejected the notion of Thain receiving a bonus that he agreed to take no end-of-the-year bonus at all.

Typically, end-of-the-year bonuses are paid to investment banking employees in the beginning of January. However, evidence suggests that on December 11, 2008 Bank of America asked Merrill Lynch's compensation committee to increase the cash portion of the bonuses to 70 percent (from 60 percent) and to pay the cash portion before December 31, yet wait to pay the 30 percent stock portion until January.[13] According to documents held by the Committee of Oversight and Government Reform, the bonuses were provided to Merrill Lynch executives on December 8, 2009. These bonuses were granted during the fourth quarter of 2009 amidst Merrill Lynch's loss of $15 billion or more as well as the announcement by the Federal Government that Merrill Lynch would be receiving an additional $10 billion in TARP funds at the end of the year.[14] Why were Merrill Lynch executives paid performance bonuses early, before year-end? Why did they receive a performance bonus at all given that the company was at risk of failing?

Bank of America claims that Thain was the sole decision maker for the time of payment of Merrill Lynch bonuses, whereas Thain claims that the decision for early bonus payments was agreed upon in writing between himself and Lewis. Thain explained, "The suggestion that Bank of America was not heavily involved in this process, and that I alone made these decisions, is simply not true."[15] It seems that the merger agreement between Bank of America and Merrill Lynch includes a non-public document, viewed by *Wall Street Journal* and the *New York Times* employees, indicating not only that Merrill Lynch was given permission to pay employee bonuses before January and before the takeover was completed, but also that Bank of America was dynamically involved in these bonus-related decisions.[16] On January 22, 2009, the *Financial Times* published an article reporting that Thain had hastened bonus payments to his employees, which, in essence, suggested that Bank of America was absolved of responsibility in the decision to pay the high bonuses.[17] Thain describes himself as "stunned" by this article. The disagreement between the CEOs came to a head when Lewis asked for Thain's resignation. Thain resigned from his position of CEO of Merrill

Lynch and was blamed not only for the collapse of Merrill Lynch but also for the bonus negotiations.[18]

The Bonus and Shareholder Disclosure Law Suit

In early 2009, the Securities and Exchange Commission (SEC) sued Bank of America for not fully disclosing knowledge of Merrill Lynch's executive bonuses to shareholders. The SEC claimed that Bank of America misled shareholders to believe that there would be no end-of-the-year bonuses for Merrill Lynch employees.[19] The SEC's case was based on the November 2008 proxy sent to shareholders, which indicated 2008 bonuses wouldn't be paid to Merrill Lynch employees without Bank of America's consent. However, the document indicating that Bank of America had consented to bonuses totaling billions of dollars was never sent to shareholders. Bank of America lawyers claim that neither "false or misleading statements" about bonus payments were made to shareholders, nor was there any law requiring the bank to reveal that Merrill Lynch's losses were increasing before January 1 when the deal was completed.[20] In February of 2009, when questioned by Congress about the Merrill Lynch executive bonuses, Lewis explained, "They [Merrill Lynch] were a public company until the first of year ... They had a separate board, separate compensation committee, and we had no authority to tell them what to do, just urged them what to do."[21]

As a resolution to the lawsuit, the SEC proposed a $33 million fine on Bank of America for their failure to disclose key information to shareholders.[22] Federal Judge Jed Rakoff renounced the SEC settlement as insufficient. Judge Rakoff's rejection of the settlement undermines the SEC as an agency and is an indication of the court's desire for the SEC to better represent investors in the regulation of financial services companies. Judge Rakoff stated that the fine against the bank, "does not comport with the most elementary notions of justice and morality" as the shareholders of Bank of America would be required to pay the penalty for the offense of which they were already victims. On February 22, 2010, Judge Rakoff "reluctantly" agreed to a revised settlement between Bank of America and the SEC in the amount of $150 million.[23] In the court's written opinion released on February 22, 2010, Judge Rakoff writes:

> The SEC and the Bank have consistently taken the position that it was, at worst, the product of negligence on the part of the Bank, its relevant executives, and its lawyers (inside and outside), who made the decisions (such as they were) to non-disclose ... In particular, it

appears that the relevant decision-makers took the position that neither the bonuses nor the mounting evidence of fourth quarter losses had to be disclosed because the bonuses were consistent with prior years' bonuses and the losses were uncertain. Despite ever-growing indications that the latter assumption was erroneous ... the relevant decision-makers stuck to their previous determinations so far as disclosure of the losses was concerned and appear never to have considered at all the impact that the accelerated payment of over $3.6 billion in bonuses might have on a company that was verging on financial ruin.[24]

With this settlement, Bank of America evaded a criminal trial. The Attorney General of New York subsequently filed a civil suit against Lewis and Chief Financial Officer, Joe Price. Lewis settled for $25 million and Price for $7.5 million, paid for by Bank of America. Both were barred from serving as an officer or director of a public company for a period of time. Bank of America eventually paid out $16.65 billion in penalties for actions related to the Merrill Lynch acquisition (and billions more for other activities overseen by Lewis).

Notes

1. *The New York Times*, "Merrill Lynch & Company Inc." Retrieved August 28, 2010 from http://topics.nytimes.com/top/news/business/companies/merrill_lynch_and_company/index.html?emc=eta2.
2. Louise Story, "For Bank of America, the Pressure Mounts over Merrill Deal," *The New York Times* (January 17, 2009).
3. Carrick Mollenkamp and Dan Fitzpatrick, "The State of Capitalism: With Feds, B of A's Lewis Met His Match," *Wall Street Journal* (November 9, 2009).
4. Kara Scannell, Liz Rappaport, and Jess Bravin, "Judge Tosses Out Bonus Deal – SEC Pact with B of A over Merrill Is Slammed; New York Weighs Charges against Lewis," *Wall Street Journal* (September 17, 2009).
5. Mollenkamp and Fitzpatrick, "The State of Capitalism."
6. Dan Fitzpatrick and Marshall Eckblad, "Lewis Voted Out as B of A Chairman," *Wall Street Journal* (April 30, 2009).
7. Mollenkamp and Fitzpatrick, "The State of Capitalism."
8. Louise Story and Julie Creswell, "For Bank of America and Merrill, Love Was Blind," *The New York Times* (February 8, 2009).
9. Susanne Craig, "Merrill's $10 Million Men – Top 10 Earners Made $209 Million in 2008 as Firm Foundered," *Wall Street Journal* (March 4, 2009).
10. Story and Creswell, "For Bank of America and Merrill, Love Was Blind."
11. Committee on Oversight and Government Reform, "Merrill Lynch Bonuses 22 Times the Size of AIG." Retrieved August 28, 2010 from http://oversight.house.gov/index.php?option=com_content&task=view&id=4021&Itemid=39.
12. Story and Creswell, "For Bank of America and Merrill, Love Was Blind."
13. Susanne Craig, "Thain Fires Back at Bank of America," *Wall Street Journal* (April 27, 2009).
14. Committee on Oversight and Government Reform, "Merrill Lynch Bonuses 22 Times the Size of AIG."
15. Ibid.
16. Ibid.; Story and Creswell, "For Bank of America and Merrill, Love Was Blind."
17. Craig, "Thain Fires Back at Bank of America."
18. Story and Creswell, "For Bank of America and Merrill, Love Was Blind."
19. Scannell et al., "Judge Tosses Out Bonus Deal."
20. Dan Fitzpatrick and Kara Scannell, "B of A Returns Fire Against Cuomo – Bank's War of Words over Merrill Deal Continues after 'Spurious' Charges," *Wall Street Journal* (September 10, 2009).
21. Craig, "Thain Fires Back at Bank of America."
22. Scannell et al., "Judge Tosses Out Bonus Deal."
23. Louise Story, "Judge Accepts S.E.C.'s Deal with Bank of America," *The New York Times* (February 22, 2010).
24. Jed S. Rakoff, "Opinion and Order," United States District Court: Southern District of New York, *Securities and Exchange Commission v. Bank of America Corporation* (February 22, 2010).

Discussion Questions

1. Do you think that the bonuses are an example of unjustified executive compensation? Why, or why not? Explain. Do the bonuses represent a larger executive compensation issue that exists in the business world? Why, or why not? Explain.

2. In your view, did Bank of America sanction the large performance bonuses paid to Merrill Lynch executives or was this merely the decision of Thain and Merrill Lynch executives? Explain.

3. Does Bank of America's acceptance of governmental bailout money affect your view of whether or not Merrill Lynch's executives' bonuses were wrong? Why, or why not? If Bank of America did not receive money from the government, would your view change? Why, or why not? Explain.

4. What theoretical perspectives from this chapter help you to best assess the facts of this case? Explain.

Case 5: Roger Boisjoly and the *Challenger* Disaster: Disloyal Employee or Courageous Whistleblower?

DENIS G. ARNOLD

In the winter of 1985 Morton Thiokol Inc. engineer Roger Boisjoly conducted post-flight analysis on the rocket boosters from NASA's STS 51-C *Discovery*. Morton Thiokol managed the reusable rocket booster program for NASA's space shuttle program, and Boisjoly was one of their leading rocket experts. The booster rockets were designed to be reusable like the shuttle itself. After each launch the rockets would detach from the shuttle and its external fuel tank and parachute back to Earth, landing in the ocean where they would be recovered by special ships. Experts at Thiokol would then examine and refurbish the rockets so that they could be used again. On this occasion Boisjoly discovered a problem. The rockets from STS 51-C exhibited signs of failed O-ring seals and what is known as "hot gas blow-by." This occurs when ignited fuel leaks from between joints on the rocket assembly. The leaking fuel acts as a blowtorch on either the shuttle itself or on the giant liquid hydrogen fuel tank. Alarmed by these findings, Boisjoly wrote to his boss R. K. Lund, Vice-President of Engineering for Morton Thiokol and reported that "we stand in jeopardy of losing a flight." A five-member Seal Erosion Task Force was assigned to address the problem. Boisjoly and the other members of the task force concluded that lower launch temperatures greatly affected the reliability of the O-ring seal. Further evidence of hot gas blow-by was detected on STS-61-A *Challenger* in October 1985. This evidence convinced the Seal Erosion Task Force that it was not safe to launch until the O-ring problem was resolved.

On January 28, 1986 STS-51-L *Challenger* was scheduled for launch with a predicted temperature of 18°F at the launch pad. This mission would carry a seven-person crew including Christa McAuliffe, a New Hampshire school teacher, who had been selected from 11,000 applicants to be the first "teacher in space." Thousands of school children in the United States would watch the launch live from their classrooms and school auditoriums. That night, during his State of the Union Address, President Ronald Reagan planned to congratulate McAuliffe and her fellow astronauts. On January 27 Boisjoly and other engineers succeeded in persuading Thiokol management to scrub the launch. This decision angered NASA rocket booster manager Larry Mulloy who applied pressure on senior managers at

Thiokol. Mulloy argued that it was not reasonable for Thiokol to change their judgment about the launch parameters of the rockets they had built for NASA. A Morton Thiokol management team comprised in part of Lund, Jerry Mason, Thiokol's Senior Vice-President of the 7,000 employee Wasatch Operations in Utah, and Joe Kilminster, Vice-President of Space Booster Programs, voted to overturn the judgment of their engineers and gave NASA permission to launch. In making the decision, Mason had told them to take off their engineering hats and put on their management hats. On January 28, approximately 73 seconds after launch, hot gas blow-by from failed O-ring seals resulted in a catastrophic explosion and the loss of the *Challenger* and its crew. The prediction of Boisjoly and the Seal Erosion Task Force team had come true.

President Reagan appointed a commission to look into the reasons for the loss of the *Challenger* and its crew. The Rogers Commission interviewed nearly everyone involved in the decision to allow the *Challenger* to launch, including Roger Boisjoly. During his interviews with the Commission, Boisjoly, and fellow engineer Arnie Thompson, truthfully reported the sequence of events leading to the disaster. In so doing they repeatedly contradicted the testimony of senior Morton Thiokol managers including Kilminster. Because Boisjoly believed senior management was engaged in a cover-up, he provided copies of memos and activity reports to the Rogers Commission that supported his and Thompson's version of the events preceding the launch of *Challenger*. Boisjoly justified his actions as follows: "I thought it was unconscionable that Morton Thiokol and NASA wouldn't tell the whole truth so that the program could go forward with proper corrective measures." As a result of the testimony of Boisjoly and Thompson, Morton Thiokol received substantial criticism from Congress, the Rogers Commission, and in the press. Senior Morton Thiokol management chastised Boisjoly and Thompson for airing the company's dirty laundry and for being disloyal employees. When he returned to work at Morton Thiokol Wasatch Operations, Boisjoly found that he was ostracized by management and removed from responsibility for the redesign of the rocket booster. He could not understand why his expertise was not being utilized in the redesign effort. Eventually he discovered that he had been intentionally isolated from NASA on the orders of Edward Garrison, Morton Thiokol's President of Aerospace Operations. Boisjoly felt that his work environment had become hostile and has said that no one at the company supported him after his testimony. The psychological strain was too much and he took sick leave and eventually resigned from Morton Thiokol. He was later diagnosed with post-traumatic stress disorder. He never worked in the aerospace industry again. However, he became something of a star on college campuses and spoke at more than 300 universities and civic organizations on corporate ethics. The American Association for the Advancement of Science awarded Boisjoly its prestigious Prize for Scientific Freedom and Responsibility for his exemplary actions.

Discussion Questions

1. In your view, was Roger Boisjoly disloyal? Why, or why not? Explain. How might Ronald Duska answer this question? Explain.
2. How would you assess the actions of the Morton Thiokol leadership team that approved the launch? Explain.
3. Given the costs to Boisjoly, why do you think he disclosed what happened to investigators? Explain.
4. Based on your reading of the selections in this chapter by Brenkert and Near and Miceli, what changes in the organizational design and management of Morton Thiokol might have prevented the disaster? Explain.

This case was prepared for teaching purposes only and is based on the following sources: *Report of the Presidential Commission on the Space Shuttle Challenger Accident*, Washington, DC, June 6, 1986.

Roger M. Boisjoly, "Ethical Decisions – Morton Thiokol and the Space Shuttle Challenger Disaster," Online Ethics Center for Engineering, May 15, 2006, National Academy of Engineering. Retrieved from www.onlineethics.org/CMS/profpractice/ppes says/thiokolshuttle.aspx.

"Memo from Roger Boisjoly on O-Ring Explosion," Morton Thiokol Inc., July 31, 1985, Online Ethics Center for Engineering, August 29, 2006, National Academy of Engineering. Retrieved from www.onlineethics.org/CMS/profpractice/exempindex/RB-intro/Erosion.aspx.

Russell P. Boisoly, Ellen Foster Curtis, and Eugene Mellican, "Roger Boisjoly and the Challenger Disaster: The Ethical Dimensions," *Journal of Business Ethics* 8 (April 1989): 217–30.

Roger M. Boisjoly, "Post Disaster Treatment," in "Ethical Decisions – Morton Thiokol and the Space Shuttle Challenger Disaster," Online Ethics Center for Engineering, May 15, 2006, National Academy of Engineering, p. 1. Retrieved from www.onlineethics.org/CMS/profpractice/ppessays/thiokolshuttle .aspx.

Douglas Martin, "Roger Boisjoly, 73, Dies; Warned of Shuttle Danger," *The New York Times* (February 3, 2012).

Case 6: Tainted Medicine

DENIS G. ARNOLD

You are a leader at a pharmaceutical firm that supplies both prescription drugs (e.g., for depression, diabetes, and migraine headaches) and over-the-counter drugs (e.g., for acid reflux, allergies, and antibacterial ointments). Seven months ago a routine FDA inspection of a company drug manufacturing plant found a series of quality control problems. FDA advised your company to investigate and fix the problems promptly. The plant employs 900 people making 20 different types of drugs for the US market.

Two days ago an express package arrived at your office from a woman named Cheryl Smith, a Manager of Quality Assurance at your company. You are meeting with other corporate leaders to discuss Smith's report. In her letter and accompanying documents Smith reports the following:

1. At the instruction of the Vice-President of Quality she led a team of investigators to the plant. She states that the problems were much more serious and widespread than the FDA investigators had discovered.
2. Among the problems she identifies are the following:
   (a) antibacterial ointment routinely contaminated with bacteria;
   (b) water used to make tablets routinely contaminated by bacteria;
   (c) erroneous drug dosing mix-ups (e.g., 20 mg doses put into 10 mg pills and vice versa);
   (d) nine different examples of regular, erroneous drug packaging mix-ups (e.g., prescription drugs packaged with over-the-counter drugs, two different

drugs mixed together in the same bottles, 25 mg doses with 10 mg labels). Production line errors make these mistakes repeatedly and they are still being shipped to customers.

3. Smith reports that Chris Brown, the Vice-President of Quality, is aware of these findings and has declined to stop production to address the problems and has not informed the FDA of the nature and extent of her findings. Smith strongly recommends that her findings be reported to the FDA, the plant shut down, and products recalled.

The meeting is called to order and Brown is asked to explain what is going on. He reports the following: (1) The company is aware of issues at the plant and has been working to resolve them quietly and with little or no disruption to production. (2) The fact that Smith went over Brown's head and contacted the others is insubordination. (3) According to Brown, Smith is overwrought and emotional and an ideal candidate for being laid off given the reduction in workforce resulting from a recent acquisition. Brown recommends letting Smith go and assures everyone that the problems at the plant are being brought under control. You have met Smith before, and while you agree that she is a sensitive and caring person, you disagree that she is "overwrought." You also believe that she is good at her job.

Discussion Questions

1. Is Smith a disloyal employee for going over Brown's head? Should she be criticized or praised, or something else, for going over Brown's head? Explain.

2. What advice would you give your colleagues regarding how to handle Smith's complaints? Do you agree that Smith should be laid off? What, specifically, would you recommend happen next? Explain.

3. Should the firm be concerned about what Smith might do if she is laid off? Why, or why not? Explain.

4

Diversity, Discrimination, and Harassment in the Workplace

4.1 INTRODUCTION

For decades women and minorities were barred from some of the most desirable institutions and positions in business. Even when declared unconstitutional or made illegal, discrimination persisted in many quarters. This discrimination has led to a widespread demand for effective policies that will provide justice for those previously and presently discriminated against. Problems of diversity and affirmative action arose in this context, and sexual harassment policies were soon to follow, with their own set of issues. More recently, discrimination against lesbian, gay, and transgender individuals has received increasing attention from governments, organizations, and the courts.

DIVERSITY IN THE WORKPLACE

Federal policies and laws have encouraged or required corporations and other institutions to advertise jobs fairly and to promote the hiring and advancement of members of groups formerly discriminated against, most notably women and minority ethnic groups. Target goals and timetables were originally imposed on corporations in some nations to ensure more equitable opportunities by counterbalancing apparently intractable prejudice and systemic favoritism. Many policies that were initiated with these lofty ambitions provoked controversy and were criticized on grounds that they established quotas that unjustifiably elevated the opportunities of members of targeted groups, discriminated against equally qualified or even more qualified members of majorities, and perpetuated racial and sexual paternalism. The term *affirmative action* has been used to refer to everything from open advertisement of positions to employment and admission quotas. Corporate planning has often adopted specific employment goals or targeted employment outcomes to eliminate the vestiges of discrimination, and these policies are ones of affirmative action. The moral problem of affirmative action is whether the goals of such policies are justified and, if so, under which conditions. At its roots, this problem is moral rather than legal, but the issues have often been played out in a legal setting.

Preferential treatment refers to hiring, promotion, or forms of admission that give preference in recruitment and ranking to groups previously and presently affected by discrimination. This preference can be in the form of goals or quotas or in the act of choosing minorities over other candidates with equal credentials. Some people may think that workplace discrimination is largely a historical phenomenon, one that does not occur in contemporary workplaces. Unfortunately, this is not the case. In the United States the Equal Employment Opportunity Commission (EEOC) sanctions companies every year for discriminatory practices. Consider just three recent examples:

159

Laudente Montoya. Laudente Montoya worked as a mechanic at J&R Well Services and Dart Energy. From his first days on the job, Mr. Montoya's supervisor called Mr. Montoya and a co-worker "stupid Mexicans," "dumb Mexicans," and "worthless Mexicans." The supervisor told Mr. Montoya that he didn't like "sp*cs" and that Mexicans were the reason Americans have swine flu. Mr. Montoya fought back. He told his supervisor that "a person in a management position in a large corporation should not talk to their employees like that." In response, the supervisor said something like "Welcome to the oil fields. That's how they talk here." According to Mr. Montoya, the supervisor did not limit his offensive comments to Hispanic employees. Mr. Montoya observed the supervisor calling other co-workers names like "n*gger," "lazy Indian," and "wagon burner." When Mr. Montoya and his co-workers complained to the area manager, a friend of the supervisor, the manager did nothing. As Mr. Montoya explained, "Working that job was one of the worst times in my life. It became so that I could hardly bring myself to go to work in the morning because I hated working with him so much. People were calling me moody. I even saw my doctor about it." Finally, Mr. Montoya and his co-workers were fed up and filed a charge of discrimination. After filing the charge, Mr. Montoya was laid off.

Contonius Gill. Contonius Gill worked as a truck driver for A.C. Widenhouse, a North Carolina-based trucking company. On the job, Mr. Gill was repeatedly assaulted with derogatory racial comments and slurs by his supervisor, who was also the facility's general manager; by the company's dispatcher; by several mechanics; and by other truck drivers – all of whom were white. Mr. Gill was called "n*gger," "monkey," and "boy." On one occasion, a co-worker approached Mr. Gill with a noose and said, "This is for you. Do you want to hang from the family tree?" White employees also asked Mr. Gill if he wanted to be the "coon" in their "coon hunt." Mr. Gill repeatedly complained about the harassment to the company's dispatcher and general manager but the harassment continued unabated. The end of the story? Mr. Gill was fired for complaining about the harassment.

Jacquelyn Hines. Jacquelyn Hines was a single mother, born and raised in Memphis, Tennessee. She didn't finish high school, but she earned her G.E.D. and worked a series of temporary jobs through various staffing agencies to support herself and her family. In 2008, she found herself working for New Breed Logistics, a supply-chain logistics company with a warehouse in Memphis. Her supervisor made a habit of directing sexually explicit comments to Jacquelyn and her female co-workers. Indeed, it wasn't only sexually explicit comments – there were lewd and vulgar gestures, and some days physical harassment as well, like the day he pressed his stomach and private parts into one woman's back. When these women asked him to "stop talking dirty to me" or "leave me alone," his response was that he "wasn't going to get into trouble, he ran the place" and if anyone complained to HR, *they* would be fired. And sure enough, that's what happened. One of Jacquelyn's co-workers was fired when she complained about the harassment by way of the company's anonymous hotline. When Jacquelyn herself stood up to her supervisor and asked him to stop, suddenly she was contacted by the temporary agency concerning alleged attendance issues (which had never been mentioned before). Her hours were cut, she lost pay, and within a week she was fired. The male co-worker who had stood up to the supervisor on behalf of his colleagues, and told him to stop making comments because the women didn't like it? He was fired, too.[1]

In recent years, companies have generally emphasized the importance of diversity as an objective, and many think that affirmative action is needed to achieve it. In this conception, affirmative action is a means to the end of achieving diversity. The corporate world seems to have come to the view that the language of "diversity" is less controversial and legally less worrisome than the language of "affirmative action." However, in many companies it is unclear whether this is merely a shift in language or a change of goals, in part because it is unclear what diversity means and how many forms of diversity are to be included – for example, racial, cultural, national, sexual, geographical, and educational. The meaning and scope of *diversity* have long been in question. Innumerable forms of diversity can be used for hiring and promotion – so many forms that no corporation is likely to cover them all. An institution may concentrate on race and sex without even considering factors such as veteran status or sexual orientation.

It is sometimes asked what it means to have an "outreach" program to achieve diversity. Clearly, outreach will vary from corporation to corporation, but it is not difficult to find many examples of outreach programs. Here, for example, is one statement in a quite detailed policy of diversity at the McGraw-Hill Company: "We sponsor and recruit prospective employees at national diversity recruiting events such as the National Black MBA Association, the National Society of Hispanic MBAs, and the National Journalist Associations. Our sponsorship includes national print advertising and job fair participation with these associations. We also sponsor various programs that attract and cultivate talented minority students to our Corporation."[2]

Preferential policies are often said to find their moral justification in the principle of compensatory justice, which requires that if an injustice has been committed, just compensation or reparation is owed to the injured person(s). Everyone agrees that if an individual has been injured by past discrimination, he or she should be compensated for the past injustice. That is, *individuals* who have been injured by past discrimination should be made whole for injuries to them. However, controversy has arisen over whether *past* discrimination against *groups* such as women and minorities justifies compensation for *current* group members. Critics of group preferential policies hold that only identifiable discrimination against individuals requires compensation.

In the first selection in this chapter, Tom L. Beauchamp discusses the voluntary preferential treatment and diversity programs that have been of special interest to senior management. He concludes that these policies can be justified under a variety of circumstances. Beauchamp does not employ arguments that compensation is owed to classes for *past* wrongs; rather, he maintains that policies of affirmative action are permissible to eliminate or alleviate *present* discriminatory practices that affect whole classes of persons (especially practices of minority exclusion). He provides factual evidence for his claim that invidious discrimination is pervasive in society. Because discrimination now prevails, Beauchamp contends that policies that may eventuate in reverse discrimination are unavoidable in reaching the end of eliminating ongoing discrimination.

The US Supreme Court has upheld some affirmative action programs and found others unsupportable. The legal problems associated with preferential and discriminatory hiring are moral in nature and turn out to be surprisingly complicated. In one landmark case the Supreme Court supported the permissibility of affirmative action. *Local 28 v. Equal Employment Opportunity Commission*, often called *Sheet Metal Workers*, held that specific numerical goals of the sort required by the lower court are justified when dealing with persistent or egregious discrimination; affirmative action plans that are intended to combat a manifest imbalance in traditionally segregated job categories thus can be shown to be justified. The Court found that the history of the Local 28 union was one of complete "foot-dragging resistance" to the idea of hiring without discrimination in their apprenticeship training programs from minority groups. The Court argued that "affirmative race-conscious relief" may be the only reasonable means to the end of assuring equality of employment opportunities and to eliminate deeply ingrained discriminatory practices and devices that have fostered racially stratified job environments to the disadvantage of minority citizens.

SEXUAL HARASSMENT

Sexual harassment is a form of sexual discrimination. Sexually harassing behaviors include unwelcome sexual remarks or communications, physical touching, and sexual advances. The conduct need not involve making a sexual act a condition of employment or promotion, and it need not be imposed on persons who are in no position to resist the conduct. Even someone who is in a strong position to resist the approach can be sexually harassed. Derogatory language, offensive touching, and sexual communications can affect a worker's performance and create a sense that the workplace is inhospitable, irrespective of an employee's ability to resist. The conduct need not be "sexual" in a narrow sense or even sexually motivated. For example, the conduct can be gender specific, involving demeaning remarks about how all women underperform in their job assignments, or are otherwise inferior to men.

A recent EEOC report found that studies consistently show that 25 percent of women in the general population have experienced sexual harassment in the workplace and that 40 percent of women report "unwanted sexual attention or sexual coercion" in the workplace.[3] The contemporary "me too" movement, where women have publicly revealed the sexually harassing behavior (sometimes sexual assault or even rape) of powerful men, has brought increased attention to harassment in recent years. Prominent and powerful men who were fired or lost their positions as a result of sexual harassment include Harvey Weinstein (Hollywood producer), Matt Lauer (co-host of the *Today* show on NBC), Roger Ailes (CEO of Fox News), Bill O'Reilly (Fox News personality), Mario Batali (chef, restaurant owner), Jerry Richardson (owner, Carolina Panthers NFL team), and Omeed Malik (managing director at Bank of America).

The landmark US Supreme Court case *Meritor Savings Bank v. Vinson* was decided in 1986. In *Meritor*, the Supreme Court extended protections against sexual harassment beyond circumstances of demanding sex acts as a condition of employment. This case, which was brought under Title VII of the US Civil Rights Act of 1964, established that a hostile or abusive work environment can result from many activities in the workplace that constitute sexual harassment.

In *Teresa Harris v. Forklift Systems*, a central issue is whether *noncoercive* comments based on employee *gender* cause an abusive work environment. In this case it was found that gender insults, gender ridicule, and sexual innuendo can constitute sexual harassment when they negatively alter the conditions of a victim's employment and constitute an abusive environment. The Court found that conduct may constitute sexual harassment even if that conduct does not involve a serious disturbance of psychological well-being or an injury. This case reaffirmed the finding in *Meritor* that "an objectively hostile or abusive environment" is enough for sexual harassment.

Case law in the United States has resulted in a multidimensional threshold for determining if a work environment is hostile. For a workplace to be sexually hostile, all of the following criteria must hold: the behavior must be sex or gender based, the victim must identify the harassment as unwelcome, the harassment must be severe or pervasive, the employer must condone the harassment (for example, by ignoring employee complaints), and the work environment must be regarded as objectively hostile by other reasonable persons (for example, co-workers, a judge, or a jury).

Crystal Liu, Elizabeth Macgill, and Apeksha Vora provide an essential roadmap for understanding sexual harassment law in the United States in their contribution "Sex Discrimination Claims under Title VII of the Civil Rights Act of 1964." Title VII was created to prevent employment discrimination on the basis of race, sex, or other protected characteristics. Discrimination can result from disparate treatment or disparate impact. A successful claimant alleging disparate treatment needs to establish that she was treated differently from similarly situated individuals based on her sex. Under the disparate treatment criterion, the plaintiff must show that the defendant acted with discriminatory intent. In response the defendant can invoke a number of defenses; the most well known is that the difference in treatment was based on a bona fide occupational qualification. The key point Liu, Macgill, and Vora make is that sexual harassment is a form of sexual discrimination. To establish a sexual harassment claim, the plaintiff must show that the alleged conduct was unwelcome, unsolicited, and motivated because of one's sex or gender. Although the most common sexual harassment claims are made by women against men, claims by men against women, or claims against a person of the same sex are also permitted under the law.

In her article in this chapter, "Reconceptualizing Sexual Harassment, Again," legal scholar Vicki Schultz takes the contemporary "me too" movement as a starting point for theorizing about the nature of sexual harassment. She argues that news reporting and popular discourse regarding the "me too" movement has tended to emphasize sexually predatory behavior, but she argues that a wealth of social science evidence makes it plain that sexual harassment is a much broader phenomenon. Schultz uses the examples of the egregious conduct of Hollywood producer Harvey Weinstein, as well as the pervasive sexual harassment that takes place at firms in Silicon Valley, to illustrate her ideas. In her view, because some men harass women and "lesser men" to preserve their dominant workplace position and related sense of masculinity, harassment is properly understood as a broader form of sex discrimination and inequality. The courts have upheld such an understanding in the United States. She goes on to argue that specific organizational conditions foster workplace-based harassment, and calls for more open and accountable organizations which are themselves intolerant of sexual harassment.

Many firms now have some form of sexual harassment training and nearly all medium and large firms have grievance policies. Corporations with sexual harassment policies for all management levels report that unwelcome comments and touching have declined significantly after initiating the policies. One reason for increased corporate interest is that corporations have been held legally liable for the behavior of their employees, even when corporate officials above the employees were unaware of the behavior.

LGBT RIGHTS AT WORK

Canada, the United Kingdom, and Australia all have federal legislation banning discrimination based on sexual orientation. However, lesbian and gay employees are not protected from discriminatory practices by federal legislation in the United States. Currently in the United States individual states and municipalities determine whether or not discrimination based on sexual orientation is legally permitted. Currently, for example, over 20 states ban employment discrimination based on sexual orientation. In some states, such as Texas, that do not ban this form of employment discrimination, individuals cities do have such bans. Given this patchwork of regulation, companies that conduct business in many states are confronted with conflicting standards.

In their article "The Social and Economic Imperative of Lesbian, Gay, Bisexual, and Transgendered Supportive Organizational Policies," Eden B. King and José M. Cortina make a strong empirical case for the existence of employment discrimination against members of the lesbian, gay, bisexual, and transgender (LGBT) community and that the existence of such discrimination causes harm to those that are discriminated against. For example, there is a considerable wage gap between heterosexual men and gay men doing comparable work – a well-established indicator of discrimination. In addition, in experimental studies, persons portrayed as having a gay or lesbian identity, particularly when that identity is associated with popular stereotypes of gay and lesbian persons, are treated differently. Heterosexuals are treated more positively than gay or lesbian persons. These surveys and studies are consistent with observations of sympathetic heterosexuals and with the self-reports of members of the LGBT community themselves. King and Cortina then argue that business support for LGBT employees makes economic as well as moral sense. With that in mind the authors conclude with a number of suggestions that would demonstrate organizational support for LGBT employees, as well as for other members of the LGBT community.

Increasingly the business community has moved in the directions that King and Cortina recommend. Companies are explicitly choosing to affirm the value of LGBT employees and customers. For example, the Human Rights Campaign (an advocacy organization) reports that in 2002 just 13 companies surveyed achieved a 100 percent rating on their annual LGBT Corporate Equality Index. By 2018 that figure had changed to 609 receiving a 100 percent rating, including 14 of the Top 20 Fortune ranked companies, such as Amazon.com, Apple, Chevron, CVS Health Corp., Ford Motor Co., and HP, Inc.[4]

In a number of instances corporations have taken controversial stands in defense of LGBT rights and values and have used their economic power to force states to abandon legislation deemed antithetical to LGBT rights and values. After the Supreme Court ruled that gay and lesbian couples had a constitutional right to marry (*Obergefell v. Hodges*, 2016), a number of states considered, and in some cases passed, "religious freedom laws" that gave individuals, companies, and organizations the right to deny gay and lesbian individuals service on the grounds that their religions forbade gay, lesbian, and bisexual relationships. However, many of these laws would permit discrimination on the basis of sexual orientation for any reason and not merely because of religious convictions. Major corporations argued against such laws and threatened economic retaliation if in fact they were enacted. Under such pressure both Arkansas and Indiana modified their laws. In Georgia the Republican governor vetoed such a law passed by the Republican legislature after significant members of the business community objected to the legislation. However, North Carolina and Mississippi did pass such laws and economic retaliation by firms and major organizations ensued. For example, North Carolina passed legislation that made it lawful for any bar, restaurant, or hotel (and most other service-related businesses) in the state to refuse service to individuals that were perceived to be LGBT. Under the law, if Apple CEO Tim Cook visited Charlotte, he could lawfully be refused hotel accommodation or entry into a restaurant or coffee shop merely because he is gay. A number of firms responded by cancelling plans to expand or open businesses in North Carolina. Particularly painful for a state that is so devoted to basketball, the National Basketball Association moved the All Star game out of Charlotte and the NCAA moved scheduled March Madness basketball tournament games out of state. Eventually the North Carolina state legislature modified the law in response to this economic pressure. Traditionally, corporations have avoided divisive political issues such as gay rights. Of course, corporations have lobbied legislatures on behalf of their economic interests and it can be argued that corporations now view their economic interests more widely. Indeed one of the arguments that corporations use is that they have significant numbers of LGBT workers, and hence they could not attract and retain valuable gay employees in states where these religious freedom laws exist. Thus, many firms have an economic interest in LGBT rights whether or not firm behavior is also motivated by a commitment to such rights.

Notes

1. Chai R. Feldblum and Victoria A. Lipnic, *Select Task Force on the Study of Harassment in the Workplace* (Washington, DC: Equal Employment Opportunity Commission, 2016).
2. www.mcgraw-hill.com/careers/diversity_recruiting_hiring.shtml.
3. Feldblum and Lipnic, *Select Task Force*.
4. Human Rights Campaign, "2018 Corporate Equality Index" (Washington, DC: Human Rights Campaign).

4.2 DIVERSITY IN THE WORKPLACE

Affirmative Action and Diversity Goals in Hiring and Promotion

TOM L. BEAUCHAMP

Since the 1960s, government and corporate policies that set goals for hiring women and minorities have encountered many criticisms. Opponents maintain that these policies establish indefensible quotas and discriminate in reverse against sometimes more qualified white males. Although some policies undoubtedly do violate rules of fair and equal treatment, I will argue that well-constructed policies that have specific, targeted goals are morally justified. These goals may be fixed in affirmative action policies, but increasingly they are fixed through diversity policies.

Two Polar Positions on Affirmative Action

I start with the relevant historical background. In 1965, President Lyndon Johnson issued an executive order that announced a toughened federal initiative requiring that employers with a history of discrimination in employment supply goals and timetables for the achievement of equal employment opportunity.[1] Since this order, several US government policies and laws have encouraged or required corporations and other institutions to advertise jobs fairly and to promote members of groups formerly discriminated, most notably women, minority ethnic groups, and the handicapped. The stated goals were to eradicate overt discrimination, redress the results of past discrimination, and smooth the course of equal opportunity in employment and admission to educational institutions. Today race and ethnicity have become the main focus of affirmative action policies, and often the exclusive focus.

These laws and related policies and reforms of practices were quickly labeled "affirmative action." Today the term "affirmative action" most commonly refers to positive steps to rank, admit, hire, or promote persons who are members of groups previously or presently discriminated against, but historically it has been used to refer to many types of practice and policy, from open advertisement of positions to quotas in employment and promotion. The term has widely, though controversially, been interpreted as synonymous with "preferential treatment."

The following introductory statement by the University of California Berkeley for its affirmative action policy for staff employment is a good example of the kind of general commitments found in many affirmative action policies as they now exist:

> The University commits itself to apply every good faith effort to achieve prompt and full utilization of minorities and women in all segments of its workforce where deficiencies exist. These efforts conform to all current legal and regulatory requirements, and are consistent with University standards of quality and excellence.[2]

This plan sets annual placement goals when the percentage of minorities or women employed in a particular job group is less than would be reasonably expected given their availability percentage in that particular job group. The placement goals are adjusted annually, and the results published in some detail.

The practice of using such goals in policies has from the beginning come into sharp conflict with a school of thought that is critical of affirmative action. Its proponents denounced preferential policies as themselves discriminatory and argued that all persons are equally entitled to a fair employment opportunity and to constitutional guarantees of equal protection in a color-blind, nonsexist society. They have argued – and still do so today – that affirmative action is partial and preferential, and therefore violates impartial principles of fair treatment and equal opportunity. Civil rights laws, from this perspective, should offer protection only to individuals who have themselves been explicitly victimized by forms of discrimination, not to groups. Corporate hiring goals and timetables therefore may function to create a reverse discrimination that decreases opportunities for populations such as nonminority males. That is, the properties of race and sex used in affirmative action policies discriminate against those who are not members of the designated race, ethnicity, or sex.

These two schools of thought often do not agree on the core meaning of the term "affirmative action," which has been defined in different ways by different parties. The original meaning of "affirmative action" was minimalist. It referred to plans to safeguard equal opportunity, to protect against discrimination, to advertise positions openly, and to create scholarship programs to ensure recruitment from specific groups. If this were all that "affirmative action" meant, few would oppose it. However, "affirmative action" has both expanded and contracted in meaning over the last quarter century. Today it is typically associated with preferential policies that target specific groups, especially women and minority groups, in order to promote the interests of members of those groups and to raise their status. Here "affirmative action" refers to positive steps to rank, admit, hire, or promote persons.

Although the meaning of "affirmative action" is still contested, I will, for present purposes, stipulate the meaning as functionally equivalent to the elements in the following policy of the IBM Company:

> To provide equal opportunity and affirmative action for applicants and employees, IBM carries out programs on behalf of women, minorities, people with disabilities, special disabled veterans and other veterans covered by the Vietnam Era Veterans Readjustment Act ... This includes outreach as well as human resource programs that ensure equity in compensation and opportunity for growth and development.[3]

Affirmative action here, as with many American corporations, means that the company extends its commitment beyond mere equal opportunity (a negative condition of nondiscrimination) to proactively recruit, hire, develop, and promote qualified women, minorities, people with disabilities, and veterans (a positive condition requiring organized action). I too will use "affirmative action" to refer to both equal opportunity provisions and positive steps taken to hire persons from groups previously and presently discriminated against, leaving open what will count as a "positive step" to remove discrimination and also leaving open precisely what "equal opportunity" means.

The two schools of thought identified thus far may not be as far apart morally as they at first appear. If legal enforcement of civil rights law could efficiently and comprehensively identify discriminatory treatment and could protect its victims, both schools would agree on the centrality of the principle of equal opportunity and would agree that the legal-enforcement strategy is preferable. However, there are at least two reasons why this solution will not be accepted, at the present time, by proponents of affirmative action. First, there is an unresolved issue about whether those in contemporary society who have been advantaged by *past* discrimination, such as wealthy owners of decades-

old family businesses, deserve their advantages. Second, there is the issue of whether *present*, ongoing discrimination can be successfully and comprehensively overcome in a timely fashion by identifying and prosecuting violators and without resorting to the outreach programs involved in affirmative action. Many believe that it takes constant vigilance to protect against discriminatory actions and ensure fair hiring and promotion.

Diversity

In many corporations the language of "diversity policy" has been either substituted for or merged with "affirmative action policy." For example, General Motors has stated its commitment to "Diversity Management" as follows:

> We believe that diversity is the collective mixture of similarities and differences. This recognizes that managing diversity includes race and gender as well as the broader aspects of age, education level, family status, language, military status, physical abilities, religion, sexual orientation, union representation, and years of service ... We remain committed to Affirmative Action as required by the Federal law. As such, we monitor our programs to determine whether recruitment, hiring and other personnel practices are operating in a nondiscriminatory manner. This process includes outreach programs designed to identify qualified individuals of any race or gender who are not fully represented in the talent pools from which we select and promote employees ... We recognize that it is essential that our work force structure reflects both the marketplace and our customers.[4]

General Motors also states that workplace diversity is of sufficient importance that it may be achieved by means of affirmative action.

Another example is the Coca-Cola Company, which worked with a task force to implement a diversity strategy "with quantifiable outcomes, timelines, and plans." The design has been to integrate diversity into the "business plan" of the company, which maintains a Diversity & Workplace Fairness Department in Human Resources. This department is "responsible for centralized strategy and monitoring of EEO issues and affirmative action plans (AAPs)." A policy initiated in 2004 was a particularly venturesome approach (later reduced and intentionally made less "aggressive"):

> Under the Diversity Goals program, all senior managers based in North America will have a portion of their incentive tied to the achievement of the

Company's diversity goals. This program tracks progress on an annual basis and was implemented in January 2004. For calendar year 2004, the program tied executive and senior manager compensation to a 2% net increase in representation of women and minorities at salary grades 10 and above, very ambitious goals for the first year of this program.[5]

Achieving diversity in a workforce or educational institution can be viewed as a means to the end of eradicating discrimination and therefore as an arm of affirmative action. However, diversity has often functioned as a goal that is independent of anti-discrimination goals, and reasons for diversity policies can be notably different from reasons for affirmative action policies. The two kinds of policy share parts of the same history and they often have overlapping goals, but they are neither synonymous in meaning nor identical in policy.

Diversity first burst into prominence because of 1970s affirmative action programs initiated in American colleges and universities that sought to bring to campus higher levels of representation of Hispanic and African-American students as well as women and minorities on the staff and faculty. Many universities altered their criteria of admission to achieve these goals, and diversity was prominently mentioned as a major goal.

In cases heard over a period of years, the United States Supreme Court has determined (as a matter of law rather than ethics, of course) that a racial or ethnic classification scheme by itself is too narrow to express a proper understanding of the goal of diversity. The desired objective of obtaining educational benefits requires consideration of properties beyond race and ethnic origin. A diversity goal for an educational environment could include many abilities, experiences, and endowments in the student body. The Court has found that diversity policies can lawfully include criteria of race and ethnicity, but only in the context of a larger set of criteria of diversity. In a controversial case about a University of Michigan Law School policy, the Court stated that race can be considered along with other factors, but only if quotas and weighted points are not parts of the admissions structure. Twenty Fortune 500 companies had filed a legal brief in support of the University of Michigan's admissions policies in the case, and Justice O'Connor in the majority opinion frequently mentioned and quoted from the brief, noting the significance of affirmative action policies well beyond higher education.[6]

The Supreme Court has brought US law to the conclusion that a diversity of abilities, backgrounds, nationalities, experiences, aptitudes, and gifts – along with ethnic and racial diversity – create a mixture that is legal and that reasonably contributes to the educational experience in an institution of higher learning. Still undecided, however, is the precise mixture of criteria of diversity that may legitimately be used. Currently what often happens in one institution in the way of a mixture does not closely resemble what happens in another, because they use disparate criteria. Corporations include a wide array of criteria when stating their diversity policies, including race, gender, ethnicity, age, conditions of disability, sexual orientation, cultural background, religion, economic status, education, and prior types of experience. These criteria are proudly mentioned in many corporate policies, but rarely are they spelled out or linked to historical discrimination. American institutions clearly are struggling with how to understand and implement criteria of diversity and with the reasons why certain criteria should or should not be adopted.

We may currently be experiencing a historical period in which diversity is gradually displacing affirmative action as the centerpiece of policies regarding underrepresented groups. More strongly put, it can be argued that, as a social matter in the United States, the demise of affirmative action began with the presidency of Ronald Reagan and was effectively transformed into diversity policy by recent social change, court cases, and new state legislation. It is too early to tell, but if affirmative action is now in its death throes, the same cannot be said about diversity policies. One way to frame the current situation is to say that many American corporations are swinging from a powerful commitment to affirmative action to a powerful commitment to affirmative diversity.

The Objectives of Corporate Policies

Many writings about corporate affirmative action programs suggest that *legal* requirements determine the *moral* obligations of corporations, but this assumption confuses ethics with law, and most forward-looking corporations have not been confused about their extra-legal moral commitments. In 1995, shortly after the United States Department of Labor gave an award to Procter & Gamble for its commitment to pursuing equal employment opportunities, Edwin L. Artzt, then chairman of the board and CEO of Procter & Gamble, said, "Affirmative action has been a positive force in our company. What's more, we have always thought of affirmative action as a starting point. We have never limited our standards for providing opportunities to women and minorities to levels mandated by law ... Regardless of what government may do, we believe we have a moral contract with all of the women and minorities in our company – a moral contract to provide equal opportunity for employment, equal opportunity for advancement, and equal opportunity for financial reward."[7] Starting from this perspective, many corporations make positive commitments, in voluntary programs, of hiring and promotions that build significantly on and move beyond what laws and federal agencies determine to be basic responsibilities.

Another moral objective of a corporate policy can be diversity itself. Corporations that fail to seek broadly for diversity will recruit narrowly and will fail to look at the full range of qualified persons in the market. This will be a moral unfairness of narrow recruiting as well as a failure to act in the company's best interest. Many corporations have reported that promoting diversity in the workforce by recruiting widely is correlated with higher quality employees, reductions in the costs of discrimination claims, a lowering of absenteeism, less turnover, and increased customer satisfaction. While the desire to achieve these goals, so stated, comes more from corporate self-interest rather than moral commitment, these reports suggest that the claims made by opponents of affirmative action that corporations lower standards and hire weaker employees under affirmative action plans have turned out not to be supported.[8]

An example is found in the Dell Computer Corporation, which announced that, by design, it had substantially increased its diversity recruiting and global diversity. Dell noted that "companies that diversify workforce and supply bases are more successful in gaining access to multicultural markets. Mutually beneficial relationships with minority suppliers open doors for Dell to market its products and services to women and minority customers, provide growth opportunities for our suppliers, and benefit our communities."[9] If many companies were today to withdraw their carefully developed affirmative action and/or diversity plans, they would violate moral commitments that have been set in place after direct negotiations with and promises made to minority groups, unions, and others. Many corporations report that they have, for moral as well as business reasons, invested heavily in eliminating managerial biases and stereotypes by training managers to hire through outreach programs.

Unintentional Discrimination and Problems of Proof

Affirmative action, and arguably diversity too, have a history in racial and sexual discrimination. In some cases there existed *intentional* forms of favoritism and exclusion, but intent to discriminate is not a necessary condition of discrimination and not a necessary condition of having a justified affirmative action or diversity policy. Institutional patterns and networks can unintentionally hold back persons. Employees are frequently hired through a network that, without design, excludes women, minority groups, or other groups. For example, hiring may occur through personal connections or by word of mouth; and layoffs may be governed by a seniority system rather than by considerations of merit and performance.[10]

The US Supreme Court has reasonably held that persons may be guilty of discriminating against the handicapped (in this particular case) when there is no "invidious animus, but rather [a discriminatory effect] of thoughtlessness and indifference – of benign neglect." The Court found that discrimination would be difficult and perhaps impossible to prove or to prevent if intentional discrimination alone qualified as discrimination.[11] The Court has also noted that discrimination is often invisible to those who discriminate as well as invisible to the public. This, in my judgment, is the main reason why reasonable target goals in affirmative action and diversity policies can be (but are not always) justifiable: They may be the only way to break down patterns of discrimination, intentional or unintentional, and bring meaningful diversity to the workplace.

Courts in the United States have on a few occasions either required or endorsed specific numerical targets on grounds that an employer had an intractable history and a bullheaded resistance to change that necessitated strong measures. The Supreme Court has never directly supported quotas using the term "quota"[12] (a term now largely displaced by "target goals," "diversity objectives," and the like), but it did at one point in its history uphold affirmative action programs that contain numerically expressed hiring formulas that are intended to reverse the patterns of both intentional and unintentional discrimination.[13] However, the Supreme Court has also clearly stated that some affirmative action programs using numerical formulas have gone too far and are not justified.[14]

The Importance of Context and Empirical Studies

Factual questions about the actual breadth and depth of discrimination at work in hiring and promotion policies (as well as in college admissions, home mortgage lending, etc.) may divide us as a society more than any other issue about the role of diversity and affirmative action. Many believe that there is a narrow sliver of discrimination that is controllable by presently available laws, whereas others believe that discrimination is deeply, and often invisibly, entrenched in society. Based on available empirical studies, discriminatory attitudes and practices are deep-seated in some institutions, while there are no such attitudes in others. In some institutions and corporations affirmative action programs are not needed today. They have achieved their goals. In others, only modest good faith programs are in order; and in still others targeted goals will continue to be necessary to break down discriminatory patterns.

Empirical studies help us understand the scope of discrimination in many American institutions and sectors. Although much has been learned through these studies about patterns of discrimination, much remains to be discovered. The hidden and subtle character of discrimination often makes it particularly difficult to study.

Conclusion

Issues of social discrimination and equality of opportunity affect all societies, and, from this perspective, problems of affirmative action could be interpreted as universal moral problems – not merely moral problems in the United States, as I have largely treated them. No well-informed person would deny that there are serious problems of discrimination in virtually every nation, in every part of the world. Both diversity and fair hiring and promotion are global problems, rising to deeply offensive levels in some countries. However, the notion of *affirmative action* has throughout its history been so closely tied to issues, laws, policies, and judicial decisions in the United States that it would be ill-advised to try to reinvent this particular concept as a global problem of social justice.

If the social circumstances of discrimination change in the future, various of my suggestions and conclusions in this article will need to be modified, perhaps substantially. I agree with critics of affirmative action that the introduction of programs of preferential treatment on a large scale runs the risk of producing economic advantages to individuals who do not deserve them, protracted court battles, a lowering of admission and work standards, increased racial and minority hostility, and the continued suspicion that well-placed minorities received their positions purely on the basis of preferential and unfair treatment. These reasons constitute a strong case *against* some affirmative action policies that set specific goals. However, this powerful case is not sufficient to overcome the still strong arguments in favor of specifically targeted affirmative action and diversity policies for those contexts in which they are still needed.

Notes

1. For historical and definitional issues, see Carl Cohen and James P. Sterba, *Affirmative Action and Racial Preference* (Oxford University Press, 2003), pp. 14, 18–20, 25, 40, 101, 200–1, 253, 279, 296.

2. University of California Berkeley, 2010–11 Staff Affirmative Action Plan. Retrieved August 1, 2011 from https://hr.berke ley.edu/news/staff-and-academic-affirmative-action-plans.

3. IBM, "Equal Opportunity." Retrieved January 15, 2017 from www.ibm.com/ibm/history/ibm100/us/en/icons/equalwork force/.

4. General Motors, "Diversity Management." Retrieved January 13, 2007 from www.gm.com/. . ./sustainability/reports/01/ social_and_community_info/social_management/diversity_ manage.html.

5. Coca-Cola Company, "Fifth Annual Report of the Task Force: December 1, 2006," pp. 36–41. Retrieved August 7, 2011 from www.coca-colacompany.com/content/dam/journey/us/en/pri vate/fileassets/pdf/unknown/unknown/task_force_report _2006.pdf.

6. *Grutter v. Bollinger*, 539 U.S. 306 (2003); and see also *Gratz v. Bollinger*, 539 U.S. 244 (2003).

7. American Council on Education, Washington, DC, "Making the Case for Affirmative Action." Retrieved January 13, 2007 from www.acenet.edu/bookstore/descriptions/makingthecase/ works/business.cfm.

8. John Yinger, *Closed Doors, Opportunities Lost* (New York: Russell Sage Foundation, 1995); Jerry T. Ferguson and Wallace R. Johnston, "Managing Diversity," *Mortgage Banking* 55 (1995): 3236L.

9. Dell Computer Corporation. Retrieved May 15, 2007 from www.dell.com/learn/us/en/uscorp1/diversity.

10. See Laura Purdy, "Why Do We Need Affirmative Action?" *Journal of Social Philosophy* 25 (1994): 133–43; Farrell Bloch, *Antidiscrimination Law and Minority Employment: Recruitment Practices and Regulatory Constraints* (University of Chicago Press, 1994); Joseph Sartorelli, "Gay Rights and Affirmative Action," in *Gay Ethics*, ed. Timothy F. Murphy (New York: Haworth Press, 1994).

11. *Alexander v. Choate*, 469 U.S. 287, at 295.

12. But the Court comes very close in *Local 28 of the Sheet Metal Workers' International Association v. Equal Employment Opportunity Commission*, 478 U.S. 421 (1986).

13. *Fullilove v. Klutznick*, 448 U.S. 448 (1980); *United Steelworkers v. Weber*, 443 U.S. 193 (1979); *United States v. Paradise*, 480 U.S. 149 (1987); *Johnson v. Transportation Agency*, 480 U.S. 616 (1987).

14. *Firefighters v. Stotts*, 467 U.S. 561 (1984); *City of Richmond v. J. A. Croson Co.*, 109 S.Ct. 706 (1989); *Adarand Constructors Inc. v. Federico Pena*, 63 LW 4523 (1995); *Wygant v. Jackson Bd. of Education*, 476 U.S. 267 (1986); *Wards Cove Packing v. Atonio*, 490 U.S. 642 (1989).

4.3 SEXUAL HARASSMENT

Sex Discrimination Claims under Title VII of the Civil Rights Act of 1964

CRYSTAL LIU, ELIZABETH MACGILL, AND APEKSHA VORA

Overview: The Title VII Statute

The Equal Pay Act of 1963 and Title VII of the Civil Rights Act of 1964 ("Title VII") marked the beginning of modern, broadly applicable anti-discrimination law.[1] Title VII prohibits employment discrimination based on sex, race, and other protected traits.[2] Although often sparking litigation, Title VII was meant "to encourage informal conciliation and to foster voluntary compliance"[3] through "the creation of antiharassment policies and effective grievance mechanisms."[4] Amended several times,[5] Title VII currently makes it unlawful for an employer:

1. to fail or refuse to hire or to discharge any individual, or otherwise to discriminate against any individual with respect to his compensation, terms, conditions, or privileges of employment, because of such individual's race, color, religion, sex, or national origin; or
2. to limit, segregate, or classify his employees or applicants for employment in any way which would deprive or tend to deprive any individual of employment opportunities or otherwise adversely affect his status as an employee, because of such individual's race, color, religion, sex, or national origin.[6]

Title VII protects both men and women from sex discrimination in the workplace. "'Race' and 'sex' are general terms that in every day usage require modifiers to indicate any relatively narrow application. We do not commonly understand 'race' to refer only to the black race, or 'sex' to refer only to the female."[7] "Sex" was amended into the statute on the last day of the debate, resulting in little to no legislative history to assist in statutory interpretation.[8] Sex discrimination claims under Title VII fall within one of two broad categories: disparate treatment and disparate impact. Disparate treatment claims require a plaintiff to show that she suffered unfavorable employment terms or conditions or was subjected to discriminatory acts[9] because of her[10] sex. Alternatively, disparate impact claims allege that while employment practices were facially neutral, they resulted in discriminatory effects on a protected class.[11]

Title VII requires that the plaintiff and her aggrievement fall within the zone of interests to file a claim.[12] Neither differences among employee interactions[13] nor adverse actions based on personal hostility[14] are actionable.

Disparate Treatment

Disparate treatment occurs when an "employer simply treats some people less favorably than others because of their race, color, religion, sex, or national origin."[15] Disparate treatment claims can be based on individual or systemic disparate treatment, including sexual harassment.[16]

Stating a Disparate Treatment Claim

In order to prevail on a Title VII disparate treatment claim based on sex, a plaintiff must establish that she was treated differently than other similarly situated individuals because of her sex.[17] Under the burden-shifting framework set forward by the Supreme Court in *McDonnell Douglas Corp. v. Green*,[18] the plaintiff bears the initial burden of demonstrating a *prima facie* case of discrimination by establishing that she was intentionally discriminated against. The burden then shifts to the defendant to provide at least one legitimate nondiscriminatory reason for the alleged action. Finally, it shifts back to the plaintiff to demonstrate that her employer's proffered reasons for the alleged action were pretextual.[19]

Defendants do not have the burden to prove that the decision was made for a nondiscriminatory reason. The *McDonnell Douglas* framework is purely procedural, "designed only to establish an order of proof and production" rather than to provide plaintiffs a substantive structural advantage.[20]

Discriminatory Intent

"[D]iscriminatory intent or motive"[21] is required to establish a disparate treatment claim, but intent need not be malicious.[22] Liability in disparate treatment cases depends on whether the employer's action was motivated by the protected trait,[23] which is proved by either direct or circumstantial evidence.[24] However, direct evidence, a showing of definitive discrimination demonstrated by explicit remarks

---

from the employer,[25] is rarely available. Instead, plaintiffs typically rely on circumstantial evidence to prove discriminatory intent.

Employer Defenses

Courts have recognized several defenses for Title VII defendants who engage in disparate treatment of employees, including bona fide occupational qualifications, mixed motives, and the *Ellerth-Faragher* affirmative defense.

Bona Fide Occupational Qualifications. When an employee's sex impacts job-related abilities, her employer can raise a bona fide occupational qualification defense (BFOQ).[26] The employer must show that its discriminatory practice relates to the "essence" of the business and bears a strong correlation to the plaintiff's capacity to do her job.[27]

Although this defense was thought to be very broad, the Supreme Court narrowed its application in *UAW v. Johnson Controls*. The Court rejected a BFOQ defense after the employer barred all fertile women of any age, marital status, or child-bearing inclination from holding a position in which they would be likely to be susceptible to lead exposure because "[f]ertile women . . . participate in the manufacture of batteries as efficiently as anyone else."[28] The targeted trait must be essential to the business as a whole and tied to the particular job in question.[29] Some courts also require the employer to show that there were no available alternatives to the institution of a discriminatory practice.[30]

An example of a bona fide occupational qualification defense is when an employer has reason to believe that its gender-based hiring policy was necessary to safeguard legitimate privacy interests of third parties, such as prisoners or psychiatric patients.[31] . . .

Individual Disparate Treatment Claims

A plaintiff can claim intentional individual discrimination due to sex, as a result of: (1) failure to hire or promote; (2) discharge; (3) disciplinary action; (4) constructive discharge; (5) compensation; or (6) employer retaliation. By establishing a *prima facie* case of disparate treatment, a plaintiff "in effect creates a presumption that the employer unlawfully discriminated against the employee."[32]

Hiring and Promotion

To establish an individual *prima facie* case of discrimination in hiring or promotion decisions, an unsuccessful applicant must demonstrate that: (1) she applied for and was qualified for a job or promotion for which the employer was seeking applicants; (2) despite the applicant's qualifications, she was

rejected for the position; and (3) after the plaintiff was rejected, the position remained open and the employer continued to seek applications from individuals with similar qualifications.[33] When an employer maintains a formal system for hiring and promoting, a plaintiff's *prima facie* case must establish that she expressed her desire for the promotion, and that she followed the formal procedures for obtaining the promotion.[34]

An employer can still argue that the decision was based on a legitimate nondiscriminatory reason. An employer is not liable if it chooses to hire an equally qualified applicant over another, barring any evidence of an unlawful motive.[35] Moreover, a "desire to hire the more experienced or better qualified applicant is a nondiscriminatory, legitimate, and common reason on which to base a hiring decision."[36] This reasoning is also applicable in a failure-to-promote case.[37] The employer cannot merely assert that it selected the "best qualified" employee. To satisfy its burden of proof, it must articulate specific reasons for its decision "so that the plaintiff will have a full and fair opportunity to demonstrate pretext."[38] Legitimate, nondiscriminatory qualifications may include seniority,[39] educational background,[40] technical training,[41] and/or job performance.[42]

Compensation

In a Title VII *prima facie* case of sex-based wage or salary discrimination, a plaintiff must show that she occupies a job similar to other higher paying jobs occupied by males.[43] The plaintiff must ultimately establish that the employer had an intent to discriminate.[44] An unlawful employment action occurs each time a person is discriminatorily compensated.[45] Unlike the Equal Pay Act, "Title VII has a relaxed standard for proving the similarity of positions."[46] Differences in pay due to negotiating power is not a defense.

Discharge

To establish a *prima facie* case for discriminatory discharge, a plaintiff must show that: (1) her performance adequately met employer expectations; (2) despite her performance, she was discharged or demoted; and (3) after her termination or demotion, the employer either sought a replacement with similar qualifications and/or replaced the plaintiff with an individual who was not a member of the plaintiff's protected class.[47]

Constructive Discharge

A constructive discharge claim arises when an employee quits due to the employer's conduct. Courts examine the circumstances surrounding an employee's decision to quit and the employer's conduct that precipitated that decision.[48] In *Pennsylvania State Police v. Suders*, a case involving workplace sexual harassment, the Supreme Court held that Title VII is violated when sexually harassing behavior in the workplace becomes so intolerable that a reasonable employee would feel compelled to resign.[49]

An employer may defend against a claim of constructive discharge due to sexual harassment using an *Ellerth-Faragher* affirmative defense. The employer must demonstrate that (1) it had implemented a policy to address complaints about sexual harassment, and (2) the plaintiff unreasonably failed to utilize this resource.[50] However, this defense is not permissible in cases where the plaintiff reasonably resigns because of an official adverse change in her employment status.[51]

Disciplinary Action

To assert a *prima facie* case of improper disciplinary action, a plaintiff must show that (1) she was qualified for the job, and (2) a similarly-situated employee engaged in identical or similar misconduct but was not punished as severely.[52]

Retaliation

Title VII prohibits an employer from taking adverse action against a job applicant or employee "because [s]he has opposed any practice made an unlawful employment practice by this subchapter, or because [s]he has made a charge, testified, assisted, or participated in any manner in an investigation, proceeding, or hearing" regarding a Title VII violation.[53] A retaliation claim may be established even if the plaintiff does not succeed on the underlying harassment claims.[54] In the retaliation context, an employer's conduct is actionable if it would have "dissuaded a reasonable worker from making or supporting a charge of discrimination."[55] To assert a *prima facie* case of retaliation under Title VII, an employee must show that: (1) she engaged in conduct protected under Title VII; (2) she suffered an adverse employment action; and (3) there was a causal connection between the protected activity and the adverse employment action.[56]

Circumstantial evidence is sufficient to establish a causal connection, such as when the employer points to certain conduct as a justification for punishing the plaintiff but does not punish other employees who have engaged in the same type of conduct.[57] ...

Systemic Disparate Treatment

Systemic disparate treatment occurs when an ongoing practice or policy has an adverse effect on a protected class.[58] Although Title VII does not require an employer to mirror the demographics of the general population in its labor force, disproportionate representation can be evidence of systemic disparate treatment.[59] However, when specific qualifications are required for a position, systemic disparate treatment cannot be proven unless the statistical evidence excludes unqualified group members.[60]

To show employer intent in these cases, plaintiffs often focus on the overall pattern of discriminatory decision-making, rather than on individual employment decisions.[61] However, assessment of individual employment decisions may reveal a general pattern of discrimination or a discriminatory policy.[62]

A claim of systemic disparate treatment can be supported by a facially discriminatory policy, statistical evidence,[63] anecdotal evidence,[64] or a combination of these factors.[65] Statistical evidence can be particularly useful, as it allows courts to infer that a pattern of adverse actions against employees of one sex is the result of discriminatory treatment.[66] To be effective, however, the statistical evidence must have a basis for comparison to the qualified labor pool.[67] Without this basis, a plaintiff must provide an appropriate benchmark against which the court may evaluate a statistical disparity.[68] Although anecdotal evidence may strengthen the evidence of disparate treatment, statistical disparities alone may establish a *prima facie* case where the disparities are gross.[69] Plaintiffs do not have to prove discrimination with scientific certainty;[70] statistical evidence showing gross disparities in the representation of characteristics, coupled with anecdotal or circumstantial evidence may be enough to establish a discriminatory pattern or practice.

In a systemic disparate treatment case seeking class-wide injunctive or declaratory relief, plaintiffs need not present evidence that each person who seeks relief was a victim of the employer's discriminatory policy.[71] Rather, plaintiffs need only prove that the company's standard operating procedure was discriminatory, which may be shown through statistics alone.[72] ...

Employer's Defense and Affirmative Action

In systemic disparate treatment cases, the employer's defense must be "designed to meet the *prima facie* case" established by the plaintiff's statistical proof because the focus of its rebuttal case "will not be on individual employment decisions."[73] To meet its rebuttal burden, the employer must demonstrate that the plaintiff's statistical evidence "is either inaccurate or insignificant."[74]

The Supreme Court has held that an employer can lawfully take race into account in preferring African-American employees as a group for admission to on-the-job training programs when that preference is designed to remedy underrepresentation in the workforce relative to the labor pool and thus is consistent with the purpose of Title VII.[75] Likewise, employers may take sex into account to address the problem of underrepresentation of women in the workforce.[76] They may also use those programs as a defense against claims of discrimination. Once a plaintiff has presented a *prima facie* case for sex discrimination alleging that he or she was passed over in favor of a protected class, the employer need only articulate the existence of an affirmative action plan to justify its adverse employment decision.[77] The plaintiff then bears the burden to prove that the affirmative action plan is invalid and thus pretextual.[78] A plan is valid as long as it was implemented to correct a manifest imbalance in the workplace and is narrowly tailored in duration and scope so as not to unnecessarily infringe upon the rights of non-minorities.[79]

Sexual Harassment

Sexual harassment is a form of sex discrimination and is thus actionable under Title VII.[80] Sexual harassment claims fall under the disparate treatment theory of Title VII and encompass both "quid pro quo" and "hostile work environment" claims.[81]

Prima Facie Case

A plaintiff asserting either claim must first establish that the defendant's alleged conduct was (a) unwelcome and unsolicited[82] and (b) motivated "because of sex." This standard does not preclude same-sex harassment claims,[83] nor does the conduct have to be motivated by sexual desire.[84]

(a) **Unwelcomeness.** To establish a *prima facie* case of sexual harassment, a plaintiff must show that the alleged conduct was unwelcome and unsolicited.[85] To show unwelcomeness, the plaintiff must show that she "neither solicited ... nor invited" the sexual advances and "regarded the conduct as undesirable or offensive."[86] The focus will be on the "plaintiff's words, deeds and deportment."[87] Importantly, the plaintiff need not show that her participation was involuntary.[88] The defendant may counter this claim by introducing evidence that the plaintiff welcomed the sexual behavior, as long as such evidence is not unfairly prejudicial.[89] Some courts have excluded evidence of a plaintiff's sexual conduct outside the workplace when offered to show welcomeness on grounds that such evidence is only marginally probative and creates a substantial risk of unfair prejudice.[90]

(b) **"Because of Sex" Rationale.** Title VII prohibits discrimination that occurs "because of [an] individual's ... sex."[91] The "because of sex" provision protects individuals of both genders.[92] The critical inquiry in the "because of sex" analysis is whether members of one sex are exposed to disadvantageous terms or conditions of employment to which members of the other sex are not exposed.[93] Even when employees of both genders are exposed to harassing conduct, female employees can be disproportionately harmed when the conduct degrades women.[94]

Types of Sexual Harassment

Although the terms "quid pro quo" and "hostile work environment" are not included in the text of Title VII,[95] the Supreme Court distinguished between quid pro quo and hostile work environment claims in *Meritor Savings Bank v. Vinson*, but ultimately determined that both of these kinds of claims are entitled to protection under Title VII.[96]

(a) **Quid Pro Quo.** To establish a *prima facie* case for "quid pro quo" harassment, a plaintiff must demonstrate that (1) she refused unwelcome sexual advances;[97] (2) she suffered from a tangible adverse employment action;[98] and (3) the defendant "explicitly or implicitly conditioned a job, a job benefit, or the absence of a job detriment" upon sexual activity.[99]

(b) **Hostile Work Environment.** A *prima facie* hostile work environment claim must establish that (1) the plaintiff was subjected to unwelcome sexual harassment; (2) the harassment was based on sex; (3) the harassment affected a "term, condition, or privilege" of the plaintiff's employment; and (4) the employer knew or should have known of the harassment but did not take prompt remedial action.[100] To determine whether the fourth prong has been satisfied, the court looks to the totality of the circumstances, including whether the harassment was frequent and/or severe; physically threatening or humiliating, as opposed to merely offensive; unreasonably interfered with work performance; and/or undermined the plaintiff's workplace competence.[101] The fourth prong also requires the harassment to be both objectively and subjectively abusive.[102]

A hostile work environment claim comprises a "series of separate acts that collectively constitute one 'unlawful employment practice'."[103] In other words, the "incidents must be more than episodic; they must be sufficiently continuous and concerted in order to be deemed pervasive."[104] In analyzing a potentially unlawful employment practice, a court will consider whether (1) the earlier and later events amounted to the same type of employment actions; (2) the events occurred relatively frequently; or (3) the events were perpetrated by the same managers.[105] Only in rare cases can a single instance of sexual harassment create a hostile work environment.[106]

Notes

1. See Lawrence Solotoff and Henry S. Kramer, *Sex Discrimination and Sexual Harassment in the Work Place* (New York: Law Journal Press, 2000), pp. 1–2.

2. See H.R. Rep. No. 88–914, at 10 (1964), reprinted in 1964 U.S. C.C.A.N. 2391, 2401; see also *Griggs v. Duke Power Co.*, 401 U.S. 424, 430 (1971) (noting congressional intent to promote parity in employment opportunities).

3. *Stache v. Intl. Union of Bricklayers Allied Craftsmen*, 852 F.2d 1231, 1234 (9th Cir. 1988), cert. denied 493 U.S. 815 (1989).

4. *Burlington Indus., Inc. v. Ellerth*, 524 U.S. 742, 764 (1998).

5. See H.R. Rep. No. 102–40, pt. 1, at 4 (1991), reprinted in 1991 U.S.C.C.A.N. 549, 550 (revealing that Congress sought to fortify "protections and remedies" available under Title VII); see also H.R. Rep. No. 92–238, at 3 (1971), reprinted in 1972 U.S.C.C.A.N. 2137, 2139 (noting that Congress sought to equip the Equal Employment Opportunity Commission with procedures necessary to counter employment discrimination).

6. 42 U.S.C. § 2000e-2(a) (West, Westlaw through P.L. 114–61 (excluding P.L. 114–52, 114–54, 114–59, and 114–60)). An employer is "a person engaged in an industry affecting commerce who has fifteen or more employees for each working day in each of twenty or more calendar weeks in the current or preceding calendar year, and any agent of such a person," with some stated exceptions. 42 U.S.C. 2000(e) (1991).

7. *Gen. Dynamics Land Sys., Inc. v. Cline*, 540 U.S. 581, 597–98 (2004).

8. Herma Hill Kay and Martha S. West, *Sex Based Discrimination: Text, Cases and Materials*, 6th ed. (Eagan, MN: Thomson West, 1996), pp. 552–53; Augustus B. Cochran, III, *Sexual Harassment and the Law* (Lawrence: University Press of Kansas, 2004), pp. 19–21.

9. Civil Rights Act of 1964, tit. VII, 42 U.S.C.A. § 2000e-2(a)(1) (West, Westlaw through P.L., 114–51).

10. For the sake of simplicity, and because the majority of Title VII sex discrimination claims are brought by women, this article will often use female pronouns to refer to the generic plaintiff. See Brenda Kruse, "Comment, Women of the Highest Court: Does Gender Bias or Personal Life Experiences Influence Their Opinions?," 36 *U. ToL. L. Rev.* 995, 1022 (2005).

11. See Civil Rights Act of 1964, tit. VII, 42 U.S.C.A. §2000e-2(k) (1)(A)(i).

12. *Thompson v. N. Am. Stainless*, 562 U.S. 170, 174–75 (2011) (maintaining a retaliation claim by an employee who alleged he was terminated after his fiancée and co-worker filed a discrimination complaint with the EEOC).

13. See *Oncale v. Sundowner Offshore Servs.*, 523 U.S. 75, 81 (1998).

14. See *Peters v. Renaissance Hotel Operating Co.*, 307 F.3d 535, 549 n.11 (7th Cir. 2002); *Grimes v. Tex. Dep't of Mental Health & Mental Retardation*, 102 F.3d 137, 143 (5th Cir. 1996).

15. *Intl. Brotherhood of Teamsters v. United States*, 431 U.S. 324, 335 n.15 (1977).

16. See *Cooper v. S. Co.*, 390 F.3d 695, 724 (11th Cir. 2004) (noting that in a "pattern and practice" disparate treatment case, the plaintiff must prove, typically through a combination of statistics and anecdotes, that discrimination is the company's standard operating procedure (citing *EEOC v. Joe's Stone Crab, Inc.*, 220 F.3d 1263, 1274 (11th Cir. 2000)), overruled on other grounds by *Ash v. Tyson Foods, Inc.*, 546 U.S. 454, 456–58 (2006).

17. See *Jespersen v. Harrah's Operating Co.*, 392 F.3d 1076, 1079 (9th Cir. 2004), aff'd en banc, 444 F.3d, 1104 (9th Cir. 2006).

18. See *McDonnell Douglas Corp. v. Green*, 411 U.S. 792, 802–804 (1973); *Cooper*, 390 F.3d, at 723–24.

19. See *McDonnell Douglas*, 411 U.S., at 802–804.

20. See *St. Mary's Honor Ctr. v. Hicks*, 509 U.S. 502, 521 (1993).

21. *Watson v. Fort Worth Bank Trust*, 487 U.S. 977, 986 (1988); *Intl. Brotherhood of Teamsters*, 431 U.S., at 335.

22. See *Jespersen*, 392 F.3d at 1079.

23. See *Raytheon Co. v. Hernandez*, 540 U.S. 44, 52 (2003).

24. See *Cooper*, 390 F.3d at 723–24.

25. See ibid., at 723 n.15.

26. See *UAW v. Johnson Controls, Inc.*, 499 U.S. 187, 204 (1991) ("[P]ermissible distinctions based on sex must relate to ability to perform the duties of the job").

27. See *W. Air Lines, Inc. v. Criswell*, 472 U.S. 400, 416–17 n.24 (1985) ("An employer asserting a BFOQ defense has the burden of proving that (1) the [discriminatory qualification] is reasonably necessary to the essence of the business, and either (2) that all or substantially all individuals excluded from the job involved are in fact disqualified, or (3) that some of the individuals so excluded possess a disqualifying trait that cannot be ascertained except by reference to age. If the employer's objective in asserting a BFOQ is the goal of public safety, the employer must prove that the challenged practice does indeed effectuate that goal and that there is no acceptable alternative which would better advance it or equally advance it with less discriminatory impact" (citing 29 C.F.R. § 1625.6(b) (1984))); *Diaz v. Pan Am. World Airways, Inc.*, 442 F.2d 385, 388–89 (5th Cir. 1971) (finding that the "cosmetic" or "soothing" effects presumably afforded to airline passengers served only by female flight attendants could not excuse the company's discriminatory refusal to hire males because the Court defined the essence of the business as safe transportation rather than maximum profit), cert. denied, 404 U.S. 950 (1971); *Weeks v. S. Bell Tel. Co.*, 408 F.2d 228, 234 (5th Cir. 1969) (finding that even if discrimination against a protected group is intended to

improve the operation of a function crucial to the enterprise, the employer must show that "all or substantially all" members of the protected group lack the required characteristic and would thus be unable to sufficiently perform that function).

28. See *UAW*, 499 U.S., at 205–206.

29. See ibid., at 201 (stating that a BFOQ defense can succeed only if the defendant objectively demonstrates that the discrimination is not only "reasonably necessary" to the "normal operation" of the "particular" business, but also relates to "job-related skills and aptitudes").

30. See, e.g., *Reed v. Cnty. of Casey*, 184 F.3d 597, 600 (6th Cir. 1999) (finding sex-based BFOQ where state law required the presence of a female prison guard when a female prisoner was in jail, and transfer of female employee from first to third shift was justified when no effective alternative existed); *Chambers v. Omaha Girls Club, Inc.*, 834 F.2d 697, 704–705 (8th Cir. 1987) (finding sex-based BFOQ where employer terminated an unmarried pregnant female employee because the primary purpose of the organization was to help teenaged girls and provide them with role models, and the job would inevitably put the employee in contact with the girls).

31. See *Olsen v. Marriott Intl., Inc.*, 75 F. Supp. 2d 1052, 1069 (D. Ariz. 1999) (stating that a privacy-based BFOQ required the defendant to show that: (1) "legitimate privacy rights of patients, clients, or inmates would be violated by hiring members of one sex to fill the position at issue"; and (2) "there are no reasonable alternatives to a sex-based policy" (quoting *Hernandez v. Univ. of St. Thomas*, 793 F. Supp. 214, 216 (D. Minn. 1992))); *Jennings v. N.Y. State Office of Mental Health*, 786 F. Supp. 376, 380–81 (S.D.N.Y. 1992) (finding that a privacy-based BFOQ required the defendant to show that: (1) it had "factual basis for believing that it is necessary" to employ a person of a particular sex in a position to "protect the privacy interests" of a third party; (2) a third party's "privacy interest is entitled to protection under the law"; and (3) "no reasonable alternatives exist to protect those interests other than the gender based hiring policy"), affirmed, 977 F.2d 731 (2nd Cir. 1992) (per curiam).

32. *Tex. Dep't of Cmty. Affairs v. Burdine*, 450 U.S. 248, 254 (1981).

33. See *McDonnell Douglas Corp.*, 411 U.S. at 802; see also *Burdine*, 450 U.S. at 254 n.6 (applying the *prima facie* elements of a race discrimination case, as articulated in *McDonnell Douglas*, to a sex discrimination case).

34. See *Williams v. Giant Food, Inc.*, 370 F.3d 423, 430–31 (4th Cir. 2004) ("If an employer has a formal system of posting vacancies and allowing employees to apply for such vacancies, an employee who fails to apply for a particular position cannot establish a prima facie case of discriminatory failure to promote. In such a circumstance, the employee's general requests for advancement are insufficient to support a claim for failure to promote. On the other hand, if the employer fails to make its employees aware of vacancies, the application requirement may be relaxed and the employee treated as if she

had actually applied for a specific position"); cf. *Smith v. J. Smith Lanier Co.*, 352 F.3d 1342, 1345 (11th Cir. 2003) (holding that expressing a general interest in being rehired without submitting an application is not enough to establish a *prima facie* case of age discrimination when a defendant employer has publicized an open position).

35. See *Evans v. Techs. Applications and Serv. Co.*, 80 F.3d 954, 960 (4th Cir. 1996).

36. *Holder v. Old Ben Coal Co.*, 618 F.2d 1198, 1202 (7th Cir. 1980); see also *Intl. Brotherhood of Teamsters v. United States*, 431 U.S. 324, 358 n.44 (1977) (naming this as one of the most common employer defenses in Title VII hiring cases).

37. See *Evans*, 80 F.3d, at 960.

38. See *Tex. Dep't of Cmty. Affairs v. Burdine*, 450 U.S. 248, 255–56 (1982).

39. See, e.g., *Dodd v. Runyon*, 178 F.3d 1024, 1028 (8th Cir. 1999) (finding no Title VII violation where failure to promote female employee was based on a seniority system that precluded postal clerks from advancing to the position of carrier).

40. See, e.g., *Stanziale v. Jargowsky*, 200 F.3d 101, 105–106 (3d Cir. 2000) (finding that employer had a legitimate, nondiscriminatory reason to pay a female employee with a post-graduate education a higher salary than the male plaintiff, who lacked even a bachelor's degree).

41. See ibid. (noting that the female sanitary inspector was more qualified because she, unlike the male plaintiff, had been certified in pesticide application and lead poisoning investigation).

42. See *Evans*, 80 F.3d, at 960 ("Job performance and relative employee qualifications are widely recognized as valid, nondiscriminatory bases for any adverse employment decision").

43. See *Sprague v. Thorn Ams., Inc.*, 129 F.3d 1355, 1363 (10th Cir. 2003) ("A female Title VII plaintiff establishes a prima facie case of sex discrimination by showing that she occupies a job similar to that of higher paid males" (quoting *Meeks v. Computer Assocs. Intl.*, 15 F.3d 1013, 1019 (11th Cir. 1994))); *E.E.O.C. v. Reichhold Chemicals, Inc.*, 988 F.2d 1564, 1569 (11th Cir. 1993). But see *Adams v. CBS Broad., Inc.*, 61 F. App'x 285, 288 (7th Cir. 2003) (noting that the Supreme Court has not articulated how the standard four-part *McDonnell Douglas* analysis should be tailored to wage discrimination claims).

44. See *Belfi v. Prendergast*, 191 F.3d 129, 140 (2nd Cir. 1999); *Reichhold Chemicals*, 988 F.2d, at 1570.

45. See 42 U.S.C.A. § 2000e-5(e)(3)(A) (West, Westlaw through P. L. 114-61 (excluding P.L. 114-52, 114-54, 114-59, and 114-60) (overturning *Ledbetter v. Goodyear Tire & Rubber Co., Inc.*, 550 U.S. 618 (2007)).

46. See *Lawrence v. CNF Transp., Inc.*, 340 F.3d 486, 492–94 (8th Cir. 2003) (finding for the plaintiff on sex discrimination claim under the Equal Pay Act and Title VII because she was paid less than her successor and was denied a benefit given to him); *Reichhold Chemicals*, 988 F.2d, at 1570.

47. See *Karpel v. Inova Health Sys. Servs.*, 134 F.3d 1222, 1227–28 (4th Cir. 1998) (outlining the *prima facie* elements of a Title VII discriminatory discharge); see also *Neuren v. Adduci*, 43 F.3d 1507, 1512 (D.C. Cir. 1995); *Cumpiano v. Banco Santander P.R.*, 902 F.2d 148, 153 (1st Cir. 1990).

48. See *Levenstein v. Salafsky*, 414 F.3d 767, 775 (7th Cir. 2005) ("We conclude that a person who is on leave with pay, with a temporary (though unsatisfying) reassignment pending an investigation of serious job misconduct, who resigns rather than waits for the conclusion of reasonable prescribed due process procedures of the institution, has not from an objective standpoint been constructively discharged"); *Pa. State Police v. Suders*, 542 U.S. 129, 134 (2004) (holding that constructive discharge is found where the plaintiff can "show that the abusive working environment became so intolerable that her resignation qualified as a fitting response").

49. *Suders*, 542 U.S., at 148.

50. See ibid., at 134.

51. See ibid.

52. See *Alexander v. Fulton Cnty.*, 207 F.3d 1303, 1336 (11th Cir. 2000).

53. 42 U.S.C.A. § 2000e-3(a) (West, Westlaw through P.L. 114–61 (excluding P.L. 114–52, 114–54, 114–59, and 114–60)).

54. *Gilooly v. Mo. Dep't of Health*, 421 F.3d 734, 739 (8th Cir. 2005).

55. *Burlington N. & Santa Fe Ry. Co. v. White*, 548 U.S. 53, 68 (2006).

56. *Gilooly*, 421 F.3d, at 739–40 (reversing summary judgment for employer as to the plaintiff's retaliation claim because the termination was based on the plaintiff's conduct during a sexual harassment investigation).

57. See *Sumner v. U.S. Postal Serv.*, 899 F.2d 203,209 (2nd Cir. 1990).

58. See *1 Aff. Action Compl. Man.* (BNA) § 2:0005, cited in *Jenson v. Eveleth Taconite Co.*, 130 F.3d 1287, 1301 (8th Cir. 1997) ("Employment policies or practices that serve to differentiate or to perpetuate a differentiation in terms or conditions of employment of applicants or employees because of their status as members of a particular group concerns a recurring practice or continuing policy rather than an isolated act of discrimination").

59. See *Intl. Brotherhood of Teamsters v. United States*, 431 U.S. 324, 340 n.20 (1977).

60. See *Hazelwood Sch. Dist. v. United States*, 433 U.S. 299, 308 n.13 (1977) (noting that a comparison to the general population was sufficient in *Intl. Brotherhood of Teamsters* because truck driving is an easily acquired skill, but teaching in a school requires special qualifications); see also *Alexander v. Fulton Cnty.*, 207 F.3d 1303, 1327–28 (11th Cir. 2000) (stating that underrepresentation of whites in sworn law enforcement positions relative to the general population was insufficient evidence of discrimination against whites because the general population is not qualified for such positions),

overruled on other grounds by *Manders v. Lee*, 338 F.3d 1304, 1328 n.52 (11th Cir. 2003).

61. See *Intl. Brotherhood of Teamsters*, 431 U.S., at 360 n.46.

62. Ibid.

63. See ibid., at 339 ("[S]tatistical analyses have served and will continue to serve an important role in cases in which the existence of discrimination is a disputed issue" (citing *Mayor of Phila. v. Educ. Equal. League*, 415 U.S. 605,620 (1974))).

64. See *Alexander*, 207 F.3d, at 1325 (stating that anecdotal evidence concerning discriminatory treatment of similarly situated co-plaintiffs or nonparties who are members of a complainant's protected group "undoubtedly are relevant to every other plaintiff's core allegation of systemic discrimination"); see also *Damon v. Fleming Supermarkets of Fla., Inc.*, 196 F.3d 1354, 1361 (11th Cir. 1999) (stating that anecdotal evidence is significant in cases of individual plaintiffs alleging individual disparate treatment).

65. See, e.g., Intl. Brotherhood of TeamstersIntl. Brotherhood of Teamsters, 431 U.S., at 338–42.

66. See ibid., at 339 n.20 (noting that statistical evidence of "longstanding and gross disparity" may suffice to establish a *prima facie* case of pattern and practice discrimination under Title VII because "absent explanation, it is ordinarily to be expected that nondiscriminatory hiring practices will in time result in a work force more or less representative of the racial and ethnic composition of the population in the community from which employees are hired").

67. See *Evans v. McClain of Ga., Inc.*, 131 F.3d 957, 963 (11th Cir. 1997) (finding no pattern or practice of discrimination where an African-American plaintiff demonstrated statistical evidence of a disproportionately low number of African-American supervisory employees but did not demonstrate statistical evidence of African-American applicants for his position as an assistant plant manager because "statistics without an analytic foundation are virtually meaningless"); see also *Krodel v. Young*, 748 F.2d 701, 709 (D.C. Cir. 1984) ("Where liability depends on a challenge to systemic employment practices, courts have required finely tuned statistical evidence, normally demanding a comparison of the employer's relevant workforce with the qualified populations in the relevant labor market").

68. See *Forehand v. Fla. State Hosp.*, 89 F.3d 1562, 1574 (11th Cir. 1996) ("Courts should adopt the benchmark which most accurately reflects the pool of workers from which promotions are granted unless that pool has been skewed by other discriminatory hiring practices").

69. See *Hazelwood Sch. Dist. v. United States*, 433 U.S., at 299, 307–308 (1977) ("Where gross statistical disparities can be shown, they alone may in a proper case constitute prima facie proof of a pattern or practice of discrimination").

70. See *Bazemore v. United States*, 478 U.S. 385, 400 (1986) ("A plaintiff in a Title VII suit need not prove discrimination with scientific certainty; rather, his or her burden is to prove discrimination by a preponderance of the evidence").

71. *Intl. Brotherhood of Teamsters*, 431 U.S., at 324, 360 (1977); cf. *Wal-Mart Stores, Inc. v. Dukes*, 131 S. Ct. 2541, 2551 (2011) ("Commonality [a requirement for class certification] requires the plaintiff to demonstrate that the class members have suffered the same injury. This does not mean merely that they have suffered a violation of the same provision of law. Title VII, for example, can be violated in many ways ... Their claims must depend upon a common contention – for example, the assertion of discriminatory bias on the part of the same supervisor. That common contention, moreover, must be of such a nature that it is capable of classwide resolution").

72. *Intl. Brotherhood of Teamsters*, 431 U.S., at 336, 339; *Beck v. Boeing Co.*, No. 02–35140, 2003 WL 683797, at *1 (9th Cir. Feb. 25, 2003).

73. *Intl. Brotherhood of Teamsters*, 431 U.S., at 46.

74. Ibid., at 360.

75. See *United Steelworkers v. Weber*, 443 U.S. 193, 208–209 (1979).

76. Ibid., at 205 n.5.

77. See *Johnson v. Transp. Agency, Santa Clara Cnty.*, 480 U.S. 616, 626 (1987).

78. See ibid., at 626–27.

79. See ibid., at 637, 640 (finding that as part of an affirmative action plan for gradual improvement in the representation of minorities and women in an agency's workforce, the agency was allowed to take the employee's sex into account in determining her eligibility for promotion); see also *United Steelworkers*, 443 U.S., at 208 (finding no Title VII violation where preferential treatment was based on an acceptable affirmative action program adopted as temporary measure to eliminate manifest imbalance in workforce); *City of Richmond v. J. A. Croson Co.*, 488 U.S. 469, 507 (1989) (finding a Title VII violation because the affirmative action program was not sufficiently tailored to remedy past discrimination).

80. Solotoff and Kramer, *Sex Discrimination and Sexual Harassment*, pp. 1–3; *Meritor Sav. Bank, FSB v. Vinson*, 477 U.S. 57, 65 (1986).

81. See *Meritor*, 477 U.S., at 65.

82. See ibid., at 68 ("The correct inquiry is whether respondent by her conduct indicated that the alleged sexual advances were unwelcome, not whether her actual participation in sexual intercourse was voluntary").

83. See *Noto v. Regions Bank*, 84 F. Appendix 399, 401–402 (5th Cir. 2003). In *Noto*, the court stated that a plaintiff could allege same-sex sexual harassment in one of three ways. "First, he can show that the alleged harasser made 'explicit or implicit proposals of sexual activity' and provide 'credible evidence that the harasser was homosexual.' Second, he can demonstrate that the harasser was 'motivated by general hostility to the presence of [members of the same sex] in the workplace.' Third, he may 'offer direct, comparative evidence about how the alleged harasser treated members of both sexes in a mixed-sex workplace'" (quoting *La Day v. Catalyst Tech., Inc.*, 302 F.3d 474, 478 (5th Cir. 2002)).

84. See *Oncale v. Sundowner Offshore Servs., Inc.*, 523 U.S. 75, 80 (1998); *EEOC v. Natl. Educ. Ass'n, Ala.*, 422 F.3d 840, 844 (9th Cir. 2005).

85. See *Meritor*, 477 U.S., at 68 ("The gravamen of any sexual harassment claim is that the alleged sexual advances were 'unwelcome'" (quoting 29 C.F.R. § 1604.11(a))).

86. *Moberly v. Midcontinent Communications*, 711 F. Supp. 2d 1028, 1038 (D.S.D. 2010) (quoting *Scusa v. Nestle U.S.A. Co.*, 181 F.3d 958, 966 (8th Cir. 1999)).

87. *Souther v. Posen Construction, Inc.*, 523 F. Appendix 352, 355 (6th Cir. 2013).

88. See note 82.

89. See EEOC, Notice No. N-915-050, *Policy Guidance on Current Issues of Sexual Harassment* (1990), www.eeoc.gov/policy/docs/currentissues.html; see generally FED. R. Evrn. 412(b)(2) ("In a civil case, the court may admit evidence offered to prove a victim's sexual behavior or sexual predisposition if its probative value substantially outweighs the danger of harm to any victim and of unfair prejudice to any party. The court may admit evidence of a victim's reputation only if the victim has placed it in controversy").

90. See FED. R. Evrn. 401, 403, 404; *Wolak v. Spucci*, 217 F.3d 157, 160 (2nd Cir. 2000) (excluding evidence of the plaintiff's history of viewing pornography outside the workplace because such evidence was of marginal probative value); *Polo-Calderon v. Corporacion Puertorriguena de Salud*, 992 F. Supp. 2d 53, 54–55 (D.P.R. 2014) (finding that the probative value of plaintiff's sexuality and texting relationships with other men did not substantially outweigh its prejudicial effect).

91. 42 U.S.C.A. § 2000e-2(a) (West, Westlaw through P.L. 114–49 (approved Aug. 7, 2015)).

92. See *Newport News Shipbuilding & Dry Dock Co. v. EEOC*, 462 U.S. 669, 682 (1983) ("Male as well as female employees are protected against discrimination"); *Phillips v. Martin Marietta Corp.*, 400 U.S. 542, 544 (1971) (per curiam) ("[Title VII] requires that persons of like qualifications be given employment opportunities irrespective of their sex").

93. See *Oncale v. Sundowner Offshore Servs., Inc.*, 523 U.S., at 75, 80 (1998).

94. See *Ocheltree v. Scallon Prods., Inc.*, 335 F.3d 325, 332 (4th Cir. 2003).

95. See 42 U.S.C.A. § 2000e-2(a) (West, Westlaw through P.L. 114–49 (approved Aug. 7, 2015)).

96. *Meritor Sav. Bank, FSB v. Vinson*, 477 U.S., at 57, 65 (1986); see also *Burlington Indus. Inc. v. Ellerth*, 524 U.S. 742, 753–54 (1998) (discussing the history of the development of quid pro quo and hostile work environment sexual harassment).

97. See *Frederick v. Sprint/United Mgmt. Co.*, 246 F.3d 1305, 1312 (11th Cir. 2001) (denying summary judgment for plaintiff who failed to demonstrate connection between alleged refusal of sexual advances and denial of promotion).

98. See *Ellerth*, 524 U.S., at 761–62 (stating that hiring, firing, failing to promote, or other significant changes in the employee's status constitute a tangible employment action).

99. See *Heyne v. Caruso*, 69 F.3d 1475, 1478 (9th Cir. 1995).

100. See *Succar v. Dade Cnty. Sch. Bd.*, 229 F.3d 1343, 1344–45 (11th Cir. 2000) (citing *Henson v. City of Dundee*, 682 F.2d 897, 903–905 (11th Cir. 1982)).

101. See *Harris v. Forklift Sys., Inc.*, 510 U.S. 17, 23 (1993); *Butler v. Ysleta Indep. Sch. Dist.*, 161 F.3d 263, 270 (5th Cir. 1998) (adding the workplace competence factor).

102. See *Harris*, 510 U.S., at 21–22 ("Conduct that is not severe or pervasive enough to create an objectively hostile or abusive work environment – an environment that a reasonable person would find hostile or abusive – is beyond Title VII's purview. Likewise, if the victim does not subjectively perceive the environment to be abusive, the conduct has not actually altered the conditions of the victim's employment, and there is no Title VII violation").

103. *Nat'l R.R. Passenger Corp. v. Morgan*, 536 U.S. 101, 117 (2002).

104. See *Lyon v. Jones*, 260 F. Supp. 2d 507, 512 (D. Conn. 2003) (quoting *Alfano v. Costello*, 294 F.3d 365, 374 (2nd Cir. 2002) (internal quotations omitted)).

105. See *Porter v. Cal. Dep't of Corr.*, 419 F.3d 885, 893 (9th Cir. 2005).

106. See, e.g., *Ferris v. Delta Airlines, Inc.*, 277 F.3d 128, 136 (2nd Cir. 2001) (noting that a single rape is "sufficiently egregious" to alter the conditions of employment).

Reconceptualizing Sexual Harassment, Again

VICKI SCHULTZ

Theory

To create lasting change requires an informed theory of sexual harassment: What *is* harassment? What is in it for the harassers? What causes harassment? To prevent it, what must change?

Two decades ago, I proposed a new theory of harassment that challenged the prevailing orthodoxy. The older view defined sexual harassment as unwanted sexual advances, typically by powerful men toward their female subordinates. I called this view the sexual desire-dominance paradigm.[1] Harassment in that paradigm is a top-down, male-to-female, *sexual* phenomenon, driven by sexual desire. It has little to do with work or workplace conditions; it is about predatory sexuality. Men merely use their positions at work, in this theory, to satisfy their urge to dominate women sexually.

My theory challenged this narrow sexual focus. In my view, sexual harassment is a means of maintaining masculine work status and identity, not expressing sexuality or sexual desire. Harassment includes not only unwanted sexual advances but also a wide range of other sexist, demeaning behaviors aimed at women and others who threaten settled gender norms. Harassment is linked to broader forms of sex discrimination and inequality, because some men harass women and "lesser men" to preserve their dominant workplace position and related sense of manhood. Sexualized behavior is often a tool of harassment, in this theory, but sexuality is not inherently degrading or discriminatory. My writing elaborated this view in the context of employment, stressing the importance of traditionally male forms of work to mainstream masculine status and selfhood. But the theory also applies more broadly to other institutions that help shape and reinforce gender identity.

This newer theory has taken hold in many quarters. First and foremost, it has been affirmed in the law. The United States Supreme Court has acknowledged explicitly that workplace harassment does not have to be explicitly "sexual" in content or motivation to be actionable,[2] and, conversely, that not all sexually tinged conduct amounts to harassment.[3] Instead, the touchstone is whether the misconduct occurs *because of sex*. Thus, the law has come to recognize that same-sex harassment is also actionable. The Equal Employment Opportunity Commission (EEOC) has also clarified that harassment includes any conduct that demeans people at work because of their sex or gender, regardless of whether it is sexual in nature.[4] Many lower courts have affirmed and elaborated on these ideas.

But the old orthodoxy still has cultural currency, and I worry that it will gain ascendancy again in the absence of vigorous public debate and education, impeding our ability to move forward with systemic change. There are signs that many people who identify with the #MeToo movement are guided, consciously or unconsciously, by the older understanding of sexual harassment. The movement was

From *The Yale Law Journal Forum* (June 18, 2018). © 2018. Reprinted with permission of the Yale Law Journal.

rekindled soon after the story broke about Harvey Weinstein, when actress Alyssa Milano asked her Twitter followers, "If you've been sexually harassed or assaulted write 'me too' as a response to this tweet."[5] Although I have found no systematic empirical research on this point, it seems clear that most of the ensuing #MeToo posts focused on specifically sexual forms of harassment and abuse, including sexual assault, and not on broader patterns of sexism and discrimination. Most of the tweets that were most frequently retweeted in the first month, for example, referenced sexual misconduct. Data visualizations of tweets in that period feature words like "sexual," "sexually," "rape," "survivor," "violence," "assault," "predator," "abuse," "exploitation" – all words associated with explicitly sexual forms of misconduct – and names like "weinstein," "harvey," "billoreilly," "trump," "louisck," "roymoorechildmolester" – all people accused of this type of conduct. A survey commissioned in February 2018, *The Facts Behind the #MeToo Movement*, also focused almost exclusively on sexualized forms of harassment, verbal and physical.

Furthermore, from the beginning, media stories reporting on the movement have, explicitly or implicitly, limited their definition of sexual harassment to unwanted sexual overtures or other specifically sexual forms of abuse – despite the fact that the legal definition of harassment covers broader forms of sex-based misconduct and has done so for twenty years. Notably, the *New York Times*, whose reporters broke the Weinstein story, has publicly defined "sexual harassment in the workplace" in explicitly sexual terms: "The *Times* uses the terms 'sexual harassment' and 'sexual misconduct' to refer to a range of behaviors that are sexual in nature and nonconsensual. The term 'sexual assault' usually signifies a felony sexual offense, like rape."[6] This definition likens workplace sexual harassment to sexual assault and rape – not to other forms of sex-based harassment and discrimination, as the legal definition does. Most press reporting and social coverage about #MeToo has tended to adopt a similarly limited sexual focus, despite two decades of efforts by feminists in law, social science, and activist circles to create a broader, more accurate picture of the harassment and discrimination most working women and LGBTQ people face.

This purely sexual lens represents a step backward, not forward. The law has come to recognize that harassment consists of many forms of sexist, hostile, and discriminatory conduct, based on sex or gender stereotypes, that go beyond sexual overtures. Recognizing these broader forms of harassment does not mean that sexual misconduct is not important. It is, of course, crucial to expose and address unwanted sexual advances and assaults in the workplace (and other realms). Sexual abuse has remained hidden in the dark shadows of organizational and social life for too long. We, as a society, must be more willing to acknowledge sexual abuse and talk about it honestly and directly, just as we do other forms of abuse, without a sense of denial, shame, or discomfort. Organizations can and should hold harassers accountable for sexual misconduct just as they do other forms of mistreatment and discrimination, without excusing it as a personal predilection or a perk of the powerful.

But targeting *only* sexual misconduct without addressing related patterns of sexism and deeper institutional dynamics has serious shortcomings – shortcomings that risk undermining the broader quest for gender equality. This point applies beyond the context of workplace harassment. The #MeToo movement has exposed sexual assaults and abuse in arenas other than workplaces, such as schools, churches, fraternities, families, and prisons. No matter where it appears, sexuality does not exist in a vacuum; sexual behavior is always a product not simply of innate individual desires, but also of institutional forces that evoke, shape, and give it meaning. Thus, regardless of whether sexual misconduct occurs at work or elsewhere, it has inevitably been facilitated and formed by these larger contextual forces. We must address these forces head-on if we are to end the full spectrum of harassment and discrimination of both the sexual and nonsexual kinds.

The Broad Range of Sex-Based Harassment

Focusing narrowly on male-to-female, unwanted sexual advances blinds us to the pervasive and pernicious *nonsexual* forms of sexism and harassment that women and others experience. Harassment does not always consist of unwanted sexual advances; a wide range of nonsexual actions is used to denigrate women and label them as "different" because of their sex.

In fact, contrary to popular perceptions, nonsexual forms of sex-based harassment and hostility are far more prevalent than unwanted sexual overtures. Harassment takes a wide variety of nonsexual forms, including hostile behavior, physical assault, patronizing treatment, personal ridicule, social ostracism, exclusion or marginalization, denial of information, and work sabotage directed at people because of their sex or gender. This harassment is not only directed at heterosexual women: men who do not conform to prescribed images of masculinity and others who threaten established gender norms are subjected to similar harassment. Research suggests that most harassment aims to shore up masculine workplace superiority, not to secure sexual gratification.[7] Most of the time, even unwanted sexual overtures are part of a broader pattern of sex-based harassment and hostility.

Years ago, I elaborated on these points, drawing examples from a wide range of industries, occupations, and jobs. By all accounts, little has changed, especially in the traditionally male-dominated industries, organizations, and jobs where harassment is most prevalent. Consider the following examples from the Hollywood film industry and the Silicon Valley technology industry. These industries profoundly impact and shape American society and attract aspirants from all different backgrounds. Both remain highly unequal along sex, gender, and other lines.

Hollywood's Harvey Weinstein

Hollywood movie mogul Harvey Weinstein is widely portrayed as the quintessential sexual predator.[8] Yet, a closer look reveals that even his predations were part of a broader campaign of nonsexual abuse, hostility, and sex discrimination. Numerous reports have described Weinstein's sexual aggressions, revealing how he preyed on young actresses and models seeking to advance in the film industry by allegedly pressuring them for sex, exposing himself, groping them and forcing himself on some of them, enticing them with promises of stardom, and threatening to ruin them if they didn't go along.

Far fewer reports have covered the nonsexual, but still utterly sexist, forms of abuse Weinstein heaped upon less influential women who worked for him. Zelda Perkins worked as Weinstein's assistant for nineteen years. She stated that Weinstein repeatedly harassed her in both sexual and nonsexual ways.[9] Not only did Weinstein work in the nude, ask to be massaged and to give her massages, and bathe in front of Perkins, he also yelled and cursed at her continually, and wore her down emotionally, especially after she had the temerity to stand up to him. Perkins says Weinstein never threatened her physically, but "she was constantly threatened 'emotionally and psychologically.'" Perkins resigned and tried to sue Weinstein for harassment, but was pressured into a secret settlement in a process she says left her broken. Afterward, Perkins could not find work anywhere in the industry and was so devastated she moved all the way to Central America to heal.

Perkins's experience was not atypical. According to a complaint filed by the New York State Attorney General after an extensive four-month investigation, Weinstein committed pervasive sexual and nonsexual harassment and discrimination against employees, creating a hostile work environment "permeated with gender-based hostility and inequality." In addition to unwanted sexual advances, Weinstein "regularly berated women using gender-based obscenities and stereotypes," yelled that they should leave and make babies since that was all they were good for, demanded to know if they had their periods, and accused them of wanting "special treatment" because of their sex. Weinstein did not target only women for such gendered opprobrium. He also used homophobic slurs and gender-based insults to degrade and scold men and to attack their masculinity.

Certain other forms of harassment, while not gendered in content, were directed only at female employees. The complaint alleges that Weinstein, a physically imposing man, "used his stature and threatening statements . . . to demean and frighten female employees . . . yelling at them for purported incompetence, cursing in their faces, threatening to end their careers, and describing his intent to harm them, all while walking into them and bringing his face only a few inches from theirs." He violently punched one employee's car seat, and backed her up against a wall while berating her. He often told employees he would kill them or their families, saying he had contacts in the Secret Service and threatening, "You don't know what I can do."

Not only did Weinstein harass employees in sexual and nonsexual ways; he also systematically discriminated against female employees in assigned duties and expectations. According to the complaint, he threatened to fire some female assistants "if they did not serve in gendered roles such as providing childcare to his young children, obtaining [his] prescriptions for medicine, and performing other domestic labor such as assisting [his] wife or one of [his] adult daughters." Weinstein similarly expected female assistants and even female executives who were trained in film production to facilitate and hide his sexual liaisons – a role that male executives were not expected to fill. One beleaguered employee complained to human resources, stating she did "not appreciate being given work my male counterparts are never asked to complete." When Weinstein berated her and retaliated against her, she left.

Harvey Weinstein's behavior was extreme, but it illustrates the way harassment works generally. Not only did Weinstein make unwanted sexual overtures, he also routinely harassed and demeaned his employees in other ways that were rooted in sexism and stereotypes. In this regard, Weinstein was far from unusual. Decades of research shows that nonsexual forms of sexism and abuse, directed at women simply because they are women, are far more prevalent than unwanted sexual advances and sexual coercion.[10] Indeed, according to one group of leading researchers, this nonsexual, but still sex-based harassment is not just a side story – it is *the* modal form of harassment against women in traditionally male-dominated job settings.[11]

Silicon Valley

While most of Weinstein's victims worked in traditionally female roles, many women who work in traditionally male jobs in similarly male-dominated industries have comparable experiences. The stories of engineer Susan Fowler and venture capital junior partner Ellen Pao illustrate how unwanted sexual advances reflect a larger culture of sexism, nonsexual harassment, and sex discrimination in the Silicon Valley technology industry.

For Susan Fowler, the engineer whose February 2017 blog post blew the lid off Uber's sexist work culture,[12] the trouble began on the first day of work, when her manager sent her chat messages saying he was looking for a woman to have sex with. The pass itself was offensive, but what proved to be even more debilitating to her and other women at Uber was the company's failure to take their complaints and concerns – and the women themselves – seriously. Fowler's complaint about her manager's behavior, like those of women before her, fell on deaf ears: upper management declined to punish a "high performer," and the human resources department instead gave Fowler a "choice" to find a new team or expect a poor performance evaluation.

When Fowler moved to a new team at Uber, the chaos and sexism there were so palpable that women fled in droves. Her director excused the exodus by saying the women "needed to step up and be better engineers," and a human resources manager suggested a low number of women should be expected in engineering "because sometimes certain people of certain genders and ethnic backgrounds were better suited for some jobs than others[.]" The company even went so far as to deny the women leather jackets that were provided to all the male engineers, saying there were too few women to justify placing an order. After being told she was "on thin ice" for reporting repeated problems to human resources and being threatened with firing, Fowler finally left Uber, like most of her other female colleagues. When she began working at Uber, women were 25 percent of her unit's engineers; by the time she left, that number had dwindled to 3 percent. At Uber, then, the initial sexual overture turned out to be only the first in a crushing series of discriminatory actions that conveyed how little women mattered to the company.

Ellen Pao's account of her problems as a junior partner at Kleiner Perkins Caufield & Byers, a leading venture capital firm, similarly begins with a sexual overture. Like Fowler's, Pao's story ends up providing a larger window into the systematic disrespect and discrimination she and other women face in venture capital and the broader tech industry.[13] On a trip abroad, a fellow junior partner told Pao that he was unhappily married and thought he and she would be "good together." He asked for her hotel room number, but when she mistakenly gave him the wrong one, he was angry the next day, having gone to the room for a rendezvous and not found her there. Over time, Pao succumbed to his entreaties and they had a brief affair.

When she broke up with him, Pao alleges the man retaliated by sabotaging her career. For five years, according to Pao, her colleague excluded her from business meetings and emails, failed to share crucial job information with her, and tried to steal companies Pao sponsored. More than once, Pao complained to senior partners about this retaliatory harassment, but they did nothing. Instead, the firm promoted the man to senior partner in the group where she worked, giving him even more control over her career. After his promotion, Pao began receiving poor performance reviews. Pao later discovered that the man had sexually harassed another female junior partner – a fact that should have lent Pao's complaint more credibility – but reporting this discovery did not vindicate Pao's reputation or prospects at Kleiner Perkins. The firm did eventually let the alleged harasser go (reportedly with a generous severance package), but it also fired Pao and hired a public relations firm to discredit her throughout Silicon Valley.

Pao's complaint and her later book make clear that the alleged sexual harassment and retaliation she faced was part of broader pattern of sexism and discrimination against women at Kleiner Perkins. Pao alleges that women were systematically excluded from events that presented business opportunities and subjected to rigged rules of the game that doomed them to failure from the start. There were male-only ski trips and dinners to which women were not invited because they would "kill the buzz," practices that prevented women (but not men) from serving on the boards of directors for the companies they sponsored,[14] and constant efforts to poach women's companies, especially when they were out on pregnancy leave. When Pao complained to her boss about these problems, he reportedly trivialized them or yelled at her and told her to drop it. Eventually, after realizing that the company was never going to change, Pao filed suit and was fired.

It is Pao's description of the "thousand paper cuts," the daily humiliations, exclusions, and slights that she and other women suffered at the hands of male higher-ups and peers at Kleiner Perkins, that most clearly reveals the ubiquity and scale of the harassment and discrimination women face in the technology industry generally. Highly educated female engineers and professionals were routinely assigned "domestic" tasks, such as taking notes at meetings, that were never asked of their male colleagues.

It is little wonder, then, that the fate of the few women employed at Kleiner Perkins resembled that of Uber's female engineers. Three years after Pao was fired, every single woman she worked with as a junior partner had left or been forced out of the firm.[15] Like their Uber counterparts, Kleiner Perkins's higher-ups attributed the decline not to sexism, but to women's biology, "maternal clocks," or "a burning desire to 'opt out'." . . .

Theoretical Implications

Not only is it inexcusable to erase the harms of nonsexual forms of harassment, but ignoring them also leads to an inadequate view of the dynamics driving harassment generally. Once we acknowledge that most harassment does not take the form of sexual overtures, it becomes clear that harassment is not and cannot be primarily a means of expressing sexual desire or sexual domination. Most of the time, harassment is not about securing sexual gratification; it's about putting women (and men who are "not man enough") down, reinforcing the existing gender order, and reaffirming threatened social identities. This happens in many realms of life, but nowhere is it more pronounced than in work or career-related settings.

For most American men, historically, labor market and workplace superiority has been crucial to hegemonic masculine identity.[16] Earning more than comparable women, holding a traditionally male job, and possessing skills and authority that women allegedly lack are all central to mainstream masculinity. Thus, it is unsurprising that women who enter traditionally male-dominated work settings are more likely to experience sex-based harassment than other women.[17] Research shows this is not simply because these women are more likely to encounter men. Rather, it is because they pose a threat to the masculine composition and image of the men's jobs and to their sense of manhood. . . .

Foundations

To have an adequate theory of harassment, it is not enough to understand what the harassers stand to gain. It is even more important to understand the industry dynamics and organizational conditions that foster and fuel harassment.

There are many such factors, but here I will stress two structural features of industries and fields in which harassment is known to flourish: sex-segregated work and subjective, unconstrained authority. . . .

On closer inspection, it is no accident that Hollywood and Silicon Valley are rife with harassment. Both industries are characterized by a high degree of sex segregation, where mostly men hold leadership positions and favored jobs, while women are greatly outnumbered or are concentrated in less highly-regarded roles. Similarly, both industries grant executives and managers vast unchecked subjective discretion to hire and promote people; success depends on navigating informal social networks and impressing high-status kingmakers who have the subjective authority to make or break careers and life prospects.

These factors – sex segregation and unconstrained, personalistic authority – set the stage for sexual harassment.

Sex Segregation

The sex segregation of work is both a cause and consequence of harassment. Sex segregation means men hold the most powerful or prized jobs, while women hold lower-status positions. This state of affairs fosters sex stereotypes – for example, a sense that men are leaders or geniuses while women are followers. Segregation primes these stereotypes, prompting the dominant group to perceive any minorities who enter their jobs as "different" and out of place, and to close ranks against them to defend their position and status. Because men's work roles still tend to afford them higher status, men's stake in preserving their superior workplace positions and associated masculinities is typically stronger than women's in preserving traditionally female jobs and related femininities. For this reason, men are more likely than women to engage in harassment and more likely to do so when they work in traditionally male-dominated settings, as discussed above.

Sex segregation also makes it more difficult for those in the minority to resist harassment. Without the power and safety that comes with more equal numbers, women and others who are harassed cannot effectively censor or counter stereotypes and cannot effectively deter, resist, or report harassment. Nor can they participate effectively in shaping the organization's cultures and norms, or in changing the organization's structures and practices in ways that foster greater inclusion and equality. Research shows that skewed numbers leave women outnumbered and vulnerable at work, left to curry favor or compete with men on an unequal basis.[18]

Harassment, in turn, further fuels sex segregation and stereotyping. By driving women away or discouraging them from male-dominated fields, and labeling the women who pursue them as different and less capable, harassment reinforces both horizontal and vertical segregation and confirms perceptions that women are not suited for traditionally "masculine" jobs or leadership roles. Similarly, by pressuring women in traditionally female-dominated jobs to tolerate sexist demands, harassment reinforces vertical sex segregation by confirming ideas that women do and should naturally submit to male authority. Thus, segregation and harassment reinforce each other in a self-perpetuating cycle.

Unconstrained, Subjective Authority

It is not only the gendered nature of the hierarchy that fuels harassment: it is also the nature of the hierarchy itself. Harassment is fueled by employment systems that give higher-ups unchecked, subjective authority to make or break other people's careers on their own subjective say-so, without the use of objective criteria or external oversight to constrain their judgments.

By unconstrained, subjective authority, I refer to the use of subjective selection systems for hiring, assigning, promoting, paying, firing, and evaluating people. First, these systems vest broad discretion in individual executives, managers, or supervisors to evaluate people based on their own personal judgment, free from external oversight or accountability. In addition, these systems are often subjective in the sense that managers deploy unmeasurable, nonobjective criteria, such as "leadership potential" or "cultural fit." Furthermore, even if some managers rely on objective criteria, the selection process may still be subjective in another sense, namely a lack of uniformity or consistency. Subjective systems typically make little or no effort to ensure that all managers use the same criteria to assess candidates or that they weigh or apply those criteria in the same way to all candidates. The result of all these factors is a lack of transparency, for candidates cannot ascertain in advance what it takes to succeed in these systems. These systems sometimes also involve an additional dimension of subjectivity: the use of tightly knit social networks to recruit and attract new talent. These networks privilege the subjective judgment of not just one executive or manager, but multiple industry insiders or peers, to recommend candidates based on their reputations or social connections. Finally, the term unconstrained, subjective authority can refer not only to subjective hiring and evaluation, but also to the unfettered authority to direct and control the day-to-day work and activities of subordinates.

It is well known that unconstrained, subjective selection systems foster discrimination. Research demonstrates that processes that give managers unfettered discretion to make decisions about employees or aspirants based on their own subjective judgment facilitate stereotyping and discrimination. Psychological research further shows that people, such as managers, whose positions give them a high degree of power to affect other people's lives by providing or withholding resources or administering punishments are more prone to engage in stereotyping, because they are less likely to attend to individuating information about them. For these reasons, the law has long recognized that without objective guideposts or oversight to ensure candidates are treated evenhandedly, managers in subjective systems often fall back on stereotypes and bias in making employment decisions.[19] Managers in these systems also tend to hire people who look like themselves to reduce uncertainty and foster trust.[20] Where employment systems lack more defined ways to evaluate skill, moreover, candidates often must depend on tight social networks to acquire jobs and advance their careers. It is well known that these networks, too, often operate to exclude women and other outsiders.[21]

Here I extend these older observations to offer a new insight: just as unfettered, subjective authority facilitates discrimination in hiring and promotion, it also fosters sex-based harassment. This is true for two different reasons. First, giving higher-ups the authority to hire, promote, and fire people based on their own subjective judgment increases their power to exercise arbitrary and abusive authority over employees. Employees have no basis for demanding accountability in the absence of any objective standards or opportunity for oversight, especially in the typical at-will employment scenario.[22] Industry cultures in which career advancement turns on connections rather than more objective credentials only intensify the problem, because they give higher-ups even more power to blackball those who cross or displease them.

But the problem is not simply that positions characterized by unchecked authority *permit* harassment and abuse; it is that they actually *encourage* it. Research shows that the nature of the authority vested in such positions inculcates in those who occupy them a sense of entitlement to wield arbitrary authority over people "beneath" them, simply by virtue of the fact that their positions give them the power to do so.[23] In one classic study, managers vested with institutional power to control employees' behavior (by firing or demoting them and paying them less) increased their attempts to control subordinates, devalued subordinates' work efforts and performance, viewed them as objects of manipulation, and desired greater social distance from them.[24] This study laid the groundwork for a metamorphic theory of power, "which asserts that through the repeated exercise of power individuals adopt more vainglorious self-concepts and as a consequence [come to] denigrate the less powerful."[25] Unchecked institutional authority, in other words, begets a growing sense of personal power and self-aggrandizement. Both formal and informal sources of authority over others can feed this sense of power.[26]

At one level, these insights simply reflect the truism that sexual harassment is about power. But what is lacking in that observation is a specification of the nature and source of that power. Men's power in the workplace is not merely attributable to higher levels of testosterone or patriarchal conditions in society at large, as is often claimed. Instead, it is attributable to the unchecked, subjective authority that is vested in many men's organizational positions by companies, industries, and the law. As Donald Trump put it, "when you're a star, they let you do it. You can do anything." Leading the Trump Organization, the Miss Universe pageant, and *The Apprentice* are what put him in the position of being a "star," not simply being male in a sexist society. Positions that grant people such unfettered subjective authority foster discrimination, harassment, and abuse.

Conclusion

The #MeToo movement has renewed women's – and all people's – dreams and demands for equal, inclusive workplaces characterized by relations of respect and solidarity, rather than discrimination and abuse. We have been here before. This time, let us not be lulled into focusing on symptoms and individual solutions. We must insist that our institutions take on the crucial tasks of dismantling sex segregation and restructuring unconstrained subjective authority in favor of more equal, open, and accountable institutions. Eliminating segregation is crucial if women and men of all types are to interact and work together as equals. Constraining subjective authority is equally important. Not only can reining in that authority reduce discrimination and stereotyping, but it can also help eliminate harassment and abuse. When bosses and benefactors no longer have carte blanche authority to make or break people's careers on their own say-so, they will have far less ability to mistreat, harass, and retaliate against the less powerful. In the name of equality, in the name of humanity, it is time to demand: no more kings; no more kingmakers.

Notes

1. Vicki Schultz, "Reconceptualizing Sexual Harassment," 107 *Yale Law Journal* 1683 (1998).
2. *Oncale v. Sundowner Offshore Servs.*, Inc., 523 U.S. 75, 80 (1998). ("[H]arassing conduct need not be motivated by sexual desire to support an inference of discrimination on the basis of sex.")
3. Ibid. ("We have never held that workplace harassment, even harassment between men and women, is automatically discrimination because of sex merely because the words used have sexual content or connotations.")
4. The EEOC's revised definition of sexual harassment, posted in guidance on its website, provides: "It is unlawful to harass a person (or applicant or employee) because of that person's sex. Harassment can include 'sexual harassment' or unwelcome sexual advances, requests for sexual favors, or other verbal of physical conduct of a sexual nature. *Harassment does not have to be of a sexual nature, however, and can include offensive remarks about a person's sex.* For example, it is illegal to harass a woman by making offensive comments about women in general." *Sexual Harassment*, US Equal Employment Opportunity Commission, www.eeoc .gov/laws/types/sexual_harassment .cfm [https://perma.cc/3QWV-4WHN] (emphasis added); see also *Harassment*, US Equal Employment Opportunity Commission, www.eeoc.gov/laws/types/harassment.cfm [https://perma.cc/6XJ5-AZ3R] ("Harassment is unwelcome conduct that is based on race, color, religion, sex (including pregnancy), national origin, age (40 or older), disability or genetic information.")
5. @Alyssa_Milano, Twitter (October 15, 2017, 1:21 p.m.) https://twitter.com/alyssa_milano /status/919659438700670976? lang=en [https://perma.cc/S3KV-NGX6]. It is important to note that Milano was picking up on work that Tarana Burke, a black feminist activist who is credited with launching the "Me Too" movement in 2007, had started. See Sandra E. Garcia, "The Woman Who Created #MeToo Long before Hashtags," *The New York Times* (October 20, 2017), www.nytimes.com/2017/ 10/20/us/me-too-movement-tarana-burke.html [https://perma .cc/Z62D-QAMJ]; cf. Angela Onwuachi-Willig, "What about #UsToo?: The Invisibility of Race in the #MeToo Movement," 128 *Yale Law Journal Forum* 105 (2018), 105–108 (describing Burke's role in the #MeToo movement).
6. Natalie Proulx, Christopher Pepper, and Katherine Shulten, "The Reckoning: Teaching about the #MeToo Movement and Sexual Harassment with Resources," *The New York Times* (January 25, 2018).
7. See, e.g., Jennifer L. Berdahl, "Harassment Based on Sex: Protecting Social Status in the Context of Gender Hierarchy," 32 *Academy of Management Review* 641 (2007), at 643 (stating that "the most common form of sexual harassment is gender harassment, which involves . . . sexist comments, jokes, and materials that alienate and demean victims based on sex rather than solicit sexual relations with them"); Jennifer L. Berdahl, "The Sexual Harassment of Uppity Women," 92 *Journal of Applied Psychology* 425, 429 (2007) (showing that "women with relatively masculine personalities experience[d] the most sexual harassment," not those with feminine attributes); Heather McLaughlin, Christopher Uggen, and Amy Blackstone, "Sexual Harassment, Workplace Authority, and the Paradox of Power," 77 *American Sociological Review* 625, 627 (2012) (collecting studies).
8. Jodi Kantor and Megan Twohey broke the Weinstein story on October 5, 2017. See Jodi Kantor and Megan Twohey, "Harvey

Weinstein Paid off Sexual Harassment Accusers for Decades," *The New York Times* (October 5, 2017), www.nytimes.com /2017/10/05/us/harvey-weinstein-harassment-allegations.html [https://perma.cc/AY97-XAH4]. Since then, news media have covered Weinstein's sexual aggressions extensively, with stories too voluminous to cite. See, e.g., Ronan Farrow, "From Aggressive Overtures to Sexual Assault: Harvey Weinstein's Accusers Tell Their Stories," *The New Yorker* (October 23, 2017), www.newyorker.com/news/news- desk/from- aggressive-overtures-to-sexual-assault-harvey-weinsteins- accusers-tell-their- stories [https://perma.cc/Q4JN-V8GQ]. Weinstein has now been arrested and charged with rape and criminal sexual assault in New York. James C. McKinley, Jr., "Harvey Weinstein Indicted on Rape and Criminal Sexual Act Charges," *The New York Times* (May 30, 2018), www.nytimes .com/2018/05/30/nyregion/weinstein-indicted-rape.html [https://perma.cc/G7YE-DGLT]; Benjamin Mueller and Alan Feuer, "Arrested on Rape Charges, Weinstein Posts $1 Million Bail," *The New York Times* (May 25, 2018), www .nytimes.com/2018/05/25/nyregion/harvey-weinstein-arrested .html [https://perma.cc/3DSN-MVKA].

9. See Matthew Garrahan, "Harvey Weinstein: How Lawyers Kept a Lid on Sexual Harassment Claims," *Financial Times* (October 23, 2017), www.ft.com/content/1dc8a8ae-b7e0- 11e7-8c12-5661783e5589 [https://perma.cc/4VZT-HVM4]; Emily Longeretta, "Harvey Weinstein's Ex Assistant Opens up about Working for 'Repulsive Monster,'" *U.S. Weekly* (December 20, 2017), www.usmagazine.com/celebrity-news/ news/harvey-weinsteins-ex-assistant-talks-working-for-repul sive-monster/ [https://perma.cc/4TX2-GLWW].

10. See Jennifer L. Berdahl and Jana L Raver, "Sexual Harassment," in *American Psychological Association Handbook of Industrial and Organizational Psychology*, vol. 3 (Washington, DC: APA, 2011), p. 646 (collecting studies); Chai R. Felblum and Victoria A. Lipnic, *Report of the Co-Chairs of the EEOC Select Task Force on the Study of Harassment in the Workplace*, Equal Employment Opportunity Commission, nn.15 and 19–20 (June 2016), www.eeoc.gov/eeoc/task_force/harassment/ report.cfm#_Toc453686302 [https://perma.cc/Z2KP-77CZ] (collecting recent studies). For one recent study, see Emily A. Leskinen, Lilia M. Cortina, and Dana B. Kabat, "Gender Harassment: Broadening Our Understanding of Sex-Based Harassment at Work," 35 *Law and Human Behavior* 25 (2011), at 37 (reporting that for women in the military and in law, sex- based or "gender harassment in the absence of unwanted sexual attention or coercion was the most common manifestation of harassment," with nine out of ten victims facing such harassment).

11. Leskinen et al., "Gender Harassment," p. 36 (showing that "gender harassment does not simply provide a backdrop for other kinds of harassment; it is the *modal form* of sex-based harassment faced by women at work").

12. Susan Fowler, "Reflecting on One Very, Very Strange Year at Uber," susanjfowler.com (February 19, 2017), www.susanjfow ler.com/blog/2017/2/19/reflecting-on-one-very-strange-year- at-uber.

13. Ellen Pao, *Reset: My Fight for Inclusion and Lasting Change* (New York: Spiegel & Grau, 2017).

14. Ibid., pp. 76–77, 120–21, 128.

15. Ibid., p. 153.

16. Hegemonic masculinity is defined as the most favored view of manhood in a particular context, and the one to which all men experience pressure to conform. It is premised on and promotes the exclusion of women and a rank ordering of men. For a clear elaboration of the concept, see David S. Cohen, "Keeping Men 'Men' and Women Down: Sex Segregation, Anti-Essentialism, and Masculinity," 33 *Harvard Journal of Law & Gender* 509, 523–25 (2010) (explaining hegemonic masculinity and collecting classic sources).

17. Berdahl, "Harassment Based on Sex," p. 647; Dana Kabat-Farr and Lilia M. Cortina, "Sex-Based Harassment in Employment: New Insights into Gender and Context," 38 *Law and Human Behavior* 58, 67–68 (2014). See generally James Gruber, "The Impact of Male Work Environments and Organizational Policies on Women's Experiences of Sexual Harassment," 12 *Gender & Society* 301 (1998).

18. Vicki Schultz, "The Sanitized Workplace," 112 *Yale Law Journal* 2061 (2003); see also Rosabeth Moss Kanter, *Men and Women of the Corporation* (New York: Basic Books, 1977), pp. 206–44; Iris Bohnet, *What Works: Gender Equality by Design* (Cambridge, MA: Harvard University Press, 2016), pp. 211–12, 230–33, 349; Robin J. Ely, "The Effects of Organizational Demographics and Social Identity on Relationships among Professional Women," 39 *Administrative Science Quarterly* 203, 224–30 (1994); and Belle Derks, Colette Van Laar, and Naomi Ellemers, "The Queen Bee Phenomenon: Why Women Leaders Distance Themselves from Junior Women," 27 *Leadership Quarterly* 456, 458–60, 464 (2016).

19. See, e.g., *Rowe v. Gen. Motors Corp.*, 457 F.2d 348, 359 (5th Cir. 1972) ("recogniz[ing] that promotion/transfer procedures which depend almost entirely upon the subjective evaluation and favorable recommendation of the immediate foreman are a ready mechanism for discrimination"). For additional cases, see Vicki Schultz, "Taking Sex Discrimination Seriously," 91 *Denver University Law Review* 995 (2015), 1063 n.364.

20. For the classic study, see Kanter, *Men and Women of the Corporation*, pp. 48–63 (discussing how managers resort to "homosocial reproduction" to reduce uncertainty); see also James N. Baron, Michael T. Hannan, G. Hsu, and O. Kocak, "In the Company of Women: Gender Inequality and the Logic of Bureaucracy in Start-up Firms," 34 *Work & Occupations* 35 (2007); Vincent J. Roscigno, Lisette M. Garcia, and Donna Bobbitt-Zeher, "Social Closure and Processes of Race/ Sex Employment Discrimination," 609 *Annals of the American Academy of Political Science* 16, 28–32 (2007); Natalie Wreyford, "Birds of a Feather: Informal Recruitment

Practices and Gendered Outcomes for Screenwriting Work in the UK Film Industry," 63 *Sociological Review* 84 (2015).

21. See, e.g., Ronald S. Burt, "The Gender of Social Capital," 5 *Rationality & Society* 10 (1998); Mia Gray, Tomoko Kurihara, Leif Hommen, and Jonathan Feldman, "Networks of Exclusion: Job Segmentation and Social Networks in the Knowledge Economy," 144 *Equal Opportunities International* 26 (2007); Mark Lutter, "Do Women Suffer from Network Closure? The Moderating Effect of Social Capital on Gender Inequality in a Project-Based Labor Market, 1929–2010," 80 *American Sociological Review* 329 (2015); Gail McGuire, "Gender, Race, Ethnicity and Networks: The Factors Affecting the Status of Employees' Network Members," 27 *Work & Occupations* 501 (2000).

22. See generally Elizabeth Anderson, ed., *Private Government: How Employers Rule Our Lives (and Why We Don't Talk about It)* (Princeton University Press, 2017), p. 37; Rachel Arnow-Richman, "Of Power and Process: Handling Harassers in an At-Will World," 128 *Yale Law Journal Forum* 85 (2018) (arguing that at-will employment, employer contracting practices, and sexual harassment law combine to produce a world in which employers tolerate sexual harassment by top-level employers).

23. Dacher Keltner, Deborah H. Gruenfeld, and Cameron Anderson, "Power, Approach, and Inhibition," 110 *Psychological Review* 265, 267, 273 (2003) (collecting studies), at 266.

24. See David Kipnis, "Does Power Corrupt?," 24 *Journal of Personality & Social Psychology* 33 (1972).

25. Keltner et al., "Power, Approach, and Inhibition," p. 266.

26. See Jeanette N. Cleveland and Melinda E. Kerst, "Sexual Harassment and Perceptions of Power: An Under-Articulated Relationship," 42 *Journal of Vocational Behavior* 49, 55–57 (1993) (explaining the sources of informal power male employees can exercise over female peers); see also Schultz, "Reconceptualizing Sexual Harassment," pp. 1751–52, 1764–65 (showing how male workers who have the ability to informally train, inform, or otherwise affect the work performance of their female peers acquire power over them).

4.4 LGBT RIGHTS AT WORK

The Social and Economic Imperative of Lesbian, Gay, Bisexual, and Transgendered Supportive Organizational Policies

EDEN B. KING AND JOSÉ M. CORTINA

The United States has enacted federal legislation prohibiting discrimination in the workplace on the basis of a variety of demographic factors. The United States has been slow, however, to enact legislation prohibiting discrimination against those who identify themselves as lesbian, gay, bisexual, or transgendered (LGBT). A substantial body of evidence has accumulated demonstrating that LGBT individuals face unequal treatment on the basis of their sexual orientation and gender identity in employment practices, and that the experience of such discrimination has consequences for well-being and organizational outcomes. Our contention is that, even in the absence of federal legislation protecting LGBT workers, organizations should institute LGBT-supportive policies. We begin by summarizing scientific evidence regarding negative attitudes and behaviors toward LGBT workers and then provide social and economic justifications for our position. We conclude by offering specific recommendations to organizations.

The Problem: Evidence of Heterosexism

Unequal treatment on the basis of sexual orientation or gender identity (i.e., discrimination) is rooted in beliefs about LGBT people (i.e., stereotypes) as well as negative attitudes toward LGBT people (i.e., prejudice). "Heterosexism"[1] encompasses both of these components and is defined as "an ideological system that denies, denigrates, and stigmatizes any nonheterosexual form of behavior, identity, relationship or community,"[2] Evidence provided below from population surveys and statistics, experimental studies, and self-report questionnaires converges on the persistence of heterosexism in American society.

From Eden B. King and José M. Cortina, "The Social and Economic Imperative of Lesbian, Gay, Bisexual, and Transgendered Supportive Organizational Policies," *Industrial and Organizational Psychology* 3, no. 1 (2010): 69–78. © 2010. Reprinted by permission.

Population Statistics and Surveys

An important set of findings regarding the status of LGBT workers in contemporary American society can be derived from nationally representative attitude surveys. Such studies typically use a random-digit dialing approach and inquire about attitudes toward LGBT individuals in a variety of contexts. Research by Gallup suggests that although the overwhelming majority of Americans (89 percent) do not oppose employment rights for gay workers,[3] responses also suggest that beliefs about homosexuality continue to be negative. When respondents were asked whether sexual relations between two adults of the same sex are "always wrong," "almost always wrong," "wrong only sometimes," or "not wrong at all," more than 50 percent of Americans chose "always wrong." This belief system may be the reason why 43 percent of respondents do not feel that gay people should be hired as elementary school teachers[4] and why feelings toward bisexual men and women may be more negative than feelings toward all other religious, racial, ethnic, and political groups except injection drug users.[5]

Another indicator of discrimination toward socially disadvantaged groups is a "wage gap." Like women and members of ethnic minority groups, LGBT individuals earn substantially lower wages than their heterosexual counterparts. The largest of these differences is for gay men. Elmslie and Tebaldi found that gay men earn up to 23 percent less than heterosexual men in the same occupation and rank.[6] In a review of nine studies and samples, Badgett and colleagues concluded that gay men earn between 10 percent and 32 percent less than similarly qualified heterosexual men.[7] Wage discrepancies are less clear cut for lesbians; in many cases, lesbians earn more than straight women. This may be because of different rates of participation in male-dominated fields or career interruptions involving children.[8]

Experimental Studies

A growing body of experimental research demonstrates that portraying individuals as having a gay or a lesbian identity correlates with differential treatment. For example, a lab study revealed that fictitious heterosexual male job applicants were rated more positively than gay and lesbian applicants with the same qualifications.[9] Similarly, an experimental field study found that ostensibly lesbian and gay job applicants encountered greater hostility than did job applicants who were presumed to be heterosexual.[10]

More recent studies suggest that heterosexism is a complex phenomenon and that the degree of discrimination toward LGBT individuals depends on several factors that are specific to the LGBT individual. In one study, participants were randomly assigned to view a male or female heterosexual or homosexual target behaving in masculine or feminine ways.[11] Ratings of the target's morality were worst when targets confirmed gender role stereotypes associated with their sexual identity; gay men who behaved in feminine ways and lesbians who behaved in masculine ways received the lowest ratings from participants who were high in prejudice. Thus, discrimination toward LGBT workers may be greatest when gender role stereotypes are enacted. Discrimination toward LGBT individuals also seems to depend on whether or not they are perceived to be "concealing" their sexual orientation. A vignette study[12] suggests that targets who conceal their sexual orientation are rated more negatively with regard to their personal characteristics than those who did not conceal their sexual orientation. Like Jean Valjean (*Les Misérables*), if LGBT workers speak, they are condemned; if they stay silent, they are damned.

Self-Report Studies

One way to assess the discrimination encountered by LGBT individuals is to directly ask both LGBT and non-LGBT about such experiences. Data from both sources indicate that heterosexism persists. Heterosexual individuals report that their nonheterosexual counterparts are likely to experience discrimination. For example, a survey of police officers suggested that many officers observed other members of the force treating homosexual members of the public more negatively than heterosexual individuals and that officers do not always take complaints from LGBT victims as seriously as those made by heterosexual victims.[13] As another example, an in-depth interview and ethnographic observational study in a baked goods company reported that overtly negative attitudes and behaviors toward LGBT workers are common. Interview quotes include statements such as "It's a sickness. Those people need help . . . They need to check their head cause there's a screw loose" and "Two lesbians raising a son? That's insane!"[14]

Arguably, even more compelling are reports of discrimination by LGBT workers themselves. A review of published studies on LGBT workplace experiences indicated that between 25 percent and 66 percent of LGBT employees reported that they had experienced discrimination, with higher rates being reported by individuals who had disclosed their sexual orientation.[15] LGB employees also report challenges developing positive relationships with their co-workers.[16] Responses to the National Survey of Midlife Development in 1995 suggest that the 8 percent of LGB individuals are approximately twice as likely as non-LGB individuals to report discrimination in the form of firing, denial of employment, or denial of a promotion.[17] Similarly, more than one third of the respondents in a national survey of 534 gay and lesbian professionals reported experiencing physical or verbal harassment on the basis of their sexual identity at work.[18]

Taken together, the results of population surveys, experimental studies, and self-report questionnaires are consistent in indicating that LGBT workers face discrimination on the basis of their sexual orientation. In the following sections, we argue that social and economic responsibilities compel organizations and organizational psychologists to create LGBT-supportive workplaces.

Why Organizations Should Respond: The Social Imperative

There is no federal legislation protecting LGBT individuals from employment discrimination in the United States. This can be contrasted with results from a recent review of the legal environment across 22 countries; 13 of these countries include sexual orientation as a protected class for employment decisions (e.g., Germany, Israel, Belgium, Canada).[19]

An analysis of congressional testimony dealing with legislation on employment discrimination toward LGBT workers highlights the justifications that are used to legitimize discrimination toward this social identity group and thus may create barriers to its passage.[20] For example, arguments that Creed and colleagues uncovered include the notion that "no one *has* to be gay," that homosexuality imposes on religious freedom, and that protection of LGBT rights in employment will increase bureaucracy and "red tape." The lack of support for LGBT workers extends beyond the federal level; only 16 states and 173 counties and cities (in which only 47 percent of Americans live) have enacted laws prohibiting discrimination on the basis of sexual identity.[21] The insufficient legal protections for LGBT workers in the United States, taken with the persistence of heterosexism, create a social responsibility for organizations to respond.

The vast and growing area of research and practice concerning corporate social responsibility (CSR) includes ongoing debate about the role of the organization in society.[22] Although it is worth noting that CSR actions have been linked with positive financial outcomes,[23] we focus for the moment on the notion that organizations share responsibility for the social good of the communities in which they operate. Historically, traditional theories of the organization were concerned with the manner in which companies affect patterns of privilege and disadvantage in society.[24] From this perspective, the organization plays an active role in shaping social hierarchies and may represent "the entities of last resort for achieving social objectives of all stripes."[25]

Consistent with this, the notion of CSR can be traced back to the philosophers of the seventeenth and eighteenth centuries (e.g., Hobbes, Locke, Rousseau) who proposed that there is a social contract between a nation and its citizens involving a shared covenant of mutual obligations. Businesses emerged as a partner in social contracts as they grew in size, were afforded many of the same protections and privileges as citizens in a series of judicial decisions, and were held accountable for compliance with rules that were not necessarily directly related to their financial earnings.[26] Indeed, incorporation is a privilege granted by the government. Incorporated entities are bestowed with benefits such as liability protection, mechanisms for raising capital, and organizational perpetuity. The taxpayer pays the costs of these benefits. In return for the privilege of incorporation, corporations have an obligation to attend to and meet the needs of the society in which they are incorporated. Integrating the notion of social contracts with stakeholder theory, Freeman argued that organizations have a responsibility to more than just their *share*holders; they also have a responsibility to a range of *stake*holders who are affected by the actions of the organization.[27]

We contend that the stakeholders with whom organizations have a social contract include LGBT workers. A recent definition of CSR relies upon a minimum behavioral standard that includes the idea that organizations "must not knowingly do anything that could harm their stakeholders," and second, that "if corporations do cause harm to their stakeholders they must then rectify it whenever the harm is discovered."[28] To meet this minimum standard of social responsibility, organizations must enact policies, practices, and procedures that prevent discrimination toward LGBT people and rectify remaining instances of heterosexism.

Reasons for Organizations to Respond: The Economic Imperative

The experience of inequitable treatment, or in the case of LGBT workers unfair treatment on the basis of sexual identity (i.e., heterosexism), has negative consequences for individuals and their organizations. One of the most consistent findings across studies on LGBT discrimination is that the experience of workplace heterosexism is correlated with attitudes about the job and the organization. For example, perceived heterosexism is negatively associated with job satisfaction,[29] organizational commitment,[30] and job anxiety.[31] Heterosexism has also been found to be associated with turnover intentions and organizational self-esteem.[32] There is also evidence that the experience of prejudice in general, and heterosexism in particular, has mental and physical health consequences. Results of a recent meta-analysis of nearly 150 studies show that perceptions of discrimination are negatively correlated with both mental and physical health.[33] Similarly, perceptions of heterosexism at work have been associated with depression and psychological distress.[34]

It is important to note that a related and critical predictor of these outcomes is "outness," or the degree to which LGBT individuals fear disclosing their sexual identities. Surveys of LGBT employees[35] suggest that openness about their sexual orientation was correlated with a range of job attitudes including affective commitment, job satisfaction, role conflict, work–family conflict, role ambiguity, and belief in the support of top management. Similarly, a national survey of LGB employees suggests that the fears associated with disclosure are correlated with job attitudes, and experienced discrimination was correlated with job satisfaction, organizational commitment, turnover intentions, opportunities for promotion, role ambiguity, role conflict, somatic complaints, depression, anxiety, and irritation.[36] Concealing one's identity has been associated with reduced task efficacy.[37] In addition, a survey of LGBT individuals indicated that utilization of avoidance strategies (i.e., continuous self-editing and half-truths to reveal nothing about one's sexual identity) was negatively associated with their ratings of work group functioning, whereas integrating strategies (i.e., explicit statement of one's sexual identity) were positively associated with group process ratings.[38] Thus, LGBT employees (and their organizations) may suffer negative consequences when they fear heterosexism as well as when they actually experience heterosexism.[39]

In addition to the outcomes of heterosexism detailed above, we also highlight the argument that employment decisions are effective only to the extent that they rely on valid predictors of performance. There is no evidence that LGBT workers perform any less well than their straight counterparts[40] or that LGBT workers differ meaningfully from non-LGBT workers on other job-related criteria. . . .

Recommendations for Organizations

The first step that organizations should take is to include LGBT employees as protected from discrimination in employment practices. Supporting this course of action, research has suggested that simply including sexual orientation in anti-discrimination statements and policies was positively related to job satisfaction and commitment among LGBT workers.[41]

As a next step, organizations should look beyond employment decisions and ensure equal treatment of heterosexual and nonheterosexual employees across organizational life. This might be accomplished by providing optional opportunities for LGBT individuals to indicate their sexual identity on anonymous engagement surveys, establishing benefits for LGBT employees and their families (e.g., domestic partner and dependent benefits), and launching diversity initiatives such as LGBT employee resource groups, diversity councils, or mentorship programs. The Human Rights Campaign recently recognized two companies as innovators in workplace equality for their establishment of programs that serve as examples of such efforts: Boeing received this award for its institution of an initiative that helps transgendered employees transition, and Kirkland & Ellis, LLP received the award for its efforts to improve the workplace climate by pairing LGBT law students with partner- and associate-level mentors. Research on the effectiveness of diversity programs with regard to gender and race suggests that diversity management may be most successful to the extent that they include "structures of responsibility" (such as diversity committees or equal employment staff members) wherein oversight and advocacy efforts can be centralized and groups and individuals held accountable.[42] Formal policies, procedures, and practices that address heterosexism throughout an organization may ultimately help to create an LGBT-supportive organizational climate,[43] which in turn is a critical determinant of the experience of LGBT employees.[44]

In addition to these steps, organizations should advocate on behalf of LGBT interests. LGBT employees may benefit from the advocacy efforts of allies for two primary reasons. First, because an LGBT identity is generally not visible, it may be difficult for LGBT workers to identify others who are also LGBT; concealability of sexual identity and orientation may be a barrier to the creation of informal social support networks and formal action committees. Second, the lack of legal protection may make it more challenging for LGBT individuals to bear the burden of advocacy compared to women, ethnic and religious minorities, and disabled and older workers. LGBT workers may be vulnerable to legally defensible retaliation and persecution should they speak out on behalf of sexual minorities. It follows that advocacy should be instigated not only by LGBT individuals but also by their allies (within their own workplaces or through external organizations) or by organizations as a whole (through charitable donations and lobbying efforts). . . .

Notes

1. Heterosexism includes stigmatization of individuals who do not identify themselves as LGBT but question their sexual identity, individuals who identify themselves as "queer," and supporters or allies of these individuals. Thus, a more inclusive acronym is LGBTQQA. Here we use the label of LGBT to be consistent with public debate and the majority of existing research, which focuses on individuals who identify themselves as LGBT.

2. G. M. Herek, "The Context of Anti-Gay Violence: Notes on Cultural and Psychological Heterosexism," *Journal of Interpersonal Violence* 5 (1990): 316–33 (p. 316).

3. Gallup, "Americans at Odds over Gay Rights" (2006). Retrieved from www.gallup.com/poll/23140/Americans-Odds -Over-Gay-Rights.aspx.

4. K. Bowman, "Gay Pride and Prejudice," *The Washington Post* (June 11, 2006), p. B2.

5. G. M. Herek, "Heterosexuals' Attitudes toward Bisexual Men and Women in the United States," *Journal of Sex Research* 39 (2002): 264–74.

6. B. Elmslie and E. Tebaldi, "Sexual Orientation and Labor Market Discrimination," *Journal of Labor Research* 28 (2007): 436–53.

7. M. V. Badgett, H. Lau, B. Sears, and D. Ho, *Bias in the Workplace: Consistent Evidence of Sexual Orientation and Gender Identity Discrimination* (Los Angeles: The Williams Institute, University of California, 2007).

8. J. Blandford, "The Nexus of Sexual Orientation and Gender in the Determination of Earnings," *Industrial & Labor Relations Review* 56 (2003): 622–42.

9. M. Horvath and A. M. Ryan, "Antecedents and Potential Moderators of the Relationship between Attitudes and Hiring Discrimination on the Basis of Sexual Orientation," *Sex Roles* 48 (2003): 115–31.

10. M. Hebl, J. M. Foster, L. M. Mannix, and J. F. Dovidio, "Formal and Interpersonal Discrimination: A Field Study Examination of Applicant Bias," *Personality and Social Psychological Bulletin* 28 (2002): 815–25.

11. K. Lehavot and A. J. Lambert, "Toward a Greater Understanding of Antigay Prejudice: On the Role of Sexual Orientation and Gender Role Violation," *Basic and Applied Social Psychology* 29 (2007): 279–92.

12. D. L. Oswald, "'Don't Ask, Don't Tell': The Influence of Stigma Concealing and Perceived Threat on Perceivers' Reactions to a Gay Target," *Journal of Applied Social Psychology* 37 (2007): 928–47.

13. M. Berstein and C. Kostelac, "Lavender and Blue: Attitudes about Homosexuality and Behavior toward Lesbians and Gay Men among Police Officers," *Journal of Contemporary Criminal Justice* 18 (2002): 302–30.

14. D. G. Embrick, C. S. Walther, and C. M. Wickens, "Working Class Masculinity: Keeping Gay Men and Lesbians Out of the Workplace," *Sex Roles* 56 (2007): 757–66.

15. J. M. Croteau, "Research on the Work Experiences of Lesbian, Gay, and Bisexual People: An Integrative Review of Methodology and Findings," *Journal of Vocational Behavior* 48 (1996): 195–209; see also B. R. Ragins, "Sexual Orientation in the Workplace: The Unique Work and Career Experiences of Gay, Lesbian, and Bisexual Workers," *Research in Personnel and Human Resources Management* 23 (2004): 37–122.

16. N. Rumens, "Working at Intimacy: Gay Men's Workplace Friendships," *Gender, Work, and Organization* 15 (2008): 9–31.

17. V. Mays and S. Cochran, "Mental Health Correlates of Perceived Discrimination among Lesbian, Gay, and Bisexual Adults in the United States," *American Journal of Public Health* 91(2001): 1869–76.

18. B. R. Ragins and J. M. Cornwell, "Pink Triangles: Antecedents and Consequences of Perceived Workplace Discrimination against Gay and Lesbian Employees," *Journal of Applied Psychology* 86 (2001): 1244–61.

19. B. Myors, F. Lievens, E. Schollaert, G. Van Hoye, S. F. Cronshaw, A. Mladinic, . . . P. R. Sackett, "International Perspectives on the Legal Environment for Selection," *Industrial and Organizational Psychology: Perspectives on Science and Practice* 1 (2008): 206–46.

20. W. E. Creed, M. A. Scully, and J. R. Austin, "Clothes Make the Person? The Tailoring of Legitimating Accounts and the Social Construction of Identity," *Organization Science* 13 (2002): 475–96.

21. J. Beatty and S. L. Kirby, "Beyond the Legal Environment: How Stigma Influences Invisible Identity Groups in the Workplace," *Employee Responsibilities and Rights Journal* 18 (2006): 29–46.

22. For a discussion, see J. D. Margolis and J. P. Walsh, "Misery Loves Companies: Rethinking Social Initiatives by Business," *Administrative Science Quarterly* 48 (2003): 268–305.

23. For example, M. Orlitzky, F. L. Schmidt, and S. L. Rynes, "Corporate Social and Financial Performance: A Meta-Analysis," *Organization Studies* 24 (2003): 403–41.

24. See C. R. Hinings and R. Greenwood, "Disconnects and Consequences in Organization Theory?" *Administrative Science Quarterly* 47 (2002): 411–21; M. Weber, *The Theory of Social and Economic Organization* (New York: Free Press, 1964).

25. Margolis and Walsh, "Misery Loves Companies," p. 296.

26. A. L. White, "Is It Time to Rewrite the Social Contract?" *Business for Social Responsibility* (2007). Retrieved May 7, 2009 from www.tellus.org/pub/Is%20It%20Time%20to%20Rewrite %20the%20Social%20Contract.pdf.

27. R. E. Freeman, *Strategic Management: A Stakeholder Approach* (Boston, MA: Pitman, 1984).

28. J. L. Campbell, "Why Would Corporations Behave in Socially Responsible Ways? An Institutional Theory of Corporate Social Responsibility," *Academy of Management Review* 32 (2007): 946–67 (p. 951).

29. S. B. Button, "Organizational Efforts to Affirm Sexual Diversity: A Cross-Level Examination," *Journal of Applied Psychology* 86 (2001): 17–28; J. M. Driscoll, F. A. Kelley, and R. E. Fassinger, "Lesbian Identity and Disclosure in the Workplace: Relation to Occupational Stress and Satisfaction," *Journal of Vocational Behavior* 48 (1996): 229–42; K. Griffith and M. R. Hebl, "The Disclosure Dilemma for Gay Men and Lesbians: 'Coming Out' at Work," *Journal of Applied Psychology* 87 (2002): 1191–99; C. R. Waldo, "Working in a Majority Context: A Structural Model of Heterosexism as

Minority Stress in the Workplace," *Journal of Counseling Psychology* 46 (1999): 218–32.

30. Button, "Organizational Efforts to Affirm Sexual Diversity."

31. Griffith and Hebl, "The Disclosure Dilemma for Gay Men and Lesbians."

32. Ragins and Cornwell, "Pink Triangles."

33. E. A. Pacoe and L. S. Richman, "Perceived Discrimination and Health: A Meta-Analysis," *Psychological Bulletin* 135 (2009): 531–54.

34. N. S. Smith and K. M. Ingram, "Workplace Heterosexism and Adjustment among Lesbian, Gay, and Bisexual Individuals: The Role of Unsupportive Social Interactions," *Journal of Counseling Psychology* 31 (2004): 57–67; D. M. Szymanski, "Examining Potential Moderators of the Link between Heterosexist Events and Gay and Bisexual Men's Psychological Distress," *Journal of Counseling Psychology* 56 (2009): 142–51; Waldo, "Working in a Majority Context."

35. For example, N. E. Day and P. Schoenrade, "Staying in the Closet versus Coming Out: Relationships between Communication about Sexual Orientation and Work Attitudes," *Personnel Psychology* 50 (1997): 147–68; N. E. Day and P. Schoenrade, "The Relationship among Reported Disclosure of Sexual Orientation, Anti-Discrimination Policies, Top Management Support, and Work Attitudes of Gay and Lesbian Employees," *Personnel Review* 29 (2000): 346–66.

36. B. R. Ragins, R. Singh, and J. M. Cornwell, "Making the Invisible Visible: Fear and Disclosure of Sexual Orientation at Work," *Journal of Applied Psychology* 92 (2007): 1103–18.

37. M. Barreto, N. Ellemers, and S. Banal, "Working under Cover: Performance-Related Self-Confidence among Members of Contextually Devalued Groups Who Try to Pass," *European Journal of Social Psychology* 36 (2006): 337–52.

38. D. Chrobot-Mason, S. B. Button, and J. D. DiClementi, "Sexual Identity Management Strategies: An Exploration of Antecedents and Consequences," *Sex Roles* 45 (2002): 321–37.

39. See Croteau, "Research on the Work Experiences of Lesbian, Gay, and Bisexual People"; B. R. Ragins, "Disclosure Disconnects: Antecedents and Consequences of Disclosing Invisible Stigmas across Life Domains," *Academy of Management Review* 33 (2008): 194–215.

40. See American Psychological Association, "Testimony of the American Psychological Association on the Employment Non-Discrimination Act" (1997). Retrieved July 15, 2008 from www.apa.org/ ppo/issues/pendatest.html; D. Hiatt and G. E. Hargrave, "Psychological Assessment of Gay and Lesbian Law Enforcement Applicants," *Journal of Personality Assessment* 63 (1994): 80–88.

41. Day and Schoenrade, "Staying in the Closet versus Coming Out."

42. A. Kalev, F. Dobbin, and E. Kelly, "Best Practices or Best Guesses? Assessing the Efficacy of Corporate Affirmative Action and Diversity Policies," *American Sociological Review* 71 (2006): 589–617.

43. See A. Huffman, K. Watrous, and E. B. King, "Diversity in the Workplace: Support for Lesbian, Gay, and Bisexual Workers," *Human Resource Management* 47 (2008): 237–53.

44. For example, E. B. King, C. Reilly, and M. R. Hebl, "The Best and Worst of Times: Dual Perspectives of Coming Out in the Workplace," *Group and Organization Management* 33 (2008): 566–601; Ragins and Cornwell, "Pink Triangles."

LEGAL PERSPECTIVES

Supreme Court of the United States, *Meritor Savings Bank, FSB v. Vinson, et al.* (1986)

Mechelle Vinson spent four years from 1974 to 1978 working at Meritor Savings Bank starting as a teller and working her way up to assistant branch manager. Sidney Taylor was her supervisor during this time. In September 1978 Vinson took sick leave for an indefinite period; in December 1978 she was discharged for excessive use of sick leave. Vincent brought suit against Taylor and the bank, claiming that during her four years at the bank she had constantly been subjected to sexual harassment by Taylor in violation of Title VII of the Civil Rights Act of 1964.

There were no issues during Vinson's probationary period. Shortly thereafter, however, Taylor invited her out to dinner and, during the course of the meal, suggested that they go to a motel to have sexual relations. At first she refused, but out of what she described as fear of losing her job she eventually agreed. Thereafter, Taylor made repeated demands upon her for sexual favors, usually at the branch, both during and after business hours. Vinson estimated that over the next several years she had intercourse with him some 40 or 50 times. In addition, Taylor fondled her in front of other employees, followed her into the women's restroom when she went there alone, exposed himself to her, and even forcibly raped her on several occasions. These activities ceased after 1977, when Vinson started going with a steady boyfriend. Finally Vinson claimed that Taylor touched and fondled other women employees of the bank.

At trial Taylor denied that any of these events had taken place. The bank denied any knowledge of alleged sexual harassment. The trial court found for Meritor Savings Bank, a result that was appealed to the Court of Appeals for the District of Columbia where the decision of the District Court was overturned. In reversing, the Court of Appeals stated that a violation of Title VII may be predicated on either of two types of sexual harassment: harassment that involves the conditioning of concrete employment benefits on sexual favors, and

harassment that, while not affecting economic benefits, creates a hostile or offensive working environment. Believing that "Vinson's grievance was clearly of the [hostile environment] type," and that the District Court had not considered whether a violation of this type had occurred the court concluded that the trial court needed to reconsider the case under the hostile environment criterion. The Appeals Court also found that the bank was liable for any sexual harassment by supervisory personnel.

In a unanimous decision upholding the Appeals Court Decision Justice William Rehnquist, writing for the Supreme Court, pointed to the existence of Equal Employment Opportunity Guidelines backed by judicial decisions that established that an employee is entitled to work in an environment free from discriminatory intimidation, ridicule, and insult. Judge Rehnquist wrote, "Since the Guidelines were issued, courts have uniformly held, and the Court agree, that a plaintiff may establish a violation of Title VII by proving that discrimination based on sex has created a hostile or abusive work environment."

Even if a person's consent was "voluntary" in the sense that the person was not forced to participate against her will, that does not mean that sexual harassment did not occur if the victim indicates that the behavior is unwelcome. What is required is the existence of a hostile environment that is severe and pervasive and so creates the conditions for an abusive employment relationship. Despite the bank's claim to the contrary, the mere existence of a grievance procedure is not sufficient to shield the employer against liability. In this case, the bank did not have a clear policy against sexual harassment and its grievance policy required employees to first complain to their supervisors – in this case Taylor. On this basis the Appeals Court decision was upheld and the case was remanded for further consideration.

Supreme Court of the United States, *Teresa Harris, Petitioner v. Forklift Systems, Inc.* (1993)

Teresa Harris worked as a manager at Forklift Systems, Inc., an equipment rental company, from April 1985 until October 1987. Charles Hardy was Forklift's president. The trial court determined that during Harris's time at Forklift, Hardy often insulted her because of her gender and often made her the target of unwanted sexual innuendoes. Hardy told Harris on several occasions, in the presence of other employees, "You're a woman, what do you know" and "We need a man as the rental manager"; at least once, he told her she was "a dumb ass woman." Again in front of others, he suggested that the two of them "go to the Holiday Inn to negotiate [Harris's] raise." Hardy occasionally asked Harris and other female employees to get coins from his front pants pocket. He threw objects on the ground in front of Harris and other women, and asked them to pick the objects up. He made sexual innuendoes about Harris's and other women's clothing. In mid-August 1987, Harris complained to Hardy about his conduct. Hardy said he was surprised that Harris was offended, claimed he was only joking, and apologized.

He also promised he would stop, and based on this assurance Harris stayed on the job. But in early September, Hardy began anew. While Harris was arranging a deal with one of Forklift's customers, he asked her, again in front of other employees, "What did you do, promise the guy . . . some [sex] Saturday night?" On October 1, Harris collected her paycheck and quit. Harris then sued Forklift, claiming that Hardy's conduct had created an abusive work environment for her because of her gender.

The District Court for the Middle District of Tennessee found against Harris arguing that Hardy's conduct did not meet the threshold for an abusive or hostile work environment. But Justice Sandra Day O'Connor, writing for the Supreme Court (9–0), stated that "When the workplace is permeated with discriminatory intimidation, ridicule, and insult, that is sufficiently severe or pervasive to alter the conditions of the victim's employment and create an abusive working environment, Title VII is violated." While not every offensive comment runs afoul of Title VII, neither does there need to tangible psychological injury. As the Court stated, Title VII comes into play before the victim suffers a nervous breakdown. The Court explicitly sought a middle ground between these two positions. The District Court was mistaken in making the criterion for an abusive work environment too strict.

A middle position is not mathematically precise but the following is a good legal standard: So long as the environment would reasonably be perceived, and is perceived, as hostile or abusive, there is no need for it also to be psychologically injurious. Whether conduct meets this condition depends on circumstances. These may include the frequency of the discriminatory conduct, its severity, whether it is physically threatening or humiliating, and whether it unreasonably interferes with an employee's work performance. The effect on the employee's psychological well-being is relevant but, like the other factors, not a necessary condition.

Using this middle standard, the Court argued that contrary to the District Court and ultimately the Appeals Court, this was not a "close case" and reversed the lower case decisions in a unanimous decision.

CASES

Case 1: Hiring Discrimination at Bass Pro Shops

SABRINA SPEIGHTS AND DENIS G. ARNOLD

Bass Pro Outdoor World, LLC is a retailer of gear for hunting, fishing, camping, and other outdoor activities. Headquartered in Springfield, Missouri, the company has 94 stores across the United States and Canada. Bass Pro was founded in 1971 and is ranked among the top 100 largest private companies in the United States employing approximately 22,000 employees and generating over $4 billion in annual sales revenue. The company represents itself as a tourist attraction and has aggressively pursued public funding for its stores. It has received more than $500 million in taxpayer subsidies. In 2017 the US Equal Employment Opportunity Commission (EEOC) reached a -$10.5 million legal settlement with Bass Pro for racial discrimination.

Title VII of the Civil Rights Act of 1964 prohibits employers from discriminating based on race or national origin and from retaliating against employees who complain of employment discrimination. The law also requires that employers maintain certain employment records. According to the EEOC, Bass Pro has been discriminating against African-American and Hispanic applicants in hiring since at least 2005, affecting over 1,000 job applicants and employees. The practices were first brought to the attention of the EEOC by a white Bass Pro manager at a Houston area store who claimed she was fired for protesting the treatment of black applicants and workers. The EEOC claims that the firm had a profile for prospective employees such that only white applicants "fit the profile." The discriminatory acts were found by EEOC to be a company-wide practice. An analysis of company records found that black employees were underrepresented in 95 percent of stores and Hispanic employees were underrepresented in 70 percent of stores.

Managers in dozens of stores across the country were alleged to have made racist remarks. For example, one manager stated that "hiring black candidates did not fit the company profile." The general manager of the Houston region reportedly told a human resources manager that "it was getting a little dark in here, you need to hire some white people." In Indiana, employees responsible for screening applicants were reported to have said "Hispanics should be shot at the border by the border patrol" and that black people steal and are not good employees. EEOC claims that managers acknowledged discriminatory practices, destroyed the applications of minorities, destroyed evidence of internal discrimination complaints, and fired or forced the resignation of those employees who protested discriminatory acts.

Mike Rowland, Bass Pro's Vice-President of Human Resources, denied the allegations by stating that stereotyping and discrimination are "contrary to our profound respect for and commitment to our team of experienced and knowledgeable associates." He further claimed that the case represented "a troubling tendency by the EEOC to stereotype those who love outdoor sports and support conservation as people who unlawfully discriminate" and that EEOC held a biased position against Bass Pro because it is a NASCAR sponsor.

According to David Lopez, General Counsel of the EEOC, "It is unlawful for employers to deny jobs to applicants based on their race or national origin and the EEOC will vigorously pursue such cases and require companies to reform their hiring practices and make victims of the discrimination whole." Bass Pro agreed to pay $10.5 million and take numerous steps to improve its record of equal opportunity recruitment, hiring, and diversity management. Part of the money will be used to provide reparations for those applicants who were discriminated against while seeking employment. The settlement will also be used to implement a comprehensive hiring program that promotes the recruitment of minority employees and requires posting job advertisements and job fairs in black and Hispanic communities. In addition to community efforts, Bass Pro is required to hire a director of diversity and inclusion who will help oversee the maintenance of applicant and employee records and oversee EEOC compliance training for employees. Bass Pro negotiated with the EEOC for many years before reaching a settlement, leading to considerable but undisclosed legal costs.

Discussion Questions

1. Why might leaders at Bass Pro think that discrimination is a useful business strategy? Explain.

2. If you worked for Bass Pro during this time period and observed some of the discriminatory practices, how would it make you feel about your job? Explain.

3. Does the defense of Bass Pro by Mike Rowland, Vice-President of Human Resources, against the EEOC seem reasonable? Are you persuaded? Why, or why not? Explain.

4. If Bass Pro had a director of diversity and inclusion since at least 2005 who ensured that applicant records were properly maintained, oversaw EEOC compliance training for employees, and oversaw the recruitment of minority candidates, how might things have turned out differently? Explain.

This case was written for classroom discussion and is based on the following sources: "America's Largest Private Companies," *Forbes* (2016). Retrieved from www.forbes.com/companies/bass-pro-shops/.

"Bass Pro to Pay $10.5 Million to Settle EEOC Lawsuit" (2017). Retrieved from https://content.govdelivery.com/accounts/USEEOC/bulletins/1acb85e.

V. Bolden-Barrett, "Bass Pro Shop Settles $10.5 M Race Discrimination Case" (2017). Retrieved from www.hrdive.com/news/bass-pro-shops-settles-105m-race-discrimination-case/447957/.

US Equal Employment Opportunity Commission (2011), "Bass Pro Failed to Hire Blacks and Hispanics at Its Stores Nationwide, EEOC Says in Suit." Retrieved from www.eeoc.gov/eeoc/newsroom/release/9-21-11.cfm.

W. Johnson, "Bass Pro, EEOC Reach Agreement on Discrimination Claims; Company Will Pay $10.5 Million," *USA Today* (July 25, 2017). Retrieved from www.usatoday.com/story/news/2017/07/25/bass-pro-eeoc-reach-agreement-discrimination-claims-company-pay-10–5-million/508002001/.

M. Perlman, "Bass Pro Accused of Racial Discrimination," *CBS News* (September 22, 2011). Retrieved from www.cbsnews.com/news/bass-pro-shops-accused-of-racial-discrimination/.

L. M. Sixel, "Bass Pro, EEOC Reach $10.5 Million Settlement," *Houston Chronicle* (July 24, 2017).

Case 2: Promotions at Uptown Bottling and Canning Company

DAVID LAWRENCE

Lincoln Grant, a 31-year-old African-American employee, has been working for six years as a technician at Uptown Bottling and Canning Co. in Baltimore, Maryland. On four separate occasions, he has unsuccessfully sought a promotion to a managerial position. As the only member in his department with a graduate degree, Grant questions how the company has treated him. He also knows that only four African-American employees have been promoted during the previous nine years, compared with 41 white employees who have been offered promotions over the same period of time. Baltimore city is more than 50 percent African-American, and the surrounding metropolitan region is about 25 percent African-American.

On one occasion, the company posted a listing for a managerial position and encouraged current employees to apply. According to the job description, eligible applicants should have at least five years of prior experience with the company and should hold a graduate degree in either business or engineering. Furthermore, each applicant would be required to take a written exam. Although Grant applied, the company awarded the position to Henry Thompson, a white male with only two years of experience and no graduate degree. Grant, as it turned out, was the only applicant with five years of prior experience and a graduate degree.

In making its final selections for jobs, Uptown Bottling and Canning considers test scores and leadership potential. Grant's test scores were significantly above average, but his supervisors told him that he lacked the leadership skills required of managers. Based on observed performance, they pointed out, Grant has never demonstrated leadership skills while working at Uptown. At the same time, Grant has also never been given any form of leadership training. Most of the 41 white employees who were promoted had been given leadership training within the first five years of their employment with the company.

Discussion Questions

1. Are the facts in this case sufficient to indicate that the Uptown Bottling and Canning Co. discriminated against Lincoln Grant on the basis of race? Why, or why not? Explain.

2. Given the promotion statistics, should the company do more to see that African-American employees are considered for both leadership training and promotions? Why, or why not? Explain.

3. Should the fact that the Baltimore area has a high percentage of African-American residents be a factor in the hiring and promotion practices at Uptown Bottling and Canning Co.? Why, or why not? Explain.

Case 3: Sexism in Silicon Valley

OSCAR JEROME STEWART AND DENIS G. ARNOLD

Gender discrimination and sexual harassment at work are not new phenomena and they remain issues across many industries, from finance, to oil and gas, to the media. However, within the high tech industry centered in Silicon Valley, there has been a significant increase in the public exposure of male executives who have engaged in sexual harassment. The casual "bro culture" that is so pervasive throughout the industry is a major part of the problem. In 2015 less than 15 percent of the technical employees in this sector were women. The Kapor Center for Social Impact *Tech Leavers Study* highlighted the systemic problems of gender discrimination and sexual harassment in the tech industry that has led many women to leave companies. It found that women experience significantly more unfair treatment than men and that sexist behavior is frequently perpetrated by senior-level employees. The *Elephant in the Valley* survey of 200+ women with 10+ years of experience working in the Silicon Valley tech sector, found that 60 percent of the women in the sample experienced unwanted sexual advances and 65 percent of those advances came from supervisors; fully 1 in 3 women felt afraid for their personal safety "because of work related circumstances."

Critics of the tech sector argue that the white, male-dominated culture of "brogrammers" has driven sexism in the industry. The industry promotes a culture of innovation and creativity in a "fun" work environment that often includes plentiful free alcohol meant to attract and retain talent. Industry observers argue that this comes at the expense of the effective policies, ethics and compliance training, and adherence to employment law typical of more traditional industries. Until recently, many women have been afraid to disclose their experiences with discrimination and harassment at work for fear of retribution. The men who discriminate and harass women are often the same men who decide whether a woman entrepreneur gets funding or whether a woman receives a choice assignment or promotion within the company. Those women who did report their experiences to the appropriate superiors were often rebuffed and sometimes lost their jobs. Women are coming forward now via alternative means such as social media, press interviews, and lawsuits.

Many of the largest tech companies in Silicon Valley have come under sustained criticism for tolerating harassment and discrimination. For example, at Google a senior software engineer claimed that she was sexually harassed repeatedly during her eight years at the company and that Google's human resources department failed to adequately address her concerns. She was eventually fired and subsequently sued the company. Former Google executive Amit Singhal resigned in 2016 after internally substantiated reports of sexual harassment. In 2018 it was revealed that Google paid Android inventor Andy Rubin $90 million to quietly leave the company after he was accused of sexual misconduct with a subordinate employee with whom he had previously been in an extramarital relationship. Journalists revealed that three other executives were given payouts when they left the firm as a result of sexual misconduct. As a result, over 20,000 Google employees walked off the job to protest Google's handling of sexual harassment cases. Employees felt that illegal, sexist behavior was being tolerated by firm leadership and that major organizational changes at Google were needed to address the problem. In response, Google CEO Sundar Pichai told employees that "I am fully committed to making progress on an issue that has persisted for far too long in our society . . . and, yes, here at Google, too."

Uber has helped define the sharing economy worldwide. Its ability to leverage innovation and to harness big data has allowed it to capitalize on demand for cheap, reliable intra-city transportation and on the contract workers who serve as drivers. Yet Uber has also tolerated a culture of pervasive sexism according to former employees and independent investigators. Dozens of employees have identified sexual harassment and gender discrimination as pervasive at Uber. Susan Fowler, a highly regarded engineer and author, who spent a year at Uber before leaving because of a culture of sexism and incompetent human resources oversight, detailed some of this behavior in an influential blog post. According to Fowler, on the first day on a new team her supervisor sent her a string of messages on company chat requesting sex. She reported the behavior to human resources who told her that he was a high performer and so would not be disciplined (despite repeated previous instances of this behavior reported by other employees). Human resources also told her that her supervisor would give her a poor performance evaluation as a result of reporting him, so she should join a different team. Moving to another part of the company and interacting with other employees gave her further insight into the pervasive sexism at Uber and as a result she left the firm.

After Fowler's well-publicized disclosures, Uber hired the law firm of former US Attorney General Eric Holder to investigate multiple allegations of misconduct at the firm. Investigations confirmed the reports of Fowler and other employees. As a result, Uber has fired more than 20 employees, including key executives and board members who were mired in discrimination or harassment scandals. CEO Travis Kalanick was forced to resign, although his actions were tied not merely to a sexist culture but to a range of other controversial actions. The company has also agreed to publish internal diversity statistics and implement a series of organizational changes designed to prevent bias and harassment moving forward.

The tech sector's venture capital industry has seen some of the most high-profile cases of sexism. Venture capitalist Justin Caldbeck, formerly of Bain Capital Ventures, Lightspeed Venture Partners, and Binary Capital, faces allegations of sexual conduct during business meetings from at least six women that span his time at all three firms. The women include Katrina Lake, the founder of an online personal shopping and styling service called Stitch Fix, Niniane Wang, former chief technology officer of Minted and co-creator of Google Desktop, and Susan Ho and Leiti Hsu, the co-founders of Journey, an online travel booking service. The allegations from the women range from propositions for sex during an interview to under-the-table groping during a funding proposal.

Lake revealed how Lightspeed enabled Caldbeck's behavior by downplaying its severity and protecting Caldbeck from being exposed or punished. After Lake reported Caldbeck's behavior to Lightspeed, the company pushed her to sign a non-disparagement agreement, which prevented her from disclosing Caldbeck's behavior. Needing to secure funding for her company, Lake signed the agreement. After Caldbeck's behavior became public, Lightspeed reported that it regretted not taking stronger action against Caldbeck. Binary Capital, on the other hand, acted more swiftly. Caldbeck resigned from the firm and penned a public letter admitting culpability, expressing regret and apologizing to women for making them feel "uncomfortable" and for leveraging his authority "in exchange for sexual gain."

Discussion Questions

1. If you are female, how might you feel about your workplace if your new boss sent you multiple chat messages on your work computer requesting sex on your first day on his team? Explain. If you're male, and you observed a female co-worker receiving such requests from your boss, how might you feel about your workplace? Explain.

2. Why might gender discrimination and sexual harassment proliferate more widely in the tech industry as opposed to some other industries? Explain.

3. How should the tech industry begin to address the pervasive culture of sexism and harassment described above? Explain.

4. What does the tech industry's problems of gender discrimination and sexual harassment have to do with the prevalence of alcohol at work and at social events in the industry? Should companies exclude alcohol from work? From social events? Explain.

5. What types of changes are needed in tech companies to successfully combat gender bias and sexual harassment? Explain.

This case was written for discussion purposes and is based on the following sources: R. Albergotti, "Silicon Valley Women Tell of VC's Unwanted Advances," *The Information* (June 22, 2017). Retrieved from www.theinformation.com/articles/silicon-valley-women-tell-of-vcs-unwanted-advances.

K. Benner, "Women in Tech Speak Frankly on Culture of Harassment," *The New York Times* (June 30, 2017). Retrieved from www.nytimes.com/2017/06/30/technology/women-entrepreneurs-speak-out-sexual-harassment.html?hp&action=click&pgtype=Homepage&clickSource=story-heading&module=first-column-region&region=top-news&WT.nav=top-news.

M. Hicks, "What the Google Gender 'Manifesto' Really Says about Silicon Valley," *The Conversation* (August 10, 2017). Retrieved from http://theconversation.com/what-the-google-gender-manifesto-really-says-about-silicon-valley-82236.

S. Levin, "Google Accused of 'Extreme' Gender Pay Discrimination by US Labor Department," *The Guardian* (April 7, 2017). Retrieved from www.theguardian.com/technology/2017/apr/07/google-pay-disparities-women-labor-department-lawsuit.

D. Primack, "How Lightspeed Responded to Caldbeck's Alleged Behavior," *Axios* (June 27, 2017). Retrieved from www.axios.com/how-lightspeed-responded-to-caldbecks-alleged-behavior-1513303291-797b3d44-6b7d-4cd1-89ef-7e35782a32e6.html.

A. Scott, F. K. Klein, and U. Onovakpuri, *Tech Leavers Study: A First-of-Its-Kind Analysis of Why People Voluntarily Left Jobs in Tech* (2017). Retrieved from Kapor Center for Social Impact website: www.kaporcenter.org/wp-content/uploads/2017/04/KAPOR_Tech-Leavers-17-0428.pdf.

C. Suddath, "Girl Code: A Big Documentary on Silicon Valley's Sexism Problem" (May 14, 2015). Retrieved from www.bloomberg.com/news/articles/2015-05-14/code-debugging-the-gender-gap-a-documentary-on-sexism-in-tech.

T. Vassallo, E. Levy, M. Madansky, H. Mickell, B. Porter, M. Leas, and J. Oberweis, "Elephant in the Valley," *Women in Tech* (2016). Retrieved from www.elephantinthevalley.com.

L. M. Segarra, "More than 20,000 Google Employees Participated in Walkout over Sexual Harassment Policy," *Fortune.com* (November 2, 2018). Retrieved from http://fortune.com/2018/11/03/google-employees-walkout-demands/.

Case 4: A Culture of Sexism and Harassment at Fox News

ROXANNE ROSS AND DENIS G. ARNOLD

Fox News is a cable news and entertainment channel with a conservative perspective. The channel was created by news mogul Rupert Murdoch in 1996 and is owned by Twenty-First Century Fox, Inc., which had earnings of $27 billion in 2016. Under the leadership of Chief Executive Officer Roger Ailes, Fox News earned 10 percent of the revenues at its parent company and reached 91 million households. The owner of Twenty-First Century Fox, Rupert Murdoch, recruited Ailes (b. 1940) in 1996 to help create Fox News and serve as the channel's CEO. Fox News surpassed CNN in viewers after five years and has been the most watched cable news network in the United States since that time.

One of the most important on-air personalities recruited by Ailes was Bill O'Reilly (b. 1949), who generated billions in revenues as the host of the most watched program on cable news. In recent years, O'Reilly's annual salary was $18.5 million. In a series of investigative reports, journalists at the *New York Times* reported that O'Reilly was a serial harasser. Five women reached separate legal settlements totaling $13 million with either O'Reilly or Fox News for harassment. These settlements, which included confidentially agreements, allowed the harassment to be hidden from public view. At least two more women have reported that they have also been harassed by O'Reilly, but chose not to pursue legal action. O'Reilly is reported to have made obscene phone calls, lewd comments, described sexual fantasies, and made unwanted sexual advances toward these women. Some of the instances of harassment were recorded. A pattern of

sexual harassment and intimidation emerges from an examination of the cases. O'Reilly would promise women career advancement, lucrative on-air spots or other perks, and big raises that were sometimes in the six-figure range. Following these promises, he would make a sexual advance. If the woman refused his advance, harsh retaliation was the result. One victim recounts O'Reilly threatening her by saying that anyone who reported his behavior would "pay so dearly that she'll wish she'd never been born." Another woman experienced a strategically planned lawsuit against her before she was able to press charges for sexual harassment. For his part, O'Reilly has maintained that he is the true victim who was targeted because of his fame and wealth.

Fox News issued the following statement in response to the allegations, "21st Century Fox takes matters of workplace behavior very seriously. Notwithstanding the fact that no current or former Fox News employee ever took advantage of the 21st Century Fox hotline to raise a concern about Bill O'Reilly, even anonymously, we have looked into these matters over the last few months and discussed them with Mr. O'Reilly. While he denies the merits of these claims, Mr. O'Reilly has resolved those he regarded as his personal responsibility. Mr. O'Reilly is fully committed to supporting our efforts to improve the environment for all our employees at Fox News."

As the furor regarding the sexual harassment settlements mounted, advertisers began pulling their advertisements from Fox and O'Reilly was subsequently fired. His severance pay was $25 million. Months after his departure from Fox it came to light that O'Reilly had recently settled a sixth lawsuit with on-air legal analyst Lis Wiehl (b. 1961) for $32 million. The behavior for which the settlement was reached included sexual harassment, sending pornography, and non-consensual sexual activity. Fox News was aware of this settlement while it negotiated its new $25 million annual contract with O'Reilly just months before his termination. O'Reilly and Fox had hoped to keep that settlement a secret.

O'Reilly's boss, and the person to whom O'Reilly's victims would ultimately have to appeal was Ailes. Numerous women at Fox News have accused Ailes of sexual harassment. Allegations include demands for sex and unwanted kissing and groping. Gretchen Carlson (b. 1966), a former news anchor with Fox, was the first to publicly disclose harassment by Ailes. In her lawsuit, Carlson claimed that Ailes had sexually harassed her and retaliated against her for refusing his advances by cutting her salary, lowering her on-air time, and canceling her daytime show, thus ending her career with Fox News. Before the show was canceled, Carlson brought up her concerns about her mistreatment in a meeting with Ailes. He responded by saying, "I think you and I should have had a sexual relationship a long time ago and then you'd be good and better and I'd be good and better." Carlson described being harassed in at least six different meetings with Ailes. Fox News anchor Megyn Kelly (b. 1970) reported that Ailes made sexual comments to her in meetings and in one case tried repeatedly to kiss her before she could get away. Numerous other alleged cases of harassment by Ailes, both at Fox News and at his previous employers, have been reported in the media. Ailes claimed that the lawsuit was a "defamatory" tactic "without merit" used by Carlson in light of the cancellation of her contract, which he attributed to low ratings. After the allegations became public, Ailes resigned. His severance agreement was worth $40 million. Fox News settled with Carlson for $20 million. Megyn Kelly moved to NBC News.

According to victims' reports, Bill Shine, the Co-President of Fox News and widely regarded as the "right-hand man" of Ailes, together with other senior leaders, concealed the numerous cases of harassment, arranged the settlements, and punished the women who tried to make their harassment known. Shine and other executives asked several on-air personalities to publicly defame Carlson in order to undermine her allegations. Shine subsequently resigned his position at Fox News in what media reports characterized as further fall-out from the harassment scandals. He later joined the Trump Administration White House as deputy chief of staff for communications.

The culture at Fox News has been characterized by former employees as a boys' club where women were denigrated, harassed, and intimidated when they resisted inappropriate behavior. Over the years, the women who endured sexual harassment often faced the end of their career with Fox News. During the first five months of 2017 alone company costs related to sexual harassment amounted to $45 million. Twenty-First Century Fox settled a shareholder lawsuit regarding the sexual harassment matter for $90 million. The lawsuit against Fox officers and directors alleged a lack of oversight and called for improved governance.

Discussion Questions

1. How would you characterize the culture at Fox News? Explain.

2. It might be argued that O'Reilly and Ailes were targeted because of their fame and wealth and only settled these cases to avoid costly litigation. How persuasive do you find this argument? Explain.

3. If you are a woman, how would you feel about working in such an environment? Explain. If you are a man, how might you feel if a female boss at your workplace acted in the same way? Explain.

4. What were the primary organizational attributes that allowed the behavior described in the case to persist? Explain

This case was written for classroom discussion and is based on the following sources: J. Stempel, "21st Century Fox in $90 Million Settlement Tied to Sexual Harassment Scandal," *Reuters* (November 20, 2017). Retrieved from www.reuters .com/article/us-fox-settlement/21st-century-fox-in-90-million-set tlement-tied-to-sexual-harassment-scandal-idUSKBN1DK2NI.

E. Steel and M. S. Schmidt, "Bill O'Reilly Settled New Harassment Claim, Then Fox Renewed His Contract," *The New York Times* (October 21, 2017). Retrieved from www .nytimes.com/2017/10/21/business/media/bill-oreilly-sexual-har assment.html.

21st Century Fox Annual Report (2016). Retrieved from www.21cf.com/sites/default/files/uploaded/investors/annual-reports/2016_21cf_annual_report.pdf.

B. Barnes, "Fox Reveals Cost of Sexual Harassment Allegations: $45 Million," *The New York Times* (May 10, 2017). Retrieved June 10, 2017 from www.nytimes.com/2017/05/10/business/media/fox-news-sexual-harassment-21st-century-fox.html.

D. Folkenflik, "Fresh Lawsuit against Ailes Slams Fox News' Response to Harassment Claims," *National Public Radio* (April 13, 2017). Retrieved June 5, 2017 from www.npr.org/sec tions/thetwo-way/2017/04/03/522436591/fresh-lawsuit-against-ailes-slams-fox-news-response-to-harassment-claims.

M. M. Grynbaum and J. Koblin, "Gretchen Carlson of Fox News Files Harassment Suit against Roger Ailes," *The New York Times* (July 6, 2016). Retrieved from www.nytimes.com/2016/07/07/business/media/gretchen-carlson-fox-news-roger-ailes-sexual-harassment-lawsuit.html.

J. Koblin, "Gretchen Carlson, Former Fox Anchor, Speaks Publicly about Sexual Harassment Lawsuit," *The New York Times* (July 12, 2016). Retrieved from www.nytimes.com/2016/07/13/business/media/gretchen-carlson-fox-news-interview.html.

E. Steel and M. S. Schmidt, "Bill O'Reilly Thrives at Fox News, Even as Harassment Settlements Add up," *The New York Times* (April 1, 2017). Retrieved from www.nytimes.com/2017/04/01/business/media/bill-oreilly-sexual-harassment-fox-news.html.

Case 5: Freedom of Expression at American Plastics Products

DAVID LAWRENCE

Barbara Hill has been employed at American Plastic Products Co. for several years. As a member of the engineering department, part of her job description included identifying defects in the equipment that formed the plastic products. She was expected to report on these defects at production meetings, which were held every morning.

In order to enter the engineering laboratory to perform this research, Barbara had to walk down a long corridor that was the only entrance to the room in which production meetings were held. As she walked down this hall every morning, she could not escape noticing pinup photographs and provocative calendars on the walls that had been placed there by male employees. Barbara complained to her supervisor, who proceeded to remove all the offending materials, including even a postcard located on a desk in an office with glass doors opening into the corridor.

The following day, as she was walking down the corridor to the laboratory, Barbara overheard a conversation between two male employees. Though not directed at her, she could not help but overhear that they were agreeing, with intensely expressed conviction, that women should not be given detail-oriented jobs, such as hers, because men are better able to focus in the workplace. Their conversation was punctuated with the language of "chicks," "bitches," and the like.

Barbara complained to her supervisor again, this time claiming that such behavior created a hostile work environment. When approached by the supervisor, the two male employees contended that they were simply expressing their political and business opinions – nothing more. The supervisor considered whether he should place the two men on probation and warn them to refrain from such conversations in the future. However, the supervisor decided to sit on this idea for a few days.

Discussion Questions

1. Should the pinup photographs and calendars have been taken down? Why or why not? Why might a supervisor deem it necessary to do so? Explain.

2. Should employees be permitted to voice their opinions at work even if other employees find them misguided or offensive? Does the right to free expression outweigh the right to a nonhostile working environment? Explain.

3. Is a workplace different from a public square with respect to the type of expression that should be permitted? Why, or why not? Explain.

This case was prepared by David Lawrence. © Tom L. Beauchamp.

Case 6: Harassment at Brademore Electric

TOM L. BEAUCHAMP

Maura Donovan is a recent graduate of UCLA who now works as a low-level administrative assistant for Keith Sturdivant at the Brademore Electric Corporation, a large Los Angeles electrical contractor. Keith interviewed and hired Maura to work directly under him.

Maura had been employed at Brademore only three weeks when Keith approached her to go out on the weekend. Maura was taken somewhat by surprise and declined, thinking it best not to mix business and pleasure. But two days later Keith persisted, saying that Maura owed him something in return for his "getting" her the job. Maura was offended by this comment, knowing that she was well qualified for the position, but Keith seemed lonely, almost desperate, and she agreed to go with him to the Annual Renaissance Fair on Saturday afternoon. As it turned out, she did not have an enjoyable time. She liked the fair but found Keith a bit crude and at times almost uncivil in the way he treated employees at the fair. She hoped he would not ask her out again.

But Monday morning he came back with the idea that they go on an overnight sailboat trip with some of his friends the next weekend. Maura politely declined. But Keith persisted, insisting that she owed her job to him. Maura found herself dreading the times she saw Keith coming down the corridor. What had been a very nice work environment for her had turned into a place of frequent dread. She spent a lot of time working to avoid Keith.

For four straight weeks, Keith came up with a different idea for how they might spend the weekend – always involving an overnight trip. Maura always declined. After the second week, she lied and told him that she was dating a number of other men. She said she was quite interested in two of these men and that she did not see any future with Keith. Keith's reaction was to become even more insistent that they had a future together and to continue to ask her out.

Keith had become quite infatuated with Maura. He watched her every movement, whenever he had the opportunity. Sometimes he openly stared at her as she walked from one office to another. He began to have sexual fantasies about her, which he disclosed to two male supervisors. However, he never mentioned to Maura that he had in mind any form of sexual relationship.

Keith's direct supervisor, Vice-President B. K. Singh, became aware of Keith's interest in Maura from two sources. First, he was told about the sexual fantasies by one of Keith's two male friends to whom Keith made the disclosures. Second, Maura had that same day come to his office to complain about what she considered sexual harassment. Mr. Singh became concerned about a possible contaminated work environment, but he did not think that he or Maura could make any form of harassment charge stick. The company had no corporate policy on harassment. Mr. Singh considered the situation to be just another case of one employee asking another out and being overly persistent. Mr. Singh decided not to do anything right away, not even to discuss the problem with Keith. He was worried that if he did take up the matter with Keith at such an early stage, he would himself be creating a hostile work environment. He believed Keith's advances would have to worsen before he should intervene or take the problem to the president.

Discussion Questions

1. If you were in Maura's position (or the equivalent position if you're male), how would you feel about your workplace? Explain.

2. Is Keith's conduct a case of sexual harassment? Is it a clear case, a borderline case, or no case at all? Explain your reasons for thinking so.

3. Is it justifiable for Mr. Singh to adopt a position of nonintervention? Why, or why not? Should he speak with Keith? What should he do to be an effective manager? Explain.

© Tom L. Beauchamp.

Case 7: Gay and Lesbian Rights at Friendly Motors
DENIS G. ARNOLD

Friendly Motors Repair Service was founded in 1992 in Houston by Paul Friendly, a military veteran, with the help of a $30,000 loan from his father. Paul repaid the loan in full with interest by 1995 and built the company into one of the largest independently owned automobile and light truck repair companies in Texas. Friendly Motors now has seven repair shops in the Houston area and is planning to expand into San Antonio. Paul

has worked hard to establish a reputation for honesty and integrity in an industry in which customers often expect to be cheated. Paul has always believed that if customers are treated fairly they will return and if employees are judged and rewarded by their work ethic and competence they will serve the company well. Nearly every race or ethnicity in Texas is represented in the workforce. The company's revenues have increased

This case was prepared for the purposes of classroom discussion. © 2011, 2018 Denis G. Arnold.

every year since he opened his first shop, but Paul is looking forward to retiring and pursuing his interests in veterans' affairs and fishing.

Over the years Paul learned that several of his mechanics are gay, including Bob who is one of the most hardworking people on his payroll and the only Friendly Motors mechanic who is a certified ASE Master Technician. Paul also knows that Brandi, one of his longest serving employees, is a lesbian. Brandi runs the repair shop with the largest revenues in the company, having built it up from being the smallest revenue generating shop. Brandi was instrumental in convincing Paul to offer the same healthcare benefits available to the spouses of employees to the same-sex partners of employees and has offered valuable advice about expansion.

Paul is nearing retirement and is considering appointing his son Mark president of Friendly Motors and turning over the business to him. Mark has successfully run the repair shop with the second largest revenues in the company for several years. Mark recently married Mary, a company accountant. Before getting married, Mark started attending Mary's evangelical church and was recently baptized as a born-again Christian. Their wedding took place at the church and was officiated by the church's senior pastor, an outspoken critic of gay, lesbian, and transgender rights. Paul has observed Mark's personal convictions about gay and lesbian employees shift in recent years from casual indifference to contempt. Mark and Mary have become increasingly outspoken about their view that gay and lesbians are sinners who must be helped to change their behavior and repent in order to be saved.

Paul worries that if he turns over the company to Mark he will fire Brandi, Bob, and other gay or lesbian employees, even though they have been loyal and productive. He knows that doing so is legal in most jurisdictions in Texas, but he doesn't believe it is the right thing to do. He suspects that Mark might even discourage gay and lesbian customers from doing business with the company. Recently he began considering promoting Brandi to president of the company instead of Mark, but he worries about whether everyone in the company would respect her authority. Not only would she be a woman running a company in a male dominated industry, but she would be a lesbian overseeing mainly straight male employees. Paul also worries that he himself might be intolerant of Mark and Mary's religious convictions regarding gays and lesbians. What, he ponders, should he do?

Discussion Questions

1. What are the ethical issues that arise in deciding between appointing Mark and Brandi as the new president of Friendly Motors? Explain.

2. Who should Paul appoint as president of the company? Why?

3. Putting aside the question of legality, what, if anything, is ethically objectionable about firing an "at-will" employee after discovering that he or she is gay or lesbian? Explain.

4. Putting aside the question of legality, what if anything, is ethically objectionable about firing an "at-will" employee for religious beliefs that are intolerant of certain employees or customers? Explain.

Case 8: A Matter of Integrity?

DENIS G. ARNOLD

The North Carolina General Assembly enacted legislation that prevented any municipality within the state, such as Charlotte, Raleigh, or Asheville, from making it illegal via local ordinances to discriminate against gay, lesbian, or transgender individuals in employment or public accommodation (e.g., hotels, bars, restaurants). In other words, under this law it would be legal in the North Carolina private sector to discriminate in employment and public accommodation (e.g., hotels, restaurants, bars, car rentals) based on the sexual orientation or gender identity of the customer or

employee. In the United States, unlike Australia, Canada, and the United Kingdom, no discrimination protections against the LGBT community are provided at the national level. At least 20 states (e.g., California, New York, Illinois) prohibit such discrimination, however, those that do not prohibit such discrimination allow local municipalities (e.g., cities and counties) to pass their own nondiscrimination regulations, thereby allowing local governments autonomy. Cities such as Dallas, TX, Nashville, TN, Louisville, KY, Atlanta, GA, and Kansas City, MO have banned such discrimination. North Carolina's House Bill 2 made it illegal for local authorities in North Carolina to protect the LGBT community from discrimination in the same way. While not stated in the legislation, one reason for permitting such discrimination is to allow business people to act in a manner consistent with their religiously grounded personal beliefs.

Imagine that you work for a large company that is considering opening a new operations facility in Charlotte, NC, one that is expected to employ 1,500 people (including transfers from company headquarters in Chicago). Your firm has a well-enforced and well-respected diversity policy that explicitly includes protections for members of the LGBT community. Some company leaders believe that the firm should not move its operations facility to Charlotte, but instead move it to a nearby state which does not permit such discrimination. They point out that such options were already determined in the site selection process. They argue that this is a matter of integrity, since the firm is explicitly committed to nondiscrimination. However, some argue that the project should go forward given the economic importance of Charlotte's new intermodal transportation hub linking trains and planes to area seaports. You, along with a number of other employees and managers, have been asked to provide your feedback on the matter.

Discussion Questions

1. What is your view of North Carolina's House Bill 2, which prevents local authorities from passing nondiscrimination legislation regarding sexual orientation or gender identity in private sector employment and public accommodation? Explain.

2. What do you recommend that your company do regarding the planned operations center? Why? Explain.

3. Do you agree, or disagree that it is "a matter of integrity" that the company publicly oppose North Carolina's new law in this case? Explain.

4. In general, do you think a company should publicly oppose government actions when such policies violate a company's own values? Why, or why not? Explain.

5

Corporate Social Responsibility

5.1 INTRODUCTION

This chapter focuses on corporate social responsibility. A socially responsible corporation is a good corporation. Over 2,000 years ago the Greeks thought they could answer questions about the goodness of things by knowing about the purpose of things. These Greek philosophers provided a functional analysis of good. For example, if one determines what a good racehorse is by knowing the purpose of racehorses (to win races) and the characteristics – for instance, speed, agility, and discipline – horses must have to win races, then a good racehorse is speedy, agile, and disciplined. To adapt the Greeks' method of reasoning, one determines what a good (socially responsible) corporation is by investigating the purpose corporations should serve in society.

THE PURPOSE OF THE CORPORATION

For many, the view that the only purpose of the corporation is to maximize profit for the owners is beyond debate and is accepted as a matter of fact. This view is most often associated with the Nobel Prize-winning economist Milton Friedman. However, it is also a feature of agency theory in finance which, at its core, holds that executives are "agents" of shareholders whose only interest is profits. Some management scholars have also adapted this perspective in arguing that corporate social responsibility should be regarded as actions that appear to benefit society but are always profitable for the firm.

Friedman has two main arguments for his position. First, shareholders are the *owners* of the corporation, and hence corporate profits *belong* to the shareholders. Managers are agents of the shareholders and have a moral obligation to manage the firm in the interest of the shareholders, that is, to maximize shareholder wealth. If the management of a firm spends corporate resources on measures to protect the environment beyond what is legally required, or provides wages and/or benefits more than those demanded by the market, or voluntarily implements human rights protections in its global operations, it is illegitimately spending shareholders' money. So too, if the management of a firm donates some of the firm's income to charitable organizations, it is seen as an illegitimate use of shareholders' money. If individual shareholders wish to donate their dividends to charity, they are free to do so, since the money is theirs. But managers have no right to donate corporate funds to charity. If society decides that private charity is insufficient to meet the needs of the poor, to maintain art museums, and to finance research for curing diseases, it is the responsibility of government to raise the necessary money through taxation. It should not come from managers purportedly acting on behalf of the corporation.

Second, shareholders are entitled to their profits as a result of a contract among the corporate stakeholders. A product or service is the result of the productive efforts of a number of parties – employees, managers, customers, suppliers, the local community, and the shareholders. Each of these stakeholder groups has a contractual relationship with the firm. In return for their services, the managers and employees are paid in the form of wages; the local community is paid in the form of taxes; and suppliers, under the constraints of supply and demand, negotiate the return for their products directly with the firm. Funds remaining after these payments have been made represent profit, and by agreement the profit belongs to the shareholders. The shareholders bear the risk when they supply the capital, and profit is the contractual return they receive for risk taking. Thus, each party in the manufacture and sale of a product receives the remuneration it has freely agreed to.

Friedman believes that these voluntary contractual arrangements maximize economic freedom and that economic freedom is a necessary condition for political freedom. Political rights gain efficacy in a capitalist system. For example, private employers are forced by competitive pressures to be concerned primarily with a prospective employee's ability to produce rather than with that person's political views. Opposing voices are heard in books, in the press, or on television so long as there is a profit to be made. Finally, the existence of capitalist markets limits the number of politically based decisions and thus increases freedom. Even democratic decisions coerce the opposing minority. Once society votes on how much to spend for defense or for city streets, the minority must go along. In the market, each consumer can decide how much of a product or service he or she is willing to purchase. Thus Friedman entitled his book defending the classical view of the purpose of the firm *Capitalism and Freedom*.

Some have criticized Friedman on the grounds that his view justifies anything that will lead to the maximization of profits including acting immorally or illegally if the manager can get away with it. We think that criticism of Friedman is unfair. In his classic article reprinted in this chapter Friedman says, in such a society, "there is one and only one social responsibility of business – to use its resources and engage in activities designed to increase its profit so long as it stays within the rules of the game, which is to say, engages in open and free competition without deception or fraud."[1]

Thus, the manager may not do anything to maximize profits. Friedman's arguments presume the existence of a robust democracy in which citizens determine the rules of the game, and businesses do not unduly influence the process via massive expenditures on political donations and lobbying the politicians who determine the rules of the game. Unfortunately, Friedman never fully elaborated on what the rules of the game are in a capitalist economy. And some of his followers have argued for tactics that strike many as unethical. For example, Theodore Levitt has argued in defense of deceptive advertising[2] and in favor of strong industry lobbying to have the government pass laws that are favorable to business and to reject laws that are unfavorable.[3] And Albert Carr has argued that business is like the game of poker and thus, just as in poker, behavior that is unethical in everyday life is justified in business.[4] One poorly understood feature of Friedman's perspective is that it has no applicability outside a democracy. In other words, his view cannot provide guidance to companies operating in China, Russia, much of Africa, the Middle East, and much of Southeast Asia.

Others have criticized Friedman on the grounds that the manager should use employees, customers, and suppliers as mere tools if by doing so he can generate profit. Thus, if wages can be cut to generate profit, they should be cut. Theoretically, that may indeed follow from Friedman's view, and some managers and CEOs even behave that way. But as a practical matter, the manager usually can generate profits only if she treats employees, customers, and suppliers well. This insight has spawned an entire field of academic study called positive organizational scholarship as well as popular books such as Jeffery Pfeiffer's *Competitive Advantage through People* and Frederick F. Reichheld's book *The Loyalty Effect*. In 1953, the US legal system acknowledged the connection between corporate philanthropy and goodwill. In the case of *A. P. Smith Manufacturing Co. v. Barlow* a charitable contribution to Princeton University was deemed to be a legitimate exercise of management authority. In the appeals case summarized in this chapter, Judge Jacobs recognized that an act that supports the public welfare can also be in the best interest of the corporation itself. The implication of this discussion is that in terms of behavior there may be no discernible difference between an "enlightened" Friedmanite and a manager who holds to the view that the purpose of the corporation involves more than the maximization of profit. The difference, to put it in a Kantian context, is in the motive. The enlightened Friedmanite treats employees well in order to generate profit. The non-Friedmanite treats employees well because it is a requirement of morality.

All business ethics scholars concur with the general public that an essential purpose of a publicly held firm is to make a profit, and thus making a profit is an obligation of the firm. Although many people also believe that the managers of publicly held corporations are legally required to maximize the profits for shareholders, this is not strictly true. Even in the most traditional interpretation managers have a fiduciary obligation to the corporation, which is then interpreted as a fiduciary obligation to shareholder interests. But many US states have laws that permit managers to take into account the needs of the other stakeholders and in Europe and Japan consideration for employees, the community, and the environment are not only permitted but are expected and often legally required.

Although managers may not be obligated to maximize profits, they certainly do have an obligation to avoid conflicts of interest where it appears that they benefit at the expense of the shareholders. Many groups that defend shareholder rights are legitimately concerned with serious issues of corporate governance. Such issues as excessive executive pay, especially when it is not linked to performance, overly generous stock options, golden parachutes in case of a hostile takeover, and the failure of executives to have to return exorbitant pay after the discovery of negligence, deception, or other misconduct, have all legitimately come under scrutiny.

As noted, the views represented by Friedman in this chapter have been criticized. Indeed, nearly all ethics and business law scholars reject his position as legally inaccurate, ethically challenged, and bad for society. In their essay in this chapter, "The Error at the Heart of Corporate Leadership," Harvard Business School professors Joseph L. Bower and Lynn S. Paine summarize many of these criticisms. They point out that the shareholder primacy view is inconsistent with corporate law because shareholders do not have the rights of the "owners" of corporations and managers are not "agents" of shareholders. Furthermore, shareholders have no accountability for firm behavior. Indeed, a firm could engage in massive consumer fraud, systematic employee abuse, and toxic environmental degradation, and shareholders would not be legally liable. Bower and Paine argue that shareholder primacy is diverting firms from innovation, strategic renewal, and sustainable firm performance.

An alternative way to understand the purpose of the corporation is to consider corporate *stakeholders*. From the stakeholders' perspective, the shareholder primacy view is problematic in that all emphasis is placed on one stakeholder – the shareholder. The interests of the other stakeholders are unfairly subordinated to the shareholders' interests. Although any person or group affected by corporate decisions is a stakeholder, most stakeholder analysis has focused on a special group of stakeholders: namely, members of groups whose existence was necessary for the firm's survival. Stakeholder theory focuses on six stakeholder groups: shareholders, employees, customers, managers, suppliers, and the local community. Managers who manage from the stakeholder perspective see their task as harmonizing the legitimate interests of the primary corporate stakeholders. In describing stakeholder management, R. Edward Freeman in his article "Managing for Stakeholders" argues that managers have an ethical duty to manage the organization for all stakeholders. Both in corporate and academic circles, stakeholder terminology has become very fashionable. For example, many corporate codes of conduct are organized around stakeholder principles.

However, theoretical problems remain. Much has been said of the obligations of managers to the other corporate stakeholders, but little has been said about the obligations of the other stakeholders, for instance, the community or employees, to the corporation. Do members of a community have an obligation to consider the moral reputation of a company when they make their purchasing decisions? Do employees have an obligation to stay with a company that has invested in their training, even if they could get a slightly better salary by moving to another corporation?

The next article in this section by Eric W. Orts and Alan Strudler argues that while stakeholder theory helps to identify legitimate interests that companies must take into account, it does not provide sufficient ethical guidance. They argue that a purely strategic or instrumental approach to stakeholders would allow a company to use unethical means to "manage" stakeholders. They also argue that since being a stakeholder is a matter of degree (e.g., employees may have more of a "stake" in a company than most community members do), and since stakeholder theory does not take into account the variety of different relationships companies have with different individuals, it is too vague to be useful. In their view stakeholder theory is no better at providing ethical guidance for managing businesses than is Friedman's shareholder view. In place of both views, they call for reflection on ethical principles that should guide managers in light of the difficult ethical problems that confront businesses. This approach is consistent with many of the readings included in the remainder of this book.

In an important new contribution to the literature, "Toward a Theory of Business," Thomas Donaldson and James Walsh take up the challenge of Orts and Strudler to develop principles to guide business. Their theoretical framework includes both empirical and normative dimensions. Importantly, their theory includes the idea of a "dignity threshold," which is the idea that a basic level of respect needs to be accorded to every business participant. This is a deontological, Kantian principle that is absent from the articles of both Friedman and Freeman. However, it is consistent with the arguments of many other articles in this book including Bowie's discussion of respect for employees in Chapter 2, Schultz's discussion of sexual harassment in Chapter 4, and Arnold's discussion of human rights and Hartman's discussion of sweatshops, both in Chapter 9. Donaldson and Walsh define business success as optimized collective value consistent with the dignity threshold. If this general aim was consistently pursued by the leaders of corporations, they argue, social welfare – that is, the overall good of societies – would be greatly enhanced.

Notes

1. M. Friedman, *Capitalism and Freedom* (University of Chicago Press, 1962), p. 126.
2. Theodore Levitt, "The Morality (?) of Advertising," *Harvard Business Review* (July–August, 1970): 84–92.
3. Theodore Levitt, "The Dangers of Social Responsibility," *Harvard Business Review* (September–October, 1958): 41–50.
4. Albert Z. Carr, "Is Business Bluffing Ethical?" *Harvard Business Review* (January–February, 1968): 143–53.

5.2 SHAREHOLDER MANAGEMENT VERSUS STAKEHOLDER MANAGEMENT

The Social Responsibility of Business Is to Increase Its Profits

MILTON FRIEDMAN

When I hear businessmen speak eloquently about the "social responsibilities of business in a free-enterprise system," I am reminded of the wonderful line about the Frenchman who discovered at the age of 70 that he had been speaking prose all his life. The businessmen believe that they are defending free enterprise when they declaim that business is not concerned "merely" with profit but also with promoting desirable "social" ends; that business has a "social conscience" and takes seriously its responsibilities for providing employment, eliminating discrimination, avoiding pollution and whatever else may be the catchwords of the contemporary crop of reformers. In fact they are – or would be if they or anyone else took them seriously – preaching pure and unadulterated socialism. Businessmen who talk this way are unwitting puppets of the intellectual forces that have been undermining the basis of a free society these past decades.

The discussions of the "social responsibilities of business" are notable for their analytical looseness and lack of rigor. What does it mean to say that "business" has responsibilities? Only people can have responsibilities. A corporation is an artificial person and in this sense may have artificial responsibilities, but "business" as a whole cannot be said to have responsibilities, even in this vague sense. The first step toward clarity in examining the doctrine of the social responsibility of business is to ask precisely what it implies for whom.

Presumably, the individuals who are to be responsible are businessmen, which means individual proprietors or corporate executives. Most of the discussion of social responsibility is directed at corporations, so in what follows I shall mostly neglect the individual proprietors and speak of corporate executives.

In a free-enterprise, private-property system, a corporate executive is an employee of the owners of the business. He has direct responsibility to his employers. That responsibility is to conduct the business in accordance with their desires, which generally will be to make as much money as possible while conforming to the basic rules of the society, both those embodied in law and those embodied in ethical custom. Of course, in some cases his employers may have a different objective. A group of persons might establish a corporation for an eleemosynary purpose – for example, a hospital or a school. The manager of such a corporation will not have money profit as his objective but the rendering of certain services.

In either case, the key point is that, in his capacity as a corporate executive, the manager is the agent of the individuals who own the corporation or establish the eleemosynary institution, and his primary responsibility is to them.

Needless to say, this does not mean that it is easy to judge how well he is performing his task. But at least the criterion of performance is straightforward, and the persons among whom a voluntary contractual arrangement exists are clearly defined.

Of course, the corporate executive is also a person in his own right. As a person, he may have many other responsibilities that he recognizes or assumes voluntarily – to his family, his conscience, his feelings of charity, his church, his clubs, his city, his country. He may feel impelled by these responsibilities to devote part of his income to causes he regards as worthy, to refuse to work for particular corporations, even to leave his job, for example, to join his country's armed forces. If we wish, we may refer to some of these responsibilities as "social responsibilities." But in these respects he is acting as a principal, not an agent; he is spending his own money or time or energy, not the money of his employers or the time or energy he has contracted to devote to their purposes. If these are "social responsibilities," they are the social responsibilities of individuals, not of business.

What does it mean to say that the corporate executive has a "social responsibility" in his capacity as businessman? If this statement is not pure rhetoric, it must mean that he is to act in some way that is not in the interest of his employers. For example, that he is to refrain from increasing the price of the product in order to contribute to the social objective of preventing inflation, even though a price increase would be in the best interests of the corporation. Or that he is to make expenditures on reducing pollution beyond the amount that is in the best interests of the corporation or that is required by law in order to contribute to the social objective of improving the environment. Or that, at the expense of corporate profits, he is to hire "hardcore" unemployed instead of better qualified available workmen to contribute to the social objective of reducing poverty.

In each of these cases, the corporate executive would be spending someone else's money for a general social interest. Insofar as his actions in accord with his "social responsibility" reduce returns to stockholders, he is spending their money. Insofar as his actions raise the price to customers, he is spending the customers' money. Insofar as his actions lower the wages of some employees, he is spending their money.

The stockholders or the customers or the employees could separately spend their own money on the particular action if they wished to do so. The executive is exercising a distinct "social responsibility," rather than serving as an agent of the stockholders or the customers or the employees, only if he spends the money in a different way than they would have spent it.

But if he does this, he is in effect imposing taxes, on the one hand, and deciding how the tax proceeds shall be spent, on the other.

This process raises political questions on two levels: principle and consequences. On the level of political principle, the imposition of taxes and the expenditure of tax proceeds are governmental functions. We have established elaborate constitutional, parliamentary, and judicial provisions to control these functions, to assure that taxes are imposed so far as possible in accordance with the preferences and desires of the public – after all, "taxation without representation" was one of the battle cries of the American Revolution. We have a system of checks and balances to separate the legislative function of imposing taxes and enacting expenditures from the executive function of collecting taxes and administering expenditure programs and from the judicial function of mediating disputes and interpreting the law.

Here the businessman – self-selected or appointed directly or indirectly by stockholders – is to be simultaneously legislator, executive, and jurist. He is to decide whom to tax by how much and for what purpose, and he is to spend the proceeds – all this guided only by general exhortations from on high to restrain inflation, improve the environment, fight poverty and so on and on.

The whole justification for permitting the corporate executive to be selected by the stockholders is that the executive is an agent serving the interests of his principal. This justification disappears when the corporate executive imposes taxes and spends the proceeds for "social" purposes. He becomes in effect a public employee, a civil servant, even though he remains in name an employee of a private enterprise. On grounds of political principle, it is intolerable that such civil servants – insofar as their actions in the name of social responsibility are real and not just window-dressing – should be selected as they are now. If they are to be civil servants, then they must be elected through a political process. If they are to impose taxes and make expenditures to foster "social" objectives, then political machinery must be set up to make the assessment of taxes and to determine through a political process the objectives to be served.

This is the basic reason why the doctrine of "social responsibility" involves the acceptance of the socialist view that political mechanisms, not market mechanisms, are the appropriate way to determine the allocation of scarce resources to alternative uses.

On the grounds of consequences, can the corporate executive in fact discharge his alleged "social responsibilities"? On the other hand, suppose he could get away with spending the stockholders' or customers' or employees' money. How is he to know how to spend it? He is told that he must contribute to fighting inflation. How is he to know what action of his will contribute to that end? He is

presumably an expert in running his company – in producing a product or selling it or financing it. But nothing about his selection makes him an expert on inflation. Will his holding down the price of his product reduce inflationary pressure? Or, by leaving more spending power in the hands of his customers, simply divert it elsewhere? Or, by forcing him to produce less because of the lower price, will it simply contribute to shortages? Even if he could answer these questions, how much cost is he justified in imposing on his stockholders, customers, and employees for this social purpose? What is his appropriate share and what is the appropriate share of others?

And, whether he wants to or not, can he get away with spending his stockholders', customers' or employees' money? Will not the stockholders fire him? (Either the present ones or those who take over when his actions in the name of social responsibility have reduced the corporation's profits and the price of its stock.) His customers and his employees can desert him for other producers and employers less scrupulous in exercising their social responsibilities.

This facet of "social responsibility" doctrine is brought into sharp relief when the doctrine is used to justify wage restraint by trade unions. The conflict of interest is naked and clear when union officials are asked to subordinate the interest of their members to some more general purpose. If the union officials try to enforce wage restraint, the consequence is likely to be wildcat strikes, rank-and-file revolts, and the emergence of strong competitors for their jobs. We thus have the ironic phenomenon that union leaders – at least in the United States – have objected to government interference with the market far more consistently and courageously than have business leaders.

The difficulty of exercising "social responsibility" illustrates, of course, the great virtue of private competitive enterprise – it forces people to be responsible for their own actions and makes it difficult for them to "exploit" other people for either selfish or unselfish purposes. They can do good – but only at their own expense.

Many a reader who has followed the argument this far may be tempted to remonstrate that it is all well and good to speak of government's having the responsibility to impose taxes and determine expenditures for such "social" purposes as controlling pollution or training the hard-core unemployed, but that the problems are too urgent to wait on the slow course of political processes, that the exercise of social responsibility by businessmen is a quicker and surer way to solve pressing current problems.

Aside from the question of fact – I share Adam Smith's skepticism about the benefits that can be expected from "those who affected to trade for the public good" – this argument must be rejected on grounds of principle. What it amounts to is an assertion that those who favor the taxes and expenditures in question have failed to persuade a majority of their fellow citizens to be of like mind and that they are seeking to attain by undemocratic procedures what they cannot attain by democratic procedures. In a free society, it is hard for "evil" people to do "evil," especially since one man's good is another's evil.

I have, for simplicity, concentrated on the special case of the corporate executive, except only for the brief digression on trade unions. But precisely the same argument applies to the newer phenomenon of calling upon stockholders to require corporations to exercise social responsibility (the recent GM crusade for example). In most of these cases, what is in effect involved is some stockholders trying to get other stockholders (or customers or employees) to contribute against their will to "social" causes favored by the activists. Insofar as they succeed, they are again imposing taxes and spending the proceeds.

The situation of the individual proprietor is somewhat different. If he acts to reduce the returns of his enterprise in order to exercise his "social responsibility," he is spending his own money, not someone else's. If he wishes to spend his money on such purposes, that is his right, and I cannot see that there is any objection to his doing so. In the process, he, too, may impose costs on employees and customers. However, because he is far less likely than a large corporation or union to have monopolistic power, any such side-effects will tend to be minor.

Of course, in practice, the doctrine of social responsibility is frequently a cloak for actions that are justified on other grounds rather than a reason for those actions.

To illustrate, it may well be in the long-run interest of a corporation that is a major employer in a small community to devote resources to providing amenities to that community or to improving its government. That may make it easier to attract desirable employees, it may reduce the wage bill or lessen losses from pilferage and sabotage or have other worthwhile effects. Or it may be that, given the laws about the deductibility of corporate charitable contributions, the stockholders can contribute more to charities they favor by having the corporation make the gift than by doing it themselves, since they can in that way contribute an amount that would otherwise have been paid as corporate taxes.

In each of these – and many similar – cases, there is a strong temptation to rationalize these actions as an exercise of "social responsibility." In the present climate of opinion, with its widespread aversion to "capitalism," "profits," the "soulless corporation," and so on, this is one way for a corporation to generate goodwill as a by-product of expenditures that are entirely justified in its own self-interest.

It would be inconsistent of me to call on corporate executives to refrain from this hypocritical window-dressing because it harms the foundations of a free society. That would be to call on them to exercise a "social responsibility"! If our institutions, and the attitudes of the public make it in their self-interest to cloak their actions in this way, I cannot summon much indignation to denounce them. At the same time, I can express admiration for those individual proprietors or owners of closely held corporations or stockholders of more broadly held corporations who disdain such tactics as approaching fraud.

Whether blameworthy or not, the use of the cloak of social responsibility, and the nonsense spoken in its name by influential and prestigious businessmen, does clearly harm the foundations of a free society. I have been impressed time and again by the schizophrenic character of many businessmen. They are capable of being extremely farsighted and clear-headed in matters that are internal to their businesses. They are incredibly shortsighted and muddle-headed in matters that are outside their businesses but affect the possible survival of business in general. This shortsightedness is strikingly exemplified in the calls from many businessmen for wage and price guidelines or controls or income policies. There is nothing that could do more in a brief period to destroy a market system and replace it by a centrally controlled system than effective governmental control of prices and wages.

The shortsightedness is also exemplified in speeches by businessmen on social responsibility. This may gain them kudos in the short run. But it helps to strengthen the already too prevalent view that the pursuit of profits is wicked and immoral and must be curbed and controlled by external forces. Once this view is adopted, the external forces that curb the market will not be the social consciences, however highly developed, of the pontificating executives; it will be the iron fist of government bureaucrats. Here, as with price and wage controls, businessmen seem to me to reveal a suicidal impulse.

The political principle that underlies the market mechanism is unanimity. In an ideal free market resting on private property, no individual can coerce any other, all cooperation is voluntary, all parties to such cooperation benefit or they need not participate. There are no values, no "social" responsibilities in any sense other than the shared values and responsibilities of individuals. Society is a collection of individuals and of the various groups they voluntarily form.

The political principle that underlies the political mechanism is conformity. The individual must serve a more general social interest – whether that be determined by a church or a dictator or a majority. The individual may have a vote and say in what is to be done, but if he is overruled, he must conform. It is appropriate for some to require others to contribute to a general social purpose whether they wish to or not.

Unfortunately, unanimity is not always feasible. There are some respects in which conformity appears unavoidable, so I do not see how one can avoid the use of the political mechanism altogether.

But the doctrine of "social responsibility" taken seriously would extend the scope of the political mechanism to every human activity. It does not differ in philosophy from the most explicitly collectivist doctrine. It differs only by professing to believe that collectivist ends can be attained without collectivist means. That is why, in my book *Capitalism and Freedom*, I have called it a "fundamentally subversive doctrine" in a free society, and have said that in such a society, "there is one and only one social responsibility of business – to use its resources and engage in activities designed to increase its profits so long as it stays within the rules of the game, which is to say, engages in open and free competition without deception or fraud."

The Error at the Heart of Corporate Leadership

JOSEPH L. BOWER AND LYNN S. PAINE

In the fall of 2014, the hedge fund activist and Allergan shareholder Bill Ackman became increasingly frustrated with Allergan's board of directors. In a letter to the board, he took the directors to task for their failure to do (in his words) "what you are paid $400,000 per year to do on behalf of the Company's owners." The board's alleged failure: refusing to negotiate with Valeant Pharmaceuticals about its unsolicited bid to take over Allergan – a bid that Ackman himself had helped engineer in a novel alliance between a hedge fund and a would-be acquirer. In presentations promoting the deal, Ackman praised Valeant for its shareholder-friendly capital allocation, its shareholder-aligned executive compensation, and its avoidance of risky early-stage research. Using the same approach at Allergan, he told analysts, would create significant value for its shareholders. He cited Valeant's plan to cut Allergan's research budget by 90 percent as "really the opportunity." Valeant CEO Mike Pearson assured analysts that "all we care about is shareholder value."

These events illustrate a way of thinking about the governance and management of companies that is now pervasive in the financial community and much of the business world. It centers on the idea that management's objective is, or should be, maximizing value for shareholders, but it addresses a wide range of topics – from performance measurement and executive compensation to shareholder rights, the role of directors, and corporate responsibility. This thought system has been embraced not only by hedge fund activists like Ackman but also by institutional investors more generally, along with many boards, managers, lawyers, academics, and even some regulators and lawmakers. Indeed, its precepts have come to be widely regarded as a model for "good governance" and for the brand of investor activism illustrated by the Allergan story.

Yet the idea that corporate managers should make maximizing shareholder value their goal – and that boards should ensure that they do – is relatively recent. It is rooted in what's known as agency theory, which was put forth by academic economists in the 1970s. At the theory's core is the assertion that shareholders own the corporation and, by virtue of their status as owners, have ultimate authority over its business and may legitimately demand that its activities be conducted in accordance with their wishes.

Attributing ownership of the corporation to shareholders sounds natural enough, but a closer look reveals that it is legally confused and, perhaps more important, involves a challenging problem of accountability. Keep in mind that shareholders have no legal duty to protect or serve the companies whose shares they own and are shielded by the doctrine of limited liability from legal responsibility for those companies' debts and misdeeds.

Moreover, they may generally buy and sell shares without restriction and are required to disclose their identities only in certain circumstances. In addition, they tend to be

From Joseph L. Bowers and Lynn S. Paine, "The Error at the Heart of Corporate Leadership," *Harvard Business Review* 95, no. 3 (May–June 2017): 50–60. Reprinted by permission.

physically and psychologically distant from the activities of the companies they invest in. That is to say, public company shareholders have few incentives to consider, and are not generally viewed as responsible for, the effects of the actions they favor on the corporation, other parties, or society more broadly. Agency theory has yet to grapple with the implications of the accountability vacuum that results from accepting its central – and in our view, faulty – premise that shareholders own the corporation.

The effects of this omission are troubling. We are concerned that the agency-based model of governance and management is being practiced in ways that are weakening companies and – if applied even more widely, as experts predict – could be damaging to the broader economy. In particular we are concerned about the effects on corporate strategy and resource allocation. Over the past few decades the agency model has provided the rationale for a variety of changes in governance and management practices that, taken together, have increased the power and influence of certain types of shareholders over other types and further elevated the claims of shareholders over those of other important constituencies – without establishing any corresponding responsibility or accountability on the part of shareholders who exercise that power. As a result, managers are under increasing pressure to deliver ever faster and more predictable returns and to curtail riskier investments aimed at meeting future needs and finding creative solutions to the problems facing people around the world.

Don't misunderstand: We are capitalists to the core. We believe that widespread participation in the economy through the ownership of stock in publicly traded companies is important to the social fabric, and that strong protections for shareholders are essential. But the health of the economic system depends on getting the role of shareholders right.

The agency model's extreme version of shareholder centricity is flawed in its assumptions, confused as a matter of law, and damaging in practice. A better model would recognize the critical role of shareholders but also take seriously the idea that corporations are independent entities serving multiple purposes and endowed by law with the potential to endure over time. And it would acknowledge accepted legal principles holding that directors and managers have duties to the corporation as well as to shareholders. In other words, a better model would be more company centered.

Before considering an alternative, let's take a closer look at the agency-based model.

Foundations of the Model

The ideas underlying the agency-based model can be found in Milton Friedman's well-known *New York Times Magazine* article of 1970 denouncing corporate "social responsibility" as a socialist doctrine. Friedman takes shareholders' ownership of the corporation as a given. He asserts that "the manager is the agent of the individuals who own the corporation" and, further, that the manager's primary "responsibility is to conduct the business in accordance with [the owners'] desires." He characterizes the executive as "an agent serving the interests of his principal."

These ideas were further developed in the 1976 *Journal of Financial Economics* article "Theory of the Firm," by Michael Jensen and William Meckling, who set forth the theory's basic premises:

- Shareholders own the corporation and are "principals" with original authority to manage the corporation's business and affairs.
- Managers are delegated decision-making authority by the corporation's shareholders and are thus "agents" of the shareholders.
- As agents of the shareholders, managers are obliged to conduct the corporation's business in accordance with shareholders' desires.
- Shareholders want business to be conducted in a way that maximizes their own economic returns. (The assumption that shareholders are unanimous in this objective is implicit throughout the article.)

Jensen and Meckling do not discuss shareholders' wishes regarding the ethical standards that managers should observe in conducting the business, but Friedman offers two views in his *Times* article. First he writes that shareholders generally want managers "to make as much money as possible while conforming to the basic rules of the society, both those embodied in law and those embodied in ethical custom." Later he suggests that shareholders simply want managers to use resources and pursue profit by engaging "in open and free competition without deception or fraud." Jensen and Meckling agree with Friedman that companies should not engage in acts of "social responsibility."

Much of the academic work on agency theory in the decades since has focused on ensuring that managers seek to maximize shareholder returns – primarily by aligning their interests with those of shareholders. These ideas have been further developed into a theory of organization whereby managers can (and should) instill concern for shareholders' interests throughout a company by properly delegating "decision rights" and creating appropriate incentives. They have also given rise to a view of boards of directors as an organizational mechanism for controlling what's known as "agency costs" – the costs to shareholders associated with delegating authority to managers. Hence the notion that a board's principal role is (or should be) monitoring management, and that boards should design executive compensation to align management's interests with those of shareholders.

The Model's Flaws

Let's look at where these ideas go astray.

1. *Agency theory is at odds with corporate law: Legally, shareholders do not have the rights of "owners" of the corporation, and managers are not shareholders' "agents."*

As other scholars and commentators have noted, the idea that shareholders own the corporation is at best confusing and at worst incorrect. From a legal perspective, shareholders are beneficiaries of the corporation's activities, but they do not have "dominion" over a piece of property. Nor do they enjoy access to the corporate premises or use of the corporation's assets. What shareholders do own is their shares. That generally gives them various rights and privileges, including the right to sell their shares and to vote on certain matters, such as the election of directors, amendments to the corporate charter, and the sale of substantially all the corporation's assets.

Furthermore, under the law in Delaware – legal home to more than half the *Fortune* 500 and the benchmark for corporate law – the right to manage the business and affairs of the corporation is vested in a board of directors elected by the shareholders; the board delegates that authority to corporate managers.

Within this legal framework, managers and directors are fiduciaries rather than agents – and not just for shareholders but also for the corporation. The difference is important. Agents are obliged to carry out the wishes of a principal, whereas a fiduciary's obligation is to exercise independent judgment on behalf of a beneficiary. Put differently, an agent is an order taker, whereas a fiduciary is expected to make discretionary decisions. Legally, directors have a fiduciary duty to act in the best interests of the corporation, which is very different from simply doing the bidding of shareholders.

2. *The theory is out of step with ordinary usage: Shareholders are not owners of the corporation in any traditional sense of the term, nor do they have owners' traditional incentives to exercise care in managing it.*

This observation is even truer today than when it was famously made by Adolf Berle and Gardiner Means in their landmark 1932 study *The Modern Corporation and Private Property*. Some 70 percent of shares in US-listed companies today are held by mutual funds, pension funds, insurance companies, sovereign funds, and other institutional investors, which manage them on behalf of beneficiaries such as households, pensioners, policy holders, and

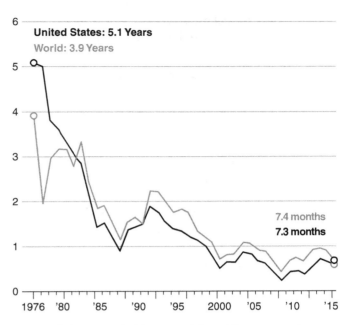

Figure 5.1 Average holding period for public company shares
Source: The World Bank, World Federation of Exchanges Database.

governments. In many instances the beneficiaries are anonymous to the company whose shares the institutions hold. The professionals who manage these investments are typically judged and rewarded each quarter on the basis of returns from the total basket of investments managed. A consequence is high turnover in shares, which also results from high-frequency trading by speculators (see Figure 5.1.)

The decisions of asset managers and speculators arise from expectations regarding share price over a relatively short period of time. As the economy passes through cycles, the shares of companies in entire industry sectors move in and out of favor. Although the shareholders of record at any given moment may vote on an issue brought before them, they need not know or care about the company whose shares they hold. Moreover, the fact that they can hedge or immediately sell their shares and avoid exposure to the longer-term effects of that vote makes it difficult to regard them as proprietors of the company in any customary sense.

The anonymity afforded the shares' beneficial owners further attenuates their relationship to the companies whose shares they own. Some 85 percent of publicly traded shares in the United States are held in the name of an institution serving as an intermediary – the so-called street name – on behalf of itself or its customers. And of the ultimate owners of those shares, an estimated 75 percent have instructed their intermediaries not to divulge their identities to the issuing company.

3. *The theory is rife with moral hazard: Shareholders are not accountable as owners for the company's activities, nor do they have the responsibilities that officers and directors do to protect the company's interests.*

The problem with treating shareholders as proprietors is exacerbated by the absence of another traditional feature of ownership: responsibility for the property owned and accountability – even legal liability, in some cases – for injuries to third parties resulting from how that property is used. Shareholders bear no such responsibility. Under the doctrine of limited liability, they cannot be held personally liable for the corporation's debts or for corporate acts and omissions that result in injury to others.

With a few exceptions, shareholders are entitled to act entirely in their own interest within the bounds of the securities laws. Unlike directors, who are expected to refrain from self-dealing, they are free to act on both sides of a transaction in which they have an interest. Consider the contest between Allergan and Valeant. A member of Allergan's board who held shares in Valeant would have been expected to refrain from voting on the deal or promoting Valeant's bid. But Allergan shareholders with a stake in both companies were free to buy, sell, and vote as they saw fit, with no obligation to act in the best interests of either company. Institutional investors holding shares in thousands of companies regularly act on deals in which they have significant interests on both sides.

In a well-ordered economy, rights and responsibilities go together. Giving shareholders the rights of ownership while exempting them from the responsibilities opens the door to opportunism, overreach, and misuse of corporate assets. The risk is less worrying when shareholders do not seek to influence major corporate decisions, but it is acute when they do. The problem is clearest when temporary holders of large blocks of shares intervene to reconstitute a company's board, change its management, or restructure its finances in an effort to drive up its share price, only to sell out and move on to another target without ever having to answer for their intervention's impact on the company or other parties.

4. *The theory's doctrine of alignment spreads moral hazard throughout a company and narrows management's field of vision.*

Just as freedom from accountability has a tendency to make shareholders indifferent to broader and longer-term considerations, so agency theory's recommended alignment between managers' interests and those of shareholders can skew the perspective of the entire organization. When the interests of successive layers of management are "aligned" in this manner, the corporation may become so biased toward the narrow interests of its current shareholders that it fails to meet the requirements of its customers or other constituencies. In extreme cases it may tilt so far that it can no longer function effectively. The story of Enron's collapse reveals how thoroughly the body of a company can be infected.The notion that managing for the good of the company is the same as managing for the good of the stock is best understood as a theoretical conceit necessitated by the mathematical models that many economists favor. In practical terms there is (or can be) a stark difference. Once Allergan's management shifted its focus from sustaining long-term growth to getting the company's stock price to $180 a share – the target at which institutional investors were willing to hold their shares – its priorities changed accordingly. Research was cut, investments were eliminated, and employees were dismissed.

5. *The theory's assumption of shareholder uniformity is contrary to fact: Shareholders do not all have the same objectives and cannot be treated as a single "owner."*

Agency theory assumes that all shareholders want the company to be run in a way that maximizes their own economic return. This simplifying assumption is useful for certain purposes, but it masks important differences. Shareholders have differing investment objectives, attitudes toward risk, and time horizons. Pension funds may seek current income and preservation of capital. Endowments may seek long-term growth. Young investors may accept considerably more risk than their elders will tolerate. Proxy voting records indicate that shareholders are divided on many of the resolutions put before them. They may also view strategic opportunities differently. In the months after Valeant announced its bid, Allergan officials met with a broad swath of institutional investors. According to Allergan's lead independent director, Michael Gallagher, "The diversity of opinion was as wide as could possibly be" – from those who opposed the deal and absolutely did not want Valeant shares (the offer included both stock and cash) to those who saw it as the opportunity of a lifetime and could not understand why Allergan did not sit down with Valeant immediately.

The Agency-Based Model in Practice

Despite these problems, agency theory has attracted a wide following. Its tenets have provided the intellectual rationale for a variety of changes in practice that, taken together, have enhanced the power of shareholders and given rise to a model of governance and management that is unrelenting in its shareholder centricity. Here are just a few of the arenas in which the theory's influence can be seen.

Executive Compensation

Agency theory ideas were instrumental in the shift from a largely cash-based system to one that relies predominantly on equity. Proponents of the shift argued that equity-based pay would better align the interests of executives with those of shareholders. The same argument was used to garner support for linking pay more closely to stock performance and for tax incentives to encourage such "pay for performance" arrangements. Following this logic, Congress adopted legislation in 1992 making executive pay above $1 million deductible only if it is "performance based." Today some 62 percent of executive pay is in the form of equity, compared with 19 percent in 1980.

Disclosure of Executive Pay

Agency theory's definition of performance and its doctrine of alignment undergird rules proposed by the SEC in 2015 requiring companies to expand the information on executive pay and shareholder returns provided in their annual proxy statements. The proposed rules call for companies to report their annual total shareholder return (TSR) over time, along with annual TSR figures for their peer group, and to describe the relationships between their TSR and their executive compensation and between their TSR and the TSR of their peers.

Shareholders' Rights

The idea that shareholders are owners has been central to the push to give them more say in the nomination and election of directors and to make it easier for them to call a special meeting, act by written consent, or remove a director. Data from FactSet and other sources indicate that the proportion of S&P 500 companies with majority voting for directors increased from about 16 percent in 2006 to 88 percent in 2015; the proportion with special meeting provisions rose from 41 percent in 2002 to 61 percent in 2015; and the proportion giving shareholders proxy access rights increased from less than half a percent in 2013 to some 39 percent by mid-2016.

The Power of Boards

Agency thinking has also propelled efforts to eliminate staggered boards in favor of annual election for all directors and to eliminate "poison pills" that would enable boards to slow down or prevent "owners" from voting on a premium offer for the company. From 2002 to 2015, the share of S&P 500 companies with staggered boards dropped from 61 percent to 10 percent, and the share with a standing poison pill fell from 60 percent to 4 percent. (Companies without a standing pill may still adopt a pill in response to an unsolicited offer – as was done by the Allergan board in response to Valeant's bid.)

Management Attitudes

Agency theory's conception of management responsibility has been widely adopted. In 1997 the Business Roundtable issued a statement declaring that "the paramount duty of management and of boards of directors is to the corporation's stockholders" and that "the principal objective of a business enterprise is to generate economic returns to its owners." Issued in response to pressure from institutional investors, the statement in effect revised the Roundtable's earlier position that "the shareholder must receive a good return but the legitimate concerns of other constituencies also must have the appropriate attention." Various studies suggest ways in which managers have become more responsive to shareholders. Research indicates, for instance, that companies with majority (rather than plurality) voting for directors are more apt to adopt shareholder proposals that garner majority support, and that many chief financial officers are willing to forgo investments in projects expected to be profitable in the longer term in order to meet analysts' quarterly earnings estimates. According to surveys by the Aspen Institute, many business school graduates regard maximizing shareholder value as their top responsibility.

Investor Behavior

Agency theory ideas have facilitated a rise in investor activism and legitimized the playbook of hedge funds that mobilize capital for the express purpose of buying company shares and using their position as "owners" to effect changes aimed at creating shareholder value. These investors are intervening more frequently and reshaping how companies allocate resources. In the process they are reshaping the strategic context in which all companies and their boards make decisions.

Taken individually, a change such as majority voting for directors may have merit. As a group, however, these changes have helped create an environment in which managers are under increasing pressure to deliver short-term financial results, and boards are being urged to "think like activists."

Value Creation or Value Transfer?

The question of whether shareholders benefit from investor activism beyond an initial bump in stock price is likely to remain unresolved, given the methodological problems plaguing studies on the subject. No doubt in some cases activists have played a useful role in waking up a sleepy board or driving a long-overdue change in strategy or management.

However, it is important to note that much of what activists call value creation is more accurately described as value transfer. When cash is paid out to shareholders rather than used to fund research, launch new ventures, or grow existing businesses, value has not been created. Nothing has been created. Rather, cash that would have been invested to generate future returns is simply being paid out to current shareholders. The lag time between when such decisions are taken and when their effect on earnings is evident exceeds the time frames of standard financial models, so the potential for damage to the company and future shareholders, not to mention society more broadly, can easily go unnoticed.

Given how long it takes to see the fruits of any significant research effort (Apple's latest iPhone chip was eight years in the making), the risk to research and innovation from activists who force deep cuts to drive up the share price and then sell out before the pipeline dries up is obvious. It doesn't help that financial models and capital markets are notoriously poor at valuing innovation. After Allergan was put into play by the offer from Valeant and Ackman's Pershing Square Capital Management, the company's share price rose by 30 percent as other hedge funds bought the stock. Some institutions sold to reap the immediate gain, and Allergan's management was soon facing pressure from the remaining institutions to accelerate cash flow and "bring earnings forward." In an attempt to hold on to those shareholders, the company made deeper cuts in the workforce than previously planned and curtailed early-stage research programs. Academic studies have found that a significant proportion of hedge fund interventions involve large increases in leverage and large decreases in investment, particularly in research and development.

The activists' claim of value creation is further clouded by indications that some of the value purportedly created for shareholders is actually value transferred from other parties or from the general public. Large-sample research on this question is limited, but one study suggests that the positive abnormal returns associated with the announcement of a hedge fund intervention are, in part, a transfer of wealth from workers to shareholders. The study found that workers' hours decreased and their wages stagnated in the three years after an intervention. Other studies have found that some of the gains for shareholders come at the expense of bondholders. Still other academic work links aggressive pay-for-stock-performance arrangements to various misdeeds involving harm to consumers, damage to the environment, and irregularities in accounting and financial reporting.

We are not aware of any studies that examine the total impact of hedge fund interventions on all stakeholders or society at large. Still, it appears self-evident that shareholders' gains are sometimes simply transfers from the public purse, such as when management improves earnings by shifting a company's tax domicile to a lower-tax jurisdiction – a move often favored by activists, and one of Valeant's proposals for Allergan. Similarly, budget cuts that eliminate exploratory research aimed at addressing some of society's most vexing challenges may enhance current earnings but at a cost to society as well as to the company's prospects for the future.

Hedge fund activism points to some of the risks inherent in giving too much power to unaccountable "owners." As our analysis of agency theory's premises suggests, the problem of moral hazard is real – and the consequences are serious. Yet practitioners continue to embrace the theory's doctrines; regulators continue to embed them in policy; boards and managers are under increasing pressure to deliver short-term returns; and legal experts forecast that the trend toward greater shareholder empowerment will persist. To us, the prospect that public companies will be run even more strictly according to the agency-based model is alarming. Rigid adherence to the model by companies uniformly across the economy could easily result in even more pressure for current earnings, less investment in R&D and in people, fewer transformational strategies and innovative business models, and further wealth flowing to sophisticated investors at the expense of ordinary investors and everyone else.

Toward a Company-Centered Model

A better model, we submit, would have at its core the health of the enterprise rather than near-term returns to its shareholders. Such a model would start by recognizing that corporations are independent entities endowed by law with the potential for indefinite life. With the right leadership, they can be managed to serve markets and society over long periods of time. Agency theory largely ignores these distinctive and socially valuable features of the corporation, and the associated challenges of managing for the long term, on the grounds that corporations are "legal fictions." In their seminal 1976 article, Jensen and Meckling warn against "falling into the trap" of asking what a company's objective should be or whether the company has a social responsibility. Such questions, they argue, mistakenly imply that a corporation is an "individual" rather than merely a convenient legal construct. In a similar vein, Friedman asserts that it cannot have responsibilities because it is an "artificial person."

In fact, of course, corporations *are* legal constructs, but that in no way makes them artificial. They are economic and social organisms whose creation is authorized by governments to accomplish objectives that cannot be achieved by more limited organizational forms such as partnerships and proprietorships. Their nearly 400-year history of development speaks to the important role they play in society. Originally a corporation's objectives were set in its charter – build and operate a canal, for example – but eventually the form became generic so that corporations could be used to accomplish a wide variety of objectives chosen by their management and governing bodies. As their scale and scope grew, so did their power. The choices made by corporate decision makers today can transform societies and touch the lives of millions, if not billions, of people across the globe.

The model we envision would acknowledge the realities of managing these organizations over time and would be responsive to the needs of all shareholders – not just those who are most vocal at a given moment. Here we offer eight propositions that together provide a radically different and, we believe, more realistic foundation for corporate governance and shareholder engagement.

1. Corporations are complex organizations whose effective functioning depends on talented leaders and managers.

The success of a leader has more to do with intrinsic motivation, skills, capabilities, and character than with whether his or her pay is tied to shareholder returns. If leaders are poorly equipped for the job, giving them more "skin in the game" will not improve the situation and may even make it worse. (Part of the problem with equity-based pay is that it conflates executive skill and luck.) The challenges of corporate leadership – crafting strategy, building a strong organization, developing and motivating talented executives, and allocating resources among the corporation's various businesses for present and future returns – are significant. In focusing on incentives as the key to ensuring effective leadership, agency theory diminishes these challenges and the importance of developing individuals who can meet them.

2. Corporations can prosper over the long term only if they're able to learn, adapt, and regularly transform themselves.

In some industries today, companies may need reinvention every five years to keep up with changes in markets, competition, or technology. Changes of this sort, already difficult, are made more so by the idea that management is about assigning individuals fixed decision rights, giving them clear goals, offering them incentives to achieve those goals, and then paying them (or not) depending on whether the goals are met. This approach presupposes a degree of predictability, hierarchy, and task independence that is rare in today's organizations. Most tasks involve cooperation across organizational lines, making it difficult to establish clear links between individual contributions and specific outcomes.

3. Corporations perform many functions in society.

One of them is providing investment opportunities and generating wealth, but corporations also produce goods and services, provide employment, develop technologies, pay taxes, and make other contributions to the communities in which they operate. Singling out any one of these as "the purpose of the corporation" may say more about the commentator than about the corporation. Agency economists, it seems, gravitate toward maximizing shareholder wealth as the central purpose. Marketers tend to favor serving customers. Engineers lean toward innovation and excellence in product performance. From a societal perspective, the most important feature of the corporation may be that it performs all these functions simultaneously over time. As a historical matter, the original purpose of the corporation – reflected in debates about limited liability and general incorporation statutes – was to facilitate economic growth by enabling projects that required large-scale, long-term investment.

4. Corporations have differing objectives and differing strategies for achieving them.

The purpose of the (generic) corporation from a societal perspective is not the same as the purpose of a (particular) corporation as seen by its founders, managers, or governing authorities. Just as the purposes and strategies of individual companies vary widely, so must their performance measures. Moreover, companies' strategies are almost always in transition as markets change. An overemphasis on TSR for assessing and comparing corporate performance can distort the allocation of resources and undermine a company's ability to deliver on its chosen strategy.

5. Corporations must create value for multiple constituencies.

In a free-market system, companies succeed only if customers want their products, employees want to work for them, suppliers want them as partners, shareholders want to buy their stock, and communities want their presence. Figuring out how to maintain these relationships and deciding when trade-offs are necessary among the interests of these various groups are central challenges of corporate leadership. Agency theory's implied decision rule – that managers should always maximize value for shareholders – oversimplifies this challenge and leads eventually to systematic underinvestment in other important relationships.

6. Corporations must have ethical standards to guide interactions with all their constituencies, including shareholders and society at large.

Adherence to these standards, which go beyond forbearance from fraud and collusion, is essential for earning the trust companies need to function effectively over time. Agency theory's ambivalence regarding corporate ethics can set companies up for destructive and even criminal behavior – which generates a need for the costly regulations that agency theory proponents are quick to decry.

7. Corporations are embedded in a political and socio-economic system whose health is vital to their sustainability.

Elsewhere we have written about the damaging and often self-destructive consequences of companies' indifference to negative externalities produced by their activities. We have also found that societal and systemwide problems can be a source of both risk and opportunity for companies. Consider Ecomagination, the business GE built around environmental challenges, or China Mobile's rural communications strategy, which helped narrow the digital divide between China's urban and rural populations and fueled the company's growth for nearly half a decade. Agency theory's insistence that corporations (because they are legal fictions) cannot have social responsibilities and that societal problems are beyond the purview of business (and should be left to governments) results in a narrowness of vision that prevents corporate leaders from seeing, let alone acting on, many risks and opportunities.

8. The interests of the corporation are distinct from the interests of any particular shareholder or constituency group.

As early as 1610, the directors of the Dutch East India Company recognized that shareholders with a ten-year time horizon would be unenthusiastic about the company's investing resources in longer-term projects that were likely to pay off only in the second of two ten-year periods allowed by the original charter. The solution, suggested one official, was to focus not on the initial ten-year investors but on the strategic goals of the enterprise, which in this case meant investing in those longer-term projects to maintain the company's position in Asia. The notion that all shareholders have the same interests and that those interests are the same as the corporation's masks such fundamental differences. It also provides intellectual cover for powerful shareholders who seek to divert the corporation to their own purposes while claiming to act on behalf of all shareholders.

These propositions underscore the need for an approach to governance that takes the corporation seriously as an institution in society and centers on the sustained performance of the enterprise. They also point to a stronger role for boards and a system of accountability for boards and executives that includes but is broader than accountability to shareholders.

In the model implied by these propositions, boards and business leaders would take a fundamentally different approach to such basic tasks as strategy development, resource allocation, performance evaluation, and shareholder engagement. For instance, managers would be expected to take a longer view in formulating strategy and allocating resources.

The new model has yet to be fully developed, but its conceptual foundations can be outlined. As shown in Table 5.1, the company-centered model we envision tracks basic corporate law in holding that a corporation is an independent entity, that management's authority comes from the corporation's governing body and ultimately from the law, and that managers are fiduciaries (rather than agents) and are thus obliged to act in the best interests of the corporation and its shareholders (which is not the same as carrying out the wishes of even a majority of shareholders). This model recognizes the diversity of shareholders' goals and the varied roles played by corporations in society. We believe that it aligns better than the agency-based model does with the realities of managing a corporation for success over time and is thus more consistent with corporations' original purpose and unique potential as vehicles for projects involving large-scale, long-term investment.

The practical implications of company-centered governance are far-reaching. In boardrooms adopting this approach, we would expect to see some or all of these features:

- greater likelihood of a staggered board to facilitate continuity and the transfer of institutional knowledge;
- more board-level attention to succession planning and leadership development;
- more board time devoted to strategies for the company's continuing growth and renewal;
- closer links between executive compensation and achieving the company's strategic goals;
- more attention to risk analysis and political and environmental uncertainty;
- a strategic (rather than narrowly financial) approach to resource allocation;
- a stronger focus on investments in new capabilities and innovation;
- more conservative use of leverage as a cushion against market volatility;

Table 5.1 Contrasting approaches to corporate governance

Theory	Shareholder-centered *Agency theory*	Company-centered theory *Entity theory*
Conception of the corporation	Legal fiction; nexus of contracts; pool of capital	Legal entity; social and economic organism; purposeful organization
Origins of the corporation	Private agreement among property owners to pool and increase capital	Created by lawmakers to encourage investment in long-term, large-scale projects needed by society
Functions of the corporation	Maximize wealth for shareholders	Provide goods and services; provide employment; create opportunities for investment; drive innovation
Purpose of specific corporations	Maximize shareholder value	Business purpose set by the particular company's board
Responsibilities to society	None (fictional entities can't have responsibilities)	Fulfill business purpose and act as a good corporate citizen
Ethical standards	Unclear: whatever shareholders want, or obey law and avoid fraud or collusion	Obey law and follow generally accepted ethical standards
Shareholders	Principals/owners of the corporation with authority over its business	Owners of shares; suppliers of capital with defined rights and responsibilities
Nature of shareholders	Undifferentiated, self-interested wealth maximizers	Diverse, with differing objectives, incentives, time horizons, and preferences
Role of directors	Shareholders' agents, delegates, or representatives	Fiduciaries for the corporation and its shareholders
Role of management	Shareholders' agents	Leaders of the organization; fiduciaries for the corporation and its shareholders
Management's objective	Maximize returns to shareholders	Sustain performance of the enterprise
Management's time frame	Present/near term (theory assumes the current share price captures all available knowledge about the company's future)	Established by the board; potentially indefinite, requiring attention to near, medium, and long term
Management performance metrics	Single: returns to shareholders	Multiple: returns to shareholders; company value; achievement of strategic goals; quality of goods and services; employee well-being
Strength	Simple structure permits clear economic argument	Consistent with law, history, and the realities facing managers
Weakness	Principles do not accord with law or good management; shareholders have power without accountability	Principles describe complex relationships and responsibilities; success is difficult to assess

- concern with corporate citizenship and ethical issues that goes beyond legal compliance.

A company-centered model of governance would not relieve corporations of the need to provide a return over time that reflected the cost of capital. But they would be open to a wider range of strategic positions and time horizons and would more easily attract investors who shared their goals. Speculators will always seek to exploit changes in share price – but it's not inevitable that they will color all corporate governance. It's just that agency theory, in combination with other doctrines of modern economics, has erased the distinctions among investors and converted all of us into speculators.

If our model were accepted, speculators would have less opportunity to profit by transforming long-term players into sources of higher earnings and share prices in the short term. The legitimizing argument for attacks by unaccountable parties with opaque holdings would lose its force. We can even imagine a new breed of investors and asset managers who would focus explicitly on long-term investing. They might develop new valuation models that take a broader view of companies' prospects or make a specialty of valuing the hard-to-value innovations and intangibles – and also the costly externalities – that are often ignored in today's models. They might want to hold shares in companies that promise a solid and continuing return and that behave as decent corporate citizens. Proxy advisors might emerge to serve such investors. . . .

Conclusion

The time has come to challenge the agency-based model of corporate governance. Its mantra of maximizing shareholder value is distracting companies and their leaders from the innovation, strategic renewal, and investment in the future that require their attention. History has shown that with enlightened management and sensible regulation, companies can play a useful role in helping society adapt to constant change. But that can happen only if directors and managers have sufficient discretion to take a longer, broader view of the company and its business. As long as they face the prospect of a surprise attack by unaccountable "owners," today's business leaders have little choice but to focus on the here and now.

Managing for Stakeholders

R. EDWARD FREEMAN

Introduction

The purpose of this essay is to outline an emerging view of business that we shall call "managing for stakeholders."[1] This view has emerged over the past 30 years from a group of scholars in a diverse set of disciplines, from finance to philosophy.[2] The basic idea is that businesses, and the executives who manage them, actually do and should create value for customers, suppliers, employees, communities, and financiers (or shareholders). And, that we need to pay careful attention to how these relationships are managed and how value gets created for these stakeholders. We contrast this idea with the dominant model of business activity, namely, that businesses are to be managed solely for the benefit of shareholders. Any other benefits (or harms) that are created are incidental.[3]

Simple ideas create complex questions, and we proceed as follows. In the next section we examine why the dominant story or model of business that is deeply embedded in our culture is no longer workable. It is resistant to change, not consistent with the law, and for the most part, simply ignores matters of ethics. Each of these flaws is fatal in the business world of the twenty-first century.

We then proceed to define the basic ideas of "managing for stakeholders" and why it solves some of the problems of the dominant model. In particular we pay attention to how using "stakeholder" as a basic unit of analysis makes it more difficult to ignore matters of ethics. We argue that the primary responsibility of the executive is to create as much value for stakeholders as possible, and that no stakeholder interest is viable in isolation of the other stakeholders. We sketch three primary arguments from ethical theory for adopting "managing for stakeholders." We conclude by outlining a fourth "pragmatist argument" that suggests we see managing for stakeholders as a new narrative about business that lets us improve the way we currently create value for each other. Capitalism is on this view a system of social cooperation and collaboration, rather than primarily a system of competition.

The Dominant Story: Managerial Capitalism with Shareholders at the Center

The modern business corporation has emerged during the twentieth century as one of the most important innovations in human history. Yet the changes that we are now experiencing call for its reinvention. Before we suggest what this revision, "managing for stakeholders" or "stakeholder capitalism" is, first we need to understand how the dominant story came to be told.

Somewhere in the past, organizations were quite simple and "doing business" consisted of buying raw materials from suppliers, converting it to products, and selling it to customers. For the most part owner-entrepreneurs founded such simple businesses and worked at the business along with members of their families. The development of new production processes, such as the assembly line, meant that jobs could be specialized and more work could be accomplished.

From Edward, R. Freedman, "Managing for Stakeholders," *Academy of Management Perspectives* (August, 2006). Reprinted by permission of the author.

New technologies and sources of power became readily available. These and other social and political forces combined to require larger amounts of capital, well beyond the scope of most individual owner-manager-employees. Additionally, "workers" or non-family members began to dominate the firm and were the rule rather than the exception.

Ownership of the business became more dispersed as capital was raised from banks, stockholders, and other institutions. Indeed, the management of the firm became separated from the ownership of the firm. And, in order to be successful, the top managers of the business had to simultaneously satisfy the owners, the employees and their unions, suppliers, and customers. This system of organization of businesses along the lines set forth here was known as managerial capitalism or laissez-faire capitalism, or more recently, shareholder capitalism.[4]

As businesses grew, managers developed a means of control via the divisionalized firm. Led by Alfred Sloan at General Motors, the divisionalized firm with a central headquarters staff was widely adapted.[5] The dominant model for managerial authority was the military and civil service bureaucracy. By creating rational structures and processes, the orderly progress of business growth could be well managed.

Thus, managerialism, hierarchy, stability, and predictability all evolved together, in the United States and Europe, to form the most powerful economic system in the history of humanity. The rise of bureaucracy and managerialism was so strong that the economist Joseph Schumpeter predicted that it would wipe out the creative force of capitalism, stifling innovation in its drive for predictability and stability.

During the last 50 years this "Managerial Model" has put "shareholders" at the center of the firm as the most important group for managers to worry about. This mindset has dealt with the increasing complexity of the business world by focusing more intensely on "shareholders" and "creating value for shareholders." It has become common wisdom to "increase shareholder value," and many companies have instituted complex incentive compensation plans aimed at aligning the interests of executives with the interests of shareholders. These incentive plans are often tied to the price of a company's stock, which is affected by many factors not the least of which is the expectations of Wall Street analysts about earnings per share each quarter. Meeting Wall Street targets and forming a stable and predictable base of quarter over quarter increases in earnings per share has become the standard for measuring company performance. Indeed, all of the recent scandals at Enron, WorldCom, Tyco, and others are in part due to executives trying to increase shareholder value, sometimes in opposition to accounting rules and

law. Unfortunately, the world has changed so that the stability and predictability required by the shareholder approach can no longer be assured.

The Dominant Model Is Resistant to Change

The Managerial View of business with shareholders at the center is inherently resistant to change. It puts shareholders' interests over and above the interests of customers, suppliers, employees, and others, as if these interests must conflict with each other. It understands a business as an essentially hierarchical organization fastened together with authority to act in the shareholders' interests. Executives often speak in the language of hierarchy as "working for shareholders," "shareholders are the boss," and "you have to do what the shareholders want." On this interpretation, change should occur only when the shareholders are unhappy, and as long as executives can produce a series of incrementally better financial results there is no problem. According to this view the only change that counts is change oriented toward shareholder value. If customers are unhappy, if accounting rules have been compromised, if product quality is bad, if environmental disaster looms, even if competitive forces threaten, the only interesting questions are whether and how these forces for change affect shareholder value, measured by the price of the stock every day. Unfortunately in today's world there is just too much uncertainty and complexity to rely on such a single criterion. Business in the twenty-first century is global and multifaceted, and shareholder value may not capture that dynamism. Or, if it does, as the theory suggests it must eventually, it will be too late for executives to do anything about it. The dominant story may work for how things turn out in the long run on Wall Street, but managers have to act with an eye to Main Street as well, to anticipate change to try and take advantage of the dynamism of business.[6]

The Dominant Model Is Not Consistent with the Law

In actual fact the clarity of putting shareholders' interests first, above that of customers, suppliers, employees, and communities, flies in the face of the reality of the law. The law has evolved to put constraints on the kinds of trade-offs that can be made. In fact the law of corporations gives a less clear answer to the question of in whose interest and for whose benefit the corporation should be governed. The law has evolved over the years to give *de facto* standing to the claims of groups other than stockholders. It has, in effect, required that the claims of customers, suppliers, local communities, and employees be taken into consideration.

For instance, the doctrine of "privity of contract," as articulated in *Winterbottom v. Wright* in 1842, has been eroded by recent developments in product liability law. *Greenman v. Yuba Power* gives the manufacturer strict liability for damage caused by its products, even though the seller has exercised all possible care in the preparation and sale of the product and the consumer has not bought the product from nor entered into any contractual arrangement with the manufacturer. *Caveat emptor* has been replaced, in large part, with *caveat venditor*. The Consumer Product Safety Commission has the power to enact product recalls, essentially leading to an increase in the number of voluntary product recalls by companies seeking to mitigate legal damage awards. Some industries are required to provide information to customers about a product's ingredients, whether or not the customers want and are willing to pay for this information. Thus, companies must take the interests of customers into account, by law.

A similar story can be told about the evolution of the law forcing management to take the interests of employees into account. The National Labor Relations Act gave employees the right to unionize and to bargain in good faith. It set up the National Labor Relations Board to enforce these rights with management. The Equal Pay Act of 1963 and Title VII of the Civil Rights Act of 1964 constrain management from discrimination in hiring practices; these have been followed with the Age Discrimination in Employment Act of 1967, and recent extensions affecting people with disabilities. The emergence of a body of administrative case law arising from labor–management disputes and the historic settling of discrimination claims with large employers have caused the emergence of a body of management practice that is consistent with the legal guarantee of the rights of employees.

The law has also evolved to try and protect the interests of local communities. The Clean Water Act of 1977 and the Clean Air Act of 1990, and various amendments to these classic pieces of legislation, have constrained management from "spoiling the commons." In a historic case, *Marsh v. Alabama*, the Supreme Court ruled that a company-owned town was subject to the provisions of the US Constitution, thereby guaranteeing the rights of local citizens and negating the "property rights" of the firm. Current issues center around protecting local businesses, forcing companies to pay the healthcare costs of their employees, increases in minimum wages, environmental standards, and the effects of business development on the lives of local community members. These issues fill the local political landscapes, and executives and their companies must take account of them.

Some may argue that the constraints of the law, at least in the United States, have become increasingly irrelevant in a world where business is global in nature. However, globalization simply makes this argument stronger. The laws that are relevant to business have evolved differently around the world, but they have evolved nonetheless to take into account the interests of groups other than just shareholders. Each state in India has a different set of regulations that affect how a company can do business. In China the law has evolved to give business some property rights but it is far from exclusive. And, in most of the European Union, laws around "civil society" and the role of "employees" are much more complex than even US law.

"Laissez-faire capitalism" is simply a myth. The idea that business is about "maximizing value for stockholders regardless of the consequences to others" is one that has outlived its usefulness. The dominant model simply does not describe how business operates. Another way to see this is that if executives always have to qualify "maximize shareholder value" with exceptions of law, or even good practice, then the dominant story isn't very useful anymore. There are just too many exceptions. The dominant story could be saved by arguing that it describes a normative view about how business should operate, despite how actual businesses have evolved.[7] So, we need to look more closely at some of the conceptual and normative problems that the dominant model raises.

The Dominant Model Is Not Consistent with Basic Ethics

Previously we have argued that most theories of business rely on separating "business" decisions from "ethical" decisions.[8] This is seen most clearly in the popular joke about "business ethics as an oxymoron." More formally we might suggest that we define:

The Separation Fallacy

It is useful to believe that sentences like "x is a business decision" have no ethical content or any implicit ethical point of view. And, it is useful to believe that sentences like "x is an ethical decision, the best thing to do all things considered" have no content or implicit view about value creation and trade (business).

This fallacy underlies much of the dominant story about business, as well as in other areas in society. There are two implications of rejecting the Separation Fallacy. The first is that almost any business decision has some ethical content. To see that this is true one need only ask whether the following questions make sense for virtually any business decision:

The Open Question Argument

1. If this decision is made for whom is value created and destroyed?

2. Who is harmed and/or benefited by this decision?
3. Whose rights are enabled and whose values are realized by this decision (and whose are not)?
4. What kind of person will I (we) become if we make this decision?

Since these questions are always open for most business decisions, it is reasonable to give up the Separation Fallacy, which would have us believe that these questions aren't relevant for making business decisions, or that they could never be answered. We need a theory about business that builds in answers to the "Open Question Argument" above. One such answer would be "Only value to shareholders counts," but such an answer would have to be enmeshed in the language of ethics as well as business. Milton Friedman, unlike most of his expositors, may actually give such a morally rich answer. He claims that the responsibility of the executive is to make profits subject to law and ethical custom. Depending on how "law and ethical custom" is interpreted, the key difference with the stakeholder approach may well be that we disagree about how the world works. In order to create value we believe that it is better to focus on integrating business and ethics within a complex set of stakeholder relationships rather than treating ethics as a side constraint on making profits. In short we need a theory that has as its basis what we might call:

The Integration Thesis
Most business decisions, or sentences about business have some ethical content, or implicit ethical view. Most ethical decisions, or sentences about ethics have some business content or implicit view about business.[9]

One of the most pressing challenges facing business scholars is to tell compelling narratives that have the Integration Thesis at their heart. This is essentially the task that a group of scholars, "business ethicists" and "stakeholder theorists," have begun over the last 30 years. We need to go back to the very basics of ethics. Ethics is about the rules, principles, consequences, matters of character, etc., that we use to live together. These ideas give us a set of open questions that we are constantly searching for better ways to answer in reasonable complete ways.[10] One might define "ethics" as a conversation about how we can reason together and solve our differences, recognize where our interests are joined and need development, so that we can all flourish without resorting to coercion and violence. Some may disagree with such a definition, and we do not intend to privilege definitions, but such a pragmatist approach to ethics entails that we reason and talk together to try and create a better world for all of us.

If our critiques of the dominant model are correct then we need to start over by reconceptualizing the very language that we use to understand how business operates. We want to suggest that something like the following principle is implicit in most reasonably comprehensive views about ethics.

The Responsibility Principle[11]
Most people, most of the time, want to, actually do, and should accept responsibility for the effects of their actions on others.

Clearly the Responsibility Principle is incompatible with the Separation Fallacy. If business is separated from ethics, there is no question of moral responsibility for business decisions. More clearly still, without something like the Responsibility Principle it is difficult to see how ethics gets off the ground. "Responsibility" may well be a difficult and multifaceted idea. There are surely many different ways to understand it. But, if we are not willing to accept the responsibility for our own actions (as limited as that may be due to complicated issues of causality and the like), then ethics, understood as how we reason together so we can all flourish, is likely an exercise in bad faith.

If we want to give up the separation fallacy and adopt the integration thesis, if the open question argument makes sense, and if something like the responsibility thesis is necessary, then we need a new model for business. And, this new story must be able to explain how value creation at once deals with economics and ethics, and how it takes account of all of the effects of business action on others. Such a model exists, and has been developing over the last 30 years by management researchers and ethics scholars, and there are many businesses who have adopted this "stakeholder framework" for their businesses.

Managing for Stakeholders

The basic idea of "managing for stakeholders" is quite simple. Business can be understood as a set of relationships among groups which have a stake in the activities that make up the business. Business is about how customers, suppliers, employees, financiers (stockholders, bondholders, banks, etc.), communities, and managers interact and create value. To understand a business is to know how these relationships work. And, the executive's or entrepreneur's job is to manage and shape these relationships, hence the title, "managing for stakeholders."

Figure 5.2 depicts the idea of "managing for stakeholders" in a variation of the classic "wheel and spoke" diagram. However, it is important to note that the stakeholder idea is perfectly general. Corporations are not the center of the

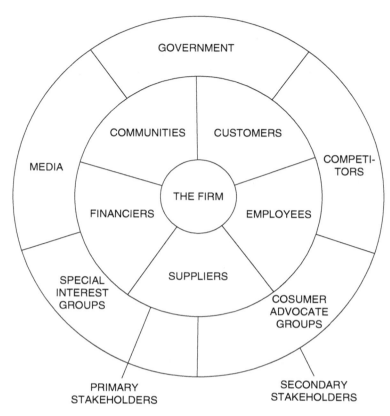

Figure 5.2 Managing for stakeholders
Source: Adapted from R. Edward Freeman, Jeffrey Harrison, and Andrew Wicks, *Managing for Stakeholders*
(New Haven, CT: Yale University Press, 2007).

universe, and there are many possible pictures. One might put customers in the center to signal that a company puts customers as the key priority. Another might put employees in the center and link them to customers and shareholders. We prefer the generic diagram because it suggests, pictorially, that "managing for stakeholders" is a theory about management and business; hence, managers and companies are in the center. But, there is no larger metaphysical claim here.

Stakeholders and Stakes

Owners or financiers (a better term) clearly have a financial stake in the business in the form of stocks, bonds, and so on, and they expect some kind of financial return from them. Of course, the stakes of financiers will differ by type of owner, preferences for money, moral preferences, and so on, as well as by type of firm. The shareholders of Google may well want returns as well as be supportive of Google's articulated purpose of "Do No Evil." To the extent that it makes sense to talk about the financiers "owning the firm," they have a concomitant responsibility for the uses of their property.

Employees have their jobs and usually their livelihood at stake; they often have specialized skills for which there is usually

no perfectly elastic market. In return for their labor, they expect security, wages, benefits, and meaningful work. Often, employees are expected to participate in the decision-making of the organization, and if the employees are management or senior executives, we see them as shouldering a great deal of responsibility for the conduct of the organization as a whole. And, employees are sometimes financiers as well, since many companies have stock ownership plans, and loyal employees who believe in the future of their companies often voluntarily invest. One way to think about the employee relationship is in terms of contracts.

Customers and suppliers exchange resources for the products and services of the firm and in return receive the benefits of the products and services. As with financiers and employees, the customer and supplier relationships are enmeshed in ethics. Companies make promises to customers via their advertising, and when products or services don't deliver on these promises, then management has a responsibility to rectify the situation. It is also important to have suppliers who are committed to making a company better. If suppliers find a better, faster, and cheaper way of making critical parts or services, then both supplier and company can win. Of course, some suppliers simply compete on price, but even so, there is a moral element of fairness and transparency to the supplier relationship.

Finally, the local community grants the firm the right to build facilities, and in turn, it benefits from the tax base and economic and social contributions of the firm. Companies have a real impact on communities, and being located in a welcoming community helps a company create value for its other stakeholders. In return for the provision of local services, companies are expected to be good citizens, as is any individual person. It should not expose the community to unreasonable hazards in the form of pollution, toxic waste, etc. It should keep whatever commitments it makes to the community, and operate in a transparent manner as far as possible. Of course, companies don't have perfect knowledge, but when management discovers some danger or runs afoul of new competition, it is expected to inform and work with local communities to mitigate any negative effects, as far as possible.

While any business must consist of financiers, customers, suppliers, employees, and communities, it is possible to think about other stakeholders as well. We can define "stakeholder" in a number of ways. First of all, we could define the term fairly narrowly to capture the idea that any business, large or small, is about creating value for "those groups without whose support, the business would cease to be viable." The inner circle of Figure 5.2 depicts this view. Almost every business is concerned at some level with relationships among financiers, customers, suppliers, employees, and communities. We might call these groups "primary" or "definitional." However, it should be noted that as a business starts up, sometimes one particular stakeholder is more important than another. In a new business start-up, sometimes there are no suppliers, and paying lots of attention to one or two key customers, as well as to the venture capitalist (financier), is the right approach.

There is also a somewhat broader definition that captures the idea that if a group or individual can affect a business, then the executives must take that group into consideration in thinking about how to create value. Or, a stakeholder is any group or individual that can affect or be affected by the realization of an organization's purpose. At a minimum some groups affect primary stakeholders and we might see these as stakeholders in the outer ring of Figure 5.2 and call them "secondary" or "instrumental."

There are other definitions that have emerged during the last 30 years, some based on risks and rewards, some based on mutuality of interests. And, the debate over finding the one "true definition" of "stakeholder" is not likely to end. We prefer a more pragmatic approach of being clear of the purpose of using any of the proposed definitions. Business is a fascinating field of study. There are very few principles and definitions that apply to all businesses all over the world. Furthermore, there are many different ways to run a successful business, or if you like, many different flavors of "managing for stakeholders." We see limited usefulness in trying to define one model of business, either based on the shareholder or stakeholder view, that works for all businesses everywhere. We see much value to be gained in examining how the stakes work in the value creation process, and the role of the executive.

The Responsibility of the Executive in Managing for Stakeholders

Executives play a special role in the activity of the business enterprise. On the one hand, they have a stake like every other employee in terms of an actual or implied employment contract. And, that stake is linked to the stakes of financiers, customers, suppliers, communities, and other employees. In addition, executives are expected to look after the health of the overall enterprise, to keep the varied stakes moving in roughly the same direction, and to keep them in balance.[12]

No stakeholder stands alone in the process of value creation. The stakes of each stakeholder group are multifaceted, and inherently connected to each other. How could a bondholder recognize any returns without management's paying attention to the stakes of customers or employees? How could customers get the products and services they need without employees and suppliers? How could employees have a decent place to live without communities? Many thinkers see the dominant problem of "managing for stakeholders" as how to solve the priority problem, or "which stakeholders are more important," or "how do we make trade-offs among stakeholders." We see this as a secondary issue.

First and foremost, we need to see stakeholder interests as joint, as inherently tied together. Seeing stakeholder interests as "joint" rather than "opposed" is difficult. It is not always easy to find a way to accommodate all stakeholder interests. It is easier to trade off one versus another. Why not delay spending on new products for customers in order to keep earnings a bit higher? Why not cut employee medical benefits in order to invest in a new inventory control system?

Managing for stakeholders suggests that executives try to reframe the questions. How can we invest in new products and create higher earnings? How can we be sure our employees are healthy and happy and are able to work creatively so that we can capture the benefits of new information technology such as inventory control systems? In a recent book reflecting on his experience as CEO of Medtronic, Bill

George summarized the managing for stakeholders mindset:[13]

> Serving all your stakeholders is the best way to produce long term results and create a growing, prosperous company . . . Let me be very clear about this: there is no conflict between serving all your stakeholders and providing excellent returns for shareholders. In the long term it is impossible to have one without the other. However, serving all these stakeholder groups requires discipline, vision, and committed leadership.

The primary responsibility of the executive is to create as much value as possible for stakeholders.[14] Where stakeholder interests conflict, the executive must find a way to rethink the problems so that these interests can go together, so that even more value can be created for each. If trade-offs have to be made, as often happens in the real world, then the executive must figure out how to make the trade-offs, and immediately begin improving the trade-offs for all sides. *Managing for stakeholders is about creating as much value as possible for stakeholders, without resorting to trade-offs.*

We believe that this task is more easily accomplished when a business has a sense of purpose. Furthermore, there are few limits on the kinds of purpose that can drive a business. Walmart may stand for "everyday low price." Merck can stand for "alleviating human suffering." The point is that if an entrepreneur or an executive can find a purpose that speaks to the hearts and minds of key stakeholders, it is more likely that there will be sustained success.

Purpose is complex and inspirational. The Grameen Bank wants to eliminate poverty. Fannie Mae wants to make housing affordable to every income level in society. Tastings (a local restaurant) wants to bring the taste of really good food and wine to lots of people in the community. And, all of these organizations have to generate profits, or else they cannot pursue their purposes. Capitalism works because we can pursue our purpose with others. When we coalesce around a big idea, or a joint purpose evolves from our day-to-day activities with each other, then great things can happen.

To create value for stakeholders, executives must understand that business is fully situated in the realm of humanity. Businesses are human institutions populated by real live complex human beings. Stakeholders have names and faces and children. They are not mere placeholders for social roles. As such, matters of ethics are routine when one takes a managing for stakeholders approach. Of course this should go without saying, but a part of the dominant story about business is that business people are only in it for their own narrowly defined self-interest. One main assumption of the managerial view with shareholders at the center is that shareholders only care about returns, and therefore their agents, managers, should only care about returns. However, this does not fit either our experiences or our aspirations. In the words of one CEO, "The only assets I manage go up and down the elevators every day."

Most human beings are complicated. Most of us do what we do because we are self-interested and interested in others. Business works in part because of our urge to create things with others and for others. Working on a team, or creating a new product or delivery mechanism that makes customer's lives better or happier or more pleasurable, all can be contributing factors to why we go to work each day. And, this is not to deny the economic incentive of getting a paycheck. The assumption of narrow self-interest is extremely limiting, and can be self-reinforcing – people can begin to act in a narrow self-interested way if they believe that is what is expected of them, as some of the scandals such as Enron have shown. We need to be open to a more complex psychology – one any parent finds familiar as they have shepherded the growth and development of their children.

Some Arguments for Managing for Stakeholders

Once you say stakeholders are persons then the ideas of ethics are automatically applicable. However you interpret the idea of "stakeholders," you must pay attention to the effects of your actions on others. And, something like the Responsibility Principle suggests that this is a cornerstone of any adequate ethical theory. There are at least three main arguments for adopting a managing for stakeholders approach. Philosophers will see these as connected to the three main approaches to ethical theory that have developed historically. We shall briefly set forth sketches of these arguments, and then suggest that there is a more powerful fourth argument.[15]

The Argument from Consequences

A number of theorists have argued that the main reason that the dominant model of managing for shareholders is a good idea is that it leads to the best consequences for all. Typically these arguments invoke Adam Smith's idea of the invisible hand, whereby each business actor pursues her own self-interest and the greatest good of all actually emerges. The problem with this argument is that we now know with modern general equilibrium economics that the argument only works under very specialized conditions that seldom describe the real world. And further, we know that if the economic conditions get very close to those needed to produce the greatest good, there is no guarantee that the greatest good will actually result.

Managing for stakeholders may actually produce better consequences for all stakeholders because it recognizes that stakeholder interests are joint. If one stakeholder pursues its interests at the expense of all the others, then the others will either withdraw their support, or look to create another network of stakeholder value creation. This is not to say that there are not times when one stakeholder will benefit at the expense of others, but if this happens continuously over time, then in a relatively free society, stakeholders will either (1) exit to form a new stakeholder network that satisfies their needs; (2) use the political process to constrain the offending stakeholder; or (3) invent some other form of activity to satisfy their particular needs.[16]

Alternatively, if we think about stakeholders engaged in a series of bargains among themselves, then we would expect that as individual stakeholders recognized their joint interests, and made good decisions based on these interests, better consequences would result than if they each narrowly pursued their individual self-interests.[17]

Now it may be objected that such an approach ignores "social consequences" or "consequences to society" and, hence, that we need a concept of "corporate social responsibility" to mitigate these effects. This objection is a vestigial limb of the dominant model. Since the only effects, on that view, were economic effects, then we need to think about "social consequences" or "corporate social responsibility." However, if stakeholder relationships are understood to be fully embedded in morality, then there is no need for an idea like corporate social responsibility. We can replace it with "corporate stakeholder responsibility," which is a dominant feature of managing for stakeholders.

The Argument from Rights

The dominant story gives property rights in the corporation exclusively to shareholders, and the natural question arises about the rights of other stakeholders who are affected. One way to understand managing for stakeholders is that it takes this question of rights seriously. If you believe that rights make sense, and further that if one person has a right to X then all persons have a right to X, it is just much easier to think about these issues using a stakeholder approach. For instance, while shareholders may well have property rights, these rights are not absolute, and should not be seen as such. Shareholders may not use their property to abridge the rights of others. For instance, shareholders and their agents, managers, may not use corporate property to violate the right to life of others. One way to understand managing for stakeholders is that it assumes that stakeholders have some rights. Now, it is notoriously difficult to parse the idea

of "rights." But, if executives take managing for stakeholders seriously, they will automatically think about what is owed to customers, suppliers, employees, financiers, and communities, in virtue of their stake, and in virtue of their basic humanity.

The Argument from Character

One of the strongest arguments for managing for stakeholders is that it asks executives and entrepreneurs to consider the question of what kind of company they want to create and build. The answer to this question will be in large part an issue of character. Aspiration matters. The business virtues of efficiency, fairness, respect, integrity, keeping commitments, and others are all critical in being successful at creating value for stakeholders. These virtues are simply absent when we think only about the dominant model and its sole reliance on a narrow economic logic.

If we frame the central question of management as "how do we create value for shareholders," then the only virtue that emerges is one of loyalty to the interests of shareholders. However if we frame the central question more broadly as "how do we create and sustain the creation of value for stakeholders" or "how do we get stakeholder interests all going in the same direction," then it is easy to see how many of the other virtues are relevant. Taking a stakeholder approach helps people decide how companies can contribute to their well-being and the kinds of lives they want to lead. By making ethics explicit and building it into the basic way we think about business, we avoid a situation of bad faith and self-deception.

The Pragmatist's Argument

The previous three arguments point out important reasons for adopting a new story about business. Pragmatists want to know how we can live better, how we can create both ourselves and our communities in ways where values such as freedom and solidarity are present in our everyday lives to the maximal extent. While it is sometimes useful to think about consequences, rights, and character in isolation, in reality our lives are richer if we can have a conversation about how to live together better. There is a long tradition of pragmatist ethics dating to philosophers such as William James and John Dewey. More recently philosopher Richard Rorty has expressed the pragmatist ideal:[18]

> pragmatists ... hope instead that human beings will come to enjoy more money, more free time, and greater social equality, and also that they will develop

more empathy, more ability to put themselves in the shoes of others. We hope that human beings will behave more decently toward one another as their standard of living improves.

By building into the very conceptual framework we use to think about business a concern with freedom, equality, consequences, decency, shared purpose, and paying attention to all of the effects of how we create value for each other, we can make business a human institution, and perhaps remake it in a way that sustains us.

For the pragmatist, business (and capitalism) has evolved as a social practice, an important one that we use to create value and trade with each other. On this view, first and foremost, business is about collaboration. Of course, in a free society, stakeholders are free to form competing networks. But the fuel for capitalism is our desire to create something of value, and to create it for ourselves and others. The spirit of capitalism is the spirit of individual achievement together with the spirit of accomplishing great tasks in collaboration with others. Managing for stakeholders makes this plain so that we can get about the business of creating better selves and better communities.[19]

Notes

1. It has been called a variety of things: "stakeholder management," "stakeholder capitalism," "a stakeholder theory of the modern corporation," and so on. Our reasons for choosing "managing for stakeholders" will become clearer as we proceed. Many others have worked on these ideas, and should not be held accountable for the rather idiosyncratic view outlined here.
2. For a stylized history of the idea, see R. Edward Freeman, "The Development of Stakeholder Theory: An Idiosyncratic Approach," in *Great Minds in Management*, ed. K. Smith and M. Hitt (Oxford University Press, 2005).
3. One doesn't manage "for" these benefits (and harms).
4. The difference between managerial and shareholder capitalism is large. However, the existence of agency theory lets us treat the two identically for our purposes here. Both agree on the view that the modern firm is characterized by the separation of decision-making and residual risk-bearing. The resulting agency problem is the subject of a vast literature.
5. Alfred Chandler's brilliant book *Strategy and Structure* (Boston, MA: MIT Press, 1970) chronicles the rise of the divisionalized corporation. For a not-so-flattering account of General Motors during the same time period, see Peter Drucker's classic work *The Concept of the Corporation* (New York: Transaction Publishers, reprint ed., 1993).
6. Executives can take little comfort in the nostrum that in the long run things work out and the most efficient companies survive. Some market theorists suggest that finance theory acts like "universal acid" cutting through every possible management decision, whether or not actual managers are aware of it. Perhaps the real difference between the dominant model and the "managing for stakeholders" model proposed here is that they are simply "about" different things. The dominant model is about the strict and narrow economic logic of markets, and the "managing for stakeholders" model is about how human beings create value for each other.
7. Often the flavor of the response of finance theorists sounds like this. The world would be better off if, despite all of the imperfections, executives tried to maximize shareholder value. It is difficult to see how any rational being could accept such a view in the face of the recent scandals, where it could be argued that the worst offenders were the most ideologically pure, and the result was the actual destruction of shareholder value (see *Breaking the Short Term Cycle* (Charlottesville, VA: Business Roundtable Institute for Corporate Ethics/CFA Center for Financial Market Integrity, 2006)). Perhaps we have a version of Aristotle's idea that happiness is not a result of trying to be happy, or Mill's idea that it does not maximize utility to try and maximize utility. Collins and Porras have suggested that even if executives want to maximize shareholder value, they should focus on purpose instead, that trying to maximize shareholder value does not lead to maximum value. See J. Collins and J. Porras, *Built to Last* (New York: HarperCollins, 2002).
8. See R. Edward Freeman, "The Politics of Stakeholder Theory: Some Future Directions," *Business Ethics Quarterly* 4 (1994): 409–22.
9. The second part of the integration thesis is left for another occasion. Philosophers who read this essay may note the radical departure from standard accounts of political philosophy. Suppose we began the inquiry into political philosophy with the question, How is value creation and trade sustainable over time? and suppose that the traditional beginning question, How is the state justified? was a subsidiary one. We might discover or create some very different answers from the standard accounts of most political theory. See R. Edward Freeman and Robert Phillips, "Stakeholder Theory: A Libertarian Defense," *Business Ethics Quarterly* 12, no. 3 (2002): 331–49.
10. Here we roughly follow the logic of John Rawls in *Political Liberalism* (New York: Columbia University Press, 1995).
11. There are many statements of this principle. Our argument is that whatever the particular conception of responsibility there is some underlying concept that is captured like our willingness or our need to justify our lives to others. Note the answer that the dominant view of business must give to questions about responsibility. "Executives are responsible only for the effects of their actions on shareholders, or only insofar as their actions create or destroy shareholder value."
12. In earlier versions of this essay in this volume we suggested that the notion of a fiduciary duty to stockholders be extended to "fiduciary duty to stakeholders." We believe that such

a move cannot be defended without doing damage to the notion of "fiduciary." The idea of having a special duty to either one or a few stakeholders is not helpful.

13. Bill George, *Authentic Leadership* (San Francisco, CA: Jossey-Bass, 2004), p. 104.

14. This is at least as clear as the directive given by the dominant model: create as much value as possible for shareholders.

15. Some philosophers have argued that the stakeholder approach is in need of a "normative justification." To the extent that this phrase has any meaning, we take it as a call to connect the logic of managing for stakeholders with more traditional ethical theory. As pragmatists we eschew the "descriptive vs. normative vs. instrumental" distinction that so many business thinkers (and stakeholder theorists) have adopted. Managing for stakeholders is inherently a narrative or story that is at once *descriptive* of how some businesses do act; *aspirational* and *normative* about how they could and should act; *instrumental* in terms of what means lead to what ends; and *managerial* in that it must be coherent on all of these dimensions and actually guide executive action.

16. See S. Venkataraman, "Stakeholder Value Equilibration and the Entrepreneurial Process," *Ethics and Entrepreneurship, The Ruffin Series* 3 (2002): 45–57; S. R. Velamuri, "Entrepreneurship, Altruism, and the Good Society," *Ethics and Entrepreneurship, The Ruffin Series* 3 (2002): 125–43; and T. Harting, S. Harmeling, and S. Venkataraman,

"Innovative Stakeholder Relations: When 'Ethics Pays' (and When It Doesn't)," *Business Ethics Quarterly* 16 (2006): 43–68.

17. Sometimes there are trade-offs and situations that economists would call "prisoner's dilemma" but these are not the paradigmatic cases, or if they are, we seem to solve them routinely, as Russell Hardin has suggested in *Morality within the Limits of Reason* (University of Chicago Press, 1998).

18. E. Mendieta (ed.), *Take Care of Freedom and Truth Will Take Care of Itself: Interviews with Richard Rorty* (Stanford University Press, 2006), p. 68.

19. The ideas in this article have had a long development time. The ideas here have been reworked from: R. Edward Freeman, *Strategic Management: A Stakeholder Approach* (Boston, MA: Pitman, 1984); R. Edward Freeman, "A Stakeholder Theory of the Modern Corporation," in T. Beauchamp and N. Bowie (eds.), *Ethical Theory and Business*, 7th ed. (Englewood Cliffs, NJ: Prentice Hall, 2005), also in earlier editions co-authored with William Evan; Andrew Wicks, R. Edward Freeman, Patricia Werhane, and Kirsten Martin, *Business Ethics: A Managerial Approach* (Englewood Cliffs, NJ: Prentice Hall, 2008); and R. Edward Freeman, Jeffrey Harrison, and Andrew Wicks, *Managing for Stakeholders* (New Haven, CT: Yale University Press, 2007). I am grateful to editors and co-authors for permission to rework these ideas here.

Putting a Stake in Stakeholder Theory

ERIC W. ORTS AND ALAN STRUDLER

Introduction

Stakeholder theory has become a vampire in the field of business ethics. It has begun to feed on any living body or idea that crosses its path. Expansive versions of stakeholder theory purport to provide a satisfactory conceptual approach for dealing with ethical problems that arise in business decision-making as well as an adequate practical guide for making these decisions. In this article, we contest this expansive view. We argue that stakeholder theory may be useful for some kinds of business decisions – especially in terms of purely strategic rather than moral thinking. We suggest also that stakeholder theory may provide useful recommendations for advances in academic theories of the firm. However, we maintain that the recent claims for stakeholder theory as providing a framework for business ethics are seriously overblown.[1]

Our objective in this article is to put a stake in stakeholder theory in the following two senses. First, we want to make

the case as strongly as possible that stakeholder theory is not a very good, reliable, or even cogent philosophical approach for dealing with many of the most difficult ethical problems in business. Given the vampiric expansion of stakeholder theory as a theory of business ethics, we aim to drive a stake into its heart: not to "kill" stakeholder theory, because we believe it to retain some useful (though limited) value, but to make it human again and to reduce its scope and ambition. We argue against the central philosophical position that presents stakeholder theory as an approach to business ethics. At most, we argue that stakeholder theory may prove useful in the identification of some relevant "interests" that may be a source of ethical claims to be considered in business decisions. However, even this "roadmap version" of stakeholder theory, we maintain, faces serious limitations with respect to both ethical scope and substance. For example, as we argued in a previous article, even roadmap versions of stakeholder theory fail to encompass at least two

From *Journal of Business Ethics* 88 (2009). Reprinted with permission.

important ethical issues relevant to business decisions: the imperative to follow the law and the imperative to take natural environmental harm seriously.[2] Stakeholder theory cannot adequately treat either of these topics because they do not reduce to a consultation of the interests of specific people who may be involved. The ethical framework and principles required to resolve these problems are much different than those that stakeholder theory can provide. In this article, we conclude that stakeholder theory as a recommended approach to deal with many of the real and everyday problems in business ethics is essentially empty of content and therefore inadequate. We suggest some alternative directions for ethical analysis that would prove more promising for some of the toughest ethical decisions in business today.[3]

We also intend to "put a stake in stakeholder theory" in a second sense. To argue that stakeholder theory is not a very useful approach to business ethics is not to deny its potential usefulness for other purposes. Stakeholder theory may remain helpful in two areas related to business: theories of the firm and strategic management. In these applications, however, any stakeholder theory requires a coherent definition of "stakeholders." Otherwise, the vagueness and overbreadth that we criticize as serious weaknesses of stakeholder theory in business ethics will also infect other potential applications.[4] As a theory of the firm or an approach to strategy, stakeholder theory may also have some ethical implications. However, the identification of ethical issues is not the equivalent to a robust ethical theory needed to address these issues.

The substantive weaknesses of stakeholder theory as applied to business ethics can be categorized as including the following problems: (1) identification and definition, (2) vagueness and overbreadth, and (3) balancing various interests and considerations in decision-making. We discuss each of these problems in turn. In the course of our analysis, we endeavor to show why stakeholder theory is not particularly useful for answering many questions of business ethics. Instead, we indicate how a properly defined and understood concept of "stakeholders" may prove helpful in terms of theories of the firm and business strategy, which may lead to posing some good and relevant ethical questions – but not answering them.

Identification and Definition: Who (or What) is a Stakeholder?

The problem of stakeholder identification has vexed stakeholder theory for decades. This problem is one primary reason to doubt the efficacy of versions of stakeholder theory in business ethics. If one cannot define the term "stakeholder," then any coherent theory collapses because of the evanescence of its central concept.

A multitude of different views of "stakeholders" advanced in the literature supports this criticism. . . . Previous literature surveys of stakeholder theories have perceived a sharp divide between what have been labeled the "narrow" and "broad" definitions of stakeholders.[5] We suggest that this divergence has occurred primarily because of two very different uses of the idea of "stakeholders." A narrow definition is consistent with an expanded theory of the firm. A broad definition recommends a potentially useful approach to business strategy. However, the two definitions of stakeholders conflict with respect to the purposes for which they are intended, and neither version is very helpful in terms of resolving everyday problems of business ethics.

The "narrow version" of stakeholders refers to theories of the firm: What groups of people are properly included within the boundaries of a business enterprise? The answer given by many economists and business theorists is that only the "owners" of the firm count.[6] Firms are managed by and on behalf of owners, and other so-called "stakeholder" groups such as creditors, suppliers, and employees who have direct contractual relationships contributing to the firm's operations are considered to be outside the scope of the firm. For business corporations, the residual owners are deemed to be the shareholders. Milton Friedman's famous argument in favor of a shareholder primacy model of the firm organized legally as a corporation enters into the discourse here. For Friedman, corporate firms should be managed for the sole objective of maximizing the economic wealth for shareholders.[7] Any other objectives – including pleas to expend the firm's assets for various motivations of "corporate responsibility" – lie outside the proper scope of the business enterprise.[8]

Narrow versions of stakeholder theory arose to contest this strict financial ownership theory of the firm. Debates then unfolded about which additional groups should be considered as "stakeholders." For example, good arguments can be advanced that employees and creditors should be included in a narrow theory of the firm. Both employees and creditors put economic resources at risk in the operations of a firm, including human as well as financial capital. Both therefore have a direct economic interest in the outcome of the firm's operations.[9]

Conceptual trouble arises, however, when the advocates of a broad version of corporate social responsibility begin to add other potentially deserving claimants into a stakeholder theory of the firm: such as the surrounding local community, the regional or national economy, global social problems, and various other groups of people who are either harmed or benefited by a firm's activities. A "stakeholder," according Freeman's influential version of this broad definition, is "any group or individual who can affect or is affected by the achievement of the organization's purpose."[10] This very expansive view – almost ecological in its scope (in the sense that "everything is connected to everything else" at some level) – provides no demarcations about who (or even what) may count as a stakeholder.

Most broad versions of stakeholder theory, we believe, are fundamentally different than narrow versions, because they were originally constructed with an entirely different objective in mind. Broad stakeholder theory is invoked for "strategic" purposes: an instrumental approach to management which presumes a basic definition of the firm.[11] "Stakeholders" in this broad sense are *outside* of the firm. This broad use of the term is therefore diametrically opposed to the narrow definitions of "stakeholders" that attempt to expand the group of relevant interests considered to be *inside* of the firm.[12]

The origins of broad versions of "stakeholders" confirm our view that a strategic purpose lies at the root of this approach. According to an early article by Freeman and Reed, the use of "stakeholder" as a term for business management first appeared in an internal memorandum at the Stanford Research Institute (SRI) in 1963. "Stakeholder analysis" was used also in the planning department of the defense contractor, Lockheed, around this time.[13] The initial definition and use of the term "stakeholder" in this strategic planning context is telling. A "stakeholder," according to an internal SRI memorandum, refers to "those groups without whose support the organization would cease to exist."[14] (Again, note that an underlying theory of the firm or organization is assumed. Stakeholder theory in this strategic sense may be used by governments, non-profit organizations, or other organizational entities – not just businesses.) Other early discussions of stakeholder theory followed this strategic focus. Beginning in 1977, for example, one of the research centers at the Wharton School convened a "stakeholder project" to develop theories that "enabled executives to formulate and implement corporate strategy in turbulent environments."[15]

From the standpoint of business ethics, one aspect of a strategic orientation toward the definition of relevant stakeholders is critical: *there is no required ethical content whatsoever!* Consider an example that may have been confronted by Lockheed. One prominent group that Lockheed depends upon is the federal government. Its lifeblood is government contracts for weapons and military technology. Strategic stakeholder theory would identify the government (and the various groups composing it) as an important

institution to influence. Identifying the government as important, however, does not provide any guidance about the *ethics* of how to interact with the government. There is nothing in a strategic version of stakeholder theory, for example, that would prevent deciding to pay bribes or lobby illegally to win contracts. Stakeholder analysis used strategically is, at least potentially, ethics free. One must look to other sources – including legal limitations as well as substantive political and ethical theories – to find the ethical constraints that Lockheed and other business firms should respect in their interactions with government and when pursuing profitable defense contracts.[16] Larger, more fundamental frameworks and principles than can be supplied by stakeholder theory are required to handle difficult problems of the proper role of business in the waging of war and the propagation of peace.[17]

The radical division between narrow and broad versions of stakeholder theory – and the quite different objectives of (1) expanding a theory of the firm and (2) constructing a framework for strategic management decision-making – suggests to us that the definition of "stakeholder" may prove to be much more trouble than it's worth for most (and perhaps all) business ethics applications.

Vagueness and Overbreadth: Good for Everyone and No One

Another way to construct our argument here is as follows. We reject stakeholder theory as an approach to business ethics on semantic grounds. For the sake of simplicity, we begin by focusing on the vagueness of the terms of stakeholder theory. We contend also that the semantic defects of stakeholder theory go beyond the vagueness of its terms.

Focus first on the vagueness of stakeholder theory. Once relevant "stakeholders" are identified (with the problems of definition discussed above), stakeholder theories of business ethics then argue that their "interests" must be "balanced." All of these terms – "stakeholders," "interests," and "balanced" – are plainly vague.

The expressed goal of stakeholder theory is to balance the interests of the stakeholders. However, this goal is doubly vague because (1) being a "stakeholder" is a matter of degree and (2) having one's interests "balanced" is also a matter of degree. This vagueness is not practically useful because it does not help decision makers identify principles or criteria by which to make their decisions. This kind of vagueness is pernicious because it tells us to balance stakeholder interests, but does not say anything about how to determine who (or what) counts as a stakeholder (vagueness as to identification) or how to determine when an appropriate balancing has occurred (vagueness as to decision-making process and criteria). This kind of vagueness, when it colors and confuses our goals, impedes rather than advances progress. It leaves us with unclear goals, no criteria for success, and thus perplexed and indecisive.

We have maintained that stakeholder theory is perniciously vague. However, we intentionally underestimated its semantic defects, for the sake of simplicity, in our argument so far. When a term is vague, we know that it refers to borderline cases in its application and we know also approximately where to find its borders.

In this context, consider stakeholder theory as a theory of the firm or as a recommended approach for strategic thinking. As a theory of the firm, vagueness about stakeholders may be helpful descriptively in the sense that the legal or economic "boundaries" of a business firm are shifting. Whether a particular person is "inside" or "outside" of the firm often depends on the question being asked.[18] However, with respect to any practical problem in business ethics, the question of "who counts" in a firm requires a response that gives a precise answer in a specific context. For example, the argument is often made that employees should have rights of representation or greater claims to profit distributions. Nothing is gained analytically to refer to vague descriptions of "stakeholders" rather than "employees." In fact, much can be lost: managers may claim that the economic interests of employees have already been "balanced off" against many other "interests" that must be considered. A common argument against stakeholder theory, in fact, has been that the "balancing of interests" may be used by managers to enrich or favor themselves at the expense of *all* of the other interests in the firm.[19]

As a matter of business strategy, perhaps vagueness is helpful in terms of the "mapping" process that we described above. However, once the various "interests" and other considerations have been identified (such as impact of a firm's operations on the natural environment or on various groups of people such as potential tort victims), then a mere "balancing" approach is insufficient. A more direct specification of principles is needed with respect to the recommended treatment of particular "interests" and other considerations. For example, consider the potential destruction of a legally protected forest which may occur if a furniture business insufficiently monitors its wood suppliers.[20] It is not enough to say that the firm's managers should "balance" this ethical concern against various other considerations (such as profits). The illegality and ethical wrongness of destroying the forest should be seen as a "trump" rather than a factor to be "balanced" or "weighed" against other factors. An ethical problem with the use of stakeholder theory, then, is that the vagueness of "balancing"

allows for a false sense of having grappled with hard problems. As an approach to business ethics, stakeholder theory can be used too easily to condone unethical behavior. Ethical constraints and principles are transmuted into mere considerations or interests to be "balanced" against other considerations and interests.

We might even go so far as to say that most versions of stakeholder theory are worse than vague. They suffer from a radical underspecificity. We know that yellowish orange is vaguely orange. However, we do not know with any specificity who is a relevant "stakeholder." Is a person downwind of a firm which pollutes the air a "stakeholder" of the firm? Some versions say "yes" and others say "no." It is unclear whether such a person is an example of a stakeholder, a vague example, or not a stakeholder at all. Our point is that this semantic difference does not really amount to much. Legal and ethical duties to this person may follow regardless of whether we label him or her as a "stakeholder."

Balancing without Objectives: An Impossible Managerial Quest

Different stakeholders have different interests. Sometimes these interests will conflict. Customers, for example, have an interest in paying a low price for a product, and shareholders have an interest in charging a high price so that their income increases. Sometimes the interests of different stakeholders will align. Lowering prices may sometimes increase the size of a firm's customer base, thus both pleasing customers and increasing profits. However, it would be wrong to contend that stakeholder interests can be always made to align. Some stakeholder theorists sing the praises of finding solutions to conflicts that improve the position of all parties, but no serious proponent of stakeholder theory argues that the relevant interests can always be made to align. What, then, does stakeholder theory advise a manager or other business decision maker to do when stakeholder interests intractably conflict? Nothing: except to say that a manager must "balance" the interest of all the stakeholders. We contend that this is unhelpful advice.

One plain meaning of the term "balance" is to make two things equal in weight. More generally, a balance is a scale which measures items in terms of some common unit, such as weight. In this sense, as Marcoux argues, to balance stakeholder interests seems to mean assigning each stakeholder's interests equal weight.[21] We agree with Marcoux that such balancing seems neither possible nor desirable in practice. The very idea of balancing stakeholder interests seems inapt because these interests themselves are often incommensurable and because assessing these interests so often involves an appeal to incommensurable values.[22]

Balancing interests, in this sense that we are considering here, involves giving equal weights to different interests. Ordinarily, if we can weigh things, then we can attach some numerical measure to their dimensions. This idea of balance seems inapt for thinking about stakeholders of a business. Consider, for example, balancing a stockholder's interest in getting enough money to develop a flourishing retirement fund against an employee dishwasher's interest in getting enough money to feed her hungry children. It seems unclear how to proceed. Their interests seem incommensurable and thus impervious to "balancing": there is no common measure that can be used to conclude that their interests are being weighed the same or indeed balanced on any other arithmetic score. The idea of "balancing stakeholder interests" emerges as a murky metaphor that does not help a business manager make choices of different courses of action or allocations of resources.

Therefore, the idea of balancing is too thin and too unrealistic to serve as a substantive norm for managerial action. It does not say enough about how managers should respond to conflicting interests or values to facilitate resolving these conflicts. Moreover, an attempt to balance too often sends one down the wrong path. For example, imagine a conflict between the majority of shareholders in a munitions firm and a minority of shareholders, all of whom are stakeholders on any account of stakeholder theory. The majority wants the firm to invest in a policy of having the nation support a genocidal regime, so that the firm might then sell munitions to this regime. The minority quite rightly opposes this policy, on the ground that it violates basic human rights. As manager of the firm, how should you think about what to do? Should you give weight to the interests of the genocidal majority? Obviously not. On a stakeholder theory, however, we do not see how one can avoid assigning weight. Its only decisional device is the balancing of interests, and evil interests are just as much interests as good interests. Stakeholder theory lacks the capacity to accommodate important moral concerns into business decision-making.

Conclusion

Stakeholder theory is alluring because it seems to solve two tough problems in one quick stroke. Each problem has moral dimensions. The first problem is stakeholder management: how to manage people fairly and effectively – with due consideration to the vital role that many people play in the life of the firm. The second problem is corporate social responsibility: what great things can and should a firm do, beyond manufacturing widgets and meeting its payroll? In order to answer these questions, a theory must tell us both

how to understand the scope and limits of a manager's duty to enhance a firm's wealth and how to understand a manager's reasons for doing good in his or her community and the world more generally.[23] Stakeholder theory does not help us to answer these larger questions of business ethics. It suffers from the intractable conceptual problems identified here, and it would be better to start from scratch: to reconsider the role of business firms in society and how ethical principles as well as economics provide a ground for understanding the role of business and the responsibilities of those who manage, own, and work for business firms. The idea of "stakeholders" and elaborate theories about them have helped us to raise some of these questions. However, at this point in history and the study of business ethics, we need to move "beyond stakeholders" to answer the most serious and toughest ethical questions surrounding business and its social obligations. A good start would be to focus on some of the most significant ethical quandaries faced in business contexts and to think through them without the artificial and unworkable constructs of various stakeholder theories.

Notes

1. The best analysis of different versions of stakeholder theory in business ethics remains T. Donaldson and L. E. Preston, "The Stakeholder Theory of the Corporation: Concepts, Evidence, and Implications," *Academy of Management Review* 20, no. 1 (1995): 65–91. By 1995, a dozen books and more than 100 articles discussed stakeholder theory (ibid., p. 65). Since then, "interest in the stakeholder concept has quickened," with an expansion of everyday use of the idea and an increasing number of academic treatments of stakeholder theory in journals and books (Andrew L. Friedman and Samantha Miles, *Stakeholders: Theory and Practice* (Oxford University Press, 2006), pp. 3, 28).

2. E. W. Orts and A. Strudler, "The Ethical and Environmental Limits of Stakeholder Theory," *Business Ethics Quarterly* 12, no. 2 (2002): 215–33.

3. In a response to our previous article, some proponents of stakeholder theory have construed our argument as focusing on the limitations of stakeholder theory as "a comprehensive moral doctrine" (R. Phillips, R. E. Freeman, and A. C. Wicks, "What Stakeholder Theory Is Not," *Business Ethics Quarterly* 13, no. 4 (2003): 479–502 (pp. 480–81); see also R. Phillips, *Stakeholder Theory and Organizational Ethics* (San Francisco, CA: Berrett-Koehler, 2003), pp. 35–38, 164–67). This is a misinterpretation of our views. Our argument is specifically with stakeholder theory as an approach to business ethics. We will argue that stakeholder theory fails not merely because its guidance is not comprehensive. It fails because it provides virtually no guidance at all.

4. Stakeholder theory – or at least the term "stakeholders" – has also been adopted in the political realm. Most famously, Tony

Blair referred to the idea of a "stakeholder society" as a part of his New Labour platform in Great Britain. See, e.g., Friedman and Miles, *Stakeholders*, p. 28; C. Stoney and D. Winstanley, "Stakeholding: Confusion or Utopia? Mapping the Conceptual Terrain," *Journal of Management Studies* 38, no. 5 (2001): 603–26 (pp. 604, 609–10). For an American contribution, see B. Ackerman and A. Alstott, *The Stakeholder Society* (New Haven, CT: Yale University Press, 1999) (proposing an $80,000 stakeholder grant to be provided to every citizen at the age of 21). Arguably, there are some links between stakeholder theories of the firm (or perhaps management strategy) and politics – with respect, for example, to employment or labor laws, as well as rules of corporate governance. However, we do not develop these potential connections here.

5. For a review of the literature recognizing "narrow" and "broad" definitions of "stakeholder theory," though drawing different conclusions, see R. K. Mitchell, B. R. Agle, and D. J. Wood, "Toward a Theory of Stakeholder Identification and Salience: Defining the Principle Who and What Really Counts," *Academy of Management Review* 22, no. 4 (1997): 853–86 (pp. 856–63). See also T. Donaldson and T. W. Dunfee, *Ties That Bind: A Social Contracts Approach to Business Ethics* (Boston, MA: Harvard Business School Press, 1999), p. 238.

6. For a strongly articulated version of this view of the firm, which argues against a broader notion of "stakeholders," see E. Sternberg, "The Defects of Stakeholder Theory," *Corporate Governance* 5, no. 1 (1997): 3–10, and *Just Business: Business Ethics in Action* (Oxford University Press, 2000). The concept of "ownership" is itself contested, but we leave this topic outside our current discussion.

7. M. Friedman, "The Social Responsibility of Business Is to Increase Its Profits," *New York Times Magazine* (September 13, 1970).

8. In Friedman's words, the proper objective of the business enterprise is "to make as much money as possible while conforming to the basic rules of society, both those embodied in law and those embodied in ethical custom" (ibid., p. 34).

9. This narrow view of stakeholder theory understood to include employees and creditors as well as equity owners of capital is associated with Max Clarkson, among others. See, e.g., M. B. E. Clarkson, "A Risk-Based Model of Stakeholder Theory," *Proceedings of the Second Toronto Conference on Stakeholder Theory*, University of Toronto (1994); see also Clarkson, "A Stakeholder Framework for Analyzing and Evaluating Corporate Social Performance," *Academy of Management Review* 20, no. 1 (1995): 92–117 (describing "primary stakeholders" in these terms and defining the firm as "a system of primary stakeholder groups, a complex set of relationships between and among interest groups with different rights, objectives, expectations, and responsibilities"), and M. M. Blair and L. A. Stout, "A Team Production Theory of Corporate Law," *Virginia Law Review* 85, no. 2 (1999): 247–328 (advancing a "team production" model of the firm including employees). For reasons of coherence as well as etymology, we

previously embraced this narrow definition of "stakeholders" (Orts and Strudler, "Ethical and Environmental Limits," pp. 217–18). One issue that we will not address here concerns the feature of "control" as well as "ownership" of a firm. Even along this dimension, however, it is not obvious that equity owners always exert a greater degree of practical control than other "stakeholders," such as employed executives or sophisticated creditors. For further discussion of the importance of various legal relationships in a theory of the firm, see E. W. Orts, "Shirking and Sharking: A Legal Theory of the Firm," *Yale Law and Policy Review* 16, no. 2 (1998): 265–329.

10. R. E. Freeman, *Strategic Management: A Stakeholder Approach* (Boston, MA: Pitman, 1984), p. 53; R. E. Freeman, J. S. Harrison, and A. C. Wicks, *Managing for Stakeholders: Survival, Reputation, and Success* (New Haven, CT: Yale University Press, 2007), p. 6.

11. Donaldson and Preston pointed out the "instrumental" and "managerial" strains in stakeholder theories, as well as competing "descriptive" and "normative" features. They observe also that some conceptions of stakeholders invoke "theories of the firm" and others do not (Donaldson and Preston, "Stakeholder Theory of the Corporation"). For an example of an "instrumental" version of stakeholder theory, see T. M. Jones, "Instrumental Stakeholder Theory: A Synthesis of Ethics and Economics," *Academy of Management Review* 20, no. 2 (1995): 404–37.

12. Some versions of stakeholder theory have tried to make this distinction (at least implicitly) and maintain an overall theoretical coherence. However, we think that this approach is difficult, if not impossible, because the different uses of "stakeholder" in a theory of the firm (narrow) and as a strategic mapping device (broad) are quite distinct and conceptually unrelated. At least, the use of "stakeholder" to refer to these very different objectives is likely to produce confusion.

13. R. E. Freeman and D. L. Reed, "Stockholders and Stakeholders: A New Perspective on Corporate Governance," *California Management Review* 25, no. 3 (1983): 88–106 (p. 89).

14. Ibid.

15. Ibid., p. 91.

16. In fact, the defense industry has adopted ethical principles tailored to some of the unique ethical considerations involved. See the statement of principles of the Defense Industry Initiative of Business Ethics and Conduct ("Statement of Purpose and Organization," www.dii.org/Statement.htm).

17. For some reflections along these lines, see, e.g., T. W. Dunfee and T. L. Fort, "Corporate Hypergoals, Sustainable Peace, and the Adapted Firm," *Vanderbilt Journal of Transnational Law* 35 (2003): 549–615; E. W. Orts, "War and the Business Corporation," *Vanderbilt Journal of Transnational Law* 35 (2002): 549–84.

18. See E. W. Orts, "The Complexity and Legitimacy of Corporate Law," *Washington and Lee Law Review* 50 (1993): 1565–623; Orts, "Shirking and Sharking," pp. 313–14.

19. See, e.g., J. R. Macey and G. P. Miller, "Corporate Stakeholders: A Contractual Perspective," *University of Toronto Law Journal* 43, no. 3 (1993): 401–24 (pp. 412, 423–24). We should note that most theories of the firm that are dominant today in both business and law schools advocate a "shareholder primacy" view against which "stakeholder theories" of the firm have often been advanced. Our argument here is not to align ourselves with "shareholder primacy" theorists or others who advocate that only strictly construed economic values should matter when making business decisions. We believe instead – consistent with many stakeholder theorists – that there are a number of serious noneconomic considerations that should inform business decisions. Our suggestion here, however, is that stakeholder theory has proven to give only relatively weak arguments against the prevailing economics-only theories of the firm.

20. See, e.g., R. Katchadourian, "The Stolen Forests," *The New Yorker* (October 6, 2008), p. 64.

21. A. Marcoux, "Business Ethics," in E. N. Zalta (ed.), *The Stanford Encyclopedia of Philosophy*, 2008 Fall Edition, http://plato.stanford.edu/archives/fall2008/entries/ethics-business/.

22. On the ubiquitous problem of incommensurable values and decision making, see N. Hsieh, "Incommensurable Values," in E. N. Zalta (ed.), *The Stanford Encyclopedia of Philosophy*, 2008 Fall Edition, http://plato.stanford.edu/archives/fall2008/entries/value-incommensurable/; A. Strudler, "Incommensurable Goods, Rightful Lies, and the Wrongness of Fraud," *University of Pennsylvania Law Review* 146, no. 5 (1998): 1529–67.

23. In addition to negative ethical constraints – such as avoiding contributions to genocide, unjust wars, or global environmental destruction – one may also ask whether there are positive duties that business firms owe when they have a "special competency" to alleviate a particularly severe problem. For an affirmative argument focusing on the specific duties of pharmaceutical firms to address problems such as AIDS, see T. W. Dunfee, "Do Firms with Unique Competencies for Rescuing Victims of Human Catastrophes Have Special Obligations? Corporate Responsibility and the AIDS Catastrophe in Sub-Saharan Africa," *Business Ethics Quarterly* 16, no. 2 (2006): 185–210. See also N. Hsieh, "The Obligations of Transnational Corporations: Rawlsian Justice and the Duty of Assistance," *Business Ethics Quarterly* 14, no. 4 (2004): 643–61.

Toward a Theory of Business

THOMAS DONALDSON AND JAMES P. WALSH

Introduction

"Law is to justice, as medicine is to health, as business is to_____."

We have asked business students and colleagues alike to fill in the blank above. The first reaction is always one of awkward silence. People are surprised that the answer does not roll off the lips. There is always a sense in the room that we should know the answer and yet, we do not. Then the answers come. A cluster of people will focus on profit, money, and wealth. Others, more expansively, will talk about value creation and prosperity. Still others will focus on the likes of coordination, exchange, production, and innovation. Some will take a decidedly macro perspective and speak about commerce, the economy, collective well-being, and society. And finally, some will shift gears and focus not on wealth but greed, not prosperity but power, not well-being but oppression. This exercise points out three challenges when we think about the nature of business. One is that we grapple with its purpose. The second is that we have a hard time disentangling our thinking about a single business enterprise from business more broadly, an agglomeration of those enterprises in their institutional and historical context. And finally, we know that business may not be an unalloyed good. All of these tensions are on display when we appraise our thinking about the place of business in society.

What is the purpose of business? While most agree that the purpose of business minimally involves the creation of value, today's discussion is haunted by a blurred double image of value. The image of what counts as value for a single firm is laid atop an image of what counts as value for business in general. We believe that these two images cannot match and that the resulting blurriness is a classic example of the composition fallacy. A fallacy of composition occurs when one assumes that the property of a part, or of all parts, can be taken to represent the whole.[1] The composition fallacy alerts us to the possibility that the attributes of a successful firm may not be the same as the attributes of

From Thomas Donaldson and James P. Walsh, "Toward a Theory of Business," *Research in Organizational Behavior* 35 (2015): 181–207. Reprinted with permission.

successful business in general. Enumerating persistent expectations and concerns about business practice, we believe that a theory of the firm is ill equipped to handle them. Working from a set of definitions that give precision to such everyday concepts as value, dignity, and business success, our goal is to develop a theory with both normative and empirical relevance. Since business works both in society and for society,[2] the theory must include both empirical and normative elements. With this work as a foundation, we then offer four central propositions about the purpose, accountability, control, and success of business. We will close with a consideration of several questions, issues, and opportunities that we are likely to face in the years ahead. While this effort is admittedly preliminary, we do hold some criteria for its success. We hope that our ideas both align with known facts about business practice and with deep, widely held intuitions about values. Beyond that, we hope that others will be moved to build upon these ideas in the coming years.

Business Matters

To begin, we want to assert that business matters. While economic historians can debate the Industrial Revolution's legacy,[3] some facts are clear. Perhaps most fundamentally, Riley observed that human life expectancy more than doubled in the past two hundred years (moving from about 30 to 65 years). He called that the "crowning achievement of the modern era."[4] To be sure, the modern era is marked by all manner of life-saving and life-enhancing achievements. Take medicine, engineering, communications, and agriculture. Would we have CT scanners, automobiles, smartphones, and drought resistant seeds without business to develop the ideas, create the products, and distribute them worldwide? Of course not. Launching a new social progress initiative, Porter and Stern looked at the cross-sectional relationship between social progress (assessing what they called basic human needs, foundations of well-being, and opportunity) and economic growth (looking at GDP per capita). Gathering data from 133 nations, they found a correlation of 0.78.[5] Economic and business activity can certainly make the world a better place. . . .

On the other hand, many fear the firm. We have been witness to what can only be called dreadful corporate behavior over the past three decades.[6] Business legitimacy, and the social trust that serves as its foundation, has been damaged. The 1981 Savings and Loan crisis shook business confidence for a time. The business scandals of 2001 and 2002, however, precipitated more than a decade-long loss of confidence in big business. The misconduct at Enron, Tyco, and WorldCom launched the trend. Such misconduct

brought us the Sarbanes–Oxley Act of 2002 and turned their disgraced CEOs – Ken Lay, Dennis Kozlowski, and Bernie Ebbers – into household names.[7] WorldCom's July 2002 bankruptcy was the world's largest at the time ($103.9 billion). These three 2001–2002 scandals, however, were just the most notorious. Looking at the data on earning restatements in the 1990–2004 time period, Coffee concluded that there was "a hyperbolic rate of increase around the turn of the millennium."[8] That is when public confidence in business really started to ebb. The concern born of the turn-of-the-century scandals was fueled anew in September 2008 with the collapse of Lehman Brothers and Washington Mutual. With asset values of $691 billion and $327.9 billion, respectively, each dwarfed WorldCom's fall and became the nation's largest and second largest bankruptcies in history.[9] As the financial crisis worsened, the US government stood behind many more troubled firms and offered billions of dollars to prevent a total economic collapse. Accounting for all of the money is a difficult task but we know, for example, that JPMorgan received $29 billion from the US government to buy the troubled Bear Stearns, AIG received at least $85 billion to stay solvent, and all manner of others (including General Motors) received portions of the $700 billion that funded the Troubled Asset Relief Program.[10]

The Gallup organization has queried the US public about its confidence in society's institutions since 1973. It reveals the contagious loss of business legitimacy that we have witnessed over the past decade or so. Legitimacy has fallen in tandem with rising expectations – society expects more from business these days than simply creating wealth. For example, a recent survey tells us that just 7 percent of the US population believes that business should only make money for its shareholders.[11] . . .

A Beleaguered Straw Man

Our extant understanding of business conduct is drawn largely from economics, specifically what is known as neoclassical economics. The economists offer us a theory of the firm, telling us why the firm exists and how commerce in a world of firms differs from commerce in a world of market exchange. Known broadly as the neoclassical theory of the firm, the power and reach of this work is impressive. Indeed, William Allen, former Chancellor of the Delaware Court of Chancery, once remarked, "One of the marks of a truly dominant intellectual paradigm is the difficulty people have in even imagining an alternative view."[12] Alternative theories have had a hard time gaining traction.

The "neoclassical" theory of the firm is really a bundle of theories, all loosely connected by their utilization of concepts drawn from this view of economics. Seeing individuals as primarily self-interested economic agents, the theories are all grounded in notions of contractual freedom, with an emphasis on prices and outputs constrained by demand. . . .

Proximate Concerns

The neoclassical theory of the firm has been under scrutiny for decades. Its salience and very success no doubt elevated its status as a high-value target for academic critics. Many of them approach the theory on its own terms, granting some of its major assumptions and challenging others. Davis, for example, questions whether shareholders truly "own" the corporation.[13] Some transfer well-known concerns about neoclassical economics to the theory of the firm. Concerns about the absence of perfect information, methodological individualism (i.e., the idea that social phenomena can best be understood as a function of individual intent and action), and the oversimplification of complex social behavior, for example, are all raised in this domain as well.[14] Others criticize the practical implications of the theory. Calling the theory's prescriptions "wrong" and "dangerous," Ghoshal and Moran argued that managers who unwittingly implement these ideas could do more harm than good.[15] Ferraro and colleagues warned us that such theories could become self-fulfilling.[16] Still others worry about the double-sided epistemic face of the theory. They worry that it can be deployed – again unwittingly – as either a positive or a normative behavioral account. The ensuing confusion does us little good.[17] To be sure, all theories have their limitations. Problems will draw earnest attempts to fix them; the theory will be refined in time. Even still, one can wonder about the ultimate utility of the ideas comprising the neoclassical theory. One can wonder how well these unalloyed ideas, perhaps even with their coming refinements, serve society.

Distal Concerns

These concerns are audible and paradoxically, sometimes inaudible. The noisy protests, attendant to the aggressive pursuit of competitive advantage and profit, are unmistakable. Taibbi, for example, began his critique of Wall Street's role in the recent financial crisis with these now infamous words:

> The first thing you need to know about Goldman Sachs is that it's everywhere. The world's most powerful investment bank is a great vampire squid wrapped around the face of humanity, relentlessly jamming its blood funnel into anything that smells like money.[18]

The toll that our recent economic problems took on the lives of everyday Americans is well known.[19] The business misbehavior that so fueled the crisis of confidence captured by the Gallup organization is well chronicled in the media. Other concerns, perhaps endemic to everyday business decision-making, may not always claim a front page headline. Newsworthy just the same, they often constitute what are known theoretically as negative externalities.

With profit the remainder as we subtract costs from revenue, a firm naturally wants to minimize its costs. Problems arise when firms pass their costs on to others. Observers of contemporary business are quite concerned about externalities. The Organisation for Economic Cooperation and Development offers a succinct definition of the phenomenon:

> Externalities refers to situations when the effect of production or consumption of goods and services imposes costs or benefits on others which are not reflected in the prices charged for the goods and services being provided.[20]

The most obvious example may be the pollution that can accompany manufacturing. While the consumers of a company's goods may not pay for the cost of this pollution, society certainly pays for it with a diminished quality of life.[21] Other examples are legion. The tobacco industry takes the lives of many of its customers.[22] In doing so, it wreaks havoc with their families and imposes a public health burden on the rest of us. The food industry contributes to childhood obesity and a near epidemic of Type II diabetes.[23]

While scandal and negative externalities sometimes garner protest, we are struck by the silence that greets so much of this news. To be sure, the financial scandals of the early 2000s contributed to the passage of the Sarbanes–Oxley Act. Scandal can fuel reform. Still, we have become desensitized to egregious firm behavior. Consider the past few years. In 2010, we learned that a Dutch court found Trafigura guilty of illegally dumping toxic waste. Instead of paying to process the waste in the Netherlands, the ship sailed to the Ivory Coast and dumped it there, sickening over 100,000 people.[24] Already under fire for hacking the phones of celebrities and politicians in search of tabloid gossip, we learned in 2011 that the News Corporation crossed a line into the world of the utterly despicable. In search of the sensational story, they hacked into the phones of terrorist bombing victims, deceased Iraqi soldiers, and even a murdered schoolgirl.[25] In 2012, HSBC paid a $1.9 billion fine after being accused of laundering money for Mexican drug traffickers and such countries as Burma, Iran, Libya, and Sudan.[26] We learned the next year (on

April 24, 2013) that the Rana Plaza garment factory building collapsed in Dhaka, Bangladesh. More than 1,100 people perished.[27] Dov Charney, the founder and long-time CEO of American Apparel, was finally deposed in 2014 after presiding over what was euphemistically called "a sexually charged workplace."[28] And finally, 2015 bore witness to two scandals of massive proportions. First, we learned that the CEO and five members of the board of directors of Petrobras, the largest company in Brazil, were forced to resign after suffering $33 billion in losses due to corruption and financial mismanagement. The scandal even found its way to the office of the country's president.[29] Second, we learned that Volkswagen cynically skirted emissions laws on 11 million vehicles in the United States, defrauding its customers and exposing the world to dangerous levels of toxic pollutants, all in its quest to become the world's largest automaker.[30] . . .

On balance, the neoclassical theory of the firm may serve business leaders fairly well. The issue is that the theory was not developed to address society's interest in business activity, the source of the distal problems we identify here. While the theory's proximate concerns are real and deserve attention, the distal questions and concerns pose problems for a theory ill equipped to handle them. We do not need a theory of the firm to address these problems; we need a theory of business. We need a theory that can answer the riddle posed at the beginning of this work: "Law is to justice, as medicine is to health, as business is to_____." . . .

Theoretical Foundations

Definitions for a Theory of Business

Any theory of business needs to focus on four key ideas. Three of these are common to the contemporary literature on corporate governance, namely, we must consider the purpose, accountability, and control of business. And given that ours is to be a normative theory as well as an empirical one, we will appraise the ultimate conduct of business – we will consider the nature of business success. With these four aspirations in mind, we offer the following definitions.

1. Business: a form of cooperation involving the Production, Exchange, and Distribution of goods and services for the purpose of achieving Collective Value.
2. Business Participant: someone who affects or is affected by the pursuit of Collective Value. Some Business Participants are identified through their membership in entities that affect or are affected by the pursuit of Collective Value.

3. Positive Value: a reason for acting where the object of the act is seen as worthy of pursuit.
4. Negative Value: a reason for acting where the object of the act is seen as aversive.
5. Intrinsic Value: a Positive Value whose worth does not depend on its ability to achieve other Positive Values.
6. Benefit: the contributions made by Business to the satisfaction of a Business Participant's Positive and Intrinsic Values, net of any aversive impact on the satisfaction of those same values.
7. Collective Value: the agglomeration of the Business Participants' Benefits, again, net of any aversive Business outcomes.
8. Dignity: an Intrinsic Value prescribing that each Business Participant be treated with respect, compatible with each person's inherent worth.
9. Dignity Threshold: the minimum level of respect accorded to each Business Participant necessary to allow the agglomeration of Benefit to qualify as Business Success.
10. Business Success: optimized Collective Value, optimized subject to clearing the Dignity Threshold. Equifinalty assumed, alternative states of Business Success are possible.

Business and Business Participants

We understand Business to include a system of production, exchange, and distribution relationships among and between the entities that constitute firms' value chains: firms themselves, civil society, institutions of government, and the communities that both sustain and benefit from business activity. All of these entities, and the individuals that comprise them, participate in business activity. However, we reserve the term "Business Participant" for those who are the ultimate bearers of value, namely, persons. Many but not all Business Participants are identified through their membership in business entities. The term, Business Participant, expansively includes anyone who affects or is affected by business. As such, our definition echoes Freeman's capacious intuition about stakeholder identification.[31] That said, we use the term "participant" and not "stakeholder" here. We do so because of the latter's longstanding association with the management of discrete business entities, not the conduct of business broadly (as we are examining here). Production is a cooperative process in which inputs generate outputs, goods or services in the world of business. Exchange is a voluntary and cooperative process in which a good or a service is given in anticipation of a return. And distribution captures both the cooperative processes by which those goods and services reach their buyers and the resulting pattern of who does or does not buy them.

It may strike some as odd that our definition of business emphasizes cooperation instead of competition. To be sure, competition plays an essential role in business. Many even see it as the heartbeat of market capitalism. Still, if we want to understand the purpose, accountability, control, and success of business, we must place competition in its proper context. Competition is significant because it serves as an important means to maximize value. However, it is not the only means to create value. The ability of groups to cooperate in competitive systems is also recognized as a critical economic success factor.[32] With competition so celebrated in contemporary society,[33] we need to be alert to goal displacement (means/ends inversion). We need to keep in mind that competition itself is not the goal of business.

Effective competition requires the social consent that we see embodied in our cooperative institutions. For example, an independent judiciary that enforces contracts and property rights and the regulatory institutions that forestall harmful monopolies together enable markets to function properly. Social contracts help to form the normative underpinnings of business.[34] We cooperatively create, manage, and participate in competitive markets to create collective value.

Positive and Negative Values

The term "value" is commonly heard in discussions of economics and business. Interestingly, it is often left undefined, or when defined, interpreted through a price mechanism or systematized preference rankings (including the analysis of indifference). In contrast, the concept of value is ubiquitous and the object of extensive analysis in moral theory. Each one of the many respected attempts to systemize morals over more than two millennia may be said to entail some definition of value, either directly or indirectly.[35] That said, nonphilosophers are often surprised not by the divergence of ethical views in moral philosophy, but by their convergence. While disagreements rage over meta-ethical issues such as moral realism (the question of whether moral qualities are reflected directly in "facts"), the more basic normative moral questions have surprisingly convergent answers. Noisy disputes about abortion, gay marriage, and the role of religion in society may command our attention, but the fact is that we all share similar views about such basic values as health, dignity, and justice.

Popularized by Rawls,[36] the term "overlapping consensus" denotes how people who support different underlying normative doctrines, including different religious doctrines, can still agree on specific principles of justice. We use it here more expansively to refer to values that are endorsed, although to varying degrees, by people with different cultural and religious views. For example, some version of the Golden Rule is found in every one of the world's major religions. Members of the United Nations General Assembly endorsed the Universal Declaration of Human Rights in 1948 without dissent. It enshrines such basic values as dignity and freedom.

We define a Positive Value as a reason for acting when the object of the act is seen as worthy of pursuit. In other words, a Positive Value is someone's reason for acting. This definition taps a deep legacy in moral philosophy, one that defines values in terms of reasons and one that relates values to human interests. By definition, some reason or other, whether good or bad, motivates intentional behavior.

In turn, a Negative Value constitutes a reason for not acting or avoiding something undesirable or aversive. It is often the negative form of a positive value. For example, the negative value of sickness finds its opposite in the positive value of health. We introduce the concept of negative and positive values in order to capture the richness of ordinary language.

A value can serve as one person's reason for acting and not another's. In other words, values can be matters of personal taste. My reason for acting in a particular instance may be to avoid buying a car, and yours may be the opposite. You may want to buy a car to stop riding a city bus; I may move to a convenient bus line in order to sell my car. Such values, whether positive or negative, are agent-specific.

Intrinsic Value

Some values are not agent-specific. Such values are Intrinsic Values. Suppose that owning more land is a value for you, and someone asks you why you value owning more land. If you attempt to give a persuasive answer, you need to appeal to a higher-order reason that is understandable to the questioner. You might reply that owning more land gives you a sense of security, with the inference that your higher-order reason is the value of security. This answer may well satisfy your questioner since both of you probably agree that security is a value. But suppose the person surprises you and follows up with another question, "Why do you value security?" Here, your reply may well be something like "I don't value security for some further reason; rather, security is something I think has intrinsic worth." In other words, you would be saying, "I think security is an intrinsic value." When something that is "worthy of pursuit" does not have its own value derived from a higher-order value, it counts as an Intrinsic Value. It is a final reason for acting. Intrinsic values, in turn, possess an "objective" normative status. Even were society to form an overlapping consensus affirming the rightness of slavery, society would be wrong. The intrinsic value of personal freedom tenders a non-relative claim.

Many if not all of our important values are dependent ultimately on higher-order values that are intrinsic in this sense. One may value wealth partly because one values the capacity to be charitable (i.e., to display beneficence). Beneficence itself, however, need not be derived from some other value. It can stand on its own two feet. Accordingly, we define an Intrinsic Value as a form of value whose worth does not depend on its ability to achieve other Positive Values. It is non-derivative. Moreover, in a world where others call us to account for our conduct, an intrinsic value can serve as a primary justification for behavior. Understandable as a good reason for any person, it constitutes a final reason for acting.

Benefit

Benefit represents the contributions made by Business to the satisfaction of a Business Participant's Values, including his or her Intrinsic Values. Because excellent production in a cooperative context (Business) is marked by the efficient production of goods and services, it follows that the values likely to be fulfilled in business are those best served by the functions of production and exchange. Such values include physical security, healthcare, personal freedom, family support, education, and charity. Indeed, while the methodological and econometric challenges are many, the current evidence seems to suggest that there is a positive relationship between wealth (looking at both GDP per capita and household income) and reported measures of well-being. The well-being measures are very abstract. Diener and colleagues and Sacks and colleagues, for example, both looked at evidence from the Gallup World Poll, where respondents appraised their lives on an 11-point scale.[37] Their assessments ranged from zero (worst possible life) to ten (best possible life). Future work will no doubt examine much more fine-grained measures of well-being. That said, we imagine that some values are difficult to serve through the production function. Love, community, virtue, self-control, integrity, friendship, self-respect, lack of prejudice, and spontaneity come to mind.

Finally, the word "satisfaction" in our definition needs some attention. Satisfaction itself has specific characteristics. First, the satisfaction of a particular value refers to the satisfaction of that value for a particular Business Participant. Second, satisfaction admits degrees. Any person's particular value may be more or less satisfied. Third, satisfaction itself can be a paradox. There may be limits to satisfaction. More satisfaction may not always be satisfying. And fourth, some values are more important to one person than another. This fact becomes important when we consider the nature of Collective Value.

Collective Value

We stated earlier that Collective Value is the agglomeration of the Business Participants' Benefits, net of any aversive Business outcomes. While the meaning of that sentence is clear, the ability to assess that statement in practice is anything but clear. Einstein reportedly said, "Not everything that counts can be counted, and not everything that can be counted counts." Not all Benefits can be easily appraised, much less combined in a fashion that allows for easy summation and comparison. The satisfaction of a set of values for an individual person, not to mention a group of people, is impossible to measure accurately on a simple numerical continuum. The chief problem is incommensurability. For example, how are we to compare Jack's utility or happiness to Jill's?[38]

Note that we use the word agglomeration and not aggregation in our definition here. Both words refer to a clustering but their ultimate coherence differs. *Merriam Webster* defines an agglomerate as a mass that is "clustered or growing together but not coherent"; the dictionary defines an aggregate as "a mass or body of units or parts somewhat loosely associated with one another." Collective Value represents an agglomeration of benefits, not an aggregation of benefits. To illustrate, consider the value expressed by a human right, say, the right to religious freedom. This is significantly different from the value expressed by beneficence. The former implies a defined minimum standard of behavior relevant to particular contexts over which the agent has no control. Beneficence, in contrast, implies a duty to go above minimum levels of prescribed behavior. It allows the duty to be exercised using considerable agent discretion in self-defined contexts. A person may value religious freedom and beneficence but it is not at all clear how we might easily combine the two into a simple summation of benefit.

We should note that while alluring, the logic of neoclassical economics fails us when we consider Collective Value. Neoclassical economics inherited its notion of value from early nineteenth-century utilitarian philosophers, developing theories of utility that could be easily mathematicized.[39] While the early notion of "utils" (units of utility) was eventually abandoned in favor of marginal utility, neoclassicists such as Jevons adopted value monism and assumed that economic activity could be subsumed (i.e., aggregated) under the banner of a single value, happiness.[40] Not so Collective Value. Those uncomfortable with value monism need to be comfortable with the consideration of an agglomeration of multiple values, and multiple values of differing character.

Dignity, the Dignity Threshold, and Business Success

If business exists to create collective value, it follows that any theory of business must be normative. A theory like this must say something about the world we hope to inhabit. We need to come to terms with how business creates value and serves society. Recognizing that aversive outcomes can attend the conduct of business, we also recognize that some aversive outcomes are simply out of bounds. Our challenge as a people is to determine just what behavior is acceptable and what is unacceptable. In legal terms, we are looking for a moral "bright line rule," one that tells us what kind of business activity is to be strictly forbidden.[41] We suggest that at a minimum, dignity establishes that decision criterion.

The idea of the dignity of the person has deep roots in moral philosophy and political action. In moral philosophy, the very possibility of realizing intrinsic values (and of moral behavior in general) presumes the inherent worth of actors capable of such achievements. In different ways, Utilitarianism, Kantian deontology, and Aristotelianism all affirm the worth of that actor who uniquely possesses the capacity to achieve the good and the right, namely, the moral person. Whether grounded in sacred notions of the divine or secular notions of agency and autonomy, every individual has what Rosen calls "an inner transcendental kernel of inalienable value."[42] Kateb, Lagon and Arend, Rosen, and Waldron all offer contemporary reviews and their own ideas about the dignity construct.[43] From them, we learn that dignity carries an action implication. Endowed with this inner "transcendental kernel," every individual is entitled to respect. Indeed, political life is judged by its affirmation and protection of human dignity.

In 1776, the US Declaration of Independence famously began with an assertion that "all men are created equal." All men – and women – are not only created equal, they must be treated as equals. They must be accorded their human dignity. Nine years later, Kant cast this kind of thinking into his categorical imperative.[44] He argued that we are always to "act so that you treat humanity, whether in your own person or in that of another, always as an end and never as a means only." This same kind of thinking was enshrined 163 years later in the Universal Declaration of Human Rights.

Without dissent, the United Nations General Assembly affirmed a document that begins with the words:

> the recognition of the inherent dignity and of the equal and inalienable rights of all members of the human family [; such dignity] is the foundation of freedom, justice and peace in the world.

Germany took this kind of aspirational thinking a step further the next year. In 1949, they affirmed the importance of human dignity in Article 1 of the Basic Law for the Federal Republic of Germany (Grundgesetz): "Human dignity shall be inviolable. To respect and protect it shall be the duty of all state authority." Theirs is not just an aspirational statement; it is an enforceable one. Thus, human dignity, with roots both in moral theory and in political action, serves as a central and even sacred Intrinsic Value to guide Business activity.

Our understanding of human dignity tells us that our fellow humans are not to be treated as mere objects or instruments in a business organization's production function. Business participants are to be treated with respect. As such, the Dignity Threshold establishes a moral foundation for business activity. The challenge, of course, is to identify what treatment does or does not clear the threshold. Since the threshold marks the minimum level of respect accorded to each Business Participant, the threshold can best be seen as prohibiting indignity. To be sure, participants can bolster another's dignity, enhancing *eudaimonia* (what the ancients called human flourishing), but at minimum, Business Participants cannot deny each other's fundamental dignity.

Borrowing language from the world of statistics, we can say that dignity is both a "categorical" and "continuous" idea. When we speak of an indignity, we speak of dignity as a categorical idea. Hold someone as a slave, for example, and regardless of how well you might treat that person, you fully deprive that person of his or her dignity. There is absolutely no dignity in slavery. Thomas Jefferson may have fathered six children with Sally Hemings but owning her as his property until the day he died, he denied her dignity.[45] Article 4 of the UN Declaration of Human Rights is unequivocal: "No one shall be held in slavery or servitude; slavery and the slave trade shall be prohibited in all their forms." The US South in the first half of the nineteenth century relied upon the institution of slavery to support its expansive system of plantation farming. Even if slavery enhanced the GDP or PPP of the region, plantation farming cannot be considered Business Success. Slavery stripped its captive people of their dignity. The institution of slavery simply does not pass the Dignity Threshold. That fact cannot be offset at a personal level by seemingly decent interpersonal treatment. The theory of business offered here directs and justifies every effort to dismantle a business system that so violates human dignity. . . .

Implications

The Purpose, Accountability, Control, and Success of Business

We opened this work by chronicling the normative pressure on firms to serve as agents of world benefit. Those who encourage businesses to change (e.g., the United Nations and the Aspen Institute) are not marked by a lack of economic sophistication but rather by a quest to honor human dignity when we produce, exchange, and distribute our goods and services. This quest inspired our attempt to develop a theory of business.

To be sure, our theory is a normative one. Looking to articulate the role that business plays in creating a good society, it cannot be otherwise. Freeman is correct.[46] The separation thesis is false. Any attempt to separate business activity from values is akin to trying to separate a vase from its shape. The same is true of business. It is impossible to jettison values from a comprehensive consideration of business practice. Business activity always reveals the values that shape it. Those values are revealed in any consideration of the purpose, accountability, control, and success of business. As such, we offer the following four propositions as corollaries to a theory of business:

- P1: The purpose of business is to optimize collective value.
- P2: Business is accountable to those who affect and are affected by its activities, those in the present, past, and future.
- P3: Business control must prohibit any assault on participants' dignity.
- P4: Optimized collective value is the mark of business success.

Three noteworthy features mark these propositions. First, we need to consider the idea of equifinality. There are many paths to business success. Second, the idea that business is accountable to business participants in the past and future, as well as to those in the present, is worthy of discussion. And finally, we need to say a word about optimization in this context.

Equifinality

One important implication of these propositions is that not all business firms need to be alike. In fact, a variety of organizations will likely achieve collective value better than a set of firms marked by cookie-cutter similarity. Consider an analogy. A coordinated team of carpenters, electricians, plumbers, masons and the like will build a better home than any one group will build on its own (or even one made by a Jack-of-all-trades artisan). And of course, it takes more than craftspeople to build a building. Bankers, lawyers, and insurance specialists, for example, enable this work too. The second implication is that the work of business needs to be coordinated. To be sure, markets facilitate coordination but those markets themselves need to be developed and sustained. Government and the not-for-profit sector play crucial roles in business too. In addition to providing the infrastructure for efficient and effective contracting among the parties, government ensures the quality of building materials, the well-being of the natural environment, the safety of the builders, and so much more. The not-for-profit sector works to both ensure that standards and safeguards of all kinds are defined and met, often before any government is involved (e.g., the National Fire Protection Association), and to make sure that society's needs are addressed (e.g., Habitat for Humanity). Any single business firm always sits in a broader ecology of business activity. The amazing, and nearly infinite, variety of firms and coordination schemes available for achieving Business Success opens the door to equifinality. Many roads can lead to the same destination

Accountability to the Past and Future, as Well as to the Present

Business participants are accountable not just to their contemporaries but to their ancestors and descendants too. That statement might strike some as very expansive, if not too expansive. To assert that business is to be accountable to those living who affect and are affected by its activity should pass without remark. To be sure, people read Freeman's definition of a stakeholder ("any group or individual who can affect or is affected by the achievement of the activities of an organization"[47]) and wonder whether a firm should really view a competitor or even a terrorist as a stakeholder.[48] Still, no one questions Freeman's implicit focus on the living.

A move to consider the unborn might raise an eyebrow at first blush, but with some reflection, we see that people do accept the idea. After all, future thinking is baked into our everyday conceptions of management. Jacques, for example, noted that a firm's senior leaders typically look 20 to 50 years into the future when they make their decisions.[49] More recently, Elkington famously defined sustainability as "meeting the needs of the present without compromising the ability of future generations to meet their own needs."[50] Legacy matters.

Indeed, a number of social psychologists are working today to understand just how people make forward-looking intergeneration resource allocation decisions.[51] However, people may not think about their predecessors' legacies. Do we owe anything to those who came before us? We say "yes." The humility that comes from an understanding of history does us good. Fundamentally, we need to appreciate that we inherit the world when we are born. We also would do well to appreciate that in time, our lives will be history too. Our legacy should be to leave the world better than we found it. . . .

Optimization

We recognize that some may question our idea that optimized collective value is the mark of business success. They might argue that just as economists problematically assumed (for decades) that humans are perfectly rational and work to optimize their economic ambitions, we might have embraced a similarly problematic idea. Adopting the idea of optimization as we do, we risk a reader dismissing our ideas of success as fantasy. Perhaps we should follow Simon's lead and develop an idea akin to his notion of satisficing.[52] Perhaps we should develop a threshold notion of "satisfactory collective value" and use it instead to define business success. There is much to be said about that kind of a well-meaning reaction. At base, however, we think it is a mistake to introduce a "good enough" criterion to any consideration of business success. *Merriam Webster* tells us that optimization is "an act, process, or methodology of making something (as a design, system, or decision) as fully perfect, functional, or effective as possible." We do well to strive for business success that is as fully perfect, functional, or effective as possible. Why should we settle for anything less?

Purpose

What is the purpose of a firm when the purpose of business is to optimize collective value? One might be tempted to reason that every firm must simply work to optimize collective value. This view, however, would evidence the division fallacy. Consider the human heart. The purpose of the heart is to pump blood. However, it is important to note that different parts of the heart, the ventricles, valves, septum, aorta and more, have their own discrete purposes. Now consider business. Just as the septum is a part of the heart that pumps blood, a firm is a part of the ecology of business that creates collective value. Few firms may be entirely focused on creating collective value. And that is fine. Still, they are not exempt from playing some role in that effort. After all, a firm is a moral entity that works in and for society. As such, a firm holds two interrelated purposes:

first, a focal purpose, a purpose that reflects its work *in* society and second, a contextual purpose, a purpose that reflects its work *for* society.

The firm's focal purpose is familiar to every business student. Fail to provide customers with a high-quality good or service at a competitive, profit-making price and the firm may well go out of business. Fail to reach those customers with an effective sales and marketing campaign, raise and manage capital, recruit and manage human resources, and efficiently manage their operations and the firm may go out of business. And to be sure, managers cannot ignore those who hold the firm's residual claims, those who hold common stock. The neoclassical economists persuasively point out that these risk-bearing shareholders are the ones most interested in maximizing the value of the entire corporation. Shareholders can keep managers ever attentive to creating sustained competitive advantage.

All of that said, the firm's contextual purpose cannot be ignored. A firm is a human creation, one designed by humans and for humans. At a minimum, all of its activities must clear the Dignity Threshold. No firm should disrespect the inherent worth, the dignity, of its many business participants. It must treat each one with respect. Moreover, no firm should forget that the final justification of its activities from a social perspective lies in its contribution to collective value.

Many firms are experimenting with aligning focal and contextual purposes in explicit ways. Indeed, such dedicated dual-purpose experimentation marks our age. Some firms, obeying the law, seek to maximize their shareholder's return. No one can complain about such firms if they clear the Dignity Threshold and recognize their broader purpose in society. Others, however, seek to make a more direct social impact as they conduct their business. Looking at what Conley and Williams called the "corporate social responsibility movement," we increasingly see firms making social investments of the kind Kofi Annan sought over 15 years ago.[53] Others firms, LinkedIn for example, have a mission infused with social purpose. Their mission is to "connect the world's professionals to make them more productive and successful"; their purpose is a lofty one – to "creat[e] economic opportunity for every member of the global workforce." Others, B Corporations, submit themselves to outside appraisal and are formally certified as committed to transparent social and environmental performance (as they do their business). Nearly 1,400 B Corps in 41 countries have been so certified as of this writing. And still others, social enterprises, commit themselves to social and economic performance but do so absent third-party certification. . . .

Notes

1. H. Hansen, "Fallacies," in E. N. Zalta (ed.), *The Stanford Encyclopedia of Philosophy*, 2015 edition, http://plato .stanford.edu/archives/sum2015/entries/fallacies/.

2. J. P. Walsh, A. D. Meyer, and C. B. Schoonhoven, "A Future for Organization Theory: Living in and Living with Changing Organizations," *Organization Science* 17 (2006): 657–71.

3. See Allen's review (R. C. Allen, "A Review of Gregory Clark's *A Farewell to Alms: A Brief Economic History of the World*," *Journal of Economic Literature* 46 (2008): 946–73) of G. Clark, *A Farewell to Alms: A Brief Economic History of the World* (Princeton University Press, 2007), for example.

4. J. C. Riley, *Rising Life Expectancy: A Global History* (Cambridge University Press, 2001), p. 1.

5. M. E. Porter and S. Stern, *Social Progress Index 2015*. Social Progress Imperative, www.socialprogressimperative.org/publi cations/.

6. H. R. Greve, D. Palmer, and J. Pozner, "Organizations Gone Wild: The Causes, Processes, and Consequences of Organizational Misconduct," *Academy of Management Annals* 4 (2010): 53–107.

7. J. C. Coates, "The Goals and Promise of the Sarbanes–Oxley Act," *Journal of Economic Perspectives* 21 (2007): 91–116.

8. J. C. Coffee, "A Theory of Corporate Scandals: Why the USA and Europe Differ," *Oxford Review of Economic Policy* 21, no. 2 (2005): 198–211 (p. 201).

9. "The 10 Largest US Bankruptcies" (2009), http://archive .fortune.com/galleries/2009/fortune/0905/gallery.largest_bank ruptcies.fortune/.

10. C. D. Block, "Measuring the True Cost of the Government Bailout," *Washington University Law Review* 88 (2010): 149–228.

11. Cone Communications, *Social Impact Study* (2013), www.con ecomm.com/research-blog/2013-cone-communications-social-impact-study#download-research.

12. W. T. Allen, "Contracts and Communities in Corporation Law," *Washington and Lee Law Review*, 50 (1993): 1395–407 (p. 1401).

13. G. F. Davis, "New Directions in Corporate Governance," *Annual Review of Sociology* 31 (2005): 143–62.

14. M. Granovetter, "Economic Action and Social Structure: The Problem of Embeddedness," *American Journal of Sociology* 91 (1985): 481–510; C. Perrow, *Complex Organizations: A Critical Essay*, 3rd ed. (New York: Random House, 1986); C. Perrow, "Economic Theories of Organization," *Theory and Society* 15 (1986): 11–45.

15. S. Ghoshal and P. Moran, "Bad for Practice: A Critique of the Transaction Cost Theory," *Academy of Management Review* 21 (1996): 13–47 (p. 13). For an elaboration of that accusation, see S. Ghoshal, "Bad Management Theories Are Destroying Good Management Practices," *Academy of Management Learning and Education* 4 (2005): 75–91.

16. F. Ferraro, J. Pfeffer, and R. I. Sutton, "Economics Language and Assumptions: How Theories Can Become Self-Fulfilling," *Academy of Management Review* 30 (2005): 8–24.

17. R. W. Coff, "When Competitive Advantage Doesn't Lead to Performance: The Resource-Based View and Stakeholder Bargaining Power," *Organization Science* 10 (1999): 119–33; T. Donaldson, "The Epistemic Fault Line in Corporate Governance," *Academy of Management Review* 37 (2012): 256–71; J. Kim and J. T. Mahoney, "A Strategic Theory of the Firm as a Nexus of Incomplete Contracts: A Property Rights Approach," *Journal of Management* 36 (2010): 806–26; L. Zingales, "In Search of New Foundations," *Journal of Finance* 55 (2000): 1623–53.

18. M. Taibbi, "The Great American Bubble Machine," *Rolling Stone* (July 13, 2009), www.rollingstone.com/politics/news/ the-great-american-bubble-machine-20100405/.

19. D. B. Grusky, B. Western, and C. Wime, *The Great Recession* (New York: Russell Sage Foundation, 2011).

20. Organisation for Economic Co-operation and Development, *Glossary of Statistical Terms – Externalities* (2014), https:// stats.oecd.org/glossary/detail.asp?ID=3215.

21. J. Brandt, J. D. Silver, J. H. Christensen, M. S. Andersen, J. H. Bønløkke, T. Sigsgaard et al., "Contribution from the Ten Major Emission Sectors in Europe and Denmark to the Health-Cost Externalities of Air Pollution Using the EVA Model System: An Integrated Modelling Approach," *Atmospheric Chemistry and Physics* 13 (2013): 7725–46.

22. J. P. Pierce, E. A. Gilpin, and W. S. Choi, "Sharing the Blame: Smoking Experimentation and Future Smoking Attributable to Joe Camel and Marlboro Advertising and Promotions," *Tobacco Control* 8 (1999): 37–44.

23. A. Lewin, L. Lindstrom, and M. Nestle, "Food Industry Promises to Address Childhood Obesity," *Journal of Public Health Policy* 27, no. 4 (2006): 327–48.

24. "Trafigura Found Guilty of Exporting Toxic Waste," *BBC News* (July 23, 2010), www.bbc.com/news/world-africa-10735255.

25. T. Watson and M. Hickman, *Dial M for Murdoch: News Corporation and the Corruption of Britain* (London: Penguin Books, 2013).

26. K. McCoy, "HSBC Will Pay $1.9 Billion for Money Laundering," *USA Today* (December 11, 2012), www.usatoday.com/story/money/business/2012/12/11/hsbc-laundering-probe/1760351/.

27. J. Burke, "Bangladesh Factory Collapse Leaves Trail of Shattered Lives," *The Guardian* (June 6, 2013), www.theguar dian.com/world/2013/jun/06/bangladesh-factory-building-col lapse-community.

28. S. Berfield, "Dov Charney's Sleazy Struggle for Control of American Apparel," *Bloomberg Businessweek* (July 9, 2014), www.bloomberg.com/news/articles/2014-07-09/american-apparel-dov-charneys-sleazy-struggle-for-control.

29. D. Iraheta, "Petrobras' Billion-Dollar Scandal: Behind the Chaos in Brazil's Biggest Company," *The World Post* (February 6, 2015), www.huffingtonpost.com/2015/02/06/pet robras-scandal-brazil_n_6615994.html/.

30. D. Hakim, A. M. Kessler, and J. Ewing, "As Volkswagen Pushed to Be No. 1, Ambitions Fueled a Scandal," *The New York Times* (September 26, 2015), www.nytimes.com/2015/09/27/business/as-vw-pushed-to-be-no-1-ambitions-fueled-a-scandal.html.

31. R. E. Freeman, *Strategic Management: A Stakeholder Approach* (Boston, MA: Pitman, 1984).

32. A. A. Lado, N. G. Boyd, and S. C. Hanlon, "Competition, Cooperation, and the Search for Economic Rents: A Syncretic Model," *Academy of Management Review* 22 (1997): 110–41; T. Markussen, E. Reuben, and J.-R. Tyran, "Competition, Cooperation and Collective Choice," *The Economic Journal* 124 (2014): F163–F195.

33. G. Stalk, "Curveball Strategies to Fool the Competition," *Harvard Business Review* 84 (2006): 114–22; G. Stalk and R. Lachenauer, "Hardball: Five Killer Strategies for Trouncing the Competition," *Harvard Business Review* (April 2004): 62–71.

34. T. Donaldson and T. W. Dunfee, "Toward a Unified Conception of Business Ethics: Integrative Social Contracts Theory," *Academy of Management Review* 19 (1994): 252–84; T. Donaldson and T. W. Dunfee, "Integrative Social Contracts Theory: A Communitarian Conception of Economic Ethics," *Economics and Philosophy* 11, no. 1 (1995): 85–112; T. Donaldson and T. W. Dunfee, *Ties That Bind: A Social Contracts Approach to Business Ethics* (Boston, MA: Harvard Business School Press, 1999); L. Sacconi, "A Social Contract Account for CSR as an Extended Model of Corporate Governance (I): Rational Bargaining and Justification," *Journal of Business Ethics* 68, no. 3 (2006): 259–81; L. Sacconi, "A Social Contract Account for CSR as an Extended Model of Corporate Governance (II): Compliance, Reputation and Reciprocity," *Journal of Business Ethics* 75, no. 1 (2007): 77–96.

35. Thomas Aquinas, *Summa theologica*, in *Basic Writings of Saint Thomas Aquinas*, ed. A. C. Pegis (New York: Random House, 1945); Aristotle, *Nicomachean Ethics*, trans. M. Ostwald (New York: Macmillan, 1962); E. Hamilton and H. Cairns (eds.), *The Collected Dialogues of Plato, Including the Letters* (Princeton University Press, 1961); Immanuel Kant, *Critique of Practical Reason and Other Writings in Moral Philosophy*, trans. L. W. Beck (University of Chicago Press, 1949); Immanuel Kant, *Foundations of the Metaphysics of Morals*, trans. L. W. Beck (New York: Library of Liberal Arts, 1959); John Stuart Mill, *Utilitarianism* (Indianapolis, IN: Hackett, 2001); G. E. Moore, *Principia Ethica* (Cambridge University Press, 1903); W. D. Ross, *The Right and the Good* (Oxford: Clarendon Press, 1930); Henry Sidgwick, *The Methods of Ethics*, 6th ed. (London and New York: Macmillan, 1901); Benedict de Spinoza, *Ethics*, ed. G. H. R. Parkinson (Oxford University Press, 2000).

36. John Rawls, *A Theory of Justice*, rev. ed. (Cambridge, MA: Harvard University Press, 1999): John Rawls, *Political Liberalism* (New York: Columbia University Press, 1993).

37. E. Diener, L. Tay, and S. Oishi, "Rising Income and the Subjective Well-Being of Nations," *Journal of Personality and Social Psychology* 104 (2013): 267–76 (p. 269); D. W. Sacks, B. Stevenson, and J. Wolfers, "The New Stylized Facts about Income and Subjective Well-Being," *Emotion* 12 (2012): 1181–87 (p. 1182).

38. D. M. Hausman, "Philosophy of Economics," in E. N. Zalta (ed.), *The Stanford Encyclopedia of Philosophy*, Winter 2013 edition, http://plato.stanford.edu/archives/win2013/entries/economics/.

39. P. Deane, *The Evolution of Economic Ideas* (Cambridge University Press, 1978).

40. W. Jevons, *The Theory of Political Economy* (London: Macmillan, 1871).

41. P. Schlag, "Rules and Standards," *UCLA Law Review* 33 (1985): 379–430.

42. M. Rosen, *Dignity* (Cambridge, MA: Harvard University Press, 2012), pp. 9, 70.

43. G. Kateb, *Human Dignity* (Cambridge, MA: The Belknap Press of Harvard University Press, 2011); M. P. Lagon and A. C. Arend, "Introduction: Human Dignity in a Neomedieval World," in *Human Dignity and the Future of Global Institutions*, ed. Lagon and Arend (Washington, DC: Georgetown University Press), pp. 1–22; Rosen, *Dignity*; J. Waldron, *Dignity, Rank, & Rights* (Oxford University Press, 2012).

44. Kant, *Foundations of the Metaphysics of Morals*, p. 54.

45. A. Gordon-Reed, *The Hemingses of Monticello* (New York: Norton and Company, 2008).

46. R. E. Freeman, "The Politics of Stakeholder Theory: Some Future Directions," *Business Ethics Quarterly* 4 (1994): 409–21.

47. Freeman, *Strategic Management*, p. 46.

48. R. Phillips, "Stakeholder Legitimacy," *Business Ethics Quarterly* 13 (2003): 25–41.

49. E. Jacques, "The Development of Intellectual Capability: A Discussion of Stratified Systems Theory," *Journal of Applied Behavioral Science* 22 (1986): 361–83.

50. J. Elkington, *Cannibals with Forks: The Triple Bottom Line of the 21st Century Business* (Gabriola Island, British Columbia: New Society Publishers, 1998), p. 55.

51. L. P. Tost, K. A. Wade-Benzoni, and H. H. Johnson, "Noblesse Oblige Emerges (with Time): Power Enhances Intergenerational Beneficence," *Organizational Behavior and Human Decision Processes* 128 (2015): 61–73; K. A. Wade-Benzoni, "A Golden Rule over Time: Reciprocity in Intergenerational Allocation Decisions," *Academy of Management Journal* 45 (2002): 1011–28; K. A. Wade-Benzoni, M. Hernandez, V. Medvec, and D. Messick, "In Fairness to Future Generations: The Role of Egocentrism, Uncertainty, Power, and Stewardship in Judgments of Intergenerational Allocations," *Journal of Experimental*

Social Psychology 44 (2008): 233–45; K. A. Wade-Benzoni, H. Sondak, and D. Galinsky, "Leaving a Legacy: Intergenerational Allocations of Benefits and Burdens," *Business Ethics Quarterly* 20 (2010): 7–34.

52. H. A. Simon, *Administrative Behavior*, 4th ed. (New York: Free Press, 1997).

53. J. M. Conley and C. A. Williams, "Engage, Embed, and Embellish Theory versus Practice in the Corporate Social Responsibly Movement," *Journal of Corporation Law* 31 (2005): 1–38; K. Annan, "The 'Unparalleled Nightmare' of AIDS." Speech to the US Chamber of Commerce, June 1, 2001, www.un.org/press/en/2001/sgsm7827.doc.htm.

LEGAL PERSPECTIVES

Supreme Court of New Jersey, *A. P. Smith Manufacturing Co. v. Barlow* (1953)

On July 24, 1951, the board of trustees of the A. P. Smith Manufacturing Company located in East Orange and Bloomfield New Jersey authorized a donation of $1,500 to Princeton University as a way of participating in Princeton's 1951 Annual Giving Campaign. In the past A. P. Smith had given funds to Upsala College and Newark University (now part of Rutgers University). In response to some stockholder complaints that such charitable donations were a misuse of corporate funds that ultimately belong to the shareholders, A. P. Smith sought a legal opinion and went to the Chancery Division where the donation was upheld. That decision was appealed directly to the New Jersey Supreme Court because of the "public importance" of the issue.

In a unanimous opinion the decision of the Chancery Division was upheld. A. P. Smith president, Hubert O'Brien, had argued that such donations were sound investments and "that the public expects corporations to aid philanthropic and benevolent institutions." Moreover O'Brien argued that such donations created goodwill and that A. P. Smith received liberally educated and well-trained workers as a result. O'Brien's position was supported by the chairman of the board of Standard Oil Corporation of New Jersey, Frank W. Abrams, and the chairman of the board of the United States Steel Corporation, Irving S. Olds. In his testimony, Mr. Olds said, "Capitalism and free enterprise owe their survival in not small degree to the existence of our private independent universities" and that if American business does not aid in their maintenance it is not "properly protecting the long-range interest of its stockholders, its employees, and its customers."

In accepting these arguments, the ruling of the court said the following about the donation to Princeton University: "There is no suggestion that it was made indiscriminately or to a pet charity of the corporate directors in furtherance of personal rather than corporate ends. On the contrary, it was made to a preeminent institution of higher learning, was modest in amount and . . . was voluntarily made in the reasonable belief that it would aid the public welfare and advance the interests of the plaintiff as a private corporation and as a part of the community in which it operates."

United States Supreme Court, *Citizens United v. Federal Election Commission* (2010)

Citizens United is a non-profit corporation that receives most of its funding from individual donations. In 2008 it wanted to have a critical documentary *Hillary: The Movie* (regarding US Senator and presidential candidate Hillary Clinton) made available on a video on demand television channel but feared that in so doing it would run afoul of the Bipartisan Campaign Reform Act (BCRA) of 2002 (popularly known as the McCain–Feingold Act) that prohibits any "electioneering communication" regarding a candidate for federal election within 30 days of the primary or 60 days of the general election. The majority in this 5 to 4 decision argued that Section 441b of the BCRA was a ban on constitutionally protected free speech because prohibiting independent corporate expenditures amounted to a ban on speech. (BCRA did permit the establishment of Political Action Committees (PACs) by a corporate entity, but not expenditures by the corporate entity itself.) Both the majority and the minority opinions agree that in a democracy political speech is particularly in need of protection and a high standard prevails with any attempt to limit it. The majority argue that corporate entities have free speech rights and cite numerous precedents to establish that legal point. However, one key Supreme Court decision, *Austin v. Michigan Chamber of Commerce* (1990), upheld a free speech restriction on the grounds of a pressing government interest in preventing "the corrosive and distorting effects of immense aggregations of wealth that are accumulated with the help of the corporate form." In rejecting the precedent of

Austin, the majority rejected the anti-distortion rationale on the following grounds: (1) *Austin* illegitimately allows the government to suppress speech merely because "the speaker is an association that has taken on the corporate form"; (2) *Buckley v. Valeo* (1976) established that the government does not have an interest "in equalizing the relative ability of individuals and groups to influence the outcomes of elections"; and (3) the fact that BCRA allows an exception for media companies is an admission of the invalidity of the anti-distortion argument. Thus, the majority concluded *Austin* should be overruled.

The four dissenting justices insist that there is settled law allowing a distinction between an individual and a corporate entity with respect to free speech rights. In defending the *Austin* precedent, Justice Stevens focused on the legitimacy of preventing "unfair influence" by corporate entities on the election process. As Justice Stevens said, "The legal structure of corporations allows them to amass and deploy financial resources on a scale few natural persons can match." There is a danger that the public will come to see the election process as dominated by corporations. The restrictions of the BCRA are necessary to "safeguard the integrity, the competitiveness and democratic responsiveness of the electoral process." Thus, the minority argue that *Austin* and BCRA should have been upheld.

United States Supreme Court, *Burwell v. Hobby Lobby Stores Inc., et al.* (2014)

Can a closely held corporation such as Hobby Lobby Stores or Conestoga Wood Specialties Corporation be required to pay for health insurance that covers "preventive care and screenings" for women, including birth control for the prevention of pregnancy, without "any cost sharing requirements" when providing that insurance is contrary to the sincerely held religious beliefs of the corporation's owners? The Supreme Court held in a 5 to 4 decision that regulations that force the provision of such products violate the Religious Freedom Restoration Act (RFRA) of 1993. The only regulation that could pass muster occurs when that regulation "constitutes the least restrictive means of serving a compelling government interest." In its decision the Court reasoned that Hobby Lobby Stores and Conestoga are "persons" entitled to the same religious freedom as actual human beings. The Court ruled that the requirement of the Affordable Care Act (ACA) that requires insurance to cover a large number of birth control methods does not meet religious freedom requirements of the RFRA. Since four of the birth control methods prevented a fertilized egg from developing any further and thus were abortifacients, such birth control methods violated the sincerely held religious beliefs of those opposed to abortion. The heavy burden rises because either the owners of the business must provide the insurance or face substantial financial penalties. The Court then argued that the ACA requirement that such insurance be mandated fails to meet the "least restrictive means" test because there are many other available ways of meeting the need for insurance coverage of such birth control methods, such as Congressional or Department Health and Human Services (HHS) provision of low cost birth control methods. Indeed HHS has already made accommodations to meet the objections of not for profits that have religious objections to the insurance mandate.

Writing on behalf of the minority in dissent, Justice Ruth Ginsburg first contended that there is no case law that gives freedom of religious expression rights to corporations. In this case the corporation should not be a considered a person. Nor should it be regarded as the type of organization provided special exemption from the preventive care requirement, namely religious organizations with shared beliefs. "Religious organizations exist to foster the interests of persons subscribing to the same religious faith. Not so of for-profit corporations. Workers who sustain the operations of those corporations commonly are not drawn from one religious community. Indeed, by law, no religion-based criterion can restrict the work force of for-profit corporations." Justice Ginsburg also pointed out that the majority decision opens the door for a corporation to claim an exemption from provisions of any law (except tax law) on grounds that the law violates a strongly held religious conviction of the owners. Moreover, this exemption is allowed regardless of the impact of such exemption on women who do not share the religious beliefs of those entitled to the exemption. The majority argued that a less restrictive alternative is to have the government pay for the preventive care and limit their decision to the four types of contraception under review. However, the minority decision argued that this is unreasonable given the possible scope of the majority decision. "Would the exemption the Court holds RFRA demands for employers with religiously grounded objections to the use of certain contraceptives extend to employers with religiously grounded objections to blood transfusions (Jehovah's Witnesses); antidepressants (Scientologists); medications derived from pigs, including anesthesia, intravenous fluids, and pills coated with gelatin (certain Muslims, Jews, and Hindus); and vaccinations (Christian Scientists, among others)?"

Johnson & Johnson: Our Credo

We believe our first responsibility is to the doctors, nurses and patients, to mothers and fathers and all others who use our products and services.

In meeting their needs everything we do must be of high quality.

We must constantly strive to reduce our costs in order to maintain reasonable prices.

Customers' orders must be serviced promptly and accurately.

Our suppliers and distributors must have an opportunity to make a fair profit.

We are responsible to our employees, the men and women who work with us throughout the world.

Everyone must be considered as an individual.

We must respect their dignity and recognize their merit.

They must have a sense of security in their jobs.

Compensation must be fair and adequate, and working conditions clean, orderly and safe.

We must be mindful of ways to help our employees fulfill their family responsibilities.

Employees must feel free to make suggestions and complaints.

There must be equal opportunity for employment, development and advancement for those qualified.

We must provide competent management, and their actions must be just and ethical.

We are responsible to the communities in which we live and work and to the world community as well.

We must be good citizens – support good works and charities and bear our fair share of taxes.

We must encourage civic improvements and better health and education.

We must maintain in good order the property we are privileged to use, protecting the environment and natural resources.

Our final responsibility is to our stockholders.

Business must make a sound profit.

We must experiment with new ideas.

Research must be carried on, innovative programs developed and mistakes paid for.

New equipment must be purchased, new facilities provided and new products launched.

Reserves must be created to provide for adverse times.

When we operate according to these principles, the stockholders should realize a fair return.

Courtesy of Johnson & Johnson.

Republic of India, The Companies Act of 2013

The India Companies Act of 2013, Chapter IX, Section 135, establishes a legal Corporate Social Responsibility (CSR) mandate for large corporations (those with annual revenue of 10 billion rupees or more). The Act makes CSR a matter of corporate governance including planning, monitoring, and reporting CSR activities. It requires that companies operating in India commit at least 2 percent of the average net profits of the preceding three years to spending on CSR or explain why they did not. In fact, the underlying premise of the CSR legislation is comply or explain. The CSR mandate applies to both domestic and foreign companies that meet the financial criteria for coverage under the Act. Companies that meet these criteria must have a board constituted CSR committee with the following responsibilities: formulate and recommend a CSR policy, recommend the amount to be spent to fulfill the goals of the policy, and monitor the implementation of the policy. Ultimately it is the responsibility to ensure that the company's CSR responsibilities are met. The Act also sets out some criteria that a CSR policy must meet. These include a list of the CSR programs or projects that a company plans to take, specify the modalities in the execution of such programs or projects, provide implementation schedules, and provide a monitoring process. The Act also has a disclosure requirement that specifies aspects of the company's CSR committee, its CSR policies and programs, and relevant financial information relating to CSR. A CSR program or project must be done in India if it is to meet the requirements of the Act. The target audience of CSR programs should be the poor and the vulnerable, but projects aimed at the general population such as consumer awareness are also acceptable.

CASES

Case 1: The 5,000 Percent Price Hike: Turing Pharmaceuticals' Acquisition of Daraprim

ROXANNE ROSS AND DENIS G. ARNOLD

There was a point in time when a patient in need of the drug Pyrimethamine (Daraprim) may have paid over 50 times more than a person who had purchased the drug one day earlier. Overnight Daraprim's price rose from $13.50 a pill to $750. The change amounted to a 5,000 percent increase. The $750 price tag bought 25 mg of the therapeutic ingredient. By weight, Daraprim was 700 times more valuable than gold and half as valuable as diamonds. An adult using the medication may require two to three pills per day for several weeks or months. The total number of pills required to treat a patient could easily be 100, entailing a cost of $75,000.

Only about 2,000 patients need Daraprim annually in the United States. Daraprim treats infections from the parasite toxoplasmosis. Many healthy individuals may unknowingly carry the parasite as it does not present symptoms to those with healthy immune systems. An estimated 20 million Americans have toxoplasmosis. Yet, those with weakened immune systems, or immunodeficiency, such as HIV-positive patients, cancer patients undergoing chemotherapy, and infants, cannot tolerate the parasite and must take Daraprim to ward off damaging effects such as brain infections and blindness.

The drug was discovered in 1952 by Gertrude Elion while working at GlaxoSmithKline. In 2009 GlaxoSmithKline charged $1 per pill before selling the rights to Daraprim to CorePharma in 2010. CorePharma increased the price to $13.50 a pill. While $13.50 was a significant price increase, once Turing Pharmaceuticals acquired Daraprim, CEO Martin Shkreli promptly implemented a 5,000 percent price hike. Outside of the United States, Daraprim still costs $1 to $2 per pill. Due to the extraordinary price increase, Shkreli and Turing Pharmaceuticals became the focus of intense public criticism. The BBC dubbed Shkreli the most hated man in America. The Infectious Diseases Society of America and the HIV Medicine Association wrote to Turing Pharmaceuticals and described the price hike as "unjustifiable for the medically vulnerable patient population" and "unsustainable for the healthcare system." Social media became ablaze with outrage directed at Shkreli and the firm.

Critics claimed that Shkreli intentionally searched for and targeted drugs where it was easy to exploit seriously ill patients. Daraprim made a prime candidate for two reasons. First, there is limited demand for the drug – around 9,000 prescriptions a year in the United States. This makes it unattractive to generic drug manufacturers whose revenue model is typically based on volume. Second, Daraprim is an essential drug. Patients with toxoplasmosis and immunodeficiency may lose vision or die without access to the drug.

Shkreli defended Daraprim's price increase by comparing the drug with cancer treatments. "These days, in modern pharmaceuticals, cancer drugs can cost $100,000 or more, rare disease drugs can cost half a million dollars. Daraprim is still underpriced, relative to its peers." Dr. Amir Attaran, health law and policy professor at the University of Ottawa, disagrees that Daraprim and cancer treatments are comparable. "They're not peers. [Shkreli] could have said, 'A bar of gold cost $1 million, so Daraprim is underpriced.' He's comparing fish and fowl." There are several important differences between cancer treatments and Daraprim. Toxoplasmosis, unlike cancer or other conditions with expensive treatments, was effectively treated with Daraprim according to health professionals. There was no need to increase the price to pay for new research into new innovations as with cancer treatments. Daraprim has also been around for many decades. Cancer treatments, on the other hand, are much newer and have not yet paid off research and development costs. Some experts argue Daraprim is more properly compared to other, older drugs such as ibuprofen or penicillin.

Since the Daraprim scandal, Shkreli stepped down as CEO of Turing for reasons unrelated to Daraprim. He was charged and subsequently convicted of securities fraud for deceiving investors in a hedge fund that he managed. After Shkreli left Turing, public outrage led to a price cut in the cost of Daraprim to $375 a pill. The figure is still considered vastly overpriced by Turing's critics. The lower price is still 27 times higher than the price of $13.50 or a 2,500% price hike. Treatment would still cost an individual patient around $37,500.

The Daraprim price hike is a well-publicized example of a larger trend in the pharmaceutical industry. The prices of older, niche drugs that have long paid off initial research and development costs are rising. Cycloserine treats drug-resistant tuberculosis and its price was recently increased by 2,000 percent. Isuprel, used for heart conditions, rose by 525 percent. The antibiotic doxycycline rose 9,100 percent from $20 a bottle to $1,849. All of these drugs, like Daraprim, were discovered over 50 years ago. Once research and development is paid off, as is the case with these older drugs, the cost to provide pharmaceuticals is much lower as manufacturing drugs is magnitudes cheaper than creating them. The low cost of manufacturing is why long-established Daraprim was sold for $1 per pill as recently as 2009. Healthcare experts believe that Turing and other firms scoured the pharmaceutical market with the intention of finding drugs where they could force patients and insurers to pay nearly whatever price they demanded given the dire and often fatal consequences for patients if they do not take the drugs.

Shkreli, like many others who defend rising drug prices, explained the increases by suggesting the money earned was going back into research and development. With Daraprim, the explanation was particularly unfounded according to medical professionals because of the efficacy of the drug (i.e., there is no need to develop a better drug for its purpose). However, research and development costs alone don't explain rising drug prices. Americans pay much higher prices than consumers in other developed countries, on average 2.5 times higher. The premium paid by Americans is often said to be for research and development costs. Yet, one study found that just 66 percent of the $116 billion extra paid for drugs by American consumers was used for research and development. In other words, in one year American healthcare consumers paid $40 billion more to pharmaceutical companies for the same drugs as citizens in other industrialized nations and the money was used for corporate expenses other than drug research and development. Such expenses might include executive compensation, billion dollar drug marketing campaigns, political donations, lobbying, or higher shareholder returns. The United States spends on average $9,000 per person on healthcare while the average for countries in the Organisation for Economic Co-operation and Development (OECD) is $3,600. Despite these disproportionate expenditures, the United States continues to perform worse than OECD averages on key health indicators such as life expectancy, infant mortality, heart attacks, and quality of care when compared to peer countries.

Discussion Questions

1. In capitalist economies, profit is a primary purpose of business. Some would argue that it is the *only* purpose of business. Shouldn't companies be praised for making as much money as possible? Wasn't CEO Martin Shkreli simply maximizing profit for Turing Pharmaceuticals? Shouldn't he be praised, rather than condemned, for his actions at Turing? Why, or why not? Explain.

2. What would Milton Friedman say about the pricing of Daraprim? Why? Explain. Do you agree with that position? Why, or why not? Explain.

3. Are essential pharmaceuticals different from other types of products (e.g., clothing, cars, or jewelry) such that their pricing should take into account considerations other than maximal profit? Why, or why not? Explain.

4. Why do you think Americans pay more for drugs than the citizens of other industrialized nations? Explain.

This case is based on the following sources: J. LaMattina, "Here's a Way for Pharma to Prevent Outrageous Generic Price Increases – and Help Its Reputation," *Forbes* (September 21, 2015). Retrieved July 30, 2017 from www.forbes.com/sites/johnlamattina/2015/09/21/heres-a-way-for-pharma-to-prevent-outrageous-generic-price-increases-and-help-its-reputation/#477451937f87.

H. Long, "What Happened to AIDS Drug That Spiked 5,000%?" *CNN Money* (August 25, 2016). Retrieved July 25, 2017 from http://money.cnn.com/2016/08/25/news/economy/daraprim-aids-drug-high-price/index.html.

L. Qiu, "Fact-Checking Martin Shkreli's Claim That Daraprim Is 'Underpriced, Relative to Its Peers,'" *PunditFact* (September 24, 2015). Retrieved July 25, 2017 from www.politifact.com/punditfact/statements/2015/sep/24/martin-shkreli/fact-checking-martin-shkrelis-claim-daraprim-under/.

Selected charts on the long-term fiscal challenges of the United States (June 2017). Retrieved from www.pgpf.org/sites/default/files/PGPF-Chart-Pack.pdf. N. Yu , Z. Helms, and P. Bach, "R&D Costs for Pharmaceutical Companies Do Not Explain Elevated US Drug Prices" (March 7, 2017). Retrieved July 25, 2017 from http://healthaffairs.org/blog/2017/03/07/rd-costs-for-pharmaceutical-companies-do-not-explain-elevated-us-drug-prices/.

Case 2: The NYSEG Corporate Responsibility Program

TOM L. BEAUCHAMP AND KELLEY MACDOUGALL

We are responsible to the communities in which we live and work and to the world community as well. We must be good citizens and support good works and charities ... We must encourage civic improvements and better health and education.[1]

Many large corporations operate consumer responsibility or community responsibility programs, which aim to return something to the consumer or to the community in which the company does business. The motivation is at least twofold: these programs create a positive image of the company, and they make life much better for various unlucky members of the community. However, these programs are not good for corporate profits. They operate at a net loss and are, in effect, a form of corporate philanthropy.

New York State Electric and Gas Corporation (NYSEG) has created a program to fulfill what its officers consider to be the company's social responsibility to its public, in particular its consumers. When this program started two decades ago, NYSEG was a New York Stock Exchange-traded public utility with approximately 60,000 shareholders. Recently, NYSEG became a subsidiary of the Energy East Corp., a superregional energy services and delivery company with more than 5,800 employees. Energy East Corp. serves 1.4 million electricity customers and 600,000 natural gas customers in the northeastern United States. It is traded on the New York Stock Exchange.

In general, eastern public utilities have not enjoyed strong returns to shareholders in recent years because of relatively mild winters, increased plant costs, and a lower electric market price. However, Energy East has been able to increase earnings per share and dividends per share every year. Operating revenues have also gone up significantly. Energy East has been aggressively attempting to increase profitability by selling power plants and focusing on energy delivery. It has expanded its services rapidly and intends to continue the expansion. NYSEG itself continues to deliver electricity to more than 800,000 customers and

natural gas to around 250,000 customers across more than 40 percent of upstate New York.

NYSEG's corporate responsibility program has not, as yet, been altered by the change to Energy East Corporation or by the relatively weak financial returns for utilities in recent years. NYSEG designed the program – and continues it today – to aid customers who are unable to pay their utility bills. The program does more than simply help customers pay their bills. It locates and attempts to remedy the root causes of bill nonpayment, which almost invariably involve financial distress. However, NYSEG attempts to reach beyond financial exigency. It seeks to rescue people in the community who are in unfortunate circumstances because of industrial injury, the ill health of a spouse or child, drug dependency, and the like. The company offers its assistance whether or not it is reasonable to suppose that the assistance provided will restore a paying customer.

To implement this plan, NYSEG has created a system of consumer advocates – primarily social workers trained to deal with customers and their problems. Since the program's 1978 inception, NYSEG has maintained a staff of several consumer representatives. Each of them handles approximately 100 cases a month, over half of which result in some form of financial assistance. The remaining cases are referred to other organizations for assistance.

The process works as follows: When the company's credit department believes that a special investigation should be made into a customer's situation, the employee refers the case to the consumer advocate. Referrals also sometimes come from human service agencies and from customers directly. Examples of appropriate referrals include unemployed household heads; paying customers who suffer serious injury, lengthy illness, or death of a wage-earner; and low-income senior citizens or those on fixed incomes who cannot deal with rising costs of living. To qualify for assistance, NYSEG requires only that the customers suffer from hardships that they are willing to work to resolve.

Consumer advocates are concerned with preventing the shutoff of service to these customers and to restore them to

This case was prepared by Tom L. Beauchamp and Kelley MacDougall, and revised by John Cuddihy and Jeff Greene. Not to be duplicated without permission of the holder of the copyright, © 1991, 1996, 2003 Tom L. Beauchamp. This case is indebted to Cathy Hughto-Delzer, NYSEG Manager, Consumer Affairs.

a condition of financial health. They employ an assortment of resources to put customers back on their feet, including programs offered by the New York State Department of Social Services and the federal Home Energy Assistance Program (HEAP), which awards annual grants of varying amounts to qualified families. In addition, the consumer advocates provide financial counseling and help customers with their medical bills and educational planning. They arrange for assistance from churches and social services, provide food stamps, and help coordinate Veterans Administration benefits.

NYSEG also created a direct financial-grants program called Project Share, which is funded by a foundation created by NYSEG and by direct contributions from NYSEG employees, retirees, and customers. The latter can make charitable donations through their bills. They are asked voluntarily to add one, two, or five extra dollars to their bill each month. This special fuel fund is intended to help customers pay for energy emergencies, repairs to heating equipment, home weatherization, and water heater replacements. Grants of up to $200 are available to households in which someone is over 60 years old, has a disability, or has a serious medical condition – and with insufficient means of paying basic bills. The special fund of money created is overseen by the American Red Cross, which receives applications, determines eligibility, and distributes the collected funds. By 2002, over $4 million has been distributed to more than 20,000 customers since Project Share began in 1982.[2]

The rationale or justification for this corporate responsibility program is rooted in the history of public utilities and rising energy costs in North America. Public utilities originally provided a relatively inexpensive product. NYSEG and the entire industry considered its public responsibility limited to the functions of providing energy at the lowest possible cost and returning dividends to investors. NYSEG did not concern itself with its customers' financial troubles. The customer or the social welfare system handled all problems of unpaid bills, which was considered strictly a matter of business.

However, the skyrocketing energy costs in the 1970s changed customer resources and NYSEG's perspective. The energy crisis caused many long-term customers to encounter difficulty in paying their bills, and the likelihood of power shutoffs increased as a result. NYSEG accepted the responsibility to assist its valued customers by creating the Consumer Advocate system. NYSEG believes that its contribution is especially important now because recent reductions in federal assistance programs have shifted the burden of addressing these problems to the private sector.

The costs of NYSEG's involvement in the program are paid for from company revenues, which in principle (and in fact) entails that returns to shareholders are lowered. However, these costs are regarded by company officers as low. The program has few costs beyond office space and the consumer advocates' salaries and benefits, which total half a million dollars. All expenses are treated as operating expenses. To augment Project Share's financial support, NYSEG shareholders have voted the program an annual, need-based grant. In the past, these shareholder gifts have ranged from $40,000 to $100,000 annually. NYSEG shareholders also fund related personnel and printing costs. The company itself has also supported Project Share through direct contributions to the Red Cross.

The company views some of the money expended for the corporate responsibility program as recovered funds because of the customers retained and the bills paid through the program. NYSEG officials assume that these charges would, under normal circumstances, have remained unpaid and would eventually have been written off as losses. NYSEG's bad-debt level is 20 percent lower than that of the average US utility company. The company believes that its corporate responsibility policy is *both* altruistic *and* good business, despite the program's maintenance costs. Though these costs well exceed recovered revenue, the service builds excellent customer relations. In other words, staffing and otherwise paying for these programs is a net financial loss for the company and its shareholders – what many businesses would call a "losing proposition" – but managers and shareholders do not (in public) complain about these unnecessary expenses, and most seem to feel good about the extra services the company provides to its customers.

It is unknown what view Energy East Corp. will ultimately take of this program, which it acquired from prior management at NYSEG. The program could be disbanded, cut back, or enlarged to serve all of Energy East's several utility services.

Notes

1. "The Johnson and Johnson Way" (from the Johnson and Johnson Company credo).
2. www.nyseg.com/nysegweb/main.nsf/doc/share and www.nyseg.com/nysegweb/faqs.nsf/pwrprtnr (posted January 2003).

Discussion Questions

1. Imagine that you are a member of a management team at Energy East that has been assigned the task of making a recommendation to executives regarding the NYSEG corporate responsibility program. Your options are to cut it, maintain it as is, or expand the program to all of Energy East. What is your recommendation? Why? Explain.

2. Would Milton Friedman and R. Edward Freeman believe that Project Share is consistent with NYSEG's fiduciary responsibility to its shareholders? Why, or why not? Explain.

3. Would John Boatright believe that Project Share is consistent with NYSEG's fiduciary responsibility to its shareholders? Why, or why not? Explain.

Case 3: H. B. Fuller in Honduras: Street Children and Substance Abuse
NORMAN E. BOWIE AND STEFANIE LENWAY

Kativo Chemical Industries, a wholly owned foreign subsidiary of H. B. Fuller, sells a solvent-based adhesive (glue) in several countries in Latin America. The brand name of the glue is Resistol. It came to H. B. Fuller's attention that large numbers of street children in the Central American country of Honduras were sniffing glue and that Resistol was among the glues being abused. Indeed all these children who sniff glue are being referred to as *Resistoleros*.

Resistol has a number of industrial uses, although one of its primary uses is in small shoe repair shops. The glue has properties that are not possible to attain with a water-based formula. These properties include rapid set, strong adhesion, and water resistance. Resistol is similar to airplane glue.

Widespread inhalant abuse among street children in Honduras can be attributed to the depth of poverty there. Honduras is one of the poorest countries in Latin America. The unemployment rate is high. Infant and child mortality rates are high, life expectancy for adults is 64 years, and the adult literacy rate is estimated to be about 60 percent. Its exports, bananas and coffee, are commodities that are subject to the vagaries of the weather and the volatility of commodity markets. Government deficits caused in part by mismanagement and corruption have prevented desirable spending on public services.

Migrants to the urban areas typically move first to cuarterias (rows) of connected rooms. The rooms are generally constructed of wood with dirt floors, and they are usually windowless. The average household contains about seven persons who live together in a single room. For those living in rooms facing an alley, the narrow way between buildings serves both as a sewage and waste disposal area and as a courtyard for as many as 150 persons.

That the name of a Fuller product should be identified with a social problem was a matter of great concern to the H. B. Fuller Company. H. B. Fuller was widely known as a socially responsible corporation. Among its achievements were an enlightened employee relations policy that included giving each employee a day off on his or her birthday and, on the tenth anniversary of employment, bonus vacation time and a substantial check so that employees could travel and see the world. H. B. Fuller contributes 5 percent of its pretax profits to charity and continually wins awards for its responsibility to the environment. A portion of its corporate mission statement reads as follows:

> H. B. Fuller Company is committed to its responsibilities, in order of priority, to its customers, employees and shareholders. H. B. Fuller will conduct business legally and ethically, support the activities of its employees in their communities, and be a responsible corporate citizen.

The issue of the abuse of glue by Honduran street children received attention in the Honduran press.

The man on the spot at Kativo was Vice-President Humberto Larach (Beto) who headed Kativo's North Adhesives Division. Beto had proved his courage and his business creativity when he was among 105 taken hostage in the Chamber of Commerce building in downtown San Pedro Sula by Honduran guerrillas from the Communist Popular Liberation Front. Despite firefights between the guerrillas and government troops, threats of

---

This case is based on a longer case with the same name authored by Norman E. Bowie and Stefanie Lenway. The full "H. B. Fuller in Honduras: Street Children and Substance Abuse" was the Case award winner in the Columbia University Graduate School of Business Ethics in Business Program.

execution, and being used as a human shield, Beto had convinced two fellow hostages to buy from Kativo rather than from a competitor. Not surprisingly, Beto had a reputation for emphasizing the importance of making the bottom line that was an important part of the Kativo corporate culture.

Initial responses to the problem were handled by officials at Kativo. These responses included requests to the press not to use "Resistolero" as a synonym for a street child glue sniffer and attempts to persuade the Honduran legislature not to require the addition of oil of mustard to its glue. Beto had requested H. B. Fuller's US headquarters to look into the viability of oil of mustard as an additive to the glue. H. B. Fuller's corporate industrial hygiene staff found evidence that indicated that oil of mustard was a carcinogen and hence was potentially dangerous to employees and consumers. Kativo officials believed that glue sniffing was a social problem and that Kativo was limited in what it could do about the problem. The solution was education.

Initially officials at H. B. Fuller headquarters in St. Paul, Minnesota, were only dimly aware of the problem. While some of these officials assisted their Kativo subsidiary by providing information on the dangers of oil of mustard, the traditional policy of H. B. Fuller was to give great autonomy to foreign-owned subsidiaries.

However, Elmer Andersen, H. B. Fuller's chairman of the board, received a letter from a stockholder who pointedly asked how a company with its enlightened business philosophy could be responsible for selling a product that was causing harm to the children of Honduras. Three years later, Vice-President for Corporate Relations Dick Johnson received a call from a stockholder whose daughter was in the Peace Corps in Honduras. The stockholder's question was how can a company like H. B. Fuller claim to have a social conscience and continue to sell Resistol which is "literally burning out the brains" of children in Latin America. Johnson knew that headquarters should become actively involved in addressing the problem. But given the nature of the problem and H. B. Fuller's policy of local responsibility, what should headquarters do?

Discussion Questions

1. To what extent can Honduran street children who obtain an H. B. Fuller product illegitimately be considered stakeholders? If they are stakeholders, how can their interests be represented? Explain.
2. What obligations does a company have to solve social problems? Explain.
3. If there is a corporate responsibility to address the issue, does the responsibility for solving this problem rest with the local subsidiary, Kativo, or with H. B. Fuller headquarters? Explain.
4. To what extent should officials at H. B. Fuller headquarters be concerned about potential criticisms that they are meddling in a problem where they don't understand the culture? Explain.

Case 4: Merck and River Blindness

DENIS G. ARNOLD

Merck & Co., Inc. is one of the world's largest pharmaceutical products and services companies. Headquartered in Whitehouse Station, New Jersey, Merck has over 90,000 employees and sells products and services in approximately 150 countries. Merck has had annual revenues in the range of $40–45 billion each year over the last two decades, is consistently a member of both the Fortune 500 and the Global 500 list of the World's Largest Corporations, and is consistently on the Fortune 100 list of the Best Companies to Work For.

In the late 1970s Merck research scientists led by William Campbell discovered a potential cure for a severely debilitating human disease known as river blindness (onchocerciasis). The disease is caused by a parasite that enters the body through the bite of black flies that breed on the rivers of Africa and Latin America. The parasite causes severe itching, disfiguring skin infections, and, finally, total and permanent blindness. In order to demonstrate that it was safe and effective, the drug needed to undergo expensive clinical trials. Executives were concerned because they knew that those who would benefit from using it could not afford to pay for the drug, even if it was sold at cost. However, Merck research scientists argued that the drug was far too promising from a medical

---

This case was prepared by Denis G. Arnold. © 2017 Denis G. Arnold.

standpoint to abandon. Merck executives had to decide whether to spend millions of dollars developing a drug that they knew patients could not afford. Eventually executives relented, hoping that a third party would step forward to pay for the drug, and a seven-year clinical trial proved the drug both efficacious and safe. A single annual dose of Mectizan, the name Merck gave to the drug, kills the parasites inside the body as well as the flies that carry the parasite. Dr. Campbell was awarded the Nobel Prize in Medicine in 2015 for his work developing Mectizan.

Once Mectizan was approved for human use, Merck executives explored third-party payment options with the World Health Organization, the US Agency for International Development, and the US Department of State without success. Four US Senators went so far as to introduce legislation to provide US funding for the worldwide distribution of Mectizan. However, their efforts were unsuccessful, no legislation was passed, and no US government funding was made available. Finally, Merck executives decided to manufacture and distribute the drug for free.

Since 1987, Merck has manufactured and distributed the medicine at no charge. The company's decision was grounded in its core values:

1. Our business is preserving and improving human life.
2. We are committed to the highest standards of ethics and integrity.
3. We are dedicated to the highest level of scientific excellence and commit our research to improving human and animal health and the quality of life.
4. We expect profits, but only from work that satisfies customer needs and benefits humanity.
5. We recognize that the ability to excel – to most competitively meet society's and customers' needs – depends on the integrity, knowledge, imagination, skill, diversity, and teamwork of employees, and we value these qualities most highly.

George W. Merck, the company's president from 1925 to 1950, summarized these values when he wrote, "Medicine is for the people. It is not for the profits. The profits follow, and if we have remembered that, they have never failed to appear. The better we have remembered that, the larger they have been."

Today, the Merck Mectizan Donation Program includes partnerships with numerous non-governmental organizations, governmental organizations, private foundations, the World Health Organization, the World Bank, UNICEF, and the United Nations Development Programme. In 1998, Merck expanded the Mectizan Donation Program to include the prevention of elephantiasis (lymphatic filariasis) in African countries where the disease coexists with river blindness. In total, approximately 250 million people in 36 countries are now treated annually with Mectizan. Merck reports that it has no idea how much the entire program has cost, but estimates that each pill is worth $1.50. Merck reports that it has provided over 2 billion treatments since 1987.

Discussion Questions

1. Given the fact that Merck is spending corporate resources to manufacture and distribute Mectizan, is the Merck Mectizan Donation Program morally justifiable? Why, or why not? Explain.
2. Would Milton Friedman approve of the Merck Mectizan Donation Program? Why, or why not? Explain.
3. Should the fact that Merck's values are clearly stated in corporate publications that are widely available to investors make a difference to someone who accepts Friedman's position? Explain.
4. What theoretical arguments from this chapter best support the existence and continuation of the Mectizan Donation Program? Explain.
5. Should Merck's Mectizan Donation Program serve as a model for other pharmaceutical companies who are in a unique position to facilitate the eradication of other diseases in the developing nations? Why, or why not? Explain.

This case is based on the following sources: Erik Eckholm, "River Blindness: Conquering an Ancient Scourge," *The New York Times* (January 8, 1989).

David Pilling, "Public Private Health Deal Aims to End Elephantiasis," *Financial Times* (London) (January 21, 2000).

Karen Lowry Miller, "The Pill Machine," *Newsweek* (November 19, 2001).

"The Merck Mectizan Donation Program." Retrieved October 3, 2002 from www.merck.com/about/featured-stories/mectizan.html.

"Mectizan Donation Program." Retrieved October 3, 2002 from www.merck.com/about/cr/mectizan/.

"MERCK Annual Report 2001." Retrieved October 3, 2002 from www.annualreports.de/documents/Merck-ar2001en.pdf.

"About Merck: Mission Statement." Retrieved October 3, 2002 from www.merck.com/about/mission.html.

"The 2002 Fortune 500." Retrieved October 3, 2002 from https://archive.fortune.com/magazines/fortune/fortune_archive/2002/02/04/317486/index.htm.

"The 2002 Global 500." Retrieved October 3, 2002 from https://fortune.com/global500/2002/.

"Best Companies to Work for." Retrieved October 3, 2002 from https://fortune.com/best-companies/2019/search/.

Case 5: From Tension to Cooperative Dialogue: Holcim

WORLD BUSINESS COUNCIL FOR SUSTAINABLE DEVELOPMENT

Holcim is one of the world's largest suppliers of cement, as well as aggregates (gravel and sand), concrete, and construction-related services. The Holcim Group, which includes Union Cement of the Philippines, has majority and minority interests in more than 70 countries on all continents.

The company has a long history of constructive engagement, particularly with local communities in many countries. A productive way of addressing specific issues that emerge from stakeholders in areas close to its operations is through the community advisory panels (CAPs). With a broad cross-section of representative voices, CAPs can directly generate substantive input from the community as well as experts in specific technical fields.

Before Holcim invested in Union in 1988, Union's relationship with external stakeholders was based on limited or selective engagement, in some cases characterized by an adversarial relationship with local communities. However, it was recognized that this did not present a supportive environment in which to maintain its license to operate.

In one instance, a flood that devastated the area close to Union's Lugait plant in 1999 became a turning point in community relations for the company. Prior to this people in the local community knew of the company, but they did not know its people. In response to the flood, Union employees volunteered assistance with provisions of food and medicine, infrastructure repair, and emotional support for victims, and in so doing opened the door to improved relations.

A community advisory panel was then created, involving company management, unions, local community representatives, non-governmental organizations, government agencies, and local government units. Membership in this committee is both by invitation from the company and nomination from either local officials or an NGO.

The mandate of this committee is to assess and validate the plants' proposals for community activities, which are identified through local stakeholder engagement processes. Projects are then carried out in collaboration with partner organizations.

For example, the "Women's Livelihood Program" trains women in sewing and production of various handicrafts. The objective is to augment the family income and help provide for family needs. To date membership to the women's livelihood program has increased from less than 50 to more than 200 and a livelihood center was constructed for production and display. This program was established in partnership with the local government, the women's association, and the Department of Social Welfare and Services.

Since the formation of the CAP committee at the Lugait plant, the relationship with the community has blossomed. The company now regularly opens its doors to the community every Friday and Saturday so that local officials, NGOs, students, and community residents can visit the plant. Similar community groups are also being organized at the other plants of Union.

CAPs are also good for business. Zita Diez, Union's CSR coordinator and Communications Manager highlights that: "At the Lugait plant, security concerns are high due to the presence of rebel groups in the area. But if you are responsible and open to discussion, then your community can actually become your first line to defense. In fact our security guard numbers have not increased but on the contrary they have reduced to about 20 percent over the last 3 years – primarily because we have improved our relationship with the community and we know that they will help 'protect' us."

In addition to helping develop community projects, strong community relations have also helped the company introduce the use of alternative fuels and raw materials (AFR). Union has held specific consultations on the topic of AFR to inform local communities and key people. As a result the company has received overwhelming support. And this is not because the community understands specifically how the AFR works but because – as surveys have shown – they know and trust the company. As a result AFR permits were received quickly.

The shift in community relations for Union Cement has not only positively impacted the community but also the company's employees who now feel and understand that they are part of a bigger community. Engagement with different stakeholder groups has led to increased awareness about environmental responsibility and the overall role the company and its employees can play in the community.

Discussion Questions

1. What would Milton Friedman think of the CAPs? Why? Explain.
2. What would R. Edward Freeman think of the CAPs? Why? Explain.
3. What would Tom Donaldson and James Walsh think of the CAPs? Why? Explain.
4. What do you think of the CAPs? Explain.

Case 6: ITC's Vocational Training Program

WORLD BUSINESS COUNCIL FOR SUSTAINABLE DEVELOPMENT

Company Background

ITC is a leading Indian multi-business conglomerate, established in 1910. Its portfolio of businesses spans fast-moving consumer goods, hotels, paperboards and packaging, agribusiness, and information technology. The Company employs about 30,000 people in the country and its value chains provide livelihoods to around 6 million people, mainly amongst the poorest in rural India.

The Skills Gap: Providing Skills and Improving Livelihood Opportunities for Millions Living in Rural Areas

It is estimated that about 12 million people join the working age group in India every year. However, the formal economy is able to provide employment to only 2 million. It is a matter of concern that this growing population of unemployed youth has high aspirations but lacks the right skills to enter the job market. This is despite the fact that there is demand for more resources in the formal sector. It is imperative, therefore, to train such unemployed youth and provide them with relevant skills. A baseline survey, carried out by ITC in ten locations where it has large operations, revealed that out of a total number of 470,000 youth in the age group of 18 to 35 years, the majority did not possess skills relevant to the job market and were hence unemployed. Only around 145,000 youths were employed in the formal sector, with 10 percent being ITC employees (about 14,000). The remaining 320,000 youths were either unemployed or operated in the informal economy with jobs that did not provide any security. For ITC, empowering the youth with relevant skills is important in order to improve production and increase benefits. ITC supports a number of initiatives for providing vocational training to youth so as to

equip them with relevant skills and increase their employability in the market. ITC's training programs, however, have a larger purpose. It is the company's driving aspiration to empower rural communities by creating sustainable livelihood opportunities through various initiatives including vocational training, employment, and entrepreneurship. In almost every location where it operates, ITC sees itself among the foremost companies in terms of excellence in production and residential facilities. In such areas, the company sees virtually two different worlds coexisting – one is the world of ITC with its factories and residential areas, and the other is the surrounding areas where communities are confronted with various challenges, especially at the level of social infrastructure. In this context, one of the challenges faced by the company is the unemployed youth who have high aspirations but not the opportunity to secure jobs to fulfill those desires.

ITC's Solution: A Vocational Training Program for the Rural Youth

In December 2013, ITC developed a vocational training program for the communities which aims at training about 10,000 people every year. The program focuses on building relevant skills that the market demands and for which there are job opportunities. The objective is to impart the relevant job skills to job seekers and make them industry-ready and employable in the manufacturing or service sectors. The program is also part of the company's affirmative action plan that focuses on the Scheduled Castes and the Scheduled Tribes (SC/ST), which are considered to be among the most socially and economically marginalized in India. The program offers training in trades including tailoring, beautician, hospitality, automotive, electrical, construction, garments, computer skills, security skills, nursing, driving, retail, marketing, and technician. The duration of the courses ranges from one to three months depending on the trade. As the company requires a very large front line sales force, ITC also accords special focus on providing skills for the fast-moving consumer goods sector. ITC trains a large number of youth, far beyond what it can absorb within the company itself. Other companies also benefit from the availability of a trained and skilled resource base.

The residential training incurs a cost of approximately US$275 per student, depending on the trade. While a major part of this cost is borne by ITC, the program requires that every youth contributes 5–10 percent to the up-front fees, depending on the trade, to ensure that there is commitment to the purpose. In total, ITC spent about US$1.7 million in the first year to set up infrastructure and run the program in all regions. ITC has divided its operations into four zones: North, West, South, and East. In each zone, the company has identified a large organization specialized in providing vocational training. The key partners identified are Pratham Foundation in the West; Don Bosco Technology Institution in the East; LabourNet in the South; and Edulever in the North. The program is first launched in ITC's factory areas, within a radius of 20 km, and then expanded as it is scaled up. ITC's partner NGO conducts a Needs Assessment Survey with the organizations operating in and around the area. Awareness camps are then held for the youth in the 18–25 age bracket to provide them with details of the training, which may be residential or non-residential. The youth then opt for the trade they are interested in. However, they have to clear an aptitude test using assessment methods developed with the NGOs. Once the assessment is completed, a match-making exercise is carried out. Depending on the results and their background, the youth may be advised to change trades.

On the completion of the classroom training, depending on the trades the youth may be placed with various organizations for 11 apprenticeship for a couple of weeks. Once the course is over, the partner organization (NGO) organizes placement camps and invites all industries in the vicinity. The intent is to establish relationships with various industries in the region, so that the skills needs can be assessed and training provided in relevant trade.

The Result

Six months after the program was launched, ITC trained nearly 2,500 youth, one quarter of them being girls. This is considered encouraging as there was no surety as to whether parents would allow their daughters to work outside their hometown. ITC has been very successful in enabling services and job linkages, as 75 percent of people who were trained by ITC have entered the formal job market.

Challenges

Willingness to relocate for training – Anecdotal data reveal that in the more prosperous parts of India (West, South), the youth are not willing to move out of their hometowns, even if there is an appropriate job opportunity. As a consequence, ITC has to arrange to train these youth in their areas of origin. In other areas such as the East, the youth (including girls) are keen to move to the more prosperous states, which was a matter of surprise for ITC.

Raising awareness – When ITC launched the program in December 2013, it witnessed a significant drop-out after the first week of training. That was a major learning for ITC, as it realized that its awareness programs were not intensive enough. The company has therefore increased its program awareness drive from half a day to three to four days in every village. ITC also telephonically connects prospective candidates and their parents to people who have already attended the program and have secured jobs.

Trade orientation – Most of the youth prefer hospitality as a trade, as it is associated with higher status jobs. However, India requires skilled labor in the construction sector, which might be associated with difficult labor conditions. ITC puts in extra efforts to convince youth that sectors like automotive or construction offer good career opportunities.

Key Success Factor

Meeting the job market needs – As the training provided by ITC is in alignment with job market requirements, most of the trained youths secure jobs in the formal sector. In addition, the partners selected by the Company have a strong network of industries and businesses, which can be leveraged for placement services.

Discussion Questions

1. Who benefits from this program and how? Explain.
2. Does this program primarily benefit Indian society? ITC? Or both? Explain.
3. Would a shareholder primacy advocate, such as Milton Friedman, support or reject this program? Why? Explain.
4. What theoretical argument made in this chapter do you believe best supports the program? Explain.
5. How is India's Companies Act of 2013 relevant to this case? Explain.

6

Ethics and Information Technology

6.1 INTRODUCTION

There is little doubt that the computer processing unit (CPU) and the Internet were two of the most significant inventions of the twentieth century. Computers and smart devices, which run on CPUs, along with the World Wide Web, allow quick and easy access to information, social interaction, and a variety of consumer activities. They also enable business firms to store and transmit large quantities of information about many aspects of the behavior of the individuals who utilize the Internet. The ways in which business works with consumer information has been transformed by the utilization of petabytes of data. In this chapter, we focus our discussion on issues regarding information technology and privacy rights. Protecting privacy was a challenge before CPUs and the Internet came into widespread use; however, information technology has vastly complicated issues regarding privacy and its protection. Information technology has changed the scale of information gathering, the kind of information that can be gathered, the scale of information exchange, and perhaps most significantly, the ease of access to personal information. It is also used by some governments to monitor and suppress political speech and dissent.

CONSUMER PRIVACY

The first three articles in this chapter document the increasingly widespread dissemination and selling of our personal information via the Internet. This includes the personal histories, credit histories, financial account data, web browsing histories, and legal actions of individuals and their family members, all of which is sold in one form or another. In the United States, the problem is exacerbated by lax regulations regarding privacy. Many websites have "opt out" privacy policies that enable you to indicate that you do not want to receive ads from the site or have your information sold to third parties. However, you must locate and select that option for each website you visit and there is little to ensure that it will be acted on promptly and thoroughly. The European Union has elected to implement a policy that better protects consumer privacy by utilizing an "opt in" strategy where citizens must choose to have their private information shared.

In his article, "The Meaning and Value of Privacy," Daniel J. Solove argues that the concept of privacy has been conceptualized incorrectly in the past. He argues that there is not one strict definition of privacy, but that privacy should instead be conceptualized as consisting of many elements. If one looks at the various problems surrounding privacy, each problem has some of these elements but not all of them. Thus, identifying something as a privacy concern is a matter of determining a kind of family resemblance. Utilizing this perspective, we would ask "Is this problem sufficiently like other well-established problems of privacy such that it counts as a privacy issue?" Solove identifies a number of elements of privacy and confidentiality, including data security and maintaining control of one's own personal information. He contends that privacy is important because it facilitates individual freedom. However, he thinks it a mistake to simply focus on the individual benefits of privacy. An exclusive focus on the individual makes privacy an easy casualty when the overall welfare of society is considered, that is, when utilitarian considerations take priority over individual rights. Privacy, he argues, is a social good, not merely an individual good, because a society that values and protects privacy better promotes overall welfare.

In his contribution to this chapter, "Information Technology, Privacy, and the Protection of Personal Data," Jeroen van den Hoven first describes two reasons for thinking that privacy is less important than it once was. First, some people claim that we should not worry about privacy since there is so much "private" information that is now public. From this perspective, defended by some business leaders, protecting privacy is essentially a lost cause. A second reason for giving up on privacy, defended by some security experts, is that the protection of society from bad actors requires that privacy be sacrificed. Despite these considerations, van den Hoven argues that there are important moral reasons for protecting privacy. One reason is to protect individuals from the use of private information to harm people through identity theft and financial fraud. Another reason is directed against the misuse of information that occurs when the information an individual willingly provides is used for unjust purposes. For example, information provided to a hospital could be used by employers to discriminate based on one's health status, or information possessed by a library could be used to criticize an individual's interests or taste. Van den Hoven uses arguments such as these to defend privacy against those who argue that it is no longer relevant.

Amitai Etzioni begins his article, "The Privacy Merchants: What Is to Be Done?," with an extensive description of the ways interested parties can obtain information about you that you believe is protected either by your own efforts or under the law. For example, your medical records are protected by law, but your visits to a medical website are not and that information is readily available by those who might want to sell you medicine or health insurance. In addition, what Etzioni calls "privacy merchants" sell information about you to the government, especially to the US federal government (e.g., the Department of Justice, the Department of Homeland Security, the Internal Revenue Service, and the Drug Enforcement Administration). What is to be done? Rejecting business self-regulation as a legitimate response to the situation, Etzioni recommends, first, that individuals must *opt in* to allow businesses with whom they do business to sell or otherwise provide information. Second, he argues that we need to rethink the distinction between sensitive information and less sensitive information. Society has tried to protect the former but has been less concerned about the latter. However, since information about less sensitive information (e.g., browsing medical websites) can provide insights into sensitive information (e.g., personal health information) he believes new regulations are needed to address these issues.

COMPLICITY

In 2006, representatives from Google, Yahoo, Cisco Systems, and Microsoft were summoned to testify before Congress regarding their complicity with the Chinese government's efforts to monitor and censor the Internet. For example, Yahoo provided Chinese authorities with information that led to the ten-year imprisonment of journalist Shi Tao. Tao's crime was to disclose Chinese censorship practices on domestic reporters to the foreign press.[1] The chair of the congressional subcommittee that held the hearings characterized the actions of the Internet companies as "sickening collaboration."[2] In their defense, Yahoo and the other companies argued that they are required to adhere to Chinese laws and that they are providing a net benefit to the Chinese people. In 2010 Google began redirecting Chinese users to its Honk Kong website where Internet searches would not be subjected to censorship. In response, the Chinese government threatened not to renew Google's Internet Content Provider (ICP) license.

In his contribution to this chapter, Jeffery D. Smith examines the recent practices of ICPs in China and concludes that ICPs are *actively* engaged in supporting the Chinese government's suppression of the rights to expression, association, and privacy. Smith argues that ICPs should be *passive* in response to the suppression of human rights. For example, he argues that ICPs should wait for court orders before complying with requests and should appeal such requests when they are made. In this way ICPs can provide Chinese citizens with many of the benefits of the Internet age without actively contributing to human rights violations. In 2018 Google disclosed its Project Dragonfly plan to offer censored Internet service in China. What is clear is that no matter how an ICP operates in China under its present form of government, it will need to comply with the demands of the government. The same is true of nearly any nation in which an ICP operates, whether democratic, communist, or totalitarian. The question of whether ICPs can operate ethically in nations where the control of the Internet facilitates the control of political dissent remains contentious.

Notes

1. Peter S. Goodman, "Yahoo Says It Gave China Internet Data," *Washington Post* (September 11, 2005).
2. Tom Zeller, "Web Firms Are Grilled on Dealings in China," *The New York Times* (February 16, 2006).

6.2 CONSUMER PRIVACY

The Meaning and Value of Privacy

DANIEL J. SOLOVE

Our privacy is under assault.[1] Businesses are collecting an unprecedented amount of personal data, recording the items we buy at the supermarket, the books we buy online, our web-surfing activity, our financial transactions, the movies we watch, the videos we rent, and much more. Nearly every organization and company we interact with now has tons of personal data about us. Companies we have never heard of also possess our profiles. Digital dossiers about our lives and personalities are being assembled in distant databases, and they are being meticulously studied and analyzed to make judgments about us: What products are we likely to buy? Are we a good credit risk? What price would we be willing to pay for certain items? How good a customer are we? Are we

likely to be cooperative and not likely to return items or complain or call customer service?

Today, government has an unprecedented hunger for personal data. It is tapping into the data possessed by businesses and other organizations, including libraries. Many businesses readily comply with government requests for data. Government agencies are mining this personal data, trying to determine whether a person might likely engage in criminal or terrorist activity in the future based on patterns of behavior, purchases, and interest.[2] If a government computer decides that you are a likely threat, then you might find yourself on a watch list, you might have difficulty flying, and there might be further negative consequences in the future.

The threat to privacy involves more than just records. Surveillance cameras are popping up everywhere. It is getting increasingly harder to have an unrecorded moment in public. In the United States, the National Security Agency is engaging in massive telephone surveillance. In the United Kingdom, millions of CCTV cameras monitor nearly every nook and cranny of public space.[3] At work, many employers monitor nearly everything – every call their employees make, every keystroke they type, every website they visit. . . .

Do People Expect Privacy Anymore?

These attitudes, however, represent a failure to understand what privacy is all about. The law often focuses on whether we expect privacy or not – and it refuses to protect privacy in situations where we do not expect it. But expectations are the wrong thing to look at. The law is not merely about preserving the existing state of affairs – it is about shaping the future. The law should protect privacy not because we expect it, but because we desire it.

Privacy is often understood narrowly, and these restrictive concepts lead to people neglecting to recognize privacy harms.[4] For example, it may be true that many businesses hold a lot of personal data about you. Does this mean you lack a privacy interest in that data? Those who view privacy narrowly as keeping information totally secret might say that you no longer have privacy in information that others possess.

But privacy is about much more than keeping secrets. It is also about confidentiality – data can be known by others, yet we have social norms about maintaining that information in confidence. For example, although librarians know information about the books we read, they understand that they have an obligation to keep the information confidential. Doctors know our medical information, but they, too, are under a duty of confidentiality.

Privacy also involves maintaining data security. Those who possess data should have an obligation to keep it secure and out of the hands of identity thieves and fraudsters. They should have an obligation to prevent data leaks.

Another dimension of privacy is having control over our information.[5] Just because companies and the government have data about you does not mean that they should be allowed to use it however they desire. We can readily agree that they should not be able to use personal information to engage in discrimination. The law can and should impose many other limits on the kinds of decisions that can be made using personal data.

Those that use data about us should have the responsibility of notifying us about the data they have and how they plan to use it. People should have some say in how their information is used. There needs to be better "data due process." Currently, innocent people are finding themselves on terrorist watch lists and with no recourse to challenge their inclusion on the list. Financial and employment decisions are made about people based on profiles and information they do not even know about.

Privacy thus involves more than keeping secrets – it is about how we regulate information flow, how we ensure that others use our information responsibly, how we exercise control over our information, how we should limit the way others can use our data.

Some argue that it is impossible for the law to limit how others use our data, but this is false. Copyright law is a clear example of the law regulating the way information is used and providing control over that data. I am not suggesting that copyright law is the answer to privacy, but it illustrates that it is possible for the law to restrict uses of data if it wants to.

We can protect privacy, even in light of all the collection, dissemination, and use of our information. And it is something we must do if we want to protect our freedom and intellectual activity in the future.

But how? The first steps involve rethinking the concept and value of privacy.

Rethinking the Concept of Privacy

We can conceptualize privacy in a different way. The philosopher Ludwig Wittgenstein argued that some concepts are best understood as family resemblances – they include things that "are *related* to one another in many different ways."[6] Some things share a network of similarities without one particular thing in common. They are related in the way family members are related. You might have your mother's eyes, your brother's hair, your sister's nose – but you all might not have one common feature. There is no common denominator. Nevertheless, you bear a resemblance to each other. We should understand privacy in this way. Privacy is not one thing, but a plurality of many distinct yet related things. . . .

According to John Dewey, philosophical inquiry begins with problems in experience, not with abstract universal principles. A theory of privacy should focus on the problems that create a desire for privacy. Privacy problems arise when the activities of the government, businesses, organizations, and other people disrupt the activities of others. Real problems exist, yet they are often ignored because they do not fit into a particular conception of privacy. Many problems are not even recognized because courts or policymakers cannot identify a "privacy" interest involved. Instead of pondering the nature of privacy in the abstract, we should begin with concrete problems and then use theory as a way to better understand and resolve these problems. In my book

Understanding Privacy I develop a framework for recognizing privacy problems, and I identify and examine sixteen such problems.

There are four basic groups of harmful activities: (1) information collection, (2) information processing, (3) information dissemination, and (4) invasion. Each of these groups consists of different related subgroups of harmful activities.

I have arranged these groups around a model that begins with the data subject – the individual whose life is most directly affected by the activities classified in the taxonomy. From that individual, various entities (other people, businesses, and the government) collect information. The collection of this information itself can constitute a harmful activity, though not all information collection is harmful. Those that collect the data (the "data holders") then process it – that is, they store, combine, manipulate, search, and use it. I label these activities "information processing." The next step is "information dissemination," in which the data holders transfer the information to others or release the information. The general progression from information collection to processing to dissemination is the data moving further away from the individual's control. The last grouping of activities is "invasions," which involve impingements directly on the individual. Instead of the progression away from the individual, invasions progress toward the individual and do not necessarily involve information.

The first group of activities that affect privacy is information collection. *Surveillance* is the watching, listening to, or recording of an individual's activities. *Interrogation* consists of various forms of questioning or probing for information.

A second group of activities involves the way information is stored, manipulated, and used – what I refer to collectively as "information processing." *Aggregation* involves the combination of various pieces of data about a person. *Identification* is linking information to particular individuals. *Insecurity* involves carelessness in protecting stored information from leaks and improper access. *Secondary use* is the use of collected information for a purpose different from the use for which it was collected without the data subject's consent. *Exclusion* concerns the failure to allow the data subject to know about the data that others have about her and participate in its handling and use. These activities do not involve the gathering of data because it has already been collected. Instead, these activities involve the way data is maintained and used.

The third group of activities involves the dissemination of information. *Breach of confidentiality* is breaking a promise to keep a person's information confidential. *Disclosure* involves the revelation of truthful information about a person that affects the way others judge her reputation. *Exposure* involves revealing another's nudity, grief, or bodily functions. *Increased accessibility* is amplifying the accessibility of information. *Blackmail* is the threat to disclose personal information. *Appropriation* involves the use of the data subject's identity to serve another's aims and interests. *Distortion* consists of disseminating false or misleading information about individuals. Information dissemination activities all involve the spreading or transfer of personal data or the threat to do so.

The fourth and final group of activities involves invasions into people's private affairs. Invasion, unlike the other groupings, need not involve personal information (although in numerous instances, it does). *Intrusion* concerns invasive acts that disturb one's tranquility or solitude. *Decisional interference* involves incursion into the data subject's decisions regarding her private affairs.

Privacy is not one thing, but many distinct but related things. For too long, policymakers and others have viewed privacy too myopically and narrowly, failing to recognize many important privacy problems. Understanding privacy in a more pluralistic manner will hopefully improve the way privacy problems are recognized and addressed.

The Social Value of Privacy

Another problem with the way privacy is often conceptualized involves how its value is assessed. Traditional liberalism often views privacy as a right possessed by individuals. For example, legal theorist Thomas Emerson declares that privacy "is based upon premises of individualism, that the society exists to promote the worth and dignity of the individual ... The right of privacy ... is essentially the right not to participate in the collective life – the right to shut out the community."[7] In the words of one court: "Privacy is inherently personal. The right to privacy recognizes the sovereignty of the individual" (*Smith v. City of Artesia*, 1989).

Framing privacy exclusively in individualistic terms often results in privacy being undervalued in utilitarian balancing, which is the predominant way policymakers resolve conflicts between various interests. When individual interests are pitted against the common good, the latter often wins out. The interests often in tension with privacy – free speech, efficient consumer transactions, or security – are frequently understood as valuable for all of society. Privacy, in contrast, is seen as a zone of respite for the sake of the individual.

There is a way, however, to justify privacy from a utilitarian basis. Pragmatist philosopher John Dewey has articulated the most coherent theory of how protecting individual rights furthers the common good. For Dewey, there is no strict dichotomy between individual and society. The individual is shaped by society, and the good of both the individual and society are often interrelated rather than antagonistic: "We cannot think of ourselves save as to some extent *social* beings. Hence we cannot separate the idea of ourselves and our own good from our idea of others and of their good."[8] Dewey contended that the value of protecting individual rights emerges from their contribution to society. In other words, individual rights are not trumps, but are protections by society from its intrusiveness. Society makes space for the individual because of the social benefits this space provides. Therefore, Dewey argues, rights should be valued based on "the contribution they make to the welfare of the community."[9] Otherwise, in any kind of utilitarian calculus, individual rights would not be valuable enough to outweigh most social interests, and it would be impossible to justify individual rights. As such, Dewey argued, we must insist upon a "social basis and social justification" for civil liberties.[10] I contend, like Dewey, that the value of protecting the individual is a social one. Society involves a great deal of friction, and we are constantly clashing with each other. Part of what makes a society a good place in which to live is the extent to which it allows people freedom from the intrusiveness of others. A society without privacy protection would be suffocating, and it might not be a place in which most would want to live. When protecting individual rights, we as a society decide to hold back in order to receive the benefits of creating the kinds of free zones for individuals to flourish.

As Spiros Simitis declares, "privacy considerations no longer arise out of particular individual problems; rather, they express conflicts affecting everyone."[11] Privacy, then, is not the trumpeting of the individual against society's interests but the protection of the individual based on society's own norms and practices. Privacy is not simply a way to extricate individuals from social control, as it is itself a form of social control that emerges from the norms and values of society.

We protect individual privacy as a society because we recognize that a good society protects against excessive intrusion and nosiness into people's lives. Norms exist not to peek into our neighbor's windows or sneak into people's houses. Privacy is thus not an external restraint on society but is in fact an internal dimension of society.[12] Therefore, privacy has a social value. Even when it protects the individual, it does so for the sake of society. It thus should not be weighed as an individual right against the greater social good. Privacy issues involve balancing societal interests on both sides of the scale.

Because privacy involves protecting against a plurality of different harms or problems, the value of privacy is different depending upon which particular problem or harm is being protected. Not all privacy problems are equal; some are more harmful than others. Therefore, we cannot ascribe an abstract value to privacy. Its value will differ substantially depending upon the kind of problem or harm we are safeguarding against. Thus to understand privacy, we must conceptualize it and its value more pluralistically. Privacy is a set of protections against a related set of problems. These problems are not all related in the same way, but they resemble each other. There is a social value in protecting against each problem, and that value differs depending upon the nature of each problem. . . .

Notes

1. This chapter adapts and discusses the ideas in my book, *Understanding Privacy* (Cambridge, MA: Harvard University Press, 2008); it was published previously in *OPEN Magazine* (October 19, 2009).
2. R. O'Harrow, *No Place to Hide* (New York: Free Press, 2005).
3. J. Rosen, *The Naked Crowd: Reclaiming Security and Freedom in an Anxious Age* (New York: Random House, 2004).
4. For example A. Westin, *Privacy and Freedom* (New York: Atheneum, 1967); R. Gavison, "Privacy and the Limits of Law," *Yale Law Journal* 89 (1980): 421–71; R. Posner, *The Economics of Justice* (Cambridge, MA: Harvard University Press, 1981); A. Etzioni, *The Limits of Privacy* (New York: Basic Books, 1999).
5. Westin, *Privacy and Freedom*; C. Fried, "Privacy: A Moral Analysis," *Yale Law Journal* 77 (1968): 475–93; A. Miller, *The Assault on Privacy: Computers, Data Banks and Dossiers* (Ann Arbor, MI: University of Michigan Press, 1971).
6. L. Wittgenstein, *Philosophical Investigations*, trans. G. E. M. Anscombe (Oxford: Basil Blackwell, 1958), § 65, original emphasis.
7. T. I. Emerson, *The System of Freedom of Expression* (New York: Random House, 1970). pp. 545, 549.
8. J. Dewey, "Ethics" (1908), in *The Middle Works of John Dewey*, ed. J. A. Boydston (Carbondale: Southern Illinois University Press, 1978), pp. 31–50, original emphasis.
9. J. Dewey, "Liberalism and Civil Liberties" (1936), in *The Later Works of John Dewey*, ed. J. A. Boydston (Carbondale: Southern Illinois University Press, 1991), p. 374.
10. Ibid., p. 375.
11. S. Simitis, "Reviewing Privacy in an Information Society," *University of Pennsylvania Law Review* 135 (1987): 707–46 (p. 709).
12. R. C. Post, "The Social Foundations of Privacy: Community and Self in the Common Law Tort," *California Law Review* 77 (1989): 957–1010 (pp. 957, 968), arguing that privacy is society's attempt to promote norms of civility).

Information Technology, Privacy, and the Protection of Personal Data

JEROEN VAN DEN HOVEN

Information technology allows us to generate, store, and process huge quantities of data. Search engines, satellites, sensor networks, scientists, security agencies, marketers, and database managers are processing terabytes of data per day. A good part of these data are about persons – about their characteristics, their thoughts, their movements, behavior, communications, and preferences – or they can be used to produce such data.[1] All countries and cultures in the present and past have constrained access to certain types of personal data in some way or the other.[2] There are etiquettes, customs, artifacts, technologies, or laws, and combinations thereof, which prevent or proscribe against the use or dissemination of personal information. Walls, curtains, doors, veils, sealed envelopes, sunglasses, clothes, locked cabinets, privacy laws, secure databases, cryptographic keys, and passwords all serve the purpose of preventing individual persons to acquire and use information about other persons. The issues are often discussed in the context of a specific social sector or professional domain, such as healthcare, social or homeland security, search engines, marketing, or policing. More specifically the issues can be concerned with camera surveillance, the monitoring of Internet communications, the retention of Internet traffic data, the disclosure of passenger lists to security agencies, the availability of individual medical information in the public health system, the linking and matching of databases in social security to detect fraud, and sifting and trawling through financial databases in order to find suspect transactions. In the near future, they may be about who has access to the scans and digital images of our brains or about who can track and trace tagged personal belongings, everyday objects, and consumer products.

Ethical issues concerning information about persons are typically cast in terms of *privacy*. Privacy is construed as a need, a right, a condition, or an aspect of human dignity. Sometimes it is construed as intrinsically valuable; sometimes it is construed as deriving its value from other sources, for example, from the fact that it is conducive to autonomy or freedom.[3] The largest part of privacy research is concerned with the moral justification of a right to privacy. There is little agreement about the most adequate moral justification, but there is consensus among privacy scholars

about the fact that privacy is important and that privacy is vague, fuzzy, and hard to explicate or pin down.[4]

In public debates about privacy at the beginning of the twenty-first century, there are roughly three positions. First, there is the view that we should stop worrying about privacy, because there is so much personal information available and everyone can know almost everything about everyone, if one would bother to make the effort.

Every credit card payment, Internet search, mobile telephone call, and every movement of a tagged object spawns data about its use and user.[5] Our life worlds have turned into ambient intelligent environments[6] which soak up, process, and disseminate personal data. There is so much information that the idea of constraining or controlling the flow in conformity with moral considerations, laws, and regulations is absurd.[7]

Second, there is the view that Western democracies cannot afford the high levels of individual privacy that they now attempt to provide. Even if it were technically feasible, high levels of privacy are undesirable. Proponents of this view often also argue along utilitarian lines that modern societies involve large numbers of free moving individuals, exhibit high degrees of mobility, social and institutional complexity, and anonymity, which facilitate free-riding in the form of criminal behaviour, fraud, and tax evasion. In order to mitigate the adverse effects of anonymity and mobility, information about individuals should be made available to governments. It is assumed that groups and communities benefit significantly from knowledge about their members. Third, another position is to argue that there are good moral reasons to protect individuals from Big Brother, data-greedy companies, and snooping fellow citizens. There are good moral reasons to justify a potent regime of individual rights which constrains access to information about individuals. . . .

The central role given to the concept of *privacy* in our thinking about the moral issues concerning the protection of personal data obfuscates practical solutions to the everyday problems we encounter in law, public policy, and software engineering concerning them. It lands us in the middle of the controversy between liberal and communitarian political philosophies and the associated conceptions of the Self.

From Jeroen Van Den Hoven and John Weckert, eds., *Information Technology and Moral Philosophy*. New York: Cambridge University Press, 2008. Reproduced with permission of the Licensor via PLSclear.

Because this controversy cannot be easily decided in the favour of either point of view, I propose to address the central question of the moral problem underlying privacy issues head on: Why should we protect personal data; what moral reasons do we have to protect personal data? I would like to construe this question on a par with questions, such as "Why should we protect nuclear reactors, medieval manuscripts, babies, and bird sanctuaries?" In each of these cases, we have good reasons to constrain access, think about visiting hours, stipulate how different persons or groups ought to behave in the vicinity of these entities, and how they may interact with them. In each of these examples, protection takes on a different form and has a different rationale. What would count as a good moral reason to protect personal data and what type of reasons would justify putting limits to the freedom of others to get access to them? This I will discuss later in the chapter. First I will discuss our long-lasting interest in personal data.

Why Personal Data Will Always Be in Demand

Personal data will always be in demand. We will continue to amass personal data in the future and questions concerning their protection are therefore unlikely to subside. First, I distinguish between reasons that governments and nongovernmental parties may have to gather information about individuals. Second, I distinguish between reasons for acquiring information about a person that are primarily directed at the interest of the data subject and reasons primarily concerned with the interests of others than the data subject. This gives us four types of reasons for data collection, which help us to understand the logic which drives the accumulation of personal data, now and in the future.

First, government agencies may want to have access to data about citizens to serve them better. In order to provide better services, they will have to know a good deal about them. Government agencies could alert individual citizens to the fact that they are entitled to benefits they did not know about. This type of proactive service delivery to citizens has become more common in recent years. In the Scandinavian countries, citizens seem to be at ease with the idea that the government thinks on their behalf about their welfare and citizens seem to be comfortable with fewer impediments for government to find out details about their individual lives.

Second, the same logic applies to commercial parties and companies. Commercial parties want to be able to serve their customers or clients better. The more they know about them, the better they can fine-tune their propositions to their preferences and needs. Attention of consumers is scarce and commercial proposals therefore need to raise the immediate interest of potential customers. Many customers have no problems with alerts by businesses which draw their attention to bargains in the areas they are interested in and many seem willing to volunteer personal information in exchange for bargains.

Third, companies or commercial parties also have strictly prudential reasons to collect or accumulate personal data, both about their customers, their partners in transactions and their employees. These reasons are not at all concerned with the interests of the data subjects. Transactions between private parties always present chances for exploitation. Other parties can break their promises, break the contract, or buy without paying. In these cases, adequate information about the partners one is dealing with, for example, information about credit risks or commercial past performance are thought to be extremely helpful in gauging the risks associated with the transaction. Perhaps even more fundamental: in order to be able to trust parties, re-identification of individual partners is a necessary condition for building up a reliable picture of someone's track record in interactions. In game theory and the study of iterated prisoners' dilemmas, the (re-)identification of players in consecutive rounds is simply assumed. In the real world, however, (re-)identification is often a practical problem. Computer applications concerning the identity and relevant properties of individuals are widely used to counter the problem of reliable identification and authentication of persons in private interactions. Information technology holds up the promise that it can deal with the knowledge deficit we are often confronted with in our dealings with strangers and people we know very little about.

The deployment of information technology in the relation between employer and employee may be accounted for in terms of the Principal–Agent theory, according to which the Principal, for example, an employer, always has the problem of making sure that the employee (the agent) is doing what he or she ought to do, when he or she is out of sight. The Principal, therefore, has to make so-called agent cost and has to monitor the agent and check what he or she is doing. This accounts for the incredible explosion of workplace monitoring and surveillance by means of logging, CCTV cameras, smart badges, and black boxes in cars.

Finally, government also has reasons to try and get information on citizens, which are not primarily and directly concerned with the individual interests of individual citizens about whom information is collected, but are primarily concerned with the public good. One of the central tasks of government is the production and maintenance of public goods. One of the central problems of the management of public goods is managing the access to public goods and more specifically the problem of excluding those who are benefiting from the public good without contributing to the maintenance and reproduction of the public good. This category of individuals is referred to as "free riders." The containment of free riders is a central task for government. Free riders can thrive and exist only if they are anonymous. If they can be identified government can affect their pay-off matrix and their self-interested calculation. Identifying information is thus very helpful to governments as managers of public goods.

These four types of "logic of the situation" explain why a range of actors in the government and the market sector will engage in massive computer-supported data collection, and will continue to do so for reasons both concerning the good of the data subject or the good of others than the data subject. They will always welcome and use new developments in information technology that may support their attempts to reach these goals.

What do people object to when they object to gathering personal data in these and other cases? We need to distinguish between different objects of concerns. When a man who enters an almost empty restaurant picks the table right next to me, there are several things I may object to. First, I may not at all be concerned with *my* personal data, but rather with *his* personal data. I may in other words not be concerned with what this person is learning about *me*, but rather with what I am learning about *him*. I just don't want to know the things that I am about to find out about him. A further concern may be the fact that my choice not to learn anything about anybody at that moment is preempted by his decision to sit next to me. I will hear what he orders, smell his aftershave, hear him turn the pages of his newspaper and hear his mobile phone conversation. A perceptual relation is imposed upon me, because he chose to move into my perceptual field without my consent. In that sense, the setting is turned into a source of personal data about the intruder. Data are stored in my brain, and I may forget about them immediately or may remember them later.

A second possible object of my discontentment in the restaurant may be that this person has manoeuvred himself into a position where he is now able to acquire data about *me*, which can be passed on – about what I was having for dinner that evening, what I was wearing, and so forth. He may decide to tell others, or, in secret, make video footage of me munching my garlic bread. Even if I would know that the merely onlooking person would not be recording or storing information in an external information carrier, or would not be able – as a result of a rare brain disease – to retain the data acquired beyond the specious present, I could still feel uncomfortable and awkward because the imposed perceptual relationship

heightens my awareness of myself and forces an external – and not freely chosen – perspective upon me.

The ethics of data protection is first and foremost about the second and third type of grievance of the lonely diner. These grievances come under the heading of informational privacy or tort privacy and need to be distinguished from the first problem sketched above (the right "to be left alone") and also from what has been termed "decisional or constitutional privacy," that is, the right to decide without government interference – for example, the right to decide in which kinds of sexual behaviour to engage between consenting adults in the privacy of one's bedroom, or to decide to have an abortion or to use contraceptives. Sandel refers to the latter as the *new privacy* and to the former as the *old privacy*.[8] In Sandel's classification, data protection is about the old privacy. Personal data are and will remain a valuable asset, but what counts as personal data? If one wants to protect X, one needs to know what X is.

Before we start answering this question a couple of things need to be observed about personal data. First of all, personal data are multiply realizable, that is, they may be stored in different places and in different media. They may be generated and acquired by different types of information processors, whether human or artificial and silicon-based, or a combination thereof. Second, data may be generated by means of a variety of methods, techniques, and artefacts. Individuals may be monitored by cameras, by persons using binoculars, by scanners which track RFID tagged items they carry around, a discussion may be overheard, or agencies may trawl and sift through databases. And, finally and importantly, data do not have a meaning separate from the context in which they are used. . . .

Moral Reasons for Protecting Personal Data

I will now discuss four types of moral reasons for engaging in data protection, that is, moral justifications for constraining actions[9] regarding identity-relevant information. These moral reasons provide the grounds to have principles like those of the 1995 EU Data Protection Act and the Organisation for Economic Co-operation and Development (OECD) principles in place. These legal regimes give to individuals autonomy and the right to control their personal data.

Information-Based Harm

The first type of moral reason for thinking about constraining the flow of identity-relevant data is concerned with the prevention of harm. Information is a very useful thing for criminals and crooks to have. A random attack in the street on an anonymous individual does not require information, but a bank robbery requires a good deal of intelligence and information, planning, and foresight. Some harms could not have been inflicted (or at least not as easily) if certain information would not have been available. Let's refer to this type of harm as "information-based harm." Cybercriminals and malevolent hackers use databases and the Internet to get information on their victims in order to prepare and stage their crimes. One of the most pressing problems is "identity theft" and identity fraud, which brings high risk of financial damages and emotional distress. One's bank account may get plundered and one's credit reports may be irreversibly tainted so as to exclude one from future financial benefits and services. Stalkers and rapists have used the Internet and online databases to track down their victims. They could not have done what they did without access to electronic resources and without accessing some of the details of their victim's lives.

In an information society, there is a new vulnerability to harm done on the basis of personal data – theft, identity fraud, or straightforward harm on the basis of identifying information. Constraining the freedom to access information of persons who could cause, threaten to cause, or are likely to cause information-based harm can be justified on the basis of Mill's Harm Principle. Protecting identifying information, instead of leaving it in the open, diminishes epistemic freedom of all to know, but also diminishes the likelihood that some will come to harm, analogous to the way in which restricting access to firearms diminishes both freedom and the likelihood that people will get shot in the street. In information societies, identity-relevant information resembles guns and ammunition. Preventing information-based harm clearly provides us with a strong moral reason to limit the access to personal data. Arguments against central databases with personal data of individual citizens in The Netherlands often makes reference to World War II when the Nazis occupied The Netherlands and found a well-organized population registration very conducive to their targeting and deportation of the Jews in Holland. It would be strange, however, to claim that the Nazis violated the *privacy* of the Jews. A better description seems to say that they used insufficiently protected personal data to take people out of their houses and send them to the concentration camps. Access to personal information made possible the most horrible of all harms. This is the first thing we want to prevent, and we do it by effectively protecting identity-relevant information. There is, of course, a broad range of harms to individuals that can be inflicted on the basis of personal information. Someone's career may be systematically corroded by the piecemeal release of selected information. This may start to add up in the eyes of others, and lead to serious reputational harm.

Another type of harm could be the harm that lies in classifying people in such a way that their chances of getting some good are diminished. Being classified as Muslim in many Western countries implies a reduced chance of getting a job. Accumulative information-based harm would refer to the releasing snippets of identity-relevant information at different occasions on the basis of which others may eventually form a rich and comprehensive picture of a person and inflict harm on him or her.

Informational Inequality

The second type of moral reason to justify constraints on our actions with identity-relevant information is concerned with equality and fairness. More and more people are keenly aware of the benefits the market for identity information can provide them with. If a consumer buys coffee at the modern shopping mall, information about that transaction is generated and added to his file or profile. Many consumers now begin to realize that every time they come to the counter to buy something, they can also *sell* something, namely, the information about their purchase or transaction, the so-called transactional data. Likewise, sharing information about ourselves on the Web with websites, browsers, and autonomous agents may pay off in terms of more and more adequate information (or discounts and convenience) later. Many privacy concerns have therefore been and will continue to be resolved in quid pro quo practices and private contracts about the use and secondary use of personal data. But, although a market mechanism for trading personal data seems to be kicking in on a global scale, not all individual consumers are aware of their economic opportunities, and if they are, they are not always in a position to trade their data or pursue their interests in a transparent and fair market environment so as to get a fair price for them. The use of RFID chips in consumer products in shops, the use of extensive cross-domain consumer profiling combined with dynamic pricing may facilitate price discrimination.

Consumers do not always know what the implications are of what they are consenting to when they sign a contract for the use of identity-relevant information. We simply cannot assume that the conditions of the developing market for identity-relevant information guarantees fair transactions by independent standards. Constraints on the flow of personal data need to be put in place in order to guarantee equality of arms, transparency, and a fair market for identity-relevant information as a new commodity.

Informational Injustice

A third and very important moral reason to justify constraints on processing of identity-relevant information is concerned with justice in a sense which is associated with the work of Michael Walzer. What is especially offensive to our sense of justice is, first, the allocation of goods internal to sphere *A* on the basis of the distributive logic associated with sphere *B*, second, the transfer of goods across the boundaries of separate spheres, and third, the dominance and tyranny of some goods over others. In order to prevent this, the "art of separation" of spheres has to be practiced and "blocked exchanges" between them have to be put in place. If the art of separation is practised effectively and the autonomy of the spheres of justice is guaranteed then "complex equality" is established. One's status in terms of the holdings and properties in one sphere is irrelevant – ceteris paribus – to the distribution of the goods internal to another sphere.

Walzer's analysis also applies to information. The meaning and value of information is local and allocation schemes and local practices that distribute access to information should accommodate local *meanings* and should, therefore, be associated with specific spheres.

Many people do not object to the use of their personal medical data for *medical* purposes, confined to the medical sphere, whether these are directly related to their own personal health affairs, to those of their family, perhaps even to their community or the world population at large, as long as they can be absolutely certain that the only use that is made of it is medical, that is, to cure people from diseases. They do object, however, to their medical data being used to classify them or disadvantage them socioeconomically, to discriminate against them in the workplace, refuse them commercial services, deny them social benefits, or turn them down for mortgages or political office.

They do not mind if their library search data are used to provide them with better *library* services, but they do mind if these data are used to criticize their tastes and character. They would also object to these informational cross-contaminations when they would benefit from them, as when the librarian would advise them a book on low-fat meals on the basis of knowledge of their medical record and cholesterol values, or when a doctor asks questions on the basis of the information that one has borrowed a book from the public library about AIDS.

We may thus distinguish a third moral reason to constrain actions regarding identity-relevant information: prevention of "informational injustice," that is, disrespect for the boundaries of what we may refer to, following Michael Walzer, as "spheres of justice" or "spheres of access." What is often seen as a violation of privacy is often more adequately construed as the morally inappropriate transfer of personal data across the boundaries of what we intuitively think of as separate "spheres of justice" or "spheres of access."[10]

A couple of illustrations are in order. When government agencies, such as social security agencies, outsource part of their operations to commercial banks, the part of the bank that will take care of the public tasks needs to be separated from the commercial branches. Software protections are put in place, referred to as "Chinese Walls," which separate the commercial from the public social security sphere. In this way, a Walzerian *blocked exchange* for personal data is implemented, and the *art of information sphere separation* is put into practice.

We have seen a similar normative logic of spheres being operative in constraining cookies to retrieve information across the boundaries of top-level domains. We do not mind if the .com site we visit collects information about our search profile on that particular site. We may not even mind if .com sites exchange information. We probably would mind if .com sites used information from .org sites or .gov sites, or vice versa. The lessons learned from the so-called DoubleClick case, where clickstream data were collected by cookies working across sites in different top-level domains seem to confirm these Walzerian intuitions about blocked exchanges between spheres.

Moral Autonomy and Moral Identification

A fourth type of moral reason for constraining the flow of identity-relevant information could be referred to as *moral autonomy*, that is, the capacity to shape our own moral biographies, to present ourselves as we think fit and appropriate, to reflect on our moral careers, and to evaluate and identify with our moral choices, without the critical gaze and interference of others and without a pressure to conform to the "normal" or socially desired identities. We want to be able to present ourselves and be identified as the ones we identify with. . . .

The conception of the person as being morally autonomous, as being the author and experimentator of his or her own moral career, provides a justification for constraining others in their attempts to engineer and directly or indirectly shape the subject's identity, either by stereotyping, or by the application of identity-management tools and techniques. Data protection laws thus justifiably provide protection against the fixation of one's moral identity by others. They do so by requiring informed consent for the processing of identity-relevant information. If there are domains where for obvious reasons individuals in well-ordered societies cannot be allowed to write their own biographies from cover to cover, they at least should be allowed to write those parts that are amenable to it and individuals should be given an opportunity to authorize the parts that were, or had to be, written by others.

A further explanation for the importance of respect for moral autonomy may be provided along the following lines. Factual knowledge of another person is always *knowledge by description*. The person himself, however, does not only know the facts of his biography, but he is the only person who is *acquainted* with the associated thoughts, desires, emotions, and aspirations. However detailed and elaborate our files and profiles on a particular individual may be, we are never able to refer to the data subject as he himself is able to do. We may only approximate his knowledge and self-understanding.

The simple identifications made on the basis of our data fall short of accepting and respecting the individual person, because they will never match the identity as it is experienced by the data subject. It fails because it does not conceive of the other on his, or her, own terms.

Because we feel we have inaccessible qualitative aspects of our own private mental states – that is, that we have hopes and purposes and there is something that it is like to have them which cannot be known from the outside – we insist on epistemic modesty on the part of others in their claims to know who we are and in their involvement in the management of our identities. Moreover, we see ourselves as our own moral projects, subject to moral development and capable of moral improvement, so the result of the management of our identities seems a premature fixation of what is an essentially dynamic project. . . .

Conclusion

I have argued that data about persons are very important and will remain important and much sought after in the future. I have argued that personal data need to be construed in a broad sense to include attributively used descriptions. I have provided four moral reasons for the protection of personal data. The first three reasons (concerning avoiding harm, preventing exploitation in markets for personal data, and preventing inequality and discrimination) can be shared by both liberals and communitarians; they both oppose inflicting harm, exploitation, and discrimination. The fourth reason, however, invokes the essentially contested liberal self. It is the liberal self that wants to decide what to think of itself and what to make of him or herself. And how others should identify him or her, preferably identify with what he himself identifies with. There is probably always over-determination of these moral reasons at stake, so that these reasons can be invoked simultaneously in the moral discussion about data protection.

This analysis opens up a space of potential agreement between parties that are usually deeply divided concerning "privacy issues." The analysis provides three central and weighty reasons to engage in the protection of personal information in the light of new technologies, which they can share. So, instead of arguing over necessary and sufficient conditions of "privacy," we can actually think about designing smart schemes of justified and implementable deontic constraints on flows of personal data.

Notes

1. There is a widely accepted convention to distinguish between data (raw data), information (meaningful data), and knowledge. My main concern here is with data or the raw material that can be used and interpreted by a variety of methods and tools to serve many different purposes. This article explores the moral foundations of data protection. In many cases, not much depends on whether we use "data" instead of "information." It is important to realize though that, even when no meaning can be assigned to data (because there is too much data, and it is too difficult to interpret them), it does make sense to think about protecting them because they may start to make sense when new tools and techniques are applied to them, or when they are combined with other data.
2. See B. Moore, *Privacy: Studies in Social and Cultural History* (New York: M. E. Sharpe, 1984).
3. See R. Gavison, "Privacy and the Limits of Law," in *Philosophical Dimensions of Privacy*, ed. F. Schoeman (Cambridge University Press, 1984), pp. 346–402; J. Wagner DeCew, *In Pursuit of Privacy: Law, Ethics, and the Limits of Technology* (Ithaca and London: Cornell University Press, 1997); B. Roessler, *The Value of Privacy* (Cambridge: Polity Press, 2005); H. Nissenbaum, "Privacy as Contextual Integrity," *Washington Law Review* 79, no. 1 (2004): 119–58; D. J. Solove, "Conceptualizing Privacy," *California Law Review* 90, no. 4 (2002): 1087–1155; J. D. Velleman, "Self to Self," *Philosophical Review* 105, no. 1 (1996): 39–76; and T. Nagel, "Concealment and Exposure," *Philosophy and Public Affairs* 27, no. 1 (1998): 3–30.
4. Wagner DeCew, *In Pursuit of Privacy*.
5. M. J. van den Hoven, "Nanotechnology and Privacy: The Instructive Case of RFID," *International Journal of Applied Philosophy* 20, no. 2 (2006): 215–28.
6. E. Aarts and J. L. Encarnacao, eds., *True Visions: The Emergence of Ambient Intelligence* (Berlin: Springer, 2006).
7. W. Safire, "Goodbye to Privacy," *The New York Times* (April 10, 2005); R. Spinello, "End of Privacy," *America* 176 (January 4–11, 1997): 9–13; J. Quittner, "The Death of Privacy," *Time* (August 25, 1997), p. 18.
8. M. J. Sandel, "Moral Argument and Liberal Toleration: Abortion and Homosexuality," *California Law Review* 77 (1989): 521–38.
9. These actions include: generation, acquisition, processing, and dissemination.

10. M. J. van den Hoven, "Privacy and the Varieties of Informational Wrongdoing," *Australian Journal of Professional and Applied Ethics* 1, no 1 (1999): 30–44; M. J. van den Hoven and R. Cushman, "Privacy, Health Care Data and Information Technology," Conference Report, *Journal of Information, Law, and Technology* 3 (1996). Available at www2.warwick.ac.uk/fac/soc/law/elj/jilt/1996 3/hoven/.

The Privacy Merchants: What Is to Be Done?

AMITAI ETZIONI

Corporate Surveillance, Tracking, Data Mining, and Profiling

Most informed citizens probably know by now that corporations collect information about them, but they may well be unaware of the extent and scope of the invasions of privacy that are now widespread. Many may be aware of tracking tools referred to as "cookies." Cookies are installed on one's computer by visited websites. They are used to identify the person and to remember his or her preferences. Some people have learned to protect themselves from such tracking by employing software that allows one to clear cookies from one's computer. However, corporations have recently begun to install "supercookies" that are very difficult to detect and, if removed, secretly reinstall themselves. As one report concluded: "This means that privacy-sensitive consumers who 'toss' their HTTP cookies to prevent tracking or remain anonymous are still being uniquely identified online by advertising companies."[1]

Major cell phone and mobile technology companies offer services that allow lovers, ex-spouses, lawyers, or anyone else to find out where a person is – and track their movements – by using the GPS capabilities of their cell phones. A German politician who inquired about location storage information discovered that over a six-month period, his longitude and latitude had been recorded over 35,000 times.

There are two kinds of corporations that keep track of what Internet users buy, read, visit, and drink, and who they call, email, date, and much else. Some merely track users' activity on their sites as part of their regular business; recording purchases and viewed products helps them increase sales. This is true for nearly every major online retailer. Other corporations make shadowing Internet users – and keeping very detailed dossiers on them – their main line of business. One can call these the "Privacy Merchants." They sell information to whoever pays the required price. One such company – Choicepoint – had records on over 220 million people. Professor Christopher Slobogin notes that the amount of information culled by corporate data miners

can provide the inquirer with a wide array of data about any of us, including basic demographic information, income, net worth, real property holdings, social security number, current and previous addresses, phone numbers and fax numbers, names of neighbors, driver records, license plate and VIN numbers, bankruptcy and debtor filings, employment, business and criminal records, bank account balances and activity, stock purchases, and credit card activity.[2]

Although several data-mining companies allow individuals to opt out of their databases, each separate company must be contacted individually, and even then information may still linger in some search results or websites. Google, for example, generally does not remove search results if the information contained is truthful and not illegal.

Privacy Merchants are limited by laws Congress (and states) have enacted that carve out subsets of data that they cannot freely trade in, especially medical and financial records. So far though, very little attention has been paid to the fact that information is fungible. Through a process that might be called "privacy violating triangulation" (PVT), one can readily derive much about a person's medical, financial, or other protected private side by using "innocent facts" not privileged by law. A piece of seemingly benign information – for instance, the number of days a person failed to show up for work, or if the person made special purchases, such as a wig – suggests volumes about one's medical condition. By building a portfolio of many such apparently innocuous facts, one could infer a great deal,

From Amitai Ezioni, "The Privacy Merchants: What Is to Be Done?" *University of Pennsylvania Journal of Constitutional Law* 14, no. 2 (2012). © 2012. Reprinted by permission of the author.

effectively violating the realm of privacy surrounding individuals' most sensitive information.

Some individuals may think that they can protect themselves from tracking and dossiers by using pseudonyms and multiple "mailboxes." However, some companies have developed software to match pseudonyms used on message boards and blogs with real names and personal email addresses. The subjects of this tracking, who are unaware that their anonymity has been stripped, include people who use online pseudonyms to discuss sensitive topics like mental illness. As Eli Pariser reports, "[s]earch for a word like 'depression' on Dictionary.com, and the site installs up to 223 tracking cookies and beacons on your computer so that other Web sites can target you with antidepressants."[3] It should be noted that the privacy of medical records is protected by law, but "visits" to medical websites or chat groups are not. . . .

Privacy Merchants in the Service of Big Brother

Even if one disregards the facts already cited, which show that corporate violations of privacy are far-reaching and chilling, one must note that the information corporations amass is available to the government. Laws may prevent the government from ordering a private company to conduct surveillance on innocent citizens not suspected of anything or from generating dossiers that the government itself is banned from generating (in other words, when corporations act as government agents, they may be subject to the same or similar limitations by which the government must abide). However, the government can and does use data already amassed by Privacy Merchants for their own sake. Nor do prevailing laws prevent private corporations from analyzing online activity with an eye towards the government's needs and shaping their privacy-violating data in ways to make them more attractive to government purchasers of their services. Indeed, because the government is such a large and reliable client, corporate databanks have a strong financial interest in anticipating its needs. The thesis that what is private does not stay private is far from hypothetical. As Chris Hoofnagle notes, even though Congress limited the executive branch's amassing of personal information in the 1974 Privacy Act, "those protections have failed to meet Congress' [sic] intent because the private sector has done what the government has been prohibited from doing."[4]

According to Daniel Solove, "for quite some time, the government has been increasingly contracting with businesses to acquire databases of personal information. Database firms are willing to supply the information and the government is willing to pay for it."[5] Solove points out that

the government can "find out details about people's race, income, opinions, political beliefs, health, lifestyle, and purchasing habits from the database companies that keep extensive personal information on millions of Americans."[6]

Hoofnagle similarly warns that "[p]rivate sector commercial data brokers have built massive data centers with personal information custom-tailored to law enforcement agents."[7] ChoicePoint, a major Privacy Merchant, has at least 35 contracts with government agencies, including the Department of Justice (through which it provides its databases to the Federal Bureau of Investigations (FBI)), as well as the Drug Enforcement Administration (DEA), the Internal Revenue Service (IRS), and the Bureau of Citizenship and Immigration Services.[8]

Another corporate data miner, Florida-based SeisInt, ran a massive database called MATRIX (Multi-State Anti-Terrorism Information Exchange) in a joint effort among several US states to coordinate counterterrorism efforts. The federal government paid $12 million to support the program, which SeisInt developed with extensive amounts of data, including individuals' "criminal histories, photographs, property ownership, SSNs, addresses, bankruptcies, family members, and credit information."[9] Even before the 9/11 attacks, the US Marshals Service alone performed up to 40,000 searches every month using private databanks.[10] The exact number of contracts the government has made with corporate data miners is unknown because many of the contracts are classified. However, one 2006 government study found that at least 52 federal agencies had launched – or were planning to launch at the time of the study – at least 199 data mining projects that rely on the services and technology of commercial databanks.[11] Other government tracking and surveillance efforts have relied on private corporations. In 2006, it was disclosed that three major telecommunications providers, AT&T, Verizon, and BellSouth, had cooperated with the National Security Agency (NSA) to provide it with the phone call records of "tens of millions of Americans" – a program which, according to one source, was "the largest database ever assembled in the world."[12] The companies, which agreed to work with the NSA, provide phone service to over 200 million Americans, leading the program significantly closer to its ultimate goal: creating a database of every phone call made within the United States. Other government projects relying on private sources include efforts by Homeland Security to secure air travel and the nation's borders and a Pentagon program which collects data on teenagers to better target military recruitment efforts.

Moreover, the trend is to extend this use, as evidenced by a 2011 FBI manual that enables agents to search for private citizens in commercial databases without prior authorization or even notification.[13] Google revealed that the US government made the most requests for Internet users' private data, with Google complying with 94 percent of those orders.[14]

One may well hold that some of the usages of private databanks by the government serve legitimate purposes, even if they are loaded with extensive dossiers on most adult Americans, rather than those for which there is some evidence or reason to suspect that they are violating the law. However, one must still note that from here on, whether such databanks are in the FBI headquarters or in some corporate office matters little. At most, they are just a click – and a payment – away.

The next segment of this article outlines differing approaches to the protection of privacy in the new world in which the traditional distinctions between public and private realms (on which many normative and legal conceptions build, in particular those that concern privacy) are much less important and are becoming still less significant. The new amalgamated social world calls for cross-realm or holistic modes of deliberations and policymaking.

The Main Alternatives

Change the Norm: A World without Privacy?

One major response to Privacy Merchants' expanding reach has been well encapsulated by the CEO of Sun Microsystems, Scott McNealy, who stated: "You have zero privacy . . . Get over it."[15] Facebook's founder, Mark Zuckerberg, argues that social norms undergirding privacy law are obsolete.[16] That is, instead of finding new ways to protect individuals from corporations, individuals should learn to accept changed – in effect, much lower – levels of privacy. He elaborated: "People have really gotten comfortable not only sharing more information and different kinds, but more openly and with more people . . . That social norm is just something that has evolved over time."[17] Zuckerberg continued: "We view it as our role in the system to constantly be innovating and be updating what our system is to reflect what the current social norms are."[18] He thus implies that the Privacy Merchants are not undermining the norm but merely accommodating their wares to already-in-place changes in norms.

As I see it, it is true that the privacy norms are eroding due to factors other than the corporate drive to use private information for profit-making, evidenced by people going on talk shows to reveal much about themselves, a form of exhibitionism. However, there can be little doubt that corporations, especially the new social media, led by Facebook, are aiding and abetting and seeking to legitimize the erosion of privacy.

The *Wall Street Journal* editorial page, which reflects that publication's philosophy, argues that the change in norms indicates that the introduction of new laws or regulations to better protect privacy is not called for.[19] L. Gordon Crovitz pointed out that, as of March 2011, more than half of Americans over age 12 have Facebook accounts. He proceeded to ask: "If most Americans are happy to have Facebook accounts, knowingly trading personal information for other benefits, why is Washington so focused on new privacy laws? There is little evidence that people want new rules."[20]

The Self-Regulation Option

The prevailing system in the United States – and the de facto prevailing system in the European Union – relies to a significant extent on self-regulation and individual choice, that is, the assumption that consumers will choose the services and products of those corporations that protect privacy at the level the consumers seek and that users can set their privacy controls to the level they prefer. And that, as a result, corporations that provide less privacy protection than the public seeks will lose business and be incentivized to enhance their privacy protection. Additionally, some scholars have argued that marketing in this vein is protected as free speech under the First Amendment, an argument not addressed in this article. These ideas are founded on the standard libertarian argument, as noted by Susanna Kim Ripken: "Respect for individual autonomy, responsibility, and decision-making is deeply entrenched in our culture and law. We believe that people can order their own economic affairs and, given sufficient information, can make their own personal assessments of the risks and benefits of transactions."[21]

None of these assumptions withstand sociological scrutiny. The thesis that consumers are rational actors who make decisions in their best interests, in line with their personal preferences and available information, has been disproven beyond reasonable doubt by the studies of behavioral economists.[22] For this very reason, transparency does not work. That is, the suggestion that if corporations simply declare what their privacy standards are, consumers could choose those that suit them, is erroneous if not misleading. The statements are written in legalese, in terms few can penetrate; the privacy settings provided are complex, cumbersome, and frequently revised – after the users have posted information on the site that they cannot erase.

Furthermore, without regulation, there is no assurance that corporations will adhere to their privacy declarations, or at least to their implied promise. This does not refer necessarily to outright false statements, but to carefully crafted yet misleading commitments to privacy that end up entrapping the consumer. . . .

Large corporations – which do business in all 50 states, as well as overseas – find it in their interest to promote regulation that would provide some modicum of privacy. This is the case because such corporations incur considerable costs when they have to adjust their way of doing business to different state laws, and deal differently in various segments of the market – some of which are more regulated than others under the current patchwork of privacy laws. Hence some large corporations once opposed to legislation now favor a federal omnibus privacy law that would simplify the patchwork of federal sector-specific laws and preempt state-specific statutes. A Microsoft white paper advised, "[F]ederal privacy legislation should pre-empt state laws that impose requirements for the collection, use, disclosure, and storage of personal information."[23] Such a law would likely set standards and ceilings (for instance, caps on damages for privacy violations), which states could not exceed. State laws demanding higher privacy standards than a federally mandated norm would be invalidated, or at least weakened significantly. Indeed, it seems they would accept only legislation that included preemption. Former CEO of eBay, Meg Whitman, explicitly testified before Congress, "Legislation without preemption would make the current situation possibly worse, not better, by creating additional uncertainty and compliance burdens."[24]

The ideal legislation, for Microsoft and similar entities, would provide "baseline privacy protection" over which companies would be encouraged to "compete on the basis of more robust privacy practices"[25] – to essentially regulate themselves. According to Microsoft Deputy General Counsel Erich Anderson's testimony before Congress, a federal law should be crafted only as "an effective *complement* to" self-regulation.[26]

State and sectoral laws have already addressed a number of privacy issues (e.g., setting limits on tracking consumers for targeted advertising) while Congress has been largely inactive in this area.[27] Hence, following a course of self-regulation would in effect reduce privacy standards in those states that lifted them and may prevent them from adding protections in the future.[28] Moreover, the corporate proposal does involve some federal legislation rather than merely relying on self-regulation. Indeed, it seems impossible to restrain the Privacy Merchants without calling in Big Brother.

Consent for Secondary Use: Opt In Rather Than Out?

A rather different approach holds that individuals who release information about themselves for a specific purpose or transaction, for example to purchase a book from Amazon, would be understood to still "own" this information, and that Amazon could use it for other purposes (or sell that information to other parties) only with the explicit consent of the consumer (rather than on the basis of a privacy statement on its websites or presumed consent). The same idea is referred to in other words, namely that consumers would have to opt in to grant secondary and additional use of private information rather than opt out. In American discourse, the term "owned" is used because information is treated as property and private information as private property. In Europe, the same idea is embraced; however, privacy is treated more as an individual right – as part of the personhood – which is violated when one's private sphere is violated.

In 1995, in an effort to establish minimum protections for Internet user privacy and establish a baseline consistency among the data protection laws of European Union (EU) member states, the European Council issued what is commonly called the "Data Protection Directive." The Directive, which scholars have called "aggressive" and "extraordinarily comprehensive,"[29] took effect in October 1998. Based on a legal tradition that "expressly recognizes the fundamental right to the protection of personal data,"[30] the Directive is credited with having established the most influential and prominent data protections in the world to date. However, it has proven difficult to ensure compliance in those countries governed by the Directive. Although the law set out ambitious goals for the standardization of privacy protection in Europe, it has been hampered from the start by significant gaps in member states' compliance and enforcement.

The Directive requires that personal data be processed "only with the consent of the data subject,"[31] with limited exceptions carved out for national security, law enforcement, and some basic state functions such as taxation. The intentionally broad language of the Directive includes – but is not limited to – such actions as collecting, storing, recording, adapting, retrieving, and erasing data; and "data" itself is defined broadly enough to include not just text, but also photographs, video, and sound. Its restrictions recognize that certain kinds of data are particularly sensitive and vulnerable to abuse; thus, it contains heightened restrictions on the processing of data which would reveal the subject's personal traits, such as race, ethnicity, religious beliefs, or health background. In most cases, collecting and passing on these kinds of information require the subject's *written* consent, or they cannot be processed.

The law also requires a degree of transparency: data processors must disclose to subjects of processing the ways in which they intend to use the data. Finally, in one of the Directive's most restrictive and controversial portions, the drafters attempted to address the "borderless" nature of the Internet and the likelihood that user data could be processed in or transmitted to countries not subject to the law's protections. To protect against this vulnerability, the Directive contains a provision requiring member states to prohibit the transfer of data to third countries that have not adopted an "adequate level of protection" for personal data.[32] However as we have seen, implementing these protections has proven difficult, and enforcement across Europe has, at best, proven inconsistent. . . .

Limiting the involuntary secondary use of private information is much more popular in Europe than in the United States, as evidenced by the Directives enacted relatively early in the Internet's lifespan, while a comprehensive American approach has yet to be articulated. The ban on involuntary secondary use burdens the consumers, who have limited capacity to evaluate various privacy statements and assurances that these are indeed heeded. They are unaware of the risks of PVT. And business lobbies tend to strenuously oppose this approach, which makes it very unlikely to be enacted in the United States or heeded in Europe. And differences in laws and enforcement levels among countries – across whose borders the same information readily flows – greatly limit the value of this way of better protecting privacy from private invasions.

Increased Public Regulation of Sensitive Information?

A limited approach to curbing Privacy Merchants entails expanding the American patchwork of sectoral laws that limit the violation of privacy in one specific area or another. As Gina Stevens catalogues, "[f]ederal laws and regulations extend protection to consumer credit reports, electronic communications, federal agency records, education records, bank records, cable subscriber information, video rental records, motor vehicle records, health information, telecommunications subscriber information, children's online information, and customer financial information."[33] One could add some more areas to this long but seemingly arbitrary list.

The patchwork of laws can be viewed as based on a rationale that treats differently three main areas – private information gleaned from public records (e.g., house ownership), relatively sensitive information (especially medical and financial), and information that is in effect deemed less sensitive (most consumer choices). The patchwork can be seen as largely based on the level of sensitivity of the information. Public records, therefore, are open for dissemination online because this information was not private in the first place; less sensitive information is considered in need of little protection because no or little harm is

inflicted when it is used by third parties; and sensitive information is protected. And to the extent that one finds that some area is not well protected, the argument runs, one can add another "patch" of legislation to cover this area.

The patchwork approach has two serious defects, one often cited and one less often noted. It is widely recognized that the patchwork lags woefully behind technological developments in the private sector. . . . Less often noted is the problem that the distinction between "sensitive" and "less sensitive" information is much less tight than it seems and is likely to further weaken in the near future. Even if sensitive information such as medical or financial records is better protected online, less sensitive – and therefore, less protected – information can reveal volumes of sensitive information through PVT. As Marcy Peek points out, "the Internet has allowed commercial decision makers to manipulate technology in such a way as to identify persons according to a multitude of variables and categories."[34] Unique IP addresses are tracked by each page people visit and ad they click on to create a detailed portrait of the offline persona. Peek explains, "[t]hrough various means such as 'cookies,' Web bugs, and personal data input such as zip codes, corporate marketers can obtain a person's demographic and other information and 'tag' an individual on the basis of such information."[35] The individual is then categorized and ranked against other users. The result is "Weblining," an online version of the offline discriminatory practice of "redlining" individuals by denying or increasing the cost of services based on their demographic. After the Fair Housing Act of 1968 prohibited redlining, which used a mortgage applicant's neighborhood to discriminate along racial lines, banks instead used other markers of race as a basis for racial discriminations; for instance, which social club people joined or church they attended. That is, an item of information that is not sensitive was used to divine another item meant to be private. The easy access to this type of non-sensitive information online streamlines this practice. . . .

All this suggests that laws that ban the use of sensitive information (without requiring any action by the millions of affected citizens), the way medical, financial, and select other records are now protected, could be reinforced by banning PVT of protected areas. That is, the wall that separates more sensitive and less sensitive information could be shored up. (Granted, the debate about what is sensitive and what is not would continue.) That is, the law would ban Privacy Merchants from using information on what one purchases (and other such "less" sensitive information) to divine one's medical condition (and other such "more" sensitive information). . . .

Conclusion

Corporations, especially those that make trading in private information their main line of business – the Privacy Merchants – are major violators of privacy, and their reach is rapidly expanding. Given that the information these corporations amass and process is also available to the government, it is no longer possible to protect privacy by only curbing the state. Suggesting that norms have changed and that people are now more willing to give up their privacy may be true, but only up to a point. The extent to which private aspects of one's medical and even financial conditions are revealed is unlikely to be widely accepted as a social good. And violation of the privacy of dissenters and, more generally, of one's political and social views (e.g., by tracking what people read) has chilling effects, whether or not the majority of the public understands the looming implications of unbounded profiling of most Americans. Self-regulation cannot come to the rescue because it assumes that individuals can sort out what corporations are doing behind the veil of their privacy statements, an unrealistic assumption. Banning the use of less sensitive information (in particular, about purchases) for divining more sensitive information (e.g., medical) – that is, outlawing Privacy Violating Triangulation – may serve, if combined with laws that add "patches" to the current patchwork of legislation, to cover new technological developments (e.g., social media). If such twin progress is possible, there will be much less reason to prevent the government from drawing on the databanks maintained by Privacy Merchants, because they would be limited to less sensitive information, and PVT of innocent Americans would be banned. Without such progress, one must assume that what is private is also public in two senses of these words: that one's privacy (including sensitive matters) is rapidly corroded by the private sector and that whatever it learns is also available to the government.

Notes

1. Ashkan Soltani et al., *Flash Cookies and Privacy* 2 (Summer Undergraduate Program in Engineering Research at Berkeley, Working Paper, 2009), http://papers.ssrn.com/sol3/papers.cfm?abstract_id=1446862 (describing how Flash cookies operate).

2. Christopher Slobogin, "Government Data Mining and the Fourth Amendment," *University of Chicago Law Review* 75 (2008): 317–41 (p. 320) (describing how the government "routinely makes use" of these "commercial data brokers").

3. Eli Pariser, "What the Internet Knows about You," *CNN* (May 22, 2011), http://articles.cnn.com/2011-05-22/opinion/pariser.filter.bubble.

4. Chris J. Hoofnagle, "Big Brother's Little Helpers: How ChoicePoint and Other Commercial Data Brokers Collect and Package Your Data for Law Enforcement," *North Carolina Journal of International Law* 29 (2004): 595–637 (p. 636).

5. Daniel Solove, *The Digital Person: Technology and Privacy in the Information Age* (New York University Press, 2004), p. 169.

6. Ibid., p. 167.

7. Hoofnagle, "Big Brother's Little Helpers," pp. 636–37.

8. Jay Stanley, *The Surveillance-Industrial Complex: How the American Government Is Conscripting Businesses and Individuals in the Construction of a Surveillance Society*, American Civil Liberties Union (2004), p. 26, www.aclu.org/FilesPDFs/surveillance_report.pdf (discussing government customers' large contracts with data companies).

9. Solove, *The Digital Person*, p. 170.

10. Slobogin, "Government Data Mining," p. 320 (highlighting the variety of data available in these banks including demographic information, net worth, employment and criminal records, and credit card activity).

11. Arshad Mohammed and Sara Kehaulani Goo, "Government Increasingly Turning to Data Mining," *Washington Post* (June 15, 2006), p. D3, www.washingtonpost.com/wp-dyn/content/article/2006/06/14/AR2006061402063.html ("It is difficult to pinpoint the number of such contracts because many of them are classified").

12. Leslie Cauley, "NSA Has Massive Database of Americans' Phone Calls," *USA Today* (May 11, 2006), p. 1A, www.usatoday.com/news/washington/2006-05-10-nsa_x.htm (internal quotation marks omitted).

13. Charlie Savage, "FBI Agents Get Leeway to Push Privacy Bounds," *The New York Times* (June 13, 2011), p. A1 ("The new rules add to several measures taken over the past decade to give agents more latitude").

14. *Transparency Report*, Google (January 2012), www.google.com/transparencyreport/governmentrequests/userdata/?p=2010-12.

15. Polly Sprenger, "Sun on Privacy: 'Get over It,'" *Wired* (January 26, 1999), www.wired.com/politics/law/news/1999/01/17538.

16. See Bobbie Johnson, "Privacy No Longer a Social Norm, Says Facebook Founder," *The Guardian* (January 10, 2010), www.guardian.co.uk/technology/2010/jan/11/facebook-privacy ("The rise of social networking online means that people no longer have an expectation of privacy, according to Facebook founder, Mark Zuckerberg").

17. Ibid. (internal quotation marks omitted).

18. Ian Paul, "Facebook CEO Challenges the Social Norm of Privacy," *PCWorld* (January 11, 2010), www.pcworld.com/article/186584/facebook_ceo_challenges_the_social_norm_of_privacy.html.

19. L. Gordon Crovitz, "The 0.00002% Privacy Solution," *Wall Street Journal* (March 28, 2011), p. A15 ("There is little evidence that people want new rules").

20. Ibid.

21. Susanna Kim Ripken, "The Dangers and Drawbacks of the Disclosure Antidote: Toward a More Substantive Approach to

Securities Regulation," *Baylor Law Review* 58 (2006): 139–204 (pp. 195–96) (footnote omitted).

22. For further discussion on this subject, see Dan Ariely, *Predictably Irrational: The Hidden Forces That Shape Our Decisions* (New York: HarperCollins, 2008), p. 243.

23. Paul M. Schwartz, "Preemption and Privacy," *Yale Law Journal* 118 (2009): 902–47 (p. 921) (internal quotation marks omitted).

24. Ibid., p. 929 (internal quotation marks omitted).

25. "The Need for a Comprehensive Approach to Protecting Consumer Privacy," Hearing on the State of Online Consumer Privacy Before the Senate Committee on Commerce, Science and Transport, 112th Congress (2011) (statement of Erich Anderson, Deputy General Counsel, Microsoft Corporation), p. 6.

26. Ibid., p. 5.

27. Raised B. 5765, Gen. Assemb., Feb. Session. (Conn. 2008). See Schwartz, "Preemption and Privacy," p. 946 ("In contrast, federal sectoral privacy law presents a more complicated situation").

28. Chris Hoofnagle, "Can Privacy Self-Regulation Work for Consumers?," *Technology / Academics / Policy* (January 26, 2011), www.techpolicy.com/CanPrivacySelf-RegulationWork-Hoofnagle.aspx (providing examples of organizations that failed to abide by their own privacy policies).

29. Julia M. Fromholz, "The European Union Data Privacy Directive," *Berkeley Technology Law Journal* 15 (2000): 461–84 (p. 462); Fred H. Cate, *Privacy in the Information Age* (Washington, DC: Brookings Institution Press, 1997), p. 36.

30. *Background: EU Data Protection Directive*, Electronic Privacy Information Center, http://epic.org/privacy/intl/eu_data_pro tection_directive.html.

31. Cate, *Privacy*, p. 37.

32. Fred H. Cate, "The EU Data Protection Directive, Information Privacy, and the Public Interest," *Iowa Law Review* 80 (1995): 431–43 (p. 437) (internal quotation marks omitted).

33. Gina Stevens, *Privacy Protections for Personal Information Online*, Congressional Research Service Report for Congress, R41756 (2011), p. 7 (footnotes omitted).

34. Marcy Peek, "Passing beyond Identity on the Internet: Espionage and Counterespionage in the Internet Age," *Vermont Law Review* 28 (2003): 91–100 (p. 94) (evaluating ways to resist discriminatory marketing in cyberspace).

35. Ibid., p. 95.

6.3 COMPLICITY

Internet Content Providers and Complicity in Human Rights Abuse

JEFFERY D. SMITH

Internet content providers (ICPs) such as Yahoo, Google, and Microsoft host popular Internet search engines and provide a wide range of information services such as email, chat rooms, blog hosting, and Web page authoring. These ICPs have recently experienced public scrutiny for their involvement in censoring information available through the Internet and disclosing sensitive information about the activities of their service subscribers. This scrutiny came to the foreground with the testimony of senior managers from Yahoo, Google, and Microsoft and Cisco Systems before the US House of Representatives Committee on International Relations on February 10, 2006. The focus of this testimony was on the compliance of ICPs in China with an elaborate system of laws and regulations that restrict Internet access within China and proscribe the Internet activity of Chinese citizens.

There are two central problems raised by these cases of Internet censorship in China. First, the regulatory efforts of the Chinese government to block access to websites, filter information, shut down information portals, and gather information about the Internet activities of particular individuals are an abridgement of basic human rights. The regulations suppress the right to expression, preclude political association, and where information is gathered to prosecute Chinese dissidents, it often interferes with the entitlement to privacy in matters of legitimate, peaceful social action.[1] Second, ICPs have been instrumental in carrying forth the directives of the Chinese government to limit the kind of information and activity of Chinese Internet users. In some cases, for example, ICPs have dutifully complied with directives to filter content from search engine queries. In other cases ICPs have turned over user information to Chinese agencies who are seeking to prosecute Chinese citizens for unlawful political speech.[2]

This essay will focus on the second problem. If one acknowledges that the rights to expression, association, and privacy are undermined by Chinese Internet censorship, then it remains an important task to determine how, and if, ICPs can legitimately do business in China without being implicated in violating these rights. Thus, while there is much to be said about the scope and justification of the human rights in question, this essay will take it for granted that there have been, and continue to be, violations of basic human rights that result from Chinese Internet censorship. I am more interested in exploring the extent to which ICPs bear moral responsibility for their compliance with Chinese directives. More specifically, these cases are an interesting opportunity to examine what it means for corporations to be *complicit* in moral wrongdoing, in this case the duty not to infringe upon the legitimate human rights of others.[3]

After an initial presentation of the extent and scope of ICP involvement in Chinese Internet censorship, I will present a conceptual examination of different forms of complicity in the infringement of human rights. I will offer a set of distinctions designed to clarify what it means to ascribe moral responsibility to corporate actors based upon their complicit involvement in activities that violate human rights. These observations will be applied to a number of recent instances drawn from ICPs and their presence in the Chinese market. I will argue in subsequent sections that while it is tempting to think of ICPs as passively involved in the violation of human rights, their behavior is more active once further details are examined. I conclude with some tentative remarks as to how ICPs can shift to a more passive presence in the Chinese Internet market that preserves their competitive position and does not assist the Chinese government in the suppression of the rights of expression, association, and privacy.

Human Rights and Multinational Business

The rights to expression, association, and privacy have been recognized as fundamental rights under international law and a growing consensus of multinational business leaders. The United Nations International Covenant on Civil and Political Rights, signed by China and ratified by the United States, explicitly acknowledges the right to expression and association in Articles 19 and 21, respectively:

Everyone shall have the right to freedom of expression; this right shall include freedom to seek, receive and impart information and ideas of all kinds, regardless of frontiers, either orally, in writing or in print, in the form of art, or through any other media of his choice.

The right of peaceful assembly shall be recognized. No restrictions may be placed on the exercise of this right other than those imposed in conformity with the law and which are necessary in a democratic society in the interests of national security or public safety, public order, the protection of public health or morals or the protection of the rights and freedoms of others.[4]

Article 22 of the International Covenant also protects association in other forms: "everyone shall have the right to freedom of association with others, including the right to form and join trade unions for the protection of his interests."[5] The International Covenant has served as the primary international instrument for the development of constitutionally recognized rights by nation-states. Its legal authority can be traced to the United Nations Universal Declaration of Human Rights, which also codifies the rights of expression and association.[6]

It is more difficult to find mention and use of the right of privacy in international law; however, a working group of the United Nations Sub-Commission on Human Rights has called for a recognition of the right to privacy in its Draft Norms of Responsibilities of Transnational Corporations and Other Business Enterprises with Regard to Human Rights.[7] This step represents a recognition among international lawyers and business leaders that the protection of privacy should be a guiding norm of multinational businesses to regulate businesses' interactions with workers, customers, and members of the community so as to assure that the content of interpersonal communication, personal data, and memberships or affiliations will not be disclosed to outside parties without due process. The United Nations Global Compact, too, has served as an international instrument to recognize and protect the human rights of various stakeholders. The Global Compact is an ongoing group of United Nations agencies, labor organizations, and business leaders that has attempted to implement the norms of the Universal Declaration of Human Rights within business contexts. The Global Compact's Business Leaders Initiative has worked diligently to articulate strategies for multinational businesses to institutionalize human rights standards in their operations, including the right to privacy.[8]

It is important to note that this legal and institutional recognition of the rights of expression, association, and privacy is not what gives these rights their moral authority.

The legal recognition of human rights is important from a practical point of view in assuring the protection of rights; however, their authority is prior to their legal protection because nation-states and corporations have a moral duty to not abridge these rights regardless of the extent to which they may, or may not, be positively recognized and protected by governments.[9]

The moral authority of human rights, including the rights of expression, association, and privacy, has been defended from a number of philosophically credible perspectives. Kantian scholars have argued that respect for personhood requires, among other things, guarantees of autonomy or the ability to fully self-determine one's life in accordance with one's own choices.[10] Human rights are one means toward securing this kind of autonomy. Libertarian and utilitarian schools of thought provide fertile ground to defend the importance of rights, especially so-called liberty rights that require noninterference by others in areas of speech, thought, and association.[11] Other scholars have more recently focused on conceptions of human well-being to defend the notion that core human goods are secured only when central human capabilities are protected. Martha Nussbaum and Amartya Sen have maintained, for instance, that human life requires physical safety, health, creativity, education, social membership, and control over the external environment. Rights are instrumental in securing these constituents of a complete life.[12]

It is not the intent of this essay to examine these philosophical justifications. It is also too large a task to systematically explore the prospects of the Draft Norms or the Global Compact in securing the rights of current and future stakeholders. My efforts in the remaining portions of this essay are instead focused on what it means for corporations to be complicit in violating these rights. In order to accomplish this task we need to first review the activities of ICPs in China that impact the rights of expression, association, and privacy and, second, develop a typology of different forms of complicity.

Internet Censorship in China

There are three primary levels at which Internet content is censored in China.[13] First, there is the censorship of content at the point where Chinese Internet access providers (IAPs) are connected to other regions of the Internet. These state-licensed IAPs sell access to this so-called international backbone of the Internet to hundreds of smaller Internet service providers (ISPs) which, in turn, sell access to individual customers. IAPs make frequent use of routers, primarily designed and sold by Cisco Systems, which screen and block specific information hosted by sources both within

and outside of China.[14] IAPs block access to specific Web addresses (URLs) or Web addresses that are known to host objectionable content. They also selectively filter content on Web pages if such content is thought to be in conflict with norms established by the Ministry of Information, its main administrative arm, the State Council of Information Office, or the propaganda agency of the Communist Party. Filtering content is more difficult to accomplish because it requires a much finer examination of the content displayed on particular Web pages on an ongoing basis, whereas blocking access to URLs can be accomplished effectively once URLs with prohibited content have been identified, collected, and passed on to ISPs.

Second, ISPs must also comply with a series of directives issued by the Ministry of Information and other state and local agencies that prohibit the hosting of content that is deemed to be harmful to state security or social stability. These orders are far-reaching. Managers of ISPs are legally required to monitor the exchange of information among their customers and routinely examine and report the content of emails, Web pages, and other forms of communication on the Internet. Dissident political activity, discussions initiated by banned organizations, references to specific historical events, and Western news sources are prime targets for ISP monitoring and censorship.

Finally, the entry of multinational ICPs into the Chinese market has brought an additional layer of censorship that essentially conditions the operation of ICPs in China upon compliance with the aims of the Ministry of Information's "Public Pledge on Self-Discipline of the Chinese Internet Industry."[15] ICPs are licensed prior to operation and are held legally responsible for all content hosted through their services, including blogs, email, personal websites, and chat rooms. Although the "Public Pledge" is not itself legally required, there are an array of specific laws that require ICPs to refrain from "disseminating pernicious information that may jeopardize state security or disrupt social stability."[16] ICPs are specifically required to delist websites and filter content that contain words, phrases, names, and addresses that are intended to be blocked at the IAP or ISP level but which may escape censorship. ICPs have discretion over how they identify sites to delist and content to filter. They also are responsible for directing internal compliance with the censorship directives of the Chinese government.

Complicity in Internet Censorship

ICPs play an increasingly central role in managing information available on the Internet. While ISPs provide access to the infrastructure of the Internet, ICPs are the primary way in which individuals search, gain access, and share information.

Accordingly, the proliferation of ICPs and the commercial opportunities for ICPs in China have produced a competitive landscape where ICPs are faced with the difficult challenge of complying with Chinese directives regarding Internet censorship or risk losing access to the most promising information systems market in the world. This reality has been mentioned time and time again by senior executives of the key ICPs like Yahoo, Google, and Microsoft.

On the assumption that there are basic human rights of expression, association, and privacy, and that the coordinated efforts of the Chinese government and ICPs constitute a violation of these rights, then it is natural to ask: To what extent, if any, are ICPs morally responsible for those violations? One common way that this type of problem is addressed in human rights circles is to probe whether we can say ICPs are *complicit* in the violation of human rights.

The International Center on Human Rights Policy holds that complicity in human rights violations involves "participating or assisting abuses committed by others," whether by armies, government agencies, or other non-governmental organizations.[17] There are numerous considerations in determining whether a corporate actor is complicit in the violation of a human right: the corporation's knowledge of the violations, their intentions, the causal significance of the corporation's activities in producing the violation, and the directness of the relationship between the corporation, the victims, and the principal perpetrators all seem like relevant pieces of information in making determinations of complicity.[18] These factors are essential in understanding the extent to which corporations can be said to participate or assist in abuse.

The Office of the United Nations High Commissioner for Human Rights (OHCHR) defines the term "complicity" in the context of applying the norms outlined in the United Nations Global Compact:

A company is complicit in human rights abuses if it authorizes, tolerates, or knowingly ignores human rights abuses committed by an entity associated with it, or if the company knowingly provides practical assistance or encouragement that has a substantial effect on the perpetration of human rights abuse. The participation of the company need not actually cause the abuse. Rather the company's assistance or encouragement has to be to a degree that, without such participation, the abuses most probably would not have occurred to the same extent or in the same way.[19]

Here complicity includes authorization, toleration, or neglect of abuses in addition to a provision of assistance to a principal perpetrator. The implication of this passage is that any one of these facilitating acts serves as a sufficient condition for a complicit violation of human rights. The OHCHR definition extends complicity beyond assistance to forbearance and involvement in practices that involve the violation of human rights. Complicity does not require the corporation to be causally implicated in the violation; that is, the complicit corporation is not necessarily one that causes the abuse but simply facilitates or accentuates a violation that might still have otherwise occurred.

To say that a corporation has been complicit in the violation of human rights is to ascribe a level of moral blameworthiness in failing to respect the basic entitlements of other human beings. The level of blame or the extent of the moral failure, however, may not rise to the level of direct violations of human rights. There is therefore a basic distinction that needs to be drawn between acts that violate human rights because of an intentional, deliberate decision to do so and acts that violate human rights because of an intentional, nondeliberate decision to do so.

All intentional actions that violate human rights can be divided into two categories: those that are performed by actors with the purpose of violating human rights and those that are performed by actors who are responding to the directives issued by other authoritative parties to engage in the violation of human rights. I will call the former category of actions *direct* acts that violate human rights and the latter category *indirect* acts that violate human rights. Direct violations are deliberate in that they are essentially characterized by the intention to deprive an individual of some human right, whereas indirect violations are nondeliberate in the sense that while they may intentionally violate a human right, they would not be performed but for adherence to a directive issued by some authoritative individual, organization, or agency.

Direct violations are non-complicit deprivations of some human right. Indirect violations are complicit deprivations because an indirect violation can be described as a knowledgeable act of tolerance, compliance, acquiescence, assistance, support, or encouragement of an authoritative directive to deprive an individual of some human right.

Within this category of indirect violations there is another important distinction to be drawn between *active* and *passive* responses to authoritative directives that deprive individuals of some human right. This difference is subtle but important. Active indirect violations are acts that take positive steps to deprive individuals of their rights where the extent and methods used in the violation are at the discretion of the secondary party. I describe such acts as *active* because the techniques used in the deprivation of rights are developed and implemented by the secondary party. There are clearly norms and implied expectations communicated by principal authorities that condition the indirect party's intentional act to implement the techniques used in depriving individuals of their rights. This is what makes this category of violations indirect; but these violations are active in the sense that indirect parties are not merely compliant with specific directives issued by the principal authority but take initiative on their own to develop policies that uphold the spirit of the principal's goal of violating some basic right. Active indirect acts involve intentional acts of assistance that qualitatively strengthen the principal authority's efforts to deprive an individual of some human right.

Passive indirect violations are indirect violations that are merely compliant to a specific directive issued by a principal authority. There is no meaningful effort at a creative implementation of some overarching norm established by the principal authority; instead, passive indirect actors remain poised simply to respond to particular edicts handed down through authoritative channels.

To illustrate this difference, consider examples from the recent past. There were a number of documented cases in apartheid South Africa where companies took positive steps to report the activities of individual employees that were seen as a challenge to the authority of the apartheid government.[20] By targeting political speech for eventual suppression by government, these South African companies can be understood as committing an indirect yet active effort to deprive individual employees of the right of expression. Consider, too, the recent revelation that Deutsche Bank branches financed the construction of certain concentration camp buildings, most notably the crematorium at Auschwitz.[21] Absent the Nazi regime, this act would not have taken place; however, within the political and business climate of the Third Reich, Deutsche Bank took active steps to enable the final solution and the deprivation of rights to life, property, and personhood. In both of these cases the companies in question exercised discretion over their relationship with the principal authority's interest in suppression of rights.

Indirect passive violations have routinely occurred. Suppose a telecommunications company responds to a specific court order to hand over individual phone records in order to facilitate an investigation as to whether someone belonged to an underground, dissident political organization. Although intentional, this act would not have occurred but for the court order. The company is merely responsive or compliant even though it can be said to facilitate the infringement of the right to association. To the extent that it facilitates the investigation and managers have knowledge of the investigation it can be said to be complicit in the violation of the right to association.

Human rights organizations extend further the class of actions that are said to be complicit. The International Council on Human Rights Policy has applied the analysis provided under the UN Global Compact to include two additional kinds of complicit acts that, I believe, are not intentional and therefore do not involve indirect violations of rights in the way I have been describing.

First, companies can be complicit in human rights abuse when they are "silent enablers" of abuse. This means that companies that engage in activities with separate, legitimate business purposes may be implicated through these activities in providing resources, technology, or expertise that are used by principal authorities to deprive individuals of their human rights. The term "silent" refers to the fact that the companies in question have knowledge, or could reasonably be expected to have knowledge, about the use of their resources, technology, or expertise in the deprivation of human rights. It is natural to describe these silent enabling acts as morally negligent as opposed to intentional because the intention to deprive an individual of some right is not a deliberate or nondeliberate intention of the company's managers. It is simply that their actions with legitimate business purposes provide the principal authority with the derivate ability to deprive individuals of their rights. This difference separates acts that silently enable human rights abuse from secondary acts that are, by definition, intentional in their deprivation of human rights. Acts that silently enable human rights violations are therefore complicit but not indirect.

The case of the Canadian oil firm Talisman Energy and its joint venture with the Sudanese government to extract and transport oil to the Red Sea serves as a nice illustration. The Canadian Foreign Ministry confirmed through various investigations that the Heglig oil field, constructed and managed by Talisman, was used by the Sudanese government to coordinate and launch military raids against Christian and tribal populations in the southern part of the country as part of Sudan's ongoing civil war.[22] Although the oil field had legitimate business purposes that were part of the explicit provisions of the joint venture, critics rightly claimed that Talisman either knew, or should have known, that the Sudanese military was using their resources as a tool to gain a geographic advantage over other factions in the civil war. To the extent that independent monitors verified that such bombing raids targeted civilian populations, it was argued that Talisman was a silent yet significant contributor to the violation of the right of noncombatants not to become military targets.

A final category of complicit acts that is often highlighted in the human rights literature concerns instances where corporations derive benefits from their engagement with a principal authority. Corporations that are derivative beneficiaries of human rights violations receive business-related benefits from actions taken by a principal authority to deprive individuals of their rights. Unocal's operations in Burma depended heavily on the existence of infrastructure and pipelines that were constructed, in part, with the use of forced labor under auspices of the Burmese government.[23] In this case Unocal knowingly tolerated the abuse of human rights as an ongoing condition of operating in the Burmese commercial environment, even though there was neither intentional assistance provided to the government (actively or passively) nor an unintentional but negligent provision of support.

This conceptual mapping has produced the following results (see Figure 6.1). Direct violations of human rights are intentional, deliberate, and have the specific purpose of depriving an individual or individuals of a right. These acts are not complicit. They are direct in that there is a principal authority that has the discretion and power to carry forth the violations. Indirect acts that result in the violation of human rights are intentional, nondeliberate and have the purpose of responding to norms established by some other principal authority. Indirect acts would not take place but for the existence of a principal authority demanding that the indirect party commit actions that result in the violation of some human right. Indirect actors are complicit in the violation of a human right because they provide practical assistance to a principal authority who directs the violation. There are active and passive secondary instances of indirect violations; the former are positive acts taken to deprive an individual of some right where the means and methods used in the deprivation are at the discretion of the secondary actor. Passive violations are merely acts of compliance with a specific order issued by the principal authority.

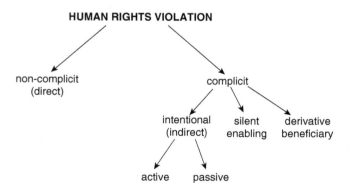

HUMAN RIGHTS VIOLATION

Figure 6.1 Classification of human rights violation

Not all complicit acts are indirect violations. Examples of these include situations where corporations enable other principal authorities to violate human rights and times when corporations benefit from ongoing human rights violations committed by principal authorities. Corporations that silently enable or derive benefit from the violation of human rights can potentially be morally negligent even though their actions do not fall into the category of indirect (intentional, nondeliberate) violations of human rights.

Complicit ICPs

The extent to which ICPs have been complicit in the violation of rights to expression, association, and privacy in China has been widely discussed. In the remaining portions of this article I will outline the nature of these complicit acts bringing to bear the aforementioned distinctions as a way of helping us understand the morally relevant features of these complicit acts. I will conclude in the following section by offering a tentative explanation as to how the different forms of complicity reviewed in this section impact the moral assessment of actions taken by ICPs in China.

The event that has garnered the most attention from critics of ICPs in China has been the case of Shi Tao, the imprisoned Chinese journalist who was found by Chinese courts to have disclosed state secrets by reporting the Communist Party's intention to limit media reports about the 15th anniversary of the Tiananmen Square massacre.[24] Shi Tao apparently took notes on a memorandum to be enforced by Chinese media agencies entitled "A Notice Regarding Current Stabilizing Work" that included recommendations that journalists not report on commemorations or other pro-democracy events at the time of the anniversary. Shi Tao sent details of this memorandum to the "Democracy Forum" under a pseudonym that was subsequently linked to Shi Tao after Yahoo provided the Chinese government the Internet protocol (IP) address from which the emails were sent. This established that Shi Tao's personal email account was accessed by a computer located in the news office of his employer, *Contemporary Business News*.[25] Once this connection was verified, the Chinese authorities also requested the content of Shi Tao's communications with the "Democracy Forum" and used this as evidence in the trial where he was convicted of "divulging state secrets abroad." He is now serving a ten-year prison sentence.

In response to the Shi Tao case, Yahoo took the official position that their managers are required to adhere to the laws, regulations, and customs of the country in which they are based. In his testimony before the US House of Representatives, Senior Vice President Michael Callahan asserted that Yahoo had no option but to conform to the requests made by Chinese law enforcement agencies for the IP addresses and user data that were eventually used in Shi Tao's case.[26] In response to criticisms leveled by human rights organizations, Yahoo has claimed that it hands over such private information only when there are specific, targeted requests made through official Chinese government channels, e.g., law enforcement agencies or courts. They also asserted that they have no way of knowing the nature of the investigations and whether there are any reliable appeal procedures for rejecting a government request for information.[27]

All of this would appear upon first blush to be an instance of what I have labeled above a passive, indirect act that violates the right of expression and privacy. Absent the government's demand for information, Yahoo would not have supplied such information. Moreover, from the perspective of Yahoo management, Yahoo was providing information in a very limited fashion, responding only to the narrow request for IP addresses and, once Shi Tao's identity had been established, specific communications of a particular user.

There are some complications with this analysis. First, although senior executives at Yahoo have confirmed that user data for Yahoo's Chinese Internet services is housed on servers in China, the information identified in court records appears to have originated from Yahoo's Hong Kong affiliate, Yahoo Holdings of Hong Kong.[28] This has led to speculation that collaboration between management in China and Hong Kong was instrumental in producing the information used to prosecute Shi Tao. Michael Callahan has denied any such information exchange between Yahoo Hong Kong and Yahoo China.[29]

If it is true that user data in Hong Kong was handed over at the request of Chinese authorities, then Yahoo's complicit action may not simply be passive in the way defined above. It could be construed as an active complicity because there is no evidence that the Chinese government either requested information on non-Chinese servers or had jurisdiction over information housed in Hong Kong. To be truly passive in their complicity Yahoo would need to demonstrate that their involvement in the investigation was specifically demanded by Chinese authorities; otherwise, the means and methods used to respond to the Chinese investigation were determined by Yahoo, rather than the principal authorities.

Second, even if this was a truly passive act of complicity with the Chinese government, Yahoo had a clear awareness of the potential problems associated with investigations of the sort illustrated in the Shi Tao case. Yahoo management clearly understood the nature of Chinese censorship of speech and the repression of political activities. While it is true that Yahoo has no way of knowing whether investigations may be criminal or political in nature, this fact provides an even stronger reason to avoid business models that may possibly implicate Yahoo in the violation of expression and privacy. Without the rule of law a company like Yahoo can easily foresee that the information gathered by the Chinese government may vary from time to time or may be arbitrary depending upon edicts of the Communist Party or the Ministry of Information. This was exactly the rationale offered by Google and Microsoft as to why they have made the decision not to offer Chinese mail, Web, and blogging services. Keeping these services in the United States has meant that user information remains located on servers outside of China.

Another set of problems has to do with the ways that Internet content in China is censored by ICPs. Here the main issue has to do with how we classify the complicity of ICPs in censorship. Are they passively responding to Chinese demands or is there an active dimension to their censorship practices?

ICPs engage in two practices that they claim are required by their operating licenses in China. First, ICPs routinely block access or "delist" websites that contain content that is deemed to be politically sensitive, destabilizing or threatening, to state security. In many cases delisting websites is redundant because such sites will be blocked by routers at the ISP and IAP level. Given the fact that ICP search engines will often display abstracted information, however, it is required that ICPs undertake their own delisting in order to prevent certain descriptions of websites from appearing before Chinese users. Examples include the *New York Times*, Radio Free Asia, Amnesty International, and Falun Gong news sites. Second, in addition to censoring certain URLs, ICPs filter content containing words or phrases that contravene norms established by the Ministry of Information. This means that websites containing dissident political themes such as Tibet, Tiananmen Square, and human rights are censored from normal search queries when those searches are performed through platforms hosted in China. When Chinese users use search phrases like "Wu Hao" (a detained filmmaker) or "June 4th 1989 crackdown" (referring to Tiananmen Square) they receive a list of Web resources and addresses that are substantially shorter than those generated by comparable searches through ICP search engines operating in other countries.[30]

Based upon studies performed by organizations such as OpenNet Imitative (ONI), Human Rights Watch, and the *Washington Post*, Yahoo, Google, and MSN all engage in delisting of URLs and Web content filtering. The extent and scope of these censorship efforts vary widely. Yahoo appears to be more aggressive in its delisting and filtering. Out of 25 URLs examined by Human Rights Watch on August 9, 2006, from stations in China, Yahoo delisted 15 sites, 14 of which were censored without explanation or notification to the user that the search result had been censored. In these nontransparent cases Yahoo's Chinese search engine simply turned up a "no results found" message in response to searches for particular URLs. Google delisted eight URLs all with a standard notification that "according to local laws, regulations, and policies, a portion of the search results do not appear." MSN was more aggressive in its delisting than Google but provided greater levels of transparency in identifying that some search results had been removed. Interestingly enough, Baidu, a main Chinese-based ICP, did not delist any of the 25 URLs on the Human Rights Watch survey; instead, Baidu simply provides a message indicating that no results have been found and a clickable URL link that is subsequently blocked by ISPs.[31]

There appears to be greater parity when looking at keyword filtering. Both Yahoo and Google filtered content from all 25 keyword searches with the addendum that some search results may not appear due to relevant laws and regulations. The number of information links available through censored searches varies according to the ICP used. In some cases the discrepancy is quite large. The keyword search for "Tibet Independence" turned up 75,200 sites in Google and 38,900 sites in Yahoo. It is difficult to determine with great accuracy the extent to which these differences result from filtering or from the search technologies employed by Google and Yahoo, respectively. Both search engines' results were dominated by pro-Chinese sources.[32]

Filtering occurs on other levels as well. MSN has taken the initiative to remove postings from blogs that use words and phrases that MSN takes to be prohibited by the spirit of the Chinese ICP licensing requirements. Google News now has a Chinese language platform that filters results that it has learned would be blocked by Chinese ISPs. Google has opted in this case not to display links to news stories or organizations that would lead to blocked searches or error pages. Google News users are neither informed that there has been blocked content nor the specific URLs or names of news organization from which the blocked content would normally appear.[33] The rationale for this move, like the rationale to filter regular Web search results, is that a limited Google presence in China is instrumental to the long-term presence of an open Internet in China. Some Internet access through non-Chinese ICPs is better than none.

Delisting and filtering sites appears to be another instance of passive complicity where ICPs are adhering to the directives issued by Chinese authorities. ICP executive leaders, such as Google's senior counsel Andrew McLaughlin and Google CEO Eric Schmidt, have stressed that absent adherence to China's censorship program it is likely that Google's services would be blocked altogether.[34] There is precedent to believe this is true. Google's US search engine and news platform were routinely inaccessible in China before the launch of Google's Chinese operations when specific licensing requirements were accepted as a condition for its operation. These requirements included delisting and filtering.[35]

The problem with classifying delisting and filtering as passive complicity is that it belies the methods used by ICPs to comply with Chinese licensing requirements. There is no official published list of URLs, words, phrases, or news stories that is handed down from Chinese officials to the managers of ICPs.[36] ICPs have developed lists of content to be censored based upon a careful extrapolation of what would fall into the broad categories of banned content identified by the Chinese government.[37] Yahoo has voluntarily signed the "Public Pledge on Self-Discipline for the Chinese Internet Industry," which specifies that Yahoo will block or filter all words, phrases, and addresses that are censored at the ISP and IAP levels. There are no guidelines, however, as to how ICPs should achieve this goal. They exercise discretion over how to monitor what is blocked by ISPs and the diagnostic tests used to determine what content Chinese routers are blocking at the point where IAPs link to the central arteries of the Internet.[38] From this effort ICPs make inferences about what content the Chinese authorities intend to block and, in turn, develop their lists of censored information. Obtaining these lists has proven to be very difficult.

ICP censorship is clearly responsive to the demands of Chinese authorities. Nonetheless, in an effort to avoid conflict with Chinese authorities and a strong motive to assure a strong competitive position within the Chinese market, American ICPs have been instrumental in improving the effectiveness of Chinese Internet censorship policies. They have deployed technology and committed resources to blocking information that has not been precisely mandated by Chinese authorities. This is an active step of complicity that requires moral justification.

A final act of complicity that should be mentioned concerns the use of Cisco Systems' routers in the maintenance of China's information networks. Cisco is not intentionally engaging in conduct that either actively or passively deprives individuals of their human rights, unless one assumes (as some have) that Cisco provides technical expertise in the use of routers for filtering purposes.[39] The act of selling network technology may be an instance of silently enabling the Chinese government to suppress rights. This may be morally negligent in that Cisco managers could foresee the use of their technology in this way. If it turns out that Cisco has intentionally designed their routers for censorship purposes, or provided technical guidance in achieving these ends, then their actions may reasonably be said to be an example of an indirect yet active violation of the rights in question. Mark Chandler, Senior Vice-President and General Counsel for Cisco Systems, has specifically denied that Cisco provides special technology or expertise for the specific purpose of filtering content or delisting URLs.[40]

Resistance through Passivity

Although I have argued that ICPs have been actively complicit in their decisions to disclose user information and filter Internet content, I have not engaged in a comparative moral assessment of active and passive varieties of what I have been calling indirect violations of human rights. Most will find the active variety more morally problematic than the passive variety. A commitment not to actively pursue methods of censorship may make the Chinese effort at censorship more difficult to accomplish. The success of the Chinese system to block all impermissible content has had, at best, mixed results; thus, if ICPs were to take a more deliberate stand to verify requests for information, explore appeal processes, wait for court orders, refrain from employing technology to enable more efficient filtering, and block URLs only upon official request, then it is more likely that ICPs could claim allegiance to the values that support basic human rights. Responding to such official requirements would help ICPs make the case that they are merely compliant actors and not assistants through their discretionary acts.

Others, including individuals representing organizations such as the Berkeley–China Internet Project and the Oxford Internet Institute, have maintained that ICPs should adopt principles that ensure greater passivity, in the technical way that I have been classifying complicit acts.[41] Greater passivity does not require inaction; indeed, refusing to initiate censorship through new technology, keeping user data offshore, waiting for written court orders, pursuing appeals, using maximal security techniques at all times, and the like, should be viewed as a kind of limited refusal to provide practical assistance in the censorship effort.

The underlying motivation for this call for greater passivity is the inability of ICPs to claim that they simply do not have a choice in how they do business in China. They are intimately familiar with the technical aspects of the Internet as well as the complicated social and political environment of China. This knowledge demands not a withdrawal from the Chinese market but a constructive engagement with it that at once refuses to provide practical assistance to censorship efforts and presses for regulatory reform through industry partners and China's trading partners. This resistance to censorship acknowledges the significance of stakeholders' rights while also accepting the claims of ICPs that their presence in China is a positive force for greater openness in an otherwise closed society.

Notes

1. For a more detailed discussion of human rights standards and their application to business, see Denis Arnold, "Human Rights and Business: An Ethical Analysis," and Bennett Freeman, "Managing Risk and Building Trust: The Challenge of Implementing the Voluntary Principles on Security and Human Rights," both in *Business and Human Rights: Dilemmas and Solutions*, ed. Rory Sullivan (Sheffield: Greenleaf Publishers, 2003).
2. Tom Zeller, "Internet Firms Are Grilled on Dealings in China," *The New York Times* (February 16, 2006). Retrieved August 15, 2006 from www.nytimes.com.
3. "Group Alleges Yahoo! Complicit in China Arrest," February 8, 2006. Retrieved September 23, 2006 from https://money.cnn.com/2006/02/08/technology/yahoo_china/index.htm.
4. International Covenant on Civil and Political Rights. Retrieved September 20, 2006 from www.ohchr.org/english/law/ccpr.htm.
5. Ibid.
6. Universal Declaration of Human Rights. Retrieved September 20, 2006 from www.un.org/Overview/rights.html.
7. David Weissbrodt and Muria Kruger, "Norms on the Responsibilities of Transnational Corporations and Other Business Enterprises with Regard to Human Rights," *American Journal of International Law* 97, no. 4 (2003): 901–22. For the complete text of the document, see the Draft Norms on the Responsibilities of Transnational Corporations and Other Business Enterprises with Regard to Human Rights. Retrieved January 3, 2007 from www1.umn.edu/humanrts/links/NormsApril2003.html.
8. United Nations Global Compact, "The Principles of the Global Compact." Retrieved November 11, 2006 from www.un.org/Depts/ptd/about-us/un-global-compact. See also Business Leader's Forum on Human Rights, "A Guide for Integrating Human Rights into Business Management," 2006. Retrieved September 2, 2006 from www.blihr.org/Pdfs/GIHRBM.pdf.
9. Arnold, "Human Rights and Business," pp. 71–75.
10. See Onora O'Neill, *Constructions of Reason: Explorations of Kant's Practial Philosophy* (Cambridge University Press, 1989), pp. 187–205; Thomas E. Hill, *Dignity and Practical Reason in Kant's Moral Theory* (Ithaca, NY: Cornell University Press, 1992), pp. 38–57; and John Rawls,

Political Liberalism (New York: Columbia University Press, 1993), pp. 289–372.

11. See John Stuart Mill, *"On Liberty" and Other Writings*, ed. Stefan Collini (Cambridge University Press, 1989) and Loren Lomasky, *Persons, Rights, and the Moral Community* (Oxford University Press, 1987).

12. Martha Nussbaum, *Women and Human Development* (Cambridge University Press, 2001) and Amartya Sen, *Development and Freedom* (New York: Random House, 1999).

13. This summary and the associated acronyms are drawn, in large part, from Human Rights Watch, "Race to the Bottom: Corporate Complicity in Chinese Internet Censorship," 18, no. 8 (August 2006): 9–24.

14. "Material Submitted for the Hearing Record," *China and the Internet: Tool for Freedom or Suppression* (Washington, DC: US Government Printing Office, 2006), pp. 181–82.

15. Human Rights Watch, "Race to the Bottom," p. 30.

16. This pledge is monitored by the Internet Society of China. See ibid., p. 12 and the Internet Society of China, "Public Pledge of Self-Regulation and Professional Ethics for China Internet Industry." Retrieved September 10, 2006 from www.isc.org.cn /20020417/ca102762.htm.

17. International Council on Human Rights Policy, "Beyond Voluntarism: Human Rights and the Developing International Legal Obligations of Companies," 2002. Retrieved October 16, 2006 from www.ichrp.org/paper_files/107_p_01.pdf.

18. Ibid., p. 121.

19. Business Leader's Forum on Human Rights, "A Guide for Integrating Human Rights into Business Management," 2006. Retrieved September 2, 2006 from www.blihr.org/Pdfs/ GIHRBM.pdf.

20. International Council on Human Rights Policy, "Beyond Voluntarism," p. 126.

21. "Holocaust Reparations: German CEOs Unlock Their Vaults," *Businessweek* (February 22, 1999). Retrieved October 27, 2006 from www.businessweek.com/1999/99_11/b3620148.htm. I owe this example to the International Council on Human Rights Policy, "Beyond Voluntarism," p. 126.

22. John Harker, "Human Security in Sudan: The Report of a Canadian Assessment Mission," Canadian Ministry of Foreign Affairs, 2000.

23. International Council on Human Rights Policy, "Beyond Voluntarism," pp. 131–32.

24. "Yahoo 'Helped Jail China Writer'," *BBC News*, September 7, 2005. Retrieved October 1, 2006 from http://news.bbc.co.uk/2/ hi/asia-pacific/4221538.stm.

25. Human Rights Watch, "Race to the Bottom," pp. 107–8.

26. Michael Callahan, Testimony before the Subcommittees on Africa, Global Human Rights, and International Operations before the Committee on International Relations, US House of Representatives, February 15, 2006, pp. 3–4.

27. Human Rights Watch, "Race to the Bottom," pp. 32–33.

28. Ibid., p. 34.

29. Michael Callahan, Testimony before the Committee on International Relations, p. 4.

30. Human Rights Watch, "Race to the Bottom," pp. 11–14. See also "The Great Firewall of China," *Washington Post* (February 18, 2006). Retrieved September 23, 2006 from www .washingtonpost.com/wpdyn/content/article/2006/02/18/ AR2006021800554.html.

31. Human Rights Watch, "Race to the Bottom," pp. 142–45.

32. Ibid.

33. Open Net Initiative, "Google.cn Filtering: How It Works," January 25, 2006. Retrieved November 27, 2006 from www .opennetinitiative.net/blog/?=87.

34. Human Rights Watch, "Race to the Bottom," p. 55.

35. Philip Pan, "U.S. Firms Balance Morality and Commerce," *Washington Post* (February 18, 2006). Retrieved September 6, 2006 from www.washingtonpost.com/wp-dyn/content/article/ 2006/02/18/AR2006021801397.html.

36. Human Rights Watch, "Race to the Bottom," p. 12.

37. Ibid., pp. 3–4.

38. Open Net Initiative, "Google.cn Filtering: How It Works."

39. Mark Chandler, Testimony before the Subcommittees on Africa, Global Human Rights, and International Operations before the Committee on International Relations, US House of Representatives, February 15, 2006, p. 1.

40. For a response, see Declan McCullah, "U.N. Blasts Cisco, Others on China Cooperation," *CNet News.com*, October 31, 2006. Retrieved November 17, 2006 from http://news.com/U.N.+blasts+ Cisco,+others+on+China+cooperation/2100–1028_ 3-6131010.html.

41. These organizations have focused their efforts on a voluntary code of conduct for ICPs. See Human Rights Watch, "Race to the Bottom," pp. 73–76.

CASES

Case 1: Privacy at MyFriends.Com

DENIS G. ARNOLD

Since the creation of the Internet, privacy policies have been an issue for many online companies, especially social networks where users can widely share information to anyone around the world. A recent and very successful start-up social network called MyFriends.com is facing a major decision about its privacy policies and practices.

Users at MyFriends.com create a profile where they can insert their private information, upload photos, and share them with their online friends. MyFriends.com also takes advantage of the applications systems where users can play games with other users, and share interests between each other. Most applications are developed by independent software developers who then make their apps available to MyFriends.com users. The applications sell the users' information, as well as that of their online friends, to advertising and Internet tracking companies. This information includes the sex, age, birthdate, address, income, shopping habits, and browsing habits of the users and their friends.

One problem is that this information is shared for all users, including those that choose the strictest level of privacy on their MyFriends.com settings. This policy option was in place for users when MyFriends.com first went online and it allowed users to communicate with their online friends while "opting out" of all sharing of their information for commercial or other purposes. Millions of users "opted out" of information sharing in this way. But because the "referrer" technology built in to most applications shares this information anyway, the strict privacy settings don't apply to the use of the apps (e.g., games, utilities, etc.) that make MyFriends.com so popular.

Senior managers at MyFriends.com have proposed three options to deal with this problem:

1. Do nothing, and allow sharing of user information for commercial purposes for all customers via applications, including those who "opted out" of information sharing when they opened their accounts.

2. Change the privacy setting options by removing the strict non-sharing option and require all users to choose between much less protective options that allow for either general information sharing about users by MyFriends.com or for information sharing about application users only.

3. Honor the strict privacy option by requiring developers to update their applications so that users who have selected to "opt out" from information sharing don't have their information shared any longer.

The managers have solicited feedback from employees and read comments by users in online forums. Most of the feedback has supported greater privacy. But enhanced user privacy will cost the company considerably more than doing nothing. They have come together to hammer out a policy. What, they ponder, should MyFriends.com do?

Discussion Questions

1. If you were an employee of MyFriends.com which of these options would you recommend and why? Explain.
2. If you were a MyFriends.com user which one of these options would you recommend and why? Explain.
3. Which policy do you believe Jeroen van den Hoven would support? Why? Which policy would Amitai Etzioni support? Why?
4. In your view, are Internet users entitled to any level of privacy with respect to their online browsing, communicating, and shopping behaviors? Why, or why not? If so, what information should be protected and by whom (e.g., firms or governments)?

Case 2: Implanting Microchips in Workers: Improving Efficiency or Invading Privacy?

OSCAR JEROME STEWART

Three Square Market is a micro market solutions company that provides self-service stores that operate within businesses as a more robust alternative to traditional vending machines. This small, Wisconsin-based company is making headlines not because of its product offerings, but because it has partnered with Swedish technology company Biohax International to become the first company in the United States to offer Radio-Frequency Identification microchip implants for its 85+ employees. Firms at the Swedish innovation hub, Epicenter, have been experimenting with these RFID microchip implants for employees since 2014. Biohax's vision for this wearable technology is to replace everything we would keep in our wallets with an implantable microchip, streamlining activity and minimizing the need for items that can get lost or stolen.

This US Food and Drug Administration approved technology is the size of a grain of rice and implants under the skin between an employee's thumb and index finger. The implant allows employees to activate certain software by holding their chip (via their hand) up to a device reader, which reads a unique number associated with that employee to activate the software at hand. The RFID readers at Three Square Market allow employees to easily purchase food in company facilities, open company doors, and login to their computers, all with a swipe of their hand. Importantly, employees at Three Square Market and its predecessors in Sweden all volunteer for the RFID microchip implant. Neither Three Square Market, nor firms at the Epicenter in Sweden, require employees to implant a RFID microchip as a part of an employment contract. After its introduction at Three Square Market, roughly two-thirds of the 80-person workforce agreed to implant the technology in their skin. For those not yet convinced, Three Square Market offers a wristband with the RFID microchip, which serves the same purpose without the implant.

Some employees and critics harbor concerns that this wearable technology will simply become a more advanced way to control employees. Currently, the technology is a "passive chip" with no power supply and thus no ability to do things such as send employers signals about its position (i.e., it has no location function). However, employers can access RFID readers to learn such information as when employees arrive (when they first use the door scanners in the morning) and when they take breaks (when they visit the vending areas throughout the day). Critics also contend that microchips have potential for health issues, such as infection, and that data privacy concerns will arise as hackers learn how to access the technology. For now, the practice is not widespread, with approximately 4,000 people worldwide having the technology implanted into their skin. However, the practice has been adapted as an option by the Swedish railway system, and Biohax is a growth orientated firm.

Discussion Questions

1. Would you accept an RFID microchip provided by your employer? Why, or why not? Explain.
2. As implantable RFID microchips develop, what other employee information might they include in the future? Do you have any significant concerns about the tracking and use of such information? If so, what are they? Explain.
3. Should employers be legally permitted to require employees to accept RFID microchips? Why or why not? Explain.
4. Would Daniel Solove object to mandatory RFID implants in workers? Why, or why not? Would he object to optional RFID implants in workers? Why, or why not?

This case was written for discussion purposes and is based on the following sources:

O. Solon, "World's Lamest Cyborg? My Microchip Isn't Cool Now – but It Could Be the Future," *The Guardian* (August 2, 2017). Retrieved from www.theguardian.com/technology/2017/aug/02/microchip-contactless-payment-three-square-market-biohax.

A. DeNisco, "Three Square Market Becomes First U.S. Company to Offer Implanted Microchips to All Employees," *TechRepublic* (July 24, 2017). Retrieved from www.techrepublic.com/article/three-square-market-becomes-first-us-company-to-offer-implanted-microchips-to-all-employees/.

M. Astor, "Microchip Implants for Employees? One Company Says Yes," *The New York Times* (July 25, 2017). Retrieved from www.nytimes.com/2017/07/25/technology/microchips-wisconsin-company-employees.html.

Case 3: Social Media and the Modern Worker: The Use of Facebook as an Organizational Monitoring and Management Tool

LORIL M. GOSSETT

Employee privacy rights on social media platforms (e.g., Facebook, Twitter, LinkedIn) is a rapidly evolving area of scholarly and legal debate. To what extent should employing organizations be allowed to monitor or restrict the information their employees share on the Internet? Does it matter if these individuals identify themselves as members of a particular firm? Does it matter if the information shared is job-related or if it is part of a worker's personal life? Does it matter if access to the website is available to the public or if it is restricted to the employee's friends and family? Where do the boundaries of organizational authority exist both outside and within cyberspace?

Companies have long employed a variety of methods to monitor the actions of their staff. In addition to surveillance cameras and software designed to track behavior on company-owned computers and phones, managers have relied on the services of third parties to monitor their employees. For example, a 2009 study revealed that 38 percent of US firms with more than 1,000 workers have hired additional staff specifically to read or otherwise analyze outbound employee email.[1] In an era where employees are increasingly geographically distributed (e.g., working at home, located in a client's office), firms are also returning to the old-school method of using private investigators to determine if their employees are actually working or instead "playing hooky" on company time.[2] While it seems clear that companies have a legitimate need to ensure their staff behave appropriately, scholars are forced to consider if there are (or should be) any limits placed on an organization's ability to monitor its workforce.

New Rules, Methods, and Questions

With the rapid growth in popularity of social media services such as Twitter, Facebook, and Myspace, companies have started to add online behavior clauses to their employment contracts.[3] In 2009, 8 percent of US firms reported firing workers specifically for violating their company's social media policy.[4] Concern over employee activity online is not strictly a US phenomenon. CareerBuilder.com found that more that 40 percent of employers in the UK had eliminated job applicants from consideration after examining their Facebook accounts.[5] Some firms have started to ask applicants to list all of their social media accounts or access them during interviews

so that the company can evaluate their content. Organizations can also subscribe to *Social Sentry*, a firm that claims it can track the social media behavior of every employee (on or off the clock) for less than $10 a person.[6]

In some instances, firms do not have to take the time or effort to monitor their workers' online behavior; the public does it for them. For example, Connor McIlvenna lost his job for posting support for the 2011 Stanley Cup riots in Vancouver on his Facebook page. His boss said he fired Connor for these comments because "I just didn't feel like what was said was appropriate, and I didn't want any affiliation towards my company with the things he said on Facebook . . . I had over 100 emails and out of the 100 emails, close to 30 of them were copies of his Facebook page which he sent out during the riots."[7] In another example of a third party employee surveillance, a TV reporter in Charlotte, North Carolina reviewed the Facebook pages of teachers employed in the local school district. The reporter then selected seven individuals whose pages contained questionable content and brought these to the attention of the school district and the public at large. While four teachers were simply reprimanded for having inappropriate material online, one male staff member was fired for commenting that he liked "chillin' wit my niggas" and because he had a suggestive exchange with a female friend accompanied by a shirtless photo of himself. Two other teachers caught in the news sting faced termination proceedings for posting comments such as "I'm teaching in the most ghetto school in Charlotte" or "I'm feeling pissed because I hate my students." The school district justified its actions by stating that "When you're in a professional position, especially one where you're interacting with children and parents, you need to be above reproach."[8]

These examples help to illustrate the growing trend of companies using social media as a way to manage both their staff and their corporate image. It has become so common that there is even a Facebook Group with over 600 members entitled "Fired by Facebook," where individuals share their stories of losing their jobs because of something they posted (or that was posted about them) on the popular website.

Some people claim that the nature of specific jobs (e.g., public school teachers) justifies more strict oversight and restriction of employee behavior online. For example, in

2011 the State of Missouri passed a law forbidding teachers from having any private or direct interaction with students on social media sites. Others have argued that in a *right to work* environment, employers should have the ability to fire any individual whose online behavior or opinions have the potential to bring negative publicity to their organization. People may be legally entitled to free speech, but they are not necessarily entitled to a job if their employer objects to what they say or do on the Internet. The following two examples can help us more carefully consider the ethical challenges associated with firms monitoring their employees' social media behavior.

A Tale of Two Ashleys

In 2010, a 22-year-old waitress in Charlotte, North Carolina (Ashley Johnson) was fired from a local restaurant after she complained about a poor tip she received on her Facebook page.[9] Ms. Johnson worked at *Brixx Wood Fired Pizza* and was upset after a customer left a $5 tip after occupying a table for three hours. When she got home from work, she posted the following comment on her personal page: "Thanks for eating at BRIXX, you cheap piece of ***[10] camper." It is important to note that Ms. Johnson's Facebook page was not available to the general public. She had limited access to her immediate friends and family (which did not include members of BRIXX management). Restaurant officials have never disclosed how they learned of Ms. Johnson's posting, other than to state that it was sent to them by a third party. However they justified the termination of her employment because they claimed Ms. Johnson had violated a clause in her employment contract that strictly forbade workers from making negative statements about the company on social media websites. BRIXX management indicated that it was forced to take action against Ms. Johnson because she, like all of its other employees, was a public ambassador of the company. "Our company social media policy clearly states that employees are not to disparage our customers, and there are consequences for those who do."

In another Facebook-related termination, a Georgia Public High School teacher (Ashley Payne) was forced to resign when an anonymous email alerted school officials to potentially offensive photos and statements on Ms. Payne's personal Facebook page. Similar to the BRIXX restaurant case discussed above, Ms. Payne had strong privacy protections on her account and did not have any students or school parents as Facebook friends. The postings in question were from a 2009 vacation Ms. Payne took to Europe which showed her holding alcoholic beverages. Additionally, Ms. Payne had a status update on her page indicating that she was going out with friends to play "Crazy Bitch Bingo," a game sponsored by an Atlanta restaurant. Once school

officials confirmed that Ms. Payne's Facebook page included the content in question, they justified requesting Ms. Payne's immediate resignation on the grounds that all teachers had been warned not to engage in "unacceptable online activities." After reviewing her Facebook account, school officials determined that Ms. Payne had violated the unacceptable activity standard because her page promoted alcohol use and contained profane language.[11]

The Georgia High School and BRIXX restaurant cases are similar in that these two employees lost their jobs because an unknown third party shared information from their Facebook pages with their employers; people who would not normally have had access to this information. Unlike the instances mentioned above, both Ms. Johnson and Ms. Payne made efforts to restrict public access to their accounts. What makes these two cases different is that Ashley Johnson's posting directly referenced the BRIXX restaurant (i.e., the tipping behavior of customers). In contrast, Ashley Payne lost her job because of issues related to her behavior outside the workplace.

Notes

1. Proofpoint Inc., "Proofpoint Survey Says: State of Economy Leads to Increased Data Loss Risk for Large Companies" (August 10, 2009). Retrieved from www.marketwire.com/press-release/Proofpoint-Survey-Says-State-Economy-Leads-Increased-Data-Loss-Risk-Large-Companies-1027877.htm.

2. Hooky Detectives, "The Sick-Day Bounty Hunters," *Bloomberg Businessweek* (December 2, 2010). Retrieved from www.bloomberg.com/news/articles/2010-12-02/the-sick-day-bounty-hunters.

3. L. Gossett and J. Kilker, "My Job Sucks: Examining Counter-Institutional Websites as Locations for Organizational Member Voice, Dissent, and Resistance," *Management Communication Quarterly* 20, no. 1 (2006): 63–90.

4. Proofpoint, "Proofpoint Survey Says."

5. "Half of Employers 'Reject Potential Worker after Look at Facebook Page,'" *The Telegraph* (January 11, 2010). Retrieved from www.telegraph.co.uk/technology/facebook/6968320/Half-of-employers-reject-potential-worker-after-look-at-Facebook-page.html.

6. C. Rubin, "Keeping Tabs on Your Employees' Facebook Activity," *INC.com* (May 30, 2010). Retrieved from www.inc.com/news/articles/2010/03/tracking-employees-on-social-media.html.

7. N. Reid, "Man Fired for Applauding Vancouver Riot on Facebook" (June 18, 2011). Retrieved from http://winnipeg.ctv.ca/servlet/an/local/CTVNews/20110618/bc_facebook_riot_comments_fired_110618/20110618/?hub=WinnipegHome.

8. A. D. Helms, "Charlotte Teachers Face Action Because of Facebook Postings," *The Herald* (November 12, 2008). Retrieved from www.heraldonline.com/news/local/article12241319.html.

9. L. Gossett, "Fired over Facebook: Issues of Employee Monitoring and Personal Privacy on Social Media Websites," in *Case Studies in Organizational Communication: Ethical Perspectives and Practices*, ed. S. May (Thousand Oaks, CA: Sage Publications), pp. 207–18.

10. Ms. Johnson's actual quote was censored by the press. As such, we can only guess at the term she used to describe her customers.

11. E. Moriarty, "Did the Internet Kill Privacy?" *CBS News* (February 6, 2011). Retrieved from www.cbsnews.com/stories/2011/02/06/sunday/main7323148.shtml.

Discussion Questions

1. Managers are responsible for maintaining a positive public image of their organization and for maintaining a civil and productive work environment for their staff. If information contained on an employee's webpage threatens the firm's culture, to what extent do managers have a moral obligation to monitor the social media behavior of their workforce?

2. According to a recent study by Dr. Chang of Boston University, some employers are requiring workers to "friend" their companies on their personal Facebook accounts as a condition of employment. Not only does this help promote the organization to their employees' own friends and families, it also provides supervisors with access to employees' Facebook accounts. Given the potential consequences to the employee, is it ethical for firms to encourage, pressure, or even require their workers to "friend" their employer?

3. If the information on the employee's webpage is protected by privacy settings or passwords, should organizations be allowed to use information gained from third parties (known or unknown) in order to determine if an employee has violated a firm's social media policy?

4. Should employers be allowed to use social media to determine if their staff members are behaving in a moral and appropriate fashion – both in their personal and professional lives? Are there any limitations to what sort of restrictions an employer can place on an employee's social media behavior?

Case 4: Facebook's Emotional Contagion Study

DENIS G. ARNOLD

In a controversial study published in the *Proceedings of the National Academy of Sciences*, researchers from Facebook and Cornell University manipulated the newsfeeds of a random sample of 689,003 Facebook users. For some users, they removed newsfeed content that contained positive words, while for other users they removed content that contained negative words. To put the experiment in straightforward terms, some users were manipulated to feel happier and others were manipulated to feel sadder. The goal was to determine if the manipulation had a corresponding negative or positive emotional impact on the users and whether or not these emotional states could be transferred by users to their Facebook friends. The degree of impact varied among users, but the results indicate that, in general, the emotions of users were successfully manipulated. The study could have shown no impact on user emotions, or a much greater impact on user emotions. The study was not restricted to adults and included Facebook users in the 13–17 age range. The researchers did not obtain informed consent from the Facebook users as is commonly required of any US based research on human subjects conducted by university researchers. Research on children normally requires special permission and compelling justification tied to public welfare. The fine print in Facebook's Data Use Policy did not inform Facebook users of the possibility of such research being undertaken until four months after the study was completed, although it did acknowledge that user data would be used by the firm to improve customer service. Even so, the document is written in dense legal language that is thousands of words in length. Few users can be expected to examine it with care before agreeing. Defenders of Facebook note that this type of research by Internet companies is commonplace, if not widely understood by users. It was mainly because the Cornell University researchers did not obtain informed consent from users that this study was particularly controversial and received widespread media attention.

Discussion Questions

1. What, if anything, is ethically objectionable about changing user newsfeeds in these ways? Explain.

2. Would you feel like Facebook was wrongfully harming you if they covertly manipulated the information you saw online in this way without disclosing this to you? Why, or why not? Explain.

3. Facebook is a for-profit company which users access and utilize for free. Shouldn't Facebook, and similar companies, be expected to manipulate consumers in ways that allow them to increase profits? Why, or why not? Explain.

4. Which theoretical perspective in this chapter best informs your thinking about this case? Explain.

This case was written for the purposes of classroom discussion and is based on the following sources: Chris Chambers, "Facebook Fiasco: Was Cornell's Study of 'Emotional Contagion' an Ethics Breach?" *The Guardian* (July 1, 2014).

Kashmir Hill, "Facebook Added 'Research' to User Agreement 4 Months after Emotion Manipulation Study," *Forbes.com* (June 30, 2014).

Gregory S. McNeal, "Controversy over Facebook Emotional Manipulation Study Grows as Timeline Becomes More Clear," *Forbes.com* (June 30, 2014). Retrieved from www.forbes.com/sites/gregorymcneal/2014/06/30/controversy-over-facebook-emotional-manipulation-study-grows-as-timeline-becomes-more-clear/#28ef331b9caa.

Case 5: Doing Business in China

DENIS G. ARNOLD

Adopted in 1948 by the United Nations in the wake of the widespread atrocities committed in World War II, the Universal Declaration of Human Rights affirms the "inherent dignity and of the equal and inalienable rights of all members of the human family." Among its 30 articles are the following:

Article 18. Everyone has the right to freedom of thought, conscience and religion; this right includes freedom to change his religion or belief, and freedom, either alone or in community with others and in public or private, to manifest his religion or belief in teaching, practice, worship and observance.

Article 19. Everyone has the right to freedom of opinion and expression; this right includes freedom to hold opinions without interference and to seek, receive and impart information and ideas through any media and regardless of frontiers.

Article 20. (1) Everyone has the right to freedom of peaceful assembly and association. (2) No one may be compelled to belong to an association.

Article 21. (1) Everyone has the right to take part in the government of his country, directly or through freely chosen representatives. (2) Everyone has the right of equal access to public service in his country. (3) The will of the people shall be the basis of the authority of government; this will shall be expressed in periodic and genuine elections which shall be by universal and equal suffrage and shall be held by secret vote or by equivalent free voting procedures.

Citizens of China are largely denied these rights. From the perspective of the ruling Communist Party, community interests supersede individual rights. Internet content providers (ICPs) that do business in China must agree to censor Internet content consistent with the demands of the Chinese government. The censorship includes search results linking to sources on political opposition to the Communist Party, facts regarding the Tiananmen Square massacre of 1989, discussion of the political controversies regarding Tibet and Taiwan, advocacy of certain religions not sanctioned by the government, and discussions of human rights. ICPs must also provide the name and locations of any users that engage in online communications deemed unacceptable, such as political dissent or criticism of government actions. With a population of 1.4 billion, China has the single largest national market in the world. Proponents of providing Internet service in China argue that firms have an obligation to shareholders to maximize profits and point out that they are merely following local laws. Critics of providing Internet service in China point out that shareholder primacy theory assumes a democratic context where citizens determine business regulations and that agreeing to these terms constitutes complicity with human rights abuses.

Discussion Questions

1. Would you be willing to accept a job at an ICP where your job responsibilities included designing and maintaining the technology necessary to censor Internet searches in China? Why, or why not? Explain.

2. If you were a leader at an ICP, would you recommend doing business in China? Why, or why not? Explain.

3. Based on his article in this chapter, what would Jeffery Smith recommend that the ICP do with respect to entering the Chinese market? Why? Do you agree or disagree with Smith? Explain.

7

Marketing Ethics

7.1 INTRODUCTION

Is it acceptable for a company to lie and use other forms of deception, such as exaggeration or concealment, in order to sell a product or service? If profits are the end, doesn't that entail that nearly any marketing methods are justified? After all, consumers have a choice about whether or not to purchase products or services. Whether or not such deception can be ethically justified, consumers face widespread deception by firms seeking to influence consumer behavior. Such deception has been documented by social scientists, journalists, public health advocates, government agencies, and even consumers themselves.

Marketing decisions include such questions as whether to place a new product on the market, how to price a product, how to advertise, and how to conduct sales. Marketing research, pricing, advertising, selling, and international marketing have all come under close ethical scrutiny in recent years. Ethical issues about marketing are often centered on obligations to disclose information. Advertising is the most visible way businesses present information to the public, but not the only or even the most important way. Sales information, annual reports, corporate social responsibility reports, public relations presentations, physician office visits by sales representatives, funding "think tanks" that support firm agendas, trade associations, and political lobbying are other vital means by which corporations manage, communicate, and limit information.

A classic defense of capitalism is that business provides the public with products that the public wants; the consumer is king or queen in the free enterprise system, and the market responds to consumer demands. This response is often said to represent the chief strength of a market economy over a collectivist system. Freedom of consumer choice is unaffected by government and corporate controls. But consider the following controversy about freedom of choice. Some years ago the US Federal Trade Commission (FTC) "reconsidered" its rule prohibiting supermarket advertising of items when those items are not in stock. The rule had been enacted to combat frustration among shoppers who found empty shelves in place of advertised goods and often wound up substituting more expensive items. FTC officials suggested that the rule may have been unduly burdensome for the supermarket industry and that "market forces" would eliminate or curtail those who dishonestly advertised. Consumer groups argued that relaxing the rule would permit more expensive stores to lure shoppers by advertising low prices leading many shoppers to spend more overall than they would have spent in a low-budget store. Mark Silbergeld of Consumers Union argued that the commission was acting in ignorance of the real purpose of supermarket advertising, which is to present a "come-on to get people into their stores."[1]

More recently, the FTC found that Volkswagen systematically deceived consumers over a seven-year period by advertising "Clean Diesel" vehicles which, in fact, produced diesel emissions harmful to human health, but which used a "defeat device" to pass emissions tests.[2] Over half a million cars were sold to consumers under this false marketing campaign, with harmful pollutants being emitted by these cars during their normal operations. It is difficult to imagine how consumers could determine that this campaign was deceptive, when the company was able to successfully deceive government inspections via the software installed in its cars.

It has been widely appreciated that this problem is only one among many that confront marketers of goods and services. Some problems are commonplace – for example, withholding vital information, distorting data, and providing payments or gifts to individuals who can influence sales. Other problems of information control are more subtle; these include the use of flashy information to entice customers, the use of corporate social responsibility reports as public relations devices, and the use of calculated "news releases" to promote products. Rights of autonomy and free choice are at the center of these discussions. In some forms, withholding information and manipulating advertising messages threaten to undermine the free choice of consumers, clients, stockholders, and even colleagues. Deceptive and misleading statements can limit freedom by restricting the range of choice and can cause a person to do what he or she otherwise would not do.

Aside from these *autonomy*-based problems, there are *harm*-based problems that may have little to do with making a choice. For example, in recent years, the pharmaceutical industry's direct-to-consumer advertising campaigns have been criticized for providing misleading information and encouraging over-medication with products that have serious, sometimes lethal, side-effects. Perhaps the most notorious recent example is the case of Merck's prescription drug Vioxx. This pain relief medication was marketed to consumers and doctors as a safe and effective painkiller suitable for use by the general population. However, the drug had serious risks, including heart attacks, which Merck attempted to suppress. Moreover, for general pain relief Vioxx was no more effective than much safer and much less expensive over-the-counter medications such as Ibuprofen. It is estimated that approximately 140,000 cases of heart disease in the United States, and as many as 56,000 premature deaths, were caused by the painkiller during the five years that it was marketed to consumers (the drug was later withdrawn from the market).[3] This controversy focused not on the freedom-based issue of the right to disseminate information, rather the controversy was regarding the public's welfare and, in particular, harm to individuals facilitated by misleading or deceptive marketing.

The root of the problem is that consumers are frequently unable to evaluate information about the variety of goods and services available to them without assistance. There is a large information asymmetry, or "knowledge gap," between consumers and marketers. Consumers frequently lack vital information, or lack the skills to evaluate goods or services. Such circumstances lead to situations in which consumers must place trust in a service agency, producer, or retailer. Many marketers are well aware of this situation and believe that they have a duty not to abuse their position of superior information. Many also engage in marketing their own trustworthiness, while simultaneously deceptively marketing a product or service. When the proclaimed trust is breached (whether intentionally or by accident), the marketer–consumer relationship is damaged.

AUTONOMY AND MARKETING

Marketing celebrates consumption and utilizes emotional appeals, persuasion, puffery, celebrity status, and a variety of other means to sell. Many critics deplore the values presented in marketing as well as the effects marketing has on consumers. Other critics are more concerned about specific practices of marketing directed at vulnerable groups such as children, the poor, and the elderly;

marketing that exploits women or uses fear appeals; advertising that uses subliminal messages; and the advertising of liquor, tobacco products, and pharmaceuticals. Although critics have long denounced misleading or information-deficient advertising, the moral concerns and concepts underlying these denunciations have seldom been carefully examined. What is a deceptive or misleading advertisement? Is it, for example, deceptive or misleading to advertise a heavily sweetened cereal as "nutritious" and "building strong bodies"? Is it deceptive to market a product that contains a single ingredient (out of several) that has been associated with lower cholesterol as a product that "prevents heart disease"? Are such advertisements forms of lying? Are they manipulative, especially when children are the primary targets or people are led to make purchases they do not need and would not have made had they not seen the advertising? If so, does the manipulation derive from some form of deception?

Control over a person is exerted through various kinds of influences, but not all *influences* actually *control* behavior. Some forms of influence are desired and accepted by those who are influenced, whereas others are unwelcome. Many influences can easily be resisted by most persons; others are irresistible to many people. Human reactions to influences such as corporate-sponsored information and advertising presentations cannot in many cases be determined or easily studied. Frank D'Andrea, Vice-President of Marketing for Schieffelin & Co., importer of Hennessy Cognac, once said that in their advertisements, "the idea is to show a little skin, a little sex appeal, a little tension."[4] This effect is accomplished by showing a scantily-clad woman holding a brandy snifter and staring provocatively in response to a man's interested glance. Hennessy tries in a subtle manner to use a mixture of sex and humor, just as Axe body wash used the technique in less than subtle ways. Other companies use rebates and coupons. All these methods are attempts to influence, and it is well known that they are at least partially successful. However, the degree of influence of these strategies and the moral acceptability of these influences have been less carefully examined.

There is a continuum of controlling influence in our daily lives, running from coercion, at the most controlling end of the continuum, to persuasion and education, both of which are noncontrolling influences. Other points on the continuum include indoctrination, seduction, and the like. Coercion requires an intentional and successful influence through a threat of harm. A coercively induced action deprives a person of freedom because it controls the person's action. Rational persuasion, by contrast, involves a successful appeal to reason to convince a person to accept freely what is advocated by the persuader. Like informing, persuading is entirely compatible with free choice.

Many choices are not substantially free, although we commonly think of them as free. These include actions under powerful family or religious influences, but also purchases made under the psychological manipulation of sophisticated marketers. Many actions fall short of ideal-free action either because the agent lacks critical information or because the agent is under the control of another person. The central question is whether actions are sufficiently or adequately free, not whether they are ideally or wholly free.

Manipulation is a general term that refers to the great gray area of influence. It is a catch-all category that suggests the act of getting people to do what is advocated without resorting to coercion but also without appealing to reasoned argument. In the case of *informational* manipulation, on which several selections in this chapter concentrate, information is managed so that the manipulated person will do what the manipulator intends. Whether such uses of information necessarily compromise or restrict free choice is an unresolved issue. One plausible thesis is that some manipulations – for instance, the use of rewards such as loyalty points earned by shopping or Internet ads which are based on a user's browsing history – are compatible with free choice, whereas others – such as deceptive offers or tantalizing ads aimed at children and adolescents – are not compatible with free choice. Alcohol and tobacco advertising aimed at teenagers and young adults have been under particularly harsh criticism, on the grounds that sex, youth, fun, and beauty are directly linked in the advertising to dangerous products, with noticeable marketing success.

As Robert L. Arrington points out in his essay, these issues raise complex questions of moral responsibility in the advertising of products. Arrington notes that puffery, subliminal advertising, and indirect information transfer are typical examples of the problem. After he examines criticisms and defenses of such practices, he analyzes four of the central concepts at work in the debate: (1) autonomous desire, (2) rational desire, (3) free choice, and (4) control. He argues that, despite certain dangers, advertising should not be judged guilty of common violations of the consumer's autonomy.

Many problems with advertising seem to fall somewhere between acceptable and unacceptable manipulation. Consider these two examples: Anheuser-Busch ran a television commercial for its Budweiser beer showing some working men heading for a brew at day's end. The commercial began with a shot of the Statue of Liberty in the background, included close-up shots of a construction crew working to restore the statue, and ended with the words "This Bud's for you; you know America takes pride in what you do." This statement may seem innocent, but the Liberty–Ellis Island Foundation accused Anheuser-Busch of a "blatant attempt to dupe [i.e., manipulate] consumers" by implying that Budweiser was among the sponsors helping repair the statue. The foundation was particularly annoyed because Anheuser-Busch had refused such a sponsorship when invited by the foundation, whereas its rival, Stroh Brewing Company, had subsequently accepted an exclusive brewery sponsorship.[5]

A second case comes from Kellogg's advertising for its All-Bran product. The company ran a campaign linking its product to the prevention of cancer, apparently causing an immediate increase in sales of 41 percent for All-Bran. Although many food manufacturers advertise the low-salt, low-fat, low-calorie, or high-fiber content of their products, Kellogg went further, citing a specific product as a way to combat a specific disease. It is illegal to make claims about the health benefits of a specific food product without Food and Drug Administration (FDA) approval, and Kellogg did not have this approval. Even so, officials at both the National Cancer Institute and the FDA were not altogether critical of the ads. On the one hand, officials at these agencies agree that a high-fiber, low-fat diet containing some of the ingredients in All-Bran does help prevent cancer. On the other hand, no direct association exists between eating a given product and preventing cancer, and certainly no single food product can function like a drug as a preventive or remedy for such a disease.

The Kellogg ad strongly suggested that eating All-Bran is what one needs to do to prevent cancer. Such a claim is potentially misleading in several respects. The ad did not suggest how much fiber people should eat, nor did it note that people can consume too much fiber while neglecting other essential minerals. Further, no direct scientific evidence linked the consumption of this product with the prevention of cancer, and this product could not be expected to affect all types of cancer. Is the Kellogg promise manipulative, or is the ad, as Kellogg claims, basically a truthful, health-promotion campaign?

One of the court cases in this chapter – *Coca-Cola Company v. Tropicana Products, Inc.* – focuses on a central question of the ethics of advertising. In this case, the two main competitors in the United States for the chilled orange juice market came into a direct conflict. The Coca-Cola Company, maker of Minute Maid orange juice, sued Tropicana Products on grounds of false advertising. Tropicana had claimed in its advertisements that its brand of orange juice is "as it comes from the orange" and the only "brand not made with concentrate and water." Coke asserted that this claim was false and that Tropicana is pasteurized and sometimes frozen prior to packaging. Coke also claimed that it had lost sales of its product as a result of this misrepresentation. The court agreed with Coke both that the company had lost sales and that consumers had been misled by Tropicana's advertising campaign.

In a second case in the legal section, the United States Court of Appeals for the Seventh Circuit took up a set of issues presented in the case *B. Sanfield, Inc. v. Finlay Fine Jewelry Corp.* The issues concerned one of the most commonly used forms of bargain advertising, which is to offer a percentage reduction from the advertiser's own former price for an article. Had the original price been a bona fide price at which the article was being offered to the public over the course of a substantial period of time, the price comparison would be a legitimate basis for an advertisement. But if the alleged "former price" was not bona fide but, rather, fictitious – for example, an inflated price that makes the subsequent offer appear to be a large reduction – then the "bargain" being advertised is itself fictitious. In this case, Sanfield (a locally owned retailer) contended that when Finlay (a nationwide retailer) advertised its jewelry at around 50 percent off the "regular" price, the ad was nothing more than a way of deceiving consumers; the "bargain" that Finlay advertised was no bargain at all, as Sanfield saw it. Sanfield believed that its business was suffering because of its competitors' misleading advertisements with phony discounting and fake percentage markdowns. Nonetheless, the court found in this case that "deception, like beauty, is in the eye of the beholder." Whether an ad is deceptive therefore turns entirely on the perception of the consumer, not the ad itself.

These examples illustrate the broad categories on the continuum of controlling influences that are under examination in this chapter. They indicate that the difference between *manipulation* and *persuasion* is the key matter. Of course, the question must be addressed whether *unjustifiably* manipulative advertising occurs frequently, or even at all.

Marketing takes many forms and includes not just advertising and "stealth" practices, such as the undisclosed use of paid experts, but nearly all forms of corporate communication. In the California Supreme Court decision *Kasky v. Nike, Inc.*, included in this chapter, it was found that corporations can be held accountable for the accuracy of statements made by public relations personnel regarding controversial issues such as their labor conditions in the factories in their supply chains. This decision, upheld by the US Supreme Court, found that such speech is commercial speech, not political speech, and as a result the courts found that firms are liable for the accuracy of their claims about such matters.

Certain segments of any given population are especially vulnerable to deceptive and manipulative marketing strategies. The elderly, children, and the economically impoverished are examples of such vulnerable groups. American children alone, for example, are targeted by at least $17 billion in marketing annually.[6] One study estimated that children view in the range of 40,000 television commercials each year.[7] Unlike previous generations, US children growing up in the twenty-first century are reached by marketers in nearly every facet of their lives. Advertisements reach them at home via television, social media apps, and web browsing; on the way to and from school via billboards and vehicle placards; and in school via paid advertisements in cafeterias and vending machines. Often the advertising is covert and arrives in the form of videos, texts, and social media celebrity endorsements which parents do not see and often cannot block. As the American Psychological Association has noted, children – especially children under the age of eight – typically lack the critical skills necessary to recognize advertisements as biased and tend to understand them as statements of fact.[8] Marketers who target children know this and use it to their advantage. Marketing to children can result in serious harms such as poor self-esteem, false notions of how to achieve happiness, a distorted worldview, a poor diet leading to obesity and serious health problems, and poor money management skills leading to indebtedness in the teen years and beyond. In his article in this chapter, "Marketing and the Vulnerable," George G. Brenkert notes that the concept of vulnerability is slippery, but he argues that we can gain enough clarity about the concept to make use of it in assessing marketing strategies. Brenkert argues that vulnerability is best understood as susceptibility to harm by others. He argues that marketing campaigns that target those, such as children, who are especially vulnerable must be designed so that those that are targeted are treated fairly. Marketing campaigns that fail to do so, he argues, are unethical.

DECEPTION AND COMMERCIAL SPEECH

In recent years the aggressive marketing of highly processed food, laden with sugar and saturated fat, has received sustained criticism of public health experts. Obesity, Type 2 diabetes, high blood pressure, heart disease, and premature death have been linked to increased consumption of such foods. In their article "The Perils of Ignoring History: Big Tobacco Played Dirty and Millions Died. How Similar Is Big Food?" Kelly D. Brownell and Kenneth E. Warner argue that many of the deceptive marketing strategies utilized by Big Food are taken from the playbook Big Tobacco. These strategies include a focus on personal responsibility for food choices, characterizing new regulation as the government usurping personal freedom, criticizing studies that show the harmful effects of such food as "junk science," emphasizing exercise over dietary choices, and engaging in sham industry self-regulation. Brownell and Warner point out that Big Food companies are more complex than Big Tobacco companies, and that many firms sell comparatively healthy products, but they also point out that the recent track record of Big Food companies raises the question of whether they will act in "honorable, health promoting ways" or resort to the fundamentally dishonest and manipulative schemes pioneered by Big Tobacco.

In response to criticism of aggressive marketing tactics many scholars and industry advocates point to the fundamental right to free speech by firms as a basis for claiming that much of the criticism of free speech is misguided. In the US context, the law differentiates between political speech and commercial speech. Political speech is protected in all but the most unusual of circumstances. Commercial speech is more narrowly protected. For example, if an automobile manufacturer were to lie about the engine performance and safety features of a vehicle, consumers would be harmed in tangible ways. For such reasons, US courts have limited the ability of firms to say anything whatsoever about their products, services, or operations. In the classic Supreme Court case *Central Hudson Gas and Electric Corp. v. Public Service Commission*, a summary of which is included in this chapter, the Court found that commercial speech that "does not accurately inform the public" or is "more likely to deceive the public than to inform it" has no grounds for constitutional protection.[9] In cases where deception is not present, the government may nonetheless regulate speech when there is a substantial public interest and when it is not more extensive than necessary to protect those interests.

In his analysis, "Persistent Threats to Commercial Speech," Jonathan H. Adler argues that while there are well-intentioned and public-spirited aims behind some free speech restrictions, other restrictions are actually economically motivated and championed by powerful corporations and industries. In such cases Adler argues that firms seek to place limits on commercial speech to protect their market position and limit competition. He characterizes this as a form of "rent-seeking," the economic term for trying to manipulate public policy in order to increase profits. He points out that because such behavior can restrict the information available to consumers, it can be harmful to society.

PHARMACEUTICAL MARKETING

Next to targeting children, one of the most controversial areas in marketing concerns the aggressive sales tactics of prescription drugs by pharmaceutical companies. The pharmaceutical industry is responsible for the creation of a wide range of drugs that have fundamentally improved the welfare of hundreds of millions of people. At the same time, pharmaceutical firms have paid out over $26 billion in settlements to federal and state authorities in the United States alone for very bad behavior, including bribing doctors to write prescriptions, faking drug studies, hiding the adverse side-effects of drugs, and pushing expensive, new drugs that result in thousands of premature deaths. At the heart of these illegal activities are marketing strategies intended to promote expensive, new drugs.

The majority of pharmaceutical marketing, amounting to approximately $26 billion, is targeted at physicians.[10] This marketing includes visits to physicians' offices by marketing representatives laden with free samples and gifts such as golf putters; lunch for the entire office staff; dinners at the best restaurants in town, typically with a presentation by a paid company spokesperson; and all-expenses-paid trips for physicians and their spouses to luxurious resorts, where they are typically offered research paid for by the company as evidence of the effectiveness of the company's latest drugs. It has also included illegal cash payments to physicians. In response to criticism of such practices, the industry trade association issued voluntary guidelines for marketing to physicians by company representatives that claim to limit the worst abuses.

In "The Drug Pushers," Carl Elliott, a medical doctor with a doctorate in philosophy, criticizes pharmaceutical companies for their aggressive marketing practices. He provides examples of the many sorts of gifts (some would say "bribes") that "drug reps" provide to physicians – expensive dinners, paid vacations, unrestricted grants – to get physicians to write more prescriptions for their companies' drugs. Elliott argues that truly innovative and safe drugs need no marketing. The billions of dollars spent annually in the United States alone to market pharmaceuticals are used, he argues, to sell "me too" drugs – drugs that companies develop mainly to take market share from a competitor's drug rather than because they provide new or innovative benefits to patients. These marketing expenditures, in turn, increase the cost of drugs and drive patient demand for unneeded medicine, thus driving up costs for individuals, employers who provide health insurance for their employees, and the state and federal governments that pay much of the cost of prescription drugs for their employees and for the poor or uninsured. An alternative to this model is to have physicians, relying on their training and experience, peer-reviewed journal articles, and non-industry-sponsored continuing medical education, determine what medications are appropriate for their patients. Elliott argues that pharmaceutical company marketing undermines the objectivity of prescribing decisions made by physicians and unduly interferes with physician–patient relationships. Further, he claims that the industry trade group's guidelines for marketing to physicians have largely been ignored.

American consumers are nearly alone among the citizens of industrialized nations in being directly targeted by prescription drug advertising. Among industrialized nations, only New Zealand also allows direct-to-consumer (DTC) advertising. In 1997 the US Food and Drug Administration altered its policy on DTC advertising in such a way as to make it possible for the widespread use of television commercials for prescription pharmaceutical advertising. Since that time the amount spent on DTC advertising has increased to over $6 billion annually. However, the practice of advertising directly to consumers has come under sustained criticism. Critics of DTC advertising argue that the practice undermines physician–patient relationships and drives up the cost of prescription drugs. In response, drug manufacturers and marketing representatives argue that DTC advertisements empower consumers and have no impact on the cost of drugs.

In the last essay in this chapter, "The Ethics of Direct to Consumer Pharmaceutical Advertising," Denis G. Arnold explains the differences between the three types of advertisements permitted by the US Food and Drug Administration. He argues that the most commonly utilized advertisements rely on biased information and peripheral, noncognitive means of persuasion and as such are manipulative. He also points out that empirical research shows that some of the largest pharmaceutical companies do not follow the industry guidelines they helped create to promote ethical DTC advertising. As a result, he argues that public policy solutions are more appropriate means of curtailing deceptive and manipulative advertising than is industry self-regulation.

Notes

1. Sari Horwitz, "FTC Considers Letting Food Stores Advertise Out-of-Stock Items," *Washington Post* (December 27, 1984), p. E1.
2. US Federal Trade Commission, "FTC Charges Volkswagen Deceived Consumers with Its 'Clean Diesel' Campaign" (March 29, 2016). Retrieved from www.ftc.gov/news-events/press-releases/2016/03/ftc-charges-volkswagen-deceived-consumers-its-clean-diesel.
3. David J. Graham et al.,"Risk of Acute Myocardial Infarction and Sudden Cardiac Death in Patients Treated with Cyclo-Oxygenase 2 Selective and Non-Selective Non-Steroidal Anti-Inflammatory Drugs: Nested Case-Control Study," *The Lancet* 365, no. 9458 (2005): 475–81.
4. As quoted in Amy Dunkin et al., "Liquor Makers Try the Hard Sell in a Softening Market," *Businessweek* (May 13, 1985), p. 56.
5. "Anheuser-Busch Sued on Ad Showing Statue of Liberty," *Wall Street Journal* (November 28, 1984), p. 43.
6. Susan Linn, *Consuming Kids: The Hostile Takeover of Childhood* (New York University Press, 2004), p. 1; Bruce Horovitz, "Six Strategies Marketers Use to Get Kids to Want Stuff *Bad*," *USA Today* (November 22, 2006).
7. American Psychological Association, "Television Advertising Leads to Unhealthy Habits in Children, Says APA Task Force" (February 23, 2004). Retrieved from www.apa.org/news/press/releases/2004/02/children-ads.
8. Ibid.
9. *Central Hudson Gas and Electric Corp. v. Public Service Commission*, 447 U.S. 557 (1980).
10. Julie M. Donohue, Marisa Cevasco, and Meredith B. Rosenthal, "A Decade of Direct-to-Consumer Advertising of Prescription Drugs," *The New England Journal of Medicine* 357 (2007): 676.

7.2 AUTONOMY AND MARKETING

Advertising and Behavior Control

ROBERT L. ARRINGTON

Consider the following advertisements:

1. "A woman in *Distinction Foundation* is so beautiful that all other women want to kill her."
2. Pongo Peach color from Revlon comes "from east of the sun . . . west of the moon where each tomorrow dawns." It is "succulent on your lips" and "sizzling on your finger tips (And on your toes, goodness knows)." Let it be your "adventure in paradise."
3. "Musk by English Leather – The Civilized Way to Roar."
4. "*Increase the value of your holdings. Old Charter Bourbon Whiskey – The Final Step Up.*"
5. Last Call Smirnoff Style: "They'd never really miss us, and it's kind of late already, and it's quite a long way, and I could build a fire, and you're looking very beautiful, and we could have another martini, and it's awfully nice just being home . . . you think?"
6. A Christmas Prayer: "Let us pray that the blessings of peace be ours – the peace to build and grow, to live in harmony and sympathy with others, and to plan for the future with confidence." New York Life Insurance Company.

These are instances of what is called puffery – the practice by a seller of making exaggerated, highly fanciful, or suggestive claims about a product or service. Puffery, within ill-defined limits, is legal. It is considered a legitimate, necessary, and very successful tool of the advertising industry. Puffery is not just bragging; it is bragging carefully designed to achieve a very definite effect. Using

Journal of Business Ethics 1 (1982): 3–12. © 1982. Reprinted by permission of Springer.

the techniques of so-called motivational research, advertising firms first identify our often hidden needs (for security, conformity, oral stimulation) and our desires (for power, sexual dominance and dalliance, adventure) and then they design ads which respond to these needs and desires. By associating a product, for which we may have little or no direct need or desire, with symbols reflecting the fulfillment of these other, often subterranean interests, the advertisement can quickly generate large numbers of consumers eager to purchase the product advertised. What woman in the sexual race of life could resist a foundation which would turn other women envious to the point of homicide? Who can turn down an adventure in paradise, east of the sun where tomorrow dawns? Who doesn't want to be civilized and thoroughly libidinous at the same time? Be at the pinnacle of success – drink Old Charter. Or stay at home and dally a bit – with Smirnoff. And let us pray for a secure and predictable future, provided for by New York Life, God willing. It doesn't take very much motivational research to see the point of these sales pitches. Others are perhaps a little less obvious. The need to feel secure in one's home at night can be used to sell window air conditioners, which drown out small noises and provide a friendly, dependable companion. The fact that baking a cake is symbolic of giving birth to a baby used to prompt advertisements for cake mixes which glamorized the "creative" housewife. And other strategies, for example involving cigar symbolism, are a bit too crude to mention, but are nevertheless very effective.

Don't such uses of puffery amount to manipulation, exploitation, or downright control? In his very popular book *The Hidden Persuaders*, Vance Packard points out that a number of people in the advertising world have frankly admitted as much:

> As early as 1941 Dr. Dichter (an influential advertising consultant) was exhorting ad agencies to recognize themselves for what they actually were – "one of the most advanced laboratories in psychology." He said the successful ad agency "manipulates human motivations and desires and develops a need for goods with which the public has at one time been unfamiliar – perhaps even undesirous of purchasing." The following year *Advertising Agency* carried an ad man's statement that psychology not only holds promise for understanding people but "ultimately for controlling their behavior."[1]

Such statements lead Packard to remark: "With all this interest in manipulating the customer's subconscious, the old slogan 'let the buyer beware' began taking on a new and more profound meaning."

B. F. Skinner, the high priest of behaviorism, has expressed a similar assessment of advertising and related marketing techniques. Why, he asks, do we buy a certain kind of car?

> Perhaps our favorite TV program is sponsored by the manufacturer of that car. Perhaps we have seen pictures of many beautiful or prestigeful persons driving it – in pleasant or glamorous places. Perhaps the car has been designed with respect to our motivational patterns: the device on the hood is a phallic symbol; or the horsepower has been stepped up to please our competitive spirit in enabling us to pass other cars *swiftly* (or, as the advertisements say, "safely"). The concept of freedom that has emerged as part of the cultural practice of our group makes little or no provision for recognizing or dealing with these kinds of control.[2]

In purchasing a car we may think we are free, Skinner is claiming, when in fact our act is completely controlled by factors in our environment and in our history of reinforcement. Advertising is one such factor. . . .

Puffery, indirect information transfer, subliminal advertising – are these techniques of manipulation and control whose success shows that many of us have forfeited our autonomy and become a community, or herd, of packaged souls? The business world and the advertising industry certainly reject this interpretation of their efforts. *Businessweek*, for example, dismissed the charge that the science of behavior, as utilized by advertising, is engaged in human engineering and manipulation. It editorialized to the effect that "it is hard to find anything very sinister about a science whose principle conclusion is that you get along with people by giving them what they want."[3] The theme is familiar: businesses just give the consumer what he/she wants; if they didn't they wouldn't stay in business very long. Proof that the consumer wants the products advertised is given by the fact that he buys them, and indeed often returns to buy them again and again.

The techniques of advertising we are discussing have had their more intellectual defenders as well. For example, Theodore Levitt, Professor of Business Administration at the Harvard Business School, has defended the practice of puffery and the use of techniques depending on motivational research.[4] What would be the consequences, he asks us, of deleting all exaggerated claims and fanciful associations from advertisements? We would be left with literal descriptions of the empirical characteristics of products and their functions. Cosmetics would be presented as facial and bodily lotions and powders which produce certain odor and color changes; they would no longer offer hope or adventure. In addition to the fact that these products would not then sell as well, they would not, according to Levitt, please us as much either. For it is hope and adventure we want when we buy them. We want automobiles not just for transportation, but for the feelings of power and status they give us. Quoting T. S. Eliot to the effect that "Human kind cannot bear very much reality," Levitt argues that advertising is an effort to "transcend nature in the raw," to "augment what nature has so crudely fashioned." He maintains that "everybody everywhere wants to modify, transform, embellish, enrich, and reconstruct the world around him." Commerce takes the same liberty with reality as the artist and the priest – in all three instances the purpose is "to influence the audience by creating illusions, symbols, and implications that promise more than pure functionality." For example, "to amplify the temple in men's eyes, (men of cloth) have, very realistically, systematically sanctioned the embellishment of the houses of the gods with the same kind of luxurious design and expensive decoration that Detroit puts into a Cadillac." A poem, a temple, a Cadillac – they all elevate our spirits, offering imaginative promises and symbolic interpretations of our mundane activities. Seen in this light, Levitt claims, "Embellishment and distortion are among advertising's legitimate and socially desirable purposes." To reject these techniques of advertising would be "to deny man's honest needs and value."

Philip Nelson, a Professor of Economics at SUNY–Binghamton, has developed an interesting defense of indirect information advertising.[5] He argues that even when the message (the direct information) is not credible, the fact that the brand is advertised, and advertised frequently, is valuable indirect information for the consumer. The reason for this is that the brands advertised most are more likely to be better buys – losers won't be advertised a lot, for it simply wouldn't pay to do so. Thus even if the advertising claims made for a widely advertised product are empty, the consumer reaps the benefit of the indirect information which shows the product to be a good buy. Nelson goes so far as to say that advertising, seen as information and especially as indirect information, does not require an intelligent human response. If the indirect information has been received and has had its impact, the consumer will purchase the better buy even if his explicit reason for doing so is silly, e.g., he naïvely believes an endorsement of the product by a celebrity. Even though his behavior is overtly irrational, by acting on the indirect information he is nevertheless doing what

he ought to do, i.e., getting his money's worth. "'Irrationality' is rational," Nelson writes, "if it is cost-free." . . .

The defense of advertising which suggests that advertising simply is information which allows us to purchase what we want, has in turn been challenged. Does business, largely through its advertising efforts, really make available to the consumer what he/she desires and demands? John Kenneth Galbraith has denied that the matter is as straightforward as this.[6] In his opinion the desires to which business is supposed to respond, far from being original to the consumer, are often themselves created by business. The producers make both the product and the desire for it, and the "central function" of advertising is "to create desires." Galbraith coins the term "The Dependence Effect" to designate the way wants depend on the same process by which they are satisfied.

David Braybrooke has argued in similar and related ways.[7] Even though the consumer is, in a sense, the final authority concerning what he wants, he may come to see, according to Braybrooke, that he was mistaken in wanting what he did. The statement "I want x," he tells us, is not incorrigible but is "ripe for revision." If the consumer had more objective information than he is provided by product puffing, if his values had not been mixed up by motivational research strategies (e.g., the confusion of sexual and automotive values), and if he had an expanded set of choices instead of the limited set offered by profit-hungry corporations, then he might want something quite different from what he presently wants. This shows, Braybrooke thinks, the extent to which the consumer's wants are a function of advertising and not necessarily representative of his real or true wants.

The central issue which emerges between the above critics and defenders of advertising is this: Do the advertising techniques we have discussed involve a violation of human autonomy and a manipulation and control of consumer behavior, *or* do they simply provide an efficient and cost effective means of giving the consumer information on the basis of which he or she makes a free choice? Is advertising information, or creation of desire?

To answer this question we need a better conceptual grasp of what is involved in the notion of autonomy. This is a complex, multifaceted concept, and we need to approach it through the more determinate notions of (a) autonomous desire, (b) rational desire and choice, (c) free choice, and (d) control or manipulation. In what follows I shall offer some tentative and very incomplete analyses of these concepts and apply the results to the case of advertising.

(a) **Autonomous Desire.** Imagine that I am watching TV and see an ad for Grecian Formula 16. The thought occurs to me that if I purchase some and apply it to my beard, I will soon look younger – in fact I might even be myself again. Suddenly I want to be myself! I want to be young again! So I rush out and buy a bottle. This is our question: Was the desire to be younger manufactured by the commercial, or was it "original to me" and truly mine? Was it autonomous or not?

F. A. von Hayek has argued plausibly that we should not equate nonautonomous desires, desires which are not original to me truly mine, with those which are culturally induced.[8] If we did equate the two, he points out, then the desires for music, art, and knowledge could not properly be attributed to a person as original to him, for these are surely induced culturally. The only desires a person would really have as his own in this case would be the purely physical ones for food, shelter, sex, etc. But if we reject the equation of the nonautonomous and the culturally induced, as von Hayek would have us do, then the mere fact that my desire to be young again is caused by the TV commercial – surely an instrument of popular culture transmission – does not in and of itself show that this is not my own, autonomous desire. Moreover, even if I never before felt the need to look young, it doesn't follow that this new desire is any less mine. I haven't always liked 1969 Aloxe Corton Burgundy or the music of Satie, but when the desires for these things first hit me, they were truly mine.

This shows that there is something wrong in setting up the issue over advertising and behavior control as a question of whether our desires are truly ours *or* are created in us by advertisements. Induced and autonomous desires do not separate into two mutually exclusive classes. To obtain a better understanding of autonomous and nonautonomous desires, let us consider some cases of a desire which a person does not *acknowledge* to be his own even though he *feels* it. The kleptomaniac has a desire to steal which in many instances he repudiates, seeking by treatment to rid himself of it. And if I were suddenly overtaken by a desire to attend an REO concert, I would immediately disown this desire, claiming possession or momentary madness. These are examples of desires which one might have but with which one would not identify. They are experienced as foreign to one's character or personality. Often a person will have what Harry Frankfurt calls a second-order desire, that is to say, a desire *not* to have another desire.[9] In such cases, the first-order desire is thought of as being nonautonomous, imposed on one. When on the contrary a person has a second-order desire to maintain and fulfill a first-order desire, then the first-order desire is truly his own, autonomous, original to him. So there is in fact a distinction between desires which are the agent's own and those which are not, but this is not the same as the distinction between desires which are innate to the agent and those which are externally induced. . . .

What are we to say in response to Braybrooke's argument that insofar as we might choose differently if advertisers gave us better information and more options, it follows that the desires we have are to be attributed more to advertising than to our own real inclinations? This claim seems empty. It amounts to saying that if the world we lived in, and we ourselves, were different, then we would want different things. This is surely true, but it is equally true of our desire for shelter as of our desire for Grecian Formula 16. If we lived in a tropical paradise we would not need or desire shelter. If we were immortal, we would not desire youth. What is true of all desires can hardly be used as a basis for criticizing some desires by claiming that they are nonautonomous.

(b) **Rational Desire and Choice.** Braybrooke might be interpreted as claiming that the desires induced by advertising are often irrational ones in the sense that they are not expressed by an agent who is in full possession of the facts about the products advertised or about the alternative products which might be offered him. Following this line of thought, a possible criticism of advertising is that it leads us to act on irrational desires or to make irrational choices. It might be said that our autonomy has been violated by the fact that we are prevented from following our rational wills or that we have been denied the "positive freedom" to develop our true, rational selves. It might be claimed that the desires induced in us by advertising are false desires in that they do not reflect our essential, i.e., rational, essence.

The problem faced by this line of criticism is that of determining what is to count as rational desire or rational choice. If we require that the desire or choice be the product of an awareness of *all* the facts about the product, then surely every one of us is always moved by irrational desires and makes nothing but irrational choices. How could we know all the facts about a product? If it be required only that we possess all of the *available* knowledge about the product advertised, then we still have to face the problem that not all available knowledge is *relevant* to a rational choice. If I am purchasing a car, certain engineering features will be, and others won't be, relevant, *given what I want in a car*. My prior desires determine the relevance of · information. Normally a rational desire or choice is thought to be one based upon relevant information, and information is relevant if it shows how other, prior desires may be satisfied. It can plausibly be claimed that it is such prior desires that advertising agencies acknowledge, and that the agencies often provide the type of information that is relevant in light of these desires. To the extent that this is true, advertising does not inhibit our rational wills or our autonomy as rational creatures.

It may be urged that much of the puffery engaged in by advertising does not provide relevant information at all but rather makes claims which are not factually true. If someone buys Pongo Peach in anticipation of an adventure in paradise, or Old Charter in expectation of increasing the value of his holdings, then he/she is expecting purely imaginary benefits. In no literal sense will the one product provide adventure and the other increased capital. A purchasing decision based on anticipation of imaginary benefits is not, it might be said, a rational decision, and a desire for imaginary benefits is not a rational desire. . . .

Some philosophers will be unhappy with the conclusion of this section, largely because they have a concept of true, rational, or ideal desire which is not the same as the one used here. A Marxist, for instance, may urge that any desire felt by alienated man in a capitalistic society is foreign to his true nature. Or an existentialist may claim that the desires of inauthentic men are themselves inauthentic. Such concepts are based upon general theories of human nature which are unsubstantiated and perhaps incapable of substantiation. Moreover, each of these theories is committed to a concept of an ideal desire which is normatively debatable and which is distinct from the ordinary concept of a rational desire as one based upon relevant information. But it is in the terms of the ordinary concept that we express our concern that advertising may limit our autonomy in the sense of leading us to act on irrational desires, and if we operate with this concept we are driven again to the conclusion that advertising may lead, but probably most often does not lead, to an infringement of autonomy.

(c) **Free Choice.** It might be said that some desires are so strong or so covert that a person cannot resist them, and that when he acts on such desires he is not acting freely or voluntarily but is rather the victim of irresistible impulse or an unconscious drive. Perhaps those who condemn advertising feel that it produces this kind of desire in us and consequently reduces our autonomy.

This raises a very difficult issue. How do we distinguish between an impulse we do not resist and one we *could* not resist, between freely giving in to a desire and succumbing to

one? I have argued elsewhere that the way to get at this issue is in terms of the notion of acting for a reason.[10] A person acts or chooses freely if he does so for a reason, that is, if he can adduce considerations which justify in his mind the act in question. Many of our actions are in fact free because this condition frequently holds. Often, however, a person will act from habit, or whim, or impulse, and on these occasions he does not have a reason in mind. Nevertheless he often acts voluntarily in these instances, i.e., he could have acted otherwise. And this is because if there *had been* a reason for acting otherwise of which he was aware, he would in fact have done so. Thus acting from habit or impulse is not necessarily to act in an involuntary manner. If, however, a person is aware of a good reason to do x and still follows his impulse to do y, then he can be said to be impelled by irresistible impulse and hence to act involuntarily. Many kleptomaniacs can be said to act involuntarily, for in spite of their knowledge that they likely will be caught and their awareness that the goods they steal have little utilitarian value to them, they nevertheless steal. Here their "out of character" desires have the upper hand, and we have a case of compulsive behavior.

Applying these notions of voluntary and compulsive behavior to the case of behavior prompted by advertising, can we say that consumers influenced by advertising, act compulsively? The unexciting answer is: sometimes they do, sometimes not. I may have an overwhelming, TV-induced urge to own a Mazda RX-7 and all the while realize that I can't afford one without severely reducing my family's caloric intake to a dangerous level. If, aware of this good reason not to purchase the car, I nevertheless do so, this shows that I have been the victim of TV compulsion. But if I have the urge, as I assure you I do, and don't act on it, or if in some other possible world I could afford an RX-7, then I have not been the subject of undue influence by Mazda advertising. Some Mazda RX-7 purchasers act compulsively; others do not. The Mazda advertising effort *in general* cannot be condemned, then, for impairing its customers' autonomy in the sense of limiting free or voluntary choice. Of course the question remains what should be done about the fact that advertising may and does *occasionally* limit free choice. We shall return to this question later.

In the case of subliminal advertising we may find an individual whose subconscious desires are activated by advertising into doing something his calculating, reasoning ego does not approve. This would be a case of compulsion. But most of us have a benevolent subconsciousness which does not overwhelm our ego and its reasons for action. And therefore most of us can respond to subliminal advertising without thereby risking our autonomy. To be sure, if some advertising firm developed a subliminal technique which drove all of us to purchase Lear jets, thereby reducing our caloric intake to the zero point, then we would have a case of advertising which could properly be censured for infringing our right to autonomy. We should acknowledge that this is possible, but at the same time we should recognize that it is not an inherent result of subliminal advertising.

(d) **Control or Manipulation.** Briefly let us consider the matter of control and manipulation. Under what conditions do these activities occur? In a recent paper on "Forms and Limits of Control" I suggested the following criteria:[11]

A person C controls the behavior of another person P *iff*

1. *C* intends *P* to act in a certain way *A*;
2. *C*'s intention is causally effective in bringing about *A*; and

3. *C* intends to ensure that all of the necessary conditions of *A* are satisfied.

These criteria may be elaborated as follows. To control another person it is not enough that one's actions produce certain behavior on the part of that person; additionally one must intend that this happen. Hence control is the intentional production of behavior. Moreover, it is not enough just to have the intention; the intention must give rise to the conditions which bring about the intended effect. Finally, the controller must intend to establish by his actions any otherwise unsatisfied necessary conditions for the production of the intended effect. The controller is not just influencing the outcome, not just having input; he is as it were guaranteeing that the sufficient conditions for the intended effect are satisfied.

Let us apply these criteria of control to the case of advertising and see what happens. Conditions (1) and (3) are crucial. Does the Mazda manufacturing company or its advertising agency intend that I buy an RX-7? Do they intend that a certain number of people buy the car? *Prima facie* it seems more appropriate to say that they *hope* a certain number of people will buy it, and hoping and intending are not the same. But the difficult term here is "intend." Some philosophers have argued that to intend *A* it is necessary only to desire that *A* happen and to believe that it will. If this is correct, and if marketing analysis gives the Mazda agency a reasonable belief that a certain segment of the population will buy its product, then, assuming on its part the desire that this happen, we have the conditions necessary for saying that the agency intends that a certain segment purchase the car. If I am a member of this segment of the population, would it then follow that the agency intends that I purchase an RX-7? Or is control referentially opaque?

Obviously we have some questions here which need further exploration.

Let us turn to the third condition of control, the requirement that the controller intend to activate or bring about any otherwise unsatisfied necessary conditions for the production of the intended effect. It is in terms of this condition that we are able to distinguish brainwashing from liberal education. The brainwasher arranges all of the necessary conditions for belief. On the other hand, teachers (at least those of liberal persuasion) seek only to influence their students – to provide them with information and enlightenment which they may absorb *if they wish*. We do not normally think of teachers as controlling their students, for the students' performances depend as well on their own interests and inclinations. . . .

Let me summarize my argument. The critics of advertising see it as having a pernicious effect on the autonomy of consumers, as controlling their lives and manufacturing their very souls. The defense claims that advertising only offers information and in effect allows industry to provide consumers with what they want. After developing some of the philosophical dimensions of this dispute, I have come down tentatively in favor of the advertisers. Advertising may, but certainly does not always or even frequently, control behavior, produce compulsive behavior, or create wants which are not rational or are not truly those of the consumer. Admittedly it may in individual cases do all of these things, but it is innocent of the charge of intrinsically or necessarily doing them or even, I think, of often doing so. This limited potentiality, to be sure, leads to the question whether advertising should be abolished or severely curtailed or regulated because of its potential to harm a few poor souls in the above ways. This is a very difficult question, and I do not pretend to have the answer. I only hope that the above discussion, in showing some of the kinds of harm that can be done by advertising and by indicating the likely limits of this harm, will put us in a better position to grapple with the question.

Notes

1. Vance Packard, *The Hidden Persuaders* (New York: Pocket Books, 1958), pp. 20–21.
2. B. F. Skinner, "Some Issues Concerning the Control of Human Behavior: A Symposium," in *Man Controlled*, ed. M. Karlins and L. M. Andrews (New York: Free Press, 1972).
3. Quoted by Packard, *Hidden Persuaders*, p. 220.
4. Theodore Levitt, "The Morality (?) of Advertising," *Harvard Business Review* 48 (1970): 84–92.
5. Phillip Nelson, "Advertising and Ethics," in *Ethics, Free Enterprise and Public Policy*, ed. Richard T. De George and Joseph A. Pichler (Oxford University Press, 1978), pp. 187–98.

6. John Kenneth Galbraith, "The Affluent Society"; reprinted in *Ethical Theory and Business*, ed. Tom L. Beauchamp and Norman E. Bowie (Englewood Cliffs, NJ: Prentice Hall, 1979), pp. 496–501.

7. David Braybrooke, "Skepticism of Wants, and Certain Subversive Effects of Corporation on American Values," in *Human Values and Economic Policy*, ed. Sidney Hook (New York University Press, 1967); reprinted in *Ethical Theory and Business*, ed. Beauchamp and Bowie, pp. 502–8.

8. F. A. von Hayek, "The Non Sequitur of the 'Dependence Effect,'" *Southern Economic Journal* (1961); reprinted in *Ethical Theory and Business*, ed. Beauchamp and Bowie, pp. 508–12.

9. Harry Frankfurt, "Freedom of the Will and the Concept of Person," *Journal of Philosophy* 68 (1971): 5–20.

10. Robert L. Arrington, "Practical Reason, Responsibility and the Psychopath," *Journal for the Theory of Social Behavior* 9 (1979): 71–89.

11. Robert L. Arrington, "Forms and Limits of Control," delivered at the annual meeting of the Southern Society for Philosophy and Psychology, Birmingham, Alabama, 1980.

Marketing and the Vulnerable

GEORGE G. BRENKERT

Introduction

Contemporary marketing is commonly characterized by the marketing concept which enjoins marketers to determine the wants and needs of customers and then to try to satisfy them. This view is standardly developed, not surprisingly, in terms of normal or ordinary consumers. Much less frequently is attention given to the vulnerable customers whom marketers also (and increasingly) target. Though marketing to normal consumers raises many moral questions, marketing to the vulnerable also raises many moral questions which are deserving of greater attention.

This paper has three objectives. First, it explores the notion of vulnerability which a target audience might (or might not) have. I argue that we must distinguish those who are specially vulnerable from normal individuals, as well as the susceptible and the disadvantaged – two other groups often distinguished in marketing literature. Second, I contend that marketing to the specially vulnerable requires that marketing campaigns be designed to ensure that these individuals are not treated unfairly, and thus possibly harmed. Third, I maintain that marketing programs which violate this preceding injunction are unethical or unscrupulous whether or not those targeted are harmed in some further manner. Accordingly, social control over marketing to the vulnerable cannot simply look to consumer injury as the measure of unfair treatment of the vulnerable.

The upshot of my argument is that, just as we have a doctrine of product liability to which marketers are accountable, we also need a corresponding doctrine of targeted consumer liability to which marketers should be held. By this I refer to the moral liability of marketers for the manner in which they market to consumers. Marketing to the specially vulnerable without making appropriate allowances for their vulnerabilities is morally unjustified.

On Being Vulnerable

The notion of vulnerability is complex and slippery. Most simply, to be "vulnerable is to be susceptible to being wounded; liable to physical hurt."[1] More generally, being vulnerable is being susceptible to some harm or other. One can be vulnerable to manmade or natural harms: one can also be vulnerable to harms from actions or omissions.[2] In each of these cases, the threatened harm is to one's "welfare" or "interests."

The vulnerability of the person who may be harmed by others may be a permanent, or temporary, condition. Clearly, vulnerability is a matter of degree. Typically only those who are subject to some substantial level of harm are referred to as "vulnerable." This vulnerability may arise due to their own peculiar characteristics, those of the agents who are said to impose the harm on them, or the system within which certain acts impose harm on them. Accordingly, vulnerability is a four-place relation: Some person (P) is vulnerable to another (moral or causal) agent (A) with respect to some harm (H) in a particular context (C). As such "vulnerability is inherently object and agent specific."[3]

The relation of vulnerability to two related concepts – susceptibility and disadvantage – used in marketing literature may serve to further clarify its nature.

Vulnerability is distinct from susceptibility, in that a person might be susceptible to something or someone and still not be vulnerable to that thing or person. "Susceptibility" merely implies that one is "capable of being affected, especially easily" by something or someone. It is true that one who is susceptible may also be vulnerable. Clearly, one who is vulnerable is susceptible. But one need not be vulnerable if one is susceptible, since one's susceptibility may not be to some harm or other. An overweight, underexercised adult might be susceptible through flattery or positive remarks to certain suggestions made by friends to exercise and moderate food intake. But this person would not, thereby, be vulnerable to such suggestions. Hence, vulnerability and susceptibility are different.

The vulnerable also differ from those with "unusual susceptibilities," a term of art in marketing for those "who have idiosyncratic reactions to products that are otherwise harmless when used by most people."[4] People who are "unusually susceptible" are those who are atypically harmed by various products. Accordingly, "unusual susceptibility" has been linked with vulnerability. However, in any ordinary sense, a person might have "unusual susceptibilities" to some experiences (e.g., changes in air pressure or moisture), the suggestions of others, clothing styles, etc., and this might not involve harm to the person but, perhaps, that person's heightened sensitivity to those influences. Further, people may be vulnerable in ways other than that they may be atypically harmed by the products they use. Vulnerable groups such as young children, the grieving, or the elderly are not necessarily atypically harmed by the products they use. Nevertheless, they are vulnerable.

Finally, the vulnerable are also distinct from the disadvantaged. Though marketers quite frequently speak of disadvantaged populations or market segments, they have given little analysis of this concept. Most discussants simply give examples of those whom they consider to be disadvantaged. This extensive, diverse, and confused list includes the poor, immigrants, the young married, teenagers, the elderly, children, racial minorities, the physically handicapped, ethnic minorities, and even women shopping for automobiles.

Generally we are told that members of this list are disadvantaged because they are impaired in their transactions in the marketplace. For some this means not getting their full consumer dollar.[5] For others this means confronting an imbalance in the marketplace.[6] Andreasen says "the disadvantaged" are "those who are unequal in the marketplace because of characteristics that are not of their own choosing, including their age, race, ethnic minority status, and (sometimes) gender."[7]

It is clear, then, that the vulnerable and the disadvantaged also constitute different, though overlapping, groups. The disadvantaged are impaired or unequal with regard to their attempt to obtain various goods and services. This may occur relative to other groups (normal consumers) competing for various goods, or to those from whom they seek to purchase those goods. On the contrary, those who are vulnerable are not vulnerable with regard to others who are competing for similar goods, but with regard to the harm they might suffer from those who market those goods to them. As such, the notion of vulnerability suggests the harm which one might receive, whether or not one is competing for a particular good, but due to the manner of obtaining some good (or service). Further, this harm need not come from paying more or being deceived. The vulnerable may get exactly what they want, but what they want may unwittingly and unfairly harm them (as well as their family and/or community).

Accordingly, the vulnerable are not simply the susceptible or the disadvantaged. They constitute a distinct group which deserves our close attention.

Vulnerability and Marketing

What moral responsibilities do marketers have when they consider marketing to the vulnerable? Since one might be said to be vulnerable in a variety of ways, and since some people might willingly place themselves in competitive situations where their vulnerabilities are exposed, we must specify the manner(s) in which various forms of vulnerability are significant from the standpoint of marketing. Otherwise, if it were morally unjustified to market to those who are vulnerable in any sense, moral marketing would not exist. It would be an oxymoron. . . .

One standard to which we might turn for the responsibilities of marketers to the vulnerable refers not to the degree of their vulnerability but to the effects on all those relevantly affected by marketing to these individuals. In short, harm to the vulnerable by marketing programs might be balanced by countervailing benefits for all other consumers and competitors. Thus, the responsibilities of marketers to the vulnerable would depend upon which course of action would maximize all relevant utilities.

However, appeal to a simple utilitarian standard is ethically unacceptable in that it would allow a few vulnerable individuals to substantially suffer because a certain action or policy maximized total utilities. For example, it might be that other marketers are more vulnerable (they might go out of business) than some of the individuals (they might be harmed by the products or the form of marketing targeting them) to whom those marketers and others sought to sell their goods. Hence, in order to protect vulnerable marketers (and their employees, suppliers, etc.), the proposed standard might permit targeting various vulnerable market segments because the total harm they sustained was less than that of those *engaged* in producing and marketing products to them. This could unleash a tide of manipulative and exploitative marketing.

Similarly, suppose that a particular means of marketing did not make allowances for the fact that those targeted were vulnerable in that they significantly lacked a capacity to make judgments regarding economic exchanges (e.g., children, the senile, or the retarded). Though the marketing efforts took advantage of this vulnerability, it nevertheless maximized total utilities. We might suppose that these customers were not dissatisfied and the marketers were pleased with their successes. To argue that this means of marketing is, nevertheless, morally acceptable runs afoul of important moral and market principles. To begin with, those targeted are not competent to evaluate the product marketed to them. They might not be aware of problems with the products they use. As such, this justification of marketing to the vulnerable permits treating some individuals simply as means to the ends of others. It denies them moral respect. It runs afoul of basic ethical and market principles, even though those targeted do not suffer a direct harm.

The difficulty with Goodin's approach is that he treats vulnerability as simply a quantitative matter without recognizing that each form of vulnerability occurs within a particular context. The market is one such context. In it some individuals may justifiably seek, in recognized forms of competition, to exploit the vulnerabilities of others. The problem with the consequential first approach is that it does not consider the nature of people's vulnerabilities except insofar as they portend certain consequences for everyone. Not the ability of the person to participate, but the effects on society are its concern. Instead, we need to be able to identify those who are specially vulnerable within a market situation, but whose vulnerability is not the occasion for justified competitive attacks. In short, we need a different approach which takes account both of the context within which marketers address the vulnerable as well as the nature of their vulnerabilities.

Marketing to the Vulnerable

The necessary features for morally (not merely legally) justified market relations are commonly stated in terms of the nature of the relations or interactions which participants in the market

enjoy.[8] Thus, we are told that among the relevant characteristics a morally justified market requires are the following: (a) Competition is free, i.e., participants in the market do so voluntarily, when each believes they can benefit; (b) Competition is open, i.e., "access to the market is not artificially limited by any power, government, or group";[9] and (c) Deception or fraud are not used in market competition.[10]

These conditions spell out some of the necessary conditions for a justified form of competition among those we may call "market participants," i.e., those who willingly and knowingly engage in market relations. The activity of these marketplace competitors is strongly determined by their need to derive a profit. To be a market participant is to place oneself in competition with other participant capitalists in which one recognizes that one may succeed or fail. It is to engage in these relations in order to produce various goods or services for sale. It is to acknowledge that all participants, including oneself, have strengths and weaknesses, formidable powers and vulnerabilities. The endeavor of each participant is to compete such that their own strengths and powers will outweigh those of others, or that their weaknesses and vulnerabilities are less significant than those of others.

Second, though these conditions are important for a morally justified market, they make no direct reference to the conditions or characteristics which those individuals who engage in market relations as ultimate consumers – call them "market clients" – must have in order to do so. However, morally and legally justified market relations also make assumptions about the nature of these participants, since not just anyone can be a market client. To take the most obvious cases, the severely mentally ill, incompetent elderly, and young children cannot be market visitors. Someone else must visit the market on their behalf.

Those who would visit the market as consumers do so not under a concern to derive a profit, but in order to satisfy various needs and wants they have. Accordingly, they must have certain market competencies such as the following: (a) They know they should shop around and are able to do so; (b) They are competent to determine differences in quality and best price; (c) They are aware of their legal rights;[11] (d) They have knowledge of the products and their characteristics; and (e) They have the resources to enter into market relations.[12]

These conditions, conjoined with the preceding, spell out essential requirements for individuals to be market clients. It is assumed that those who fulfill these conditions are able to protect their own interests and that their self-interested behavior in the market will work towards greater wealth or well-being for all. Accordingly, when these conditions are fulfilled (ceteris paribus), market relations between market participants and clients will be fair or just. Thus, these conditions for market clients (or consumers) have been recognized not simply as moral restrictions, but also as the source of various legal regulations regarding children, the elderly, and the grieving.

Third, the preceding market client conditions are not fulfilled by consumers wholly independently of marketers. On the contrary, marketers seek to foster the fulfillment of these conditions. "Ultimately," a marketing text reminds us, "the key objective [for marketers] must be to influence customer behavior."[13] Thus, marketers extend credit or loans to prospective individuals so that they may have the needed resources to enter the market. They advertise to foster the knowledge and desire of their products. They seek to identify unfulfilled needs, wants, and interests among potential consumers or clients and endeavor to find ways to satisfy them. Marketers seek to draw into the market those who might not otherwise enter the market, or do so only in different ways and under different conditions. Thus, one marketing researcher comments that "marketers have failed to develop strategies designed to attract the elderly consumer market."[14] In short, marketers create not only products to sell to market clients (consumers), but seek to create consumers (clients) out of ordinary, nonmarket interested people. This is not to say that they create consumers out of whole cloth, as it might seem that they do a product. Nor is it to say that they are always successful, or that whenever a person becomes a market client it is because of some specific action of a marketer. Still, marketers not only create products for consumers, but they also have a hand in creating consumers for their products.

In these various efforts, the marketer has a number of advantages over even the most reasonable consumer (client). These include greater knowledge of the product; expertise on how to market to individual customers and targeted groups; knowledge of what interests, fears, wants, and/or needs motivate various market segments; and resources to bring that knowledge to bear on behalf of persuading a customer to buy a product. Indeed, the marketer may be aware of attributes of potential consumers of which they are themselves unaware. These special characteristics, powers, and abilities of marketers create special responsibilities for them in the relationships they create with consumers.[15]

Fourth, when marketers, or market participants, compete with each other, the fact that one has a vulnerability may be viewed as an opportunity for another who seeks to take advantage of that vulnerability. There are, obviously, legal and moral limits here. If one firm has temporarily lost its security force and its headquarters are unguarded one evening, this does not imply that another firm may use that opportunity to sneak into those headquarters to steal important files. Thus, competing firms ought not to try to exploit those vulnerabilities which would require illegal or immoral acts. On the other hand, vulnerabilities linked to market performance may be the occasion for other firms to try to outperform the vulnerable firm when the acts involved do not transgress the preceding limits. Accordingly, if market participants fail to compete aggressively out of laziness or are indifferent to quality differences, they may be harmed as a result. This is acceptable to the market, since it is intended to encourage participant competitiveness.

However, when a marketer confronts a market client, i.e., an ordinary consumer, the situation is different. Individuals must fulfill the above conditions to be market clients. Those that do so may also be lazy shoppers or indifferent to quality differences. As a consequence, they too may suffer. This is also acceptable within the market. However, some individuals may suffer not through such circumstances, but because they fail to fulfill, in ways which render them specially vulnerable, various conditions to be market clients.

I suggest that we may initially characterize this specially vulnerable group as being constituted by those individuals who are particularly susceptible to harm to their interests because the qualitatively different experiences and conditions that characterize them (and on account of which they may be harmed) derive from factors (largely) beyond their control.

Accordingly, there are three conditions for the specially vulnerable:

1. They are those, in contrast to other normal adults, who are characterized by qualitatively different experiences, conditions, and/or incapacities which impede their abilities to participate in normal adult market activities. These characteristics may render them vulnerable in any of four different ways:

   (a) They may be *physically vulnerable* if they are unusually susceptible due to physical or biological conditions to products on the market, e.g., allergies or special sensitivity to the chemicals or substances which are marketed.

   (b) They may be *cognitively vulnerable* if they lack certain levels of ability to cognitively process information or to be aware that certain information was being withheld or manipulated in deceptive ways. Children, the senile elderly, and even those who lack education and shopping sophistication have been included here.[16]

(c) They may be *motivationally vulnerable* if they could not resist ordinary temptations and/or enticements due to their own individual characteristics. Under the motivationally vulnerable might be brought the grieving and the gravely ill.[17]

(d) They may be *socially vulnerable* when their social situation renders them significantly less able than others to resist various enticements, appeals, or challenges which may harm them. Some of those who have been included here are certain groups of the poor, the grieving, and new mothers in developing countries.

2. The qualitatively different conditions and incapacities of specially vulnerable individuals are ones they possess due to factors (largely) beyond their control. In addition, they may be largely unaware of their vulnerability(ies). In either case, they are significantly less able (in any normal sense) to protect themselves against harm to their interests as a result. Thus, the allergic, the child, the elderly, and the grieving all experience their vulnerabilities due to reasons (largely) beyond their control. In certain situations this may also be true of various racial groups. The fact that these factors are largely beyond their control may be due to the weaknesses or inabilities these individuals themselves possess, due to the greater power of marketers which render their characteristics specially weak or incapable, or due to the system within which they find themselves.

3. These special conditions render them particularly susceptible to the harm of their interests by various means which marketers (and others) use but which do not (similarly) affect the normal adult. In short, it is the combination of their special characteristics and the means or techniques which marketers use that render them specially vulnerable. This emphasizes the relational nature of vulnerability.

As so identified, the specially vulnerable are significantly less able than others to protect their own interests and, in some cases, even to identify their own interests. Consequently, they are considerably less able to take appropriate measures to satisfy or fulfill those interests. Central to these difficulties is the special liability (or susceptibility) they have to be swayed, moved, or enticed in directions which may benefit others but which may harm their interests.

Accordingly, when market participants face individuals who do not qualify or pass a certain threshold for market competition, the latter are unable to protect their interests in a manner comparable to that of ordinary market clients. If the fulfillment of these conditions or threshold is required to be treated as a market client, then these individuals may not morally be treated as other clients in the market. Further, when this situation arises because these individuals have special vulnerabilities then to market to them in ways which take advantage of their vulnerabilities, i.e., to seek to engage them in the competitive effort to sell them goods through the weaknesses characterizing their vulnerabilities, is to treat them unfairly. Regardless of whether they are actually harmed, they are being taken advantage of. They have little or no control over these features of their behavior. The fact that they may take fun or pleasure in being targeted by marketers is, then, irrelevant since they do not qualify as market clients.[18] And it is this situation which has been cited as one of the criteria for determining unfairness in advertising, i.e., advertising (or marketing) makes unfair claims when those claims "cause especially vulnerable groups to engage in conduct deleterious to themselves."[19]

Consequently, since moral marketing must exclude treating customers unfairly, marketers need to "qualify" those they propose to target as genuine market clients before they introduce marketing campaigns which target them. This might involve helping them to become qualified consumers, avoiding marketing to them, or marketing to them in ways which are compatible with their limited abilities and characteristics.

As such, moral marketing requires a theory of targeted consumer liability analogous to the product liability, to which marketers are presently held responsible. A theory of targeted consumer liability would elaborate on and operationalize the conditions noted above under which individuals may play full roles as market clients as well as what lesser roles they may play. In each case, it would tell us what relationships marketers might have with them.

Implications

What are the implications of the preceding analysis? A first interpretation might be that marketers may not market to the specially vulnerable at all. This is mistaken. There are obviously cases in which those who are specially vulnerable, e.g., the elderly or the grieving, require various products and services and would benefit from learning about them. The preceding argument contends that any marketing to the vulnerable cannot morally be undertaken in a way which trades upon their vulnerabilities.

In cases when the special vulnerability is temporary, measures could be taken to restrain marketing to them until after such period. Accordingly, the legislatures of some states have introduced and/or passed legislation prohibiting lawyers from "soliciting the business of victims until 30 days after accidents, wrongful deaths, and workplace injuries."[20]

Similarly, for the grieving, some have suggested that "insurance companies may need to be restricted through legislation regarding the nature of their contacts with those in grief; specifically, the payoff of a life insurance policy should not be accompanied by an immediate attempt to encourage the survivor to reinvest. A period of time (i.e., at least a month) should elapse before the insurance company initiates a sales contact."[21] When it is desirable that individuals in this group have certain products or services prior to the vulnerability-creating situation's abating, other arrangements can be made for advisors to the specially vulnerable to be present or for restraints on marketing to them.

The situation is different when the vulnerability is not temporary or relatively short-term. In such cases, marketers may not target those who are specially vulnerable in ways such that their marketing campaign depends upon the vulnerabilities of that specially vulnerable group. That is, in the case of the specially vulnerable, no significant aspect of a marketing campaign may rely upon the characteristics that render those individuals specially vulnerable in order to sell a product. Hence, because children are cognitively vulnerable due to their undeveloped abilities, any marketing to children must be done in ways which do not presuppose those vulnerabilities. As such, the FCC's limit on the amount of advertising on children's television programming does not directly address this issue. Instead, the content of those advertisements must be monitored so that children's special vulnerabilities are not taken advantage of. The removal of ads for vitamins and drugs from children's television programming does directly respond to the present point.[22] However, it does not go far enough. Since young children do not understand the purpose of ads,[23] they do not fulfill the qualifications of market clients. Accordingly, it is mistaken to speak of restrictions on marketing to the vulnerable (and particularly children) as violating their rights as consumers.[24] Since vulnerable children do not qualify as market clients or consumers, they cannot be said to have consumers' rights.

Admittedly, vulnerable individuals such as children will witness marketing to competent market clients. There is no way to stop this. Nor is it desirable to try to do so. But this does not mean that marketers can invoke images, symbols, etc., which are designed to persuade or influence this group of noncompetent vulnerable individuals to purchase products (or influence those who do) through the very characteristics which render them unfit to be market clients.

Accordingly, it is not morally acceptable to market goods to specially vulnerable individuals with the intention that they bring pressure to bear on genuine market clients to buy those products and with the expectation that those genuine clients will curb any problems which the use or possession of those products by the specially vulnerable would raise. Such marketing continues to target those who are not fully competent market clients. Further, to depend upon others to prevent harm which the marketing techniques may potentially engender through the purchase of various products is to seek to escape from the responsibility marketers have for the consequences of their actions. It is a case of displaced moral responsibility.

However, the interpretation of the above argument is still incomplete. What about those cases in which marketing takes place to genuine market clients, but the campaigns are (unavoidably) witnessed by the specially vulnerable who positively react upon these campaigns and seek out the marketers' products? Let us assume that R. J. Reynolds's use of "Old Joe" is such an example.[25]

If the effects on the specially vulnerable in such cases were not harmful, then few moral problems would be raised. However, when they are harmful, one must ask whether there are other means of marketing the product which would not have these secondary effects? If marketers, as other individuals, are under the general obligation of doing no harm, or minimizing harm, then they should seek to alter those marketing methods even if the harm is an indirect result of the marketer's intentions. On the other hand, if it is not possible to alter the marketing methods, then means might be sought to limit the exposure of those who are specially vulnerable to these marketing measures. In short, moral marketing requires some response other than simply ignoring the harm done to the vulnerable.

I suggest, then, that a more complete account of marketers and the vulnerable is that marketers may not market their products to target groups (specially vulnerable or not) in such a way that their marketing campaigns significantly affect vulnerable groups through their vulnerabilities. That is, there is nothing in the preceding that says that we must limit the effects of marketers' programs to their intentional aims with regard to a particular target segment. When significant spillover effects arise, they too must be taken into account. In effect, this would be to apply a form of strict targeted consumer liability.

Finally, is it morally justified to use marketing techniques which take advantage of the vulnerabilities of the specially vulnerable but which promote products which members of this group are widely acknowledged to need? For example, may marketers use techniques which young children cannot understand in order to get them to exercise properly or to eat a healthy diet? Or, may marketers use fear appeals to get the elderly to use their medications in a proper manner? Bailey has suggested that public service appeals might use fear appeals to warn certain groups of the elderly about dangers to them.[26] But this misses the point three ways. First, if the use of such appeals violates those who have been rendered specially susceptible to it, then they ought not to be used for good (public service messages) or bad (confidence games) or even ordinary marketing. Second, if some of the elderly are so specially susceptible to messages including fear, then the use of ordinary messages concerning their problems should also reach them. Fear is not needed; they are already concerned about the content of the appeal. Third, public service messages are one kind of "communication," whereas those messages which seek to sell a product or a service are very different. Since the marketing concept speaks of marketers seeking to satisfy consumer needs, some seek to use this to slide over into the public message realm. However, this is a slide that rests on an equivocation: public messages solely for the good of the recipient and private messages for the good of the sender, which may also be good for the recipient. In short, if a group is specially vulnerable, the use of unfair techniques which would not ultimately cause them harm is still the use of techniques which treat such individuals unfairly through manipulating them through their vulnerabilities. Only in very special circumstances should such marketing techniques be employed. . . .

Notes

1. C. L. Barnhart, ed., *American College Dictionary* (New York: Random House, 1956).

2. R. E. Goodin, *Protecting the Vulnerable: A Reanalysis of Our Social Responsibilities* (University of Chicago Press, 1985), p. 110.

3. Ibid., p. 112.

4. F. W. Morgan, D. K. Schuler, and J. J. Stoltman, "A Framework for Examining the Legal Status of Vulnerable Consumers," *Journal of Public Policy & Marketing* 14, no. 2 (1995): 267–77 (p. 267).

5. A. R. Andreasen, *The Disadvantaged Consumer* (New York: Free Press, 1975), p. 6.

6. J. A. Barnhill, "Market Injustice: The Case of the Disadvantaged Consumer," *Journal of Consumer Affairs* 6, no. 1 (1972): 78–83; F. W. Morgan and E. A. Riordan, "The Erosion of the Unusual Susceptibility Defense: The Case of the Disadvantaged Consumer," *Journal of the Academy of Marketing Science* 11, no. 2 (1983): 85–96.

7. A. R. Andreasen, "Revisiting the Disadvantaged: Old Lessons and New Problems," *Journal of Public Policy & Marketing* 12 (1993): 270–75 (p. 273).

8. I wish to capture here not the ideal market, but a morally justified imperfect market, filled with real participants. Further, I do not attempt to state all the necessary conditions for a capitalist market system, but only to highlight those most important for present purposes.

9. R. T. DeGeorge, *Business Ethics* (New York: Macmillan, 1982), p. 101.

10. M. Friedman, *Capitalism and Freedom* (University of Chicago Press, 1962).

11. R. Schnapper, "Consumer Legislation and the Poor," *Yale Law Journal* 76, no. 4 (1967): 745–92.

12. I intend that this allows for the use of credit, loans, and the like.

13. H. Assael, *Marketing: Principles & Strategy*, 2nd ed. (Fort Worth, TX: The Dryden Press, 1993), p. 592.

14. J. M. Bailey, "The Persuasibility of Elderly Consumers," *Current Issues in Research in Advertising* 10, no. 1 (1987): 213–47 (p. 213).

15. It is conceivable that they could transform the vulnerabilities of a normal consumer into special vulnerabilities.

16. Andreasen writes that "the swindler finds particularly good customers among the disadvantaged, since he expects the consumer not to understand much about contracts and 'formalities,' such as confessions of judgment, and to be unlikely to read legal language carefully or to peruse contracts disguised as receipts" (Andreasen, *Disadvantaged Consumer*, p. 204).

17. Vulnerability, in the grieving, involves a transformation of the self that forces people to face new consumer of market roles when they are least prepared to do so because of the associated stresses. See J. W. Gentry, P. F. Kennedy, K. Paul, and R. P. Hill, "The Vulnerability of Those Grieving the Death of a Loved One: Implications for Public Policy," *Journal of Public Policy & Marketing* 13, no. 2 (1994): 128–42 (p. 129). This state involves "traumatic confusion" (ibid.); a passage between two worlds; a "marginalized experience often accompanied by isolation and suspension of social status" (ibid.).

18. See McNeal, who notes the objection that limiting the market exposure of children would rob them of "the joy of being a consumer" or "the fun and pleasure that comes with being a consumer" (J. U. McNeal, *Children as Consumers* (Lexington, MA: Lexington Books, 1987), pp. 183–84).

19. D. Cohen, "The Concept of Unfairness as It Relates to Advertising Legislation," *Journal of Marketing* 38 (1974): 8–13 (p. 13). Among the members of these specially vulnerable groups which may be treated unfairly by marketers Cohen lists "children, the Ghetto Dweller, the elderly, and the handicapped" (ibid., p. 11).

20. R. Ferrar, "Bill Seeks to Reduce 'Ambulance Chasing,'" *Knoxville News Sentinel* (January 18, 1996), p. A3.

21. Gentry et al., Vulnerability," p. 139.

22. S. S. Guber and J. Berry, *Marketing to and through Kids* (New York: McGraw-Hill, 1993), p. 145.

23. Cf. McNeal, *Children as Consumers*, p. 186.

24. Cf. ibid., p. 185.

25. There is much dispute over whether this is the case. For present purposes I will assume that R. J. Reynolds has not directly targeted children.

26. Bailey, "Persuasibility of Elderly Consumers," p. 242.

7.3 DECEPTION AND COMMERCIAL SPEECH

The Perils of Ignoring History: Big Tobacco Played Dirty and Millions Died. How Similar Is Big Food?

KELLY D. BROWNELL AND KENNETH E. WARNER

In December 1953, the CEOs of the major tobacco companies met secretly in New York City. Their purpose was to counter the damage from studies linking smoking to lung cancer. A year earlier *Reader's Digest* – then the public's leading source of medical information – had printed an article entitled "Cancer by the Carton."[1] After it appeared, cigarette sales plummeted for two years, the first such decline of the century except during the Great Depression. Working closely with John Hill, the founder of the public relations giant Hill & Knowlton, the industry created "A Frank Statement to Cigarette Smokers" and paid to have it published in 448 newspapers on January 4, 1954. To give the industry a human face, the statement included the signatures of the nation's top tobacco executives and assured Americans that "we accept an interest in people's health as a basic responsibility, paramount to every other consideration in our business." Furthermore, they promised that "we always have and always will cooperate closely with those whose task it is to safeguard the public's health."[2]

The "Frank Statement" was a charade, the first step in a concerted, half-century-long campaign to mislead Americans about the catastrophic effects of smoking and to avoid public policy that might damage sales. Unearthed later, industry documents showed the repeated duplicity of its executives. Everything was at stake. The industry wanted desperately to prevent, or at least delay, shifts in public opinion that would permit a barrage of legislative, regulatory, and legal actions that would erode sales and profits.

Today another industry is under attack for marketing products perceived by some to damage health, and it also faces legislative, regulatory, and legal threats that could fundamentally alter how it does business. Schools are banning soft drinks and snack foods; legislation requiring calorie labels on restaurant menus has been passed at state and local levels and is being considered nationally; restrictions in food marketing practices have been proposed around the world; and even radical measures such as taxing snack foods are part of the national debate. Such actions invite comparison of the food and tobacco industries, exemplified by a *Fortune*

magazine cover story in 2003 entitled "Is Fat the Next Tobacco?" The cover depicted a French fry lying in an ashtray as if it were a cigarette. The article did what is now common – debate the parallels between tobacco and food in the context of culpability for health damage and ask whether Big Food should be sued for the same reasons that Big Tobacco was.

There are, of course, differences between food and tobacco as substances. The most obvious is that humans must eat to maintain health and life, whereas the unnecessary activity of smoking is, in the words of former Secretary of Health, Education and Welfare Joseph Califano, "slow-motion suicide." Moreover, selling tobacco to children is illegal, but there currently are no restrictions on food sales. Tobacco has a well-chronicled addictive process, whereas research on food and addiction is just now maturing. And although the fight against tobacco coalesced around a single product made by a few companies, food and its industries are far more complex.

The more important issue is whether tobacco history is instructive in addressing the problems created by unhealthy diets. A half-century of tobacco industry deception has had tragic consequences: Since the "Frank Statement," approximately 16 million Americans have died from smoking, and millions more have suffered from debilitating diseases ranging from emphysema to heart disease. Had the industry come clean in 1954 – matching deeds with promises – many of these deaths would almost certainly have been prevented. No one knows how many. Perhaps 3 million. Maybe 5 million. Maybe 7 million – just in the United States. An honest approach by industry might have saved more lives than any public health measure taken during the past 50 years. Furthermore, if industry had made good faith efforts globally, rather than exploit and addict the developing world, the benefits could have been stunning.

Food, physical inactivity, and obesity may be in the same league. An astonishing two-thirds of the US adult population is overweight or obese.[3] As with smoking, social justice issues are prominent, given that obesity rates are highest in

The Milbank Quarterly 87, no. 1 (2009). © 2009 Milbank Memorial Fund. Reprinted by permission of Blackwell Publishing Ltd.

the poorest segments of the population.[4] But weight issues are hardly unique to the United States. The World Health Organization has declared obesity a global epidemic, now surpassing hunger as the chief nutrition problem, even in some developing countries.[5]

Obesity rates are especially troubling in children, rising at three times the rate of increase in adults.[6] Indeed, the term *adult onset diabetes* has now been scrapped and replaced with *Type 2 diabetes* because children as young as eight are developing the disease. Canadian researchers conducted a 15-year follow-up of children diagnosed with Type 2 diabetes and found an alarming rate in *young* adults of blindness, amputation, kidney failure requiring dialysis, pregnancy loss, and death.[7] Health experts now are asking whether America's children will be the first in the nation's history to live shorter lives than their parents.[8]

Such statistics worry people, leading the press, parent groups, school officials, nutrition experts, healthcare providers, and government leaders to conclude that something must be done. Caught in the crosshairs, the food industry is reacting, sometimes with heavy ammunition. As an example, in response to menu-labeling initiatives, the restaurant industry has sued New York City, used its political might to weaken legislation in California, and successfully encouraged federal legislators to introduce weak national legislation that would preempt states and cities from acting more aggressively.

There are striking similarities, and some differences, in the way the food and tobacco industries have responded to public mistrust, damning scientific evidence, and calls for legal and legislative actions. As an important example of the similarities, food companies have issued their own versions of frank statements, stating their concern with the public's well-being and pledging to make changes to benefit public health. In this article we discuss what can be learned from tobacco and propose what might be done to avoid the repetition of a deadly history.

A Crossroads for Food

The food industry is on the defensive, hit hard by nutrition groups and public health professionals, the press, parent groups, child advocacy organizations, and state and national legislators sponsoring bills that could have a powerful impact on business. Popular books like *Fast Food Nation*[9] and movies like *Supersize Me* have sensitized the public to industry practices. In turn, the industry has had to react to claims that it seduces children into a lifestyle of unhealthy eating, infiltrates schools, buys loyalty from scientists, and pressures administration officials into accepting weak and ineffective nutrition policies.[10]

To the extent that these charges are fair, the analogy with the tobacco experience is inescapable. Seducing children? There is no better example than Joe Camel. Buying the loyalty of scientists? It happened time and again with tobacco. Using pressure to stall or prevent needed policy change? Few industries have been more effective than tobacco.[11]

A first step is to understand the industry players. Unlike tobacco, with one major product and a handful of companies producing it, food involves an immense array of products made by thousands of companies worldwide. The industry is diverse and fragmented in some ways, counting as its players a local baker making bread for a few stores; a family running a convenience store; an organic farmer; mega companies like Kraft, McDonald's, and Coca-Cola; and even Girl Scouts selling cookies. The same company making fried foods laden with saturated fat might also sell whole-grain cereal.

In other ways, the industry is organized and politically powerful. It consists of massive agribusiness companies like Cargill, Archer Daniels Midland, Bunge, and Monsanto; food sellers as large as Kraft (so big as to own Nabisco) and Pepsi-Co (owner of Frito-Lay); and restaurant companies as large as McDonald's and Yum! Brands (owner of Pizza Hut, Taco Bell, KFC, and more). These are represented by lobbyists, lawyers, and trade organizations that in turn represent a type of food (e.g., Snack Food Association, American Beverage Association), a segment of the industry (e.g., National Restaurant Association), a constituent of food (e.g., Sugar Association, Corn Refiners Association), or the entire industry (e.g., Grocery Manufacturers of America).

Common to all these players is an arresting logic: to successfully address the obesity epidemic, the nation must consume fewer calories, which means eating less food. Marion Nestle estimates that the number of daily calories created for the American food supply rose from 3,300 per person in 1970 to 3,800 in the late 1990s, far in excess of what the average person needs to maintain a healthy weight.[12] If consumers' demand for food were to reflect what they needed to maintain a healthy weight, the market would contract. A shrinking market for all those calories would mean less money – a lot less.

Of course there will always be a need for food – people cannot stop eating. But the *types* and *amounts* of food people eat must change dramatically if there is to be any hope of curbing obesity and other problems associated with unhealthy eating. The foods most at risk happen to be those most processed, dense in calories, highest in profit margin, and sold mainly by the major industry players.

Industry stands at a crossroads where one turn would mean fighting change, defending practices like targeting children, forestalling policy changes, and selling as much product as possible no matter the consequences, and the other would require retooling, working with the public health community, selling far fewer harmful products, and promoting healthier options with much greater urgency. Adopting the first option while laying claim to the second was the path taken by the tobacco industry. Is the food industry different, or is history repeating itself, this time with another substance?

The Playbook

The tobacco team had a playbook – a master plan and script that directed the behavior of industry executives, lobbyists, lawyers, scientists, and government officials friendly to the industry. In *A Question of Intent*, a former FDA commissioner, David Kessler wrote:

> Devised in the 1950s and '60s, the tobacco industry's strategy was embodied in a script written by the lawyers. Every tobacco company executive in the public eye was told to learn the script backwards and forwards, no deviation was allowed. The basic premise was simple – smoking had not been proved to cause cancer. Not proven, not proven, not proven – this would be stated insistently and repeatedly. Inject a thin wedge of doubt, create controversy, never deviate from the prepared line. It was a simple plan and it worked.[13]

The food industry appears to have a strategy as well, repeatedly carried to the public by spokespersons from food companies, trade associations, and their political allies. As noted by Brownell and Horgen and by Nestle regarding the food industry specifically and by Mooney and by Michaels about industries in general,[14] its main features are the following:

- Focus on personal responsibility as the cause of the nation's unhealthy diet.
- Raise fears that government action usurps personal freedom.
- Vilify critics with totalitarian language, characterizing them as the food police, leaders of a nanny state, and even "food fascists," and accuse them of desiring to strip people of their civil liberties.
- Criticize studies that hurt industry as "junk science."
- Emphasize physical activity over diet.
- State there are no good or bad foods; hence no food or food type (soft drinks, fast foods, etc.) should be targeted for change.

- Plant doubt when concerns are raised about the industry.

These points play well in America – personal responsibility and freedom are central values – but they obscure the reality that some of the most significant health advances have been made by population-based public health approaches in which the overall welfare of the citizenry trumps certain individual or industry freedoms. Can one reasonably defend half a million deaths per year from cigarettes by provoking fears that freedom and choice are threatened by actions that might adversely affect the industry? In addition, disputing science has been a key strategy of many industries, including tobacco.[15] Beginning with denials that smoking causes lung cancer and progressing to attacks on studies of secondhand smoke, the industry instilled doubt. Likewise, groups and scientists funded by the food industry have disputed whether the prevalence figures for obesity are correct, whether obesity causes disease, and whether foods like soft drinks cause harm.[16]

Public Relations and Framing

A great deal of influence rests in the hands of parties who control the framing of a health issue. That is, a problem framed as a matter of personal irresponsibility will be addressed differently from one for which other factors, such as corporate misbehavior, environmental toxins, or infectious agents, are responsible. The tobacco industry devoted considerable resources to public relations as its primary weapon to influence public opinion and neutralize calls for government intervention.

The food industry, its trade associations, and its political front groups have been similarly aggressive in attempting to shape public and legislator opinion. At the heart of this strategy is a script built on values of personal responsibility.

The Personal Responsibility Script

At the 1996 shareholders' meeting of cigarette and food manufacturer RJR Nabisco, a woman in the audience asked company chairman Charles Harper whether he would want people smoking around his children and grandchildren. Mr. Harper responded, "If the children don't like to be in a smoky room ... they'll leave." When the woman responded, "An infant cannot leave a room," Mr. Harper answered, "At some point they learn to crawl, okay? And then they begin to walk."[17] Personal responsibility has been invoked to shield the food industry from criticism, legislation, and litigation. Legislation sponsored by Congressman Ric Keller (R-FL) in 2004 to ban lawsuits claiming health damages against fast-food restaurants is typical in emphasizing personal behavior: "We've got to get back to those old-fashioned principles of personal responsibility, of common sense, and get away from this new culture where everybody plays the victim and blames other people for their problems."[18] When asked about the role of restaurants in contributing to the obesity problem, Steven Anderson, president of the National Restaurant Association stated, "Just because we have electricity doesn't mean you have to electrocute yourself."[19]

These assertions illustrate the execution of an organized corporate strategy that shifts responsibility from the parties who make and market products to those who use them.[20] A variety of corollary messages are also typical of industry framing, namely, that companies offer choices and pleasure, emphasize moderation, and do not encourage consumers to overuse their products.

Industry Self-Regulation as a Defense against Government Action

Industries under threat often claim that self-regulation is sufficient and that they deserve the public's and government's trust. Then they launch highly publicized pledges for change. Beginning with the "Frank Statement" made by tobacco companies in 1954 in which companies pledged, among other things, to "cooperate closely with those whose task it is to safeguard the public health," the industry did its best to fight calls for strict regulation. A modern-day version is the Philip Morris television campaign focused on preventing youth from smoking. An outside evaluation found that it did no such thing and in fact might affect children in ways that would make them *more* likely to smoke.[21] Nonindustry antismoking efforts, in comparison, have been successful with both youth and adult smokers.[22]

The food industry is in full-scale pursuit of self-regulatory authority.[23] The American Beverage Association, in association with the Alliance for a Healthier Generation,[24] announced that it would reduce sales of traditional carbonated soft drinks in schools. Left untouched was an array of beverages whose sales are increasing (e.g., sports drinks), compared with the traditional carbonated beverages whose sales are declining. Another example is the announcement by a coalition of major food companies and the Council of Better Business Bureaus that their child-marketing practices would change.[25]

The impact of these pledges on children's dietary practices has not been established objectively, but to the extent the tobacco experience applies, there is reason to be on high alert. The child market for the food companies is enormous. American children, counting only those aged five to fourteen, spend $20 billion annually and influence the spending of $200 billion to $500 billion more. Some ad agencies specialize in children's television marketing and others in product placements in children's media, handbooks, and conferences on child marketing, and prizes for the best marketing campaigns.

Corporate Social Responsibility

Businesses often invest in their communities because it is considered good public relations and is used to burnish the company image. Contributing to the community thus can be especially important to companies battling tarnished reputations. Corporate social responsibility investments can also pay dividends in buying loyalty, or at least stifling opposition, from groups that might otherwise oppose a company's business practices.

For decades, the tobacco industry used perceptions of social responsibility to great effect. Contributions to minority and women's organizations offered implicit encouragement of leaders to target concerns other than smoking. Leaders of African-American communities faced a very real conflict: either to help the community by accepting money or to speak out about the disproportionate toll of tobacco on the health of minority populations. Women's groups, heavily supported by Big Tobacco and buoyed by support for events like the Virginia Slims Tennis Tour, were silent on the rapidly escalating epidemic of lung cancer in women, focusing instead on breast cancer and other problems.[26]

In addition to women's tennis, the tobacco companies have supported dance troupes, museums, and orchestras. Hard-pressed to fund their endeavors, members of the nation's cultural elite become vulnerable to the seduction of tobacco money and show their appreciation in statements of support for their benefactors' good deeds. In 2000, Philip Morris spent $115 million on worthy social causes, including, in addition to the arts, supplying flood victims with clean water and sheltering women who were victims of abuse. The company spent $150 million on a national TV advertising campaign touting its beneficence. It is noteworthy that such "corporate social responsibility" comes cheap. Philip Morris's spending on good deeds that year constituted one-half of 1 percent of the company's $23 billion in domestic tobacco revenues.[27]

The food industry also does its share of charitable work and has developed inroads in key social institutions such as hospitals and schools. Ronald McDonald houses are one example. Fast-food restaurants also can be found in the lobbies of many of the nation's leading hospitals,[28] including McDonald's franchises in the lobbies of the Cleveland Clinic and the Children's Hospital of Philadelphia. One study found that 59 of 200 hospitals with pediatric residencies had fast-food restaurants and that families who made outpatient pediatric visits were four times more likely to eat fast food (at any time of the day) if they visited a hospital with a fast-food restaurant.[29] Likewise, schools remain a branding and sales opportunity for the beverage industry at the same time it pledges to protect children.[30]

Influencing Government and Key Organizations

The Influence of Government

Decades ago, Big Tobacco adopted a political strategy quite similar to that now employed by the food industry, with tobacco industry spokespeople, paid scientists, and consultants attempting to influence many key decision-making bodies. Little appreciated today is that the government gave the tobacco industry veto power over the membership of the advisory committee that eventually produced the first surgeon general's report on smoking and health, published in 1964.[31]

The tobacco industry's insider roles have had a profound impact on public policy. As the former FDA commissioner David Kessler explained:

> When we launched our investigation of tobacco at the Food and Drug Administration, we had no idea of the power wielded by the tobacco companies. But we soon learned why the tobacco industry was for decades considered untouchable. Tobacco employed some of the most prestigious law firms in the country and commanded the allegiance of a significant section of the Congress. It also had access to the services of widely admired public figures ranging from Prime Minister Margaret Thatcher to Senator Howard Baker.[32]

Kessler also noted the influence of the food industry when the FDA addressed issues of food labeling. The beef industry fought the FDA on labeling of fat and promoted a higher number than the FDA's proposed standard for how many calories a day the average person is expected to consume. Kessler recounted:

> From the White House, the pressure moved down to the Office of Management and Budget, which had the power to block our regulations. As required, we had submitted draft after draft of the final rule to OMB and often had it returned to us with industry-sought changes. More than once, OMB's wording had been taken almost verbatim from food industry comments we had already carefully considered.[33]

In dealing with the obesity issue, one of Tommy Thompson's early acts as Secretary of Health and Human Services (DHHS) in George W. Bush's administration was to meet with the board of directors of the Grocery Manufacturers of America (GMA), the world's largest food industry trade association. According to a GMA press release, Thompson applauded the industry for its efforts to deal with obesity, and when asked how to deal with critics who believed that the industry should change its practices, he encouraged the industry to "go on the offensive."[34]

Thompson figured prominently in another case in which public health and food industry priorities were at odds. In February 2003, the World Health Organization released a draft report outlining a global strategy to address issues of diet and physical activity.[35] Making recommendations considered tame by many, the report advocated such measures as reducing the intake of sugar and fat and creating a safer nutrition environment for children in schools. Six words in that report, "limit the intake of 'free' sugars," stimulated a remarkable series of events. Free sugars are those added to foods – obvious ones like soft drinks, candy, and desserts but also foods less often thought of as sugar rich, including soups, ketchup, beef stew, and yogurt.

The food industry went to work within days of the draft's release. The sugar industry, through the Sugar Association, enlisted the support of officials high in the US government and led a vigorous attack on both the report and the WHO.[36] Beginning with letters to the WHO's director general, the Sugar Association criticized both the science and the process by which the report was prepared and asked that it be stopped, or at the very least, delayed. Not receiving the desired response, the industry quickly raised the stakes when two US senators, Larry Craig and John Breaux, cochairs of the "U.S. Senate Sweetener Caucus," implored Thompson to use his "personal intervention" in blocking the report.

Thompson attempted to deliver. A DHHS assistant secretary sent a 28-page, single-spaced report to the WHO picking at the science and making the same three points promoted by the industry: personal responsibility should be the emphasis; there should be a stronger focus on physical activity; and there are no good and bad foods. Thompson dispatched this assistant to Geneva at the time of a key WHO meeting, pressuring constituent countries to block the report.

The Sugar Association simultaneously played its ultimate card. Expressing concern for "the hard working sugar growers and their families," its president again wrote the WHO, vowing to use "every avenue possible to expose the dubious nature" of the report, "including asking Congressional appropriators to challenge future funding of the U.S.'s $406 million contributions . . . to the WHO." This is the WHO that deals with AIDS, malnutrition, infectious disease, bioterrorism, and more, threatened because of its stance on sugar.

The tobacco history is similar. In its first-ever use of its international treaty-making authority, the WHO proposed, and eventually received, near-universal approval to adopt the Framework Convention on Tobacco Control (FCTC), an international treaty that would, among other things, result in higher cigarette prices, the abolition of most tobacco advertising, and global cooperation in combating cigarette smuggling.[37] The multiyear effort to develop the FCTC encountered serious opposition from only a handful of countries, with the US delegation leading the charge. The United States' vocal resistance was noteworthy in that the convention would have limited impact on this country, which had already achieved much success in tobacco control. Rather, the convention would attack the spread of tobacco in poor and middle-income countries, the principal targets of the industry's plans for future expansion. Success in the latter endeavor, of course, would affect the financial well-being of major multinational companies like Altria (parent of Philip Morris).

The FCTC experience gave the US administration a black eye and fed perceptions that business interests are more important to the United States than the health of developing countries. The global community adopted the FCTC with such strong unanimity, however, that even the United States voted in favor, but only after the failure of its last-minute efforts to subvert the agreed-upon document. Nearly all the countries that approved the FCTC at the May 2003 World Health Assembly subsequently ratified the convention, making the FCTC one of the most widely and rapidly adopted treaties in history. As of August 2008, 160 countries had ratified the treaty. The United States remains one of the few holdouts. In fact, the Bush administration did not even forward the treaty to the Senate for its consideration.

The United States found itself similarly isolated in its attack on the WHO's diet and nutrition recommendations. Skewered by the international press and unsupported by food industry giants located outside the country (like Nestle and Unilever), the administration and industry nonetheless maintained their stance.

The idea that industry interests should trump public health has been institutionalized in regulatory agencies like the US Department of Agriculture (USDA) by means of a "rotating door" that leads to the regulatory agency's "capture" by industry.[38] While working to promote healthy eating, the USDA at the same time has as its main objective the promotion of American agriculture (selling more food), so

one goal typically prevails over the other when the two conflict. There is a long history of USDA leaders and leaders of other agencies being recruited from food and agriculture industries and then returning to businesses like lobbying firms when their government service ends. Tommy Thompson, a former secretary of DHHS, is now a partner with Akin Gump, a law firm that defended tobacco companies and food companies like Archer Daniels Midland. Daniel Glickman went to the same firm after serving as secretary of the USDA.

Disputing Science, Planting Doubt, Creating Conflicts of Interest

Industry must often contend with research that questions the safety and healthfulness of its products and the impact of practices such as marketing. There is a long history, in both the tobacco and food industries, of their seeking to influence science.

Scientists, Conflicts of Interest, and Industry Front Groups

From the early days of research showing the harmful effects of tobacco on health, the industry paid prominent scientists to conduct studies and to act as advisors and consultants with the intent of countering the potentially damaging scientific evidence.[39] This practice continues today.[40] Michaels, Kessler, and Mooney all note that this may well be a deliberate strategy to buy loyalty and to instill doubt: to confuse the public, give ammunition to political allies, and stall or prevent government action.[41] A case in point is the tobacco industry's behavior in undermining the science with respect to secondhand smoke.[42]

Similar concerns have been raised about the food industry.[43] Many of the major food companies have advisory boards composed of the field's most visible academics, pay scientists as consultants, and fund research. The question is what industry "buys" with these transactions. It is possible some scientists and professional organizations are not affected, but for others (1) the conduct or interpretation of science becomes biased; (2) scientists or professional organizations issue statements and take positions more favorable to industry; (3) well-placed scientists help industry in key strategic roles (e.g., membership on the Dietary Guidelines Committee); and (4) industry uses the funding of research as evidence it is seeking the "truth" about the dangers of its products.[44] Common sense argues that industry would not spend the money if there were no return, but more important are the data addressing the issue.

One example is the research on the connection between the consumption of soft drinks and health. A meta-analysis of available research showed clear relationships among the consumption of soft drinks, poor nutrition, and negative health outcomes.[45] Within this meta-analysis, which was not funded by industry, those studies with stronger methods were more likely to show these negative outcomes. Furthermore, a comparison of studies funded or not funded by industry showed that the former were more likely to find results favorable to industry. An analysis of studies of the health effects of secondhand smoke produced similar findings.[46]

The soft drink industry, through the American Beverage Association (ABA), responded swiftly by supporting a group of researchers to conduct another review of the link between soft drinks and body weight. Two of the authors had conducted multiple industry-funded studies in the past, and one was employed by the ABA when the study was published. This study found that the consumption of soft drinks is not related to negative outcomes.[47]

There are a few signs that this conflict of interest may improve. "Sunlight" being trained on the issue by the press may shame conflicted scientists and professional organizations into behaving differently. A highly visible case occurred when the press documented that a prominent obesity researcher was paid by the restaurant industry to write a brief in its legal case opposing menu-labeling regulations in New York City.[48]

Improvements also may follow when scientists recognize that the field's response to conflicts – disclosure – may actually make the situation worse. Cain, Loewenstein, and Moore found that an audience hearing information from a source who discloses a conflict of interest discounts what they hear, but only to a small extent.[49] The source, however, feels emboldened to present his or her views more strongly, ultimately making the conflicted source more, rather than less, credible. This phenomenon may apply to organizations as well as to individuals, and as noted earlier, prominent organizations such as the American Dietetic Association and the Obesity Society receive considerable funding from industry.

Industry front groups provide another parallel between the industries. The tobacco industry created organizations that appeared at first glance to be grassroots groups seeking to protect smokers' rights and to fight off government intrusion.[50] An industry, of course, has the right to promote its positions, but when money flows through such organizations, their nature and intent are not apparent to the general public. The food industry also funds groups with names that would not necessarily alert the public to the industry connection. The Center for Consumer Freedom is an example. Such front groups attack and instill doubt in published

science and the scientists who do research, in concert with the industry script.[51]

Product Marketing and "Safer" Products

Another similarity between tobacco and food companies is the introduction and heavy marketing of "safer" or "healthier" products. When cigarette sales dropped in the early 1950s owing to health concerns, the industry introduced "safer" cigarettes that gave health-conscious smokers an alternative to quitting.[52] Filtered cigarettes, sold with the explicit message that filters removed dangerous substances while preserving flavor, were marketed aggressively. Cigarette consumption then resumed its upward trajectory, and within a decade, filtered cigarettes came to dominate the market. Ironically, the filter of the first highly successful brand of filtered cigarettes, Kent, added to the smoking experience yet another dangerous substance: the asbestos in its filter.[53]

Fifteen years later, industry addressed the widespread fear of smoking by introducing low-tar and low-nicotine cigarettes. Advertising explicitly conveyed the message that these new "light" cigarettes were safer. An ad for True cigarettes read, "All the fuss about smoking got me thinking I'd either quit or smoke True. I smoke True." Within a decade this new product dominated the market. Moreover, the cigarette companies enjoyed a windfall because they retained customers while selling them a product that required many of them to smoke even more cigarettes to accumulate their accustomed intake of nicotine. Industry analysts have observed that low-tar and low-nicotine cigarettes were designed as public relations devices, not harm reduction products.[54] The industry knew that the cigarettes generated official machine-measured tar and nicotine yields far lower than they would when smoked by human beings (due to the location of ventilation holes, designed so that they would be blocked when held by fingers, but not blocked when held at their very tip by a testing machine). Yet even today, smokers of "lights" believe, erroneously, that their risk of death from smoking is substantially below that of smokers of "full-flavor" cigarettes.[55] Smokers of low-tar cigarettes, who frequently pull harder on their cigarettes, are now developing cancers farther down in the lung than was the case with traditional cigarettes.[56] These "safer" products have had disastrous results for public health.[57]

For many years the food industry has marketed both products with smaller amounts of those ingredients thought to cause harm (e.g., sugar, fat, salt, trans fats) and products supplemented or fortified with ingredients purported to improve health (e.g., vitamins and minerals, oat bran, whole grains). Fueled in part by lax government regulation of marketing and health claims, there has been an explosion of such products in recent years. Some examples:

- Removing trans fats is a positive development, but the degree of health benefit depends on what is used as a replacement (saturated fats are more damaging replacements than polyunsaturated or monounsaturated fats).
- A KFC ad campaign depicted an African-American family in which the father was told by the mother that "KFC has 0 grams of trans fat now." The father, in the presence of children, shouts, "Yeah baby! Whoooo!!" and then begins eating the fried chicken with abandon. Does such an ad imply it is now fine to eat fried chicken and potentially increase consumption in ways that contribute to obesity (there is no calorie advantage of switching one fat for another)?
- General Mills has an aggressive marketing and packaging campaign to tout the fact that its cereals are made with whole grains, including high-sugar products like Lucky Charms and Cinnamon Toast Crunch. Whether consumers, responding to the General Mills campaign, would overestimate the benefit of the grain change and increase their consumption of such cereals is not known.

At the center of this issue is whether industry can be trusted to make changes that benefit the public good and can be responsible with the accompanying marketing. The tobacco history is clear and is captured in this quotation: "If the past 50 years have taught us anything, it is that the tobacco industry cannot be trusted to put the public's interest above their profits no matter what they say."[58] Where does the food industry fit in this picture? A number of motives encourage industry to introduce products perceived to be safer and healthier, including the possibility that consumers will buy these products in increasing numbers; public relations; less exposure to litigation; and a convincing case that industry can self-regulate, making government intervention unnecessary. These apply to both tobacco and food.

Objective evaluations will be needed to establish whether the "better for you" products promoted by the food industry are actually better for consumers' health. In addition, the validity of inferences that consumers draw from marketing of such products and consumers' actual responses will need to be evaluated objectively. A product slightly improved but marketed to imply a large benefit could lead consumers to eat more and hence have a damaging impact overall. These needs for evaluation, and possibly regulation, duplicate those identified by an Institute of Medicine committee regarding the contemporary proliferation of novel nicotine and tobacco products, all marketed as reducing risk.[59]

The food industry could indeed improve its products in ways that will be beneficial to the public's health. We suggest that the industry adopt marketing approaches that are consistent with the goal of serving the public's health.

A Question of Priorities

Today 50 Americans will be murdered; 89 will take their own lives; 40 will succumb to HIV/AIDS; and 112 will die from motor vehicle injuries. This sums to 291 deaths, compared to the 1,200 people who will die as a result of their smoking. But one act might have saved even more lives: an honest approach by the industry, one consistent with the industry's pledge in the 1954 "Frank Statement" and precisely opposite the disastrous route it chose to follow.[60]

Food industry versions of the "Frank Statement" and its aftermath are unacceptable. Americans now realize there is a serious problem with the nation's diet, physical activity, and weight. There is growing awareness of who is selling what and to whom they are selling, coupled with mounting insistence on corporate accountability. . . .

In the 1950s, cigarette advertisements claimed, "More doctors smoke Camel than any other cigarette." Ronald Reagan was well known for his endorsement of Chesterfield cigarettes. The world was not then aware of the havoc that cigarettes could visit on the body. Only recently have we become truly aware of the catastrophic impact of the modern food and physical activity environment. Now we must wonder how history will view Shaquille O'Neal promoting Burger King, Britney Spears and Beyoncé Knowles working with Pepsi, and Cedric the Entertainer, Michael Jordan, Kobe Bryant, Serena and Venus Williams, and Donald Trump all endorsing McDonald's.

To protect profits, the food industry must avoid perceptions that it is uncaring and insensitive, ignores public health, preys on children, intentionally manipulates addictive substances, and knowingly, even cynically, contributes to death, disability, and billions in healthcare costs every year. Stated another way, it cannot afford to look like tobacco. Whether it *is* like tobacco is a question of central importance.

The food industry is more complex than tobacco, with scores more players and thousands more products. Some companies, such as fruit and vegetable sellers, promote inherently good products, while some like the candy companies do the opposite. Most companies, especially the major players such as Nestle, Unilever, and Kraft (the world's three largest food companies), do a great deal of both. Such companies have many ways to leave a better health footprint on the world (reformulating their products, selling fewer calorie-dense foods and more healthy choices, curtailing marketing to children, and withdrawing from schools). The question is whether they will behave in honorable, health-promoting ways or will sink to the depths occupied by tobacco. . . .

Notes

1. R. Norr, "Cancer by the Carton," *Reader's Digest* (December, 1952), pp. 7–8.

2. Tobacco Industry Research Committee, "A Frank Statement to Cigarette Smokers" (1954). Retrieved from http://legacy .library.ucsf.edu/cgi/getdoc? tid=zep91f00&fmt=pdf&ref=results.

3. C. L. Ogden, M. D. Carroll, M. A. McDowell, and K. D. Flegal, "Obesity among Adults in the United States – No Statistically Significant Change since 2003–2004," *NCHS Data Brief* no. 1 (2007). Hyattsville, MD: National Center for Health Statistics.

4. S. Kumanyika, "Nutrition and Chronic Disease Prevention: Priorities for US Minority Groups," *Nutrition Reviews* 64, no. 2, pt. 2 (2006): S9–S14.

5. World Health Organization, *Global Strategy on Diet, Physical Activity and Health* (2004). Geneva. Retrieved from www.who .int/dietphysicalactivity/strategy/eb11344/strategy_english_ web.pdf.

6. C. L. Ogden, M. D. Carroll, and K. M. Flegal, "High Body Mass Index for Age among U.S. Children and Adolescents, 2003– 2006," *Journal of the American Medical Association* 299 (2008): 2401–5.

7. H. Dean and B. Flett, "Natural History of Type 2 Diabetes Diagnosed in Childhood: Long-Term Follow-up in Young Adult Years." Paper presented at the annual meeting of the American Diabetes Association, San Francisco, June 2002.

8. S. J. Olshansky, D. J. Passaro, R. C. Hershow, J. Layden, B. A. Carnes, J. Brody, L. Hayflick, R. N. Butler, D. B. Allison, and D. S. Ludwig, "A Potential Decline in Life Expectancy in the United States in the 21st Century," *New England Journal of Medicine* 352, no. 11 (2005): 1138–45.

9. E. Schlosser, *Fast Food Nation: The Dark Side of the All American Meal* (New York: Houghton Mifflin, 2001).

10. K. D. Brownell and K. B. Horgen, *Food Fight: The Inside Story of the Food Industry, America's Obesity Crisis, and What We Can Do about It* (New York: McGraw-Hill, 2004); M. Nestle, *Food Politics: How the Food Industry Influences Nutrition and Health* (Berkeley: University of California Press, 2002).

11. Advocacy Institute, *Smoke & Mirrors: How the Tobacco Industry Buys & Lies Its Way to Power & Profits* (Washington, DC, 2008).

12. Nestle, *Food Politics*.

13. D. A. Kessler, *A Question of Intent: A Great American Battle with a Deadly Industry* (New York: Public Affairs, 2001), p. xiii.

14. Brownell and Horgen, *Food Fight*; Nestle, *Food Politics*; C. Mooney, *Republican War on Science* (New York: Basic Books, 2006); D. Michaels, *Doubt Is Their Product: How Industry's Assault on Science Threatens Your Health* (Oxford University Press, 2008).

15. Advocacy Institute, *Smoke & Mirrors*; T. McGarity and W. Wagner, *Bending Science: How Special Interests Corrupt Public Health Research* (Cambridge, MA: Harvard University Press, 2008); Michaels, *Doubt Is Their Product*; Mooney, *Republican War on Science*.

16. For example, R. A. Forshee, P. A. Anderson, and M. L. Story, "Sugar-Sweetened Beverages and Body Mass Index in Children and Adolescents: A Meta-Analysis," *American Journal of Clinical Nutrition* 87 (2008): 1662–71; Grocery Manufacturers of America, Press release, September 25, 2003. Retrieved from www.gmabrands .com/news/docs/Testimony .cfm?docid=1209.

17. RJR Nabisco, Annual Meeting of Shareholders (proceedings), Winston-Salem, NC, April 17, 1996, pp. 61–62. Retrieved from http://legacy.library.ucsf.edu/action/document/page? tid=ygk01d00&page=61.

18. CNN, Interview with Congressman Ric Keller, March 10, 2004. Retrieved from http://transcripts.cnn.com/TRANSCRIPTS/ 0403/10/ltm.02.html.

19. J. Holguin, "Battle of the Widening Bulge: Lawyers Who Battled Big Tobacco Size up Fast Food Industry," August 8, 2002. Retrieved from www.cbsnews.com/stories/2002/08/08/ eveningnews/main518023.shtml.

20. J. S. Hacker, *The Great Risk Shift: The New Economic Insecurity and the Decline of the American Dream* (Oxford University Press, 2006).

21. E. M. Sebrie and S. A. Glantz, "Attempts to Undermine Tobacco Control: Tobacco Industry 'Youth Smoking Prevention' Programs to Undermine Meaningful Tobacco Control in Latin America," *American Journal of Public Health* 97 (2007): 1357–67; M. Wakefield, Y. Terry-McElrath, S. Emery, H. Saffer, F. J. Chaloupka, G. Szczypka, B. Flay, P. M. O'Malley, and L. D. Johnston, "Effect of Televised, Tobacco Company-Funded Smoking Prevention Advertising on Youth Smoking-Related Beliefs, Intentions, and Behavior," *American Journal of Public Health* 96 (2006): 2154–60.

22. A. Hyland, M. Wakefield, C. Higbee, G. Szczypka, and K. M. Cummings, "Anti-Tobacco Television Advertising and Indicators of Smoking Cessation in Adults: A Cohort Study," *Health Education Research* 21 (2006): 348–54; K. E. Warner, "Tobacco Policy Research: Insights and Contributions to Public Health Policy," in *Tobacco Control Policy*, ed. K. E. Warner (San Francisco, CA: Jossey-Bass), pp. 3–86.

23. L. Sharma, S. Teret, and K. D. Brownell, "Self-Regulation and the Food Industry: Successes, Failures, and Needed Directions." Unpublished paper, 2008.

24. Alliance for a Healthier Generation, "Announcement of School Beverage Guidelines," May 3, 2006. Retrieved from

www.healthiergeneration.org/uploadedFiles/For_Schools/
School_Beverage_Guide lines/Beverage%20MOU.pdf.

25. Council of Better Business Bureaus, Press release: "Better Business Bureau Announces Food and Beverage Advertising Commitments from 11 Industry Leaders," July 18, 2007. Retrieved from www.bbb.org/alerts/article.asp?ID=779.

26. Advocacy Institute, *Smoke & Mirrors*.

27. K. E. Warner, "What's a Cigarette Company to Do?" *American Journal of Public Health* 92 (2002): 897–900.

28. P. Cram, B. K. Nallamothu, A. M. Fendrick, and S. Saint, "Fast Food Franchises in Hospitals" (letter), *Journal of the American Medical Association* 287 (2007): 2945–46; H. B. Sahud, H. J. Binns, W. L. Meadow, and R. E. Tanz, "Marketing Fast Food: Impact of Fast Food Restaurants in Children's Hospitals," *Pediatrics* 118 (2006): 2290–97.

29. Sahud et al., "Marketing Fast Food."

30. For example, American Beverage Association, "Questions and Answers: Beverages in Schools" (2009). Retrieved from www.ameribev.org.

31. Public Health Service, *Smoking and Health: Report of the Advisory Committee to the Surgeon General of the United States* (1964). Washington, DC: US Department of Health, Education and Welfare, Public Health Service, Center for Disease Control. PHS Publication no. 1103.

32. Kessler, *A Question of Intent*, p. xii.

33. Ibid., p. 58.

34. Grocery Manufacturers of America, Press release, November 12, 2002. Retrieved from www.gmabrands.com/news/docs/NewsRelease.cfm?DocID=1028.

35. World Health Organization, *Global Strategy on Diet, Physical Activity and Health* (Geneva: WHO, 2004).

36. K. D. Brownell and M. Nestle, "The Sweet and Lowdown on Sugar," *The New York Times* (January 23, 2004), Op-Ed.

37. World Health Organization, *WHO Framework Convention on Tobacco Control* (2003). Geneva. Retrieved from https://apps.who.int/iris/bitstream/handle/10665/42811/9241591013.pdf;jsessionid=22A46C3FB974F9305A686B19657D97A5?sequence=1.

38. T. Makkai and T. Braithwaite, "In and Out of the Revolving Door: Making Sense of Regulatory Capture," *Journal of Public Policy* 12 (1992): 61–78.

39. K. M. Cummings, A. Brown, and R. O'Connor, "The Cigarette Controversy," *Cancer Epidemiology, Biomarkers & Prevention* 16 (2007): 1070–76.

40. J. Barnoya and S. A. Glantz, "The Tobacco Industry's Worldwide ETS Consultants Project: European and Asian Components," *European Journal of Public Health* 16 (2006): 69–77; S. G. Mars and P. M. Ling, "Meanings and Motives: Experts Debating Tobacco Addiction," *American Journal of Public Health* 98 (2008): 1793–802; S. F. Schick and S. A. Glantz, "Old Ways, New Means: Tobacco Industry Funding of Academic and Private Sector Scientists since the Master Settlement Agreement," *Tobacco Control* 16 (2007): 157–64.

41. Michaels, *Doubt Is Their Product*; Kessler, *A Question of Intent*; Mooney, *Republican War on Science*.

42. McGarity and Wagner, *Bending Science*; E. K. Tong and S. A. Glantz, "Tobacco Industry Efforts Undermining Evidence Linking Secondhand Smoke with Cardiovascular Disease," *Circulation* 116 (2007): 1845–54.

43. Brownell and Horgen, *Food Fight*; M. Nestle, "Food Company Sponsorship of Nutrition Research and Professional Activities: A Conflict of Interest?" *Public Health Nutrition* 4 (2001): 1015–22; Nestle, *Food Politics*.

44. McGarity and Wagner, *Bending Science*.

45. L. R. Vartanian, M. B. Schwartz, and K. D. Brownell, "Effects of Soft Drink Consumption on Nutrition and Health: A Systematic Review and Meta-Analysis," *American Journal of Public Health* 97 (2007): 667–75.

46. A. Misakian and L. Bero, "Publication Bias and Research on Passive Smoking: Comparison of Published and Unpublished Studies," *Journal of the American Medical Association* 280 (1998): 250–53.

47. Forshee et al., "Sugar-Sweetened Beverages and Body Mass Index."

48. R. Nichols, "On the Side: Obesity Expert Sides with Chain Restaurants," *Philadelphia Inquirer* (February 21, 2008); S. Saul, "Conflict on the Menu," *The New York Times* (February 16, 2008); K. Stark, "Obesity Case Raises Questions about the Influence of Money on Science," *Philadelphia Inquirer* (February 15, 2008).

49. D. M. Cain, G. Loewenstein, and D. A. Moore, "The Dirt on Coming Clean: Perverse Effects of Disclosing Conflicts of Interest," *Journal of Legal Studies* 34 (2005): 1–25.

50. Advocacy Institute, *Smoke & Mirrors*; D. E. Apollonio and L. A. Bero, "The Creation of Industry Front Groups: The Tobacco Industry and 'Get Government Off Our Back,'" *American Journal of Public Health* 97 (2007): 419–27.

51. McGarity and Wagner, *Bending Science*; Michaels, *Doubt Is Their Product*.

52. K. M. Cummings, A. Brown, and C. E. Douglas, "Consumer Acceptable Risk: How Cigarette Companies Have Responded to Accusations That Their Products Are Defective," *Tobacco Control* 15, suppl. 4 (2006): 84–89.

53. J. Slade, "Nicotine Delivery Devices," in *Nicotine Addiction: Principles and Management*, ed. C. T. Orleans and J. Slade (Oxford University Press, 1993), pp. 3–23.

54. P. W. Pollay and T. Dewhirst, "Marketing Cigarettes with Low Machine-Measured Yields," in *Risks Associated with Smoking Cigarettes with Low Machine-Measured Yields of Tar and Nicotine*. Smoking and Tobacco Control Monograph no. 13, ed. D. R. Shopland, D. M. Burns, N. L. Benowitz, and R. H. Amacher (Bethesda, MD: US Department of Health and Human Services, Public Health Service, National Institutes of Health, National Cancer Institute, NIH Publication no. 02-5074, 2001), pp. 199–235. Retrieved from https://cancercontrol.cancer.gov/brp/tcrb/monographs/13/m13_7.pdf.

55. S. Shiffman, J. L. Pillitteri, S. L. Burton, J. M. Rohay, and J. G. Gitchell, "Smokers' Beliefs about 'Light' and 'Ultra Light' Cigarettes," *Tobacco Control* 10, suppl. 1 (2001): 17–23; N. D. Weinstein, "Public Understanding of Risk and Reasons for Smoking Low-Yield Products," in *Risks Associated with Smoking Cigarettes*, ed. Shopland et al., pp. 193–98.

56. D. R. Brooks, J. H. M. Austin, R. T. Heelan, M. S. Ginsberg, V. Shin, S. H. Olson, J. E. Muscat, and S. D. Stellman, "Influence of Type of Cigarette on Peripheral versus Central Lung Cancer," *Cancer Epidemiology Biomarkers and Prevalence* 14 (2005): 576–81.

57. K. E. Warner, "Will the Next Generation of 'Safer' Cigarettes Be Safer?" *Journal of Pediatric Hematology and Oncology* 27 (2005): 543–50.

58. Cummings et al., "The Cigarette Controversy," p. 1070.

59. K. Stratton, P. Shetty, R. Wallace, and S. Bondurant, eds., *Clearing the Smoke: Assessing the Science Base for Tobacco Harm Reduction* (Washington, DC: National Academies Press, 2001).

60. K. M. Cummings, C. P. Morley, and A. Hyland, "Failed Promises of the Cigarette Industry and Its Effect on Consumer Misperceptions about the Health Risks of Smoking," *Tobacco Control* 11, suppl. 1 (2002): 110–17.

Persistent Threats to Commercial Speech

JONATHAN H. ADLER

Free speech may be under fire in America today, but not at One First Street. Under Chief Justice Roberts, the Supreme Court has been quite protective of speech. From offensive protests and lies about military service, to violent video games and campaign-related expenditures, the Supreme Court has continued to expand the range of expression protected by the First Amendment. Commercial speech is no exception.

Over the past two decades, the Supreme Court has consistently protected commercial speech under the First Amendment. Existing commercial speech jurisprudence recognizes the consumer and citizen interests that justify safeguarding the free flow of information about products and services. If anything, the degree of protection most commercial speech retains is on the rise.

While commercial speech enjoys a substantial degree of protection, there are threats on the horizon. In this brief essay, I will focus on two. The first threat comes from speech regulation that is driven by rent-seeking. Economic interests regularly seek to restrict commercial speech as a way of suppressing competition, often by prohibiting or limiting the disclosure of factually true information about products or services. Regulation of advertising and other communication about products and services is an effective way to control the underlying market and pursue competitive advantage.

The second threat comes from compelled commercial speech. Governments at all levels routinely impose speech requirements, such as mandatory labels or other disclosures, for a variety of reasons. Examples of such requirements range from mandatory nutrition labels and mandatory energy efficiency disclosures for motor vehicles and appliances, to disclosure requirements on imported meat, debt-relief advisors, and attorney advertising.

At present, such requirements are often subject to minimal scrutiny in federal court. This makes compelled commercial speech an attractive means for suppressing competition or otherwise utilizing government regulation to enhance corporate power or advance other interests. The relative ease with which disclosure and labeling requirements are imposed threatens core First Amendment values and undermines the robust protection of commercial speech more generally. . . .

Protecting Commercial Speech

The Supreme Court first extended constitutional protection to commercial speech in the 1970s. Since then, the Court has consistently held that "[t]he fact that the speech is in aid of a commercial purpose does not deprive [the speaker] of all First Amendment protection."[1] Indeed, the Court has noted repeatedly that a "consumer's concern for the free flow of commercial speech often may be far keener than his concern for urgent political dialogue."[2]

In its first decisions protecting commercial speech, the Court emphasized the value of information about goods and services to consumers.[3] As the Court explained in *Virginia State Board of Pharmacy v. Virginia Citizens Consumer Council*:

So long as we preserve a predominantly free enterprise economy, the allocation of our resources in large

Excerpted from *Journal of Law and Policy* 25. © 2016. Reprinted by permission of the author.

measure will be made through numerous private economic decisions. It is a matter of public interest that
those decisions, in the aggregate, be intelligent and well
informed. To this end, the free flow of commercial
information is indispensable.[4]

On this basis, the Court concluded that commercial
speech should be protected by the First Amendment, but
not to quite the same degree as core protected speech, such
as political speech. Less explicit in the Court's decisions was
the recognition that commercial speech can also serve to
advance the broader interests of democratic self-governance. Yet as the Court noted in *Virginia State Board*, much
commercial speech is also "indispensable to the formation of
intelligent opinions as to how that system ought to be
regulated or altered," and thus helps to "enlighten public
decision-making in a democracy."[5]

In the 1980 case, *Central Hudson Gas and Electric v. Public
Service Commission*,[6] the Court outlined a form of inter-
mediate scrutiny for analyzing government restrictions on
commercial speech:

> For commercial speech to come within [the First
> Amendment], it at least must concern lawful activity
> and not be misleading. Next, we ask whether the
> asserted governmental interest is substantial. If both
> inquiries yield positive answers, we must determine
> whether the regulation directly advances the govern-
> mental interest asserted, and whether it is not more
> extensive than is necessary to serve that interest.[7, 8]

Since then, the degree of protection afforded to commercial expression has, if anything, increased. Several Justices
have suggested *Central Hudson* should be revisited. Perhaps
more significantly, on more than one occasion, the Court's
decisions have seemed to apply greater protections to commercial speech regulations than *Central Hudson*'s stated test
requires. For these reasons, commercial speech has seemed
fairly secure in the Supreme Court. . . .

Speech Regulation as Rent-Seeking

Commercial speech is an important means for producers and
sellers to communicate information about the products and
services that they offer. Such communications extend well
beyond the price and availability of products, however.
Advertising and other commercial speech sends explicit and
implicit messages about product quality and desirability. Such
speech is used to appeal to existing consumer preferences as
well as to shape such preferences over time. As discussed above,
advertising and other commercial speech also incorporate

cultural and normative messages that both help develop
brand identity and create or support affinity groups, which
may or may not be centered around specific products or
brands.

Just as commercial speech is an effective means for producers and sellers to communicate with consumers, restrictions on commercial speech are a powerful means of
restraining competition and privileging the interests of
some producers and sellers over others. For this reason, it
should not be surprising at all that corporate interests have
often sought to regulate commercial speech as a means of
obtaining a competitive advantage. In this regard, support
for commercial speech regulation can be a form of "rent-
seeking." If a new product has a feature or characteristic that
differentiates it from those of existing products, incumbent
producers may seek to restrict or alter communication about
those characteristics, perhaps by placing limits on how products may be described or characterized. Such use of speech
regulation has a long and sordid history.

Commercial speech is essential for producers to differentiate their products from competitors in the minds of
consumers and citizens. This is particularly true of new
entrants to the market that lack the brand identification,
distribution networks, and brand loyalty of more established brands. To protect themselves (and their existing
market share), incumbents are often eager to limit the
communication of their competitors, through traditional
and untraditional channels alike. Incumbent firms may
also benefit from across-the-board restrictions on advertising, as this may reduce the ability of new entrants to attract
market share.

Consider recent controversies over labeling within the
dairy industry, where some dairy farmers, with the aid of
biotechnology companies, have sought to restrict commercial
speech regarding the hormones used to increase milk production.[9] Bovine somatotropin (BST) is a naturally occurring
growth hormone that affects the amount of milk a dairy
cow will produce.[10] In an effort to increase milk production,
scientists learned how to synthesize BST through modern
genetic engineering techniques.[11] The result is recombinant
bovine somatotropin (rBST), which increases milk production in treated cows. This can increase the efficiency of dairy
production, particularly in larger firms.[12]

Although the use of rBST is controversial, the US Food
and Drug Administration (FDA) maintains that milk produced from cows treated with rBST is not appreciably different from milk from untreated cows, and certainly no less
safe.[13] Indeed, the FDA declared that any suggestion that
there is a meaningful difference in milk from treated and

untreated cows would be "false and misleading."[14] Despite these assurances, some consumers and producers were unconvinced.[15] In response to such concerns, the state of Vermont sought to require labeling of milk and other dairy products from cows treated with rBST, but these regulations were struck down in federal court.[16]

Some dairy farms oppose the use of rBST, either because they believe such treatments are "unnatural," are inhumane, or perhaps even dangerous.[17] Some milk producers may also believe that they can obtain a larger market share by appealing to consumers who prefer "organic" products or otherwise do not wish to consume products that were produced with the aid of modern biotechnology. Not only do such producers refuse to treat their cows with rBST, they would also like to inform consumers of this fact, such as by adding a voluntary "rBST free" or "No rBST" label to their products. Prominent companies, such as Ben & Jerry's ice cream, supported this effort.[18]

Dairy farmers who use rBST understandably object to any implication that their milk may be less desirable, or even less safe. For this reason, many dairy producers (and the producers of rBST) sought to impose limits on such claims by non-rBST-using producers.[19] Rather than defend the safety and quality of their product in an open marketplace, or supporting a broader public education program about the technology and its uses, these producers sought to squelch claims made by their competitors.[20]

In some states, dairy producers went even further, seeking to prevent any rBST-related claims on product labels. In Ohio, for example, the State Department of Agriculture adopted a rule that considered any dairy product label that included phrases such as "rBST free" or "Hormone Free" to be misleading.[21] Insofar as all dairy cows have hormones, the regulators may have had a point. Nonetheless, these requirements went well beyond any need to prevent consumer deception. The clear purpose of these restrictions was to protect favored dairy farmers by preventing their competitors from using commercial speech to disclose factually true information about their products and to encourage consumers to believe that these facts might be a reason to purchase their products.

These restrictions prompted a First Amendment challenge.[22] The US Court of Appeals for the Sixth Circuit recognized these restrictions for what they were, and pared back the legal requirements.[23] Were it not for the constitutional protection of commercial speech, however, Ohio's rules would have been upheld, and conventional dairy producers would have been able to squelch the communication of dissenting views within the commercial marketplace.

Nonetheless, some regulatory constraints on the ability of dairy and other producers to differentiate their products on value-based grounds remain.[24]

Limitations on commercial speech by competitors may harm consumers too. Such restrictions limit the information available to consumers, and may even impair efforts to protect public health or advance other social goals. Consider the case of reduced-risk tobacco products and smoking alternatives. Not all tobacco products present the same risks to consumers, and some smoking alternatives – such as electronic cigarettes and vaping devices – appear to present a tiny fraction of the risks posed by cigarettes. For this reason, many public health professionals believe that convincing smokers to switch to alternative products would help improve public health and reduce the death toll tobacco continues to inflict on American society.

Under the Family Smoking Prevention and Tobacco Control Act,[25] the makers and sellers of tobacco products and tobacco substitutes, such as electronic cigarettes, are extremely limited in their ability to inform consumers about the relative risks of competing products. Federal law prohibits the sale of any tobacco product containing a label which claims, implicitly or explicitly, that the product presents a lower risk of tobacco-related diseases, that the product contains a reduced level of a substance or is free of a substance, or that uses descriptors such as "light," or "low."[26] Tobacco products, which, under current regulations, include tobacco alternatives such as electronic cigarettes, can only be marketed as "reduced risk" products with FDA approval.[27] Although these regulations restrict purely factual claims that are supported by a fair amount of peer-reviewed scientific research, they have withstood legal challenge thus far.[28]

The nation's largest tobacco producer, Altria (aka Philip Morris), lobbied for and supported the federal statute limiting the disclosure and promotion of scientific information on the relative risks proposed by different sorts of tobacco products and their alternatives.[29] At least one opponent labeled the bill the "Marlboro Protection Act."[30] As the dominant cigarette manufacturer – and a firm well-positioned to make inroads into markets for tobacco alternatives provided that competitors are hamstrung by regulatory limitations on advertising and promotion – Altria benefited from limitations on commercial speech. Yet such limitations on speech, insofar as they inhibit consumer education about the relative risks of various products, can have negative consequences on public health. This is nothing new, however, as the tobacco industry long ago discovered that limitations on advertising – and limitations on comparative health claims in particular – is an effective means of suppressing competition and inhibiting consumer education about the potential health risks of their products.

It may be tempting to think that restrictions on commercial speech typically involve well-intentioned and public-spirited efforts to counteract firms' profit-seeking behavior. This is undoubtedly true in some cases. Yet, as the above examples illustrate, some restrictions on commercial speech are motivated by economic concerns and represent efforts to obtain competitive advantage through government intervention in the marketplace. Insofar as such measures restrict information that could lead consumers to choose less dangerous products, the consequences of such regulations are more than economic.

The Myth of a Consumer "Right-to-Know"

Policymakers often advocate the use of mandatory disclosure or other forms of speech compulsion as an alternative to traditional forms of product regulation. In some cases, the argument for mandating disclosure of product characteristics can be based upon health risks or consumer protection concerns. In other cases, mandatory product disclosures are grounded on the assertion that there is a consumer "right-to-know" about any product characteristics in which some set of consumers may have a particular interest. This idea of a consumer right-to-know is itself a significant threat to commercial speech, particularly when combined with the false idea that the free flow of commercial information is advanced by mandatory disclosure.

Information about products and services can often improve consumer decision-making. Disclosure requirements may empower consumers to protect themselves from health or other risks posed by particular products. For instance, food content requirements help those with allergies or particular dietary needs avoid those ingredients that may cause them harm. Mandatory disclosures may also help address the problem of information asymmetries, and may help increase consumer welfare as a result.

While information often has value, it is a mistake to assume that more information is always better. Just as a consumer may have too little information, a consumer may also have too much. "Information overload" is a real phenomenon. Consumers have "limited time and cognitive energy" for the consideration and analysis of information about products and services.[31] Mandating the disclosure of additional information, such as the pages of information contained in a pharmaceutical insert, may not actually increase consumer understanding. In some cases, the surfeit of information may actually make it more difficult for some consumers to understand which information is most important, such as which potential risks of a product are those with which the consumer should be most concerned.

Mandating the additional disclosure of information, if not justified by independent interests such as a need to protect consumers from unwitting harms, may actually harm consumer welfare. Indeed, mandating excessive information disclosure may actually result in the communication of less substantive content to consumers and reduced consumer understanding. Factually true disclosures may also mislead consumers into thinking that information subject to such disclosure is more important than other product or service attributes that will actually have a greater effect on consumer welfare.[32] . . .

Notes

1. *United States v. United Foods*, 533 U.S. 405, 410 (2001).
2. See, e.g., *Sorrell v. IMS Health Inc.*, 564 U.S. 552, 566 (2011) (quoting *Bates v. State Bar of Ariz.*, 433 U.S. 350, 364 (1977)).
3. See *Virginia State Board of Pharmacy v. Virginia Citizens Consumer Council, Inc.*, 425 U.S. 748 (1976); *Bigelow*, 421 U.S., at 818. The Court had noted the value of commercial speech in earlier cases. See, e.g., *Pittsburgh Press v. Pittsburgh Commission on Human Relations*, 413 U.S. 376, 388 (1973) (noting that "the exchange of information is as important in the commercial realm as in any other").
4. *Virginia State Board*, 425 U.S. The opinion also noted that commercial speech "is indispensable to the proper allocation of resources in a free enterprise system, it is also indispensable to the formation of intelligent opinions as to how that system ought to be regulated or altered."
5. *Virginia State Board*, 425 U.S.
6. See *Central Hudson Gas and Electric v. Public Service Commission of New York*, 447 U.S. 557 (1980).
7. Ibid., at 566.
8. *Obergefell v. Hodges*, 135 S. Ct. 2584 (2015).
9. See David Barboza, "Monsanto Sues Dairy in Maine over Label's Remarks on Hormones," *The New York Times* (July 12, 2003). Retrieved from www.nytimes.com/2003/07/12/business/monsanto-sues-dairy-in-maine-over-label-s-remarks-on-hormones.html.
10. See US Food and Drug Administration, Interim Guidance on the Voluntary Labeling of Milk and Milk Products from Cows That Have Not Been Treated with Recombinant Bovine Somatotropin, 59 Fed. Reg. 6279-04, 6279-80 (February 10, 1994) [hereinafter FDA Guidance]. Retrieved from https://milk.procon.org/sourcefiles/fdaguidebst1994.pdf.
11. See Christopher L. Culp, "Sacred Cows: The Bovine Somatotropin Controversy," in *Environmental Politics: Public*

Costs, Private Rewards, ed. Michael S. Greve and Fred L. Smith, Jr. (New York: Praeger, 1992), pp. 47, 48 (noting that rBST was first synthesized in 1973).

12. Ibid., at pp. 55–56.

13. US Food and Drug Administration, "Bovine Somatotropin (BST)." Retrieved from www.fda.gov/AnimalVeterinary/SafetyHealth/ProductSafetyInformation/ucm055435.htm (last updated October 19, 2016).

14. See FDA Guidance.

15. See, e.g., Organic Consumers Association, "Study Shows Consumer Concern over Bovine Growth Hormone-Tainted Milk" (September 17, 2003). Retrieved from www.organicconsumers.org/old_articles/rbgh/rbgh_tainted_milk.php (showing public concern about use of hormones in milk production).

16. See *International Dairy Foods Association v. Amestoy*, 92 F.3d 67, 69–74 (2nd Cir. 1995).

17. One prominent concern is that there is a higher rate of infection in cows treated with rBST due to the increased milk production resulting from such treatment. See "About rbGH," Center for Food Safety. Retrieved from www.centerforfoodsafety.org/issues/1044/rbgh/about-rbgh.

18. See, e.g., Ben & Jerry's, "rBGH." Retrieved from www.benjerry.com/values/issues-we-care-about/rbgh (explaining company's opposition to the use of rBST); Sarah Lozanova, "Back to Basics: When Ben & Jerry's Dropped rBGH," *Triple Pundit* (April 6, 2015). Retrieved from www.triplepundit.com/special/disrupting-short-termism/back-to-basics-when-ben-jerrys-dropped-rgbh (discussing ice-cream maker's decision to source from farms not treating cows with rBST).

19. See Keith Schneider, "F.D.A. Warns the Dairy Industry Not to Label Milk Hormone-Free," *The New York Times* (February 8, 1994). Retrieved from www.nytimes.com/1994/02/08/us/fda-warns-the-dairy-industry-not-to-label-milk-hormone-free.html (noting that the FDA directive against hormone-free labels was "requested by some states and the dairy industry").

20. See Stephen J. Hedges, "Monsanto Having a Cow in Milk Label Dispute," *Chicago Tribune* (April 15, 2007). Retrieved from www.chicagotribune.com/news/ct-xpm-2007-04-15-0704140151-story.html.

21. See Peggy Hall, "Federal Court Decided Ohio Dairy Labeling Case," Ohio Agricultural Law Blog (October 4, 2010). Retrieved from https://ohioaglaw.wordpress.com/2010/10/04/federal-court-decides-ohio-dairy-labeling-case/ (quoting Ohio Admin. Code § 901:11-8-01 (repealed 2012)).

22. *International Dairy Foods Association v. Boggs*, No. 2:08-CV-628, 2:08-CV-629, 2009 WL 937045, at *2–4 (S.D. Ohio, April 2, 2009).

23. See *International Dairy Foods Association v. Boggs*, 622 F.3d 628, 635–40 (6th Cir. 2010) (holding that the Ohio rule banning claims such as "rBST free" is more extensive than necessary to protect against consumer deception, and thus cannot survive *Central Hudson* scrutiny).

24. See FDA Guidance.

25. Family Smoking Prevention and Tobacco Control Act of 2009, Public Law No. 111-31, 123 Stat. 1776 (2009).

26. 21 U.S.C. § 387(k) (2009).

27. See 21 U.S.C. § 387k(g)(1).

28. See, e.g., *Discount Tobacco City & Lottery, Inc. v. United States*, 674 F. 3d 509, 518 (6th Cir. 2012) (rejecting, *inter alia*, First Amendment challenges to federal tobacco regulations).

29. See Duff Wilson, "Philip Morris's Support Casts Shadow over a Bill to Limit Tobacco," *The New York Times* (March 31, 2009). Retrieved from www.nytimes.com/2009/04/01/business/01tobacco.html; C. Stephen Redhead and Vanessa K. Burrows, "FDA Tobacco Regulation: The Family Smoking Prevention and Tobacco Control Act of 2009" (Congressional Research Service, 2009).

30. See Mike Enzi, "HELP Committee Passes a 'Marlboro Protection Act,'" *The Hill* (August 1, 2007). Retrieved from https://thehill.com/blogs/congress-blog/politics/27745-help-committee-passes-a-marlboro-protection-act-sen-mike-enzi.

31. See David Weil, Archon Fung, Mary Graham, and Elena Fagotto, "The Effectiveness of Regulatory Disclosure Policies," *Journal of Policy Analysis and Management* 25 (2006): 155–81 (p. 156).

32. For example, warnings on trace levels of mercury in fish may take consumer attention away from the health benefits of consuming fish high in omega-3 fatty acids. In this way, such warnings can actually work against efforts to improve public health. See, e.g., Joshua T. Cohen, "Matters of the Heart and Mind: Risk–Risk Tradeoffs in Eating Fish Containing Methylmercury," *Risk in Perspective* (January 2006), at pp. 1, 2–3. Retrieved from https://cdn1.sph.harvard.edu/wp-content/uploads/sites/1273/2013/06/RISK_IN_PERSP_JANUARY2006.pdf (suggesting that warnings about the danger of mercury contamination in fish to pregnant women could have the negative effect of decreasing intake of beneficial omega-3 oils, also found in fish).

7.4 PHARMACEUTICAL MARKETING

The Drug Pushers

CARL ELLIOTT

Back in the old days, long before drug companies started making headlines in the business pages, doctors were routinely called upon by company representatives known as "detail men." To "detail" a doctor is to give that doctor information about a company's new drugs, with the aim of persuading the doctor to prescribe them. When I was growing up, in South Carolina in the 1970s, I would occasionally see detail men sitting patiently in the waiting room outside the office of my father, a family doctor. They were pretty easy to spot. Detail men were usually sober, conservatively dressed gentlemen who would not have looked out of place at the Presbyterian church across the street. Instead of bibles or hymn books, though, they carried detail bags, which were filled with journal articles, drug samples, and branded knick-knacks for the office.

Today detail men are officially known as "pharmaceutical sales representatives," but everyone I know calls them "drug reps." Drug reps are still easy to spot in a clinic or hospital, but for slightly different reasons. The most obvious is their appearance. It is probably fair to say that doctors, pharmacists, and medical-school professors are not generally admired for their good looks and fashion sense. Against this backdrop, the average drug rep looks like a supermodel, or maybe an A-list movie star. Drug reps today are often young, well-groomed, and strikingly good-looking. Many are women. They are usually affable and sometimes very smart. Many give off a kind of glow, as if they had just emerged from a spa or salon. And they are always, hands down, the best-dressed people in the hospital.

Drug reps have been calling on doctors since the mid-nineteenth century, but during the past decade or so their numbers have increased dramatically. From 1996 to 2001 the pharmaceutical sales force in America doubled, to a total of 90,000 reps. One reason is simple: good reps move product. Detailing is expensive, but almost all practicing doctors see reps at least occasionally, and many doctors say they find reps useful. One study found that for drugs introduced after 1997 with revenues exceeding $200 million a year, the average return for each dollar spent on detailing was $10.29. That is an impressive figure. It is almost twice the return on investment in medical-journal advertising, and more than seven times the return on direct-to-consumer advertising.

But the relationship between doctors and drug reps has never been uncomplicated, for reasons that should be obvious. *The first duty of doctors, at least in theory, is to their patients.* Doctors must make prescribing decisions based on medical evidence and their own clinical judgment. Drug reps, in contrast, are salespeople. They swear no oaths, take care of no patients, and profess no high-minded ethical duties. Their job is to persuade doctors to prescribe their drugs. If reps are lucky, their drugs are good, the studies are clear, and their job is easy. But sometimes reps must persuade doctors to prescribe drugs that are marginally effective, exorbitantly expensive, difficult to administer, or even dangerously toxic. Reps that succeed are rewarded with bonuses or commissions. Reps that fail may find themselves unemployed.

Most people who work in healthcare, if they give drug reps any thought at all, regard them with mixed feelings. A handful avoid reps as if they were vampires, backing out of the room when they see one approaching. In their view, the best that can be said about reps is that they are a necessary by-product of a market economy. They view reps much as NBA players used to view Michael Jordan: as an awesome, powerful force that you can never really stop, only hope to control.

Yet many reps are so friendly, so easygoing, so much fun to flirt with that it is virtually impossible to demonize them. How can you demonize someone who brings you lunch and touches your arm and remembers your birthday and knows the names of all your children? After a while even the most steel-willed doctors may look forward to visits by a rep, if only in the self-interested way that they look forward to the UPS truck pulling up in their driveway. A rep at the door means a delivery has arrived: takeout for the staff, trinkets for the kids, and, most indispensably, drug samples on the house. Although samples are the single largest marketing expense for the drug industry, they pay handsome dividends: doctors who accept samples of a drug are far more likely to prescribe that drug later on. . . .

The King of Happy Hour

Gene Carbona was almost a criminal. I know this because, 30 minutes into our first telephone conversation, he told me, "Carl, I was almost a criminal." I have heard ex-drug reps speak bluntly about their former jobs, but never quite so cheerfully and openly. These days Carbona works for the *Medical Letter*, a highly respected non-profit publication (Carbona stresses that he is speaking only for himself), but he was telling me about his 12 years working for Merck and then Astra Merck, a firm initially set up to market the Sweden-based Astra's drugs in the United States. Carbona began training as a rep in 1988, when he was only 11 days out of college. He detailed two drugs for Astra Merck. One was a calcium-channel blocker he calls "a dog." The other was the heartburn medication Prilosec, which at the time was available by prescription only. Prilosec is the kind of drug most reps can only dream about. The industry usually considers a drug to be a blockbuster if it reaches $1 billion a year in sales. In 1998 Prilosec became the first drug in America to reach $5 billion a year. In 2000 it made $6 billion. Prilosec's success was not the result of a massive heartburn epidemic. It was based on the same principle that drove the success of many other 1990s blockbusters, from Vioxx to Viagra: the restoration of an ordinary biological function that time and circumstance had eroded. In the case of Prilosec, the function was digestion. Many people discovered that the drug allowed them to eat the burritos and curries that their gastrointestinal systems had placed off-limits. So what if Prilosec was $4 a pill, compared with a quarter or so for a Tagamet? Patients still begged for it. Prilosec was their savior. Astra Merck marketed Prilosec as the "purple pill," but, according to Carbona, many patients called it "purple Jesus."

How did Astra Merck do it? Prilosec was the first proton pump inhibitor (a drug that inhibits the production of stomach acid) approved by the Food and Drug Administration, and thus the first drug available in its class. By definition this gave it a considerable head start on the competition. In the late 1990s Astra Merck mounted a huge direct-to-consumer campaign; ads for the purple pill were ubiquitous. But consumer advertising can do only so much for a drug, because doctors, not patients, write the prescriptions. This is where reps become indispensable.

Many reps can tell stories about occasions when, in order to move their product, they pushed the envelope of what is ethically permissible. I have heard reps talk about scoring sports tickets for their favorite doctors, buying televisions for waiting rooms, and arranging junkets to tropical resorts. One rep told me he set up a putting green in a hospital and gave a putter to any doctor who made a hole in one. A former rep told me about a colleague who somehow managed to persuade a pharmacist to let him secretly write the prescribing protocol for antibiotic use at a local hospital.

But Carbona was in a class of his own. He had access to so much money for doctors that he had trouble spending it all. He took residents out to bars. He distributed "unrestricted educational grants." He arranged to buy lunch for the staff of certain private practices every day for a year. Often he would invite a group of doctors and their guests to a high-end restaurant, buy them drinks and a lavish meal, open up the club in back, and party until 4:00 a.m. "The more money I spent," Carbona says, "the more money I made." If he came back to the restaurant later that week with his wife, everything would be on the house. "My money was no good at restaurants," he told me, "because I was the King of Happy Hour."

My favorite Carbona story, the one that left me shaking my head in admiration, took place in Tallahassee. One of the more important clinics Carbona called on was a practice there consisting of about 50 doctors. Although the practice had plenty of patients, it was struggling. This problem was not uncommon. When the movement toward corporate-style medicine got under way, in the 1980s and 1990s, many doctors found themselves ill-equipped to run a business; they didn't know much about how to actually make money. ("That's why doctors are such great targets for Ponzi schemes and real-estate scams," Carbona helpfully points out.) Carbona was detailing this practice twice a week and had gotten to know some of the clinicians pretty well. At one point a group of them asked him for help. "Gene, you work for a successful business," Carbona recalls them saying. "Is there any advice you could give us to help us turn the practice around?" At this point he knew he had stumbled upon an extraordinary opportunity. Carbona decided that the clinic needed a "practice management consultant." And he and his colleagues at Astra Merck knew just the man: a financial planner and accountant with whom they were very friendly. They wrote up a contract. They agreed to pay the consultant a flat fee of about $50,000 to advise the clinic. But they also gave him another incentive. Carbona says, "We told him that if he was successful there would be more business for him in the future, and by 'successful,' we meant a rise in prescriptions for our drugs."

The consultant did an extremely thorough job. He spent 11 or 12 hours a day at the clinic for months. He talked to every employee, from the secretaries to the nurses to the doctors. He thought carefully about every aspect of the practice, from the most mundane administrative details to big-picture matters such as bill collection and financial strategy. He turned the practice into a profitable, smoothly running financial machine. And prescriptions for Astra Merck drugs soared.

When I asked Carbona how the consultant had increased Astra Merck's market share within the clinic so dramatically, he said that the consultant never pressed the doctors directly. Instead, he talked up Carbona. "Gene has put his neck on the line for you guys," he would tell them. "If this thing doesn't work, he might get fired." The consultant emphasized what a remarkable service the practice was getting, how valuable the financial advice was, how everything was going to turn around for them – all courtesy of Carbona. The strategy worked. "Those guys went berserk for me," Carbona says. Doctors at the newly vitalized practice prescribed so many Astra Merck drugs that he got a $140,000 bonus. The scheme was so successful that Carbona and his colleagues at Astra Merck decided to duplicate it in other practices.

I got in touch with Carbona after I learned that he was giving talks on the American Medical Student Association lecture circuit about his experiences as a rep. At that point I had read a fair bit of pharmaceutical sales literature, and most of it had struck me as remarkably hokey and stilted. Merck's official training materials, for example, instruct reps to say things like, "Doctor, based on the information we discussed today, will you prescribe Vioxx for your patients who need once-daily power to prevent pain due to osteoarthritis?" So I was unprepared for a man with Carbona's charisma and forthright humor. I could see why he had been such an excellent rep: he came off as a cross between a genial con artist and a comedic character actor. After two hours on the phone with him I probably would have bought anything he was selling.

Most media accounts of the pharmaceutical industry miss this side of drug reps. By focusing on scandals – the kickbacks and the fraud and the lavish gifts – they lose sight of the fact that many reps are genuinely likeable people. The better ones have little use for the canned scripts they are taught in training. For them, effective selling is all about developing a relationship with a doctor. If a doctor likes a rep, that doctor is going to feel bad about refusing to see the rep, or about taking his lunches and samples but never prescribing his drugs. As Jordan Katz, a rep for Schering-Plough until two years ago, says, "A lot of doctors just write for who they like."

A variation on this idea emerges in *Side Effects*, Kathleen Slattery-Moschau's 2005 film about a fictional fledgling drug rep. Slattery-Moschau, who worked for nine years as a rep for Bristol-Myers Squibb and Johnson & Johnson, says the carefully rehearsed messages in the corporate training courses really got to her. "I hated the crap I had to say to doctors," she told me. The heroine of *Side Effects* eventually decides to ditch the canned messages and stop spinning her product. Instead, she is brutally honest. "Bottom line?" she says to one doctor. "Your patients won't shit for a week." To her amazement, she finds that the blunter she is, the higher her market share rises. Soon she is winning sales awards and driving a company BMW.

For most reps, market share is the yardstick of success. The more scripts their doctors write for their drugs, the more the reps make. Slattery-Moschau says that most of her fellow reps made $50,000 to $90,000 a year in salary and another $30,000 to $50,000 in bonuses, depending on how much they sold. Reps are pressured to "make quota," or meet yearly sales targets, which often increase from year to year. Reps who fail to make quota must endure the indignity of having their district manager frequently accompany them on sales calls. Those who meet quota are rewarded handsomely. The most successful reps achieve minor celebrity within the company.

One perennial problem for reps is the doctor who simply refuses to see them at all. Reps call these doctors "No Sees." Cracking a No See is a genuine achievement, the pharmaceutical equivalent of a home run or a windmill dunk. Gene Carbona says that when he came across a No See, or any other doctor who was hard to influence, he used "Northeast–Southwest" tactics. If you can't get to a doctor, he explains, you go after people surrounding that doctor, showering them with gifts. Carbona might help support a little league baseball team or a bowling league. After a while, the doctor would think, Gene is doing such nice things for all these people, the least I can do is give him 10 minutes of my time. At that point, Carbona says, the sale was as good as made. "If you could get ten minutes with a doctor, your market share would go through the roof." For decades the medical community has debated whether gifts and perks from reps have any real effect. Doctors insist that they do not. Studies in the medical literature indicate just the opposite. Doctors who take gifts from a company, studies show, are more likely to prescribe that company's drugs or ask that they be added to their hospital's formulary. The pharmaceutical industry has managed this debate skillfully, pouring vast resources into gifts for doctors while simultaneously reassuring them that their integrity prevents them from being influenced. For example, in a recent editorial in the journal *Health Affairs*, Bert Spilker, a vice-president for PhRMA, the pharmaceutical trade group, defended the practice of gift giving against critics who, he scornfully wrote, "fear that physicians are so weak and lacking in integrity that they would 'sell their souls' for a pack of M&M candies and a few sandwiches and doughnuts."

Doctors' belief in their own incorruptibility appears to be honestly held. It is rare to hear a doctor – even in private, off-the record conversation – admit that industry gifts have made a difference in his or her prescribing. In fact, according to one small study of medical residents in the *Canadian Medical Association Journal*, one way to convince doctors that they cannot be influenced by gifts may be to give them one; the more gifts a doctor takes, the more likely that doctor is to believe that the gifts have had no effect. This helps explain why it makes sense for reps to give away even small gifts. A particular gift may have no influence, but it might make a doctor more apt to think that he or she would not be influenced by larger gifts in the future. A pizza and a penlight are like inoculations, tiny injections of self-confidence that make a doctor think, I will never be corrupted by money.

Gifts from the drug industry are nothing new, of course. William Helfand, who worked in marketing for Merck for 33 years, told me that company representatives were giving doctors books and pamphlets as early as the late nineteenth century. "There is nothing new under the sun," Helfand says. "There is just more of it." The question is: Why is there so much more of it just now? And what changed during the past decade to bring about such a dramatic increase in reps bearing gifts?

An Ethics of Salesmanship

One morning last year I had breakfast at the Bryant-Lake Bowl, a diner in Minneapolis, with a former Pfizer rep named Michael Oldani. Oldani grew up in a working-class family in Kenosha, Wisconsin. Although he studied biochemistry in college, he knew nothing about pharmaceutical sales until he was recruited for Pfizer by the husband of a woman with whom he worked. Pfizer gave him a good salary, a company car, free gas, and an expense account. "It was kind of like the Mafia," Oldani told me. "They made me an offer I couldn't refuse." At the time, he was still in college and living with his parents. "I knew a good ticket out of Kenosha when I saw one," he says. He carried the bag for Pfizer for nine years, until 1998.

Today Oldani is a Princeton-trained medical anthropologist teaching at the University of Wisconsin at Whitewater. He wrote his doctoral dissertation on the anthropology of pharmaceutical sales, drawing not just on ethnographic fieldwork he did in Manitoba as a Fulbright scholar but also on his own experience as a rep. This dual perspective – the view of both a detached outsider and a street-savvy insider – gives his work authority and a critical edge. I had invited Oldani to lecture at our medical school, the University of Minnesota, after reading his work in anthropology journals. Although his writing is scholarly, his manner is modest and self-effacing, more Kenosha than Princeton. This is a man who knows his way around a diner.

Like Carbona, Oldani worked as a rep in the late 1980s and the 1990s, a period when the drug industry was undergoing key transformations. Its ethos was changing from that of the country-club establishment to the aggressive, new-money entrepreneur. Impressed by the success of AIDS activists in pushing for faster drug approvals, the drug industry increased pressure on the FDA to let companies bring drugs to the market more quickly. As a result, in 1992 Congress passed the Prescription Drug User Fee Act, under which drug companies pay a variety of fees to the FDA, with the aim of speeding up drug approval (thereby making the drug industry a major funder of the agency set up to regulate it). In 1997 the FDA dropped most restrictions on direct-to-consumer advertising of prescription drugs, opening the gate for the eventual Levitra ads on Super Bowl Sunday and Zoloft cartoons during daytime television shows. The drug industry also became a big political player in Washington: by 2005, according to the Center for Public Integrity, its lobbying organization had become the largest in the country.

Many companies started hitting for the fences, concentrating on potential blockbuster drugs for chronic illnesses in huge populations: Claritin for allergies, Viagra for impotence, Vioxx for arthritis, Prozac for depression. Successful drugs were followed by a flurry of competing me-too drugs. For most of the 1990s and the early part of this decade, the pharmaceutical industry was easily the most profitable business sector in America. In 2002, according to Public Citizen, a non-profit watchdog group, the combined profits of the top 10 pharmaceutical companies in the Fortune 500 exceeded the combined profits of the other 490 companies.

During this period reps began to feel the influence of a new generation of executives intent on bringing market values to an industry that had been slow to embrace them. Anthony Wild, who was hired to lead Parke-Davis in the mid-1990s, told the journalist Greg Critser, the author of *Generation Rx*, that one of his first moves upon his appointment was to increase the incentive pay given to successful reps. Wild saw no reason to cap reps' incentives. As he said to the company's older executives, "Why not let them get rich?" Wild told the reps about the change at a meeting in San Francisco. "We announced that we were taking off the caps," he told Critser, "and the sales force went nuts!"

It was not just the industry's ethos that was changing; the technology was changing, too. According to Oldani, one of the most critical changes came in the way that information was gathered. In the days before computers, reps had to do a lot of legwork to figure out whom they could influence. They had to schmooze with the receptionists, make friends with the nurses, and chat up the pharmacists in order to learn which drugs the local doctors were prescribing, using the right incentives to coax what they needed from these informants. "Pharmacists are like pigeons," Jamie Reidy, a former rep for Pfizer and Eli Lilly, told me. "Only instead of bread crumbs, you toss them pizzas and sticky notes."

But in the 1990s, new information technology made it much simpler to track prescriptions. Market-research firms began collecting script-related data from pharmacies and hospitals and selling it to pharmaceutical companies. The American Medical Association collaborated by licensing them information about doctors (including doctors who do not belong to the AMA), which it collects in its "Physician Masterfile." Soon reps could find out exactly how many prescriptions any doctor was writing and exactly which drugs those prescriptions were for. All they had to do was turn on their laptops and download the data.

What they discovered was revelatory. For one thing, they found that a lot of doctors were lying to them. Doctors might tell a rep that they were writing prescriptions for, say, Lipitor, when they weren't. They were just being polite, or saying whatever they thought would get the rep off their back. Now reps could detect the deception immediately. (Even today many doctors do not realize that reps have access to script-tracking reports.)

More important, script-tracking helped reps figure out which doctors to target. They no longer had to waste time and money on doctors with conservative prescribing habits; they could head straight to the "high prescribers," or "high writers." And they could get direct feedback on which tactics were working. If a gift or a dinner presentation did not result in more scripts, they knew to try another approach.

But there was a rub: the data were available to every rep from every company. The result was an arms race of pharmaceutical gift giving, in which ways to exert influence. If the Eli Lilly rep was bringing sandwiches to the office staff, you brought Thai food. If GSK flew doctors to Palm Springs for a conference, you flew them to Paris. Oldani used to take residents to major league baseball games. "We did beer bongs, shots, and really partied," he told me. "Some of the guys were incredibly drunk on numerous occasions. I used to buy half barrels for their parties, almost on a retainer-like basis. I never talked product once to any of these residents, and they took care of me in their day-to-day practice. I never missed quota at their hospital."

Oldani says that script-tracking data also changed the way that reps thought about prescriptions. The old system of monitoring prescriptions was very inexact, and the relationship between a particular doctor's prescriptions and the

work of a given rep was relatively hard to measure. But with precise script-tracking reports, reps started to feel a sense of ownership about prescriptions. If their doctors started writing more prescriptions for their drugs, the credit clearly belonged to them. However, more precise monitoring also invited micromanagement by the reps' bosses. They began pressuring reps to concentrate on high prescribers, fill out more paperwork, and report more frequently back to management.

"Script tracking, to me at least, made everyone a potentially successful rep," Oldani says. Reps didn't need to be nearly as resourceful and street savvy as in the past; they just needed the script-tracking reports. The industry began hiring more and more reps, many with backgrounds in sales (rather than, say, pharmacy, nursing, or biology). Some older reps say that during this period the industry replaced the serious detail man with "Pharma Barbie" and "Pharma Ken," whose medical knowledge was exceeded by their looks and catering skills. A newer, regimented style of selling began to replace the improvisational, more personal style of the old-school reps. Whatever was left of an ethic of service gave way to an ethic of salesmanship.

Doctors were caught in a bind. Many found themselves being called on several times a week by different reps from the same company. Most continued to see reps, some because they felt obligated to get up to speed with new drugs, some because they wanted to keep the pipeline of free samples open. But seeing reps has a cost, of course: the more reps a doctor sees, the longer the patients sit in the waiting room. Many doctors began to feel as though they deserved whatever gifts and perks they could get because reps were such an irritation. At one time a few practices even charged reps a fee for visiting.

Professional organizations made some efforts to place limits on the gifts doctors were allowed to accept. But these efforts were halfhearted, and they met with opposition from indignant doctors ridiculing the idea that their judgment could be bought. One doctor, in a letter to the *American Medical News*, confessed, "every time a discussion comes up on guidelines for pharmaceutical company gifts to physicians, I feel as if I need to take a blood pressure medicine to keep from a having a stroke." In 2001 the AMA launched a campaign to educate doctors about the ethical perils of pharmaceutical gifts, but it undercut its message by funding the campaign with money from the pharmaceutical industry.

Of course, most doctors are never offered free trips to Monaco or even a weekend at a spa; for them an industry gift means a Cialis pen or a Lexapro notepad. Yet it is a rare rep who cannot tell a story or two about the extravagant gifts doctors have requested. Oldani told me that one doctor asked him to build a music room in his house. Phyllis Adams, a former rep in Canada, was told by a doctor that he would not prescribe her product unless her company made him a consultant. (Both said no.) Carbana arranged a $35,000 "unrestricted educational grant" for a doctor who wanted a swimming pool in his back yard. "It was the Wild West," says Jamie Reidy, whose frank memoir about his activities while working for Pfizer in the 1990s, *Hard Sell: The Evolution of a Viagra Salesman*, recently got him fired from Eli Lilly. "They cashed the check, and that was it. And hopefully they remembered you every time they turned on the TV, or bought a drink on the cruise, or dived into the pool."

The trick is to give doctors gifts without making them feel that they are being bought. "Bribes that aren't considered bribes," Oldani says. "This, my friend, is the essence of pharmaceutical gifting." According to Oldani, the way to make a gift feel different from a bribe is to make it personal. "Ideally, a rep finds a way to get into a script-writer's psyche," he says. "You need to have talked enough with a script-writer – or done enough recon with gatekeepers – that you know what to give." When Oldani found a pharmacist who liked to play the market, he gave him stock options. When he wanted to see a resistant oncologist, he talked to the doctor's nurse and then gave the oncologist a $100 bottle of his favorite cognac. Reidy put the point nicely when he told me, "You are absolutely buying love."

Such gifts do not come with an explicit quid pro quo, of course. Whatever obligation doctors feel to write scripts for a rep's products usually comes from the general sense of reciprocity implied by the ritual of gift giving. But it is impossible to avoid the hard reality informing these ritualized exchanges: reps would not give doctors free stuff if they did not expect more scripts.

My brother Hal, a psychiatrist currently on the faculty of Wake Forest University, told me about an encounter he had with a drug rep from Eli Lilly some years back, when he was in private practice. This rep was not one of his favorites; she was too aggressive. That day she had insisted on bringing lunch to his office staff, even though Hal asked her not to. As he tried to make polite conversation with her in the hall, she reached over his shoulder into his drug closet and picked up a couple of sample packages of Zoloft and Celexa. Waving them in the air, she asked, "Tell me, Doctor, do the Pfizer and Forest reps bring lunch to your office staff?" A stony silence followed. Hal quietly ordered the rep out of the office and told her to never come back. She left in tears.

It's not hard to understand why Hal got so angry. The rep had broken the rules. Like an abrasive tourist who has not caught onto the code of manners in a foreign country, she had said outright the one thing that, by custom and common agreement, should never be said: that the lunches she brought were intended as a bribe. What's more, they were a bribe that Hal had never agreed to accept. He likened the situation to having somebody drop off a bag of money in your garage without your consent and then ask, "So what about our little agreement?"

When an encounter between a doctor and a rep goes well, it is a delicate ritual of pretense and self-deception. Drug reps pretend that they are giving doctors impartial information. Doctors pretend that they take it seriously. Drug reps must try their best to influence doctors, while doctors must tell themselves that they are not being influenced. Drug reps must act as if they are not salespeople, while doctors must act as if they are not customers. And if, by accident, the real purpose of the exchange is revealed, the result is like an elaborate theatrical dance in which the masks and costumes suddenly drop off and the actors come face to face with one another as they really are. Nobody wants to see that happen.

The New Drug Reps?

Last spring a small group of first-year medical students at the University of Minnesota spoke to me about a lecture on erectile dysfunction that had just been given by a member of the urology department. The doctor's PowerPoint slides had a large, watermarked logo in the corner. At one point during the lecture a student raised his hand and, somewhat disingenuously, asked the urologist to explain the logo. The urologist, caught off-guard, stumbled for a moment and then said that it was the logo for Cialis, a drug for erectile dysfunction that is manufactured by Eli Lilly. Another student asked if he had a special relationship with Eli Lilly. The urologist replied that yes, he was on the advisory board for the company, which had supplied the slides. But he quickly added that nobody needed to worry about the objectivity of his lecture because he was also on the advisory boards of the makers of the competing drugs Viagra and Levitra. The second student told me, "A lot of people agreed that it was a pharm lecture and that we should have gotten a free breakfast."

This episode is not as unusual as it might appear. Drug company-sponsored consultancies, advisory-board memberships, and speaking engagements have become so common, especially among medical-school faculty, that the urologist probably never imagined that he would be challenged for lecturing to medical students with materials produced by Eli Lilly. According to a recent study in the *Journal of the American Medical Association*, nine out of ten medical students have been asked or required by an attending physician to go to a lunch sponsored by a drug company. As of 2003, according to the Accreditation Council for Continuing Medical Education, pharmaceutical companies were providing 90 percent of the $1 billion spent annually on continuing medical education events, which doctors must attend in order to maintain their licensure.

Over the past year or two pharmaceutical profits have started to level off, and a backlash against reps has been felt; some companies have actually reduced their sales forces. But the industry as a whole is hiring more and more doctors as speakers. In 2004, it sponsored nearly twice as many educational events led by doctors as by reps. Not long before, the numbers had been roughly equal. This raises the question: Are doctors becoming the new drug reps?

Doctors are often the best people to market a drug to other doctors. Merck discovered this when it was developing a campaign for Vioxx, before the drug was taken off the market because of its association with heart attacks and strokes. According to an internal study by Merck, reported in the *Wall Street Journal*, doctors who attended a lecture by another doctor subsequently wrote nearly four times more prescriptions for Vioxx than doctors who attended an event led by a rep. The return on investment for doctor-led events was nearly twice that of rep-led events, even after subtracting the generous fees Merck paid to the doctors who spoke.

These speaking invitations work much like gifts. While reps hope, of course, that a doctor who is speaking on behalf of their company will give their drugs good PR, they also know that such a doctor is more likely to write prescriptions for their drugs. "If he didn't write, he wouldn't speak," a rep who has worked for four pharmaceutical companies told me. The semi-official industry term for these speakers and consultants is "thought leaders," or "key opinion leaders." Some thought leaders do not stay loyal to one company but rather generate a tidy supplemental income by speaking and consulting for a number of different companies. Reps refer to these doctors as "drug whores."

The seduction, whether by one company or several, is often quite gradual. My brother Hal explained to me how he wound up on the speakers' bureau of a major pharmaceutical company. It started when a company rep asked him if he'd be interested in giving a talk about clinical depression to a community group. The honorarium was $1,000. Hal thought, Why not? It seemed almost a public service. The next time, the company asked him to talk not to the public but to practitioners at a community hospital. Soon company reps were making suggestions about content. "Why don't you mention the side-effect profiles of the different antidepressants?" they asked. Uneasy, Hal tried to ignore these suggestions. Still, the more talks he gave, the more the reps became focused on antidepressants rather than depression. The company began giving him PowerPoint slides to use, which he also ignored. The reps started telling him, "You know, we have you on the local circuit giving these talks, but you're medical-school faculty; we could get you on the national circuit. That's where the real money is." The mention of big money made him even more uneasy. Eventually the reps asked him to lecture about a new version of their antidepressant drug. Soon after that, Hal told them, "I can't do this anymore."

Looking back on this trajectory, Hal said, "It's kind of like you're a woman at a party, and your boss says to you, 'look, do me a favor: be nice to this guy over there.' And you see the guy is not bad-looking, and you're unattached, so you say, 'Why not? I can be nice.'" The problem is that it never ends with that party. "Soon you find yourself on the way to a Bangkok brothel in the cargo hold of an unmarked plane. And you say, 'Whoa, this is not what I agreed to.' But then you have to ask yourself, 'When did the prostitution actually start? Wasn't it at that party?'"

Thought leaders serve an indispensable function when it comes to a potentially very lucrative marketing niche: off-label promotion, or promoting a drug for uses other than those for which it was approved by the FDA – something reps are strictly forbidden to do. The case of Neurontin is especially instructive. In 1996 a whistleblower named David Franklin, a medical-science liaison with Parke-Davis (now a division of Pfizer), filed suit against the company over its off-label promotion of this drug. Neurontin was approved for the treatment of epilepsy, but according to the lawsuit, Parke-Davis was promoting it for other conditions – including bipolar disorder, migraines, and restless leg syndrome – for which there was little or no scientific evidence that it worked. To do so the company employed a variety of schemes, most involving a combination of rep ingenuity and payments to doctors. Some doctors signed ghostwritten journal articles. One received more than $300,000 to speak about Neurontin at conferences. Others were paid just to listen. Simply having some of your thought leaders in attendance at a meeting is valuable, Kathleen Slattery-Moschkau explains, because they will often bring up off-label uses of a drug without having to be prompted. "You can't get a better selling situation than that," she says. In such circumstances all she had to do was pour the wine and make sure everyone was happy.

The litigation over Neurontin cost Pfizer $430 million in criminal fines and civil damages for the period 1994 to 2002. It was well worth it. The drug's popularity and profitability soared. In spite of the adverse publicity, Neurontin generated more than $2.7 billion in revenues in 2003, more than 90 percent of which came from off-label prescriptions.

Of course, sometimes speakers discover that the drug they have been paid to lecture about is dangerous. One of the most notorious examples is Fen-Phen, the diet-drug combination that has been linked to primary pulmonary hypertension and valvular heart disease. Wyeth, the manufacturer of Redux, or dexfenfluramine – the "Fen" in Fen-Phen – has put aside $21 billion to cover costs and liabilities from litigation. Similar events played out, on a lesser scale, with Parke-Davis's diabetes drug Rezulin, and Wyeth's pain reliever Duract, which were taken off the market after being associated with life-threatening complications.

And what about reps themselves? Do they trust their companies to tell them about potential problems with their drugs? Not exactly. As one veteran rep, voicing a common sentiment, told me, "Reps are the last to know." Of course, for a rep to be detailing a drug enthusiastically right up to the day it is withdrawn from the market is likely to erode that rep's credibility with doctors. Yet some reps say they don't hear about problems until the press gets wind of them and the company launches into damage control. At that point, Slattery-Moschau explains, "Reps learn verbatim how to handle the concern or objection in a way that spins it back in the drug's favor."

Some believe that the marketing landscape changed dramatically for both reps and doctors in 2002, after the Office of the Inspector General in the Department of Health and Human Services announced its intention to crack down on drug companies' more notorious promotional practices. With the threat of prosecution in the air, the industry began to take the job of self-policing a lot more seriously, and PhRMA issued a set of voluntary marketing guidelines.

Although most reps agree that the PhRMA code has changed things, not all of them agree that it changed things for the better. Some say that as long as reps feel pressure to meet quota, they will find ways to get around the rules. As one former rep pointed out, not all drug companies belong to PhRMA, and those that don't are, of course, not bound by PhRMA's guidelines. Jordan Katz says that things actually got worse after 2002. "The companies that tried to follow the guidelines lost a ton of market share, and the ones who didn't gained it," he says. "The bottom line is that if you don't pay off the doctors, you will not succeed in pharmaceuticals. Period."

The Ethics of Direct to Consumer Pharmaceutical Advertising

DENIS G. ARNOLD

Customers in the United States and New Zealand are alone among the citizens of industrialized nations in being directly targeted by prescription drug advertising that touts the benefits of specific drugs. This may change in the future as the pharmaceutical industry is lobbying the European Union to allow the practice. In 1997 the US Food and Drug Administration (FDA) altered its policy on direct-to-consumer (DTC) advertising in such a way as to make it possible for the widespread use of television commercials for prescription pharmaceutical advertising. Since that time spending on direct-to-consumer advertising has increased substantially. However, the practice of advertising directly to consumers has come under sustained criticism. Critics of DTC advertising argue that the practice undermines physician–patient relationships and drives up the cost of prescription drugs. In response, drug manufacturers and their trade group the Pharmaceutical Research and Manufacturers of America (PhRMA) argue that DTC advertisements empower consumers and have no impact on the cost of drugs. Furthermore, the pharmaceutical industry is currently engaged in a lobbying campaign in the European Union to allow individual companies to market their drugs to European consumers.[1] In this article it is argued that branded DTC advertising is unethical because it illegitimately manipulates consumers, increases risks to patients, and drives up overall healthcare costs. However, it is also argued that genuinely non-branded DTC advertising by the pharmaceutical industry is ethically permissible and can play a beneficial role in the healthcare marketplace for both patients and the pharmaceutical industry.

Pharmaceutical firms currently spend $6 billion in the United States on DTC advertising, six times in inflation adjusted dollars the $760 million spent in 1997.[2] Hollywood studios spend less than half of that to market

From Denis G. Arnold, ed., *Ethics and the Business of Biomedicine* (Cambridge University Press, 2009). Revised and updated in 2017. Reprinted with permission.

all their films in a year. Many pharmaceutical firms spend more marketing drugs than they do researching and developing new drugs. DTC advertisements target a range of symptoms and disorders. Examples include depression, anxiety, osteoporosis, attention deficit disorder, erectile dysfunction, heartburn, obesity, diabetes, arthritis, high cholesterol, insomnia, acne, "dry eye disease," and "restless leg syndrome."

The FDA's 40 person Division of Marketing, Advertising, and Communications is responsible for policing over 50,000 advertisements every year. The FDA distinguishes between three varieties of DTC advertising. First, "product claim" advertisements refer to drugs by name and include its use or claims about its effectiveness. Such advertisements are supposed to provide a "fair balance" of information about the product. Second, "reminder" advertisements include the product name but are not allowed to make usage claims. Historically targeted at physicians, such advertisements are intended to remind the target audience of the availability of the product and build brand recognition. For this reason they are exempted from having to include warnings regarding adverse effects. The FDA reports that, increasingly, such advertisements are "testing the limits of what might be considered a product claim" and that they serve "no useful purpose in the DTC arena."[3] Third, "help seeking" advertisements discuss diseases or disorders and recommend that consumers consult their physicians to obtain more information. Because these advertisements do not tout particular products, they are not regulated by the FDA. The FDA routinely issues citations for DTC advertising and statutory and regulatory violations. The most common violations include "minimization or omission of risk information, overstatement of effectiveness or safety, misleading comparative claims, and promotion for uses that are not in the product labeling."[4]

The Debate over DTC Advertising

The pharmaceutical industry argues that DTC advertisements play a valuable role in educating consumers. For example, PhRMA literature states that "DTC advertising's overarching purpose is to inform and educate consumers about treatable conditions, the symptoms that may help them identify diseases, and available therapies."[5] Hank McKinnell, former Chairman of the Board and Chief Executive Officer of Pfizer, argues that DTC advertising should not be understood as advertising at all, but rather as education. He writes,

DTC advertising can be a powerful public good – making people familiar with various therapies and promoting the primacy of the doctor–patient relationship. Good DTC communication should encourage people to talk with their physicians about their medical conditions. DTC advertising should help demystify sensitive medical problems and encourage people to seek treatment even for conditions stigmatized by society. For all these reasons, I prefer to describe our efforts as DTC education.[6]

While preliminary research has been undertaken regarding both consumer and physician attitudes toward DTC advertising, most researchers believe that the impact of such advertising is not well understood. For example, one recent study concluded as follows, "We still know very little about the effects of DTC advertising, especially its impact on consumer behavior (as opposed to attitudes and knowledge) and, ultimately, on consumer health."[7]

Critics of DTC advertising raise numerous objections to the practice. First, it is claimed that DTC advertising undermines patient–physician relationships.[8] One way it is alleged to do so is by persuading consumers to believe that they need a particular drug to be normal, just as other marketing campaigns persuade consumers that men need to give women diamonds in order to have normal, intimate relationships. Many of these consumers, in turn, place pressure on physicians to prescribe specific medications, even when such medications are not the physicians' preferred method of treatment. And in many cases physicians acquiesce to such pressure. One physician described the experience as follows. "As my patients' ideas about the best approach to their medical care became increasingly influenced by the drug advertisements, I would try to help them understand how this process serves the drug companies' interests, not their health. Often I was successful, but once it became clear that a patient was unwilling or unable to reconsider, I often gave in (unless there was a real danger . . .)."[9] Busy physicians who want their patients to leave happy may not have the time to talk through alternative treatment options such as lifestyle changes or generic alternatives, especially in the face of a patient determined to have the advertised brand. Second, DTC advertising is alleged to encourage the overmedication of consumers since the overall message of such advertisements is that drugs, and not lifestyle changes, are the best solution for such comparatively normal experiences as anxiety, sleeplessness, and mild depression.[10] Third, DTC advertising is alleged to needlessly increase the cost of pharmaceuticals. Critics argue that DTC advertising is unnecessary, since it is the proper role of physicians and not patients qua consumers to determine whether or not a specific drug regimen is ultimately warranted. This unnecessary expense is passed on to consumers via higher drug prices and to employers, governments, and individual purchasers via higher insurance premiums.[11]

The pharmaceutical industry is well aware of these criticisms and has deployed considerable resources to counter them. As we have seen, industry representatives argue that DTC advertisements are to be praised insofar as they play an important role in educating consumers regarding healthcare options. Far from encouraging inappropriate pressure on physicians, the industry argues that DTC advertisements encourage patients to partner with physicians in making healthcare decisions. As one Pfizer policy analyst argues:

> Given sufficient and accurate information about options – information greatly enhanced by DTC advertising – a consumer knows better than anyone else whether he or she would prefer a product with fewer unpleasant side effects even a slightly higher risk of some serious event. Consumers who are not professionally trained in health care are not so foolish as to discard the expert advice of medical professionals. Valuing and using technical experts is not the same, however, as electing to abdicate decision making to them. Rather, the ideal – and the emerging model – is a full partnership between patient and health care professional.[12]

According to this view, DTC advertising enhances patient autonomy and thus improves healthcare. In response to the second major criticisms of DTC, namely, that it increases the costs of pharmaceuticals, PhRMA points out that DTC advertising represents a small portion of the total cost of drugs and that little evidence supports the claim that DTC advertising has a direct, causal connection to increased drug prices.[13] Finally, in response to the claim that DTC advertising encourages the overuse of prescription drugs, PhRMA cites a recent study that found underuse of medications where medications were appropriate treatment.[14]

There is a typical and seldom recognized feature of the arguments of both critics and defenders of DTC advertising. In both cases, there is normally a failure to distinguish between "product claim" and "reminder" advertisements on the one hand, and "help-seeking" advertisements on the other hand. The distinctions between these classes of advertisements are important, since in the former case the advertisements mention specific drugs while in the latter case they do not. What we shall call "branded" advertisements carry with them specific mention of brand name drugs such as Vioxx, Paxil, or Effexor, whereas non-branded advertisements do not carry with them the names of specific drugs although they may include the name of the pharmaceutical company that sponsors the non-branded advertisement. This distinction is of vital importance for any analysis of the ethics of DTC advertising since the arguments for and against DTC advertising do not necessarily apply equally to each category of advertisement. For example, the criticism that DTC advertisements place pressure on physicians to prescribe specific medication doesn't apply to non-branded DTC advertisements. So too, a defense of DTC advertisements that appeals to the undertreatment of certain conditions where medication is appropriate fails to undermine criticism of the use of branded advertisements that target, e.g., routine anxiety or ennui.

Assessing the Ethical Legitimacy of DTC Advertising

Reminder Advertisements

According to the FDA, reminder advertisements include the name of the drug product but do not include indications or any recommendation regarding the use of the product.[15] There are no legal restrictions on where such advertisements can be placed or how much money can be spent on them. Examples of reminder advertisements include Schering-Plough's early Claritin "blue skies" campaign; GlaxoSmithKline and Bayer's placement of advertisements for Levitra on the final table of the World Series of Poker, on the stairs and escalators of Alltel Stadium in Jacksonville, Florida for the Super Bowl, and in 15-second television commercials; and Pfizer's sponsorship of Mark Martin's Nascar number six Ford Viagra car and its 15-second and 30-second "wild thing" television commercials. From the perspective of pharmaceutical company marketing executives, the advantage of reminder advertisements directed at consumers is that they are not subject to the same legal restrictions as product claim advertisements. The primary marketing purpose of this advertisement is to build brand awareness. However, because the advertisements contain little more than the product's name and an association of the product with a particular image, representation, or sport, it is implausible to characterize the advertisements as educating consumers.

To its credit, PhRMA partly acknowledges this point in its "Guiding Principles" for ethical consumer advertising (discussed below). One of its principles states that "DTC television advertising that identifies a product by name should clearly state the health conditions for which the medicine is approved and the major risks associated with the medicine being advertised."[16] This voluntary restriction on broadcast reminder advertisements should be welcomed. Nonetheless, the principle is too narrowly defined allowing, as it does, print and other forms of reminder advertisements. Non-broadcast advertisements do not differ from broadcast advertisements in any substantive way that would justify permitting them to continue being used to build brand identity. In other words, if there are ethically sound reasons for banning broadcast reminder advertisements then, barring an argument to the contrary, there are ethically sound reasons for banning all reminder advertisements. PhRMA should articulate a plausible justification for permitting non-broadcast reminder advertisements or ban such advertisements as well. Given that all reminder advertisements are commonly understood within the advertising industry to build brand awareness of a product, rather than to educate consumers regarding the range of appropriate therapies for specific medical conditions, it is difficult to imagine how such advertisements could be ethically justified.

Product Claim Advertisements

Let us now examine the ethical legitimacy of "product claim" advertisements. Let us do so by considering the impact of such advertisements relative to two contested matters. First, the impact of such advertisements on healthcare costs. Second, the role of such advertisements in promoting consumer education regarding medical conditions and their treatments.

The pharmaceutical industry consistently denies that DTC advertising raises the price of prescription pharmaceuticals. In defense of this position they argue that there is no evidence to support the claim that rapidly increasing numbers of DTC advertisements are causally related to rising drug prices. That this would be the case is not surprising, since such a causal connection would be difficult to document. Nonetheless, the billions of dollars spent annually in the United States on DTC advertising must be accounted for somehow. There are a limited number of sources for such money. The three most obvious and sustainable of these include cuts in other areas of corporate spending such as research and development or wages and benefits, lower return on equity to shareholders, or increased revenues from drug sales. It is not unreasonable to think that a significant portion of the cost of DTC advertising is passed on to consumers via higher drug prices. However, even if it could be made clear that DTC advertising causes the price of prescription drugs to rise, this would not by itself constitute an objection to DTC advertising. Additional arguments would be needed. For example, it would need to be argued that pharmaceutical companies, rather than governments, have an ethical obligation to ensure that prices for innovative, new drugs do not exceed certain limits. While such a claim may be plausibly developed, grounded perhaps in a recognition of efficacious and life-improving drugs as social goods, that is not a position that will be argued for in the

space of this essay. Alternatively, it could be argued that some DTC advertising uses manipulative marketing techniques to increase spending on pharmaceuticals. If increased spending can be tied to the intentional manipulation of consumers, then there would be good reason for arguing that the increased costs are illegitimate. This is the strategy that will be utilized in the remainder of this section.

DTC advertising may have adverse effects on the cost of healthcare by simply increasing unnecessary spending on pharmaceuticals. Many of the drugs pitched by pharmaceutical companies in DTC advertisements are no better than much less expensive drugs already available. Consider, for example, the antihistamine Claritin manufactured by Schering-Plough. This drug was one of the first to be marketed to consumers after the change in FDA rules regarding DTC advertising. Despite the existence of equally good or better, but much less expensive, allergy medications, DTC advertisement driven patient spending on Claritin rose to $2.6 billion in 2000. Numerous prescription drugs with equally unremarkable profiles in comparison to their much less expensive competitors have been marketed via DTC advertising. Among the most well known of these are the cox-2 inhibitors Vioxx (manufactured and marketed by Merck) and Celebrex (manufactured and marketed by Pfizer), and the nonsteroidal anti-inflammatory Relafen (manufactured and marketed by SmithKline Beecham). For general pain relief cox-2 inhibitors are no more effective than much safer and much less expensive over-the-counter medications such as Ibuprofen. However, they have much more serious side-effects. It is estimated that approximately 140,000 cases of heart disease in the United States, and as many as 56,000 premature deaths, were caused by Vioxx during the five years that it was marketed to consumers (the drug was later withdrawn from the market).[17]

Product claim advertisements for such drugs often lead patients to believe that only the advertised drug will do. One physician characterized his interactions with his patients, in the wake of the Claritin campaign, in the following terms:

> It certainly convinced many of my patients that they needed not just any allergy medicine, but Claritin and only Claritin. They resisted the idea that there were equally good and perhaps better ways to relieve their allergy symptoms than a new (and therefore less well tested) drug. Moreover, they were unconcerned about Claritin's cost (more than $2.10 per day): most had prescription drug coverage as part of their health insurance.[18]

This anecdotal evidence is supported by a recent study that concluded that "Patients' requests for medicines are a powerful driver of prescribing decisions."[19] The aggregate impact of millions of patients exerting similar influence over physicians is a substantial and scientifically unwarranted increase in the cost of healthcare. Editors at the *Canadian Association of Medicine Journal* concluded that if DTC advertising were to be introduced in Canada, prescription drug costs to the government would increase on an annual basis by $CAN1.2 billion.[20] While some of that spending would be on drugs that patients need and which are the best available for the price, much of the spending would be on expensive "me too" drugs, or on drugs that medicalize normal human experience. Consumer driven spending on such drugs has amounted to additional billions of dollars being spent on healthcare in the United States. These increased costs are primarily borne by public and private health insurance companies, employers, and subscribers via higher premiums, and taxpayers. There is, of course, shared responsibility for these increased costs. The US government permits the use of such advertisements, patients pressure physicians to provide them with branded drugs, physicians often acquiesce to such pressure, and insurance companies may not adequately dissuade patients from choosing expensive drugs. Nonetheless, because pharmaceutical companies develop and aggressively market these drugs in a manipulative manner, they bear a disproportionate level of responsibility for these increased healthcare costs.

Expenditures on such drugs are objectionable primarily when those expenditures are the result of manipulative advertising campaigns for brand name products. Manipulation has both a metaphorical and nonmetaphorical usage.[21] It is in the nonmetaphorical sense that we say that one manipulates a complicated object or system such as a magnetic resonance imaging machine. Such manipulation typically involves a sophisticated understanding of the object to be manipulated. Interpersonal manipulation is similar in that it typically involves a complex understanding of the agents involved, or of relevant feature of human psychology in general, as well as an instrumental treatment of those agents. Manipulation of this sort, as contrasted with rational persuasion, is characterized by the skillful control of circumstances and information in a manner intended to alter the judgment or behavior of a person in a manner consistent with the preferences of the person, group, or organization responsible for the manipulative activity. In such cases one does not merely seek to provide straightforward reasons for an agent to act in a particular way, one seeks to engineer that outcome via peripheral means and regardless of the victim's judgment. The carefully crafted manner in which influence is brought to bear on victims of manipulation often involves deceptive practices that are themselves objectionable.

Manipulation is *prima facie* wrong because it treats the subjects of manipulation as mere tools, as objects lacking the rational capacity to choose for themselves how they shall act. The Kantian origins of this concept of respect for persons are well known. In this view, all persons possess dignity, or intrinsic value, and this dignity must be respected.[22] The obligation that we respect others requires that we not use people as a means only, but instead that we treat other people as capable of autonomous, principled action. The pharmaceutical industry explicitly denies that it uses manipulative or even persuasive, mass market advertising to sell drugs to consumers. As we have seen, the pharmaceutical industry argues repeatedly and consistently that it is in the business of educating consumer about healthcare choices.

Product claim advertisements are properly characterized as manipulative for several reasons. First, it is clear that many product claim advertisements make use of peripheral techniques that appeal to emotion and unreflective dispositions rather than a central route of rational persuasion. Social scientists who work with the elaboration likelihood model of persuasion refer to an elaboration continuum with the central, analytic route having high cognitive elaboration and the peripheral route having low or no cognitive elaboration.[23] When product claim advertisements make use of images such as a cartoon moth lulling restless sleepers into a sound slumber (Lunesta), men with horns sprouting from their temples (Viagra), and friendly Hollywood stars such as Sally Field giving medical advice (Boniva), they are making use of low elaboration models of persuasion. In other words, they are working to persuade consumers to seek these drugs using the standard low elaboration techniques of persuasive advertising.

Given the pervasiveness of peripheral advertising techniques in the United States, and the apparent widespread acceptance of such techniques, it is worth considering why the pharmaceutical industry does not openly defend its right to advertise to consumers in this way. The reason, of course, is that there is also widespread acceptance of the view that pharmaceuticals are different in important ways from soap, automobiles, clothing, jewelry, and even over-the-counter drugs. Prescription pharmaceuticals are different in kind from consumer goods. Indeed, they can usefully be characterized as a hazardous substance along with hazardous materials such as arsenic, toluene, and plutonium insofar as they (a) are potentially harmful to human health and (b) are products that require specialized scientific or technical knowledge in order to be used safely. It is this quality of pharmaceuticals that is the statutory basis for the criteria used to distinguish prescription pharmaceuticals from over-the-counter pharmaceuticals in US law. The 1951 Durham-Humphrey Amendment to the Food, Drug, and Cosmetic Act specifies that drugs that can only be used safely under the supervision of a physician require a prescription. Prescription pharmaceuticals differ from other consumer goods in that they have been determined by scientific experts to require the supervision of a physician for their effective and safe use. Physicians themselves need to be familiar with the physician package insert (PI) provided by the drug manufacturers in compliance with FDA guidelines, which indicate usage and proper dosage, detail known side-effects, and specify drug interactions, among other important details. These inserts are written in technical language intended to be understood by physicians, and are not typically intelligible to non-physicians. Without knowledge of these technical details, as well as the clinical and scientific knowledge necessary to interpret these details, consumers are not in a position to determine whether or not such drugs are appropriate for their personal use, and if so whether other available drugs are more appropriate for medical or economic reasons. There is then a compelling public safety argument against branded DTC advertising.

The second reason for characterizing DTC advertising as manipulative is that it is implausible, on any reasonable definition of education, to characterize non-cognitive persuasion as education. Since these advertisements are defended as educational, and given that they do not meet minimum standards of education, it is reasonable to characterize this defense of DTC advertising as an attempt to manipulate consumers into believing a proposition that is not true. Pharmaceutical companies must characterize their branded DTC advertising as purely educational because there is no plausible case to be made in defense of the use of peripheral marketing techniques to increase sales of prescription drugs.

In reply, defenders of DTC advertising argue that DTC advertisements enhance consumer autonomy and empower patients to communicate with physicians regarding their healthcare needs. This claim is unpersuasive in the case of branded advertisements for several reasons. First, the advertisements themselves do not provide sufficient information to assess the efficacy of the drug in relation to the consumer's current health. Second, the information that is presented is almost always biased in favor of the drug being pitched. Third, the vast majority of consumers lack the sophisticated knowledge of medicine necessary to assess the claims being made to determine whether or not the claims have validity.

While it is important to distinguish individual advertising campaigns from one another and to assess their accuracy on an individual basis, there is significant evidence that branded DTC campaigns constitute intentionally manipulative and misleading efforts to persuade consumers to purchase branded drugs rather than genuine educational campaigns. Indeed, a major FDA survey found that most physicians believe that DTC advertisements provide unbalanced information regarding the risks and benefits of the drugs they are selling.[24] According to the FDA:

> Seventy percent (70%) of primary care physicians said that DTC advertising confuses their patients either "a great deal" (28%) or "somewhat" (42%) about the relative risks and benefits of prescription drugs, whereas about 60 percent of specialists rated the confusion as either "a great deal" (24%) or "somewhat" (36%). Seventy-five percent (75%) of physicians of both categories indicated that DTC advertising causes patients to believe either "a great deal" (32%) or "somewhat" (43%) that drugs work better than they actually do.[25]

This should not be surprising, for a full accounting of the risks and benefits of a drug cannot be depicted in broadcast advertisements and are difficult to communicate in print advertisements. Recall that the FDA approved product claim broadcast advertisements so long as such advertisements refer consumers to print advertisements where "adequate provision" of the adverse risks of such drugs are explained in detail. The difficulty here is that the print advertisements do not meet the adequate provision requirement. To provide consumers with the requisite information such advertisements would need to be intelligible to a significant majority of the adult population in the United States. A study by the American Association of Retired Persons found that one-third of 1,310 adults failed to notice the fine print, and of those who did notice it one-third read the fine print.[26] The study did not assess comprehension of the fine print by the approximately one-fifth of adults surveyed who actually read that fine print. However, a Kaiser Family Foundation survey of 1,872 adults found that 70 percent of those shown advertisements reported that they had learned little or nothing about the condition requiring treatment.[27] Finally, the authors of a recent study found that of 69 print advertisements that were studied all required a college or graduate level education in order to be understood.[28] Just 27 percent of the adult population in the United States is college educated.[29] These surveys confirm what common sense would suggest, namely, that most DTC advertising is unsuccessful at educating consumers about diseases, the appropriate use of the advertised drugs, and their risks. DTC advertising seems instead to play the role described in a pharmaceutical trade magazine, namely, to "ensur[e] that patients walk out of the doctor's office with a prescription for a particular brand, rather than for a competitor's product or for some other form of therapy."[30]

DTC advertising that was genuinely educational would provide consumers with objective and impartial information about the drug being advertised. At a minimum, this would include a description of the disease or ailment that the drug is approved to treat, an accurate and balanced account of the drug's risks and benefits in relation to other available medications, available non-drug therapies, and a cost comparison for the consumer *qua* patient in relation to other available medications. Branded "product claim" advertisements typically cannot fulfill these educational goals because the purpose of such advertisements is not to provide patients *qua* consumers with the information they need to have informed conversations with their physicians regarding possible treatment regimens. Rather, the goal of such advertisements is to have patients communicate a preference for a particular brand to the physician, with the well-founded assumption that the physician will comply at least some of the time. Branded advertisements that purport to be educational, but actually pitch specific products are manipulative insofar as they use patients as tools to secure prescriptions from doctors for the advertised drugs. It is, of course, within the power of physicians to deny these requests when they are not in the best interest of their patients. However, pharmaceutical companies rely on the fact that many physicians may themselves be persuaded by demanding patients in conjunction with pharmaceutical marketing representatives. The claim that physicians are themselves capable of being manipulated into prescribing particular drugs should not be surprising to anyone familiar with the ways in which pharmaceutical companies spend $22 billion annually on marketing directly to physicians.[31]

Is Self-Regulation the Solution?

In response to widespread criticism of DTC advertising the industry trade group PhRMA issued "Guiding Principles" for ethical consumer advertising. These principles were interpreted in the media as an effort by the industry to prevent further government regulation of DTC advertising in the United States. According to PhRMA, the principles are intended to ensure that DTC advertisements educate patients and consumers. Significantly, the chief ethics officers and the CEOs of major companies have certified that their companies are in compliance with the principles.[32] Researchers recently studied actual compliance with the principles by companies in the pharmaceutical industry. Researchers found that for one class of heavily advertised pharmaceuticals (those for erectile dysfunction), Pfizer, Eli Lilly, Bayer, GlaxoSmithKline, Schering-Plough, and Merck routinely violated the principles over the four-year period of study.[33] Of the nine principles assessed in the study, only one was followed by all companies all of the time. Four of the principles were never followed by any of the companies over a four-year period. For example, one of the principles requires that companies include in their advertisements information about the availability of other treatment options for the condition such as diet and lifestyle changes. The study documented that this was never done by any company in any television or print advertisement, or on the company sponsored drug webpages, during the four-year period of the study. Recall that these principles were written by the pharmaceutical industry and that executives at leading companies voluntarily pledged to follow these principles.

At present, PhRMA invites public comment on compliance with the Guiding Principles (submitted by fax and conventional mail only). This material is collected and distributed to individual companies who in turn are encouraged to respond to individual commentators. PhRMA does not make public the comments they, or the companies, identified, or the company responses. When researchers attempted to file comments with PhRMA in order to learn more about company advertising practices they discovered that the facsimile (fax) machine number that PhRMA published online for the purpose of submitting comments was not connected to a fax machine.[34] The researchers then submitted comments via the United States Postal Service and confirmed that the comments were received by PhRMA at their Washington, DC office. PhRMA never responded to the comments nor did any company.

In a follow-up study, the same researchers found that the public disclosure of firm non-compliance with the "Guiding Principles" did not improve firm compliance with the standards.[35] In other words, even after PhRMA and the companies acknowledged the results of the study, firms continued to violate the "Guiding Principles" – ten years in succession. The researchers point out that since there is no penalty for non-compliance, this should not be surprising. Industry self-regulation is better understood as a means of placating stakeholders and blocking additional government regulation than a substitute for actual government regulation. If PhRMA is to be taken seriously as an organization whose purpose is, in part, to self-regulate the pharmaceutical industry it needs to implement a serious mechanism for tracking compliance with its guidelines and codes by signatory companies, report its findings to the public, and disavow the marketing practices of those signatory companies that violate its guidelines. If companies can publicly commit to adhering to PhRMA's DTC advertising guidelines, while at the same time running broadcast advertisements that violate the guidelines, both the guidelines and PhRMA will rightly be regarded as lacking credibility.

In the European Union regulators could avoid such deceptive self-regulation by retaining current bans on DTC advertising. In the United States, a complete legislative ban is unlikely to survive court challenges mounted on constitutional free speech grounds. Are there any alternatives that would result in genuine healthcare education?

"Help-Seeking" Advertisements and Genuine Health Education

Despite objections to "product claim" advertisements, and in spite of the industry's failure to self-regulate, there is way for companies to utilize DTC advertising without resorting to deception and manipulation. Non-branded, "help-seeking" advertisements have the potential to play genuinely educational roles while at the same time enhancing the revenues of pharmaceutical companies. This could be accomplished with careful, non-branded advertisements that do two things. First, describe an ailment or disease, such as diabetes, hypertension, or osteoporosis. Second, invite consumers interested in learning more about symptoms and treatments of the disease to consult a webpage or call a toll free number to obtain a brochure. The information obtained from these sources would be the same and would contain the following information:

- detailed description of the disease or ailment;
- available non-drug therapies;
- a description of available medications, including an accurate and balanced account of the risks and benefits;
- a cost comparison of medications in relation to other available medications.

Consumers who had access to such information would be genuinely empowered to have informed conversations with their physicians regarding the problem for which they are seeking help and available treatment options.

Companies with pharmaceuticals that are competitive on the basis of therapeutic and economic value would have a clear incentive for producing such non-branded DTC advertisements. However, it is reasonable to suppose that companies with weaker or inferior products may not produce genuinely objective informational brochures and webpages if they believe doing so will undermine their profitability. There is merit to this concern, but there is also a ready solution to the problem. The responsibility for overseeing the design of non-branded DTC brochures and webpages

could be turned over to the National Library of Medicine at the National Institutes of Health. The National Library of Medicine would have the responsibility of overseeing the content and distribution of the information and its operations could be funded by the companies running the help-seeking advertisements. Such a strategy is consistent with concern for the well-being of patients, as well as fair and honest competition among pharmaceutical companies in the healthcare marketplace.

Skeptics would likely point out that it is unlikely that companies would voluntarily agree to outsource this component of their advertising to medical and communications professionals working on behalf of the public. If such a policy were to be enacted in the United States, the skeptic might argue it would likely need to be the result of regulatory changes. However, it remains open to companies supportive of genuine healthcare education, and with the managerial leadership necessary to act with integrity, to voluntarily support such a program.

Notes

1. Les Toop and Dee Mangin, "Industry Funded Patient Information and the Slippery Slope to New Zealand," *British Medical Journal* 335 (October 2007): 694–95.
2. Denis G. Arnold and James L. Oakley, "Self-Regulation in the Pharmaceutical Industry: The Exposure of Children and Adolescents to Erectile Dysfunction Commercials," *Journal of Health Politics, Policy & Law* (2018).
3. Rachel Behrman, "The Impact of Direct-to-Consumer Advertising on Seniors' Health and Health Care Costs," Hearing before the Special Committee on Aging, US Senate, 109th Congress, 1st Session, Washington, DC, September 29, 2005, p. 3.
4. Thomas Abrams, "The Regulation of Prescription Drug Promotion," in *Ethics and the Pharmaceutical Industry*, ed. Michael A. Santoro and Thomas M. Gorrie (Cambridge University Press, 2005), p. 162.
5. PhRMA, "Pharmaceutical Marketing & Promotion Q&A: Tough Questions, Straight Answers," p. 10. Retrieved from www.phrma.org/files/Tough_Questions.pdf.
6. Hank McKinnell, *A Call to Action: Taking Back Health Care for Future Generations* (New York: McGraw-Hill, 2005), p. 181.
7. John E. Calfee, "Public Policy Issues in Direct-to-Consumer Advertising of Prescription Drugs" (July 8, 2002), p. 46. Retrieved from https://journals.sagepub.com/doi/abs/10.1509/jppm.21.2.174.17580?journalCode=ppoa.
8. See, for example, Barbara Mintzes, "Direct to Consumer Advertising Is Medicalising Normal Human Experience," *British Medical Journal* 324 (April 13, 2002): 908; John Abramson, *Overdosed America: The Broken Promise of American Medicine* (New York: HarperCollins, 2005), ch. 10;

and Jerry Avron, *Powerful Medicines: The Benefits, Risks, and Costs of Prescription Drugs* (New York: Random House, 2007), p. 289.

9. Abramson, *Overdosed America*, p. 155.

10. See, for example, Matthew F. Hollon, "Direct-to-Consumer Advertising: A Haphazard Approach to Health Promotion," *Journal of the American Medical Association* 293, no. 16 (2005): 2030–33 (p. 2031) and "Direct-to-Consumer Marketing of Prescription Drugs: Creating Consumer Demand," *Journal of the American Medical Association* 281, no. 4 (1999): 382–84; R. L. Kravitz, R. M. Epstein, M. D. Feldman et al., "Influence of Patients' Requests for Direct-to-Consumer Advertised Antidepressants: A Randomized Controlled Trial," *Journal of the American Medical Association* 293, no. 16 (2005): 1995–2002.

11. See, for example, Abramson, *Overdosed America*, pp. 158–59; Avron, *Powerful Medicines*, pp. 288–90.

12. Alison Keith, "Information Matters: The Consumer as the Integrated Health Care System," in *Prescription Drug Advertising: Empowering Consumers through Information.* Published by Pfizer as part of the series *Economic Realities in Health Care Policy* 2, no. 1 (East Brunswick, NJ: Pfizer, 2001). Retrieved from www.pfizer.com/about/public_policy/resources.jsp.

13. PhRMA, "Pharmaceutical Marketing & Promotion Q&A," p. 6.

14. Ibid., p. 8.

15. US Food and Drug Administration, Division of Drug Marketing, Advertising, and Communications, "Prescription Drug Advertising and Promotional Labeling," *Center for Drug Evaluation and Research Handbook*, p. 8. Created April 16, 1998; revised November 7, 2006. Retrieved from www.fda.gov/cder/ddmac/FAQS.HTM#reminder.

16. "PhRMA Guiding Principles: Direct to Consumer Advertisements about Prescription Medicines." Retrieved from http://phrma-docs.phrma.org/files/dmfile/PhRMA_Guiding_Principles_2018.pdf.

17. D. J. Graham, D. Campen et al., "Risk of Acute Myocardial Infarction and Sudden Cardiac Death in Patients Treated with Cyclo-Oxygenase 2 Selective and Non-Selective Non-Steroidal Anti-Inflammatory Drugs: Nested Case-Control Study," *The Lancet* 365 (2005): 475–81.

18. Abramson, *Overdosed America*, p. 152.

19. B. Mintzes, M. L. Barer, R. L. Kravitz et al.,"Influence of Direct to Consumer Pharmaceutical Advertising and Patients' Requests on Prescribing Decisions: Two Site Cross Sectional Survey," *British Medical Journal* 324 (2002): 279.

20. "Ads and Prescription Pads," *Canadian Medical Association Journal* 169, no. 5 (September 2, 2003): 381.

21. Joel Rudinow makes this point in "Manipulation," *Ethics* 88 (1978): 338–47 (p. 339). The overall account of manipulation provided here follows my argument in Denis G. Arnold,

"Coercion and Moral Responsibility," *American Philosophical Quarterly* 38, no. 1 (2001): 53–67. See also Michael Kligman and Charles Culver, "An Analysis of Interpersonal Manipulation," *Journal of Medicine and Philosophy* 17 (1992): 173–97 (pp. 186–87).

22. For discussion of a contemporary Kantian view of respect for persons, see Joseph Raz, *Value, Respect, and Attachment* (Cambridge University Press, 2001), esp. ch. 4. For detailed discussion of the concept of dignity as it is used here, see Thomas E. Hill, Jr., *Dignity and Practical Reason* (Ithaca, NY: Cornell University Press, 1992), pp. 202–3.

23. For an overview of this literature, see R. E. Petty and D. T. Wegener, "The Elaboration Likelihood Model: Current Status and Controversy," in *Dual Process Theories in Social Psychology*, ed. S. Chaiken and Y. Trope (London: Guilford Press, 1999), pp. 41–72.

24. Kathryn J. Aikin, John L. Swasy, and Amie C. Braman, "Patient and Physician Attitudes and Behaviors Associated with DTC Promotion of Prescription Drugs: Summary of FDA Survey Research Results, Final Report," November 19, 2004. Retrieved from www.fda.gov/cder/ddmac/researchka.htm.

25. Ibid., p. 73.

26. "Free Rein for Drug Ads? A Slowdown in FDA Review Has Left Consumers More Vulnerable to Misleading Messages," *Consumer Reports*, February 2002. Retrieved from www.consumerreports.org:80/cro/health-fitness/drugs-supplements/drug-ads-203/overview/index.htm.

27. Ibid.

28. K. A. Kaphingst, R. E. Rudd, W. Dejong, and L. H. Daltroy, "Literacy Demands of Product Information Intended to Supplement Television Direct-to-Consumer Prescription Drug Advertisements," *Patient Education and Counseling* 55 (2004): 293–300.

29. Nicole Stoops, US Census Bureau, *Educational Attainment in the United States: 2003* (Washington, DC, June 2004). Retrieved from www.census.gov/prod/2004pubs/p20-550.pdf.

30. "Free Rein for Drug Ads?"

31. Julie M. Dononue, Marisa Cevasco, and Meredith B. Rosenthal, "A Decade of Direct-to-Consumer Advertising of Prescription Drugs," *New England Journal of Medicine* 357 (2007): 673–81 (p. 676).

32. PhRMA Office of Accountability, "Report of Second Survey of Signatory Companies" (2006). Retrieved from www.phrma.org/office_of_accountability.

33. Denis G. Arnold and James Oakley, "The Politics and Strategy of Industry Self-Regulation: The Pharmaceutical Industry's Principles for Ethical Direct-to-Consumer Advertising as a Deceptive Blocking Strategy," *Journal of Health Politics, Policy and Law* 38, no. 3 (2013): 505–44.

34. Ibid.

35. Arnold and Oakley, "Self-Regulation in the Pharmaceutical Industry."

LEGAL PERSPECTIVES

United States Court of Appeals for the Seventh Circuit, *B. Sanfield, Inc. v. Finlay Fine Jewelry Corp.* (1999)

Sanfield and Finlay Fine Jewelry Corp. (Finlay) both sell gold earrings, gold chains, gold bangles, and gold charms. Sanfield is a locally owned retailer with one store in Rockford, Illinois. Finlay has multiple outlets including two in Rockford. Finlay prices these gold jewelry items at 5.5 times higher than their costs, Finlay frequently sells these items at a 40–60 percent discount from this original price. Sanfield brought suit against Finlay for false and deceptive advertising because Finlay never expected, and almost never marketed and sold jewelry, at the regular, non-discounted list price. Sanfield argued that in fact the true regular price was the discounted price. However, this "discounted" price was higher than the regular price charged by other retail jewelers. Through the enticement of large discounts consumers were attracted to Finlay's stores where they were deceived into paying non-competitive prices for jewelry and more than they would have paid at Sanfield.

In addition there are a number of state laws and the Federal Lanham Act that were consistent with Sanfield's reasoning. For example, Illinois has a law specifying that it is deceptive to compare the discounted price of an item with the regular price unless the seller has either (1) sold a substantial number of that item at a price equal to or greater than the regular price; or (2) has offered the item openly and actively at the regular price for a reasonably substantial time in a good faith effort to sell the item at the regular price.

The Appeals Court rejected the District Court's claim that these regulations could be ignored and, in particular, the District Court's reasoning in this regard. The District Court held that "Deception, like beauty, is in the eye of the beholder. If consumers generally understand that a retailer makes little or no concerted effort to sell at a stated regular price, then stating the price as regular would be neither deceptive nor misleading." The Appeals Court found that the District Court's logic was faulty for two reasons. First, "it disregards the judgment of state and federal regulators as to the deceptive potential" of the term "regular price." Second, "in elevating subjective consumer perceptions to preeminence, the [lower] court's approach appears to demand proof of actual consumer deception before an act is deemed deceptive. To that extent, it is at least in part inconsistent with the federal and state statutes alike, neither of which focuses strictly on actual perception to the exclusion of practices which are likely to mislead." The Appeals Court determined that whether or not state and federal regulations were violated must be determined at trial and remanded the case (returned it to a lower court for reconsideration).

United States Court of Appeals for the Second Circuit, *Coca-Cola Company v. Tropicana Products, Inc.* (1982)

In 1982 Tropicana Products, Inc. (Tropicana) ran a television ad for its "Premium Pack" orange juice. The commercial shows former Olympic athlete Bruce Jenner squeezing an orange while saying, "It's pure pasteurized juice as it comes from the orange," and then shows Jenner pouring the freshly squeezed juice into a Tropicana carton while the audio states, "It's the only leading brand not made with concentrate and water." Shortly thereafter, Coca-Cola brought suit under the Lanham Act against Tropicana for using "a false description or representation in connection with goods placed in commerce." Coca-Cola claimed that the Tropicana ad is false because "it incorrectly represents that Premium Pack orange juice contains unprocessed fresh-squeezed juice when in fact the juice is pasteurized (heated to about 200 degrees Fahrenheit) and sometimes frozen prior to packaging." The District Court had rejected a preliminary injunction against Tropicana that would prevent it from showing the ad.

The granting of an injunction requires that the plaintiff (Coca-Cola) show that it will be harmed if the injunction is not granted. Citing previous cases where market studies were used as evidence that some consumers were misled by the advertising in those cases, the Court said, "Applying the same reasoning in the instant case, if consumers are misled by Tropicana's commercial, Coca-Cola probably would suffer irreparable injury." As the Court explained, Coca-Cola and Tropicana are the leading competitors for the chilled, ready to serve orange juice market. If consumers were deceived into thinking that Premium Pack was a better product because it contained only fresh-squeezed unprocessed juice, Coca-Cola would likely lose market share and be harmed as a result. The Court also ruled that Coca-Cola was likely to prevail in its false advertising claim because Tropicana's claims were blatantly false, given that both pasteurization and freezing took place. The Appeals Court reversed the District Court and granted an injunction preventing the airing of the Tropicana ad.

Supreme Court of California, *Kasky v. Nike, Inc.* (2002)

As early as October 1996 with a report on the television news program *48 Hours*, and continuing at least through November and December of 1997 various persons and organizations alleged that in the factories where Nike products are made workers were paid less than the applicable local minimum wage; required to work overtime; allowed and encouraged to work more overtime hours than applicable local law allowed; subjected to physical, verbal, and sexual abuse; and exposed to toxic chemicals, noise, heat, and dust without adequate safety equipment, in violation of applicable local occupational health and safety regulations.

In response to this adverse publicity, Nike made statements to California consumers that were allegedly false and misleading. Specifically, Nike said that workers who make Nike products are protected from physical and sexual abuse, that they are paid on average double the applicable local minimum wage, that they receive a "living wage," and that they receive free meals and healthcare. Nike made these statements in press releases, in letters to newspapers, in a letter to university presidents and athletic directors, and in other documents distributed for public relations purposes. Nike also bought full-page advertisements in leading newspapers to publicize a report based on an investigation by former ambassador to the United Nations Andrew Young that found no evidence of illegal or unsafe working conditions at Nike factories in China, Vietnam, and Indonesia. Kasky alleges that these statements were false or misleading.

The Court focused on whether Nike's alleged false statements are commercial or noncommercial speech. Resolution of this issue is important because commercial speech receives a lesser degree of constitutional protection than many other forms of expression, and because governments may entirely prohibit commercial speech that is false or misleading. The United States Supreme Court has not adopted an all-purpose test to distinguish commercial from noncommercial speech under the First Amendment to the Constitution. The Appeals Court did argue that a close reading of the High Court's commercial speech decisions suggests that it is possible to formulate a limited-purpose test based on three elements: the intended speaker, the intended audience, and the content of the message. The Court then argued that the three elements are met.

The first element – a commercial speaker – is satisfied because the speakers – Nike and its officers and directors – are engaged in commerce. The second element – an intended commercial audience – is also satisfied. Nike's letters to university presidents and directors of athletic departments were addressed directly to actual and potential purchasers of Nike's products. College and university athletic departments are major purchasers of athletic shoes and apparel. In addition Nike's press releases and letters to newspaper editors, although addressed to the public generally, were also intended to reach and influence actual and potential purchasers of Nike's products. Specifically, Kasky had alleged that Nike made these statements about its labor policies and practices to maintain and increase its sales and profits.

The third element – representations of fact of a commercial nature – is also present. The Court said, "In describing its own labor policies, and the practices and working conditions in factories where its products are made, Nike was making factual representations about its own business operations. In speaking to consumers about working conditions and labor practices in the factories where its products are made, Nike addressed matters within its own knowledge. The wages paid to the factories' employees, the hours they work, the way they are treated, and whether the environmental conditions under which they work violate local health and safety laws, are all matters likely to be within the personal knowledge of Nike executives, employees, or subcontractors." Thus, Nike was in a position to readily verify the truth of any factual assertions it made on these topics.

Because Nike was acting as a commercial speaker, because its intended audience was primarily the buyers of its products, and because the statements consisted of factual representations about its own business operations, the Court concluded that the statements were commercial speech for purposes of applying state laws designed to prevent false advertising and other forms of commercial deception. The Court went on to point out that the Supreme Court has indicated that false and misleading speech has no constitutional value in itself and is protected only in circumstances and to the extent necessary to give breathing room for the free debate of public issues. The Court then concluded, "Because the messages in question were directed by a commercial speaker to a commercial audience, and because they made representations of fact about the speaker's own business operations for the purpose of promoting sales of its products, we conclude that these messages are commercial speech for the purpose of applying state laws barring false and misleading commercial messages." The verdict was upheld in federal courts. In the end Nike settled with Kasky for an undisclosed amount, but the more important outcome is that firms are legally liable for false statements about working conditions in their supply chains.

United States Supreme Court, *Central Hudson Gas and Electric Corp. v. Public Service Commission* (1980)

In the midst of the 1970s energy shortage in the United States, the Public Service Commission of the State of New York banned Central Hudson Gas and Electric Corporation from promoting the use of electricity in its marketing campaigns. The justification was that "the interconnected utility system in New York State does not have sufficient fuel stocks or sources of supply to continue furnishing all customer demands for the 1973–1974 winter." The Commission's order explicitly permitted "informational" advertising designed to encourage "*shifts* of consumption" from peak demand times to periods of low electricity demand. Central Hudson Gas and Electric Corporation challenged the order in court, arguing that the Commission had restrained commercial speech in violation of the First and Fourteenth Amendments. Historically, the US Supreme Court found that the Constitution accords a lesser protection to commercial speech than to other constitutionally guaranteed expression such as political speech. In this case it developed a three-part test for appropriate government restrictions on commercial speech. Speech can be restricted if any of the following conditions hold. First, the speech is related to illegal activity. Second, the speech is misleading. Third, the speech substantially advances a public interest and at the same time is narrowly tailored to serve the government's interest. The Court found that while energy conservation was in the public interest, the Public Service Commission ban was not sufficiently tailored to meeting that interest. It therefore decided in favor of Central Hudson Gas and Electric Corporation in this case. The three-part test of restrictions on commercial speech has been an important precedent which most courts have followed since this landmark decision.

CASES

Case 1: Advice for Sale: How Companies Pay TV Experts for On-Air Product Mentions

JAMES BANDLER

In November, *Child* magazine's Technology Editor James Oppenheim appeared on a local television show in Austin, Texas, and reviewed educational gadgets and toys. He praised "My ABC's Picture Book," a personalized photo album from Eastman Kodak Co.

"Considering what you showed me, kids' games really don't have to be violent," said the anchor for KVUE, an ABC affiliate and the no. 1-rated television station in its market.

"If . . . you're not careful, they will be," Mr. Oppenheim replied. "That's why I've shown you some of the best."

There was one detail the audience didn't know: Kodak paid Mr. Oppenheim to mention the photo album, according to the company and Mr. Oppenheim. Neither Mr. Oppenheim nor KVUE disclosed the relationship to viewers. During the segment, Mr. Oppenheim praised products from other companies, including Atari Inc., Microsoft Corp., Mattel Inc., Leapfrog Enterprises Inc., and RadioShack Corp. All paid for the privilege, Mr. Oppenheim says.

One month later, Mr. Oppenheim went on NBC's *Today* show, the US's biggest national morning news program, which is part of NBC's news division. "Kodak came out with a great idea," he said to host Ann Curry, before proceeding to talk about the same product he'd been paid to discuss on KVUE. Ms. Curry called it a "nice gift for a little child." Kodak says it didn't pay for the *Today* show mention. But neither Mr. Oppenheim nor NBC disclosed the prior arrangement to tout the product on local TV.

In the *Today* segment, Mr. Oppenheim talked about products made or sold by 15 companies. Nine were former clients, and eight of those had paid him for product placement on local TV during the preceding year.

KVUE says it didn't know about Mr. Oppenheim's business deal. An NBC spokeswoman says the network is looking into what it knew about Mr. Oppenheim's relationship with Kodak and the other manufacturers.

Mr. Oppenheim is part of a little-known network that connects product experts with advertisers and TV shows.

The experts pitch themselves to companies willing to pay for a mention. Next, they approach local-TV stations and offer themselves up to be interviewed. Appearances frequently coincide with trade shows, such as the Consumer Electronics Show, or holidays, including Christmas or Valentine's Day.

The segments are often broadcast live via satellite from a trade event and typically air during regular news programming in a way that's indistinguishable from the rest of the show. One reviewer may conduct dozens of interviews with local stations over the course of a day in what the industry calls a "satellite media tour." While this circuit is predominantly focused on the local television market, the big prize for marketers is a mention on national television shows, which carry far more clout with viewers.

The familiar faces on this circuit include Mr. Oppenheim, *Today* Tech Editor Corey Greenberg, and trend spotter Katlean de Monchy. They are among an army of experts who have risen to prominence as news organizations everywhere, seeking to expand their audiences, have branched into reviewing consumer products ranging from home furnishings to personal finance.

A longstanding principle of journalism holds that reporters cannot have financial relationships with the people or companies they cover. TV shows present these gurus' recommendations as unbiased and based solely on their expertise. But that presentation is misleading if the experts have been paid to mention products on network or local TV.

Mr. Oppenheim's pitch is typical. Late last year, he invited electronics and game companies to join two satellite tours, according to a copy of his solicitation. "We expect these tours to sell out fast," Mr. Oppenheim wrote, "so please contact us as soon as possible to reserve a spot." The

$12,500 fee per company, he explained, covered development, production, and "spokesperson expenses."

On his website, Mr. Oppenheim used to describe himself as a consumer advocate. "My pledge is to tell the unvarnished truth about the products reviewed," he wrote. "The good, the bad, and the ugly." He recently changed his biographical description to "technology expert and industry spokesperson."

In an interview, Mr. Oppenheim says getting paid by the companies he reviews on local television doesn't influence his judgment. He says his main purpose is to educate the public about nonviolent games. Renting studio and satellite time, he says, is expensive. Mr. Oppenheim says he, too, needs to be paid.

"My motives are the highest: to get information out to parents about what they can be doing to advance children through technology," he says.

Mr. Oppenheim has a different set of standards when it comes to getting paid to go on national television. He says he notifies clients in writing that his *Today* appearances are off-limits, in part because the show bars such payments. According to a copy of Mr. Oppenheim's pitch, his tour "does not run on the *Today* show."

Kodak, one of the companies that hired Mr. Oppenheim, is happy with its relationship with the reviewer but thinks their financial relationship ought to have been disclosed, according to spokesman Mike McDougal. Mr. McDougal says disclosing the payments is the responsibility of local television stations.

Some production companies say they inform stations about the financial relationship beforehand. By contrast, Frank Volpicella, executive news director of KVUE, the station which hosted Mr. Oppenheim last year, says it didn't know about the payments and wouldn't have aired the segment if it had.

"There's an appearance that he compromised his integrity by promoting a product in which he has a financial interest," Mr. Volpicella says.

NBC, the General Electric Co. unit that broadcasts the *Today* show, says it tightened its conflicts-of-interest policies after receiving questions about the matter from the *Wall Street Journal*. It now specifically says any payments for local-TV appearances via satellite tours should be disclosed to the network.

David McCormick, executive producer for broadcast standards at NBC, says an expert might be allowed to talk about a product on *Today* even if he had a financial conflict. "Some products that they might talk about might be quite topical," Mr. McCormick says, "and to avoid them would be peculiar." In this case, Mr. McCormick says he believes Mr. Oppenheim picked the Kodak photo album on its merits.

The use of TV consumer experts is the latest way marketers have tried to disguise their promotions as real news, often with the aid of media outlets. Magazines accept "advertorials" designed to look like editorial features, not ads. TV stations often use "video news releases" produced by companies, which are designed to look like news segments. Last week, the Federal Communications Commission told broadcasters they must inform viewers about the origins of these video releases.

For advertisers, these techniques help keep their messages from getting lost in an increasingly crowded sea of ads. An example is the camera maker Olympus Optical Corp. Along with Canon Inc. and Nikon Inc., it paid last year to be on a satellite tour operated by DWJ Television that featured John Owens, the editor-in-chief of *Popular Photography & Imaging* magazine, according to Michael Friedman, DWJ's executive vice-president. The DWJ tour was timed to coincide with a 2004 photography trade show. Chris Sluka, an Olympus spokesman, says the tour "secured me some broadcast coverage that's hard to get in a cluttered atmosphere." He says local stations probably wouldn't air the segments if they knew manufacturers paid to be mentioned. "I know when these are pitched, they're pitched as news," he says.

For example, KFMB Local 8, a CBS affiliate in San Diego, aired an interview with Mr. Owens from that tour but didn't disclose the payments. Fred D'Ambrosi, news director at KFMB, says the station assumed Mr. Owens's magazine paid for the tour. He says the station will do a better job finding out who the actual sponsors are in the future.

Mr. Owens also didn't disclose the financial ties when he went on CBS's *Early Show* in December and talked about Nikon and Canon products, among others. Leigh Farris, a spokeswoman for CBS News, says the network is revising its rules to include such conflicts of interest.

Mr. Owens didn't respond to repeated requests seeking comment. Mr. Friedman says Mr. Owens wouldn't endorse products he didn't believe in.

While most satellite media tours take place on local television, the biggest prize is a mention on a national television show. The publicity value of a brief *Today* appearance is estimated at about $250,000, according to Multivision Inc., a company that tracks TV broadcasts. Multivision bases its estimate on ad rates, audience size, and other factors. *Today* is watched by an average of 6.1 million people each weekday. A mention on a local news show is valued at anywhere from a few hundred to a few thousand dollars, depending on audience size.

The exact relationship between paid local tours and mentions on national television is unclear. Many reviewers say national shows are off-limits because of stricter ethics rules enforced by top news organizations.

But some advertisers say one of the key reasons they pay for local media tours is the hope – and sometimes the expectation – that they'll get a mention on the national shows, even if there isn't an explicit financial arrangement to do so.

For several years, Walmart Stores Inc.'s Sam's Club paid trend and fashion expert Katlean de Monchy to get its jewelry mentioned on local TV. Ms. de Monchy's company, Nextpert News, charges $25,000 for a "special option" that includes Ms. de Monchy touting products on local shows, according to a copy of one of its pitches.

Then in January, Ms. de Monchy appeared as a guest on a *Good Morning America* segment explaining how to replicate fashions worn at the Golden Globe awards. "It's the accessories that really caught my eye, though. A lot of bling-bling," Ms. de Monchy told host Diane Sawyer, singling out a pair of diamond earrings available at Sam's Club.

Dee Breazeale, Sam's Club's vice-president and divisional merchandise manager for jewelry, says the company didn't pay to get on ABC's *Good Morning America* but that the mention was "the icing on the cake." Ms. Breazeale adds that Sam's Club would probably not hire Ms. de Monchy if the payments were disclosed, because that would make her appearance seem too much like an infomercial. Ms. Breazeale says the paid segments are more effective than buying an ad. "It brings [the product] more to life," she says.

During the same *Good Morning America* segment, Ms. de Monchy showed off a pair of pointy-toed pumps, sold by another paying customer, shoe retailer DSW. Mike Levison, DSW's vice-president of marketing, says he believed his company paid to get on *Good Morning America* as part of the satellite tour. With 10 being the ultimate marketing coup, he described the appearance as a "9 or 10."

A third client, prom-dress maker Faviana International Inc., had two dresses mentioned on the show. Omid Morady, a principal at Faviana, says getting on *Good Morning America* was the main appeal of hiring Ms. de Monchy and was part of his contract. "Millions of people see it," he says. "It creates more credibility with customers."

Ms. de Monchy did not respond to requests for comment. David Post, executive producer for Ms. de Monchy's company, says the payments help defray their company's high production expenses, which include hiring models. He says Nextpert doesn't recommend particular items and adds that

Good Morning America is "absolutely not in the tour. It's as clear as a bell."

Asked why the paying relationships weren't disclosed on local TV, Mr. Post says: "It's soft news . . . we would never do anything on drugs or political issues; it's like where do you get a prom dress." He says TV stations wouldn't air the segments if they weren't newsworthy.

Bridgette Maney, a spokeswoman for *Good Morning America* says ABC, a unit of Walt Disney Co., requires that regular contributors disclose conflicts of interest. She says Ms. de Monchy isn't a regular contributor. "We were unaware of her affiliation with these other companies," Ms. Maney says. "Now that we're aware of it I do not think she'll be on the program."

One of the most coveted TV consumer experts is Corey Greenberg, the *Today* show's main tech-product reviewer. He came to NBC in 2000 with little television experience. Previously, he was a well-regarded editor and writer at a number of audio-equipment magazines.

Quick on his feet, witty, and able to talk about complicated technology in a simple way, Mr. Greenberg quickly became a regular, doing dozens of segments a year. NBC pays Mr. Greenberg a nominal fee per segment and also gave him the title of Tech Editor.

Mr. Greenberg has charged companies $15,000 per tour to get their products on local news programs, according to a copy of one of his contracts. Mr. Greenberg says paying clients he has mentioned on local shows include Sony Corp., Hewlett-Packard Co., Seiko Epson Corp., and Energizer Holdings Inc.

Mr. Greenberg has also appeared on national shows, including *The Wall Street Journal Report with Maria Bartiromo*, a weekly syndicated business program produced by CNBC, a division of NBC. In a February broadcast about digital music, Mr. Greenberg mentioned products made by Apple Computer Inc. and Creative Technology Ltd. Mr. Greenberg says Apple was a client more than a year ago. He did paid work for Creative last November, both sides say. Neither relationship was disclosed on CNBC.

"It should have been disclosed. He was bound by our policies, which require contributors to disclose such payments to the network," says Amy Zelvin, a CNBC spokeswoman. Mr. Greenberg says he didn't solicit the appearance and was invited by CNBC to talk about that topic.

Rachel Branch, a Sony public-relations official, says one of the things Sony likes about Mr. Greenberg is his credibility. "Viewers like him because he's able to communicate about a product without showing bias," she says. Mr. Greenberg also comes cheaper than some of his competitors, Ms. Branch adds, without elaborating.

Mr. Greenberg defends his local paid work, saying he's providing valuable news to consumers. He says he wouldn't do paid work for a product he didn't believe in. Mr. Greenberg says his business resembles a magazine that collects money from advertisers and then reviews products marketed by the same companies. He says he can maintain a wall between his business and editorial practices. "I am a one-man magazine," he says.

Mr. Greenberg says he labors to keep his *Today* appearances distinct from the paid work. He says on *Today* he is giving specific recommendations; on satellite tours, Mr. Greenberg says, he talks generally about gadget-related issues, such as battery life. As a general rule, he says he won't mention a product on *Today* until 6 months after a paid mention. He says he's rebuffed "high five-figure" offers "to place a product on *Today*."

Mr. McCormick, the NBC executive, says the network has "a lot of confidence" in Mr. Greenberg.

Executives at some companies have the impression there is a connection between Mr. Greenberg's paid tours and his *Today* appearances. Jacqueline E. Burwitz, vice-president of investor relations for Energizer, said she's "absolutely sure" that when

Energizer hired Mr. Greenberg for a local tour in late 2003, the company believed he would mention its products on *Today*.

A few weeks after the local tour, Mr. Greenberg mentioned Energizer's lithium batteries on *Today*.

"So, buy them," said the *Today* host Ms. Curry.

"Exactly," said Mr. Greenberg.

Neither NBC nor Mr. Greenberg mentioned that he had recently been hired by Energizer.

Discussion Questions

1. Are the stealth marketing practices described in this case ethically legitimate means of marketing to consumers? Why, or why not? Explain.

2. Should consumer experts be required to disclose their financial relationships with manufacturers when they appear on television? Why, or why not? Explain. If so, who should enforce such a requirement?

3. In your judgment, how would Arrington evaluate the stealth marketing practices described in this essay? Explain. Do you tend to agree or disagree with this assessment? Explain.

Case 2: Hucksters in the Classroom

WILLIAM H. SHAW AND VINCENT BARRY

Increased student loads, myriad professional obligations, and shrinking school budgets have sent many public school teachers scurrying for teaching materials to facilitate their teaching.

They don't have to look far. Into the breach has stepped business, which is ready, willing, and able to provide print and audiovisual materials for classroom use. These industry-supplied teaching aids are advertised in educational journals, distributed directly to schools, and showcased at educational conventions. Clearasil, for example, distributes a teaching aid and color poster called "A Day in the Life of Your Skin." Its message is hard to miss: Clearasil is the way to clear up your pimples. Domino's Pizza supplies a handout that is supposed to help kids learn to count by tabulating the number of pepperoni wheels on one of the company's pizzas. Chef Boyardee sponsors a study program on sharks based on its "fun pasta," which is shaped like sharks and pictured everywhere on its educational materials.

The list goes on. General Mills supplies educational pamphlets on Earth's "great geothermic 'gushers'" along with the company's "Gushers" snack (a candy filled with liquid). The pamphlets recommend that teachers pass the "Gushers" around and then ask the students as they bite the candy, "How does this process differ from that which produces erupting geothermic phenomena?" In an elementary school in Texas, teachers use a reading program called "Read-A-Logo." Put out by Teacher Support Software, it encourages students to use familiar corporate names such as McDonald's, Hi-C, Coca-Cola, or Cap'n Crunch to create elementary sentences, such as, "I had a hamburger and a Pepsi at McDonald's." In other grade schools, children learn from Exxon's Energy Cube curriculum that fossil fuels pose few environmental problems and that alternative energy is costly and unattainable. Similarly, materials from the American Coal Foundation teach them that the "earth could benefit rather than be harmed from increased carbon

From William H. Shaw and Vincent Barry, *Moral Issues in Business*, 10th ed. (Belmont, CA: Wadsworth, 2007).

dioxide." Courtesy of literature from the Pacific Lumber Company, students in California learn about forests; they also get Pacific Lumber's defense of its forest-clearing activities: "The Great American Forest . . . is renewable forever." At Pembroke Lakes elementary school in Broward County, Florida, 10-year-olds learned how to design a McDonald's restaurant and how to apply and interview for a job at McDonald's, thanks to a seven-week company-sponsored class intended to teach them about the real world of work.

"It's a corporate takeover of our schools," says Nelson Canton of the National Education Association. "It has nothing to do with education and everything to do with corporations making profits and hooking kids early on their products." "I call it the phantom curriculum" adds Arnold Fege of the National PTA, "because the teachers are often unaware that there's subtle product placement." There's nothing subtle, however, about the product placement in *Mathematics Applications and Connections*, a textbook used by many sixth graders. It begins its discussion of the coordinate system with an advertisement for Walt Disney: "Have you ever wanted to be the star of a movie? If you visit Walt Disney–MGM Studios Theme Park, you could become one." Other math books are equally blatant. They use brand-name products like M&Ms, Nike shoes, and Kellogg's Cocoa Frosted Flakes as examples when discussing surface area, fractions, decimals, and other concepts.

All this is fine with Lifetime Learning Systems, a marketing firm that specializes in pitching to students the products of its corporate customers. "[Students] are ready to spend and we reach them," the company brags, touting its "custom-made learning materials created with your [company's] specific marketing objectives in mind." Today's 43 million schoolchildren have tremendous buying power. Elementary schoolchildren spend $15 billion a year and influence another $160 billion in spending by parents. Teenagers spend $57 billion of their own money and $36 billion of their families' money. It's not surprising, then, that many corporations clearly see education marketing as a cost-effective way to build brand loyalty.

Corporate America's most dramatic venture in the classroom, however, began in 1990, when Whittle Communications started beaming into classrooms around the country its controversial Channel One, a television newscast for middle- and high-school students. The broadcasts are 12 minutes long – 10 minutes of news digest with slick graphics and 2 minutes of commercials for Levi's jeans, Gillette razor blades, Head & Shoulders shampoo, Snickers candy bars, and other familiar products. Although a handful of states have banned Channel One, 40 percent of American teens see it every school day.

Primedia, which now owns Channel One, provides cash-hungry schools with thousands of dollars' worth of electronic gadgetry, including TV monitors, satellite dishes, and video recorders, if the schools agree to show the broadcasts. In return, the schools are contractually obliged to broadcast the program in its entirety to all students at a single time on 90 to 95 percent of the days that school is in session. The show cannot be interrupted, and teachers do not have the right to turn it off.

For their part, students seem to like Channel One's fast-paced MTV-like newscasts. "It was very interesting and it appeals to our age group," says student Angelique Williams. "One thing I really like was the reporters were our own age. They kept our attention." But educators wonder how much students really learn. A University of Michigan study found that students who watched Channel One scored only 3.3 percent better on a 30-question test of current events than did students in schools without Channel One. Although researchers called this gain so small as to be educationally unimportant, they noted that all the Channel One students remembered the commercials. That, of course, is good news for Primedia, which charges advertisers $157,000 for a 30-second spot. That price sounds high, but companies are willing to pay it because Channel One delivers a captive, narrowly targeted audience.

That captive audience is just what worries the critics. Peggy Charren of Action for Children's Television calls the project a "great big, gorgeous Trojan horse . . . You're selling the children to the advertisers. You might as well auction off the rest of the school day to the highest bidders." On the other hand, Principal Rex Stooksbury of Central High School in Knoxville, which receives Channel One, takes a different view. "This is something we see as very, very positive for the school," he says. And as student Danny Diaz adds, "We're always watching commercials" anyway.

Discussion Questions

1. Have you had any personal experience with industry-sponsored educational materials? What moral issues, if any, are involved in the affiliation between education and commercial interests? Does commercial intrusion into schools change the nature of education? What values and beliefs does it instill in children? Explain.

2. Do you think students have a right to an education free of commercial indoctrination? If you were a parent of school-age children, would you be concerned about their exposure to commercials and corporate propaganda? Explain.

3. What are the primary justifications for the use of commercial advertising in schools? Explain. What are the primary ethical reasons for thinking that the use of commercial advertising in schools is wrong? Explain.

4. If you were a member of the governing body for an educational system, such as a school board in the United States, contemplating the use of either industry-sponsored materials or Channel One, how would you vote? Why? Explain.

Case 3: The Exposure of Children to Erectile Dysfunction Advertising

DENIS G. ARNOLD

Television commercials for impotence pills are ubiquitous in the United States. In one of the most inventive marketing campaigns of the last 20 years, large pharmaceutical firms rebranded impotence as "erectile dysfunction" (ED) and successfully marketed three blockbuster drugs: Viagra (sildenafil citrate) manufactured and marketed by Pfizer; Cialis (tadalafil) manufactured and marketed by Eli Lilly; and Levitra (vardenafil) manufactured by Bayer Healthcare and jointly marketed by Bayer Healthcare, GlaxoSmithKline, and Schering Plough/Merck (Schering-Plough merged with Merck in 2009). For the last 15 years Viagra alone has generated annual revenues of $1.5–2 billion ($26.5 billion total) for Pfizer. A primary means of marketing these drugs has been the use of television commercials. Since 2010 Viagra and Cialis have consistently been among the top pharmaceuticals brands advertised on television, with Cialis routinely being among the top three in annual commercial buys and Viagra among the top five to ten.

All ED advertisements are sexually themed. In one Viagra commercial the narrator says, "Remember that guy who used to be called 'Wild Thing'? The guy who wanted to spend the entire honeymoon indoors? Remember the one who couldn't resist a little mischief? Yeah, that guy. He's back." In the background a pair of devil horns rise from a man's head and the narrator describes the man as a "Wild Thing." In another Viagra commercial, a blonde woman with bare shoulders, lying on a bed says, "So guys, it's just you and your honey. The setting is perfect. But then erectile dysfunction happens again . . . Plenty of guys have this issue – not just getting an erection, but keeping it." In another ad a woman in a football jersey, laying on a bed, says "Viagra helps guys with ED get and keep an erection." All product claim ads for pharmaceuticals are required by federal regulations to indicate the potential side-effects of the drug. For ED drugs this includes the narrator stating that side-effects might include headache, flushing, upset stomach, abnormal vision, and "erections lasting more than four hours."

According to the *Wall Street Journal*, in one December alone, Viagra aired an ad around 9:00 p.m. during *Prancer*, a G-rated movie which is about a young girl who nurses one of Santa's reindeers back to health; a Levitra ad appeared during an afternoon showing of the family comedy *Pee-wee's Big Adventure*; and a Cialis advertisement was run during a showing of the holiday classic *Miracle on 34th Street*. ED commercials routinely appear during college and professional sports broadcasts. Parents have taken notice. Kelly Simmons, executive vice-president and chief creative officer at Tierney Communications in Philadelphia reported, "My 6-year-old daughter turned to me and said, 'What's a four-hour erection?' How do you explain it?" Dr. Ethan Weiss, a cardiologist at the University of San Francisco School of Medicine was watching a baseball game with his daughter when a Viagra commercial aired. "My 11 year old daughter just asked what the Viagra ad was about. Not sure how to respond." ED advertising has been criticized by the American Academy of Pediatricians which found that "Ads for ED drugs give children and teens inappropriate messages about sex and sexuality at a time when they are not being taught well in school sex education programs." The American Academy of Pediatricians recommended that ED ads be broadcast only after 10:00 p.m. The Families for ED Decency Advertising Act would have restricted ED advertising to between 10:00 p.m. and 6:00 a.m. In 2005 US representatives Jim Moran of Virginia and John J. Duncan Jr. of Tennessee introduced the Families for ED Decency Advertising Act (H.R. 1420) in the 109th Congress. The act would have restricted the hours during which erectile dysfunction advertising may be broadcast to between 10:00 p.m. and 6:00 a.m. Subsequently the Pharmaceutical Research and Manufacturers of America (PhRMA), the pharmaceutical industry's trade and lobbying association, introduced "Guiding Principles" for direct to consumer advertising and pledged to voluntarily limit ED and other adult themed advertisements to broadcast times where 90 percent of the audience is 18 or older. The CEOs and the Chief Compliance

Officers have gone so far as to certify, via PhRMA, that they are meeting the standard. As a result of this promise, H.R. 1420 was allowed to die in subcommittee after Representative Moran received a commitment from pharmaceutical company executives to meet this standard.

As it turns out, the industry never followed its own standard. Utilizing data from the AC Nielsen company, the same data marketing agencies use for selecting where to place commercials, academic researchers documented that for every single quarter over a ten-year period the ED advertising for all brands failed by a wide margin to meet the 90 percent adult standard. An "impression" is a single commercial view, so if a family of five is watching television together there would be five impressions of one commercial. During this time period there were well over 100 billion impressions of sexually explicit ED commercials seen by children. Even after the research was published and acknowledged by the companies and PhRMA in press releases, violation of the standard continued. The companies made no significant changes to the placement of the commercials and children continue to be routinely exposed to ED advertisements. There are no penalties or sanctions for violating the industry standards.

Discussion Questions

1. Do you agree with the critics of erectile dysfunction advertisements that children should not be routinely exposed to such advertisements? Why, or why not? Explain.

2. How would you assess the behavior of pharmaceutical firms discussed in this case? Explain.

3. Why do you think the pharmaceutical industry created "Guiding Principles" for direct-to-consumer advertising that it does not actually follow? Explain.

4. How does George Brenkert's analysis in "Marketing and the Vulnerable" apply to this case? Explain?

5. How does Denis Arnold's analysis in "The Ethics of Direct to Consumer Advertising" apply to this case? Explain.

This case is based on the following sources: Stuart Elliott, "Viagra and the Battle of the Awkward Ads," *The New York Times* (April 25, 2004).

Avery Johnson, "New Impotence Ads Draw Fire – Just Like the Old Ones," *Wall Street Journal* (February 16, 2007).

John LaMattina, "New Viagra TV Ad Should Be Dropped," *Forbes* (October 6, 2014).

Victor C. Strasburger, "Policy Statement: Children, Adolescents, and Advertising," *Pediatrics* 118 (2006): 2563–69.

Gilbert Fuld et al., "Policy Statement: Sexuality, Contraception, and the Media," *Pediatrics* 126 (2013): 576–82.

"Worldwide Revenue of Pfizer's Viagra from 2003 to 2017," *Statista* (2018). Retrieved from www.statista.com/statistics/264827/pfizers-worldwide-viagra-revenue-since-2003/.

Denis G. Arnold and James Oakley, "The Politics and Strategy of Industry Self-Regulation: The Pharmaceutical Industry's Principles for Ethical Direct-to-Consumer Advertising as a Deceptive Blocking Strategy," *Journal of Health Politics, Policy & Law* 38 (2013): 505–44.

Denis G. Arnold and James Oakley, "Self-Regulation in the Pharmaceutical Industry: The Exposure of Children and Adolescents to Erectile Dysfunction Commercials," *Journal of Health Politics, Policy & Law* (2018).

Case 4: Kraft Foods, Inc.: The Cost of Advertising on Children's Waistlines

PAULINE HWA, TIMOTHY HOUSMAN, AND JAMES S. O'ROURKE

The room fell silent as Dr. Ellen Wartella, Dean of the College of Communications at the University of Texas at Austin, gave Kraft executives her opinions on a presentation they had just made regarding Kraft and advertising to children. Wartella characterized Kraft's online marketing as "indefensible" and concluded that Kraft's claim that it was not advertising to children under the age of six was "at best disingenuous and at worst a downright lie."[1] The executives in the room were visibly shaken by her comments.

In late 2003, Kraft formed the Worldwide Health & Wellness Advisory Council, comprising ten nutritionists and media experts, including Wartella, to investigate allegations that Kraft had been knowingly advertising unhealthy foods and to help address the rise in obesity, among other

---

This case was prepared by Research Assistants Pauline Hwa and Timothy Housman under the direction of James S. O'Rourke, Concurrent Professor of Management, as the basis for class discussion rather than to illustrate either effective or ineffective handling of an administrative situation. Information was gathered from corporate as well as public sources. © 2006 Eugene D. Fanning Center for Business Communication.

health issues.[2] The pressure for Kraft to review its advertising policies came amidst increasing criticism from congressional panels, parent groups, and other concerned citizens, that food corporations, such as Kraft Foods and McDonald's Corporation, have been knowingly targeting young children (up to age 12) in their advertising campaigns. The concern surrounding childhood obesity stems from statistics showing a 200 percent increase in childhood obesity since the 1980s. Between the 1960s and the 1980s, the percentage of overweight children hovered around 6 percent, but in the last two decades, this rate has leapt to 16 percent.[3] Despite this, Kraft decided to keep marketing to children under 12. One Kraft executive admitted, "We didn't want to give up the power of marketing to kids."[4]

This "power" is villainizing the company, however. Currently, Kraft is a trusted brand, but that reputation is already slipping. According to the Reputation Quotient study conducted in 2005 by research firm Harris Interactive, Kraft is ranked in the 50th slot.[5] While this is a small drop from the 48th spot Kraft held the previous year, it is a far distance from the 8th position occupied by competitor General Mills. This survey is based on consumer perception of various factors, including a company's quality of products and services, social responsibility, and vision and leadership. Depending on what Kraft chooses to do about its food marketing issue, the company may rise higher in subsequent Reputation Quotient studies, or it may fall further down.

Kraft Foods is a company that values quality and safety in its products. One of Kraft's key strategies is to "build superior consumer brand value" through "great-tasting products, innovative packaging, consistent high quality, wide availability, helpful services and strong brand image."[6] With products in more than 99 percent of US households, Kraft certainly has earned the trust of its consumers.[7] With the recent feedback from the Health and Wellness Advisory Council and public concerns about childhood obesity due to aggressive food marketing, however, Kraft must take action before it loses consumers' loyalty and trust in its products.

Kraft Foods, Inc.

Kraft Foods, Inc., the largest food and beverage company in North America, has grown considerably from its humble beginnings in 1903. With only $65, a rented wagon, and a horse named Paddy, J. L. Kraft started the company by purchasing cheese from a wholesale market and reselling it to local merchants.[8] These cheeses were packaged with Kraft's name. A decade later, Kraft improved the cheese by processing the product, which prolonged its shelf life. The processed cheese became such a success that a patent for the "Process of Sterilizing Cheese and an Improved Product Produced by Such Process" was issued to Kraft in 1916.[9] Over the years, the company went on to create other new cheese products that are familiar to homes today including *Velveeta* and *Cheez Whiz*, as well as expanding beyond cheese to introduce salad dressings, packaged dinners, barbecue sauce, and other products.

Tobacco giant Philip Morris acquired General Foods Corporation in 1985 and then Kraft three years later for $12.9 billion.[10] Through the acquisition of these two major food companies, Philip Morris formed Kraft General Foods, which put products such as *Velveeta*, *Post* cereals, *Oscar Mayer*, and *Jell-O* pudding all under the same food division. Kraft General Foods further expanded its household reach by acquiring Nabisco, home of well-known brands including *Oreo* cookies, *Ritz* crackers, and *Planters* nuts in 2000. The next big step for Kraft occurred in 2001 when Philip Morris conducted an initial public offering of Kraft's shares (NYSE: KFT). The following year, Philip Morris changed its name to Altria Group. Altria Group was the parent company to Kraft Foods until it spun off Kraft in 2007.

Kraft's Troubles in Advertising

There are many reasons why Kraft should be concerned about further criticism of its advertising practices. As a leader in the food industry, Kraft is both large and very visible, and the company has experienced repeated controversy and criticism of its advertising campaigns over the years. A few recent issues include:

- Kraft's advertisement of *Post* cereal in *National Geographic Kids* was not focused on the food but rather on the premium of Postokens instead, which is a violation of the Children's Advertising Review Unit's Self-Regulatory Guidelines for Children's Advertising.[11]
- Kraft had previously announced its intention to reduce portion size and then later backed out of that commitment, saying that consumers wanted to choose their portion sizes for themselves.[12]
- Kraft pulled an *Oreo* commercial directed at teenagers that promoted a "slothlike" lifestyle because the company realized that such an ad would hurt its image and instead opted for promoting "a more active lifestyle."[13]

Obesity in the Courts: The McLawsuit

The food industry became visibly worried about food marketing and childhood obesity in 2002. It was then that

McDonald's Corporation faced a lawsuit, *Pelham v. McDonald's Corporation*, in which the company was charged with marketing food products that contribute to the rise of obesity in children and teenagers. Although the judge threw out the class-action lawsuit against McDonald's, he made it very clear that he supports the plaintiffs' position. He encouraged them to redraft and refile the suit with stronger evidence, and went so far as to provide advice on what to look for. One of his recommendations was to show how McDonald's advertising campaigns encouraged over-consumption by promoting its food products for "everyday" eating.[14]

McDonald's Corporation still stands behind their standards in marketing to children. According to David Green, Senior Vice-President of Marketing for McDonald's, even though 20 percent of McDonald's commercials are targeted at children, the company follows a strict set of guidelines. The Golden Arches Code, according to company spokesmen, "conforms with the major network Broadcasting Standards and the guidelines of the Children's Unit of the National Advertising Division Council of Better Business Bureaus Inc., as well as establishing additional standards applicable only to McDonald's advertising."[15] Green says that the Golden Arches Code "states that in our advertising we should never promote the sale of food items to children that might be too large for them to consume realistically at one sitting nor should children be depicted as coming to McDonald's on their own, as they must always be accompanied by an adult."

A month prior to *Pelham v. McDonald's Corporation*, Sam Hirsch, the attorney who filed the suit for the overweight children and teenagers, had filed another class-action suit against McDonald's and other leading fast-food establishments.[16] This suit was filed not only against McDonald's Corporation, but also Burger King, Kentucky Fried Chicken, and Wendy's. Observers speculated the driving force behind these two suits was the prospect of a large financial settlement. Hirsch remained adamant about his clients' intentions, saying "we are not looking to get rich from a large money settlement. We are proposing a fund that will educate children about the nutritional facts and contents of McDonald's food."[17] These suits intensified fears in the food industry of a future of "tobacco-like" litigation against restaurants and food manufacturers.[18]

In January 2005, the second US Circuit Court of Appeals reinstated claims that McDonald's falsely advertised the health benefits of its fast food, a violation of the New York Consumer Protection Act.[19] Unquestionably, the plaintiffs had the full attention of quick service restaurant operators and food manufacturers worldwide.

Studies Show . . .

Fewer Ads

In July 2005, the Federal Trade Commission (FTC) released its findings that children today watch fewer food commercials than they did almost three decades ago. Children today watch 13 food advertisements on television per day, a significant reduction from the 18 television commercials per day in 1977.[20] The FTC also reported that kids today are exposed to fewer ads for cereal, candy, and toys but more ads for restaurants and fast-food chains, other television shows, movies, video games, and DVDs. Wally Snyder, president of the American Advertising Federation, believed this study was proof that food marketing is not culpable for the rise of obesity in children, which he blamed on a "lack of exercise and moderation in the diet."

More Ads

A year later in 2004, the Kaiser Family Foundation released a study with contrary information, claiming "the number of ads children see on TV has doubled from 20,000 to 40,000 since the 1970s, and the majority of ads targeted to kids are for candy, cereal, and fast food."[21] The study suggested that this increase in food advertising was correlated to the rise in obesity in children aged 6 to 11. In 1963–70, only 4.2 percent of children in this age group were listed as overweight compared with 1999–2000, when the number spiked to 15.3 percent.

The Tie-Breaker

Perhaps because of the conflicting findings or because of rising concerns about food marketing to children and its effects, Congress requested a study of its own from the National Academy of Sciences, which was created by the federal government to advise on scientific issues.[22] In December 2005, The Institute of Medicine (IOM), a private, non-governmental division of the National Academy of Sciences, released the latest study on the subject, *Food Marketing to Children and Youth: Threat or Opportunity?* Based upon individual findings, the IOM committee responsible for the study came to the following five conclusions:[23]

Broad Conclusions

1. Along with many other intersecting factors, food and beverage marketing influences the diets and health prospects of children and youth.
2. Food and beverage marketing practices geared to children and youth are out of balance with healthful diets and contribute to an environment that puts their health at risk.

3. Food and beverage companies, restaurants, and marketers have underutilized potential to devote creativity and resources to develop and promote food, beverages, and meals that support healthful diets for children and youth.

4. Achieving healthful diets for children and youth will require sustained multisectoral and integrated efforts that include industry leadership and initiative.

5. Public-policy programs and incentives do not currently have the support or authority to address many of the current and emerging marketing practices that influence the diets of children and youth.

The study also suggested there was "strong evidence" that food marketing influences the preferences, purchase requests, and short-term consumption of children between the ages of 2 and 11. This information combined with the fact that a "preponderance of television food and beverage advertising relevant to children and youth promotes high-calorie and low-nutrient products, it can be concluded that television advertising influences children to prefer and request high-calorie and low-nutrient foods and beverages."[24] Wartella, who served not only on Kraft's advisory council but also as a member of the committee that produced the IOM study, said "We can't any more argue whether food advertising is related to children's diets. It is."[25]

The IOM's recommendations for the food industry included promoting and supporting healthier products and working with government, public health, and consumer goods "to establish and enforce the highest standards for the marketing" of food and beverage products to children.[26] In general, many food companies had already started programs to promote healthier products. The problem was with the latter recommendation in marketing standards. IOM believed this meant licensed characters should be "used only for the promotion of foods and beverages that support healthful diets for children and youth."[27] Most companies, Kraft included, were reluctant to give this up. Licensed characters were typically familiar faces to children. How does a company replace a spokesperson or promoter that already has the trust of the audience, is affordable, and will never get into any real-life trouble?

The Announcement

In January 2005, Kraft announced that it would stop advertising certain products to children under 12. These products include regular *Kool-Aid* beverages, *Oreo* and *Chips Ahoy* cookies, several *Post* children's cereals, and some varieties of its *Lunchables* lunch packages.[28] These favorites will still be found in stores, but Kraft said it will no longer be targeting children with television, radio, and print ads for these products. The initial cost of implementing these new guidelines included an estimated $75 million in lost profits, though this figure continued to change several times.[29] While this estimate may seem high, Michael Mudd, a member of Kraft's obesity strategy team said, "If the tobacco industry could go back 20 or 30 years, reform their marketing, disarm their critics, and sacrifice a couple of hundred million in profits, knowing what they know today, don't you think they'd take that deal in a heartbeat?"[30] Kraft, learning the lessons of Philip Morris, was eager for the deal.

Shortly after Kraft made its announcement, however, the company joined competitors General Mills and Kellogg to form a lobbying group to keep the government from regulating food marketing to children. The group's mission statement states its belief that "there is not a correlation between advertising trends and recent childhood obesity."[31] General Mills had always argued for this point. In fact, instead of stopping ads to children, Tom Forsythe, General Mills Vice-President, announced that the company "launched a vigorous defense of cereal," to support its health benefits.[32] The company also decided to promote "balanced moderation and exercise," believing that such lifestyle choices affect obesity as much as food selection.[33] Thus, General Mills's participation in this group was expected, but for Kraft, joining this group appeared to be a hypocritical move. David S. Johnson, Kraft's Chief of North America, defended the action, "We believe self-regulation of the marketing of food products can and does work, and we are collaborating with the industry to strengthen efforts in this area."[34]

Conclusion

Since the announcement, Kraft has still struggled with child advertising and obesity issues. Margo G. Wootan, Director of Nutrition for the Center for Science in the Public Interest, has called Kraft's new marketing plan only "a really good step forward."[35] The problem is that there will always be critics who will demand for more. For instance, although Kraft has taken a huge leap in minimizing television, radio, and print ads, the company has yet to act on Wartella's criticism for its online advertising.

Kraft has spent a great deal of time to respond to critics and potential threats of government regulation. What Kraft really needs at this point is to put the focus back on its customers and communicate with them. The question is how to go about doing this without appearing to go back on its promises of not saturating the market with advertisements.

Notes

1. Sarah Ellison, "Why Kraft Decided to Ban Some Food Ads to Children," *Wall Street Journal* (November 1, 2005).
2. http://164.109.46.215/newsroom/09032003.html.
3. www.childstats.gov/americaschildren/index.asp.
4. Ellison, "Why Kraft Decided to Ban Some Food Ads to Children."
5. www.foodprocessing.com/industrynews/2006/018.html.
6. http://kraft.com/profile/company_strategies.html.
7. www.altria.com/about_altria/01_00_01_kraftfoods.asp.
8. http://kraft.com/profile/factsheet.html.
9. http://kraft.com/100/founders/JLKraft.html.
10. www.altria.com/about_altria/1_2_5_1 altriastory.asp.
11. www.caru.org/news/2004/kraft.asp.
12. Patricia Callahan and Delroy Alexan, "As Fat Fears Grow, Oreo Tries a New Twist," *Chicago Tribune* (August 22, 2005).
13. Ibid.
14. Benjamin Weiser, "Your Honor, We Call Our Next Witness: McFrankenstein," *The New York Times* (January 26, 2003).
15. "McLibel" Case–Green, David B., Witness Statement, www.mcspotlight.org/people/witnesses/advertising/green.html.
16. Summons, http://news.findlaw.com/cnn/docs/mcdonalds/barbermcds72302cmp.pdf.
17. Jonathan Wald, "McDonald's Obestiy Suit Tossed," *CNNmoney.com* (February 17, 2003), http://money.cnn.com/2003/01/22/news/companies/mcdonalds/.
18. Reuters article: http://onenews.nzoom.com/onenews_detail/0,1227,218579-1-6,00.html.
19. www.law.com/jsp/article.jsp?id=1106573726371.
20. Caroline E. Mayer, "TV Feeds Kids Fewer Food Ads, FTC Staff Study Finds," *Washington Post* (July 15, 2005).
21. "Ads Rapped in Child Obesity Fight," www.cbsnews.com/stories/2004/02/24/health/main601894.shtml.
22. www.nationalacademies.org/hmd/~/media/Files/Report%20Files/2005/Food-Marketing-to-Children-and-Youth-Threat-or-Opportunity/KFMOverviewfinal2906.pdf.
23. Institute of Medicine, *Food Marketing to Children and Youth: Threat or Opportunity?* 2006, Box 7-1, p. 317.
24. Ibid., p. 322.
25. Sarah Ellison and Janet Adamy, "Panel Faults Food Packaging for Kid Obesity," *Wall Street Journal* (December 7, 2005).
26. Institute of Medicine, *Food Marketing to Children and Youth*, pp. 325–26.
27. Ibid., p. 326.
28. "Kraft to Curb Some Snack Food Advertising," *Associated Press* (January 12, 2005), http://msnbc.msn.com/id/6817344/.
29. Ellison, "Why Kraft Decided to Ban Some Food Ads to Children."
30. Ibid.
31. Callahan and Alexan, "As Fat Fears Grow, Oreo Tries a New Twist."
32. Ellison and Adamy, "Panel Faults Food Packaging for Kid Obesity."
33. Sarah Ellison, "Divided, Companies Fight for Right to Plug Kids' Food," *Wall Street Journal* (January 26, 2005).
34. Callahan and Alexan, "As Fat Fears Grow, Oreo Tries a New Twist."
35. Caroline E. Mayer, "Kraft to Curb Snack-Food Advertising," *Washington Post* (January 12, 2005).

Discussion Questions

1. Who are the stakeholders in this case? What are the ethical issues in this case, and how do they relate to each stakeholder group? Explain.
2. What should Kraft do to maintain the declining trust of consumers? Explain.
3. Should the public believe in Kraft's commitment to limit food marketing to children? Why, or why not? Explain.
4. What are Kraft's options concerning its marketing tactics? Make a list of the main options. Next, identify the options that you think are ethically appropriate taking into account the interests of the different stakeholders. Explain your reasons of selecting these options.

Case 5: Let Them Drink Soda: Coca-Cola's Effort to Influence Public Health Research

ROXANNE ROSS AND DENIS G. ARNOLD

A 16 ounce coke has 52 grams (equivalent to a quarter cup or 13 teaspoons) of sugar and 201 calories. Approximately one in four Americans drink over 200 calories a day from sugar sweetened soda. The predominant source of calories in teen diets are sugary beverages, averaging at 226 calories per day. These calories quickly add up. For example, if a person goes over their needed daily calories by a single 16 ounce coke each day, he or she would gain

© 2017 Denis G. Arnold.

approximately 20 pounds a year or about an extra pound every 17 days. Women should consume no more than 25 grams (6 teaspoons) of added sugar a day, and men should consume no more than 36 grams (9 teaspoons). That means for a woman who drinks a 16 ounce coke each day, she consumes over double the recommended maximum amount of sugar. The health consequences of excess consumption of added sugars are widely known and supported by empirical evidence. Unlike sugars consumed in fruit and dairy, excess consumption of any form of added sugar such as corn syrup, cane sugar, or even honey, are linked with health problems such as obesity, liver disease, type 2 diabetes, heart disease, and gout. Each year, $190 billion is spent in the United States alone treating obesity related health conditions. If American obesity related healthcare were its own company, it would be the 13th largest, based on revenue, in the world. The amount spent in the United States on obesity related treatments is equivalent to the GDP of Greece.

Despite the well-established health consequences of excess sugar consumption, one exercise scientist, Dr. Steven Blair, famously announced "there's virtually no compelling evidence" that consumption of sugary drinks and junk foods is the cause of the obesity epidemic. Rather, Dr. Blair says that an inactive lifestyle should be targeted to fix the obesity problem and that cutting calories hasn't been a successful way to fix obesity. Dr. Blair made this statement in a promotional video for a non-profit research group called Global Energy Balance Network. Soda fans might have rejoiced if it wasn't later discovered that the non-profit organization received in total about $4 million in funding from the beverage giant, Coca-Cola. In 2008, Coca-Cola gave several health scientists $1.5 million each to start the Global Energy Balance Network.

Recently, soda consumption is in decline. Over the last 20 years, soda consumption fell by over 25 percent. Schools are banning soda and several cities flirted with imposing a soda tax. Coca-Cola and other soda companies are fighting back with lobbying, marketing tactics, and large donations to health organization (e.g., the American Beverage Association donated $10 million to the Children's Hospital in Philadelphia). Critics charge that Coca-Cola's sponsorship of the Global Energy Balance Network was a thinly veiled effort to regain consumer interest in soda through pro-soda rhetoric grounded in poor science.

Founders of the Global Energy Balance Network, Dr. Steven Blair and Dr. James Hill, made no mention of their corporate sponsorship until another researcher, Dr. Yoni Freedhoff, asked them to disclose their funding source. Only after Dr. Freedhoff's request did the organization disclose that Coca-Cola was a major sponsor. Dr. Hill responded by saying their objective as an organization was independent of its funders. The Global Energy Balance Network later disbanded, and some of the funds were returned to Coca-Cola. The University of Colorado housed Dr. Hill and returned nearly $1 million to Coca-Cola. The University of South Carolina housed Dr. Blair and has not returned any money to the soda company.

The revelation of the relationship between Coca-Cola and the non-profit resulted in significant criticism from the scientific community and public health experts. Dr. Marion Nestle, professor of public health at New York University, commented, "The Global Energy Balance Network is nothing but a front group for Coca-Cola. Coca-Cola's agenda here is clear: Get these researchers to confuse the science and deflect attention from dietary intake." Dr. Barry Popkin, professor of global nutrition at the University of North Carolina at Chapel Hill, likened the strategy to tactics used by the tobacco industry. "Essentially, Coke is following the strategy used by the tobacco industry as they tried to create doubt among the general public and also politicians. It was very effective in the fights to regulate cigarettes and we have learned from this that it is essential to address these attempts and uncover what they are very rapidly."

Discussion Questions

1. Why do you believe Coca-Cola provided $4 million in funding to the Global Energy Balance Network? Explain.

2. How would you assess Coca-Cola's actions from an ethical perspective? Explain.

3. How does the analysis by Kelly Brownell and Kenneth Warner, in their article "The Perils of Ignoring History," apply to this case? Which points of their analysis are most salient and why? Explain.

4. Doesn't Coca-Cola have a right to provide funds to whomever it likes? Are Coca-Cola's critics being unfair to the company? Why, or why not? Explain.

This case was written for classroom discussion and is based on the following sources: "Added Sugars," *American Heart Association* (February 1, 2017). Retrieved July 17, 2017 from www.heart.org/HEARTORG/HealthyLiving/HealthyEating/Nutrition/Added-Sugars_UCM_305858_Article.jsp.

A. O'Connor, "Coca-Cola Funds Scientists Who Shift Blame for Obesity Away from Bad Diets" (August 9, 2015). Retrieved July 20, 2017 from https://well.blogs.nytimes.com/2015/08/09/coca-cola-funds-scientists-who-shift-blame-for-obesity-away-from-bad-diets/.

M. Sanger-Katz, "The Decline of 'Big Soda,'" *The New York Times* (October 2, 2015). Retrieved from www.nytimes.com/2015/10/04/upshot/soda-industry-struggles-as-consumer-tastes-change.html.

"Sugary Drinks and Obesity Fact Sheet" (September 18, 2012). Retrieved July 20, 2017 from www.hsph.harvard.edu/nutritionsource/sugary-drinks-fact-sheet/.

J. Walters, "Nutrition Experts Alarmed by Nonprofit Downplaying Role of Junk Food in Obesity," *The Guardian* (August 11, 2015). Retrieved from www.theguardian.com/society/2015/aug/11/obesity-junk-food-exercise-global-energy-balance-network-coca-cola.

Case 6: Merck & Company: The Vioxx Recall

MIKE HANAHOE, MIKE GOOD, JAKE KULZER, TERRY GRIFFITH, STEVE MANLOVE, AND DENIS G. ARNOLD

On the afternoon of September 23, 2004, Raymond V. Gilmartin, president, chairman, and chief executive officer of Merck and Co., Inc. sat in his office intently focused on reviewing the firm's strategic direction. Gilmartin had guided Merck and Co. through unprecedented growth within the pharmaceutical industry. During the 1990s Merck launched six blockbuster drugs, which drove the increased revenue, stock, and value of the company. Merck had been the darling of Wall Street and earned an irreproachable ethical reputation in a risky and complex market.

However, the company had recently lost its market leadership position and fallen to number six within the industry. Five patents had recently expired, significantly impacting its revenue stream. To complicate matters, Merck had to cancel development of two important research and initiatives regarding depression and diabetes. The depression drug failed a critical clinical trial, and the diabetes drug increased the risk of cancer when tested in laboratory animals. Merck had been positioning the two drugs as the next blockbusters to propel Merck back into a leadership position. The product pipeline, which was once continuously stocked, was not meeting Gilmartin's expectations.[1] However, Merck had recently dedicated its newest research facility near Harvard Medical School. It would facilitate research for the treatment of Alzheimer's disease, cancer, and obesity. One of Merck's main revenue generating drugs was Vioxx (rofecoxib), a drug marketed to the general public for pain relief. This single drug brought in revenues of $2.5 billion a year.

What Gilmartin did not anticipate was the news Peter Kim, Merck's President of Research Laboratories, would deliver that afternoon. Kim called to inform Gilmartin that outside investigators had recommended Merck discontinue the APPROVe (Adenomatous Polyp Prevention on Vioxx) study. APPROVe was a long-term study on the drug Vioxx's (rofecoxib) efficacy in reducing the size and frequency of colon polyps. In parallel Merck had decided to utilize the study to determine whether Vioxx produced increased cardiovascular risk to its users. There were strong theoretical reasons for thinking it would, and academic medical doctors researching the issue had found that this was the case. However, Merck had vehemently defended the drug. The results of the APPROVe study demonstrated that Vioxx increased risk of heart attack for patients who had regularly used the prescription for greater than 18 months.

The results of the APPROVe study added credence to the external researchers' accusations and required Merck to make some critical decisions. Merck had spent nearly $500 million on marketing Vioxx to US consumers as a general pain relief and anti-inflammation drug. The APPROVe study was being used to determine if it was effective for another purpose. Gilmartin now had to determine the appropriate response. Based on US Food and Drug Administration (FDA) regulations, Merck was under no obligation to withdraw the product from the market or conduct a full-scale recall. Updating the FDA on the new clinical findings and amending the prescription warning criteria was all that was required. Gilmartin stated that his commitment was "to make a decision about Vioxx totally in the interest of the patients' safety."[2]

On September 30, 2004, Gilmartin informed the FDA of Merck's intention to recall Vioxx from the market. Withdrawing the drug would have unprecedented financial and legal ramifications. Critics alleged that the drug should never have been widely marketed to the general public in the first place, since the drug was no better for average patients

This case was prepared for educational purposes by Mike Hanahoe, Mike Good, Jake Kulzer, Terry Griffith, and Steve Manlove under the supervision of Denis Arnold © 2007.

than over-the-counter pain relievers like aspirin, but was far more expensive and had serious side-effects resulting in heart attacks and premature deaths for tens of thousands of patients.

The Vioxx Story

In 1994 Merck scientists discovered Vioxx, one of a new class of painkillers called COX-2 inhibitors. COX-2 inhibitors reduce pain and inflammation without causing ulcers and gastrointestinal bleeding, side-effects often seen from nonsteroidal anti-inflammatory drugs (NSAIDs), such as ibuprofen (Advil). These older painkillers such as aspirin and Aleve, known generically as naproxen, block two enzymes – COX-1 and COX-2 – that are involved in inflammation and pain. Blocking COX-1 can damage the stomach and intestines, but it also may prevent blood clots. Vioxx and another drug, Pfizer Inc.'s Celebrex, were designed to block only COX-2.

From the earliest stages, companies developing COX-2 inhibitors faced a dilemma. The drugs seemed to offer clear benefits to arthritis and other pain sufferers, who couldn't stand the stomach damage of aspirin, naproxen, or ibuprofen, but that was a relatively small market. The real bonanza lay with the general mass of pain patients, who were using cheap and effective over-the-counter pain relievers.[3] However, COX-2 inhibitors did not work better than those pain relievers, were much more expensive, and required a prescription. In addition, early studies indicated that they increased the risk of adverse cardiovascular events such as heart attacks.

Merck was facing the loss of patent protection on its largest revenue-producing drugs over the next five years and needed a new blockbuster. Merck felt that it would be difficult to penetrate the pain management market if patients did not receive a cardiovascular benefit provided by COX-1 inhibitors. Merck underwent trials attempting to prove that there was a clear benefit to the stomach without increased risk to the heart. Study participants were not able to take aspirin, and Merck researchers were concerned that "there is a substantial chance that significantly higher rates" of heart problems in the Vioxx control group. This concern was voiced in early 1997 by a Merck official who said that "thrombotic events" will "kill [the] drug."[4]

By 1998 Merck had completed the multiphase development and research for Vioxx. They submitted a New Drug Application (NDA) for Vioxx to the FDA. The mood at Merck was upbeat. Recent drug releases had propelled Merck's stock to new highs. With the successful release of Vioxx, Merck intended to take a leadership position in the long-term anti-inflammatory drug market. However, in the autumn of 1998, a group of University of Pennsylvania researchers discovered that COX-2 inhibitors interfere with enzymes thought to play a key role in preventing cardiovascular disease. Merck vehemently opposed the study and said that it found the evidence to be inconclusive.[5] That year Merck's net income was $5.24 billion, making them the number one pharmaceutical company in the world.

During the following year there were three important events for Merck: The first was the initiation of the Vioxx Gastrointestinal Outcomes Research (VIGOR) trial, the purpose of which was to show that Vioxx posed less gastrointestinal risk than older NSAIDs. In the study patients were given high doses of Vioxx and not allowed to take aspirin. It excluded patients at risk for heart problems. The second event occurred in May 1999. The FDA approved Vioxx for marketing. It took only six months of review, whereas the typical drug review periods for drugs from other pharmaceutical companies typically averaged two years. This quick turnaround is alleged to be the result of a "cozy" relationship between Merck and the FDA's Center for Drug Evaluation and Research (CDER) and the payment of a large fee. Merck touted its release as "the biggest, fastest, and best launch ever." Merck marketed Vioxx directly to consumers with tremendous success. The third was the impending retirement of Dr. Edward Scolnick, head of Merck Research Laboratories. Scolnick was leaving just as Merck was facing several looming drug patent expirations. Its drug development pipeline was dwindling, and Merck found itself banking on only a small number of potential new drug releases – the most significant of which was Vioxx.

In February 2000, the Merck-sponsored APPROVe trial was initiated. As noted above, the purpose of the study was to show whether the use of Vioxx would reduce colon polyps. If successful, Merck could request FDA approval to market the drug for this purpose. This study was unique in that it was the first true controlled study comparing Vioxx with a placebo instead of another drug. In March, the VIGOR results were published internally. The study showed Vioxx patients suffered fewer stomach problems, but more blood clot problems. The heart attack rate was five times higher than the placebo. This significant disparity caused Scolnick to write an internal email confirming cardiovascular events "are clearly there." Dr. Scolnick went on to say that he wanted more data before results were presented publicly. The research chief recalled that some of his greatest drugs had side-effects. He wrote, "We have a great drug, but just like angioedema with Vasotec, seizures with Primaxin, and myopathy with Mevacor, there is always a hazard. The class will do well and so will we."[6]

In a news release later in March, no mention of the cardiovascular events was included. Merck maintained that the VIGOR results were consistent with expectations. A month later another news release touted "No difference in the incidence of cardiovascular events" between Vioxx and older painkillers. The *New England Journal of Medicine* published the VIGOR study results in November of the same year. The article was authored by academic researchers, some of whom received funding from Merck. The paper discussed Vioxx's benefits to the digestive system and the cardiac problems. In addition, the paper maintained that patients who were not at high risk for heart problems did not show an increase in heart problems.

The pressures of the dwindling drug pipeline were taking their toll on Dr. Scolnick, however. Several potential "inside" successors had left the company, complaining of an "emperor's new clothes" mentality that was developing in Scolnick's wake. Despite these problems, Merck's net income was up $930 million to $6.82 billion, and their stock was selling at $93.63 a share, up 38 percent from the previous year. This year would prove to be Merck's high mark in both market share and stock price. At year-end, Peter Kim joined Merck as head of its internal research operations.

By early 2001 the VIGOR results caused the debate to shift to whether the drug was fundamentally safe. In February, an advisory committee recommended that the FDA require a label warning of the possible link to cardiovascular problems. Merck ignored the recommendation, approaching the same committee later that month in order to convince them to allow Merck to drop an unrelated digestive tract warning.[7] In the end, a compromise was reached with the warning label showing good news about fewer stomach problems and bad news about possibly more heart attacks and strokes. The FDA warned Merck to stop misleading doctors about Vioxx's effect on the cardiovascular system, requiring them to send doctors a letter "to correct false or misleading impressions and information" about Vioxx's effect on the cardiovascular system.[8]

By year-end Merck's net income was $7.28 billion. Expiring patents, as well as overall market conditions were blamed for a decline in the stock price. The impact of the Vioxx concerns had yet to reach Wall Street or the general population. In April 2002, Merck was spending more than $100 million a year in direct-to-consumer advertising, pitching Vioxx not only to the small percentage of the US population that might benefit from the drug, but to the entire population as a safe pain reliever. This investment in television and print advertising was successfully sustaining Vioxx's "blockbuster" status. Merck went on the offensive, taking on the critics of Vioxx's safety rather than warning consumers about the safety problems.

Criticisms Mount

One of the first critics to go public was Dr. Gurkirpal Singh from Stanford University. A prominent COX-2 researcher, he gave lectures sponsored by Merck and said he repeatedly asked Merck for more safety data. When the company refused his request, Dr. Singh added a portion to his presentation depicting a man hiding under a blanket. This was aimed to represent missing safety data. Merck cancelled several lectures by Dr. Singh. Merck executive Dr. Louis Sherwood called Dr. James Fries, who was Dr. Singh's boss at Stanford Medical School, at home on a Saturday. Sherwood told Fries that Dr. Singh was "irresponsibly anti-Merck and anti-Vioxx." He suggested that if this continued, there would be consequences for Dr. Singh, Dr. Fries and Stanford. The veiled threat was to cut off research funding to Stanford's research programs. A similar threat was made to Dr. M. Thomas Stillman of the University of Minnesota. When he discussed data on high blood pressure and swelling as a result of Vioxx in his lectures, he was fired from the Merck-sponsored lecture program. Sherwood made similar calls to medical school officials at six other universities where faculty were critical of Vioxx, including Dr. Stillman's boss the University of Minnesota and to Harvard's teaching hospital. When news of the threats was brought to the attention of CEO Gilmartin, he responded that Merck had a "deep and abiding commitment to the highest ethical standards in all our dealings with physicians and other healthcare providers."

At the end of 2002, Edward Scolnick retired as President, Merck Research Laboratories. As planned, Peter Kim was named his successor. Merck had failed to launch any significant new drugs, and patents continued to expire on their existing products. Merck's net income was down $130 million. In 2003, Merck suspended research on four costly Phase III drug trials. By year-end, Merck's net income was $6.83 billion (down $320 million) and their stock was selling at $46.20, down 18 percent from the previous year.

The FDA approved Vioxx for the treatment of juvenile rheumatoid arthritis in August of 2004. Since this indication involves using the product for children, Vioxx was put through a particularly rigorous review. On August 25, 2004, an FDA researcher presented the results of a data analysis of 1.4 million patients, which concluded that

Vioxx users were more likely to suffer a heart attack than those taking Celebrex or older NSAIDs. Though the evidence was now mounting, Merck relentlessly stuck to its guns and issued a news release strongly disagreeing with the FDA study. "Merck stands behind the efficacy, overall safety and cardiovascular safety of Vioxx."

Resolution

Merck pulled Vioxx from the market on September 30, 2004. By this time, Merck had spent more than $500 million on direct-to-consumer advertising of Vioxx to the general public. Twenty million Americans had taken the drug and it was making as much as $2.5 billion a year for Merck. Merck lost $33 billion in market capitalization (33 percent of its total) over the next several days. On December 7, 2004, Merck's stock was selling at $27.89 a share, down 60 percent since the first of the year.

Dr. David Graham, Associate Director for Science and Medicine in FDA's Office of Drug Safety, published research in a prestigious medical journal documenting that Vioxx caused approximately 140,000 cases of heart disease in the United States, and at least 56,000 premature deaths. In testimony before Congress he stated that "Vioxx is a terrible tragedy and a profound regulatory failure ... FDA and its Center for Drug Evaluation and Research [CDER] are broken." CDER "views the pharmaceutical industry it is supposed to regulate as its client, over values the benefits of the drugs it approves and seriously under values, disregards and disrespects drug safety."[9] Merck settled lawsuits by 47,000 groups of plaintiffs for $4.85 billion. In a settlement with the US Department of Justice, Merck agreed to pay $950 million and plead guilty to a criminal offense. Tony West, Assistant Attorney General for the Civil Division of the Department of Justice, stated "As this plea agreement and civil settlement make clear, we will not hesitate to pursue those who skirt the proper drug approval process and make misleading statements about the safety and efficacy of their products."[10]

Notes

1. John Simons, "Will Merck Survive Vioxx?" *Fortune* (November 1, 2004).
2. Ibid.
3. Anna Wilde Mathews and Barbara Martinez, "Warning Signs: Merck Knew Vioxx Dangers at Early Stage," *Wall Street Journal* (November 1, 2004).
4. Ibid.
5. Simon, "Will Merck Survive Vioxx?"
6. Anna Wilde Mathews and Barbara Martinez, "Warning Signs: E-mails Suggest Merck Knew Vioxx's Dangers at Early Stage," *Wall Street Journal* (November 1, 2004).
7. Rita Rubin, "How Did Vioxx Debacle Happen?" *USA Today* (October 12, 2004).
8. Ibid.
9. D. J. Graham, D. Campen et al., "Risk of Acute Myocardial Infarction and Sudden Cardiac Death in Patients Treated with Cyclo-Oxygenase 2 Selective and Non-Selective Non-Steroidal Anti-Inflammatory Drugs: Nested Case-Control Study," *The Lancet* 365 (2005): 475–81; United States Senate Finance Committee, Testimony of David J. Graham, MD, MPH, November 18, 2004.
10. Eric Platt, "Merck to Pay Nearly $1 Billion to Settle Viox Probe," *Business Insider* (November 22, 2011). Retrieved from www.businessinsider.com/merck-to-pay-nearly-1-billion-to-settle-vioxx-probe-2011-11.

Discussion Questions

1. What, if anything, was ethically wrong about Merck's marketing of Vioxx? Explain.

2. Should a pharmaceutical company control the information physicians disclose about their products when those physicians are hired as consultants? Why, or why not? Explain.

3. Merck spent $500 million dollars advertising Vioxx to the general public before the company pulled the drug off the market because of adverse health outcomes. Should pharmaceutical companies market prescription drugs directly to consumers? Why, or why not? Explain.

4. The US Congress has considered legislation that would ban direct-to-consumer advertising on new classes of drugs until their safety can be better assessed and doctors have had an opportunity to learn about the new drug. This law would have prevented Merck from marketing Vioxx to consumers for one or more years after it was introduced. Proponents argue that this policy will promote patient welfare, whereas critics argue that it unjustly limits free speech. Do you support such legislation? Why, or why not? Explain.

Case 7: Pfizer: Repeat Offender

LAKEISHA GILES, SUSAN SWAN, AND SHANNAN WOOTEN

Introduction

Pfizer, Inc., founded in 1849 by Charles Pfizer and Charles Erhart, is "the world's largest research-based biopharmaceutical company, which discovers, develops, manufactures, and markets prescription medicines for humans and animals" (Pfizer.com). The company, based in New York City, is ranked number two for 2010 in pharmaceutical sales in the world by Fortune 500 behind only Johnson & Johnson. Overall, the company is ranked number 40 overall on the Fortune 500. Pfizer's values state that it is committed to "upholding the highest ethical standards in everything from research and development to sales and marketing" (www.pfizer.com/about/).

Drug approval for the pharmaceutical industry is strictly regulated by the Center for Drug Evaluation and Research (CDER), which is part of the US Food and Drug Administration (FDA). The CDER "evaluates new drugs before they can be sold" and ensures that the drugs "work correctly and that their health benefits outweigh their known risks" (FDA.gov). The entire pharmaceutical industry has been heavily scrutinized in recent years for marketing practices, paying kick-backs to doctors, and questionable clinical trials. In fact, seven of the world's top drug companies "have paid a total of $7 billion in fines and penalties" since 2004.[1] At the forefront of the controversy is Pfizer, which has been repeatedly charged with violations of US law in marketing its products.

Off-Label Marketing of Neurontin

In spite of Pfizer's commitment to uphold high ethical standards in every area of the business, they have encountered controversy, lawsuits, and criminal charges repeatedly in recent years. In 2002, Pfizer subsidiary Pharmacia & Upjohn Company LLC pleaded guilty to illegally marketing the drug Genotropin for unapproved or off-label uses. This instance was self-reported by Pfizer and resulted in a $34.7 million fine. The illegal marketing is alleged to have taken place before Pfizer's acquisition of Pharmacia. This case did not receive much attention in the news media.

In 2000, Pfizer acquired Warner-Lambert including the Parke-Davis division which manufactured Neurontin. Prior to the acquisition the FDA had approved Neurontin to be used only as an adjunctive epileptic drug. The FDA's approval specified that the only approved use of the drug was as an add-on drug in the event the primary anti-epileptic medication was not effective. Although patents were filed claiming Neurontin could be used in the treatment of other disorders including mania and bipolar disease, no New Drug Application (NDA) was ever filed with the FDA for approval for these additional uses. Near the time that the patent for Neurontin was to expire, Parke-Davis/Warner-Lambert was facing substantial costs to conduct studies necessary to have the drug approved for other uses. The company knew that they alone would bear the brunt of this added cost while generic competitors would soon be able to reap the benefits of their investment.

Rather than spend the money for additional studies, the decision was made to focus on heavily marketing Neurontin through a publication strategy, which marketed the drug for off-label uses. Parke-Davis/Warner-Lambert took advantage of a small loophole in FDA regulations that allowed them to distribute articles written by independent third parties that described the off-label benefits of Neurontin. Since no such independent articles existed Parke-Davis hired writers to create the articles and specialists to become the ghost writers of the articles which would be published in medical journals. Additionally, Parke-Davis paid physicians to promote Neurontin for off-label uses by recommending its use and for ordering the prescriptions themselves. Parke-Davis used various methods to pay the doctors including hiring them as consultants and paying them to attend conferences about the off-label uses of Neurontin (FDA.gov). Parke-Davis also paid physicians to conduct studies where they prescribed patients Neurontin in higher doses than approved by the FDA all to prove that higher doses were safe and effective. The studies were never deemed of scientific value nor were the results presented to the FDA.

Soon after the acquisition of Warner-Lambert and its Parke-Davis division, a class-action suit was filed in US District Court against Pfizer alleging the off-label marketing of Neurontin for higher doses and uses other than those approved by the FDA. This suit was brought on as a whistleblower lawsuit filed by a former Parke-Davis employee. In 2004, Warner-Lambert pleaded guilty to two felony

This case was written by LaKeisha Giles, Susan Swan, and Shannan Wooten for the purposes of classroom discussion and is reprinted by permission. © Denis G. Arnold, 2011.

counts of marketing a drug for uses unapproved by the FDA. As a result of the agreement Pfizer paid $430 million in criminal fines and civil penalties and assured prosecutors that they would no longer promote drugs for unapproved uses. The criminal fines of $430 million paid due to off-label marketing of Neurontin were minor in comparison to the revenues generated by the medication. In 2003 and 2004 the gross revenue from the sale of this drug exceed $2.7 billion each year. Pfizer lost exclusivity on the medication in 2005 but still generated greater than $400 million in sales each year through 2007 and $387 million in 2008. It was later discovered that "before the ink was dry on their plea" Pfizer sales representatives were already involved in off-label marketing with four other drugs: Bextra, Geodon, Zyvox, and Lyrica.[2]

Off-Label Marketing of Bextra

Although the troubles for Pfizer began in 2002 with lawsuits stemming from off-label marketing of Neurontin, the lawsuit that thrust them unwillingly into the spotlight involved Bextra and did not begin until 2006. The looming lawsuits were foreshadowed by similar lawsuits filed against their competitor, Merck & Co, which manufactured Vioxx. Vioxx is a non-steroidal anti-inflammatory drug (NSAID) that was withdrawn in 2004 due to safety concerns. The drug, meant for treating patients with osteoarthritis and rheumatoid arthritis, was withdrawn due to concerns of increased risk of heart attack and stroke. Merck was accused of marketing the drug for uses that were not approved by the Food and Drug Administration. David Graham, an FDA employee, stated that "Vioxx killed some 60,000 patients – as many people as died in the Vietnam War."[3]

Pfizer's drug Bextra was the main competitor of Vioxx; however, Pfizer did not pull Bextra from the market until April of 2005 (seven months after the removal of Vioxx) and not until the FDA forced them to do so. In 2001 the FDA approved an NDA for Bextra (valdecoxib) for the treatment of osteo- and rheumatoid arthritis and Primary dysmenorrhea (extremely painful menstrual cramps), but denied it for treatment of acute pain. It was deemed "not safe for patients at high risk of heart attacks and strokes."[4] In fact, clinical trials had proven that Bextra could cause heart damage. The drug was also found to have a connection "with a rare skin condition" called Stevens–Johnson syndrome.[5] Despite this, Pfizer illegally marketed the drug for the treatment of all types of pain, which critics believed put the lives of many patients at risk. Once the FDA approves drugs, doctors are allowed to prescribe them for any use. However, the actual maker of the drug can't legally market them for anything other than approved uses.

Felony charges against Pfizer stemmed from a violation of the Food, Drug and Cosmetic Act for misbranding Bextra with the intent to defraud or mislead. Under this act, companies must specify the intended uses of a product to the FDA when it fills out its NDA. Once the FDA approves the drug the law prohibits the drug from being marketed or promoted for any use outside of those approved by the FDA. From 2002 through April 2005, Pfizer knowingly used both false and misleading claims to promote Bextra for unapproved uses and for dosages above the approved level. First, the company's marketing team created sales materials to promote Bextra for unapproved uses, such as surgical pain. "Market research was commissioned to test the sales materials" and Pfizer allowed the promotion of Bextra for the unapproved purposes to continue.[6] Pfizer's marketing team produced promotional material that illegally stated that one intended use of Bextra was for acute pain. The Pfizer sales team marketed Bextra to hospitals for the treatment of acute pain but did not explain the increased risk of heart damage. The doctors were told that the risks were the same as those of sugar pills.[7]

Secondly, the sales representatives were encouraged and allowed to promote Bextra directly to physicians for unapproved uses and dosages. Furthermore, so-called advisory boards, consultant meetings, and other forums and remuneration, were used to promote Bextra to medical prescribers for unapproved uses and dosages and with false and misleading claims to safety and efficacy.[8] One way this was done was by sending them on trips to lavish resorts for consultant meetings. Pfizer paid more than $5 million to physicians to entice them to come to seminars at resorts. Finally, Pfizer caused false claims to be submitted to government healthcare programs for uses that were not medically accepted and therefore not covered by the government programs such as Medicaid and Medicare.

The federal government's investigation into Pfizer was initiated by whistleblower lawsuits. The first of the whistleblower lawsuits was filed by one of Pfizer's sales representatives John Kopchinski. He began questioning the marketing of Bextra and was fired, which is a violation of the anti-retaliation provision of the federal False Claims Act. Kopchinski filed a qui tam lawsuit in 2003, which sparked the interest of state and federal investigators. A qui tam lawsuit is a provision of the False Claims Act that allows a private citizen, the whistleblower, to file suit on behalf of the government against federal contractors committing fraud against the government. The individual filing suit, the Relator, stands to receive a portion of the settlement (USDOJ.gov).

The Largest Penalty in US History

In September 2009, after a federal investigation into their "fraudulent marketing of drugs" Pfizer was ordered to pay $2.3 billion to resolve criminal and civil allegations.[9] At the time, this was the largest penalty paid by any corporation. Pharmacia & Upjohn, a subsidiary of Pfizer, pleaded guilty to a felony violation for the off-label promotion of Bextra. Pfizer's settlement was the largest combined federal and state health-care fraud settlement not only in the history of the healthcare industry, but also in the history of corporate wrongdoing. The fine was "the largest ever imposed in the USA for any matter" according to the Justice Department.[10] The lawsuit included $1.3 billion in criminal charges involving Bextra and $1 billion in civil charges which stemmed from accounts from whistle-blowers contending that the drugs Lyrica, Zyvox, Geodon, and nine others were marketed for purposes "other than those approved by the Food and Drug Administration."[11] According to the terms of the Pfizer civil settlement agreement, $102 million will be divided among six whistleblowers. Kopchinski will receive $51.5 million.[12] The fine was surpassed in 2011 when GlaxoSmithKline, another pharmaceutical company, agreed to a $3 billion fine for illegal activities.

Pfizer's marketing actions also violated the Pharmaceutical Research and Manufacturers of America (PhRMA) "Code on Interactions with Healthcare Professionals" which Pfizer had pledged to follow but systematically violated. The code states that "in interacting with the medical community, we are committed to following the highest ethical standards as well as all legal requirements." In 2010 Pfizer Chairman and CEO Jeffrey Kindler was elected Board Chairman of PhRMA by its members.

A CNN special report revealed that the company that was actually charged and fined by the government was a subsidiary of Pfizer. Pharmacia & Upjohn Co., Inc. was created on March 27, 2007, the "same day Pfizer lawyers and prosecutors agreed that the company would plead guilty in a kickback case against a company Pfizer had acquired a few years earlier."[13] A company that has been convicted of major healthcare fraud loses its Medicare and/or Medicare billing eligibility for all of its products. Prosecutors agreed that this could lead to the downfall of Pfizer and in turn create hardships for users of Pfizer drugs, a loss of employment for employees that were not involved in the fraud, and financial loss to investors. So, a deal was cut to file the criminal charges against Pharmacia & Upjohn Co., Inc. leaving Pfizer free to continue providing medication to Medicare and Medicaid patients. Pharmacia & Upjohn Co., Inc. is merely a shell corporation that has never produced anything. Then two years later the shell company pleaded guilty again to criminal charges in the Bextra case.[14]

Pfizer entered into a five-year Corporate Integrity Agreement (CIA) after the settlement of the most recent lawsuit. To comply with this agreement Pfizer must allow all internal and external investigators to conduct audits to monitor the company's marketing activities. The agreement requires Pfizer to become more accountable and transparent in all aspects of their business. To ensure adherence the Audit Committee of Pfizer's board of directors must reevaluate the compliance program each year and sign off on the effectiveness of the program. Pfizer's senior executives, including the CEO, also have to sign off on the effectiveness of the program. This move ensures that the executives and the board can no longer deny responsibility for the activities of the marketing department. Pfizer is required to notify doctors about the settlement and create processes and procedures that allow them to report inappropriate behavior by any of Pfizer's employees. If Pfizer fails to comply with its obligations, it risks exclusion from federal healthcare programs and monetary penalties.[15]

Although Pfizer pleaded guilty to criminal charges in many of the lawsuits, the company denied wrongdoing in most of the civil cases. The company never took full responsibility for its actions. In response to the settlement, Senior Vice-President Amy Schulman simply stated "We regret certain actions taken in the past, but are proud of the action we've taken to strengthen our internal controls and pioneer new procedures."[16]

Notes

1. David Evans, "Pfizer Broke the Law by Promoting Drugs for Unapproved Uses," *Bloomberg.com* (November 9, 2009). www .bloomberg.com/apps/news?pid=20601109&sid=a4yV1 nYxCGoA.
2. Ibid.
3. Matthew Herper, "David Graham on the Vioxx Verdict," *Forbes.com* (August 19, 2005). www.forbes.com/2005/08/19/ merck-vioxx-graham_cx_mh_0819graham.html.
4. Drew Griffin and Andy Segal, "Feds Found Pfizer Too Big to Nail," *CNN* (April 2, 2010). www.cnn.com/2010/HEALTH/04/ 02/pfizer.bextra/index.html.
5. Shannon Pettypiece and Tony Capaccio, "Pfizer Agrees to $2.3 Billion Payment, Plea in Probe" (Update 1), *Bloomberg Businessweek* (September 2, 2009).
6. US Department of Health & Human Services and US Department of Justice, "Pfizer Factsheet" (2009).
7. Evans, "Pfizer Broke the Law by Promoting Drugs for Unapproved Uses."
8. US Department of Health & Human Services and US Department of Justice, "Pfizer Factsheet."
9. Griffin and Segal, "Feds Found Pfizer Too Big to Nail."
10. Cary O'Reilly and Tony Capaccio, "Pfizer Agrees to Record Criminal Fine in Fraud Probe" (Update 1), *Bloomberg Businessweek* (September 2, 2009).

11. Ibid.
12. Rita Rubin, "Pfizer Fined $2.3 Billion for Illegal Marketing in Off-Label Drug Case," *USA Today* (September 3, 2009).
13. Griffin and Segal, "Feds Found Pfizer Too Big to Nail."
14. Ibid.
15. US Department of Health & Human Services and US Department of Justice, "Pfizer Factsheet."
16. Rubin, "Pfizer Fined $2.3 Billion for Illegal Marketing in Off-Label Drug Case."

Discussion Questions

1. Based on what you have learned thus far about Pfizer's actions, what is the best explanation for their repeated fraudulent marketing of pharmaceuticals? Was it poor management? Was it disregard for the law? Was it simply a decision based on a cost–benefit analysis? Or was it something else? Explain.

2. How would you characterize the ethical culture of Pfizer? Does it seem like managers were expected to follow industry and federal guidelines? Why, or why not? How might the culture be changed to improve compliance?

3. To what extent do you believe that pharmaceutical industry self-regulatory guidelines are a good way to ensure that companies engage in ethical marketing practices? Does it matter if there is no means of enforcing the industry standards? Why, or why not?

8

Environmental Sustainability

8.1 INTRODUCTION

The current human population of Earth is approximately 7 billion and is estimated to reach 9.3 billion by 2050.[1] According to the World Bank, 2.4 billion people live on less than $2 a day. A total of 4 billion live on less than $3,000 per year. In 1987 the World Commission on Environment and Development issued a report highlighting the challenges of economic development in light of the negative impact of growing human populations, along with increased natural resource consumption and pollution.[2] The Brundtland Report, as it has come to be known, defined sustainable development as that which "meets the needs of the present without compromising the ability of future generations to meet their own needs," emphasizing that development must take into consideration the limits of environmental resources. What this entails for business activity and governmental policy is contested. Many companies now incorporate claims about the importance of sustainability into their mission statements or public relations releases. Sustainability is often taken to refer to a concern for "people, the planet, and profitability," which is to say it combines considerations of the traditional issues of business ethics, such as concern for the welfare of employees or impact on the community, with environmental conservation, and profitability. Often, however, "sustainability" is used as shorthand for "environmental sustainability" and it is that topic that is the concern of this chapter.

It is now widely recognized that we are in an environmental crisis. There is nearly unanimous agreement that the Earth is getting warmer, and the consensus in the scientific community is that human activity, especially through activities that emit hydrocarbons, is the chief cause of climate change. However, climate change is only the most prominent of the environmental issues facing us. Some species of fish, such as Atlantic cod, have been overfished to the extent that vast areas of the ocean that once contained millions of the species are now largely devoid of them. Other fish popular with consumers, such as Chilean sea bass, swordfish, and orange roughy, are near extinction. Scientists predict that if present practices continue, all fisheries will collapse – falling below a critical mass that will not allow recovery – by 2048.[3] The dangers confronting fish populations are but one example of concerns about the future extinction of many plants and animals. In the United States and in most other nations old-growth forests, and the unique animal species that depend on such habitats for their survival, continue to be lost. The International Union for Conservation of Nature, the global scientific organization that tracks the status of known species, estimates that 20 percent of animal and plant species are at risk of extinction because of ecosystem loss and climate change. Deforestation and changing weather patterns also contribute to the process of desertification (the process whereby fertile land becomes desert). The declining supply of freshwater is yet another concern. Overdevelopment in the US Southwest and in Southern California has severely taxed the available water supply. The situation in the Southwest is similar to that in many parts of the world. Some believe that future wars will be fought over access to adequate water supplies. Prices for commodities such as rice, corn, and wheat have risen steeply as a result of increased demand to feed the nearly 7 billion people on Earth and changing weather patterns due to climate change. Lastly, the steep rise of fuel over the past several years has awakened everyone to concerns about the future supply of oil and the changes we must make as the supply of oil inevitably declines.

In Europe, dealing with the environmental crisis is addressed at the highest levels of the European Union (EU). The EU has decreed that capitalism, and hence business practices within capitalism, should be environmentally sustainable. Financial success by itself is no longer sufficient. The sustainable corporation must be financially successful, but it must also be environmentally friendly and socially responsible. Thus, in the EU, environmentally friendly business practices are considered a moral norm and consequently a moral obligation. Although the United States has not made sustainable business a matter of public policy, many business leaders have argued that business must take a leadership role in responding to the environmental crisis. For example, Nike CEO Mark Parker has famously stated that "Sustainability is our generation's defining issue."

SUSTAINABILITY AND NATURAL CAPITALISM

Views expressed on climate change science may be divided into three broad categories. First, there is the peer-reviewed research that appears in leading scientific journals. This work is typically vetted by editors and external peer reviewers who have expertise on the precise issues being addressed. The editorial boards of these journals are populated by senior academic and government scientists. Second, there are summaries of such research, concurring statements, and policy statements prepared for use by policymakers and the general public by teams of scientists. This includes the work of the Intergovernmental Panel on Climate Change as well as that of the American Association for the Advancement of Science, the National Research Council of the National Academy of Sciences, and the European Science Foundation. Third, there are opinion pieces in newspapers, blogs, industry-sponsored position papers, and even vanity journals published with the intention of advancing an ideological perspective rather than advancing science.[4]

Critics of the view that there is a consensus on climate change typically appeal to sources in the third category. Instead of advancing their position via credible scientific papers, critics typically broadcast their message through the pronouncements of think tanks and self-proclaimed experts. In fact, according to one review of this debate, nearly all climate change skeptics are "economists, business people or politicians, not scientists."[5] In their article, "Meet the Global Warming Skeptics," the magazine New Scientist examines the connections of many of the prominent climate change skeptics. They note that the Competitive Enterprise Institute, a free-market lobby organization, is made up of two lawyers, an economist, a political scientist, a graduate in business studies, and a mathematician. Similarly, the American Enterprise Institute, another free-market lobbying organization, has only one natural scientist, a chemist. Both of these lobby groups were funded by ExxonMobil, as were the George C. Marshall Institute and the International Policy Network, leading think tanks promoting global climate change skepticism.[6] The tobacco industry used similar techniques in an effort to promote their agenda and undermine public health efforts regarding the dangers of smoking.[7] Indeed, former US Senator and former US Undersecretary of State Timothy Wirth argues that climate change deniers "patterned what they did after the tobacco industry. Both figured, sow enough doubt, call the science uncertain and in dispute. That's had a huge impact on both the public and Congress."[8]

But is there really a consensus in the scientific literature regarding climate change? Are climate scientists really in agreement on this question? What evidence is there for such conclusions? Before answering these questions, it will be helpful to briefly review some recent history. In the 1980s scientists noticed that the Earth's climate was changing. In the late 1980s the Intergovernmental Panel on Climate Change (IPCC) was formed in order to investigate these changes.[9] The IPCC quickly gained credibility by offering cautious conclusions concerning climate change that were grounded in rigorous scientific studies.[10] The third IPCC climate change report, released in 2001, confirmed that the majority of earth scientists were convinced that climate change was happening and that the release of anthropogenic greenhouse gases (GHGs) such as carbon dioxide and methane was the main cause. Does the peer-reviewed scientific literature support these conclusions? It does so unequivocally. In an important study of the scientific literature Naomi Oreskes examined 928 articles on climate change published in peer-reviewed journals between 1993 and 2003.[11] She found that *none* of these articles disagreed with the main conclusions of the IPCC. According to Oreskes, "there is a scientific consensus on the reality of anthropogenic climate change. Climate scientists have repeatedly tried to make this clear. It is time for the rest of us to listen."[12]

More recently researchers surveyed earth scientists with academic affiliations along with those at state geologic surveys, at US federal research facilities, and at US Department of Energy national laboratories about their views on climate change.[13] Of the 3,146 earth scientists who completed the survey 90 percent believe that global temperature levels have risen in comparison to pre-1800s levels.[14] Among those surveyed "the most specialized and knowledgeable respondents (with regard to climate change) are those who listed climate science as their area of expertise and who also have published more than 50% of their recent peer-reviewed papers on the subject of climate change."[15] Of these specialists, 96.2 percent (76 of 79) believe that global temperature levels have risen in comparison to pre-1800s levels and 97.4 percent (75 of 77) believe that "human activity is a significant contributing factor in changing mean global temperatures."[16]

The two areas of expertise in the survey with the smallest percentage of participants indicating that they believed that climate change resulted from anthropogenic activity were those in economic geology, the study of the earth for economic gain, with 47 percent (48 of 103), and meteorology, which tends to focus on short-term climate patterns, with 64 percent (23 of 36).[17] The researchers reach the following conclusion: "It seems that the debate on the authenticity of global warming and the role played by human activity is largely nonexistent among those who understand the nuances and scientific basis of long-term climate processes."[18]

It is not surprising then that the findings of the IPCC regarding global climate change have been endorsed by most major scientific organizations including the Academies of Science for the G8+5 in a joint statement.[19] This includes the National Science academies of Brazil, Canada, China, France, Germany, India, Italy, Japan, Mexico, Russia, South Africa, the United Kingdom, and the United States. Additionally, the IPCC's findings have received concurring assessments from the American Association for the Advancement of Science, the National Research Council, the European Science Foundation, the American Geophysical Union, the European Federation of Geologists, the European Geosciences Union, the Australian Meteorological and Oceanographic Society, the American Meteorological Society, the Australian Meteorological and Oceanographic Society, the American Chemical Society, the American Physical Society, the American Statistical Association, and others.[20] In 2007 a group of 27 corporations and environmental organizations formed the United States Climate Action Partnership (USCAP) in response to inaction at the national level regarding climate change policy. USCAP has persistently called for national legislation that would require significant reductions in greenhouse gas emissions. *The Economist* magazine – whose normal editorial stance is consistent with Milton Friedman's stockholder view – published a special 15-page report on how businesses are responding to climate change.[21] The article pointed out that "very few serious business-men will say publicly either that climate change is not happening or that it is not worth tackling."[22]

Leading global companies have also recognized that a scientific consensus exists regarding anthropogenic climate change and have taken proactive measures to address greenhouse gas emissions. These include Alcan, Alcoa, BP, BHP Billiton, Dow Chemical, Iberdrola, Novo Nordisk, Scottish Power, Royal Dutch Shell, STMicroelectronics, and Weyerhaeuser, among others.[23] As early as 1997 then Alcoa chairman and CEO Paul O'Neil recognized the scientific consensus on climate change and directed his team to reduce greenhouse gas emissions.[24] (O'Neil later served as US Treasury Secretary from 2001 to 2002.) During his tenure as President of Shell Oil Company John Hofmeister criticized those who still argue that the science is unclear. "We have to deal with greenhouse gases," he said at a 2006 speech at the National Press Club. "From Shell's point of view, the debate is over. When 98 percent of scientists agree, who is Shell to say, 'Let's debate the science'?" On another occasion he stated that "It's a waste of time to debate it. Policymakers have a responsibility to address it. The nation needs public policy. We'll adjust."[25] John Chambers, chairman and CEO of Cisco has said that "It [climate change] is not a question of if. It is," adding "There is no doubt in hardly any of the well-educated minds that if we don't act quickly, we are going to have a tremendous problem on our hands."[26] According to Chambers,[27] "Mitigating the impacts of climate change is critical to the world's economic and social stability."[28]

The view that businesses have an obligation to respond to improve their environmental performance has become increasingly accepted. In the 1990s business contributions to a more sustainable environment began to emerge. Many practices of business had been wasteful and inefficient. Business leaders saw that waste had a financial cost and thus eliminating waste, through recycling or alternative product development, was a good way to be more environmentally friendly and more profitable, not only in the long run but immediately. Even now there are many areas in which business could change its practices and be more profitable as a result. For instance, many escalators run day and night, yet there is technology that would have them on standby until an electronic eye sensed someone approaching. A similar technology would allow lights to be turned off in hallways and other public areas until people were actually present in the public space. In Europe, hotels commonly utilize key activated energy management systems to conserve energy, but the technology is rarely present in US hotels (the technology makes it nearly impossible for lights to be left on when a guest is not in a room). Recently there has been a revolution in building design. For example, replacing incandescent bulbs with long-lasting and low power consuming LED bulbs saves energy and money over the long run. Many new buildings are also being designed with skylights to supplant or reduce the need for daytime lights. These technologies allow businesses to be more sustainable. However, what precisely is meant by sustainability remains a contested issue.

What constitutes sustainable development? How is it to be achieved? In his contribution to this chapter Alan Holland points out that sustainability is often discussed in terms of passing on to future generation the same amount of capital as the present generation enjoys despite growing human populations. On a weak account of sustainability, human-made capital (for example, solar panels) can be substituted for natural capital (for example, coal) whereas a strong account of sustainability maintains that naturally occurring capital should not be regarded as substitutable and should therefore be preserved in the interest of future generations. However, should nature merely be regarded as "capital" in the economic sense or does it have noneconomic value as well? And doesn't the very idea of natural capital often involve the destruction of nature to get at the capital (for example, mining)? Holland raises these issues and points to the need for careful reflection on the context in which human population growth, economic development, and the environment can be debated.

The next essay in this chapter is written by three of the leading figures in the business sustainability movement who together have extensive and successful business and engineering experience. Paul Hawken, Amory Lovins, and L. Hunter Lovins envision a new industrial revolution in which coal and oil have been phased out as energy sources and human populations have reoriented industries as if ecosystem health and atmospheric stability mattered. They call this new economic system "natural capitalism" and in their essay of the same name they highlight four changes to business as usual that can lead to this new way of doing business. These include radically increased resource productivity, redesigning industrial systems to mimic nature in closed cycles that produce little or no waste, a focus on service relationships rather than consumption, and investments in natural capital that help reverse decades of harm to our planet. Leadership in Energy and Environmental Design (LEED) is an internationally recognized green building certification system that companies like Avon, Bank of America, and PepsiCo are using to help design or retrofit buildings in a manner that is more consistent with natural capitalism than traditional capitalism. Case studies on Interface and Frito-Lay included in this chapter highlight such proactive corporate responses to the global environmental crisis.

The essay by Joseph DesJardins takes on a more critical view of sustainability. DesJardins argues that the concept of sustainability is often misused in academic scholarship and in the business world. He argues against attempts to convert sustainability, on the one hand, into a narrow concept of risk management or, on the other hand, into a broader concept of social responsibility. Instead, he argues that it is essential that business sustainability focuses on how firms can meet both present and future needs without jeopardizing future generations via the destruction of the biosphere.

CORPORATE ENVIRONMENTAL MISCONDUCT

Just as there are financial incentives for improving environmental performance, there can be financial incentives for ignoring or neglecting environmental protection and defeating regulations intended to protect humans from harmful environmental damage. This idea is well illustrated by case studies in this chapter that focus on the cruise industry's troubled environmental record and the actions of Texaco over a 20-year period in the Amazon jungle of Ecuador. Large corporations have a distinctive capacity to impact both public opinion and environmental regulation. In his essay in this chapter, Denis G. Arnold describes how corporate political activity has been utilized by companies and trade associations in the fossil fuel industry to distort public understanding of climate change by funding "think tanks" and other organizations that deceptively misrepresent, or simply lie about, the scientific consensus on climate change. The ultimate goal of this political activity is to defeat regulations intended to prevent harmful climate change. Ostensibly, these deceptive practices are undertaken in the interest of short-term profits. However, Arnold argues that such corporate political activity is actually inconsistent with the shareholder primacy theory of the firm that is grounded upon respect for the rights of citizens to determine business regulations via their elected representatives. The final essay in this chapter, by Jacob Vos, explains the disturbing practice of corporate "greenwashing," which is the practice of falsely representing a firm's operations or products as environmentally responsible. Vos cites numerous examples of greenwashing in his article, examines why greenwashing occurs, and provides some potential solutions to this deceptive corporate practice. The case studies on Tesla and Volkswagen provide contrasting examples of corporate sustainability practices. Tesla's business model is grounded in environmental sustainability, whereas Volkswagen utilized greenwashing to misrepresent its environmental performance.

This chapter also includes summaries of two landmark environmental law cases from the US Supreme Court. The 1998 case *United States v. Best Foods et al.* deals with the issue of whether a parent corporation may be held liable for the polluting activities of one of its subsidiaries. The Court maintained that liability depends on the level of active participation and control by the corporation, especially where wrongful purposes are involved (most notably fraud). This opinion explores several levels of corporate responsibility to avoid disposal of hazardous materials. The 2001 case *Whitman v. American Trucking Associations, Inc.* concerns the issue of whether the administrator of the US Environmental Protection Agency may take into consideration the cost to businesses of implementing congressionally mandated environmental standards. In this case, trucking companies sought to weaken the enforcement of enhanced air quality standards. In ruling against the trucking companies the Court maintained that in most cases involving congressional legislation the costs of implementation may not be taken into account. This case illustrates an increasingly rare business response to the environmental crisis that focuses on defeating legislation intended to protect the environment and human health. As we have seen, an alternative response is to seek proactive solutions that are simultaneously environmentally and economically sustainable.

Notes

1. Justin Gillis and Celia W. Dugger, "U.N. Forecasts 10.1 Billion People by Century's End," *The New York Times* (May 3, 2011).
2. The World Commission on Environment and Development, *Our Common Future* (1987).
3. Cornelia Dean, "Study Sees 'Global Collapse' of Fish Species," *The New York Times* (November 2, 2006).
4. For an overview of the climate change denial industry, see Sharon Begley, "The Truth about Denial," *Newsweek* (August 13, 2007): www.newsweek.com/id/32482; and "Meet the Global Warming Skeptics," *New Scientist* (February 12, 2005): 40. For an example of a vanity journal publication on climate change, see "Environmental Effects of Increased Atmospheric Carbon Dioxide," *Journal of American Physicians and Surgeons* 12, no. 2 (Fall, 2007). Retrieved April 12, 2009 from www.jpands.org/vol12no3/robinson.pdf. This journal is not listed in major scientific databases such as PubMed or ISI Web of Knowledge. However, the article is featured prominently on the pages of the Heartland Institute, a "free market" think tank and a center of climate change skepticism. See www.heartland.org/_template-assets/docu ments/publications/gwreview_oism600.pdf, retrieved April 12, 2009.
5. Fred Pearce, "Climate Change: Menace or Myth," *New Scientist* 2486 (February 12, 2005): 38.
6. "Meet the Global Warming Skeptics," 40.
7. For an overview, see, for example, Allan M. Brandt, *The Cigarette Century: The Rise, Fall, and Deadly Persistence of the Product That Defined America* (New York: Basic Books, 2009). Creationists use similar methods to cast doubt on Darwinian evolutionary theory. For an assessment of their arguments, see, for example, Philip Kitcher, *Abusing Science: The Case against Creationism* (Cambridge, MA: MIT Press, 1983).
8. Begley, "The Truth about Denial."
9. Spencer R. Weart, *The Discovery of Global Warming* (Cambridge University Press, 2003), p. 160.
10. Ibid., p. 162.
11. Naomi Oreskes, "Beyond the Ivory Tower: The Scientific Consensus on Climate Change," *Science* 306 (2004): 1686.
12. Ibid. See also Naomi Oreskes and Erik M. Conway, *Merchants of Doubt: How a Handful of Scientists Obscured the Truth on Issues from Tobacco Smoke to Global Warming* (New York: Bloomsbury, 2010).
13. Peter Doran and Maggie Kendall Zimmerman, "Examining the Scientific Consensus on Climate Change," *EOS* 20, no. 3 (January 20, 2009): 21–22.
14. Ibid., p. 21.
15. Ibid.
16. Ibid.
17. Ibid.
18. Ibid.

19. "Joint Science Academies' Statement: Climate Change Adaptation and the Transition to a Low Carbon Society" (June 2008). Retrieved from www.nationalacademies.org/includes/climatechangestatement.pdf.

20. Links to the original documents may be found at Wikipedia contributors, "Scientific Opinion on Climate Change," *Wikipedia, The Free Encyclopedia*. Retrieved March 24, 2009 from http://en.wikipedia.org/w/index.php? title=Scientific_opinion_on_climate_change&oldid=278716034.

21. "Cleaning Up: A Special Report on Business and Climate Change," *The Economist* (June 2, 2007).

22. Ibid., p. 3.

23. *Businessweek*, "The Race against Climate Change: How Top Companies Are Reducing Emissions of CO_2 and Other Greenhouse Gases" (December 12, 2005).

24. Alcoa, *1997 Annual Report*, p. 4.

25. Associated Press, "Shell Oil Chief: U.S. Needs Global Warming Plan" (September 8, 2006). Retrieved from www.msnbc .msn.com/id/14733060/.

26. Michael Kanellos, "Cisco CEO Takes Jab at Climate Change Deniers," *CNET News* (February 20, 2008). Retrieved from www.cnet.com/news/cisco-ceo-takes-jab-at-climate-change-deniers/.

27. Antony Savvas, "NASA and Cisco Build Climate Change Reporting Platform," *ComputerWeekly.com* (March 4, 2009). Retrieved from www.computerweekly.com/Articles/2009/03/04/235132/nasa-and-cisco-build-climate-change-report ing-platform.htm.

28. Components of this introduction are drawn from Denis G. Arnold, "Climate Change and Ethics," in *The Ethics of Global Climate Change* (Cambridge University Press, 2011).

8.2 SUSTAINABILITY AND NATURAL CAPITALISM

Sustainability

ALAN HOLLAND

Introduction: Birth of the Idea

The twentieth century saw unprecedented environmental change, much of it the cumulative and unintended result of human economic activity. In the judgment of many, this change – involving the exhaustion of natural resources and sinks, extensive pollution, and unprecedented impacts upon climate, life-forms, and life-sustaining systems – is undermining the conditions necessary for the economic activity to continue. In a word, present patterns of economic activity are judged to be "unsustainable."

An initial response was to suggest that human society would have to abandon the attempt to improve the human condition through economic growth, and settle instead for zero growth. The response was naturally unwelcome, both to political leaders anxious to assure voters of better times to come, and to businesses anxious to stay in business. Its logic, moreover, is open to question. For even if we accept that economic growth has been the chief cause of environmental degradation, it does not follow that abandoning growth is the remedy. If zero growth led to global war, for example, there would be environmental

degradation, and zero growth to boot. And genetic technology holds out the hope, at least, that we might provide for human needs with decreasing impact on the natural environment, and even reverse some of the degradation that has already occurred.

This is the hope expressed by the idea of "sustainable development" – or "sustainability," for short. The origin of the idea is commonly dated to a report produced by the International Union for the Conservation of Nature in 1980. Over the ensuing years, and especially since the publication of the Brundtland Report,[1] it has come to dominate large areas of environmental discourse and policymaking. Replacing more confrontational discourse between advocates of economic development, and those increasingly concerned over its environmental consequences, Brundtland advanced the (conciliatory) proposition that the needs of the poor (among the declared aims of economic development) were best met by sustaining environmental capacity (among the declared aims of environmentalism). Development, it was suggested, could be pursued to the extent that it was compatible with sustaining environmental capacity. On the

From Dale Jamieson, ed., *A Companion to Environmental Philosophy*. © 2003. Reprinted by permission of Wiley Blackwell.

assumption that environmental capacity can be expressed in terms of the capacity to satisfy human needs, this was formulated as a principle of "sustainable development" – "development that meets the needs of the present without compromising the ability of future generations to meet their own needs."[2]

There are formal analogies between the principle of sustainability, so framed, and J. S. Mill's (1806–73) principle of liberty, which licenses the pursuit of liberty insofar as this is compatible with a similar liberty for all. The principle of sustainability in effect licenses the pursuit of quality of life insofar as this is compatible with a similar quality of life for all (including future people). Such a principle appears to safeguard the future of the environment, too. But far from abandoning the aim of economic growth, Brundtland foresees "a new era of economic growth" and believes such growth is "absolutely essential" for the relief of poverty. On the other hand it holds that growth is not sufficient to relieve poverty, and sees the need for what it calls a "new development path," one that sustains environmental capacity. Its approach is notably human-centered, and aside from one reference to a "moral reason" for conserving wild beings, the deep ecology perspective is absent. The loss of coral reefs, for example, is lamented simply on the grounds that they "have generated an unusual variety of toxins valuable in modern medicine"; and hope is expressed that "The Earth's endowment of species and natural ecosystems will soon be seen as assets to be conserved and managed for the benefit of all humanity." Sustainable development is understood as development that sustains human progress into the distant future. At the same time, the human-centered reasons that are given are often as much moral as prudential. Poverty is declared to be an "evil in itself" and a strong thread of the argument centers on a concern that current economic activity imposes costs on the future: "We borrow environmental capital from future generations."[3] In this way Brundtland clearly links issues of intragenerational equity with those of intergenerational equity. The implications for environmental protection, however, are less clear. Environmentalists may welcome the recognition that it is not environmental protection that stands in the way of future development so much as the fallout from existing patterns of development. But the fundamental issue is whether the protection that the environment requires serves to determine the "new development path," or whether it is the new development path that dictates the nature of the environmental protection required. In the latter event, it makes a difference – or rather it makes all the difference – what conception of the human good is to govern the development path in question.

Reception of the Idea

In the world of policy, the concept of sustainability has been assimilated with remarkable speed, determining much of the agenda of the United Nations conference on Environment and Development held in Rio de Janeiro in 1992. Agenda 21, a program to which governments all over the world have committed themselves, represents the agenda for putting sustainability into practice. At the local level, too, many sensible schemes are being put into operation in the name of sustainability, often under the auspices of Agenda 21, and the term figures increasingly as an overriding objective of environmental organizations, whether inside or outside the remit of government.

However, the appearance of consensus even at the highest policy levels continues to be accompanied by a sustained chorus of skepticism and suspicion. Environmentalists are suspicious that what is billed as a constraint on business as usual will turn out to be a cover for business as usual. Vandana Shiva comments on the paradox that development and growth – creatures of the market economy – are being offered as a cure for the very ecological crisis that they have served to bring about.[4] "Nature shrinks as capital grows," she writes: the market destroys both the economy of nature, and non-market "survival economies."[5] Business interests, on the other hand, are suspicious that the constraint on business as usual might be a cover for no business at all. The sustainability agenda is also a fertile source of suspicion between North and South – the poorer countries suspecting that the constraint on development now judged to be necessary as a result of patterns of economic activity from which they received little or no benefit is being used to justify a constraint on *their* development. This was already a key issue ahead of the first ever world conference on Environment and Development held in Stockholm in 1972.[6] ...

Objectives

For those who accept the need for a new, sustainable, development path, two immediate questions must be faced: (1) What values are affirmed by sustainability? (2) Are they all consistent?

The values most evident among the arguments advanced for sustainability are justice, well-being, and the value of nature "in its own right." The point of most interest to environmentalists is how far the claims of nature are going to be served by policies designed to secure human well-being and justice. For it is no foregone conclusion that some preordained "harmony" must obtain between these objectives. But equally of interest is the relation between sustainability and the pursuit of justice, both intragenerational and intergenerational. Sustainable development is sometimes defined as non-declining consumption per capita. However, non-declining per capita consumption is compatible with enormous per capita inequalities. And while it is true that a commitment to intergenerational equity appears logically to imply a commitment to intragenerational equity, realization of these two aims might in practice conflict. The opportunity costs of measures to "save" the environment that benefit future generations might happen to fall upon today's poor; and this just makes the point that although the poor suffer most from environmental degradation, because they depend more heavily than the rich on natural, as opposed to human-made resources, it does not follow that they will benefit most from its restoration. But if environmental protection is not sufficient to ensure social justice, i.e., to help today's poor, is it not at least necessary? A skeptic might wonder whether environmental damage – e.g., damage that results from development – is not also at least as necessary a condition of social justice. The relation between environmental protection and the well-being of future humans is also not straightforward. Environmental protection does not guarantee the well-being of future humans, without many enabling factors being in place. Whether it is necessary depends on how environmental protection is understood. If it is explained as "maintaining the capacity of the environment to serve human interests," then indeed the connection is assured – by fiat. But if environmental protection is given a more radical slant – allowing nature to "go its own way," for example – then again, it might be environmental damage that is required to ensure the well-being of future humans.

Whether long-term human economic interests and the long-term integrity of the natural world really do coincide is one of the deep underlying problems of the sustainability debate. Of particular interest in this connection is the way that the sustainability debate itself has prompted searching critiques of the growth model, and questionings of the relation between growth and the human good. Increasingly, the distinction is drawn between economic growth, on the one hand, and development on the other, the latter denoting a richer register of human aspiration. Amartya Sen, for example, has explained development as "a process of expanding the capabilities of people," a notion that is intended to include expanded autonomy and greater access to justice.[7] There are in fact sound conceptual reasons for claiming that human well-being, if this is understood as implying a conscious state of sensitivity, cannot be intelligibly specified without reference to external circumstances, including states

of the natural world. Peace of mind is simply not an option if a baby is crying, or people are starving. And there are conceptions of the human good that make a concern for nature for its own sake a contributing or even constitutive factor in human well-being. In this way human interest and ecological integrity do not just happen to coincide, but exhibit an interlocking conceptual relationship. This prompts a more hopeful line of thought – that human aspirations for a better quality of life might be met even though there is decreasing reliance upon economic growth as such, and therefore decreasing impact on non-human life-forms. At least on one scenario, then, the leading objectives of sustainability might after all be made consistent.

A further question is how sustainability compares with environmental objectives of longer standing that it has tended to supplant, such as (a) nature conservation, (b) land health, and (c) ecological integrity.

Nature Conservation. Writing in the 1991 annual report of the Council for the Protection of Rural England, its Chairman David Astor voiced the opinion that "The great pioneers of CPRE in the 1920s did not use the term sustainable development but that is exactly what they stood for." But one might well take issue with this claim. For among these traditional nature conservationists one finds a concern for natural features that are indigenous, rare, venerable, fragile and irreplaceable. It is not clear, however, that a single one of these categories would be guaranteed a place on a sustainability program.

Land Health. Aldo Leopold's notion of land health – "the capacity of the land for self-renewal" – on the other hand, comes much closer. It embraces cultivated as well as natural landscapes and, like sustainability, anticipates the idea of future capacity. But one difference is suggested by an analogy with the human body. We can function in pretty much the normal way (sustain our activities) with spectacles, dentures, and a walking-stick. But the conditions which these aids help us surmount are incapacities. The same goes for agricultural systems, which can continue to function provided humans continue to supply the necessary fertilizers, etc., but it does not exactly have the capacity for self-renewal (as specified in Leopold's definition of land health). It is not clear that sustainability requires land health as such.

Integrity. The contrast between the goal of sustainability and that of ecological integrity – understood as a condition of minimum human disturbance – appears at first sight more marked. But the prospects for compatibility depend on which of two questions are asked. The first question is: How much integrity do we need? There are those who believe that a tolerable human future actually requires the maintenance of substantial portions of the globe relatively free of human influence. But whether they are right depends upon the character of the human future being envisaged; and it is hard to avoid the suspicion that certain sustainable futures at any rate would feature a natural world containing only species that can abide, or avoid, the human footprint. The second question is: How much freedom from human disturbance do non-human species need? This way lies a brighter prospect for the compatibility of the sustainability and ecological agendas. But its realization depends on whether human society is prepared to ask the question, and act on the answer.

The Criteria

The issue of what will count as achieving sustainability, and what criterion will be used to map the new development path, is absolutely crucial. It will in effect determine the sustainability agenda. By far the most developed suggestions for measuring progress towards sustainability have come from economists and in a number of countries many so-called "green accounting" schemes are in operation. At the heart of the economic approach to sustainability is the concept of capital. The modeling of nature on the analogy of financial "capital," capable of yielding "interest," arises readily from earlier notions of "sustainable yield," found in resource economics. Applied to nature generally, the proposed criterion states that if each generation bequeaths at least as much capital to the next generation as it receives, then this will constitute a sustained development path. (Economists appear not to be deterred from using the model despite there being no clear sense in which nonrenewable resources can "yield" interest.)

The theory proceeds to mark a distinction between two kinds of capital – natural and human-made.[8] Human-made capital comprises all artifacts, as well as human and social capital – people, their skills, intelligence, virtues, and institutions. Natural capital comprises all naturally occurring organic and inorganic resources, including not just physical items but also genetic information, biodiversity, life-support systems, and sinks. This distinction in turn generates two versions of the criterion: so-called "weak sustainability," which stipulates an undiminished capital bequest irrespective of how it is composed; and so-called "strong sustainability," which stipulates an undiminished bequest of natural capital.

The distinguishing feature of weak sustainability is indifference between natural and human-made capital, provided only that human needs continue to be met. It is often alleged, but on not very good textual evidence, that advocates of weak sustainability are committed to unlimited substitutability between natural and human-made capital. What they are committed to, as economists, is that the value of all kinds of capital is comparable. But this is quite different from the claim that the valued *items* can be substituted: a visit to the cinema might cost as much as a good meal, but it doesn't follow that it can replace a good meal. Moreover, advocates of strong sustainability, if they are committed to the principles of neoclassical economics, must also hold that the value of human-made and natural capital is comparable in terms of economic value; for this is ultimately reducible to the preferences of rational economic agents, and therefore capable of being expressed in monetary terms. Indeed, it is just this feature of the account that makes it possible for the level of capital to be measured, and therefore possible for there to be a criterion of sustainability. The distinguishing feature of strong sustainability is that it is not indifferent between natural and human-made capital, but requires natural capital to be maintained. So it requires natural capital to be maintained not only where substitution by human-made capital is not possible (this much weak sustainability would agree with, since if natural capital cannot be substituted its loss would be a loss to total capital, which weak sustainability does not allow), but crucially, where it is possible.

The impact of weak sustainability is not insignificant. Although it allows environmental loss to be offset against other kinds of economic gain, it at least acknowledges that environmental loss harbors economic loss, and must therefore be taken into account rather than regarded as an "externality" – something which purely economic accounting can afford to ignore. From the environmentalist perspective, however, the most obvious defect of weak sustainability is that it appears to countenance severing the connection between sustainability and environmental protection. It permits the natural environment to be degraded provided that human well-being can still be secured. But it should be noted that if the claim made by some advocates of strong sustainability is correct, and the presence of substantial features of the natural world is indispensable for human well-being, then certainly it will justify the claim that the level of natural capital should be maintained. But, far from justifying strong sustainability as a distinct position from weak, it actually shows that it is redundant.

The advantages of the economic approach are several:

1. It highlights the fact that environmental conservation carries economic costs and burdens; also – and crucially – that economic benefits carry environmental costs.
2. It offers a way of measuring the benefits of environmental conservation against those gained from other forms of expenditure, e.g., military, health.
3. It makes the case for compensating forgone income – e.g., "debt-for-nature" swaps (though this runs up against the problem that compensating "poor" countries may mean "compensating" individually rich people).
4. It offers a way of measuring the effectiveness of any conservation policy or program, which, however unclear its methods or contested its results, is vital for any durable program of implementation.
5. The concept of "natural capital" in particular makes the point that we should not regard our use of environmental resources as if we were living off *income*.

But how plausible is it to construe nature as capital? The account of the economists faces moral, methodological, ecological, and conceptual difficulties.

The moral objection, first, is that the natural world is not simply a resource but, for example, contains sentient creatures who have claims to moral consideration. An alternative, or additional, point is that the natural world embodies values other than its value to humans, values that are inherent rather than instrumental. A third objection stems from resistance to the idea that all values are commensurable, and especially resistance to the idea that they can be assessed according to a common economic numeraire [such as money].

Among methodological objections is the problem of how markets distorted by sociopolitical power structures can adequately reflect resource scarcity; and more generally, how the value of items and processes that span centuries can be adequately assessed according to the parochial and quotidian values of the day. Besides being presumptuous, the difficulty is that the slightest difference in evaluative criteria here and now – say a 1 percent difference in the "discount rate" – will have enormous and amplified effects hereafter.

Among ecological objections is the difficulty of mapping ecological realities – involving processes that are episodic, non-linear, unstable, and unpredictable – with economic indicators and criteria. A further objection to the resource approach is that it suppresses recognition of the historical character of the biosphere. Even where there is recognition that the biosphere is the result of complex events spanning many centuries, this tends to be construed as merely a technical problem of restoration. Time and historical process is construed, in other words, as nothing more than a technical constraint on the preservation of natural capital – an approach which completely misses what is at stake in loss of biodiversity. Irreversibility, too, is seen as an annoying impediment to the maintenance of capital, instead of being seen for what it is – the very stuff of natural process.

There are also severe conceptual difficulties. First, the concepts "natural world" and "natural capital" have quite different connotations. Natural capital is the natural world construed as an "asset": it is the natural world just insofar as it represents its capacity to service human needs. Large portions of the natural world therefore do not count as natural capital – for example, events such as volcanic eruptions and hurricanes, and species such as mosquitoes and locusts. On the one hand, degradation seems to abound: stunted tree development associated with deteriorating soil quality; premature leaf drop associated with air pollution; fish and aquatic mammals disappearing from rivers; thousands of miles of coral reef bleached or dying in the wake of 1998's highest sea temperatures on record. But the situation from the point of view of natural capital is far from clear. Is this a description of a decline in natural capital? The capacity of the natural world to serve human well-being appears unabated – perhaps *because* we have, for example, more efficient ways of destroying locusts. Hence, the economic criterion appears unable to identify what has gone wrong. If this is true, it cannot possibly function as a guide to the path that will put it right.

A second point is that the extent of natural capital depends on the availability of human-made capital. For our vulnerable ancestors, much of the natural world needed to be – and was – destroyed. Much else needed to be transformed – by fire, cultivation, and domestication. The implication is that natural capital relies so extensively on human-made capital for its capacity to be realized that it is by and large meaningless to talk of natural capital in abstraction from the human-made capital that mediates its use. Reflections of this kind lead Dale Jamieson to remark that "it is quite difficult to distinguish natural from human produced capital."[9] If this is true, then it will also be "quite difficult" to specify the requirements for strong sustainability. The amount of natural capital available simply cannot be judged independently of reference to human-made capital.

A third problem concerns the notion of substitution; for, levels of capital are supposed to be judged depending upon whether substitutions can or cannot be made. But the question whether A can or cannot be substituted for B is not intelligible in isolation; it depends on context – the purpose for which the substitution is made, the degree of precision required, and so forth.[10] Nor is it clear, in any case, how far these are empirical as opposed to normative questions. However, the real problem is not the proposed substitution between natural and human-made capital; it is the proposed substitution of capital for nature. Natural capital is not the yield of nature; on the contrary, it tends to be yielded through the destruction of nature.

One, final, difficulty with the economic approach is how we are to know, at any particular point along the "new development path," what the overall trajectory of the path is likely to be, and what "next step" will contribute to it. The source of the difficulty is both causal and epistemological, because each possible next step will have different outcomes, and these will rapidly become impossible to predict. It is hard to see how a sustainable path could be identified in any other way than retrospectively. This suggests that the condition or state of sustainability cannot be understood in terms of purely economic criteria, i.e., as measurable by any kind of efficiency or optimizing outcomes. It appears rather as an inter-temporal and path-dependent process which can only be maintained by procedures and traditions that are self-critical, self-renewing, and sensitive to distributional and historical concerns.

Implementation

A "new ethic," and new technologies, might both be seen as possible ingredients of a "new development path," but they cannot be realized in a vacuum. They require the presence of certain sorts of social and political institution, and above all a citizenry that is attuned to the demands of the new development path. Unfortunately, certain characteristics of the present global economy, for example, the mobility of labor and capital, and the centralization of knowledge and power, make transitions to environmental sustainability and to redistributive social and economic policies hard to envisage. The interests of multinational corporations, even though they put on a green costume and may sincerely speak of feeding the hungry, are not best served by widening access to natural resources and helping the hungry to feed themselves. Developments in science and technology, e.g., nuclear and genetic research programs, point to a similar conclusion. They are becoming less, rather than more, socially accountable, as their research agendas fall increasingly into private hands. The future looks set to belong to powerful and well-financed minorities rather than being held in common – the "common future" to which Brundtland aspired. For these reasons, the notion of a "technical solution" had best not be too readily dismissed, since from one perspective it appears

the most likely eventuality. From the spinning jenny to the information revolution, technology has shown a remarkable ability to lead society by the nose. In accordance with such reflections, it is now being increasingly recognized that "social" or "cultural" sustainability is likely to be crucial to the achievement of any kind of sustainability at all. Among the key elements of cultural sustainability that will need to be in place are: (a) resilient political institutions; (b) effective regulation; (c) appropriate social skills and habits; (d) accountable science and technology; and (e) a climate of trust.

There are signs that the sustainability agenda itself may be capable of provoking certain sorts of political institution and vision, just as much as it requires them for its implementation. The very idea of intergenerational justice, for example, at least complements and may well presuppose and inspire notions of cross-generational community that are by no means new, but have been somewhat muted in the face of prevailing utilitarian and individualistic ideologies. In modern times they reach back at least to the eighteenth-century Irish philosopher Edmund Burke's notion of a diachronic community, a "partnership ... not only between those who are living, but between those who are living, those who are dead, and those who are to be born." Skeptics doubt whether such a community can enjoy reciprocal relations, or shared values. But such doubts appear misplaced. Later generations can reciprocate by honoring their predecessors or striving to fulfill their hopes. And the importance of shared values can be overrated: absence of dissent and lack of change over time are more symptomatic of a moribund than a healthy community. ...

Conclusion

Sustainable development may be summarily defined as development of a kind that does not prejudice future development. It is intended to function essentially as a criterion for what is to count as acceptable environmental modification. Although we may not be able to predict future human needs with any precision, we can be sure that any future human development will require resources, sinks, and life-sustaining systems. We may be reasonably sure therefore that measures taken to minimize human impact on resources and sinks, and to minimize changes to life-support functions, will be steps toward sustainability thus understood. We can also be sure that measures taken to secure these environmental targets require a supporting social fabric. At the same time, it must not be forgotten that what any generation bequeaths to its successors is a package, including not only "costs," but also "benefits," such as technological expertise and other forms of human and social "capital," without which natural resources, sinks, and services would not have the value to humans that they do. But perhaps most crucial of all, its actions also shape and determine the very conditions under which succeeding generations will live. Hence, the question of whether any society is on a sustainable trajectory is at best an extremely complex one, and may well be in principle impossible to compute. What then, should we make of the attempts, especially by economists, to provide just such computations? It is true that environmental degradation has economic costs, and that these costs are a telling symptom of our environmental predicament. But it does not follow that these are the only costs, or that economic values can successfully measure these costs – for a variety of reasons. These include doubts about the various methodologies deployed, and difficulties of principle – about how to cost moral concerns, or how to cost features of the social fabric, such as a Royal Commission on Environmental Pollution, or the environmental habits of Swedish citizens. Above all, if our assessment of economic value is determined by the very economic system whose credentials are in question, it is hard to see how the translation of that value system into the environmental sphere can yield a just estimate of environmental value, or enforce the re-evaluation of environmental goods, as it is supposed to do.

The real importance of sustainability may lie in providing a new conceptual context within which issues of growth and environment can be debated, and in provoking us to reassess our notions of quality of life and environment. It answers also to a need visceral as well as pragmatic, to do something in the face of loss. But as a guiding principle, it must be judged ultimately unsatisfying. It seems too closely locked in to conceptions of the world – a storehouse that must be kept filled, a machine that must be maintained – that are themselves no longer sustainable. In the wake of Darwin, the world looks much more like an open-ended historical process ill-suited for filling or maintaining. Our more modest task is how not to blight the interlocking futures of the human and the natural community that we have the power profoundly to affect but lack the capacity and the wisdom to manage.

Notes

1. World Commission on Environment and Development, *Our Common Future* [Brundtland Report] (Oxford University Press, 1987).
2. Ibid., p. 8.
3. Quotations from ibid., pp. 1, 4, 13, 151, 160, 8, respectively.
4. See Shiva's brief but probing essay on sustainability: V. Shiva, "Recovering the Real Meaning of Sustainability," in *The Environment in Question*, ed. D. Cooper and J. Palmer (London: Routledge, 1992), pp. 187–93 (p. 188).
5. Ibid., p. 189.
6. H. H. Landsberg, "Looking Backward: Stockholm 1972," *Resources for the Future* 106 (1992): 2–3 (p. 2).
7. Amartya Sen, *On Ethics and Economics* (Oxford: Blackwell, 1987).
8. D. Pearce, A. Markandya, and B. B. Barbier, *Blueprint for a Green Economy* (London: Earthscan, 1989), pp. 34–35.
9. Dale Jamieson, "Sustainability and Beyond," *Ecological Economics* 24 (1998): 183–92 (p. 185).
10. Alan Holland, "Substitutability: or, Why Strong Sustainability Is Weak and Absurdly Strong Sustainability Is Not Absurd," in *Valuing Nature? Economics, Ethics and the Environment*, ed. J. Foster (London: Routledge, 1997), pp. 119–34.

Natural Capitalism: The Next Industrial Revolution

PAUL HAWKEN, AMORY LOVINS, AND L. HUNTER LOVINS

Imagine for a moment a world where cities have become peaceful and serene because cars and buses are whisper quiet, vehicles exhaust only water vapor, and parks and greenways have replaced unneeded urban freeways. OPEC has ceased to function because the price of oil has fallen to five dollars a barrel, but there are few buyers for it because cheaper and better ways now exist to get the services people once turned to oil to provide. Living standards for all people have dramatically improved, particularly for the poor and those in developing countries. Involuntary unemployment no longer exists, and income taxes have largely been eliminated. Houses, even low-income housing units, can pay part of their mortgage costs by the energy they *produce*; there are few if any active landfills; worldwide forest cover is

From Paul Hawken, Amory B. Lovins, and L. Hunter Lovins, *Natural Capitalism* (Little, Brown, 1999). Reprinted by permission of the authors in care of The Spieler Agency, New York, Little Brown and Company, an imprint of Hachette Book Group, Inc., and Taylor & Francis Book Group.

increasing; dams are being dismantled; atmospheric CO_2 levels are decreasing for the first time in two hundred years; and effluent water leaving factories is cleaner than the water coming into them. Industrialized countries have reduced resource use by 80 percent while improving the quality of life. Among these technological changes, there are important social changes. The frayed social nets of Western countries have been repaired. With the explosion of family-wage jobs, welfare demand has fallen. A progressive and active union movement has taken the lead to work with business, environmentalists, and government to create "just transitions" for workers as society phases out coal, nuclear energy, and oil. In communities and towns, churches, corporations, and labor groups promote a new living-wage social contract as the least expensive way to ensure the growth and preservation of valuable social capital. Is this the vision of a Utopia? In fact, the changes described here could come about in the decades to come as the result of economic and technological trends already in place.

This article is about these and many other possibilities.

It is about the possibilities that will arise from the birth of a new type of industrialism, one that differs in its philosophy, goals, and fundamental processes from the industrial system that is the standard today. In the next century, as human population doubles and the resources available per person drop by one-half to three-fourths, a remarkable transformation of industry and commerce can occur. Through this transformation, society will be able to create a vital economy that uses radically less material and energy. This economy can free up resources, reduce taxes on personal income, increase per-capita spending on social ills (while simultaneously reducing those ills), and begin to restore the damaged environment of the earth. These necessary changes done properly can promote economic efficiency, ecological conservation, and social equity.

The industrial revolution that gave rise to modern capitalism greatly expanded the possibilities for the material development of humankind. It continues to do so today, but at a severe price. Since the mid-eighteenth century, more of nature has been destroyed than in all prior history. While industrial systems have reached pinnacles of success, able to muster and accumulate human-made capital on vast levels, *natural capital*, on which civilization depends to create economic prosperity, is rapidly declining, and the rate of loss is increasing proportionate to gains in material well-being. *Natural capital* includes all the familiar resources used by humankind: water, minerals, oil, trees, fish, soil, air, et cetera. But it also encompasses living systems, which include grasslands, savannas, wetlands, estuaries, oceans, coral reefs, riparian corridors, tundras, and rainforests. These are deteriorating worldwide at an unprecedented rate. Within these ecological communities are the fungi, ponds, mammals, humus, amphibians, bacteria, trees, flagellates, insects, songbirds, ferns, starfish, and flowers that make life possible and worth living on this planet.

As more people and businesses place greater strain on living systems, limits to prosperity are coming to be determined by natural capital rather than industrial prowess. This is not to say that the world is running out of commodities in the near future. The prices for most raw materials are at a twenty-eight-year low and are still falling. Supplies are cheap and appear to be abundant, due to a number of reasons: the collapse of the Asian economies, globalization of trade, cheaper transport costs, imbalances in market power that enable commodity traders and middlemen to squeeze producers, and in large measure the success of powerful new extractive technologies, whose correspondingly extensive damage to ecosystems is seldom given a monetary value. After richer ores are exhausted, skilled mining companies can now level and grind up whole mountains of poorer-quality ores to extract the metals desired. But while technology keeps ahead of depletion, providing what appear to be ever-cheaper metals, they only appear cheap, because the stripped rainforest and the mountain of toxic tailings spilling into rivers, the impoverished villages and eroded indigenous cultures – all the consequences they leave in their wake – are not factored into the cost of production.

It is not the supplies of oil or copper that are beginning to limit our development but life itself. Today, our continuing progress is restricted not by the number of fishing boats but by the decreasing numbers of fish; not by the power of pumps but by the depletion of aquifers; not by the number of chainsaws but by the disappearance of primary forests. While living systems are the source of such desired materials as wood, fish, or food, of utmost importance are the *services* that they offer, services that are far more critical to human prosperity than are nonrenewable resources. A forest provides not only the resource of wood but also the services of water storage and flood management. A healthy environment automatically supplies not only clean air and water, rainfall, ocean productivity, fertile soil, and watershed resilience but also such less-appreciated functions as waste processing (both natural and industrial), buffering against the extremes of weather, and regeneration of the atmosphere.

Humankind has inherited a 3.8-billion-year store of natural capital. At present rates of use and degradation, there will be little left by the end of the next century. This is not only a matter of aesthetics and morality, it is of the utmost practical concern to society and all people. Despite reams of press about the state of the environment and rafts of laws attempting to prevent further loss, the stock of natural capital is plummeting and the vital life-giving services that flow from it are critical to our prosperity.

Natural capitalism recognizes the critical interdependency between the production and use of human-made capital and the maintenance and supply of natural capital. The traditional definition of capital is accumulated wealth in the form of investments, factories, and equipment. Actually, an economy needs four types of capital to function properly:

- human capital, in the form of labor and intelligence, culture, and organization
- financial capital, consisting of cash, investments, and monetary instruments
- manufactured capital, including infrastructure, machines, tools, and factories
- natural capital, made up of resources, living systems, and ecosystem services

The industrial system uses the first three forms of capital to transform natural capital into the stuff of our daily lives: cars, highways, cities, bridges, houses, food, medicine, hospitals, and schools.

The climate debate is a public issue in which the assets at risk are not specific resources, like oil, fish, or timber, but a life-supporting system. One of nature's most critical cycles is the continual exchange of carbon dioxide and oxygen among plants and animals. This "recycling service" is provided by nature free of charge. But today carbon dioxide is building up in the atmosphere, due in part to combustion of fossil fuels. In effect, the capacity of the natural system to recycle carbon dioxide has been exceeded, just as overfishing can exceed the capacity of a fishery to replenish stocks. But what is especially important to realize is that there is no known alternative to nature's carbon cycle service.

Besides climate, the changes in the biosphere are widespread. In the past half century, the world has a lost a fourth of its topsoil and a third of its forest cover. At present rates of destruction, we will lose 70 percent of the world's coral reefs in our lifetime, host to 25 percent of marine life. In the past three decades, one-third of the planet's resources, its "natural wealth," has been consumed. We are losing freshwater ecosystems at the rate of 6 percent a year, marine ecosystems by 4 percent a year. There is no longer any serious scientific dispute that the decline in every living system in the world is reaching such levels that an increasing number of them are starting to lose, often at a pace accelerated by the interactions of their decline, their assured ability to sustain the continuity of the life process. We have reached an extraordinary threshold.

Recognition of this shadow side of the success of industrial production has triggered the second of the two great intellectual shifts of the late twentieth century. The end of the Cold War and the fall of communism was the first such shift; the second, now quietly emerging, is the end of the war against life on earth, and the eventual ascendance of what we call natural capitalism.

Capitalism, as practiced, is a financially profitable, non-sustainable aberration in human development. What might be called "industrial capitalism" does not fully conform to its own accounting principles. It liquidates its capital and calls it income. It neglects to assign any value to the largest stocks of capital it employs – the natural resources and living systems, as well as the social and cultural systems that are the basis of human capital.

But this deficiency in business operations cannot be corrected simply by assigning monetary values to natural capital, for three reasons. First, many of the services we receive from living systems have not known substitutes at any price; for example, oxygen production by green plants. This was demonstrated memorably in 1991–93 when the scientists operating the $200 million Biosphere 2 experiment in Arizona discovered that it was unable to maintain life-supporting oxygen levels for the eight people living inside. Biosphere 1, a.k.a. Planet Earth, performs this task daily at no charge for 6 billion people.

Second, valuing natural capital is a difficult and imprecise exercise at best. Nonetheless, several recent assessments have estimated that biological services flowing directly into society from the stock of natural capital are worth at least $36 trillion annually. That figure is close to the annual gross world product of approximately $39 trillion – a striking measure of the value of natural capital to the economy. If natural capital stocks were given a monetary value, assuming the assets yielded "interest" of $36 trillion annually, the world's natural capital would be valued at somewhere between $400 and $500 trillion– tens of thousands of dollars for every person on the planet. That is undoubtedly a conservative figure given the fact that anything we can't live without and can't replace at any price could be said to have an infinite value. ...

Conventional Capitalism
Following Einstein's dictum that problems can't be solved within the mind-set that created them, the first step toward

any comprehensive economic and ecological change is to understand the mental model that forms the basis of present economic thinking. The mind-set of the present capitalist system might be summarized as follows:

- Economic progress can best occur in free-market systems of production and distribution where reinvested profits make labor and capital increasingly productive.
- Competitive advantage is gained when bigger, more efficient plants manufacture more products for sale to expanding markets.
- Growth in total output (GDP) maximizes human well-being.
- Any resource shortages that do occur will elicit the development of substitutes.
- Concerns for a healthy environment are important but must be balanced against the requirements of economic growth, if a high standard of living is to be maintained.
- Free enterprise and market forces will allocate people and resources to their highest and best uses.

The origins of this worldview go back centuries, but it took the industrial revolution to establish it as the primary economic ideology. This sudden, almost violent, change in the means of production and distribution of goods, in sector after economic sector, introduced a new element that redefined the basic formula for the creation of material products: Machines powered by water, wood, charcoal, coal, oil, and eventually electricity accelerated or accomplished some or all of the work formerly performed by laborers. Human productive capabilities began to grow exponentially. What took two hundred workers in 1770 could be done by a single spinner in the British textile industry by 1812. With such astonishingly improved productivity, the labor force was able to manufacture a vastly larger volume of basic necessities like cloth at greatly reduced cost. This in turn rapidly raised standards of living and real wages, increasing demand for other products in other industries. Further technological breakthroughs proliferated, and as industry after industry became mechanized, leading to even lower prices and higher incomes, all of these factors fueled a self-sustaining and increasing demand for transportation, housing, education, clothing, and other goods, creating the foundation of modern commerce.

The past two hundred years of massive growth in prosperity and manufactured capital have been accompanied by a prodigious body of economic theory analyzing it, all based on the fallacy that natural and human capital have little value as compared to final output. In the standard industrial model, the creation of value is portrayed as a linear sequence of extraction, production, and distribution: Raw materials are introduced. (Enter nature, stage left.) Labor uses technologies to transform these resources into products, which are sold to create profits. The wastes from production processes, and soon the products themselves, are somehow disposed of somewhere else. (Exit waste, stage right.) The "somewheres" in this scenario are not the concern of classical economics: Enough money can buy enough resources, so the theory goes, and enough "elsewheres" to dispose of them afterward.

This conventional view of value creation is not without its critics. Viewing the economic process as a disembodied, circular flow of value between production and consumption, argues economist Herman Daly, is like trying to understand an animal only in terms of its circulatory system, without taking into account the fact it also has a digestive tract that ties it firmly to its environment at both ends. But there is an even more fundamental critique to be applied here, and it is one based on simple logic. The evidence of our senses is sufficient to tell us that all economic activity – all that human beings are, all that they can ever accomplish – is embedded within the workings of a particular planet. That planet is not growing, so the somewheres and elsewheres are always with us. The increasing removal of resources, their transport and use, and their replacement with waste steadily erodes our stock of natural capital.

With nearly ten thousand new people arriving on earth every hour, a new and unfamiliar pattern of scarcity is now emerging. At the beginning of the industrial revolution, labor was overworked and relatively scarce (the population was about one-tenth of current totals), while global stocks of natural capital were abundant and unexploited. But today the situation has been reversed: After two centuries of rises in labor productivity, the liquidation of natural resources at their extraction cost rather than their replacement value, and the exploitation of living systems as if they were free, infinite, and in perpetual renewal, it is people who have become an abundant resource, while *nature* is becoming disturbingly scarce.

Applying the same economic logic that drove the industrial revolution to this newly emerging pattern of scarcity implies that, if there is to be prosperity in the future, society must make its use of *resources* vastly more productive – deriving four, ten, or even a hundred times as much benefit from each unit of energy, water, materials, or anything else borrowed from the planet and consumed. Achieving this degree of efficiency may not be as difficult as it might seem because from a materials and energy perspective, the economy is massively inefficient. In the United States, the materials used by the metabolism of industry amount to more than twenty times every citizen's weight per day – more than one million pounds per American per year. The global flow of matter, some 500 billion tons per year, most of it wasted, is largely invisible. Yet obtaining, moving, using, and disposing of it is steadily undermining the health of the planet, which is showing ever greater signs of stress, even of biological breakdown. Human beings already use over half the world's accessible surface freshwater, have transformed one-third to one-half of its land surface, fix more nitrogen than do all natural systems on land, and appropriate more than two-fifths of the planet's entire land-based primary biological productivity. The doubling of these burdens with rising population will displace many of the millions of other species, undermining the very web of life.

The resulting ecological strains are also causing or exacerbating many forms of social distress and conflict. For example, grinding poverty, hunger, malnutrition, and rampant disease affect one-third of the world and are growing in absolute numbers; not surprisingly, crime, corruption, lawlessness, and anarchy are also on the rise (the fastest-growing industry in the world is security and private police protection); fleeing refugee populations have increased throughout the nineties to at least tens of millions; over a billion people in the world who need to work cannot find jobs, or toil at such menial work that they cannot support themselves or their families; meanwhile, the loss of forests, topsoil, fisheries, and freshwater is, in some cases, exacerbating regional and national conflicts.

What would our economy look like if it fully valued *all* forms of capital, including human and natural capital? What if our economy were organized not around the lifeless abstractions of neoclassical economics and accountancy but around the biological realities of nature? What if Generally Accepted Accounting Practice booked natural and human capital not as a free amenity in putative inexhaustible supply but as a finite and integrally valuable factor of production? What if, in the absence of a rigorous way to practice such accounting, companies started to act *as if* such principles were in force? This choice is possible and such an economy would offer a stunning new set of opportunities for all of society, amounting to no less than the *next industrial revolution*.

Capitalism as if Living Systems Mattered

Natural capitalism and the possibility of a new industrial system are based on a very different mind-set and set of values than conventional capitalism. Its fundamental assumptions include the following:

- The environment is not a minor factor of production but rather is "an envelope containing, provisioning, and sustaining the entire economy."

- The limiting factor to future economic development is the availability and functionality of *natural capital*, in particular, life-supporting services that have no substitutes and currently have no market value.

- Misconceived or badly designed business systems, population growth, and wasteful patterns of consumption are the primary causes of the loss of natural capital, and all three must be addressed to achieve a sustainable economy.

- Future economic progress can best take place in democratic, market-based systems of production and distribution in which *all* forms of capital are fully valued, including human, manufactured, financial, and natural capital.

- One of the keys to the most beneficial employment of people, money, and the environment is radical increases in resource productivity.

- Human welfare is best served by improving the quality and flow of desired services delivered, rather than by merely increasing the total dollar flow.

- Economic and environmental sustainability depends on redressing global inequities of income and material well-being.

- The best long-term environment for commerce is provided by true democratic systems of governance that are based on the needs of people rather than business.

This article introduces four central strategies of natural capitalism that are a means to enable countries, companies, and communities to operate by behaving as if all forms of capital were valued. Ensuring a perpetual annuity of valuable social and natural processes to serve a growing population is not just a prudent investment but a critical need in the coming decades. Doing so can avert scarcity, perpetuate abundance, and provide a solid basis for social development; it is the basis of responsible stewardship and prosperity for the next century and beyond.

1. **Radical Resource Productivity.** Radically increased resource productivity is the cornerstone of natural capitalism because using resources more effectively has three significant benefits: It slows resource depletion at one end of the value chain, lowers pollution at the other end, and provides a basis to increase worldwide employment with meaningful jobs. The result can be lower costs for business and society, which no longer has to pay for the chief causes of ecosystem and social disruption. Nearly all environmental and social harm is an artifact of the uneconomically wasteful use of human and natural resources, but radical resource productivity strategies can nearly halt the degradation of the biosphere, make

it more profitable to employ people, and thus safeguard against the loss of vital living systems and social cohesion.

2. **Biomimicry.** Reducing the wasteful throughput of materials – indeed, eliminating the very idea of waste – can be accomplished by redesigning industrial systems on biological lines that change the nature of industrial processes and materials, enabling the constant reuse of materials in continuous closed cycles, and often the elimination of toxicity.

3. **Service and Flow Economy.** This calls for a fundamental change in the relationship between producer and consumer, a shift from an economy of goods and purchases to one of service and flow. In essence, an economy that is based on a flow of economic services can better protect the ecosystem services upon which it depends. This will entail a new perception of value, a shift from the acquisition of goods as a measure of affluence to an economy where the continuous receipt of quality, utility, and performance promotes well-being. This concept offers incentives to put into practice the first two innovations of natural capitalism by restructuring the economy to focus on relationships that better meet customers' changing value needs and to reward automatically both resource productivity and closed-loop cycles of materials use.

4. **Investing in Natural Capital.** This works toward reversing worldwide planetary destruction through reinvestments in sustaining, restoring, and expanding stocks of natural capital, so that the biosphere can produce more abundant ecosystem services and natural resources.

All four changes are interrelated and interdependent; all four generate numerous benefits and opportunities in markets, finance, materials, distribution, and employment. Together, they can reduce environmental harm, create economic growth, and increase meaningful employment.

Resource Productivity

Imagine giving a speech to Parliament in 1750 predicting that within seventy years human productivity would rise to the point that one person could do the work of two hundred. The speaker would have been branded as daft or worse. Imagine a similar scene today. Experts are testifying in Congress, predicting that we will increase the productivity of our resources in the next seventy years by a factor of four, ten, even one hundred. Just as it was impossible 250 years ago to conceive of an individual's doing two hundred times more work, it is equally difficult for us today to imagine a

kilowatt-hour or board foot being ten or a hundred times more productive than it is now.

Although the movement toward radical resource productivity has been under way for decades, its clarion call came in the fall of 1994, when a group of sixteen scientists, economists, government officials, and businesspeople convened and, sponsored by Friedrich Schmidt-Bleek of the Wuppertal Institute for Climate, Environment, and Energy in Germany, published the "Carnoules Declaration." Participants had come from Europe, the United States, Japan, England, Canada, and India to the French village of Carnoules to discuss their belief that human activities were at risk from the ecological and social impact of materials and energy use. The Factor Ten Club, as the group came to call itself, called for a leap in resource productivity to reverse the growing damage. The declaration began with these prophetic words: "Within one generation, nations can achieve a ten-fold increase in the efficiency with which they use energy, natural resources and other materials."

In the years since, Factor Ten (a 90 percent reduction in energy and materials intensity) and Factor Four (a 75 percent reduction) have entered the vocabulary of government officials, planners, academics, and businesspeople throughout the world. The governments of Austria, the Netherlands, and Norway have publicly committed to pursuing Factor Four efficiencies. The same approach has been endorsed by the European Union as the new paradigm for sustainable development. Austria, Sweden, and OECD environment ministers have urged the adoption of Factor Ten goals, as have the World Business Council for Sustainable Development and the United Nations Environment Programme (UNEP). The concept is not only common parlance for most environmental ministers in the world, but such leading corporations as Dow Europe and Mitsubishi Electric see it as a powerful strategy to gain a competitive advantage. Among all major industrial nations, the United States probably has the least familiarity with and understanding of these ideas.

At its simplest, increasing resource productivity means obtaining the same amount of utility or work from a product or process while using less material and energy. In manufacturing, transportation, forestry, construction, energy, and other industrial sectors, mounting empirical evidence suggests that radical improvements in resource productivity are both practical and cost-effective, even in the most modern industries. Companies and designers are developing ways to make natural resources – energy, metals, water, and forests – work five, ten, even one hundred times harder than they do today. These efficiencies transcend the marginal gains in performance that industry constantly seeks as part of its evolution. Instead, *revolutionary* leaps in design and technology will alter industry itself … Investments in the productivity revolution are not only repaid over time by the saved resources but in many cases can *reduce* initial capital investments.

When engineers speak of "efficiency," they refer to the amount of output a process provides per unit of input. Higher efficiency thus means doing more with less, measuring both factors in physical terms. When economists refer to efficiency, however, their definition differs in two ways. First, they usually measure a process or outcome in terms of expenditure of money – how the market value of what was produced compares to the market cost of the labor and other inputs used to create it. Second, "economic efficiency" typically refers to how fully and perfectly market mechanisms are being harnessed to minimize the monetary total factor cost of production. Of course it's important to harness economically efficient market mechanisms, and we share economists' devotion to that goal. But to avoid contusion, when we suggest using market tools to achieve "resource productivity" and "resource efficiency," we use those terms in the engineering sense.

Resource productivity doesn't just save resources and money; it can also improve the quality of life. Listen to the din of daily existence – the city and freeway traffic, the airplanes, the garbage trucks outside urban windows – and consider this: The waste and the noise are signs of inefficiency, and they represent money being thrown away. They will disappear as surely as did manure from the nineteenth-century streets of London and New York. Inevitably, industry will redesign everything it makes and does, in order to participate in the coming productivity revolution. We will be able to see better with resource-efficient lighting systems, produce higher-quality goods in efficient factories, travel more safely and comfortably in efficient vehicles, feel more comfortable (and do substantially more and better work) in efficient buildings, and be better nourished by efficiently grown food. An air-conditioning system that uses 90 percent less energy or a building so efficient that it needs no air-conditioning at all may not fascinate the average citizen, but the fact that they are quiet and produce greater comfort while reducing energy costs should appeal even to technophobes. That such options save money should interest everyone.

The unexpectedly large improvements to be gained by resource productivity offer an entirely new terrain for business invention, growth, and development. Its advantages can also dispel the long-held belief that core business values and environmental responsibility are incompatible or at odds. In fact, the massive inefficiencies that are causing environmental degradation almost always cost more than the measures that would reverse them.

But even as Factor Ten goals are driving reductions in materials and energy flows, some governments are continuing to create and administer laws, policies, taxes, and subsidies that have quite the opposite effect. Hundreds of billions of dollars of taxpayers' money are annually diverted to promote inefficient and unproductive material and energy use. These include subsidies to mining, oil, coal, fishing, and forest industries as well as agricultural practices that degrade soil fertility and use wasteful amounts of water and chemicals. Many of these subsidies are vestigial, some dating as far back as the eighteenth century, when European powers provided entrepreneurs with incentives to find and exploit colonial resources. Taxes extracted from labor subsidize patterns of resource use that in turn displace workers, an ironic situation that is becoming increasingly apparent and unacceptable, particularly in Europe, where there is chronically high unemployment. Already, tax reforms aimed at increasing employment by shifting taxes away from people to the use of resources have started to be instituted in the Netherlands, Germany, Britain, Sweden, and Denmark, and are being seriously proposed across Europe.

In less developed countries, people need realistic and achievable means to better their lives. The world's growing population cannot attain a Western standard of living by following traditional industrial paths to development, for the resources required are too vast, too expensive, and too damaging to local and global systems. Instead, radical improvements in resource productivity expand their possibilities for growth, and can help to ameliorate the polarization of wealth between rich and poor segments of the globe. When the world's nations met in Brazil at the Earth Summit in 1992 to discuss the environment and human development, some treaties and proposals proved to be highly divisive because it appeared that they put a lid on the ability of nonindustrialized countries to pursue development. Natural capitalism provides a practical agenda for development wherein the actions of both developed and developing nations are mutually supportive.

Biomimicry

To appreciate the potential of radical resource productivity, it is helpful to recognize that the present industrial system is, practically speaking, a couch potato: It eats too much junk food and gets insufficient exercise. In its late maturity, industrial society runs on life-support systems that require enormous heat and pressure, are petrochemically dependent and materials-intensive, and require large flows of toxic and hazardous chemicals. These industrial "empty calories" end up as pollution, acid rain, and greenhouse gases, harming environmental, social, and financial systems. Even though all the reengineering and downsizing trends of the past decade were supposed to sweep away corporate inefficiency, the US economy remains astoundingly inefficient: It has been estimated that only 6 percent of its vast flows of materials actually end up in products. Overall, the ratio of waste to the *durable* products that constitute material wealth may be closer to one hundred to one. The whole economy is less than 10 percent – probably only a few percent – as energy-efficient as the laws of physics permit.

This waste is currently rewarded by deliberate distortions in the marketplace, in the form of policies like subsidies to industries that extract raw materials from the earth and damage the biosphere. As long as that damage goes unaccounted for, as long as virgin resource prices are maintained at artificially low levels, it makes sense to continue to use virgin materials rather than reuse resources discarded from previous products. As long as it is assumed that there are "free goods" in the world – pure water, clean air, hydrocarbon combustion, virgin forests, veins of minerals – large-scale, energy- and materials-intensive manufacturing methods will dominate, and labor will be increasingly marginalized. In contrast, if the subsidies distorting resource prices were removed or reversed, it would be advantageous to employ more people and use fewer virgin materials.

Even without the removal of subsidies, the economics of resource productivity are already encouraging industry to reinvent itself to be more in accord with biological systems. Growing competitive pressures to save resources are opening up exciting frontiers for chemists, physicists, process engineers, biologists, and industrial designers. They are reexamining the energy, materials, and manufacturing systems required to provide the specific qualities (strength, warmth, structure, protection, function, speed, tension, motion, skin) required by products and end users and are turning away from mechanical systems requiring heavy metals, combustion, and petroleum to seek solutions that use minimal inputs, lower temperatures, and enzymatic reactions. Business is switching to imitating biological and ecosystem processes replicating natural methods of production and engineering to manufacture chemicals, materials, and compounds, and soon maybe even microprocessors. Some of the most exciting developments have resulted from emulating nature's life-temperature, low-pressure, solar-powered assembly techniques, whose products rival anything human-made. Science writer Janine Benyus points out that spiders make silk, strong as Kevlar but much tougher, from digested crickets and flies, without needing boiling sulfuric acid and high-temperature extruders. The abalone generates an inner shell twice as tough as our best ceramics, and diatoms make glass, both processes employing seawater with no furnaces. Trees turn sunlight, water, and air into cellulose, a sugar stiffer and stronger than nylon, and bind it into wood, a natural composite with a higher bending strength and stiffness than concrete or steel. We may never grow as skillful as spiders, abalone, diatoms, or trees, but smart designers are apprenticing themselves to nature to learn the benign chemistry of its processes.

Pharmaceutical companies are becoming microbial ranchers managing herds of enzymes. Biological farming manages soil ecosystems in order to increase the amount of biota and life per acre by keen knowledge of food chains, species interactions, and nutrient flows, minimizing crop losses and maximizing yields by fostering diversity. Meta-industrial engineers are creating "zero-emission" industrial parks whose tenants will constitute an industrial ecosystem in which one company will feed upon the nontoxic and useful wastes of another. Architects and builders are creating structures that process their own wastewater, capture light, create energy, and provide habitat for wildlife and wealth for the community, all the while improving worker productivity, morale, and health. High-temperature, centralized power plants are starting to be replaced by smaller-scale, renewable power generation. In chemistry, we can look forward to the end of the witches' brew of dangerous substances invented this century, from DDT, PCB, CFCs, and Thalidomide to Dieldrin and xenoestrogens. The eighty thousand different chemicals now manufactured end up everywhere, as Donella Meadows remarks, from our "stratosphere to our sperm." They were created to accomplish functions that can now be carried out far more efficiently with biodegradable and naturally occurring compounds.

Service and Flow

Beginning in the mid-1980s, Swiss industry analyst Walter Stahel and German chemist Michael Braungart independently proposed a new industrial model that is now gradually taking shape. Rather than an economy in which *goods* are made and sold, these visionaries imagined a *service economy* wherein consumers obtain *services* by leasing or renting goods rather than buying them outright. (Their plan should not be confused with the conventional definition of a service economy in which burger-flippers outnumber steelworkers.) Manufacturers cease thinking of themselves as sellers of products and become, instead, deliverers of service, provided by long-lasting, upgradable durables. Their goal is selling results rather than equipment, performance and satisfaction rather than motors, fans, plastics, or condensers.

The system can be demonstrated by a familiar example. Instead of purchasing a washing machine, consumers could pay a monthly fee to obtain the *service* of having their clothes cleaned. The washer would have a counter on it, just like an office photocopier, and would be maintained by the manufacturer on a regular basis, much the way mainframe computers are. If the machine ceased to provide its specific service, the manufacturer would be responsible for replacing or repairing it at no charge to the customer, because the washing machine would remain the property of the manufacturer. The concept could likewise be applied to computers, cars, VCRs, refrigerators, and almost every other durable that people now buy, use up, and ultimately throw away. Because products would be returned to the manufacturer for continuous repair, reuse, and remanufacturing, Stahel called the process "cradle-to-cradle."

Many companies are adopting Stahel's principles. Agfa Gevaert pioneered the leasing of copier services, which spread to the entire industry. The Carrier Corporation, a division of United Technologies, is creating a program to sell coolth (the opposite of warmth) to companies while retaining ownership of the air-conditioning equipment. The Interface Corporation leases the warmth, beauty, and comfort of its floor-covering services rather than selling carpets.

Braungart's model of a *service economy* focuses on the nature of material cycles. In this perspective, if a given product lasts a long time but its waste materials cannot be reincorporated into new manufacturing or biological cycles, then the producer must accept responsibility for the waste with all its attendant problems of toxicity, resource overuse, worker safety, and environmental damage. Braungart views the world as a series of metabolisms in which the creations of human beings, like the creations of nature, become "food" for interdependent systems, returning to either an industrial or a biological cycle after their useful life is completed. To some, especially frugal Scots and New Englanders, this might not sound a novel concept at all. Ralph Waldo Emerson once wrote, "Nothing in nature is exhausted in its first use. When a thing has served an end to the uttermost, it is wholly new for an ulterior service." In simpler times, such proverbial wisdom had highly practical applications. Today, the complexity of modern materials makes this almost impossible. Thus, Braungart proposed an Intelligent Product System whereby those products that do not degrade back into natural nutrient cycles be designed so that they can be deconstructed and completely reincorporated into *technical nutrient* cycles of industry.

Another way to conceive of this method is to imagine an industrial system that has no provision for landfills, outfalls, or smokestacks. If a company knew that nothing that came into its factory could be thrown away, and that everything it produced would eventually return, how would it design its components and products? The question is more than a theoretical construct, because the earth works under precisely these strictures.

In a *service economy*, the product is a means, not an end. The manufacturer's leasing and ultimate recovery of the product means that the product remains an asset. The minimization of materials use, the maximization of product durability, and enhanced ease of maintenance not only improve the customer's experience and value but also protect the manufacturer's investment and hence its bottom line. *Both* producer and customer have an incentive for continuously improving resource productivity, which in turn further protects ecosystems. Under this shared incentive, both parties form a relationship that continuously anticipates and meets the customer's evolving value needs – and meanwhile rewards both parties for reducing the burdens on the planet.

The service paradigm has other benefits as well: It increases employment, because when products are designed to be reincorporated into manufacturing cycles, waste declines, and demand for labor increases. In manufacturing, about one-fourth of the labor force is engaged in the fabrication of basic raw materials such as steel, glass, cement, silicon, and resins, while three-quarters are in the production phase. The reverse is true for energy inputs: Three times as much energy is used to extract virgin or primary materials as is used to manufacture products from those materials. Substituting reused or more durable manufactured goods for primary materials therefore uses less energy but provides more jobs.

An economy based on a service-and-flow model could also help stabilize the business cycle, because customers would be purchasing flows of services, which they need continuously, rather than durable equipment that's affordable only in good years. Service providers would have an incentive to keep their assets productive for as long as possible, rather than prematurely scrapping them in order to sell replacements. Over- and undercapacity would largely disappear, as business would no longer have to be concerned about delivery or backlogs if it is contracting from a service provider. Gone would be end-of-year rebates to move excess automobile inventory, built for customers who never ordered them because managerial production quotas were increased in order to amortize expensive capital equipment that was never needed in the first place. As it stands now, durables manufacturers have a love-hate relationship with durability. But when they become service providers, their long- and short-term incentives become perfectly attuned to what customers want, the environment deserves, labor needs, and the economy can support.

Investing in Natural Capital

When a manufacturer realizes that a supplier of key components is overextended and running behind on deliveries, it takes immediate action lest its own production lines come to a halt. Living systems are a supplier of key components for the life of the planet, and they are now falling behind on their orders. Until recently, business could ignore such shortages because they didn't affect production and didn't increase costs. That situation may be changing, however, as rising weather-related claims come to burden insurance companies and world agriculture.

If the flow of services from industrial systems is to be sustained or increased in the future for a growing population, the vital flow of life-supporting services from living systems will have to be maintained and increased. For this to be possible will require investments in natural capital.

As both globalization and Balkanization proceed, and as the per capita availability of water, arable land, and fish continue to decline (as they have done since 1980), the world faces the danger of being torn apart by regional conflicts instigated at least in part by resource shortages or imbalances and associated income polarization. Whether it involves oil or water, cobalt or fish, access to resources is playing an ever more prominent role in generating conflict.

Societies need to adopt shared goals that enhance social welfare but that are not the prerogatives of specific value or belief systems. Natural capitalism is one such objective. It is neither conservative nor liberal in its ideology, but appeals to both constituencies. Since it is a means, and not an end, it doesn't advocate a particular social outcome but rather makes possible many different ends. Therefore, whatever the various visions different parties or factions espouse, society can work toward resource productivity now, without waiting to resolve disputes about policy.

Is It Time to Jump Off the Sustainability Bandwagon?

JOSEPH DESJARDINS

In their 1987 report, *Our Common Future*, the United Nations World Commission on Environment and Development (the "Brundtland Commission") called for a new model of global economic development. The Brundtland Report offered what has become the conventional definition of sustainable development as development that "meets the needs of the present without compromising the ability of future generations to meet their own needs."[1] The Brundtland Report addressed economic development in global terms because the economic, environmental, and ethical challenges it addressed were global in scope. Yet while this original application was at the macro-economic level, the Brundtland Report was also intended to have significant implications for business at the micro level.

Almost 30 years after the Brundtland Report, "sustainable" is regularly used today to modify an innumerable range of distinct and diverse activities, ranging from agriculture and architecture to zoning and zoos. Similarly, the noun "sustainability" has become a generic stand-alone concept, as well as a term modified by such diverse adjectives as economic, environmental, social, ecological, corporate, financial, global, human, and organizational.[2]

Sustainability has become ubiquitous within business, with virtually every division including management, marketing, investing, accounting, strategy, and operations developing sustainable models and practices. It is difficult to find a major corporation that does not issue an annual sustainability report; by one account 95 percent of the Global 250 issue annual sustainability reports.[3] Cottage industries have arisen in such areas as sustainability consulting, ranking, investing and measurement. Major consulting firms including Ernst & Young, Deloitte, Accenture, PwC, and KPMG, and countless advocacy groups and NGOs have created significant business ventures in sustainability consulting, advising businesses on

From *Business Ethics Quarterly* 26, no. 1 (2016): 117–35. © Society for Business Ethics, 2016, published by Cambridge University Press. Reproduced with permission of the Licensor through PLSclear.

how to become more sustainable. *Forbes* magazine, in conjunction with Global Knights Capital, publishes an annual ranking of the top 100 sustainable firms, the "Global100." Virtually every brokerage and investment firm offers a sustainable portfolio, with the Dow Jones Sustainability Index perhaps the most widely used sustainability investing guide. Similar to the Global 100, the Global Reporting Initiative (GRI) has created a sustainability measurement and assessment tool that is widely used by business and NGOs throughout the world. Another well-known major benchmarking framework is the "triple bottom line" (TBL), now widely cited in management literature and in sustainability consulting.

It is prudent to be cautious whenever a concept, especially one that claims significant ethical implications, becomes so popular among such a wide range of people and institutions. While I believe that the original Brundtland idea of sustainable development has the potential to do much good in guiding business practice, I believe that this potential is being undermined by the systematic misuse, misunderstanding, and flawed application of the concept in many business settings. Under the guise of sustainability, business is being asked to do both less than and more than what should be required by the commitment to sustainable development. As a result, serious ethical and practical questions that must be addressed before sustainability can become a meaningful business strategy go unanswered. The question needs to be asked: "Is it time for business to jump off the sustainability bandwagon?"

Brundtland's Ethical Foundations

The Brundtland Commission's concern with sustainable development arose at a time in which evidence was mounting that worldwide economic development, then understood almost exclusively in terms of GDP *growth*, was approaching the bio-physical limits imposed by the biosphere in which that growth occurred. The Brundtland Commission argued that a model of economic development in which undifferentiated growth is taken as the end of economic activity and in which less developed countries were advised simply to "get richer," was failing to address the real needs of hundreds of millions of people while at the same time placing long-term environmental productivity in jeopardy. The Brundtland Report was instrumental in shifting attention away from an exclusively quantitative interpretation of economic development to one that stressed the qualitative dimension.

Some considerable ethical foundations are implicit in this discussion. As the Brundtland Commission pointed out, the goal of economic development should be to "improve the lot" of all people, but not simply by helping them "get richer," but by meeting the needs of the hundreds of millions of people who lack adequate food, water, shelter, and security. Economic activity that did not meet human needs, or that compromised the productive capacity of the Earth's biosphere so that future needs could not be met, was unacceptable.

Thus, along with economic development and environmental protection, ethical considerations were a part of their work from the beginning. As articulated by the Brundtland Commission, both the economic and the environmental aspects of sustainable development are means to the end of human well-being, specifically meeting human needs in both present and future. Accordingly, while the concept of sustainable development is commonly said to encompass three dimensions – the "three pillars" of economics, environment, ethics – the ethical dimension is better understood as the foundation upon which both economic and environmental policy rests.

The Brundtland Report was not a treatise in philosophy, so we should not expect to find a sophisticated treatment of ethics presented. But we can plausibly sketch its ethical foundations. The Brundtland Report is an essay in distributive justice, specifically judging the distribution of economic goods and services by how well it meets the needs of the least advantaged. The Brundtland Report is also an essay in intergenerational justice in that it is concerned with justice not only to presently living humans, but to future generations as well.

It is this focus on the satisfaction of needs rather than of expressed preferences, which distinguishes Brundtland's qualitative interpretation of economic development from the quantitative and utilitarian interpretations of economic growth found in standard market accounts. The standard interpretation of economic development as economic growth seeks an increase in overall wealth as a measure of overall happiness. By focusing on the needs of the least advantaged, Brundtland's distributive justice offers an alternative to the collectivist utilitarianism of growth-based economics.

There is also an environmental ethics implicit in this framework. In the vocabulary of the discipline, sustainable development's environmentalism is anthropocentric and conservationist. From the perspective of sustainable development, the value of the natural world derives from how it serves human needs and how effectively and efficiently these resources are used in this capacity. It is an ethics of environmental stewardship rather than environmental preservation. Consistent with the prevailing economic growth model, but differing from those who attribute an intrinsic value to the natural world, this account is anthropocentric in that the value of the natural world derives from how it is used to serve human ends.[4] It is conservationist in that it advocates a more conservative stewardship of those resources than is found in the prevailing model, which has given little or no notice to the environmental context for economic growth. We can therefore summarize these ethical foundations as (1) a needs-based account of intergenerational distributive justice, and (2) an anthropocentric, conservationist environmental ethics.

These starting points have significant philosophical pedigrees and are not without problems. But if only on an intuitive level, the ethical foundations of the Brundtland Report are appealing and this intuitive appeal likely explains much of the widespread acceptance of the idea of sustainable development. Basic needs have an ethical priority over desires or preferences; the needs of future generations deserve moral consideration; the needs of both present and future people are being jeopardized by an economic model that is putting the Earth's productive capacity at risk.

Asking Sustainability to Do Too Little: Sustainable Development as Risk Management

Sustainable development is, thus, a normative concept, suggesting a direction or norm that should guide practical decision-making in public policy and economics. Building from this starting point, the appeal to sustainability plays a justificatory and *normative* role in most contemporary business settings where to describe an activity as sustainable is to justify and approve it. To characterize something as sustainable is also to provide a motivational component: it is a commendable thing; people get credit for doing it. Conceptually, of course, this need not be true. Beside this normative connotation, "sustainability" also has a *descriptive* connotation in which it means simply the capacity to continue long term. To be sustainable in this descriptive sense is to be capable of continuing over an extended period. We could, for example, talk of the sustainability of predatory lending, Ponzi schemes, excessive executive compensation, or of the war on terror.

This ambiguity helps us recognize that the normative force of "sustainable" will come from the concept it modifies. Sustainable *development* is normative in that it refers to economic activity that serves the ethical end of human well-being, and *sustainable* development seeks to do this in a stable and ongoing manner.

Whenever the adjective "sustainable" is divorced from "development," and turned into the noun "sustainability," we are well advised to look deeper and ask *what* is to be sustained and ask *why* should it be sustained? In the words of philosopher J. L. Austin, "sustainable" is a "substantive-hungry" word, calling out for a noun to be characterized and when turned into a noun itself, it becomes misleading if not meaningless.[5]

Much of the appeal of sustainability within business contexts can be explained by a failure to distinguish descriptive from normative uses of the term. The attractiveness that sustainability holds for many businesses lies in the fact that it is interpreted in the descriptive sense and thus interpreted as little more than a risk management strategy. When used only in this descriptive sense, a claim that some business activity is sustainable is no more deserving of ethical approbation than a criminal who claims that his Ponzi scheme is sustainable. One can readily find many such examples, but I will mention only two. Ernst & Young promotes their sustainability consulting by appeal to "improved reputation," "access to capital," "increased efficiencies," as well as "avoiding and mitigating environmental and social risks."[6]

The Dow Jones Sustainability Index (DJSI), as another example, is even more explicit in this regard.

> Corporate Sustainability is a business approach that creates long-term shareholder value by embracing opportunities and managing risks deriving from economic, environmental and social developments.[7]

DJSI's European partner, RobecoSAM, elaborates on this description further:

> No doubt contemporary business is confronted with a broad range of environmental risks, ranging from climate change to resource depletion, and social risks, ranging from labor supply to corruption within a supply chain. Risk management is a challenge for all firms and effective managers analyze the environmental and social risks facing the firm.[8]

But managing risks in order to increase the likelihood of financial success is an altogether different normative foundation than the ethics implicit in the Brundtland Commission vision. Depending on the firm and its activities, long-term economic survival may, or may not, contribute to sustainable development in an ethical sense. A descriptively sustainable business may, or may not, conform to sustainable development's ethical norm of meeting needs without compromising ongoing environmental productivity. Treating sustainability as a risk management strategy therefore asks business to do too little in serving the ethical ends of sustainable development.

An important thing to note about this risk management interpretation of sustainability is that it assumes a link between beneficial (or at least benign) environmental initiatives and economic success, the former being a means to the end of the latter.[9] Thus, the ethical status of the risk management approach will stand or fall on the depth of the connection between normatively sustainable activities and business success.

Two questions follow from the alleged connection between environmental responsibility and risk management. Is it true, in fact, that long-term shareholder value will be served, and risks mitigated, by adopting the type of sustainable practices envisioned in the Brundtland Report? Second, even if this is true, are there other more cost-effective means for attaining those same risk management goals? To secure a connection between normatively sustainable activities and long-term business success – to successfully manage risks by adopting environmentally sounds practices – the answer to the first question must be "yes," and to the second question "no." If long-term shareholder value is not served by the type of environmentally sustainable activity envisioned by Brundtland, then the risk management advice would be for business to move in other directions, likewise, if a business can find more cost-effective means than the sustainable approach for attaining that end.

We should also recognize that these are empirical not conceptual questions. They cannot be answered by definition, in principle, for all firms in all situations. Because this connection is empirical, one can imagine cases in which an environmental responsibility runs counter to the firm's long-term self-interest. It will all depend on the particular firm, its products and services, the industry in which it exists, and the environmental impact of the individual firm, the industry and, in fact, the entire surrounding economy and ecosystem.

To the degree that certain products or industries are destructive of the biosphere's ability to support human life, they will need to change and that product or industry will be threatened by a move towards sustainable development. After all, the force of the Brundtland Commission recommendations was that the status quo was unsustainable. One could imagine many individual firms, if not entire industries, that will and should face great risks from the environmentally sustainable economy. To the degree that present production and consumption patterns, particularly those found in consumer-driven industrial economies, are causing environmental deterioration, the status quo is exactly what needs to change.

Promoting business sustainability simply as a risk management strategy suggests that any firm can become sustainable. Of course, one way to mitigate risks created by

environmental challenges would be to adopt more environmentally benign practices and evolve into a new type of firm. But this is only one way. We cannot assume that every firm or every industry can or will adapt in this way. Other risk management strategies, not the least of which involves corporate political activity such as lobbying, funding climate change deniers, and otherwise participating in the political arena to counter the sustainable development agenda, are open to firms threatened by a sustainable future.

To restate, when we hear talk about "sustainability," we should always be prepared to ask "*What* is being sustained?" and most importantly, "How does that product, that firm, that industry, contribute to an economically just future by meeting present and future needs in an environmentally sound manner?" Without an answer to this question, the normative and ethical justification of an appeal to sustainability is lost. Treating sustainability simply as a risk management strategy divorces the concept from its ethical foundations and thus expects too little of business.

Asking Sustainability to Do Too Much: Sustainable Development as Social Development

If treating sustainability as a risk management strategy asks too little of business, much of what passes as sustainability among its advocates asks too much. The ethical dimension of sustainability is narrower than what is often claimed, especially as it is thought to apply to business. I will also argue that the environmental dimension is much more narrow than often construed.

Over time the ethical responsibilities underlying the original Brundtland Commission recommendations have morphed into a more general prescription for "social" responsibility.

One can find many examples of this over-extension. I'll mention only three. The first comes from the Global Reporting Initiative (GRI). GRI is the foremost advocate for corporate sustainability reporting that works closely with various United Nations programs and is the leading example of sustainability measurement. GRI has created a Sustainability Reporting Framework to help businesses measure their sustainability performance by providing "metrics and methods for measuring and reporting sustainability-related impacts and performance."[10]

GRI adopts the common practice of dividing sustainability into the "three pillars" of an economic, environmental, and ethical dimension. The economic dimension of the GRI framework consists of metrics that measure "the organization's impacts on the economic conditions of its stakeholders, and on economic systems at local, national, and global levels." The environmental dimension "concerns the organization's impact on living and non-living natural systems, including land, air, water and ecosystems [and] covers impacts related to inputs (such as energy and water) and outputs (such as emissions, effluents and waste)."[11] "Impact" is a vague term and can suggest a very wide range of responsibilities. But while these are broad interpretations of what is involved in economic and environmental aspects of sustainability, they are not as broad as the ethical dimension. According to the GRI:

> The social dimension of sustainability concerns the impacts the organization has on the social systems within which it operates. The Social Category includes the sub-Categories: Labor Practices and Decent Work; Human Rights; Society; Product Responsibility. Most of the content in the sub-Categories is based on internationally recognized universal standards or other relevant international references.[12]

These standards includes the United Nations' "Universal Declaration of Human Rights"; the "International Covenant on Civil and Political Rights"; the "International Covenant on Economic, Social, and Cultural Rights"; various International Labour Organization (ILO) declarations on workplace rights, as well as responsibilities to local community engagement, initiatives to counter corruption and anti-competitive behavior, commitments to product safety, ethical marketing, and ethical sourcing. How broad is this conception? The Universal Declaration of Human Rights includes rights to, among other things, "rest and leisure," and a right to "enjoy the arts," and the International Covenant on Economic, Social, and Cultural Rights includes rights "to form and join labor unions," a "right to strike," a right to "free education," "social security," and "paid parental leave." In short, the ethical dimension described by the GRI might fairly be described as a generic theory of corporate social responsibility and looks very similar to the range of topics covered in a typical business ethics course.

The Corporate Knights Global 100 ranking, similar to the GRI framework, also incorporates many thoughtful and imaginative environmental measures, including metrics for energy, carbon, water, and waste productivity (revenues generated per unit of energy and water used and per unit of carbon and waste produced). Among the Global 100's social metrics are percentage of tax paid, ratio of CEO to average worker salary, stability of pension funds, workplace safety rates, employee turnover, and diversity of leadership.

Consider also how sustainability has been interpreted by some business-related professional societies. The Society of

Human Resource Managers (SHRM) advocates for a sustainable workplace which is to "include examining employee carbon footprint, offering occupational wellness programs and stress-reducing strategies (e.g., nap rooms, on-site massages and stretch breaks), and providing wellness-related benefits such as on-site gyms. Maintaining a sustainable workplace also means minimizing external environmental impact – for example, by purchasing repurposed and recycled materials, minimizing unnecessary employee travel, and reducing energy and water consumption."[13] The American Institute of CPAs (AICPA), for example, straightforwardly identifies sustainability with corporate social responsibility. Their explanation of sustainability is:

> Sometimes used interchangeably with the term corporate social responsibility, the most widely accepted definition of sustainability that has emerged over time is the "triple bottom-line" consideration of 1) economic viability, 2) social responsibility, and 3) environmental responsibility.[14]

To say that these applications of sustainability ask business to do too much is to say that many of them are not an essential part of an environmentally sustainable economy. However, not every socially responsible act, nor every environmentally responsible act, belongs as a part of the sustainability agenda. One could imagine a society, even a global one, in which present and future needs were met in an environmentally safe way without also recognizing widespread commitments to civil rights, labor rights, or other socially desirable ends.

In these and many other cases, the Brundtland understanding of sustainable development has evolved from a model of global economic development into a wider understanding of a "social development" or "social sustainability." The United Nations now regularly uses the phrase "social development," in contexts wherever sustainable development and "sustainability" is used. For example, on the United Nations website, sustainable development is now characterized in the following way:

> Defined as "development that meets the needs of the present without compromising the ability of future generations to meet their own needs" (World Commission on Environment and Development, 1987), sustainable development has emerged as the guiding principle for long-term global development. Consisting of three pillars, sustainable development seeks to achieve, in a balanced manner, economic development, social development and environmental protection.[15]

There is a plausible historical explanation for this evolution. Agenda 21, the development plan that came out of the United Nations Conference on Environment and Development (the "Rio Summit") in 1992, five years after the Brundtland Report, began to focus on some of the environmental, social, and political conditions that are necessary to secure needs. So, for example, if present and future needs include food and water, then fertile soil, prevention of desertification, and access to drinking water are some of the secondary goods essential to secure basic needs. But the understanding of social development has continued to expand. Given the United Nations' own agenda for a wide range of human rights, including the Declaration of Human Rights and International Covenant on Economic, Social, and Cultural Rights, it is not surprising that that institution would seek to broaden the normative implication of sustainable development. The United Nations' goal of making the world a better place is simply broader than the Brundtland Commission's goal of sustainable development.

But consider what has happened here. The Brundtland Commission Report called for a new model of *economic* development on the grounds that the present economic growth model's disregard for environmental factors was jeopardizing its ability to meet human needs, both in the present and future. The end was intergenerational justice and the means was a more environmentally conservative economy. Today, those ethical ends have been transformed into a generic social agenda – something called "social development" – that stands as one of three equal foundational "pillars" of a single concept: sustainability.

Once again we find a tendency to divorce the modifier "sustainable" from any specific noun and turn it into the stand-alone concept of "sustainability." This suggests that sustainability can be achieved only if we adopt a particular social vision – something called "social development," a vision that includes labor rights, rights to leisure and the arts, paid parental leave, free education, controlled CEO pay, etc. But why assume that this social vision is connected in any way with the concept of sustainability, in either the normative or descriptive sense? One can understand why economic development cannot be sustainable over the long term without certain environmental conditions, but there is little reason to think that society cannot be sustainable over the long term without an entire array of social and ethical goods. At the very least, these are altogether different questions. ...

Asking Sustainability to Do Too Much: Sustainable Development as Environmental Ethics

If expansion of the ethical dimension of sustainable development into a general social development is confusing,

expanding it into a more general concept of environmental sustainability can actually detract from the sustainable development agenda. From the start, many environmentalists were skeptical of the sustainability movement, criticizing Brundtland's conservationist approach for failing to acknowledge important environmental goods, duties, and virtues.[16]

At its core, the environmental pillar of sustainable development rests on a conservationist environmentalism, which treats the natural world as a means to human ends, important ends to be sure, but human ends nonetheless. This conservationist agenda emphasizes such environmental responsibilities as protection of clean air and water, conservative use of non-renewable resources and a shift towards renewable energy sources. Basic needs such as food, water, shelter, health and responsibility to future generations give rise to a concern with such issues as pollution, desertification, renewable energy, resource use, climate change.

Not all environmentalists would agree with this emphasis. The so-called "deep ecology" movement rejects as "shallow" the conservationist approach that underlies Brundtland in favor of a broader biocentric and preservationist agenda. Biocentric environmentalists, for example, those who believe that non-human animals deserve ethical consideration, reject the anthropocentric approach to environmentalism that is embedded in sustainable development. Preservationists who believe that there is an intrinsic value in the natural world, whether it lies in the moral status of animals, the aesthetic or spiritual values of wilderness areas, or in the diversity of species, reject the conservationist approach which values nature only instrumentally.

In many contemporary settings the anthropocentric and conservationist foundations for sustainable development are often replaced by conceptions of sustainability that encompass the entire biocentric and preservationist range of environmental concerns. In much the same way that the ethical dimension has morphed into generic social development, or social sustainability, the environmental dimension has morphed into a generic environmental sustainability. One can find some very good and focused work on the environmental responsibilities of sustainable business by such institutional players as the GRI, the World Bank, Global Knights, and others. But one will also find a common tendency to expand the range of environmental responsibilities to include almost any human impact on the natural environment. The GRI, for example, describes the environmental dimension this way:

The environmental dimension of sustainability concerns the organization's impact on living and non-living natural systems, including land, air, water and ecosystems. The Environmental Category covers impacts related to inputs (such as energy and water) and outputs (such as emissions, effluents and waste). In addition, it covers biodiversity, transport, and product and service-related impacts, as well as environmental compliance and expenditures.[17]

Many of the specific metrics developed by GRI are reasonable, emphasizing a concern with standard conservationist issues of resource use and pollution. But the description of "impact on living and non-living natural systems" is too general. In particular, the implicit suggestion seems to be that any human impact on the natural world is, if not environmentally wrong, at least something to be avoided or minimized. Any and every human activity will impact the natural world and expecting any organization to limit, or measure, such impacts seems to ask too much, especially if this requires making a trade-off with meeting present human needs.

The case against collapsing the environmental dimension of sustainable development into a more generic environmental sustainability parallels the case against collapsing the ethical dimension into a more generic social development or social sustainability. The underlying rationales and ends are different, and there are philosophical, conceptual, and practical reasons not to confuse the two.

Like social sustainability, environmental sustainability is conceptually confusing. What, exactly, is to be sustained by environmental sustainability? The Earth and its natural environment existed for billions of years before humans evolved and will exist for untold eons after them. If anything is sustainable regardless of any and all human acts, it is the natural environment. Drawing any practical or ethical conclusions from a generic idea of environmental sustainability is nonsensical without an account of what elements of the natural environment should be sustained, and why. The sustainable development agenda answers these questions by connecting the natural world to human needs. In this context, environmental sustainability is based on a conservationist ethic in which the natural world can and should be used, prudently and efficiently, to meet human needs. Arguments can and have been made to support a wider biocentric and preservationist agenda. As Brundtland acknowledged, good reasons beyond utility can be given for protecting many endangered species and preserving biodiversity and wilderness areas for their own sake. They are just different arguments from those that support sustainable development and they should not be confused with, or smuggled into, the sustainable development agenda. ...

Perhaps nowhere can the tensions between the ethical dimension of sustainable development and a broader environmentalism be seen than in the area of food and agriculture. The production, distribution, and access to food and water, food and water quality and safety, food types (meat? beef? organic? local? processed?), diet and nutrition, cultural aspects of food, and food and such technologies as genetically modified organisms, synthetic biology (synthetic meat!), synthetic fertilizers and pesticides all raise issues at the boundary of sustainable development and a broader environmentalism.

As Brundtland reminds us, the green revolution of the twentieth century allowed food production to outpace global population growth. Global food production today remains highly dependent on irrigation, synthetic chemicals, fossil fuels, factory farms and fisheries, and GMOs. Given that we are barely meeting the food needs of the present by using such technologies – if in fact we are meeting those needs – it is unrealistic to think that moving to a more environmentally benign agriculture, at least in the short term, would result in anything other than widespread starvation and malnourishment.

Yet there are risks to present and future human beings associated with most elements of modern, high-tech agricultural practices. Many legal pesticides have been known to cause cancer in animals, and have been associated with various forms of cancer, birth defects or other reproductive harms, and are known to impair child development. Several studies found a mixture of pesticide residues in the blood and urine of almost 100 percent of all persons sampled.[18] Given these considerable risks, a plausible case can and has been made that the present generation is compromising the ability of future generations to meet their food needs with such practices. Yet, there is equally strong evidence that changing such practices will compromise the present generation's ability to meet their needs.

But just at this point where more analysis and evaluation is needed, these discussions can be overwhelmed and debate silenced by wider environmental objections to technology-intensive agriculture. These objections range from loss of biodiversity, habitat and natural areas, mistreatment of animals, threats to native species, to the creation of non-natural "Frankenfoods," the concentration of power in the hands of a few global corporations, harm to local rural or indigenous communities, and lack of transparency in product labeling.

An example of where these tensions have virtually shut down debate is the case of so-called "golden rice." Vitamin A deficiency (VAD), which can lead to blindness and death, is a common occurrence among undernourished populations.

The World Health Organization estimates that as many as 190 million children were affected by VAD in 2009.[19] Golden rice is a genetically modified rice that contains genes that synthesize beta-carotene, making the rice a significant source of vitamin A. Because rice is an inexpensive, readily available, and familiar food in many of the regions where VAD is prevalent, golden rice would seem an ideal solution to meet the needs of some of the world's poorest and malnourished people. Yet, because it is a GMO food opposition among many environmentalists has essentially put an end to golden rice production in many of the world's poorest regions. Greenpeace, for example, calls golden rice "environmentally irresponsible."

On sustainable development grounds, at least a plausible case can be made to support policies and actions in all of these areas that are in tension with more biocentric, preservationist environmentalism. Collapsing sustainable development's conservationist approach into a generic environmentalism cloaks the real tensions that can occur, it often silences the conservationist agenda by branding it as "environmentally irresponsible," it can dissuade those firms and industries which might otherwise support the sustainable development agenda, and it can obstruct the needed work that remains to be done. …

A potential middle ground between the conservationist approach embedded in sustainable development and the preservationist approach of many environmentalists might still be found. While sustainable development cannot support preserving natural systems in some unchanged steady-state, the rate of human-caused change does seem to matter for the conservationist agenda. For example, climates do change, species do become extinct, and ecosystems do get disrupted naturally. But this does not mean that any and all change, especially at any rate over any time frame, is without danger. The rate and extent of present climate change, species extinction, and ecosystem disruption may well be occurring in ways that meeting both present and future needs are compromised.

Thus, we might conclude that a more cautionary approach to disrupting ecosystems can be justified on prudential grounds, but it is a cautionary approach that can be overridden when such disruption does serve human needs. So, for example, disrupting the world's climate by emitting large amounts of carbon dioxide from coal-fired power plants is one thing ethically if those plants serve basic human needs in poor countries; it might be a different matter ethically when those plants serve the consumerist preferences in an industrialized country.

I should be clear that my position does not imply that any disruptions or destructions of natural systems are justified as long as they serve any human ends, nor that the status quo of industrial agriculture should always trump a more biocentric and preservationist agenda. But the tensions and trade-offs between the conservationist environmentalism implicit in Brundtland and a wider biocentric, preservationist environmentalism will require both normative and empirical analysis. My contention is that this needed analysis can be lost when the Brundtland approach is uncritically absorbed into a far-ranging notion of environmental sustainability.

Notes

1. World Commission on Environment and Development, *Our Common Future* (Oxford University Press, 1987), p. 15. Hereafter WCED.

2. One sustainable management textbook, *Sustainability: Essentials for Business*, cites over 500 different uses and definitions of sustainability or activities modified by the word sustainable: Scott T. Young and Kanwalroop Kathy Dhanda, *Sustainability: Essentials for Business* (Thousand Oaks, CA: Sage, 2012).

3. Ernst Ligteringen, keynote speech at the GRI Global Conference on Sustainability and Reporting, May 22, 2013, as reported in Ernst & Young, *Sustainability Reporting: The Time Is Now*, p. 13. Retrieved January 15, 2016 from www.globalreporting.org/resourcelibrary/2013-GRI-Global-Conference-in-Review.pdf.

4. The Brundtland Report did acknowledge that there are other reasons to adopt a wider environmentalism. "But utility aside, there are also moral, ethical, cultural, aesthetic, and purely scientific reasons for conserving wild beings" (WCED, para. 53).

5. Austin was concerned with the misuse of the words "real" and "reality." Describing something as real calls out for further information. Real what? A real duck as opposed to a decoy? Real cream, as opposed to artificial? Removed from specific contexts, "reality" is meaningless. So, too, I would claim about sustainable and sustainability. J. L. Austin, *Sense and Sensibilia* (Oxford University Press, 1964), chap. 7.

6. *The Value of Sustainability Reporting: A Study Conducted by Ernst and Young and the Boston College Center for Corporate Citizenship* (2013), p. 3. Retrieved January 15, 2016 from www.ey.com/Publication/vwLUAssets/EY_Value_of_Sustainability_Reporting/%24File/EY-Sustainability.pdf.

7. Dow Jones Sustainability Indexes, *Annual Review* (2002), p. 3. Retrieved January 15, 2016 from www.sustainability-indices.com/images/review-presentation-2002.pdf.

8. Robesco statement on "Corporate Sustainability." Retrieved January 15, 2016 from https://assessments.robecosam.com/documents/DJSI_FAQ_2016.pdf.

9. Importantly, this is why a risk management strategy differs from making the so-called "business case" for sustainability. The latter case accepts the ends of environmental protection while making a financial case to strive for that end. The former case judges

whether the end of environmental protection is worth the risk taken to achieve it and is open to the possibility that it is not. This distinction is similar to the distinction between cost–benefit and cost-effective strategies. In one case – cost-effective and the business case for sustainable practices – the ends are granted and we look for best means; in the other – cost–benefit and risk management – the ends themselves are determined by the best costs/risks ratio.

10. Global Reporting Index G4: *Sustainability Reporting Guidelines 2015*, p. 3. Retrieved January 19, 2016 from www.ey.com/Publication/vwLUAssets/G4-Sustainability-Reporting-Guidelines/$FILE/G4-Sustainability-Reporting-Guidelines.pdf.

11. Ibid., p. 52.

12. Ibid., p. 64.

13. Society for Human Resource Management, "Sustainable Workplace Practices." Retrieved October 12, 2015 from www.shrm.org/templatestools/hrqa/pages/sustainableworkplacepracticesandhowtheybenefit-thebottomline.aspx#sthash.Y8HffmhY.dpuf.

14. American Institute of CPAs, "Sustainability Accounting and Reporting." Retrieved January 18, 2016 from www.aicpa.org/interestareas/businessindustryandgovernment/resources/sustainability/sustainability-accounting.html.

15. Retrieved November 11, 2014 from www.un.org/sustainabledevelopment/development-agenda/.

16. See, for example, Holmes Rolston, *Conserving Natural Value* (New York: Columbia University Press, 1994), pp. 84–88.

17. GR4 guidelines (May 2013), p. 54.

18. The known cancer and reproductive claims are from Office of Environmental Health and Hazard Assessment, *List of chemicals known to the state to cause cancer or reproductive toxicity* (Sacramento, CA: California Environmental Protection Agency, 1998). The residue claim is from G. Solomon et al., *Pesticides and Human Health: A Resource for Health Care Professionals* (Santa Monica, CA: Physicians for Social Responsibility, 2000), p. 9, which cites three separate scientific studies.

19. Staff, "Global Prevalence of Vitamin A Deficiency in Populations at Risk 1995–2005," WHO Global Database on Vitamin A Deficiency (Geneva: World Health Organization, 2009).

8.3 CORPORATE ENVIRONMENTAL MISCONDUCT

Corporate Responsibility, Democracy, and Climate Change

DENIS G. ARNOLD

The Earth's climate is changing as a result of steadily increasing greenhouse gas (GHG) emissions and deforestation. Scientists warn that if these activities are not curbed the changes to the Earth's climate will cause substantial economic, social, and environmental harm both in the lifetime of present generations and to future generations. GHG emissions are the result of a market failure, and collective governmental action is required to correct the market failure and protect Earth's atmosphere. In the United States context, legislative proposals to curb GHG emissions have been unsuccessful. A major cause of this failure has been corporate political activity intended to defeat such legislative efforts. Little attention has been paid to the question of whether corporate efforts to defeat climate change legislation can be ethically justified. This article develops a series of six propositions that are used collectively to assess the moral legitimacy of corporate political activity aimed at defeating climate change. The question that motivates this article is a simple one: Can corporate political activity to defeat climate change legislation be ethically justified?

Harmful Climate Change

Steadily increasing CO_2 and other GHG emissions are accumulating in Earth's atmosphere, trapping heat that would otherwise dissipate into space via the greenhouse effect. This is supplemented by deforestation that results in a loss of carbon sinks and causes carbon to be released into the atmosphere. The existence of anthropogenic climate change has been understood by climate scientists since the 1980s and was the basis for the creation of the Intergovernmental Panel on Climate Change (IPCC) in 1988.[1] The discovery of anthropogenic climate change can be traced to the subsequent release of the IPCC's 2001 scientific report.[2] This report documented increased atmospheric CO_2 and other sources of climate change and the impact of these emissions on global mean temperature changes. While the evidence

From *Business and Human Rights Journal* 1, no. 2 (2016): 255–75. Reprinted with permission of Cambridge University Press.

has grown stronger since that time, it is important for our purpose to acknowledge the date by which the relevant scientific communities had achieved consensus regarding climate change. Thus:

1. The scientific community has understood with reasonable certainty since at least 2001 that anthropogenic climate change is occurring.

At the same time, scientists have identified a series of harmful impacts on present and future human populations resulting from climate change. These include water scarcity, drought, heat waves, forest fires, increased global distribution of tropical diseases, increased intensity of storms, rising sea levels, and the inundation of low lying coastal regions.[3] These impacts of a changing climate will have direct, negative impacts on human populations and will have an especially harmful impact on the ability of the least economically well off to attain basic human rights.[4] In terms of the current global population, the 4 billion people living on less than $9.05 a day[5] are most vulnerable, but wealthier populations living in the areas most negatively impacted by sea-level rise also confront prospective risks to the attainment of human rights. Without substantial alterations to present practices, harm to persons will be more widespread in future generations. While not the focus of our present analysis, ecosystems and non-human species will also be adversely impacted in ethically significant ways.[6] Thus:

2. Climate change will result in significant harm to human populations, both the current generation and future generations, and to the ecosystems that we inhabit.

Market Failures and Legislative Corrections

Human actions in the form of economic activity aimed at wealth enhancement are the driving force behind increased GHGs in Earth's atmosphere in relation to global historical averages. The atmosphere is a public (or collective) good in that the utilization of the good by one person does not limit or constrain the utilization of the good by other persons regardless of their willingness to pay for the maintenance of the atmosphere.[7] GHG emissions are a negative externality, that is, firms and their customers do not bear all the social costs of emitting GHGs. In this case, the social costs of climate change are not priced into the cost of the goods or services. As a result, there is a market failure. "Greenhouse gas emissions constitute the greatest market failure the world has seen."[8] Markets do not price GHG emissions in ways that account for their negative impact on the atmosphere. Thus:

3. GHG emissions are negative externalities requiring market corrections in order to preserve public goods.

Many individuals have responded to climate change by altering their behavior in order to reduce their personal responsibility for GHG emissions or by advocating for changes at a local level aimed at reducing GHG emissions and deforestation.[9] However, such activity is radically insufficient for addressing a vast market failure that is global in scale and transgenerational in its impact. Because markets currently misprice GHG emissions by failing to take into account the negative impact of emissions on the atmosphere, national and international level actions are needed. National policies and international agreements among nations are required to adequately respond to the scope of the problem. These policies need to facilitate a shift to "natural capitalism" and environmentally sustainable economic development.[10]

Individuals express wants and preferences in the marketplace, and this is quantifiable and therefore measurable in monetary terms. Consumers have limited ability to express pro-environmental preferences in the market for several reasons. First, there is often an asymmetry in information regarding negative externalities between consumers and the firms that produce the goods or services. For example, many consumers are unaware that the atmospheric lifetime of specific GHGs can be hundreds of years or longer,[11] although corporate scientists and leaders in the transportation and energy sectors, for example, are knowledgeable about these technical aspects of GHG life cycles. Second, "greenwashing" by firms, that is, the practice of falsely representing products or a firm as environmentally sustainable in order to deceive consumers into purchasing goods and services, leads consumers to believe that their purchasing choices are environmentally sustainable when they are not. Third, many consumers lack the ability to pay sustainability premiums for products and services that have lower carbon footprints than conventional products but which cost more to produce (e.g., wind- or solar-generated energy in comparison to coal-generated energy).

Even in the absence of asymmetric information, greenwashing, and an inability to pay, marketplace preferences do not always reflect the environmental and social values of citizens, especially values regarding public goods.[12] Routines and habits, together with limited consumer choices, can lead individuals to knowingly utilize high levels of carbon-based energy despite a preference against doing so. For example, parents may elect to drive a conventional minivan with poor fuel efficiency because reliable, easily accessible public transportation is not available and because hybrid minivans are not a viable consumer option in their national market. Individuals may make such consumer choices while they strongly support regulatory measures to limit carbon-based fuel consumption and to promote alternative energy sources. This is a view recognized even by theorists with strong libertarian and market-orientated perspectives, such as Cass Sunstein. "As consumers, people make choices that diverge from the choices they make as citizens. The appropriate kind and degree of environmental protection raises issues to be discussed by citizens offering reasons for one or another view. This democratic conception of environmental protection competes with the market-orientated view."[13] In democratic nations, citizens express environmental and social welfare values, and especially values regarding public goods, in the political arena. Thus:

4. Limiting GHG emissions to reduce harm to present and future generations is a political problem primarily at the national level of government (including international treaties negotiated by national governments).

Corporate Responsibility

Corporate social responsibility (CSR) is most often described as an activity that benefits society but is not legally required.[14] Instrumental corporate responsibility is the view that CSR can only be justified when it is profitable for the firm.[15] With respect to corporate sustainability, theorists of instrumental CSR hold that "green management matters only if it yields more green."[16] That is, environmental sustainability is justified only when it is profitable for the firm. This conception of corporate ethical obligations regarding social welfare and environmental sustainability is grounded in shareholder primacy ideology, the idea that the only obligation of the executive is to maximize profits for shareholders while adhering to the law and avoiding deception. This theoretical account of markets, the purpose of firms, and legitimate business conduct emanates from the Chicago School of economics.[17] This shareholder primacy view is grounded in the rights of investors to residual earnings and the positive impact corporations have on social utility. In this view, managers who expend corporate resources on activities that are not focused on corporate profits are, in effect, undemocratically redistributing investor resources. Typically, defenders of this view adhere to broadly libertarian beliefs regarding markets, emphasizing minimal regulations, private property rights, and freedom, especially the freedom to enter into contracts. This consolidation of economic, legal, and management theory has been characterized as a "unified normative theory of markets, firms and business practices."[18] According to this theory, executives agree to follow the laws determined by the democratic process, thereby garnering moral legitimacy grounded in respect for a democratic system of government. Substantial market failures are addressed via regulation, leaving firm managers free to pursue strategies that promote fiduciary obligations to shareholders.

5. The shareholder primacy theory of the firm is grounded upon respect for the rights of citizens to determine business regulations via their elected representatives.

Shareholder primacy is espoused by many economists, as well as business school faculty influenced by such economists and the MBA graduates produced by those business schools. This position has been criticized by scholars on numerous grounds,[19] but our purpose is not to assess the merits of this position but rather to understand the implications of this position in assessing corporate ethical obligations regarding climate change.

Corporate Political Activity

Given the threat that GHG emissions pose to the atmosphere, and so to the welfare of present and future generations, one might expect significant support for legislative action in the United States and other democratic nations. However, in the United States in particular, political inertia has resulted in a lack of legislative action to combat climate change. Stephen Gardiner identifies three reasons for this inertia.[20] First, it is claimed that the economic cost of changing "business as usual" development strategies utilizing fossil fuel exploitation outweighs the benefits of shifting to alternative models of sustainable development that do not rely primarily on fossil fuels. Gardiner points out that such a perspective reflects a fundamental misunderstanding of the economic threats posed by climate change. Second, there are psychological limitations to our ability to take in and process complex, analytical data. There are also psychological limits to how much we can be "worried" about, with more immediate concerns more often receiving priority. Third, from a psychological perspective, the present generation is not readily able to take into account the impact of its activity on future generations. Each of these reasons is compelling, and each likely plays some role in the creation of political inertia. However, there is a fourth explanation for political inertia that merits attention and analysis: corporate political activity aimed at stopping legislative action to reduce GHG gas emissions and move economies toward sustainable capitalism.

Corporate political activity (CPA) can be broadly understood as firm actions intended to influence or control political actors and institutions. In his classic study of corporate political influence, Charles Lindblom argues that corporations in democracies exert power over governments in two primary ways.[21] First, corporations and their surrogates exert ideological power by shaping public preferences. Second, corporations exert political power through political action committees and paid lobbyists. Lindblom's conclusions are well supported by social science data compiled in the United States and Great Britain.[22] Meta-analysis of CPA studies demonstrates that CPA has a positive relationship to firm financial performance.[23]

One of the primary components of CPA is domain maintenance, which focuses firm resources on "threats to the legitimacy of organizational methods, regardless of the perceived legitimacy of its goals and purposes."[24] The shift to a sustainable economy is clearly a threat to the methods of traditional firms in the energy sector as well as other industries that are heavily reliant on fossil fuels such as transportation.[25] Firms have used a variety of CPA strategies to deflect challenges to their methods of doing business. Here, it will be sufficient to focus on three methods of domain maintenance directly linked to legislative efforts to combat climate change: disinformation, political contributions, and the co-optation of environmental legislation.

Corporate support for the spread of disinformation regarding climate change science has directly contributed to political inaction by creating unfounded doubt regarding the scientific basis of anthropogenic climate change. The disinformation campaigns of firms and trade groups intended to undermine legislation to reduce GHG emissions and encourage alternative energy development have been well documented.[26] Climate change was sufficiently well understood in 1982 that in-house scientists at Exxon (now ExxonMobil) confirmed for company executives that the scientific consensus regarding increased CO_2 levels in the atmosphere was correct and that the climatic effects of increased atmospheric CO_2 would include significant increases in global average temperatures resulting in alterations to the biosphere harmful to human populations.[27] Exxon scientists developed models to confirm these findings and published their results.[28] However, the firm's strategy shifted from planning for inevitable changes in energy policy in the United States and elsewhere to a systematic policy of disinformation and denial just as the IPCC was confirming the serious threat climate change posed to humanity.[29]

Corporations and business trade associations have also provided financial support to climate change deniers seeking elected office. For example, for the 113th Congress alone corporations and trade associations made $641 million in contributions to climate change-denying candidates.[30] If

over time increasing scientific certainty and pressure by environmental activists leads to legislative action, business interests seek to co-opt and weaken the legislation to make it compatible with their perceived interests.[31] With a myopic focus on short-term, quarterly profit statements, many executives fail to imagine alternative paths for their businesses that are compatible with a sustainable future. Thus:

6. Corporate political activity is a primary reason for political inertia regarding climate change legislation.

Corporate political activity has been successful in defeating climate change legislation in the United States. But can CPA aimed at defeating legislation intended to correct the "the greatest market failure the world has seen" be ethically justified? To be clear, the question of ethical justification is distinct from the question of whether or not CPA constitutes lawful speech. The question of whether different forms of CPA, and in particular disinformation campaigns, are lawful speech hinges on current court interpretations.[32] Under current law, political contributions and co-optation without undue influence, such as bribes, are lawful practices. With respect to disinformation campaigns, their lawfulness depends on whether the courts interpret them as commercial speech or political speech and, if interpreted as commercial speech, whether or not that speech is found to be truthful or fraudulent.[33] These questions are distinct from the question of whether or not CPA directed at defeating climate change legislation is ethically justifiable.

Proponents of shareholder primacy theory maintain that firm managers have no obligations to society other than adhering to the law (Proposition 5 above). However, we have seen that CPA has been utilized to prevent legislative responses to GHG emissions (Proposition 6 above). The legislative process is the only mechanism for solving this market failure in democratic nations (Proposition 4 above). To defend the use of corporate resources to prevent climate change legislation in the name of shareholders contradicts the theoretical basis of shareholder primacy management and instrumental corporate responsibility. The ideal of representative democracy that is an essential feature of the shareholder primacy view, one where citizens determine the rules of the game, addressing significant market failures when they arise, and companies adhere to those rules while maximizing wealth for shareholders, is incompatible with the reality of modern interest group politics. One way of understanding democracy is in terms of plural interest groups competing for political influence. In this view, the democratic process comprises shifting coalitions of interest groups that reflect the interests of their members. The disproportionately influential role that corporations and their surrogates play in shaping the rules of the game is largely ignored by proponents of the shareholder primacy view. In the United States, for example, polls consistently find that a large majority of Americans believe that corporations exert too much political influence.[34] CPA has been utilized to combat the efforts of citizens to correct market failures.

Corporate political activity aimed at defeating climate change illustrates an important weakness of shareholder primacy theory, namely, its inability to account for a political system in which corporate interests can block legislative attempts to correct market failures and in effect determine for themselves the "rules of the game" which they are to follow. CPA aimed at preventing legislative action regarding climate change cannot be justified with present theoretical resources regarding the legitimate role of corporations in society. The silence of scholars who adapt the shareholder primacy perspective regarding the use of CPA to prevent grave harm to the welfare of present and future generations is striking.

Conclusion

Let us take stock of the proceeding analysis. Six propositions have been presented:

1. The scientific community has understood with reasonable certainty since at least 2001 that anthropogenic climate change is occurring.
2. Climate change will result in significant harm to human populations, both the current generation and future generations, and to the ecosystems that we inhabit.
3. GHG emissions are negative externalities requiring market corrections in order to preserve public goods.
4. Limiting GHG emissions to reduce harm to present and future generations is a political problem primarily at the national level of government (including international treaties negotiated by national governments).
5. The shareholder primacy theory for the firm is grounded on respect for the rights of citizens to determine business regulations via their elected representatives.
6. Corporate political activity is a primary reason for political inertia regarding climate change legislation.

Because Proposition 6 is inconsistent with Proposition 5, it is appropriate to conclude that corporations and business trade associations act irresponsibly and illegitimately when they utilize CPA to defeat climate change legislation. This type of irresponsibility may be lawful, but, just as pro-social, "beyond compliance" corporate behavior is lawful, so are

many forms of harmful, anti-social, and anti-democratic corporate behavior. The fact that CPA aimed at defeating climate change cannot be justified utilizing the dominant "unified normative theory of markets, firms, and business practices" in democratic societies provides evidence that efforts to combat such corporate political activity are justified. We began this article by asking whether corporate political activity to defeat climate change legislation can be ethically justified. The results of our analysis is "no" because theories of the firm and its legitimate role in society cannot provide an ethical basis for such activity.

Notes

1. United Nations General Assembly, *Protection of Global Climate for Present and Future Generations of Mankind*, A/RES/43/53, December 6, 2008.
2. Intergovernmental Panel on Climate Change (IPCC), *Climate Change 2001: The Scientific Basis* (Cambridge University Press, 2001); Joint Science Academies, "Global Response to Climate Change" (2005). Retrieved November 23, 2015 from http://nationalacademies.org/onpi/06072005.pdf; Spencer R. Weart, *The Discovery of Global Warming* (Cambridge University Press, 2003), p. 160.
3. IPCC, *Climate Change 2001*; Mark Lynas, *Six Degrees: Our Future on a Hotter Planet* (Washington, DC: National Geographic Books, 2008).
4. Simon Caney, "Climate Change, Human Rights, and Moral Thresholds," in *Climate Ethics: Essential Readings*, ed. Stephen M. Gardiner, Simon Caney, Dale Jamieson, and Henry Shue (Oxford University Press, 2010), pp. 163–77.
5. Denis G. Arnold and Andrew Valentin, "Corporate Social Responsibility at the Base of the Pyramid," *Journal of Business Research* 66 (2013): 1904–14.
6. Clare Palmer, "Does Nature Matter? The Place of the Nonhuman in the Ethics of Climate Change," in *The Ethics of Global Climate Change*, ed. Denis G. Arnold (Cambridge University Press, 2011), pp. 272–91.
7. Paul A. Samuelson, "The Pure Theory of Public Expenditure," *Review of Economics and Statistics* 36 (1954): 387–89.
8. Nicholas Stern, *The Global Deal: Climate Change and the Creation of a New Era of Progress and Prosperity* (Philadelphia, PA: Public Affairs, 2009), p. 11.
9. Sarah Krakoff, "Parenting the Planet," in *The Ethics of Global Climate Change*, ed. Arnold, pp. 145–69.
10. Edward B. Barbier and Anil Markandya, *A New Blueprint for a Green Economy* (New York: Routledge, 2013); Joseph DesJardins, "Is It Time to Jump Off the Sustainability Bandwagon?" *Business Ethics Quarterly* 26 (2016): 117–35; Paul Hawken, Amory B. Lovins, and L. Hunter Lovins, *Natural Capitalism: The Next Industrial Revolution* (Boston: Little, Brown, 1999).
11. Susan Solomon, ed., *Climate Change 2007: The Physical Science Basis*. Working Group I Contribution to the Fourth

Assessment Report of the IPCC, vol. 4 (Cambridge University Press, 2007), sec. 2.10.2.

12. Norman E. Bowie, "Morality, Money, and Motor Cars," in *Business, Ethics and the Environment: The Public Policy Debate*, ed. W. Michael Hoffman, Robert Frederick, and Edward S. Petry (New York: Quorum Books, 1990), pp. 89–97; Marc A. Cohen and John W. Dienhart, "Citizens, Kant and Corporate Responsibility for the Environment," in *Kantian Business Ethics: Critical Perspectives*, ed. Denis G. Arnold and Jared Harris (Northampton, MA: Edward Elgar, 2012), pp. 96–114; Mark Sagoff, *The Economy of the Earth* (Cambridge University Press, 1988).

13. Cass R. Sunstein, *Free Markets and Social Justice* (Oxford University Press, 1997), p. 378.

14. Herman Aguinis and Ante Glavas, "What We Know and Don't Know about Corporate Social Responsibility: A Review and Research Agenda," *Journal of Management* 38 (2012): 932–68.

15. Abigail McWilliams and Donald Siegel, "Corporate Social Responsibility: A Theory of the Firm Perspective," *Academy of Management Review* 26 (2001): 117–27.

16. Donald Siegel, "Green Management Matters Only If It Yields More Green: An Economic/Strategic Perspective," *Academy of Management Perspectives* 23, no. 1 (2009): 5–16 (p. 5).

17. Henry Hansmann and Reinier Kraakman, "End of History for Corporate Law," *The Georgetown Law Journal* 89 (2000): 439–68; Joseph Heath, Jeffrey Moriarty, and Wayne Norman, "Business Ethics and (or as) Political Philosophy," *Business Ethics Quarterly* 20 (2010): 427–52.

18. Heath et al., "Business Ethics and (or as) Political Philosophy."

19. Thomas M. Jones and Will Felps, "Shareholder Wealth Maximization and Social Welfare: A Utilitarian Critique," *Business Ethics Quarterly* 23 (2013): 207–38; Lynn A. Stout, *The Shareholder Value Myth: How Putting Shareholders First Harms Investors, Corporations, and the Public* (San Francisco, CA: Berrett-Koehler, 2012).

20. Stephen Gardiner, *A Perfect Moral Storm: The Ethical Tragedy of Climate Change* (Oxford University Press, 2011), pp. 191–96.

21. Charles E. Lindblom, *Politics and Markets: The World's Political-Economic Systems* (New York: Basic Books, 1977).

22. Neil J. Mitchell, *The Conspicuous Corporation: Business, Public Policy, and Representative Democracy* (Ann Arbor, MI: University of Michigan Press, 1997).

23. Sean Lux, T. Russell Crook, and David J. Woehr, "Mixing Business with Politics: A Meta-Analysis of the Antecedents and Outcomes of Corporate Political Activity," *Journal of Management* 37 (2010): 223–47.

24. Barry D. Baysinger, "Domain Maintenance as an Objective of Business Political Activity: An Expanded Typology," *Academy of Management Review* 9 (1984): 248–58 (p. 254).

25. Denis G. Arnold and Keith Bustos, "Business, Ethics, and Global Climate Change," *Business and Professional Ethics Journal* 22, no. 2/3 (2005): 103–30.

26. David Hasemyer and John H. Cushman, Jr., "Exxon Sowed Doubt about Climate Science for Decades by Stressing Uncertainty," *Inside Climate News* (October 22, 2015); James Hoggan and Richard Littlemore, *Climate Cover-Up: The Crusade to Deny Global Warming* (New York: Greystone Books, 2009); Naoli Oreskes and Erik M. Conway, *Merchants of Doubt: How a Handful of Scientists Obscured the Truth on Issues from Tobacco Smoke to Global Warming* (London: Bloomsbury, 2010).

27. Lisa Song, Neela Banerjee, and David Hasemyer, "Exxon Confirmed Global Warming Consensus in 1982 with In-House Climate Models," *Inside Climate News* (September 22, 2015).

28. Martin I. Hoffert, Brian P. Flannery, Andrew J. Callegari, C. T. Hsieh, and Warren Wiscombe, "Evaporation-Limited Tropical Temperatures as a Constraint on Climate Sensitivity," *Journal of the Atmospheric Sciences* 40 (1983): 1659–68; Brian P. Flannery, "Energy Balance Models Incorporating Transport of Thermal and Latent Energy," *Journal of the Atmospheric Sciences* 41 (1984): 414–21.

29. Hasemyer and Cushman, "Exxon Sowed Doubt about Climate Science."

30. Brant Olson, Daniel Kessler, Antonia Bruno, and Duncan Magidson, "How Big Business Is Funding Climate Change Denial in the 113th Congress and Why They Should Stop," *Forecast the Facts Action and SumOfUs* (September 2014). Retrieved November 23, 2015 from https://s3.amazonaws.com/s3.forecastthefacts.org/images/disruptdenialreport.pdf.

31. Judith A. Layzer, "Deep Freeze: How Business Has Shaped the Global Warming Debate in Congress," in *Business and Environmental Policy: Corporate Interests in the American Political System*, ed. Michael E. Kraft and Sheldon Kamieniecki (Cambridge, MA: MIT Press, 2007), pp. 93–126.

32. Margaret M. Blair, "Of Corporations, Courts, Personhood, and Morality," *Business Ethics Quarterly* 25 (2015): 415–31.

33. David Hess and Thomas W. Dunfee, "The Kasky-Nike Threat to Corporate Social Reporting: Implementing a Standard of Optimal Truthful Disclosure as a Solution," *Business Ethics Quarterly* 17 (2007): 5–32.

34. Businessweek/Harris Poll, "How Business Rates: By the Numbers" (2000). Retrieved November 23, 2015 from www.bloomberg.com/news/articles/2000-09-11/business-week-harris-poll-how-business-rates-by-the-numbers; Hart Research Associates, "Protecting Democracy from Unlimited Corporate Spending" (June 2010). Retrieved November 23, 2015 from www.pfaw.org/sites/default/files/citupoll-pfaw.pdf.

Actions Speak Louder than Words: Greenwashing in Corporate America

JACOB VOS

Forty years ago, people may not have cared about which companies used the most carbon-neutral manufacturing processes, or which used non-biodegradable packaging. Things have changed. Now green is everywhere – green cars, green packaging, green buildings. This green wave of current environmentalist thought stemmed from the likes of Thoreau and Muir, while the old guard of environmental thought stemmed from the utilitarian approach favored by Theodore Roosevelt, where the wild lands existed to be tamed.[1] Though the environmentalist movement was slow to start, it began to pick up steam with the publication of *Silent Spring*.[2] Being green started to become synonymous with good business. Companies are now able to capitalize on their new green-collar jobs and biodegradable packaging. However, green manufacturing techniques can only take a company so far. To borrow from the introduction of *Green to Gold*:

> Our economy and society depend on natural resources. To over simplify, every product known to man came from something mined or grown. The [Note] you're reading was once a tree; the ink these words are printed in began life as soybeans. The environment provides critical support to our economic system – not financial capital, but natural capital.[3]

When, as is often the case, a company's practices don't match up to the image they would like to have, they start to engage in greenwashing.

The term "greenwashing" stems from "whitewashing." While whitewashing a fence may bring up sentiments of down-home Americana,[4] when applied to corporations its meaning is more sinister: "a deliberate concealment of someone's mistakes or faults."[5] Greenwashing is defined as "disinformation disseminated by an organization so as to present an environmentally responsible public image."[6] Large corporations are most commonly accused of greenwashing. The charges usually stem from some environmental stance a corporation publicizes without putting its rhetoric into practice; talking the talk without walking the walk. Most corporations do not greenwash their reputations by lying outright. Rather, they bend the truth or misrepresent their ecological stances. The deception often lies in the emphasis corporations place on their ecological projects, rather than in the existence of the projects themselves.

Part I will discuss the history and present state of corporate greenwashing, further illustrating the phenomenon with specific examples. Part II examines why greenwashing occurs, and takes into account the actions of consumers, investors, and the greenwashing companies themselves. Part III examines greenwashing's impact on both the environment and on the fabric of society. Finally, Part IV marches out various ways we can address the problem of greenwashing, including implementable legal, legislative, and societal changes.

I. Greenwashing: Past and Present

Greenwashing is a relatively new strategy for corporations. The environment did not have a significant impact on the practice of marketing until the 1970s.[7] "The reasons for this limited impact range from environmental regulations being limited in scope and influence to society being ambiguous with respect to environmentalism and corporate social responsibility."[8] In addition, there was no coercive or regulatory influence motivating ecologically oriented marketing strategies.[9] This changed in the 1980s, when administrations like the EPA and laws like the Endangered Species Act and Superfund came into play.[10] Both the federal government and the general public began to pay attention to companies' environmental practices. Eventually, becoming environmentally friendly, or at least *appearing* environmentally friendly, started to look good for a company's bottom line. This stood as a shift from the traditional corporate response to allegations of environmental unfriendliness, which had been to deny problems, avoid responsibility, and avoid controls.[11] For example, CFC manufacturers denied their role in ozone depletion for over 14 years after scientists discovered connections between their products and the destruction of the ozone.[12] During that period of denial, "chlorine built up in the atmosphere and depletion of the ozone layer accelerated worldwide."[13]

From *Notre Dame Journal of Ethics and Public Policy* 23 (2009). Reprinted by permission of the author. Originally printed as a Student Note.

Now, green corporations are all the rage, and more and more companies are advertising their green stances. "But too many," said Michael Brune, executive director for the Rainforest Action Network, "are seeking maximum accolades for minimum change."[14] For example, Ford Motors gets a lot of mileage out of running advertisements for its lines of hybrid and flex fuel cars.[15] Brune argues that "[y]ou look beyond the green sheen, and Ford's actions don't match its rhetoric."[16] The rhetoric looks like this: "William Clay Ford Jr., chairman of Ford Motor, stares out from the television screen and pledges that the automaker is 'dramatically ramping up its commitment' to environmentally safer cars like gasoline-electric hybrids."[17] However, the rhetoric doesn't tell the whole story, which includes the move in 2003 where Ford "dropped its promise to increase average fuel efficiency on its sport utility fleet."[18] Likewise, "[i]n 2004, the company joined other automakers in suing to block a California law that would limit emissions of gases linked to global warming."[19]

Toyota, another major auto manufacturer, has received major accolades for its popularization of hybrid vehicles with the launch and promotion of the Prius, a gas-electric hybrid.[20] Toyota claims that "the Prius emits 80 percent less harmful gases than the most efficient standard vehicles."[21] Additionally, the Prius gets much better mileage than most standard vehicles due to its hybrid engine.[22] Left unsaid in Toyota's touting of the Prius is that "[t]he average fuel efficiency of the carmaker's vehicles has fallen to 27.5 miles per gallon, or eight liters every 100 kilometers, from 30 miles per gallon in 1985, because it sells more pickup trucks and SUVs, according to EPA statistics."[23] By greenwashing its reputation through the Prius, Toyota can draw attention away from its worsening fuel efficiency record.

General Motors is the world's number one manufacturer of motor vehicles, and motor vehicles are the number one source of air pollution and consume one-third of the world's oil.[24] The health costs attributable to vehicle emissions in the United States alone are $25 billion per year.[25] GM has a program of planting a tree for each car sold in its Geo division, a practice that sounds extremely eco-friendly.[26] However, to counter the amount of carbon dioxide produced by a single Geo car, GM would have to plant 734 trees over the lifetime of each vehicle.[27] GM has also lobbied against fuel efficiency and has supported political organizations which give campaign contributions to political candidates who oppose tighter emissions standards.[28] Against this background, that single tree planted for every Geo sold starts to materialize as a worthless gesture toward environmentalism, and a clear move toward the greenwashing of GM's reputation.

Auto manufacturers aren't the only culprits; power companies have also jumped onto the greenwashing bandwagon with both feet. Pacific Gas and Electric, of *Erin Brockovich* fame, has been running ads like: "Green is a city with country air" and "Green is 4 wheels on the road versus 400."[29] These ads are run despite the company's "history of environmental degradation" and "slow and litigious reaction to rectifying its past mistakes."[30] Aliza Wasserman, founder of letsgreenwashthiscity.org, a website that exposes instances of corporate greenwashing, took aim at PG&E's Climate Smart program, which encourages customers to pay an extra $4.31 per month to offset their carbon emissions.[31] Wasserman argued that PG&E has "launch[ed] an environmental project that relies on the consumer making the choice rather than the company taking on the responsibility to improve its operations."[32] If a company can get a green reputation without taking on any of the financial burden itself, so much the better. …

Generally speaking, the practice of greenwashing can be broken down into three types: confusion, fronting, and posturing:

> Confusion flows naturally from the complex nature of the corporate form, reliance on decentralized decision making, and the practices of managerial winking. Fronting is accomplished through the representations of retained counsel, compliance officers, ethics officers, and ethics communities. Posturing seeks to convince internal customers, as much as external stakeholders, of the organization's collective commitment to ethics.[33]

These techniques allow a corporation to clean up its act in the face of the media. Indeed,

> [t]he very firms that wash their reputations through public relations, complex front coalitions, sponsored "think tanks," and who publicly lead the fight against global warming, nuclear waste, and water pollution, remain some of the worst corporate offenders. The appearance of environmental leadership, for example, like the appearance of corporate compliance, may actually serve to decrease care levels. Corporations can rely on their reputations for compliance and social responsibility with lesser scrutiny.[34]

II. Why Greenwashing Occurs

Greenwashing occurs for a number of reasons, but the most important are economic. More and more consumers and investors are mindful of the environmental ethics of the companies they support. Paradoxically, an extension of traditional business ethics leads one to the conclusion that corporations can be ethically led to greenwash their reputations. As the argument goes, greenwashing is still ethical since greenwashing claims are generally true, even though they may give a consumer a distorted image of a corporation. Furthermore, since greenwashing improves a corporation's bottom line, traditional business ethics proclaim the tactic a resounding success, since a corporation's goal under traditional business ethics is to maximize its profits while staying within the rules of "the game." Section A will examine how consumer choices prompt corporations to greenwash, while section B will discuss how corporations can ethically justify greenwashing to themselves and their employees.

A. The Bottom Line

The lion's share of greenwashing efforts are motivated by the simple fact that, generally speaking, companies gain a market advantage if they can project an earth-conscious image. Consumers are starting to pay attention. More and more surveys reveal a "growing segment of consumers who either reward or intend to reward firms that address environmental concerns in their business and marketing practices and who punish firms that appear to ignore the environmental imperatives."[35] Consumers tend to take a particularly hard look at industries regarded as heavy polluters, like the auto and oil industries. Corporations in high-pollution fields "don't want to be caught not talking about these issues, because they are a key part of them," said John Stauber, co-founder of the Center for Media and Democracy, which analyzes the truthfulness of advertising and marketing claims.[36] Even in other industries, normative pressures within the institutional environment push companies toward committing to environmental policies, since once a group of visible companies commit to environmental policies, others will follow suit as a sort of benchmarking.[37] If a company is the first to take steps toward stewardship, they can improve their market share through differentiation.[38] Finally, pressures can also come from external organizations like watchdog groups, which exert public pressure on companies to commit to protecting the environment.[39]

As a result of these pressures, more and more companies are moving toward green marketing campaigns. According to GE's global executive director of advertising and branding, Judy Hu, "Green is green as in the color of money. It is about a business opportunity, and we believe we can increase our revenue behind these Ecomagination products and services."[40] As mentioned earlier, the move toward green marketing coincided with society's concern with the harms large corporations were inflicting on the environment. While academics framed the issue as green versus greed, environmental interests and profits became aligned.[41] Studies like Ajay and Anil Menon's *Environmental Marketing Strategy: The Emergence of Corporate Environmentalism as Market Strategy* have shown that creating social good and making a profit are often interwoven.[42]

However, the rationale underpinning the greenwashing movement is the realization that a corporation does not need to actually *create* social good in order to reap the benefits of a green reputation. If companies' actions matched up with all of their rhetoric, greenwashing would not be an issue. However, if a company can reap the benefits of a green reputation without actually spending the time or money to substantially change its practices, it reaps all of the benefits without any of the associated costs.

One of the most common forms of greenwashing occurs when corporations release environmental policy statements – broad, high-minded statements proclaiming a corporation's commitment to preserving the environment. The impression, as described by DuPont's Paul Tebo, is that "[o]nce you go public, it's no longer voluntary."[43] These statements can positively influence public perceptions of a company's commitment to environmental protection and sustainable development, "possibly even resulting in increased market share and improved stakeholder relations. And, there is little downside to making a public commitment."[44] Tebo's interpretation of environmental policy statements is exceedingly idealistic. Since environmental policy statements rarely include any specifics regarding the implementation of the policy, they tend to bring about good publicity without actually obligating the corporation to change anything. Without specific commitments, the corporation putting forth the statement is not bound to any benchmarks which might be used to measure its progress toward its goal. For example, BP's Indonesian environmental policy states that "[o]ur project is committed to working toward the goals of no harm to people, no accidents and no damage to the environment."[45] Since no endeavor which requires natural resources can have "no damage to the environment," the fact that BP is "working toward" such an impossible goal allows it to duck any allegations of specific environmental problems by pointing to its laudable goals and policies.

B. The Corporate Ethics of Greenwashing

Lots of greenwashing comes from companies following the classical model of business, which holds that "there is one and only one social responsibility of business – to use its resources and engage in activities to increase its profits so long as it stays within the rules of the game, which is to say, engages in open and free competition without deception or fraud."[46] Since greenwashing is not deceptive in the classic sense, and since it falls well short of fraud, it is arguably ethical under the classical model of business ethics. Under the classical model, environmental ethics don't even enter the picture. This model "denies that business has any direct environmental responsibility."[47] It also means that when it comes to a showdown between what is good for business and what is good for the environment, the environment always loses. "For the entire range of issues in which economic growth competes with environmental or ecological ends, the classical model necessarily locates corporate responsibility on the side of economic growth."[48]

Another, slightly more flexible version of corporate theory holds that corporations are loyal to their stakeholders.[49] Stakeholders have been defined as "any group or individual who can affect or is affected by the achievement of the organization's objectives" or "groups or individuals who 'have an interest in the actions of an organization and … the ability to influence it.'"[50] Stakeholders in a corporation generally include stockholders, employees, the local community, the media, and perhaps even the environment itself.

Corporations greenwash in order to play to their stakeholders in a number of different ways. Some green ad campaigns are targeted at a corporation's employees. For example, Alcan, a Canadian aluminum producer, hired CGCom, an advertising firm, to produce a series of green ads for the company. The company's president doesn't pretend that the ads will help Alcan sell more aluminum; his primary audience was internal. "Every time we survey our 70,000 employees, we hear that they want to be proud of our environmental leadership," he said. "Outsiders may not remember the Alcan ads a few months down the road, but our employees will remember them with pride."[51] Most greenwashing ad campaigns are run to influence the media. Oil companies like Exxon, under attack for reaping windfall profits from soaring fuel prices, are trying to position themselves as part of the solution to energy problems rather than the cause.[52] Manufacturers of green products are recognizing that they can burnish their image even as they promote their products, and realize larger payoffs from their efforts.[53]

How companies view their stakeholders affects how they conduct business.[54] Firms seen as leaders in the environmental field view environmental management as an important business function.[55] When viewed under the stakeholder theory of corporations, these corporations view the environment as an active stakeholder and conduct their businesses accordingly. Firms that fit the reactive profile, the environmental followers, only saw the media as an important stakeholder when it came to

environmental policy.[56] "[R]eactive firms appear to be more concerned about being caught doing something wrong by a reporter than about being caught by a regulator."[57] If an environmental crisis were to occur, reactive firms would not (and proactive firms would) be able to demonstrate due diligence.[58]

Ironically enough, for some of these reactive firms, "hypocrisy is the first step toward meaningful change."[59] If firms begin talking the environmental talk, it may not be long until they're walking the walk. To some, this may be looking at greenwashing in an overly charitable light, but big changes need to begin with small steps. Stakeholders can move firms toward the switch from rhetoric to action through the various pressures they can apply.

III. Greenwashing's Impact

While the environmental impact of greenwashing may be the most obvious, the social impact of greenwashing is no less important. Though it may not be fraud, greenwashing is, at its heart, the product of corporations which willingly mislead the public. This deception, once uncovered, bothers a lot of people, and for good reason. "Truthful advertising about goods and services is an unequivocal social good. It reduces uncertainty and improves the quality of decisionmaking. It facilitates search, promotes competition, and increases the likelihood of consumer satisfaction."[60]

Part of the problem is moral. James Nash argues that "[a]ll creatures are entitled to moral consideration."[61] Though the taking of life is inevitable – it forms the basis of our model of the ecosystem – it is not without moral cost. Another, similar ethical model holds that we must have a moral consideration of "the systems that together comprise the biosphere."[62] In fact, most ethical models give ethical standing, if not to individual animals, at least to the integrity of ecosystems. By obfuscating the damage they do to ecosystems, greenwashing corporations attempt to hide their moral wrongs. If and when this subterfuge is uncovered, people become even more disillusioned with corporate America.

Another disconnect lies at the center of what a business *is*. Paul Hawken argues:

> The ultimate purpose of a business is not, or should not be, simply to make money. Nor is it merely a system of making and selling things. The promise of business is to increase the general well-being of humankind through service, a creative invention and ethical philosophy. Making money is … totally meaningless.[63]

While Hawken's perspective may strike a chord with many consumers, very few companies appear to be following his business model. Fortunately, some successful companies are attempting to increase the general well-being of humankind instead of simply trying to increase profits. Take Clif Bar, for example. Founder Gary Erickson has taken the company from his mom's kitchen to a 150 million dollar corporation.[64] A corporation which runs on biodiesel, and does not tout the fact that it supports sustainable farming and uses organic ingredients.[65] Greenwashing isn't even a remote concern, since Clif Bar does not advertise.[66] Companies like Clif Bar show that it's possible to sustain economic growth without misleading customers or destroying ecosystems. If more companies follow their lead, they can collectively combat the skepticism and disillusionment currently confronting big business.

IV. Addressing Greenwashing

Now that I have identified the problem, it is time to start pinning down some possible solutions. Much of the pressure on companies should come from the companies' stakeholders. If they talk, companies will listen.

> NGOs, customers, and employees increasingly ask pointed questions and call for action on a spectrum of issues. To give just one example, HP says that in 2004, $6 billion of new business depended in part on answers to customer questions about the company's environmental and social performance – up 660 percent from 2002.[67]

A number of legal recourses are also available. Section A will discuss the use of various citizen suit provisions incorporated into pieces of environmental legislation. Section B will discuss the need for the implementation of verifiable reporting schemes to give the public a clear picture of companies' environmental track records. Section C will propose additional environmental legislation. Section D takes a broader view, discussing the adoption of a neoclassical model of business ethics in order to stem the tide of greenwashing. Finally, section E looks at the enactment of environmental and ethical policy statements as a way to move toward a neoclassical model of business ethics.

A. Citizen Suits

One of the most obvious responses to greenwashing resonates within the battle cry of the tort lawyer: "Sue the bastards."

> Private groups can use the courts to pursue better environmental quality in three main ways: (1) by

suing polluters to recover monetary damages caused by the pollution, (2) by suing public officials entrusted with responsibility for implementing the laws to force compliance with Congressional or Constitutional requirements, and (3) by suing polluters for the purpose of bringing them into compliance with the law.[68]

Most environmental protection legislation includes a citizen suit provision of one sort or another. Since the government may not have the resources required to prosecute each and every violation, it has, in essence, allowed concerned citizens and non-governmental organizations to take the place of the government prosecutors. Who can bring suit varies depending on the statute, whether it's the Clean Water Act, the Clean Air Act, CERCLA, RCRA, or some other act. The provisions are far-ranging, and "allow a private citizen more than a challenge to arbitrary agency action; citizen suit provisions essentially confer 'private attorney general' status, allowing a citizen to proceed on behalf of the general public."[69]

Under many of these provisions, making out a case is relatively easy. For example, the CWA allows for citizen suits if a company exceeds its permitted discharge amounts, a fairly common offense:

> It is relatively easy, with minimum training, for a citizen to check and compare the facility permits with the discharge reports if the citizen (or community group) suspects that violations may be causing undue pollution. If there is a violation, the citizen should be able to establish liability at the summary judgment phase of a case simply by submitting the permit and the discharge monitoring reports indicating a discharge beyond permit limitations.[70]

However, considerable vigilance is required just to get the ball rolling. "Regardless of whether the enforceable requirement is easy to isolate or more difficult, the community must first become aware of a risk to the public and associate the risk with a suspected violation."[71] Considering the proliferation of greenwashing tactics, the local community may not even be aware that they have a pollution problem.

In addition to enforcement actions against regulated entities, citizen suit provisions allow action-forcing suits against regulatory officials for failure to perform nondiscretionary duties.[72] These suits have a beneficial side-effect of drawing more media and public attention to the case, hopefully prompting a speedier remedy to the problem.

Though citizens filing suit under these provisions have a lot going in their favor, there are some limitations on citizen suits. Citizens must serve the Environmental Protection Agency, the state in which the violation occurred, and the alleged violator notice of the intent to sue and then wait 60 days before suing, unless the violation involves substances which present an imminent hazard.[73] The Attorney General and Environmental Protection Agency administrator have 45 days to review settlement to see if they agree with it.[74] Finally, citizen suits are barred if a federal judicial suit or administrative action has been filed against the alleged violator for the same violation.[75]

Remedies for these suits can include injunctive relief, penalties (which can be up to $75,000 per day, per violation) and attorney's fees.[76] The plaintiff's bar has already landed some heavy blows. "W.R. Grace, which once had a multi-billion dollar market capitalization, was driven into bankruptcy in 2001 by an avalanche of asbestos-related lawsuits."[77] Others are on the horizon. "A class action lawsuit for Hurricane Katrina victims was filed against ten oil and gas companies for destroying wetlands that might have reduced the severity of the floods."[78]

B. Verifiable Reporting

As things currently stand, consumers and investors are generally left to trust or distrust corporations' self-reports of their environmental practices. Unless a citizen suit, media report, or administrative action uncovers some sort of wrongdoing, the corporations themselves provide the majority of the information. While self-reporting of a corporation's environmental impact is to be encouraged, it's almost worthless unless there is a way to verify the accuracy of the reports.[79] "The growing wisdom is that companies must produce verified accountability reports – verified reports by auditors specializing in social accounting and auditing."[80] In addition, "[a] good environmental report should discuss the important aspects of the company's footprint. It should use quantitative metrics and cover core issues such as air emissions, water pollution, hazardous waste disposal, energy consumption, greenhouse gas emissions, and notices of legal violations."[81] These reports would not just help consumers and investors become better informed; they would help the companies as well – "If for no other reason, with accusations of greenwashing and evidence of its practice, decisions to defer third-party auditing or to forgo the requirement entirely strongly undermine an appearance of legitimacy."[82] If corporations accused of greenwashing are able to prove that there is action behind their rhetoric, their trustworthiness is enhanced and they can reap the public benefits of having a reputation for being both trustworthy *and* green.

C. Enact and Enforce Environmental Legislation

Environmental regulation is a prime example of an instance where private market pressures are not helpful in bringing about an optimum balance between current needs and the protection of future resources. The market can be helped along by environmental legislation if the legislation turns over the right information to the market. If verifiable reporting is required by law, consumers can make informed choices about the products they buy and the companies they support. As we have seen, consumers and investors are making green choices, but the problem has been getting accurate information to them through the screen of disinformation and greenwashing that gets in the way. It would not be difficult for legislation to enact reporting schemes along with any emissions regulations that may be otherwise implemented. Furthermore, when armed with this information, the public will be more apt to take advantage of citizen suit provisions in environmental legislation.

D. Adopt a Neoclassical Model of Business Ethics

If we take the long view for a moment, it becomes clear that the real change that needs to occur in order to stop greenwashing is a shift from a classical to a neoclassical model of business ethics. As discussed earlier, the classical model of business ethics views a maximization of investment returns while playing within the rules of the game as a corporation's sole goal.[83] In contrast, the neoclassical model of corporate social responsibility holds that "corporations ought to seek profits while nevertheless obeying a 'moral minimum.' ... A moral minimum is incorporated into the 'rules of the game' and becomes part of standard business practice."[84] This moral minimum can take a number of different forms. This moral content could include avoiding intervention in the political process for the purpose of defeating or weakening environmental legislation, for example. If environmental concerns are integrated within the moral minimum, they become part of a business' social responsibility.[85]

Likewise, societal marketing has started to develop, which suggested that "marketers should balance three considerations in formulating and implementing marketing strategies: company profits, consumer needs and satisfaction, and society's interests."[86] This balancing act brings up the idea that society's interests should be viewed on a longer time scale, and the best plan for making immediate profits may actually work against humans' longer-term interests.

It shouldn't be presumptuous or particularly leftist to suggest that "effective policy should appeal to the interests, albeit long-term, of human beings."[87] Though it sounds noble to try to protect the panda bear or spotted owl, it is tough to persuade corporations, voters, or any other stakeholders to protect the environment for the intrinsic value of the environment. It is not impossible, but it is difficult. However, if we argue that the environment should be protected for the sake of our grandchildren, people start to listen. One way to incorporate this theory of business ethics is to talk about avoidance of harm to ecosystems, rather than merely to individual living organisms.[88] Sustaining ecosystems is clearly in humankind's best interests. Put another way, "[a] helpful image for understanding these responsibilities is to think of natural resources as capital. Our economic goal should be maximum sustainable yield in which we live off of the income generated by that capital without depleting the investment itself."[89]

The focus of neoclassic businesses should change from the growth of resources to the development of resources.[90] "Developing" resources includes extracting as much benefit from the available resources as possible – allowing our utilization of resources to catch up to our needs, instead of allowing our consumption of resources to increase. It allows companies to move toward sustainability, which would "meet … the needs of the present without compromising the ability of future generations to meet their own needs."[91]

E. Corporate Codes of Ethics

A common greenwashing technique is employed through corporations' publication of their corporate codes of ethics or codes of environmental ethics. More often than not, these public commitments elicit favorable articles in the press. However, since the commitments rarely outline specific steps the corporation plans to take in furtherance of their broad goals, the policy statements don't cost the corporations anything. Though the publication of corporate codes of ethics often gives companies an opportunity to greenwash their reputations, corporate codes of ethics can also serve as a tool to change a corporation's practices.

Perhaps surprisingly, codes of ethics can have a significant impact on the behavior of a corporation's management.[92] A code of ethics is "a written, distinct, and formal document which consists of moral standards used to guide employee or corporate behaviour."[93] A review of how ethical codes affect behavior suggested that "it is those areas of activity which are 'grey' and not 'black and white' (e.g. fraud or theft) where the code would potentially influence behaviour."[94] Greenwashing is likely one of those grey areas,

where the information disseminated by the corporation isn't necessarily fraud, but the ethics of the practice is still on shaky grounds at best.

Environmental policy statements go hand-in-hand with corporate codes of ethics. Environmental policy statements, like codes of ethics, are not required by law; they are voluntary statements which make a public commitment to maintaining environmentally friendly practices.[95] Industry-wide pressures move companies toward voluntary commitments to policy statements, so it's unsurprising that policy statements are often very similar across a certain industry.[96] However, the statement does not always lead to making commitments to specific policies that would aid in the implementation of the overreaching environmental policy.[97] Corporate policy statements don't vary much between industry sectors, but policy *implementation* does.[98] When examined in context, this isn't particularly surprising:

> The environmental literature specifies the following drivers for environmental management: regulation, the degree of stakeholder pressure, economic advantage, and mimetic pressures from the institutional environment. These drivers can be generalized to the industry level. For example, large companies in the same industry face the same environmental regulations and the same types of stakeholder pressure, engage in the same type of industrial activity as defined by their products and services, and can easily imitate each others' practices.[99]

Since there is no mechanism to track commitment to environmental policies, the implementation of policies and a company's commitment to them are very separate things, and can vary widely.[100] Studies have shown that without explicit sanctions, self-regulation is not consistent, and companies in the same industry will commit to different levels of environmental protection.[101] For example, companies in the services sector "have fewer economic incentives and disincentives to implement environmental change and … companies in this industry sector would therefore be less likely [than companies in the oil, gas, and manufacturing industries] to implement environmental policies."[102] The service companies were just as likely to commit to the environmental policies, but less likely to take concrete steps to implement them.[103] …

Notes

1. Brian Tokar, *Earth for Sale: Reclaiming Ecology in the Age of Corporate Greenwash* (Cambridge, MA: South End Press, 1997), p. 6.

2. Rachel Carson, *Silent Spring* (Boston, MA: Houghton Mifflin, 1962).

3. Daniel C. Esty and Andrew S. Winston, *Green to Gold: How Smart Companies Use Environmental Strategy to Innovate, Create Value, and Build Competitive Advantage* (New Haven, CT: Yale University Press, 2006), p. 3.

4. See, e.g., Mark Twain, *The Adventures of Tom Sawyer* (1876), chap. 2.

5. "Whitewash," in *Compact Oxford English Dictionary*, 3rd ed., ed. Catherine Soanes (2005).

6. "Greenwash," in *Concise Oxford English Dictionary*, 10th ed., ed. Judy Pearsall (2003).

7. Ajay Menon and Anil Menon, "Environmental Marketing Strategy: The Emergence of Corporate Environmentalism as Market Strategy," *Journal of Marketing* 61 (1997): 51–67 (p. 52).

8. Ibid.

9. Ibid.

10. Ibid., p. 53.

11. Jed Greer and Kenny Bruno, *Greenwash: The Reality behind Corporate Environmentalism* (New York: Third World Network, 1996), p. 14.

12. Ibid., pp. 14, 37.

13. Ibid., p. 14.

14. Claudia Deutsch, "It's Getting Crowded on the Environmental Bandwagon," *The New York Times* (December 22, 2005), p. C5.

15. Ibid.

16. Ibid.

17. Peter Robison and Gregory Viscusi, "Ecologists Unmoved by 'Green' Wave in Advertising," *International Herald Tribune* (January 18, 2006), p. 19.

18. Ibid.

19. Ibid.

20. The Prius became the most popular car in Silicon Valley as of July 2007. See Matthew Sparkes, "Prius Most Popular Car in Silicon Valley," *treehugger.com* (July 22, 2007). Retrieved from www.treehugger.com/cars/prius-most-popular-car-in-silicon-valley.html.

21. Robison and Viscusi, "Ecologists Unmoved."

22. See Marshall Loeb, "Don't Be Fuelish: Try a Hybrid," *Record* [Bergen County, NJ] (May 14, 2008), p. B02.

23. Robison and Viscusi, "Ecologists Unmoved."

24. Greer and Bruno, *Greenwash*, p. 161.

25. Ibid., p. 162.

26. Ibid.

27. Ibid.

28. Ibid.

29. Amanda Witherell, "Green Is the Color of Money," *Good Magazine* (May–June 2007). Retrieved from http://www.goodmagazine.com/section/Features/green_is_the_color_of_money.

30. Ibid.

31. Ibid.

32. Ibid.

33. William S. Laufer, "Social Accountability and Corporate Greenwashing," *Journal of Business Ethics* 43 (2003): 253–61 (p. 257).

34. Ibid.

35. Menon and Menon, "Environmental Marketing Strategy," p. 51.

36. Wendy Melillo and Steve Miller, "Companies Find It's Not Easy Marketing Green," *Brandweek* (July 24, 2006), p. 8. Retrieved from www.brandweek.com/bw/news/recem_display.jsp?vnu_content_id=1002878049

37. Catherine A. Ramus and Ivan Montiel, "When are Corporate Environmental Policies a Form of Greenwashing?," *Business & Society* 44 (2005): 377–414 (p. 386).

38. Ibid., p. 388.

39. Ibid., p. 385.

40. Melillo and Miller, "Companies Find It's Not Easy Marketing Green," p. 36.

41. See Menon and Menon, "Environmental Marketing Strategy," pp. 53–54.

42. Ibid., p. 64.

43. Esty and Winston, *Green to Gold*, p. 211.

44. Ramus and Montiel, "When are Corporate Environmental Policies a Form of Greenwashing?," p. 378.

45. BP Indonesia, "Environmental Policy" (2008). Retrieved March 9, 2009 from www.bp.com/sectiongenericarticle.do?categoryId=9004784&contentId=7008767. The rest of the statement is similarly vague.

46. Milton Friedman, *Capitalism and Freedom* (University of Chicago Press, 1962), p. 133.

47. Joe DesJardins, "Corporate Environmental Responsibility," *Journal of Business Ethics* 17 (1998): 825–38 (p. 827).

48. Ibid., p. 828.

49. Not to be confused with the narrower category of stockholders.

50. Irene Henriques and Perry Sadorsky, "The Relationship between Environmental Commitment and Managerial Perceptions of Stakeholder Importance," *Academy of Management Journal* 42 (1999): 87–99 (p. 89, quoting R. Edward Freeman, *Strategic Management: A Stakeholder Approach* (London: Pitman, 1984), p. 46; Grant T. Savage, Timothy W. Nix, Carlton J. Whitehead, and John D. Blair, "Strategies for Assessing and Managing Organizational Stakeholders," *The Executive* 5 (1991): 61–75 (p. 61)).

51. Deutsch, "It's Getting Crowded on the Environmental Bandwagon."

52. Ibid.

53. Ibid.

54. See generally Henriques and Sadorsky, "The Relationship between Environmental Commitment and Managerial Perceptions of Stakeholder Importance."

55. Ibid., p. 95.

56. Ibid.

57. Ibid., pp. 95–96.

58. Ibid., p. 95.

59. Witherell, "Green Is the Color of Money."

60. Lillian R. BeVier, "Competitor Suits for False Advertising under Section 43(a) of the Lanham Act: A Puzzle in the Law of Deception," *Viginia Law Review* 78 (1992): 1–48 (p. 14).

61. Larry L. Rasmussen, *Earth Community, Earth Ethics* (Maryknoll, NY: Orbis Books, 1996), p. 107 (citing James Nash, *Loving Nature* (Nashville, TN: Abingdon Press, 1991), p. 181).

62. Rasmussen, *Earth Community, Earth Ethics*, p. 108.

63. Paul Hawken, "A Teasing Irony," in *Business and the Environment: A Reader*, ed. Richard Welford and Richard Starkey (Washington, DC: Taylor & Francis, 1996), pp. 5–16 (p. 5).

64. Witherell, "Green is the Color of Money."

65. Ibid.

66. Ibid.

67. Esty and Winston, *Green to Gold*, p. 9.

68. Wendy Naysnerski and Tom Tietenberg, "Private Enforcement of Federal Environmental Law," *Land Economics* 68 (1992): 28–48 (p. 28).

69. Eileen Gauna, "Federal Environmental Citizen Provisions: Obstacles and Incentives on the Road to Environmental Justice," *Ecology Law Quarterly* 22 (1995): 1–87 (p. 4).

70. Ibid., p. 47 (internal citations omitted).

71. Ibid., p. 46.

72. Ibid., p. 70.

73. Naysnerski and Tietenberg, "Private Enforcement of Federal Environmental Law," p. 31.

74. Ibid.

75. Ibid.

76. Ibid., p. 32.

77. Esty and Winston, *Green to Gold*, p. 79.

78. Ibid.

79. See generally Laufer, "Social Accountability and Corporate Greenwashing"; Ramus and Montiel, "When are Corporate Environmental Policies a Form of Greenwashing?"

80. Laufer, "Social Accountability and Corporate Greenwashing," p. 259.

81. Esty and Winston, *Green to Gold*, p. 226.

82. Ibid.

83. See discussion in Part II.B.

84. DesJardins, "Corporate Environmental Responsibility," p. 828.

85. Ibid., p. 829.

86. Menon and Menon, "Environmental Marketing Strategy," p. 54.

87. DesJardins, "Corporate Environmental Responsibility," p. 830.

88. Ibid.

89. Ibid., p. 832.

90. Ibid., p. 831.

91. Ibid. (quoting World Commission on Environment and Development, *Our Common Future* [Brundtland Report] (Oxford University Press, 1987), p. 43).

92. M. Schwartz, "The Nature of the Relationship between Corporate Codes of Ethics and Behaviour," *Journal of Business Ethics* 32 (2001): 247–62.

93. Ibid., p. 248.

94. Ibid., p. 253.

95. Ramus and Montiel, "When are Corporate Environmental Policies a Form of Greenwashing?," pp. 377–78.

96. Ibid., p. 400.

97. Ibid.

98. Ibid., p. 378.

99. Ibid., pp. 379–80 (internal citations omitted).

100. Ibid., p. 378 (citing Monika L. Winn and Linda C. Angell, "Towards a Process Model of Corporate Greening," *Organization Studies* 21 (2000): 1119–47).

101. Ramus and Montiel, "When are Corporate Environmental Policies a Form of Greenwashing?," p. 382.

102. Ibid., p. 408.

103. Ibid.

LEGAL PERSPECTIVES

United States Supreme Court, *United States v. Best Foods et al.* (1998)

The Comprehensive Environmental Response, Compensation, and Liability Act of 1980 (CERCLA) was enacted in response to the serious environmental and health risks posed by industrial pollution. CERCLA is a comprehensive statute that grants the President of the United States broad power to command government agencies and private parties to clean up hazardous waste sites. If it satisfies certain statutory conditions, the United States may, for instance, use the "Hazardous Substance Superfund" to finance cleanup efforts, which it may then replenish by suits brought under §107 of the Act against, among others, "any person who at the time of disposal of any hazardous substance owned or operated any facility." The term "person" is defined in CERCLA to include corporations and other business organizations.

The question before the Court was whether "a parent corporation that actively participated in, and exercised control over, the operations of a subsidiary may, without more, be held liable as an operator of a polluting facility owned or operated by the subsidiary." The Court held that a corporate parent that actively participated in, and exercised control over, the operations of the facility itself may be held directly liable in its own right as an operator of the facility. The Court recognized the general established principle of corporate law that a corporation could not be held liable for the action of its subsidiaries. As the Court said, "Thus it is hornbook law that 'the exercise of the "control" which stock ownership gives to the stockholders ... will not create liability beyond the assets of the subsidiary ... But there is an equally fundamental principle of corporate law, applicable to the parent–subsidiary relationship as well as generally, that the corporate veil may be pierced and the shareholder held liable for the corporation's conduct when, *inter alia*, the corporate form would otherwise

be misused to accomplish certain wrongful purposes, most notably fraud, on the shareholder's behalf.'"

The Court then considers the following case: CERCLA liability may turn on operation as well as ownership, and nothing in the statute's terms bars a parent corporation from direct liability for its own actions in operating a facility owned by its subsidiary. Thus, a publicly held corporation may not own a subsidiary but nonetheless in some important way operate that facility. When such a condition occurs we do not have a case of derivative liability because it is the owner's actions in operating the facility that creates the liability. "The fact that a corporate subsidiary happens to own a polluting facility operated by its parent does nothing, then, to displace the rule that the parent 'corporation is [itself] responsible for the wrongs committed by its agents in the course of its business.'"

The Court recognizes that much hinges on what is meant by "operating a facility." What a court looks to are the common norms that determine what counts as operating a facility. As the Court said, "Just as we may look to such norms in identifying the limits of the presumption that a dual officeholder acts in his ostensible capacity, so here we may refer to them in distinguishing a parental officer's oversight of a subsidiary from such an officer's control over the operation of the subsidiary's facility. ... The critical question is whether, in degree and detail, actions directed to the facility by an agent of the parent alone are eccentric under accepted norms of parental oversight of a subsidiary's facility." The decision that a parent company that operates a subsidiary is liable for its actions, even though it does not own the facility, was unanimous.

United States Supreme Court, *Whitman v. American Trucking Associations, Inc.* (2001)

In this case the Supreme Court needed to determine (1) whether §109(b)(1) of the Clean Air Act (CAA) delegates legislative power to the Administrator of the Environmental Protection Agency (EPA) and (2) whether

the Administrator may consider the costs of implementation in setting national ambient air quality standards (NAAQS) under §109(b)(1). As to whether the EPA had been granted legislative power under the law, Justice

Scalia, writing for the Court, wrote that the EPA was not and could not be granted legislative power under the law and that the District Court had erred in thinking otherwise. Interpreting Article 1, Section 1 of the Constitution, Scalia pointed out that the text permits no delegation of legislative powers and that this interpretation has been repeatedly upheld by the courts: "we have repeatedly said that when Congress confers decision making authority on agencies Congress must lay down by legislative act an intelligible principle to which the person or body authorized to act is directed to conform." Scalia then indicated that the governing standard was to be "sufficient but not more than necessary" based on the meaning of "at a level requisite to protect public health." The EPA did not have discretion to set a different standard.

On the question of cost, the Supreme Court upheld the District Court's determination that costs of implementation could not be considered when setting national ambient air quality standards. First the Court argues that the language of the law is clear; costs are not to be considered. Second, an examination of the history of the Act indicates that the issue of the cost of implementation including the impact on whole industries was considered but that Congress had made its decision that the standards were to be set independent of the costs of implementation. What about a situation where the costs of implementation are more detrimental to the public health than the standards that are set would be to the improvement of public health? Congress provided for that exigency. Thus, the Supreme Court upheld the District Court's opinion that the costs of implementation could not be considered in the making of ambient clean air standards.

CASES

Case 1: The Cruise Industry: Exotic Promises and Toxic Waters

DENIS G. ARNOLD, TODD JOHNSON, AND GEOFFREY CELLA

Often described as "floating cities," cruise ships are marketed as opportunities for travelers to visit exotic destinations, enjoy the natural environment, experience "once in a lifetime" scenery, and relax with a myriad of leisure activities. Passengers are encouraged to enjoy outdoor pursuits such as swimming, snorkeling, scuba diving, interacting with dolphins, kayaking, rafting, fishing, surfing, and site seeing. The cruise industry is experiencing rapid growth, and the size of ships is steadily increasing with newer ships now able to accommodate more than 7,000 passengers.

According to Oceana, an organization that "campaigns to protect and restore the world's oceans," cruise liners can generate in excess of 30,000 gallons of sewage, or "black water," 250,000 gallons of water from sinks, showers, laundries, etc., known as "gray water," 7,500 gallons of oily bilge water, and 7–10 tons of garbage and solid waste in a single day. A study by the Alaska Department of Environmental Conservation concluded that of 42 samples of discharged water taken from various cruise companies voyaging in Alaskan waters, nine exceeded the fecal (human solid waste) bacterial standards by 50,000 times, and only one sample was in full compliance with all regulations. According to Daniel Rieger, of the German environmental association NABU (Nature and Biodiversity Conservation Union), "Ships cause not only greenhouse gas emissions, but also sulphur oxides, nitrogen oxides and particulate matter. Per day one cruise ship emits as much particulate matter as a million cars. So 30 cruise ships pollute as much as all the cars in the United Kingdom" (see Coldwell, 2017 in the sources).

Royal Caribbean Cruises Ltd. is the second largest cruise company in the world with current net income of $1.28 billion and revenues of $8.5 billion. The company, headquartered in Miami, Florida, is publicly traded. It owns and operates Royal Caribbean International, Celebrity Cruises, and Azamara Club Cruises. It also has joint ventures with the German company TUI Cruises, the Spanish Pullmantur, and the Chinese Sky Sea Cruises. With whole and partial ownership of 49 vessels, cruises under the Royal Caribbean umbrella reach over 500 destinations in over 100 different countries.

The Royal Caribbean Cruise's *Code of Business Conduct and Ethics* states the company's priority to "Commit to a comprehensive environmental protection program focusing on the key elements of reduction of waste, recycling, and proper disposal." Despite this public commitment, from 1998 to 2000 the company was required to pay $30,500,000 in fines to state and national agencies for intentional and illegal environmental pollution and subsequent attempted cover-ups. The first offense resulted in a $1 million fine, for falsifying records regarding oil-water discharged into the waters off the coast of Miami, Florida, by the *Nordic Empress* cruise ship. A second $8 million fine resulted from similar activity off the coast of Puerto Rico by five different ships, *Sovereign of the Seas*, *Monarch of the Seas*, *Song of America*, *Nordic Prince*, and *Nordic Empress*. Royal Caribbean was placed on five years' probation by the US District Court for the Southern District of Florida in Miami. In addition to acknowledging the dumping itself, employees on the ships admitted to falsifying the records and lying to the Coast Guard to conceal the dumping. In the following year the company was fined $18 million because of similar activities, including illegal dumping by *Grandeur of the Seas*, *Majesty of the Seas*, *Monarch of the Seas*, *Nordic Empress*, *Nordic Prince*, *Song of America*, *Song of Norway*, *Sovereign of the Seas*, and *Sun Viking*. Many of these ships were found guilty of bypassing mandated water purification systems for oily water, dumping human wastewater and other chemicals directly into the waters in which it sailed, fabricating relevant records, and providing false testimony to government officials.

A subsequent fine of $3.5 million resulted from a 2000 plea agreement with the state of Alaska, for dumping oil, waste, dry-cleaning chemicals, and other toxins into the state's waters. The majority of each of the fines over this span were the result of deliberate and repeated attempts to cover up the activities when investigated by the US Coast Guard, the Environmental Protection Agency, and state environmental protection agencies, and not for the environmental damage itself. In June 2008 Royal Caribbean's

---

This case was written for the purpose of classroom discussion by Denis G. Arnold, Todd Johnson, and Geoffry Cella. © 2017 Denis G. Arnold.

Rhapsody of the Seas discharged 20,000 gallons of wastewater into the Chatham Strait in Alaska. More recently, Royal Caribbean ships were among the 19 cruise ships from across the industry that committed 49 violations of Alaska state environmental protection laws between 2010 and 2014 (more recent violations are not publicly available). These included illegal emissions of unburned fuel, soot, carbon, and other particulate matter from exhaust stacks. Royal Caribbean is not the only cruise ship company producing serious and harmful environmental pollution.

Carnival Corporation & PLC is the largest cruise company in the world, with recent net income of $2.8 billion against annual revenues at $16.4 billion. In 2017, Princess Cruise Lines Ltd., a division of Carnival Corp., was ordered to pay a $40 million penalty of the US Department of Justice after investigations determined that the company had deliberately and illegally dumped onboard waste into the waters it cruised. Engineering officers for Princess Cruises had created a "magic pipe" that served to bypass pollution measuring and prevention equipment. This allowed for the unchecked release of contaminants into the ocean. The illegal activity was brought to the attention of authorities by a whistleblower and investigations determined that illegal discharges had been occurring since at least 2005. In Britain a 2017 investigation found air quality on the deck of the cruise ship *Oceana*, the same air being breathed by sunbathing passengers, to be worse than the most polluted cities in the world due to the emissions from the burning of heavy fuel oil (also known as bunker fuel). *Oceana* is a ship in the fleet of P&O Cruises, Britain's largest cruise line and a subsidiary of Carnival Corp.

In all, the cruise line industry has been penalized by an estimated $53,000,000 on fines owing to environmental degradation, and cover-ups of such behavior, since 1992, with Royal Caribbean and Carnival Corp. responsible for approximately 75 percent of that total. Critics charge that the companies engage in cost–benefit analysis to determine whether or not it is more costly to properly and lawfully dispose of waste or to foul waters and harm ocean life and pay fines and legal fees when they are caught. They also point out that at present there are no federal regulations prohibiting many of the worst types of pollution produced by cruise ships.

Environmental regulation of the cruising industry remains limited and companies are not held accountable for most of the environmental damage caused by their ships. In general, it is difficult to supervise and regulate the activities of cruise ships for at least two reasons. First, many cruise ships are flagged, or registered, in nations other than those from which they sail in order to avoid more demanding statutes and regulations including environmental laws. For example, the large majority of ships sailing from the United States or the United Kingdom are flagged in the Bahamas, Bermuda, Panama, or Malta. Second, many cruise ships travel in international waters, where no immediate oversight is present, and most laws protecting the environment are inapplicable. The US Clean Water Act, for example, is designed to regulate land-based activities, whereas the cruise ships' discharges are water-based. The Clean Cruise Ship Act is a law designed to close many of these loopholes in the United States and to establish national standards and prohibitions for discharges from cruise vessels. It has been repeatedly introduced in the US Congress in recent years but is opposed by industry and has not been enacted.

Discussion Questions

1. Given that Royal Caribbean and Carnival Corp. use images of excursions in pristine waters in their marketing campaigns to attract customers, how should one ethically assess their illegal dumping of human waste and toxic pollutants into those same waters? Explain.

2. Given that illegal activities and subsequent fines continue to occur despite the numerous punishments already handed out, what responsibility, if any, do customers have to help reduce the environmental pollution of cruise ships? Explain.

3. Why do you believe the harmful pollution by the cruise industry still takes place? Explain.

4. Is ocean cruising environmentally sustainable in your view? Why, or why not? If you answered no, how might it be made environmentally sustainable? Explain.

5. What are the best moral arguments *supporting* the Clean Cruise Ship Act to make certain levels of air and water discharges from cruise ships illegal? What are the best moral arguments *opposing* them? Explain.

The case is based on the following sources: R. Trigaux, "To Keep Waters Pristine, Punish the Polluters," *St. Petersburg Times* (May 19, 2002).

E. Strickland, "Making a Stink: What Effect Does Ship Waste Have on Our Coastal Waters? As New Orleans Embraces the Cruise Line Industry, It's Time to Ask the No. 1 Question about No. 2," *Gambit Weekly* (November 11, 2003). Retrieved February 15, 2007 from www.bestofneworleans.com/dispatch/2003–11-18/cover_story.html.

M. O'Rourke, "Cruise Line Forced to Address Pollution," *Risk Management* 51 (July 1, 2004), p. 8.

"Pollution and Environmental Violations and Fines, 1992–2007" (only those reported in the media or public documents). Retrieved February 15, 2007 from www.cruise junkie.com/enviro fines.html.

"Corporate Governance – Code of Business Conduct and Ethics." Retrieved February 15, 2007 from www.rclcorporate .com/wp-content/uploads/GCE-Code-of-Business-Conduct-2018.pdf.

"Plan a Cruise > Activities." Retrieved February 15, 2007 from www.royalcaribbean.com/findacruise/experiencetypes/home.do; jsessionid=0000hfqnfoilghcBjIVE7jeyEGq:10ktdmlju?cS=NAVBAR.

"Oceana." Retrieved February 16, 2007 from http://oceana.org/ index.php?id=1769&no_cache=1.

S.1359 – Clean Cruise Ship Act of 2013; 2016 Cruise Ship Report Card. Retrieved September 2, 2017 from https://foe .org/cruise-report-card/.

J. Brooks, "DEC Reveals Extent of Cruise Pollution" (August 12, 2015). Retrieved September 7, 2017 from http://juneauempire.com/ state-local/2015–08-12/dec-reveals-extent-cruise-pollution?page=2.

W. Coldwell, "Air on Board Cruise Ships 'Is Twice as Bad as at Piccadilly Circus'" (July 3, 2017). Retrieved September 6, 2017 from www.theguardian.com/travel/2017/jul/03/air-on-board-cruise-ships-is-twice-as-bad-as-at-piccadilly-circus.

"Cruise Line Ordered to Pay $40 Million for Illegal Dumping of Oil Contaminated Waste and Falsifying Records" (April 19, 2017). Retrieved September 7, 2017 from www.justice.gov/opa/pr/cruise-line-ordered-pay-40-million-illegal-dumping-oil-contaminated-waste-and-falsifying.

"Cruise Ships." Retrieved September 2, 2017 from https://foe .org/projects/oceans-and-forests/cruise-ships/.

"Events at Sea by Rhapsody of the Seas." Retrieved September 7, 2017 from www.cruisejunkie.com/Ships/RCI/Events_by_Rhapsody .html.

J. Flechas and C. Herrera, "Carnival Corp Ship Caught in Pollution Scheme. Now They're Paying $40 Million for It" (December 1, 2016). Retrieved September 6, 2017 from www.mia miherald.com/news/business/tourism-cruises/article118245433. html.

"Royal Caribbean Cruises Ltd (RCL.N) Financials" (n.d.). Retrieved September 6, 2017 from www.reuters.com/finance/ stocks/financial-highlights/RCL.N.

Case 2: Texaco in the Ecuadorean Amazon

DENIS G. ARNOLD

Ecuador is a small nation on the northwest coast of South America. During nearly its entire history, Ecuador has been one of the least politically stable South American nations. In 1830 Ecuador achieved its independence from Spain. Ecuadorean history since that time has been characterized by cycles of republican government and military intervention and rule. The period from 1960 to 1972 was marked by instability and military dominance of political institutions. From 1972 to 1979 Ecuador was governed by military regimes. In 1979 a popularly elected president took office, but the military demanded and was granted important governing powers. The democratic institutional framework of Ecuador remains weak. Decreases in public sector spending, increasing unemployment, and rising inflation have hit the Ecuadorean poor especially hard. World Bank estimates indicate that in 1994, 35 percent of the Ecuadorean population lived in poverty, and an additional 17 percent were vulnerable to poverty.

The Ecuadorean Amazon is one of the most biologically diverse forests in the world and is home to an estimated 5 percent of Earth's species. It is home to cicadas, scarlet macaws, squirrel monkeys, freshwater pink dolphins, and thousands of other species. Many of these species have small populations, making them extremely sensitive to disturbance. Indigenous Indian populations have lived in harmony with these species for centuries. They have fished and hunted in and around the rivers and lakes; and they have raised crops of cacao, coffee, fruits, nuts, and tropical woods in *chakras*, models of sustainable agroforestry.

Ten thousand feet beneath the Amazon floor lies one of Ecuador's most important resources: rich deposits of crude oil. Historically, the Ecuadorean government regarded the oil as the best way to keep up with the country's payments on its $12 billion foreign debt obligations. For 20 years American oil companies, led by Texaco, extracted oil from beneath the Ecuadorean Amazon in partnership with the government of Ecuador. (The United States is the primary importer of Ecuadorean oil.) They constructed 400 drill sites and hundreds of miles of roads and pipelines, including a

---

This case was written by Denis G. Arnold for the purposes of classroom discussion. © 2017 Denis G. Arnold.

primary pipeline that extends for 280 miles across the Andes. Large tracts of forest were clear-cut to make way for these facilities. Indian lands, including *chakras*, were taken and bulldozed, often without compensation. In the village of Pacayacu the central square is occupied by a drilling platform.

Officials estimate that the primary pipeline alone has spilled more than 16.8 million gallons of oil into the Amazon over an 18-year period. Spills from secondary pipelines have never been estimated or recorded; however, smaller tertiary pipelines dump 10,000 gallons of petroleum per week into the Amazon, and production pits dump approximately 4.3 million gallons of toxic production wastes and treatment chemicals into the forest's rivers, streams, and groundwater each day. (By comparison, the Exxon Valdez spilled 10.8 million gallons of oil into Alaska's Prince William Sound.) Significant portions of these spills have been carried downriver into neighboring Peru.

Critics charge that Texaco ignored prevailing oil industry standards that call for the reinjection of waste deep into the ground. Rivers and lakes were contaminated by oil and petroleum; heavy metals such as arsenic, cadmium, cyanide, lead, and mercury; poisonous industrial solvents; and lethal concentrations of chloride salt, and other highly toxic chemicals. The only treatment these chemicals received occurred when the oil company burned waste pits to reduce petroleum content. Villagers report that the chemicals return as black rain, polluting what little freshwater remains. What is not burned off seeps through the unlined walls of the pits into the groundwater. Cattle are found with their stomachs rotted out, crops are destroyed, animals are gone from the forest, and fish disappear from the lakes and rivers. Health officials and community leaders report adults and children with deformities, skin rashes, abscesses, headaches, dysentery, infections, respiratory ailments, and disproportionately high rates of cancer. In 1972 Texaco signed a contract with the military regime in power requiring it to turn over all of its operations to Ecuador's national oil company, Petroecuador, by 1992. Petroecuador inherited antiquated equipment, rusting pipelines, and uncounted toxic waste sites. Independent estimates place the cost of cleaning up the production pits alone at $600 million. From 1995 to 1998 Texaco spent $40 million on cleanup operations in Ecuador. In exchange for these efforts the government of Ecuador relinquished future claims against the company. However, the citizens of Ecuador in the regions in which Texaco operated over 20 years did not release the

company from liability for the environmental and health impacts of their operations.

Numerous international accords – including the 1972 Stockholm Declaration on the Human Environment signed by over 100 countries, including the United States and Ecuador – identify the right to a clean and healthy environment as a fundamental human right and prohibit both state and private actors from endangering the needs of present and future generations. Ecuadorean and Peruvian plaintiffs, including several indigenous tribes, have filed billion-dollar class-action lawsuits against Texaco in US courts under the Alien Tort Claims Act (ACTA). Enacted in 1789, the law was designed to provide noncitizens access to US courts in cases involving a breach of international law, including accords. Texaco maintains that the case should be tried in Ecuador. However, Ecuador's judicial system does not recognize the concept of a class-action suit and has no history of environmental litigation. Furthermore, Ecuador's judicial system is notoriously corrupt (a poll by George Washington University found that only 16 percent of Ecuadoreans have confidence in their judicial system) and lacks the infrastructure necessary to handle the case (e.g., the city in which the case would be tried lacks a courthouse). Texaco defended its actions by arguing that it is in full compliance with Ecuadorean law and that it had full approval of the Ecuadorean government.

In May 2001 US District Judge Jed Rakoff rejected the applicability of the ACTA and dismissed the case on grounds of *forum non conveniens*. This was a victory for Texaco, who argued that the case should be tried in Ecuador. Judge Rakoff agreed and wrote in his decision that since "no act taken by Texaco in the United States bore materially on the pollution-creating activities," the case should be tried in Ecuador and Peru. In October 2001 Texaco completed a merger with Chevron Corporation. In 2002 the US Court of Appeals for the Second Circuit upheld Judge Rakoff's decision. The plaintiffs then sued Chevron in Ecuador. After years of additional litigation, in 2011 the plaintiffs won a $9.5 billion judgment against Chevron in an Ecuadorean court. Chevron did not deny the pollution had taken place, but maintained that it was not legally liable. Chevron challenged the Ecuadorean court verdict in US courts on the grounds that the New York based lawyer who represented the plaintiffs committed fraud by colluding with some of the expert witnesses who assessed damages and other means. The US Supreme Court agreed with Chevron in 2016 and prevented collection of the Ecuadorean court judgment. In the meantime, the Ecuadorean plaintiffs, with different legal teams, have sued Chevron in Canada, Brazil, and Argentina, hoping still to hold it accountable for the negative environmental and health impacts they attribute to the company's failure to meet prevailing oil industry environmental standards for 20 years.

Discussion Questions

1. It is widely believed that Texaco did not operate in Ecuador with prevailing oil industry standards regarding environmental protection. On the other hand, Ecuador had essentially no laws regarding environmental protection that Texaco violated during most of the time that it operated in Ecuador. In your view, did Texaco do anything wrong in Ecuador? Why, or why not? Explain.

2. Given the fact that Texaco operated in partnership with the Ecuadorean government (to which it paid revenues), are Texaco's activities in the Amazon morally justified? Does it matter that a non-democratic, military regime was in power in Ecuador for most of this period? Why, or why not? Explain.

3. Does Texaco (now Chevron) have a moral obligation to provide additional funds and technical expertise to clean up areas of the Amazon it is operationally, if not legally, responsible for polluting? Does it have a moral obligation to provide medical care for the residents of the Amazon region who are suffering from the effects of the pollution? Why, or why not? Explain.

4. Does the example of Texaco's actions in Ecuador indicate a need for enforceable regulations governing transnational corporate activity? Why, or why not? Explain.

5. Chevron has spent tens of millions, and perhaps hundreds of millions of dollars, on legal fees and public relations costs related to this case over the years. It has also received many years of negative publicity as a result of its operations in Ecuador and is likely to do so in the future. From the standpoint of managing stakeholder relationships and social risk on behalf of a firm, what lessons would you draw from the case? Explain.

This case is based on the following sources: James Brooke, "New Effort Would Test Possible Coexistence of Oil and Rain Forest," *The New York Times* (February 26, 1991).

Dennis M. Hanratty, ed., *Ecuador: A Country Study*, 3rd ed. (Washington, DC: Library of Congress, 1991).

Anita Isaacs, *Military Rule and Transition in Ecuador, 1972–92* (University of Pittsburgh Press, 1993).

Ecuador Poverty Report (Washington, DC: World Bank, 1996).

Joe Kane, *Savages* (New York: Vintage Books, 1996).

"Texaco on Trial," *Nation* (May 31, 1999). "Texaco and Ecuador," *Texaco: Health, Safety & the Environment* (September 27, 1999). Retrieved December 16, 1999 from www.texaco.com/she/index.html.

Aguinda v. Texaco Inc., 142 F. Supp. 2d 534 (S.D.N.Y. 2001).

"Jungle Justice," *Businessweek* (March 10, 2011). © 2012.

Case 3: Interface Corporation and Sustainable Business

JOSEPH DESJARDINS

Carpet manufacturing would not normally be thought of as an environmentally praiseworthy industry. Most carpet fibers are derived from petroleum, a nonrenewable resource, and synthesized with fiberglass and PVC – two known carcinogens – to create the fibers used to manufacture carpeting. The carpeting is then dyed, and the waste produced from this process contains various toxins and heavy metals. Carpet manufacturing factories are heavy industrial producers of CO_2 emissions. Used carpets, especially nylon-based products, are not recycled and therefore end up in landfills. This carpet waste is often toxic and nonbiodegradable.

Reflecting on the environmental record of the carpeting industry, Ray Anderson, the founder, CEO, and chairman of Interface, a $1 billion-a-year carpeting and floor-covering corporation, suggested that "In the future, people like me will go to jail." That now seems unlikely given recent changes at Interface. Over the last decade under Anderson's leadership, Interface has become a leader in the movement to make business environmentally sustainable.

"Sustainability" and "sustainable development" have become something of a mantra among many in the environmental community. The concept of sustainable business can be traced to a UN report authored by then-Prime Minister

Gro Brundtland of Norway in which sustainability was defined as the ability "to meet the needs of the present without compromising the ability of future generations to meet their own needs." Since the mid-1990s, Anderson has moved to make Interface a model of sustainable business practices.

Perhaps the most significant change at Interface involves a redefinition of their business. Interface is making a transition from selling carpeting to leasing floor-covering services. On a traditional business model, carpet is sold to consumers who, once they become dissatisfied with the color or style or once the carpeting becomes worn, dispose of the carpet in landfills. There is little incentive here to produce long-lasting or easily recyclable carpeting. Once Interface shifted to leasing floor-covering services, incentives were created to produce long-lasting, easily replaceable and recyclable carpets. Interface thereby accepts responsibility for the entire life cycle of the product it markets. Because the company retains ownership and is responsible for maintenance, Interface strives to produce carpeting that can be easily replaced in sections rather than in its entirety, that is more durable, and that can eventually be remanufactured. Redesigning their carpets and shifting to a service lease has also improved production efficiencies and reduced material and energy costs significantly. Consumers benefit by getting what they truly desire at lower costs and fewer burdens.

But Interface has also committed itself to wider-ranging changes. Interface has set seven distinct corporate goals on its road to sustainability. One goal is to continue to redesign their business to focus on delivering services rather than material. This produces incentives to create products that are long-lasting and recyclable rather than products with "planned obsolescence." A second goal is to eliminate, and not simply reduce, all forms of waste. A third goal is to make any and all products that are emitted from the production process non-toxic. Fourth, Interface seeks to reduce energy use and move to renewable and nonpollution sources of energy. Their fifth goal is to "close the loop" of the production process, so that everything that comes out of the process can be recycled back into productive uses. Sixth, Interface strives for resource efficiencies, seeking to transport information rather than products and people. This goal encourages plants to be located near suppliers and retailers and supports information technology, videoconferencing, email, and telecommuting. Finally, Interface is committed to raising community awareness of natural systems and our impact upon them.

Discussion Questions

1. Some critics argue that sustainability is popular only because it allows industrialized countries to believe, falsely, that consumer-driven lifestyles can continue indefinitely. In what ways do you believe your own lifestyle is sustainable? Unsustainable?

2. Should manufacturers be legally liable for "cradle to grave" responsibility for their products? Should manufacturers be responsible to recycle their products after consumers are finished with them? Who should pay for disposal of consumer goods at the end of their product life?

3. What government policies might encourage other businesses to follow Interface's lead? What government policies hinder such activities?

4. What responsibilities, if any, do we have to future generations? How might these responsibilities change contemporary business?

Case 4: What Does It Mean to Be Truly Green? Environmental Sustainability at Frito-Lay North America

DENIS G. ARNOLD AND SAMANTHA PAUSTIAN-UNDERDAHL

Former President and CEO of Frito-Lay, Al Carey, pledged that his company would be the most environmentally sustainable company on the planet. "Our goal," he said, "is to become the preeminent green company. Not the preeminent company in the food industry, the preeminent green company."[1] But what does it mean to be "the preeminent green company?" What has Frito-Lay achieved thus far on this front? And how should it proceed in order to achieve this goal? Frito-Lay North America is presently the largest division of PepsiCo Americas Foods – one of PepsiCo's three global units. (Carey is currently CEO of the North American division of PepsiCo.) Frito-Lay primarily

This case was written for the purposes of classroom discussion by Denis Arnold and Samantha Paustian-Underdahl. © 2011, 2017 Denis G. Arnold.

operates in the United States, with its headquarters in Plano, Texas. The company employs over 50,000 people and is the world's biggest producer of snack foods. Frito-Lay consistently earns approximately 30 percent of PepsiCo's $60+ billion in revenues and over 40 percent of its operating profits.

Indra Nooyi has served as the Chief Executive Officer of PepsiCo since 2006 and is consistently ranked at the top of annual lists of the most powerful women in American business. Nooyi has given PepsiCo a strategic advantage in the area of sustainability. Nooyi has embraced the concept of sustainability in a broad sense via the corporate philosophy of "Performance with Purpose." This philosophy has three planks that supplement PepsiCo's economic focus and impacts. The three planks are:

Human Sustainability – how we work to *nourish* people with our products

Environmental Sustainability – how we work to *replenish* the environment

Talent Sustainability – how we work to *cherish* people[2]

To meet the goal of human sustainability Frito-Lay has taken steps to improve the healthfulness of its products. Frito-Lay now offers a line of 100-calorie-portion Mini-Bites, a line of vegetable crisps called Flat Earth, a line of nut and fruit snacks called True North, and low-sodium and baked versions of its potato chips, corn chips, and tortilla chips. In 2004 Frito-Lay removed trans fatty oils (partially hydrogenated oils) from all of its products. According to the American Heart Association trans fats reduce good HDL cholesterol and increase bad LDL cholesterol levels thereby increasing the risk of heart disease and stroke.[3] While the company is working to produce healthier snack options, Frito-Lay remains the world's top producer of salty snacks, including corn chips and potato chips.[4] Researchers believe that the increase in the consumption of salty snacks, candy, and soft drinks throughout the past three decades may be one reason for the rise in obesity rates.[5] Recent statistics show that nearly 65 percent of American adults are overweight or obese[6] and close to 30 percent of children between the ages of 6 and 19 are overweight or at risk of being overweight.[7] As the world's top producer of salty snacks, Frito-Lay must consider how to further increase its human sustainability initiatives.

PepsiCo has had a reputation for hiring and promoting racial and ethnic minorities that began at least as early as the 1940s; PepsiCo has long been regarded as a national leader in creating a respectful workplace for minorities and for promoting equal opportunity.[8] More recently it has developed an outstanding reputation protecting and promoting the interests of women, gays and lesbians, and disabled individuals. PepsiCo regularly appears near the top of the Fortune 50 Best Companies for Minorities and has received numerous awards from organizations across the planet for its support of diversity and inclusiveness in its global operations.[9] Frito-Lay embraces this corporate culture and has been recognized with regional and national awards honoring its respect for diversity. These awards include the Corporation of the Year Award by the National Minority Supplier Development Council, the Corporation of the Year Award from the Women's Business Council, and the Sharing Success Award for "Best of the Decade Performance" in Minority and Women Business Development from *Minority Business News*.[10]

PepsiCo's status as a corporate leader regarding environmental protection and conservation is still developing. When asked about PepsiCo's commitment to "green" initiatives Nooyi responded as follows:

Our goal is to make sure that when it comes to water and energy, we replenish the environment and leave it in a net zero state. So across the world we have unleashed the power of our people to come up with ideas to reduce, recycle, replenish the environment and we are making great progress by reducing how much water we use in our manufacture and the carbon footprint that we put on the environment. As a consequence, what we are seeing is an incredible investment in all these environment initiatives. But is otherwise really in two ways, one is tangible financial investment, second is a huge return on investment and because new employees are usually idealistic young people who just graduated from college. They want to come to a company to work for a purpose, that is wise about the next generation.[11]

Since her appointment as CEO Nooyi has increased public awareness of environmental sustainability initiatives at PepsiCo and broadened their application to all major divisions of the organization, including receiving the prestigious US Environmental Protection Agency (EPA) and US Department of Energy joint Energy Star Partner of the Year Award for Energy Management for ten years in a row. However, the efforts to reduce pollution and waste, and to make the most efficient use of natural resources, began many years ago at Frito-Lay.

Origins of Environmental Sustainability: Compliance and Efficiency

Environmental sustainability is fully integrated into the operations of Frito-Lay, beginning with the Senior Vice-

President for Operations and extending to plant environmental managers and distribution center resource conservation champions. Much of the responsibility for environmental sustainability at Frito-Lay falls to David Haft, Senior Vice-President for Productivity, Sustainability, and Quality. Haft reports that at "Frito-Lay, when we talk about environmental sustainability, we look across the entire supply chain. So we start out with raw materials and packaging, and we work with potato growers, corn farmers, oil manufacturers, packaging film suppliers." And we ask, "Are they operating their business in a sustainable manner and are they doing things for us that support our sustainability agenda?"[12,13]

One of the greatest threats to Frito-Lay's continued success has been the increasing cost of water, energy, and agricultural commodities such as corn and potatoes. The prices of water used in manufacturing, natural gas and electricity used to power facilities, and diesel fuel to power its truck fleet continue to rise. Since 2012 the price of corn per bushel has fluctuated from a high of $8.395 to a low of $2.805. Higher corn prices are partly due to the increased demand for corn to produce ethanol. Since corn is one of Frito-Lay's key raw materials, the increase in corn prices could negatively affect their margins. Moreover, Frito-Lay has faced challenges of high operational costs because of the increased cost of water and electricity in the United States and elsewhere.

With 37 manufacturing plants in the United States and Canada, and one of the largest corporate truck fleets in the United States, Frito-Lay produced significant water and air emissions (PepsiCo itself has the largest truck fleet in the United States). Partly in response to the Clean Air Act Amendments of 1990, Frito-Lay initiated a program in their factories that utilized "green teams" to ensure that all facilities were in strict compliance with local, state, and federal environmental regulations. As a result of these actions managers noticed cost savings as a result of increased efficiency in the use of natural resources. Given the substantial cost savings, leaders at Frito-Lay decided that additional resources should be channeled into water and energy conservation. In 1997 a productivity and safety enhancement program known as "Starfleet" was put in place. This program utilizes teams of specialists from across the organization to determine and implement best practices in manufacturing, safety, fleet operations, sales, and other areas. A natural resources team was established with the task of utilizing best practices to achieve enhanced efficiency and cost savings. This team quickly took advantage of "low hanging fruit" such as installing more efficient light bulbs, minimizing wastewater, and implementing additional measures to increase productivity. The team then became more innovative and began to search for the technology necessary to further enhance productivity.

When the Starfleet team realized that the technology did not exist to further enhance productivity an engineer was assigned to develop solutions. It became evident by 2000 that one person could not do this work alone. At that time, Haft reports, senior operations managers were thinking "Look, if we think one person can go invent all this themselves, we're kidding ourselves. We're going to have to go ahead and invest the resources and funding to make this a bigger program." The team identified resource-conservation BHAGs ("big hairy audacious goals," popularized by management theorists Jim Collins and James Porras in 1996) including a 50 percent reduction in water usage, a 30 percent reduction in thermal fuel usage, and a 25 percent reduction in electricity consumption. The ultimate goals were energy and water conservation and cost savings of millions of dollars. To achieve these efficiency goals, and to realize the cost savings, money had to be invested in personnel and in facilities, equipment, and fleet modifications. Frito-Lay CFO David Rader was convinced, but he needed to be sure that then PepsiCo CFO Indra Nooyi was supportive as well. In a now famous 2000 meeting Rader pitched the proposal to Nooyi. Her response was immediate and positive. She allowed the Frito-Lay team to increase capital expenditures on water and energy quickly, without requiring a lengthy study period or further research. Indeed, her quick approval of the plan so surprised Haft that after the meeting he asked Rader, "Was that a yes? Can we do that?"[14]

Frito-Lay immediately put together a team of engineers to work on the technical aspects of water and energy conservation. In addition, Frito-Lay regularly consulted with world-class experts such as the Southwest Research Institute, Joel Swisher of the Rocky Mountain Institute (RMI), and university faculty when they required additional technical expertise. The challenge was significant because, according to Haft, the quality of Frito-Lay's products could not be diminished by the new production technologies. The results included a variety of means for increasing water and energy efficiency. Low-water corn processing, recycling water from starch recovery systems, and other measures have reduced water consumption by three billion gallons annually. Electricity usage was cut by natural daylighting, photovoltaic (solar powered) electricity generation, and co-generation of heat and electricity. Natural gas consumption was reduced by making nearly every heat exchanger and boiler at Frito-Lay more efficient and by implementing innovations such as potato stack heat recovery systems that captured the heat generated in the manufacturing of potato chips and channeled that energy for other uses within the plant. At the San

Antonio plant, heat released from a toaster oven was used to provide the energy for a Doritos fryer. In other plants, potato chip stack heat recovery was used to heat buildings or water. Ninety-eight percent of oil used in the fryers was either absorbed or recovered and recycled. The recycling process took the oil at the end of its run, moved it to a holding tank where it was nitrogen blanketed, and then blended the oil back into the process.

Across the organization real time-actionable information was utilized to measure production efficiency via scorecards. Haft reports that "we're kind of a scorecard crazy company. We love to scorecard everything … What we do is we look at the technology that every plant in the company has in place and we look at the products they make because different products use different amounts of water, gas, and electricity." For example, with respect to water they want to know "if you did everything perfectly for the products you're making, how many gallons of water you should've used yesterday? So we scorecard that on a period every four-week basis and we actually develop our financial plans using these scorecards to continue pressing up to 95% efficiency." Another way that water, electricity, and natural gas were conserved was via the use of utility walls at all plants. These are large, flat screen monitors that track water and energy use. According to Haft, every day at Frito-Lay's plants a team of technicians gathered to review the plant's resource consumption data for the past 24 hours. "They compare their site's performance to their site's goals, and if they identify variances, they quickly develop and implement an action plan to fix the issue."

From 2001 to the present annual capital expenditures on energy and water conservation ranged between $16 million and $23 million. Annual returns on these capital investments ranged between $6 and $8 million, or approximately 25 percent annually. Resource specialists from across Frito-Lay operations utilized budgets, scorecards, and audits to execute goals. Employees were rewarded for meeting goals with bonuses and other incentives. By 2006, relative to a 1999 baseline, Frito-Lay had reduced annual water consumption by 35 percent, natural gas consumption by 24 percent, and electricity consumption by 21 percent, with estimated annual cost savings of $50 million. Then in 2008 FLNA saw a reduction in water consumption by 39 percent, natural gas consumption by 30 percent, and electricity consumption by 22 percent, with estimated annual cost savings of $60 million. Its current target goals are a 75 percent reduction in water consumption, 50 percent reduction in natural gas, 45 percent reduction in electricity, and 25 percent reduction in diesel relative to total 1999 consumption.

Fleet Operations and Packaging

Frito-Lay operates the eighth largest private over-the-road fleet in North America with over 1,000 tractors and 4,000 trailers driving 130 million over-the-road miles each year (PepsiCo, including all its divisions, operates the single largest private fleet in the United States). In addition, they operate 14,000 route vans, 3,000 24-foot box trucks, and 650 sales cars. The semi-trailer trucks operated between 37 plants and 200 distribution centers of between 25,000 and 100,000 square feet in size. Frito-Lay also operated 14,000 bin locations. These are "very small unmanned warehouses out in very rural areas" utilized by route sales representatives. Frito-Lay salespeople serviced 19,000 supermarkets, 7,000 mass merchandisers (e.g., Target and Walmart), 1,000 club stores (e.g., Sam's Club and Costco), and 250 street routes serving smaller stores. In 2006 Frito-Lay targeted diesel fuel consumption for reduction. Fuel consumption for the over-the-road fleet has been reduced by 6 percent or more by enhancing trailer aerodynamics via low drag mud flaps and trailer belly flaring. Frito-Lay buys 1,000 trucks a year and is working with truck manufacturers to improve fuel efficiency by using lightweight composite materials and reducing engine size. These innovative practices can enhance fuel efficiency from 10 mpg to 16–18 mpg, an improvement of 60–80 percent. In 2009 Frito-Lay introduced 1,200 Sprinter delivery vans to its national fleet. The Sprinter vans utilized a 3.0L diesel engine to achieve an average 17 mpg and 20 percent reduction in vehicle CO_2 emissions.[15] Frito-Lay also recently completed the conversion of its 650 vehicle sales fleet to hybrid vehicles. In 2012, and again in 2015, the US Environmental Protection Agency awarded Frito-Lay the SmartWay Excellence Award for superior environmental performance in shipping and logistics and in 2016 it received the Advanced Clean Transportation Fleet Award.

The cartons carried by Frito-Lay's fleet have been designed to precisely accommodate the bags of snacks or other products being shipped, and the cartons were also designed to fit precisely into delivery vehicles so no space is wasted and efficiency is maximized. The cartons are produced with over 99 percent recycled paper and are themselves reused multiple times. Between 98 percent and 99 percent of cartons are returned for reuse. According to Haft, "we reuse our cartons until they fall apart." That program alone saves 4 to 5 million trees each year while providing Frito-Lay with $100 million dollars in annual cost savings, reports Haft. Frito-Lay is also being innovative in the design of product packaging. In 2009 they introduced 100 percent biodegradable snack packaging comprising paper, polylactic acid (corn lacquer), and an ultra-thin layer of aluminum that serves as a barrier for moisture and oxygen. Because the technology did not yet exist, Frito-Lay developed the technology in-house on its own initiative.

Second Generation Environmental Sustainability: Embracing Net Zero and Carbon Emission Reductions

In 2007 Frito-Lay committed to building all new facilities in compliance with the US Green Building Council's Leadership in Energy and Environmental Design (LEED) Green Building Rating System at the Silver level or better. In 2009 Frito-Lay's retrofitted global headquarters in Plano, Texas received LEED Gold certification.[16] In manufacturing plants and distribution facilities across the United States and Canada Frito-Lay implemented measures to reduce energy and water consumption. Nowhere is this more evident than in Casa Grande, Arizona. Haft and his team were brainstorming about how they might push the sustainability envelope when they realized that they had the capability to take a plant off the grid for water, gas, and electricity. Haft presented the concept to Nooyi as something to consider in five to seven years if they needed a new plant. According to Haft, Nooyi decided she wanted an existing plant re-engineered in this way as soon as possible. Haft explains their reasoning in this way:

> We feel we need to have the answers to the problems of the future before they become problems. If we wait around for natural gas to be $25Mcf or electricity to be 30 cents a kilowatt hour, or they tell you that you can't get water anymore, you gotta big problem. If we can solve this today and [provide] proof at scale, we can replicate these technologies as situations arise.

Frito-Lay hired the National Renewable Energy Laboratory to produce a feasibility study in which they would determine the optimal combination of renewable energy that would provide 100 percent of Frito-Lay plant energy at minimal life cycle cost. Once the study was submitted, an existing plant in Casa Grande, Arizona was designated as Frito-Lay's first Net Zero plant. That site was chosen in part because it was a medium sized plant with lower operating costs than bigger plants. These reduced costs made the project less risky. Solar concentration fields were installed to produce electricity for the plant. However, because solar power cannot provide energy 24 hours a day, seven days a week, additional alternative

energy production was needed. Haft had a biomass boiler installed that provides all the steam and the remaining electricity needs for the plant. Frito-Lay owns 162 acres bordering the plant and this land is utilized to grow hay for the biomass generator. Membrane bioreactors are used to treat wastewater allowing for the recycling of 75–95 percent of water used in the manufacturing process. Joel Swisher, formerly of the Rocky Mountain Institute and currently Director of Technical Services and Chief Technology Officer for Camco North America, a major climate change and sustainability consulting company, consulted for Frito-Lay while at RMI. Swisher believes that the Casa Grande plant's net zero goal "pushes designers to get out of the typical engineer's incremental-thinking box, to look for advanced technology solutions, and to find design synergies that can lead to breakthroughs in cost and performance."[17]

While the costs of the improvements to the Casa Grande plant were all borne by Frito-Lay, the company welcomes governmental incentives for energy and water conservation. In Connecticut, as a result of the state's Energy Independence Act, grants are being provided to get companies off the power grid because of increased demand and limited supply. With the additional support of the Department of Energy's Industrial Technology Program, Frito-Lay received $1.7 million to subsidize the new $10 million co-generation system that supplies nearly all power to its Killingly, Connecticut plant. The 5 megawatt cogeneration system uses waste heat from the ovens to produce steam that in turn generates the electricity for the 300,000 square foot plant. The plant used 250,000 pounds of potatoes and corn to produce snack foods for the New England region.[18] Frito-Lay has also received a $700,000 grant from the State of California Energy Commission toward a $5 million investment in a 5-acre solar concentration field in its Modesto, California plant. At the Modesto plant solar energy produced steam that is used to heat cooking oil to make Sun Chips and other products, thus greatly reducing the need for natural gas.

The recent modifications to the Killingly, Connecticut plant reduces greenhouse gas emissions by 5 percent at the facility. Frito-Lay has been working to reduce carbon emissions since 1999 when it joined EPA's Climate Wise program. By 2010 the company had reduced greenhouse gas emissions by 14 percent per pound of product. Frito-Lay is also a member of EPA's Climate Leader's Program. According to the EPA, "Climate Leaders is an EPA industry-government partnership that works with companies to develop comprehensive climate change strategies. Partner

Table 8.1 Categories of GHG emissions

Category	Level of control or influence	Examples
Scope 1: Direct GHG Emissions	Owned or controlled by company	Generation of heat, electricity, steam; processing and manufacturing; and transportation
Scope 2: Electricity Indirect GHG Emissions	Purchased by company for use in company owned or controlled facilities	Electricity
Scope 3: Other Indirect GHG Emissions	Relevant to business	Raw material extraction or production; employee business travel and commuting; use of sold products; waste disposal; outsourced operations, etc.

Source: World Business Council of Sustainable Development and World Resources Institute, *The Greenhouse Gas Protocol: A Corporate Accounting and Reporting Standard*. Revised 1234 Edition, March 2004, pp. 24–33. http://pdf.wri.org/ghg_protocol_2004.pdf (accessed December 2009).

companies commit to reducing their impact on the global environment by completing a corporate-wide inventory of their greenhouse gas emissions based on a quality management system, setting aggressive reduction goals, and annually reporting their progress to EPA. Through program participation, companies create a credible record of their accomplishments and receive EPA recognition as corporate environmental leaders."[19] GHG emissions are commonly divided into three categories or scopes (see Table 8.1).

According to the EPA, PepsiCo has purchased renewable energy certificates (RECs) to offset 100 percent of its scope 2 electricity generation emissions under EPA's Green Power Partnership.

Frito-Lay's commitment to environmental sustainability has been recognized and rewarded by the US government. For example, EPA's National Environmental Performance Track program recognizes individual facilities for excellence in environmental sustainability above and beyond legal compliance. Prior to the termination of the program in May 2009, Frito-Lay had eight plants admitted to the program. In 2009 PepsiCo received EPA's Green Power Leadership Award for Best Promotional Campaign by a Green Power Purchaser. The award was given for Frito-Lay's marketing of Sun Chips, which are made in the Modesto plant with solar power and packaged in biodegradable bags. After the introduction of the new bags into the marketplace, consumers complained that the bags were too noisy. Frito-Lay withdrew the bags from the marketplace, reengineered the bags, and quietly reintroduced the quieter bags. As noted above, from 2007 to 2017 parent company PepsiCo received the Environmental Protection

Agencies Award for Sustained Excellence in Energy Management.

What Does It Mean to Be Sustainable?

Historically, environmental sustainability at Frito-Lay has been a function of the operations program. More recently, Carey and Rader asked Haft to think about ways in which an operations program could be extended to all aspects of the business. Haft notes that Frito-Lay can sensibly be divided into four segments: make, move, sell, and support. "We make product. We move the product. We sell the product. Or we support those that are doing that." But how should sustainability be incorporated into each of these segments? Should Frito-Lay product-design teams only design products that can be produced in an energy efficient manner? Should new plants be located close to potato and corn suppliers to reduce the amount of energy needed to get commodities to the plant? With respect to its workforce, should Frito-Lay be trying to reduce employee travel to conserve fuel and reduce emissions? Should it subsidize energy efficient transportation to and from work? Should it encourage employees to become involved in environmental protection initiatives in their local communities? Should common carriers that deliver goods to Frito-Lay plants be asked to embrace energy efficiency?

In terms of production, many of Frito-Lay's products are produced by co-packers. These are the 35 companies that produce Frito-Lay products outside the company's core expertise. These include dips, salsa, and cookies. Frito-Lay is considering partnering with the co-packers to help them reduce the consumption of water, natural gas, electricity, and diesel fuel. But where should the capital come from and who should benefit from the savings? With respect to equipment manufacturing, Frito-Lay orders energy and water efficient ovens, fryers, and packaging machinery but should they also be asking suppliers about the energy efficiency of their plants, their carbon footprint, their raw material sources, and their shipping methods? What about the direct suppliers of packing material, cornmeal, vegetable oil, potato flakes, and other raw materials? Should Frito-Lay require that they meet strict energy and water efficiency standards?

Senior leadership at Frito-Lay is consulting with academic and industry sustainability experts in order to determine how to proceed. Joel Swisher believes that Frito-Lay has "outperformed most other companies in terms of direct greenhouse gas emission reductions in FLNA operations through the many engineering improvements that have been implemented and continue to be designed. In terms of offset programs," he notes that "their main effort has been a large procurement of renewable energy certificates (RECs) that represents a legitimate offset of emissions from (scope 2) emissions related to the electricity use that the RECs cover." Swisher points out that "they have not purchased offsets that would cover their scope 1 GHG emissions" but they "have the opportunity to produce their own offsets by developing renewable energy to replace or offset (fossil fuel-fired) grid energy and GHG emissions, through internal projects and investment." For example, he points out that if Frito-Lay "were to use biomass fuel from internal and nearby external sources to generate zero-carbon electricity in excess of its plant's own needs, they could potentially sell surplus power to the grid, backing out some amount of gas- or coal-fired power at the margin. By reducing grid emissions, this type of project creates a GHG offset, or at least comparable value by reducing the utility buyer's emissions."

Another unique opportunity identified by Swisher is "to close the loop between engineering solutions and brand value in a marketing-led company. Typically, sustainability efforts are stuck in the 'payback trap,' where every new initiative is subject to budget constraints and cost-effectiveness calculations based on conservative estimates of cost savings. However, as a marketing-led company [Frito-Lay] is beginning to recognize that their success in sustainability adds to brand value and justifies a commitment of resources as a marketing initiative." According to Swisher, "Once sustainability is seen in this light and begins to compete successfully for resources that would otherwise go to traditional marketing efforts, such as another Super Bowl commercial, the company can begin to escape the 'payback trap' and ramp

up sustainability investments in ways that are not possible in most companies."

Sustainability expert Daniel Fogel, founder and chairman of environmental sustainability consulting firm EcoLens, also believes Frito-Lay is on the right path.[20] EcoLens consults with major corporations, governments, and universities regarding best practices in environmental sustainability. EcoLens customers include Lockhead Martin, General Electric Duke Energy, Wachovia Bank, and Pfizer, among many others, but has not consulted for Frito-Lay. According to Fogel, Frito-Lay should continue to take its lead from nature which "has a unique ability to replenish itself and to create no waste." Fogel believes that the more Frito-Lay "operate[s] as a biological system the 'greener' they will be." More specifically, he believes that the company should continue to "identify ways to radically increase the productivity of natural systems such as water, fossil fuels, and crops that go into their products" and reduce "the degradation of our world by physical means including how they distribute products and how they build their factories." Finally, Fogel believes that the company should continue to "evaluate their products in light of this lens of promoting health."

How should Frito-Lay move forward in order to execute its pledge to be, in the words of former CEO Al Carey, "the preeminent green company" in any industry? What specific goals should they pursue in the future? How should "the preeminent green company" engage its co-packers on environmental sustainability? What unique challenges confront a snack food company that seeks to be green? What does it mean to be truly green?

Notes

1. Benjamin Fry, "Frito-Lay CEO Talks Sustainability," *KSMU News* (April, 2009). Retrieved August 15, 2009 from http://ksmu.org/content/view/4381/66/.
2. PepsiCo, "We Call It Performance with a Purpose," *PepsiCo Corporate Citizenship 2008*, Retrieved June 18, 2009 from www.pepsico.com/PEP_Citizenship/sustainability/Gri_v10b.pdf.
3. American Heart Association, Learn and Live, "Trans Fat." Retrieved July 25, 2009 from www.americanheart.org/presenter.jhtml?identifier=3045792.
4. Frito-Lay Inc., "Company Profile, June 19, 2008," Datamonitor Report via Business Source Complete. Retrieved June 22, 2009 from https://connect2.uncc.edu/ehost/,DanaInfo=web.ebscohost.com+pdf?vid=5&hid=108&sid=347c2103-cfec-473b-bd6d-704ae3f55fdb%40sessionmgr110.
5. S. J. Nielson, A. M. Siega-Riz, and B. M. Popkin, "Trends in Food Locations and Sources among Adolescents and Young Adults," *Preventive Medicine* 35 (2002): 107–13.

6. K. M. Flegal, M. D. Carroll, C. L. Ogden, and C. L. Johnson, "Prevalence and Trends in Overweight among US Adults, 1999–2000," *JAMA* 288 (2002): 1723–27.

7. C. L. Ogden, K. M. Flegal, M. D. Carroll, and C. L. Johnson, "Prevalence and Trends in Overweight among US Children and Adolescents, 1999–2000," *JAMA* 288 (2002): 1728–32.

8. PepsiCo, "Our Commitment to Diversity," *PepsiCo Corporate Citizenship 2008*. Retrieved June 18, 2009 from www.pepsico .com/Purpose/Diversity-and-Inclusion/Commitment.html.

9. Cora Daniels, "50 Best Companies for Minorities," *Fortune* (June 28, 2004). Retrieved June 18, 2009 from https://archive .fortune.com/magazines/fortune/fortune_archive/2004/06/28/ 374393/index.htm.

10. Frito-Lay, "About Us, Corporate Awards." Retrieved December 1, 2009 from www.fritolay.com/about-us/corpo rate-awards.html.

11. Indra Nooyi, interview by Jim Cramer, *CNBC'S Mad Money* with Jim Cramer, CNBC, July 24, 2007. Retrieved June 18, 2009 from www.cnbc.com/id/19940404/site/14081545.

12. David Haft, personal interview with author, May 16, 2008. (Interview included use of "Frito-Lay Planet Sustainability" slides.)

13. Frito-Lay Inc., "Company Profile, June 19, 2008."

14. Betsy Morris, "The Pepsi Challenge," *CNN Money* (February 19, 2008). Retrieved September 21, 2008 from https://money .cnn.com/2008/02/18/news/companies/morris_nooyi.for tune/index.htm; Haft, personal interview.

15. Thi Dao, "Frito-Lay Augments Fleet with Higher-MPG Sprinters," *Automotive Fleet* (April 2009). Retrieved June 18, 2009 from www.automotive-fleet.com/146219/green-fleet-frito-lay-augments-fleet-with-higher-mpg-sprinters.

16. Greener Buildings, "Frito-Lay HQ, 2 REI Stores and 3 Transwestern Buildings Attain LEED Ratings," *GreenerBuildings.com* (October 30, 2009). Retrieved December 10, 2009 from www.greenerbuildings.com/news/2009/10/30/ frito-lay-hq-2-rei-stores-and-3-transwestern-buildings-attain-leed-ratings.

17. Joel Swisher, personal interview (December 8, 2009).

18. "Commitment to a Culture of Conservation," *Combined Cycle Journal*, Second Quarter (2009): 154–57. Retrieved December 2009 from www.ccj-online.com/2q-2009/frito-lay-cogen-com mitment-to-a-culture-of-conservation/.

19. US Environmental Protection Agency, *Draft Recommendations for Climate Leaders Program Enhancements* (October 1, 2009). Retrieved December 2009 from https:// nepis.epa.gov/Exe/ZyPDF.cgi/P1007UYW.PDF? Dockey=P1007UYW.PDF.

20. Daniel S. Fogel, personal interview (November 21, 2009).

Discussion Questions

1. Which of the four central strategies of natural capitalism described by Hawken, Lovins, and Lovins seems to best describe Frito-Lay's operations? Cite specific examples to illustrate your points.

2. How would you assess Frito-Lay's success to date in being the "preeminent green company" in any industry? What does it mean to be truly green? Explain.

3. On a broader concept of sustainability, how would you assess Frito-Lay's social sustainability? What about PepsiCo? Can a company that specializes in salty snacks and sugary drinks really be socially sustainable? Why, or why not? Explain.

4. Do you believe that Frito-Lay's sustainability initiatives give them an advantage over their competition? Why, or why not? Explain.

5. DesJardins is critical of firms that use "sustainability" as a general category for business ethics, diversity management, CSR, stakeholder relations, and environmental sustainability practices and policies. How might he assess PepsiCo's use of sustainability to include diversity management and the healthfulness of the products that Frito-Lay and its parent company produce and sell? Explain. How would you assess PepsiCo's broad use of the term sustainability? Explain.

Case 5: Driving Sustainability at Tesla

GEOFFREY CELLA AND DENIS G. ARNOLD

Tesla, Inc. is a multifaceted corporation currently operating in the automotive and energy generation and storage industries. Named after Nicola Tesla, the visionary inventor and Thomas Edison contemporary, Tesla is best known for its visually appealing and environmentally friendly electric luxury vehicles.

Since its inception in 2003, Tesla has become a global leader in the sustainable energy, with far-reaching effects across many industries. Headquartered in Palo Alto, California, the company posted annual revenues of $7 billion in 2016 and is publicly traded on the NASDAQ Stock Exchange.

Tesla, Inc. began as Tesla Motors, Inc., a company with the goal of transforming the automotive industry by creating fully electric vehicles with functionality and style. The brainchild of Elon Musk, a modern-day visionary, Tesla's original goal was "to accelerate the advent of sustainable transport by bringing compelling mass market electric cars to market as soon as possible." Understanding the limitations of an emerging automobile company, Tesla adopted a production and pricing strategy that placed initial emphasis on high-end and profitable vehicles. Output would move towards more economically priced offerings as production efficiencies were realized. The initial rollout of the Tesla Roadster sports car was followed by the Model S luxury sedan, Model X luxury SUV, and Model 3 luxury midsized vehicle. With each passing year, the electric vehicles coming from Tesla move closer towards a zero-emissions vehicle with accessibility for the masses.

The company itself was originated due to lack of environmental progress and initiative within the automobile industry. From the beginning, Musk's goal was to challenge the petroleum-dependent strategies of traditional automobile manufacturers. By design, the technology created by Tesla has been critical to the ecological transformation of the automobile industry. These patented achievements are revolutionary and the firm has not been able to meet the high demand for its automobiles, but Elon Musk's mission for Tesla was more than just financial. In 2014, Elon Musk and Tesla removed intellectual property restrictions on patented technology in the interest of advancing electric vehicle development across the industry. Influenced by the open source movement of the Palo Alto tech community, Tesla hopes for rapid expansion of the sustainable transportation market through shared information. This institutional selflessness may be a lightning rod for investor complaints, but it highlights the critical mission in which Tesla is engaged: environmentally sustainable automotive transport.

In 2016, Tesla acquired SolarCity, the leader in residential and commercial solar power systems. By targeting SolarCity, Tesla displays a vested interest in the future need for emission-free energy generation and storage. Pairing the two companies has created the world's only integrated sustainable energy company. Under the Tesla umbrella, energy from the sun can now be collected, stored, and transferred to its automobiles. SolarCity's transformative product line includes solar roofing and the Powerwall 2 residential energy storage system. Now backed by the strong brand confidence of Tesla, increased household adoption of sustainable energy systems is anticipated. This acquisition illustrates a commitment to sustainability more generally and not only within the automotive industry.

Tesla vehicles are all built using lithium-ion batteries, a disruptive technology that allows for the expansive mileage range of its vehicles. With the evolution of Tesla Motors to Tesla, Inc., additional environmentally conscious projects began to take shape. Battery storage, supercharging, and solar collection projects help Tesla to avoid the criticism that its electronic vehicles were simply agents of pollution redistribution from roadways to power generation facilities. Supercharging stations, or electric "gas" stations, are being constructed throughout Asia, North America, Europe, and the Middle East. According to quarterly reports, Tesla expects to have over 5,000 available superchargers in North America. Locations will be strategically determined to maximize geographic coverage. Current charging stations pull energy from local grid networks, often reliant on carbon emitting power plants. In the future, Musk envisions solar generated, battery powered charging stations, further reducing the environmental footprint of its vehicles.

After the inauguration of Donald Trump as the 45th president of the United States, Elon Musk agreed to serve on two of the president's economic advisory councils: the Strategic and Policy Forum and the Manufacturing Council. As a result, Musk faced criticism from many sectors of American society who believed he was lending support to a president with little regard for environmental protection among many other concerns. In response to critics, Musk said that he hoped to use this platform to convince President Trump to take environmental sustainability more seriously at the federal level. On June 1, 2017, President Trump announced his intention to withdraw the United States from the Paris Climate Accord, the main outcome of the United Nations Climate Change Conference in Paris in December 2015. The US delegation to the conference in the Obama administration was instrumental in the details of the final accord and pledged to adhere to the purely voluntary agreement. Effective since November 2016, the accord is a promise among all nations (except war-torn Syria) to monitor greenhouse emissions to mitigate global warming with the goal of keeping the global average temperature "well below" 2° C (3.6° F) above pre-industrial levels and try further to limit temperature rise to 1.5° C (2.7° F). There is a consensus among scientists that increases in global average temperatures above 2.0° C would have extremely harmful economic and health impacts on human populations globally. Trump's decision was a clear signal to Elon Musk and other advisors that the president was not heeding their advice. Musk responded on

Twitter: "Am departing presidential councils. Climate change is real. Leaving Paris is not good for America or the world." Disney CEO Robert Iger followed Musk's lead and also resigned from the Strategic and Policy Forum to protest Trump's decision to withdraw the United States from the accord.

Discussion Questions

1. How would you assess the environmental sustainability of Tesla relative to the automobile industry in general? Explain.

2. Which of the four central strategies of natural capitalism described by Hawken, Lovins, and Lovins seems to best describe Tesla's business model? Explain. Is there possibly a different, fifth strategy that would better explain Tesla's business model? If so, explain.

3. Do you agree with Elon Musk's decision to resign in protest from President Trump's councils? Why, or why not? Explain.

4. What reasons might politicians have for failing to take steps to stop the looming threat of a warming planet and changing climatic conditions? Think about reasons other than a denial of the overwhelming scientific consensus that anthropogenic climate change is taking place. What might some of those reasons be? Explain.

This case is based on the following sources: M. Astor, "Paris Climate Agreement to Take Effect Nov. 4" (October 6, 2016). Retrieved September 7, 2017 from https://apnews.com/9daff3d1c8c9413f99224d5057f0b096/paris-climate-agreement-take-effect-30-days.

"About Tesla" (n.d.). Retrieved September 2, 2017 from www.tesla.com/about.

P. A. Eisenstein, "Tesla's Master Sustainability Plan Goes Well Beyond Cars" (July 21, 2016). Retrieved September 2, 2017 from www.nbcnews.com/tech/tech-news/tesla-s-master-sustainability-plan-goes-well-beyond-cars-n614256.

R. Ferris, "Tesla Will Double Number of Supercharger Stations in 2017" (April 24, 2017). Retrieved September 6, 2017 from www.cnbc.com/2017/04/24/tesla-will-double-number-of-supercharger-stations-in-2017.html.

R. Greenspan, "Tesla Motors, Inc. Corporate Social Responsibility, Stakeholders" (February 21, 2017). Retrieved September 2, 2017 from http://panmore.com/tesla-motors-inc-stakeholders-corporate-social-responsibility.

S. Hanley, "Elon Musk Says All Tesla Supercharger Locations Will Use Solar Power Soon (#ElonTweets)" (June 10, 2017). Retrieved September 6, 2017 from https://cleantechnica.com/2017/06/10/elon-musk-says-tesla-supercharger-locations-will-use-solar-power-soon-elontweets/.

E. Musk, "The Secret Tesla Motors Master Plan (Just between You and Me)" (July 2, 2006). Retrieved September 6, 2017 from www.tesla.com/blog/secret-tesla-motors-master-plan-just-between-you-and-me.

E. Musk, "All Our Patent Are Belong to You" (June 12, 2014). Retrieved September 6, 2017 from www.tesla.com/blog/all-our-patent-are-belong-you.

E. Musk, "The Mission of Tesla" (November 19, 2013). Retrieved September 6, 2017 from www.tesla.com/blog/mission-tesla.

L. Shen, "Elon Musk Leaves President Trump's Advisory Council after Paris Agreement Exit" (June 1, 2017). Retrieved September 7, 2017 from http://fortune.com/2017/06/01/elon-musk-trump-paris-agreement/.

"Tesla and SolarCity" (November 1, 2016). Retrieved September 5, 2017 from www.tesla.com/blog/tesla-and-solarcity.

Tesla Inc. (TSLA.OQ), "Financials" (n.d.). Retrieved September 6, 2017 from www.reuters.com/finance/stocks/financial-highlights/TSLA.OQ.

The Socially Responsible Investor, "Tesla: Social Responsibility Scorecard Shows Strengths and Weaknesses" (January 6, 2015). Retrieved September 2, 2017 from https://seekingalpha.com/article/2801365-tesla-social-responsibility-scorecard-shows-strengths-and-weaknesses?page=2.

Case 6: The Dirty Truth: Volkswagen's Diesel Deception

ROXANNE ROSS AND DENIS G. ARNOLD

Diesel engines are more fuel-efficient then gasoline engines and produce fewer carbon dioxide (CO_2) emissions. CO_2 is the main greenhouse gas causing global climate change. In the 1990s there was a push for greater utilization of diesel engines in order to reduce greenhouse gases emissions. Diesel became another environmentally conscious vehicle option, aimed at buyers who might otherwise consider a Toyota Prius or other electric or hybrid vehicles. In Europe, approximately 50 percent of vehicles are powered by diesel engines. In general, trucks, boats, buses, and other commercial vehicles use diesel instead of gasoline engines. The perceived benefits of diesel engines have led to tax reductions on the fuel. Some automobile manufacturers have marketed a new generation of "clean diesel" light duty cars.

Although initially well received, diesel engines turned out to be more harmful than anticipated. Diesel exhaust emits nitrogen oxide that converts into nitrogen dioxide. Nitrogen dioxide is responsible for the brown smog that surrounds many cities. The nitrogen oxide and nitrogen dioxide particles, together known as NOx, are smaller than 2.5 micrometers (or one-thirtieth the diameter of a human hair) and are absorbed through the lungs, penetrating deep into living tissues and organs. The NOx particles exacerbate problems such as asthma, bronchitis, emphysema, heart attacks, and contribute to premature death. The sulfur dioxide (SO_2) in diesel fuel emissions is the major cause of acid rain that harms plants and animals. Given these considerations, diesel engines are no longer seen as an answer to the pollution problems caused by transportation. Rather, diesel engines trade less carbon dioxide emissions and greater fuel efficiency for more emission of particulates that are harmful to the health of humans and other living beings.

Volkswagen was created in the late 1930s as part of a movement during the Third Reich to increase the number of German families with cars. The intention was to create a "people's car." The phrase became the company's namesake with "volk" translating as people and "wagon" translating as car. Currently, Volkswagen owns 12 subsidiaries including Audi, Bentley, Lamborghini, and Porsche. Volkswagen has factories in 31 nations and sells its products in 153 nations. Globally, the company employs 590,000 people and manufactures 41,000 vehicles each day. Volkswagen was known for producing and marketing "clean diesel" engines, yet the car manufacturer struggled to have success in the US market. While half of cars in Europe have diesel engines, less than 1 percent of vehicles are diesel in the United States. The main reason is that the United States has some of the strictest laws regarding automobile air pollution in the world. Volkswagen sought to develop a cleaner diesel engine in order improve their sales in the US market. However, diesel engines that met US emissions standards were not feasible given the company's timeline and research and design budget.

As an alternative to producing clean diesel engines that met US environmental standards, engineers secretly installed a "defeat device" in many vehicle models such as the Volkswagen Passat, Jetta, Golf, and Beetle models and the Audi A3, A6, A7, A8, Q5 and Q7 models. The defeat device is computer software that cheated on government emissions tests. The devices sensed when emissions tests were being conducted and would switch the vehicle to a driving mode that released less noxious emissions but had poor engine performance. When back on the road, the device would switch off thereby releasing more noxious emissions but achieving improved engine performance. For seven years Volkswagen marketed these vehicles as "clean diesel," falsely comparing the environmental impact of driving a diesel Volkswagen to riding a bike. Globally, 11 million vehicles had the defeat device installed with 590,000 of these vehicles sold in the United States since 2008.

The deception continued until a team of researchers at West Virginia University tested the pollution from the diesel engines. They found the engines emitted 10 to 40 times more pollutants during on-road driving than in off-road laboratory testing and that the on-road emissions did not meet US standards. Because of the illegal software, an estimated 10,000 to 40,000 extra tons of NOx have been released into the air in the United States alone. Each ton of NOx pollution is associated with $7,300 in health related costs. The total extra healthcare costs in the United States from the defeat devices is estimated to be over $100 million with an estimated 8 to 34 premature deaths caused by the extra emissions. Damages are much more extensive in Europe where there are more of these diesel vehicles with cheating software. Travis Bradford, a sustainability expert at Columbia University, stated that Volkswagen, "literally stole public property. They took air that could have been cleaner and available to all the people in the U.S. because they wanted to sell cars."

The year after the scandal broke Volkswagen was profitable with over $5 billion in net income. The company's chief finance officer, Hans Pötsch, explained why the scandal occurred by saying, "There was not one single mistake, but rather a chain of errors that was never broken." He further elaborated by claiming that a small group of engineers were mainly to blame. According to an internal audit, no one in senior leadership knew about the defeat devices. Yet two anonymous sources found a PowerPoint for an executive meeting that contained information about installing the illegal software nearly a decade before it was discovered. Martin Winterkorn, CEO of Volkswagen during the scandal, maintained that he did not know about the emissions cheating. However, Volkswagen confirmed that Winterkorn received a memo about the issue but said he may not have read it. Because of the illegal software Winterkorn stepped down from his position.

Six other executives faced criminal charges for their involvement in the scandal. One of those charged was Oliver Schmidt, the Volkswagen liaison with US regulators. Schmidt was arrested at Miami International Airport as he attempted to board a flight to Germany. He and other executives were charged with conspiracy to defraud the United States, defrauding customers, and violating the Clean Air Act. Others charged were not arrested as they were in Germany. German prosecutors believed at least 37 people were involved in the scandal. None of the charged individuals were on the company's management board, which shelters Volkswagen from being sued by shareholders.

Federal prosecutors charged Volkswagen with conspiracy to defraud the US government and violating the Clean Air Act. The Clean Air Act makes it illegal to intentionally violate the Environmental Protection Agency's emissions standards. Volkswagen pleaded guilty to violating these laws. The guilty plea is notable as many large corporations have been able to evade guilt by entering into "deferred prosecution agreements" where the firm agrees to pay certain penalties and conditions, but avoids an admission of guilt. Volkswagen reached a $4.3 billion settlement with the US Department of Justice. In the settlement, the company agreed to probation and monitoring for three years. In total, Volkswagen currently anticipates around $23.9 billion in costs related to the scandal. However, this projection may underestimate legal costs. In the United States, the Federal Trade Commission filed a four-count civil complaint alleging that the company falsely advertised its diesel engines as "clean diesel." The FTC is seeking more than $15 billion in damages.

Discussion Questions

1. Why do you believe Volkswagen engaged in this deceptive, greenwashing behavior rather than developing truly innovative engine technology that has less negative environmental impacts than traditional engines and does not have the harmful health impacts of their diesel engines? Explain.

2. Is it plausible to you that executives knew nothing about the "defeat device" and the deceptive marketing campaign? Why, or why not? Explain.

3. Volkswagen has deceptively marketed technology that was widely adapted in Europe, leading to lower air quality and negative health impacts in major European cities such as London, Paris, and Milan. How would you assess Volkswagen's actions from an ethical standpoint? Explain.

4. What recommendations do you have to address the organizational culture and leadership issues at Volkswagen that led to the greenwashing behavior? Explain.

This case was written for classroom discussion and is based on the following sources: W. Boston, H. Varnholt, and S. Sloat, "Volkswagen Blames 'Chain of Mistakes' for Emissions Scandal," *Wall Street Journal* (December 10, 2015). Retrieved from www.wsj.com/articles/vw-shares-up-ahead-of-emissions-findings-1449740759.

T. Bowler, "Volkswagen: From the Third Reich to Emissions Scandal. BBC News" (October 2, 2015). Retrieved from www.bbc.com/news/business-34358783.

J. Ewing, "Engineering a Deception: What Led to Volkswagen's Diesel Scandal," *The New York Times* (March 16, 2017). Retrieved from www.nytimes.com/interactive/2017/business/volkswagen-diesel-emissions-timeline.html.

T. Grescoe, "Opinion: The Dirty Truth about 'Clean Diesel,'" *The New York Times* (January 2, 2016). Retrieved from www.nytimes.com/2016/01/03/opinion/sunday/the-dirty-truth-about-clean-diesel.html.

S. Hall, "Volkswagen Scandal Causes Small but Irreversible Environmental Damage," *Scientific American* (September 29, 2015). Retrieved June 29, 2017 from www.scientificamerican.com/article/vw-scandal-causes-small-but-irreversible-environmental-damage/.

Jamie Butters, Steven Raphael, and Margaret Cronin Fisk, "Volkswagen Pleads Guilty in U.S. Emissions-Cheating Scandal," *Bloomberg.com* (March 10, 2017). Retrieved from www.bloomberg.com/news/articles/2017-03-10/volkswagen-pleads-guilty-in-u-s-emissions-cheating-scandal.

N. E. Selin, "One of the Biggest Consequences of the Volkswagen Diesel Scandal," *Fortune* (September 30, 2015). Retrieved June 29, 2017 from http://fortune.com/2015/09/30/volkswagen-diesel-scandal-consequences/.

H. Tabuchi, J. Ewing, and M. Apuzzo, "6 Volkswagen Executives Charged as Company Pleads Guilty in Emissions Case," *The New York Times* (January 11, 2017). Retrieved from www.nytimes.com/2017/01/11/business/volkswagen-diesel-vw-settlement-charges-criminal.html.

Sara Randazzo and Mike Spector, "FTC Sues Volkswagen over Advertising of Diesel Vehicles," *Wall Street Journal* (March 29, 2016). Retrieved from www.wsj.com/articles/ftc-sues-volkswagen-over-advertising-of-diesel-vehicles-1459262536.

9

Ethical Issues in International Business

9.1 INTRODUCTION

Contemporary business takes place in an era of economic globalization, one in which the everyday purchases of consumers in industrialized nations – items such as shirts, avocados, smart phones, and gasoline – typically originate in foreign nations. Production supply chains span the globe and the factories and farms that supply Western consumers exist in nations with a variety of forms of government. These include republics, parliamentary democracies, communist governments, monarchies, and dictatorships. Most developing nations have extensive labor and environmental laws, but few of these nations have the governance capacity to enforce those laws. This means that transnational corporations and other business enterprises are typically free to take advantage of not just low wages, but reduced costs that result from lax health and safety standards for workers and weak environmental controls. There are, then, a multitude of environments in which firms operate globally. The variety of these political environments creates significant ethical complexities for firms and their managers and leaders.

In some instances what is considered right or acceptable in one country is considered wrong or unacceptable in another. Facilitation payments to low-level government officials, the treatment of women as second-class citizens, and religious intolerance are examples. In addition, many of the problems that occur in one country have an impact on other nations. Two important examples concern two very different problems – maintaining the integrity of financial markets and protecting the world environment. Global financial markets are tied to one another in such a way that widespread fraud in US markets, for example, has a direct impact on Asian and European markets. So, too, the phenomenon of anthropogenic climate change is inherently global in scope – Chinese carbon emissions have a direct impact on the United States and vice versa. Thus, we are all forced to think internationally whether we want to or not.

There is plenty to think about. Bribery, extortion, and the issue of facilitating payments remain common problems. These practices have been shown to undermine fundamental human rights. When firms try to take advantage of lower costs, whether it be low wages, lax health and safety standards, or lax environmental protection, they are often accused of harmful exploitation. Consumers in developed countries have become increasingly aware of the "sweatshop" conditions under which many of the goods they purchase are manufactured and assembled. In 2013 over 1,100 garment workers died in a factory disaster in Bangladesh while making inexpensive clothing for Western companies and their customers. Most of these workers were young women, no older than the average college student. Their deaths were universally attributed to the incessant demand for cheap labor by Western companies in combination with poor local governance. Many critics of international business argue that companies that utilize suppliers in developing nations have an obligation to respect basic norms of decency in their global operations and supply chains.

RELATIVISM VS. HUMAN RIGHTS

There are a variety of opinions regarding what is acceptable conduct in international business, and some doubt whether there are any universal norms for ethical business practice. An international company involved in business abroad must confront the question, When in Rome, should I behave as the Romans do? For the purposes of this discussion, the home country of a business firm is where it has its headquarters or where it has its charter of incorporation. A host country is any other country where that firm does business.

When the norms of the home country and the norms of the host country are in conflict, a transnational corporation has four options: (1) follow the norms of the home country because that is how things are normally done or because of national allegiance; (2) follow the norms of the host country to show proper respect for the host country's culture; (3) follow whichever norm is most profitable; (4) follow whichever norm is morally best. (The four alternatives are not mutually exclusive.)

To choose option (4) requires an appeal to international moral norms for business practice. In his article Norman E. Bowie shows the importance of establishing the existence and content of these international norms. Bowie bases his argument for international norms on three considerations. First, widespread agreement already exists among nations, as illustrated by the large number of signatories to the United Nations Declaration of Human Rights and by the existence of a number of international agreements establishing norms of business practice. The United Nations' "Protect, Respect and Remedy Framework for Business and Human Rights," endorsed by nearly all nations, is the most important example of the latter. Business executives have also undertaken efforts to establish international ethical norms such as the Caux Roundtable Principles of Business, an earlier effort by business leaders to establish basic ethical norms for international business. Second, Bowie argues that certain moral norms must be endorsed if society is to exist at all. Corporations ought to accept the moral norms that make society and hence business itself possible. This argument is a powerful response to the view known as ethical relativism. *Ethical relativism* asserts that whatever a country says is right or wrong for a country, *really* is right or wrong for that country. But if there are ethical norms that must be adopted if a country is to exist at all, then obviously the rightness of these norms is not justified by being endorsed in any particular country.

Third, Bowie uses certain Kantian arguments to show that business practice presupposes certain moral norms if it is to exist at all. Bowie refers to these norms as the *morality of the marketplace*. For example, there must be a moral obligation for business to keep its contracts if business is to exist at all. Bowie's argument is not merely theoretical. Russia has had difficulty in adopting a capitalist economy because business persons and business firms were either unwilling or unable to pay their bills. Extortion and governmental cronyism are widespread in Russia. Dissidents and reporters who document government corruption are often killed. Without judicial institutions to enforce legitimate contracts and hold parties accountable for agreements, business practice is fragile at best.

Many argue that the notion of human rights provides a set of universal standards that both individuals and organizations, including business organizations, should respect. After all, nearly all countries in the world belong to the United Nations and thus have in principle endorsed the UN Declaration of Human Rights. (We acknowledge that countries differ on the interpretation and implementation of these rights.) However, as Thomas Donaldson has pointed out, there are three distinct ways to honor human rights: (1) to avoid depriving; (2) to help protect from deprivation; and (3) to aid the deprived.[1] Donaldson maintains that while human rights should be honored in all three senses, it is not clear that it is the obligation of business to honor all human rights in all three ways. For example, if a right to an education is a human right, that does not mean that it is the obligation of a corporation to provide it.

Working out what is morally required for firms engaged in international business is a complex activity. In his article "Corporate Human Rights Obligations," Denis G. Arnold reviews arguments supporting corporate human rights obligations in light of the United Nations' "Protect, Respect and Remedy Framework for Business and Human Rights" which was formally adopted in 2011. He describes the different forms transnational corporations (TNCs) take and explains why TNCs are properly understood as moral agents responsible for their policies and practices. He goes on to explain different theoretical justifications for corporate human rights obligations. The third section articulates and responds to objections to the idea that corporations have human rights obligations. In particular, Arnold considers and rejects the position of "shareholder primacy" theorists such as Milton Friedman (see Chapter 5) whose position appears to hold that profits should trump human rights in business. Arnold's main conclusion is that there are multiple, compelling, and overlapping justifications of corporate human rights obligations.

The discussion of "when in Rome should we do as the Romans do?" has legal ramifications as well. What about the rights of foreigners who are injured abroad by US corporations? Do they have any rights to relief in American courts? Normally, they do not under the doctrine of *forum non conveniens* (it is not the convenient forum). It makes more practical sense for foreigners to seek relief in the country where the injury took place. But in *Dow Chemical Company and Shell Oil Company v. Domingo Castro Alfaro et al.*, the Supreme Court of Texas disagreed. The Texas Supreme Court in a majority opinion pointed out that the chief effect of the doctrine of *forum non conveniens* was to give an unjust advantage to multinationals. However, *forum non conveniens* is still the prevailing law in most states.

Recently, foreign nationals have sued American companies alleging human rights abuses. One landmark case, *John Doe I, et al., v. Unocal Corp, et al.*, granted summary judgment on behalf of Unocal in a case involving alleged human rights violations in Myanmar (formerly Burma). The government of Myanmar supplied labor to Unocal that the plaintiffs claimed was forced labor or slavery. The Court found that Unocal knew about and benefited from forced labor in Myanmar. But Unocal was not a willing partner, since it could not control the Myanmar military and thus was not liable under federal law. However, the US Court of Appeals disagreed in part and argued that trial against Unocal could go ahead on the issues of whether Unocal aided and abetted the Myanmar military in subjecting workers to forced labor. Unocal eventually settled with the plaintiffs out of court and further legal action was suspended.

Most recently, the US Supreme Court decided in *Kiobel v. Royal Dutch Petroleum Co.* that, in current US law, there is a presumption against holding corporations legally liable in US courts for their actions in sovereign foreign countries. The Supreme Court did allow that under unique circumstances such liability was still possible. Summaries of each of these important legal cases are provided later in this chapter.

Note

1. Thomas Donaldson, *The Ethics of International Business* (Oxford University Press, 1989).

SWEATSHOPS AND BRIBERY

Perhaps the international business ethics issue that has received the most attention on college campuses in recent years is the issue of sweatshops. Companies that make university branded apparel worn by college teams and sold in campus bookstores, online, and/or via company owned and operated stores through licensing agreements, have been accused of utilizing sweatshop labor in their supply chains. Pressure from student activists on college campuses and other critics of sweatshops have resulted in changes to global supply chain management. Mattel, Gap, Adidas, and Nike have implemented significant social responsibility programs to ensure that the rights of workers in their global supply chains are better protected. Not all activists are satisfied with these programs, but there can be no doubt that the negative publicity associated with abusive working conditions has led to significant improvements in the labor practices of many transnational companies.

Monitoring is not limited to individual companies. The Fair Labor Association is made up of industry and human rights representatives. This group was created by a presidential task force and includes such companies as Adidas, Nike, New Balance, Hanesbrands, Hugo Boss, Patagonia, and Under Armour.

Not everyone is so quick to condemn the practices of transnational companies for poor working conditions and wages in their supply chains. Some economists and libertarian theorists have spoken out claiming that the wages paid to the workers of foreign suppliers in the third world are hardly immoral but rather represent an increase in their standard of living. Defenders of sweatshops argue that transnational companies are wrong to improve working conditions and wages because doing so will lead to lower employment in developing nations. They argue that labor markets alone should determine wages and working conditions because that will always result in optimal utility or social welfare. In contrast, scholars who emphasize human dignity and human rights claim that transnational companies have a moral obligation to ensure that their suppliers follow local labor laws, meet minimum safety standards, and provide a living wage for employees. In her contribution to this chapter, "Sweatshops," Laura P. Hartman provides an overview of the issues and arguments regarding the obligations of companies for the working conditions in their global supply chains. Hartman emphasizes that many firms have exhibited "positive ethical deviancy" and made strides in improving working conditions in their suppliers. However, Richard M. Locke sounds a cautionary note in his contribution to this chapter. Locke has conducted research in the supply chains of major international companies and argues there are limits on what improvements firms can make on their own. In "Can Global Brands Create Just Supply Chains?" he discusses the roles of companies, as well as local governments, consumers, and non-governmental organizations in realizing justice in supply chains.

One international norm is the prohibition against bribery. Such a norm received legal recognition in the United States with the passage of the Foreign Corrupt Practices Act (FCPA) in 1977. That Act, which was amended in 1988, makes it illegal for US companies to pay bribes to do business abroad. Spokespersons for some American businesses have long criticized the law on the grounds that it puts American firms at a competitive disadvantage. Other countries operate under no such restrictions. Although the United States did take the lead in this respect, more and more organizations are passing rules outlawing bribery. For example, the European Union has done so.

Another criticism of the FCPA was that it was an example of American moral imperialism – a charge that is often leveled against American regulations. However, in this case, the charge of moral imperialism is false, since the FCPA does not force other countries or the multinationals of other countries to follow America's lead. It simply requires US companies to follow American moral norms with respect to bribery when doing business abroad.

A third criticism of the FCPA is more telling, however. That criticism is that the Act does not adequately distinguish among gift giving, facilitating payments, bribery, and extortion. The FCPA does allow for facilitating payments, and that allowance was expanded when the law was amended in 1988. However, the law does not sufficiently distinguish between bribery and extortion. The chief difference between bribery and extortion is who initiates the act. A corporation pays a bribe when it offers to pay or provide favors to a person or persons of trust to influence the latter's conduct or judgment. A corporation pays extortion money when it yields to a demand for money to have accomplished what it has a legal right to have accomplished without the payment. The difference between extortion and a facilitating payment is one of degree. It is also often difficult to distinguish a gift from a bribe.

In his essay, "Corruption and the Multinational Corporation," David Hess explains the connection between bribery and human rights violations. He argues that anti-corruption laws, policies, and practices should be regarded as part of the human rights movement because corruption is a major impediment to the realization of internationally recognized human rights. But, as he explains, there is also a pragmatic case for anti-bribery policies. In other words, implementing anti-corruption policies and practices can improve the long-term financial performance of a firm. Hess goes on to provide practical guidance on how to implement anti-corruption policies and procedures in international business. One of the most important recent cases of corruption is Walmart's systematic bribery scheme in Mexico. Hess uses this important case to illustrate many of his conclusions. The case is also included as a case study in this chapter.

Globalization and the increase in international business competition it brings forth continue to spark a number of debates in international business ethics. Multinationals need to find a way to harmonize the core values of the firm with universal ethical norms. At the same time, they need to respect the legitimate ethical norms and values of the countries in which they do business. The effort to be an ethical and profitable business at home becomes even more complicated when a business enters the international arena.

9.2 RELATIVISM VS. HUMAN RIGHTS

Relativism and the Moral Obligations of Multinational Corporations

NORMAN E. BOWIE

In this essay, I will focus on the question of whether US multinationals should follow the moral rules of the United States or the moral rules of the host countries (the countries where the US multinationals do business). A popular way of raising this issue is to ask whether US multinationals should follow the advice "When in Rome, do as the Romans do." In discussing that issue I will argue that US multinationals would be morally required to follow that advice if the theory of ethical relativism were true. On the other hand, if ethical universalism is true, there will be times when the advice would be morally inappropriate. In a later section, I will argue that ethical relativism is morally suspect. Finally, I will argue that the ethics of the market provide some universal moral norms for the conduct of multinationals.

Relativism

Cultural relativism is a descriptive claim that ethical practices differ among cultures; that, as a matter of fact, what is considered right in one culture may be considered wrong in another. Thus the truth or falsity of cultural relativism can be determined by examining the world. The work of anthropologists and sociologists is most relevant in determining the truth or falsity of cultural relativism, and there is widespread consensus among social scientists that cultural relativism is true.

This piece is composed of selections from Norman Bowie, "The Moral Obligations of Multinational Corporations," in *Problems of International Justice* (ed. Steven Luper-Foy; Voulder, CO: Westview Press, 1988) and Norman Bowie, "Relativism, Cultural and Moral," in *The Blackwell Encyclopedic Dictionary of Business Ethics* (ed. Patricia Werhane and R. Edward Freeman; Cambridge, MA: Blackwell, 1997). Reprinted with permission of the author and Blackwell Publishers.

Moral relativism is the claim that what is really right or wrong is what the culture says is right or wrong. Moral relativists accept cultural relativism as true, but they claim much more. If a culture sincerely and reflectively adopts a basic moral principle, then it is morally obligatory for members of that culture to act in accordance with that principle.

The implication of moral relativism for conduct is that one ought to abide by the ethical norms of the culture where one is located. Relativists in ethics would say, "One ought to follow the moral norms of the culture." In terms of business practice, consider the question, Is it morally right to pay a bribe to gain business? The moral relativists would answer the question by consulting the moral norms of the country where one is doing business. If those norms permit bribery in that country, then the practice of bribery is not wrong in that country. However, if the moral norms of the country do not permit bribery, then offering a bribe to gain business in that country is morally wrong. The justification for that position is the moral relativist's contention that what is really right or wrong is determined by the culture.

Is cultural relativism true? Is moral relativism correct? As noted, many social scientists believe that cultural relativism is true as a matter of fact. But is it?

First, many philosophers claim that the "facts" aren't really what they seem. Early twentieth-century anthropologists cited the fact that in some cultures, after a certain age, parents are put to death. In most cultures such behavior would be murder. Does this difference in behavior prove that the two cultures disagree about fundamental matters of ethics? No, it does not. Suppose the other culture believes that people exist in the afterlife in the same condition that they leave their present life. It would be very cruel to have one's parents exist eternally in an unhealthy state. By killing them when they are relatively active and vigorous, you insure their happiness for all eternity. The *underlying* ethical principle of this culture is that children have duties to their parents, including the duty to be concerned with their parents' happiness as they approach old age. This ethical principle is identical with our own. What looked like a difference in ethics between our culture and another turned out, upon close examination, to be a difference based on what each culture takes to be the facts of the matter. This example does, of course, support the claim that as a matter of fact ethical principles vary according to culture. However, it does not support the stronger conclusion that *underlying* ethical principles vary according to culture.

Cultures differ in physical setting, in economic development, in the state of their science and technology, in their literacy rate, and in many other ways. Even if there were universal moral principles, they would have to be applied in these different cultural contexts. Given the different situations in which cultures exist, it would come as no surprise to find universal principles applied in different ways. Hence we expect to find surface differences in ethical behavior among cultures even though the cultures agree on fundamental universal moral principles. For example, one commonly held universal principle appeals to the public good; it says that social institutions and individual behavior should be ordered so that they lead to the greatest good for the greatest number. Many different forms of social organization and individual behavior are consistent with this principle. The point of these two arguments is to show that differences among cultures on ethical behavior may not reflect genuine disagreement about underlying principles of ethics. Thus it is not so obvious that any strong form of cultural relativism is true.

But are there universal principles that are accepted by all cultures? It seems so; there does seem to be a whole range of behavior, such as torture and murder of the innocent, that every culture agrees is wrong. A nation-state accused of torture does not respond by saying that a condemnation of torture is just a matter of cultural choice. The state's leaders do not respond by saying, "We think torture is right, but you do not." Rather, the standard response is to deny that any torture took place. If the evidence of torture is too strong, a finger will be pointed either at the victim or at the morally outraged country: "They do it too." In this case the guilt is spread to all. Even the Nazis denied that genocide took place. What is important is that *no* state replies that there is nothing wrong with genocide or torture.

In addition, there are attempts to codify some universal moral principles. The United Nations Universal Declaration of Human Rights has been endorsed by the member states of the UN, and the vast majority of countries in the world are members of the UN. Even in business, there is a growing effort to adopt universal principles of business practice. The United Nations has formally endorsed the "Protect, Respect and Remedy Framework for Business and Human Rights" (discussed in the next reading) which outlines specific, universal standards for human rights. This standard was produced in conjunction with a variety of business organizations and was grounded in many previous agreements on international business codes of ethics produced by various industries and in consultation with many corporations.[1] The Caux Roundtable, a group of corporate executives from the United States, Europe, and Japan, has sought worldwide endorsement of a set of principles of business ethics. Thus there are a number of reasons to think that cultural relativism, at least with respect to basic moral principles, is not true, that is, that it does not accurately describe the state of moral agreement that exists globally. This is consistent with maintaining that cultural relativism is true in the weak form, that is, when applied only to surface ethical principles.

But what if differences in fundamental moral practices among cultures are discovered and seem unreconcilable? That would lead to a discussion about the adequacy of moral relativism. The fact that moral practices do vary widely among countries is cited as evidence for the correctness of moral relativism. Discoveries early in the century by anthropologists, sociologists, and psychologists documented the diversity of moral beliefs. Philosophers, by and large, welcomed corrections of moral imperialist thinking, but recognized that the moral relativist's appeal to the alleged truth of cultural relativism was not enough to establish moral relativism. The mere fact that a culture considers a practice moral does not mean that it is moral. Cultures have sincerely practiced slavery, discrimination, and the torture of animals. Yet each of these practices can be independently criticized on ethical grounds. Thinking something is morally permissible does not make it so.

Another common strategy for criticizing moral relativism is to show that the consequences of taking the perspective of moral relativism are inconsistent with our use of moral language. It is often contended by moral relativists that if two cultures disagree regarding universal moral principles, there is no way for that disagreement to be resolved. Since moral relativism is the view that what is right or wrong is determined by culture, there is no higher appeal beyond the fact that culture endorses the moral principle. But we certainly do not talk that way. When China and the United States argue about the moral rights of human beings, the disputants use language that seems to appeal to universal moral principles. Moreover, the atrocities of the Nazis and the slaughter in Rwanda have met with universal condemnation that seemed based on universal moral principles. So moral relativism is not consistent with our use of moral language.

Relativism is also inconsistent with how we use the term "moral reformer." Suppose, for instance, that a person from one culture moves to another and tries to persuade the other culture to change its view. Suppose someone moves from a culture where slavery is immoral to one where slavery is morally permitted. Normally, if a person were to try to convince the culture where slavery was permitted that slavery was morally wrong, we would call such a person a moral reformer. Moreover, a moral reformer would almost certainly appeal to universal moral principles to make her argument; she almost certainly would not appeal to a competing cultural standard. But if moral relativism were true, there would be no place for the concept of a moral reformer.

Slavery is really right in those cultures that say it is right and really wrong in those cultures that say it is wrong. If the reformer fails to persuade a slaveholding country to change its mind, the reformer's antislavery position was never right. If the reformer is successful in persuading a country to change its mind, the reformer's antislavery views would be wrong – until the country did in fact change its view. Then the reformer's antislavery view would be right. But that is not how we talk about moral reform.

The moral relativist might argue that our language should be reformed. We should talk differently. At one time people used to talk and act as if the world were flat. Now they don't. The relativist could suggest that we can change our ethical language in the same way. But consider how radical the relativists' response is. Since most, if not all, cultures speak and act as if there were universal moral principles, the relativist can be right only if almost everyone else is wrong. How plausible is that?

Although these arguments are powerful ones, they do not deliver a knockout blow to moral relativism. If there are no universal moral principles, moral relativists could argue that moral relativism is the only theory available to help make sense of moral phenomena.

An appropriate response to this relativist argument is to present the case for a set of universal moral principles, principles that are correct for all cultures independent of what a culture thinks about them. This is what adherents of the various ethical traditions try to do. The reader will have to examine these various traditions and determine how persuasive she finds them. In addition, there are several final independent considerations against moral relativism that can be mentioned here.

First, what constitutes a culture? There is a tendency to equate cultures with national boundaries, but that is naïve, especially today. With respect to moral issues, what do US cultural norms say regarding right and wrong? That question may be impossible to answer, because in a highly pluralistic country like the United States, there are many cultures. Furthermore, even if one can identify a culture's moral norms, it will have dissidents who do not subscribe to those moral norms. How many dissidents can a culture put up with and still maintain that some basic moral principle is the cultural norm? Moral relativists have had little to say regarding criteria for constituting a culture or how to account for dissidents. Unless moral relativists offer answers to questions like these, their theory is in danger of becoming inapplicable to the real world.

Second, any form of moral relativism must admit that there are some universal moral principles. Suppose a culture does not accept moral relativism, that is, it denies that if an entire culture sincerely and reflectively adopts a basic moral principle, it is obligatory for members of that culture to act in accord with that principle. Fundamentalist Muslim countries would reject moral relativism because it would require them to accept as morally permissible blasphemy in those countries where blasphemy was permitted. If the moral relativist insists that the truth of every moral principle depends on the culture, then she must admit that the truth of moral relativism depends on the culture. Therefore the moral relativist must admit that at least the principle of moral relativism is not relative.

Third, it seems that there is a set of basic moral principles that every culture must adopt. You would not have a culture unless the members of the group adopted these moral principles. Consider an anthropologist who arrives on a populated island: How many tribes are on the island? To answer that question, the anthropologist tries to determine if some people on some parts of the island are permitted to kill, commit acts of violence against, or steal from persons on other parts of the island. If such behavior is not permitted, that counts as a reason for saying that there is only one tribe. The underlying assumption here is that there is a set of moral principles that must be followed if there is to be a culture at all. With respect to those moral principles, adhering to them determines whether there is a culture or not.

But what justifies these principles? A moral relativist would say that a culture justifies them. But you cannot have a culture unless the members of the culture follow the principles. Thus it is reasonable to think that justification lies elsewhere. Many believe that the purpose of morality is to help make social cooperation possible. Moral principles are universally necessary for that endeavor.

The Morality of the Marketplace

Given that the norms constituting a moral minimum are likely to be few in number, it can be argued that the argument thus far has achieved something – that is, multinationals are obligated to follow the moral norms required for the existence of a society. But the argument has not achieved very much – that is, most issues surrounding multinationals do not involve alleged violations of these norms. Perhaps a stronger argument can be found by making explicit the morality of the marketplace. That there is an implicit morality of the market is a point that is often ignored by most economists and many business persons.

Although economists and business persons assume that people are basically self-interested, they must also assume that persons involved in business transactions will honor their contracts. In most economic exchanges, the transfer of product for money is not simultaneous. You deliver and I pay or vice versa. As the economist Kenneth Boulding put it: "without an integrative framework, exchange itself cannot develop, because exchange, even in its most primitive forms, involves trust and credibility."[2]

Philosophers would recognize an implicit Kantianism in Boulding's remarks. Kant tried to show that a contemplated action would be immoral if a world in which the contemplated act was universally practiced was self-defeating. For example, lying and cheating would fail Kant's tests. Kant's point is implicitly recognized by the business community when corporate officials despair of the immoral practices of corporations and denounce executives engaging in shady practices as undermining the business enterprise itself.

Consider what John Rawls says about contracts:

Such ventures are often hard to initiate and to maintain. This is especially evident in the case of covenants, that is, in those instances where one person is to perform before the other. For this person may believe that the second party will not do his part, and therefore the scheme never gets going. ... Now in these situations there may be no way of assuring the party who is to perform first except by giving him a promise, that is, by putting oneself under an obligation to carry through later. Only in this way can the scheme be made secure so that both can gain from the benefits of their cooperation.[3]

Rawls's remarks apply to all contracts. Hence, if the moral norms of a host country permitted practices that undermined contracts, a multinational ought not to follow them. Business practice based on such norms could not pass Kant's test.

In fact, one can push Kant's analysis and contend that business practice generally requires the adoption of a minimum standard of justice. In the United States, a person who participates in business practice and engages in the practice of giving bribes or kick-backs is behaving unjustly. Why? Because the person is receiving the benefits of the rules against such activities without supporting the rules personally. This is an example of what John Rawls calls freeloading. A freeloader is one who accepts the benefits without paying any of the costs.

In everyday life an individual, if he is so inclined, can sometimes win even greater benefits for himself by taking advantage of the cooperative efforts of others. Sufficiently many persons may be doing their share so that when special circumstances allow him not to contribute (perhaps his omission will not be found out), he gets the best of both worlds. ... We cannot preserve a sense of justice and all that this implies while at the same time holding ourselves ready to act unjustly should doing so promise some personal advantage.[4]

This argument does not show that if bribery really is an accepted moral practice in country X, that moral practice is wrong. What it does show is that practices in country X that permit freeloading are wrong and if bribery can be construed as freeloading, then it is wrong. In most countries I think it can be shown that bribery is freeloading, but I shall not make that argument here.

The implications of this analysis for multinationals are broad and important. If activities that are permitted in other countries violate the morality of the marketplace – for example, undermine contracts or involve freeloading on the rules of the market – they nonetheless are morally prohibited to multinationals that operate there. Such multinationals are obligated to follow the moral norms of the market. Contrary behavior is inconsistent and ultimately self-defeating.

Our analysis here has rather startling implications. If the moral norms of a host country are in violation of the moral

norms of the marketplace, then the multinational is obligated to follow the norms of the marketplace. Systematic violation of marketplace norms would be self-defeating. Moreover, whenever a multinational establishes businesses in a number of different countries, the multinational provides something approaching a universal morality – the morality of the marketplace itself. If Romans are to do business with the Japanese, then whether in Rome or Tokyo, there is a morality to which members of the business community in both Rome and Tokyo must subscribe – even if the Japanese and Romans differ on other issues of morality.

Notes

1. C. Langlois and B. B. Schlegelmilch, "Do Corporate Codes of Ethics Reflect National Character? Evidence from Europe and the United States," *Journal of International Studies* 21 (1990): 519–39.
2. Kenneth E. Boulding, "The Basis of Value Judgments in Economics," in *Human Values and Economic Policy*, ed. Sidney Hook (New York University Press, 1967), p. 68.
3. John Rawls, *A Theory of Justice* (Cambridge, MA: Harvard University Press, 1971), p. 569.
4. Ibid., p. 497.

Corporate Human Rights Obligations

DENIS G. ARNOLD

In 2011 the United Nations formally endorsed the "Protect, Respect and Remedy Framework for Business and Human Rights." This framework holds that:

1. states have a duty to protect against the human rights violations of their citizens by third parties including corporations and other business enterprises;
2. corporations and other business enterprises have an obligation to respect human rights; and
3. as a part of the duty to protect, states have an obligation to provide effective remedy when human rights abuses by corporations and other business organizations occur.

The "Protect, Respect and Remedy Framework" has been formally endorsed by the Organisation for Economic Co-operation and Development (OECD), a group of 35 leading industrialized nations including the United States, United Kingdom, Canada, Australia, Germany, France, and Japan

focused on economic development and prosperity. Nonetheless, the claim that corporations have human rights obligations remains contentious and can be fraught with confusion. The aim of this article is to synthesize existing corporate human rights theory and respond to objections to the idea that transnational corporations (TNCs) have human rights obligations. We proceed in three stages. First, because it is sometimes claimed that corporations are not the sort of entity that can have human rights obligations the first section describes the different forms TNCs take and explains why TNCs are properly understood as intentional organizations that are morally responsible for their policies and practices. The second section takes up the question of human rights obligations directly by reviewing and explaining different theories of corporate human rights obligations. The third section articulates and responds to objections to the idea that corporations have human rights obligations.

Excerpted from Denis G. Arnold, "Corporations and Human Rights Obligations," *Business and Human Rights Journal* 1, no. 2 (2016): 255–75.

The main conclusion of this article is that there are multiple, compelling, and overlapping justifications of corporate human rights obligations.

Corporate Moral Agency

How can TNCs have moral obligations, in addition to legal obligations? In what sense can TNCs be said to have moral responsibility, in additional to legal culpability? To answer this question, we need to examine the ontological status of corporations. A common refrain in much management, finance, and economics literature, and some legal scholarship, is that TNCs are mere legal fictions established for the purpose of enhancing the economic interests of investors and do not possess the agency necessary to be duty bearers. But as we shall see, there are good reasons for thinking that this view is mistaken. While there are compelling reasons for claiming that corporations are moral agents,[1] that position remains contentious.[2] The aim of this section is to explain why TNCs are properly understood to have the ontological status necessary to be duty bearers that are morally, and not just legally, responsible for corporate policies and practices. The aim of this section, then, is to explain the idea of *corporate moral agency* as applied to TNCs.[3]

Forms of TNCs

To begin, let us consider the corporate form. A variety of types and sizes of companies operate internationally. Small or medium-sized firms may have supply chains that extend across national boundaries, or may service foreign customers, but are based in one nation. Larger organizations that have operations and employees in many nations are the primary subject of analysis in this article. Bartlett and Ghoshal provide a conceptual framework for understanding the different types of organizational structures of large firms operating in an international context.[4] In recent history, they argue, there have been three main types of organizational structures. First, there are multinational companies characterized by a decentralized governance structure with self-sufficient companies operating in host nations. The strategy of multinational companies is based on sensitivity and *responsiveness* to national contexts, and knowledge acquired and retained within national units. Second, there are global companies that are characterized by the centralized governance of a parent company operating from a home nation. The strategy of global companies is characterized by the *efficient* deployment of a uniform strategy in host nations, and knowledge acquired and retained by the center. Finally, there are international companies that are characterized by a combination of centralized and decentralized

core competencies. International companies utilize a strategy of *leveraging* parent company competencies grounded in knowledge acquired centrally and distributed overseas.[5]

Bartlett and Ghoshal argue that in order for modern, transnational companies to adapt to a global marketplace and remain competitive they need to be responsive to national contexts, efficient in their global operations, and capable of leveraging parent company competencies. That is, they argue that companies need to adapt key attributes from each of the three types of companies operating globally in order to be economically successful. In this article the phrase "transnational corporations" is utilized to encompass multinational companies, global companies, and international companies, as well as the model of transnational companies that Bartlett and Ghoshal advise general managers to adapt. Each type of company is transnational in the sense that the scope of company operations, customer base, or supply chains extend across national boundaries and often into regulatory and governance gaps. While characteristics described by Bartlett and Ghoshal are important for understanding the differences between the varieties of companies operating internationally, and the strategic advantages and disadvantages of each variety, the differences are insignificant for clarifying the human rights and other obligations of businesses.

Each type of company described by Bartlett and Ghoshal directs the behavior and operations of subsidiaries in host nations. Multinational companies may grant more autonomy to subsidiary companies than global companies, but each type of company has the ability to direct subsidiary operations via an internal decision structure and a transnational ethical infrastructure. The internal decision structure includes hierarchical lines of organizational responsibility, rules of procedure, and corporate policies.[6] The ethical infrastructure of a company includes corporate ethics and compliance managers, employee training, company values statements, employee assessment and incentives linked to policies and values, and communications about ethics and compliance.[7] The existence of internal decision structures and ethical infrastructures helps us to understand how companies can exhibit intentionality[8] and why it is reasonable to hold both companies and their executive leadership teams accountable for organizational behavior including ethical transgressions. We refer to *corporate* moral agents, to delineate moral agents with internal decision structures comprised of human persons from other types of moral agents.

Intentionality, in the sense relevant here, is understood as the ability to plan future actions in a coordinated manner.[9] More specifically, plans have two distinct features: (1)

they are typically partial or incomplete and need to be filled in over time; (2) plans typically have a hierarchical structure in which some plans are embedded in other plans. This type of intentionality exists at both the individual, group, and organizational level, but at the group and organizational level planning is accompanied by coordination. Understanding how organizations such as companies exhibit intentionality is important for understanding claims regarding corporate moral agency and organizational normative legitimacy.

Corporate Intentionality

Consider this conception of intentionality as it applies to corporations and other organizations. TNCs routinely utilize planning, along with analysis, and assessment, to achieve strategic goals that allow them to remain competitive and provide value to their customers. Long-term planning is an important component of strategic management and is routinely taught in business schools. Consider the example of a company implementing a new anti-corruption program in all of its global operations. Bribery anywhere in the world is illegal for all companies conducting business in the United States under the Foreign Corrupt Practices Act and in the United Kingdom under the Bribery Act (consistent with the OECD Convention on Combating Bribery of Foreign Officials in International Bribery Transactions). Utilizing the ability of TNCs to adhere to legal regulations is helpful because it illustrates how companies can and do meet one type of obligation: namely, the obligation to obey the law. The orthodox view of the purpose of the firm holds that the function of executives and managers is to maximize economic value for firm owners while adhering to the law. However, almost no management, finance, or economics scholars explicitly defend the idea that companies should violate the law in the interest of additional wealth creation. Conventions and laws make bribery illegal because bribery is widely understood to undermine economic development, human rights, and democracy. Transparency International, the respected anti-corruption organization, succinctly summarizes the reasons that bribery has been made illegal via regulations and conventions:

> Corruption impedes investment, undermines economic growth, diverts humanitarian assistance and reduces market opportunities for legitimate business. When government is for sale, it destroys public trust in democratic institutions and denies citizens, businesses, taxpayers, and consumers the benefit of open markets and fair competition. Corruption disproportionately burdens the poor, diverting scarce resources that could otherwise

help lift millions out of poverty. It raises the costs of education, nutrition, clean water, and health care, often denying citizens these essential public services.[10]

Bribery is also related to human rights. As Mary Robinson has noted, "When individuals and families have to pay bribes to access food, housing, property, education, jobs and the right to participate in the cultural life of a community, basic human rights are clearly violated."[11]

How might a TNC intentionally implement an anti-corruption policy? Such a process might look like the following: First, executives form a committee to oversee this process. The committee might include the company's chief ethics officer and representatives from the general counsel's office, internal auditing, human resources, and representatives from divisions operating in nations with high levels of corruption. Coordination is accomplished in the different departments and divisions of the company and its subsidiaries. For example, the corporate ethics office develops the principles and practices that will guide company behavior, the training of employees, and coordinates the production of an anti-bribery handbook that described various scenarios and appropriate responses in each of the nations or regions in which the company operates. Human resources crafts disciplinary procedures for employees who violate the policy. Corporate communications ensures that all employees are informed of the anti-bribery policy, together with sanctions for violations, and so on. The coordination requirement is satisfied insofar as each person is aware of the subplans of other members of the group necessary for the execution of the plan. Again, the required level of knowledge will vary between individuals. Presumably each employee of the company will need to be made aware of both the anti-bribery policy and the corresponding disciplinary policy. Further plans may still need to be negotiated, such as incentives to help convince employees to comply with the new policy and appropriate responses for non-compliance. These negotiations regarding subplans may continue after the group has begun to carry out their plan. If the criteria of intentionality are met in these ways, it is proper to say that company has a collective intention to create and institute a new anti-bribery program.

It might be argued that multinational companies, where subsidiaries exhibit more autonomy, would find the process of implementing a global anti-corruption policy more challenging than global companies because parent companies in multinationals exhibit less control than global companies where parent companies retain greater control. However, multinational companies have the advantage over global companies of deep knowledge of local contexts that may better facilitate education and training of subsidiary employees relative to the local context of corruption. In other words, both types of companies have strengths and weaknesses with regard to implementing standards globally. Transnational companies that are both responsive to national contexts and capable of leveraging parent company expertise in training, evaluation, monitoring, and enforcement of employee compliance with anti-corruption policies may have an advantage in the successful implementation of anti-corruption policies. However, each of the company structures in Bartlett and Ghoshal's typology is compatible with the development and implementation of corporate ethics policies.

It is because the implementation of company policies and practices are intentional in the way that has been described here that it is proper to hold companies and their leaders morally responsible for corporate activity. However, in addition to intentionality and an internal decision structure, a further condition must be met if corporations are to be regarded as agents that are morally responsible for practices and policies independently of individual directors, executives, and employees. Corporations must be capable of reflectively endorsing or rejecting existing practices and strategies. Corporations that are capable of evaluating past decisions and existing practices, of determining whether those corporate intentions ought to remain in place, or whether they should be modified or eliminated in favor of alternative plans and strategies, are capable of the requisite reflective decision-making and are properly understood as moral agents.

Meeting human rights obligations can be understood as a central element of the ethics and compliance programs of TNCs, just as implementing anti-corruption programs are for many companies. It might be thought that because TNCs have human rights obligations, they should also be understood as rights bearers.[12] Agency is not, however, a sufficient condition for personhood. As explained in the following section, persons in the ontological (not legal) sense have freedom of the will, the capacity to gain meaning, personal satisfaction, and happiness, from the pursuit of plans and life projects, and the moral status of ends in themselves. These characteristics are not shared by corporations, but these characteristics are essential features of moral justifications of human rights. This unique status of human persons is recognized in the Universal Declaration of Human Rights which is explicitly grounded in the "dignity and worth of the human person" and which makes repeated use of the concept of human dignity. Mere agents, in contrast, possess none of these qualities. For example, a sophisticated computer that exhibited agency but did not have freedom of the will, nor the capacity to gain meaning, personal satisfaction, and happiness, from the pursuit of plans and life projects, would not qualify as person entitled to human rights, even if it was granted the status of legal personhood.

To sum up, TNCs are properly understood as corporate moral agents capable of being duty bearers and entities morally responsible for their actions because they have internal decision structures comprised of human agents, including the ethical infrastructure of the firm, corporate intentions understood primarily as plans, and the capacity for reflective assessment of corporate plans and practices.

Corporate Human Rights Obligations

There are a variety of ways of conceptualizing corporate human rights obligations, and different ways of thinking about human rights naturally entail different sets of human rights obligations. Much of the apparent disagreement regarding corporate human rights obligations reflects differences in the types of rights at issue and in the way scholars conceptualize the responsibilities of corporations to preserve or promote justice. Unpacking these distinctions will go some way toward providing clarity regarding corporate human rights obligations.

Human Rights as Moral Rights

Moral rights are most often grounded in considerations regarding the nature of humanity. Here the central concern focuses on what is required to live a functional human life given that humans are self-governing beings, physically vulnerable and susceptible to harm, and with basic needs such as for adequate food, water, and shelter. The most common accounts of the moral basis of human rights developed by philosophers over the last 30 years have emphasized the centrality and importance of autonomy or agency. There are two, compatible ways in which this basis for moral rights has been defended. First, the *intrinsic* account, which has a lineage that extends to Kant, emphasizes that self-governing beings possess a unique dignity that rights serve to protect.[13] On this account, rights confer the moral status of inviolability that is independent of the general good of society.[14] Rights are not moral goods in need of our protection merely because of the ends they allow persons to achieve, rather rights are moral goods that should be protected because they confer upon persons the status of ends in themselves. As such, when a person's rights are violated a wrong has been committed regardless of other considerations. Second, an *instrumental* account of human rights is concerned with the ability of people to pursue practical interests and long-term projects in the interest of achieving happiness, satisfaction, or meaning.[15] Here the argument is that to achieve a fulfilling human life, rights need to be protected. On an instrumental account rights are derivative of other values, such as the goods of happiness, freedom, or self-realization.[16] In the case of both accounts of moral human rights presented here, it is proper to ascribe responsibility, and potentially blame, to individuals, organizations, or institutions that violate the rights of individuals.

I have previously argued that agentic accounts of human rights provide an appropriately deep foundation for corporate human rights obligations, particularly when limited in scope to basic rights such as liberty, physical security, and subsistence.[17] Basic rights are those rights that are necessary for the attainment of other rights; they are rights required for a decent human life.[18] Basic rights take the form of side-constraints that bound the moral space in which corporations may legitimately pursue economic ends. Basic human rights obligations for corporations might include ensuring that workers are not subject to forced labor, human trafficking, corporal punishment, imprisonment, discrimination, suppression of their freedom to organize, or death or injury resulting from poor safety standards. It might also mean that local communities are not exposed to harmful pollutants and that the natural environment is not so adversely impacted as to undermine health or the utilization of natural resources for economic and physical subsistence. Putting the issue in the form of an interrogative can help to provide focus and clarity: If an agentic account of human rights is correct, how could managers of companies, or their agents, be exempt from meeting the obligation not to violate the human rights of individuals with whom they interact or impact in their operations? The fact that corporations are legal entities with proscribed economic aims and legal protections makes it challenging to hold firms legally liable for human rights violations, especially in nations with significant governance gaps, but this does not alter the force of morally grounded human rights obligations.[19] Since TNCs are moral agents that have specific relationships with employees, contractors, customers, and the individual members of communities in which they operate, those individuals with whom they have relationships, or upon whom they have a direct impact (e.g., via water or air pollution) have legitimate claims on TNCs to meet basic human rights duties.

Human Rights as Political Rights

As we have seen, both agentically grounded and social contract models provide a moral grounding for corporate human rights obligations. Political accounts of human rights, on the other hand, eschew moral justifications and instead appeal to the role rights play in the international political sphere.[20] Political accounts of human rights focus on theoretical or actual agreements among nations and supranational organizations such as the United Nations and the International Labour Organization. The historical function of international human rights law has been to provide universal standards for the treatment of individuals by national governments. In practice, the current international human rights legal system includes, at a minimum, the Universal Declaration of Human Rights, the International Covenant on Economic, Social and Cultural Rights, the International Covenant on Civil and Political Rights, and the International Labour Conventions.[21] While moral rights may be used to justify some or all of international human rights law, international human rights can be justified independently of a direct correlation to morally justified human rights.[22]

Transnational corporations operate in a multitude of political jurisdictions and so are subject to a multitude of legal frameworks. Laws regarding such matters as the treatment of customers, the treatment of employees, and environmental protection vary significantly in different host nations. In the case of developing economies, consumer protection, worker safety, and environmental safeguards are often poorly developed and enforced. The law enforcement infrastructure and judicial apparatus necessary to ensure compliance is often weak, understaffed, and underfunded. Transnational companies operating in such nations are often free to determine for themselves whether or not they will adhere to host nation laws. Observers of a post-Westphalian international system note an increase in the influence and power of corporations and an inability on the part of governments to appropriately govern corporate operations and impacts. For example, Stephen Kobrin argues that "the shift from a state-centric to multi-actor system associated with the emergence of a transnational world order has fragmented political authority and blurred the once distinct line between the public and private spheres: both have led to an expanded conception of the rights and duties of non-state actors."[23]

It is because of actual corporate human rights abuses, and not merely the potential for such abuses, that the United Nations developed and approved the "Protect, Respect and Remedy Framework for Business and Human Rights," introduced at the beginning of this article, and its accompanying *Guiding Principles on Business and Human Rights* (2011). The *Guiding Principles* require that "Business enterprises should respect human rights. This means that they should avoid infringing on the human rights of others and should address adverse human rights impacts with which they are involved."[24] While not currently a legally binding set of obligations, the corporate responsibility to respect human rights enunciated in the *Guiding Principles* is a major development insofar as it expands the international human rights regime to include corporations and other businesses enterprises within its domain. The human rights referenced by the *Guiding Principles* are broader than basic moral rights, and their justification is grounded in both the legitimacy of the process by which they were determined and the political agreements that were a part of that process. These rights are compatible with moral rights, but not equivalent to morally grounded human rights.

Significantly for understanding the normative legitimacy of the *Guiding Principles*, business organizations were active in development of the "Protect, Respect and Remedy Framework." The tripartite framework and the *Guiding Principles* were expressly endorsed by the International Organisation of Employers, the International Chamber of Commerce, and the Business and Industry Advisory Committee to the OECD. These organizations, and other business organizations and specific companies, also played a consulting role during the six-year development process of the tripartite framework. It is also important to keep in mind that employer representation has been a formal component of the ILO governance structure since its inception in 1919 and as such played a formal role in the development of the ILO Conventions.

Objections: Shareholder Primacy

The conventional Anglo-American story regarding the normative obligations of corporate managers that is assumed in much of the economics, finance, and management literature holds that it is the obligation of managers to maximize profits for shareholders (or private equity holders) while adhering to the law. Sometimes it is added that corporations should also avoid deception, although this is typically stipulated as an aside and not explained or defended by proponents of the "shareholder primacy" perspective.[25] Proponents of this view typically emphasize the importance of protecting property rights and the positive impact corporations have on social utility. They argue that managers who expend corporate resources on activities that are not focused on corporate profits are, in effect, undemocratically redistributing investor resources. They endorse the idea that managers are agents of shareholders who must always act on behalf of shareholder interests. A bedrock assumption upon which shareholder ideology rests is that the corporation is operating in a democratic context. It is only by assuming that citizens determine the regulatory framework of business (the "rules of the game") that proponents of shareholder primacy and instrumental corporate social responsibility (CSR) have any basis for defending the idea that firms need only adhere to the law to retain normative legitimacy.[26]

Proponents of this view typically adhere to broadly libertarian beliefs regarding markets emphasizing minimal regulations, private property rights, freedom, especially the freedom to enter into contracts, weak labor protections, and free trade among nations. The ideological bedfellow of the shareholder primacy view is the instrumental theory of corporate responsibility. Instrumental, or economic, CSR holds that corporations should engage in pro-social or ethical conduct only when doing so will improve the return on investment of the financiers of the organization.[27] Proponents of this perspective are committed to the view that TNCs should meet human rights standards only when doing so generates more revenue than not meeting human rights standards. If violating human rights standards is more profitable, then from this perspective that is the obligation of TNC managers.

The shareholder primacy ideology has been soundly criticized by management and legal scholars,[28] but it has received less explicit attention in the context of international business and human rights.[29] One might think that a view that was defended by influential scholars would have a firm grounding in a well-developed theory of the legitimacy of corporate practices in a global economic system, but this is not the case. Consider just two of the difficulties with the shareholder position as applied to the human rights context: faulty assumptions regarding institutional frameworks and the lack of democratic governments in many nations in which TNCs operate.

Faulty Assumptions Regarding Institutional Frameworks

The shareholder primacy ideology is grounded in a faulty interpretation of corporate law, namely, that the sole obligation of TNC executives and managers is to maximize economic value. Lynn Stout points out that, contrary to the shareholder primacy ideology, corporate law in the United States gives directors and executives wide discretion with regard to corporate objectives via the business judgment rule.[30] In practice this entails that managers have the legal right to take into account the impact of the actions of their companies on other stakeholders and on society in general. Pressure from Wall Street analysts, major investors, and poorly designed executive incentive structures can encourage a myopic focus on short-term stock performance and disregard for social considerations such as human rights, but this is not a legal requirement and many US companies are managed in a way that balances the interests of multiple stakeholders. In the United Kingdom, the revised Companies Act requires that directors take into account the interests of the company's employees, "the impact of the company's operations on the community and the environment," the need to maintain "a reputation for high standards of business conduct," and the need to act fairly.[31] More generally, 15 of 27 member states of the European Union have national policy frameworks for promoting CSR. The European Commission, the executive governing body of the European Union, has recommended that all member states implement such frameworks.[32]

Many of the nations in which TNCs conduct business lack important democratic institutions such as equal voting rights, multiple political parties, democratic elections, politically neutral militaries, and an independent judiciary. According to Freedom House, 56 percent of the world's sovereign states and colonial units – home to 60 percent of the world's population – lack civil or political freedom.[33] Thirty-six percent of nations including China and Russia are not electoral democracies. The shareholder primacy view presumes the existence of electoral democracies, and the civil and political rights that facilitate political speech and activity, so that citizens can regulate business activity.[34] The shareholder primacy view is inapplicable in other political contexts. However, international business is conducted in all nations and a theory of the firm that cannot provide guidance to companies operating in unfree or partially free nations can provide no guidance for TNCs operating in a global economy.

Regulatory and Governance Gaps

In non-democratic nations, as well as in many electoral democracies, there are regulatory and governance gaps pertaining to business operations. A regulatory gap refers to a substantive lack of regulation regarding some type of business activity. In this context, the gaps we are concerned with are those that permit harm to human welfare (e.g., gaps in the protection of internationally recognized labor rights, or in environmental laws that protect water and air quality, or in financial regulations preventing usurious loans). Such gaps should be filled by regulations that better protect citizens from exploitation and the degradation of the environments in which they live. Many developing nations have such regulatory gaps that companies have historically utilized to advance profit maximization.[35] Governance gaps involve institutional failures to enforce existing regulations regarding business activity or to create regulations intended to protect human rights.[36] This may be the result of political turmoil, weak or corrupt governments, or a lack of institutional resources necessary to police and enforce existing regulations. Governance gaps are present in many developing nations and in Russia and former Soviet bloc nations. Governance gaps often prevent the enforcement of regulations intended to protect citizens from physical harm or deprivation and the degradation of the natural environments in which citizens live and upon which they depend upon for their livelihood.

TNCs exploit governance gaps when they or their suppliers violate local laws in their business operations with the knowledge that local authorities are unable or unwilling to adequately enforce existing regulations. The violation of local labor and environmental laws often results in human rights abuses such as forced labor, human trafficking, corporal punishment of workers, false imprisonment, discrimination, suppression of the freedom to organize, and death or injury as a result of poor working conditions or exposure to harmful environmental pollutants. A failure to adhere to host nation laws and regulations can result in costs savings, faster turn-around time for production orders, increased access to markets, or greater sales. Violation of the law may be routine and incorporated into the business strategy of a transnational company, or it might be the decision of one or more subsidiaries of a multinational company with a decentralized and nationally self-sufficient organizational structure, or it may be undertaken by suppliers who are not carefully monitored by a company.

It is difficult to assess how widespread the practice of violating host nation laws may be among transnational companies, their subsidiaries, and suppliers. Recently the United States Securities and Exchange Commission stepped up enforcement of the US Foreign Corrupt Practices Act. Bribery is typically illegal in the host nations where it takes place but governance gaps result in lax enforcement by authorities. Among the 60 companies that the US Securities and Exchange Commission has taken enforcement actions against recently for corruption are US-based General Electric for corruption in Iraq; Eli Lily for corruption in Russia, Brazil, China, and Poland; Pfizer for corruption in Bulgaria, China, Croatia, the Czech Republic, Kazakhstan, Russia, and Serbia; Johnson & Johnson for corruption in Poland, Romania, and Iraq; IBM for corruption in China; KBR and its former parent Halliburton for corruption in Nigeria; London-based Diageo for corruption in India and Thailand; French-based Alcatel-Lucent for corruption in Costa Rica; and the German company Siemens for corruption in Indonesia. Corruption and bribery are unique in that the violation of host nation laws also violates US law (as well as the 2010 UK Bribery Act) providing an incentive for companies to maintain an active compliance and corruption prevention program. The violation of labor and environmental laws in host nations does not normally also violate US, UK, or European Union laws and as result companies have less incentive for compliance with these laws. As discussed above, there are also many political contexts in which regulatory gaps exist and where human rights violations are legally permitted and where TNCs' human rights violations are not at the same time violations of the law.

The logic of the shareholder primacy perspective encourages the exploitation of regulatory and governance gaps. First, governance and regulatory gaps often exist in non-democratic nations where the shareholder primacy ideology is inapplicable because it is predicated on the existence of democratic governments where citizens freely determine business regulations through their elected representatives.[37] Second, in developing nations that are also democracies, but with weak governance institutions, the relentless pursuit of profit advocated by the shareholder ideology implicitly advocates illegal activity when such activity is profitable and governments are unable to enforce existing regulations. Proponents of the shareholder primacy ideology have been conspicuously silent on the question of what obligations transnational companies have when, for example, labor and environmental laws go unenforced in developing nations. Gond, Palazzo, and Basu argue that the logic of shareholder primacy and instrumental corporate responsibility is consistent with the institutional logic of the Italian Mafia which has a similar focus on extreme profits and the exploitation of governance gaps.[38]

Notes

1. Thomas Donaldson, *Corporations and Morality* (Englewood Cliffs, NJ: Prentice-Hall, 1982); P. A. French, "The Corporation as a Moral Person," *American Philosophical Quarterly* 16 (1979): 207–15; D. G. Arnold, "Corporate Moral Agency," *Midwest Studies in Philosophy* 30 (2006): 279–91.
2. Amy J. Sepinwall, "Denying Corporate Rights and Punishing Corporate Wrongs," *Business Ethics Quarterly* 25, no. 4 (2015): 517–34.
3. It is important to clarify from the outset that the position defended in this article is not that corporations are "moral persons," as nearly all scholars of corporate ontology deny that corporations are persons and have done so for at least 20 years – ever since the leading proponent of that view, Peter French, repudiated the idea that ontologically corporations are "moral persons" and modified his view to one in which corporations are properly understood as "moral agents" (P. A. French, "Integrity, Intentions, and Corporations," *American Business Law Journal* 34 (1996): 141–56; Arnold, "Corporate Moral Agency"). Discussions of the ontological status of corporations and moral responsibility are distinct from discussion of the legally granted artificial personhood that allows the corporation to be legally distinct from its shareholders and to have

certain legal rights such as property ownership. In the United States, corporations have been recognized as legal persons since the Supreme Court's decision in *Santa Clara County v. Southern Pacific Railroad Company*, 118 U.S. 394, 397 (1886). For discussion of the current legal status of corporate persons, including corporate rights, see M. M. Blair, "Of Corporations, Courts, Personhood, and Morality," *Business Ethics Quarterly* 25 (2015): 415–31.
4. Christopher A. Bartlett and Sumantra Ghosal, *Managing across Borders: The Transnational Solution*, 2nd ed. (Boston, MA: Harvard Business School Press, 2002).
5. Ibid., pp. 16–18.
6. French, "The Corporation as a Moral Person."
7. A. E. Tenbrunsel, K. Smith-Crowe, and E. E. Umphress, "Building Houses on Rocks: The Role of the Ethical Infrastructure in Organizations," *Social Justice Research* 16 (2003): 285–307; L. K. Treviño and K. A. Nelson, *Managing Business Ethics* (New York: John Wiley, 2010).
8. French, "Integrity, Intentions, and Corporations"; Arnold, "Corporate Moral Agency."
9. Michael E. Bratman, *Intention, Plans, and Practical Reason* (Cambridge, MA: Harvard University Press, 1987); Michael E. Bratman, "Intention and Personal Policies," *Philosophical Perspectives* 3 (1989): 443–69.
10. Transparency International, *Mission and History* (2015). Retrieved October 17, 2015 from www.transparency-usa.org/archive/who/mission.html.
11. Transparency International, *Global Corruption Report* (London: Pluto Press, 2004), p. 7.
12. John D. Bishop, "The Limits of Corporate Human Rights Obligations and the Rights of For-Profit Corporations," *Business Ethics Quarterly* 22, no. 1 (2012): 119–44.
13. Alan Gewirth, *Human Rights: Essays on Justification and Applications* (University of Chicago Press, 1982); Immanuel Kant, *Foundations of the Metaphysics of Morals* (New York: Macmillan, 1990; originally published in 1785); Thomas Nagel, "Personal Rights and Public Space," *Philosophy & Public Affairs* 24 (1995): 83–107; Robert Nozick, *Anarchy, State, and Utopia* (New York: Basic Books, 1974).
14. Nagel, "Personal Rights and Public Space."
15. James Griffin, *On Human Rights* (Oxford University Press, 2008); L. E. Lomasky, *Persons, Rights, and the Moral Community* (Oxford University Press, 1987).
16. Nagel, "Personal Rights and Public Space," p. 86.
17. D. G. Arnold, "Transnational Corporations and the Duty to Respect Basic Human Rights," *Business Ethics Quarterly* 20 (2010): 371–99; D. G. Arnold, "Global Justice and International Business," *Business Ethics Quarterly* 32 (2013): 125–43; D. G. Arnold and A. Valentin, "CSR at the Base of the Pyramid: Exploitation, Empowerment, and Poverty Alleviation," *Journal of Business Research* 66 (2013): 1904–14.
18. Henry Shue, *Basic Rights: Subsistence, Affluence, and U.S. Foreign Policy*, rev. ed. (Princeton University Press, 1996).

19. Peter T. Muchlinski, *Multinational Enterprises and the Law*, 2nd ed. (Oxford University Press, 2007), pp. 507–36.

20. John Rawls, *Law of Peoples* (Cambridge, MA: Harvard University Press, 1999); Charles R. Beitz, *The Idea of Human Rights* (Oxford University Press, 2009); Allen Buchanan, *The Heart of Human Rights* (Oxford University Press, 2013).

21. While the ILO Conventions are not a part of the International Bill of Human Rights, they are an important element of the international human rights legal system and are particularly important to discussions of corporate human rights obligations because employers' representatives (along with workers' representatives and government representatives) are a formal component of the ILO governance structure. The United Nations' "Protect, Respect and Remedy Framework" expressly refers to both the International Bill of Rights and the ILO Conventions.

22. Buchanan, *The Heart of Human Rights*, pp. 14–22.

23. S. J. Kobrin, "Private Political Authority and Public Responsibility: Transnational Politics, Transnational Firms, and Human Rights," *Business Ethics Quarterly* 19 (2009): 349–74 (p. 353).

24. United Nations, *Guiding Principles on Business and Human Rights: Implementing the United Nations "Protect, Respect and Remedy" Framework*. HR/PUB/11/04 (New York and Geneva: United Nations, 2011), p. 13.

25. T. M. Jones and W. Felps, "Shareholder Wealth Maximization and Social Welfare: A Utilitarian Critique," *Business Ethics Quarterly* 23 (2013): 207–38; L. A. Stout, *The Shareholder Value Myth: How Putting Shareholders First Harms Investors, Corporations, and the Public* (San Francisco, CA: Berrett-Koehler, 2012).

26. D. G. Arnold, "Libertarian Theories of the Corporation and Global Capitalism," *Journal of Business Ethics* 48 (2003): 155–73.

27. J. Gond, G. Palazzo, and K. Basu, "Reconsidering Instrumental Corporate Social Responsibility through the Mafia Metaphor," *Business Ethics Quarterly* 19 (2009): 57–85; A. McWilliams and D. Siegel, "Corporate Social Responsibility: A Theory of the Firm Perspective," *Academy of Management Review* 26 (2001): 117–27; A. McWilliams, D. S. Siegel, and P. M. Wright, "Corporate Social Responsibility: Strategic Implications," *Journal of Management Studies* 43 (2006): 1–18.

28. S. Ghoshal, "Bad Management Theories Are Destroying Good Management Practices," *Academy of Management Learning & Education* 4 (2005): 75–91; Jones and Felps, "Shareholder Wealth Maximization and Social Welfare"; Stout, *The Shareholder Value Myth*.

29. Florian Wettstein, *Multinational Corporations and Global Justice: Human Rights Obligations of a Quasi Governmental Institution* (Stanford University Press, 2009).

30. Stout, *The Shareholder Value Myth*.

31. United Kingdom, Companies Act 2006, 172(1).

32. European Union Commission, *A Renewed EU Strategy 2011–14 for Corporate Social Responsibility* (Brussels: EU Commission, 2011).

33. Freedom House, *Freedom in the World* (2016). Retrieved from https://freedomhouse.org/report/freedom-world/freedom-world-2016.

34. Arnold, "Libertarian Theories of the Corporation and Global Capitalism."

35. Ibid.; Wesley Cragg, "Business and Human Rights: A Principle and Value Based Analysis," in *The Oxford Handbook of Business Ethics*, ed. George Brenkert and Tom Beauchamp (Oxford University Press, 2009), pp. 267–304.

36. United Nations Special Representative of the Secretary-General on the Issue of Human Rights and Transnational Corporations and Other Business Enterprises, "Promotion and Protection of Human Rights," United Nations Doc. E/CN.4/2006/97 (February 22, 2006); United Nations Special Representative of the Secretary-General on the Issue of Human Rights and Transnational Corporations and Other Business Enterprises, "Protect, Respect and Remedy: A Framework for Business and Human Rights," United Nations Doc. A/HRC/8/5 (April 7, 2008).

37. Arnold, "Libertarian Theories of the Corporation and Global Capitalism."

38. Gond et al., "Reconsidering Instrumental Corporate Social Responsibility."

9.3 SWEATSHOPS AND BRIBERY

Sweatshops

LAURA P. HARTMAN

By common agreement, a sweatshop is a workplace that provides low or subsistence wages under harsh working conditions, and/or an oppressive environment. Some observers see these work environments as essentially acceptable if the laborers freely contract to work in such conditions. For others, to call a workplace a sweatshop implies

From Robert W. Kolb, ed., *Encyclopedia of Business Ethics and Society* (Sage, 2007). Reproduced with permission of Sage Publications, Inc. in the format Other Published Product via Copyright Clearance Center.

that the working conditions are illegitimate and immoral. The US General Accounting Office would hone this definition to US workplaces to include those environments where an employer violates more than one federal or state labor, industrial homework, occupational safety and health, workers' compensation, or industry registration laws. The AFL-CIO Union of Needletrades, Industrial and Textile Employees would expand on that to include workplaces with systematic violations of global fundamental workers' rights. The Interfaith Center on Corporate Responsibility (ICCR) defines sweatshops much more broadly than either of these; even where a factory is clean, well organized, and harassment free, the ICCR considers it a sweatshop if its workers are not paid a sustainable living wage. The purpose of reviewing these varied definitions is to acknowledge that, by definition, sweatshops are defined as oppressive, unethical, and patently unfair to workers.

Sweatshops exist in all countries, including the United States, and have a lengthy history. One finds sweatshops in certain countries where there are no laws protecting workers from oppressive working conditions, as well as in those countries where the conditions allowed by the local laws remain substandard according to international laws. However, if by definition sweatshops involve the violation of laws, then no *legal* sweatshops can exist in those jurisdictions where there are significant worker protection laws.

However, strict labor laws, effective labor unions, and the growth of employee mobility and opportunity have attempted to eliminate sweatshops in developed countries. The vast majority of sweatshops currently are found in economically underdeveloped countries, especially those with large pools of unskilled labor, high unemployment, and few regulatory constraints. In an unregulated environment, the more broad definitions apply to include workplaces where the owner is not violating any local laws but instead is perhaps violating international standards of human rights, such as provisions found in the United Nations Universal Declaration of Human Rights. But in those developing countries, the incentives and circumstances arguably leave employers with few options. To attract purchasers for their goods, suppliers must keep labor costs low and, therefore, pay workers on a "piece rate" basis rather than hourly, where workers' wages are based on the number of items they produce during a particular time period. Consequently, the longer and harder an employee works, the more he or she will be paid. In some circumstances, since the piece rate is so low, workers have no choice but to contribute extraordinary hours to merely survive, hence the ICCR's emphasis on subsistence wages as the primary element of a modern-day sweatshop.

Why do sweatshops exist, if their mistreatment of workers is so unquestionable and where countries in the developed world have put into place significant worker protections? In fact, there remain persuasive reasons why we have them in our global economy and even why we should permit them. Though some are present simply because there are those in human society who will abuse their power at the expense of those without power, there are far more that exist because they play a role in the economic cycle of development. There are two fields of thought in connection with their continued existence.

First, free-market economists suggest that sweatshops represent the cheapest and most efficient means for developing countries to expand export activities and to improve their economies, benefiting stakeholders, including the employees subject to the challenging conditions. In fact, they would argue that the *only* path to economic development for these poorer countries may lie in their ability to compete effectively – perhaps exclusively – on a world scale. This economic growth brings more jobs, which will cause the labor market to tighten, which in turn will force companies to improve conditions to attract workers. In fact, several commentators argue that encouraging greater global production will create additional opportunities for expansion domestically, providing a positive impact on more stakeholders. Moreover, if the suppliers raise wages to at least subsistence levels, they will need to raise their prices to the contracting retailers, who will then arguably seek lower prices elsewhere – and find them, otherwise known as the "race to the bottom." Though an unpopular sentiment with the general consuming public, and often characterized by the polarizing and volatile name "prosweatshops," many economists argue that the maintenance of sweatshop conditions is therefore supported by economic theory.

The second field of thought with regard to the continuation of these conditions is based on the contention that the current situation is perceived as "bad" only when considered through the perspective of those in developed economies. Where individual workers are faced with the choice of no job or a job that pays a subsistence wage, the workers will opt for the job. Similarly, when parents are faced with wages that do not allow them to feed, clothe, or house their entire family, they do not consider child labor to be unethical. Instead, it is often the only means by which the family can reap sufficient income with which to feed that child. Accordingly, if regulations or other strictures are imposed that demand conditions similar to those in developed countries, the multinationals will have no incentive to house their operations or to seek suppliers in developing countries, and will accordingly remain in their home countries, depriving the workers in the developing countries these positions.

Similarly, along this line of thinking, some philosophers assert that, as long as the worker has freely chosen the position, it is ethnocentric, paternalistic, and imperialistic to then impose alternative values. No one is forcing the worker to work under these conditions; therefore, the conditions should be permitted. If no worker would accept these conditions, the employer would be forced to ameliorate them.

On the other hand, labor advocates state that this argument contains a fallacy of choice. A worker forced to choose between accepting a position under substandard conditions to feed his family or declining the position and watching his family starve does not have true freedom of choice. They contend that it is precisely the imposition of Western expectations of free choice and the empowered worker that create a false analysis of the circumstances under which these workers accept the positions. While those in developed economies might be able to envision declining a job if the position described is unsuitable, in those environments where unemployment is exceptionally high and no public system of welfare or education exists, workers may not perceive that they have that option. The learned helplessness, whether actual or perceived, prevents the workers from impacting their environments to proceed down the route described by the economists.

Moreover, the traditional concept of free trade fails to provide social clauses for the protection of workers serving that trade environment and should therefore be curtailed. While free trade agreements encourage multinational companies to do business with developing economies, thereby increasing the gross national product of those economies, it is argued that these agreements are at the expense of (or "on the backs of") the workforces involved. In addition, these advocates suggest that allowing this economic process to take its course may not necessarily lead to the result articulated by the free-market economists and, similarly, voluntarily improving legal compliance, wages, and working conditions will not inevitably lead to the negative consequences the free-market advocates threaten.

There are innumerable examples of questionable sweatshop labor practices. Included below are discussions of four major areas of concern – child labor, wage rates and work hours, worker health and safety, and worker constraints and treatment – to provide a taste of the nature of sweatshop problems. To avoid confusion throughout the above debate and to raise the discussion above mere terminological discussions, it therefore remains critical to develop a deeper understanding of the meaning of the term *sweatshop* and the conditions to which it refers, even if the resulting definition remains a stipulative one.

Basic Human Rights

Any exploration of sweatshops would be incomplete without a discussion of the basic human rights that ethicists contend to be inalienable, though the determination of which rights would so qualify is far from resolved. To effectively consider the definitions mentioned above, it is important to stipulate the standards to which one should hold a multinational and its product or service supply chain. Yet the identification of global fundamental workers' rights is a challenge not only because of the debate that rages with regard to universalism versus relativism but also because of the challenge of determining the degree of protection. For instance, even if there was agreement that employers should pay a living wage to their workers, there is no agreement with regard to the determination of how to determine what that wage should be.

One scholarly analysis reviewed a variety of global labor standards to determine whether in this array of emerging standards there existed any such norms with respect to labor standards. The following basic labor rights were determined to have *relatively* universal acknowledgment in the range of codes and documents reviewed for that study:

- Just and favorable working conditions, including a limit to the number of hours a human should have to work each day and a healthy working environment.
- Minimum age and working conditions for child labor.
- Nondiscrimination requirements regarding the relative amount that a worker should be paid and the right to equal pay for equal work.
- Freedom from forced labor.
- Free association, including the right to organize and to bargain collectively in contract negotiations.

Thus, there is an argument that, at least in theory, there is some agreement about what rights *ought* to be respected. On the other hand, however, as mentioned above, there remains broad disagreement with regard to the parameters of fundamental human rights and this study suggests but one option for their identification. A cursory review of conditions around the world reveals that, though perhaps accepted by some as basic human rights, these standards are not necessarily respected as such.

Child Labor

As discussed briefly, there may be persuasive reasons why parents might encourage their children to work. However, in developing countries, children may begin work at ages as young as 3 years and often in unhealthy conditions. The labor that exists almost always precludes children from obtaining an education, as children often work on a full-time basis. In extreme cases, children are forced into slavery, often in the guise of indentured servitude or apprenticeship training. When referring to the nature of children's work, the International Labour Organization (ILO) Bureau of Statistics reports that most children working as paid employees are paid much less than the prevailing rates in their localities, even when compared with the legal minimum wages – receiving only one-sixth of the minimum rate in one survey finding; also the younger the working child, the lower the wage payment.

On average, girls work longer hours than boys but are paid less than their working brothers doing the same type of work, and children are generally not paid for overtime work. The ILO reports that, in the Philippines, more than 60 percent of working children are exposed to hazardous working conditions and 40 percent of those exposed experience serious injuries or illnesses including those that result in amputations and loss of body parts. Because work takes children out of school, more than half of the child labor force will never be literate. And because of substandard working conditions, child employees will grow less than those who didn't work as children and the child workers' bodies will be smaller, even into adulthood. By the time child laborers reach adulthood, most will irrevocably be sick or deformed; the children are unlikely to live to be 50 years old.

As horrendous as these conditions appear, many ask whether there are always better alternatives. Free-market economists point out that, in many circumstances, the wages these children earn are what pays for their food each night. If the children are denied jobs in communities where welfare systems are not in place, their very existence may be threatened. Often suppliers respond to multinational corporations' concerns by summarily and immediately terminating young workers, even when the local law would allow their employment. The impact of this dismissal on the children's survival may be devastating. In addition, if children are not permitted to work in mainstream ventures, they are often forced into the underground professions involving drugs and prostitution to help support themselves and their families. Until such time as welfare systems become prevalent throughout the developing countries, the answer to the question of children in the workplace is not an obvious one.

Wages and Hours

Sweatshop employees are often paid very low wages and are required to work very long hours, sometimes with no provision for overtime. Alternatively, if they refuse to work overtime in some circumstances, they may lose the pay already earned. The piece rate production quotas are often so high that workers are unable to leave the work floor to eat or use the restroom for fear of falling below quota, which often results in a loss of pay for those pieces submitted. The wage levels are far below the wages paid for similar types of employment in developed countries, even after restating wages in terms of country-specific purchasing power. An example of very low wages comes from a study of Honduran labor. In Honduras, workers earn only an average of $24.27 per week. However, basic necessities for a Honduran family cost $22.75 per week, which leaves an average family's wage earner with only $2.05 for transportation, school expenses, clothing, and other items. According to the National Labor Committee, El Salvadoran workers producing NBA jerseys make fewer than three jerseys per hour at $0.24 per jersey, which then sell for $140 in the United States. This $0.60 per hour is only about one-third of the Salvadoran cost of living.

Under some extraordinary circumstances, workers are expected to pay for the opportunity to work; at some factories, workers must pay work deposits and monthly tool deposits. Recovery of deposits generally depends on how long workers stayed at the factory. In one factory, workers lost their deposits if they did not stay at the factory for at least two years. Similar conditions have existed in Saipan, where workers were forced to pay a recruitment fee of $2,000 to $7,000 before they could begin working.

Frequently, minimum wage and maximum work hours laws have been enacted but have not been effectively enforced. In China, workers at one factory reported that they regularly work 16-hour days, 7 days a week during peak production times, despite Chinese labor laws that establish a maximum 49-hour workweek.

Health and Safety

Working conditions in sweatshops may seriously threaten worker health and safety. The ILO and the World Health Organization have concluded that the shift of industrial production to developing countries will *increase* the global occurrence of occupational disease and injury. In El Salvador, for example, workers at one factory had to endure intense heat, poor ventilation, contaminated drinking water, and a limit on bathroom breaks of one per day. As punishment for breaking rules, workers were forced to stand in direct sunlight. Children who work often encounter some of the worst health and safety conditions. Workers in sweatshops are often missing key pieces of safety equipment such as face masks to ensure safe breathing or work in environments with insufficient means of emergency exit since employers may lock the doors and windows to prevent theft during working hours.

Sweatshop employers frequently impose and brutally enforce rigid constraints on their workers. Neil Kearney, the general secretary of the International Textile, Garment and Leather Workers' Federation, explains that in the garment industry workplace management by terror is standard practice. Workers are routinely verbally abused, shoved, beaten, and kicked, even when pregnant. Kearney claims that attempts to unionize are met with the utmost brutality, sometimes with murder. Although illegal, Mexican *maquiladora* factory (operations that assemble imported materials for export) operators require women to take pregnancy tests or prove they are menstruating as a condition of employment, and women thought to be pregnant are not hired. In El Salvador, women who work in manufacturing industries have been required to take company-provided birth control pills daily in the presence of their supervisors.

Finally, forced labor continues to exist in certain countries. A study from the ILO reports that at least 12.3 million workers are trapped in situations involving forced labor around the world. Forced economic exploitation occurs in sectors such as agriculture, construction, brickmaking, and informal apparel and footwear manufacturing and does not seem to discriminate between men and women as does much of traditional apparel and footwear manufacturing, where one finds significantly more women and children involved than men. Forced labor also includes forced commercial sexual exploitation, which involves almost entirely women and girls. In addition, children younger than 18 years make up 40–50 percent of forced laborers.

Next Steps

In the apparel industry in particular, the process of internal and external monitoring has matured such that it has become the norm at least to self-monitor, if not to allow external third-party monitors to assess compliance of a supplier factory with the code of conduct of a multinational corporation or with that of NGOs. Though a number of factors affected this evolution, one such factor involved pressure by American universities on their apparel suppliers, which resulted in two multistakeholder efforts – the Fair Labor Association, primarily comprising and funded by the multinational retailers, and the Worker Rights Consortium, originally perceived as university driven. Through a cooperative effort of these two organizations, large retailers such as Nike and Adidas have not only allowed external monitoring but Nike has now published a complete list of each of its suppliers.

As discussed above, a common response to the criticisms of these types of labor practices is to note that, no matter how well-meaning and accurate the criticisms, there is simply no viable alternative for people in many developing nation labor markets. Free-market or neo-classical economists contend stridently that this is not necessarily the case. They concur that attempts to redress sweatshop conditions must take into account the pressures of globalization and the poor economic conditions of developing nations. But as long as significant global disparities in wages and working conditions exist among nations, labor practices that are unacceptable in one nation may be used in other nations to secure contracts with multinational corporations (the race to the bottom). Second, in the current global regulatory environment, nations are not permitted to impose import bans on sweatshop-based goods since the World Trade Organization's (WTO) current interpretation of its rules declares such practices protectionist.

Multinational corporations such as those discussed above seek to avoid these negative outcomes by embracing the positive consequences to a proactive response to questions regarding global labor practices. Employees who are treated with respect tend to be more loyal and productive workers; consumers in industrialized countries increasingly prefer to purchase goods and services from companies that treat workers with respect; and potential employees increasingly care about the ethical reputations of the companies with whom they take a job, raising the cost of low-reputation companies to hire high-quality employees. These forward-thinking organizations can be categorized as exhibiting "positive deviancy" with respect to their labor practices.

Nike and Adidas represent several examples of positive ethical deviancy among firms that have been subject to previous criticism by the media or NGOs for their treatment of workers. In actuality, intense media scrutiny often forces firms to be creative in their responses to common globalization challenges. For example, after years of sustained criticism of supplier labor practices by NGOs, Nike CEO Philip Knight accepted responsibility in 1998 at the corporate level for the poor treatment of workers by Nike suppliers. Knight explained that, as of the day of his pronouncement, Nike was committed to increasing minimum age requirements for workers in factories, improving factory health and safety conditions so that they comply with US standards, expanding worker education programs, increasing support for microenterprise loan programs, and involving NGOs in the factory monitoring process.

Though these and other multinational corporations – including Dow Chemical, Chiquita, and Levi Strauss & Co. – are often viewed as positive deviants from the current norms among their peers, their efforts have not only garnered attention but will also serve as models for other organizations with regard to the appropriate treatment of their workers and of those of their suppliers, while remaining sustainable from a long-term perspective. There is no *one* solution to sweatshops and other labor challenges posed by contemporary corporate globalization. However, the programs and initiatives that have successfully been implemented by positive ethical deviants can be used as a basis for other multinational corporations to develop their own economically enhancing and ethical labor programs and initiatives that demonstrate respect for the most basic human rights while remaining profitable.

Can Global Brands Create Just Supply Chains?

RICHARD M. LOCKE

When Jia Jingchuan, a 27-year-old electronics worker in Suzhou, China, sought compensation for the chemical poisoning he suffered at work, he appealed neither to his employer nor to his government. Instead, he addressed the global brand that purchased the product he was working on. "We hope Apple will heed to its corporate social responsibility."

In the past, his appeal would probably have fallen on deaf ears. But today, throughout the world, buyers in many industries have acknowledged a degree of responsibility for workplace conditions in supplier factories and pledged to ensure that the goods they eventually market are not made under abusive, dangerous, environmentally degrading, or otherwise unethical conditions. These businesses have committed to using private, voluntary regulation to address labor issues traditionally regulated by government or unions. And for the most part, the companies have acted on these commitments.

But have these private efforts improved labor standards? Not by much. Despite many good faith efforts over the past 15 years, private regulation has had limited impact. Child labor, hazardous working conditions, excessive hours, and poor wages continue to plague many workplaces in the developing world, creating scandal and embarrassment for the global companies that source from these factories and farms.

That is my reluctant conclusion after a decade studying this issue. Before I turned my attention to global labor standards, I was a student of labor and politics in Western Europe and the United States. I came to the idea of private regulation with the hope that it might be a new, suppler way of ensuring workers fair compensation, healthy and safe conditions, and rights of association.

To test that hope, I began studying Nike because I was impressed with its commitment to labor standards. After several years of effort, with many conversations and visits to corporate headquarters, I convinced the company to share its factory audit reports and facilitate visits to its suppliers. Eventually my case study evolved into a full-fledged research project involving the collection, coding, and analysis of thousands of factory audit reports; more than 700 interviews with company managers, factory directors, NGO representatives, and government labor inspectors; and field research in 120 factories in 14 different countries. What began as a study of one company (Nike) in a particular industry (athletic footwear) grew to include several global corporations competing in different industries, with different supply chain dynamics, operating across numerous national boundaries.

But what started in hope ended in disappointment. While I continue to think that companies have a large responsibility for ensuring good labor standards, I also have a renewed appreciation for the older idea that ensuring fair treatment for workers – including real rights of association – is a public responsibility.

Private, Voluntary Regulation

The challenge of improving global labor standards begins with the complexity of today's supply chains.

Consider the production of consumer electronics. Raw materials for electronic components are extracted, often under harsh working conditions, from mines in Asia and Africa. These materials are refined and processed in Asia and then sold to Western and Asian companies that manufacture component parts such as computer chips, batteries, cameras, and circuit boards. These parts are then assembled, primarily in China, in large factory complexes that employ hundreds of thousands of workers. The final products are shipped back to consumer markets that are located principally in developed economies. The shelf life of these devices is relatively short, and the e-waste generated by consumers who dispose of their phones and other portable devices in exchange for newer models is, in turn, shipped back to Asia and Africa.

These new supply chains reflect a shift both in the geography of global manufacturing – from the advanced industrial states to developing countries – and in the organization of production. In the past, most brands relied on manufacturers and suppliers located within their home countries or else were vertically integrated multinational corporations that owned their subsidiaries in foreign markets. Today, lead firms are coordinating the production of thousands of independent suppliers located for the most part in developing countries.

Such changes have had profound implications for labor regulation. For most of the twentieth century, labor standards were regulated largely on a national basis, through a mixture of laws, union–management negotiations, and company policies. Internationally, the conventions and technical services of the International Labour Organization (ILO) provided an additional source of moral authority and advice, though the ILO lacked significant enforcement power. The emergence of global supply chains stretching across national borders, from richer to poorer countries, presented a forceful challenge to this model of regulation.

In many cases, the governments of the developing countries hosting these new factories lacked the institutional capacity to regulate labor, health, safety, and environmental standards. Moreover, they often intentionally overlooked their own laws for fear of driving up costs and thereby repelling foreign investment, jobs, and tax revenues.

In the 1990s, in an initial effort to fill the regulatory void, NGOs and others pushed to include "social clauses" within global trade agreements. These same groups sought to mobilize consumers in developed countries who would in turn pressure developing countries to enforce labor laws. These efforts failed: they were blocked by developing-country governments, which argued that such standards were protectionism with a moral face. Efforts by the ILO and the United Nations to promote core labor standards through the establishment of Decent Work Conventions (2008) and the Global Compact (2000) also had limited impact because they too lacked enforcement powers.

In the absence of an enforceable system of global justice, private, voluntary regulation became the dominant approach, promoted by labor rights NGOs and global corporations alike.

Private, voluntary regulation comes in many forms. The most familiar is a corporate code of conduct. A global brand – Nike, HP, Apple – develops standards for working conditions, wages, hours, and health and safety and requires that its suppliers accept those standards. Private audits are then used to assess factories for compliance with those codes of conduct. In some cases, outside certifiers label products "sweat free" or "fair trade," thus signaling to consumers that the products are made under fair or sustainable conditions.

Heated debates have raged over the specifics of these programs: which standards should be included in codes of conduct; how factory auditors are trained and selected; how information generated from factory audits is shared. Yet regardless of the mission, good will, leadership, organizational design, and even resources underlying private initiatives, they have all produced limited or mixed results.

Consider Nike. A series of public relations nightmares in the 1990s – involving underpaid workers in Indonesia, child labor in Cambodia and Pakistan, and poor working conditions in China and Vietnam – tarnished Nike's image. At first, Nike managers took a defensive position, insisting that they were not the employers of the abused workers. But by 1992 Nike formulated its code of conduct, requiring its suppliers to observe some basic labor standards. After initial efforts fell short, Nike substantially expanded its compliance staff, invested heavily in the training of its own staff and that of its suppliers, developed more rigorous auditing protocols, internalized much of the auditing process, worked with third-party social auditing companies to double check its own internal audits, and spent millions of dollars to improve working conditions at its supplier factories. My research collaborators and I found Nike auditors and compliance staff to be serious, hardworking, and moved by genuine concern for workers and their rights.

Given all that Nike invested in staff, time, and resources, one might expect that conditions at their supplier factories improved significantly. But while some factories appear to have been substantially or fully compliant with Nike's code of conduct, others have suffered from persistent problems with wages, work hours, and employee health and safety.

Such disappointing results are common all over the world, in every industry.

"Capability Building": Promise and Peril

As the shortcomings of the compliance model grew increasingly apparent, analysts and practitioners began to embrace an alternative approach built around the concept of capability building.

The capability-building model starts with the observation that factories throughout the developing world often lack the resources, technical expertise, and management systems necessary to address the root causes of compliance failures. Whereas the compliance model sought to deter violations by policing and penalizing factories, capability building aims to prevent violations by providing the skills, technology, and organizational skills that enable factories to enforce labor standards on their own. By providing suppliers with the technical know-how and management systems required to run more efficient businesses, this approach aims to improve these firms' financial situations, thus allowing them to invest in higher wages and better working conditions. At the same time, to keep these factories running "high-performance" operations, management must also train shop-floor workers to help identify persistent quality problems.

Capability-building programs envision a mutually reinforcing cycle in which more efficient plants invest in their workers, who, in turn, promote improvement throughout the factory, rendering these facilities yet more efficient and thus capable of producing high-quality goods on time and at cost while also respecting corporate codes of conduct.

According to proponents of this model, the "good" factory auditor behaves very much like the "good cop": tough but sensitive to specific situations, using his or her discretion to promote problem solving and rehabilitation rather than focusing on coercion and punishment.

These initiatives represent some of the most innovative practices taking place in the arena of private governance. Yet the capability-building model has also generated very mixed results that raise serious questions about the extent to which it can lead to sustained and broadly diffused improvements of working conditions and labor rights.

Some of the inconsistent results can be explained simply by the way capability-building programs have been implemented. Programs that involve frequent interactions between buyers and suppliers as well as a buyer's commitment to invest in long-term, mutually beneficial relations with suppliers work better than those that entail limited interactions, one-shot training sessions, and no sense among the suppliers of long-term commitment.

But, those differences aside, some of the limitations appear deeply rooted in assumptions of the model itself.

One key assumption is that technical upgrading automatically leads to better working conditions. Perhaps because industrial upgrading can at times lead to skill development, supply chain observers often believe such upgrades also yield better wages and working conditions for factory employees.

Yet there are two fundamental problems with this assumption. First, little empirical evidence suggests that it is true. In their 2010 study of global production networks in India, Anne Posthuma and Dev Nathan found that economic upgrading has not improved conditions for lower-tier workers and may reduce job security.[1]

Second, this assumption overlooks the fact that the enforcement of some labor standards may have little to do with the profitability or technical sophistication of suppliers, but instead hinges on other social and political factors. For instance, standards regarding freedom of association have less to do with suppliers' policies than with workers' political rights. Such standards therefore cannot be enforced effectively one factory at a time, no matter how well managed or technically sophisticated these factories are.

A second assumption of the capability-building model has to do with its simplistic notion of actor interests. Many capability-building initiatives fail to register the divergent (and at times competing) interests of the players involved.

Consider the global brands and buyers. They want high-quality products delivered as quickly and cheaply as possible. They also fear that harsh working conditions could, if discovered, create scandal and hence risk to their reputation. Yet because they are competing with one another, they are unwilling to pay extra for improved working conditions, which could lead to price increases that threaten market share.

Even when individual buyers or brands invest in "supplier responsibility" programs – and many of them do – some of their upstream business practices drive their suppliers into production schemes that undermine these very same corporate responsibility efforts.

Global brands and buyers pressure their suppliers to reduce costs, manufacture on shorter deadlines, and produce a greater variety of products in smaller batches. Suppliers respond to these demands by paying their workers low wages, limiting their benefits, and insisting on excessive work hours.

Workers and developing country governments also express contradictory interests. Governments have an interest in asserting their sovereignty and protecting the rights and welfare of their citizens. But even those with the institutional capacities to enforce their own laws often refuse to do so, or they grant manufacturers regulatory exemptions in order to create more hospitable business environments. And workers, preferring factory jobs to whatever work was available in their home villages, are often willing to toil long hours under stressful conditions. At the same time, they want to be treated fairly, to be paid for their overtime, and to avoid situations that threaten their safety and health.

The capability-building models assume a win-win scenario in which improvements in some part of the supply chain – say, increased efficiencies at supplier factories – will translate into gains for all actors involved. But these gains rarely are evenly distributed; they often accumulate to the most powerful link in a particular supply chain.

A third assumption of many capability-building programs is that management techniques produce consistent outcomes regardless of the local context. This ignores how initiatives are shaped by social, historical, and cultural legacies.

These assumptions have led in many cases to an overly technocratic approach to capability building, with poor results. Investments in production, work organization, and management can translate into some improvements in working conditions. But, as HP's Focused Improvement Supplier Initiative illustrates, when suppliers were not convinced that investments in capability building will deliver concrete economic gains, their commitment was limited. Some suppliers involved in the Initiative could not even recall the content of their training workshops. Vietnamese suppliers who took part in the ILO's Factory Improvement Program cherry picked components of the trainings they were interested in (productivity and quality) and ignored the rest (workplace relations).

A Tale of Two Factories

If there is a role for capability-building programs in improving labor conditions in global supply chains, clarifying how their costs and gains are distributed among workers, suppliers, and brands is key. We must also ask whose capabilities – and which ones – are most in need of development.

The story of two Mexican Nike suppliers is instructive. The two factories – which, owing to nondisclosure agreements, cannot be named – have many similarities. Both operate in the same political and economic environment and are subject to the same labor regulations; both make apparel; both produce more or less the same products for Nike and other brands; both are subject to the same code of conduct; both interface with the same Nike office in Mexico City, which is responsible for coordinating orders and compliance visits to the factories; and both employ unionized labor.

The two factories received comparable scores when audited by Nike's compliance staff. However, they pursued very different approaches under Nike's capability-building plan. One factory, let's call it Plant A, empowered shop-floor workers by giving them voice. The other, Plant B, aimed to reduce worker voice and discretion. At Plant A, management invested in training and allowed employees to work in autonomous cells. These workers often took initiative to solve production-related problems. "We want people here to feel important," factory owners reported during our interviews. In contrast, at Plant B, workers were seen as an "input" to be controlled, a "cost" to be reduced. When we asked the head of operations at Plant B what would happen if he could not continue to lower labor costs in the factory, he replied, "In that case we will move back to Asia."

At Plant A, relations between management and Nike's local staff were collaborative and open. Nike managers would visit Plant A about once a month, and the owners of Plant A were frequently spotted in Nike's regional office. Nike staff and plant managers went out for dinner and played golf together. Whenever an issue related to workplace standards arose, Nike compliance specialists and Plant A management worked together to quickly remediate it.

Nike production and quality managers also were instrumental in supporting Plant A in its shift to lean manufacturing, a system of production that enhances productivity and quality by reorganizing the flow of work, reducing inventory and waste, and promoting worker skill and voice. Nike not only provided information and technical advice but also moral support in the form of an implicit agreement to continue sourcing from the plant as it struggled through its transition. In interviews, managers at Plant A indicated that they saw Nike as a partner with whom they could collaborate to improve both productivity and working conditions.

The relationship between Nike's regional office and Plant B management was more formal and distant. Plant B received fewer visits to its facilities (which were farther from Mexico City) and thus much of the communication between the local Nike office and Plant B occurred over the phone or through email. Management at Plant B saw Nike as a buyer whose requirements and deadlines it needed to respect in order to receive future orders. Nike's local staff, in turn, viewed Plant B as a technically excellent manufacturer whose commitment to labor standards was weak.

Conditions for workers varied significantly. At Plant A, workers averaged higher wages than at Plant B, reported a greater sense of participation in decisions affecting production goals, and described their work experience as more collaborative. And at Plant A, overtime was voluntary.

In their study of supplier–buyer relations in China, Stephen Frenkel and Duncan Scott found that brands develop two distinct types of compliance relationships with their suppliers: a hands-on, cooperative relationship or a less trusting, arm's-length "compliance" relationship.[2]

The arm's-length relationship between Plant B and Nike is the more common variety. Brands and suppliers in compliance relationships are often locked in a low-trust trap in which suppliers claim that brands are sending them mixed messages, insisting on shorter deadlines, better quality, and lower prices while at the same time policing and admonishing them for poor working conditions. Brands, in turn, argue that problems associated with both production and labor standards are the result of their suppliers' shortsightedness and lack of professionalism.

The experience at Plant A shows a way out of this trap. Plant A's model promises benefits for everyone involved, including workers. But sustaining the model, let alone diffusing it, is a challenge. And that challenge has as much to do with the business practices of global buyers and large retailers as with supply chain dynamics. Until these broader practices are reformed, Plant A will remain the exception rather than the rule.

Retailer and Consumer Pressure

Focusing interventions on the suppliers' factories ostensibly makes sense: this is where most labor standards violations occur. But many of those violations are in large part the result of policies and practices designed and implemented upstream by large retailers and global buyers. For example, an internal Nike report states:

> One of the biggest root causes of excessive overtime in apparel manufacturing is the large number of styles factories produce. Every time a factory has to change a style, it reduces productivity and overall efficiency, adding to the total number of hours of work requested. Our analysis shows that, among the variables we have direct control over, asking factories to manufacture too many styles is one of the highest contributors to factory overtime in apparel.[3]

Indeed, my colleagues and I often heard plant managers lament that several of their labor problems, especially excessive working hours and mandatory overtime, were due to late or changed orders from Nike.

This is not just a Nike problem. After years of analyzing audit reports, visiting factories, and interviewing hundreds of company managers, NGO leaders, local officials, and union leaders throughout the world, I have come to understand that poor working conditions and weak labor standards are not only – or even primarily – the result of misguided managerial practices and behavior in the plants. Rather, they stem from global buyers' responses to dynamic market conditions.

The consumer electronics industry perhaps best illustrates the problem. These days, electronics brands primarily serve individual consumers rather than governments or institutional users, and keeping consumers interested is especially tough. Brands feel forced to constantly create new gadgets that will attract buyers, and the result has been dramatically shortened product life cycles.

In order to maximize market share over such short life cycles, large retailers engage in constant promotions that rapidly erode selling prices. Price erosion, along with pressure to carry a broad product assortment, means that retailers do not like to carry large inventories. Instead, they opt for more frequent shipments, often by air cargo, to meet consumer demand. This reduces costly inventory and keeps their shelves well stocked with successful, high-selling products.

At the same time, however, this practice puts an enormous strain on contract manufacturers to deliver smaller, more customized batches of products as quickly and cheaply as possible. This balancing act is complicated by the concentration of electronics retail channels that has occurred in recent years. The top four US consumer electronics and computer retailers control close to 75 percent of their respective markets. Concentrated buying power allows retailers to maintain margins, thus forcing price drops on the brands. Retailers also seek to differentiate their own products from their competitors' in order to prevent consumers from shopping around for lower prices, a process facilitated by the Internet. Again, the pressure falls on suppliers and workers.

Public–Private Partnerships That Work

The limitations of private initiatives will come as no surprise to critics of voluntary regulation. Critics of private compliance and technocratic capability-building initiatives have long argued that they are designed not to protect labor rights or improve working conditions but rather to limit the liability of global brands and prevent damage to their reputations.

Some of these critics contend that private, voluntary regulation is not simply ineffective and self-serving but also pernicious, displacing and undermining more thorough government regulation. Former US Secretary of Labor Robert Reich nicely summarizes this line of argument:

> A declaration of corporate commitment to social virtue may ... forestall government legislation or regulation in an area of public concern where one or more companies have behaved badly, such as transporting oil carelessly and causing a major oil spill or flagrantly failing to respect human rights abroad. The soothing promise of responsibility can deflect public attention from the need for stricter laws and regulations or convince the public that there's no problem to begin with.[4]

Improving global working conditions requires government action, since only the state has the authority and legitimacy to enforce labor legislation and to promote and protect citizens' rights. Thus, even as manufacturing stretches across national borders, the fate of workers remains tied to their home countries' institutions.

But private, voluntary regulatory efforts do not necessarily crowd out or undermine state enforcement of labor laws and employment standards. Under certain circumstances, private projects can complement and even enhance government enforcement. For instance, Nike's private compliance program works best in countries with more developed labor inspection schemes and strong rule of law.

Other researchers working on both labor and environmental standards have found similar results. According to David Graham and Ngaire Woods, governments in developed and developing countries can enhance the effectiveness of corporate self-regulation by insisting upon – and perhaps even legislating – greater transparency and accountability among global buyers and their suppliers.[5] Those governments can demand that the rights of workers to organize and mobilize be protected. Only in these circumstances can the promise of private, voluntary regulation be fulfilled.

Earlier I suggested that national governments, especially in developing countries, have declined to regulate labor standards as a consequence of competition for investment. However, recent research shows that national governments – even in poor countries with few natural resources – have far more ability to impose their will on foreign investors than was previously believed. Where buyers and suppliers

have incentives to circumvent regulations that increase their costs, national governments are best positioned to prevent defections by individual firms and ensure that all producers within the same national or regional economy adhere to common standards. Yet how does one promote this type of government intervention in a world of global supply chains?

In explaining the features of what they call "experimentalist governance," Charles Sabel and Jonathan Zeitlin describe a process in which government agencies collaborate with the private companies they regulate in order to develop broad goals and metrics.[6] These goals and metrics are then used to promote responsiveness to variation in local circumstances, learning and diffusion of best practices across private and public actors, and ever-increasing compliance with government regulations. Using this framework, European governments have been able to foster enhanced environmental standards both within the European Union and among developing countries supplying forestry products to Europe.

Aseem Prakash and Matthew Potoski describe a similar process within the United States, in which innovative state-level policies, such as lenient penalties in exchange for transparency and self-disclosure, have encouraged private firms to enhance their compliance with environmental regulations.[7] These sorts of innovations are not limited to the United States and Europe but have also emerged in several developing countries, including Argentina, Brazil, Cambodia, and India.

In each of these cases, national governments were able to promote labor and environmental standards by reconciling the competing interests of, and resolving the collective action problems among, offending private firms. This process involved not traditional command-and-control government regulation (deterrence) but rather a mix of carrots (capability building and technical assistance programs) and sticks (threatening sanctions and closing off "low road" options).

We need more analysis of innovative public regulation, but we already know that laws and government institutions are critical to the success of private initiatives seeking to improve labor conditions in global supply chains.

Notes

1. A. Posthuma and D. Nathan, *Labour in Global Production Networks* (Oxford University Press, 2010).
2. Stephen Frenkel and Duncan Scott, "Compliance, Collaboration, and Codes of Labor Practice: The Adidas Connection," *California Management Review* 45 (2002): 29–49.
3. Nike Inc., *Corporate Responsibility Report* (Beaverton, OR: Nike, 2010).

4. Robert Reich, *Supercapitalism* (New York: Alfred A. Knopf, 2007), p. 170.
5. David Graham and Ngaire Woods, "Making Corporate Self-Regulation Effective in Developing Countries," *World Development* 34 (2006): 868–83.
6. Charles F. Sabel and Jonathan Zeitlin, "Experimentalist Governance," in *The Oxford Handbook of Governance*, ed. David Levi-Faur (Oxford University Press, 2012), pp. 169–84.
7. Aseem Prakash and Matthew Potoski, *The Voluntary Environmentalists* (Cambridge University Press, 2006).

Corruption and the Multinational Corporation

DAVID HESS

In a recent address, Pope Francis stated that corruption "ends up being paid for by the poor." His quote reflects the realization that corruption is not a victimless crime, but that corruption is a significant impediment to the realization of human rights in developing countries. This realization has helped create a global anti-corruption norm,[1] and has created a sea change in the treatment of corruption in international business over the last 20 years.

Corruption refers to the abuse of a position of trust or responsibility (such as that held by a public official) for purposes of private gain.[2] In this essay, the primary focus is on corruption in the form of bribery – the payment of something of value by a business to a person in a position of trust or responsibility in return for an abuse of that position that results in benefits to the business. By participating in such corrupt transactions, especially in developing countries, corporations are not simply following local business practices, but are contributing to a system that leads to systematic human rights abuses.

This essay provides an overview of the harms of corruption, and the role of corporations to combat corruption in their operations. The first part below sets out the relationships between corruption and recent developments in the area of business and human rights. The next part outlines the efforts to criminalize bribery in international business throughout the world. This essay then presents the "business case" for corporations to fight corruption. Then, the essay discusses the guidance available to help corporations prevent the use of corrupt payments by their employees and agents. The next part describes the efforts of corporations to use collective action strategies to reduce the level of corruption in the institutional environment surrounding their operations.

Business, Human Rights, and Corruption

In recent years there has been a dramatic increase in the efforts to provide guidance to businesses on their responsibilities to respect human rights in their operations around the world. Currently, there are two primary international soft law initiatives that shape corporations' responsibilities towards human rights – the United Nations *Guiding Principles on Business and Human Rights* and the United Nations *Global Compact*. This section provides a brief overview of those initiatives and discusses the impact of corruption on those initiatives.

The leading framework for understanding businesses' obligations towards human rights is the 2011 United Nations *Guiding Principles on Business and Human Rights* (UNGPs). The UNGPs provide guidance to corporations on operationalizing the 2008 United Nations' "Protect, Respect and Remedy Framework for Business and Human Rights." The United Nations' three pillar approach sets out the responsibilities of government and business. Under the first pillar, the primary duty for protecting human rights rests with the state. Under the second pillar, business has a responsibility to "respect" human rights, which means corporations should "avoid infringing on the human rights of others and should address adverse human rights impacts with which they are involved." To meet these responsibilities, corporations should conduct a risk management process referred to in the UNGPs as "due diligence." This involves a corporation assessing any current or potential negative human rights impacts related to their operations, taking efforts to prevent or mitigate any negative impacts, continued monitoring of the situation, and reporting on those efforts and outcomes. Under the third pillar, both the state and business have an obligation to provide human rights abuse victims with access to remedies, including both judicial and non-judicial remedies.

The UN Global Compact (UNGC) – which predates the UNGPs – was the first major attempt to create a universal framework for business and human rights and was officially launched in 2000. In its initial version, the UNGC established nine general principles to guide business conduct. These principles were divided into the areas of human rights, labor rights, and the environment. In 2004, after the adoption of the UN Convention against Corruption in the prior year, the UNGC added a tenth principle on combating corruption. The tenth principle states, "Businesses should work against corruption in all its forms, including extortion and bribery."

Corruption should be considered part of the business and human rights movement. First, corruption is a significant impediment to the realization of human rights recognized under the Universal Declaration of Human Rights (UDHR), the International Covenant on Economic, Social, and Cultural Rights (ICESCR), and the International Covenant on Civil and Political Rights (ICCPR). International law scholar James Gathii makes the point this way:

> Corruption affects human rights in a variety of ways. For example, the rights to food, water, education, health, and the ability to seek justice can be violated if a bribe is required to gain access to these basic rights. Corruption by high-level government officials can siphon millions of dollars of the country's wealth, which in turn handicaps the government from fulfilling its duty to protect, ensure, and respect the rights guaranteed to its people.[3]

Second, corruption impacts the ability of corporations to successfully implement social initiatives designed to improve a corporation's performance on the UNGC's other nine principles, or to respect human rights under the UNGPs. As one commentator stated, "If ending corruption is not treated as a prerequisite to all corporate [CSR] efforts, CSR practitioners will continue to work upon a foundation of quicksand."[4]

The recent Rana Plaza tragedy illustrates both of these concerns. Rana Plaza was a building that housed garment factories in Bangladesh. In April 2013, the building collapsed and caused the death of over 1,100 workers and severe injuries to 2,500 additional workers. Subsequent reports showed that the building was several stories higher than allowed by the building code, was made with substandard materials, and was designed for retail space not factories.[5]

Corruption allows factories such as Rana Plaza to violate building codes and remain open when they should have failed building inspections.[6]

To avoid another Rana Plaza tragedy, or any other human rights violation, corporations rely heavily on audits of garment factories. The audits are intended to identify safety violations in the factories and other violations of corporations' human rights policies. Unfortunately, in countries with high levels of corruption, there are reports of bribery impacting the quality of the audits. For example, a bribe payment – suggested by either the auditor or the factory manager – may cause the auditor to fail to report a deficiency at the factory.[7] Likewise, the factory may hire "consultants" to help them receive a passing grade from the auditor, which allows the factory to be one-step removed from any corrupt transaction that prevents corrective action.

International Efforts to Criminalize Bribery

Although the Foreign Corrupt Practices Act (FCPA) in the United States has criminalized any business person's payment of bribes to foreign government officials since 1977, for over two decades the law was rarely enforced and had little impact. In addition, in that time period, other countries did not adopt similar legislation. In fact, many countries allowed bribe payments to foreign officials to be deducted as a business expense on their tax filings. In short, corruption was viewed as an internal governance matter for that country, and there were no home country consequences for a corporation that paid a bribe.

This began to change in the mid-1990s as policymakers gained a better understanding of the impact of corruption on poverty and economic development. One major development occurred in 1997 when the OECD adopted the *Convention on Combating Bribery of Foreign Public Officials*. This convention required signatory countries to criminalize the payment of bribes to public officials and to prohibit practices that allow the concealment of bribe payments (e.g., off-the-books accounts). Then, in 2003, the global anti-corruption norm fully developed with the adoption of the United Nations *Convention against Corruption*. The United Nations convention is far-reaching and requires states to take action to prevent corruption in the public sector and the private sector, and to criminalize corruption if it does occur. Since the convention, many countries – including Brazil, China, India, and the United Kingdom – have adopted new anti-bribery laws.

Since the adoption of these conventions, there have been several high-profile investigations and prosecutions of corporations for corruption. In 2006, the largest engineering company based in Europe, Siemens AG, pled guilty to violating anti-bribery laws and paid $1.6 billion in fines to the US and German governments.[8] Over many years, Siemens paid bribes in multiple countries and utilized secret bank accounts to reduce the risks of getting caught. One manager stated that he oversaw an annual bribery budget of $40 to $50 million for several years, and bribe payments were referred to as "NA," which was an abbreviation of a German phrase for "useful money."[9] The company did not always directly pay the bribes, but paid fees to consultants knowing that the consultants would bribe government officials. Overall, the company made approximately $1.4 billion in bribe payments between 2001 and 2007. Although this culture of corruption at the company began before Germany adopted laws prohibiting the payment of bribes to foreign government officials, Siemens continued to pay bribes after the change in the law because, as one manager stated, employees believed they had to pay them or else "we'd ruin the company."[10]

In a matter that began as an FCPA investigation in 2012 and still has not been resolved at the time of this writing, Walmart was accused of paying bribes in Mexico.[11] Walmart was alleged to have paid bribes to Mexican officials to gain priority access to government services, to build stores without the appropriate licenses or impact assessments, and to obtain building permits on land that had been designated as a sensitive archeological zone due to its proximity to Mayan pyramids.[12] Furthermore, it was alleged that Walmart officials in the United States became aware of the wrongful payments, but failed to take corrective action.[13] According to the *New York Times* journalists that investigated the story:

> Wal-Mart de Mexico was not the reluctant victim of a corrupt culture that insisted on bribes as the cost of doing business. Nor did it pay bribes merely to speed up routine approvals. Rather, Wal-Mart de Mexico was an aggressive and creative corrupter, offering large payoffs to get what the law otherwise prohibited. It used bribes to subvert democratic governance – public votes, open debates, transparent procedures. It used bribes to circumvent regulatory safeguards that protect Mexican citizens from unsafe construction. It used bribes to outflank rivals.[14]

Although the case has not yet been settled Walmart has spent over $800 million on internal investigations and compliance program improvements between 2012 and 2016.[15]

These, and many other prosecutions, have focused corporations on the need to prevent bribe payments. The criminal law has given corporations a strong incentive to fight corruption, but, as outlined in the next section, there is also a business case for combating corruption.

The Business Case for Combating Corruption

In addition to the ethical concerns over the negative impact of corruption on society (including the realization of human rights) and the legal obligation to avoid the use of corrupt payments, there is also the business case for combating corruption. Due to the business case, more investors are incorporating anti-corruption matters into their initiatives and interactions with companies. For example, equity indexes focused on sustainability, such as the FTSE4Good and the Dow Jones Sustainability Index (DJSI), include a corporation's handling of corruption matters (e.g., company policies and reported incidents) in their inclusion criteria. One investor group, the International Corporate Governance Network (ICGN), listed the following reasons why investors should care about anti-corruption:[16]

- "At a macroeconomic level, corruption greatly reduces efficiency by distorting competition and depriving buyers of economically superior products at the most competitive prices."
- "Corruption destabilises the political process and promotes conflict," which "raises the cost of doing business and deters investment."
- For companies that have been disadvantaged by competitors paying bribes, "this directly reduces returns, even in some cases threatening commercial survival."
- For companies that pay bribes, they can suffer legal fines, damage to reputation, debarment, imprisonment for executives, and other penalties.
- "Companies with a reputation for weak anti-corruption controls, or which are found to have 'skeletons in the closet' during pre-merger due diligence, can find that deals are re-priced or even called off."
- "[A] corporate culture that tolerates corrupt payments is also one that is much more likely to tolerate, or fail to prevent, financial fraud, theft of company assets and other actions that will directly harm shareholders."

Further explaining the business case, another investment management company stated:

> By diverting capital away from its "highest and best uses" towards those that offer the richest illicit rewards, corruption not only distorts competition, but breeds corporate cultures that promote circumvention of the law, undermines the rule of law and creates the conditions for companies to mistreat shareholders just as they do other business partners. This is plainly not in the interests of long-term investors and their clients.[17]

Combating Corruption and Corporate Social Responsibility

The emergence of a global anti-corruption norm has also spread to many corporate social responsibility (CSR) initiatives. Combating corruption is not simply a legal requirement, but a social responsibility of corporations. Corporations are a crucial actor in the fight against corruption in international business. They have the ability to determine where their employees or agents are at the greatest risk of paying bribes. The corporations must then take action to prevent corrupt payments, which requires them to adopt effective compliance and ethics programs (and to continually improve those programs), implement appropriate internal controls, review employee incentive plans (e.g., an employee should not be punished for losing a contract due to a refusal to make a wrongful payment), and manage its ethical corporate culture as it relates to these issues.

A corporation cannot fight the supply side of corruption alone. Corporations need assurances that their competitors are also taking appropriate action, and not simply adopting "paper" compliance programs.[18] A corporation will have a difficult time maintaining its commitment to combating corruption if it believes it is losing business to competitors that are paying bribes. It is a collective action problem; all corporations must refuse to pay bribes. Thus, CSR initiatives should work to help corporations implement best practices to prevent the use of wrongful payments by its employees or agents, and to help ensure that all corporations in that industry or geographic location are equally committed to combating corruption.

This part will consider how anti-corruption is treated under two major corporate social responsibility initiatives – the UN Global Compact and the Global Reporting Initiative (GRI). As stated above, shortly after the UN Convention against Corruption, the UN Global Compact was amended to include its tenth principle against corruption. Likewise, the GRI – the leading standards for sustainability reporting by organizations – did not include bribery in its initial set of guidelines in the 1990s, but included the issue in subsequent versions.[19]

In connection with Transparency International, the UN Global Compact published the report *Business against Corruption: A Framework for Action* in 2011. To combat corruption, the report recommended that companies follow the six steps in its management model:

1. Commit
   a. Company leadership must communicate a clear policy of zero tolerance of bribery to all employees. In addition, leadership must demonstrate a commitment to this policy by adopting and implementing anti-corruption practices, and avoiding any exceptions to the policy, or leaving codes of conduct up to interpretation based on the local business environment.
2. Assess
   a. Companies should assess its operations for the areas with the greatest risks of corruption. The company should also regularly re-assess those risks to determine if company policies are successful, or if circumstances have changed.
3. Define
   a. The company should define its goals and select indicators to help determine if it has reached its goals. This step also involves developing strategies and policies to achieve its goals, including compliance and ethics programs. The company's goals should include not just its own employees, but also ensuring that the company's business partners are aware of, and comply with, the company's expectations.
4. Implement
   a. Codes of conduct and ethics and compliance programs must be integrated into the company's other management systems. This may include actions such as adapting human resources policies, developing new training programs, and setting up mechanisms for employees to report wrongdoing.
5. Measure
   a. The company must monitor its progress and collect data on the indicators it selected.
6. Communicate
   a. The company should communicate its efforts and performance to interested stakeholders. The Global Reporting Initiative, described below, is one way to communicate with stakeholders.

More detail, especially on steps one though five, can be found in guidance on corporate compliance and ethics programs, especially programs designed especially for anti-bribery. One such guide is Transparency International's *Business Principles for Countering Bribery* (originally published in 2003, and revised in 2013). The *Business Principles* provide implementation guidance on steps similar to the six listed above. Importantly, the *Business Principles* encourage corporations to adopt policies and procedures to cover all aspects of the risks of making corrupt payments, including conflicts of interest, bribes, political contributions, charitable contributions, facilitation payments, and gifts, hospitality, and expenses. Charitable contributions are included because

Table 9.1 GRI Corruption Reporting Guidelines

(1) The company's "management approach." This is narrative description of the policies and procedures the company uses to manage issues related to corruption, including its policies and practices on:

    a. Risk assessments for different regions and activities.

    b. Conflicts of interests for employees and business partners.

    c. Ensuring that charitable donations are not used for corrupt purposes.

    d. Communications and trainings for employees, business partners, and other relevant person that may create a risk of corrupt payments for the company.

    e. The company's participation in collective action initiatives (e.g., multi-stakeholder initiatives) on combating corruption.

(2) The corporation's operations that were assessed for risks related to corruption, and any significant risks that the corporation identified.

(3) Any confirmed incidents of corruption that the corporation identified, and the actions the corporation took in response (e.g., employees dismissed or disciplined, cancellation of contracts with business partners).

(4) Any legal cases brought against the company or its employees for corruption.

---

they are a common way that employees or agents attempt to disguise corrupt payments. For example, in 2004, Schering-Plough Corporation reached a settlement agreement with the Securities Exchange Commission (SEC) on allegations that the company made donations to a Polish charity headed by a government official in exchange for gaining the official's help in securing government purchases of the company's pharmaceutical products.[20] In 2016, Nu Skin reached a settlement agreement with the SEC on allegations that its Chinese subsidiary made a contribution to a charity of a government official's choosing in return for ending a government agency investigation into regulatory violations.[21] Facilitation payments are payments to government officials for the business to obtain a routine service that the official has an existing duty to provide. For example, a government official may wrongfully refuse to issue the business a regulatory permit – even though the business has a legal right to the permit – until the business provides the official with bribe payment. Although such payments are technically legal under the FCPA, many other countries prohibit facilitation payments due to their contribution to a system of corruption.[22] In fact, the vast majority of US corporations' codes of conduct prohibit such payments.[23]

In 2016, the International Organization for Standardization issued *ISO 37001-Anti-Bribery Management Systems*. This standard provides guidance for corporations on adopting, monitoring, and improving the appropriate anti-bribery controls, and, similar to other ISO standards, creates the opportunity for a third party to certify that the company is in compliance with the standard.

The governments in other countries may also provide guidance to their companies. In the United Kingdom, a company accused of paying a bribe through an employee or agent is allowed the defense against liability that it had "adequate procedures" in place to prevent bribery. Thus, the UK government has issued a set of principles – similar to the management model above – on its expectations for appropriate adequate procedures that a company should adopt. In the United States, it is not a defense for a corporation to have adopted a compliance program, but prosecutors consider the effectiveness of such a program when deciding whether or not to file a criminal complaint against the company, or when negotiating a settlement agreement with the company. In 2012, the Department of Justice issued *A Resource Guide to the U.S. Foreign Corrupt Practices Act*, which includes a section on the "Hallmarks of an Effective Compliance Program." The *Guide* also points out that when evaluating a corporation's compliance program, the prosecutors will not have "formulaic requirements," but will use a "common sense" approach that focuses on the following three factors:

- "Is the company's compliance program well designed?
- Is it being applied in good faith?
- Does it work?"[24]

Step 6 in the management model described above requires a corporation to communicate its efforts to interested stakeholders. The Global Reporting Initiative provides guidance on how to structure those communications (Table 9.1). In the current set of GRI standards, corporations are required to report on anti-corruption matters only if the corporation determines that corruption is a "material" issue for it.[25] For example, corruption would be a material issue for a corporation with significant operations in countries with high levels of corruption, or at least, high levels of

Table 9.2 Anti-Bribery Reporting Indicators

"B" designates a "basic" indicator and "D" designates a "desired" indicator.

Commitment & Policy

B1 Publicly stated commitment to work against corruption in all its forms, including bribery and extortion

B2 Commitment to be in compliance with all relevant laws, including anti-corruption laws

D1 Publicly stated formal policy of zero-tolerance of corruption

D2 Statement of support for international and regional legal frameworks, such as the UN Convention against Corruption

D3 Carrying out risk assessment of potential areas of corruption

D4 Detailed policies for high-risk areas of corruption

D5 Policy on anti-corruption regarding business partners

Implementation

B3 Translation of the anti-corruption commitment into actions

B4 Support by the organization's leadership for anti-corruption

B5 Communication and training on the anti-corruption commitment for all employees

B6 Internal checks and balances to ensure consistency with the anti-corruption commitment

D6 Actions taken to encourage business partners to implement anti-corruption commitments

D7 Management responsibility and accountability for implementation of the anti-corruption commitment or policy

D8 Human Resources procedures supporting the anti-corruption commitment or policy

D9 Communications (whistleblowing) channels and follow-up mechanisms for reporting concerns or seeking advice

D10 Internal accounting and auditing procedures related to anti-corruption

D11 Participation in voluntary anti-corruption initiatives

Monitoring

B7 Monitoring and improvement processes

D12 Leadership review of monitoring and improvement results

D13 Dealing with incidents

D14 Public legal cases regarding corruption

D15 Use of independent external assurance of anti-corruption programs

---

corruption in that corporation's industry. For all other companies, disclosure on these matters is voluntary.

In 2009, the UN Global Compact and Transparency International issued *Reporting Guidance on the 10th Principle Against Corruption*. The indicators for anti-bribery that corporations should report against are listed in Table 9.2.

Collective Action

The previous sections focused on corporate actions to ensure that the corporation is not a party to a transaction involving bribe payments. The criminal law provides incentives for corporations to monitor the behavior of its employees and agents, and various CSR initiatives provide guidance for corporations on how to best design and implement anti-bribery management programs. Corporations, however, should go beyond ensuring that they are not a party to a bribe payment, and also work to reduce the level of corruption in the institutional environment surrounding their operations. Such efforts will reduce the demand for bribes

and help ensure that the corporation's competitors are not paying bribes. Thus, many corporations are working with the local government and non-governmental organizations to develop solutions to reduce corruption through collective action. Depending on the circumstances, the collective action measures can focus on bringing transparency to government–business interactions, reducing the opportunities for government officials to demand bribes, reforming legal and regulatory requirements, and helping support integrity initiatives in the government.

As an example, Hess provides a brief description of the Maritime Anti-Corruption Network (MACN), which works to reduce bribes, extortion, and facilitation payments in the shipping industry.

In addition to promoting improved corporate practices to resist corruption (e.g., compliance programs and financial controls), the network also seeks to improve the operating environment where bribes are demanded. MACN "works to raise awareness, report on corruption incidents and trends, and engage in and catalyze collective action by business, government, international organizations, and civil society to drive tangible improvements in the operating environment and promote a culture of integrity." In the operating environment, MACN takes actions designed to improve the capacity of all stakeholders to adopt anti-corruption management programs and adopt organizational cultures of integrity, and to "[s]trengthen governance frameworks and accountability across the maritime sector." The collective action works of MACN begin with "root cause analyses" and then "develop solutions that are both beneficial to all [stakeholders] and realistic to implement." Examples of implemented solutions include new regulations implemented by the local government, new standard operating procedures, and formalized grievance mechanisms.[26]

Another example is the Extractive Industries Transparency Initiative (EITI). Under the EITI, companies in the oil, gas, and mining industries publish information on any payments they make to the local government. The local government is also required to make disclosures on their receipts. This allows outsiders to monitor the payments to ensure that the government is properly using the funds. Although companies may lose some strategic business advantages to competitors and other governments with which they must negotiate, by disclosing their contract terms, this disadvantage is outweighed by the potential to reduce corruption and avoid what is often referred to as the "resource curse" (where a country with significant natural resources ends up with low economic growth and high levels of poverty due to corruption in government).

In recent years there has been a dramatic shift in the fight against corruption and the emergence of what some commentators refer to as a global anti-corruption norm. Corporations are actively involved in reducing the supply side of corruption by adopting compliance programs and internal controls, but they are also working to help reduce the demand side of corruption through collective action strategies.

Notes

1. E. Spahn, "Implementing Global Anti-Bribery Norms: From the Foreign Corrupt Practices Act to the OECD Anti-Bribery Convention to the U.N. Convention against Corruption," *Indiana International & Comparative Law Review* 23 (2013): 1–33.

2. P. M. Nichols, "The Business Case for Complying with Bribery Laws," *American Business Law Journal* 49 (2012): 325–68.

3. J. T. Gathii, "Defining the Relationship between Human Rights and Corruption," *University of Pennsylavania International Law Journal* 31 (2009): 125–201 (p. 126).

4. M. A. Arafa, "Battling Corruption within a Corporate Social Responsibility Strategy," *Indiana International & Comparative Law Review* 21 (2011): 397–420 (p. 408).

5. D. Hess, "Business, Corruption, and Human Rights: Towards a New Responsibility for Corporations to Combat Corruption," *Wisconsin Law Review*, forthcoming.

6. See S. N. Mawla et al., *The Readymade Garment Sector: Governance Problems and Way Forward* (Transparency International Bangladesh, October 31, 2013); J. Chalmers, "How Textile Kings Weave a Hold on Bangladesh," *Reuters* (May 2, 2013).

7. Hess, "Business, Corruption, and Human Rights."

8. C. O'Rielly and K. Matussek, "Siemens to Pay $1.6 Billion to Settle Bribery Cases," *Washington Post* (December 16, 2008).

9. S. Schubert and T. C. Miller, "At Siemens, Bribery Was Just a Line Item," *The New York Times* (December 20, 2008).

10. Ibid.

11. N. Bishara and D. Hess, "Human Rights and a Corporation's Duty to Combat Corruption," in *Law, Business and Human Rights*, ed. R. C. Bird, D. Cahoy, and J. D. Prenkert (Northhampton, MA: Edward Elgar, 2014), pp. 71–93.

12. D. Barstow, "Wal-Mart Hushed up a Vast Mexican Bribery Case," *The New York Times* (April 21, 2012), p. A1; D. Barstow and A. X. V. Bertrab, "The Bribery Aisle: How Wal-Mart Got Its Way in Mexico," *The New York Times* (December 17, 2012), p. A1.

13. A. D. Westbrook, "Does the Buck Stop Here? Board Responsibility for FCPA Compliance," *University of Toledo Law Review* 48 (2017): 493–518.

14. Barstow and Bertrab, "The Bribery Aisle."

15. Westbrook, "Does the Buck Stop Here?"

16. Quoted in D. Hess, "Enhancing the Effectiveness of the Foreign Corrupt Practices Act through Corporate Social Responsibility," *Ohio State Law Journal* 73 (2012): 1121–44 (p. 1128; citations omitted).

17. Quoted in ibid., p. 1129.

18. D. Hess, "Combating Corruption in International Business: The Big Questions," *Ohio Northern Law Review* 41 (2015): 679–96.

19. D. Hess and T. W. Dunfee, "Taking Responsibility for Bribery: The Multinational Corporation's Role in Combating Corruption," in *Business and Human Rights: Dilemmas and Solutions*, ed. R. Sullivan (Sheffield: Greanleaf Publishing, 2003), pp. 260–71.

20. *In the Matter of Schering-Plough Corp.*, SEC Admin. Proc. File No. 3-11517 (June 9, 2004).

21. *In the Matter of Nu Skin Enterprises, Inc.*, SEC Admin. Proc. File No. 3-17556 (September 20, 2016).

22. P. M. Nichols, "Are Facilitation Payments Legal?" *Virginia Journal of International Law* 54 (2013): 127–55.

23. D. Hess, "Catalyzing Corporate Commitment to Combating Corruption: Understanding the Role of the Public Sector in Private Anti-Corruption Initiatives," *Journal of Business Ethics* 88 (2009): 781–90.

24. US Department of Justice and Securities and Exchange Commission, *A Resource Guide to the U.S. Foreign Corrupt Practices Act* (Washington, DC, 2012), p. 56.

25. Global Reporting Initiative, *GRI 205: Anti-Corruption 2016* (Amsterdam: GRI, 2016).

26. Hess, "Business, Corruption, and Human Rights."

LEGAL PERSPECTIVES

Supreme Court of Texas, *Dow Chemical Company and Shell Oil Company v. Domingo Castro Alfaro et al.* (1990)

Domingo Castro Alfaro was employed by Standard Fruit Company. He, along with 81 other Costa Ricans and their wives, brought suit against Dow Chemical Company and Shell Oil Company because these companies had provided Standard Fruit with dibromochloropropane (DBCP), a pesticide that caused Alfaro and his co-plaintiffs severe medical problems including sterility. Defendants argued that the case involving Costa Ricans should not be tried in the United States because of the doctrine of *forum non conveniens.* *Forum non conveniens* is a common-law concept that says that when there is a conflict as to where a case should be tried, the case should be tried in the place where it is most convenient. In the initial trial, the case was dismissed on the *forum non conveniens* principle. The plaintiffs then filed an appeal. The Court of Appeals ruled that the case against Dow Chemical and Shell Oil could not be dismissed on the grounds of *forum non conveniens* and that the trial should be held in Texas. That decision, in turn, was appealed to the Texas Supreme Court.

In a majority decision, the Texas Supreme Court upheld the Court of Appeals. The decision rested on a complex legal argument as to whether a statute, Section 71.031 of the Civil Practice and Remedies Code, effectively outlawed the use of *forum non convenience* in the State of Texas. That section states:

(a) An action for damages for the death or personal injury of a citizen of this state, of the United States, or of a foreign country may be enforced by the courts of this state, although the wrongful act, neglect or default causing the death or injury takes place in a foreign state or country if:

    (1) a law of the foreign state or country or of this state gives a right to maintain an action for damages for the death or injury;

    (2) an action is begun in this state within the time provided by the laws of this state for beginning the action; and

    (3) in the case of a citizen of a foreign country, the country has equal treaty rights with the United States on behalf of its citizens …

The question at law was whether the word "may" in (a) allowed the Court to relinquish jurisdiction under *forum non conveniens.* A majority found that on the basis of an analysis of the law, amendments to the law, and court precedents, an allowance to relinquish jurisdiction was not permitted.

Judge Doggett, one of the concurring judges, was explicitly concerned about some of the ethical issues raised in this case and wrote his own concurring opinion challenging the defenders of *forum non conveniens.* One of the defenses of *forum non conveniens* is based on the notion of "judicial comity." That doctrine gives deference to foreign courts in these matters. However, Judge Doggett points out that actually judicial comity would be shown if *forum non convenience* were outlawed. After all, if the trial were held in Costa Rica the liability for Dow and Shell would be very much reduced. *Forum non conveniens* is often used as a device by transnational companies to avoid being held responsible for their acts and that many developing countries are tired of having products such as DBCP used in their countries when they are banned in developed countries. Judge Doggett put his position this way:

The doctrine of *forum non conveniens* is obsolete in a world in which markets are global and in which ecologists have documented the delicate balance of all life on this planet. The parochial perspective embodied in the doctrine of *forum non conveniens* enables corporations to evade legal control merely because they are transnational. This perspective ignores the reality that actions of our corporations affecting those abroad will also affect Texans. Although DBCP is banned from use within the United States, it and other similarly banned chemicals have been consumed by Texans eating foods imported from Costa Rica and elsewhere.

United States Court of Appeals, Ninth Circuit, *John Doe I, et al. v. Unocal Corp., et al.* (2002)

This case involves a suit on behalf of villagers from the Tenasserim region of Myanmar (formerly Burma) against Unocal for the alleged forced labor, murder, rape, and torture against these villagers committed by the Myanmar military. The suit against Unocal is based on Unocal's knowledge that the Myanmar military was committing these human rights violations as it provided security for a Unocal natural gas project in the region. The grounds for bringing such a suit by foreign nationals in a US court was the Alien Tort Claims Act (ATCA) of 1789.

The Court overturned a district court's grant of Unocal's motion for summary judgment (a summary judgment is a decision of the court for or against one party without having a trial). The ATCA grants aliens (foreign nationals) the right to sue where there are allegations that Americans have violated the "law of nations" or what we now refer to as human rights. The Court maintained that forced labor is a violation of the "law of nations." In examining the allegations that Unocal aided and abetted the Myanmar military the Court said the following: "We hold that the standard for

aiding and abetting under the ATCA is … knowing practical assistance or encouragement that has a substantial effect on the perpetration of a crime. We further contend that a reasonable factfinder could find that Unocal's conduct met this standard." Allegations of Unocal's aiding and abetting were provided by witness accounts, including accounts by the plaintiffs that they were forced to clear the right of way for the pipeline and to build helipads before construction for the project began. Others contended that they were "pipeline porters" who performed menial tasks such as hauling materials and cleaning the army camps for soldiers guarding the pipeline. The Court also concluded that there was evidence that Unocal provided practical assistance in the form of money or food to provide security as well as providing photos, surveys, and maps as aids to the military. The Court concluded: "Unocal knew or should reasonably have known that its conduct – including the payments and instructions where to provide security and build infrastructure – would assist or encourage the Myanmar Military to subject Plaintiffs to forced labor."

United States Supreme Court, *Kiobel v. Royal Dutch Petroleum Co.* (2013)

The petitioners in this case were a group of Nigerian nationals living in the United States who had been admitted as refugees and are now permanent residents. Previously they had resided in Ogoniland, Nigeria, an area where Royal Dutch Petroleum had drilling facilities. Royal Dutch Petroleum's drilling activities were extremely controversial. Among other Ogoni complaints was the significant environmental damage the drilling activities caused. The petitioners alleged that Royal Dutch Petroleum enlisted the Nigerian government to protect its facilities. In doing so the Nigerian military and police forces had attacked Ogoni villages, beating, raping, arresting, and sometimes killing residents as well as looting and destroying property. The petitioners alleged that Royal Dutch Petroleum had aided and abetted these atrocities by providing food, transportation, and compensation as well as allowing the Nigerian military to use company property as a base for their attacks. The petitioners brought suit under the Alien Tort Statute (ATS) enacted in 1789. That Act allowed aliens, persons from countries other than

the United States, to file civil suits in US district courts when torts committed in violation of the law of nations* had been committed. In the initial filing, Royal Dutch Shell was charged with seven violations of the law of nations. Four of the seven charges were dismissed on the grounds that the facts were not sufficient to sustain a violation of the law of nations.

The Second Circuit dismissed the entire case on the basis that the law of nations does not recognize corporate liability. Initially the Supreme Court was to address that question alone, but later it widened the scope of the case to "Whether and under what circumstances the ATS allows courts to recognize a cause of action occurring within a sovereign other than the United States." The Court did not question whether the plaintiffs had a proper claim under ATS but whether the reach of ATS extended to an action in a sovereign foreign country (whether ATS applied extraterritorially).

The Court raised the following considerations against extraterritoriality. (1) There is a recognized presumption against extraterritoriality because the courts are reluctant to interfere when our laws would be in conflict with the laws of other countries or when extraterritoriality would undercut the foreign policy of the United States; (2) that ATS was never intended to have extraterritorial reach, that one of the chief reasons for its being was to address piracy on the high seas. The Court then concluded in a unanimous decision as follows:

> On these facts all the relevant conduct took place outside the United States. And even where the claims touch and concern the territory of the United States they must do so with sufficient force to replace the presumption against extraterritorial application … Corporations are often present in many countries and it would reach too far to say that mere corporate presence suffices. If Congress were to determine

otherwise, a statute more specific than ATS would be required.

It should be pointed out that although all nine judges accepted the decision, four judges rejected the reasoning. Justice Breyer did not appeal to the presumption against extraterritoriality, but rather that "the parties and relevant conduct lacked sufficient ties to the United States for the ATS to provide jurisdiction."

As a result of this decision the attempt to use ATS to sue corporations for violations of international norms or the law of nations appears to have come to an end.

* Duhaime's *Law Dictionary* defines the "law of nations" as "the body of rules that nations in the international community universally abide by, or accede to, out of a sense of legal obligation and mutual concern."

The United Nations, *Global Compact*

The Global Compact's ten principles in the areas of human rights, labor, the environment, and anti-corruption enjoy universal consensus and are derived from:

The Universal Declaration of Human Rights
The International Labour Organization's Declaration on Fundamental Principles and Rights at Work
The Rio Declaration on Environment and Development
The United Nations Convention against Corruption

The Global Compact asks companies to embrace, support, and enact, within their sphere of influence, a set of core values in the areas of human rights, labor standards, the environment, and anti-corruption:

Human Rights

Principle 1: Businesses should support and respect the protection of internationally proclaimed human rights; and
Principle 2: make sure that they are not complicit in human rights abuses.

Labor Standards

Principle 3: Businesses should uphold the freedom of association and the effective recognition of the right to collective bargaining;

Principle 4: the elimination of all forms of forced and compulsory labor;
Principle 5: the effective abolition of child labor; and
Principle 6: the elimination of discrimination in respect of employment and occupation.

Environment

Principle 7: Businesses should support a precautionary approach to environmental challenges;
Principle 8: undertake initiatives to promote greater environmental responsibility; and
Principle 9: encourage the development and diffusion of environmentally friendly technologies.

Anti-Corruption

Principle 10: Businesses should work against all forms of corruption, including extortion and bribery.

Sources: University of Minnesota Human Rights Library, www1.umn.edu/humanrts/links/NormsApril2003.html (retrieved May 20, 2007).

United Nations, www.unglobalcompact.org/AboutThe GC/TheTenPrinciples/index.html (retrieved May 20, 2007).

The United Nations, *Protect, Respect and Remedy Framework for Business and Human Rights*

I. The State Duty to Protect Human Rights

A. Foundational Principles

1. States must protect against human rights abuse within their territory and/or jurisdiction by third parties, including business enterprises. This requires taking appropriate steps to prevent, investigate, punish and redress such abuse through effective policies, legislation, regulations and adjudication.

2. States should set out clearly the expectation that all business enterprises domiciled in their territory and/or jurisdiction respect human rights throughout their operations.

B. Operational Principles

General State Regulatory and Policy Functions

3. In meeting their duty to protect, States should:
   (a) Enforce laws that are aimed at, or have the effect of, requiring business enterprises to respect human rights, and periodically to assess the adequacy of such laws and address any gaps;
   (b) Ensure that other laws and policies governing the creation and ongoing operation of business enterprises, such as corporate law, do not constrain but enable business respect for human rights;
   (c) Provide effective guidance to business enterprises on how to respect human rights throughout their operations;
   (d) Encourage, and where appropriate require, business enterprises to communicate how they address their human rights impacts.

The State–Business Nexus

4. States should take additional steps to protect against human rights abuses by business enterprises that are owned or controlled by the State, or that receive substantial support and services from State agencies such as export credit agencies and official investment insurance or guarantee agencies, including, where appropriate, by requiring human rights due diligence.

5. States should exercise adequate oversight in order to meet their international human rights obligations when they contract with, or legislate for, business enterprises to provide services that may impact upon the enjoyment of human rights.

6. States should promote respect for human rights by business enterprises with which they conduct commercial transactions.

Supporting Business Respect for Human Rights in Conflict-Affected Areas

7. Because the risk of gross human rights abuses is heightened in conflict-affected areas, States should help ensure that business enterprises operating in those contexts are not involved with such abuses, including by:
   (a) Engaging at the earliest stage possible with business enterprises to help them identify, prevent and mitigate the human rights-related risks of their activities and business relationships;
   (b) Providing adequate assistance to business enterprises to assess and address the heightened risks of abuses, paying special attention to both gender-based and sexual violence;
   (c) Denying access to public support and services for a business enterprise that is involved with gross human rights abuses and refuses to cooperate in addressing the situation;
   (d) Ensuring that their current policies, legislation, regulations and enforcement measures are effective in addressing the risk of business involvement in gross human rights abuses.

Ensuring Policy Coherence

8. States should ensure that governmental departments, agencies and other State-based institutions that shape business practices are aware of and observe the State's human rights obligations when fulfilling their respective mandates, including by providing them with relevant information, training and support.

9. States should maintain adequate domestic policy space to meet their human rights obligations when pursuing business-related policy objectives with other States or

business enterprises, for instance through investment treaties or contracts.

10. States, when acting as members of multilateral institutions that deal with business-related issues, should:

    (a) Seek to ensure that those institutions neither restrain the ability of their member States to meet their duty to protect nor hinder business enterprises from respecting human rights;

    (b) Encourage those institutions, within their respective mandates and capacities, to promote business respect for human rights and, where requested, to help States meet their duty to protect against human rights abuse by business enterprises, including through technical assistance, capacity-building and awareness-raising;

    (c) Draw on these Guiding Principles to promote shared understanding and advance 13.

II. The Corporate Responsibility to Respect Human Rights

A. Foundational Principles

11. Business enterprises should respect human rights. This means that they should avoid infringing on the human rights of others and should address adverse human rights impacts with which they are involved.

12. The responsibility of business enterprises to respect human rights refers to internationally recognized human rights – understood, at a minimum, as those expressed in the International Bill of Human Rights and the principles concerning fundamental rights set out in the International Labour Organization's Declaration on Fundamental Principles and Rights at Work.

13. The responsibility to respect human rights requires that business enterprises:

    (a) Avoid causing or contributing to adverse human rights impacts through their own activities, and address such impacts when they occur;

    (b) Seek to prevent or mitigate adverse human rights impacts that are directly linked to their operations, products or services by their business relationships, even if they have not contributed to those impacts.

14. The responsibility of business enterprises to respect human rights applies to all enterprises regardless of their size, sector, operational context, ownership and structure. Nevertheless, the scale and complexity of the means through which enterprises meet that responsibility may vary according to these factors and with the severity of the enterprise's adverse human rights impacts.

15. In order to meet their responsibility to respect human rights, business enterprises should have in place policies and processes appropriate to their size and circumstances, including:

    (a) A policy commitment to meet their responsibility to respect human rights;

    (b) A human rights due diligence process to identify, prevent, mitigate and account for how they address their impacts on human rights;

    (c) Processes to enable the remediation of any adverse human rights impacts they cause or to which they contribute.

B. Operational Principles

Policy Commitment

16. As the basis for embedding their responsibility to respect human rights, business enterprises should express their commitment to meet this responsibility through a statement of policy that:

    (a) Is approved at the most senior level of the business enterprise;

    (b) Is informed by relevant internal and/or external expertise;

    (c) Stipulates the enterprise's human rights expectations of personnel, business partners and other parties directly linked to its operations, products or services;

    (d) Is publicly available and communicated internally and externally to all personnel, business partners and other relevant parties;

    (e) Is reflected in operational policies and procedures necessary to embed it throughout the business enterprise.

Human Rights Due Diligence

17. In order to identify, prevent, mitigate and account for how they address their adverse human rights impacts, business enterprises should carry out human rights due diligence. The process should include assessing actual and potential human rights impacts, integrating and acting upon the findings, tracking responses, and communicating how impacts are addressed. Human rights due diligence:

    (a) Should cover adverse human rights impacts that the business enterprise may cause or contribute to through its own activities, or which may be directly linked to its operations, products or services by its business relationships;

(b) Will vary in complexity with the size of the business enterprise, the risk of severe human rights impacts, and the nature and context of its operations;

(c) Should be ongoing, recognizing that the human rights risks may change over time as the business enterprise's operations and operating context evolve.

18. In order to gauge human rights risks, business enterprises should identify and assess any actual or potential adverse human rights impacts with which they may be involved either through their own activities or as a result of their business relationships. This process should:

(a) Draw on internal and/or independent external human rights expertise;

(b) Involve meaningful consultation with potentially affected groups and other relevant stakeholders, as appropriate to the size of the business enterprise and the nature and context of the operation.

19. In order to prevent and mitigate adverse human rights impacts, business enterprises should integrate the findings from their impact assessments across relevant internal functions and processes, and take appropriate action.

(a) Effective integration requires that:

(i) Responsibility for addressing such impacts is assigned to the appropriate level and function within the business enterprise;

(ii) Internal decision-making, budget allocations and oversight processes enable effective responses to such impacts.

(b) Appropriate action will vary according to:

(i) Whether the business enterprise causes or contributes to an adverse impact, or whether it is involved solely because the impact is directly linked to its operations, products or services by a business relationship;

(ii) The extent of its leverage in addressing the adverse impact.

20. In order to verify whether adverse human rights impacts are being addressed, business enterprises should track the effectiveness of their response. Tracking should:

(a) Be based on appropriate qualitative and quantitative indicators;

(b) Draw on feedback from both internal and external sources, including affected stakeholders.

21. In order to account for how they address their human rights impacts, business enterprises should be prepared to communicate this externally, particularly when concerns are raised by or on behalf of affected stakeholders. Business enterprises whose operations or operating contexts pose risks of severe human rights impacts should report formally on how they address them. In all instances, communications should:

(a) Be of a form and frequency that reflect an enterprise's human rights impacts and that are accessible to its intended audiences;

(b) Provide information that is sufficient to evaluate the adequacy of an enterprise's response to the particular human rights impact involved;

(c) In turn not pose risks to affected stakeholders, personnel or to legitimate requirements of commercial confidentiality.

Remediation

22. Where business enterprises identify that they have caused or contributed to adverse impacts, they should provide for or cooperate in their remediation through legitimate processes.

Issues of Context

23. In all contexts, business enterprises should:

(a) Comply with all applicable laws and respect internationally recognized human rights, wherever they operate;

(b) Seek ways to honour the principles of internationally recognized human rights when faced with conflicting requirements;

(c) Treat the risk of causing or contributing to gross human rights abuses as a legal compliance issue wherever they operate.

24. Where it is necessary to prioritize actions to address actual and potential adverse human rights impacts, business enterprises should first seek to prevent and mitigate those that are most severe or where delayed response would make them irremediable.

III. Access to Remedy

A. Foundational Principle

25. As part of their duty to protect against business-related human rights abuse, States must take appropriate steps to ensure, through judicial, administrative, legislative or other appropriate means, that when such abuses occur within their territory and/or jurisdiction those affected have access to effective remedy.

B. Operational Principles

State-Based Judicial Mechanisms

26. States should take appropriate steps to ensure the effectiveness of domestic judicial mechanisms when addressing business-related human rights abuses, including considering ways to reduce legal, practical and other relevant barriers that could lead to a denial of access to remedy.

State-Based Non-Judicial Grievance Mechanisms

27. States should provide effective and appropriate non-judicial grievance mechanisms, alongside judicial mechanisms, as part of a comprehensive State-based system for the remedy of business-related human rights abuse.

Non-State-Based Grievance Mechanisms

28. States should consider ways to facilitate access to effective non-State-based grievance.

29. To make it possible for grievances to be addressed early and remediated directly, business enterprises should establish or participate in effective operational-level grievance mechanisms for individuals and communities who may be adversely impacted.

30. Industry, multi-stakeholder and other collaborative initiatives that are based on respect for human rights-related standards should ensure that effective grievance mechanisms are available.

Effectiveness Criteria for Non-Judicial Grievance Mechanisms

31. In order to ensure their effectiveness, non-judicial grievance mechanisms, both State-based and non-State-based, should be:

(a) legitimate: enabling trust from the stakeholder groups for whose use they are intended, and being accountable for the fair conduct of grievance processes;

(b) Accessible: being known to all stakeholder groups for whose use they are intended, and providing adequate assistance for those who may face particular barriers to access;

(c) Predictable: providing a clear and known procedure with an indicative time frame for each stage, and clarity on the types of process and outcome available and means of monitoring implementation;

(d) Equitable: seeking to ensure that aggrieved parties have reasonable access to sources of information, advice and expertise necessary to engage in a grievance process on fair, informed and respectful terms;

(e) Transparent: keeping parties to a grievance informed about its progress, and providing sufficient information about the mechanism's performance to build confidence in its effectiveness and meet any public interest at stake;

(f) Rights-compatible: ensuring that outcomes and remedies accord with internationally recognized human rights;

(g) A source of continuous learning: drawing on relevant measures to identify lessons for improving the mechanism and preventing future grievances and harms.

Operational-level mechanisms should also be:

(h) Based on engagement and dialogue: consulting the stakeholder groups for whose use they are intended on their design and performance, and focusing on dialogue as the means to address and resolve grievances.

Source: United Nations Human Rights Council, *Guiding Principles on Business and Human Rights: Implementing the United Nations "Protect, Respect and Remedy" Framework*, A/HRC/17/31 (March 21, 2011), p. 13.

The United Kingdom Bribery Act (2010) and the United States Foreign Corrupt Practices Act (1977)

The Bribery Act is the United Kingdom's (UK) response to the Organisation for Economic Co-operation and Development's 1997 Convention on Combating Bribery of Foreign Public Officials in International Business Transactions. The Act places strict liability on companies and the only defense to avoid liability is to have strong, effective, and up-to-date policies and procedures to prevent bribery. Penalties for individuals include the possibility of up to ten years in prison and unlimited fines. The companies also face the possibility of unlimited fines. The Act has extraterritorial reach, as it applies to all UK companies operating abroad and to any overseas companies with a presence in the UK. A foreign subsidiary of a UK company can bring liability on the parent company when, in performing services for the parent company, it engages in bribery. Under the Act facilitating payments remain illegal. The UK Bribery Act has significant differences from the United States Foreign Corrupt Practices Act (FCPA) which made it illegal to make payments to foreign government officials for the purpose of obtaining or retaining business. The FCPA does allow for payments to facilitate routine government actions such as issuing otherwise lawful permits, licenses, or documents. Conformity with the FCPA is not sufficient to avoid liability under the UK Bribery Act because such conformity does not guarantee that a company's procedures are strong, effective, and up to date. Moreover, the UK Bribery Act covers business transactions not covered by the FCPA such as the receipt of a bribe. The UK Bribery Act applies to the private sector as well as the public sector (private to private bribery), and it makes no provision for promotional expenses. Finally, the UK Bribery Act is more strict than the FCPA with respect to outlawing facilitating payments and the possible prison sentence for violations of the Act is twice that of the FCPA.

CASES

Case 1: Foreign Assignment

THOMAS DUNFEE AND DIANA ROBERTSON

Sara Strong graduated with an MBA from UCLA four years ago. She immediately took a job in the correspondent bank section of the Security Bank of the American Continent. Sara was assigned to work on issues pertaining to relationships with correspondent banks in Latin America. She rose rapidly in the section and received three good promotions in three years. She consistently received high ratings from her superiors, and she received particularly high marks for her professional demeanor.

In her initial position with the bank, Sara was required to travel to Mexico on several occasions. She was always accompanied by a male colleague even though she generally handled similar business by herself on trips within the United States. During her trips to Mexico she observed that Mexican bankers seemed more aware of her being a woman and were personally solicitous to her, but she didn't discern any major problems. The final decisions on the work that she did were handled by male representatives of the bank stationed in Mexico.

A successful foreign assignment was an important step for those on the "fast track" at the bank. Sara applied for a position in Central or South America and was delighted when she was assigned to the bank's office in Mexico City. The office had about 20 bank employees and was headed by William Vitam. The Mexico City office was seen as a preferred assignment by young executives at the bank.

After a month, Sara began to encounter problems. She found it difficult to be effective in dealing with Mexican bankers – the clients. They appeared reluctant to accept her authority, and they would often bypass her in important matters. The problem was exacerbated by Vitam's compliance in her being bypassed. When she asked that the clients be referred back to her, Vitam replied, "Of course, that isn't really practical." Vitam made matters worse by patronizing her in front of clients and by referring to her as "my cute assistant" and "our lady banker." Vitam never did this when only Americans were present and in fact treated her professionally and with respect in internal situations.

Sara finally complained to Vitam that he was undermining her authority and effectiveness; she asked him in as positive a manner as possible to help her. Vitam listened carefully to Sara's complaints, then replied, "I'm glad that you brought this up, because I've been meaning to sit down and talk to you about my little game playing in front of the clients. Let me be frank with you. Our clients think you're great, but they just don't understand a woman in authority, and you and I aren't going to be able to change their attitudes overnight. As long as the clients see you as my assistant and deferring to me, they can do business with you. I'm willing to give you as much responsibility as they can handle your having. I *know* you can handle it. But we just have to tread carefully. You and I know that my remarks in front of clients don't mean anything. They're just a way of playing the game Latin style. I know it's frustrating for you, but I really need you to support me on this. It's not going to affect your promotions. You just have to act like it's my responsibility." Sara replied that she would try to cooperate, but that basically she found her role demeaning.

As time went on, Sara found that the patronizing actions in front of clients bothered her more and more. She spoke to Vitam again, but he was firm in his position and urged her to try to be a little more flexible, even a little more "feminine."

Sara also had a problem with Vitam over policy. The Mexico City office had five younger women who worked as receptionists and secretaries. They were all situated at work stations at the entrance of the office. They were required to wear standard uniforms that were colorful and rather sexy. Sara protested the requirement that uniforms be worn because (1) they were inconsistent with the image of the banking business and (2) they were demeaning to the women who had to wear them. Vitam just curtly replied that he had received a lot of favorable comments about the uniforms from clients of the bank.

Several months later, Sara had what she thought would be a good opportunity to deal with the problem. Tom Fried, an executive vice-president who had been a mentor for her since she arrived at the bank, was coming to Mexico City; she arranged a private conference with him. She described her problems and explained that she was not able to be effective in this environment and that she worried that it would have a negative effect on her chance of promotion within the bank. Fried was very careful in his response. He spoke of certain "realities" that the bank had to respect, and he urged her to "see it through" even though he could understand how she would feel that things weren't fair.

Sara found herself becoming more aggressive and defensive in her meetings with Vitam and her clients. Several clients asked that other bank personnel handle their transactions. Sara has just received an Average rating, which noted "the beginnings of a negative attitude about the bank and its policies."

Discussion Questions

1. What obligations does an international company have to ensure that its employees are not harmed, for instance, by having their chances for advancement limited by the social customs of a host country? Explain.

2. What international ethical standard, if any, is being violated by Security Bank of the American Continent? Explain.

3. Has the bank made the correct decision by opting to follow the norms of the host country in this case? Explain.

4. What steps should be taken on the part of the transnational companies and their employees to avoid or resolve situations in which employees are offended or harmed by host country practices? Explain.

5. In this situation does ethics require respect for Mexican practices, or does it require respect for Sara Strong? Are these incompatible?

Case 2: Blood, Sweat, and Tears: Child Labor in the Chocolate Supply Chain

ROXANNE ROSS AND DENIS G. ARNOLD

Before chocolate bars are savored by consumers, the core ingredient makes a long voyage that often originates in the Ivory Coast (Côte d'Ivoire) or Ghana. Over 70 percent of cocoa is produced between the two countries. Chocolate is a guilty pleasure for many, but it may be so described for reasons other than expected. Chocolate is brought to market, in part, by children who work long hours at the cocoa farms of Africa for little or no pay. The Fair Labor Association documented youth younger than age 15 working on cocoa farms that are thought to supply to Nestlé, Hershey, Mars, and Cargill, among other companies. Some children work on their family farms. Other children were trafficked to work as slaves on cocoa farms. Reports from investigative journalists describe children carrying bags of cocoa beans upwards of 100 pounds on their backs. Many have never gone to school. They are whipped and beaten. Children report being forced to work up to 14-hour days. Those who try to escape risk having their feet sliced open to keep them from running away. According to a study by Tulane University, over 2 million children work in hazardous conditions in cocoa production between the two countries.

There are many reasons why people say child slavery continues to fuel the $100 billion chocolate industry. The Ivorian government says the problem stems from political instability in the region. Others say local governments are not taking child slavery seriously enough. The anti-human-trafficking unit in the Ivory Coast has an annual budget of just $7,700. Regardless, poverty is a central feature of the problem. The per capita GDP in the Ivory Coast is $3,600 and in Ghana it is $4,400. These are among the lowest 25 percent per capita GDPs globally. Nick Weatherill, executive director of the International Cocoa Initiative commented on the matter, "It is clearly a complex problem that has its roots in poverty, and rural poverty no less. And if the problem is rooted in poverty, then the solution, in a way, is as complex as poverty eradication."

Lawmakers attempted to reform the industry by requiring chocolate companies to certify and label their products as produced without the use of child slave labor. This legislation passed the US House of Representatives, but under lobbying pressure from the chocolate industry a similar bill was never introduced in the US Senate. Instead, lawmakers and chocolate companies negotiated a voluntary protocol, called the Harkin-Engel Protocol, signed by leaders of the chocolate industry, members of Congress, representatives of non-governmental organizations, and other leaders. The protocol is aimed at fulfilling the International Labour Organization's "Convention

This case was written for the purpose of classroom discussion by Roxanne Ross and Denis G. Arnold. © 2017 Denis G. Arnold.

concerning the Prohibition and Immediate Action for the Elimination of the Worst Forms of Child Labour" (No. 182) ratified by 181 countries including the United States, United Kingdom, Canada, Australia, Ivory Coast, and Ghana. The protocol requires poverty relief efforts, an audit system, and public reporting by African governments. The protocol established a deadline to eradicate child slavery, but the target date for meeting that deadline has continually been moved back many years. To meet the deadline, over 1 million children would need to be taken out of hazardous working conditions. The Tulane University study estimated 97 percent of farmers were not reached by current reform efforts.

Discussion Questions

1. What specific human rights norms are relevant to this case? Explain.
2. Who is responsible for stopping child abuse and child slavery in the production of cocoa? Explain. Which actors do you believe would be most *effective* at stopping the problem? Explain.
3. Do you think chocolate manufacturers should be required to certify and label their products as produced without the use of child slave labor? Why, or why not? Explain.
4. What do you think would have happened if the law had passed requiring chocolate to be labeled as slave labor free? Might this have driven up the cost of chocolate products? Would consumers behave differently? Would companies behave differently? Why, or why not? Explain.

This case is based on the following sources: W. Bertrand and E. de Buhr, "2013/14 Survey Research on Child Labor in West African Cocoa Growing Areas" (July 30, 2015). Retrieved August 18, 2017 from www.childlaborcocoa.org/images/Payson_Reports/Tulane% 20University%20-%20Two-Page%20Summary%20of%20Research %20Findings%20-%2030%20July%202015.pdf.

J. S. Clarke, "Child Labour on Nestlé Farms: Chocolate Giant's Problems Continue," *The Guardian* (September 2, 2015). Retrieved August 18, 2017 from www.theguardian.com/global-development-professionals-network/2015/sep/02/child-labour-on-nestle-farms-chocolate-giants-problems-continue.

D. McKenzie and B. Swails, "Child Slavery and Chocolate: All Too Easy to Find," *CNN* (January 19, 2012). Retrieved August 18, 2017 from http://thecnnfreedomproject.blogs.cnn.com/2012/01/ 19/child-slavery-and-chocolate-all-too-easy-to-find/.

B. O'Keefe, "Inside Big Chocolate's Child Labor Problem," *Fortune* (March 1, 2016). Retrieved August 18, 2017 from http:// fortune.com/big-chocolate-child-labor/.

"The Human Cost of Chocolate," *CNN* (January 16, 2012). Retrieved August 18, 2017 from http://thecnnfreedomproject .blogs.cnn.com/2012/01/16/chocolate-explainer/.

CIA, *The World Factbook* (n.d.). Retrieved August 22, 2017 from www.cia.gov/library/publications/the-world-factbook/ran korder/2004rank.html.

Case 3: Chrysler and Gao Feng: Corporate Responsibility for Religious and Political Freedom in China

MICHAEL A. SANTORO

Introduction

For multinational corporations, doing business in China presents many complex ethical issues. The Gao Feng incident exemplifies the challenging decisions that confront corporate executives trying to run a business in a country run by a totalitarian government that violates the human rights of its own citizens.

The Gao Feng Incident

In May 1994, Gao Feng, a devout Christian, was arrested in Beijing for planning a private worship service and candlelit vigil to commemorate the fifth anniversary of the Tiananmen Square massacre. Gao was a 26-year employee of Beijing Jeep, Chrysler's joint venture with the Chinese government. Gao was accused of violating Chinese laws against the practice of religion outside of a state-authorized venue.

Technically, Gao appears to have violated Chinese law. Article 36 of the Chinese Constitution nominally provides for freedom of religious belief. However, the government restricts religious practice to government-sanctioned organizations in order to control the growth and scope of activity of religious groups. State Council Regulation 145, signed into law by then Premier Li Peng in January 1994, requires all places of worship to register with government religious affairs bureaus and come under the supervision of official "patriotic" religious organizations. There are almost 85,000 approved venues for religious activities in China. Many religious groups, however, have been reluctant to comply with the regulation either out of principled opposition to state control of religion or due to fear of adverse consequences if they reveal, as the regulations require, the names and addresses of church leaders.

The Universal Declaration of Human Rights, endorsed by a resolution of the United Nations General Assembly in 1948, contains the following relevant provisions:

Article 18: Everyone has the right to freedom of thought, conscience and religion; this right includes freedom to change his religion or belief, and freedom, either alone or in community with others and in public or private, to manifest his religion or belief in teaching, practice, worship and observance.

Article 19: Everyone has the right to freedom of opinion and expression; this right includes freedom to hold opinions without interference and to seek, receive and impart information and ideas through any media and regardless of frontiers.

Article 20: (1) Everyone has the right to freedom of peaceful assembly and association. (2) No one may be compelled to belong to an association.

According to press reports, Gao remained under administrative detention for five weeks. He was never formally charged. In early July, Gao returned to work at Beijing Jeep and told his supervisor that the Chinese Public Safety Bureau had imprisoned him for over a month. Chrysler asked Gao to produce proof of his detention. The Chinese police gave Gao a note that said that he had been detained for three days and then released without trial.

Beijing Jeep's general manager was faced with a tough decision. The Chinese joint venture partner was pressuring Chrysler to fire Gao Feng. If he did not fire him, millions of dollars of Chrysler's invested capital in China would be put at risk. If, however, Chrysler fired Gao Feng, the company would become complicit in the violation of his right to religious freedom and political expression.

The commercial interests at stake for Chrysler cannot be ignored. One of the keys to success in the Chinese markets is good relations with the Communist Party, which keeps rigid control over the economy. Multinational corporations spend years cultivating good *guanxi* or connections in China. They are thus extremely vulnerable to retaliation. Even powerful corporations such as Motorola, Hewlett-Packard, and General Motors are well aware that they

could jeopardize billions of dollars of investments if they take a position on human rights that angers the Chinese government. At the time of the Gao Feng incident, for example, Chrysler was very aware that failure to accede to the government's request could result in losing a valuable minivan contract to its German competitor Daimler-Benz. (US-based Chrysler subsequently merged its worldwide businesses with Germany-based Daimler-Benz.) As a consequence, the basic instinct of most foreign business people in China is to stay as far away from the subject of human rights as possible. However, when a situation like the Gao Feng incident arises, corporate executives must make a decision and take action. Avoidance is simply not an option.

The Decision

Put yourself in the position of Chrysler's general manager. How would you handle the situation? Would you fire Gao Feng? Would you refuse to fire him? Is there some other course of action you would consider?

Would it be a sign of "cultural imperialism" if Chrysler refused to fire Gao Feng? After all, didn't Gao Feng violate Chinese law on the practice of religion? Does it matter that the enforcement of the law would appear to be in violation of the Universal Declaration of Human Rights?

How much should you factor in the financial consequences of your decision? What if your refusal to fire Gao Feng cost Chrysler millions of dollars in potential profits? Is there some way of handling the situation that would minimize the potential financial consequences?

When asked how he would handle the Gao Feng scenario, one executive with many years of business experience in China replied as follows: "The first thing I would do is to tell my secretary to hold my calls and then I would close my door to think. Because this would be a very serious situation, which, if not handled properly, could have serious repercussions for my company. I would take this very seriously."

Outcome

Chrysler, presumably reasoning that Gao Feng had no documented reason for failing to report to work for the bulk of the time he was missing, fired him for poor attendance. Gao Feng's case became widely publicized when the advocacy group Human Rights Watch took up his cause. Due to the personal intervention of Chrysler's chairman, Robert J. Eaton, Gao was eventually reinstated, but his case dramatically illustrates the moral and financial pitfalls of operating in a country where there are serious and pervasive human rights abuses.

Gao's freedom was, however, short-lived once the publicity surrounding his case subsided. A few months after his reinstatement at Chrysler, Gao was rearrested and without benefit of a legal proceeding sent to a re-education through labor camp. Gao Feng was again released in 1998 following the highly publicized visit of an interdenominational group of clergy appointed by President Clinton to investigate religious freedom in China.

Discussion Questions

1. Was Chrysler's decision to fire Gao Feng right? Why, or why not? Explain.
2. What other options did Chrysler have in this situation? Explain.
3. Should Chrysler lobby the Chinese government to change its laws regarding religious freedom? Why, or why not? Explain.

Case 4: Should Walmart Do More? A Case Study in Global Supply Chain Ethics

ELLERY HANLIN, AMY LAMBERT, CHRIS M. MILLER, JOEL RIDDLE, RITCHEY YOUNG, AND DENIS G. ARNOLD

> Respect for the Individual
> Service to our Customers
> Strive for Excellence
>
> —Sam Walton

Walmart's global procurement organization was formed in 2002 and took ownership of Walmart's global factory certification program, which had existed for ten years and managed the ethical conduct of Walmart's supply chain. By 2005, this program, renamed the Ethical Standards Program, was one of the largest, most extensive efforts by a multinational firm to enforce ethical conduct throughout its supply chain. In July 2006, global procurement organization president and CEO Lawrence Jackson announced that Walmart had conducted 13,600 factory audits in 2005 – more than any other multinational firm.[1] He pointed out that the program collaborated with suppliers, even training and assisting them in their compliance with ethical standards.

In a cover story entitled "Secrets, Lies, and Sweatshops: How Chinese Suppliers Hide the Truth from U.S. Companies" *Businessweek* reported that a Walmart supplier in China falsified reports and faked inspections to defy both local labor laws and Walmart's own standards.[2] Around the same time a class-action lawsuit was filed by the Washington, DC-based advocacy group International Labor Rights Fund. Filed on behalf of Walmart employees from Bangladesh, China, Indonesia, Nicaragua, and Swaziland, the lawsuit accused Walmart of knowingly allowing their code of conduct to be broken by overseas suppliers. Specifically, the lawsuit complained that employees were paid less than the minimum wage, did not receive equitable

compensation for overtime, were denied the right to associate freely, and suffered abusive managers and working conditions.[3]

WalMart's Ethical Standards Program

The *Businessweek* article focused on Ningbo Beifa Group, a Chinese supplier to Walmart of pens, highlighters, and other writing instruments. After failing three of Walmart's audits, Beifa feared losing its largest customer permanently. Out of desperation, Beifa resorted to hiring a "consulting firm," who advised the company to cover up its practices through fake documentation and forcing employees to display ethical labor practices on the days of audit.[4]

The *Businessweek* article was certainly not the first time Walmart had received widespread negative publicity about its supply chain practices. As far back as 1992, NBC's *Dateline* accused Walmart of not monitoring its Asian suppliers' illegal use of child labor and sweatshops. Nearly 14 million Americans tuned into the broadcast, the highest rated episode of the season, and Americans were shocked by the images of 11-year-old children sewing garments in sweatshops. Consumers had long associated Walmart with Sam Walton's American values, and many now questioned these values. Walmart's then president and CEO, David D. Glass, responded by rejecting the accusations, claiming they had recently audited the factories in question and had not discovered inappropriate use of child labor.[5]

While Mr. Glass maintained his position that Walmart monitored its suppliers closely, the *Dateline* broadcast was a wake-up call that Walmart needed to actively promote an ethical code of conduct. With that realization, he set forth the initiative to begin a Factory Certification Program, including written Standards for Suppliers.[6] These standards were based on Walmart's core values laid out by its founder, Sam Walton. While this laid an ethical foundation for Walmart to build on, its scope was limited to the areas of China and Bangladesh (the two countries highlighted in the *Dateline* broadcast) and addressed labor issues such as safety, compensation, working hours, and minimum age standards. While the program included an audit plan, it did not include a comprehensive plan to actively build relationships with its suppliers.[7]

Since 1992, Walmart's Factory Certification Program has expanded to all its suppliers, domestic and global. The scope of the program now covers issues such as protecting the natural environment, freedom of association and collective bargaining, and rights of foreign contract workers.[8]

Not only has Walmart expanded the scope of the program's geographic boundaries and guidelines, it has evolved its approach. Many suppliers did not even fully understand the laws and regulations in the country where they operated, much less Walmart's comprehensive standards. Beginning in 2003, Walmart began a program to build relationships with its suppliers and train their managers on how to operate in compliance with Walmart's ethical standards.[9] In its "2005 Report on Ethical Sourcing," Walmart referred to this as a change from a "policing approach to a coaching approach." In addition, Walmart very clearly communicates its standards on its corporate website.

Jackson stated his strong belief in the program's success in his message appended to Walmart's "2005 Report on Ethical Sourcing." In addition to performing over 13,000 audits in 2005, Walmart trained over 11,000 suppliers on ethical practices regarding health, safety, the natural environment, and labor. This increased from 8,000 trained suppliers in 2004. Walmart has also segmented its suppliers by level of risk and focused its auditing efforts on higher-risk companies. Furthermore, high-risk suppliers are subject to unannounced audits, which contributed 20 percent of the audits in 2005. Still, Walmart acknowledges the challenges of hidden violations in its "2005 Report on Ethical Sourcing." Walmart has reacted to this issue through information gathering and further collaboration, but as the Beifa incident shows, this may not sufficiently uncover hidden violations.

The Challenges of Overseas Audits

In recent years, society has demanded answers from American importers for the abusive work conditions of their overseas suppliers. In order to address these accusations, many corporations developed auditing systems and long codes of ethics. While there is evidence that substantial improvements have been made, it is clear that many companies have simply improved their ability to conceal abuse.[10] Some auditors estimate that as many as half of all contract factories in China are committing some kind of deception. As a result, the positive assurances of certain corporations on behalf of supply chain partners are often based on faulty information.[11]

Some of the most common methods for misleading labor auditors include keeping double books, training employees to provide scripted responses that cover up legal and company code violations, and maintaining hidden production away from the factory itself. Factory managers are reluctant to explain their methods, and many corporations are reluctant to persuade them for fear of negative publicity. The few details that have leaked out include factory managers retaining teams of employees that falsify records and forge documents.[12] Some companies even go so far as to use bribery to assure a successful audit.[13]

When questioned, overseas factory managers complain about the pressure put on them to meet production quotas and deadlines at the lowest possible cost while absorbing the added costs of compliance. For many of these factories, failing an audit means the loss of a contract and potential bankruptcy. On the other hand, compliance is costly and often requires a cultural transformation. Faced with those choices, many factory owners resort to illegal activities. As one Asian manager put it, "We are under enormous stress, customers place late orders, they change their orders part way through manufacturing, and they pay their bills late. At the same time, they ask us to provide better training for our staff, better health and safety, and better accommodation. We just can't do it all."[14]

So far, the answer has not been more auditing. As the level and number of audits increases, the time of auditors has been spread over more and more factories. Additionally, those auditors want to avoid embarrassing public relations fiascos for their employers, often issuing only warnings or even turning a blind eye. Even as auditors get more effective, factories employ "consultants" that help them beat audits. They see the cost of these consultants as less than the cost for compliance.

John and Jane Doe et al. v. Walmart Stores Inc.

On September 13, 2005, the International Labor Rights Fund (ILRF) filed a class-action lawsuit in the Los Angeles Superior Court on the grounds that Walmart had a breach of contract violation with employees of overseas suppliers. ILRF's complaint laid out the case that Walmart's

"Standards for Suppliers" created a contractual obligation between Walmart and overseas contractors. As a result of failing to enforce those standards, the ILRF argued that Walmart was violating the contract at the cost of working conditions for thousands of workers around the globe. The Executive Director of ILRF, Terry Collingsworth, claimed that the lawsuit was filed in California because Walmart had violated that state's laws regarding employment standards. In addition, he reported that the lawsuit could not be filed in the employees' local countries because they would face the threat of arrest, physical attacks, and hostile judicial systems that favor corporations. Mr. Collingsworth said, "Our premise here is that Walmart and many other companies issued these codes of conduct as public relations devices. They never expected that someone would take it seriously and use it as an affirmative tool to actually make them do what they promised to do."[15]

In the end, however, the US Court of Appeals for the Ninth Circuit ruled that Walmart had no legal duty to protect foreign workers in its supplier factories from the violation of local labor laws or human rights abuses. As a result, the lawsuit was dismissed and Walmart was not held to be legally liable for the alleged maltreatment of workers in its global supply chains.

Notes

1. Walmart Stores, "2005 Report on Ethical Sourcing" (July 31, 2006). Retrieved November 28, 2006 from www.walmart stores.com.
2. Dexter Roberts, Pete Engardio, Aaron Bernstein, and Stanley Holmes, "Secrets, Lies, and Sweatshops: How Chinese Suppliers Hide the Truth from U.S. Companies," *Businessweek* (November 27, 2006).
3. Steven Greenhouse, "Suit Says Walmart is Lax on Labor Abuses Overseas," *The New York Times* (September 14, 2006). Retrieved November 28, 2006, via LexisNexis.
4. Roberts et al., "Secrets, Lies, and Sweatshops."
5. Thomas Hayes, "Walmart Disputes Report on Labor," *The New York Times* (December 24, 1992). Retrieved November 28, 2006, via LexisNexis.
6. Walmart Stores, "2005 Report on Ethical Sourcing."
7. Ibid.
8. Ibid.
9. Ibid.
10. Roberts et al., "Secrets, Lies, and Sweatshops."
11. Lauren Foster and Alexandra Harney, "Why Ethical Sourcing Means Show and Tell," *Financial Times* (April 22, 2005). Retrieved November 28, 2006, via LexisNexis.
12. Ibid.
13. Roberts et al., "Secrets, Lies, and Sweatshops."
14. Foster and Harney, "Why Ethical Sourcing Means Show and Tell."
15. Keith Ecker, "Labor Group Holds Walmart to Code of Conduct," *Corporate Legal Times* (November, 2005). Retrieved November 28, 2006, via LexisNexis.

Discussion Questions

1. Given international human rights standards, are Walmart's critics correct in believing that Walmart has an ethical obligation to ensure that the factories in its supply chain adhere to local labor laws and treat employees in an ethically appropriate manner? Why, or why not? Explain.

2. Should Walmart do more to ensure that the factories in its supply chain adhere to local labor laws and treat employees in an ethically appropriate manner? If so, what should they do and why? If not, why not? Explain.

3. What obligations, if any, do consumers have regarding working conditions in supply chain factories that make the items that they purchase? Explain.

Case 5: The Hidden Price of Low Cost: Subcontracting in Bangladesh's Garment Industry

VIJAY PADMANABHAN, DOROTHÉE BAUMANN-PAULY, AND SARAH LABOWITZ

Garment Production in Bangladesh

Bangladesh specializes in high-volume, low-cost production of technically simple garments, utilizing the world's largest low-cost labor pool. Minimum and average wages in Bangladesh are lower than in competitor countries, and wages are growing at a comparatively slower pace.[1] This cost advantage has catapulted Bangladesh into the position of the world's second largest national exporter of garments behind China.[2] As exports have skyrocketed, the garment sector has become the most significant industry in the country, accounting for 80 percent of its export income.[3]

Bangladeshi manufacturers use low-cost labor to overcome significant infrastructure hurdles that raise the cost of production. The World Economic Forum's Global Competitiveness Report ranks Bangladesh's infrastructure 127 out of the 144 nations surveyed.[4]

The government of Bangladesh careens from crisis to crisis, led by a fierce rivalry between the two major political parties.[5] Political unrest is a regular feature of the Bangladeshi system, with "hartals" or strikes creating impediments to production.[6] Corruption is endemic to Bangladesh, with Transparency International ranking Bangladesh 145 out of 175 countries in its most recent survey of global corruption.[7] Unrest and corruption create significant business uncertainty in Bangladesh, and have prevented the government from investing adequately in infrastructure improvements needed to improve competitiveness.

Basic Black

Basic Black's Business Model

Basic Black is a medium-sized American discount clothing brand specializing in "fast fashion," targeting the growing demographic of Americans who prefer fashion-forward clothing that emulates the latest trends at mainstream prices, generally through the use of low-cost, offshore labor. It sells a full line of men's, women's, and children's basics, including T-shirts, dress shirts, sweaters, jeans, and dresses. Basic Black markets its clothing through large discount retailers, trumpeting "the latest fashion at yesterday's prices." This niche has led Basic Black to grow by leaps and bounds over the past ten years. In 2016 the company recorded $2.7 billion in sales revenue, a 14 percent increase from 2015.

Basic Black prioritizes low-cost, high-volume, and quick turn-around production in its sourcing relationships. Like most Western brands, Basic Black does not manufacture any of its own clothes. Actual production is handled by independent companies based in Asia, Central America, and Turkey under terms laid out in supplier agreements. Basic Black prefers this "asset light" model to owning its own factories for production because it frees the company to concentrate on high-value added tasks like design and marketing, while contracting-out low-value tasks like cutting and sewing to its overseas business partners.

Basic Black sources more than 50 percent of the total volume of its clothes in Bangladesh. In particular, it has developed a close relationship with Raz Fashions. That relationship is subject to a supplier agreement between the companies that prohibits Raz from using subcontractors without Basic Black's approval to fulfill its orders.

Basic Black's Subcontracting Surprise

Nicole Walker is the Sourcing Manager for Basic Black. Walker supervises the relationships between Basic Black and its overseas suppliers. One morning in mid-April 2017 in her office in New York, Walker received a phone call from the quality management team of Basic Black. They informed her that a quality manager who had recently visited Raz Fashions discovered that Raz had subcontracted a significant portion of a recent order placed by Basic Black. Upon investigation, the manager learned that some parts of the production had been moved to a different facility, Leila Emporium. This was done without obtaining Basic Black's permission and was therefore in direct violation of the supplier agreement between the companies.

Upon receiving this information, Walker immediately met with Rosanna Cabot, Basic Black's Chief Sustainability Officer, and Evan Jones, its Chief Executive Officer, to discuss next steps. Cabot reminded Walker that the prohibition on unauthorized subcontracting was placed into all supplier agreements to allow Basic Black to have complete visibility into its supply chain. Without having inspected and assessed Leila Emporium, Basic Black has no idea what conditions workers face at the facility, or whether it is capable of performing work to Basic Black's specifications and standards, and within its time frames.

Jones, Walker, and Cabot are worried about the reputational risks to their business if human rights violations surface at Leila Emporium and the lack of control in their supply chain if orders are being subcontracted without their knowledge. Cabot, the sustainability manager, pushed for Jones to punish Raz Fashions, either by terminating the supplier relationship as provided in the contract, or by placing the company on probation, with the risk of termination for further violations. Walker, the sourcing manager, on the other hand, reminded Jones that, outside this episode, Basic Black has enjoyed an excellent business relationship with Raz Fashions. Raz produces high-volume, high-quality, low-cost garments for Basic Black – production that would be difficult to replicate elsewhere. Thus, she urged caution before disrupting such an important supplier relationship.

Walker and Cabot decided they would travel to Bangladesh themselves to investigate why Raz had decided to subcontract in direct violation of the supplier agreement, and to create a plan of action to respond to the violation.

Addressing the Human Rights Challenge of Production in Bangladesh

From an economic perspective, the rise of the garment export sector has been a huge boon to Bangladesh. It has been a major driver in reducing poverty in the country and increasing life expectancy, literacy, and per capita food intake. Women in particular have been economic beneficiaries of the industry's presence in Bangladesh. Most garment workers are women and industry jobs provide women an opportunity to work outside the home.

But the nature of garment production in Bangladesh results in risks to the human rights of workers. Because the primary driver of the industry's success is the low cost of labor, there is significant downward pressure on wages and working conditions. For years, labor groups and non-governmental organizations (NGOs) have pointed to rampant human rights violations in Bangladesh's garment industry.[8] In particular, most workers do not receive a living wage; forced overtime and child labor are rampant; and many factories do not meet the bare minimum of Western safety requirements, with too often deadly results.[9]

Few checks on the mistreatment of workers exist in Bangladesh. The country has lax labor laws and has been reluctant to raise standards to international levels. Garment manufacturers enjoy considerable influence with lawmakers, stemming from their preeminent role in the country's economy. The two main industry associations, Bangladesh Garment Manufacturers and Exporters Association (BGMEA) and Bangladesh Knitwear Manufacturers and Exporters Association (BKMEA) have in the past used their influence to block legislation that would impose meaningful oversight over the industry.[10] The regulations that exist are largely unenforced because the government lacks an adequate number of labor inspectors for a garment sector of its size. Labor inspectors are not paid well and are susceptible to bribery to supplement their salaries.[11]

Unions are exceedingly weak in Bangladesh. Despite labor law reform in 2013,[12] the government has been slow to bring its laws into compliance with international norms protecting workers' freedom of association. Labor leaders have been harassed and even subjected to violence or death as a consequence of their organizing activities.[13] The plentiful, low-skilled labor within the country provides a strong disincentive to organize, as manufacturers are able to easily replace workers who complain about conditions.

In recent years, a number of high-profile incidents have exposed the unsafe and even deadly conditions for workers in Bangladeshi garment factories. In November 2012, the Tazreen garment factory caught fire and 112 of its workers were killed. Another 200 workers were injured.[14] The most dramatic industrial incident in Bangladesh is the April 2013 collapse of Rana Plaza, a building housing five garment factories and other commercial facilities, in which more than 1,100 workers were killed.[15] The eight-story structure was built in violation of Bangladeshi building codes, with numerous illegal floors added on top of the original, legally constructed floors; the added floors contained heavy industrial machines and generators for which adequate structural support did not exist.[16] Before the collapse, a building inspector found cracks in the building and ordered the building to be evacuated. Factory owners overruled that decision and forced workers, many of whom were subsequently killed or injured, to enter the building.[17]

In the wake of Rana Plaza, two major remedial frameworks were launched by foreign brands and retailers: the Accord on Fire and Building Safety in Bangladesh, which involves local authorities, unions, NGOs, and the International Labour Organization,[18] and the Alliance for Bangladesh Worker Safety.[19] While these systems have established systems of factory monitoring and worker training, they encompass less than 2,000 of the estimated 5,000–6,000 garment factories that operate in Bangladesh.[20]

Predating Tazreen and Rana Plaza, an audit system arose in response to sweatshop scandals in the 1990s.[21] This system, run primarily by Western brands and retailers and implemented by numerous organizations in Bangladesh, oversees conditions for workers in Bangladeshi factories with direct relationships with foreign brands and retailers. It generally involves:

1. a code of conduct to govern the labor practices of Bangladeshi manufacturers with direct relationships with the buyer;
2. an audit regime to uncover violations of the code; and
3. mechanisms for companies to work with primary manufacturers to address code violations, or to terminate relationships in the case of the most egregious violations.

For Western brands, the appeal of the audit system lies in its potential to reduce business risks associated with poor conditions in supplier factories. Brand reputations are sullied by an association with human rights violations in the production of garments. Reputational harm has the potential to lead to consumer boycotts and investor actions protesting the conditions in which clothes are made. Western companies may also incur financial costs associated with compensation for workers whose human rights were violated in the production of their clothes.[22]

From the perspective of Bangladeshi manufacturers, the code and audit system is complex and costly. Standards differ from company to company and the large number of audits increases production costs for manufacturers as a result of disrupted production and remediation of adverse audit findings, whose costs are borne by the manufacturer, not the brand or retailer. At the same time, the prices manufacturers can charge have generally decreased.

The audit system can be an effective means to identify and correct some risks to workers, especially those related to occupational safety and health or wage and hour violations. But the cycle of auditing and remediation rarely addresses the root causes of persistent non-compliance, especially the sourcing practices of buyers and weak governance. While the Accord and the Alliance resulted in large groups of companies working together with outside unions and NGOs against common standards for building and fire safety, these initiatives rely on longstanding principles of auditing and remediation.

The Problem of Unauthorized Subcontracting

One of the most significant limitations of the audit system is the fact that it excludes factories that are outside the relatively small network of direct suppliers and that are essential to Bangladesh's ability to meet demand for high volumes of low-cost garments. After the Rana Plaza collapse, many Western brands were unaware that their orders were produced at the factories in the complex because of the extensive use of unauthorized subcontracting by manufacturers in Bangladesh. While the lead contractors with direct relationships with Western companies are subject to the code and audit system, companies further down the subcontracting often are invisible to Western brands.

There are many economic drivers behind subcontracting in Bangladesh's garment sector. First, the Bangladeshi export system rewards companies that demonstrate high order and export volumes with access to capital. Capital is critical to financing factory improvements and increasing production capacity. This system creates a strong incentive for manufacturers to take on a volume of orders that is greater than their total capacity. When production capacity is exceeded, the manufacturers of record subcontract production to smaller manufacturers to meet deadlines. For example, a factory with a capacity of 100,000 pieces will take on orders of ten times that volume, do the highest value work itself, and subcontract the remainder to smaller factories.

Second, subcontracting allows lead contractors to complete orders on time when Bangladesh's many infrastructure limitations result in unexpected delays in production. Transportation delays, blackouts, and political strikes, among other things, frequently delay the production and transport of garments. When that occurs, subcontracting is essential to meet the tight deadlines imposed by Western companies.

Third, subcontractors are willing to take on work at a lower price-per-unit than lead contractors. The result is a strong financial incentive to subcontract to increase margins for lead contractors.

Fourth, subcontractors also benefit from the arrangement. Lead contractors assume full responsibility for all aspects of production, from obtaining materials through to cutting, stitching, and assembly; to finally packaging and transporting garments. Many aspects of this chain are capital intensive and technically complicated and thus beyond the capacity of the smallest manufacturers. These small factories are economically viable because lead contractors take on the legal and financial responsibilities associated with production.

For the most part, Western brands have benefited from subcontracting. It lowers the price of goods and ensures that they arrive on time despite the multitude of infrastructure-related delays that plague manufacturing in Bangladesh. Subcontracting does not inherently increase human rights risks and can be a good way to increase efficiency and lower costs, when done with transparency and oversight. But the human rights risks associated with production outside the audit system, and the resulting business risks, have led many Western brands to formally ban subcontracting without the brand's approval in their supplier agreements. The efficiency gains from subcontracting for lead manufacturers often outweigh the risks of being detected and the practice persists throughout the industry. Officially banning non-transparent subcontracting has at this point merely resulted in a hidden production system that is removed from any form of oversight.

The Relationship between Basic Black and Raz Fashions

The Supplier Agreement

Basic Black's supplier agreement with Raz Fashions is typical of the agreements it makes with its Bangladeshi suppliers. The underlying principle in the agreement is flexibility, which allows Basic Black to be responsive to the rapid fluctuations in consumer demand that is the hallmark of "fast fashion." Some key provisions of the supplier agreement are produced here:

1. The supplier relationship between Basic Black and Raz Fashions is "on demand." Basic Black will notify Raz Fashions of the quantity, specifications, price-per-unit, and expected delivery times of orders at its convenience. Raz Fashions will have the option with each order of: (a) accepting the terms of the order request as provided; or (b) rejecting the order. Any modifications of the supplier order by Raz Fashions will be treated as a "rejection" for purposes of this contract.

2. Raz Fashions may not subcontract any of its obligations or duties without the express written consent of Basic Black. Where consent is granted, Raz Fashions remains responsible and liable to Basic Black for the actions of its subcontractors.

3. Basic Black shall have the right to immediately cancel and terminate the agreement with Raz Fashions based upon its failure to perform or comply with any of the terms and conditions of the agreement.

Spring is typically the slow season for Basic Black T-shirts. Over the past five spring seasons, the company has sold an average of just 500,000 T-shirts, far below its performance in the other quarters of the year. But in 2015, Basic Black unveiled a new style and fabric for its staple "V-neck, slim fit" T-shirt. The new fabric, a mix of cotton and polyester, absorbs sweat and is form-fitting. The T-shirt was featured in a major fashion magazine as "the perfect T-shirt," which resulted in a dramatic increase of sales in the first quarter of 2015, creating optimism in the company that it would be able to drastically increase T-shirt sales in the spring in comparison to past years.

On March 1, 2015, Walker, the sourcing manager, placed an order with Raz Fashions for 1,000,000 black, V-neck, slim fit T-shirts due on April 15, 2015. This order represented a 200 percent increase over the order placed on March 1, 2014. Despite this dramatic increase in production, Walker did not increase the time allotted to make the T-shirts, or increase their per-unit-price, hoping that Raz Fashions would accept the terms of the order. When they did, she asked no further questions about how Raz would meet the order. Walker later explained, "It's not my business how Raz Fashions accomplishes its orders so long as they meet the terms of our agreement. It's unseemly for me to police the inner workings of a contract manufacturer."

On March 15, 2015, Walker added another 500,000 units to her order due on April 15, to respond to even stronger-than-expected demand. Raz accepted the production request. While the order was pending, Basic Black's auditors in Bangladesh noticed minor but consistent quality differences in finished T-shirts at the packaging stage of production. This discrepancy led to the discovery that Raz had subcontracted a portion of its production for Basic Black to Leila Emporium. While the auditors were investigating, Basic Black fixed the quality issue and managed to produce all of the T-shirts on time and in good condition. Walker received the auditors' report concerning Raz and Leila on April 15, after the quality issues had been resolved.

Walker and Cabot Visit Raz Fashions

In Dhaka, Walker meets with Nazim Raz, the owner of Raz Fashions. Walker sets out for Raz the evidence collected by the auditors and asks, "Why did you violate the terms of our contract? We value our business relationship with Raz Fashions, but the prohibition on subcontracting without prior approval is non-negotiable for us."

Raz does not deny sending a portion of the Basic Black order to Leila Emporium. Rather, he lays out for Walker the reasons he resorted to subcontracting:

1. While the supplier agreement with Basic Black does not guarantee future orders or production lead times, Raz Fashions makes projections on demand based on past practice. "I have to keep my production lines busy at all times in order to stay profitable given the low margins with which I operate," he explains. "In the spring, I have agreements with four other Western brands because I need the work to stay busy during the traditional slow season and to keep my workers." Raz tells Walker that when Basic Black drastically increased the number of units ordered in spring 2015 without providing additional time or money for overtime, he was overcommitted for the period.

2. These problems were compounded, Raz explains, when the V-neck stitching came apart in the first batch of T-shirts stitched, revealing a deficiency in the ordered material. "I ordered higher quality material straight away, but port workers were on strike."

3. Subcontracting resolved his problems, Raz finished. "I knew my good friends at Leila had excess capacity. If they produced half the T-shirts, I would be able to finish on time. And Leila charges a lower per-unit price than what it costs me to make a T-shirt myself. Reducing the cost of production allowed me to generate a profit despite the expense of purchasing extra fabric."

While Walker was sympathetic to Raz's situation, she could not understand why he accepted Basic Black's supply request in the first place. After all, the contract allows Raz to decline production requests. Raz replied, "What choice did I really have? If I declined your orders, my competitors would have stepped in and promised to complete the orders on time and at cost. I then risk losing Basic Black's business altogether, and without it, my business is sunk."

Based on the visit, Walker must decide how Basic Black will respond to the violation of the supplier agreement by Raz Fashions.

Notes

1. See ILO Research Note (November 2014), www.ilo.org/wcmsp5/groups/public/—asia/—ro-bangkok/documents/genericdocument/wcms_223988.pdf.

2. World Trade Organization, *International Trade Statistics 2014: Merchandise Trade*, Table II.57, www.wto.org/english/res_e/statis_e/its2014_e/its14_merch_trade_product_e.htm.

3. International Labour Organization, "Improving Working Conditions in the Ready Made Garment Industry: Progress and Achievements" (2016), www.ilo.org/dhaka/Whatwedo/Projects/WCMS_240343/lang–en/index.htm. See also Serajul Quadir, "Bangladesh Eyes Fivefold Increase in Readymade Garment Exports to Canada," *Reuters* (April 19, 2015), https://ca.finance.yahoo.com/news/bangladesh-eyes-fivefold-increase-readymade-garment-exports-canada-145927478–finance.html.

4. World Economic Forum, *Reports: Bangladesh* (2015), http://reports.weforum.org/global-competitiveness-report-2014–2015/economies/#economy=BGD.

5. See, e.g., Victor Mallet, "Bangladesh: A Dangerous Rivalry," *Financial Times* (April 12, 2015), www.ft.com/content/03a9b202-deac-11e4-b9ec-00144feab7de.

6. McKinsey & Co., *Bangladesh's Ready-Made Garments Landscape: The Challenge for Growth* (New York: McKinsey & Co., 2011), p. 16.

7. Transparency International, *Corruption Perceptions Index 2014*, www.transparency.org/cpi2014/results.

8. See, e.g., Human Rights Watch (HRW), *"Whoever Raises Their Head Suffers the Most": Workers' Rights in Bangladesh's Garment Factories* (2015) ("HRW Report"); Business and Human Rights Resource Centre (BHRRC), "The Rana Plaza Building Collapse in Bangladesh: One Year On" (2014), www.business-humanrights.org/en/the-rana-plaza-building-collapse-in-bangladesh-one-year-on. The extent of human rights violations is in part related to the size of Bangladesh's informal economy: see generally ILO, *Bangladesh: Seeking Better Employment Conditions for Better Socioeconomic Outcomes* (Geneva: ILO, 2013).

9. See generally HRW Report; Centre for Research on Multinational Corporations (SOMO), *Fact Sheet: Child Labour in the Textile & Garment Industry* (March 2014).

10. Transparency International Bangladesh, *Readymade Garments Sector: Problems of Good Governance and Way Forward* (October 31, 2013), pp. 15–19, https://blog.transparency.org/wp-content/uploads/2014/04/2013_TIB_GarmentSector ExecSum_EN.pdf.

11. Ibid., pp. 36–38.

12. See ILO, "ILO Statement on Reform of Bangladesh Labour Law" (July 22, 2013), www.ilo.org/global/about-the-ilo/news room/statements-and-speeches/WCMS_218067/lang–en/index.htm.

13. HRW, "Bangladesh: Protect Garment Workers' Rights. Factory Owners Use Beatings, Threats to Kill, to Stop Labor Organizers" (February 6, 2014), www.hrw.org/news/2014/02/06/bangladesh-protect-garment-workers-rights.

14. See BHRRC, "Lawsuit against Tazreen Fashions (re Factory Fire in Bangladesh)," www.business-humanrights.org/en/lawsuit-against-tazreen-fashions-re-factory-fire-in-bangladesh; Joseph Allchin, "In Bangladesh, Charging of Garment Factory Owner Spurs Hope of New Era of Accountability," *Time* (February 12, 2014), http://time.com/6607/bangladesh-tazreen-factory-owner-charged/.

15. See generally "Timeline: Deadly Factory Accidents in Bangladesh," *CBC News* (October 9, 2013), www.cbc.ca/news2/interactives/timeline-bangladesh/; "Bangladesh Factory Death Toll Soars Past 1,100," *CBC News* (May 11, 2013), www.cbc.ca/news/world/bangladesh-factory-death-toll-soars-past-1-100-1.1370852.

16. Julfikar Ali Manik and Jim Yardley, "Building Collapse in Bangladesh Leaves Scores Dead," *The New York Times* (April 24, 2013), www.nytimes.com/2013/04/25/world/asia/bangladesh-building-collapse.html; Associated Press, "Bangladesh Factory Collapse Blamed on Swampy Ground and Heavy Machinery," *The Guardian* (May 24, 2013), www.theguardian.com/world/2013/may/23/bangladesh-factory-collapse-rana-plaza.

17. HRW Report; Associated Press, "Bangladesh Factory Collapse Blamed on Swampy Ground and Heavy Machinery."

18. Accord on Fire and Building Safety in Bangladesh, http://bangladeshaccord.org/.

19. Alliance for Bangladesh Worker Safety, www.bangladeshwor kersafety.org/about/about-the-alliance. For a comparison of the Alliance and Accord initiatives, see Sarah Labowitz and Dorothee Baumann-Pauly, *Business as Usual Is Not an Option: Supply Chains and Sourcing after Rana Plaza* (2014), pp. 53–56, www.stern.nyu.edu/experience-stern/about/departments-centers-initiatives/centers-of-research/business-human-rights/activities/supply-chains-sourcing-after-rana-plaza.

20. Labowitz and Baumann-Pauly, *Business as Usual Is Not an Option*, p. 6.

21. Ibid., p. 28.

22. For instance, Benetton agreed to contribute over US$1 million to a fund established by action group Avaaz: see Avaaz, "Victory with Benetton," https://secure.avaaz.org/campaign/en/benetton_thank_you/.

Discussion Questions

1. How can Basic Black respond to the violation of the supplier agreement by Raz Fashions? Could it be the right answer to shift production out of Bangladesh entirely?

2. Are there ways in which Basic Black is responsible for the decision of Raz Fashions to resort to unauthorized subcontracting? Could the supplier agreement, or Basic Black's ordering practices, be modified in ways that would reduce the pressures on Raz to subcontract? Would those steps be consistent with business interests?

3. How does the audit model employed by Basic Black work and not work here? Are there alternative models of responsibility that would better protect workers' rights?

4. Is Basic Black meeting its obligations to respect human rights in accord with the United Nations' "Protect, Respect and Remedy Framework for Business and Human Rights"? Why, or why not? Explain.

Case 6: FIFA's Red Card: Corruption and World Cup Soccer

ROXANNE ROSS AND DENIS G. ARNOLD

Soccer (or football outside the United States) is immensely popular. The World Cup is the most watched sporting event in the world, with more viewers than the Olympics. The last World Cup tournament attracted 3.2 billion viewers, approximately half of the world's population. The non-profit organization that organizes international soccer operations is the Fédération Internationale de Football Association, more commonly referred to as FIFA. Approximately 209 national associations participate in FIFA.

Ninety percent of FIFA revenue is from the World Cup, which is held every four years. The most recent World Cup cycle grossed $4.8 billion against expenses of $2.2 billion. As the organizing body, FIFA's revenue comes from TV rights, marketing rights and sponsorship, tickets, license rights, and hospitality of tournament guests. FIFA profits were $2.6 billion. Profits earned from the World Cup are intended to be used for soccer development funds supporting youth teams, lower division leagues, and soccer infrastructure in developing countries.

While overseeing one of the world's most beloved sports, FIFA faces harsh criticism for the pervasive corruption of its senior officials. The suspected misconduct inspired an early morning raid at FIFA's headquarters in Zurich. The raid was orchestrated by the US government with the help of Swiss police. Seven FIFA officials were arrested that morning on suspicion of accepting $150 million in bribes. Agents of Russia and Qatar are alleged to have paid bribes to FIFA officials in order to host the World Cup. In addition, sports marketing firms and apparel companies are alleged to have bribed FIFA officials to obtain lucrative contracts.

The US indictment alleges members of FIFA's leadership accepted over $150 million in bribes over a 20-year period. Forty people were charged in connection to corruption at FIFA. The 47-count indictment included racketeering, conspiracy, money laundering, and wire fraud. In particular, the Swiss investigation focused on bribery related to determining future hosts for the World Cup. The US investigation centered on the fact that the alleged illegal activities were planned in the United States and American banks were used to transfer illicit funds. However, because the US Foreign Corrupt Practices Act focuses primarily on the bribery of public officials, bribery was not among the charges brought by US prosecutors.

Chuck Blazer, former general secretary of the Confederation of North, Central America and Caribbean Association Football, cooperated with US prosecutors after being charged with accepting bribes. His statements revealed that he and others accepted money to vote for South Africa and Morocco during the 2010 and 1998 World Cup selection processes. Blazer's statements, along with other evidence, exposed a long history of buying votes for marketing rights. Because the tournament attracts billions of viewers, many companies jockey for the right to attach their name to the World Cup. The most recent game generated $1.47 billion from marketing revenue from these sponsors. Blazer said he and others accepted bribes for CONCACAF Gold Cup broadcasting rights in 1996, 1998, 2000, 2002, and 2003 (the Gold Cup is awarded every two years in North America, Central America, and the Caribbean). Reports also indicate that the Swiss marketing firm International Sports and Leisure Company won World Cup marketing rights in the 1990s through buying votes. Additionally, Alejandro Burzaco, the owner of the marketing company Torneos y Competencias, paid senior officials $110 million to maintain control of media rights. Burzaco eventually turned himself in and plead guilty to racketeering conspiracy, wire fraud conspiracy, and money laundering conspiracy.

Bribery problems extended to referees as well. An Asian crime syndicate paid referees to fix games in order to profit from sports betting. Unlike many other countries, sports betting is legal in parts of Asia. Football 4 U International was a front for the match fixing organization that was the main culprit involved with the bribing. Some referees were offered as much as $400,000 by the organization, and at least 15 matches were suspected to have been rigged including World Cup qualifying games. There is also evidence that Football 4 U was responsible for making death threats, selecting referees despite having no authority to do so, and offering bribes to those willing to comply. FIFA did little to follow up on match fixing cases. They technically have no legal authority over referees. As such, the full extent of match fixing is difficult to gauge. Still, FIFA neither banned nor accused any referees even though they acknowledged the match fixing had likely occurred.

Although FIFA members were previously accused of misconduct, the accusations by the US Department of Justice were unique because they were the first to take meaningful action against FIFA. Former head of FIFA security, Chris Eaton, commented by saying, "The fact is there's been no jurisdiction that was able to take a report, or to take action, or to coordinate a global action such as the U.S. has done today. We're seeing for the first time a very powerful jurisdiction take action against a very powerful, opaque organization." FIFA had virtual impunity until the US and Swiss investigations were launched, as no other government was willing or able to take action despite longstanding knowledge of corruption.

Despite being the most powerful member, former president Sepp Blatter was not charged for any crimes. Still, Blatter was ousted during the beginning of his fifth term by FIFA's ethics committee. The committee banned Blatter for eight years for making a "disloyal payment" of $2 million to another member. Even though Blatter wasn't charged, some of those involved maintain Blatter was responsible for the misconduct. As president of FIFA, many argue Blatter should have done more to curtail or eliminate rampant corruption.

FIFA's most vulnerable stakeholders bore the brunt of the corruption. The youth leagues, lower-division leagues, and workers involved in preparing for the tournaments unduly suffered because of FIFA's carelessness or malevolence. The money FIFA generates is supposed to be reinvested to help support soccer development for the youth and lower-division leagues. Each federal association receives about $2 million from a World Cup game that is to be used for these purposes. Yet infrastructure for players is often dilapidated. Some players are not provided enough food to properly sustain themselves during matches, and some youth leagues play with poor quality used equipment because they are so underfunded. Others negatively affected are the migrant construction workers building the stadium in Qatar who face many human rights violations. Their working arrangements are described as a form of modern slavery. Workers can be forced to stay in Qatar, are underpaid, live in deplorable conditions, and are often grossly indebted to their employers. Every day about 2.7 workers die building World Cup facilities. Critics of FIFA say they failed both to adequately address human rights violations and to react appropriately once human rights violations were revealed. Qatar was well known to violate internationally recognized workers' rights before it made its bid to host the World Cup.

The reaction to the scandals from sponsors has been mixed. Sony, Emirates, and Castrol did not renew their contract. Coca-Cola, Adidas, and Visa voiced concerns but have not otherwise acted. Regarding workers' conditions in Qatar, top sponsors voiced concerns but did not withdraw their support. Several sponsors maintained that the responsibility was on FIFA to work with the Qatari government to remedy the situation. The top sponsors paid on average $30 million annually for the last World Cup. A third of FIFA revenue comes from sponsors. Only 12 out of 34 sponsorship slots were filled a year before the competition, an unusually low figure.

To many observers, FIFA's widespread corruption was enabled by a lack of oversight, transparency, responsiveness, and accountability on the part of senior leadership and the organization as a whole. According to a report, 41 percent of FIFA member associations do not publish any detailed information about their organization including finances, statutes, ethical codes, or organizational activity. Eighty percent of FIFA's 209 federal associations do not publish financial reports of any kind. Deborah Unger of Transparency International's Corruption in Sport Initiative stated, "If you have a look at FIFA's accounts, you do not know where all the money went. You don't know how much the senior executives get. They're very very lump-sum broad accounts." Because FIFA has a long history of misconduct, many believe little will change. However, the unprecedented actions taken by the US and Swiss prosecutors suggest the possibility of reform.

Discussion Questions

1. Why do you believe corruption at FIFA has taken place for so long? Explain.
2. Who was harmed by the corruption at FIFA? Explain.

3. Do you believe that the US Foreign Corrupt Practices Act should be modified so that, in addition to it being illegal to bribe public officials, it is also illegal to bribe the executives of non-profit organizations such as FIFA? Why, or why not? Explain.

4. If you were in charge of revamping FIFA to root out corruption, what changes in the organization would you implement to achieve that end? Explain.

This case is based on the following sources: "2014 FIFA World Cup™ Reached 3.2 Billion Viewers, One Billion Watched Final" (December 16, 2015). Retrieved July 3, 2017 from www.fifa.com/worldcup/news/2014-fifa-world-cuptm-reached-3-2-billion-viewers-one-billion-watched–2745519.

Amnesty International, *The Ugly Side of a Beautiful Game* (London: Amnesty International, 2015).

"FIFA Corruption Crisis: Key Questions Answered," *BBC News* (December 21, 2015). Retrieved July 3, 2017 from www.bbc.com/news/world-europe-32897066.

M. J. Garcia and C. Borbély, "Report on the Inquiry into the 2018/2022 FIFA World Cup™ Bidding Process," *The New York Times* (June 27, 2017). Retrieved July 3, 2017 from www.nytimes.com/interactive/2017/06/27/sports/soccer/document-World-Cup-Garcia-Report.html.

M. Heywood, D. Unger, and B. Wheatland, *The Transparency International Football Governance League Table* (Berlin: Transparency International, 2015).

D. Hill and J. Longman, "Fixed Soccer Matches Cast Shadow over World Cup," *The New York Times* (May 31, 2014). Retrieved July 11, 2017 from www.nytimes.com/2014/06/01/sports/soccer/fixed-matches-cast-shadow-over-world-cup.html.

"One Year before the World Cup, FIFA is Shunned by Sponsors," *The Economist* (June 15, 2017). Retrieved July 13, 2017 from www.economist.com/news/business/21723430-it-recently-replaced-officials-serving-its-ethics-committee-one-year-world-cup.

E. Perez and Shimon Prokupecz, "FIFA Arrests: U.S. Charges 16 FIFA Officials," *CNN* (December 3, 2015). Retrieved July 3, 2017 from https://edition.cnn.com/2015/12/03/sport/fifa-corruption-charges-justice-department/index.html.

G. Smith, "Another Report Damns Qatar's Treatment of World Cup Workers," *Fortune* (March 31, 2016). Retrieved July 12, 2017 from https://fortune.com/2016/03/31/qatar-world-cup-workers/.

S. Wade, "The Biggest Victims of the FIFA Scandal Speak Out," *Business Insider* (May 31, 2015). Retrieved July 12, 2017 from www.businessinsider.com/the-biggest-victims-of-the-fifa-scandal-speak-out-2015-5.

Case 7: Walmart de México: Millions in Bribes Fuel Growth

ROXANNE ROSS AND DENIS G. ARNOLD

Over two thousand years ago the city of Teotihuacán was one of the most prosperous metropolises of Mesoamerica's Golden Age. At its peak, 200,000 residents lived in relative abundance supported by sophisticated comforts such as a spring water irrigation system, obsidian darts and spears crafted from nearby deposits and used as trade goods, and imports such as chocolate and cotton. The jewels of the city were two impressive pyramids, among the largest built in Mesoamerica. The pyramids still stand today among many other important ancient buildings and together they constitute Mexico's most important archaeological site. Tourists from around the world flock to this UNESCO World Heritage Site. Today, amidst the mountainous terrain is a strangely familiar sight. Just a mile away from the pyramids, where there was previously an alfalfa field, there is now a large Walmart store. Congested traffic surrounds the store producing air pollution that harms the stone pyramids and other ancient buildings.

Zoning regulations intended to protect the pyramids should have prevented Walmart from building on the site. Teotihuacán city officials had worked for years on a zoning plan that would protect the pyramids, and the final plan prohibited commercial construction on the alfalfa field. However, the final step in the legal process of implementing the zoning plan was to publish the complete plan in a government newspaper. Walmart sought out and bribed a government official with $52,000 to redraw the zoning map to allow the store to be built on the field before sending it to the newspaper. Soon after the illegally altered map was published, Walmart broke ground on the site in the face of fierce, local opposition including street protests, sit-ins, and hunger strikes.

Walmart brought in bulldozers to start construction excavation on grounds bearing ancient relics. Normally, construction with bulldozers is prohibited. Development near historical sites must be conducted with picks and shovels to protect any artifacts found. Walmart also avoided an archaeological survey of the land before building. If historical pieces are discovered in the survey, construction could be stopped permanently. Walmart obtained the scores of permits required in an unusually short period of time and the store was built quickly.

Protestors believed the company was using bribery to get its way. The protestors' claims were corroborated by Sergio Cicero, a former executive at Walmart de México. Cicero admitted that bribery by Walmart offices were commonplace in violation of the US Foreign Corrupt Practices Act. He reported that bribes were used to circumvent legal obstacles, such as environmental regulations and zoning restrictions, so that Walmart could expand in Mexico at a pace ahead of its competition. The payments were concealed using fraudulent accounting, often labeled as external consulting fees. According to Cicero, Walmart de México perfected the art of bribery throughout its Mexican operations. According to news reports, Walmart de México paid out $24 million in bribes.

Individuals bribed by Walmart in order to build the Teotihuacán store included the mayor, the director of the urban planning, city staff with the responsibility of issuing permits, and the agency responsible for protecting anthropological and historical remains in Mexico, the Instituto Nacional de Antropolígía e Historia (INAH). Walmart also paid local church members to form a counter protest to show support for building the store. The mayor and INAH were recipients of some of the larger payments, receiving over $100,000 and $81,000 respectively. Bribery was utilized not just to build near the pyramids of Teotihuacán, but to build at least 19 other stores in Mexico.

Cicero reported that former CEO of Walmart de México, Eduardo Castro-Wright, was heavily involved in the use of bribes to fuel growth. The payments markedly increased when Castro-Wright joined Walmart de México and dropped off when he left. Cicero claimed Castro-Wright used illegal payments to achieve aggressive growth rates in Mexico. Currently Mexico is home to approximately 20 percent of all Walmart stores. Over 209,000 Mexican citizens work for Walmart de México, making it the largest private employer in the country. Because of his success at growing Walmart de México, Castro-Wright was promoted to vice-chairman of parent company Walmart in the United States.

Cicero had notified corporate headquarters of the violations of the Foreign Corrupt Practices Act in 2004. Walmart's inquiry was first conducted by a former member of the FBI, but was later turned over to the general counsel of Walmart de México. As such, the investigation was effectively conducted by the entity being investigated. Those in charge of the Walmart de México investigation explained Cicero's allegations by suggesting the former executive was attempting to tarnish Walmart de México's name. They also suggested that Cicero himself was using the bribes to embezzle millions from Walmart. Evidence for these claims has not been presented, and the explanation would not itself absolve senior leadership from responsibility for authorizing the bribes. Walmart ceased investigation in 2006 and declined to report the violations to the US Department of Justice at that time or otherwise make them public.

The New York Times broke the story in late 2012 in a two-part, Pulitzer Prize winning investigative report. Castro-Wright retired form Walmart soon thereafter. Walmart's shares fell 5 percent, a $10 billion decrease. The firm subsequently spent approximately $800 million internally on investigations and improved ethics and compliance controls. Internal investigations led to revelations of Walmart's use of bribery in China, India, and Brazil. An investigation undertaken by the US Department of Justice has yet to be resolved. Because Walmart covered up the allegations, it may have no legal liability for the most serious cases of bribery. This is because the most serious allegations were only revealed after the five-year statute of limitations under the Foreign Corrupt Practices Act had expired, making the case more challenging for the Department of Justice.

Walmart responded to the revelations of corruption by stating that they would cooperate with the investigation by the Department of Justice. In a press release Walmart stated, in part:

> Acting with integrity is the essence of our corporate culture. We have the same high standards of integrity for every associate – regardless of his or her position – and everyone is held accountable for those standards. In a large global enterprise such as Walmart, sometimes issues arise despite our best efforts and intentions. When they do, we take them seriously and act as quickly as possible to understand what happened. We take action and work to implement changes so the issue doesn't happen again. That's what we're doing today.

Discussion Questions

1. From an ethical perspective, how would you assess Walmart de México's actions in Teotihuacán? Explain.
2. How would you assess Walmart's global ethics and compliance programs before the New York Times

reported to the public on Walmart de México's actions? Explain.

3. What do you make of Walmart's explanation that "sometimes issues arise despite our best efforts and intentions" and that "everyone is held accountable" by way of explaining the bribery scheme in Mexico? Explain.

4. Do you believe that the five-year statute of limitations on the Foreign Corrupt Practices Act ought to be extended or eliminated? Why, or why not? Explain.

This case was written for classroom discussion and is based on the following sources: D. Barstow, "At Walmart in Mexico, a Bribe Inquiry Silenced," *The New York Times* (April 21, 2012). Retrieved from www.nytimes.com/2012/04/22/business/at-wal-mart-in-mexico-a-bribe-inquiry-silenced.html.

D. Barstow and A. Xanic von Bertrab, "How Walmart Used Payoffs to Get Its Way in Mexico," *The New York Times* (December 17, 2012). Retrieved from www.nytimes.com/2012/12/18/business/walmart-bribes-teotihuacan.html.

M. Cartwright, "Teotihuacán" (February 17, 2015). Retrieved August 16, 2017 from www.ancient.eu/Teotihuacán/.

T. Hsu, "Walmart Responds to Report Saying It Squashed Mexico Bribery Probe," *Los Angeles Times* (April 22, 2012). Retrieved August 21, 2017 from www.latimes.com/business/la-fi-mo-walmart-mexican-bribery-20120422-story.html.

A. Viswanatha and D. Barrett, "Walmart Bribery Probe Finds Few Signs of Major Misconduct in Mexico," *Wall Street Journal* (October 19, 2015). Retrieved August 21, 2017 from www.wsj.com/articles/wal-mart-bribery-probe-finds-little-misconduct-in-mexico-1445215737.

Tom Schoenberg, "Wal-Mart Close to Resolving Bribery Probe for $300 Million," *Bloomberg.com* (May 9, 2017). Retrieved August 21, 2017 from www.bloomberg.com/news/articles/2017-05-09/wal-mart-said-close-to-resolving-bribery-probe-for-300-million.

10

Ethical Markets

10.1 INTRODUCTION

Free markets are those where supply and demand for goods, services, and labor determine prices and wages. Free markets rely on enforceable property rights and are commonly regarded as an essential feature of capitalism, yet perfectly free markets exist in no nation. All legal markets are regulated rendering them partially free. Without regulation markets would grow unstable and collapse. Consider, for example, financial markets, which include products like stocks, bonds, and derivatives, securities exchanges for the sale of these products, and banks, insurers, and credit rating agencies that facilitate such market exchanges. Without the regulation of financial markets, and regulators to enforce these laws, investors would lose confidence in financial products, demand would dry up, and markets would cease to function. The question for any modern nation is not "Should markets be regulated?" but "How should markets be regulated?" Government regulation can be efficient or cumbersome, it can promote economic growth or stifle growth, and can be used to provide incentives for the development of necessary products and services (e.g., life-saving drugs or sustainable energy) or disincentives for harmful economic activities (e.g., worker fatalities and environmental pollution). Markets can promote efficiency and wealth creation, but the regulation of markets serves to protect other important values such as human dignity, justice, democracy, and a sustainable planet.

Economists emphasize monetary value and many economists assume that maximizing wealth will produce maximal social welfare. However, many of these economists are unable to conceptualize and utilize other values in their research. For example, from the perspective of the Kantian tradition in ethics, basic human dignity, and the corresponding practical instantiation of human dignity in the form of basic human rights, cannot be properly monetized. This is because humanity, via the individual capacity for moral self-governance, is an end in itself – as Kant famously put this point, persons have value "beyond all price." For this reason, scholars, politicians, and ordinary citizens hold that the regulation of markets is needed to help protect the dignity of persons. Dignity is widely regarded as an essential human value outside of economics. Another value that economics has historically had great difficulty in recognizing is ecological value, that is, the value of nature independent of the monetary value of its constituent elements (e.g., lumber, fossil fuels, or fisheries), or its monetary real estate value, in market exchanges. The global environment sustains human populations, but markets can produce harmful outcomes (negative externalities in economic terms) such as the degradation of the Earth's atmosphere and oceans, widespread deforestation, ecosystem destruction, and species extinctions. The very real trends in environmental degradation (discussed in Chapter 8) require a more complex conception of the value of nature than economics has historically been able to provide.

This chapter has as its focus the ethical boundaries that should be placed on markets. What goods and services can be legally bought and sold? For example, should sex, synthetic recreational drugs, children, or electoral votes be legally available for sale in market economies? What about the pricing of lawful goods? Should pharmaceutical companies with patents be able to price life-saving drugs at whatever level the company deems appropriate? In cases of natural disasters, such as hurricanes, should retailers of life-sustaining goods (e.g., baby food, water, or portable generators) be allowed to raise their prices to levels only the very rich can afford? The case study "Should Everything Be for Sale?" introduces some of these issue in practical terms, while the case study "Like Taking Candy from a Baby? Mylan's Pricing of the EpiPen" facilitates a deep assessment of the problems associated with the accessibility of life-saving drugs to all US citizens.

This chapter also takes up the regulation of financial markets. To what extent should government regulations protect individual investors vs. promoting aggressive growth and profit strategies for financial firms? Deregulating financial markets is commonly advocated by industry trade groups and Wall Street investment banks in order to reduce costs. They claim that financial professionals will watch out for the interests of individual investors. However, repeated major financial crises suggest that *caveat emptor* (buyer beware) is a better characterization of Wall Street values. These conflicting perspectives are represented in the case study "The Big Fix: How Big Banks Colluded to Rig Interest Rates," as well as other case studies in this chapter.

SHOULD EVERYTHING BE FOR SALE?

In her contribution to this chapter, "Noxious Markets," Deborah Satz explains why markets in certain goods and services should be regarded as harmful or pernicious and thereby prohibited or heavily regulated. She provides a conceptual scheme for identifying such markets. In her view, noxious markets are ones where there are problems regarding the standing of the parties before, during, and after the exchange. Such problems often undermine the equality of citizens in a democracy. For example, a grain market which leaves some people starving as a result of prices set through supply and demand, or markets in child labor which preclude access to childhood education result in severe inequality among citizens. Likewise, she argues that there is an important reason for blocking the sale of votes in a democracy. Namely, permitting the sale of votes would give the rich even more power over the poor who would be the most likely to sell their votes. In her rich and nuanced discussion, she takes up other controversial markets such as "blood diamonds," human reproduction, and primary education. She concludes her contribution with a discussion of the legitimacy of limiting the scope of property rights and blocking certain markets altogether.

Libertarians typically reject restrictions on property rights, or what can be owned, oppose regulation, and defend maximally free markets. They emphasize individual freedom as the supreme value, and typically minimal attention to other values. From this perspective, everything, or nearly everything should be available for purchase in markets. Jason Brennan and Peter M. Jaworski adapt such a pro-commodification perspective in their contribution to this chapter "Markets without Limits." They claim that if it is ethically permissible for you to do something for free, then it is also ethically permissible for you to do it for money. They take on two controversial examples to illustrate their position: markets in babies and markets in votes. According to Brennan and Jaworski, markets in babies are appropriate. Because they recognize that children are not legal property, their claim is actually that parents should be able to sell parental rights and thereby transfer the child to the purchaser(s). They qualify this view by stipulating that the purchaser(s) must meet a basic test for parental fitness before the sale and transfer is permitted to go through. On their view, then, a parent that feels overwrought by parenting duties, or who needs an infusion in cash, can identify a qualified buyer and sell his or her parental rights in the market, and then permanently transfer one or more children to the new owner. Their view on markets in voting is similar: since we can vote for free, we should be able to sell our votes to the highest bidder.

Not all libertarians agree with Brennan and Jaworski's position. James Stacey Taylor is a libertarian scholar who has defended liberal markets in his own work. However, Taylor finds the arguments of Brennan and Jaworski unpersuasive. In his contribution to this chapter, "Markets in Utopia," he argues that Brennan and Jaworski put so many restrictions on their pro-commodification arguments that it turns out to be a tepid claim that has none of the bravado they seem to attribute to their argument. Taylor argues that their view boils down to this: If it is morally permissible to give away a good or service, then it could also be morally permissible to sell in those situations where the market for that good or service is not noxious in the sense utilized by Satz. In other words, according to Taylor, the pro-commodification arguments of Brennan and Jaworski are applicable only in a utopian society that does not presently exist.

Questions regarding the ethical limits of markets can be theoretically challenging, but they are also a feature of everyday public policy debates in societies across the world and merit our careful attention.

PRICE GOUGING

Severe storms, hurricanes, and tropical cyclones are increasing in intensity as the Earth's climate warms. The severe flooding and high winds that accompany these extreme events cause massive flooding and property damage. People living in affected areas are often left homeless, or in flooded homes with no electricity. Hospitals and clinics can no longer see patients, restaurant and grocery store services are severely curtailed, and subsistence supplies are scare. However, these circumstances represent an opportunity for large and small companies alike to make huge profits by drastically raising prices on scarce products and services. In a capitalist economy, is there anything wrong with raising prices as high as possible for such goods and services? Or imagine a firm has the patent on a life-saving drug for which there is no competition. In capitalist society, shouldn't the firm be praised for raising prices as high as possible in order to make more profits for investors and executives? Most defenders of shareholder primacy and free markets answer these questions with an unwavering affirmative response. On the other hand, critics argue that such "price gouging" is immoral because it wrongfully exploits vulnerable people. Because of this, many jurisdictions have laws prohibiting price gouging.

Matt Zwolinski is a libertarian theorist who defends price gouging in this chapter. In "The Ethics of Price Gouging," Zwolinski argues that the common moral condemnation of price gouging is mistaken and that most laws prohibiting price gouging are unjust. His account is grounded in the view that mutually advantageous exploitation is not wrong, since both parties benefit. In such cases, one party is vulnerable because of their circumstances and lack of wealth, while a second party is in a position to sell the vulnerable party valuable goods and services that are at present scarce. Since scarcity drives up prices for goods in demand, it is reasonable to offer the vulnerable party the good or services at much higher prices. The buyer benefits from acquiring needed goods, while the seller benefits from the increased prices brought on by scarcity and high demand. Jeremy Snyder provides a contrasting set of arguments in his contribution to this chapter, "What's the Matter with Price Gouging?" Snyder's Kantian analysis argues that price gouging is disrespectful of persons because it undercuts equitable access to essential goods. His position stands in opposition to that of Zwolinski and he concludes that most versions of price gouging laws are not merely just, but are necessary to maintain democratic equality. Both Zwolinski and Snyder emphasize pricing in the midst of natural disasters in their discussions of price gouging. However, price gouging can take place in other contexts and one of the most contentious is the pricing of life-saving drugs where the producer holds an exclusive patent and the government places no limit on pricing. The case study "Like Taking Candy from a Baby? Mylan's Pricing of the EpiPen" takes up price gouging in this context.

FINANCIAL SERVICES

The financial crisis of 2008–2009 was caused by a combination of reckless consumer borrowing, predatory lending by mortgage originators, the deceptive bundling and selling of risky or "toxic" mortgages by banks to third-party investors as high grade investments, and the false representation of those loans as high quality by credit rating agencies. Executives were rewarded for making high-risk bets with investor assets when they succeeded, but were not penalized when the bets caused massive losses. In addition, the US Congress – heavily influenced by lobbyists representing large financial service companies – removed financial regulations designed to protect investors that had been in place since the Great Depression of the mid-1930s. According to the Federal Deposit Insurance Corporations, in the United States 531 banks have failed since 2008 while only 23 banks failed in the previous eight years.[1] Some experts put the total global cost of the financial crisis at $15 trillion.[2] In the five years following the crisis the US unemployment rate was between 8 and 10 percent while the Euro Area unemployment rate hovered between 9 and 12 percent. The global financial crisis that has developed during the last several years raises a wide variety of ethically significant questions regarding trust and regulation in financial services. The case study "The Big Fix: How Big Banks Colluded to Rig Interest Rates" illustrates the fact that these issues persist beyond the financial crisis. The case focuses on the price fixing of interest rates by mega banks in the face of lax government regulation.

At the core of most ethical issues between financial professionals, their clients, and the public are fiduciary duties, that is, duties that have been entrusted to finance professionals based on a relationship of trust. Most unethical practices in finance stem from breaches of these relationships of trust. In his contribution to this chapter, "Ethical Issues in Financial Services," John R. Boatright begins by discussing some of the unethical practices that are commonly observed in the financial services industry. These include deception; churning, or the inappropriate trading of a client's assets to generate broker income; and recommending unsuitable securities and financial products for clients. One of the most significant breaches of trust in financial services is the practice of predatory lending which involves deceptively selling unsuitable products to clients. This practice is the focus of the case study "Predatory Lending at Countrywide Financial." Boatright argues that financial service professionals have a moral obligation to refrain from such behavior. He then turns his attention to insider trading where he argues that the fiduciary duties of managers and other insiders to shareholders provide a strong basis for a prohibition on insider trading. The case study "Martha Stewart Living Omnimedia, Inc.: An Accusation of Insider Trading" provides a valuable tool for assessing in practical terms the ethics and legality of insider trading.

Not everyone agrees that insider trading should be illegal. Some economists, for example, argue that insider trading does not harm anyone while benefiting those who trade on inside information. Libertarians defend small government and minimal regulation and most advocate industry self-regulation rather than government regulation. In his contribution to this chapter, "The Moral Problem of Insider Trading," Alan Strudler analyzes the act of insiders buying or selling shares of a company based on information they gained from having access to confidential company information not available to the general public. Strudler argues that the ethical wrong in insider trading is best understood as an unconscionable contract between the insider and shareholders. Since shareholders would never agree to such a contractual relationship he argues that insider trading is deceptive and should be illegal. But should "outsiders" be permitted to trade on information obtained from "insiders"? In the 1997 US Supreme Court decision *United States, Petitioner v. James Herman O'Hagan*, reprinted in the legal perspectives section of this chapter, insider trading was found to be illegal when it involves the misappropriation of confidential information by an outsider, not directly employed by the company in question. It is enough, the Court ruled, if the outsider has fiduciary ties to the company and makes inappropriate use of confidential information.

Notes

1. FDIC, "Failed Bank List." Retrieved November 15, 2017 from www.fdic.gov/bank/individual/failed/banklist.html.
2. Al Yoon, "Total Global Losses from Financial Crisis: $15 Trillion," *Wall Street Journal* (October 1, 2012).

10.2 SHOULD EVERYTHING BE FOR SALE?

Noxious Markets

DEBORAH SATZ

Abstract Markets versus Noxious Markets

What is wrong with markets in everything? What is it about the nature of particular exchanges that concerns us, to the point that markets in some goods appear to be clearly undesirable? How should our social policies respond to such markets? Where and for what reasons is it appropriate to regulate a market, and when should we seek to block it? These are the difficult but important questions that this essay attempts to answer.

Several brief clarifications about my scope and aims here. First, my project does not involve an overall assessment of "the market system."[1] Markets allow people to accomplish many important social and individual tasks under modern conditions of interdependence and diversity. The point of my inquiry is not to raise general questions about the market system or about markets in the abstract. Rather, I am concerned here with the differing characteristics of very particular market exchanges: in human body parts, child labor, toxic waste, sex, and life-saving medicines. Markets in these goods provoke reservations even among those who are otherwise great enthusiasts about the market system. ...

A market exchange based in desperation, humiliation, or begging or whose terms of remediation involve bondage or servitude is not an exchange between equals. On my view,

lurking behind many, if not all, noxious markets are problems relating to the *standing* of the parties before, during, and after the process of exchange.

I will argue in this essay that some markets are noxious and need to be blocked or severely constrained if the parties are to be equals in a particular sense, as citizens in a democracy. In making this argument I draw on the writings of Adam Smith and other classical political economists. These thinkers recognized that markets require certain background conditions – specification of and enforcement of entitlements and property rights – in order to support relations of freedom and equality. The markets of the classical political economists were populated not by the abstract individuals with given wants that tend to characterize contemporary economic theory, but by landless peasants and wasteful landlords and by impoverished workers who stood in asymmetrical power relations with their employers. Moreover agents' preferences, capacities, and relationships were understood to be shaped by the structure and nature of particular markets. Like these theorists, the approach to markets I defend recognizes market heterogeneity and stresses the need to consider other values besides efficiency and distributional equality narrowly conceived.

Noxious Markets: The Basic Parameters

I begin with a characterization of four parameters in terms of which we can differentiate the markets that people find especially objectionable from other types of markets. Several of these parameters are *internal* to the perspective of economics in that scoring high on them will often undermine efficiency. However, there are also political and moral rationales for limiting noxious markets. That is why the addition of more markets is not always the appropriate response to a noxious market. In some cases our goal should be to curtail a particular noxious market, not to make it work better.

The first two parameters characterize the *consequences* of particular markets.

1. Some markets produce extremely *harmful outcomes.* That is, the operation of some markets leads to outcomes that are deleterious, either for the participants themselves or for third parties. Consider market exchanges that lead to the depletion of the natural resource base of a country or to the fueling of a genocidal civil war. Or consider a stock market transaction that wipes out a person's resources.

Of course, many markets have harmful outcomes without eliciting our revulsion; we think that the ups and downs of prices come with the territory. But some market outcomes are so negative, so extremely harmful that they almost always evoke a strong reaction. How harmful is that? Following up on a suggestion by Ravi Kanbur, we might consider as a natural starting point for answering this question a market whose operation leaves a person destitute. For example, a grain market whose operation leaves some people starving because they cannot afford the price at which grain is set through supply and demand is bound to make us feel uncomfortable.

Yet markets can also be extremely harmful to individuals in ways that go beyond destitution. Amartya Sen usefully distinguishes between two types of interests that people have: *welfare interests* concern a person's overall good, and *agency interests* concern a person's ability to participate in deciding matters that bear on that good.[2] These interests are interdependent, but they are distinct. (A benign dictator, for example, could meet all my basic welfare interests.) We can define a set of *basic* interests for people, interests in minimum levels of well-being and agency, and define extremely harmful market outcomes as outcomes that leave these basic interests unsatisfied. The idea of basic interests is meant to capture the idea that there are universal features of an adequate and minimally decent human life, a "line beneath which no one is to be allowed to sink."[3]

2. In addition to leading to extreme individual harms, certain markets can also be *extremely harmful for society*. The operation of these markets can undermine the social framework needed for people to interact *as equals*, as individuals with equal standing. There are, of course, running disagreements among philosophers concerning the meaning of "interact as equals," as well as the scope of this ideal. I take the content of this ideal to be given by the preconditions necessary for individuals to make claims on one another and interact without having to beg or to push others around. Markets help enable this ideal, as the basis of market claims is reciprocal self-interest of the parties.[4] But they can also undermine it. Consider markets that operate to undermine the capacities that a person needs to claim her rights or to participate in society; this is a problem with child labor markets and bonded labor. Or consider that particular markets may condition people to be docile or servile, shape them into passive accepters of a status quo. Whereas contemporary economics sees the capacities and preferences of agents in a market as givens, particular markets – think of media, education, and caregiving – shape us. Moreover they may shape us in ways that are in tension with a society of equals.

A special case is a market that is harmful for the standing of the parties as equal citizens in a democracy. This case ratchets up from the more minimal notion of equal standing: it has to do with the equality of individuals as co-deliberants and co-participants in making laws that apply to themselves. This kind of equality presupposes additional constraints on markets and their scope.

The next two parameters characterize the *sources* of particular markets, the underlying condition of the market agents:

3. Some markets are characterized by *very weak or highly asymmetric knowledge and agency* on the part of market participants. All real markets, of course, involve imperfect information. But in some cases this imperfect information is apt to produce extremely harmful consequences. This may be most likely in cases where there is a significant time lag between the initiation and the completion of a transaction. It is hard to predict one's future preferences. Consider the case of a woman selling her ability to have a child. In this case we might suspect that a woman who has never been pregnant cannot really know the consequences of selling the right to the child she bears.

Of course the fact that a contract has potential risks for an agent does not mean that the contract should not bind the agent, or else most contracting would fail. Nevertheless information failures are relevant to our assessment of particular markets in the face of harmful outcomes; in particular

Table 10.1 What makes a market noxious?

Source: Weak Agency	Source: Vulnerability
Inadequate information about the nature of and/or consequences of a market; others enter the market on one's behalf	Markets in a desperately needed good with limited suppliers; markets with origins in poverty and destitution; markets whose participants have very unequal needs for goods being exchanged
Outcome: Extreme Harms for Individual	*Outcome: Extreme Harms for Society*
Produces destitution; produces harm to the basic welfare and/or agency interests of the individual	Promotes servility and dependence; undermines democratic governance; undermines other regarding motivations

such failures serve to block justifications of a market transaction that appeal simply to the fact that it was chosen. Thus if agency is weak in surrogacy contracts, and a surrogate is now devastated by the thought of giving up the child she has borne, we will be less likely to think that we can justify enforcement of the contract simply on the basis that there was an agreement.

Although the majority of troubling markets characterized by weak agency involve extremely harmful outcomes, it is possible to be concerned by such markets even in the absence of harms. In this category would fall product markets that target young children; markets involving the production, purchase, and dissemination of information that fail to present relevant alternative points of view about a pressing political issue; and markets whose products are based on deception, even when there is no serious harm.

Agency problems also arise in markets in which one of the affected parties is not directly involved in the transaction but depends on others to transact for her. In such cases we cannot be certain that the party herself actually benefits from the transaction. In the majority of cases of child labor, for example, parents are transacting on behalf of the children whose time and labor are traded. Many forms of child labor give little or no benefit to the working child and in some cases significantly interfere with the child's ability to grow up into a healthy functioning adult. Other markets in which some of the affected parties are not directly involved as participants include markets in a nation's important scarce natural resources (such as timber in a rainforest), which can affect subsequent generations and others around the globe.

4. Some markets reflect the *underlying* extreme *vulnerabilities* of one of the transacting parties. Rousseau wrote that no citizen should "be wealthy enough to buy another, and none poor enough to be forced to sell himself."[5] When people come to the market with widely varying resources or widely

different capacities to understand the terms of their transactions, they are unequally vulnerable to one another. In such circumstances the weaker party is at risk of being exploited. For example, when a desperately poor person agrees to part with an asset at a fire sale price, even if the exchange improves his well-being we are rightly concerned with the fact that his circumstances made him willing to accept an offer for his asset that no one with a decent alternative would ever accept. When a person enters a contract from a position of extreme vulnerability he is likely to agree to almost any terms that are offered. Other examples of markets that exploit the vulnerability of transacting agents include markets in urgently needed goods where there is only a small set of suppliers and markets where the participants have highly unequal needs for the goods being exchanged.

Some markets not only *reflect* the different and unequal underlying positions of market agents but may also *exacerbate* them by the way they operate. For example, in Bangladesh a recent famine arose when the price of the main food, rice, rose very rapidly and became too expensive for the poor to purchase. By contrast, rich households were insulated from the risks of rising prices because they generally receive rice from their tenants as payment for the use of land so that they have rice for their own needs and surplus to sell.

So we have two dimensions regarding the source of a market and two dimensions regarding the consequences of a market that can be used to think about the acceptability of particular markets (see Table 10.1).

High scores along one of these dimensions, or several of them together, can make any market appear "noxious" to us. Consider the market in diamonds, whose sale is used to fund brutal civil wars. Many people find such a market abhorrent. On the analysis offered here, the best way to understand our negative reaction to this market has to do with its *extremely harmful* outcome – prolonging a bloody civil war in which thousands or tens of thousands die, hence the term "*blood diamonds*" – and with the *weak agency* of so many who are affected by the markets that fuel that war. Our discomfort with such markets doesn't seem to have anything to do with the social meaning of diamonds and little to do with the underlying income inequality of buyer and sellers.

Markets can damage important relationships people have with one another by allowing people to segment and opt out of a common condition. A central feature of most noxious markets on my approach has to do with their effects on the relationships between people, particularly the horizontal relationship of equal status. For two people to have equal status they need to see each other as legitimate sources of independent claims and they need to each have the capacity to press their claims without needing the other's permission to do so. This requires that each have rights and liberties of certain kinds as well as very specific resources, such as a level of education.

Equal status stands opposed to the ideas of caste, hereditary privilege, and unequal birthright. It insists that all individuals have an equal moral worth. Although it is perhaps possible to interpret this idea of equal status in economic terms, it is not easy to see how this would be done. Equal income and wealth by themselves do not entail equal status, as I stressed in my discussion of people with disabilities who have been marginalized from social positions and from public spaces.

Why not let people enter into labor contracts that involve bondage or contracts that grant labor bondage as remediation in the case of default? These were once common practices; such practices are compatible with both libertarian choice theory and welfare economics. But those who think that the problem with a market in bonded labor is its incompatibility with a conception of equal human status have reason to prohibit such contractual arrangements.

Equal Status in a Democracy

Social rights in their modern form imply an invasion of contract by status, the subordination of market price to social justice, the replacement of the free bargain by the declaration of rights.[6]

The preconditions for equal status as citizens in a democracy are more demanding than those needed for people to interact in horizontal relationships based on their reciprocal self-interest and equal moral worth. According to the conception of citizenship developed by the British social theorist T. H. Marshall, citizenship not only includes formal legal freedoms, but also a set of social rights with respect to healthcare, education, housing, and a decent minimum of income. These latter rights, he claimed, are needed to make one a full member of one's society. I think Marshall is correct: an equal right to vote has little effective meaning if some voters are too badly educated to read a ballot; citizenship means little for the destitute if society is so structured that they have no opportunity to share in society's benefits.

According to Marshall's view, the status of equal citizenship requires that all have (1) equal basic political rights and freedoms, including rights to speech and participation in the political process; (2) equal rights and freedoms within civil society, including rights to own property; and (3) equal rights to a threshold of economic welfare and to "share to the full in the social heritage and to live the life of a civilized being according to the standards prevailing in the society."[7]

Marshall viewed citizenship as a given status, not a privilege that depends on individual virtue or achievement. Citizenship gives to all within its ambit a single set of rights, irrespective of their wealth or family origin. While markets can be supportive of equal citizenship understood in this sense, whether or not they are so depends on the background circumstances, property rights, and regulations within which they operate. Someone who is desperately poor might agree to an exchange that requires her to function as an around-the-clock domestic servant or to bond her labor to obtain a loan at usurious rates that she can never hope to repay. The fate of such a person may be little different from that of a serf under feudalism.

In thinking about the preconditions of equal citizenship, it is important to think in terms of general social practices and not acts. For example, there may seem to be no problem with allowing a single person to work for whatever wages and hours she chooses, yet the existence of minimum wages and maximum hours laws may be necessary to preserve a threshold of economic welfare "according to the standards prevailing in the society,"[8] and to enhance the bargaining power of the poorest people in society to protect them from exploitation and abuse. Or consider another example: even if it makes sense in an individual instance for a poor family to put its children to work, when child labor is adopted as a widespread social practice it drives down adult wages, making it virtually impossible for poor parents to refrain from sending their children to work. Rather than seeing a person's market choices as exogenous variables, the choices we actually have open to us may depend on other market choices being blocked.

The transfer of income and wealth will not always be sufficient to maintain the conditions for citizen's equality; here the insights of specific egalitarians like Michael Walzer, Elizabeth Anderson, and Michael Sandel are important.

Consider the case of distributing primary and secondary school education through a market. Lack of education is an extremely harmful outcome in terms of democratic citizenship: a very poorly educated person will be incompetent as a juror and a voter and have little or no access to the basic opportunities and liberties associated with full membership in her society. But giving money, even a great deal of money, to a child who has not been educated will not compensate for her lack of education, even if cash is what she (as an adult) now herself prefers. Not only does it not replace the personal and social development that education might have enabled for her, but it does not turn her into a citizen who can participate competently and meaningfully in democratic self-governance. ...

These are all reasons for *not* distributing primary and secondary education solely through a market system, but enforcing it as a mandatory requirement. If our concern is with avoiding outcomes that undermine the conditions for citizens to interact as equals, then there is a powerful argument for guaranteeing access to a certain level of goods – education, healthcare, opportunities, rights, liberties, and physical security – even if some citizens would prefer to trade and sell these goods, or the opportunity to access these goods, to the highest bidder. While markets can supplement the supply of these goods in many cases, my point is that access to these goods should not depend only on individual preferences or income. The conditions for equal citizenship cannot be cashed out in terms of a generic good like money or utilitarian welfare; in addition to some level of income, they require that some goods be distributed in kind and that, in some cases, the distribution be more or less equal.

At the same time I would not defend the distribution of education or healthcare in terms of the idea that these goods are corrupted through sale. A public right to education is in theory compatible with the existence of a complementary or supplementary private education system. Instead my argument draws on Marshall's suggestion that some goods function as prerequisites for *full inclusion* in society, for counting as an equal member. A person who lacks a certain level of education or access to medical care or physical security is not only ill-equipped to navigate her own life and values, but also faces substantial impediments to participation in the economy and to participating in public debates about social choices. Such a person is vulnerable to exploitation and manipulation by others and dependent on luck or the will of benefactors to meet her basic needs.

In addition to supplementing market distributions in goods such as education and healthcare, we may have reason to *block certain market exchanges altogether* if citizens are to

be equals. Consider votes in a democracy. No one defends the outright sale of voting, even though it can be argued that such sale is consistent with efficiency and freedom. The interesting question is why. I think there are two main answers to this question, associated with two different ideals of democratic citizenship.

The first answer points out that the regulative idea of democracy is that citizens are equals engaged in a common cooperative project of governing themselves together. Thus citizens participate with others on an equal footing in deciding on the laws and policies that will govern them. A market in votes would have the predictable consequence of giving the rich disproportionate power over others since the poor would be far more likely than the rich to sell their political power. Indeed one rationale for secret ballots is to make contracts about votes unenforceable, thus protecting the poor and vulnerable from pressure to sell. If political, regulatory, judicial, and legal decision mechanisms were literally up for sale, this would concentrate political power in the hands of a few.

A second answer pushes in a more republican direction, interpreting democracy not merely as government among equals but as a means of determining the common good. On this view of democracy, *votes are acts of political co-deliberation.* Even if a vote market were not monopolized by the rich, we would still have a reason to proscribe vote trading on the grounds that voting is not about the aggregation of private interests; it is an act undertaken only after collectively deliberating about what is in the common good. Distributing votes according to preferences views citizens as consumers, not co-deliberators.

Both conceptions of democracy require that some markets be blocked and others be highly regulated. Both conceptions would block markets in votes, judicial offices, legislative offices, and voluntary slavery. Moreover, both conceptions would regulate markets governing the production and distribution of political information and markets governing access to legislative office and the opportunities associated with political influence, although to varying degrees. But these two conceptions might well differ on the treatment of military service as a market good. On the republican conception of democracy, there is something deeply troubling about the ways in which today's volunteer army shares some attributes with a mercenary army. Rather than seeing military service as an obligation of citizenship, today's soldiers are drawn from a small segment of the population that is largely working class.

Just as democracies made up of equal citizens require blocks on markets in votes or people, a related argument might be made that some markets need to be blocked or highly regulated if people are to develop the *capacities* that they need to participate effectively in civil and political society. Human beings are malleable in a way that goods such as apples are not.[9] We do not usually need to worry about the noneconomic effects of a market on the apples exchanged, but we do need to worry about whether a particular kind of market produces or supports passivity, alienation, or a ruthless egoism. Labor markets may be structured so as to accustom people to being pushed around and managed by others. Widespread markets in women's reproductive or sexual capacities (including quid pro quo sexual harassment contracts) might amplify gender inequalities by entrenching and deepening negative stereotypes about women. Unregulated education markets are compatible with children being treated as and raised as servile dependents. We need to pay special attention to cases like these, for they pose potential threats to the stable reproduction of democratic citizenship over time. Indeed the democratic state has an interest in withholding its support from institutions that cultivate subordination and servitude, even if those institutions are not strictly illegal.

Regulating Markets, Blocking Markets

How should we decide what approach to take to a noxious market? Obviously which policies it makes sense to adopt depends on the source of the market's noxiousness, which of the four parameters is in play. We need to tailor our response to the particular problems with that market. For example, if weak agency is the problem with a particular market, then we may want to undertake measures that increase information. If underlying vulnerability is a problem, we may want to redistribute income or create supplementary alternatives to market provision. Regulating a market is often the best way to address a market's noxiousness. At the same time, some problems with a market may be best addressed by closing off the ability of agents to trade in that market at all. Some markets undermine the social context in which people are able to interact on terms of equality.

In such cases we need to address not merely distributions, but also the underlying property rights of the transacting agents. To illustrate this, let's look briefly at child labor. In our world child labor often arises on the basis of destitution. But even in a world without destitution child labor would be problematic. Although many libertarian economists often view freedom as the freedom to participate in the market, they are often blind to the fact that individuals are not born with all the required capacities for exercising agency and making choices (including market choices) already

developed. The achievement of even a minimal threshold level of decision-making powers requires support from a variety of sources, including parents and the state: nurturing, help in developing the capacities for understanding and weighing alternatives, help in developing the ability to see oneself as an agent worthy of having choices, and attaining an adequate level of education. Child labor fails to promote and often blocks the development of these capacities.

Notes

1. Ravi Kanbur, "On Obnoxious Markets," in *Globalization, Culture and the Limits of the Market: Essays in Economics and Philosophy*, ed. Stephen Cullenberg and Prasanta Pattanaik (Oxford University Press, 2004), p. 44.
2. Amartya Sen, *On Ethics and Economics* (Oxford: Blackwell, 1987).
3. Henry Shue, *Basic Rights: Subsistence, Affluence and U.S. Foreign Policy* (Princeton University Press, 1996), p. 18. The language of human rights tries to capture the idea of some universal basic interests whose protection is especially urgent.
4. Adam Smith stressed this point in his famous remarks on the human tendency "to truck, barter, and exchange":

   When an animal wants to obtain something … it has no other means of persuasion but to gain the favor of those whose services it requires. A puppy fawns upon its dam, and a spaniel endeavors by a thousand attractions to engage the attention of his master who is at dinner, when it wants to be fed by him. Man sometimes uses the same arts with his brethren, and … endeavors by every servile and fawning attention to obtain their good will … But man has almost constant occasion for the help of his brethren, and it is in vain for him to expect it from their benevolence only. He will be more likely to prevail if he can … show them that it is for their own advantage to do for him what he requires of them … It is not from the benevolence of the butcher, the brewer, or the baker that we expect our dinner, but from their regard to their own interest. We address ourselves, not to their humanity, but to their self-love … Nobody but a beggar chooses to depend chiefly upon the benevolence of his fellow-citizens.

   Quotation from Adam Smith, *An Inquiry into the Nature and Causes of the Wealth of Nations* (Indianapolis, IN: Liberty Classics, 1976; originally published in 1776), pp. 118–19.
5. Jean-Jacques Rousseau, *Social Contract and Discourses* (London: J. M. Dent; originally published in 1762), p. 34.
6. T. H. Marshall, "Citizenship and Social Class," in *Class, Citizenship and Social Development: Essays by T. H. Marshall* (University of Chicago Press, 1977), p. 122.
7. Ibid., p. 78.
8. Ibid.

9. Labor markets may be highly constitutive in their effects on the parties involved. As we saw, Adam Smith conjectured that a worker who spends her life engaged in menial, servile tasks in which she has no voice or authority is not likely to develop the capacities she needs to function as an active citizen. (Nor is she likely, given the chance, to be a loyal employee. Indeed a large body of research shows that high worker effort and loyalty require substantial departures from the treatment of labor as a pure commodity.)

Markets without Limits

JASON BRENNAN AND PETER M. JAWORSKI

We're going to spend some time clarifying just what our thesis is and what the commodification debate is about. We need to do so in part because many of the people who participate in the debate get the debate confused. Simply by clarifying what's at stake, we'll take care of perhaps half of the cases we've seen the anti-commodification critics complain about.

Our Thesis

No one thinks that literally everything and anything should be for sale under any circumstances, no matter what. Everyone thinks there are at least some cases in which certain things should not be for sale.

Despite this admission, our title *Markets without Limits* is not misleading. There is an important sense in which we do advocate markets with unlimited scope. Our view of the scope of the market can be summarized as follows:

Markets without Limits:
   If you may do it for free, then you may do it for money.

To put it in a more long-winded way, if you may have, use, possess, and dispose of something (that does not belong to someone else) for free, then – except in special circumstances – it is permissible for you to buy and sell it. Another way of expressing our thesis is that the market does not *transform* what were permissible acts into impermissible acts. It does not *introduce* wrongness where there was not any already. Yet another way of expressing this is that, in the debate on commodification, to produce a successful argument for a limit on markets, the fact that something is on the market must cause or contribute to the wrongness. It must feature in an explanation for why it is wrong.

To illustrate these ideas, consider the following two markets:

1. Child Porn. A market in which people sell pornographic images of young children.

2. Nukes. A market in which arms dealers sell nuclear weapons.

We agree that child porn and nuclear weapons should not be for sale. But the problem with these markets isn't the markets themselves – it's that the items for sale should not be possessed, period. It's wrong to possess child pornography even if you acquired it for free. The wrongness of markets in child pornography does not originate in the market, but in the existence of the traded item in the first place.

We think the same goes for nuclear weapons, though this claim is more controversial, and we will not defend it here. We think no country should have nuclear weapons. But suppose we are wrong – suppose relatively peaceful countries like England and France may permissibly have nuclear weapons, even if Myanmar and the average citizen may not. If so, then our view is that England and France may sell nuclear weapons to one another, but not to Myanmar or the average citizen.

So, we agree that buying and selling is wrong in cases 1 and 2, but this is because *possessing* the items in question is wrong, not because buying and selling introduce wrongness where there was none to begin with. That it's wrong to buy and sell these items is a trivial consequence of their being wrong to *have*.

Thus, we agree to the following principle:

The Principle of Wrongful Possession:
   If it is inherently morally wrong for someone to possess (do, use) X, then (normally) it is morally wrong for that person to buy or sell X.[1]

As far as we can tell, everyone in this debate agrees to the Principle of Wrongful Possession. It follows trivially, on that principle, that if someone inherently shouldn't have something, then he or she should not sell it or buy it. Because child porn shouldn't exist, it also shouldn't be for sale.

Excerpts from "If You May Do It for Free, You May Do It for Money" (Chapter 2) in *Markets Without Limits* by Jason Brennan and Peter M. Jaworski. © 2016. Reproduced with permission of Routledge in the format Educational/Instructional Program via Copyright Clearance Center.

Similarly, consider the case of dog fighting. For the sake of argument, let's agree that dog fighting wrongfully mistreats dogs. If so, then we agree that people shouldn't sell tickets to dog fights or bids on dog fights. But, again, the reason people shouldn't sell dog fight tickets is that dog fights shouldn't exist. It would be wrong to host dog fights *for free*. Selling tickets doesn't *introduce* wrongness where there wasn't any to begin with.

Or, to take another obvious example, it's wrong to pay someone to murder someone else, but that's just because it's wrong to murder people, period. Perhaps paying someone to kill another person might *amplify* the wrongness, under certain circumstances, of killing, but it's not that the market in killing introduces wrongness into what was otherwise a permissible act. …

Or, as a final example … we agree that it's wrong for students to buy essays from AstonishingPapers.com and then submit those papers as if they were their own. But the problem here isn't the *buying*. It's that the students plagiarize. We've both seen plenty of students plagiarize essays they acquired for free. The market in academic dishonesty is wrong only because academic dishonesty is wrong. A fortiori, if the students purchased papers from AstonishingPapers.com without any intention to pass these papers in as their own, they would do nothing wrong at all. But if the students acquired those same papers for free and then passed them in as their own, they would act wrongly. Thus, imagine that we decided, as an experiment, to pay AstonishingPapers to write a five-page essay on some silly topic, such as "the importance of purple fruit." We have no intention of submitting this work as our own; we just want to see what they come up with. If we never try to pass off someone else's work as our own, then it is perfectly permissible to buy a paper from them. …

Baby Buying

A famous photograph published in 1948 in the Valparaiso *Vidette-Messenger*, shows four unkempt, bewildered children, ages 2–6, sitting beside a sign: "Children for Sale: Inquire Within." Their mother, Lucille Chalifoux, stands above them, covering her face in shame. Perhaps the photo was staged. The original caption explains that Chalifoux and her husband – who, by all accounts, were irresponsible, neglectful, and abusive parents – decided to sell the children after years of economic desperation. A recent news report claims that the children were, in some sense, sold – the Chalifouxes did indeed give up their parental rights, at least de facto, in exchange for money. Some of the children went to abusive and exploitative homes; some did not.[2]

Was it wrong to "sell" the children? If so, was the problem the actual "selling," or was it rather the negligent way the parents gave up their parental rights? …

Babies are not the kind of thing you can own. They are not property, the way a guitar or even a dog can be property. One might say that it follows straightforwardly that babies cannot be bought and sold.

However, the question of "baby selling" is not really about whether we can buy and sell babies as if they were property. Instead, the interesting question in the commodification debate is whether it is permissible to buy and sell *adoption rights*.

Biological parents generally have some sort of presumptive guardianship rights over their biological children. Parents have the right to live with their children, raise them as they see fit, and so on, within certain limits. These rights are of course not absolute. Parents who are abusive or negligent can and should forfeit their guardianship rights, that is, their rights to parent their children. Guardianship comes with responsibilities and limits: parents must provide adequately for their children, and they cannot just do anything they want to their children.

Note that guardianship rights are not only something one can forfeit, but something one can relinquish. Parents can voluntarily relinquish their guardianship rights over their children. Moreover, they usually have wide latitude to instead imbue others with those rights. So, for instance, in the hit movie *Juno*, pregnant teen Juno not only decides to relinquish guardianship rights over her baby, but specifically chooses Vanessa. However, even here, almost everyone accepts that there are limits to whom we can choose as adoptive parents. It was permissible for Juno to give Vanessa the baby, but it would not be permissible for her to give the baby to a known pedophile.

Our thesis, recall, is that if you may give something to someone, you may sell that thing to him or her. If you may take something from someone for free, then you may buy that thing from him or her. Let's apply that kind of reasoning here. Some people object to markets in adoption rights. But, for their objection to genuinely be about *markets* in adoption rights, they need to hold that (1) there are cases where it is permissible to transfer adoption rights for free, without the exchange of money, but (2) it would be inherently wrong in those cases to transfer adoption rights for money.

We think the interesting moral questions about markets in adoption rights aren't really about the *markets* per se. Instead, we see two major moral questions:

1 When, if ever, is it permissible for a person to relinquish, voluntarily and without compensation, his or her parental rights over a child?
2 What conditions and factors, independent of the willingness and ability to buy adoption rights, make a potential parent *fit* to adopt a child?

In our view, the ethics of adoption markets just reduces to the answers to these questions. Markets themselves play no explanatory role in explaining when it is wrong to buy and sell adoption rights.

We don't ourselves have an answer to the first question, and it's not essential that we do. Suppose you think parents may voluntarily relinquish their parental rights only if they are in distress. Our response would be that if that view is correct, then only parents in distress may sell parental rights. Or, suppose you think, as many of our left-liberal colleagues do, that new biological parents may always voluntarily relinquish their parental rights, provided they can find a suitable home for their children, or find a suitable governmental or non-governmental agency that will in turn ensure their offspring's welfare. Our response would be that if that view is correct, then any parents meeting those conditions may sell their parental rights. Or, suppose you think that parents may *never* voluntarily relinquish their parental rights. Our response would be that, if so, then they may never sell rights to adopt, but that's not because *selling* per se is wrong. Rather, it's because they may not *give* these rights away, period.

As for the second question: Some potential parents are unfit and so should not be allowed to adopt or care for children. Others are fit and should be allowed to adopt or care for children. We do not ourselves have any fully developed theory of parental fitness, though there are philosophers and others who work on explaining this distinction. We accept commonsense ideas, such as that pedophiles should not be allowed to adopt or care for children. We also accept the commonsense idea that we ourselves are fit enough to be parents – our children should not be taken away from us, and we should be allowed to adopt. But beyond uncontroversial claims like these, we do not have a fully worked out theory.

However, let's just say that there is such a theory, the Correct Theory of Fitness, that explains which would-be parents are fit to adopt, and which are not. We don't ourselves know what the Correct Theory of Fitness is, and we don't ourselves know if anyone else knows what it is. However, presumably there is some truth of the matter here.

Now, according to the Correct Theory of Fitness, some would-be parents are fit to adopt. Others are not. Our view is that the question of who may *buy* adoption rights reduces to

this Correct Theory of Fitness. It is permissible for you to buy adoption rights, so long as you are a fit parent, as judged by the Correct Theory of Fitness. If, according to the Correct Theory of Fitness, you are fit to adopt a child for free, then, we hold, you may pay as much as you'd like to adopt that child.

Our main concern for markets in adoption or guardianship rights is just that babies not go to unfit parents. But this is a question of the design and regulation of the market, not an inherent problem with the market that can never be solved. ...

Vote Selling

The Ethics of Vote Selling Just Is the Ethics of Voting

For $50, would you vote Republican? Most people would recoil at such an offer. They believe it's inherently wrong to buy or sell votes.[3] In fact, of all the "contested commodities" we've discussed ... markets in votes might be the most contested.

When it comes to buying and selling votes, as with everything else, our thesis is, "If you can do it for free, you can do it for money." Vote selling is not in principle wrong. It has no inherent moral status. Vote selling cannot *transform* otherwise morally acceptable actions into wrongful actions. If it's morally permissible for you to vote a certain way for free, then it's permissible to vote that way for payment. If it's morally acceptable for someone to vote a certain way for free, then it's morally acceptable for you to pay her to vote that way.[4] There are cases where it's wrong for you to accept money to vote a certain way, but, in those cases, you shouldn't vote that way for free either.

There are many reasons why people oppose the commodification of votes. Perhaps the most important of these objections are that if votes are for sale, this will cause the wrong people to have too much power, cause people to use power badly, or cause people to vote in ways that harm others. We share these concerns. But, we will argue, these concerns do not justify the view that vote buying and selling are always wrong. At most, they justify the view that paying people to vote *badly* is wrong.

Imagine someone said, "If people are allowed to buy and sell sandwiches, a man who wants his wife dead might pay a cook for a poisoned sandwich. Therefore, sandwiches shouldn't be for sale." Or, suppose someone said, "If people are allowed to buy and sell sandwiches, a rich evil person might buy all the food in the world, put it in one big sandwich, and then laugh gleefully while everyone starves. We can't let that happen. Therefore, sandwiches shouldn't be for sale."

Both of these arguments are crazy. Sure, if sandwiches are for sale, these horrible things *could* happen, though the latter scenario is extremely improbable. But the proper response is not to conclude that sandwiches are the kind of thing that cannot be bought or sold. Rather, we conclude that it's fine to sell sandwiches, but not poisoned sandwiches. It's fine to buy a sandwich, but not to buy up all the food and then cause mass starvation.

Yet, when it comes to voting, people have the opposite reaction. They say, "If people are allowed to buy and sell votes, someone might pay someone else to vote in harmful ways. Therefore, votes shouldn't be for sale." They're right that these things might happen. But, as with the commodification of sandwiches, isn't the most obvious response that it's wrong to pay people to vote in harmful ways, but it's fine to sell *good* votes?

Our view is that the ethics of vote selling just is the ethics of voting. That is, in our view, there are rightful and wrongful ways to vote. Citizens do not have a specific moral duty to vote – there are a great many ways for them to discharge any duties they might have to serve the common good or to "do their part." However, people who do choose to vote have moral obligations to vote responsibly, to take the proper care to form their political beliefs in a rational manner on the basis of proper social scientific evidence, and to vote for what they justifiedly believe will best serve justice, in light of how they justifiedly expect others to vote and behave. In short, we endorse the following principle:

> *The Principle of Ethical Voting:* People who choose to vote must vote for candidates or policies they justifiedly expect to best promote justice; otherwise, they must abstain.

Note that this principle doesn't say it should be illegal for people to vote badly, or that people shouldn't possess the right to vote unless they vote well. It just says that it's morally wrong to vote in certain ways.

Given this background commitment, we then endorse the following view of vote selling and buying:

> *Permissible Vote Selling:* So long as a person conforms to the Principle of Ethical Voting, she may sell her vote.
>
> *Permissible Vote Buying:* It is permissible to buy votes from anyone who will conform to the Principle of Ethical Voting. Also, if you are justified in believing that voting for a particular candidate or position will serve the right ends of government, you may pay other people to vote for that candidate or position, even if those people are not themselves justified in believing

that such votes will serve the right ends of government.

In short, we think many cases of vote selling are wrong, but in such cases the problem isn't really with the vote selling, but with the way people vote, period.[5] The problem is that vote selling induces people to do something they shouldn't do, period. …

What Is Good Voting?

Voting is an ethical issue. The way we vote can make government better or worse, and in turn, make people's lives go better or worse. Bad choices at the polls can destroy economic opportunities, produce crises that lower everyone's standards of living, lead to unjust and unnecessary wars (and thus to millions of deaths), lead to sexist, racist, and homophobic legislation, help reinforce poverty, produce overly punitive criminal legislation, and worse.

Voting is not like choosing what to eat off a restaurant's menu. If a person makes bad choices at a restaurant, at least only she bears the consequences of her actions. Yet when voters make bad choices at the polls, everyone suffers. Irresponsible voting can harm innocent people.

With that in mind, we'll first articulate a theory of what it means for a person to vote well, and then articulate an argument for that theory.

Brennan's Principle of Ethical Voting holds that a voter votes well if and only if she votes for a person or policy that she *justifiedly* believes will promote the right ends of government. Notice the term "*justifiedly.*" The theory does not merely say that voters must believe that they are voting for candidates or policies that will promote the right ends of government. It is not sufficient for them to vote in a public-spirited way. Rather, they should be *epistemically justified* in believing they are voting for the right ends of government.

A belief is epistemically justified when a person has sufficiently strong evidence to warrant the belief. …

Good Voting, Commodified

We have a very restrictive, stringent view of the ethics of voting, combined with a more permissive view of the ethics of buying and selling votes. In contrast, most people have a very permissive view of the ethics of voting combined with a restrictive, stringent view of the ethics of buying and selling votes.

Most people in the United States and Canada subscribe to what Brennan has previously called the "Folk Theory of Voting Ethics."[6] According to this view, people have a moral duty to vote, but few if any duties attach to the act of voting itself. People have no duty to be informed, to process political information in a rational way, or to vote for just outcomes. Instead, it's morally permissible (if not admirable) to be utterly reckless with their vote. However, the Folk Theory of Voting Ethics also holds that it's wrong to buy and sell votes, period. So, the Folk Theory allows you to vote however you'd like, so long as you do it for free.

We find the Folk Theory puzzling. Consider three situations:

1. *Ignorant Ignacio:* Ignacio knows almost nothing about politics. He has never studied economics or political science. Come Election Day, he watches 30-second advertisements from two major candidates. He feels in his gut that one of the candidates has better ideas than the others, and votes for those candidates, and votes accordingly.
2. *Careless Carla:* Carla knows almost nothing about politics. She has never studied economics or political science. Come Election Day, she shows up at the polls, and sees a list of names she doesn't recognize for an office (the "comptroller") whose function she can't begin to guess. She picks the name she thinks sounds the most regal.
3. *Lackadaisical Loren:* Loren is a prominent political philosopher and political economist who has written some of the world's most important books and articles on voting. Loren has a thorough understanding of the social sciences, and has as much a claim to having sound political ideas as any person alive. Still, Loren doesn't vote, in large part because he recognizes his individual vote has almost no chance of making a difference. On Election Day, his friend and colleague Jason pays Loren $200 to vote his conscience.

According to the Folk Theory of Voting Ethics, Ignacio and Carla did nothing wrong. Their actions might not be particularly admirable, but they aren't blameworthy either. Loren and his friend Jason, however, acted badly, and they should feel bad. Perhaps they should even go to jail.

But this seems puzzling. After all, Ignacio and Carla had no clue what they're doing, while Loren voted for what he justifiedly believed would serve the right ends of government. For all Ignacio and Carla know, they're voting for terrible candidates who will produce bad outcomes for all. In contrast, Loren has every reason to expect that the candidates he supports will produce good and just outcomes. According to Brennan's Principle of Ethical Voting, Ignacio and Carla shouldn't vote at all, for free or for money. But according to that principle, Loren is a *good voter*. If Jason pays Loren to vote, what Jason has done is paid to get Loren to vote the way people ought to vote.

People might worry that if votes were commodified, malevolent rich people – you can insert here George Soros or the Koch brothers, depending on your political predilection – would then buy up votes for their own nefarious ends. For instance, suppose there are two presidential candidates, Al and Bob. Suppose Al and Bob are identical in all respects, except for how they intend to deal with climate change. Suppose that the evidence overwhelmingly favors Al's position; in fact, the evidence is so strong that no person could be justified in advocating Bob's position. But now suppose that either George Soros or the Koch brothers – again, pick your favorite villain here – pays the majority of voters to vote for Bob. We agree that it is wrong for Soros or the Koch brothers to buy these votes, and that it is wrong for people to sell them. But we also think it would be wrong for people to vote for Bob *for free*, because doing so violates the Principle of Ethical Voting. We don't see this as being a case where commodification introduced wrongness where there wasn't any.

On the other hand, suppose you know that many careless, ignorant voters are going to vote for a harmful candidate. They will not be convinced by evidence and argument. However, suppose you could pay them to vote for what you justifiedly believe, on the basis of sound reasoning with good evidence, is the best candidate. If you do so, you make it much more likely that we'll all enjoy a good outcome. The Folk Theory of Voting Ethics holds that you did something wrong. But we think your behavior is admirable. You did a major public service – you paid for justice out of your own pocket.

The Inalienability Objection

One common argument against vote selling holds that the right to vote is inalienable, just like a right to basic liberty in the person or to free speech are inalienable. The right to vote is not like a property right to a car. You may sell a car, but you may not sell yourself into slavery. You may not sell away your right to free speech. Some kinds of rights can't be sold. The right to vote is one of those rights.

The problem with this argument is that it misunderstands what's being debated. The question we've been discussing so far is not whether a person should literally be allowed to purchase additional rights to vote. If Jaworski were to pay Brennan to vote a certain way, it's not as though Jaworski would literally come to have two votes while Brennan would then have zero. He wouldn't pay Brennan to literally transfer his right to vote the way he might buy a deed to a house. Rather, what happens in traditional vote buying and selling is that one person pays a second person to perform a certain action. Paying someone to vote is not like buying a house, and so doesn't mean that the seller loses the right to vote.

In the same way, suppose the University of Toronto pays Brennan or the College of New Jersey pays Jaworski to give a guest lecture on commodification. When we agree to give such lectures, we thereby accept certain constraints about what we'll talk about. For instance, we thereby agree not to surprise our audiences with lectures on how to distinguish speed, thrash, power, hair, black, nu, and death metal. But we don't thereby alienate our rights of free speech or transfer them to these universities. So, the worry about the inalienability of voting rights is irrelevant to the question of whether it's permissible to pay someone to vote a certain way.

Now, we could of course imagine a legal system in which the right to vote could literally be bought and sold like a car. Rather than simply paying others to vote a certain way, a citizen might buy extra rights to vote. Under that system, perhaps George Soros might come to have 1,000,000 votes all to himself, while 999,999 citizens end up with no votes at all. If the claim that the right to vote is inalienable is correct, it follows that this legal system is unjust, and that people

should not buy and sell their rights to vote. However, notice that even here, the problem is not about commodification per se. If voting rights are inalienable, one may not sell these rights *because* one may not give them away, period.

Notes

1. Deirdre McCloskey, *If You're So Smart: The Narrative of Economic Expertise* (University of Chicago Press, 1990), p. 1
2. https://tucson.com/news/local/sold-as-kids-their-lives-now-converge/article_f4fe5e61-f226-5a63-96f9-270154a02545.html.
3. Debra Satz, *Why Some Things Should Not Be for Sale* (Oxford University Press, 2012), p. 102; Michael Sandel, *What Money Can't Buy* (New York: Farrar, Straus & Giroux, 2012), pp. 104–5.
4. This essay incorporates material and ideas from Jason Brennan, *The Ethics of Voting* (Princeton University Press, 2011), pp. 135–60. The thesis defended here ("If you can do it for free, you can do it for money") is a generalization of the view of vote commodification that Brennan defended in this earlier work.
5. For an even more radical defense of vote buying and selling than we offer here, see Christopher Freiman, "Vote Markets," *Australasian Journal of Philosophy* 92 (2014): 759–74.
6. Brennan, *Ethics of Voting*, p. 3.

Markets in Utopia

JAMES STACEY TAYLOR

In *Markets without Limits* Jason Brennan and Peter Jaworski defend the view that "If you may do it for free, then you may do it for money."[1] At first, this appears to be a highly controversial claim. There are, after all, many things that it seems that people may "use, possess, and dispose of …" for free, but which it would appear to be morally impermissible for them to sell.[2] It seems, for example, that while it is morally permissible for a parent to give her child up for adoption for free, it would be morally impermissible for her to sell adoption rights to him or her to the highest bidder. Similarly, while it seems that it is morally permissible for a person to cast his vote for a political candidate for free, it appears that it would be morally impermissible for him to cast it for her solely because she had paid him to do so.

Despite its controversial appearance Brennan's and Jaworski's view is correct. However, this does not mean that markets in, for example, adoption rights and political votes are morally permissible in any existing society. This is because Brennan's and Jaworski's arguments only establish

that in *certain* situations it would be morally permissible to have markets in goods and services that it is morally permissible to give away. And if we are living in a different situation than one of those situations then even though it is true that persons may exchange parental rights and political votes for money in *some* situations this does not show that these market transactions are permissible in our actual situation.

This essay is divided into three parts. In part one I will clarify Brennan's and Jaworski's pro-market thesis. In part two I argue that while it is morally permissible for persons to cast their votes for free, in certain situations it would be morally impermissible to allow the buying and selling of votes for money. In part three I outline a way in which Brennan and Jaworski could respond to my argument in part two. I accept that this possible response would successfully defend their view that political votes may be exchanged for money. I argue, however, that the success of this response shows that their view is much less controversial than it first appears – and, indeed, that it could be readily accepted by even those who, like Debra Satz, oppose noxious markets. Moreover, not only is Brennan's and Jaworski's view not as robust a defense of commodification as it might initially seem, but, I will argue, it fails to provide us with *any* practical answers as to whether or not particular markets in certain goods or services are morally permissible.

Clarifying Brennan's and Jaworski's Thesis

Brennan and Jaworski write that their view is "If you may do it for free, then you may do it for money." In other words, if you may do it for free, then there are no good ethical reasons that you should not do it for money. But this is plainly false. Imagine that you have promised to drive a friend to the airport for free next Friday. Friday arrives, and, knowing that your friend was relying on your promise and so now has no other means of transport, you tell her that you will only take her if she pays you a nominal fee of $20. However, since you are obligated by your prior promise to take her to the airport for free, it is morally impermissible for you to make your driving her to the airport conditional upon payment. Of course, you could still accept payment from her for taking her to the airport if she offers, but given your prior obligation to her you cannot make your taking her there conditional upon payment. In this case, then, while you can take her there for free you cannot take her there *for* money.[3]

Given that Brennan's and Jaworski's initial way of stating their thesis is so readily falsified, charity requires that it be understood differently. Fortunately, Brennan and Jaworski provide an alternative understanding of their thesis: "that the market does not transform what were permissible acts into impermissible acts."[4] This way of formulating their thesis avoids the above objection. If you promise your friend that you will take her to the airport for free you are obligated not to make doing so conditional upon her paying you. But even if you do subsequently require that she pay you to take her to the airport, this payment would not render your act of taking her to the airport impermissible. The morally condemnable act would be breaking your promise and requiring payment, not the act of taking her to the airport. The payment would not transform the permissible act of taking your friend to the airport into an impermissible act. (Nor would it transform the permissible act of your friend accepting a ride from you to the airport into an impermissible act.) Thus, if a type of service can be provided without payment (e.g., driving someone to the airport), then the same type of service could be provided for payment. Similarly, if a type of good could be provided without payment (e.g., a person could give up her parental rights for free), then it could also be provided for payment (e.g., she could sell her parental rights to a willing buyer). Brennan's and Jaworski's thesis is, thus,

that if it is morally permissible to provide a *type* of good or service for free then it is also morally permissible to provide that *type* of good or service for payment.

An Argument against Markets in Votes

Since it is morally permissible for a person to vote for a particular political candidate for free, Brennan and Jaworski argue that it is also morally permissible for him to vote for her for payment. Similarly, they claim, if it is morally permissible for someone to vote for a particular political candidate for free, then it is morally permissible for someone else to pay him to vote for her.

Brennan and Jaworski do not defend an "outright" market in political votes.[5] Instead, they defend a market in political votes that are cast for candidates or policies that the persons who choose for whom the vote is cast "justifiedly expect to best promote justice."[6] Provided that the purchased votes are cast in accordance with this requirement Brennan and Jaworski believe that it would be morally permissible to buy and sell them. They also do not defend the view that a person can sell her right to vote. Instead, they defend the view that persons can be paid to cast their votes in the way that the buyer of those votes decides.

But even with these restrictions in place there is reason to believe that a market in votes would be morally impermissible. Market transactions are often justified on the grounds that they are positive-sum games; that (ex ante) they make both the buyer and the seller better off. A market in votes could thus be justified on the grounds that if a person bought a vote she would (ex ante) be better off because she would value the vote more than the cash that she exchanged for it, and if a person sold a vote she would (ex ante) be better off as she would prefer the cash she received for the vote to the vote itself.[7] (This seems to be the argument that James Tobin was alluding to when he wrote that "Any good second year graduate student in economics could write a short examination paper proving that voluntary transactions in votes would increase the welfare of the sellers as well as the buyers."[8]) Yet despite the intuitive appeal of this argument, it will not work in all situations. Consider, for example, a situation in which there are a small number of wealthy and politically active persons in the national electorate and a much larger number of poorer persons. Imagine that in this situation the poor support candidate A, while the wealthy support candidate B. (In all cases support for the candidates is based on justified views concerning which one would best promote justice.) Moreover, the members of the electorate are all rational and self-interested, and they value their votes only instrumentally as means of influencing the outcome of the election. Finally, imagine that the election is based on a plurality voting system (each voter has the right to cast one vote) and that to win the election a candidate must secure a majority of the votes cast. If a market in votes was prohibited then to be elected candidate B would either have to adjust her policies to appeal to the (majority) of voters who would otherwise prefer candidate A, or else she and her supporters would have to convince the supporters of candidate A that her policies were superior to his.

If, however, a market in votes was allowed then candidate B would not need to appeal to the supporters of candidate A. To see this, let us consider the reasoning processes that would occur to both the prospective sellers and the prospective buyers of votes. Let us begin with that of the prospective vote sellers. Note first that no individual vote is likely to make any difference to the outcome of a national electoral contest such as that between A and B. A rational voter would thus realize that since this is so it would not matter for whom her vote was cast. She would also realize both that other prospective vote sellers would see that they would be rational to sell their votes as well, and that since a candidate only needs 50.01 percent of the votes cast there would be an oversupply of votes in the market. She would thus rush to sell her vote before the demand for them was met. Moreover, since she realizes that her vote is unlikely to make any difference to the electoral outcome she would be willing to sell it to anyone who would be willing to buy it, whether she agreed with their policies or not. Given that votes are fungible she would only be able to compete with other prospective vote sellers on price. And since she realizes that this would be true for the other sellers, she would reduce her price to just marginally above the transaction costs that she would incur in selling it. The price of votes in a competitive market would thus be very low. Since this is so, the prospective vote sellers would be more likely to be the poor (who support candidate A) than the rich (who support candidate B).

Given the assumptions outlined above the poor would be willing to sell their votes cheaply to either candidate A or candidate B. Now recall that A's supporters are the poor and that B's are the rich. By hypothesis, then, B is better capitalized than A. Since the prospective vote sellers would be indifferent to whom they sold their votes, and since the cost of each individual vote would be low, the candidate with the greater wealth would win the election. If candidate A realized that candidate B was better capitalized than he was, then, he would realize that he would lose the election. He would thus decide to conserve his resources, refrain from buying votes, and concede defeat. This would grant candidate B a *de facto* monopoly on the purchase of votes. The supporters of B could thus easily buy enough votes to secure her electoral victory – and so B could simply ignore the views of A's supporters.

With this analysis in place let us return to the pro-market argument mentioned above: namely, that a market in votes could be justified as both vote buyers and vote sellers would ex ante expect to be made better off through their trades. Allowing a vote market in the situation outlined above would lead to the *de facto* disenfranchisement of A's supporters. On the (reasonable) assumption that they would object to such disenfranchisement, one would not be able to infer from the fact that they voluntarily sold their votes that A's supporters were made better off through so doing. This is because they were only made better off through selling their votes *relative to the situation in which they could have sold their votes but refrained from so doing.* That this is so does not show that allowing a market in votes improved their situation *when compared to the situation in which such a market was prohibited.* It is perfectly possible that a person (such as the typical supporter of candidate A) could prefer to sell her vote if a market in votes was allowed rather than not do so, but still prefer that the market not be allowed to a situation where it was allowed (and in which she sold her vote). The pro-market argument outlined above (i.e., that it can be inferred from the presence of vote-trading that allowing a market in votes has increased the well-being of both the vote buyers and vote sellers) is thus mistaken.[9]

Note that the concern expressed here is not that a market in votes would enable "malevolent rich people" to "buy up votes for their own nefarious ends."[10] Candidate B and her supporters are justified in believing that their preferred policies would promote justice. Rather, the concern is that in this situation the typical prospective vote seller would be made worse off (i.e., through frustrating their preferences concerning both the vote market itself and the election of her preferred candidate) through the introduction of a market in votes. To put this in Satz's terms, in the situation outlined above the introduction of a market in votes would frustrate the agency interests of those who were *de facto* disenfranchised by this. These persons would be placed into a situation where it would be rational for them to abdicate from participating in deciding on matters that bear on their overall good (e.g., the political distribution of goods in society). In addition to this harm that would be imposed on individual vote sellers, the introduction of a market in votes would also, in Satz's terms, be *"extremely harmful for society"* for it would "undermine the social framework needed for people to interact *as equals.*"[11] In particular, through effectively disenfranchising the poor and providing political privilege to the rich a market in votes would, in the situation outlined above, be "harmful for the standing of the parties as equal citizens in a democracy."[12] Finally, since the oversupply of votes relative to the demand for them would lead vote sellers to sell at a price that is just marginally above their transaction costs, this market would reflect the vulnerability of the prospective vote sellers.[13] A market in votes in the situation outlined above would thus meet the conditions for it to be a "noxious" market.[14] In this situation, then, while it would be morally permissible for votes to be cast without payment it would not be morally permissible to allow them to be cast for payment.

A Possible Response – and a Utopian Fantasy

Brennan and Jaworski could respond that this objection to the sale of votes fails to be an objection to their thesis in the same way that the above example of the request for payment for the promised free ride to the airport fails to be an objection to their (clarified) thesis. Their view is not that goods or services that could permissibly be given away for free could also permissibly be sold in *any* circumstances. Instead, their view is merely that if a good or service is of a type that it is morally permissible to give away for free then it is of a type that it would be morally permissible to sell in *some* situations. Noting that there are some *other* situations (e.g., when you have promised your friend a free ride, or the voting situation outlined above) in which it would *not* be morally permissible to exchange money for a good that it would be morally permissible to give away for free does not falsify their view. Even though there might be *some* situations where it would be morally impermissible to exchange, for example, airport rides or votes for cash, this does not show that it would *never* be morally permissible to exchange airport rides or votes for cash. The harms that are associated with a market in votes in the situation outlined above might not, for example, transpire if this market occurred in a society whose voting members enjoyed economic equality and prosperity. And even in a society whose voting members were not economically equal, it is possible that a vote market could be regulated in such a way that the harms that were associated with this market in the situation above could be avoided. Perhaps, for example, only a small number of votes could be sold so that the transactions in them would be unlikely to affect the outcome of the election, or perhaps only the very wealthy would be allowed to sell their votes.

This is certainly a reasonable response. But the point of the above discussion of vote markets was not to argue against the commodification of voting. Instead it was to emphasize that to make their position defensible Brennan and Jaworski must concede that in some circumstances it would not be morally permissible to exchange for money a good or service that it would be morally permissible to give away for free. In what circumstances, then, would it not be morally permissible to exchange for money a good or service that it would be morally permissible to give away for free? The above objection to markets in votes provides us with an answer. Given the circumstances in which that market took place (a small number of wealthy people, and a large number of poor people) it would impose harms on the individual vote sellers and also on society as a whole. From this, we conclude that the circumstances in which Brennan and Jaworski would agree that it is morally impermissible to exchange for money a good or service that it would be morally permissible to give away for free would be those in which the commodification of the good or service in question would, overall, be harmful (or, in Satz's terms, "noxious"). But once this concession is brought to the fore, Brennan's and Jaworski's pro-commodification view is rather mild: namely, that if it is morally permissible to give away a good or service, then it could also be morally permissible to sell in those situations where the market for that good or service would *not* be noxious.

This is not an uncontroversial view. It would, for example, be rejected by anyone who believed that there are certain goods or services whose nature precludes the moral permissibility of their sale, even though it does not preclude the permissibility of their being given away or the *possibility* of their commodification.[15] But it would not be rejected by persons who object to markets in certain goods or services (e.g., parental rights, kidneys, sex, or votes) at particular times and in particular places on the grounds that the overall consequences of these particular markets would be harmful. Brennan's and Jaworski's approach to assessing the moral permissibility of particular markets is thus compatible with that of Satz. Satz does not, for example, object to (e.g.) the buying and selling of diamonds per se, but only to the buying and selling of diamonds when doing so funds (and thereby prolongs) a bloody civil war.[16] Her objection to this market in diamonds could be endorsed by Brennan and Jaworski. The fact that this particular diamond trade funds a civil war would be a circumstance in which, while it would be morally permissible to give away diamonds for free, it would not be morally permissible to sell them.

Brennan and Jaworski could thus agree with Satz that if the commodification of a particular good or service would, overall, be harmful in a particular situation, then that good or service should not be commodified in that situation. Similarly, Satz could agree with Brennan and Jaworski that if it would be morally permissible to give away a good or service for free, and if this would not be harmful, then it would be morally permissible to do this. She could thus agree that in some special set of circumstances all goods and services could be commodified. To see this, imagine a utopian world in which everyone could have immediate and free access to any type of good or service that they desired, and that everyone had morally appropriate attitudes towards everyone else. In this utopian world there would be no desperate exchanges, for there would be no economic desperation. In this world any good or service that could be given away for free could be commodified without any overall harmful effects. There would thus be no noxious markets. In this world persons who traded away adoption rights over their children would not do so out of morally relevant economic desperation, but solely because they valued something other than raising their children themselves.[17] The adverse effects of a market in votes that would occur in the situation outlined above would not transpire in this utopian world for there would be no morally relevant disparities in wealth. And since persons would not have any morally inappropriate attitudes towards each other in this world markets in sex would not lead to the degradation of those who voluntarily decided (without any morally relevant financial pressure) to operate as sex workers. In this world of abundance and morally appropriate attitudes no harms could result from cash-based exchanges. In this utopian world, if it is morally permissible to give away a good or service, then it would always be morally permissible to buy (or sell) it. And so, in the special circumstances of this world, Satz could endorse Brennan's and Jaworski's pro-commodification position.

But this utopian world is not ours. In our world we have to assess whether allowing a market in a good or service that had hitherto been market inalienable would, overall, be harmful or not in any given situation. That under some circumstances (e.g., the utopian world outlined above) it is morally permissible to buy and sell those goods and services that it is morally permissible to give away (or accept) for free tells us little about whether markets in certain goods are morally permissible in the *actual* situations in which their institution has been proposed. The real question, then, is not whether it *could* be morally permissible to buy and sell certain goods or services but whether it *is* morally permissible to do so in a certain place at a certain time. There is, for example, nothing morally objectionable about a trade in diamonds per se, but it is morally impermissible to trade in diamonds when this trade fuels a bloody civil war. Thus, while Brennan and Jaworski have provided a persuasive defense of commodification in the abstract, their arguments do little to undermine the claim that certain market transactions are as noxious as their opponents claim.

Notes

1. Jason Brennan and Peter M. Jaworski, *Markets without Limits: Moral Virtues and Commercial Interests* (New York: Routledge, 2016), p. 10.
2. Ibid.
3. A version of this clarification was offered in James Stacey Taylor, "What Limits Should Markets Be without?" *Business Ethics Journal Review* 4, no. 7 (2016): 41–46 (pp. 44–45).
4. Brennan and Jaworski, *Markets without Limits*, p. 10.
5. Debra Satz, *Why Some Things Should Not Be for Sale* (Oxford University Pres, 2012), p. 102.
6. Brennan and Jaworski, *Markets without Limits*, p. 184.
7. See Christopher Freiman, "Vote Markets," *Australasian Journal of Philosophy* 92 (2014): 759–74 (p. 761).
8. James Tobin, "On Limiting the Domain of Inequality," *Journal of Law and Economics* 13 (1970): 263–77 (p. 269). Quoted by Satz, *Why Some Things Should Not Be for Sale*, p. 96.
9. A version of this objection to markets in votes was developed in James Stacey Taylor, "How Not to Argue for Markets, or, Why the Argument from Mutually Beneficial Exchange Fails," *Journal of Social Philosophy* 48 (2017): 165–79.
10. Brennan and Jaworski, *Markets without Limits*, p. 189.
11. Satz, *Why Some Things Should Not Be for Sale*, p. 95.
12. Ibid.
13. Ibid., p. 97.
14. Ibid., p. 94.
15. Brennan and Jaworski attribute this position to Elizabeth Anderson, claiming that her objection to prostitution is based on the view that markets in sex are "essentially disrespectful even if these markets do not involve exploitation, harm, rights violations, etc" (*Markets without Limits*, p. 75). But Anderson explicitly rejects this view, writing that "My arguments … do not show that the sale of sexual services cannot have a legitimate place in a just society," going on to endorse the possibility of for-profit sex therapy. See her *Value in Ethics and Economics* (Cambridge, MA: Harvard University Press, 1993), p. 156.
16. Satz, *Why Some Things Should Not Be for Sale*, p. 98.
17. In which case it is plausible that this trade would be good for the children, provided that the adoptive parents would be endorsed by the Correct Theory of Fitness. Brennan and Jaworski, *Markets without Limits*, p. 179.

10.3 PRICE GOUGING

The Ethics of Price Gouging

MATT ZWOLINSKI

Introduction

In 1996, Hurricane Fran struck North Carolina, leaving over a million people in the Raleigh-Durham area without power. Without any way of refrigerating food, infant formula, or insulin, and without any idea of when power would be restored, people were desperate for ice, but existing supplies quickly sold out. Four young men from Goldsboro, which was not significantly affected by the storm, rented refrigerated trucks, bought 500 bags of ice for $1.70 per bag, and drove to Raleigh. The price they charged for the ice was $12 per bag – more than seven times what they paid for it.

This kind of behavior is often referred to as "price gouging." Many states, North Carolina included, prohibit it by law. And even when it is not legally prohibited, it is generally thought to be exploitative and immoral. The purpose of this essay is to explore the philosophical issues surrounding price gouging, and to argue that the common moral condemnation of it is largely mistaken. The core of my argument will be that standard cases of price gouging provide great benefit to those in desperate need, that they tend to lack the morally objectionable features often ascribed to them such as coercion and exploitation, and that attempts to prohibit the practice will harm individuals who are already vulnerable and can least afford to bear further harm. ...

The Concept of Price Gouging

A fruitful place to begin a conceptual analysis of price gouging is with the language of the statutes which prohibit it. Approximately 34 states, however, have laws against price gouging, a survey of which reveals that gouging is generally defined in terms of three elements.

1. Period of Emergency: Almost all anti-gouging laws specify that they apply only to actions taken during times of disaster or emergency.[1]
2. Necessary Items: Most laws further specify that their restrictions apply only to certain classes of items, generally those which are necessary for survival or for coping with serious problems caused by the disaster. California, for instance, is typical in limiting its scope to items which

are "consumer food items or goods, goods or services used for emergency cleanup, emergency supplies, medical supplies, home heating oil, building materials, housing, transportation, freight, and storage services, or gasoline or other motor fuels."[2]
3. Price Ceilings: The definitive feature of anti-gouging laws is the limit they set on the maximum price that can be charged for specified goods. Such limits are set either by prohibitions on "unreasonable," "excessive," or "unconscionable" price increases, or by specific limits on the percentage increase in price allowed after the onset of the emergency.[3] In the most extreme laws, the maximum allowable percentage increase is set at zero.[4]

This preliminary analysis leaves a number of important questions unresolved, such as what ought to count as an emergency, which kinds of items are "necessary," and which of the varying methods of determining unacceptable price hikes should be employed. These complexities will be explored to some extent in the remainder of this essay. For the most part, however, the argument that follows will be broad enough that the differences between various conceptions of price gouging will not matter. *Any* conception of price gouging which fits the general outline above is vulnerable to the kinds of criticism that I will make below. ...

The Moral Status of Laws against Price Gouging

The argument in this section is designed to show that laws against price gouging are morally unjustified. That is, it attempts to show that we *do not* have all-things-considered good moral reasons to pass, maintain, or support such laws, and that we *do* have all-things-considered good moral reason to repeal them. Moreover, it is designed to show that such laws are unjustified *whatever* one might think about the moral status of price gouging itself. Even if price gouging is morally reprehensible, there is good reason not to prohibit it by law.

One difficulty with anti-gouging laws is that there is no unproblematic way of defining the practice of price gouging for legal purposes. Laws which prohibit "unconscionable" or

Business Ethics Quarterly 18, no. 3 (2008): 347–78. © 2008 Society for Business Ethics, published by Cambridge University Press. Reproduced with permission of the Licensor through PLSclear.

"unreasonable" exchanges, for instance, present serious problems of interpretation and predictability given the difficulty of assigning clear and shared meanings to these terms. Even those whose full-time occupation is interpreting, applying, and working with the law have grave difficulty understanding precisely what these terms mean. There is little hope, then, that ordinary merchants or individuals who begin selling goods for the first time in the wake of a disaster will be able to form a clear understanding of what the law requires of them. Without such an understanding, these individuals will be unable to predict how the law will respond to their behavior, and unable to plan their economic activity accordingly. This is objectionable both on grounds of efficiency and fairness.

Laws which prohibit price increases above a specified level (including zero) fare better on the dimension of clarity, but run into other difficulties as a result of the inflexible nature of the limits they set. Many such laws, for instance, take no account of increased costs which the sellers might face as a result of the same disaster which put their customers in difficulty. This raises problems from both fairness and consequentialist perspectives. In terms of fairness, it is not clear why the merchant should be forced to absorb the increased costs in order to benefit her customers, especially if we think that those merchants exercised good foresight and responsibility in obtaining a ready stock of goods which might be necessary in the case of a disaster. It is true that we might plausibly think that society as a whole bears some responsibility for protecting its members in time of crisis, but placing the whole of this responsibility on one class of persons seems an affront to fairness. In addition, the *consequences* of not allowing merchants to make up for increased costs are likely to be bad – for merchants, of course, but for customers as well. For, while the statutes under consideration punish selling items at above a certain specified level of price, they do not punish those who choose not to sell at all. Rather than continuing to sell needed goods such as generators, then, merchants might respond to anti-gouging statutes by closing up shop altogether. Because of the law, merchants will lose out on potential profits and customers will lose out on the opportunity to decide for themselves whether the goods they could have bought would have been worth the higher price. ...

Whatever else one might think about price gouging, the standard cases – those not involving deception, misinformation, or other extraneous factors – are clearly beneficial to both parties participating in the exchange. Even if the price they are being charged is exceptionally high and more than consumers would ideally like to pay, the fact that they are willing to pay it shows that they nevertheless value the good they are purchasing more than the money they are giving up for it. And assuming they are not misinformed, deceived, or irrational, there is no reason to think that they are *wrong* in assigning these relative values. Not only will the exchange satisfy their subjective preferences, but there is every reason to think that it will make them better off from an objective point of view as well. The goods that they are purchasing are, after all, genuinely *important*. And while the price of generators might rise dramatically in the wake of a disaster which knocks out power to a certain population, so too does the *need* people have for generators. Their willingness to pay the higher price is a reflection of this increased need, and not the product of mistake or irrationality.

Of course, one might insist that consumers are not benefiting *enough* from the exchange. Perhaps merchants have a moral duty of beneficence to sell needed goods to consumers at something less than the market-clearing price. Or perhaps there is some moral notion of a "fair" price which price gouging merchants are violating. One could grant all that has been said above, in other words, and still hold that merchants who charge the market-clearing price for necessary goods in the wake of a disaster are *exploiting* their customers.

I am not convinced by the accounts of exploitation on which such an argument would rely, and will have more to say about this in the next section. For our present purposes, however, we can grant the wrongfulness of this kind of exploitation and simply point out that this wrongfulness is insufficient warrant for prohibiting price gouging by law. For many of the very same concerns which underlie our objection to exploitation also count against any attempt to prohibit mutually beneficial but exploitative exchanges.

If, for instance, we object to exploitation because it sets back the interests of the exploited person, we can note that the prohibition of price gouging sets back their interests even more. To see this, we need simply to think about how anti-gouging laws work. When such laws have any effect at all, it is because they require merchants to sell goods at below the market-clearing price. The market-clearing price is the price at which the quantity supplied is equal to the quantity demanded. If prices are set above the market-clearing price, there will be insufficient demand for merchants to sell all their goods, and a surplus will result. If, on the other hand, prices are set below the market-clearing price as anti-gouging statutes require, there will be *too much* demand for available supply. There will, in other words, be a shortage of the relevant goods. This point is established both by widely accepted economic theory and by experiences with price caps such as those established during the oil crisis of the late 1970s. The existence of shortages, in turn, means that many consumers who would like to buy goods – even at the illegal market-clearing price – will be unable to do so. Because they are prevented from engaging in the economic exchanges they desire, they are made worse off. And because the goods affected by price gouging laws are *necessary* goods that are especially important for their health and well-being, they are probably made *significantly* worse off.

If, on the other hand, one's reasons for objecting to exploitation are of a deontological rather than a consequentialist nature, then a parallel argument can be made regarding the relevant deontological considerations. Exploitation might plausibly be argued to manifest a lack of respect for the personhood of those who are exploited. But laws against price gouging both manifest and encourage similar or greater lack of respect. They manifest a lack of respect for both merchants and customers by preventing them from making the autonomous choice to enter into economic exchanges at the market-clearing price. They send the signal, in effect, that *your* decision that this exchange is in your best interest is unimportant, and that the law will decide for you what sorts of transactions you are allowed to enter into. And they encourage a lack of respect for buyers by making it more likely that their needs will be *neglected* by those who are in a position to help them. This is because anti-gouging laws lead to shortages not just in the literal sense in which the supply is completely consumed with leftover demand unsatisfied, but also in a broader sense in which others who could supply the needed goods choose not to. The world never literally runs out of ice, generators, or sandbags in the wake of disaster. Such goods exist, and could be brought to the people who need them if those who possessed them were sufficiently motivated to do so. And whatever our moral attitude toward the fact might be, it is nevertheless a fact that the potential for high profits is one of the most effective ways available of so motivating individuals. Laws which prohibit the reaping of such high profits lead many individuals who would have done something to help to do nothing instead. As a result, disaster victims' needs are not exploited, but they are not satisfied either. They are simply ignored. This is a less obvious way of failing to value the humanity of such persons, but it is a failure nonetheless, and one which I am sure most persons would be willing to trade for the disrespect involved in mutually beneficial exploitation, if given the choice. ...

Against the Permissibility of Gouging – Exploitation
The second and much more prevalent concern about price gouging is that it is wrongfully exploitative. We have already examined the concept and possible moral wrongness of mutually beneficial exploitation in section two of this essay. The core of this concern is that it is unfair for sellers to take advantage of buyers' vulnerability in order to derive disproportionate benefit to themselves, even if buyers are benefiting from the exchange as well.

There are, however, some puzzles about the wrongness of mutually beneficial exploitation, at least when it is supposed to lead us to think that there is something *especially* wrong with acts of price gouging, as compared with the actions of most non-gougers.

The puzzles have to do with an incoherence in our thinking about what morality requires of us in terms of aiding those in distress. On the one hand, to the extent that we hold that price gougers are guilty of mutually beneficial exploitation, we hold that they are acting wrongly even though their actions bring *some* benefit to disaster victims. On the other hand, many of *us* do *nothing* to relieve the suffering of most disaster victims, and we generally do not view ourselves as acting wrongly in failing to provide this benefit – or, at least, we do not view ourselves as acting *as* wrongly as price gougers. How can it make sense to hold these two attitudes simultaneously?

The puzzle is one way of bringing out what Wertheimer calls the "nonworseness claim." That claim holds that in cases where A has a right not to transact with B, and where transacting with B is not worse for B than not transacting with B at all, then it cannot be seriously wrong for A to engage in this transaction, even if its terms are judged to be unfair by some external standard.[5]

From a consequentialist moral framework, the nonworseness claim seems obviously true. But the point is meant to have traction for deontological theories as well. If B's need places a claim on A for help, then it is puzzling how it could be worse by any moral standard – respect for persons, responsiveness to moral reasons, and so on – for A to provide some help than it is for him to provide none. On the face of it, those who ignore the needs of the vulnerable altogether treat them with *less* respect than those who do *something* to help. ...

The Signaling Function of Prices
The final argument in support of the permissibility of price gouging draws on Hayek's work on the information-conveying function of the price system. For Hayek, as for others in the Austrian tradition of economics, the *imperfect* nature of market competition is a crucially important fact for understanding the nature of markets. It is precisely because we do *not* live in a competitive equilibrium where supply is precisely equal to demand that prices and market competition are important. In the real world, as opposed to the world

of equilibrium models, facts are constantly changing. People's desires change, the quantity and quality of available resources change, and so on. When this happens, the natural reaction of prices is to change accordingly. In so doing, prices convey information to market actors about the new relative supply and demand of goods, and at the same time provide them with an incentive to alter their behavior in light of that new information.

In the case of price gouging, the higher prices charged for ordinary goods serve as a signal to both consumers and suppliers of that good. We have already seen, in the section above, how prices can serve as a signal to consumers. To illustrate the theoretical point with a real-world example, however, we can look at the case of hotels in Florida which were charged with price gouging in the wake of Hurricane Charley. According to charges filed by the state Attorney General, one hotel in West Palm Beach charged three individuals a rate of over $100 per night for a room, more than double their advertised rate of less than $50 per night. "Families putting their lives back together," the Attorney General wrote, "should not have to worry about price gouging."[6]

But the higher prices did more than simply increase the profits of the hotel owner. They also sent a signal to consumers to economize, and in so doing *helped* many families. The lower the price of hotel rooms, the higher people's demand for them. As prices increased, people looked for other ways to satisfy their needs. As one commentator pointed out, a family that might have chosen to rent separate rooms for parents and children at $50 per night will be more likely to rent only one room at the higher price, and a family whose home was damaged but in livable condition might choose to tough it out if the cost of a hotel room is $100 rather than $50.[7] Thus, while the increase in price does not literally increase the supply of hotel rooms, it increases the *available* supply – as a result of consumers' economizing behavior, more hotel rooms are available to individuals and families who need them most.

Prices also send signals to increase supply in more direct ways. If ice can be bought for $1.70 per bag in Goldsboro and sold for $12 in Raleigh, this tells people that Raleigh needs Goldsboro's ice, and that there is a substantial profit to be made in getting it there. Prices convey information about where there is high demand for goods, and supply a built-in incentive for individuals to meet that demand. The four men discussed at the beginning of this essay were probably not moved to drive to Raleigh by altruistic motives. But in doing so, they did something to help alleviate the shortage of ice

that Raleigh was facing. And if they hadn't been arrested for price gouging, others who heard about the profits they were making presumably would have followed suit. As more people brought needed supplies to Raleigh, competition would cause the price to decrease, and a new and lower equilibrium would be approximated.

The lesson we can draw from Hayek's insight is that markets are dynamic, and that our moral intuitions often fail to consider this dynamism. When we think about price gouging we often imagine a small, fixed supply of resources being distributed among a group of people. If a high price is charged, the rich will get the goods, and the rest won't. From all appearances, those who bought ice from the four men in Raleigh were in a zero-sum game with each other – one could win only if another lost – and the price gougers were taking advantage of this vulnerability. This seems to violate the most basic of moral standards – if *we* were desperately in need of ice, we would not want others to profit from our misery. In a static world, price gouging seems to be a clear-cut violation of the Golden Rule.

But here, as with many other cases involving markets, our intuitive moral response is driven too much by what we can visualize, and not enough by what is harder to see. It is easy for us to visualize the zero-sum relation between the individuals fighting over a small immediate supply of ice. It is more difficult for us to see the way in which the market forces at work in that scenario operate to increase supply and to spur the discovery and improvisation of substitutes, such that what is zero-sum in the microcosm is positive-sum in the macrocosm. ...

Notes

1. Anti-gouging statutes are generally triggered by an official proclamation of emergency, and last either the length of the emergency or for some specified time – Kansas, for instance, specifies that its law shall be in effect for either the time during which the declaration of emergency is in effect, or for a period of 30 days after the event that triggered the declaration, whichever is longer. See K.S.A. 50-6, 107. Michigan is an exception to this general rule, as it requires no triggering event and simply has general prohibitions on excessive price increases or profits. See UDAP Statute MCL 445.903(1)(z).

2. Cal. Penal Code §396. The District of Columbia, Hawaii, and Mississippi, however, are among the states which have laws that are not limited to necessary or disaster-related items, but extend to any good and/or service. See D.C. Code §28.4101–4102, Haw. Rev. Stat. §209.9 and Miss. Code Ann. §75-24-25.

3. Massachusetts, Virginia, Florida, Indiana, and New York are among the states which prohibit the sale of goods at "unconscionably high prices" or "grossly excessive prices" in the

wake of an emergency. See 940 Mass. Code Reg. 3.18, Va. Code Ann §59.1-526 (Supp. 2005), Fla. Stat. Ann §501.160(2) (West 2002 and Supp. 2005), Ind Code Ann. §4-6-9.1-2 (West 2005), and N.Y. Gen. Bus. Law §396-r(1) (McKinney 1996 & Supp. 2005). Arkansas and California are examples of states which set a percentage cap (both use 10 percent) on price increases in the wake of a disaster. See Ark. Code Ann. §4-88-33 (2001 & Supp. 2005) and Cal. Penal Code §396 (West 1999 & Supp. 2006). Most states that use a percentage cap also allow that cap to be exceeded if the cause of the price increase can be directly attributed to increases in cost to the seller.

4. Georgia, Louisiana, Mississippi, and Connecticut all have laws prohibiting any price increase for certain goods in the wake of a disaster. See Ga. Code Ann. §10-1-393.4(a)(1995), La. Rev. Stat. Ann. §29:732(2005), Miss. Code Ann. §75-24-25(2003), and Conn. Gen. Stat. §42-232(1991). Louisiana's code is, for reasons which are at least understandable if not correct, one of the harshest laws on the book, stipulating that criminal gouging offenses which result in property damage in excess of $5,000 can be punishable by up to five years imprisonment at hard labor.

5. A. Wertheimer, *Exploitation* (Princeton University Press, 1996), p. 189.

6. O. Crist, "Attorney General Charges Two Florida Hotels with Price Gouging" (2004). Retrieved November 27, 2007 from http://myfloridalegal.com/852562220065EE67.nsf/0/A15CA108ECBF1DDE85256EF30054D0FC?Open&Highlight=0,gouging, palm,beach.

7. T. Sowell, "Price Gouging in Florida," *Jewish World Review* (September 28, 2004). Retrieved November 15, 2007 from www.jewishworldreview.com/cols/sowell091404.asp.

What's the Matter with Price Gouging?

JEREMY SNYDER

Prices for essential goods are likely to increase when a disaster strikes, should that event decrease available supplies of these goods, increase demand, or both. Sometimes these price increases are condemned as "price gouging" or "profiteering." Such labels are not intended as simply descriptions of price increases; rather, they carry a strong negative moral valence. In many cases, the moral wrong of these price increases is identified as wrongfully gaining from another's misfortune. Consider the common view that "[t]hings like selling generators for four and five times their cost is not free enterprise, that's taking advantage of other people's misery."[1] In other cases, price gouging is condemned as unfairly taking advantage of others' needs, language that is often associated with exploitation.

But it isn't clear from these kinds of sentiments when a price increase amounts to price gouging or why, if at all, certain price increases following disasters are morally worrisome. Moreover, there are many reasons to think that price increases can create a net benefit for a community following a disaster. As one critic of anti-price gouging legislation puts it:

> Price to the left of the intersection of the supply-and-demand curve and you are guaranteed to vaporize whatever you are attempting to keep inexpensive. The reason that gasoline is disappearing from service stations across the nation is because station owners aren't gouging with sufficient gusto. Whether out of a misguided sense of kindness, concern about what politicians might think, fear of bad press, or the desire to keep customers happy, they are pricing below what the market would otherwise bear and, as a result, their inventory has disappeared. Now, how are the poor being helped by service stations closing down for lack of fuel? Gas at $6 a gallon, after all, is better than gas unavailable at any price.[2]

Price increases lead to rationing by consumers and encourage increased production of scarce goods. If the aim of anti-gouging legislation is to prevent vendors from profiting too much from a supply disruption, then achieving this aim may come at the cost of a swift return to normal market conditions.

In this essay, I discuss what moral wrongs, if any, are most reasonably ascribed to accusations of price gouging. ...

Price Gouging in the Law

At present, 32 states and the District of Columbia have passed some form of anti-gouging legislation. Although there is no federal anti-gouging law in the United States, a bill targeting fuel price increases passed the House of Representatives in 2007. In order to develop a better sense of what actions raise worries about price gouging, I will briefly examine this body of legislation.

Anti-gouging legislation is typically triggered by the declaration of a state of emergency or disaster. This

From *Business Ethics Quarterly* 19, no. 2 (2009).

declaration may be made by the state governor, local officials, or even the President. In substantially fewer cases, anti-
gouging legislation requires a declaration by public officials
in addition to a declaration of emergency. The duration of
the activation of anti-gouging controls can vary from the
length of the declaration of a disaster to a fixed length of time
or some mix of the two.

Laws against price gouging limit price increases for goods
during their period of activation. For the most part, price
increases are allowed when they reflect increases in the cost
of doing business following the disaster and, to some extent,
changes in the market. For example, the Federal Trade
Commission defined price gouging as occurring when "a
firm's average monthly sales price for gasoline in a particular
area is higher than for a previous month, *and* where such
higher prices are not substantially attributable to *either* (1)
increased costs, or (2) national or international market
trends."[3] In many cases, these caps seek to factor in changes
in the market and costs by allowing the price of goods to
increase a certain percentage above the pre-disaster price.
Otherwise, vague language prohibiting "unconscionable" or
"gross" increases in prices is used.[4] At their most extreme,
anti-gouging legislation may forbid *any* increase in the
prices of goods beyond those justified by higher business
costs. These more extreme restrictions are unusual and at
present limited to Georgia, Louisiana, Mississippi, and
Connecticut.[5]

Anti-gouging laws can be tied to all goods and services
following activation of anti-gouging statutes[6] or limited to
specific, essential goods. What counts as an essential good is
often left undefined but can explicitly include dwelling units,
gasoline, food, water, supplies for home repair, and pharmaceuticals. Florida Statute 501.160, for example, states that
following a state of emergency, it is unlawful "for a person or
her or his agent or employee to rent or sell or offer to rent or
sell at an unconscionable price within the area for which the
state of emergency is declared, any essential commodity
including, but not limited to, supplies, services, provisions,
or equipment that is necessary for consumption or use as a
direct result of the emergency."

Price Gouging and Respect for Others

If there is something morally wrong with price gouging, it is
not that gouging causes direct harms or economic inefficiency. In fact, a critique of price gouging will need to
confront the positive moral value of the efficiencies and
rationing effect created by price increases.

As I have noted, many anti-gouging laws are limited to
price increases on certain goods that are tied to basic human

needs. I believe that this characteristic of anti-gouging legislation offers an important insight regarding what is
morally objectionable about price gouging. As not all types
of price increases trigger the worry about gouging, it is not
price increases themselves that motivate this concern.
Rather, I would like to argue, it is price increases that undermine equitable access to certain, essential goods that motivate the worry about price gouging.

Put another way, worries about price gouging are engaged
when price increases cut off poor consumers from necessary
goods, not when price increases are unfair. We might think
that price increases following a disaster are unfair in the
sense that they allow for a large shift in the social surplus
of the interaction in the favor of the vendor. If the normally
functioning market serves as a benchmark for a fair transaction and fair distribution of the social surplus generated by
that transaction, then the disaster shifts the equilibrium
point between supply and demand in such a way that the
vendor can now charge unfair prices for her products.[7]

To see that it is not fairness, per se, that motivates concerns over price gouging, consider an example. An ava-
lanche outside of an exclusive ski resort blocks the only
road to the resort on New Year's Eve. Because this road is
blocked, a group of wealthy revelers at the resort no longer
have access to a resupply of champagne that was to be used
to celebrate the New Year. While there is food, drink, and
shelter to meet everyone's essential needs until the road is
cleared, there is far too little champagne on hand to ensure
that everyone will be able to make a toast at midnight.
Because of the high value placed on participating in the
midnight toast by the resort's wealthy patrons, the owners
of the limited remaining supply of champagne are able to
clear unusually high profits by selling their supplies.

The actions of these vendors could certainly be considered unfair by the lights of the normally functioning market.
But to label these actions as a case of price gouging strains
the normal use of the term.[8] Consider that the language
surrounding gouging typically focuses on the vulnerability
created by the disaster and the desperation of consumers to
meet their basic needs. As the Attorney General of Texas put
it, following gouging accusations in the wake of Hurricane
Ike, "They took advantage of the fear and the needs of people
who were evacuating the Gulf Coast region, and they jacked
up prices."[9] Price hikes for gasoline following that same
hurricane again focus on the absolute needs of consumers:
"It's sad to think that merchants would take advantage of
people who are already struggling to fill their gas tanks just
to get from home to work or from home to church and
back."[10] While the would-be champagne drinkers may be

desperate to participate in the New Year's toast and willing to pay unusually high prices to do so, their desperation is of an entirely different kind than that which normally motivates the charge of gouging. It is the desperation of individuals for essential goods, rather than simply the unfairness of the transaction, that motivates accusations of price gouging following a disaster.

Having located the wrongness of price gouging in access to essential goods, we can now say more about the duty that price gouging violates. To be specific, I would like to argue that price increases following a disaster can undermine equitable access to the goods essential to minimal human functioning. When price increases do so, they violate the norm of equal respect for persons. Respect for persons is often understood in terms of a duty to treat others as ends in themselves. More specifically, this respect is expressed both through recognizing that human animals are capable of forming and acting on a conception of the good life but need material support in order to do so.[11]

Proponents of various ethical theories can agree that basic respect for human persons will entail two components: Negatively, we should not interfere with others as they live out their conception of the good life given reciprocal respect and non-interference. Positively, we should aid others in forming and living out their conception of the good life, particularly by ensuring that they have the minimal means of developing such a conception. An attitude of respect for others will be expressed through our actions, including non-interference, positive support, and other expressions of the equal value of all human persons.[12]

At first glance, it would seem that placing limits on the functioning of the market through anti-gouging legislation would run counter to the goal of respecting others' freedom to pursue their conception of the good life. In the first place, I have discussed how price increases efficiently bring new supplies of essential goods into the market and help ration existing supplies. In this way, free markets serve as a means of supplying the goods essential to forming and acting on a conception of the good life.

Second, in their ideal form, markets carry their own value as institutions that protect and enlarge human freedom. By offering a space in which consumers can freely negotiate, consummate, and exit exchanges, markets ensure that consumers are not beholden to any particular vendor in their pursuit of the good life. Adam Smith specifically defends markets in terms of their historical role in undermining the oppressive feudal system of production.[13] Under a feudal system, serfs are tied to single masters and denied the freedoms of movement and exit created by a well-functioning market. Without the freedom to exit from the feudal relationship, the serf is condemned to take whatever terms of exchange are offered by her master. In a market, on the other hand, the "tradesman or artificer derives his subsistence from the employment, not of one, but of a hundred or thousand different customers. Though in some measure obliged to them all, therefore, he is not absolutely dependent on any one of them."[14] Markets guarantee legal protections for persons so that the equal right to make exchanges is enshrined as an entitlement, creating political equality between richer and poorer.[15] The moral concern that justifies the idealized institution of the market, then, is an interest in providing the material means to and institutional protection of individual freedom.

Conditions following a disaster can be highly non-ideal for a market, however, at least from the perspective of a stable balance between supply and demand. A disaster potentially results in a reduction of supply and spike in demand for some or all essential goods. While price increases reflect a new, post-disaster balance between supply and demand, over the short term this new equilibrium point can be particularly disruptive to the lives of the poorest members of a community. Until the pricing signals created by the new equilibrium increase supplies of essential goods, prices will remain high and supplies may be insufficient to meet demand. This gap between supply and demand is morally troubling because the goods in question are essential to minimal human functioning and may be out of reach for the poorest members of the affected community. While price increases in a free market represent one means of restoring supplies and rationing existing stocks of essential goods, anti-gouging legislation offers an alternative approach to this problem. ...

Avoiding Price Gouging in Practice

A vendor concerned about the effects of unconstrained price increases on equitable access to essential goods might respond by retaining pre-disaster prices for his poorest customers while allowing price increases for the remainder. That is, instead of allowing price increases according to the market, a vendor might adjust prices according to each consumer's ability to pay. This response would have the benefit of protecting the vendor against committing the moral wrongs I have described while preserving some of the price signaling and rationing effects of price increases.

In practice, vendors will face a range of difficulties should they attempt to price goods according to consumers' ability to pay. A great deal of information will often not be available to the merchant, particularly the means available to customers for purchasing essential goods. While some vendors in smaller communities will be intimately familiar with the needs and vulnerabilities of their customers, typically this will not be the case, particularly if the vendor enters the market from outside of the community in response to a disaster.

Given this problem, legislators and vendors can take two steps in order to avoid the moral wrong that I have argued is associated with price gouging. First, legislators can adopt a typical strategy found in existing state price gouging legislation and limit price increases to the going market rate prior to the disaster, plus increases for additional costs and risks to the vendor. When legislation of this kind has not been enacted within a community, individual vendors should still take it upon themselves to moderate their price increases. The aim of this moderation is to prevent vendors from receiving windfall profits in the face of the desperate need of their individual customers. By raising prices only to reflect changes in costs and risks in the post-disaster market, vendors maintain their own access to essential goods without unduly worsening others' access.

This strategy presumes that the going fair market price enabled members of the community generally to meet their essential needs prior to the disaster. Of course, this is an imperfect strategy since some persons will be priced out of competitive markets for essential goods even under normal conditions. If the local market prior to the disaster does not provide access to essential goods for a large portion of the community prior to the disaster, then this benchmark for setting prices should be discarded. This problem demonstrates that pre-disaster prices can serve as a useful shortcut under conditions of uncertainty only; these prices do not carry normative weight of their own. Nonetheless, a competitive market, in conjunction with a social safety net to make up for those priced out of the market, will serve as a useful mechanism for distributing goods essential to basic functioning.

Because the exchanges under discussion are mutually advantageous, there is good reason to allow for prices to exceed slightly the pre-disaster rate. As I have noted, price increases following a disaster have the positive effect of increasing supplies, encouraging rationing, and discouraging waste. Insofar as the prices charged by merchants aim at these goals, they can also serve the goal of equitable access to essential goods. Therefore, limited price increases even beyond those justified by increased costs and risks can be justified. Otherwise, price increases merely promote the vendor's self-interest at the cost of the basic needs of those around her.

While even limited price increases achieve a rationing effect, they will typically need to be supplemented with non-price rationing mechanisms, such as caps on purchases. As a second step, legislators should impose caps on the purchase of essential goods in order to ration these goods without distributing them according to ability to pay. When these caps are not mandated by law, individual vendors should impose caps on the sale of their own stocks of essential goods. The limits placed by these caps should depend on supplies and demand for essential goods following a disaster and the needs of the local population. For example, rationing of generators will not be necessary in a post-disaster setting where ample electricity remains available. Therefore, attention to the context in which the disaster takes place will be essential to the proper execution of this step. ...

Conclusions

If my account of the wrongness of price gouging is correct, it supports three major conclusions. First, the moral wrongs associated with price gouging should be understood generally as failures of respect for others. Vendors who ration scarce essential goods according to ability to pay undercut the goal of equitable access to essential goods within their community. This failure of respect takes place in a setting where the vendor owes a specified duty of beneficence to her customers and alternative means of achieving price signaling (through modest price increases) and rationing (through purchasing caps) are available.

Second, price gouging is only possible in transactions involving some good essential to living a distinctly human life. Price increases for diamonds, for example, are not instances of price gouging under my account. Moral wrongs, such as unfairness, may accompany price increases for nonessential goods. These wrongs, however, are distinct from the wrongs I have ascribed to price gouging.

Finally, the potential for price gouging will depend on the extent and strength of non-market social institutions for distributing essential goods. If these institutions are in place prior to a disaster and survive that event, price gouging is unlikely to occur even if vendors freely raise their prices in the post-disaster market. Individuals are more highly susceptible to price gouging in communities where entitlements to essential goods are weak or non-existent. Therefore, the moral wrong of price gouging cannot be reduced merely to price increases for essential goods following a disaster, even if these prices cannot be justified by increased costs. ...

Notes

1. J. Taylor Rushing, "Storms Stir up Price Gouging," *Florida Times-Union* (September 18, 2004), p. A-1.
2. Jerry Taylor, "Gouge on," National Review Online (September 2, 2005). www.nationalreview.com/2005/09/gouge-jerry-taylor/.
3. Federal Trade Commission, *Investigation of Gasoline Price Manipulation and Post-Katrina Gasoline Price Increases* (2006). www.ftc.gov/reports/060518PublicGasolinePricesInvestigationReportFinal.pdf, p. 137.
4. See, for example, Michigan (Mich. Stat. Ann. §445.903(z)), Missouri (15 CSR §60-8.030), and Texas (Tex. Bus & Com. Code §17.46(b)(27)).
5. See Geoffrey Rapp, "Gouging: Terrorist Attacks, Hurricanes, and the Legal and Economic Aspects of Post-Disaster Price Regulation," *Kentucky Law Journal* 94 (2005–2006): 535–60.
6. For example, California, Connecticut, the District of Columbia, Hawaii, and Mississippi make general prohibitions against price increases. California prohibits price increases generally for consumer goods and services (Cal. Pen. Code §396), Connecticut includes any item (Conn. Gen. Stat. §42-230), DC any merchandise or service (D.C. Code §28.4101 to 4102), Hawaii any commodity (Haw. Rev. Stat. §209-9), and Mississippi all goods and services (Miss. Code Ann. §75-24-25).
7. Alan Wertheimer, *Exploitation* (Princeton University Press, 1996).
8. If one feels that "price gouging" can appropriately apply to the champagne example, we can discriminate between two senses of price gouging. "Fairness gouging" can apply to price increases on all goods following a disaster or other market disruption while "needs gouging" will be limited to price increases on essential goods. As I argue, "needs gouging" is at the heart of the moral wrong that is typically associated with gouging.
9. Janet Elliott, "Two Hotels Face Lawsuits for Raising Rates," *The Houston Chronicle* (October 3, 2008).
10. "Go after Those Who May Be Price Gouging," *The Jackson Sun* (September 17, 2008).
11. Thomas Hill, *Autonomy and Self-Respect* (Cambridge University Press, 1991). The goods essential to minimal human functioning are supported through various non-essential goods. For this reason, I will also discuss non-essential goods like electrical generators, gasoline, and ice that are, in many communities, instrumental to the durability of essential goods such as food, water, and adequate shelter. Insofar as the essential goods are relevant to the wrongness of gouging, these non-essential goods will be relevant as well.
12. Elizabeth Anderson, *Value in Ethics and Economics* (Cambridge, MA: Harvard University Press, 1993).
13. Debra Satz, "Liberalism, Economic Freedom, and the Limits of Markets," *Social Philosophy and Policy* 24 (2007): 120–40.
14. Adam Smith, *An Inquiry into the Nature and Causes of the Wealth of Nations*, ed. R. H. Campbell, Andrew Skinner, and W. B. Todd (Oxford University Press, 1976), p. 420.
15. Elizabeth Anderson, "Ethical Assumptions in Economic Theory: Some Lessons from the History of Credit and Bankruptcy," *Ethical Theory and Moral Practice* 7 (2004): 347–60.

10.4 FINANCIAL MARKETS

Ethical Issues in Financial Services

JOHN R. BOATRIGHT

Some cynics jokingly deny that there is any ethics in finance, especially on Wall Street. This view is expressed in a thin volume, *The Complete Book of Wall Street Ethics*, which claims to fill "an empty space on financial bookshelves where a consideration of ethics should be."[1] Of course, the pages are all blank! However, a moment's reflection reveals that finance would be impossible without ethics. The very act of placing our assets in the hands of other people requires immense trust. An untrustworthy stockbroker or insurance agent, like an untrustworthy physician or attorney, finds few takers for his or her services. Financial scandals shock us precisely because they involve people and institutions that we should be able to trust.

Finance covers a broad range of activities, but the two most visible aspects are financial markets, such as stock exchanges, and the financial services industry, which includes not only commercial banks, but also investment banks, mutual fund companies, pension funds, both public and private, and insurance. Less visible to the public are the

From John R. Boatright, *Ethics and the Conduct of Business*, 6th ed. 2009. Adapted by permission of Pearson Education Inc., Upper Saddle River, NJ.

financial operations of a corporation, which are the responsibility of the chief financial officer (CFO). ...

Financial Services

The financial services industry still operates largely through personal selling by stockbrokers, insurance agents, financial planners, tax advisors, and other finance professionals. Personal selling creates innumerable opportunities for abuse, and although finance professionals take pride in the level of integrity in the industry, misconduct still occurs. However, customers who are unhappy over failed investments or rejected insurance claims are quick to blame the seller of the product, sometimes with good reason.

For example, two real estate limited partnerships launched by Merrill Lynch & Co. lost close to $440 million for 42,000 investor-clients.[2] Known as Arvida I and Arvida II, these highly speculative investment vehicles projected double-digit returns on residential developments in Florida and California, but both eventually stopped payments to investors. In the end, each $1,000 unit of Arvida I was worth $125, and each $1,000 unit of Arvida II, a mere $6.

The Arvida partnerships were offered by the Merrill Lynch sales force to many retirees of modest means as safe investments with good income potential. The brokers themselves were told by the firm that Arvida I entailed only "moderate risk," and company-produced sales material said little about risk while emphasizing the projected performance. Left out of the material was the fact that the projections included a return of some of the investors' own capital, that the track record of the real estate company was based on commercial, not residential projects, and that eight of the top nine managers of the company had left just before Arvida I was offered to the public.

This case raises questions about whether investors were deceived by the brokers' sales pitches and whether material information was concealed. In other cases, brokers have been accused of churning client accounts in order to generate higher fees and of selecting unsuitable investments for clients. Other abusive sales practices in the financial services industry include twisting, in which an insurance agent persuades a policy holder to replace an older policy with a newer one that provides little if any additional benefit but generates a commission for the agent, and flipping, in which a loan officer persuades a borrower to repay an old loan with a new one, thereby incurring more fees. In one case, an illiterate retiree, who was flipped ten times in a four-year period, paid $19,000 in loan fees for the privilege of borrowing $23,000.

This section discusses three objectionable practices in selling financial products to clients, namely, deception, churning, and suitability.

Deception

The ethical treatment of clients requires salespeople to explain all of the relevant information truthfully in an understandable, nonmisleading manner. One observer complains that brokers, insurance agents, and other salespeople have developed a new vocabulary that obfuscates rather than reveals.

> Walk into a broker's office these days. You won't be sold a product. You won't even find a broker. Instead, a "financial adviser" will "help you select" an "appropriate planning vehicle," or "offer" a menu of "investment choices" or "options" among which to "allocate your money." ... [Insurance agents] peddle such euphemisms as "private retirement accounts," "college savings plans," and "charitable remainder trusts." ... Among other linguistic sleights of hand in common usage these days: saying tax-free when, in fact, it's only tax-deferred; high yield when it's downright risky; and projected returns when it's more likely in your dreams.[3]

Salespeople avoid speaking of commissions, even though they are the source of their compensation. Commissions on mutual funds are "front-end" or "back-end loads"; and insurance agents, whose commissions can approach 100 percent of the first year's premium, are not legally required to disclose this fact – and they rarely do. The agents of one insurance company represented life insurance policies as "retirement plans" and referred to the premiums as "deposits."[4]

Deception is often a matter of interpretation. Promotional material for a mutual fund, for example, may be accurate but misleading if it emphasizes the strengths of a fund and minimizes the weaknesses. Figures of past performance can carefully be selected and displayed in ways that give a misleading impression. Deception can also occur when essential information is not revealed. Thus, an investor may be deceived when the sales charge is rolled into the fund's annual expenses, which may be substantially higher than the competition's, or when the projected hypothetical returns do not reflect all charges. As these examples suggest, factually true claims may lead typical investors to hold mistaken beliefs. Deception aside, what information ought to be disclosed to a client? The Securities Act of 1933 requires the issuer of a security to disclose all material information, which is defined as information about which an average prudent investor ought reasonably to be informed or to which a reasonable person would attach importance in determining a course of action in a transaction. The rationale for this provision of the Securities Act is both fairness to investors, who have a right to make decisions with adequate information, and the efficiency of securities markets, which requires that investors be adequately informed. Most financial products, including mutual funds and insurance policies, are accompanied by a written prospectus that contains all of the information that the issuer is legally required to provide.

In general, a person is deceived when that person is unable to make a rational choice as a result of holding a false belief that is created by some claim made by another. That claim may be either a false or misleading statement or a statement that is incomplete in some crucial way.

Consider two cases of possible broker (mis)conduct:

1. A brokerage firm buys a block of stock prior to issuing a research report that contains a "buy" recommendation in order to ensure that enough shares are available to fill customer orders. However, customers are not told that they are buying stock from the firm's own holdings, and they are charged the current market price plus the standard commission for a trade.
2. A broker assures a client that an Initial Public Offering (IPO) of a closed-end fund is sold without a commission and encourages quick action by saying that after the IPO is sold, subsequent buyers will have to pay a 7 percent commission. In fact, a 7 percent commission is built into the price of the IPO, and this charge is revealed in the prospectus but will not appear on the settlement statement for the purchase.

In the first case, one might argue that if an investor decides to purchase shares of stock in response to a "buy" recommendation, it matters little whether the shares are bought on the open market or from a brokerage firm's holdings. The price is the same. An investor might appreciate the opportunity to share any profit that is realized by the firm (because of lower trading costs and perhaps a lower stock price before the recommendation is released), but the firm is under no obligation to share any profit with its clients. On the other hand, the client is buying the stock at the current market price and paying a fee as though the stock were purchased at the order of the client. The circumstances of the purchase are not explained to the client, but does the broker have any obligation to do so? And would this knowledge have any effect on the client's decision?

In the second case, however, a client might be induced to buy an initial offering of a closed-end mutual fund in the mistaken belief that the purchase would avoid a commission charge. The fact that the commission charge is disclosed in the prospectus might ordinarily exonerate the broker from a charge of deception except that the false belief is created by the broker's claim, which, at best, skirts the edge of honesty. Arguably, the broker made the claim with an intent to deceive, and a typical, prudent investor is apt to feel that there was an attempt to deceive.

Churning

Churning is defined as excessive or inappropriate trading for a client's account by a broker who has control over the account with the intent to generate commissions rather than to benefit the client. Although churning occurs, there is disagreement on the frequency or the rate of detection. The brokerage industry contends that churning is a rare occurrence and is easily detected by firms as well as clients. No statistics are kept on churning, but complaints to the SEC and various exchanges about unauthorized trading and other abuses have risen sharply in recent years.

The ethical objection to churning is straightforward: It is a breach of a fiduciary duty to trade in ways that are not in a client's best interests. Churning, as distinct from unauthorized trading, occurs only when a client turns over control of an account to a broker, and by taking control, a broker assumes a responsibility to serve the client's interests. A broker who merely recommends a trade is not acting on behalf of a client or customer and is more akin to a traditional seller, but a broker in charge of a client's portfolio thereby pledges to manage it to the best of his or her ability.

Although churning is clearly wrong, the concept is difficult to define. Some legal definitions offered in court decisions are: "excessive trading by a broker disproportionate to the size of the account involved, in order to generate commissions,"[5] and a situation in which "a broker, exercising control over the frequency and volume of trading in the customer's account, initiates transactions that are excessive in view of the character of the account."[6] The courts have held that for churning to occur a broker must trade with the intention of generating commissions rather than benefiting the client. The legal definition of churning contains three elements, then: (1) the broker controls the account; (2) the trading is excessive for the character of the account; and (3) the broker acted with intent.

The most difficult issue in the definition of churning is the meaning of "excessive trading." First, whether trading is excessive depends on the character of the account. A client who is a more speculative investor, willing to assume higher risk for a greater return, should expect a higher trading volume. Second, high volume is not the only factor; pointless trades might be considered churning even if the volume is relatively low. Third, churning might be indicated by a pattern of trading that consistently favors trades that yield higher commissions. Common to these three points is the question of whether the trades make sense from an investment point of view. High-volume trading that loses money might still be defended as an intelligent but unsuccessful investment strategy, whereas investments that represent no strategy beyond generating commissions are objectionable, no matter the amount gained or lost.

An SEC report concluded that the compensation system in brokerage firms was the root cause of the churning problem.[7] The report identified some "best practices" in the industry that might prevent churning, including ending the practice of paying a higher commission for a company's own products, prohibiting sales contests for specific products, and tying a portion of compensation to the size of a client's account, regardless of the number of transactions. However, an SEC panel concluded that the commission system is too deeply rooted to be significantly changed and recommended better training and oversight by brokerage firms.

Suitability

In general, brokers, insurance agents, and other salespeople have an obligation to recommend only suitable securities and financial products. However, suitability, like churning, is difficult to define precisely. The rules of the National Association of Securities Dealers include the following:

> In recommending to a customer the purchase, sale, or exchange of any security, a member shall have reasonable grounds for believing that the recommendation is suitable for such customer upon the basis of the facts, if any, disclosed by such customer as to his other security holding and as to his financial situation and needs.[8]

The most common causes of unsuitability are (1) unsuitable types of securities, that is, recommending stocks, for example, when bonds would better fit the investor's objectives; (2) unsuitable grades of securities, such as selecting lower-rated bonds when higher-rated ones are more appropriate; (3) unsuitable diversification, which leaves the portfolio vulnerable to changes in the markets; (4) unsuitable trading techniques, including the use of margin or options, which can leverage an account and create greater volatility and risk; and (5) unsuitable liquidity.

Limited partnerships, for example, are not very marketable and are thus unsuitable for customers who may need to liquidate the investment.

The critical question, of course, is, When is a security unsuitable? Rarely is a single security unsuitable except in the context of an investor's total portfolio. Investments are most often deemed to be unsuitable because they involve excessive risk, but a few risky investments may be appropriate in a well-balanced, generally conservative portfolio. Furthermore, even an aggressive, risk-taking portfolio may include unsuitable securities if the risk is not compensated by the expected return.

Ensuring that a recommended security is suitable for a given investor thus involves many factors, but people in the financial services industry offer to put their specialized knowledge and skills to work for us. We expect suitable recommendations from physicians, lawyers, and accountants. Why should we expect anything less from finance professionals?

Insider Trading

Financial transactions typically take place in organized markets, such as stock markets, commodities markets, futures or options markets, currency markets, and the like. These markets presuppose certain moral rules and expectations of moral behavior. The most basic of these is a prohibition against fraud and manipulation, but, more generally, the rules and expectations for markets are concerned with fairness, which is often expressed as a level playing field. The playing field in financial markets can become "tilted" by many factors, including unequal information, bargaining power, and resources.

Insider trading is commonly defined as trading in the stock of publicly held corporations on the basis of material, non-public information. In a landmark 1968 decision, executives of Texas Gulf Sulphur Company were found guilty of insider trading for investing heavily in their own company's stock after learning of the discovery of rich copper ore deposits in Canada.[9] The principle established in the *Texas Gulf Sulphur* case is that corporate insiders must refrain from trading on information that significantly affects stock price until it becomes public knowledge. The rule for corporate insiders is, reveal or refrain!

Much of the uncertainty in the law on insider trading revolves around the relation of the trader to the source of the information. Corporate executives are definitely "insiders," but some "outsiders" have also been charged with insider trading. Among such outsiders have been a printer who was able to identify the targets of several takeovers from legal documents that were being prepared; a financial analyst who uncovered a huge fraud at a high-flying firm and advised his clients to sell; a stockbroker who was tipped off by a client who was a relative of the president of a company and who learned about the sale of the business through a chain of family gossip; a psychiatrist who was treating the wife of a financier who was attempting to take over a major bank; and a lawyer whose firm was advising a client planning a hostile takeover.[10] The first two traders were eventually found innocent of insider trading; the latter three were found guilty (although the stockbroker case was later reversed in part). From these cases, a legal definition of insider trading is slowly emerging.

The key points are that a person who trades on material, non-public information is engaging in insider trading when (1) the trader has violated some legal duty to a corporation and its shareholders; or (2) the source of the information has such a legal duty and the trader knows that the source is violating that duty. Thus, the printer and the stock analyst had no relation to the corporations in question and so had no duty to refrain from using the information that they had acquired. The stockbroker and the psychiatrist, however, knew or should have known that they were obtaining inside information indirectly from high-level executives who had a duty to keep the information confidential. The corresponding rule for outsiders is: Don't trade on information that is revealed in violation of a trust. Both rules are imprecise, however, and leave many cases unresolved.

Arguments against Insider Trading

The difficulty in defining insider trading is due to disagreement over the moral wrong involved. Two main rationales are used in support of a law against insider trading. One is based on property rights and holds that those who trade on material, non-public information are essentially stealing property that belongs to the corporation. The second rationale is based on fairness and holds that traders who use inside information have an unfair advantage over other investors and that, as a result, the stock market is not a level playing field. These two rationales lead to different definitions, one narrow and the other broad. On the property rights or "misappropriation" theory, only corporate insiders or outsiders who bribe, steal, or otherwise wrongfully acquire corporate secrets can be guilty of insider trading. The fairness argument is broader and applies to anyone who trades on material, non-public information no matter how it is acquired.

Inside Information as Property.

One difficulty in using the property rights or misappropriation argument is to determine who owns the information in question. The main basis for recognizing a property right in trade secrets and confidential business information is the investment that companies make in acquiring information and the competitive value that some information has. Not all insider information fits this description, however. Advance knowledge of better-than-expected earnings would be an example. Such information still has value in stock trading, even if the corporation does not use it for that purpose. For this reason, many employers prohibit the personal use of any information that an employee gains in the course of his or her work. This position is too broad, however, since an employee is unlikely to be accused of stealing company property by using knowledge of the next day's earning report for any purpose other than stock trading.

A second difficulty with the property rights argument is that if companies own certain information, they could then give their own employees permission to use it, or they could sell the information to favored investors or even trade on it themselves to buy back stock. Giving employees permission to trade on insider information could be an inexpensive form of extra compensation that further encourages employees to develop valuable information for the firm. Such an arrangement would also have some drawbacks; for example, investors might be less willing to buy the stock of a company that allowed insider trading because of the disadvantage to outsiders. What is morally objectionable about insider trading, according to its critics, though, is not the misappropriation of a company's information but the harm done to the investing public. So the violation of property rights in insider trading cannot be the sole reason for prohibiting it. Let us turn, then, to the second argument against insider trading, namely, the argument of fairness.

The Fairness Argument.

Fairness in the stock market does not require that all traders have the same information. Indeed, trades will take place only if the buyers and sellers of a stock have different information that leads them to different conclusions about the stock's worth. It is only fair, moreover, that a shrewd investor who has spent a lot of time and money studying the prospects of a company should be able to exploit that advantage; otherwise there would be no incentive to seek out new information. What is objectionable about using inside information is that other traders are barred from obtaining it no matter how diligent they may be. The information is unavailable not for lack of effort but for lack of access. Poker also pits card players with unequal skill and knowledge without being unfair, but a game played with a marked deck gives some players an unfair advantage over others. By analogy, then, insider trading is like playing poker with a marked deck.

The analogy may be flawed, however. Perhaps a more appropriate analogy is the seller of a home who fails to reveal hidden structural damage. One principle of stock market regulation is that both buyers and sellers of stock should have sufficient information to make rational choices. Thus, companies must publish annual reports and disclose important developments in a timely manner. A CEO who hides bad news from the investing public, for example, can be sued for fraud. Good news, such as an oil find, need not be announced until a company has time to buy the drilling rights, and so on; but to trade on that information before it is public knowledge might also be described as a kind of fraud.

Insider trading is generally prosecuted under SEC Rule 10b-5, which merely prohibits fraud in securities transactions. In fraudulent transactions, one party, such as the buyer of the house with structural damage, is wrongfully harmed for lack of knowledge that the other party concealed. So too – according to the fairness argument – are the ignorant parties to insider-trading transactions wrongfully harmed when material facts, such as the discovery of copper ore deposits in the *Texas Gulf Sulphur* case, are not revealed.

The main difficulty in the fairness argument is to determine what information ought to be revealed in a transaction. The reason for requiring a homeowner to disclose hidden structural damage is that doing so makes for a more efficient housing market. In the absence of such a requirement, potential home buyers would pay less because they are not sure what they are getting, or they would invest in costly home inspections. Similarly – the argument goes – requiring insiders to reveal before trading makes the stock market more efficient.

The trouble with such a claim is that some economists argue that the stock market would be more efficient without a law against insider trading.[11] If insider trading were permitted, they claim, information would be registered in the market more quickly and at less cost than the alternative of leaving the task to research by stock analysts. The main beneficiaries of a law against insider trading, critics continue, are not individual investors but market professionals who can pick up news "on the street" and act on it quickly. Some economists argue further that a law against insider trading preserves the illusion that there is a level playing field and that individual investors have a chance against market professionals.

Economic arguments about market efficiency look only at the cost of registering information in the market and not at possible adverse consequences of legalized insider trading, which are many. Investors who perceive the stock market as an unlevel playing field may be less inclined to participate or will be forced to adopt costly defensive measures. Legalized insider trading would have an effect on the treatment of information in a firm. Employees whose interest is in information that they can use in the stock market may be less concerned with information that is useful to the employer, and the company itself might attempt to tailor its release of information for maximum benefit to insiders. More importantly, the opportunity to engage in insider trading might undermine the relation of trust that is essential for business organizations.[12] A prohibition on insider trading frees employees of a corporation to do what they are supposed to be doing – namely, working for the interests of the shareholders – not seeking ways to advance their own interests.

The harm that legalized insider trading could do to organizations suggests that the strongest argument against legalization might be the breach of fiduciary duty that would result. Virtually everyone who could be called an "insider" has a fiduciary duty to serve the interests of the corporation and its shareholders, and the use of information that is acquired while serving as a fiduciary for personal gain is a violation of this duty. It would be a breach of professional ethics for a lawyer or an accountant to benefit personally from the use of information acquired in confidence from a client, and it is similarly unethical for a corporate executive to make personal use of confidential business information.

The argument that insider trading constitutes a breach of fiduciary duty accords with recent court decisions that have limited the prosecution of insider trading to true insiders who have a fiduciary duty. One drawback of the argument is that "outsiders," whom federal prosecutors have sought to convict of insider trading, would be free of any restrictions. A second drawback is that insider trading, on this argument, is no longer an offense against the market but the violation of a duty to another party. And the duty not to use information that is acquired while serving as a fiduciary prohibits more than insider trading. The same duty would be violated by a fiduciary who buys or sells property or undertakes some other business dealing on the basis of confidential information. That such breaches of fiduciary duty are wrong is evident, but the authority of the SEC to prosecute them under a mandate to prevent fraud in the market is less clear.

The *O'Hagan* Decision. In 1997, the US Supreme Court ended a decade of uncertainty over the legal definition of insider trading. The SEC has long prosecuted insider trading using the misappropriation theory, according to which an inside trader breaches a fiduciary duty by misappropriating confidential information for personal trading. In 1987, the

High Court split 4–4 on an insider-trading case involving a reporter for the *Wall Street Journal* and thus left standing a lower court decision that found the reporter guilty of misappropriating information.[13] However, the decision did not create a precedent for lack of a majority. Subsequently, lower courts rejected the misappropriation theory in a series of cases in which the alleged inside trader did not have a fiduciary duty to the corporation whose stock was traded. The principle applied was that the trading must itself constitute a breach of fiduciary duty. This principle was rejected in *U.S. v. O'Hagan*.[14]

James H. O'Hagan was a partner in a Minneapolis law firm that was advising the British firm Grand Metropolitan in a hostile takeover of Minneapolis-based Pillsbury Company. O'Hagan did not work on Grand Met business but allegedly tricked a fellow partner into revealing the takeover bid. O'Hagan then reaped $4.3 million by trading in Pillsbury stock and stock options. An appellate court ruled that O'Hagan did not engage in illegal insider trading because he had no fiduciary duty to Pillsbury, the company in whose stock he traded. Although O'Hagan misappropriated confidential information from his own law firm – to which he owed a fiduciary duty – trading on this information did not constitute a fraud against the law firm or against Grand Met. Presumably, O'Hagan would have been guilty of insider trading only if he were an insider of Pillsbury or had traded in Grand Met stock.

In a 6–3 decision, the Supreme Court reinstated the conviction of Mr. O'Hagan and affirmed the misappropriation theory. According to the decision, a person commits securities fraud when he or she "misappropriates confidential information for securities trading purposes, in breach of a fiduciary duty owed to the source of the information." Thus, an inside trader need not be an insider (or a temporary insider, like a lawyer) of the corporation whose stock is traded. Being an insider in Grand Met is sufficient in this case to hold that insider trading occurred. The majority opinion observed that "it makes scant sense" to hold a lawyer like O'Hagan to have violated the law "if he works for a law firm representing the target of a tender offer, but not if he works for a law firm representing the bidder." The crucial point is that O'Hagan was a fiduciary who misused information that had been entrusted to him. This decision would also apply to a person who receives information from an insider and who knows that the insider source is violating a duty of confidentiality. However, a person with no fiduciary ties who receives information innocently (by overhearing a conversation, for example) would still be free to trade.

Conclusion

Ethical issues in finance are important because they bear on our financial well-being. Ethical misconduct, whether it be by individuals acting alone or by financial institutions, has the potential to rob people of their life savings. Because so much money is involved in financial dealings, there must be well-developed and effective safeguards in place to ensure personal and organizational ethics. Although the law governs much financial activity, strong emphasis must be placed on the integrity of finance professionals and on ethical leadership in our financial institutions. Some of the principles in finance ethics are common to other aspects of business, especially the duties of fiduciaries and fairness in sales practices and securities markets. However, such activities as insider trading raise unique issues that require special consideration.

Notes

1. Jay L. Walker [pseudonym], *The Complete Book of Wall Street Ethics* (New York: William Morrow and Company, 1987).
2. Mark Maremont, "Burned by Merrill," *Businessweek* (April 25, 1994): 122–25.
3. Ellen E. Schultz, "You Need a Translator for Latest Sales Pitch," *Wall Street Journal* (February 14, 1994), p. C1.
4. Michael Quint, "Met Life Shakes up Its Ranks," *The New York Times* (October 29, 1994), p. C1.
5. *Marshak v. Blyth Eastman Dillon & Co., Inc.*, 413 F. Supp. 377, 379 (1975).
6. *Kaufman v. Merrill Lynch, Pierce, Fenner & Smith*, 464 F. Supp. 528, 534 (1978).
7. Report of the Committee on Compensation Practices, issued by the Securities and Exchange Commission (April 10, 1995).
8. *NASD Rules of Fair Practice*, art. III, sec. 2.
9. *SEC v. Texas Gulf Sulphur*, 401 F.2d 19 (1987).
10. *Chiarella v. U.S.*, 445 U.S. 222 (1980); *Dirks v. SEC*, 463 U.S. 646 (1983); *U.S. v. Chestman*, 903 F.2d 75 (1990); *U.S. v. Willis*, 737 F. Supp. 269 (1990); *U.S. v. O'Hagan*, 117 S.Ct. 2199 (1997).
11. Henry Manne, *Insider Trading and the Stock Market* (New York: Free Press, 1966).
12. This point is argued in Jennifer Moore, "What Is Really Unethical about Insider Trading?" *Journal of Business Ethics* 9 (1990): 171–82.
13. *Carpenter et al. v. U.S.*, 484 U.S. 19 (1987).
14. *U.S. v. O'Hagan*.

The Moral Problem of Insider Trading

ALAN STRUDLER

Insider trading is a crime that can have sensational results. Its perpetrators risk finding themselves behind bars for many years and vilified in popular opinion, while their firms and the people heavily invested in them risk financial ruin. Even so, doubt may be raised about our understanding of insider trading, a doubt that should prompt concern about the justice of insider trading prosecution and about the harsh moral judgments people often make of insider traders. The doubt comes from trying to identify the moral wrong in insider trading.

Perhaps the most influential insider trading case is *SEC v. Texas Gulf Sulphur*, in which officers of Texas Gulf Sulphur learned of their company's rich ore strike in Canada and traded on this information before the news became public. These officers, who engaged in securities transactions on the basis of material, non-public information, are paradigm insider traders. It is clear that they committed a legal wrong. We will find more challenging the matter of identifying the moral wrong in their conduct.

Harm

The argument from harm maintains that insider trading is wrong because of the social harm it causes, given that we understand "causing harm" expansively, as causing a failure to attain optimal social welfare or social good.

In a securities market there are winners and losers, people who get good prices and people who get bad prices. Other things equal, the person with the best information about what is being bought or sold stands in the best position to find bargains and get the best price. Competing against corporate insiders, who possess superior information, thus increases the risk that one loses. Ordinary traders will balk at the risk of trading against insiders, and insider trading, then, will undermine confidence in securities markets and deter investment, increasing the price a firm must pay to raise capital and hindering both a firm's development and a society's economic growth more generally, according to the argument from harm. As a society, we have good moral reason to protect ourselves against this kind of economic harm, and laws prohibiting insider trading afford the relevant protection. On this view, insider trading is wrong because it fails a cost/benefit test, depriving us of a peculiar kind of benefit, a social good whose continued existence requires the cooperation of many people in maintaining a credible securities market.

An empirical claim forms the core of the argument from harm: that insider trading will significantly deter investment. Influential research lends some support to this claim. A leading article on insider trading compares the cost of capital (the price that firms must pay to raise money in a securities market) in (mostly developing) countries both before and after they begin enforcing insider trading laws, and concludes that because this cost generally decreases after insider trading laws are enforced, social welfare improves when insider trading diminishes. Does the article show that insider trading is socially harmful? Its authors acknowledge that they locate no causal link between insider trading and changes in social welfare, but merely non-causal correlation. Even the best social science research, then, expresses no confidence about whether insider trading deters investment in ways that prove socially harmful. Moreover, there is good reason to wonder whether insider trading will deter investment. Securities traders are accustomed to the idea that other traders may possess advantages in information, even if it is not inside information, and hardly seem deterred by this idea. Most investors do not believe that the quality of their information is as good as Warren Buffet's, or the stock market wizards at Goldman Sachs. If the investment public is willing to trade against Warren Buffet and the wizards at Goldman Sachs, perhaps it will not be deterred by the prospect of trading against corporate insiders, either.

In addition to doubt about the harm insider trading causes, there are other reasons for skepticism about the argument from harm: Credible economic arguments purport to show that insider trading, if it causes some harm, also creates benefits; perhaps these benefits are more significant than any harms that insider trading causes. Some scholars find these benefits in the idea that insider trading facilitates getting insider information to market quickly. Arguably when market information improves, so does market performance. One

From Chapter 13, "The Moral Problem of Insider Trading," in *The Oxford Handbook of Business Ethics*, ed. George G. Brenkert and Tom Beauchamp (Oxford University Press, 2009), pp. 388–89 and 398–405. By permission of Oxford University Press, Inc.

may also argue that insider trading benefits the firm and hence society more generally by providing a cheap compensation device: If a firm gives its employees the valuable perquisite of a right to trade insider information, it costs the firm nothing. An entirely different but equally plausible argument that insider trading is socially beneficial focuses on the costs of law enforcement. The argument is simple. If we as a society need not pay the costs of enforcing laws against insider trading, we save money.

There are, then, arguments both that insider trading harms us and arguments that it benefits us. Which, if any, of these arguments should prevail in our decision-making about insider trading? Scholars who examine the issue say that the economic considerations for and against insider trading seem both closely balanced and to rest on speculative assumptions. We should worry, then, about accepting either the idea that insider trading is generally beneficial or that it is harmful. There exists no measure for the magnitudes of alleged harms and benefits, and nobody knows that a reliable measure will ever emerge. So we do not know how to balance the good consequences of insider trading (if they exist) against the bad (if they exist).

Deception

Courts have always seen insider trading as a kind of fraud, viz., securities fraud. Historically, wrongful deception forms the heart of fraud. Hence, we might look to the wrong in wrongful deception as the explanation of the wrong in insider trading. Recall *Texas Gulf Sulphur*. On the deception account, they deceived shareholders by buying stock from them while concealing material, non-public information relevant to the valuation of the securities. Deception can be understood as inherently wrong, apart from any harm it causes.

The deception account of insider trading has its problems. Most salient is the elusiveness of any deception that occurs in insider trading. Recall, again, the Texas Gulf Sulphur officers. As a matter of fact, these officers were responsible for a number of misstatements that appeared in the press and misled the trading public about their discoveries of ore, and these statements were used at trial against the officers. Yet insider trading law requires no false or misleading statement for a finding of liability. The law is clear that if corporate insiders trade on material, non-public information while silently failing to disclose the basis of their trade, their silence may ground a conviction. Even if Texas Gulf Sulphur officers had made no false or misleading statements about their ore find, they might nonetheless have been convicted of insider trading. But on what grounds? If deception is at the core of insider trading, whom do silent officers deceive and how do they do it? How can silence, saying nothing, be deceptive?

Suppose that officers have a moral obligation to inform shareholders of significant firm developments before they trade on firm stock. Then before making a trade, they have an obligation to say, if true, that there has been an important strike. By their silence, they license the inference that no new strike occurred. Had the officers discharged their obligations, shareholders would have had very different beliefs – fewer relevantly false beliefs – about the firm. Perhaps that suffices to show that they deceive shareholders. We may distinguish between deception as it ordinarily occurs, which involves a discrete deceptive act, and a failure of candor, which need involve no discrete deceptive act. We may then criticize a firm's officers for their failure of candor. We may say that sometimes minimal decency requires not merely that one not conceal the truth, but instead that one reveal the truth.

In a competitive business environment, however, one need not always be entirely candid. Suppose that you work for The Walt Disney Company, which assigns you the task of purchasing land for a new theme park. You need to acquire one more plot of land to complete your assignment. On that plot sits the home of a savvy used car salesman. Should you disclose to the homeowner what Disney intends to do with his land, or even that you work for Disney? If you disclose, you risk that the homeowner, knowing how valuable the land is to Disney, will insist on an unfairly high price, and you will have no choice except to pay it. I suggest that although it would plainly be wrong for you to lie to the homeowner about what you will do with the land, morality does not require you to be forthcoming. Honesty does not require full disclosure in a competitive business environment, even when a failure to disclose denies benefits to others. How, then, do we know how much information a firm's officers should disclose?

The judgment that the officers' stock sale is deceptive, even in our expansive interpretation of that term, makes little sense unless one also finds that they fail in some duty to disclose the truth. So the deception account leaves us with a crucial but seemingly unanswerable question: What is the moral basis for this duty to disclose?

Unfairness

The argument from unfairness contends that insider traders get an unfair advantage over people with whom they engage in securities transactions and that their trades are therefore wrong on grounds of justice. The supposed unfair advantage is in their use of insider information, which stock market competitors lack. The unfairness argument looks at the comparative position of buyer and seller of stock and declares these positions unacceptable on grounds of justice.

The unfairness argument against insider trading identifies the relevant unfairness in terms of an acute inequality of information separating buyer and seller in a securities transaction. There are certainly cases, outside the securities realm, in which an asymmetry casts doubt on the legitimacy of a sales transaction. Typically, these cases involve dishonesty. Hence, if you have a car that has a massively defective engine, or if your house has a cracked foundation, it seems wrong not to disclose the fact to a prospective buyer. One might think that the asymmetry of information that separates insider traders and parties on the other end of a securities transaction is similarly problematic.

But not all asymmetries of information are unacceptable. Suppose that Edna, an engineering genius, studies internal combustion engines for years, and finds a deep design flaw in Toyota's favorite engine. She alone knows that soon most Toyotas in the world will cease functioning abruptly, as their engines melt, creating billions of dollars of liability for Toyota, and ruining its name and stock value. So Edna short-sells the stock. Even though there is an acute asymmetry of information between Edna and those at the other end of her securities transactions, she does nothing wrong. Not all acute asymmetries of information in securities transactions present unfairness. Why, then, should one think that an acute asymmetry arising from inside corporate information in a securities transaction is a problem?

One might try to bolster the unfairness argument by identifying the unfairness in insider trading not in terms of a simple asymmetry of information between the buyer and seller of a security, but instead in terms of an asymmetry stemming from wrongly unequal access. Put more simply, the argument is that insider trading is unfair because one party trades on information stolen from the firm. The argument relies on the idea that inside information is owned by the firm. When Texas Gulf Sulphur officers use their inside information about an ore strike to get a bargain in Texas Gulf Sulphur stock, they use valuable information that belongs not to them, but to their firm. They steal something valuable, information that belongs to the firm, and hence to its shareholders. They have no right to use the information. When they do so, they act unfairly and hence wrongly.

The soundness of the argument depends on contingencies regarding certain contracts. Suppose that a firm's board of directors, operating in a different legal regime from the United States, legally tells managers that as a reward for their excellent performance, it grants them the right to trade on insider information. Indeed, the firm might even warn prospective shareholders of its policy to grant employees this right. It would seem that these managers do not steal anything when they trade on inside information: the owners agree to their use of the property. Thus, this version of the unfairness argument has limited scope. It cannot show that it is always wrong, either legally or morally, for insiders to trade on material, non-public information, but only that it is wrong in the absence of bona fide agreements to allow insider trading. As it stands, the argument fails to find anything inherently wrong with insider trading.

But the argument might be strengthened by showing the impossibility of bona fide agreements to engage in insider trading. There are many examples of agreements that neither society nor the courts will accept as bona fide. No matter how lucrative, we would not recognize contracts that require a person to enter slavery, even with an apparently benign slaveholder. Less extreme, we do not accept agreements in which employees trade their most basic legal rights, for example the right to complain about mistreatment, for higher wages. Trying to understand the depth of our abhorrence for these agreements is both very challenging and very interesting. Why not just let the market work and allow people to enter into whatever contracts they wish? This much seems clear: Slavery contracts, like all abusive labor contracts, make the slave unconscionably vulnerable to the choices of the slaveholder; they set up the slave for wrongful treatment; they create an exploitative relationship. An agreement for slavery can work only through society's participation as the ultimate sanction for and enforcer of the agreement. We as a society have the right to choose not to facilitate an agreement that makes a party so vulnerable to abuse, even if we think it likely that the slave would somehow come out ahead through the agreement.

There is a lesson here for insider trading. Even if we do not know that insider trading is harmful, we know that it makes people vulnerable to financial calamity. The prospect of insider trading gives corporate insiders a reason to manipulate stock prices, creating short-term gains in corporate profits that will allow insiders to sell their own stock at a large profit but harm the firm, other shareholders, and the public in the long term. We do not know, as a matter of fact, how much market manipulation would occur under an insider trading regime, or whether its costs would be economically "outweighed" by its benefits. We do know, however, that if we as a society sanction the practice of insider trading, it will give corporate insiders new and powerful reasons to engage in market manipulation, an unacceptably exploitative practice that can devastate its victims. The problem with allowing insider trading, then, is not simply in the harm it might cause, but in the exploitative relations it fosters. We as a society have no more reason to facilitate the exploitative relations in insider trading than to facilitate exploitative labor practices, even if some people are willing to gamble that they will prosper under exploitation. Insider trading is wrong as a matter of principle.

Sources: *SEC v. Texas Gulf Sulphur Co.*, 401 F.2nd 833 (2nd Cir. 1968) (en banc), cert. denied, 394 U.S. 976.

Utpal Battacharya and Hazem Daouk, "The World Price of Insider Trading," *Journal of Finance* 57 (2002): 75–108.

Victor Brudney, "Insiders, Outsiders and the Informational Advantages under the Federal Securities Laws," *Harvard Law Review* 93 (1979): 322–76.

Frank H. Easterbrook and Daniel R. Fischel, *The Economic Structure of Corporate Law* (Cambridge, MA: Harvard University Press, 1991).

Henry G. Manne, *Insider Trading and the Stock Market* (New York: Free Press, 1966).

Andrew Metrick, "Insider Trading," in *The New Palgrave Dictionary of Economics*, 2nd ed., ed. Larry Blume and Steven Durlauf (Basingstoke: Palgrave Macmillan, 2008).

Jennifer Moore, "What Is Really Unethical about Insider Trading?" *Journal of Business Ethics* 9 (1990): 171–82.

Seana Shiffrin, "Paternalism, Unconscionability Doctrine, and Accommodation," *Philosophy & Public Affairs* 29 (2000): 205–51.

LEGAL PERSPECTIVE

United States Supreme Court, *United States, Petitioner v. James Herman O'Hagan* (1997)

Justice Ruth Bader Ginsburg wrote the opinion of the Court. James O'Hagan was a partner in the law firm of Dorsey & Whitney in Minneapolis, Minnesota. In July 1988, Grand Metropolitan PLC (Grand Met), based in London, retained Dorsey & Whitney as local counsel to represent Grand Met regarding a potential purchase of the Pillsbury Company, headquartered in Minneapolis. O'Hagan did no work on the Grand Met representation, but learned of the potential purchase from his colleagues. O'Hagan purchased a large quantity of common stock and call options for Pillsbury stock. After Grand Met announced its tender offer in October, O'Hagan sold his Pillsbury call options and common stock, making a profit of more than $4.3 million. The Securities and Exchange Commission (SEC) investigated and issued a 57-count indictment alleging that O'Hagan defrauded his law firm and Grand Met by using for his own trading purposes material, non-public information regarding Grand Met's planned purchase of Pillsbury. According to the indictment, O'Hagan used these profits to conceal his previous embezzlement of unrelated client trust funds. A jury convicted O'Hagan on all 57 counts, and he was sentenced to a 41-month term of imprisonment. O'Hagan appealed the decision.

At issue is whether or not the "misappropriation theory" of securities fraud on which the prosecution relied was appropriate. The Supreme Court found that criminal liability under §10(b) of the Securities Exchange Act of 1934 may be predicated on the misappropriation theory which prohibits: "(1) using any deceptive device (2) in connection with the purchase or sale of securities, in contravention of rules prescribed by the [SEC]." The provision, as written, does not confine its coverage to deception of a purchaser or seller of securities; rather, the statute reaches any deceptive device used "in connection with the purchase or sale of any security."

Under the traditional theory of insider trading a corporate insider trades in the securities of his corporation utilizing non-public information and thereby breaches a fiduciary duty to shareholders. The misappropriation theory applies to those outside a corporation, to corporate "outsiders" who breach a duty to the source of the confidential information and is intended to protect the integrity of securities markets. Writing for the Court, Judge Ginsburg stated that "Under this theory, a fiduciary's undisclosed, self serving use of a principal's information to purchase or sell securities, in breach of a duty of loyalty and confidentiality, defrauds the principal of the exclusive use of that information ... the misappropriation theory premises liability on a fiduciary turned trader's deception of those who entrusted him with access to confidential information." The traditional theory and the misappropriation theory are, in the view of the SEC and the Supreme Court, complementary means of protecting the integrity of securities markets consistent with the Securities Exchange Act. As such, the Court ruled against O'Hagan and the misappropriation theory was upheld as a valid application of existing regulation.

CASES

Case 1: Should Everything Be for Sale?

DENIS G. ARNOLD

Rand, Leslie, and Irina are members of an entrepreneurship club at their university. They are nearing graduation and have been brainstorming to come up with ideas to start a business. They decided to each come up with an idea that promised to make them the most amount of money in the shortest amount of time. They got together one Saturday afternoon with other members of their club to share their ideas.

1. Rand pitched the idea of selling fake pot, or synthetic cannabinoids, that mimic the experience of smoking marijuana. He pointed out that doing so was legal in many jurisdictions including states where real marijuana remains illegal, that demand was high, and that it could be packaged as incense or herbal tea, and sold at a high profit margin. Rand said he had some friends from his dormitory that were chemistry majors that would be willing to work on the formula in exchange for cash and product and that Chinese suppliers would manufacture what they formulated cheaply. The one downside he could think of was that since their product would not undergo any kind of safety testing, the potential adverse side-effects were unknown. He acknowledged that there were many media accounts of users of synthetic cannabinoids experiencing a racing heartbeat, vomiting, hallucinations, and in some cases lashing out in physical assaults or committing suicide, but he thought these incidents were uncommon. Club members pointed out that real marijuana did not produce the same negative symptoms.

2. Leslie pitched the idea of starting an Internet business called OrgansForSale.com to link people in developed nations who need a kidney or cornea transplant with people in developing nations who are willing to sell one of their kidneys or eyes. The kidney or eye purchaser would get information about the age, blood type, health, and general location of the seller, but would need to pay the company a large commission to be put in touch with the seller's agent. The buyer would then arrange for travel to the seller's home country and arrange for

transplant services in private hospitals. The buyer would pay the seller a fee brokered by local agents who better understood the local market price for human organs. Leslie pointed out that no one would be forced to sell an organ by the company, but she acknowledged that they would have no way of knowing why individuals were selling organs or whether they were pressured to do so locally. It was pointed out by another club member, who had done a research paper on the topic, that husbands sometimes pressured their wives into making organ donations and that the desperately poor were the most likely donors. It was also pointed out that healthcare after the organ was removed was typically very poor for the sellers, that their health deteriorated, and they sometimes died from complications months later.

3. Irina pitched the idea of an escort service using college women who needed extra cash to cover the cost of tuition. She noted that several women on campus already danced at a local "strip club" and that she could approach them first and then talk to their friends about joining the service. She made it clear that the women would be encouraged to provide sexual services to their clients, but that strictly speaking this was not a job requirement. She mentioned that her roommate worked in the financial aid office, and she thought that she could easily target students who were in financial need with the help of her friend. The company would create an Internet presence and would set up the "dates" and take a set fee from the women for each date that it facilitated. She said this idea had the advantage of not needing foreign suppliers or agents and could be started up sooner. Irina acknowledged that there was no way to guarantee the safety of the women while they were on their "dates," but she pointed out that this was true for people who met at online dating websites as well. Club members pointed out the escorts would be employees, so that they would not merely be facilitating a date but selling employee services.

The entrepreneurship club members decided to meet again next week to discuss these business propositions.

This case was written for the purposes of classroom discussion. © 2017 Denis G. Arnold.

Discussion Questions

1. Imagine that you are a member of the entrepreneurship club. Which, if any, of these business ideas would you be willing to get involved with as a partner? Which, if any, of these business ideas would you *not* be willing to get involved with? Explain.

2. What consequences for all relevant parties would each business likely have if it was undertaken? Explain.

3. Are all parties appropriately respected in each business proposed? Explain.

4. Does the impact on employees, customers, or third parties of the product or service you sell matter to you? Why, or why not? Explain.

5. Would Debra Satz support any or all of these business plans? Why, or why not? Explain. Would Brennan and Jaworski support any or all of these business plans? Why, or why not? Explain.

Case 2: Like Taking Candy from a Baby? Mylan's Pricing of the EpiPen

ROXANNE ROSS AND DENIS G. ARNOLD

Allergies affect the lives of 40 percent of children and 30 percent of adults. They are the most common health problem for children in the United States. Some allergies result in severe reactions that can be deadly. Food and medicine allergies, along with insect bites, are the main cause of most fatal allergic reactions. About 200,000 visits to the emergency room are made per year for food allergies alone, and the number of deadly food allergies is rising. People with these potentially life-threatening allergies may go into anaphylactic shock when they come into contact with the allergen. During anaphylactic shock, the person suffers difficulty breathing, rashes, hives, asthma attacks, and/or low blood pressure. If untreated, anaphylactic shock can result in death from asphyxiation.

Anyone with a severe allergy, or any parent of a child with such an allergy, is most likely familiar with the EpiPen, or the EpiPen Jr., which has dosage appropriate for children. The patent for the EpiPen is currently owned by the drug company Mylan. The auto-injector was invented in the 1970s for military purposes related to chemical warfare. An EpiPen is a potentially life-saving device that the consumer uses to self-administer epinephrine, also called adrenaline, during anaphylactic shock. Epinephrine increases the chance of survival by stabilizing the patient and allowing him or her to make it to a hospital for further treatment. A key feature of the EpiPen is that it allows an average person to safely deliver the correct dosage of the medication, whether to oneself, to another adult, or to a child. Children with severe peanut or dairy allergies, for example, will typically die without immediate EpiPen Jr. injections. The EpiPen drug and device combination was first approved for sale by the Food & Drug Administration (FDA) in 1987.

The rights to the EpiPen changed owners several times during the following decades. Most recently in 2007 a German company, Merck KGaA, sold the rights to manufacture the product to Mylan. Prior to 2007, EpiPen sales were approximately $200 million annually. In 2008 the auto-injector sold for around $100 dollars for a two pack; however, Mylan has dramatically increased the price since that time. Over the following ten years prices rose six to seven times to between $600 and $700. Profits on the auto-injector rose from 57 percent to 75 percent after price increases. Epinephrine expires yearly and needs to be replaced even if not used. The people most harmed by the EpiPen price increases are those who don't have insurance or third parties to negotiate prices for them. Mylan now earns over $1 billion a year from EpiPen sales. In total, the company's annual revenue hovers around $10 billion with the EpiPen accounting for approximately 10 percent of the company's revenue.

Politicians, consumers, and even employees of Mylan, have voiced concern over the drastic price increases. Many expressed the concern that it causes people to push their luck with the expiration date or go without the product altogether. Despite public outrage, the prices have not gone down. Mylan has a near monopoly over the device. Because the product is potentially life-saving, consumer demand remains stable despite high prices. Mylan's prices also cannot be undercut by competitors because of the barriers to entry caused by the drug approval process. The company claims just over 90 percent of the market share of

---

epinephrine injector sales. Part of the reason for the near monopoly is that the FDA delayed the release of other epinephrine injectors because of safety problems. Other devices are years away from approval. Mylan's patent will run out in 2025. However, it may be able to engage in "product-hopping" and thereby block generic competition. This is a borderline legal trick whereby a drug company reformulates a product with no benefit to patients, obtains a new patent, and then withdraws the original formulation extending their monopoly control and pricing.

The EpiPen price increases were accompanied by increases in executive compensation at Mylan. CEO Heather Bresch saw her annual pay grow by over 600 percent from $2.45 million in 2007, when Mylan first acquired EpiPen, to over $18.9 million after the price hikes. Mylan board chairman Robert Coury was provided with a $97.6 million compensation package. Mylan's compensation program sparked disapproval from a majority of shareholders who have twice voted to reject these compensation levels. Coury has also been criticized for his use of Mylan corporate jets to fly his son to music concerts. However, because the shareholder recommendations are advisory, the Mylan board, led by Coury, does not have to carry out investor wishes.

For many years mid-level executives at Mylan spoke out against the price hikes which some regarded as morally unjustifiable profiteering that potentially placed the lives of patients with limited financial means at risk. When employees challenged Coury about the price hikes in a meeting, Coury was unsympathetic. In an interview with the *New York Times*, one executive reported a meeting with employees in which Coury raised both his middle fingers and used expletives to convey his view that anyone who criticized Mylan could go screw themselves. He repeatedly directed the comment to Mylan employees, Congress, Wall Street, and the FDA.

The controversial price of EpiPens led to a Congressional hearing. CEO Bresch defended the firm's practices on the grounds that her obligation was to her shareholders and not customers or the public. She faced criticism from Democrats and Republicans alike. Mylan was investigated by the US Department of Justice for overcharging Medicaid for the injector. Reports suggest that Mylan overcharged Medicaid by $1.27 billion. The company falsely classified the product as a generic drug which enabled them to reimburse Medicaid at a lower rebate rate. At the time, no such generic drug existed for the EpiPen. Mylan agreed to pay $465 million for the deception.

Despite receiving this negative attention, Mylan has done little to lower the price of EpiPen. It has, however, offered a coupon to reduce the cost to consumers paying full retail price for the product. Many health policy experts argue that at the root of the problem are structural flaws in the US pharmaceutical industry that cannot be fixed with consumer outrage alone. Other nations pay significantly less for EpiPens (e.g., EpiPens cost $69 in the United Kingdom and under $100 in France). The UK price is so much lower because the British government negotiates a cap on drug prices with drug companies. The United States has no such regulatory mechanism regarding pricing which means that in the United States unlimited price hikes are legal.

Discussion Questions

1. Mylan's CEO and board chairman argue that their responsibility is to maximize shareholder value and not concern themselves with the affordability of EpiPens. Do you agree with that claim? Why, or why not? Explain.

2. What role, if any, do you think the pay incentives Mylan's CEO and board chairman received played in driving up the cost of the EpiPen? Explain.

3. From an ethical standpoint, how would you assess Mylan's pricing of the EpiPen and its response to critics? Explain.

4. What concepts, ideas, or arguments of Deborah Satz's do you think are most important for understanding the ethical legitimacy of Mylan's actions as described in this case? Why? Explain. How might Brennan and Jaworski respond? Explain. Whose views do you believe are most correct? Explain.

5. Do you believe that the US regulation of the pharmaceutical industry should be modified to put price limits on life-saving products such as the EpiPen? Why, or why not? Explain.

This case is based on the following sources: "Allergy Facts and Figures" (n.d.). Retrieved June 4, 2017 from www.aafa.org/page/allergy-facts.aspx.

C. Duhigg, "Outcry over EpiPen Prices Hasn't Made Them Lower," *The New York Times* (June 4, 2017). Retrieved June 4, 2017 from www.nytimes.com/2017/06/04/business/angry-about-epipen-prices-executive-dont-care-much.html.

E. Emanuel, "Don't Only Blame Mylan for $600 EpiPens," *Fortune* (September 8, 2016), Retrieved July 10, 2017 from https://insiders.fortune.com/dont-only-blame-mylan-for-600-epipens-6ad0065373e0.

D. McLaughlin, S. Forden, and J. Hopkins, "Mylan Faces U.S. Antitrust Investigation on EpiPen," *Bloomberg.com* (January 30, 2017). Retrieved June 4, 2017 from www.bloomberg.com/news/articles/2017-01-30/mylan-faces-u-s-antitrust-investigation-on-epipen-practices.

A. Melin, E. Proper, and C. Koons, "Mylan Shareholders Reject Drugmaker's Executive Pay Package," *Bloomberg.com* (June 22, 2017). Retrieved July 17, 2017 from www.bloomberg.com/news/articles/2017-06-22/mylan-shareholders-reject-drugmaker-s-2016-executive-pay-plan.

J. Paton and N. Kresege, "Why the $600 EpiPen Costs $69 in Britain," *Bloomberg.com* (September 29, 2016). Retrieved June 4, 2017 from www.bloomberg.com/news/articles/2016-09-29/epipen-s-69-cost-in-britain-shows-other-extreme-of-drug-pricing-itnvgvam.

L. Ramsey, "The Strange History of the EpiPen, the Device Developed by the Military That Turned into a Billion-Dollar Business, " *Business Insider* (August 27, 2016). Retrieved July 17, 2017 from www.businessinsider.com.au/the-history-of-the-epipen-and-epinephrine-2016-8.

Case 3: The Big Fix: How Big Banks Colluded to Rig Interest Rates

DENIS G. ARNOLD

One of the world's most important numbers is also one of the least recognized. Most people have never heard of LIBOR; however, the figure influences over $300 trillion in financial accounts worldwide. LIBOR stands for the London Interbank Offered Rate. It is the average interest rate at which banks report that they can borrow funds from each other. Every day by 11:00 a.m. London time, a panel of banks scattered around the globe submit an estimate to the British Bankers' Association (BBA). The BBA throws out the highest and lowest 25 percent of the estimates and then averages the remaining middle 50 percent. The rate is calculated for 10 different currencies and 15 different borrowing periods. LIBOR is the foundation for interest rates in the derivatives market. It also influences prime mortgages, subprime mortgages, credit cards, bonds, and private student loans. LIBOR is the most commonly utilized figure for calculating short-term interest rates globally. However, it is also utilized as one measure of a bank's financial health.

The mundane, daily routine that determines LIBOR was utilized in an illegal and well-organized scheme to manipulate and control the rate for financial gain. Traders, brokers, and LIBOR estimate submitters worked together to manipulate the rate since at least 2005, although by some accounts LIBOR manipulation began much earlier in 1991. Traders from banks such as Citigroup, JPMorgan, Barclays, and Royal Bank of Scotland were caught using an online chat and secret codes to orchestrate the rate fixing. The alliance of traders called themselves "The Cartel." In total, over 30 individuals participated in the collusion. Those involved manipulated LIBOR both up and down depending on their position in the market at the time. Tiny fluctuations in the rate carry significant weight for traders. It is commonplace for a one basis point (0.01 percent) shift to mean a difference in the millions of dollars. Much of the rate fixing was related to assets held in the derivatives market. The Cartel also coordinated bids for euros and dollars in order to exert control over the foreign exchange market. Barclays submitted deceitfully low estimates to appear more financially stable. During the Great Recession of 2007–2008, the banking industry saw high borrowing cost estimates as a sign that a bank was failing. Knowing this, Barclays submitted inaccurate, low estimates to falsely bolster its reputation.

Those clearly harmed by LIBOR manipulation included the traders and investors who were not involved in the collusion, but who happened to have an opposing position to those who were involved. For every dollar made in the derivatives market, there is a dollar lost. Money gained from the manipulation of LIBOR came at a cost to someone else. Home owners with adjustable rate mortgages were also affected. The manipulation both lowered and raised rates for homeowners depending on when they acquired their loans. Those obtaining home equity loans, new mortgages, or private student loans were also affected. However, because banks are more likely to pass high borrowing costs down to consumers, lower borrowing costs trickle down to consumers to a lesser extent. As a result, industry experts believe consumers ended up paying higher rates on average.

LIBOR was easy to manipulate because of a lack of government regulation and oversight. The employees submitting the numbers worked for the same banks that were financially dependent on LIBOR. At times, traders offered to pay co-workers to report certain numbers. Regulators in the United States, the United Kingdom, the European Union, Canada, Switzerland, and Japan launched investigations into the collusion. Twenty banks were named for involvement in the scandal. As a result, the banks faced felony charges and paid out over $9 billion in fines. Deutsche Bank, Citigroup, JPMorgan Chase, Royal Bank of Scotland, HSBC, UBS, Barclays, and others were identified as participants by regulators.

Former UBS and Citigroup trader Thomas Hayes was the first individual charged for his role as a leader of the collusion. Hayes coordinated the rate fixing with employees at ten different firms. He was charged with eight counts of conspiracy and sentenced to 11 years in prison. More recently three Barclays bankers were convicted of similar crimes. Several bank CEOs issued statements in response to the scandal. CEO Michael Corbat at Citigroup promised reform: "We will learn from this experience … Fostering a culture of ethical behavior has been, and continues to be, a top priority for Citi." JPMorgan CEO Jamie Dimon blamed the problem on a few bad apples by commenting, "The lesson here is that the conduct of a small group of employees, or of even a single employee, can reflect badly on all of us, and have significant ramifications for the entire firm." UBS chairman Axel Weber and CEO Sergio Ermotti echoed Dimon's sentiment in a joint statement in which they attributed the collusion to "a small number of employees." In reference to his actions, Hayes has stated that "everything I did was with complete transparency. Everything I did my managers knew about … sometimes going up all the way to the CEO."

Discussion Questions

1. Whose financial interests seem to have been primarily served by LIBOR price fixing? Explain.
2. Who do you believe is primarily to blame for LIBOR price fixing? The colluding employees? The banks they worked for? Governments? Explain.
3. Does it seem plausible to you that the collusion and manipulation of LIBOR could take place within banks for years, perhaps decades, without managers and executives being aware? Why, or why not? Explain.
4. The financial services industry persistently argues against the need for more regulation, and for the repeal of existing financial regulation. In general, libertarians and others who support "free markets" oppose financial regulation and support the idea of banks "self-regulating" by governing their own actions, either individually or as an industry. What lessons regarding financial services regulation do you take from the LIBOR scandal? Explain.

This case is based on the following sources: J. Colombo, "This New Libor 'Scandal' Will Cause a Terrifying Financial Crisis," *Forbes* (June 3, 2014). Retrieved July 29, 2017 from www.forbes.com/sites/jessecolombo/2014/06/03/this-new-libor-scandal-will-cause-a-terrifying-financial-crisis/#4f0fb4fa3bd8.

P. Crowe, "Wall Street Gets Slammed with $5.8 Billion in Fines for Rate Rigging," *Business Insider* (May 20, 2015). Retrieved July 29, 2017 from www.businessinsider.com/libor-rigging-criminal-charges-and-fines-2015-5.

James McBride, "Understanding the Libor Scandal" (October 12, 2016). Retrieved July 29, 2017 from www.cfr.org/backgrounder/understanding-libor-scandal.

J. Kasperkevic, "Lawsuit Accusing 16 Big Banks of Libor Manipulation Reinstated by US Court," *The Guardian* (May 23, 2016). Retrieved July 29, 2017 from www.theguardian.com/business/2016/may/23/libor-manipulation-lawsuit-hsbc-barclays-ubs-bank-of-america-deutsche.

Marion Dakers and Tim Wallace, "US and UK Bank Libor Fines" (May 27, 2015). Retrieved July 29, 2017 from http://cloud.highcharts.com/show/urolaj/1.

C. Needham, "Libor Manipulation and Its Consequences." Report prepared for Library of the European Parliament (2012). Retrieved July 29, 2017 from www.europarl.europa.eu/RegData/bibliotheque/briefing/2012/120343/LDM_BRI%282012%29120343_REV2_EN.pdf.

Case 4: Predatory Lending at Countrywide Financial

REBECCA GLAVIN AND DENIS G. ARNOLD

Angelo Mozilo and David Loeb founded Countrywide Financial Corporation in 1986. Countrywide, a mortgage bank, did not take deposits from customers like commercial banks. Instead, Countrywide financed loans via short-term commercial borrowing.[1] Countrywide's services extended to all aspects of the industry including broker-dealer services, short-term debt special purpose vehicles, insurance, real estate closing, and loan servicing.[2] In 2006, Countrywide

This case was written for the purposes of classroom discussion by Rebecca Glavin under the supervision of Denis Arnold. Revised by Denis Arnold in 2017. © 2011, 2017 Denis G. Arnold.

had a pretax income of $4.3 billion and revenue of $11.4 billion. In early 2007, the company had assets of $200 billion and employed 62,000 employees in 900 offices. Since he became executive chairman in 1999, Mozilo earned $410 million in compensation. However, by June 2007 Countrywide's foreclosure rate on loans was at 25 percent, a 167 percent increase over the previous year, and its loan defaults were rising.[3] In 2009 Bank of America announced that it would acquire Countrywide for $4 billion in stock, just a sixth of the $1.5 trillion valuation Countrywide enjoyed in the previous year.[4] Despite the massive devaluation, Mozilo was awarded an additional $112 million in severance compensation. But Countrywide's position was much worse than expected. It is estimated that acquiring Countrywide has cost Bank of America well over $40 billion in legal penalties, legal fees, and real estate losses since the acquisition. What happened?

Countrywide's stated mission was to improve people's lives through homeownership. Mozilo famously stated that, "Homeownership is not a privilege but a right!"[5] Born in the Bronx to Italian immigrants with little formal education, Mozilo claimed that his work helped those who were "disenfranchised" as he once was. However, a 1992 report by the Federal Reserve Bank of Boston claimed that Countrywide systematically discriminated against African-American and Hispanic borrowers. Countrywide then sought to increase loans to minorities. Between 1992 and 1994 the number of Countrywide loans to Hispanics and African-Americans increased 163 percent and 325 percent respectively. In order to increase its lending capabilities to these segments of the market, Countrywide increased subprime lending. Subprime borrowers do not have sufficient credit history or documentation of financial resources to be granted prime borrower status. As a result, they pay much higher interest rates and fees.

Countrywide's incentive structure for its sales force reinforced the sale of subprime loans. If a mortgage broker sold a Countrywide subprime loan, the broker received 0.5 percent of the loan's value in commission. However, if the broker sold an Alt-A (alternative documentation) loan, which lives between a prime loan and a subprime in terms of quality, the broker received a 0.2 percent in commission. On a $400,000 house this difference amounted to a $20,000 commission versus an $8,000 commission. David Sambol, an executive at Countrywide, is described as frequently exclaiming, "Price any loan!" Sambol's statement implied that at Countrywide, every borrower was qualified, no matter how risky.[6] The higher the risk of the loan, the greater the prepayment penalties were for a borrower, and thus, the larger the profit margin for Countrywide. In 2007, Countrywide's profit margins for prime loans were 1.07 percent as opposed to the 1.84 percent for subprime loans. Countrywide could bundle subprime loans and sell them to investors on Wall Street for higher prices than they could sell prime loans thereby earning greater revenues. The prepayment penalties and higher interest rates associated with subprime loans created higher cash inflows for investors.[7]

Countrywide's subprime strategy was based on two assumptions: that home prices would continue to increase and that even if one borrower happened to default on his/her loan, most borrowers would not default. Many mortgage companies used mathematical formulas to price loans that assumed housing prices would always increase. These assumptions were proven false. With a decline in the housing market came an increase in the number of defaults and foreclosures on homes. As subprime homeowners continued to default on more loans, Countrywide was left with greater losses. In emails Mozilo refers to some of the company's subprime mortgages as "poison" due to the absence of a mandatory down payment from customers. Mozilo also wrote, "we have no way, with reasonable certainty, to assess the real risk of holding these loans on our balance sheet … the bottom line is that we are flying blind on how these loans will perform in a stressed environment of higher unemployment, reduced values and slowing home sales."[8] As foreclosures and defaults increased, banks and companies' abilities to attain short-term financing became more difficult. This included Countrywide which needed cash infusions to survive. In August 2008 Bank of America contributed $2 billion to Countrywide in exchange for partial ownership of the company in. Then in January 2009 Bank of America purchased Countrywide and its loan portfolio for an additional $4 billion.

By the end of 2008, housing prices had drastically decreased and at least 8.3 million borrowers' homes were worth less than their mortgages. According to First America, this number would increase by another 2.2 million households if home prices fell by another 5 percent.[9] With so many Countrywide mortgages "underwater," and foreclosure rates increasing by the day, state governments began filing lawsuits against Countrywide for predatory lending. Attorney General Richard Blumenthal of Connecticut explained why, "Countrywide conned customers into loans that were clearly unaffordable and unsustainable, turning the American Dream of homeownership into a nightmare. When customers defaulted, the company bullied them into solutions doomed to fail … The company broke promises that homeowners could refinance, condemning them to hopelessly unaffordable loans."[10]

Two examples of Countrywide's predatory lending practices were its use of interest only and option Adjustable-Rate Mortgages (ARMs), also known as payment option mortgages, or "pick-a-pay."[11] Both Interest only and Option ARMs are attractive to borrowers because they start with low payments, making homeownership seem more attainable; yet, payments increase after a set date. These mortgages reset to higher interest rates in order to not only "make up" the lost money, but also produce a profit for the mortgage company. Many Countrywide borrowers did not fully understand the terms of their loans, and their mortgages reset before they had anticipated. For example, Edward Marini, a disabled, 63-year-old Vietnam veteran, took out a $280,000 refinance mortgage for his New Jersey home in 2003. Edward explains, "The way I understood it was that I would have a really low payment for five years."[12] Edward's payment was $1,300, but in 2005, he learned that his mortgage was going to reset to $3,800 starting in 2006, which was two years before he was told it would. Edward's disability payment, his sole income, was $550 less than his monthly mortgage payment. He said, "I didn't think they would even pull this kind of stuff on someone who is on a fixed income." Like Edward, many Countrywide borrowers were unaware of the risks associated with their option ARM loans. Borrowers claim they were misled by dishonest terms and a lack of transparency on Countrywide's part and they would not have agreed to the terms of their mortgages had they fully understood them.

Eleven states filed lawsuits against Countrywide for predatory lending, alleging that the company broke state banking and consumer protection laws. Although the suits were originally filed by each state separately, California, Illinois, Connecticut, Florida, North Carolina, Michigan, Ohio, Iowa, Washington, Arizona, and Texas agreed to settle the suit jointly. The National Conference of State Legislatures describes Predatory Lending practices as follows:

(a) Loan flipping – repeatedly refinancing loans, charging high fees each time.
(b) Excessive fees and "packing" – adding fees far exceeding those justified on economic grounds, often through loan terms, such as the financing of points, fees and prepayment penalties, single-premium insurance (to cover the balance of the loan should a borrower die, paid in one sum and added to the amount financed), and balloon payments (those due at the end of a loan that are significantly higher than monthly payments).
(c) Asset-based lending – lending based on a borrower's overall assets, rather than income and ability to repay.
(d) Outright fraud and abuse.[13]

The allegations laid out in the suit against Countrywide included, "viewing borrowers as nothing more than the means for producing more loans … with little or no regard to borrower's long term ability to afford them and to sustain homeownership," and also "misleading marketing practices designed to sell risky and costly loans to homeowners, the terms and dangers of which they [borrowers] did not understand."[14] Examples of Countrywide's false advertising included:

(a) advertising that it was the nation's largest lender and could be trusted by customers; (b) encouraging borrowers to refinance or obtain purchase money financing with complicated mortgage instruments … by emphasizing the very low initial "teaser" or "fixed" rates while obfuscating or misrepresenting the later steep monthly payments and interest rate increases … and (c) routinely soliciting borrowers to refinance only a few months after Countrywide or the loan broker with whom it had "business partnerships" had sold them the loan.[15]

Because Bank of America acquired Countrywide, all lawsuits, fines, and settlements became the responsibility of Bank of America. Bank of America agreed to settle the lawsuit against Countrywide for $8.5 billion, which was intended to assist homeowners whose homes had been foreclosed, or were close to being foreclosed. In 2012 Bank of America entered into a $1 billion settlement as a result of Countrywide issuing loans to unqualified buyers. Also in 2012 the bank paid out $11.8 billion in a settlement for foreclosure abuse that included activities at Countrywide. The *Wall Street Journal* puts Bank of America's Countrywide losses at more than $40 billion.[16] Mozilo earned at least $522 million since 1999. In 2010 he agreed to pay $67.5 million in penalties to the US Securities and Exchange Commission of which Bank of America paid $20 million as part of a Countrywide indemnification agreement. Mozila also agreed to be permanently banned from serving as an officer or director at a public company. Nonetheless, he kept $474.5 million of the compensation he received, or an average of $47.45 million per year.

Notes

1. Connie Bruck, "Angelo's Ashes: The Man Who Became the Face of the Financial Crisis," *The New Yorker* (June 29, 2009).
2. Gretchen Morgenson, "Inside the Countrywide Lending Spree," *The New York Times* (August 26, 2007).
3. Ibid.
4. Bruck, "Angelo's Ashes."

5. Ibid.

6. Ibid.

7. Gretchen Morgenson, "Inside the Countrywide Lending Spree," *The New York Times* (August 26, 2007).

8. Ibid.

9. Edward Robinson, "Subprime Swindlers Reconnect to Homeowners in Scams (Update1)," *Bloomberg.com* (March 27, 2009).

10. Ibid.

11. Ruth Simon, "Corporate News: Defaults Rising Rapidly for 'Pick-a-Pay' Option Mortgages," *Wall Street Journal* (April 30, 2008).

12. Ibid.

13. National Conference of State Legislature, "Mortgage Lending Practices: Subprime and Predatory Mortgage Lending." Retrieved from www.ncsl.org/default.aspx?TabId=12511 (last updated June 12, 2008).

14. *The People of the State of California v. Countrywide Financial Corporation.* Complaint filed in the Superior Court of the State of California for the County of Los Angeles, June 24, 2008.

15. Ibid.

16. Dan Fitzpatrick, "BofA's Blunder: $40 Billion-Plus," *Wall Street Journal* (July 1, 2012).

Discussion Questions

1. Do you think mortgage loan officers have an obligation to explain the terms of loans to customers, and generally look out for their customers' interests, or do you believe the primary responsibility for understanding the financial product lies with customers? Explain.

2. What are the factors that allowed Countrywide to engage in predatory lending? What role did incentives play? Explain.

3. Many employees who issued mortgages for companies such as Countrywide had no training, no college education, and no prior experience in the financial services industry. Do you believe that there should be a federal requirement that employees who work as mortgage loan officers receive training and meet certain ethics standards in their dealing with customers? Why, or why not? Explain.

4. Mozilo helped build Countrywide from scratch, employed thousands, personally earned over $522 million during just the last ten years of his tenure at Countrywide, and managed to sell the company before the true costs of its actions were known, thereby transferring legal liability to Bank of America. Is he a good business person? Why, or why not? Explain. What does it mean to be a good business person? Explain.

5. In your view, what are the primary factors that led to the collapse of Countrywide and to the massive costs to Bank of America that resulted? Explain.

Case 5: Martha Stewart Living Omnimedia, Inc.: An Accusation of Insider Trading

JOHN R. BOATRIGHT

On December 27, 2001, Martha Stewart was en route with a friend from her home in Connecticut to a post-Christmas holiday in Mexico when her private plane landed for refueling in San Antonio, Texas.[1] While standing on the tarmac, she listened to a telephone message from her assistant, Ann Armstrong, reporting a call from Peter Bacanovic, her stockbroker at Merrill Lynch. The message relayed by her assistant was brief: "Peter Bacanovic thinks ImClone is going to start trading down." Stewart immediately returned the call, and at some point during the 11-minute conversation was put through to her broker's office at Merrill Lynch. Bacanovic was on vacation in Florida, and so she talked instead with his assistant, Douglas Faneuil. Faneuil later testified that, on orders from Bacanovic, he told Stewart that he had no information on the company but that the Waksal family was selling their shares in ImClone. Although Stewart denied being told this, she instructed Faneuil to sell all of her ImClone stock. Her 3,928 shares sold within the hour at an average price of $58.43 a share, netting her approximately $228,000. Stewart then made one more phone call, to Sam Waksal's office, leaving a message that Waksal's secretary scribbled as "Martha Stewart something is going on with ImClone and she wants to know what." During her vacation in Mexico, she reportedly told her friend, "Isn't it nice to have brokers who tell you those things?"

From John R. Boatright, *Ethics and the Conduct of Business*, 6th ed. (2009). Reprinted by permission of Pearson Prentice Hall, Inc., Upper Saddle River, NJ.

Martha Stewart became a national celebrity and self-made billionaire through her print and television presence and the many household products bearing her brand name. After a brief career on Wall Street as a stockbroker, she started a successful catering business that led to a succession of books on cooking and household decorating. The magazine *Martha Stewart Living* followed, along with a television series and a partnership with Kmart. In 1999, her company, Martha Stewart Living Omnimedia (MSLO) went public, with Stewart as the CEO and chairman. MSLO was unique in that Martha Stewart herself was the company's chief marketable asset.

Sam Waksal was the founder, president, and CEO of ImClone Systems, Inc., a biopharmaceutical company that sought to develop biologic compounds for the treatment of cancers. Martha Stewart and Sam Waksal were close friends, having been introduced in the early 1990s by Stewart's daughter Alexis, who had dated Waksal for a number of years. It was also through Alexis that her mother and Waksal came to know Peter Bacanovic, who attended Columbia University in the mid-1980s while Alexis was enrolled at nearby Barnard College. Bacanovic worked briefly at ImClone before joining Merrill Lynch in 1993 as a broker, and Stewart and Waksal became two of his most important clients. Waksal helped Stewart achieve an advantageous split from her then-publisher Time Warner in 1997, and in gratitude, she invested an initial $80,000 in ImClone stock. With a net worth of over $1 billion, her investment in 2001 represented three-hundredths of 1 percent of her total holdings.

In 2001, the future of ImClone rested on the uncertain prospects of a single drug, Erbitux, for the treatment of advanced colon cancer. Erbitux was a genetically engineered version of a mouse antibody that showed great promise in early tests. In October, ImClone submitted a preliminary application to the Food and Drug Administration (FDA) for approval of Erbitux. This application was merely the first step that allowed the FDA to determine whether the research submitted by the company was sufficiently complete to begin a full FDA review. A decision on the application was expected by the end of December. On December 28, 2001, ImClone announced that the FDA had found the application to be incomplete and would not proceed to the next stage. After the news was announced, ImClone stock dropped 16 percent to $46 a share. The previous day, on the morning of December 27, Sam Waksal and his daughter asked Peter Bacanovic to sell all of their ImClone shares held at Merrill Lynch, which were worth over $7.3 million. Merrill Lynch sold the ImClone stock of the daughter for approximately $2.5 million but declined to sell Sam Waksal's shares, citing concern about insider trading. An attempt by Waksal to have his shares transferred to his daughter so that they could be sold by her failed. Separately, Sam Waksal's father sold shares worth more than $8 million, and smaller amounts were sold by another daughter and a sister of Sam Waksal.

The Securities and Exchange Commission (SEC) quickly opened an investigation into suspected insider trading in ImClone stock. Faneuil later testified that Bacanovic initially told him that dumping Stewart's stock was part of a tax-loss selling plan. After being informed by Faneuil that Stewart had made a profit, Bacanovic changed the story, explaining that Stewart had placed a stop-loss order to sell the stock if it dropped below $60 a share. Stewart affirmed to federal investigators that she had given this instruction to Bacanovic and gave as a reason that she did not want to be bothered about the stock during her vacation. This conversation, she claimed, was with Bacanovic, though she had in fact talked only with Faneuil. She also said that she was unable to recall whether Sam Waksal had been discussed in the December 27 telephone conversation or whether she had been informed about stock sales by the Waksal family. Before meeting with investigators, Stewart accessed the phone message log on her assistant's computer and changed the entry "Peter Bacanovic thinks ImClone is going to start trading downward" to "Peter Bacanovic re imclone," but afterwards told her assistant to restore the original wording. Meanwhile, Bacanovic altered a worksheet that contained a list of Stewart's holdings at Merrill Lynch with notations in blue ballpoint ink to include "@$60" by the entry for ImClone. An expert later testified in court that the ink for this entry was different from that used in the other notations.

In March 2003, Sam Waksal pleaded guilty to charges of securities fraud for insider trading, obstruction of justice, and perjury. He was later sentenced to seven years and three months in prison and ordered to pay $4 million. The Department of Justice accepted a proposal from Martha Stewart's attorneys that she plead guilty to a single felony count of making a false statement to federal investigators that would probably avoid any prison time. However, Stewart decided that she could not do this and would take her chances in court. A justice department official said, "We had no desire to prosecute this woman" but indicated that the lying was too egregious to ignore.[2] Stewart and Bacanovic were charged with conspiracy, obstruction of justice, and perjury – but not insider trading. On March 5, 2004, a jury found both parties guilty. Stewart and Bacanovic were each sentenced to five months in prison, five months of home confinement, and two years of probation. Stewart was fined $30,000 and Bacanovic, $4,000. By selling her ImClone stock when she did, Stewart avoided a loss of approximately $46,000. She estimated the total loss from her legal troubles to be $400 million, including a drop in the value of MSLO stock and missed business opportunities.

In June 2003, the SEC brought a civil action for insider trading, which was separate from the criminal charges of which Stewart was found guilty. To convict Stewart of insider trading, the SEC would have to show that she had received material non-public information in violation of a fiduciary duty. The information that she received from Faneuil in the December 27 phone call was that the members of the Waksal family were selling their ImClone stock. Neither Faneuil nor Bacanovic had information about the FDA rejection of the Erbitux application that prompted the sell-off. Neither one had a fiduciary duty to ImClone. However, Bocanovic owed a fiduciary duty to Merrill Lynch that he breached in ordering that information about the Waksal's sales conveyed to Stewart. Merrill Lynch had an insider trading policy that prohibited the disclosure of material non-public information to anyone who would use it to engage in stock trading. A confidentiality policy also prohibited employees from discussing information about a client with other employees except on a "strict need-to-know basis," and further stated, "We do not release client information, except upon a client's authorization or when permitted or required by law."

Since the information that the Waksals were selling was obtained by Bacanovic in his role as their broker, he breached his duty to Merrill Lynch. However, Martha Stewart denied that she was aware that Bacanovic was their broker. Moreover, as a former stockbroker who understood the law on insider trading, she knew that she could not act on information received from an insider like Waksal. But could she trade on information provided by Bacanovic, even if he was violating a fiduciary duty to Merrill Lynch? Stewart was apparently unconcerned about her first interview with federal investigators because, according to a close associate, "All she thought they wanted to talk about was whether Waksal himself had tipped her about the F.D.A. decision. She knew she was in the clear on that one."[3]

On August 7, 2007, the SEC announced a settlement with Martha Stewart and Peter Bacanovic.[4] Stewart agreed to pay a $195,000 penalty and accept a five-year ban on serving as an officer or director of a public company. Bacanovic was ordered to pay $75,000; he had previously received a permanent bar from work in the securities industry. The SEC's Director of Enforcement declared, "It is fundamentally unfair for someone to have an edge on the market just because she has a stockbroker who is willing to break the rules and give her an illegal tip. It's worse still when the individual engaged in the insider trading is the Chairman and CEO of a public company."

Notes

1. Information on this case is taken from the following sources: *United States of America v. Martha Stewart and Peter Bacanovic*, United States District Court, Southern District of New York, Superseding Indictment S1 03 Cr. 717 (MGC); US Securities and Exchange Commission, Plaintiff against Martha Stewart and Peter Bacanovic, Defendants, United States District Court, Southern District of New York, Complaint 03 CV 4070 (NRB); Jeffrey Toobin, "Lunch at Martha's," *The New Yorker* (February 3, 2003), pp. 38–41; Jeffrey Toobin, "A Bad Thing," *The New Yorker* (March 22, 2004), pp. 60–72.
2. Toobin, "A Bad Thing."
3. Ibid.
4. US Securities and Exchange Commission, "Martha Stewart and Peter Bacanovic Settle SEC's Insider Trading Charges," Press release 2006.

Discussion Questions

1. What are the main ethical issues in the case? Explain.
2. What, if anything, did Sam Waksal do wrong? Be as specific as possible. What, if anything, ought he have done differently? Explain.
3. What, if anything, did Martha Stewart do wrong? Be as specific as possible. What, if anything, ought she have done differently? Explain.
4. What, if anything, did Peter Bacanovic do wrong? Be as specific as possible. What, if anything, ought he have done differently? Explain.
5. Do you believe that insider trading is ethically wrong? Why, or why not? Explain. Do you believe insider trading should be illegal? Why, or why not? Explain.

11

Economic and Global Justice

11.1 INTRODUCTION

Economic disparities among individuals and nations have generated heated controversy over schemes for distributing and taxing income and wealth. The data show why these controversies exist. According to the US National Bureau of Economic Research, in the United States adults in the top 1 percent averaged 81 times the income of those in the bottom 50 percent. Those in the bottom half of income distribution in the United States earned just 12 percent of overall income distribution.[1] In the United Kingdom, the wealthiest 10 percent owned 45 percent of household wealth while the bottom 50 percent owned 9 percent of household wealth according to the UK Office for National Statistics.[2] Such disparities in income result in debates regarding the justification of public policies regarding taxation, minimum wages, gender equity, executive compensation, and international trade agreements.

Well-reasoned and systematic answers to these questions are grounded in theories of justice – that is, theories of how social and economic benefits, protections, services, and burdens should be distributed. In Chapter 1 we briefly analyzed some problems of ethical theory and justice. In the present chapter, the major distinctions, principles, and methods of moral argument in theories of justice are treated. The first four essays address which general system of social and economic organization is most just. The next two essays address justice in relation to economic globalization. Case studies illustrate these problems with practical examples.

THEORIES OF DISTRIBUTIVE JUSTICE

What a person deserves or is entitled to is often decided by specific rules and laws, such as those governing taxation, unemployment security, the provision of healthcare, and provisions for old age such as social security benefits in the United States or state pensions in the United Kingdom. These rules may be evaluated, criticized, and revised by reference to moral principles such as equality of persons, nondiscriminatory treatment, property ownership, protection from harm, compensatory justice, and retributive justice. The word *justice* is used broadly to cover both these principles and specific rules derived from the same principles, but developed for specific situations.

Economists have sometimes complained about philosophical approaches to justice on the grounds that a "fair price" or "fair trade" is not a matter of moral fairness: prices may be low or high, affordable or not affordable, but not fair or unfair. It is simply unfortunate, not unfair, if one cannot afford to pay for something or if another person is paid 100 times what you are paid. The basis of this exclusion of price as a consideration of justice is the market-established nature of prices and salaries. To speak of "unfair" prices, trade, or salaries is to express a negative opinion, of course; but these economists reason that from a market perspective any price is fair as long as it is determined by a fair market. Salaries must be treated in the same way, according to many economists.

However, such an economist would be missing the point. Philosophical approaches to justice ask whether the market itself is a fair arrangement. If so, what makes it fair? If not, what makes it unfair? If coercion is used in the market to set prices, is this unfair, or does it render the market not a free market? If healthcare and education are distributed nationally or internationally with vast inequality, can high prices on essential items such as healthcare and university tuition be fair? If a transnational company has a monopoly on an essential food or drug, is there no such thing as a price that is too high? These questions of fairness fall under the topic of distributive justice. The very idea of a "fair market" requires philosophical justification and is not the product of economic analysis. Economists and others that fail to understand this fail to understand the nature of justice.

The term *distributive justice* refers to the proper distribution of social benefits and burdens. A theory of distributive justice attempts to establish a connection between the properties or characteristics of persons and the morally correct distribution of benefits and burdens in society. *Egalitarian* theories emphasize equal access to primary goods (see John Rawls's essay); *libertarian* theories emphasize rights to social and economic liberty and deemphasize collective control (see Robert Nozick's essay); *utilitarian* theories emphasize a mixed use of such criteria resulting in the maximization of both public and individual interests (see Peter Singer's essay).

Systematic theories of justice attempt to elaborate how people should be compared and what it means to give people what they are due. Philosophers attempt to achieve the needed precision by developing material principles of justice, so called because they put material content into a theory of justice. Each material principle of justice identifies a relevant property on the basis of which burdens and benefits should be distributed. The following list includes the major candidates for the position of principles of distributive justice.

1. To each person an equal share.
2. To each person according to individual need.
3. To each person according to that person's rights.
4. To each person according to individual effort.
5. To each person according to societal contribution.
6. To each person according to merit.

A theory of justice might accept more than one of these principles. Some theories accept all six as legitimate. Many societies use several, in the belief that different rules are appropriate to different situations.

UTILITARIAN THEORY

In utilitarianism (which is examined in detail in Chapter 1), problems of justice are viewed as one part of the larger problem of maximizing value, and it is easy to see how a utilitarian might use all these material principles to this end. The ideal distribution of benefits and burdens is simply the one having this maximizing effect. According to utilitarian Peter Singer, in his essay in this chapter, a heavy element of political planning and economic redistribution is required to ensure that justice is done. Because utilitarianism was treated in Chapter 1, detailed considerations in this introduction will be focused on egalitarian and libertarian theories.

EGALITARIAN THEORY

Equality in the distribution of social benefits and burdens has a central place in several influential ethical theories. For example, in utilitarianism different people are equal in the value accorded their wants, preferences, and happiness, and in Kantian theories all persons are considered equally worthy and deserving of respect as ends in themselves. Egalitarian theory treats the question of how people should be considered equal in some respects (for example, in their basic political and moral rights and obligations), yet unequal in others (for example, in wealth and social burdens such as taxation).

John Rawls's Theory. The most influential theory of justice of the twentieth and twenty-first centuries is John Rawls's *A Theory of Justice*. Rawls's theory maintains that all economic goods and services should be distributed equally except when an unequal distribution would work to everyone's advantage (or at least to the advantage of the worst off in society). Rawls presents this egalitarian theory as a direct challenge to utilitarianism. He argues that social distributions produced by maximizing utility permit violations of basic individual liberties and rights. Being indifferent to the distribution of satisfactions among individuals, utilitarianism permits the infringement of people's rights and liberties to produce a proportionately greater utility for all concerned.

In the most important contribution to theories of justice in the modern era, Rawls defends a hypothetical social contract procedure that is strongly indebted to what he calls the "Kantian conception of equality." Valid principles of justice are those to which all persons would agree if they could freely and impartially consider the social situation. Impartiality is guaranteed by a conceptual device Rawls calls the "veil of ignorance." Here each person is imagined to be ignorant of all his or her particular characteristics, for example, the person's sex, race, IQ, family background, and special talents or handicaps. Theoretically, this veil of ignorance would prevent the adoption of principles biased toward particular groups of persons.

Rawls argues that under these conditions people would unanimously agree on two fundamental principles of justice. The first requires that each person be permitted the maximum amount of basic liberty compatible with a similar liberty for others. The second stipulates that once this equal basic liberty is assured, inequalities in social primary goods (for example, income, rights, and opportunities) are to be allowed only if they benefit everyone. Rawls considers social institutions to be just if and only if they conform to these principles of the social contract. He rejects a more radical egalitarianism, arguing that inequalities that render everyone better off by comparison to being equal are desirable.

Rawls formulates what is called the *difference principle*: Inequalities are justifiable only if they maximally enhance the position of the "representative least advantaged" person, that is, a hypothetical individual particularly unfortunate in the distribution of fortuitous characteristics or social advantages. Rawls is unclear about who might qualify under this category, but a worker incapacitated from exposure to asbestos and living in poverty clearly would qualify. Formulated in this way, the difference principle could allow, for instance, extraordinary economic rewards to business entrepreneurs, venture capitalists, and corporate takeover artists if the resulting economic situation were to produce improved job opportunities and working conditions for the least advantaged members of society, or possibly greater benefits for pension funds holding stock for the working class.

The difference principle rests on the moral viewpoint that because inequalities of birth, historical circumstance, and natural endowment are undeserved, persons in a cooperative society should make more equal the unequal situation of its naturally disadvantaged members.

LIBERTARIAN THEORY

What makes a libertarian theory *libertarian* is the priority given to distinctive procedures or mechanisms for ensuring that liberty rights are recognized in social and economic practice, typically the rules and procedures governing economic acquisition and exchange in capitalist or free-market systems.

The Role of Individual Freedom. The libertarian contends that it is a basic violation of justice to ensure equal economic returns in a society. In particular, individuals are seen as having a fundamental right to own and dispense with the products of their labor as they choose, even if the exercise of this right leads to large inequalities of wealth in society. Equality and utility principles, from this perspective, sacrifice basic liberty rights to the larger public interest by exploiting one set of individuals for the benefit of another. The most apparent example is the coercive extraction of financial resources through taxation.

Robert Nozick's Theory. Libertarian theory is defended in this chapter by Robert Nozick, who refers to his view as an "entitlement theory" of justice. Nozick argues that a theory of justice should work to protect individual rights and should not propound a thesis intended to "pattern" society through arrangements such as those in socialist and (impure) capitalist countries in which governments take pronounced steps to redistribute wealth.

Nozick's libertarian position rejects all distributional patterns imposed by material principles of justice. He is thus committed to a form of *procedural* justice. That is, for Nozick there is no pattern of just distribution independent of fair procedures of acquisition, transfer, and rectification; in this view he is joined by Milton Friedman (see Chapter 5). Their claims have been at the center of controversy over the libertarian account, and competing theories of justice often react to their uncompromising commitment to pure procedural justice.

Nobel Prize-winning economist and philosopher Amartya Sen identifies difficulties with each of these approaches to justice. He argues that Rawls's focus on the importance of primary goods (e.g., basic rights and liberties, freedom of movement, and income and wealth) for the pursuit of a good life masks important differences in the capabilities of individuals to utilize such primary goods. In Sen's view, the libertarian's near exclusive focus on liberty, via the individual's *control* of personal decisions, fails to adequately address actual *outcomes* that are influenced by these same factors. Sen points out that as a result of personal characteristics, deprivation, the influence of social and physical environments, and disability, there is great variation among individuals both with regard to how they can utilize primary goods and the outcomes of personal decisions. However, he believes that both Rawls and libertarians are correct in emphasizing the importance of rights, something utilitarianism is notoriously bad at accommodating without utilizing tortuous reasoning. Given that the entire field of economics is grounded in utilitarianism, he takes this to be an indictment of much contemporary work in economics, especially welfare economics, which focuses on the distributions of goods and resources in society. Sen argues that an alternative theoretical framework is needed.

Sen's alternative is his *capabilities* approach which emphasizes the capability of individuals to function well as humans. Sen's essay in this chapter emphasizes both capabilities and functionings. The concept of "functioning" concerns those things that a person values doing or being, such as pursuing an advanced education, being healthy, or having self-respect. The concept of "capability" refers to the freedom to achieve various functionings. Sen's thesis is that his capabilities approach provides a better evaluative framework for assessing social welfare than the other approaches discussed in this chapter, both in developed nations, but especially in developing nations. On his account, governmental institutions should be designed to facilitate the capability of citizens to function well.

CAPITALISM: IS THERE JUSTICE BEYOND THE FREE MARKET?

Many philosophers argue that an adequate theory of economic justice must recognize a set of individual rights that is more inclusive than those acknowledged in theories of capitalist markets. *Capitalism* is here understood as a market-based economic system governed by capital, that is, the wealth of an individual or an establishment accumulated by or employed in its business activities. Entrepreneurs and the institutions they create generate the capital with which businesses provide goods, services, and payments to workers. Defenders of capitalism argue that this system maximally distributes social freedoms and desirable resources, resulting in the best economic outcomes for everyone in society. All libertarians, but also many utilitarians, egalitarians, and communitarians, have defended capitalism using this general conception.

Critics of capitalism believe that owners and managers unfairly allocate high wages for themselves while distributing only low wages to workers, who are not able to move freely from one job to another in many capitalist markets. Critics of capitalism generally acknowledge that capitalists do often take significant economic risks (a justification advanced for their higher wages); however, critics maintain that capitalists rarely have to assume the burdens of deprivation that workers do. The avoidance of deprivation is a major reason why some writers propose interventions in capitalist markets; they seek to secure stronger economic rights for workers – such as a higher minimum wage, continuous health insurance, and unemployment insurance (or protections against economic disaster in the circumstance of job layoffs).

Critics of capitalism argue that its proponents must answer the following questions: Why should we assume that people's economic rights extend only to the acquisition and dispensation of private property according to free-market rules? Is it not equally plausible to posit more substantive moral rights in the economic sphere – say, rights to healthcare, decent levels of education, decent standard of living, and limits on compensation?

The capitalist ideal is widely agreed to be plausible for free transactions among informed and consenting parties who start as equals in the bargaining process. However, this conception has come under significant criticism in circumstances in which contractual bargaining among equals is impossible or unlikely. Contracts, voting privileges, individuals investing in the stock market, and family relationships may involve bluffing, differentials of power and wealth, manipulation, and the like. These factors can and often do work systematically to disadvantage vulnerable individuals. For example, over the course of time in the working of capitalist markets, one group in society may gain considerable wealth and political influence, by comparison with other groups in society. Even if the *transactions* leading to this imbalance may have been legitimate, the *outcome* may not be acceptable. If an individual's bargaining position has been deeply eroded, does he or she have a right to protection from social inequalities that have emerged? If he or she is destined to poverty as a result of social conditions, is there a legitimate claim of justice, as several authors in this chapter propose?

If people have a right to a minimal level of material means (a right libertarians do not acknowledge), it seems to many writers that their rights are violated whenever economic distributions leave persons with less than that minimal level. A commitment to individual economic rights, then, may go hand in hand with a theory of justice that requires a more activist role for government. This may be true even if one starts with free-market assumptions. Many philosophers agree with libertarian premises that economic freedom is a value deserving of respect and protection, but they disagree with the claim that the principles and procedures of unmitigated capitalist markets adequately protect the basic values of individual and public welfare.

In reaction to these problems, some reject the pure procedural commitments of pure capitalist (often libertarian or utilitarian) theories and replace them with a principle specifying human need as the relevant respect in which people are to be compared for purposes of determining social and economic justice. Much turns here on how the notion of need is defined and implemented. For purposes of justice, a principle of need would be least controversial if it were restricted to fundamental needs. If malnutrition, bodily injury, and the withholding of certain information involve fundamental harms, we have a fundamental need for nutrition, healthcare facilities, and education. According to theories based on this material principle, justice places the satisfaction of fundamental human needs above the protection of economic freedoms or rights (or at least at the same level of importance).

This construal of the principle of need has been used to support rights that reach well beyond capitalism. Yet there may be room for reconciliation between the principle of need and the principles that underlie capitalist systems. Many advanced industrial countries have the capacity to produce more than is strictly necessary to meet their citizens' fundamental needs. One might argue that *after* everyone's fundamental needs have been satisfied, *then* justice requires no particular pattern of distribution. For example, some current discussions of the right to healthcare and the right to a job are rooted in the idea of meeting basic medical and economic needs – but *only basic* needs. In this way, a single unified theory of justice might require the maintenance of certain patterns in the distributions of basic goods (for example, a decent minimum level of income, education, and healthcare) while allowing the market to determine distributions of goods beyond those that satisfy fundamental needs.

This approach accepts a two-tiered system of access to goods and services: (1) social coverage for basic and catastrophic needs and (2) private purchase of other goods and services. On the first tier, distribution is based on need, and everyone's basic needs are met by the government. Better services may be made available for purchase in an economic system on the second tier. This proposal seems to present an attractive point of convergence and negotiation for libertarians, utilitarians, and egalitarians. It provides a premise of equal access to basic goods while allowing additional rights to economic freedom. Theories such as utilitarianism may also find the compromise particularly attractive because it serves to minimize public dissatisfaction and to maximize community welfare. The egalitarian finds an opportunity to use an equal-access principle, and the libertarian retains free-market production and distribution. However, the system would involve compromise by proponents of each of these theories of justice.

GLOBAL JUSTICE

Concerns regarding the global distribution of economic resources have come to dominate much of the most interesting work by theorists of justice in recent years. The facts that inform much of this debate over global justice are increasingly well known. Nearly 1 billion people are malnourished and without access to safe drinking water. Approximately 50,000 human deaths per day are attributable to poverty-related causes.[3] This remains true despite the fact that Article 25 of the Universal Declaration of Human Rights (included in this chapter) stipulates that all people have "the right to a standard of living adequate for . . . health and well-being, for themselves and their families."[4]

Current foreign direct investment (FDI) outflows are approximately $1.7–2 trillion, up from $53 billion in 1980.[5] Approximately one-third of that investment is finding its way into developing economies. This remarkable increase in FDI is one indicator of a steady increase in economic globalization. Trade economists typically argue that such FDI enhances job creation in the world's poorest nations. Using broadly utilitarian reasoning, they argue that the exploitation by multinational corporations of cheap labor supplies, abundant natural resources, and lax regulatory regimes allows developing countries to expand export activities and to improve their economies. This economic growth brings much-needed jobs, which cause labor markets to tighten, which eventually force corporations to improve working conditions in order to attract workers. As wages rise, workers spend more and local economies expand, thus creating more jobs and wealth.

Critics of economic globalization argue that rather than improving overall welfare, economic globalization increases inequality and poverty by depressing the wages of the poor and middle class while enhancing the wealth of economic elites, thus increasing the gap between the "haves" and the "have nots." In their view, economic globalization undermines rather than enhances human rights. Further, they argue that workers are often treated as disposable tools, and local environments are often polluted in ways that harm human welfare and inhibit future well-being. Critics of "neoliberal" strategies for alleviating global poverty point out that the global labor supply is so vast that the theoretically sound idea that tighter labor markets alone will lead to improved working conditions is, in terms of practicality, implausible. In his contribution to this chapter, economist Martin Wolf argues that most critics of globalization are wrong. He argues that both the number and the percentage of the world's population in poverty has declined since 1980 as a result of economic globalization. Broadly construed, Wolf argues, the economic welfare of the world's population has improved as a result of globalization.

In his essay "Globalization Moralized" Richard W. Miller complicates the neoliberal narrative that economic globalization typically improves the welfare of people in developing nations. He argues that individuals, firms, and governments in developed nations take unfair advantage of people in developing nations in the process of production and in the institutional frameworks that regulate international trade. More specifically, he argues that firms wrongfully exploit workers in developing nations by taking unfair advantage of their desperate circumstances without giving due consideration to basic human dignity. He also argues that developed nations unjustly utilize coercion to inhibit the ability of developing nations to use many of the tools available to them to facilitate their own economic growth. He argues that developed nations and their citizens have a duty to give up many of the consequent benefits of these exploitative relationships by promoting the interests of the global poor. The debate between Wolf and Miller reflects current public policy debates among the citizens and politicians of most developed nations regarding international trade.

CONCLUSION

Each of the theorists considered in this chapter capture some intuitive convictions about justice. Rawls's difference principle, for example, describes a widely shared belief about justified inequalities. Nozick's theory makes a strong appeal in the domains of property rights and liberties. Utilitarianism is widely used in Western nations in the development of public policy. Sen's and Miller's arguments are consistent with many international agreements and protocols such as the Universal Declaration of Human Rights.

Perhaps, then, there are several equally valid, or at least equally defensible, theories of justice. There could be, based on this analysis, libertarian societies, egalitarian societies, utilitarian societies, and a cosmopolitan global community, as well as societies based on mixed theories or derivative theories of taxation and redistribution. The unique circumstances regarding a nation's stage of economic development, the historical period, and the threats and opportunities a nation faces, may shape the type of just institutions and frameworks that it adapts. However, this possibility raises other problems in ethical theory discussed in Chapter 1 – in particular, relativism and moral disagreement, and before this conclusion is accepted, the details of the arguments in this chapter's selections should be carefully assessed.

Notes

1. US National Bureau of Economic Research, *NBER Digest*, "New Evidence on Income Inequality," February 2017.
2. UK Office of National Statistics, *Wealth in Great Britain Wave 4, 2012 to 2014.* "Total Wealth in Great Britain, 2012 to 2014," December 18, 2015.
3. Thomas Pogge, "Priorities of Global Justice," reprinted in the 9th edition of this textbook.
4. United Nations Universal Declaration of Human Rights, reprinted in this chapter.
5. United Nations Conference on Trade and Development, *World Investment Report 2017.*

11.2 ECONOMIC JUSTICE

An Egalitarian Theory of Justice

JOHN RAWLS

The Role of Justice

Justice is the first virtue of social institutions, as truth is of systems of thought. A theory however elegant and economical must be rejected or revised if it is untrue; likewise laws and institutions no matter how efficient and well-arranged must be reformed or abolished if they are unjust. Each person possesses an inviolability founded on justice that even the welfare of society as a whole cannot override. For this reason justice denies that the loss of freedom for some is made right by a greater good shared by others. It does not allow that the sacrifices imposed on a few are outweighed by the larger sum of advantages enjoyed by many. Therefore in a just society the liberties of equal citizenship are taken as settled; the rights secured by justice are not subject to political bargaining or to the calculus of social interests. The only thing that permits us to acquiesce in an erroneous theory is the lack of a better one; analogously, an injustice is tolerable only when it is necessary to avoid an even greater injustice. Being first virtues of human activities, truth and justice are uncompromising.

These propositions seem to express our intuitive conviction of the primacy of justice. No doubt they are expressed too strongly. In any event I wish to inquire whether these contentions or others similar to them are sound, and if so how they can be accounted for. To this end it is necessary to work out a theory of justice in the light of which these assertions can be interpreted and assessed. I shall begin by considering the role of the principles of justice. Let us assume, to fix ideas, that a society is a more or less self-sufficient association of persons who in their relations to one another recognize certain rules of conduct as binding and who for the most part act in accordance with them. Suppose further that these rules specify a system of cooperation designed to advance the good of those taking part in it. Then, although a society is a cooperative venture for mutual advantage, it is typically marked by a conflict as well as by an identity of interests. There is an identity of interests since social cooperation makes possible a better life for all than any would have if each were to live solely by his own efforts. There is a conflict of interests, since persons are not indifferent as to how the greater benefits produced by their collaboration are distributed, for in order to pursue their ends they each prefer a larger to a lesser share. A set of principles is required for choosing among the various social arrangements which determine this division of advantages and for underwriting an agreement on the proper distributive shares. These principles are the principles of social justice: They provide a way of assigning rights and duties in the basic institutions of society and they define the appropriate distribution of the benefits and burdens of social cooperation. ....

The Main Idea of the Theory of Justice

My aim is to present a conception of justice which generalizes and carries to a higher level of abstraction the familiar theory of the social contract as found, say, in Locke, Rousseau, and Kant. In order to do this we are not to think of the original contract as one to enter a particular society or to set up a particular form of government. Rather, the guiding idea is that the principles of justice for the basic structure of society are the object of the original agreement. They are the principles that free and rational persons concerned to further their own interests would accept in an initial position of equality as defining the fundamental terms of their association. These principles are to regulate all further agreements; they specify the kinds of social cooperation that can be entered into and the forms of government that can be established. This way of regarding the principles of justice I shall call justice as fairness.

Thus we are to imagine that those who engage in social cooperation choose together, in one joint act, the principles which are to assign basic rights and duties and to determine the division of social benefits. Men are to decide in advance how they are to regulate their claims against one another and what is to be the foundation charter of their society. Just as each person must decide by rational reflection what constitutes his good, that is, the system of ends which it is rational for him to pursue, so a group of persons must decide once and for all what is to count among them as just and unjust. The choice which rational men would make in this hypothetical situation of equal liberty, assuming for the present that this choice problem has a solution, determines the principles of justice.

In justice as fairness the original position of equality corresponds to the state of nature in the traditional theory of the social contract. This original position is not, of course, thought of as an actual historical state of affairs, much less as a primitive condition of culture. It is understood as a purely hypothetical situation characterized so as to lead to a certain conception of justice. Among the essential features of this situation is that no one knows his place in society, his class position or social status, nor does any one know his fortune in the distribution of natural assets and abilities, his intelligence, strength, and the like. I shall even assume that the parties do not know their conceptions of the good or their special psychological propensities. The principles of justice are chosen behind a veil of ignorance. This ensures that no one is advantaged or disadvantaged in the choice of principles by the outcome of natural chance or the contingency of social circumstances. Since all are similarly situated and no one is able to design principles to favor his particular condition, the principles of justice are the result of a fair agreement or bargain. For given the circumstances of the original position, the symmetry of everyone's relations to each other, this initial situation is fair between individuals as moral persons, that is, as rational beings with their own ends and capable, I shall assume, of a sense of justice. The original position is, one might say, the appropriate initial status quo, and thus the fundamental agreements reached in it are fair. This explains the propriety of the name "justice as fairness":

It conveys the idea that the principles of justice are agreed to in an initial situation that is fair. The name does not mean that the concepts of justice and fairness are the same, any more than the phrase "poetry as metaphor" means that the concepts of poetry and metaphor are the same.

Justice as fairness begins, as I have said, with one of the most general of all choices which persons might make together, namely, with the choice of the first principles of a conception of justice which is to regulate all subsequent criticism and reform of institutions. Then, having chosen a conception of justice, we can suppose that they are to choose a constitution and a legislature to enact laws, and so on, all in accordance with the principles of justice initially agreed upon. Our social situation is just if it is such that by this sequence of hypothetical agreements we would have contracted into the general system of rules which defines it.

. . . It may be observed, however, that once the principles of justice are thought of as arising from an original agreement in a situation of equality, it is an open question whether the principle of utility would be acknowledged. Offhand it hardly seems likely that persons who view themselves as equals, entitled to press their claims upon one another, would agree to a principle which may require lesser life prospects for some simply for the sake of a greater sum of advantages enjoyed by others. Since each desires to protect his interests, his capacity to advance his conception of the good, no one has a reason to acquiesce in an enduring loss for himself in order to bring about a greater net balance of satisfaction. In the absence of strong and lasting benevolent impulses, a rational man would not accept a basic structure merely because it maximized the algebraic sum of advantages irrespective of its permanent effects on his own basic rights and interests. Thus it seems that the principle of utility is incompatible with the conception of social cooperation among equals for mutual advantage. It appears to be inconsistent with the idea of reciprocity implicit in the notion of a well-ordered society. Or, at any rate, so I shall argue.

I shall maintain instead that the persons in the initial situation would choose two rather different principles: The first requires equality in the assignment of basic rights and duties, while the second holds that social and economic inequalities, for example inequalities of wealth and authority, are just only if they result in compensating benefits for everyone, and in particular for the least advantaged members of society. These principles rule out justifying institutions on the grounds that the hardships of some are offset by a greater good in the aggregate. It may be expedient but it is not just that some should have less in order that others may prosper. But there is no injustice in the greater benefits earned by a few provided that the situation of persons not so fortunate is thereby improved. The intuitive idea is that since everyone's well-being depends upon a scheme of cooperation without which no one could have a satisfactory life, the division of advantages should be such as to draw forth the willing cooperation of everyone taking part in it, including those less well situated. Yet this can be expected only if reasonable terms are proposed. The two principles mentioned seem to be a fair agreement on the basis of which those better endowed, or more fortunate in their social position, neither of which we can be said to deserve, could expect the willing cooperation of others when some workable scheme is a necessary condition of the welfare of all. Once we decide to look for a conception of justice that nullifies the accidents of natural endowment and the contingencies of social circumstance as counters in the quest for political and economic advantage, we are led to these principles. They express the result of leaving aside those aspects of the social world that seem arbitrary from a moral point of view. . . .

The Original Position and Justification

. . . The idea here is simply to make vivid to ourselves the restrictions that it seems reasonable to impose on arguments for principles of justice, and therefore on these principles themselves. Thus it seems reasonable and generally acceptable that no one should be advantaged or disadvantaged by natural fortune or social circumstances in the choice of principles. It also seems widely agreed that it should be impossible to tailor principles to the circumstances of one's own case. We should insure further that particular inclinations and aspirations, and persons' conceptions of their good, do not affect the principles adopted. The aim is to rule out those principles that it would be rational to propose for acceptance, however little the chance of success, only if one knew certain things that are irrelevant from the standpoint of justice. For example, if a man knew that he was wealthy, he might find it rational to advance the principle that various taxes for welfare measures be counted unjust; if he knew that he was poor, he would most likely propose the contrary principle. To represent the desired restrictions one imagines a situation in which everyone is deprived of this sort of information. One excludes the knowledge of those contingencies which sets men at odds and allows them to be guided by their prejudices. In this manner the veil of ignorance is arrived at in a natural way. . . .

Two Principles of Justice

I shall now state in a provisional form the two principles of justice that I believe would be chosen in the original position. . . .

The first statement of the two principles reads as follows.

First: each person is to have an equal right to the most extensive basic liberty compatible with a similar liberty for others.

Second: social and economic inequalities are to be arranged so that they are both (a) reasonably expected to be to everyone's advantage, and (b) attached to positions and offices open to all. . . . [The Difference Principle]

By way of general comment, these principles primarily apply, as I have said, to the basic structure of society. They are to govern the assignment of rights and duties and to regulate the distribution of social and economic advantages. As their formulation suggests, these principles presuppose that the social structure can be divided into two more or less distinct parts, the first principle applying to the one, the second to the other. They distinguish between those aspects of the social system that define and secure the equal liberties of citizenship and those that specify and establish social and economic inequalities. The basic liberties of citizens are, roughly speaking, political liberty (the right to vote and to be eligible for public office) together with freedom of speech and assembly; liberty of conscience and freedom of thought; freedom of the person along with the right to hold (personal) property; and freedom from arbitrary arrest and seizure as defined by the concept of the rule of law. These liberties are all required to be equal by the first principle, since citizens of a just society are to have the same basic rights.

The second principle applies, in the first approximation, to the distribution of income and wealth and to the design of organizations that make use of differences in authority and responsibility, or chains of command. While the distribution of wealth and income need not be equal, it must be to everyone's advantage, and at the same time, positions of authority and offices of command must be accessible to all. One applies the second principle by holding positions open, and then, subject to this constraint, arranges social and economic inequalities so that everyone benefits.

These principles are to be arranged in a serial order with the first principle prior to the second. This ordering means that a departure from the institutions of equal liberty required by the first principle cannot be justified, or compensated for, by greater social and economic advantages. The distribution of wealth and income, and the hierarchies of authority must be consistent with both the liberties of equal citizenship and equality of opportunity.

It is clear that these principles are rather specific in their content, and their acceptance rests on certain assumptions that I must eventually try to explain and justify. A theory of justice depends upon a theory of society in ways that will become evident as we proceed. For the present, it should be observed that the two principles (and this holds for all formulations) are a special case of a more general conception of justice that can be expressed as follows.

All social values – liberty and opportunity, income and wealth, and the bases of self-respect – are to be distributed equally unless an unequal distribution of any, or all, of these values is to everyone's advantage.

Injustice, then, is simply inequalities that are not to the benefit of all. Of course, this conception is extremely vague and requires interpretation.

As a first step, suppose that the basic structure of society distributes certain primary goods, that is, things that every rational man is presumed to want. These goods normally have a use whatever a person's rational plan of life. For simplicity, assume that the chief primary goods at the disposition of society are rights and liberties, powers and opportunities, income and wealth. These are the social primary goods. Other primary goods such as health and vigor, intelligence and imagination, are natural goods; although their possession is influenced by the basic structure, they are not so directly under its control. Imagine, then, a hypothetical initial arrangement in which all the social primary goods are equally distributed: everyone has similar rights and duties, and income and wealth are evenly shared. This state of affairs provides a benchmark for judging improvements. If certain inequalities of wealth and organizational powers would make everyone better off than in this hypothetical starting situation, then they accord with the general conception.

Now it is possible, at least theoretically, that by giving up some of their fundamental liberties men are sufficiently compensated by the resulting social and economic gains. The general conception of justice imposes no restrictions on what sort of inequalities are permissible; it only requires that everyone's position be improved. . . .

Now the second principle insists that each person benefit from permissible inequalities in the basic structure. This means that it must be reasonable for each relevant representative man defined by this structure, when he views it as a going concern, to prefer his prospects with the inequality to his prospects without it. One is not allowed to justify differences in income or organizational powers on the ground that the disadvantages of those in one position are outweighed by the greater advantages of those in another. Much less can infringements of liberty be counterbalanced in this way. Applied to the basic structure, the principle of utility would have us maximize the sum of expectations of representative men (weighted by the number of persons they represent, on the classical view); and this would permit us to compensate for the losses of some by the gains of others. Instead, the two principles require that everyone benefit from economic and social inequalities. . . .

The Tendency to Equality

I wish to conclude this discussion of the two principles by explaining the sense in which they express an egalitarian conception of justice. Also I should like to forestall the objection to the principle of fair opportunity that it leads to a callous meritocratic society. In order to prepare the way for doing this, I note several aspects of the conception of justice that I have set out.

First we may observe that the difference principle gives some weight to the considerations singled out by the principle of redress. This is the principle that undeserved inequalities call for redress; and since inequalities of birth and natural endowment are undeserved, these inequalities are to be somehow compensated for. Thus the principle holds that in order to treat all persons equally, to provide genuine equality of opportunity, society must give more attention to those with fewer native assets and to those born into the less favorable social positions. The idea is to redress the bias of contingencies in the direction of equality. In pursuit of this principle greater resources might be spent on the education of the less rather than the more intelligent, at least over a certain time of life, say the earlier years of school.

Now the principle of redress has not to my knowledge been proposed as the sole criterion of justice, as the single aim of the social order. It is plausible as most such principles are only as a *prima facie* principle, one that is to be weighed in the balance with others. For example, we are to weigh it against the principle to improve the average standard of life, or to advance the common good. But whatever other principles we hold, the claims of redress are to be taken into account. It is thought to represent one of the elements in our conception of justice. Now the difference principle is not of course the principle of redress. It does not require society to try to even out handicaps as if all were expected to compete on a fair basis in the same race. But the difference principle would allocate resources in education, say, so as to improve the long-term expectation of the least favored. If this end is attained by giving more attention to the better endowed, it is permissible; otherwise not. And in making this decision, the value of education should not be assessed only in terms of economic efficiency and social welfare. Equally if not more important is the role of education in enabling a person to enjoy the culture of his society and to take part in its affairs, and in this way to provide for each individual a secure sense of his own worth.

Thus although the difference principle is not the same as that of redress, it does achieve some of the intent of the latter principle. It transforms the aims of the basic structure so that the total scheme of institutions no longer emphasizes social efficiency and technocratic values. . . .

The natural distribution is neither just nor unjust; nor is it unjust that men are born into society at some particular position. These are simply natural facts. What is just and unjust is the way that institutions deal with these facts. Aristocratic and caste societies are unjust because they make these contingencies the ascriptive basis for belonging to more or less enclosed and privileged social classes. The basic structure of these societies incorporates the arbitrariness found in nature. But there is no necessity for men to resign themselves to these contingencies. The social system is not an unchangeable order beyond human control but a pattern of human action. In justice as fairness men agree to share one another's fate. In designing institutions they undertake to avail themselves of the accidents of nature and social circumstance only when doing so is for the common benefit. The two principles are a fair way of meeting the arbitrariness of fortune; and while no doubt imperfect in other ways, the institutions which satisfy these principles are just. . . .

There is a natural inclination to object that those better situated deserve their greater advantages whether or not they are to the benefit of others. At this point it is necessary to be clear about the notion of desert. It is perfectly true that given a just system of cooperation as a scheme of public rules and the expectations set up by it, those who, with the prospect of improving their condition, have done what the system announces that it will reward are entitled to their advantages. In this sense the more fortunate have a claim to their better situation; their claims are legitimate expectations established by social institutions, and the community is obligated to meet them. But this sense of desert presupposes the existence of the cooperative scheme; it is irrelevant to the question whether in the first place the scheme is to be designed in accordance with the difference principle or some other criterion.

Perhaps some will think that the person with greater natural endowments deserves those assets and the superior character that made their development possible. Because he is more worthy in this sense, he deserves the greater advantages that he could achieve with them. This view, however, is surely incorrect. It seems to be one of the fixed points of our considered judgments that no one deserves his place in the distribution of native endowments, any more than one deserves one's initial starting place in society. The assertion that a man deserves the superior character that enables him to make the effort to cultivate his abilities is equally problematic, for his character depends in large part upon fortunate family and social circumstances for which he can claim no credit. The notion of desert seems not to apply to these cases. Thus the more advantaged representative man cannot say that he deserves and therefore has a right to a scheme of cooperation in which he is permitted to acquire benefits in ways that do not contribute to the welfare of others. There is no basis for his making this claim. From the standpoint of common sense, then, the difference principle appears to be acceptable both to the more advantaged and to the less advantaged individual. . . .

Background Institutions for Distributive Justice

The main problem of distributive justice is the choice of a social system. The principles of justice apply to the basic structure and regulate how its major institutions are combined into one scheme. Now, as we have seen, the idea of justice as fairness is to use the notion of pure procedural justice to handle the contingencies of particular situations. The social system is to be designed so that the resulting distribution is just however things turn out. To achieve this end it is necessary to get the social and economic process within the surroundings of suitable political and legal institutions. Without an appropriate scheme of these background institutions the outcome of the distributive process will not be just. Background fairness is lacking. I shall give a brief description of these supporting institutions as they might exist in a properly organized democratic state that allows private ownership of capital and natural resources. . . .

In establishing these background institutions the government may be thought of as divided into four branches.[1] Each branch consists of various agencies, or activities thereof, charged with preserving certain social and economic conditions. These divisions do not overlap with the usual organization of government but are to be understood as different functions. The allocation branch, for example, is to keep the price system workably competitive and to prevent the formation of unreasonable market power. Such power does not exist as long as markets cannot be made more competitive consistent with the requirements of efficiency and the facts of geography and the preferences of households. The allocation branch is also charged with identifying and correcting, say by suitable taxes and subsidies and by changes in the definition of property rights, the more obvious departures from efficiency caused by the failure of prices to measure accurately social benefits and costs. To this end suitable taxes and subsidies may be used, or the scope and definition of property rights may be revised. The stabilization branch, on the other hand, strives to bring about reasonably full employment in the sense that those who want work can find it and the free choice of occupation and the deployment of finance are supported by strong effective demand. These two branches together are to maintain the efficiency of the market economy generally.

The social minimum is the responsibility of the transfer branch. ... The essential idea is that the workings of this branch take needs into account and assign them an appropriate weight with respect to other claims. A competitive price system gives no consideration to needs and therefore it cannot be the sole device of distribution. There must be a division of labor between the parts of the social system in answering to the common sense precepts of justice. Different institutions meet different claims. Competitive markets properly regulated secure free choice of occupation and lead to an efficient use of resources and allocation of commodities to households. They set a weight on the conventional precepts associated with wages and earnings, whereas a transfer branch guarantees a certain level of well-being and honors the claims of need. ...

It is clear that the justice of distributive shares depends on the background institutions and how they allocate total income, wages and other income plus transfers. There is with reason strong objection to the competitive determination of total income, since this ignores the claims of need and an appropriate standard of life. From the standpoint of the legislative stage it is rational to insure oneself and one's descendants against these contingencies of the market. Indeed, the difference principle presumably requires this. But once a suitable minimum is provided by transfers, it may be perfectly fair that the rest of total income be settled by the price system, assuming that it is moderately efficient and free from monopolistic restrictions, and unreasonable externalities have been eliminated. Moreover, this way of dealing with the claims of need would appear to be more effective than trying to regulate income by minimum wage standards, and the like. It is better to assign to each branch only such tasks as are compatible with one another. Since the market is not suited to answer the claims of need, these should be met by a separate arrangement. Whether the principles of justice are satisfied, then, turns on whether the total income of the least advantaged (wages plus transfers) is such as to maximize their long-run expectations (consistent with the constraints of equal liberty and fair equality of opportunity).

Finally, there is a distribution branch. Its task is to preserve an approximate justice in distributive shares by means of taxation and the necessary adjustments in the rights of property. Two aspects of this branch may be distinguished. First of all, it imposes a number of inheritance and gift taxes, and sets restrictions on the rights of bequest. The purpose of these levies and regulations is not to raise revenue (release resources to government) but gradually and continually to correct the distribution of wealth and to prevent concentrations of power detrimental to the fair value of political liberty and fair equality of opportunity. For example, the progressive principle might be applied at the beneficiary's end.[2] Doing this would encourage the wide dispersal of property which is a necessary condition, it seems, if the fair value of the equal liberties is to be maintained.

Notes

1. For the idea of branches of government, see R. A. Musgrave, *The Theory of Public Finance* (New York: McGraw-Hill, 1959), chap. 1.
2. See Meade, *Efficiency, Equality, and the Ownership of Property* (London: Allen & Unwin, 1964), pp. 56 ff.

The Entitlement Theory

ROBERT NOZICK

The term *distributive justice* is not a neutral one. Hearing the term "distribution," most people presume that some thing or mechanism uses some principle or criterion to give out a supply of things. Into this process of distributing shares some error may have crept. So it is an open question, at least, whether *re*distribution should take place; whether we should do again what has already been done once, though poorly. However, we are not in the position of children who have been given portions of pie by someone who now makes last-minute adjustments to rectify careless cutting. There is no *central* distribution, no person or group entitled to control all the resources, jointly deciding how they are to be doled out. What each person gets, he gets from others who give to him in exchange for something, or as a gift. In a free society, diverse persons control different resources, and new holdings arise out of the voluntary exchanges and actions of persons. . . .

The subject of justice in holdings consists of three major topics. The first is the *original acquisition of holdings*, the appropriation of unheld things. This includes the issues of how unheld things may come to be held, the process, or processes, by which unheld things may come to be held, the things that may come to be held by these processes, the extent of what comes to be held by a particular person, and so on. We shall refer to the complicated truth about this topic, which we shall not formulate here, as the principle of justice in acquisition. The second topic concerns the *transfer of holdings* from one person to another. By what processes may a person transfer holdings to another? How may a person acquire a holding from another who holds it? Under this topic come general descriptions of voluntary exchange, and gift and (on the other hand) fraud, as well as reference to particular conventional details fixed upon in a given society. The complicated truth about this subject (with placeholders for conventional details) we shall call the principle of justice in transfer. (And we shall suppose it also includes principles governing how a person may divest himself of a holding, passing it into an unheld state.)

If the world were wholly just, the following inductive definition would exhaustively cover the subject of justice in holdings.

1. A person who acquires a holding in accordance with the principle of justice in acquisition is entitled to that holding.
2. A person who acquires a holding in accordance with the principle of justice in transfer, from someone else entitled to the holding, is entitled to the holding.
3. No one is entitled to a holding except by (repeated) applications of 1 and 2.

The complete principle of distributive justice would say simply that a distribution is just if everyone is entitled to the holdings they possess under the distribution. . . .

Not all actual situations are generated in accordance with the two principles of justice in holdings: the principle of justice in acquisition and the principle of justice in transfer. Some people steal from others, or defraud them, or enslave them, seizing their product and preventing them from living as they choose, or forcibly exclude others from competing in exchanges. None of these are permissible modes of transition from one situation to another. And some persons acquire holdings by means not sanctioned by the principle of justice in acquisition. The existence of past injustice (previous violations of the first two principles of justice in holdings) raises the third major topic under justice in holdings: the rectification of injustice in holdings. If past injustice has shaped present holdings in various ways, some identifiable and some not, what now, if anything, ought to be done to rectify these injustices? . . .

Historical Principles and End-Result Principles

The general outlines of the entitlement theory illuminate the nature and defects of other conceptions of distributive justice. The entitlement theory of justice in distribution is *historical*; whether a distribution is just depends upon how it came about. In contrast, *current time-slice principles* of justice hold that the justice of a distribution is determined by how things are distributed (who has what) as judged by some *structural* principle(s) of just distribution. A utilitarian who judges between any two distributions by seeing which has the greater sum of utility and, if the sums tie, applies some fixed equality criterion to choose the more equal distribution, would hold a current time-slice principle of justice. As would someone who had a fixed schedule of trade-offs between the sum of happiness and equality. According to a current time-slice principle, all that needs to be looked at, in judging the justice of a distribution, is who ends up with what; in comparing any two distributions one need look only at the matrix presenting the distributions. No further information need be fed into a principle of justice. It is a consequence of such principles of justice that any two structurally identical distributions are equally just. . . .

Most persons do not accept current time-slice principles as constituting the whole story about distributive shares. They think it relevant in assessing the justice of a situation to consider not only the distribution it embodies, but also how that distribution came about. If some persons are in prison for murder or war crimes, we do not say that to assess the justice of the distribution in the society we must look only at what this person has, and that person has, and that person has, . . . at the current time. We think it relevant to ask whether someone did something so that he deserved to be punished, *deserved* to have a lower share. . . .

Patterning

. . . Almost every suggested principle of distributive justice is patterned: to each according to his moral merit, or needs, or marginal product, or how hard he tries, or the weighted sum of the foregoing, and so on. The principle of entitlement we have sketched is *not* patterned. There is no one natural dimension or weighted sum or combination of a small number of natural dimensions that yields the distributions generated in accordance with the principle of entitlement. The set of holdings that results when some persons receive their marginal products, others win at gambling, others receive a share of their mate's income, others receive gifts from foundations, others receive interest on loans, others receive gifts from admirers, others receive returns on investment, others make for themselves much of what they have, others find things, and so on, will not be patterned. . . .

To think that the task of a theory of distributive justice is to fill in the blank in "to each according to his _____" is to be predisposed to search for a pattern; and the separate treatment of "from each according to his _____" treats production and distribution as two separate and independent issues. On an entitlement view these are *not* two separate questions. Whoever makes something, having bought or contracted for all other held resources used in the process (transferring some of his holdings for these cooperating factors), is entitled to it. . . .

So entrenched are maxims of the usual form that perhaps we should present the entitlement conception as a competitor. Ignoring acquisition and rectification, we might say:

> From each according to what he chooses to do, to each according to what he makes for himself (perhaps with the contracted aid of others) and what others choose to do for him and choose to give him of what they've been given previously (under this maxim) and haven't yet expended or transferred.

This, the discerning reader will have noticed, has its defects as a slogan. So as a summary and great simplification (and not as a maxim with any independent meaning) we have:

From each as they choose, to each as they are chosen.

How Liberty Upsets Patterns

It is not clear how those holding alternative conceptions of distributive justice can reject the entitlement conception of justice in holdings. For suppose a distribution favored by one of these nonentitlement conceptions is realized. Let us suppose it is your favorite one and let us call this distribution D_1; perhaps everyone has an equal share, perhaps shares vary in accordance with some dimension you treasure. Now suppose that Wilt Chamberlain is greatly in demand by basketball teams, being a great gate attraction. (Also suppose contracts run only for a year, with players being free agents.) He signs the following sort of contract with a team: In each home game, 25 cents from the price of each ticket of admission goes to him. (We ignore the question of whether he is "gouging" the owners, letting them look out for themselves.) The season starts, and people cheerfully attend his team's games; they buy their tickets, each time dropping a separate 25 cents of their admission price into a special box with Chamberlain's name on it. They are excited about seeing him play; it is worth the total admission price to them. Let us suppose that in one season 1 million persons attend his home games, and Wilt Chamberlain winds up with $250,000, a much larger sum than the average income and larger even than anyone else has. Is he entitled to this income? Is this new distribution D_2, unjust? If so, why? There is *no* question about whether each of the people was entitled to the control over the resources they held in D_1; because that was the distribution (your favorite) that (for the purposes of argument) we assumed was acceptable. Each of these persons *chose* to give 25 cents of their money to Chamberlain. They could have spent it on going to the movies, or on candy bars, or on copies of *Dissent* magazine, or of *Monthly Review*. But they all, at least 1 million of them, converged on giving it to Wilt Chamberlain in exchange for watching him play basketball. If D_1 was a just distribution, and people voluntarily moved from it to D_2, transferring parts of their shares they were given under D_1 (what was it for if not to do something with?), isn't D_2 also just? If the people were entitled to dispose of the resources to which they were entitled (under D_1) didn't this include their being entitled to give it to, or exchange it with, Wilt Chamberlain? Can anyone else complain on grounds of justice? Each other person already has his legitimate share under D_1. Under D_1, there is nothing that anyone has that anyone else has a claim of justice against. After someone transfers something to Wilt Chamberlain, third parties *still* have their legitimate shares; *their* shares are not changed. By what process could such a transfer among two persons give a rise to a legitimate claim of distributive justice on a portion of what was transferred, by a third party who had no claim of justice on any holding of the others *before* the transfer? To cut off objections irrelevant here, we might imagine the exchanges occurring in a socialist society, after hours. After playing whatever basketball he does in his daily work, or doing whatever other daily work he does, Wilt Chamberlain decides to put in *overtime* to earn additional money. (First his work quota is set; he works time over that.) Or imagine it is a skilled juggler people like to see, who puts on shows after hours. . . .

The general point illustrated by the Wilt Chamberlain example is that no end-state principle or distributional patterned principle of justice can be continuously realized without continuous interference with people's lives. Any favored pattern would be transformed into one unfavored by the principle, by people choosing to act in various ways; for example, by people exchanging goods and services with other people, or giving things to other people, things the transferrers are entitled to under the favored distributional pattern. To maintain a pattern one must either continually interfere to stop people from transferring resources as they wish to, or continually (or periodically) interfere to take from some person's resources that others for some reason chose to transfer to them. . . .

Patterned principles of distributive justice necessitate *re*distributive activities. The likelihood is small that any actual freely arrived-at set of holdings fits a given pattern; and the likelihood is nil that it will continue to fit the pattern as people exchange and give. From the point of view of an entitlement theory, redistribution is a serious matter indeed, involving, as it does, the violation of people's rights. (An exception is those takings that fall under the principle of the rectification of injustices.) . . .

Locke's Theory of Acquisition

. . . [Let us] introduce an additional bit of complexity into the structure of the entitlement theory. This is best approached by considering Locke's attempt to specify a principle of justice in acquisition. Locke views property rights in an unowned object as originating through someone's mixing his labor with it. This gives rise to many questions. What are the boundaries of what labor is mixed with? If a private astronaut clears a place on Mars, has he mixed his labor with (so that he comes to own) the whole planet, the whole uninhabited universe, or just a particular plot? Which plot does an act bring under ownership? . . .

Locke's proviso that there be "enough and as good left in common for others" is meant to ensure that the situation of others is not worsened. . . .

. . . I assume that any adequate theory of justice in acquisition will contain a proviso similar to [Locke's]. . . .

I believe that the free operation of a market system will not actually run afoul of the Lockean proviso. . . . If this is correct, the proviso will not . . . provide a significant opportunity for future state action.

Rich and Poor

PETER SINGER

One way of making sense of the nonconsequentialist view of responsibility is by basing it on a theory of rights of the kind proposed by John Locke or, more recently, Robert Nozick. If everyone has a right to life, and this right is a right *against* others who might threaten my life, but not a right *to* assistance from others when my life is in danger, then we can understand the feeling that we are responsible for acting to kill but not for omitting to save. The former violates the rights of others, the latter does not.

Should we accept such a theory of rights? If we build up our theory of rights by imagining, as Locke and Nozick do, individuals living independently from each other in a "state of nature," it may seem natural to adopt a conception of rights in which as long as each leaves the other alone, no rights are violated. I might, on this view, quite properly have maintained my independent existence if I had wished to do so. So if I do not make you any worse off than you would have been if I had had nothing at all to do with you, how can

I have violated your rights? But why start from such an unhistorical, abstract and ultimately inexplicable idea as an independent individual? We now know that our ancestors were social beings long before they were human beings, and could not have developed the abilities and capacities of human beings if they had not been social beings first. In any case we are not, now, isolated individuals. If we consider people living together in a community, it is less easy to assume that rights must be restricted to rights against interference. We might, instead, adopt the view that taking rights to life seriously is incompatible with standing by and watching people die when one could easily save them. . . .

The Obligation to Assist

The Argument for an Obligation to Assist

The path from the library at my university to the Humanities lecture theatre passes a shallow ornamental pond. Suppose that on my way to give a lecture I notice that a small child has

From Peter Singer, "Rich and Poor," in *Practical Ethics* (Cambridge University Press, 2011), pp. 191–215. © Peter Singer, 1980, 1993, 2011, published by Cambridge University Press. Reprinted with permission of the publisher.

fallen in and is in danger of drowning. Would anyone deny that I ought to wade in and pull the child out? This will mean getting my clothes muddy, and either cancelling my lecture or delaying it until I can find something dry to change into; but compared with the avoidable death of a child this is insignificant.

A plausible principle that would support the judgment that I ought to pull the child out is this: if it is in our power to prevent something very bad happening, without thereby sacrificing anything of comparable moral significance, we ought to do it. This principle seems uncontroversial. It will obviously win the assent of consequentialists; but nonconsequentialists should accept it too, because the injunction to prevent what is bad applies only when nothing comparably significant is at stake. Thus the principle cannot lead to the kinds of actions of which nonconsequentialists strongly disapprove – serious violations of individual rights, injustice, broken promises, and so on. If a nonconsequentialist regards any of these as comparable in moral significance to the bad thing that is to be prevented, he will automatically regard the principle as not applying in those cases in which the bad thing can only be prevented by violating rights, doing injustice, breaking promises, or whatever else is at stake. Most nonconsequentialists hold that we ought to prevent what is bad and promote what is good. Their dispute with consequentialists lies in their insistence that this is not the sole ultimate ethical principle: that it is *an* ethical principle is not denied by any plausible ethical theory.

Nevertheless the uncontroversial appearance of the principle that we ought to prevent what is bad when we can do so without sacrificing anything of comparable moral significance is deceptive. If it were taken seriously and acted upon, our lives and our world would be fundamentally changed. For the principle applies, not just to rare situations in which one can save a child from a pond, but to the everyday situations in which we can assist those living in absolute poverty. In saying this I assume that absolute poverty, with its hunger and malnutrition, lack of shelter, illiteracy, disease, high infant mortality and low life expectancy, is a bad thing. And I assume that it is within the power of the affluent to reduce absolute poverty, without sacrificing anything of comparable moral significance. If these two assumptions and the principle we have been discussing are correct, we have an obligation to help those in absolute poverty which is no less strong than our obligation to rescue a drowning child from a pond. Not to help would be wrong, whether or not it is intrinsically equivalent to killing. Helping is not, as conventionally thought, a charitable act which it is praiseworthy to do, but not wrong to omit; it is something that everyone ought to do.

This is the argument for an obligation to assist. Set out more formally, it would look like this.

First premise: If we can prevent something bad without sacrificing anything of comparable significance, we ought to do it.
Second premise: Absolute poverty is bad.
Third premise: There is some absolute poverty we can prevent without sacrificing anything of comparable moral significance.
Conclusion: We ought to prevent some absolute poverty.

The first premise is the substantive moral premise on which the argument rests, and I have tried to show that it can be accepted by people who hold a variety of ethical positions.

The second premise is unlikely to be challenged. Absolute poverty is, as [Robert] McNamara put it, "beneath any reasonable definition of human decency" and it would be hard to find a plausible ethical view which did not regard it as a bad thing.

The third premise is more controversial, even though it is cautiously framed. It claims only that some absolute poverty can be prevented without the sacrifice of anything of comparable moral significance. It thus avoids the objection that any aid I can give is just "drops in the ocean" for the point is not whether my personal contribution will make any noticeable impression on world poverty as a whole (of course it won't) but whether it will prevent some poverty. This is all the argument needs to sustain its conclusion, since the second premise says that any absolute poverty is bad, and not merely the total amount of absolute poverty. If without sacrificing anything of comparable moral significance we can provide just one family with the means to raise itself out of absolute poverty, the third premise is vindicated.

I have left the notion of moral significance unexamined in order to show that the argument does not depend on any specific values or ethical principles. I think the third premise is true for most people living in industrialized nations, on any defensible view of what is morally significant. Our affluence means that we have income we can dispose of without giving up the basic necessities of life, and we can use this income to reduce absolute poverty. Just how much we will think ourselves obliged to give up will depend on what we consider to be of comparable moral significance to the poverty we could prevent: color television, stylish clothes, expensive dinners, a sophisticated stereo system, overseas holidays, a (second?) car, a larger house, private schools for our children.... For a utilitarian, none of these is likely to be of comparable significance to the reduction of absolute poverty; and those who are not utilitarians surely must, if they subscribe to the principle of universalizability, accept that at least *some* of these things are of far less moral significance than the absolute poverty that could be prevented by the money they cost. So the third premise seems to be true on any plausible ethical view – although the precise amount of absolute poverty that can be prevented before anything of moral significance is sacrificed will vary according to the ethical view one accepts.

Objections to the Argument

Taking Care of Our Own. Anyone who has worked to increase overseas aid will have come across the argument that we should look after those near us, our families and then the poor in our own country, before we think about poverty in distant places.

No doubt we do instinctively prefer to help those who are close to us. Few could stand by and watch a child drown; many can ignore a famine in Africa. But the question is not what we usually do, but what we ought to do, and it is difficult to see any sound moral justification for the view that distance, or community membership, makes a crucial difference to our obligations.

Consider, for instance, racial affinities. Should whites help poor whites before helping poor blacks? Most of us would reject such a suggestion out of hand, [by appeal to] the principle of equal consideration of interests: people's needs for food has nothing to do with their race, and if blacks need food more than whites, it would be a violation of the principle of equal consideration to give preference to whites.

The same point applies to citizenship or nationhood. Every affluent nation has some relatively poor citizens, but absolute poverty is limited largely to the poor nations. Those living on the streets of Calcutta, or in a drought-stricken region of the Sahel, are experiencing poverty unknown in the West. Under these circumstances it would be wrong to decide that only those fortunate enough to be citizens of our own community will share our abundance.

We feel obligations of kinship more strongly than those of citizenship. Which parents could give away their last bowl of rice if their own children were starving? To do so would seem unnatural, contrary to our nature as biologically evolved beings – although whether it would be wrong is another question altogether. In any case, we are not faced with that situation, but with one in which our own children are well fed, well clothed, well educated, and would now like new bikes, a stereo set, or their own car. In these circumstances any special obligations we might have to our children have been fulfilled, and the needs of strangers make a stronger claim upon us.

The element of truth in the view that we should first take care of our own lies in the advantage of a recognized system of responsibilities. When families and local communities look after their own poorer members, ties of affection and personal relationships achieve ends that would otherwise require a large, impersonal bureaucracy. Hence it would be absurd to propose that from now on we all regard ourselves as equally responsible for the welfare of everyone in the world; but the argument for an obligation to assist does not propose that. It applies only when some are in absolute poverty, and others can help without sacrificing anything of comparable moral significance. To allow one's own kin to sink into absolute poverty would be to sacrifice something of comparable significance; and before that point had been reached, the breakdown of the system of family and community responsibility would be a factor to weigh the balance in favor of a small degree of preference for family and community. This small degree of preference is, however, decisively outweighed by existing discrepancies in wealth and property.

Property Rights. Do people have a right to private property, a right which contradicts the view that they are under an obligation to give some of their wealth away to those in absolute poverty? According to some theories of rights (for instance, Robert Nozick's) provided one has acquired one's property without the use of unjust means like force and fraud, one may be entitled to enormous wealth while others starve. This individualistic conception of rights is in contrast to other views, like the early Christian doctrine to be found in the works of Thomas Aquinas, which holds that since property exists for the satisfaction of human needs, "whatever a man has in superabundance is owed, of natural right, to the poor for their sustenance." A socialist would also, of course, see wealth as belonging to the community rather than the individual, while utilitarians, whether socialist or not, would be prepared to override property rights to prevent great evils.

Does the argument for an obligation to assist others therefore presuppose one of these other theories of property rights, and not an individualistic theory like Nozick's? Not necessarily. A theory of property rights can insist on our *right* to retain wealth without pronouncing on whether the rich *ought* to give to the poor. Nozick, for example, rejects the use of compulsory means like taxation to redistribute income, but suggests that we can achieve the ends we deem morally desirable by voluntary means. So Nozick would reject the claim that rich people have an "obligation" to give to the poor, in so far as this implies that the poor have a right to our aid, but might accept that giving is something we ought to do and failure to give, though within one's rights, is wrong – for rights is not all there is to ethics.

The argument for an obligation to assist can survive, with only minor modifications, even if we accept an individualistic theory of property rights. In any case, however, I do not think we should accept such a theory. It leaves too much to chance to be an acceptable ethical view. For instance, those whose forefathers happened to inhabit some sandy wastes around the Persian Gulf are now fabulously wealthy, because oil lay under those sands; while those whose forefathers settled on better land south of the Sahara live in absolute poverty, because of drought and bad harvests. Can this distribution be acceptable from an impartial point of view? If we imagine ourselves about to begin life as a citizen of either Kuwait or Chad – but we do not know which – would we accept the principle that citizens of Kuwait are under no obligation to assist people living in Chad?

Population and the Ethics of Triage. Perhaps the most serious objection to the argument that we have an obligation to assist is that since the major cause of absolute poverty is overpopulation, helping those now in poverty will only ensure that yet more people are born to live in poverty in the future.

In its most extreme form, this objection is taken to show that we should adopt a policy of "triage." The term comes from medical policies adopted in wartime. With too few doctors to cope with all the casualties, the wounded were divided into three categories: those who would probably survive without medical assistance, those who might survive if they received assistance, but otherwise probably would not, and those who even with medical assistance probably would not survive. Only those in the middle category were given medical assistance. The idea, of course, was to use limited medical resources as effectively as possible. For those in the first category, medical treatment was not strictly necessary; for those in the third category, it was likely to be useless. It has been suggested that we should apply the same policies to countries, according to their prospects of becoming self-sustaining. We would not aid countries which even without our help will soon be able to feed their populations. We would not aid countries which, even with our help, will not be able to limit their population to a level they can feed. We would aid those countries where our help might make the difference between success and failure in bringing food and population into balance.

Advocates of this theory are understandably reluctant to give a complete list of the countries they would place into the "hopeless" category; but Bangladesh is often cited as an example. Adopting the policy of triage would, then, mean cutting off assistance to Bangladesh and allowing famine, disease and natural disasters to reduce the population of that country (now around 80 million) to the level at which it can provide adequately for all.

In support of this view Garrett Hardin has offered a metaphor: we in the rich nations are like the occupants of a crowded lifeboat adrift in a sea full of drowning people. If we try to save the drowning by bringing them aboard our boat will be overloaded and we shall all drown. Since it is better that some survive than none, we should leave the others to drown. In the world today, according to Hardin, "lifeboat ethics" apply. The rich should leave the poor to starve, for otherwise the poor will drag the rich down with them. . . .

Anyone whose initial reaction to triage was not one of repugnance would be an unpleasant sort of person. Yet initial reactions based on strong feelings are not always reliable guides. Advocates of triage are rightly concerned with the long-term consequences of our actions. They say that helping the poor and starving now merely ensures more poor and starving in the future. When our capacity to help is finally unable to cope – as one day it must be – the suffering will be greater than it would be if we stopped helping now. If this is correct, there is nothing we can do to prevent absolute starvation and poverty, in the long run, and so we have no obligation to assist. Nor does it seem reasonable to hold that under these circumstances people have a right to our assistance. If we do accept such a right, irrespective of the consequences, we are saying that, in Hardin's metaphor, we would continue to haul the drowning into our lifeboat until the boat sank and we all drowned.

If triage is to be rejected it must be tackled on its own ground, within the framework of consequentialist ethics. Here it is vulnerable. Any consequentialist ethics must take probability of outcome into account. A course of action that will certainly produce some benefit is to be preferred to an alternative course that may lead to a slightly larger benefit, but is equally likely to result in no benefit at all. Only if the greater magnitude of the uncertain benefit outweighs its uncertainty should we choose it. Better one certain unit of benefit than a 10 percent chance of 5 units; but better a 50 percent chance of 3 units than a single certain unit. The same principle applies when are we trying to avoid evils.

The policy of triage involves a certain, very great evil: population control by famine and disease. Tens of millions would die slowly. Hundreds of millions would continue to live in absolute poverty, at the very margin of existence. Against this prospect, advocates of the policy place a possible evil which is greater still: the same process of famine and disease, taking place in, say, 50 years' time, when the world's population may be three times its present level, and the number who will die from famine, or struggle on in absolute poverty, will be that much greater. The question is: How probable is this forecast that continued assistance now will lead to greater disasters in the future?

Forecasts of population growth are notoriously fallible, and theories about the factors which affect it remain speculative. One theory, at least as plausible as any other, is that countries pass through a "demographic transition" as their standard of living rises. When people are very poor and have no access to modern medicine their fertility is high, but population is kept in check by high death rates. The introduction of sanitation, modern medical techniques and other improvements reduces the death rate, but initially has little effect on the birth rate. Then population grows rapidly. Most poor countries are now in this phase. If standards of living continue to rise, however, couples begin to realize that to have the same number of children surviving to maturity as in the past, they do not need to give birth to as many children as their parents did. The need for children to provide economic support in old age diminishes. Improved education and the emancipation and employment of women also reduce the birth rate, and so population growth begins to level off. Most rich nations have reached this stage, and their populations are growing only very slowly.

If this theory is right, there is an alternative to the disasters accepted as inevitable by supporters of triage. We can assist poor countries to raise the living standards of the poorest members of their population. We can encourage the governments of these countries to enact land reform measures, improve education, and liberate women from a purely childbearing role. We can also help other countries to make contraception and sterilization widely available. There is a fair chance that these measures will hasten the onset of the demographic transition and bring population growth down to a manageable level. Success cannot be guaranteed; but the evidence that improved economic security and education reduce population growth is strong enough to make triage ethically unacceptable. We cannot allow millions to die from starvation and disease when there is a reasonable probability that population can be brought under control without such horrors.

Population growth is therefore not a reason against giving overseas aid, although it should make us think about the kind of aid to give. Instead of food handouts, it may be better to give aid that hastens the demographic transition. This may mean agricultural assistance for the rural poor, or assistance with education, or the provision of contraceptive services. Whatever kind of aid proves most effective in specific circumstances, the obligation to assist is not reduced.

One awkward question remains. What should we do about a poor and already overpopulated country which, for religious or nationalistic reasons, restricts the use of contraceptives and refuses to slow its population growth? Should we nevertheless offer development assistance? Or should we make our offer conditional on effective steps being taken to reduce the birth rate? To the latter course, some would object that putting conditions on aid is an attempt to impose our own ideas on independent sovereign nations. So it is – but is this imposition unjustifiable? If the argument for an obligation to assist is sound, we have an obligation to reduce absolute poverty; but we have no obligation to make sacrifices that, to the best of our knowledge, have no prospect of reducing poverty in the long run. Hence we have no obligation to assist countries whose governments have policies which will make our aid ineffective. This could be very harsh on poor citizens of these countries – for they may have no say in the government's policies – but we will help more people in the long run by using our resources where they are most effective.

Freedom and the Foundations of Justice

AMARTYA SEN

Let me begin with a parable. Annapurna wants someone to clear up the garden, which has suffered from past neglect, and three unemployed laborers – Dinu, Bishanno, and Rogini – all very much want the job. She can hire any one of them, but the work is indivisible and she cannot distribute it among the three. Annapurna would get much the same work done for much the same payment from any of them, but being a reflective

From Amartya Sen, *Development as Freedom* (New York: Anchor Books, 1999), pp. 54–55, 74–77. Used by permission of Alfred A. Knopf, an imprint of the Knopf Doubleday Publishing Group, a division of Penguin Random House LLC. All rights reserved.

person, she wonders who would be the right person to employ.

She gathers that while all of them are poor, Dinu is the poorest of the three; everyone agrees on that fact. This makes Annapurna rather inclined to hire him ("What can be more important," she asks herself, "than helping the poorest?").

However, she also gathers that Bishanno has recently been impoverished and is psychologically most depressed about his predicament. Dinu and Rogini are, in contrast, experienced in being poor and are used to it. Everyone agrees that Bishanno is the unhappiest of the three and would certainly gain more in happiness than the other two. This makes Annapurna rather favorable to the idea of giving the job to Bishanno ("Surely removing unhappiness has to be," she tells herself, "the first priority").

But Annapurna is also told that Rogini is debilitated from a chronic ailment – borne stoically – and could use the money to be earned to rid herself of that terrible disease. It is not denied that Rogini is less poor than the others (though certainly poor) and also not the unhappiest since she bears her deprivation rather cheerfully, used – as she has been – to being deprived all her life (coming from a poor family, and having been trained to reconcile herself to the general belief that, as a young woman, she must neither grumble nor entertain much ambition). Annapurna wonders whether, nevertheless, it might not be right to give the job to Rogini ("It would make the biggest difference," she surmises, "to the quality of life and freedom from illness").

Annapurna wonders what she really should do. She recognizes that if she knew only the fact that Dinu is the poorest (and knew nothing else), she would have definitely opted for giving the work to Dinu. She also reflects that had she known only the fact that Bishanno is the unhappiest and would get the most pleasure from the opportunity (and knew nothing else), she would have had excellent reasons to hire Bishanno. And she can also see that if she was apprised only of the fact that Rogini's debilitating ailment could be cured with the money she would earn (and knew nothing else), she would have had a simple and definitive reason for giving the job to her. But she knows all the three relevant facts, and has to choose among the three arguments, each of which has some pertinence.

There are a number of interesting issues of practical reason in this simple example, but the point I want to emphasize here is that the differences in the principles involved relate to the particular information that is taken to be decisive. If all the three facts are known, the decision rests on which information is given the most weight. The principles thus can best be seen in terms of their respective "informational bases." Dinu's income-egalitarian case focuses on income poverty; Bishanno's classical utilitarian case concentrates on the metric of pleasure and happiness; Rogini's quality-of-life case centers on the kinds of life the three respectively can lead. The first two arguments are among the most discussed and most used in the economic and ethical literatures. I shall present some arguments for the third.

Well-Being, Freedom, and Capability

I have tried to argue for some time now that for many evaluative purposes, the appropriate "space" is neither that of utilities (as claimed by welfarists), nor that of primary goods (as demanded by Rawls), but that of the substantive freedoms – the capabilities – to choose a life one has reason to value.[1] If the object is to concentrate on the individual's real opportunity, to pursue her objectives (as Rawls explicitly recommends), then account would have to be taken not only of the primary goods the persons respectively hold, but also of the relevant personal characteristics that govern the *conversion* of primary goods into the person's ability to promote her ends. For example, a person who is disabled may have a larger basket of primary goods and yet have less chance to lead a normal life (or to pursue her objectives) than an able-bodied person with a smaller basket of primary goods. Similarly, an older person or a person more prone to illness can be more disadvantaged in a generally accepted sense even with a larger bundle of primary goods.

The concept of "functionings," which has distinctly Aristotelian roots, reflects the various things a person may value doing or being. The valued functionings may vary from elementary ones, such as being adequately nourished and being free from avoidable disease, to very complex activities or personal states, such as being able to take part in the life of the community and having self-respect.

A person's "capability" refers to the alternative combinations of functionings that are feasible for her to achieve. Capability is thus a kind of freedom: the substantive freedom to achieve alternative functioning combinations (or, less formally put, the freedom to achieve various lifestyles). For example, an affluent person who fasts may have the same functioning achievement in terms of eating or nourishment as a destitute person who is forced to starve, but the first person does have a different "capability set" than the second (the first *can* choose to eat well and be well nourished in a way the second cannot).

This is not the occasion to go much into the technicalities of representation and analysis of functionings and capabilities. The amount or the extent of each functioning enjoyed by a person may be represented by a real number, and when this is done, a person's actual achievement can be seen as a *functioning vector.* The "capability set" would consist of the alternative functioning vectors that she can choose from. While the combination of a person's functionings reflects her actual *achievements*, the capability set represents the *freedom* to achieve: the alternative functioning combinations from which this person can choose.

The evaluative focus of this "capability approach" can be either on the *realized* functionings (what a person is actually able to do) or on the *capability set* of alternatives she has (her real opportunities). The two give different types of information – the former about the things a person does and the latter about the things a person is substantively free to do. Both versions of the capability approach have been used in the literature, and sometimes they have been combined.

According to a well-established tradition in economics, the real value of a set of options lies in the best use that can be made of them, and – given maximum behavior and the absence of uncertainty – the use that is *actually* made. The use value of the opportunity, then, lies derivatively on the value of the one element of it (to wit, the best option or the actually chosen option).[2] In this case, the focusing on a *chosen functioning vector* coincides with concentration on the *capability set*, since the latter is judged, ultimately, by the former. . . .

Individual functionings can lend themselves to easier interpersonal comparison than comparisons of utilities (or happiness, pleasures, or desires). Also, many of the relevant functionings – typically the non-mental characteristics – can be seen distinctly from their mental assessment. The variability in the conversion of means into ends (or into freedom to pursue ends) is already reflected in the extents of those achievements and freedoms that may figure in the list of ends. These are advantages in using the capability perspective for evaluation and assessment.

However, interpersonal comparisons of *overall* advantages also require "aggregation" over heterogeneous components. The capability perspective is inescapably pluralist. First, there are different functionings, some more important than others. Second, there is the issue of what weight to attach to substantive freedom (the capability set) vis-à-vis the actual achievement (the chosen functioning vector). Finally, since it is not claimed that the capability perspective exhausts all relevant concerns for evaluative purposes (we might, for example, attach importance to rules and procedures and not just to freedoms and outcomes), there is the underlying issue of how much weight should be placed on the capabilities, compared with any other relevant consideration.

Is this plurality an embarrassment for advocacy of the capability perspective for evaluative purposes? Quite the contrary. To insist that there should be only one homogeneous magnitude that we value is to reduce drastically the range of our evaluative reasoning. It is not, for example, to the credit of classical utilitarianism that it values only pleasure, without taking any direct interest in freedom, rights, creativity, or actual living conditions. To insist on the mechanical comfort of having just one homogeneous "good thing" would be to deny our humanity as reasoning creatures. It is like seeking to make the life of the chef easier by finding something which – and which *alone* – we all like (such as smoked salmon, or perhaps even French fries), or some one quality which we must all try to maximize (such as the saltiness of the food). . . .

Notes

1. See my " Equality of What?" in *Tanner Lectures on Human Values*, vol. I, ed. S. McMurrin (Cambridge University Press, 1982; Salt Lake City: University of Utah Press); reprinted in my *Choice, Welfare and Measurement* (Cambridge, MA: MIT Press, 1982); also in John Rawls, Charles Fried, Amartya Sen, and Thomas C. Schelling, *Liberty, Equality and Law*, ed. S. McMurrin (Cambridge University Press; Salt Lake City: University of Utah Press, 1987), and in Stephen Darwall, ed., *Equal Freedom: Selected Tanner Lectures on Human Values* (Ann Arbor: University of Michigan Press, 1995). See also my "Public Action and the Quality of Life in Developing Countries," *Oxford Bulletin of Economics and Statistics* 43 (1981): 287–319; *Commodities and Capabilities* (Amsterdam: North-Holland, 1985); "Well-Being, Agency and Freedom," *Journal of Philosophy* 82 (1985): 169–221; (jointly with Jean Dreze) *Hunger and Public Action* (Oxford: Clarendon Press, 1989); and "Capability and Well-Being," in *The Quality of Life*, ed. Martha Nussbaum and Amartya Sen (Oxford: Clarendon Press, 1993).

2. This approach is called "elementary evaluation" of the capability set; the nature and scope of elementary evaluation is discussed in my *Commodities and Capabilities*. See also G. A. Cohen's argument for what he calls "midfare," in "On the Currency of Egalitarian Justice," *Ethics* 99 (1989): 906–44; "Equality of What? On Welfare, Goods and Capabilities," *Louvain Economic Review* 56 (1990): 357–82; and *Self-Ownership, Freedom, and Equality* (Cambridge University Press, 1995). See Richard Arneson, "Equality and Equality of Opportunity for Welfare," *Philosophical Studies* 56 (1989): 77–93, and "Liberalism, Distributive Subjectivism, and Equal Opportunity for Welfare," *Philosophy and Public Affairs* 19 (1990): 158–94.

11.3 GLOBAL JUSTICE

Why Globalization Works

MARTIN WOLF

Globalization has dramatically increased inequality between and within nations, even as it connects people as never before. A world in which the assets of the 200 richest people are greater than the combined income of the more than 2 billion people at the other end of the economic ladder should give everyone pause.

> Jay Mazur, president of the Union of Needletrades, Industrial and Textile Employees.[1]

Jay Mazur is not alone. Ignacio Ramonet has written on similar lines, in *Le Monde Diplomatique*, that:

the dramatic advance of globalization and neoliberalism ... has been accompanied by an *explosive growth in inequality* and a return of mass poverty and unemployment. The very opposite of everything which the modern state and modern citizenship is supposed to stand for.

The net result is a *massive growth in inequality*. The United States, which is the richest country in the world, has more than 60 million poor. The world's foremost trading power, the European Union, has over 50 million. In the United States, 1 percent of the population owns 39 percent of the country's wealth. Taking the planet as a whole, the combined wealth of the 358 richest people (all of them dollar billionaires) is greater than the total annual income of 45 percent of the world's poorest inhabitants, that is, 2.6 billion people.[2]

Let us, for a moment, ignore the assumption that the number of poor (how defined?) in two of the richest regions in the world tells one anything about global inequality, or about poverty for that matter, or even about inequality within the United States and the European Union. Let us also ignore the comparison between the *assets* of one group of people, the richest, and the *incomes* of another, the poor, which is a comparison of apples and oranges. (In order to obtain the permanent incomes of the rich, one would need to divide the value of their assets by at least 20.) These absurdities merely make Ramonet's diatribe representative of the empty rhetoric of many critics of globalization. But the questions that underlie his remarks need to be tackled.

Here are seven propositions that can be advanced about what has happened in the age of so-called neoliberal globalization over the past two decades.

First, the ratio of average incomes in the richest countries to those in the poorest has continued to rise.

Second, the absolute gap in living standards between today's high-income countries and most developing countries has also continued to rise.

Third, global inequality among individuals has risen.

Fourth, the number of people in extreme poverty has risen.

Fifth, the proportion of people in extreme poverty in the world's population has also risen.

Sixth, the poor of the world are worse off not just in terms of incomes, but in terms of a wide range of other indicators of human welfare.

Seventh, income inequality has risen in every country and particularly in countries most exposed to international economic integration.

In the rest of this essay I will consider what we know about these propositions and how the answers relate to international economic integration. Before examining them, however, we need to ask what matters to us. Most of the debate has been either about whether inequality has risen between the world's rich and poor or about whether the number of people in income poverty has risen. But critics of globalization have themselves often rightly argued that there is more to life than income. What is most important must be the living standards of the poor, not just in terms of their incomes, narrowly defined, but in terms of their health, life expectancy, nourishment, and education.

Equally, we need to understand that rises in inequality might occur in very different ways. Three possibilities come to mind at once; a rise in the incomes of the better off, at the expense of the poor; a rise in the incomes of the better off, with no effects on the welfare of the poor; or rises in incomes of the better off that, in various ways, benefit the poor, but not by proportionately as much as they benefit the better off. It seems clear that the first of these is malign, the second desirable, unless the welfare of the better off counts for

From Martin Wolf, *Why Globalization Works* (New Haven: Yale University Press, 2004). Reprinted with permission of Yale University Press.

nothing, and the third unambiguously desirable, though one might wish more of the gains to accrue to the poor. True egalitarians would differ on these judgments, of course. Indeed, an extreme egalitarian might take the view that a world in which everybody was an impoverished subsistence farmer would be better than the world we now have, because it would be less unequal. Most people – including, I imagine, many protestors against globalization – would regard this as crazy. Few are that egalitarian. Most people are not even as egalitarian as the late philosopher John Rawls, who argued that inequality was permissible only to the extent that it benefited the poor.

We need to be equally careful in considering the role of globalization in relation to inequality and poverty. International economic integration may affect global inequality in several different ways. Here are a few possibilities: it may increase inequality by lowering the incomes of the poor; it may raise the incomes of the better off, without having any impact on the incomes of the poor; it may raise the incomes of the poor by proportionately less than it raises the incomes of the better off; or it may raise the incomes of the poor by proportionately more than it raises those of the better off. Only the first is unambiguously bad, but all of the first three would be associated with increasing inequality. Yet both of the last two mean higher living standards for the poor.

Again, it may not be globalization, as such, that delivers these outcomes, but a combination of globalization with nonglobalization. Globalization may raise incomes of globalizers, while nonglobalization lowers the incomes of nonglobalizers. Then an era of globalization may be associated with rising inequality that is caused not by globalization, but by its opposite, the refusal (or inability) of some countries to participate.

The most important questions to bear in mind in the discussions below are, therefore, these. Is human welfare, broadly defined, rising? Is the proportion of humanity living in desperate misery declining? If inequality is rising, are the rich profiting at the expense of the poor? Is globalization damaging the poor or is it rather nonglobalization that is doing so? To answer all these questions, one must start at the beginning, with economic growth.

Economic Growth and Globalization

In the mid-1970s I was the World Bank's senior divisional economist on India during the country's worst post-independence decade. After a spurt of growth in the early phase of its inward-looking development, growth in incomes per head had ground virtually to a halt. Hundreds of millions of people seemed, as a result, to be mired in

hopeless and unending poverty. In a book published in 1968, a well-known environmentalist doomsayer, Paul Ehrlich, had written the country off altogether.[3] For a young man from the UK, work in India as an economist was both fascinating and appalling: so much poverty; so much frustration; so much complacency. Yet I was convinced then, as I am now, that, with perfectly feasible policy changes, this vast country could generate rapid rates of economic growth and reductions in poverty. No iron law imposed levels of real output (and so real incomes) per head at only 10 percent of those in high-income countries.

Since those unhappy days, India has enjoyed the fruit of two revolutions: the green revolution, which transformed agricultural productivity; and a liberalizing revolution, which began, haltingly, under Rajiv Gandhi's leadership, in the 1980s and then took a "great leap forward" in 1991, in response to a severe foreign exchange crisis, under the direction of one of the country's most remarkable public servants, Manmohan Singh, the then finance minister. Slowly, India abandoned the absurdities of its pseudo-Stalinist "control raj" in favor of individual enterprise and the market. As a result, between 1980 and 2000, India's real GDP per head more than doubled. Stagnation has become a thing of the past.

India was not alone. On the contrary, it was far behind a still more dynamic and even bigger liberalizing country – China, which achieved a rise in real incomes per head of well over 400 percent between 1980 and 2000. China and India, it should be remembered, contain almost two-fifths of the world's population. China alone contains more people than Latin America and sub-Saharan Africa together. Many other countries in East and South Asia have also experienced rapid growth. According to the 2003 Human Development Report from the United Nations Development Programme, between 1975 and 2001, GDP per head rose at 5.9 percent a year in East Asian developing countries (with 31 percent of the world's population in 2000). The corresponding figure for growth of GDP per head for South Asia (with another 22 percent of the world's population) was 2.4 percent a year. Between 1990 and 2001, GDP per head rose at 5.5 percent a year in East Asia, while growth rose to 3.2 percent a year in South Asia.

Never before have so many people – or so large a proportion of the world's population – enjoyed such large rises in their standards of living. Meanwhile, GDP per head in high-income countries (with 15 percent of the world's population) rose by 2.1 percent a year between 1975 and 2001 and by only 1.7 percent a year between 1990 and 2001. This then was a period of partial convergence: the incomes of poor developing countries, with more than half the world's population, grew substantially faster than those of the world's richest countries.

This, in a nutshell, is why Mazur and the many people who think like him are wrong. Globalization has not increased inequality. It has reduced it, just as it has reduced the incidence of poverty. How can this be, critics will demand? Are absolute and proportional gaps in living standards between the world's richest and poorest countries not rising all the time? Yes is the answer. And is inequality not rising in most of the world's big countries? Yes, is again the answer. So how can global inequality be falling? To adapt Bill Clinton's campaign slogan, it is the growth, stupid. Rapid economic growth in poor countries with half the world's population has powerful effects on the only sort of inequality which matters, that among individuals. It has similarly dramatic effects on world poverty. . . .

What, the reader may ask, has this progress to do with international economic integration? In its analysis of globalization, published in 2002, the World Bank divided 73 developing countries, with aggregate population, in 1997, of 4 billion (80 percent of all people in developing countries), into two groups: the third that had increased ratios of trade to GDP, since 1980, by the largest amount and the rest.[4] The former group, with an aggregate population of 2.9 billion, managed a remarkable combined increase of 104 percent in the ratio of trade to GDP. Over the same period, the increase in the trade ratio of the high-income countries was 71 percent, while the "less globalized" two-thirds of countries in the sample of developing countries experienced a decline in their trade ratios.

The average incomes per head of these 24 globalizing countries rose by 67 percent (a compound rate of 3.1 percent a year) between 1980 and 1997. In contrast, the other 49 countries managed a rise of only 10 percent (a compound rate of 0.5 percent a year) in incomes per head over this period. . . .

What then do we learn from the success of the countries picked out as globalizers by the World Bank? We can say, with confidence, that the notion that international economic integration necessarily makes the rich richer and the poor poorer is nonsense. Here is a wide range of countries that increased their integration with the world economy and prospered, in some cases dramatically so. A subtler question is precisely what policies relatively successful developing countries have followed. Critics are right to argue that success has not required adoption of the full range of so-called neoliberal policies – privatization, free trade, and capital-account liberalization. But, in insisting upon this point, critics are willfully mistaking individual policy trees for the market-oriented forest. What the successful countries all

share is a move toward the market economy, one in which private property rights, free enterprise, and competition increasingly took the place of state ownership, planning, and protection. They chose, however haltingly, the path of economic liberalization and international integration. This is the heart of the matter. All else is commentary. . . .

Growth and Inequality

Now what does the performance of those who have succeeded in growing through economic integration mean for inequality? Inequality is a measure of relative incomes. If the average real incomes of poor countries containing at least half of the world's population have been rising faster than those of the relatively rich, inequality among countries, weighted by population, will have fallen. This will be true even if the ratio of the incomes of the world's richest to the world's poorest countries and the absolute gaps in average incomes per head between rich countries and almost all developing countries have risen (as they have).

These two points may need a little explanation. First, compare, say, the United States with China. Between 1980 and 2000, according to the World Bank, Chinese average real incomes rose by about 440 per cent. Over the same period, US average real incomes per head rose by about 60 percent. The ratio of Chinese real incomes per head, at purchasing power parity, to those of the United States rose, accordingly, from just over 3 percent in 1980 to just under 12 percent in 2000. This is a big reduction in relative inequality. But the absolute gap in real incomes between China and the United States rose from $20,600 to $30,200 per head (at PPP). The reason is simple: since China's standard of living was, initially, about a thirtieth of that of the United States, the absolute gap could have remained constant only if China's growth had been 30 times faster than that of the United States. That would have been impossible. If China continues to grow faster than the United States, however, absolute gaps will ultimately fall, as happened with Japan in the 1960s and 1970s.

Second, while the *ratio* of the average incomes per head in the richest country to those in the world's least successful countries is rising all the time, the *proportion* of the world's population living in the world's poorest countries has, happily, been falling. Thirty years ago, China and India were among the world's poorest countries. Today, the poorest seems to be Sierra Leone, a country with a population of only 5 million. China's average real income per head is now some ten times higher than Sierra Leone's. The largest very poor country today is Nigeria, with a population of 127 million in 2000 and a real income, at PPP, just a fortieth of that of the United States (and a fifth of China's). Again, this means that rising ratios between the average incomes of the world's richest and poorest countries are consistent with declining inequality among countries, weighted by their populations. Moreover, it is also perfectly possible for inequality to have risen in every single country in the world (as Mazur alleges, wrongly) while global inequality has fallen. Unless the increase in inequality among individuals within countries offsets the reduction in population-weighted inequality among countries, not only inequality among (population-weighted) countries, but also inequality among individuals will have declined. . . .

Growth and Poverty

On all measures, global inequality rose until about the early 1980s. Since then, it appears, inequality among individuals has declined as a result of the rapid growth of much of Asia and, above all, China. But it is also important to understand what drove the long-term trend toward global inequality over almost two centuries. It is the consequence of the dynamic growth that spread, unevenly, from the UK in the course of the nineteenth and twentieth centuries. In the process a growing number of people became vastly better off than any one had ever been before, but few can have become worse off. Such dynamic growth is bound to be uneven. Some regions of the world proved better able to take advantage of the new opportunities for growth, because of superior climates, resources and policies. In just the same way, some parts of countries, particularly huge countries such as China or India, are today better able to take advantage of new opportunities than others. To bemoan the resulting increase in inequality is to bemoan the growth itself. It is to argue that it would be better for everybody to be equally poor than for some to become significantly better off, even if, in the long run, this will almost certainly lead to advances for everybody.

For this reason, it makes more sense to focus on what has happened to poverty than to inequality. Again, the statistical debate is a vexed one. But some plausible conclusions can be reached.

The World Bank has, for some time, defined extreme poverty as an income of a dollar a day at 1985 international prices (PPP). Bourguignon and Morrison also used that figure in an analysis of extreme poverty since 1820, on the same lines as their analysis of inequality.[5] It comes to three intriguing conclusions. First, the number of desperately poor people rose from about 900 million in 1820 to a peak of from 1.3 to 1.4 billion between 1960 and 1980, before falling, modestly, to just under 1.3 billion in 1992. Second, the proportion of the world's population living on less than a dollar a day fell dramatically, over time, from over 80

percent in 1820, a time when living on the margins of subsistence was the norm, to about two-thirds at the beginning of the twentieth century, to close to 50 percent by 1950, then 32 percent in 1980 and, finally, 24 percent by 1992. The contrast between rising numbers and falling proportions of the world's population in extreme poverty reflects the race between higher output and rising population, particularly in poor countries. In 1820, the world's population was a little over a billion. By 1910 it was 1.7 billion and by 1992 it had risen to 5.5 billion.

Again, the results from Bourguignon and Morrison are cause for qualified optimism. From being universal, extreme poverty has become, if not rare, the affliction of less than a quarter of a vastly increased human population. . . .

Professors Thomas Pogge and Sanjay Reddy, also of Columbia University, like Professor Sala-I-Martin, argue that the Bank's numbers, if not necessarily too optimistic, are unsoundly based. They suggest, in particular, that this admittedly heroic attempt to compare poverty across the globe with the use of one measuring rod ($1.08 a day at PPP, in 1993 prices) is fundamentally flawed, in three ways. First, the international poverty line used by the Bank "fails to meet elementary requirements of consistency." As a result, "the Bank's poverty line leads to meaningless poverty estimates." Second, "the Bank's poverty line is not anchored in any assessment of the basic resource requirements of human beings." And third, "the poverty estimates currently available are subject to massive uncertainties because of their sensitivity to the values of crucial parameters that are estimated on the basis of limited data or none at all."[6]

Let us grant most of this. It is evident that converting national data with PPP exchange rates that are themselves both averages for economies and variable from year to year is a rough-and-ready procedure, to put it mildly. Equally, the dollar-a-day line is both inherently arbitrary and bound to mean different things in different countries. It is also true, as Pogge and Reddy argue, that PPP adjustments, which are largely for the relative price of nontradable services, will create large, and growing, mismeasurement of the real incomes of the poor, since the latter consume commodities more intensively than the better off. That could well justify higher poverty lines. At the same time, it might mean that the rate of decline in poverty is higher than estimated by the Bank, since relative prices of commodities normally fall in fast-growing countries.

The big question, however, is whether it would be easy to do better. Pogge and Reddy suggest that the exercise should be conducted in terms not of arbitrary levels of income, but of capabilities – "calories and essential nutrients." They argue that "the income persons need to avoid poverty at some particular time and place can then be specified in terms of the least expensive locally available set of commodities containing the relevant characteristics needed to achieve the elementary human capabilities."[7] This sounds straightforward. In fact, long experience suggests that reaching agreement on such poverty levels across countries is nigh on impossible.

Pogge and Reddy provide a warning. All poverty estimates are inherently arbitrary. Certainly, there is no good reason to believe in anybody's estimates of the levels of poverty at any moment. Trends are another matter. It is certain that the share of those in extreme (absolute, as opposed to relative) income poverty in the world's population has fallen enormously over the last two centuries, a decline that has, equally certainly, continued since 1980. It is almost equally certain that the numbers in extreme income poverty fell in East Asia over the past few decades and particularly over the past two. That is likely, though less certain, for India. Encouragingly, both China and India show enormous declines in estimates of numbers in extreme poverty on their different national measures (about 100 million for India, between 1980 and 2000, and 220 million for China, between 1978 and 1999, despite large increases in population in both countries over this period). Given these changes in East and South Asia, it is plausible, though not certain, that numbers in absolute income poverty declined worldwide. What is more than merely plausible is the proposition that, where numbers in extreme poverty have declined, the cause has been accelerated growth. This is as true of regions within countries (especially where mobility is hindered, as in China) as among them.

Poverty and Human Welfare

In the absence of any of the internationally comparable measures of capabilities that Pogge and Reddy call for, one has to look at other supporting evidence. It is here that we find unambiguous good news. For it is clear that human welfare has improved greatly in recent decades.[8] As an independent analyst, Indur Goklany, persuasively argues, it is possible, in addition, for people to enjoy better health and longer lives, at lower incomes, than before.[9] This is the result of technological and organizational improvements that have come from the world's rich countries. In 1913, life expectancy at birth in the United States was 52 years. US GDP per head, at PPP, was then about 50 percent higher than China's would be in 2000, and 150 percent higher than India's. Yet, in 2000, life expectancy in China was 70 and in India 63. In 1900, Sweden seems to have had the world's highest life expectancy, at 56. In 2000, only very poor countries, mostly in Africa, had life

expectancy as low as (or lower than) this. As Goklany shows, the curve relating life expectancy to average GDP per head has shifted upward over time. Similarly, the curve relating infant mortality to incomes has shifted downward over time. Much the same desirable pattern can be observed for the relationship between other indicators of human welfare and income.

In the developing world as a whole, life expectancy rose by 4 months each year after 1970, from 55 years in 1970 to 64 years in 2000. It rose from 49 in 1970 to 62 in South Asia and from 59 to 69 in East Asia. Tragically, life expectancy fell in 32 countries in the 1990s, mostly because of the AIDS epidemic, or the gross incompetence (or worse) of governments, as in North Korea and Zimbabwe. It also fell because of Western hysteria about DDT, which removed the only effective way of controlling that dreadful curse, malaria. Improvements in life expectancy have meant a decline in global inequality as well. In 1950, average life expectancy in developing countries was two-thirds of the levels in high-income countries (44 and 66 years of age, respectively). By 2000, it was 82 percent (64 and 78).

Meanwhile, in the developing world as a whole, infant mortality rates have fallen from 107 per thousand in 1970 to 87 in 1980 and 58 in 2000. In East Asia, the region with the fastest-growing economy, they have fallen from 56 in 1980 to 35 in 2000. In South Asia, infant mortality fell from 119 in 1980 to 73 in 2000. In sub-Saharan Africa progress was, once again, slower. But infant mortality fell even there, from 116 in 1980 to 91 in 2000.

Losing a child must inflict the sharpest grief human beings can suffer. The decline in infant mortality is thus a tremendous blessing in itself. So, too, is the rise in life expectancy. But these improvements also mean that it makes sense to invest in education. The world increasingly produces smaller families with much better-educated children. On average, adult literacy in developing countries rose from 53 percent in 1970 to 74 percent in 1998. By 2000, adult male illiteracy was down to 8 percent in East Asia, though it was still 30 percent in sub-Saharan Africa and (a real scandal this) 34 percent in South Asia. Adult female illiteracy was more widespread than that for men, but was also improving. Between 1990 and 2000, female illiteracy fell from 29 percent to 21 percent in East Asia. In South Asia, it fell from 66 percent to 57 percent (an even worse scandal than the low rate for men), while in sub-Saharan Africa it fell from 60 to 47 percent. Illiteracy is much lower among the young. This guarantees that rates will continue to fall, as time passes.

The reduction in fertility rates has also been remarkable. In the developing world as a whole, births per woman (the fertility rate) have fallen from 4.1 in 1980 to 2.8 in 2000. In

East Asia, the fertility rate, down from 3.0 to 2.1, is already at close to the replacement rate. In Latin America, the fertility rate has fallen from 4.1 to 2.6. Even in South Asia it has fallen from 5.3 in 1980 to 3.3 in 2000. Again, progress has been slowest in sub-Saharan Africa, where the birth rate has only fallen from 6.6 in 1980 to 5.2 in 2000. But, in all, these reductions tell us of improved control by women of their fertility, of fewer children with more parental investment in each and of far stronger confidence that children will survive to maturity. The demographic transition that is now under way in the developing world is immensely encouraging. It is also an indication – as well as a source – of rising welfare.

Now, let us look at hunger. Growth in food production has substantially outpaced that of population. Between 1961 and 1999, the average daily food supply per person increased 24 percent globally. In developing countries, it rose by 39 percent, to 2,684 calories. By 1999, China's average daily food supply had gone up 82 percent, to 3,044 calories, from a barely subsistence level of 1,636 in 1961. India's went up by 48 percent to 2,417 calories, from 1,635 calories in 1950–51. According to estimates by the United Nations Food and Agricultural Organization, the average active adult needs between 2,000 and 2,310 calories per person. Thus the developing-country food supply has gone, on average, from inadequate to adequate. Hunger persists. But the FAO estimates that the number of people suffering from chronic undernourishment fell from 920 million in 1969–71 to 790 million in 1997–99, or from 35 to 17 percent of the population of developing countries. Trends in sub-Saharan Africa, the continent that did not grow, were far worse. Between 1979–81 and 1997–99, the share of the population that was undernourished declined from 38 to 34 percent, but absolute numbers, in a rapidly growing population, rose from 168 million to 194 million.

Now, turn to what has become one of the most controversial indicators: child labor. One would expect that more prosperous parents, with fewer children, who are also expected to live longer, would wish to see their children being educated rather than at work. So, happily, it has proved. The proportion of children aged 10 to 14 in the labor force has, according to the World Bank, fallen from 23 percent in all developing countries in 1980 to 12 percent in 2000. The fall in East Asia has, once again, been astonishing, from 26 to 8 percent. In South Asia, it has fallen from 23 to 15 percent. In sub-Saharan Africa, the decline has been less impressive, from 35 to 29 percent. China's transformation has been breathtaking, with a fall from 30 percent in 1980 to just 8 percent in 2000. In lagging India, the fall was from 21 to 12 percent. Thus, just as one would expect, countries whose economies have done well in the era of globalization have been ones in which parents have chosen to withdraw their children from the labor force. Parents have never put their children to work out of indifference or malevolence, but only out of necessity.

Finally, let us remember some of the other features of the last two decades: the worldwide shift to democracy, however imperfect; the disappearance of some of the worst despotisms in history; the increase in personal economic opportunity in vast swaths of the world, notably China and India; and the improving relative position of women almost, although not quite, everywhere.

All these are very encouraging trends. People in developing countries and, particularly, in the fast-growing ones are enjoying longer and healthier lives than before. They are better fed and better educated. They treat their fewer children better. All these good things have not happened only because of rising incomes. Learning from the high-income countries has helped. Developing countries are reaching higher levels of social progress at lower levels of income than the high-income countries of today. But, as one would expect, social progress has been greatest where incomes have risen fastest. It remains "the growth, stupid."

Conclusion

Let us return then to the propositions with which this exploration of growth, poverty and inequality began. Here they are, together with what we now know.

First, the ratio of average incomes in the richest countries to those in the very poorest has continued to rise in the age of globalization. Response: correct.

Second, the absolute gap in living standards between today's high-income countries and the vast proportion of developing countries has continued to rise. Response: also correct and inevitably so, given the starting point two decades ago.

Third, global inequality among individuals has risen. Response: false. Global inequality among individuals has, in all probability, fallen since the 1970s.

Fourth, the number of people in extreme income poverty has also risen. Response: probably false. The number of people in extreme poverty may well have fallen since 1980, for the first time in almost two centuries, because of the rapid growth of the Asian giants.

Fifth, the proportion of people in extreme poverty in the world's population has also risen. Response: false. The proportion of the world's population in extreme poverty has certainly fallen.

Sixth, the poor of the world are worse off not just in terms of incomes, but in terms of a wide range of indicators of human welfare and capability. Response: unambiguously false. The welfare of humanity, judged by life expectancies, infant mortality, literacy, hunger, fertility and the incidence of child labor has improved enormously. It has improved least in sub-Saharan Africa, partly because of disease and partly because of the continent's failure to grow.

Seventh, income inequality has risen in every country and particularly in countries most exposed to international economic integration. Response: false. Income inequality has not risen in most of the developing countries that have integrated with the world economy, though it has risen in China. Inequality has apparently risen in the high-income countries, but the role of globalization in this change is unclear and, in all probability, not decisive.

We can also make some propositions of our own. Human welfare, broadly defined, has risen. The proportion of humanity living in desperate misery is declining. The problem of the poorest is not that they are exploited, but that they are almost entirely unexploited: they live outside the world economy. The soaring growth of the rapidly integrating developing economies has transformed the world for the better. The challenge is to bring those who have failed so far into the new web of productive and profitable global economic relations.

Notes

1. Jay Mazur "Labor's New Internationalism," *Foreign Affairs* 79 (January–February, 2000): 79–93.
2. Ignacio Ramonet, *Le Monde Diplomatique* (May 1998). Cited in Xavier Sala-I-Martin, "The Myth of Exploding Income Inequality in Europe and the World," in *Europe and Globalization*, ed. Henryk Kierzkowski (Basingstoke: Palgrave Macmillan, 2002), p. 11.
3. Paul Ehrlich, *The Population Bomb* (New York: Ballantine Books, 1968).
4. World Bank, *Globalization, Growth and Poverty: Building an Inclusive World Economy* (Washington, DC: World Bank, 2002), table 1.1, p. 34.
5. François Bourguignon and Christian Morrison, "Inequality among World Citizens," *American Economic Review* 92, no. 4 (2002): 727–44.
6. See Thomas W. Pogge and Sanjay G. Reddy, "Unknown: The Extent, Distribution and Trend of Global Income Poverty" (July 16, 2003), mimeo, pp. 1–2.
7. Ibid., p. 12.
8. Where not otherwise indicated, data in this section come from World Bank, *World Development Indicators 2002* (Washington, DC: World Bank, 2002).
9. Indur M. Goklany, "The Globalization of Human Well-Being," *Policy Analysis No. 447*, Cato Institute, Washington, DC, August 22, 2002.

Globalization Moralized

RICHARD W. MILLER

In every era, the bare statement that countries are economically interdependent, engage in commerce and protect property has left out facts with a vital bearing on international justice. Paradigmatically, commerce in slaves was not mere commerce: the slave trade and slavery were wrong, everyone had a duty to help end these wrongs, and no one had a just complaint against losing the right to own humans. Ours *is* an era in which abject suffering, on the one hand, and resources for relieving it, on the other, are concentrated in different countries. For example, in 2006, 37 percent of the world's people lived in countries with per capita gross national income of less than $905 (the World Bank's "low income" threshold), where one in nine people died before the age of five, usually of readily treatable infectious diseases, and health expenditures averaged about $27 per person. In contrast, 16 percent of the world's people lived in countries with per capita income greater than $11,116 (the "high income" threshold), where the before five death rate was a sixteenth as great (0.7 percent) and health expenditures averaged about $3,979 per person.[1] Everyone ought to be appalled by the fact that so many suffer in a world in which such suffering is not inevitable.

This essay will scrutinize processes and institutions that sustain and regulate globalization, i.e., the dramatically increased economic integration into worldwide market processes at all levels of production, exchange and finance of developing as well as developed countries starting in the last quarter of the twentieth century. I will argue that indivi-

From Richard W. Miller, *Globalizing Justice: The Ethics of Poverty and Power* (Oxford University Press, 2010), pp. 58–67, 69–70, 73–75, 77–79. Reprinted with permission of the publisher.

duals, firms and governments in developed countries currently take advantage of people in developing countries in both the process of production, exchange and finance and the institutional framework that regulates it, and that they have a duty to give up consequent benefits, promoting the interests of the global poor.

The flawed processes will be normal and pervasive features of globalization, not the inevitable isolated wrongs. However, this critique will not condemn globalization as a whole, insisting that the world would be better off without it. Export-led growth, which contributes to and depends on globalization, has been the only path by which developing countries have substantially reduced poverty. Through this escape route, the number of people living in abysmal poverty has declined by hundreds of millions since 1980 (almost entirely in East and South Asia, and mostly in China).[2] The irresponsibilities that I will emphasize in this essay consist of making improper use of the desperate neediness of people in developing countries, not imposing it on them.

The Moral Flaw: Taking Advantage

According to the critique I will present, affluent people in developed countries have duties to respond to globalization with measures that would strengthen developing economies because otherwise they take advantage of people in developing countries. A person takes advantage of someone if he derives a benefit from her difficulty in advancing her interests in interactions in which both participate, in a process that shows inadequate regard for the equal moral importance of her interests and her capacity for choice. In the case of globalization, the central difficulties are bargaining weaknesses due to desperate neediness.

Using someone's weakness to get one's way always stands in need of justification, to reconcile it with respect for the weaker person. In such conduct, rather than basing participation on willing cooperation, one overrides the will of another, who is forced to defer by her circumstances. Rather than allowing her an equal capacity to assert her interests, one makes use of her inferior capacity in order to extract benefits from her that advance one's own goals. In the absence of further justification, such conduct fails to express an appreciation of the equal worth of others, and, instead, uses them as means, human tools subordinate to one's purposes.

However, there are justifications that reconcile the use of others' weaknesses with respect for them, so that taking advantage of someone's weakness does not involve taking advantage of him. These justifications involve excessive costs to stronger parties of avoiding the use of weakness, in the case at hand or relevantly similar cases in general, excessive costs to the weaker parties or those at least as needy, and the need to take advantage of weakness to correct for the shortsightedness, moral insensitivity or outright injustice of other parties. In assessing processes characteristic of globalization, it will be important to consider whether justifications of these kinds are available, so that the underlying reason to condemn, the fact that agents based in developed countries make use of bargaining weakness in developing countries, is not decisive. However, one purported justification for using others' weakness is so familiar in debates over globalization that it ought to be debunked at the outset. The fact that the weaker party is better off than she would have been in the absence of interaction with the stronger party is quite insufficient to show that the stronger party did not wrong her by taking advantage of her. That is why the criticism of globalizing agents for taking advantage of people in developing countries is quite compatible with the view that those with a just complaint against their activity are better off for contact with them.

Suppose that I am lost in a desert, about to die of thirst, when a man on a camel appears out of the shimmering haze and convinces me that he will lead me to a well next to his home, if I agree to be his servant for life, making the beds and cleaning the toilets of his palace. He assures me that once I accompany him to the oasis, I will not be able to survive without continually exchanging my services for sustenance. I would agree, and would be better off on account of my encounter with him. But he does wrong in exacting the bargain. He has taken advantage of me, benefiting from my inferior capacity to pursue my interests in our interaction due to the urgency of my need, doing so in conduct that displays an inadequate appreciation of my equal moral worth. This is not to say that it would have been all right for him to have turned away on catching sight of me, leaving me in the lurch. If he does, he does not take advantage of me. But there are other ways of doing wrong. By leaving me in the lurch, he violates the duty of nearby rescue. There would be no objection to his asking for some payment for his services. Perhaps he makes a living by rescuing lost travelers. But the right response for him is to extract less than the most the other would provide if noninteraction were the only alternative, pursuing an outcome that the other would accept if bargaining power were not crippled by urgency.

If one puts aside the question of whether a prohibitive law would be desirable, a modern capitalist society is also a setting for clear examples of taking advantage of weakness that wrongs while bettering. The dentist who triples his normal fee for a procedure when someone from another town walks into his office driven by excruciating pain and the billionaire seeking land for a third summer home who extracts every dollar he can gain from a poor farmer's desperation to sell are so far beyond the justifications for using another's weakness that their conduct is clearly to be condemned as wrong. That nonworsening is not decisive is also strongly confirmed by judgments of other processes of taking advantage, turning on other weaknesses. A militarily brilliant despot who extracts harsh tribute to sustain a luxurious court does wrong in benefiting from the weakness of his subjects, even if in his absence they would suffer a worse fate of chaotic anarchy. A Victorian husband who relies on sexist discrimination in opportunities for employment and terms of divorce to insure his wife's self-abnegating deference does wrong even if in his absence her life would be worse. In all of these interactions, stronger parties make some contribution to the lives of weaker parties. Yet the benefits of the interaction to the stronger parties also derive, in significant part, not from contribution to the others but from the others' difficulties in advancing their interests by means of the interaction. This is why the mutually beneficial interaction is appropriately condemned as unfair, in the absence of further justification.

In emphasizing wrongdoing in which the weaker party is not made worse off, I do not mean to set aside the badness of the situation of people in developing countries as irrelevant to the critique of globalization. To the contrary, when a person takes advantage of another's weakness in an economic interaction that does not worsen her, the further, moral judgment that he takes advantage of *her* typically depends on the badness of the outcome for her. It is usually hard to tell whether one is taking advantage of another's weak capacity to advance her interests through bargaining or simply taking part in a normal and legitimate process of advancing one's personal goals. So the burdensomeness of monitoring whether one benefits from others' bargaining weakness and the risks of serious loss as a result of needless scruples are apt to be excessive unless attention is restricted to cases in which the other party's fate is bad. In addition, in market interactions, there is a danger that excessive restraint in profit-seeking will destroy efficiency and economic expansion which the weak need, a danger not apt to be worth its risks when outcomes would otherwise be good for both the strong and weak (as opposed to being bad but better than the fate that was avoided).

To avoid these dangers, one should adopt this working assumption in the moral scrutiny of globalization: no one takes advantage of another in an interaction involving no force or deception by either party in which both parties do better and neither ends up badly. Even though the critique of globalization is not based on worsening, it is important that

billions of participants in global interactions end up very badly indeed.

In this critique, I will locate major unmet transnational responsibilities in two aspects of globalization. The first corresponds to the familiar charge that transnational corporations exploit. In transnational processes of production, trade and investment, people in developed countries currently take advantage of bargaining weaknesses of individuals desperately seeking work in developing countries, in ways that show inadequate appreciation of their interests and capacities for choice. Responding to this moral flaw, a citizen of a developed country ought to use benefits derived from this use of weakness to relieve the underlying neediness. The other aspect corresponds to familiar charges of inequity in the institutional framework that regulates world trade and finance. The multinational arrangements that sustain globalization depend on tainted deliberations in which the governments of developed countries take advantage of the weak capacity to resist their threats of governments of developing countries. Citizens of developed countries should support arrangements that would be the outcome of responsible deliberations based on relevant shared values, a shift that would entail giving up large current advantages to promote the interests of people in developing countries.

Exploitation

The most striking feature of globalization is the vast expansion of exports to developed countries of goods and profits due to manufacturing in developing countries, often through local employment by transnational firms based in developed countries, often through their contracts with local suppliers, and always facilitated by transnational firms' engagement in building up the infrastructure of developing countries. In 2000, the current dollar value of manufactured goods imported from low and middle income countries by high income OECD countries was 3.7 times the current dollar value in 1990, as compared to a ratio of 1.7 in the values of total high income country imports in those years. Those imports from low and middle income countries had risen to 16 percent of high income country merchandise imports, from 7 percent in 1990.[3] By 2005, the proportion had further increased to 21 percent.[4] Opportunities to profit from this expansion are a major source of the growth of foreign direct investment in developing countries: from 1990 to 2005, foreign direct investment in low and middle income countries grew elevenfold (nearly thirteenfold in lower middle income countries), as compared to a fourfold increase in high income countries.[5] These steep increases significantly depend on taking advantage of poor people in developing countries, a defect generating duties of repair.

The great expansion of exports and investments involving manufacturing in developing countries reflects the cheapness of the wages and working conditions that are accepted by competent, hardworking people there. At the turn of the twentieth century, hourly labor costs in manufacturing were a tenth of US costs in Malaysia, a thirtieth in Thailand, a sixtieth in China and India.[6] As fans of globalization remind us, people seek work in the sweatshops of globalizing firms because the alternatives are even worse: grinding rural poverty, horrors of unemployment, or lower wages and harsher working conditions in local firms producing for local markets. These hard facts of life in developing countries benefit globalizing firms. Typical job-seekers in such a market are in no position to hold out for terms of employment that sustain a life fully worthy of human dignity. They would not respect themselves and their dependents if they jeopardized their chances of escaping worse misery by holding out for non-misery. They compete with others driven by similarly desperate needs – directly in the local labor market and indirectly with desperately poor people abroad to whom direct investment could shift in pursuit of cheaper labor inputs. Transnational firms are subject to competitive pressure as well, but it is less intense. The capacity to establish and coordinate production and sales on a worldwide scale, efficiently and reliably, is limited to relatively few firms, while the global reservoirs of desperate job-seekers are vast.

This is not to say that the special difficulty of using labor for profit in a developing country plays no independent role in explaining lower wages in developing countries. Supplies and repairs may be less prompt and reliable; advanced and efficient techniques may not fit local skills; international coordination and shipment to distant markets have costs, even in the era of globalization, and may be hampered by problems of communication and tenuous networks of acquaintance; burdensome regulations and corruption may add to costs. If such difficulties were the whole story, then the inequalities in the price paid for labor would correspond to equality in the ratio between the price of labor and the value it adds. But there are stark international inequalities of the second kind, as well, which explain the steep increase in the flow of manufactured goods from developing countries. According to an extensive survey by the World Bank of labor costs in manufacturing per worker per year and value added in manufacturing per worker per year at the end of the twentieth century, the ratio of labor cost to value added in the United States was 0.36 – i.e., it took $0.36 in wages and benefits to add a dollar of value. The ratio was significantly less in a number of countries playing a large role in US imports and investments, for example, 0.19 in Thailand, 0.23 in the Philippines, 0.25 in China, 0.27 in Malaysia and 0.29 in Mexico.[7] Moreover, these ratios for manufacturing as a whole substantially underestimate the special productivity of transnational investment in manufacturing in developing countries and the savings due to importing manufactured goods from developing countries; for globalized manufacturing favors especially labor intensive processes that do not depend on elaborate and advanced local technology, such as stitching garments, assembling components and milling textiles. For an assessment of the productivity of globalized manufacturing, we should turn to the experts, executives in charge of making profits. That elevenfold increase in foreign direct investment reflected appreciation of exceptional revenue-productivity of labor which transnational employers use in developing countries, not the view that low wages barely balance the difficulties of production.

Because they flee from worse alternatives, those who are employed in the burgeoning export sector accept, even actively seek, work that is stultifying, without anyone's forcing them to accept these terms of employment. In this sense, they voluntarily consent to these terms. (In another usage, which can be revealing, their agreement is not fully voluntary, since it is forced on them by their circumstances. For present purposes, I will put this more demanding construal to one side.) In the course of an eminent book-length defense of globalization, Jagdish Bhagwati insists that this voluntary acceptance blocks the charge that the employer exploits. For example, he emphasizes the role of voluntary consent to very long hours, among workers whose hourly wages are very low, in his gloss on this *New York Times* report on women who had fled dire rural poverty to work in a leather-stitching operation in southern China:

> We chatted with several women as their fingers flew over their work.
> "I start at about 6.30 after breakfast, and go on until 7 p.m.," explained one shy teenage girl. "We break for lunch and I take half an hour off then."
> "You do this six days a week?" "Oh no. Every day."
> "Seven days a week?"
> "Yes." She laughed at our surprise. "But then I take a week or two off at Chinese New Year to go back to my village."
> The others we talked to all seemed to regard it as a plus that the factory allowed them to work long hours.[8]

Bhagwati says, of the workers in this factory, "[L]ike many of us who work long hours, they are not being exploited; they drive themselves." Assimilation of the worklife of that child to the worklife of a University Professor at Columbia must be unintended, but it *is* clear from the *Times* report that the workers have made their labor contract voluntarily, i.e., without anyone's forcing them to do so. So the same example shows that such voluntary engagement is compatible with exploitation in one usage: deriving benefits from the bargaining weakness of another, which leads her to enter arrangements involving drudgery or penury that are not fully worthy of human dignity. Presumably, in his denial of exploitation, Bhagwati has another usage in mind, even more morally loaded. The assertion of exploitation, in this usage, alleges that a process of exploiting someone in the first sense derives benefits in a way that is incompatible with adequate appreciation of the moral worth of her interests and of her capacity for choice. Exploitation in the first sense is a matter of taking advantage of someone's bargaining weakness; exploitation in the second sense involves something more, taking advantage of a person by taking advantage of her bargaining weakness. Strictly speaking, only the second usage condemns. But it is also quite compatible with voluntary acceptance. The wanderer saved in the desert voluntarily agreed to be exploited, in the second sense as well as the first.

Do transnational corporations exploit workers in developing countries in the second sense, as well as the first? Sometimes, they do, creating a duty to improve wages and working conditions to avoid the wrongdoing of exploitation in the second sense ("immoral exploitation" as one might call it). Even when they do not, this is not, by any means, the end of the significance of exploitation in the first sense ("mere exploitation" as one might call it) for the critique of globalization. Mere exploitation at the point of production gives rise to a series of moral demands, moving from initiatives by the employing firm at the site of production, to regulation by the government of the country where production takes place, to collective negotiations of governments over the international framework of globalization, to a political duty of people in developed countries to relieve desperate neediness in developing countries.

Exploitation in the first sense is a *prima facie* reason for ascribing exploitation in the second sense. To derive benefits from another's bargaining weakness through an arrangement that is stultifying is only compatible with adequate respect for her interests and capacity for choice on account of special, exculpatory reasons. Voluntary consent by the employee and her improvement as compared with opportunities available from other sources have turned out to be insufficient reasons. But others might work. In particular, costs of avoiding mere exploitation can be reasons why it is not immoral.

Of course, no grave loss is entailed by any particular decision by a transnational manufacturer to avoid taking advantage of someone's bargaining weakness, by hiring her on terms that she would rightly regard as satisfactory rather than merely better than extremely bad alternatives. However, duties of responsible participation in transactions, like duties of beneficence, are determined by principles to be assessed in light of the impact of enduring conformity on people's lives, not just in light of the impact of conformity on particular occasions. And a moral principle requiring individual firms, on their own initiative, to avoid benefiting from bargaining weaknesses in employing people in stultifying work arrangements would have excessive costs, both for firms that seek to fulfill this obligation and for potential employees.

In the management of an investment, it is none too easy to draw the line between benefits of bargaining weakness and compensation for special difficulties of production in developing countries. The burdens of scrupulous self-monitoring are heavy, and, at best, would produce extremely fallible assessments. If a firm were to avoid all significant risks of taking advantage of bargaining weakness, it would have to withdraw from developing countries or so severely jeopardize its profit margin that its operations in developing countries are apt to fail. This would only make life worse for job-seekers in developing countries. If a firm is much more scrupulous than most who would seek to engage in the same type of production in the same labor market, i.e., if it tolerates much greater risks to revenue to avoid taking advantage of bargaining weaknesses, then less scrupulous rivals will expand at its expense. Again, needy people in developing countries lose, as well as the scrupulous self-monitor.

More moderate self-monitoring avoids these costs. A conscientious manager should ask herself whether she really has reason to believe that net revenues will be jeopardized if she finds arrangements that are easier on workers or pay more, and should try to improve benefits if the answer is "No." As in the case of sympathy, undue anxieties will make this a hard principle to live up to. So it ought to be affirmed and promoted, for example, by the pressures epitomized in organized consumer boycotts, and the humane managers who live up to the principle ought to be admired. No one is reasonable to reject a moral code that requires at least this much. Exploitation that could be mitigated by such conscientious management is immoral and should be changed at the firm's own initiative, in the interest of those who are exploited. The leather goods factory in China might or might not pass this moral test. One doesn't know enough to tell, from the evidence Bhagwati provides.

In addition, sometimes and to some extent, morally relevant costs to individual firms and actual and potential employees of avoiding mere exploitation can be eliminated by government imposition of minimum labor standards. By imposing such measures, the government of a developing country takes over burdensome responsibilities for monitoring and information-gathering and protects firms from loss due to competition from sub-minimal operations within the borders. If the line is properly drawn, the dangers to vulnerable people in the country of driving out employers by raising costs will be sufficiently contained. Those dangers can be further reduced by international coordination of labor standards. Such political measures change the terms of moral judgment. If labor standards eliminating relevant costs of reducing mere exploitation are in place, then exploitation that once was mere becomes immoral, a violation of duties to actual and potential employees, not just duties to obey the law.

The great limit to this remedy is a risk of disaster for the vulnerable when minimal standards are imposed. The higher the minimum, the greater the danger that the needy will be hurt by stunted growth of economic opportunities. Faced with the new balance sheets, firms may take their business elsewhere, perhaps to developed countries, which are still the predominant sites for production. These dangers are greatest in the countries where needs are greatest, because these are the countries in which local infrastructure, skills and supplies are least inviting and structural unemployment is most burdensome and pervasive. . . .

The limited scope of the responsibility to avoid immoral exploitation makes it important to scrutinize a different aspect of globalization, where the imprint of superior power is very large, more easily discerned, and subject to potentially demanding prohibitions of political injustice. This is the political process in which governments of developed and developing countries have agreed to the institutional framework on which globalization relies.[9]

Inequitable Frameworks

Globalization is not just a matter of interactions among firms, workers and consumers. It has required coordinated activities among governments, in which they commit themselves to enduring constraints on their legitimate sovereign prerogatives in joint decisions that provide a suitable framework for the deepening integration of developed and developing economies. More specifically, it has required the coordinated reduction of barriers to international trade in goods and services and to international flows of capital epitomized by the arrangements negotiated in the Uruguay Round, administered by the World Trade Organization.

This trade and investment framework has been shaped by threats of exclusion or discrimination, through which major developed countries take advantage of the especially urgent need of developing countries for access to developed countries' markets. In the Uruguay Round negotiations, from 1981 to 1994, the United States frequently used threats of devastating trade discrimination – for example, US Trade Representative Carla Hills's flamboyant warning that if others held out the United States would start "trade wars over all sorts of silly things,"[10] or Secretary of State James Baker's more measured but no less ominous intimation, "we hope that this follow-up liberalization will occur in the Uruguay Round. If not, we might be willing to explore a 'market liberalization club' approach, through minilateral arrangements or a series of bilateral agreements."[11] The resulting regime has been sustained by similar bullying. For example, after a coalition of developing countries united in insistence on an end to rich-country farm subsidies in the Cancun WTO conference of 2003, Robert Zoellick, the US Trade Representative (who was to become President of the World Bank four years later), noted that "the transformation of the WTO into a forum for the politics of protest . . . dismayed" the United States, and announced an American commitment "in our hemisphere, and with sub-regions or individual countries . . . to move towards free trade with can-do countries" excluding the "won't do" countries that had held out for an end to the subsidies.[12] As intended, the threat led countries such as Costa Rica, highly dependent on access to US markets and without good alternatives, to cave in and leave the coalition.

Presumably, the bullying trade representatives believe that if they did not use fear to steer the negotiations, interest groups seeking protection from market forces, including political elites and their clients in many developing countries, would, instead, carry the day, making matters worse for all. Even if this is true, developed countries wrong the global poor, taking advantage of them, if the outcome seriously departs from what could result from reasonable deliberations, i.e., negotiations in which the mutually respectful offering and assessment of reasons for alternative proposals leads to the willing acceptance of a shared commitment by all. If a trade regime essentially depends on concessions that responsible representatives of some countries could only make under pressure of need, rather than in mutual accommodation to relevant justifications, then it is a means by which the strong take advantage of the weak. Thus, an account of reasonable deliberations over a trade and investment framework is the proper basis for assessing the justice of the current arrangements. . . .

To begin describing the basic shape of trade justice: a trade regime that all responsible representatives can willingly accept must be justifiable to each citizenry as advancing their good on the whole. More precisely, this must be possible if trade-external considerations are put to one side and relevant adjustments have been made for past departures from reasonableness. In accepting the regime, a government binds itself not to exercise legitimate prerogatives in excluding and regulating trade and investment. Except as a reflection of trade-external commitments or correction of past unreasonableness, the report, "We willingly agreed to set aside your prerogatives in an arrangement that does you no good," is an admission of irresponsibility on the part of the negotiating team to the citizenry they represent.

The requirement of some benefit for each citizenry (relative to a suitably corrected baseline) attends to the interests of the most prosperous parties as well as the poorest. However, so long as this requirement is met, the vulnerabilities of a poor country should have special standing, even if it is not one of the poorest. Suppose that a responsible representative is faced with a proposed regime in which suffering among the people she represents is extensive and plausibly foreseen to be substantially greater than in an alternative providing her country with greater trade access to other countries, permitting wider recourse by her government to measures it regards as useful means of overcoming economic burdens, or providing more resources for alleviating harms of disruption from imposed trade policies. As a responsible representative of her citizenry, she must count this as a serious reason not willingly to accept the proposal. International reciprocity of reasons must also be observed. So the representative must take account of similar concerns to avoid suffering among their people on the part of other representatives, giving them weight appropriate to the seriousness of the concern. As a result of this combination of national and transnational responsibilities, the basic tendency of reasonable trade deliberations will be a trade regime whose allocation of openness to goods, exemptions from constraints and mitigation of burdens of disruption due to trade most favors the countries where there is the most need for growth through trade, for policy instruments for development and for mitigation of disruption and other burdens of exposure to global markets. In short, in the absence of serious reasons to the contrary, the poor will be favored – for reasons of justice, not beneficence.

Conflicting considerations of need and vulnerability can make this standard hard to apply. For example, an alternative that would facilitate a great many escapes from destitution in China might disrupt more urgently needed development among far fewer, much poorer people in Southeast Asia and sub-Saharan Africa. Here, asking what pattern one would prefer behind a veil of ignorance is a helpful device for taking proper account of the seriousness of the competing concerns. Even though there is no duty to

implement a comprehensive global standard of justice that one would choose behind a veil of ignorance of where one lives, the veil of ignorance device is useful at specific junctures of responsible global decision-making at which the impact of specific kinds of choices on certain interests of participants is impartially assessed, as one aspect of the justification that respects the interests and autonomy of all.

It might seem that any departure from a pattern of utter openness of developed countries to goods from developing countries is precluded, as irresponsible, by these considerations. After all, the inhibition of export-led growth in developing countries condemns people to recurrent fatigue, constant threats of bad health, and constraining isolation. Even in China, already the site of stupendous export-led growth, over 100 million people were undernourished, in the first years of the twenty-first century, over 200 million lived on less than $1.25 a day, there were a mere 1.5 physicians per 1,000 people, highly concentrated in urban areas, and those in the countryside had to make do with a highly inferior share of transportation resources that involved 24 motor vehicles per 1,000 Chinese in 2005.[13] The cost of thwarted escape from such destitution is much more serious than the worst suffering imposed in developed countries by uninhibited entry of goods from developing countries, namely, the displacement of middle-aged workers in industries that cannot compete. . . .

Governments of developed countries have special responsibilities to their especially vulnerable citizens. Faced with a free-trade agreement that would improve economic life in the United States on the whole but devastate industrial cities in the Midwest, the United States government might, in principle, be reasonable in seeking more protection, even at the cost of slowing the escape from dire poverty in China and Brazil. If the government were to tell Americans whose morally serious interests were in jeopardy, "We agreed to let in these goods to enable needier people abroad to escape from poverty," those at risk in the Midwest have a morally relevant response: "You should treat our interests with special concern, rather than absorbing them in impartial global concern for suffering due to trade arrangements as soon as over-all national benefit is achieved." (That they have a legitimate fear of serious harm, not just a desire for greater benefits, is important. The representative of a developed country would not be irresponsible in telling the citizenry, "We could have held out for an even better deal, but this would have required other countries to accept substantial suffering that this agreement avoids.")

However, developed countries and their citizens must live up to all their political responsibilities in reasonable deliberations. Duties of good faith among representatives make it hard for governments of developed countries responsibly to maintain that imports from developing countries are to be inhibited to protect vulnerable people within their borders. In pressing for liberalization in the world at large, developed countries propose that considerable disruption is worth the gains in developing countries. It would show bad faith not to swallow the same medicine at home. In addition, what counts as a gain in productivity and growth that justifies displacement through *domestic* policies should count as adequate in judging the domestic effects of international trade policies as well. Developed countries, especially the United States, are, domestically, receptive to "creative destruction" through displacement.

A Shortfall in Equity

The WTO, like the GATT regimes that it transformed, is officially committed to the pursuit of reciprocal reductions in barriers to free trade, modified as needed to guard against severe disruption of economic life in member countries and to respect the special needs and vulnerabilities of developing countries.

Far from indicting this broad official commitment, the criterion of reasonable deliberations confirms and specifies it. Similarly, reasonable deliberations over the institutional framework for international finance and payments would support the IMF's official general commitment to combine a goal of facilitating monetary measures needed to sustain international trade and investment with special concern for damage from disruptive fluctuations and currency and fiscal crises, which especially afflicts the people of developing countries. The current epidemic of inequity in the global frameworks for trade and finance is a pervasive failure actually to implement such general commitments in specific measures that reasonable deliberations could justify.

An assessment of this shortfall cannot be certain and precise, since estimates depend on controversial empirical claims. Still, there is little room for doubt that the outcome of reasonable deliberations would be very different from the current outcome of bullying.

Distorting the Basic Shape. Current arrangements drastically depart from the general rule of openness by richer countries to imports from poorer countries. In 2000, developing countries' exports faced trade barriers in high-income countries that were, on average, three times higher (value-weighted) than the barriers faced by other high-income countries. The barriers that the United States imposed on goods from the least developed countries were ten times higher than the barriers faced by high income country exporters.[14] Indeed, the poorest countries lost out on

balance in the Uruguay Round on account of barriers to their exports and requirements of bureaucratic procedures and patent constraints. The most widely cited estimate of the initial impact on the poorest countries is a net loss of $600 million a year among the 48 poorest.[15] If developed countries' tariffs on imports from developing countries were eliminated, benefits to developing countries of this improved access might well exceed $100 billion a year.[16] There is little reason to suppose that significant rich-country restriction of this access could be justified without violations of reciprocity in reasons.

Non-Reciprocal Reasoning. Violation of reciprocity is a basis for the most pervasive criticisms of the trade regime, objections to rich-country agricultural subsidies. In 2005, the governments of developed countries gave subsidies to their farms (often inefficient farms owned by rich people) of $280 billion, a sum equaling a third of the value of these countries' farm product and substantially exceeding the total GDP of the 50 poorest countries, where one in eight people lived.[17] These subsidies shield rich-country farms from the pressures of market competition on which the governments of rich countries generally insist in trade negotiations. Granted, a country could reasonably resist abandonment of its farm subsidies by appealing to considerations of cultural continuity, national independence in provision of vital needs or stability in families' economic lives. But whatever the role of thriving farms in continuity, independence and stability in developed countries, they are much more important to continuity, independence and stability in developing countries. And extensive farm subsidies in developed countries destroy farming life in developing countries, undermining all of these values, by choking off opportunities to compete in world markets. Because of subsidies to US cotton farming which amounted to $3.9 billion in 2001, the United States, the world's largest cotton exporter, doubled exports in a three-year period of slumping prices, from 1998 to 2001. The cost to people in poor countries of the skewing of competition by US cotton subsidies was about $300 million a year in Africa alone.[18]

Blocked Options for Development. While much more could be done to mitigate the human costs of trade liberalization, they can hardly be eliminated. This makes it all the more important to consider whether the current extent of mandated liberalization of developing economies deprives them of policy options that informed and responsible governments would seek to preserve.

No country has ever successfully developed without relying on measures to manage damage and increase advantages from world trade that are banned by rules that were instituted by the Uruguay Round, through dire threats overcoming heated resistance.[19] In 1960–78, the heyday of those currently banned measures (such as export subsidies and high tariff walls protecting vulnerable economic sectors), population-weighted average annual growth of per capita GDP was 2.8 percent among Latin American countries; in 1978–98, when such state-direction was replaced by direction by world markets, first through structural adjustment conditions imposed, on US initiative, by the IMF and World Bank, then through the trade, investment and property rights regime administered by the WTO, growth declined to 0.8 percent. The comparable figures for Asia are a decline from 4.0 percent to 3.6 percent, for Africa, a decline from 1.5 percent to 0.1 percent.[20] According to Rodriguez and Rodrik's incisive analysis of the major international studies of the relationship between economic growth and policy-induced liberalization in the last quarter of the twentieth century, the causal contribution of trade liberalization to economic growth in developing countries was, on average, nil – despite the tumultuous instability that liberalization policies introduced into millions of lives.[21]

Given the state of the evidence and the profound importance of the outcome for the peoples of developing countries, responsible governments of developing countries in the current world trade regime have reason to complain of being prevented from using plausible development strategies, which may be the best in their situations. Any major strategy for development is a gamble.[22] Those whose futures will be shaped by the gamble ought to have the main voice in choosing which bet to place. Since the right package of policies is extremely hard to discover and almost certainly varies from region to region and time to time, the exclusion of a wide range of plausible strategies also has a familiar epistemic cost of regimentation: it eliminates needed experimentation. The prohibition of these development strategies was, at the very least, an objectionable constraint, and may have been a disaster. . . .

Notes

1. World Bank, *World Development Indicators 2008* (Washington, DC: World Bank, 2008), tables 1.1, 2.15, 2.21.
2. Comparing world poverty in 2005 with world poverty in 1981, Shaohua Chen and Martin Ravallion, the chief poverty researchers at the World Bank, estimate that there were 505 million fewer people living below $1.25 a day at 2005 purchasing power parity – their proposed revision, in light of improved purchasing power estimates, of the World Bank poverty threshold whose familiar, imprecise label is "a dollar a day." The decline in China was 627 million. There was a decline of 123 million in East Asia outside of China, 35 million in India, 12 million in the rest of South Asia, and 1 million in the Middle East and North Africa, accompanied by increases elsewhere, vast in sub-Saharan Africa (182 million). There was a worldwide increase of 56 million in the number living below $2.00 a day (the threshold corresponding to the median national poverty line among developing countries) from which China was a signal exception, with a decline of 499 million. See Shaohua Chen and Martin Ravallion, *The Developing World Is Poorer than We Thought, but No Less Successful in the Fight against Poverty* (Washington, DC: World Bank, 2008), pp. 34 ff.
3. See World Bank, *World Development Indicators 2002* (Washington, DC: World Bank, 2002), tables 4.6, 6.3.
4. See World Bank, *World Development Indicators 2008*, tables 4.5, 6.4.
5. See World Bank, *World Development Indicators 2007* (Washington, DC: World Bank, 2007), table 6.8.
6. See Paul Collier and David Dollar, *Globalization, Growth and Poverty* (Washington, DC: World Bank, 2002), p. 45.
7. World Bank, *World Development Indicators 2006* (Washington, DC: World Bank, 2006), table 2.6.
8. Quotation from Nicholas Kristof and Sheryl WuDunn, "Two Cheers for Sweatshops," *The New York Times Magazine* (September 24, 2000), in Jagdish Bhagwati, *In Defense of Globalization* (Oxford University Press, 2004), p. 175.
9. In connecting economic exploitation with taking advantage of others' bargaining weakness and in creating space for morally acceptable exploitation, my account parallels Allen Wood's illuminating discussion in "Exploitation," *Social Philosophy and Policy* 12 (1993): 135–58. There, Wood characterizes exploitation as one person's extracting a benefit from another by using her weakness or vulnerability in accordance with his plans (pp. 141–3). He takes this feature to be, in itself, a reason to criticize a relationship, but not a decisive one: other features can make exploitation morally acceptable all told. The main differences derive from the broader scope of the crucial benefiting-from-weakness in Wood's account and from his view that it generates an ineradicable taint of degradation. Wood says that the planned derivation of benefit from another's weakness or vulnerability, even "as doctors do when they treat patients," is, as such, degrading (p. 153). Although, as in the standard medical case, other aspects may make the interaction all right all told, the "inevitably exploitive side" should still occasion "profound moral ambivalence" (p. 153). These implausible assessments, which would give oncologists a (non-compelling) reason to be dealers in dispensable trinkets instead, result from putting people's difficulties in asserting their will in interaction with others on a par with difficulties that they overcome through interaction with others. Desperation can make it hard to hold out in bargaining or can be an expression of vulnerability to a need that one satisfies through bargaining. Only the former is an aspect of exploitation, on my view. Moreover, justifications deriving from burdens of avoiding exploitation sometimes reconcile it with respect for the other's

capacity for choice, so that the morally well-ordered process of mere exploitation merits unambivalent acceptance. Bhagwati's unambivalent encomium to the leather goods factory may or may not fit the facts that shape the responsibilities in play, but it is not inherently misguided. (Some parts of Wood's rich essay are more receptive to these views.)

10. Jarrod Wiener, *Making Rules in the Uruguay Round of the GATT* (Aldershot: Dartmouth Publishing Company, 1995), p. 186.

11. Ernest Preeg, *Traders in a Brave New World* (University of Chicago Press, 1995), p. 80. Preeg also notes similar threats to organize a "GATT for the like-minded" (US Trade Representative Brock, p. 48) and "if insignificant progress is made . . . to explore regional and bilateral agreements with other nations" (President Reagan, p. 51) and describes the crucial role of threatened trade discrimination in advancing US proposals on intellectual property rights ("[Recalcitrant] developing countries came to realize that a multilateral agreement in the GATT could be the lesser evil to unilateral U.S. demands outside the GATT," p. 67). Preeg was a member of the US delegation to the Uruguay Round. His history of the negotiations is accompanied, on the back cover, by praise from Carla Hills and from Arthur Dunkel, the director general of GATT for most of this period.

12. Robert Zoellick, "America Will Not Wait for the Won't-Do Countries," *Financial Times* (September 22, 2003), sec. 1, p. 23.

13. See Chen and Ravallion, "The Developing World Is Poorer than We Thought," p. 34; World Bank, *World Development Indicators 2008*, tables 2.18, 2.15, 3.13.

14. See United Nations Development Programme, *Human Development Report 2005* (New York: United Nations, 2005), p. 127.

15. See United Nations Development Programme, *Human Development Report 1997* (New York: United Nations, 1997), p. 82.

16. As always, estimates are sensitive to assumptions in the underlying models. The models most commonly used to estimate the effects of alternative trade regimes make simplifying assumptions, known to be false, that the amount of employment in each country would be unaffected and that there would be no gains in productivity through economies of scale and learning by doing. The correction of such assumptions can greatly increase projected benefits. For example, Santiago Fernandez de Cordoba and David Vanzetti estimate that gains to developing countries under a proposal that would reduce tariffs on manufactures imposed by developed countries to an average of 0.8 percent, while reducing developing countries' tariffs to an average of 5.3 percent, would amount to $28 billion a year according to a standard model that assumes fixed employment; the gains would amount to $87 billion on the plausible assumption that expanded production in developing countries could make use of a current large reserve of under-used unskilled labor. See Santiago Fernandez de Cordoba and David Vanzetti, "Now What? Search for a Solution to the WTO Industrial Tariff Negotiations," in *Coping with Trade Reforms*, ed. Santiago Fernandez de Cordoba and Sam Laird (Geneva: UNCTAD, 2005), pp. 30, 39 ff.

17. See OECD, *Agricultural Policies in OECD Countries at a Glance 2006* (Paris: OECD, 2006), p. 19; UNCTAD, *The Least Developed Countries Report 2006* (Geneva: UNCTAD, 2006), Annex: Basic Data on the Least Developed Countries, table 1.

18. See Oxfam, *Cultivating Poverty: The Impact of U.S. Cotton Subsidies on Africa* (2002), https://policy-practice.oxfam.org.uk/publications/cultivating-poverty-the-impact-of-us-cotton-subsidies-on-africa-114111, pp. 2, 11. More precisely, the loss and subsidy figures are for the 2001–2002 "marketing year."

19. See Dani Rodrik, *The Global Governance of Trade as if Development Really Mattered* (New York: United Nations Development Programme, 2001) for a cogent account of these departures from free trade orthodoxy.

20. See Branko Milanovic, *The Two Faces of Globalization* (Washington, DC: World Bank, 2002), www.worldbank.org/research/inequality/pdf/naiveglob1.pdf, p. 14.

21. See Francisco Rodriguez and Dani Rodrik, *Trade Policy and Economic Growth: A Skeptic's Guide to the Cross-National Evidence* (Cambridge, MA: National Bureau of Economic Research, 1999), www.nber.org/papers/w7081.

22. For a vivid account of the repeated past failures of the consensus among developed-country experts about the best path to development, see William Easterly, *The Elusive Search for Growth* (Cambridge, MA: MIT Press, 2001).

LEGAL PERSPECTIVE

Universal Declaration of Human Rights

Preamble

Whereas recognition of the inherent dignity and of the equal and inalienable rights of all members of the human family is the foundation of freedom, justice and peace in the world,

Whereas disregard and contempt for human rights have resulted in barbarous acts which have outraged the conscience of mankind, and the advent of a world in which human beings shall enjoy freedom of speech and belief and freedom from fear and want has been proclaimed as the highest aspiration of the common people,

Whereas it is essential, if man is not to be compelled to have recourse, as a last resort, to rebellion against tyranny and oppression, that human rights should be protected by the rule of law,

Whereas it is essential to promote the development of friendly relations between nations,

Whereas the peoples of the United Nations have in the Charter reaffirmed their faith in fundamental human rights, in the dignity and worth of the human person and in the equal rights of men and women and have determined to promote social progress and better standards of life in larger freedom,

Whereas Member States have pledged themselves to achieve, in co-operation with the United Nations, the promotion of universal respect for and observance of human rights and fundamental freedoms,

Whereas a common understanding of these rights and freedoms is of the greatest importance for the full realization of this pledge,

Now, Therefore THE GENERAL ASSEMBLY proclaims THIS UNIVERSAL DECLARATION OF HUMAN RIGHTS

as a common standard of achievement for all peoples and all nations, to the end that every individual and every organ of society, keeping this Declaration constantly in mind, shall strive by teaching and education to promote respect for these rights and freedoms and by progressive measures, national and international, to secure their universal and

effective recognition and observance, both among the peoples of Member States themselves and among the peoples of territories under their jurisdiction.

Article 1

All human beings are born free and equal in dignity and rights. They are endowed with reason and conscience and should act towards one another in a spirit of brotherhood.

Article 2

Everyone is entitled to all the rights and freedoms set forth in this Declaration, without distinction of any kind, such as race, colour, sex, language, religion, political or other opinion, national or social origin, property, birth or other status. Furthermore, no distinction shall be made on the basis of the political, jurisdictional or international status of the country or territory to which a person belongs, whether it be independent, trust, non-self-governing or under any other limitation of sovereignty.

Article 3

Everyone has the right to life, liberty and security of person.

Article 4

No one shall be held in slavery or servitude; slavery and the slave trade shall be prohibited in all their forms.

Article 5

No one shall be subjected to torture or to cruel, inhuman or degrading treatment or punishment.

Article 6

Everyone has the right to recognition everywhere as a person before the law.

Article 7

All are equal before the law and are entitled without any discrimination to equal protection of the law. All are entitled to equal protection against any discrimination in violation of

United Nations Department of Public Information, "Universal Declaration of Human Rights," www.unhchr.ch/udhr/lang/eng.htm (accessed March 19, 2003).

this Declaration and against any incitement to such discrimination.

Article 8

Everyone has the right to an effective remedy by the competent national tribunals for acts violating the fundamental rights granted him by the constitution or by law.

Article 9

No one shall be subjected to arbitrary arrest, detention or exile.

Article 10

Everyone is entitled in full equality to a fair and public hearing by an independent and impartial tribunal, in the determination of his rights and obligations and of any criminal charge against him.

Article 11

(1) Everyone charged with a penal offence has the right to be presumed innocent until proved guilty according to law in a public trial at which he has had all the guarantees necessary for his defence.

(2) No one shall be held guilty of any penal offence on account of any act or omission which did not constitute a penal offence, under national or international law, at the time when it was committed. Nor shall a heavier penalty be imposed than the one that was applicable at the time the penal offence was committed.

Article 12

No one shall be subjected to arbitrary interference with his privacy, family, home or correspondence, nor to attacks upon his honour and reputation. Everyone has the right to the protection of the law against such interference or attacks.

Article 13

(1) Everyone has the right to freedom of movement and residence within the borders of each state.

(2) Everyone has the right to leave any country, including his own, and to return to his country.

Article 14

(1) Everyone has the right to seek and to enjoy in other countries asylum from persecution.

(2) This right may not be invoked in the case of prosecutions genuinely arising from non-political crimes or from acts contrary to the purposes and principles of the United Nations.

Article 15

(1) Everyone has the right to a nationality.

(2) No one shall be arbitrarily deprived of his nationality nor denied the right to change his nationality.

Article 16

(1) Men and women of full age, without any limitation due to race, nationality or religion, have the right to marry and to found a family. They are entitled to equal rights as to marriage, during marriage and at its dissolution.

(2) Marriage shall be entered into only with the free and full consent of the intending spouses.

(3) The family is the natural and fundamental group unit of society and is entitled to protection by society and the State.

Article 17

(1) Everyone has the right to own property alone as well as in association with others.

(2) No one shall be arbitrarily deprived of his property.

Article 18

Everyone has the right to freedom of thought, conscience and religion; this right includes freedom to change his religion or belief, and freedom, either alone or in community with others and in public or private, to manifest his religion or belief in teaching, practice, worship and observance.

Article 19

Everyone has the right to freedom of opinion and expression; this right includes freedom to hold opinions without interference and to seek, receive and impart information and ideas through any media and regardless of frontiers.

Article 20

(1) Everyone has the right to freedom of peaceful assembly and association.

(2) No one may be compelled to belong to an association.

Article 21

(1) Everyone has the right to take part in the government of his country, directly or through freely chosen representatives.

(2) Everyone has the right of equal access to public service in his country.

(3) The will of the people shall be the basis of the authority of government, this will shall be expressed in periodic and genuine elections which shall be by universal and

equal suffrage and shall be held by secret vote or by equivalent free voting procedures.

Article 22

Everyone, as a member of society, has the right to social security and is entitled to realization, through national effort and international co-operation and in accordance with the organization and resources of each State, of the economic, social and cultural rights indispensable for his dignity and the free development of his personality.

Article 23

(1) Everyone has the right to work, to free choice of employment, to just and favourable conditions of work and to protection against unemployment.

(2) Everyone, without any discrimination, has the right to equal pay for equal work.

(3) Everyone who works has the right to just and favourable remuneration ensuring for himself and his family an existence worthy of human dignity, and supplemented, if necessary, by other means of social protection.

(4) Everyone has the right to form and to join trade unions for the protection of his interests.

Article 24

Everyone has the right to rest and leisure, including reasonable limitation of working hours and periodic holidays with pay.

Article 25

(1) Everyone has the right to a standard of living adequate for the health and well-being of himself and of his family, including food, clothing, housing and medical care and necessary social services, and the right to security in the event of unemployment, sickness, disability, widowhood, old age or other lack of livelihood in circumstances beyond his control.

(2) Motherhood and childhood are entitled to special care and assistance. All children, whether born in or out of wedlock, shall enjoy the same social protection.

Article 26

(1) Everyone has the right to education. Education shall be free, at least in the elementary and fundamental stages. Elementary education shall be compulsory. Technical and professional education shall be made generally available and higher education shall be equally accessible to all on the basis of merit.

(2) Education shall be directed to the full development of the human personality and to the strengthening of respect for human rights and fundamental freedoms. It shall promote understanding, tolerance and friendship among all nations, racial or religious groups, and shall further the activities of the United Nations for the maintenance of peace.

(3) Parents have a prior right to choose the kind of education that shall be given to their children.

Article 27

(1) Everyone has the right freely to participate in the cultural life of the community, to enjoy the arts and to share in scientific advancement and its benefits.

(2) Everyone has the right to the protection of the moral and material interests resulting from any scientific, literary or artistic production of which he is the author.

Article 28

Everyone is entitled to a social and international order in which the rights and freedoms set forth in this Declaration can be fully realized.

Article 29

(1) Everyone has duties to the community in which alone the free and full development of his personality is possible.

(2) In the exercise of his rights and freedoms, everyone shall be subject only to such limitations as are determined by law solely for the purpose of securing due recognition and respect for the rights and freedoms of others and of meeting the just requirements of morality, public order and the general welfare in a democratic society.

(3) These rights and freedoms may in no case be exercised contrary to the purposes and principles of the United Nations.

Article 30

Nothing in this Declaration may be interpreted as implying for any State, group or person any right to engage in any activity or to perform any act aimed at the destruction of any of the rights and freedoms set forth herein.

CASES

Case 1: Sapora's Patriarchal Society

SASHA LYUTSE, TOM L. BEAUCHAMP, AND DENIS G. ARNOLD

Sapora, a large Pacific Rim island, has for years been a leading industrial, commercial, and financial center with a flourishing market and growing trade. GlobeCom, an American telecommunications firm long established in Sapora, has decided to expand its Sapora branch and the volume of business it does with local Saporan companies. Ties with local businesses have flourished quickly, and an extremely profitable business relationship has developed. Sapora has rapidly become a major training ground for GlobeCom managers, and successful tenure in Sapora is viewed as a key step on the way to the top of GlobeCom.

Sapora, however, is a traditionally patriarchal society, and its businessmen at the executive level are just that: men. Female executives in the workplace are a rarity, and there is seldom, if ever, a managerial track available to women. Women are often given positions largely designed to make the office more comfortable, such as serving tea and performing basic services. Women are discouraged from aiming at executive positions and are not invited to afterwork social functions that play a vital role in successful employee and corporate bonding – an entrenched aspect of Sapora's business culture. The overwhelmingly male majority of Saporan customers, suppliers, and government officials are also uncomfortable doing business with foreign women, preferring to work with men.

Although GlobeCom abides by strict US gender equality laws in its American branches, its human resource managers who send executives abroad hesitate to violate the unwritten laws and cultural mores of Sapora. They have found over time that female managers working in Sapora tend to be less successful than males; they have a more difficult time dealing with local businesses and are generally offered fewer business opportunities than their male counterparts. Resource managers, who are responsible for the efficacy of the GlobeCom workforce, both domestically and abroad, are sending fewer and fewer women to fill open posts in Sapora.

The American woman's inability to obtain the necessary first-hand experience in dealing with Saporan businesses has become a career handicap. Female employees have found that while in the beginning they move up the company ranks fairly easily in GlobeCom's American branches, they eventually hit a career ceiling because they lack the formative, career-building experience their male counterparts receive in Sapora. It would be difficult, however, to persuade GlobeCom that female managers can succeed in Sapora's culture, which in many subtle and overt ways discourages gender equality.

Discussion Questions

1. Should GlobeCom do business in a country with a patriarchal society? In responding, imagine that GlobeCom could not survive if it stopped doing business in Sapora.

2. Assuming that GlobeCom's female employees are unable to obtain the necessary experience and suffer a career disadvantage because of the situation in Sapora, should the company use some form of compensation (for example, a bonus) to offset the career handicap? Would such compensation be demeaning?

3. What should US gender equality look like in light of GlobeCom's problem?

This case was written by Sasha Lyutse under the supervision of Tom L. Beauchamp and revised by Denis G. Arnold. Sapora is fictional, but the case is based in an existing country that is a powerful player in international markets. © 2017 Denis G. Arnold.

Case 2: Cocaine at the Fortune 500 Level

TOM L. BEAUCHAMP AND DENIS G. ARNOLD

Roberto, a pure libertarian in moral and political philosophy, is deeply impressed by his reading of Robert Nozick's account of justice. He lives in Los Angeles and teaches philosophy at a local university. Roberto is also a frequent user of cocaine, which he enjoys immensely and provides to friends at parties. Neither he nor any of his close friends are addicted. Over the years Roberto has become tired of teaching and now has an opportunity, through old friends who live in Peru, to become a middleman in the cocaine business. Although he is disturbed about the effects cocaine has in some persons, he has never witnessed these effects firsthand. He is giving his friends' business offer serious consideration.

Roberto's research has told him the following: The United States is the largest market for cocaine in the world. Selling cocaine is estimated to be a $94–143 billion plus industry according to Global Financial Integrity, a Washington, DC based non-profit organization that provides analysis designed to help developing nations deal with illicit financial activity. Although he is interested primarily in a Peruvian connection, his research has shown conclusively that the Colombian cartel alone has historically been large enough to place it among the Fortune 500 corporations. According to the United Nations Office on Drugs and Crime's *World Drug Report* (2016), cocaine production in Peru and Bolivia represents about 50 percent of the world's cocaine base; the remaining 50 percent is produced in Columbia. Cocaine is one of Latin America's largest export goods, accounting for 17 percent of the gross domestic product of Peru and experiencing a resurgence of production in Columbia since the end of that nation's long, bloody civil war.

Former Peruvian President Alan Garcia once described cocaine as Latin America's "only successful multinational." It can be and has been analyzed in traditional business categories, with its own entrepreneurs, chemists, laboratories, employment agencies, small organizations, distribution systems, market giants, growth phases, and so forth. Cocaine's profit margins have narrowed in some markets, while expanding in others. It often seeks new markets in order to expand its product line. For example, in the mid-1980s "crack," a potent form of smoked cocaine, was moved heavily into new markets in Europe. Between the mid-1960s and the late 1990s the demand for cocaine grew dramatically (weathering some up and down markets) because of successful supply and marketing. Demand for cocaine in North America peaked around 1998 with 7 million consumers, before declining. However, demand remains strong with over 5 million current consumers in North America according to the 2016 *World Drug Report*. Demand in Europe also remains strong with over 4 million cocaine consumers. Consumer demand in all other regions of the world has increased significantly in recent years. For example, in South America there were just over 3 million consumers in 1998 while currently there are nearly 5 million consumers. Meanwhile, consumption in Asia has grown from less than 200,000 in 1998 to nearly 1.5 million consumers currently.

Roberto sees the cocaine industry as not being subject to taxes, tariffs, or government regulations other than those pertaining to its illegality. It is a pure form of the free market in which supply and demand control transactions. This fact about the business appeals to Roberto, as it seems perfectly suited to his libertarian views. He is well aware that there are severe problems of coercion and violence in some parts of the industry, but he is certain that the wealthy clientele whom he would supply in Los Angeles would neither abuse the drug nor redistribute it to others who might be harmed. He also sees growth opportunities in the Pacific Rim region. Roberto is confident that his Peruvian associates will be honest with him and that he can avoid problems of violence, coercion, and abusive marketing. However, he has recently read a newspaper story that cocaine-use emergencies – especially those involving cocaine-induced heart attacks – continue to be a serious public health problem. It is only this fact that has given him pause before deciding whether or not to enter the cocaine business. He views these health emergencies as unfortunate but not unfair outcomes of the business. Therefore, it is his humanity and not his theory of justice that gives him pause.

This case was prepared by Tom L. Beauchamp with help from Jeff Greene and Sasha Lyutse, and subsequently revised by Denis G. Arnold. © 2017 Denis G. Arnold.

Discussion Questions

1. Would a libertarian – such as Roberto – say that the cocaine business is not unfair so long as no coercion is involved and the system is a pure function of supply and demand? What specific claims by Nozick support your view? Explain.

2. Does justice demand that cocaine be outlawed, or is this not a matter of justice at all? Are questions of justice even meaningful when the activity is beyond the boundaries of law? Explain.

3. Is the distinction Roberto draws between what is unfortunate and what is unfair relevant to a decision about whether an activity is just? Why, or why not. Explain.

Case 3: Surviving (?) on a Minimum Wage

NORMAN E. BOWIE AND DENIS G. ARNOLD

Rainie Sherr of South Scranton, Pennsylvania, works in a fast food restaurant for the minimum wage of $7.25 an hour. This is a welcome change from the previous three years during which time she and her children got by on public welfare. She began working in fast food as a 16-year-old teenager for $3.35 an hour. Twenty-eight years later, at age 44, and the single mother of a 12-year-old son and a 7-year-old daughter, she is struggling to pay the bus fare she needs to get to work

If Rainie worked her normal 36 hours a week, her monthly salary would be just over $1,000 before taxes. She receives $60 a month in child support, and government assistance raises her total monthly income to $1,985. That amount includes food stamps and $710 in Social Security disability payments because her daughter has medical problems. Of course, as is common with hourly workers, sometimes her hours are cut. In the previous week, she lost 12 hours. A housing subsidy keeps her contribution to her monthly rent at $250.

According to one study, a full-time, minimum wage worker supporting himself or herself and another adult without any public assistance could not afford the average cost for food and rent in Lackawanna County. For Lackawanna County, which includes South Scranton, the monthly cost of living for adults with children varied from $3,154 for a single adult with one school age child, to $5,685 for an adult with three young children. Another way of looking at this is through a "self-sufficiency wage" – a measure that calculates how much a person must earn, including various tax credits, to survive without public assistance. In Lackawanna County, a single adult with one child would need $16.91 an hour while an adult with three children would need $30.12 an hour.

Twenty-eight states currently have a higher minimum wage than the federal minimum wage of $7.75 an hour. Pennsylvania is not one of them. The national minimum wage has lost 30 percent of its purchasing power since 1968 according to an analysis by the National Employment Law Project. Not surprisingly, there is pressure to raise the minimum wage as high as $15 per hour. Seattle and San Francisco have already done so, while California and New York State have mandated a graduated increase over several years to a $15 minimum wage. On the other hand, governors in Illinois and New Jersey have vetoed similar legislation on the grounds that such an increase would curtail economic growth in their states.

Critics of proposals to raise the minimum wage argue that such an increase would help some, but would hurt many others because employers would hire fewer people, or would replace workers with robots or other technological innovations. Some studies support the critics, while others do not. A recent study of 137 different minimum wage increases in the United States "found little change in employment in the five years after a minimum-wage increase." According to this analysis, on average workers made more and employment levels remained constant.

As the politicians and scholars debate, Rainie Sherr, who cannot afford a car, uses a $13 toboggan to get her groceries home. Her goal is to earn enough to purchase a car to drive to work, something that she hopes would allow her to get a better paying job.

Discussion Questions

1. Do you think you could provide adequate food, housing, energy, clothing, transportation, and healthcare, for yourself and two children, where you currently live, working 24–36 hours a week for $7.25 an hour ($9,048–$13,572 a year)? Why, or why not? What if you worked 40 hours a week and

This case was written by Norman E. Bowie and Denis G. Arnold for the purposes of classroom discussion and draws from Terrie Morgan-Besecker, "Minimum Wage Earners Struggle to Survive," *Scranton Times Tribune* (December 22, 2013) and Arindrajit Dube, "Minimum Wage and Job Loss," *The New York Times* (July 20, 2017). © 2017 Denis G. Arnold.

earned $15,080 for the year? Could you provide for yourself and two children then? Why, or why not?

2. Do minimum wage earners such as Rainie Sherr earn a just wage? Why, or why not? Explain your answer utilizing theoretical resources from the readings in this chapter.

3. In your view, does the fact that workers like Rainie Sherr need government support to provide for their families' basic needs indicate that the government indirectly subsidizes companies by providing additional income in the form of rent relief, food stamps, and other government programs? Why, or why not? If you answered affirmatively, what is your assessment of the legitimacy of such indirect subsidies for companies? Explain. What is your assessment of the companies themselves if you believe they rely on such subsidies? Explain.

4. Do you believe that minimum wages should be increased to bring them more in line with self-sufficiency wages, despite the claims of those who argue that increasing wages reduces employment by driving up the costs to employers? Why, or why not? Explain your answer utilizing theoretical resources from the readings in this chapter.

Case 4: Wages of Failure: The Ethics of Executive Compensation

JULIAN FRIEDLAND

For the last couple of weeks General Global, a prominent multinational electronics and telecommunications company, was being scolded by editorials in the mainstream press. Its departing CEO, Bill Hogson, had exited with two years' pay and bonuses totaling $100 million after working barely a year. Hogson had presided over a tumultuous and lackluster year for which most of General Global executives thought he was to blame. Hogson was finally choosing to step down after a bitter power struggle involving his firing of several top executives, many of whom were now being rehired by the board. The press saw Hogson's generous exit compensation for doing a poor job as a testament to the dauntless greed infecting the highest levels of corporate America.

Hogson's replacement was Janice White, the previous CFO whom Hogson had fired only a month earlier. In the face of mounting public outrage over exorbitant executive compensation packages for poor leadership, White has asked the board to base her yearly compensation solely on performance. This was a clear break from General Global's policy of paying the average of industry standards. But White felt this change was necessary to send a strong message to the stakeholders that she too would share the burden should the company have to further tighten its belt. Several hundred employees had already been laid off, and many considered that unfair since those layoffs represented the lion's share of Hogson's stratospheric exit package.

Initially, White's request for a merit-based salary seemed a laudable act of courage and integrity. But when a decision had to be made on whether or not to grant her request, several concerns arose at the meeting:

1. Should all the top executives also be paid accordingly?
2. Should there be a cap on total yearly compensation?
3. Would making such changes put the company at a disadvantage when competing for the best talent?
4. Could such changes make the company less stable?

Some thought it would make little sense to base the CEO's salary on performance without doing the same for all executives. But doing so might prove difficult since it is not always clear how responsible each and every one is for the company's successes and failures. The CEO, however, sets the agenda and direction of each fiscal year and, thus, seems ultimately most responsible for the consequences. So, paying her according to merit did not necessarily require everyone else to be paid that way as well.

What about a cap on total yearly compensation? Critics in the press argued that no individual should be making $50 million a year, even if deserved. That money could always be better spent elsewhere in year-end bonuses for employees, increasing stock value, etc. But any such cap might make it more difficult to compete for the best talent in the future. It was important to remember that the millions earned in executive compensation were always reinvested into the economy, which in turn benefited everyone.

Perhaps a compromise was reachable between these conflicting concerns. Basing CEO compensation entirely on performance but without caps would keep the company's talent searches competitive by preserving the specter of achieving great wealth. At the same time, it would inspire the CEO to do the best job possible since she would thereby have more to lose by performing poorly.

This case is written by Julian Friedland. © 2006 Center for Business and Society, Leeds School of Business, University of Colorado, Boulder, Colorado, USA.

Furthermore, this solution would promote loyalty across the company since everyone would know that even the CEO's salary would be on the chopping block if profits faltered. Still, there was one last, important concern. Making such a radical change might actually risk long-term stability. If, for example, White underperformed one year, she would likely redouble her efforts in order to compensate for that personal loss of wealth. But what if, despite her efforts, she underperformed the next year as well? Would she be as likely to leave before inflicting further damage on the company? Without a lucrative exit package, she might very well choose to stay on board longer despite her poor track record, to the detriment of the company. High exit compensation packages have the virtue of allowing poor leaders to resign earlier rather than later, sparing the company any further poor decision-making.

It is one thing to inspire the CEO to outdo herself, but quite another to give her hope against hope. No company should seek to motivate an underperforming leader to stay on. Unfortunately, given the political influence of the CEO in the corporation, top executives and shareholders cannot always be relied upon to fire that person. It can often take several years of failure to muster enough courage in the ranks to do so. As General Global's last CEO proved, many executives risked losing their own jobs in the process with no certainty of ever regaining them. Hence there was perhaps an advantage to giving a CEO the luxury of a lucrative exit package in order to increase the chances that, if need be, she might choose to step down, without bringing the company down with her.

Was the answer then to simply deny Janice White's seemingly noble request for performance-based pay? Or would it make sense to accept her request but preserve a relatively high exit package that could double or even triple her compensation for a disappointing performance? Or would that create a disincentive to perform well? This was turning out to be a much more confounding dilemma than it seemed at first. A decision needs to be made nonetheless. What should it be?

Discussion Questions

1. Do you think executive compensation is generally appropriate or inflated in the United States? Why or why not?
2. Is performance-based pay an attractive solution? Are there any other alternatives to keep from rewarding failure? What are the costs and benefits to these solutions?
3. Are the long-term effects of CEO performance always clear at the end of each fiscal year?
4. Can certain performance-based pay plans make it less likely for CEOs to artificially inflate stock value in the short term? If so, how? If not, why not?

Case 5: SC Johnson: Pyrethrum Sourcing from Kenya
WORLD BUSINESS COUNCIL FOR SUSTAINABLE DEVELOPMENT

Flowers grown by subsistence farmers in the highlands of Kenya are the key active ingredient for value-added products found in households around the world. Pyrethrum, a unique daisy, is the source for a naturally occurring insecticide that degrades quickly back into the earth. Over the past 30 years, US company SC Johnson has become one of the biggest single end users of natural pyrethrins, for RAID™ household insecticide products.

The Pyrethrum Board of Kenya (PBK), a parastatal agency that controls and operates the entire pyrethrum business in Kenya, manages the country's total supply of pyrethrum through a network of farmer cooperatives. SC Johnson has worked directly with PBK since 1970. This relationship has extended considerably beyond that of a normal supplier–purchaser relationship, characterized increasingly by a strong degree of knowledge and technology exchange.

In the early days there was a focus on exchanging skills and knowledge pertaining to crop husbandry and education and training. The focus of the efforts shifted however in the last ten years, predominantly as a result of shortages experienced, as well as the increasing competitiveness of synthetic pyrethroids.

Initially SC Johnson was sourcing primarily natural pyrethrins; however, during the early 1980s, as a result of the supply shortage of pyrethrum, SC Johnson turned to synthetic pyrethroids, which had improved in quality, become less costly, and maintained consistently adequate supply levels. A supplier was identified in Japan, which provided very high levels of customer service, efficiency, and professionalism that made them an appealing supplier. However, the company maintained a preference for using natural pyrethrins and felt strongly about maintaining the relationship established with PBK. The challenge then was to help PBK to reach higher standards as a supplier. Among the issues of greatest importance was PBK's ability to provide a reliable, consistent supply level of pyrethrum. SC Johnson introduced its Quality Assurance Audit to PBK in 1995 and at this time their processes were significantly below established criteria to be considered an SC Johnson "Partner in Quality." Efforts were then directed at helping PBK reach this global standard.

SC Johnson has helped PBK develop planning and forecasting abilities through sharing of best practice examples and ongoing advice regarding establishment and maintenance of a safety stock to help offset harvest shortages. SC Johnson has also provided technical assistance to PBK. The company has provided bioefficacy testing protocols and tools to allow for a better comparison of results between products tested at PBK in Kenya and at SC Johnson in the United States. In addition, SC Johnson has also collaborated in the development of up-to-date analytical chemistry methods that have aided in the identification of new and different pyrethrum extracts.

As a result of this long-term capacity building effort, there has been a notable improvement in product quality and a rise in production standards. PBK have made continuous improvements in their quality control programs, and they have passed supplier audits from SC Johnson as well as by European buyer Aventis. Standards continue to rise and PBK is now seeking International Organization for Standardization (ISO) certification.

In summary:

- Project: Supply chain capacity building and technical assistance program.
- Drivers: Effort to secure high quality raw material supply to avoid use of synthetic alternatives.
- Training/assistance: Planning and forecasting; plant husbandry; customer service; bio-efficacy testing.
- Status: PBK recognized SC Johnson "Partner in Quality."
- Employment: 300,000 jobs industry wide; 680 jobs with PBK.
- Industry level economic impact: US$25 million in export sales value to Kenya.
- Regional level economic impact: 3 percent of profits going to payment for infrastructure.
- Farmer level environmental impact: 900,000 Kenyans gaining access to monetized economy through pyrethrum.
- Social impacts: Industry is funding schooling for more than 30,000 children.
- Environmental impacts: Perennial crop rotation helps maintain soil in 17,600 to 32,000 hectares on Kenyan highlands; little chemical, fossil fuel, fertilizers, or herbicides are necessary; pyrethrum crop does not require irrigation. Relies on natural rainfall.

Discussion Questions

1. How does SC Johnson benefit from working with PBK? Explain.
2. How do the Kenyan people benefit from working with SC Johnson? Explain.
3. How does this case relate to Sen's capabilities approach? Explain. How does the case relate to Miller's analysis of the relationship between companies and consumers in the developed world and the poor in the developing world? Explain.

INDEX

A.C. Widenhouse, 160
A.P. Smith Manufacturing Co.
    v. Barlow, 260
abstract markets, 496
act utilitarians, 18–19
actions (business)
    complicit, 282–84
    Kantian, 21–23
    and prudentiality, 3–4
advertising
    and behavior control, 302–8
    in direct-to-consumer advertising,
        340–43
    pharmaceutical industry, 337–46
affirmative action. *See also* hiring
    defined, 159
    and diversity in hiring and promotion,
        165–69
    Supreme Court decisions on, 161
Affordable Care Act, 260
Age Discrimination in Employment Act
    (1967), 222
agency theory. *See also* stakeholders, busi-
    ness theory
    corporate leadership and, 211–16
    difficulty of balancing interests, 232–33
    distal concerns, 237–38
    environmental, 409–10
    human rights and, 443–44
    market interests and, 497–98
    narrow and broad definitions of, 230–31
    neoclassical nature of, 237
    proximate concerns with, 237
    vagueness of, 231–32
agglomeration, 240
aggregation, 265
agreement view (executive compensation),
    118–19
Ailes, Roger, 199
Alcatel-Lucent, 446
Alcoa, 100
Alder, J., 300
Alien Tort Claims Act, 418
alignment
    and agency theory, 214
    and CEO pay, 121–22

ethical culture systems, 98
    and performance management systems,
        104–5
Allen, W., 237
Allergan, 211, 214, 216
American Beverage Association, 321
American Eagle Distribution Company, 84
American Express, 104
American Greetings Corporation, 260
Andreasen, A.R., 309, 314
Anheuser-Busch, 298
applied ethics, 7
appropriation (information), 265
Arend, A.C., 241
Aristotle, 28
Arnold, D., 302, 373, 434
Arrington, R., 298
Arthur Andersen, 25
Arvida partnerships, 521
asbestos litigation, 5
audits (international), 480
*Austin v. Michigan Chamber of
    Commerce*, 260
Austin, J.L., 392
automobile industry
    corporate social responsibility in,
        477–79
    General Motors, 67, 124–25, 140, 166,
        221, 405
    greenwashing in, 405
    Tesla, 427–29
    Volkswagen, 429–31
autonomous desire, 305
autonomy
    and behavior control, 304–8
    in direct-to-consumer advertising, 339
    in marketing ethics, 296
    moral, 271–72
    and right to know, 73–74
aviation industry, 76

B. Sanfield Inc. v. Finlay Fine Jewelry Corp,
    299, 346
backdating, 24–25
Baier, A. C., 110
Bailey, J. M., 313

Bank of America, 153–55, 538
Bartlett, C. A., 441–43
Basic Black, 482–83, 484–86
Bass Pro Shops, 198
Bass, B. M., 92
Basu, K., 447
Bathsheba Syndrome, 109
BB&T bank, 3
Beauchamp, T., 161
Beazer Homes USA, 23
behavior control
    and advertising, 302–8
    and contract at will, 58–59
    and marketing, 297
behavioral ethics, 106
beneficence, 240
benefit, 240
benevolence, 15
Bennis, W., 93
Bentham, Jeremy, 16, 18
Berle, A., 213
Bextra, 366
biomimicry (natural capitalism), 387–88
Bliss, Dave, 107
blocking markets
    in democracy, 500–1
    in globalization, 578
    noxious, 501
board of directors
    CEO independence and, 118
    and corporate social responsibility, 215
    and executive bad behavior, 109
    and executive pay, 89–90
Boatright, J., 44, 207, 495
Bognanno, M. L., 122
Boisjoly, Roger, 156–57
Bok, S., 125, 127
bona fide agreements (insider trading), 529
bona fide occupational qualification (legal
    defense), 171
Boulding, K., 439
Bourguignon, F., 567
Bower, J., 206
Bowie, N., 42, 125, 433
Braungart, Michael, 388–89
Braybrooke, D., 304

breach of confidentiality, 265
Brenkert, G., 91, 299
Brennan, J., 493, 507–12
bribery. *See also* corruption
    conditional nature of, 8
    corporate intentionality and, 442
    effort to criminalize, 460–61
    reporting, 464
    sweatshops and, 448–53
    Walmart, 490
Bribery Act (2010), 442, 446, 474
British Petroleum, 86–87, 101, 406
Brooks, D., 107
Brotman, Jeffrey, 49–50
Brown and Williamson, 141
Brown, M. E., 93
Browne, Lord John, 101, 108
Brownell, K., 300, 317
Brundtland Commission, 390–97
Brundtland Report (1987), 375–76
Brune, M., 405
BST (hormone), 326–27
Bureau of Statistics (International Labour
    Organization), 451
Burns, J. M., 92
Burwell v. Hobby Lobby Stores, Inc., 260
business exploitation
    of developing countries, 572–75
    gaps in law, 446–48
    in price gouging, 513–14
Business Principles for Countering Bribery
    (report), 462
business theory. *See also* agency theory
    and CSR, 238–43
    foundations of, 238–42
    of the good, 17
    implications of, 242–43
Byham, W., 102
Byrne, J., 100–1

Cain, D.M., 321
capability building model, 455–57, 545,
    562–63
capital (environmental sustainability), 378
capitalism
    economic justice and, 546–47
    human-made, 383–85
    natural, 381–83, 385–90
Carbona, Gene, 331–32
Carnoules Declaration, 386
Carr, A., 205
Cartel, The, 535
Cascio, W., 42–43, 207
case law, 4

categorical imperative, 22–23
Caux Roundtable Principles of Business,
    433, 438
censorship (Internet), 279–89
Center for Consumer Freedom, 321
*Central Hudson Gas and Electric Corp
    v. Public Service Commission*, 300,
    326, 348
CEO (chief executive officer)
    cult of, 110
    social responsibilities of, 208–11
    stakeholder management responsibil-
        ities, 225–26
    susceptibility to bad behavior, 107–9
CEO pay. *See* executive compensation
Challenger, 156–57
Chamberlain, Wilt, 556–57
Chevron Oil, 5
children
    baby buying, 503–4
    forced labor of, 451, 476–77, 479, 498,
        501, 569
    industry charity to, 319
    industry self-regulation to, 318
    marketing to, 299–300
    mortality rates in developing coun-
        tries, 568
    obesity in, 315–16, 355–58
    on-air product mentions, 349
    pornography, 502
    selling of, 493–94
    television advertising towards, 352–55,
        357–58
    Vioxx and, 363
    vulnerability of, 309, 313
Chinese business practices, 294
Chiquita, 453
choice
    free, 306–7, 450
    rational desire and, 305–6
ChoicePoint, 274
Chrysler, 477–79
churning, 523
Cicero, Sergio, 490
Cisco Systems, 262–63, 279, 286–87, 372
Citicorp, 96
*Citizens United v. Federal Election
    Commission*, 260
Ciulla, J., 88–89
Civil Rights Act (1964), 56, 162, 170–74
Clean Air Act (1990), 222, 413, 422, 430–31
Clean Cruise Ship Act, 416
Clean Water Act (1977), 222, 408
climate change, 370–72, 383, 398–99

Coca-Cola Co. v. Tropicana Products Inc.,
    298, 346–47
Coca-Cola Company, 167, 346–47, 359–60
codes of conduct
    ethical, 103
    greenwashing the, 410
    Royal Caribbean, 415–16
    voluntary international, 454–55
    Walmart, 479–80
coercion and employment-at-will princi-
    ple, 71
Coffee, J. C., 236
cognitive dissonance, 110
cognitive vulnerability, 311
Cohen, M., 45
collective value, 240–41, 243
Collins, J., 102
collusion, 535–36
commercial speech
    consumers' right-to-know and, 328
    court protection of, 326
    deception in, 315–23
    regulations of, 326–28
    restrictions on, 348
common morality theory, 30–32
communitarianism, 116
community advisory panels, 258–59
company-centered model, 216–20
competition
    capability building model and, 455
    effectiveness of, 239
    in ethical marketing, 310, 311
    in virtue ethics, 29
Competitive Advantage Through People
    (Pfeiffer), 206
*Complete Book of Wall Street Ethics,
    The* (Walker), 521
complicity (foreign government), 262–63,
    279–89
Comprehensive Environmental Response
    Compensation and Liability Act
    (1980), 413
compulsive behavior, 306
conceptual approach (ethics), 6
conceptual clarity (disagreement), 10
confirmation bias, 110
conformity bias, 107
Conley, J. M., 243
consumer choice, 18
consumer electronics industry
    dynamic market conditions in, 457
    supply chains in, 454
Consumer Financial Protection Bureau,
    40–41

consumer privacy. *See* privacy
contract at will, 56–61
contracting defects, 115
Convention against Corruption, 460
Convention on Combating Bribery of
    Foreign Public Officials, 460
conventional capitalism, 383–85
Cooper, Cynthia, 139–40
corporate culture
    bad behavior of, 236–38
    safety and, 76
    Wells Fargo, 149–52
corporate governance models
    agency theory, 211–16
    company-centered, 216–20
corporate political activity
    environmental, 400–2
    human rights and, 393–94
corporate social responsibility (CSR)
    and agency theory, 211–16, 220–23,
        230–33, 236–38
    business theory and, 238–43
    company-centered model, 216–20
    as corporate framing strategy, 318–19
    corruption and, 462–64
    defined, 188
    ethical culture and moral responsibil-
        ity, 207
    and profits, 207–11
    H.B. Fuller, 255–56
    Holcim Group, 258–59
    India Companies Act (2013), 260
    ITC, 259–60
    Johnson & Johnson, 260
    Merck, 256–57
    New York State Electric and Gas
        Corporation, 253–54
    on greenhouse gases, 400
    stakeholders and, 204–7, 223–25
    Turing Pharmaceutical, 251–52
corruption. *See also* bribery
    business case for combating, 461
    corporate social responsibility and,
        462–64
    defined, 459
    human rights, 459–60
    laws to prevent, 460
    public/private collective action on,
        464
Cortina, J., 163–64
Costco, 42–43, 49–54, 229
costs
    in consumer electronics industry, 457
    of contract at will, 60

in direct-to-consumer advertising,
    338–39
and product claim advertisements,
    340–41
transaction, 74
Council for the Protection of Rural
    England, 377
Countrywide Financial, 536–38
Cowherd, D. M., 122
Crovitz, L. G., 275
cruise ship industry, 415–16
cult of the CEO, 110
cultural systems
    capability building model and, 456
    and community advisory panels, 258–59
    ethical, 98–102, 207
    orientation/training programs, 103
    performance management, 103–5
    policies and codes, 103
    relativism of, 436
    relativism of beliefs, 7–9
    relativism of standards in, 437–38
    selection, 102
    values and mission statements, 102

Daraprim, 251–52
data mining, 273–74
data protection and privacy, 267–72
Data Protection Directive (1998), 276–77
Davis, G. F., 237
de Monchy, Katlean, 351
deception
    commercial speech limits and, 315–23
    financial services, 521–22, 528
    vulnerability, 110, 300
decisional interference (information), 265
Declaration of Independence, 241
Deepwater Horizon, 86–87
Delaney amendment, 70
delisting (website), 285
Dell Computer Corporation, 168
democracy
    global shift towards, 569
    market equality in, 499–501
deontological theories, 93–94, 180, 241,
    See also Kantianism
Department of Agriculture, 320
Department of Health and Human
    Services, 319, 337
descriptive approach (ethics)
    defined, 6
    ethical egoism, 13–15
    psychological egoism, 11–13
desert argument, 113–14, 119–20

desire
    autonomous, 305
    rational, 305–6
DesJardins, J., 373
detail men, 330
Dewey, John, 264, 265–66
Diageo, 446
Diener, E., 240
difference principle, 544, 552–53
dignity and business success, 241–42
direct acts (complicit), 282, 284
direct cause concept, 69–70
direct-to-consumer advertising
    paid experts, 349–52
    pharmaceutical industry, 301–2,
        337–46
    school supplies, 352–53
disadvantaged versus vulnerability, 309
discrimination
    at Bass Pro Shops, 198
    and hazards, 80
    mortgage lending, 537
    sexism, 109
    sexism and patriarchy, 583
    sexism in London, 83
    systemic disparate treatment, 172–73
    toward employees, 48
    towards LGBT community, 186–88
    trade wars as, 575
    unintentional, 168
discriminatory intent, 171
disparate treatment, 170, 171–72
distortion (information), 265
distributive justice theories, 542–43,
    553–54
diversity
    and affirmative action, 165–69
    Alcoa, 100
    corporate outreach for, 160–61
    federal policies for, 159–60
    organizational policies for, 166–68
Dodd-Frank Act (2011), 91
dominant theory. *See* agency theory
Donaldson, T., 433
Dow Chemical Company, 453, 467
*Dow Chemical Company and Shell Oil
    Company v. Domingo Castro Alfaro*,
    434, 467
Dow Corning, 5
Dow Jones Sustainability Index, 392
Draft Norms of Responsibilities of
    Transnational Corporations and
    Other Business Enterprises, 280
Dreher, B., 50–51

due process and employment-at-will principle, 62–67
Dunfee, T., 465
Dunlap, Al, 29, 93, 100–1
Durham-Humphrey Amendment (1951), 342
Duska, R., 90
Dutch East India Company, 218

eBay, 276
economic justice. *See also* justice
    capitalism, 546–47
    distributive theories, 542–43
    and drug trade, 584
    egalitarianism, 544, 549–54
    entitlement theory, 554–57
    global, 547–48
    libertarianism, 545, 561–63
    trade, 575–77
    utilitarianism, 543, 557–61
effectiveness
    of cooperation over competition, 239
    ethical, 93
efficiency
    capability building model and, 455–57
    corruption and, 461
    at Costco, 229
    in natural capitalism, 387
    in utilitarianism, 16–17
egalitarianism, 115–16, 543, 544, 549–54,
    See also equality
egoism, 11–15
Ehrenberg, R., 122
Eli Lily, 446
Elkington, J., 243
Elliott, C., 301
Elo TouchSystems Inc., 4
Em Kay Equities, 145–46
Emerson, T., 265
employees. *See also* whistleblowing
    Costco benefits, 52
    decency towards in discount stores,
        49–54
    Global Compact on, 469
    harassment and discrimination
        toward, 48
    health and safety of, 44–45, 47–48,
        68–80, 84, 85–87
    hiring and firing of, 43–44, 56–61,
        84–85
    privacy of, 48
    respect-for-persons principle, 45–47
    social media monitoring of, 291–92
    worker notification, 72–75

employment-at-will principle, 43, 47, 62–67
Enron, 24–25, 89, 107, 236
entitlement theory, 26, 108, 545, 554–57
*Environmental Marketing Strategy:
    The Emergence of Corporate
    Environmentalism as Market
    Strategy* (Menon), 406
environmental sustainability
    and agency theory, 237–38
    in the Amazon, 417–19
    background of, 375–76
    Brundtland Commission and, 390–97
    business misconduct, 373–74, 398–402,
        404–10
    business obligation to, 372–73
    climate change, 370–72
    crisis, 369–70
    criteria for, 378–80
    cruise ship industry, 415–16
    defined, 369
    equity indexes, 461
    Global Compact on, 469
    hypocritical leadership and, 101
    implementation of, 380
    laws for, 222
    natural capitalism and, 381–90
    objectives, 376–78
    reception of, 376
    strong versus weak, 378
    and a theory of business, 242–43
environmental sustainability examples
    Frito-Lay, 420–26
    General Electric Company, 99
    Interface Corporation and, 419–20
    Tesla, 427–29
    Volkswagen, 429–31
EpiPen, 533–34
Epstein, R., 43
Equal Employment Opportunity
    Commission, 159, 162, 194–95
Equal Pay Act (1963), 170, 222
equality. *See also* egalitarianism
    democratic, 499–501
    difference principle and, 544
    globalization and, 564–65, 566–67,
        575–77
    informational, 270
    market, 499–501
    price gouging undermines, 517–18
ethical egoism, 13–15
ethical relativism, 433, 436–40
ethical theory
    approaches to the study of, 6–7
    defined, 1–2

ethical theory and business practices
    basic terms of, 1–3
    Brundtland Commission environmental, 391–92, 395–97
    market regulation, 492–93
    problems with, 7–15
    salesmanship and, 333–35
Etzioni, A., 262
executive compensation. *See also* wages,
    CEO pay
    and agency theory, 215
    agreement view, 117, 118–19
    and contractual freedom to do, 114
    communitarianism, 116
    complexity of, 113
    Costco, 52
    Countrywide Financial, 538
    desert argument, 113–14, 117, 119–20
    distributive justice, 115–16
    EpiPen, 534
    ethical, 89–90
    Merrill Lynch and Bank of America,
        153–55
    moral issues in, 112–13, 586–87
    utility maximization, 114–15, 118, 120–22
experts (direct-to-consumer advertising),
    349–52
exploitation
    of gaps in law, 446–48
    price gouging and, 513–14
    of the vulnerable, 514, 572–75
Extractive Industries Transparency
    Initiative, 465
Exxon, 401

Facebook, 34–35, 275, 291–92, 293–94
Factor Ten Club, 386, 387
factual beliefs
    in normative ethical theory deci-
        sions, 35
    relativism of, 8–9
Fair Housing Act (1968), 277
fairness
    of contract at will, 56–57
    in distributive justice, 543
    insider trading and, 524–25, 528–29
    price gouging and, 513, 517–18
false attribution error, 109
False Claims Act (1986), 91, 366
false consensus effect, 110
Family Smoking Prevention and Tobacco
    Control Act, 327
Federal Trade Commission, 295, 357, 517
Fen-Phen, 337

Ferraro, F., 237
financial crisis. *See* great recession
financial services industry
    analysis of Costco and Walmart, 50–51
    churning in, 523
    collusion in, 535–36
    deception in, 521–22
    insider trading, 523–26, 527–31, 539–41
    predatory lending, 536–38
    suitability of offerings in, 523
firing
    and contract at will, 58
    disparate treatment in, 171
    employees, 43–44
    over brand choices, 84–85
Fishman, Charles, 49–54
Fogel, F., 426
Folk Theory of Voting Ethics, 505–6
Food and Drug Administration
    Bextra, 366
    influence of, 319
    milk hormones and, 326
    Neurontin, 365–66
    pharmaceutical industry and, 333,
        337–38, 339, 342
    Vioxx, 364
food industry
    buying research and development, 320–21
    child labor in, 476–77
    cigarette, 321–22
    Frito-Lay, 420–26
    and global hunger, 569
    government influence by, 319–20
    obesity in, 315–17, 322–23
    public relations of, 317–18
Foreign Corrupt Practices Act (1977), 435,
    442, 446, 460, 474
foreign direct investment, 547–48
forum non conveniens, 467
Fox News, 199
Framework Convention on Tobacco
    Control, 320
framing strategy (marketing defense)
    corporate social responsibility as, 318–19
    government influence as, 319–20
    personal responsibility script as, 317–18
    safer products as, 321–22
    scientific disputes as, 320–21
    self-regulation as, 318
Frank Statement to Cigarette Smokers,
    A (article), 315
Frankfurt, H., 305
Franklin, David, 336
free choice

behavior control and, 306–7
    sweatshops and, 450
free markets
    drug trade and, 584
    and economic justice, 546–47
    shortfall in equity in global, 578
    sweatshop advantages, 449
    without limits, 502–3
free riders, 269
freeloader, 439
Freeman, R. E., 206, 238, 242
Frenkel, S., 457
Friedman, Milton, 48, 204–7, 212–13
Frito-Lay, 420–26

Galanti, Richard, 50, 51, 52
Galaxywire, 81–82
Galbraith, J. K., 304
Gao Feng, 477–79
Gardiner, S., 400
garment industry
    corruption in, 460
    international costs, 482–86
    sweatshops in, 434–50
Gathii, J., 460
General Electric Company, 99, 446
General Motors, 67, 124–25, 140, 166,
    221, 405
Gewirth, A., 70
Ghoshal, S., 237, 441–43
gifts
    bribery and, 462
    pharmaceutical, 333–36
Gill, Contonius, 160
Gilmartin, Raymond, 361–62
GlaxoSmithKline, 91–92, 142–43, 251
Glen, M., 124–25
Glickman, Daniel, 320
Global 100, 391
Global 100 ranking, 394
Global Compact, 280, 283, 459–60, 462, 469
Global Energy Balance Network, 360
Global Reporting Initiative, 391, 393–94,
    396, 463–64
globalization. *See also* international
    business
    economic growth and, 565–66
    human welfare and, 568–69
    inequality in, 564–65, 566–67, 579
    morality of, 578
    poverty and, 567–68
Goklany, I., 568
golden rice, 396–97
Golden Rule, 45–46, 239

Gond, J., 447
good voting
    commodified, 505–7
    defined, 505
good will (Kantian), 22–23
Google, 196, 262–63, 273, 279, 282, 286
Gordon, I., 50–51
governance
    democratic equality and, 500–1
    distributive justice theories, 553–54
    gaps in, 446–48
Graham, D., 458
great recession, 3, 23, 236, 495, 536–38
Greenberg, Corey, 351–52
greenhouse gases, 371, 398–402, 424–25
Greenpeace, 10
greenwashing, 404–10
Grocery Manufacturers of America, 319
Gross National Income (global), 570
Guiding Principles (pharmaceutical adver-
    tising), 343–44, 354
Guiding Principles on Business and Human
    Rights (2011), 444, 459

H. B. Fuller, 255–56
Hansen, H., 235
harm. *See also* safety
    information-based, 269–70, 296
    insider trading causing, 527–28
    marketing, 313–15
    markets without limits and, 502–3
    noxious markets causing, 497
    tobacco causing, 327–28
    Vioxx causing, 361–64
harassment. *See also* sexism and sexual
    harrassment
    toward employees, 48
    at Uber, 148
Harrison, D. A., 93
Hartman, L., 448
Hawken, P., 373, 407
Hayek, F. A., 514–16
hazards
    discrimination because of, 80
    and employee safety, 44–45
    and federal regulations, 69
    prescription pharmaceutical as, 341–42
    right to know about, 72–75
health
    basic international norms on, 451–52
    employees, 44–45, 47–48
    and employment-at-will principle,
        68–75
    smoking, 84

Health and Wellness Advisory Council, 355–56
hedge fund interventions, 216
hedonic calculus, 18
Heifetz, R.A., 92
help seeking advertisements, 343–46
Hess, D., 436
heterosexism, 186–88
high-reliability organizations, 76–77
Hill, T. E., 47
Hines, Jacquelyn, 160
hiring. See also affirmative action
    Bass Pro Shops, 198
    CE utility maximization and pay, 120–22
    disparate treatment in, 171, 172–73
    employees, 43–44
    quotas, 168
Hirsch, Sam, 357
Hitler problem, 92–93
Hobbes, Thomas, 14, 30, 188
Hobby Lobby Stores, 260
Hoffman-LaRoche, 43
Holcim Group, 258–59
Holland, A., 372
Hollander, E. P., 95
Holmes, S., 229
Hoofnagle, C., 274
Hopkins, A., 76–77
Horgan, K. B., 317
hostile work environment, 173
housing bubble, 23
human rights. See also Protect, Respect and Remedy Framework
    basic international, 450–52
    corruption and, 459–60
    ethical theories based on, 25–28
    Global Compact on, 469
    in international garment industry, 482–86
    international human rights and, 440–65
    United Nations Declaration, 433
human-made capitalism, 378, 379, 383–85
Hume, David, 16, 30

IBM
    affirmative action policy goals, 166
    corruption in, 446
identification (information), 265
ImClone Systems, 539–41
Immelt, Jeffrey, 12, 99
impartiality
    Kantian, 24–25
    moral point of view, 34

imperfect information, 60
incentive compatibility, 115
increased accessibility (information), 265
India Companies Act (2013), 260
indirect acts (complicit), 283, 284
indirect information advertising, 304
insecurity (information), 265
insider trading, 495–96, 523–26, 527–31
instant entitlement bias, 108
Institute of Medicine, 357–58
Integration Thesis, 223
integrity
    in environmental sustainability, 377
    in normative ethical theory decisions, 35–36
integrity theory
    components of, 129
    duties of employees in, 129–30
    principle of positional responsibility, 130–36
intentionality (corporate), 441–43
Interface Corporation, 419–20
Interfaith Center on Corporate Responsibility, 449
Intergovernmental Panel on Climate Change, 370–71, 398–99
internalization, 96–97
international business. See also globalization
    capability building model, 455–57
    corruption in, 459
    drug trade and, 584
    economic justice in, 547–48, 587–88
    exploitation by, 572–75
    human rights obligations, 440–65, 477–79
    relativism of moral standards, 436–40
    retailer and consumer pressure in, 457
    supply chains in, 453–55, 457
    universal moral norms and, 434–53
International Corporate Governance Network, 461
International Council on Human Rights, 282, 283
International Covenant on Civil and Political Rights, 280, 394, 460
International Covenant on Economic, Social, and Cultural Rights, 460
International Labor Rights Fund, 480–81
International Labour Organization, 451–52, 454
international law (defined), 4
Internet
    content providers, 263, 279–89

foreign government complicity and, 262–63
    privacy issues and, 261–62
    service providers, 281
interrogation, 265
intrinsic value, 239–40
intrusion (information), 265
ITC, 259–60

J&R Well Services and Dart Energy, 160
Jacques, E., 243
Jaworski, P., 493, 507–12
Jefferson, Thomas, 98
Jensen, M., 212–13, 216
John and Jane Doe et al. v. Walmart Stores, 480–81
John Doe, et al., v. Unocal, 434, 468
Johnson & Johnson, 93, 108, 260, 446
Johnson Controls, 80
Johnson, Lyndon, 165
just procedures, 32
just results, 32
justice. See also economic justice
    in Brundtland Report, 391
    in executive compensation, 115–16
    in normative ethical theory, 32–33
    informational, 270–71
    and public morality, 2
justification
    of due process absence in employment-at-will, 67
    for employment-at-will, 63–65
    and moral philosophy, 2
    of right to know, 73–74
    and rights-based theories, 28
    for taking advantage of developing country, 571–72

Kalanick, Travis, 147–48
Kanbur, R., 497
Kantianism, 6, 20–25, 33, 45–46, 433, 439–40, See also deontological theories
Kasky v. Nike, Inc., 299
Kateb, G., 241
Katz, J., 337
KBR, 446
Kearney, Neil, 452
Kelleher, Herb, 98
Kellogg, 298
Kendrick, Kenneth, 138, 140
Kessler, D., 317, 319, 320
keyword filtering, 284–86
kidney sale, 20

King, E., 163–64
Kiobel v. Royal Dutch Petroleum, 434, 468–69
Knight, Philip, 453
knowledge gap, 296, 497
Kolb, R., 90
Kozloff, E., 50
Kraft General Foods, 355–56, 358
Kresge, Stanley, 5–6

labor. *See* employees
Ladd, J., 125–26
Lagon, M. P., 241
Lanham Act, 346
law
    and agency theory, 213, 221–22
    and contract at will, 56
    anti-corruption, 474
    corporate political activity to influence, 400–2
    diversity rulings in, 167
    and due process, 62–67
    and employee firing, 44
    employee loyalty, 91
    environmental greenwashing, 408–9
    insider trading, 523–24, 525
    international business exploitation of gaps in, 446–65
    LGBT community protection, 164, 186
    minimum wage and work hours, 451, 575
    morality and, 4–5
    in occupational health and safety, 69
    price gouging, 512–14, 515, 516–17
    privacy merchants and, 274–78
    private regulations and labor, 457–58
    religious freedom, 164
    self-regulation of, 275–76
    social control and, 58
    statutory, 4
    and whistleblowing, 142–43
Lay, Kenneth, 107, 139
leadership
    bad behavior and, 106–10
    in CSR company-centered model, 217
    ethical culture and, 88–89, 98–100
    hypocritical, 101
    nature of good, 92–95
    neutral/silent, 101–2
    unethical, 100–1, 147–48, 149–52
Leadership in Energy and Environmental Design, 373
Leopold, Aldo, 377
Levi Strauss & Co., 453
Levine, D. I., 122

Levitt, T., 304
LGBT community
    discrimination toward, 48
    rights at work, 164, 186–89
libertarianism
    and free trade in drugs, 584
    justice and, 543, 561–63
    sale of votes and, 493
    self-regulation and, 275–76
    theory of, 545
LIBOR (London Interbank Offered Rate), 535–36
Lindblom, C., 401
Liu, C., 162–63
Local 28 v. Equal Employment Opportunity Commission (Sheet Metal Workers), 161
Locke, John, 26, 188, 549, 557
Locke, R., 453
Loewenstein, G., 321
Longenecker, C. O., 109
loss aversion, 107
Lott, Trent, 93
Lovins, A., 373
Lovins, H., 373
loyalty (whistleblowing), 129–36
Loyalty Effect, The (Reichheld), 206
Ludwig, D. C., 109

MacCarthy, M., 69
Maccoby, M., 94
Macgill, E., 162–63
macho culture, 83
Maitland, I., 65
manipulation (marketing), 297–99, 303, 307–8, 341–42
Maritime Anti-Corruption Network, 464
market morality, 439–40
market regulation. *See also* self-regulation
    baby buying and, 503–4
    democratic, 499–501
    ethical limits of, 493–94
    financial services and, 495–96, 520–31
    in libertarian utopia, 507–12
    marketing to children, 358
    noxious markets and, 496–99, 501
    price gouging and, 494–95, 512–20
    principle of wrongful possession, 502–3
    utopian vote selling and ethics, 507–12
    vote selling and ethics, 504–7
marketing ethics
    concept of, 295–302
    greenwashing, 404–10
    pharmaceutical, 330–37

and the vulnerable, 308–15
Markets Without Limits (Brennan and Jaworski), 502, 507
Marlboro Protection Act, 327
Marriott Corporation, 3
Marsh v. Alabama, 222
Marshall, T.H., 499–500
MATRIX (database), 274
Mazur, J., 564
McCain-Feingold Act (2002), 260
McClelland, D. C., 94
McDonald's Corporation, 356–57
McDonnell Douglas Corp v. Green, 170
McGarity, T. O., 74
McGraw-Hill Company, 161
McKinnell, H., 338
McNealy, Scott, 275
Means, G., 213
Mectizan, 257
Merck, 12, 256–57, 296, 331–32, 361–64
Meritor Savings Bank v. Vinson, 162, 173, 192
Merrill Lynch, 153–55, 521
Miceli, M., 91
Michaels, D., 317, 320
Microsoft, 276, 279, 282
Milgram, S., 106
Mill, John Stuart, 16, 18, 93–94, 376
Miller Brewing Co., 84–85
Miller, R., 548
minimum wage
    law, 451, 575
    survival on, 585
misappropriation theory, 524, 531
mission statements, 102
Montoya, Laudette, 160
Mooney, C., 317, 320
Moore, D. A., 321
moral disagreement methods, 9–11
moral equilibrium, 108
moral license, 108
morality
    compensation and, 108
    of corporate diversity programs, 167–68
    defined, 1
    and ethical theory, 1–2
    executive compensation, 586–87
    globalization, 578
    human rights and, 443–44
    international business obligations to, 440–65
    law and, 4–5
    marketing and, 308–15
    of the marketplace, 433

morality (cont.)
    point of view, 33–34
    of protecting personal data, 269–72
    prudence and, 2–3
    rationalization in, 108–9
    reformers in, 438
    relativism of, 436–39
    and responsibility in ethical culture, 207
    and the rule of conscience, 5–6
    standards, 94–95
Moran, P., 237
Moriarty, J., 90
Morrison, C., 567
Morton Thiokol, 156–57
motivation
    in virtue ethics, 28–29
    vulnerability and, 312
Motorola, 21
Mr. Oppenheim, 349–50
multiculturalism
    and common morality theory, 30–31
    and ethical theory, 7–9
    and rights-based theories, 28
multinational corporations. *See* interna-
    tional business
MyFriends.com (fictitious business), 289
Mylan, 533–34

Nabisco, 317–18
Nanus, B., 93
NASA, 77, 156–57
Nash, J., 407
National Labor Relations Act (1935),
    56, 222
National Library of Medicine, 344
natural capitalism, 378, 379, 381–90
natural rights, 26
Navient, 40–41
Near, J., 91
negative obligations, 27
negative value, 239
Nelson, K., 89, 96, 207
Nelson, P., 304
neoclassical theory. *See* agency theory
Nestle, M., 317
Neurontin, 336–37, 365–66
New Breed Logistics, 160
New York State Electric and Gas
    Corporation, 253–54
Nike, 452, 453, 454–55, 456–57
nonworseness claim, 514
Nooyi, I., 421
normative ethical theory
    common morality theory and, 30–32

defined, 6–7
    justice theories and, 32–33
    Kantianism and, 20–25
    moral point of view and, 33–34
    multi-step decision procedure, 34–36
    relativism and, 7–8
    rights theories and, 25–28
    utilitarianism and, 16–20
    virtue ethics and, 28–29
noxious markets
    basic parameters of, 497–99
    regulation of, 501
    versus abstract markets, 496
Nozick, Robert, 26, 71, 545, 584
nuclear power industry
    safety, 76
    whistleblowing, 124
nuclear weapons, 502

obesity
    child, 315–16, 355–58
    and Coca-Cola, 359–60
    corporate strategy of, 318
    epidemic of, 316
    Frank Statement, 322
    Kraft General Foods, 355–58
objectivity
    and moral disagreements, 10
    and relativism, 7–9
obligation
    in common morality theory, 30
    Kantian, 22
    and rights-based theories, 26–27
    utilitarian, 557–61
Occupational Safety and Health Act
    (1970), 69
Office of the United Nations High
    Commissioner for Human
    Rights, 282
Oishi, S., 240
Oldani, Michael, 333–35
O'Neill, Paul, 100
Open Question Argument, 222–23
opt in/out (information sharing), 276–77
optimization (collective value), 243
O'Reilly, Bill, 199
Oreskes, N., 371
Organisation for Economic Co-operation
    and Development, 237, 252, 440, 474
organizational culture
    defined, 95–96
    multisystem framework of, 97–98
    socialization and internalization, 96–97
    strong versus weak, 96

    and whistleblowing, 136–38
organizational training
    affirmative action and discrimination,
        167–68
    LGBT community, 189
orientation/training programs, 103
original position (egalitarian), 551–52
Orts, E., 207
outsourcing
    morals of, 81–82
    tax breaks to prevent, 85–86
overconfidence, 107–8, 110
overlapping consensus, 239
overpopulation, 560–61

Packard, V., 303
Pain, L., 206
Palazzo, G., 447
Pariser, E., 274
Parke-Davis, 333, 336
participant. *See* stakeholders
Payne v. Western & Atlantic, 56, 57
Peanut Corporation of America, 138
Peek, M., 277
Pelham v. McDonald's Corporation, 356–57
Pennsylvania State Police v. Suders, 172
performance management systems, 103–5
personal positivity bias, 110
personal responsibility script, 317–18
petroleum industry, 467–69
Pfeffer, J., 237
Pfizer, 336–37, 339, 365–67, 446
pharmaceutical industry
    biomimicry in, 388
    Daraprim, 251–52
    direct to consumer advertising, 337–46
    drugs reps, 330–37
    marketing targets, 300–2
Pharmaceutical Research and
    Manufacturers of America, 337,
    339–40, 343–44, 355, 367
Physician Masterfile, 334
Plato, 28
pluralistic utilitarians, 17
Pogge, T., 567–68
political action committee, 260
political speech, 300
Porter, M. E., 236
positive obligations, 27
positive organizational scholarship, 206
positive value, 239
Potoski, M., 458
Potter v. Village Bank of New Jersey, 145–46
poverty

global economic growth and, 565–66, 567–68
globalization and, 564–65, 578
human welfare and, 568–69
minimum wage survival and, 585
Prakash, A., 458
predatory lending, 495, 536–38
preferences (utilitarian), 17
preferential policies
and affirmative action, 165
and principle of compensatory justice, 161
Prentice, R., 89
Prescription Drug User Fee Act (1992), 333
prescriptive approach (ethics), 6–7
price gouging, 494–95, 512–20
Price, Sol, 49–50
Price, T. L., 95
pricing strategy (Costco), 51
Prilosec, 331
Princeton University, 260
Principal-Agent theory, 268
Principle of Ethical Voting, 505, 508–10
principle of positional responsibility
implications of, 132
nature of, 130–32
scope of, 132–33
stringency of, 133–36
principle of redress, 552
principle of utility, 16
privacy
and complicity, 262–63, 279–89
data protection and, 267–72
employee, 48
and the Internet, 261–62
meaning and value of, 263–66
social media and, 291–92
triangulation and, 274
Privacy Act (1974), 274
privacy merchants, 273, 274–78
private regulations
capability building model and, 455–57
international business, 453–55
international supply chains, 453–58
profiling, 273–74
Project Share, 254
Protect, Respect and Remedy Framework, 433, 438, 440–41, 444, 445, 459, 470–73, See also human rights
Prudence, self-interest
and agency theory, 214
and CEO pay, 118
corporate differing from shareholders, 218–20

and egoism, 15
morality and, 2–3
psychological egoism, 11–13
public health research, 359–60
Public Interest Disclosure Act (1999), 91
public morality, 2
public relations, 317–19
public speech, 300
public/private distinction
data privacy and, 274–75
and employment-at-will principle, 66–67
of information in China, 279–89
insider trading, and public shares, 214, 523–24
puffery, 302–3

quotas (hiring), 168

radical resource productivity (natural capitalism), 386–87
Radin, T., 44
Ramonet, I., 564
rationality
and desire, 305–6
morality and, 33, 108–9
Rawls, John, 239, 439–40, 544
Reddy, S., 567–68
regulation. See market regulation
relativism
of judgments, 9
and objectivity of beliefs, 7–9
of standards, 9, 436–40
religious freedom laws, 164
Religious Freedom Restoration Act (1993), 260
reminder advertisements, 339–40
rent-seeking (commercial speech), 326–28
Reporting Guidance on the 10th Principle Against Corruption, 464
reputational losses (contract at will), 59
Resistol, 255–56
respect
Kantian, 20–23
price gouging and, 517–18
roots in moral philosophy, 241
respect-for-persons principle, 45–47
responsibility principle, 223
retaliation
disparate treatment in, 172
international business, 478
whistleblowing, 142–43
RFID, 290
right to know, 72–75, 328

rights
political, 444–45
privacy, 261–62
property, 559–60
shareholders, 215
rights-based theories, 25–28
Riley, J. C., 236
Ripken, S. K., 275
risk
and contract at will, 59
and employment-at-will principle, 70–72
prescription drug, 342–43
sustainable development and, 392–93
river blindness, 256–57
Roche, James, 125
Rorty, R., 227
Rose, Tim, 52
Rosen, M., 241
Rousseau, Jean Jacques, 188
Rowley, Coleen, 139–40
Royal Dutch Shell, 372, 468–69
rule of conscience, 5–6
rule utilitarians, 18–19

S.C. Johnson, 587–88
Sabel, C., 458
Sacks, D. W., 240
safety. See also harm
basic international norms on, 451–52
in British Petroleum, employees, 44–45, 47–48, 86–87
and employment-at-will principle, 68–75
food, 326–27
in high risk industries, 75–80
as marketing strategy, 321–22
and right-to-know, 328
salesmanship
doctors involved in, 335–37
and ethics, 333–35
Sam's Club, 49–54
Sandal, M. J., 269
Sarbanes-Oxley Act (2002), 91, 103, 128, 207, 236
satisfaction, 240
Satz, D., 493, 510–11
scandals. See also sweatshops
environmental sustainability, 373–74, 398–402, 404–10
Fen-Phen, 337
fueling reform, 237–38
international soccer, 487–88
pharmaceutical, 331–32

Scanlon, T. M., 67
Schultz, Howard, 52
scientific approach (ethics), 6
Scott, D., 457
SEC v. Texas Gulf Sulphur, 523, 527
secondary use (information), 265
second-order desire, 305
Security Pacific Corporation, 24
SeisInt, 274
selection cultural systems, 102
self-interest. *See also* prudence
　　bias, 108
　　insider trading and, 525
　　in international supply chains, 456
self-regulation. *See also* market regulation
　　and global exploitation, 574
　　pharmaceutical direct-to-consumer
　　　advertisement, 343–46
　　and whistleblowing, 137–38
Sen, Amartya, 377, 497, 545
Separation Fallacy, 222, 242
service and flow economy (natural capital-
　　ism), 388–90
sexism and sexual harrassment. *See also*
　　harrassment
　　Bathsheba Syndrome, 109
　　in City of London, 83
　　and Civil Rights Act, 170–74
　　and disparate treatment, 173–74
　　as form of discrimination, 162–63
　　at Fox News, 199
　　in international business, 475–76
　　law, 162–63
　　and patriarchy, 583
　　in Silicon Valley, 197
shareholders
　　and agency theory, 211–16, 220–23
　　and corporate social responsibility to
　　　environment, 400
　　primacy ideology, 445–47
Shearer, C., 124–25
Shell Oil Company, 467
Shi Tao, 284–85
Shiva, V, 376
Shkreli, Martin, 251–52
shrinkage, 52
Side Effects (film), 332
Siemens AG, 446, 461
Silbergeld, M., 295
silent enablers, 283
Simitis, S., 266
Simon, H. A., 243
Sinegal, Jim, 49–51, 52, 229
Singh, Gurkirpal, 363

Skinner, B. F., 303
Slattery-Moschau, K., 332
Slobogin, C., 273
Smith, Adam, 14–15
Smith, Howard III, 260
Smith, J., 263
smoking, 84
Snyder, J., 495
social science
　　business affecting, 236, 237–38
　　and public morality, 2
society
　　effects of vote selling on, 510
　　executive responsibility to, 445–46
　　harmful markets and, 497
　　internalization in, 96–97
　　orientation/training programs, 103
　　privacy in, 265–66, 275–76
　　and purpose of business, 243
　　sustainability and development, 393–95
soft drink industry, 320–21
SolarCity, 428
Solove, D., 261–62, 274
Southwest Airlines, 21, 98
specialty vulnerability, 311–12
specification (common morality theory), 31
Spilker, B., 332
Stahel, Walter, 388–89
stakeholders. *See also* participant, agency
　　theory
　　greenwashing and, 407
　　in normative ethical theory deci-
　　　sions, 35
　　stakeholder capitalism, 220–23
　　versus stockholders, 204–7
statutory law, 4
Stauber, J., 406
Stern, S., 236
Stevens, G., 277
Stevenson, B., 240
Stewart, Martha, 539–41
Stockholm Declaration on the Human
　　Environment, 418
Strudler, A., 207
subliminal advertising, 306–7
substance abuse, 255–56
sugar industry, 319–20, 359–60
Sun Microsystems, 275
Sunbeam, 100–1
supply chains
　　Costco and Walmart, 52
　　unauthorized subcontracting in, 484
　　Walmart, 479–81
surveillance, 265, 273–74

sustainability. *See* environmental
　　sustainability
Sutcliffe, K. M., 76, 77
Sutton, R. I., 237
sweatshops, 434–50, 573–74, *See also* scandals

Taibbi, M., 237
Talisman Energy, 283
tax breaks, 85–86
Tay, L., 240
Taylor, J. S., 494
Tebo, P., 406
technology industry
　　ethics in, 261–66
　　sexism in, 197
telecommunications industry, 274
teleological theories, 93–94
television advertising
　　erectile dysfunction, 354–55
　　paid expert product mentions, 349–50
　　paid local tours and, 350
　　school supplies, 352–53
Teresa Harris v. Forklift Systems, 162, 193
Tesla, 427–29
Texaco, 417–19
Theory of Justice (Rawls), 544
theory of the good, 17
Thompson, Tommy, 319, 320
Three Square Market, 290
Title VII (Civil Rights Act), 170–74, 222
tobacco industry, 315–16, 317–18, 320, 321,
　　327–28
Tobin, J., 508
Tolstedt, Carrie, 150
total shareholder return, 215
Toyota, 405
transaction costs, 74
transnational corporations. *See* interna-
　　tional business
Transparency International, 442, 462, 464,
　　482, 488
Trevino, L., 89, 93, 207
triage ethics, 560–61
triple bottom line (sustainability), 391
Tropicana Products, 346–47
Trump, Donald, 85, 428
Turing Pharmaceutical, 251–52
Tyco, 108, 236

Uber, 147–48, 196–97
ultimate moral standards, 8–9
Union Pacific railroad, 77
unions
　　and contract at will, 60–61

and employment-at-will principle, 43, 47
lack of at Costco and Walmart, 52–53
United Nations Environment Programme, 386
United Nations World Commission on Environment and Development. *See* Brundtland Commission
United States v. Best Foods, 413
United States v. O'Hagan, 496, 525–26, 531
Universal Declaration of Human Rights, 241–42, 280, 294, 394, 433, 437, 443, 444, 449, 460, 469, 478, 547, 548, 580–82
universalizability
    Kantian, 23
    moral point of view, 33
universities and sweatshops, 452
Unocal Corporation, 24, 284, 434, 468
utilitarianism
    and dignity, 241
    and distributive justice, 543
    and economic justice, 557–61
    and egoism, 14–15
    and Kantianism, 33
    as normative principle, 6
    in normative ethical theory, 16–20
    privacy and, 265–66
    and right to know, 74–75
Utilitarianism (Mill), 16
utilities industry, 253–54, 348, 405
utility
    of contract at will, 57–60
    maximization, 114–15, 118, 120–22

value
    collective, 240–41
    and mission statements, 102
    positive, 239–40
    of privacy, 265–66
Van Buren, P., 141
van den Hoven, J., 262
veil of ignorance, 544
venture capital sexism, 197
Vioxx, 361–64
Virginia State Board of Pharmacy v. Virginia Citizens Consumer Council, 326

virtue ethics, 28–29, 227
vocational training program, 259–60
Volkswagen, 296, 429–31
voluntary behavior, 306
von Hayek, F. A., 305
Vora, A., 162–63
Vos, J., 373
voting
    folk theory of, 505–6
    good, 505–7
    inalienability objection to commodification, 506–7
    principle of ethical, 505
    utopian argument against markets in, 507–12
vulnerability
    and business exploitation, 514
    deception, 110, 300
    defined, 308–9
    marketing and, 309–11
    markets exploiting, 498
    physical, 311
    price gouging targeting and, 494
    specialty, 311–12
    and taking advantage of developing countries, 570, 576–77
    temporary, 313

wages. *See also* executive compensation
    basic international norms on, 451
    disparate treatment in, 171
    LGBT community, 187
    minimum, 451, 575, 585
Waldron, J., 241
Wall Street. *See* financial services industry
Walmart, 42–43, 49–54, 229, 351, 461, 479–81, 490
Walton, Sam, 49
Warner, K., 300
Warthen v. Toms River Community Memorial Hospital, 145
Waskal, Sam, 539–41
Watkins, Sherron, 139–40
weak agency, 497–98
weblining, 277
Weick, K., 76, 77
Welch, Jack, 99

Wells Fargo, 149–52
Werhane, P., 44, 69
Wertheimer, A., 514
Whirlpool Corporation, 72
whistleblowing. *See also* employees
    complex nature of, 128–29
    employee loyalty and, 129–36
    ethics of, 90–92
    integrity theory and, 129–36
    management and, 138–43
    organizational design and, 136–38
    Pfizer, 366
    Potter v. Village Bank of New Jersey, 145–46
    Warthen v. Toms River Community Memorial Hospital, 145
Whitman v. American Trucking Associations Inc., 374, 413–14
Whitman, Meg, 276
Wigland, Jeff, 141
Wild, Anthony, 333
Williams, C. A., 243
Winter, D. G., 94
Winterbottom v. Wright, 222
Wittgenstein, Ludwig, 264
Wolf, M., 548
Wolfers, J., 240
Wood, H. G., 62
Woods, N., 458
worker notification, 72–75
World Bank, 565–66, 567, 573
World Business Council for Sustainable Development, 386
World Cup (soccer), 487–88
World Health Organization, 319–20, 397
World Trade Organization, 452, 577
WorldCom, 236
Wyatt, John, 51
Wyeth, 337

Yahoo, 262–63, 279, 282, 284–86

Zeitlin, J., 458
Zellner, W., 229
Zuckerberg, Mark, 275
Zwolinski, M., 494–95